D1379914

Handbook of
CAREER
STUDIES

To Michael, Tim, and Barbara: You did it first.

Handbook of
CAREER
STUDIES

Edited by
Hugh Gunz · Maury Peiperl
University of Toronto   *IMD*

SAGE Publications
Los Angeles • London • New Delhi • Singapore

For information:

Sage Publications, Inc.
2455 Teller Road
Thousand Oaks, California 91320
E-mail: order@sagepub.com

Sage Publications Ltd.
1 Oliver's Yard
55 City Road
London EC1Y 1SP
United Kingdom

Sage Publications India Pvt. Ltd.
B 1/I 1 Mohan Cooperative Industrial Area
Mathura Road, New Delhi 110 044
India

Sage Publications Asia-Pacific Pte. Ltd.
33 Pekin Street #02-01
Far East Square
Singapore 048763

Printed in the United States of America

Library of Congress Cataloging-in-Publication Data

Handbook of career studies/[edited by] Hugh Gunz, Maury Peiperl.
    p. cm.
Includes bibliographical references and index.
ISBN 978-0-7619-3039-6 (cloth)
    1. Career development. 2. Vocational guidance. I. Gunz, Hugh. II. Peiperl, Maury.

HF5549.5.C35H357 2008
331.702—dc22   2007004812

This book is printed on acid-free paper.

07 08 09 10 11 10 9 8 7 6 5 4 3 2 1

Acquisitions Editor:	Al Bruckner
Editorial Assistant:	MaryAnn Vail
Production Editor:	Melanie Birdsall
Copy Editor:	QuADS Prepress (P) Ltd.
Typesetter:	C&M Digitals (P) Ltd.
Proofreader:	Sue Irwin
Indexer:	Kathy Paparchontis
Cover Designer:	Michelle Kenny
Marketing Manager:	Nichole M. Angress

CONTENTS

FOREWORD

CAREER RESEARCH

Some Personal Perspectives

EDGAR H. SCHEIN

In this overview foreword, I do not wish to repeat or elaborate on the excellent historical chapter provided by Moore, Gunz, and Hall but rather to make some comments based on my personal experiences in doing research on career dynamics and on my reactions to perusing this rather monumental *Handbook*. The issues I will raise are exemplified by various specific chapters but I will deliberately *not* comment on individual chapters. This brief essay is not a critique as much as a set of reactions based on half a century of observation.

GROWTH AND DIVERSIFICATION

The first comment to be made is that the field of career studies has grown and diversified to an incredible degree. One need only peruse the table of contents of this volume to see both the depth and breadth of what is today labeled career studies. This is a healthy trend that reflects how much more important "careers" have become as the world has become more global, complex, diverse, and, most important, individualistic. With economic development comes individualism (Hofstede & Bond, 1988) and with that comes a decline in organizations managing the careers of their members. It is a normal evolution to be talking more about individuals being responsible for their own career partly because the reality for organizations is that they cannot predict or control career paths in the way that they used to be able to do.

With the diversification of topics, we also see a diversification of research approaches—an inevitable and healthy trend. As one peruses the various chapters, it is striking how people from very different disciplines have entered the fray. There are the usual psychologists and sociologists, but increasingly we see an interest in careers from anthropology and from broader-based management scholars. Especially welcome is a more case-based clinical approach that reveals some of the inner dynamics of careers over time (Schein, 2001). Such an approach allows the reader to become familiar not only with the individual experience of careers but with the nature of the work itself, something that is often neglected in career studies.

The career field has grown enormously since those early efforts in the 1960s by Thompson, Dalton, Derr, Driver, Bailyn, Van Maanen, Schein, Louis, Bray, Storey, Harrell, and many others, but it is far from integrated. Rather, a few paradigms built on individual developmental theories such as those of Super and Holland have dominated the field. Such lack of integration is not in itself a problem, but the disregard of researchers in one paradigm for the relevant work of researchers in another paradigm is a problem when each set of researchers presents their work as the final and correct analysis of a particular area. This *Handbook* is clearly an effort to overcome such provincialism, and the editors have commissioned a very useful set of integrative chapters for Part III. What lack of integration and pluralism of paradigms remains is but a reflection of the growing diversity that a popular field inevitably reflects.

CAREER DYNAMICS AT DIFFERENT STAGES AND AGES

Career research has broadened in several significant ways. At one time, it was just about selection coming out of the research on how to select pilots in World War I. This was an age where testing was coming into its own, so testing for selection when one had a clear criterion—a job with certain specific characteristics—was enormously successful. For a long time, the field limited itself to studying just careers where the job requirements were clear, such as accounting. And if the job could not be described, one could at least compare whether the profile of interests that a career candidate exhibited matched the profile of successful people in that career. The Strong Interest Inventory dominated the field.

As the many chapters in this *Handbook* show, we now have more occupations to think about, and the whole testing and selection model, though still alive and well, has been supplemented by many other approaches to studying careers. In particular, in the selection of managers, researchers have had to acknowledge that it is not very clear what managers are supposed to do and what skill set will make the doing of it effective, so it is hard to design a test for managerial career success. We still try with various "competency" models, but the list of competencies is itself growing into hundreds, which should warn us that this approach may not be significantly better than the old aptitude testing approach. As organizations become more complex, more different kinds of careers become possible, and as more women enter careers, more patterns of career growth become visible, most notably Bailyn's concept of "slow burn" (Bailyn, 1993).

With the evolution beyond the selection models also came the recognition that there were issues of mid-career and late career that needed research attention. The earliest research saw the career as an occupational label. As the reader of this *Handbook* will see, career dynamics within an occupation are increasingly becoming an important focus and the moving from one career to another or retiring altogether poses many important practical as well as psychological problems that are now receiving more research attention.

SOCIOECONOMIC VARIATION AND LATE CAREERS

Mid-career and late career studies such as those reviewed in this *Handbook* reflect yet another way in which the career field has grown and diversified. As the reader will find, we now have research on a wide variety of careers reflecting different socioeconomic levels, cultures, gender, and age cohorts. Expanding our understanding of the socioeconomic variations seems to me to be crucial in that the concept of career must be seen as independent of occupation, especially middle-class and professional occupations. There was a tradition in the Chicago School of Sociology under Everett Hughes that studied criminals, prostitutes, janitors, jazz musicians, cops, assembly line workers, and other representatives of the "underclasses" in our society, but for a long time, this kind of research lay dormant and is only now reappearing.

Finally, it should be noted that we are discovering with the increase in longevity that between retirement at 60 or 65 and death, there is room for an entire other career that people are living. And this is not about moving to a sunshine state and playing golf. It is about people discovering new talents and new opportunities, about finding that staying occupationally active is good for physical health, and about a whole new industry arising to educate so-called retirees in new life routines.

Conclusion

The good news is that the field of career studies is alive and well, growing rapidly, and moving forward with enthusiasm. This *Handbook* is testament to that reality and an excellent reference for those interested in knowing more about it. What I have tried to do in this foreword is to provide some perspective and to highlight some issues that are emerging as the career field leaves adolescence and appears fully grown on the research stage.

References

Bailyn, L. (1993). *Breaking the mold.* New York: Free Press. (2nd ed., 2006)

Hofstede, G., & Bond, M. H. (1988). The Confucius connection: From cultural roots to economic growth. *Organizational Dynamics, 16*(4), 4–21.

Schein, E. H. (2001). Clinical inquiry and research. In P. Reason & H. Bradbury (Eds.), *Handbook of action research: Participative inquiry and practice* (pp. 228–237). Thousand Oaks, CA: Sage.

PREFACE

How does one come to edit a work like a *Handbook of Career Studies?* In one sense the answer is simple: We were asked to do it. Al Bruckner, of Sage Publications, approached one of us (Gunz) out of the blue with the proposition: How would you feel about editing a handbook on careers? And because we had been planning for many years to develop some kind of synthesis of the careers field, but had never quite figured out what it should be, this seemed the ideal opportunity. Gunz contacted Peiperl, Peiperl swallowed hard and agreed, and that was that.

But in another sense, it was, perhaps appropriately for a book on careers, a product of our backgrounds. Although both of us share a fascination with career studies, our own careers have been somewhat unusual for business academics working in the field. Gunz is a chemist by training and a former Shell technologist; Peiperl is an engineer and an ex-IBMer. Admittedly, we both legitimized ourselves, so to speak, by completing our PhDs in social science disciplines. But perhaps because of our initial education, we both tend to view the field from a perspective that is not that of someone trained ab initio in one of the social sciences. For the field of career studies has something of the Rorschach test about it. As we discuss in the Introduction (Chapter 1), it is broad almost to the point at which it is not a field at all but a perspective on social enquiry.

We explain in Chapter 1 what we think that perspective is. Suffice it to say for the moment that it is, as Michael Arthur, Tim Hall, and Barbara Lawrence point out in their 1989 *Handbook of Career Theory*, one that covers virtually all the social sciences and a fair proportion of the humanities. So you can see in the inkblots of careers pretty much what you want to see. If you are a vocational psychologist, you are naturally likely to see careers first as being about choosing occupations; if you are a sociologist you are equally likely to see careers as fundamental to the way societies reproduce themselves. And so on. Once you have been working in the field for some years, however, your view may broaden, so that it is perhaps no accident (as we shall see later in this *Handbook*) that it is senior careers scholars who typically lead the way in arguing for integration across the disciplines.

But if you are a chemist or an engineer, you lack the strong particular perspective that an initial training in a particular social science would have afforded, so your view of the inkblots is likely to be unpredictable and somewhat catholic. Someone says to you, "Careers are about occupational choice," and you reply, "How fascinating!" Someone else says, "Careers are about the social reproduction of societies," and you reply, "Of course, how intriguing!" This does not, obviously, lead to a profound understanding of every possible perspective on career; that would be a presumptuous claim. But it *does* create fertile ground for wanting to work with people who really do combine between them such a breadth of understanding, which is to say, editing a *Handbook.*

Not that such a truly comprehensive project is possible, of course, without producing a whole set of volumes each the size of this or larger, and probably not even then. But we have tried at least to be as representative as we could of the main currents in the field and to bring together as many of the leading thinkers as we could, knowing that, inevitably, we were leaving out others. We apologize both to our readers and to those omitted scholars for these gaps. But we have found this journey utterly absorbing and fascinating and we hope you do, too. We have learned an immense amount from our authors about the state of the field of career studies; we can never thank them enough for their ideas, their unflagging hard work, and especially their patience.

There are many others who helped us with this project. First among them are our wives, Elizabeth Badley and Jennifer Georgia, both of whom have quite overwhelming enough professional lives without husbands endlessly going on about their *Handbook*. We thank them profusely for putting up with it, and us, anyway. Gunz, in particular, is profoundly grateful to the Peiperl household for acting as such gracious hosts during what must have seemed to them interminable editing sessions.

We learned a great deal about editing from, and, in fact, would never have embarked on this *Handbook*, without the interest and support of Michael Arthur, Tim Hall, and Barbara Lawrence, whose original *Handbook* helped to define the field.

In addition to her role as author, Celia Moore assisted in many ways, not least in acting as rapporteur to the meeting of Part III authors in Lausanne, Switzerland, a meeting that would not have been possible without the financial support and hospitality of Dr. Peter Lorange and the faculty and staff of IMD, and especially the organizational efforts of Sonia Klose. We are also most grateful to Al Bruckner and MaryAnn Vail of Sage Publications for suggesting the project in the first place and helping us see it through to completion. The production phase of the book was orchestrated patiently and meticulously by Melanie Birdsall, for whom nothing was too much trouble however late the editors were in discovering things they should have noticed much sooner. Mike Badley made available to us, free of charge, the outstanding software package *Unite-It,* which facilitated enormously the business of planning and controlling such a complex project—in particular, keeping track of the myriad versions of each chapter, no matter who was editing it, or where. Finally, Slavka Murray kept things running smoothly in Gunz's department at the University of Toronto, which made his frequent absences on editing sessions in Maryland and Switzerland feasible.

To all who worked with us and helped us on this project, we offer our profound thanks. The chapter authors as well as the editors will welcome readers' comments. The editors, of course, accept responsibility for any shortcomings.

—*HPG*
—*MAP*
Bougy-Villars, Switzerland
September 2006

1

INTRODUCTION

HUGH GUNZ

MAURY PEIPERL

The fascination of careers as an object of study comes from their pervasiveness as individual and social phenomena. We all have careers; but more than this, there is very little in the field of organization studies that is not affected by the simple observation that people, unlike organizations or societies, are mortal or, at least, that they have very different life spans from organizations or societies. They make their way through life, their abilities, knowledge, and interests changing as they mature and age, within social contexts that shape them and that they play their part in shaping. The study of careers, to paraphrase one of its founders, Everett Hughes, is both of how the individual makes sense of his or her passage through life and also of what this reveals about what Hughes refers to as "the nature and 'working constitution' of a society."

It is now approaching 20 years since Michael Arthur, Tim Hall, and Barbara Lawrence published the *Handbook of Career Theory* (Arthur, Hall, & Lawrence, 1989b). A landmark work, it marked the culmination of the period, starting in the mid-1970s, during which career studies became established within the more general field of organization studies. Since the 1970s, wrote the editors, "career theory has 'gone legitimate.' We (people who study careers) have become established. We have become a *field*" (p. xv). Like all good handbooks, it defined the field, made authoritative statements about the state of scholarship in its various branches, and proposed agendas for future research. Little wonder that it has been a sourcebook for research ever since, its chapters still regularly cited by scholars from many disciplines.

However, the world is, in many ways, a different place from that of the late 1980s, when that *Handbook* was written, and these changes have had their impact on the nature of careers or at least on the ways in which they are conceived. Most obviously, economic fluctuations through the mid-1980s and early 1990s have had lingering effects on labor markets, calling into question many of the apparent certainties about work careers that the post–World War II generation had grown up with. This period was eventually followed by an atypically long-lasting boom that created jobs, many of which were of very different kinds from those that had gone before. The so-called "new economy" or "knowledge economy," many observers argued, was so different from the "old economy" that the very nature of work and career needed to be drastically rethought. Later, when the "tech boom" was followed by the Asian crisis of the late 1990s and the technology "bust" of the early 2000s, the uncertainties of a decade earlier (and for those with longer time horizons, the uncertainty that typified most of human experience) became firmly—one could argue, permanently—reestablished in the consciousness of people and labor markets the world over.

These changes have had their impact on the thinking of careers scholars (and, of course, practitioners) in the past decade and a half. But other scholarly agendas have risen to prominence as well—for example, network phenomena (with mentoring being a particularly popular subtopic), links between firm strategy and the career histories of top managers, and the emergence (or at least, greater recognition) of "nontraditional" careers. In other words, important, career-related work is going on in many different areas of organizational scholarship. But even a cursory look across these areas reveals that despite the obvious possibilities, there is little cross-fertilization happening.

APPROACHES TO A HANDBOOK

What was so remarkable about the 1989 *Handbook* was its highly creative approach. The editors did not start with a preconceived view of the structure of the careers field but allowed it to emerge from the "review chapters with a point of view" (p. xvii) of Part I. To the extent that the editors did provide structure, it was in their choice of authors for these reviews. Part II of the work was written by scholars who had not thus far been associated with the field and who were asked to "think out loud about concepts from their field that potentially would be useful to people studying careers" (p. xvii). Finally, the editors "asked four leading scholars of organizations to take the rich harvest of ideas in Parts I and II and simply 'play' with them" (p. xvii).

The book that emerged, therefore, was in very great measure a particular creation of a particular group of authors working together on a particular project. That great strength, of course, was also the problem in producing a second edition. Even assuming that the same group of authors could be assembled, what would such a revision look like? Was it not much more likely that an entirely different work would emerge? And if so, could it genuinely be called a second edition, as opposed to a different handbook? The editors were never able to resolve this dilemma and thus decided not to pursue such a venture (though not for want of opportunity or of interest on the part of careers scholars).[1]

We recount this story to explain why the present volume is not, and was never intended to be, a revision of the 1989 *Handbook*. Partly because the field has matured even more in the intervening years and partly because of our own predilections, we chose an entirely different approach, in many ways a much more conventional one. Whereas the 1989 *Handbook* allowed the shape of the field to emerge from the work of its many authors, we started by imposing a structure. Admittedly, it was a highly inductive process: We took what we believed to be the main themes currently being addressed in the field and invited the leading experts in each to contribute a chapter. But the choices about what to include and what to leave out were ours, and to that extent, we must stand accused of placing a shape on the field with which by no means everyone will agree. For some, the omissions will be glaring. For others, the inclusion of certain topics will be baffling. All we can say in reply is this: There is no consensus that we have detected about what is "in" the field of career studies and what is not (more about this below). Because of this, we have devoted one chapter to a discussion of the structure of the field (Chapter 3); in that chapter, we discuss the different approaches that have been taken and outline our own particular perspective.

STUDYING CAREERS

Like numerous topics in psychology, sociology, and organization studies, the subject of careers is one with which many, if not most, people identify. In some ways, this makes it more, rather than less, difficult to frame the field in a way that is both inclusive and rigorous. We will delve into the history and structure of the careers field more deeply in Chapters 2 and 3, but it is important at the outset to specify what we mean, and do not mean, by the term *career studies.*

The word *career* itself comes from a number of Romance language derivatives of the late Latin *carraria,* a carriage-road or road (*Oxford English Dictionary [OED],* 1989). As a noun, it has had a number of meanings, many of them pertaining to racecourses and the path followed by a horse. These live on in the usage of *career* as a verb: "to gallop, run or move at full speed" (*OED,* 1989). However, even by the end of the 16th century, the noun had also taken on a figurative meaning, as a "rapid and continuous 'course of action, uninter-rupted procedure'" (*OED,* 1989). But it was not until the beginning of the 19th century that the Duke of Wellington refers in a letter to his corre-spondent's "diplomatic career" and the poet (and Shakespearian forger) W. H. Ireland writes about "that great statesman's public career" (*OED,* 1989). Gradually, this meaning evolved into the sense of career as "a course of professional life or employment, which affords opportunity for progress or advancement in the world" (*OED,* 1989).

Career, for many, is inextricably bound up with work. Indeed, there are implications in the definitions provided by the *OED* that it is not just any work but professional work and that it is about getting ahead ("progress," "advancement"). Although we will not restrict ourselves in this volume to such specific implications, we do find that people talk about their careers as profession-als: lawyers, engineers, administrators, or foot-ballers. They tend not to talk about their careers as amateurs: avocational photographers, actors in community theater, local league footballers, or gardeners. It is as if in everyday life, *career* means something one is serious about, as opposed to those things that one does for the love of doing them but without getting paid for doing so.

There is at least one tradition in career schol-arship, originating from the Chicago school of sociology (Barley, 1989, although, as Becker, 2003, points out, not all members regarded it as a "school"), which defines career much more broadly than this. For these scholars, the term meant not just work, let alone professional work,

but some significant aspect of a person's life history. They famously studied the careers of, for example, drug users, taxi dancers, and tubercu-losis patients. Career, for them, was in a very gen-eral sense a passage through life, and it marked a perspective that, although often remarked on now (Moore, Gunz, and Hall, Chapter 2), is rarely found in the so-called career literature.

Indeed, what is commonly recognized as "career literature" covers but a small portion of the research and scholarship that impinge on the phenomenon of career. There is scarcely a corner of scholarship on people or organizations in which the concept of career does not put in an appearance. Arthur, Hall, and Lawrence (1989a, pp. 9–10) list some of the many fields that draw on the concept, including psychology, social psychology, sociology, anthropology, econom-ics, political science, history, and geography. Similarly, careers pervade the management literature. A brief and highly selective list of the disciplines that have contributed to the careers field would have to include the following:

- Sociologists interested in intergenerational mobility and societal life-changes, the struc-ture and behavior of business elites specifi-cally, and the social origins and demography of managers in general
- Organizational demographers studying the fac-tors underlying promotion rates and mobility
- Labor economists investigating the structure of inter- and intrafirm labor markets
- Organizational theorists working on the struc-ture of careers within and between organizations
- Developmental psychologists investigating the life stages through which people pass
- Educational and vocational psychologists invol-ved in training and counseling
- Social psychologists and sociologists with an interest in patterns of work experience and the interaction among the many roles that people experience, sequentially and in parallel
- Sociologists and social psychologists with an interest in comparative studies of careers in dif-ferent societies and in the impact of new organi-zational forms on careers in developed societies
- Strategic management and finance scholars studying the impact of managerial background on the strategic behavior of companies and their experience with capital markets

Career, then, is an extraordinarily pervasive concept. We are clearly getting into difficult territory here: If a term becomes too broad, as, for example, Wilensky (1964) and, later, Freidson (1986) argued was a risk with the label "professional," it ceases to be useful. Indeed, Barley (1989, p. 45) suspects that Wilensky (1960) thought that the very broad definition of career used by the Chicago sociologists risked precisely this fate. Boundaries have their drawbacks (Gunz, Peiperl, and Tzabbar, Chapter 24), but they are necessary for any kind of intellectual progress (Zerubavel, 1995). What exactly is it that we are talking about when we use the label "career"? Can we be more precise than simply saying that it is something encountered in pretty much every branch of the social science and management literatures?

The perspective taken in this volume is to focus on career as it relates to the world of work. This, of course, begs the question of what we mean by *work*. To avoid the dangers of infinite regression, we shall confine ourselves to the relatively simplistic definition of work as that which one does to make a living. It is simplistic in the sense that it ignores all the concomitants of work—for example, its role in establishing an identity within society or of providing structure to one's life (the loss of both, of course, being a major explanation for the devastation many experience on unemployment or retirement; Feldman, Chapter 9). It does, however, provide some sense of bounds to our venture.

This is not to say that we ignore the rest of life as it is lived but rather that it is not the primary focus of the book. For example, family life impinges on, and is impinged on by, work (Greenhaus and Foley, Chapter 8; Valcour, Bailyn, and Quijada, Chapter 11), and the same holds for ethnicity (Prasad, D'Abate, and Prasad, Chapter 10) and age (Feldman, Chapter 9). But it is the *work-related* implications of these phenomena on which we focus rather than on the phenomena (family, ethnicity, and age) themselves.

We adopt as our working definition of career that of the 1989 *Handbook*: "the evolving sequence of a person's work experiences over time" (Arthur et al., 1989a, p. 8). It has the virtue of being succinct and of leaving the matter open as to whether we are interested in experiences as the person experiences them (the so-called

subjective career; Hughes, 1937) or as others see them (the "objective career") and whether we are interested in the person as an individual or in the institutions through which he or she passes in the course of life (and in so doing, transforms and is transformed by them to a greater or lesser extent). As Arthur et al. (1989a) point out,

> Careers reflect the relationships between people and the providers of official position, namely, institutions or organizations, and how these relationships fluctuate over time. Seen in this way, the study of careers is the study of both individual and organizational change (Van Maanen, 1977a) as well as of societal change. (p. 8)

This definition suggests that career studies may not be a field at all but *a perspective on social enquiry*. Its central concept is *the effect on people of the passage of time*. We may be interested in the passage of time retrospectively, as in the way in which biography traces someone's pathway through life or demography examines the aggregate biographies of the members of some population of interest. Our interest may be longitudinal, as in the massive study conducted by Douglas Bray and his colleagues on AT&T managers (Bray, Campbell, & Grant, 1974). Or it may be prospective, as in research on career choice, in which one tries to predict the success in a given occupation of a young person with a given set of characteristics or the impact on someone's career of being adopted as a protégé by a given mentor. Finally, it may be both retrospective and prospective, as in the way in which strategic management includes the variable "background" when it tries to understand the impact of different CEOs or combinations of top management team members on the future behavior of the companies they manage. But whichever way one looks at it, career and the passage of time are inextricably entangled.

This volume, then, at one level is about "the evolving sequence of a person's work experiences over time." But at another, it is an exploration of what one sees when one looks at people, networks, organizations, institutions, or societies through a lens that focuses on the passage of time. This is a broad canvas indeed; but it is one with a clear structure, once you know where to look for the structure. As we shall briefly preview here (but do so in greater detail in the introductions to each part and section of the book), the range of phenomena that can be examined through this lens is vast, as is the literature that documents them.

It is also a remarkably old canvas. Its history is often traced to a ferment of activity in the mid-1970s, some associated with a cluster of scholars mainly based in Boston at institutions such as MIT and Harvard, and led by figures such as Edgar Schein and Donald Super, and some with a group organized by George Milkovich at Cornell. It would be invidious to try to list the names of those involved, if only because there were so many. Suffice it to say that it was during this time that a great many highly influential books and studies were published, perhaps the best known being the ones by Schein (1978), Hall (1976), Dyer (1976), and Van Maanen (1977b), from which a considerable volume of scholarship has descended.

Yet, as we shall see later, this was by no means the beginning. As Schein points out in the Afterword to this volume, the scholars we have just listed owe a great debt to Everett Hughes in particular and the sociologists of the Chicago school in general, working from the 1920s until the 1960s; also important was the work of Donald Super (who, with Schein and others, had been active in the career field long before the 1970s) and of Douglas Bray at AT&T. But even this is an oversimplification. Schein remarks (Moore, Gunz, and Hall, Chapter 2) that when he joined the field in the late 1950s, he encountered two quite distinct scholarly traditions associated with career, which he labeled psychological and sociological, each completely oblivious of the other (arguably, they still are; Peiperl and Gunz, Chapter 3). The psychological tradition he traced to scholars such as Strong, Super, Osipow, and Holland and the sociological to Hughes, Becker, Goffman, and White.

Yet, as Moore, Gunz, and Hall point out (Chapter 2), the tradition can be traced back considerably further than the names listed in the previous paragraph. Weber, Durkheim, Freud, and many others wrote about career, often in surprisingly contemporary terms. Max Weber, for example, wrote about organizational careers when he described the way in which people were selected for advancement in rational-legal organizations. It could be argued that Freud's ideas about the sexual development of the individual represent an early example of a scientific analysis of the individual career. It may be true to say that the application of the word *career* to a series of work-related experiences was an early 19th-century happening, at least in the English language, but the phenomenon to which the label is now attached is not. Indeed, the melancholy philosopher Jaques's soliloquy on the seven ages of man in Shakespeare's *As You Like It* (Act II; Scene vii) is but an Elizabethan take on a theme that is as old as mankind.

This should not surprise us if we recall the unifying concept that, we argued above, defines career: the effect on people of the passage of time. Clearly, it would be stretching things somewhat to argue that the field of career studies was founded by Shakespeare, however apt his observations might be to 21st-century life. Our point is simply that of Hughes (1937) that everyone has a career and that in living those careers we give form to and, over time, change the institutions through which we pass.

It is not easy to get a clear picture of the size of the field of career studies, if only because it covers so much territory. One very crude indicator of the level of interest is the number of articles published in peer-reviewed journals that list the keyword "career." In the social science publications indexed by the CSA Illumina database (www.csa.com), the number with the keyword "career" has steadily increased. For articles and dissertations, this trend has been both in absolute and in relative terms (Figures 1.1 and 1.2), although books seem to have experienced a surge in the late 1970s (Derr and Briscoe, Chapter 29) and early 1980s.

To get a better sense of the significance of these figures, we can compare them with the number of peer-reviewed articles published on other topics. In the period 2001 to 2005, more than 21,000 peer-reviewed articles had the keyword "career," very comparable with the total number on the ever-popular subject of motivation (25,000).[2] Emotion, a topic of growing interest, totaled a little more than 13,500 papers during this time, and even leadership, perhaps the most managerially significant of them all, accounted for under 79,000 articles (1.85% of all social science articles).

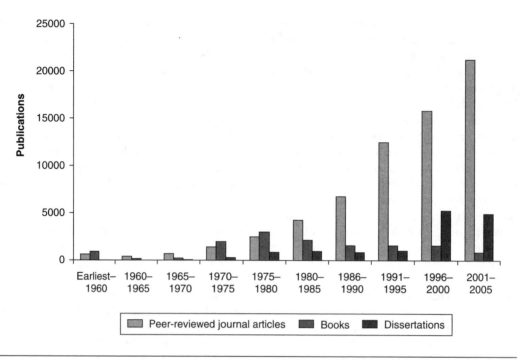

Figure 1.1   Publications With the Keyword "Career"

SOURCE: CSA Illumina.

NOTE: The date ranges (overlapping until 1985 and non-overlapping thereafter) are dictated by the CSA Illumina search engine's date selections.

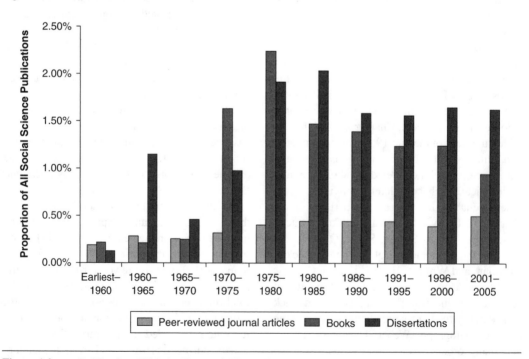

Figure 1.2   Publications With the Keyword "Career," as a Proportion of All Social Science Publications

SOURCE: CSA Illumina.

NOTE: The date ranges (overlapping until 1985 and non-overlapping thereafter) are dictated by the CSA Illumina search engine's date selections.

The field of career studies, then, provides a key perspective on the study of people and organizations, and it is one that is of lively scholarly interest. How did we approach the task of documenting it?

PURPOSE AND CONSTRUCTION OF THIS HANDBOOK

Our aim in this volume is to provide a focus and a reference point for this interest. Although career studies, like organization studies generally, continues to change and evolve, there is a current need, we believe, for a volume that brings together what is currently known about careers. This book is thus in part a repository of knowledge that, although we cannot claim it to be totally comprehensive, goes well beyond what has heretofore been available. In addition, many of the contributors to this *Handbook* have tried to build some links across the field's many subtopics and to look ahead to where career phenomena and research about them are going. In the process, the questions often asked by newcomers to a field, such as "Who is doing what within the field of career studies? What are the current lively issues that are attracting the attention of scholars?" as well as questions that are more the province of those currently active in careers research, such as "Where does the field seem to be going? What *should* be attracting attention, but isn't?" have become nearly as important to us as the basic question "What is known about careers?"

As we remarked above, the world has moved on since the 1989 *Handbook* was published. Regardless of what one takes as one's starting point for career studies, it is unarguable that what a number of writers were describing in the 1980s as a "mature" field has been prolific in its output since then. This emboldened us to take a different approach to laying out the present *Handbook:* We took as our starting point the assertion that what may have been mature then is even more so now, with no signs of senescence setting in yet. There are now a great many recognizable threads in the literature within the overarching field of career studies, so we set about the massive—and arguably hubristic—task of organizing them by first listing them.

In Chapter 3, where we examine the structure of the field in greater depth, we label this approach "taxonomic." We distinguish there between two approaches that have been taken to describing career studies, the other being what we term "topological." Taxonomic approaches are those that attempt to divide the field into subfields, while topological approaches distinguish between different themes in the literature by plotting them on a chart, the dimensions of which are derived from a particular theoretical perspective. As we shall see, no two taxonomies of the field of career studies that we have found have agreed with each other to any great extent: Each has its unique topics and leaves out others. This raises the obvious question, If there is so little consensus in the field about which topics belong "inside" it, what makes us think that we are any more correct than anyone else in the selection that we made for this volume? Indeed, to return to our theme above, do we have any business labeling such a disparate selection of themes a "field"?

There are, of course, no good answers to these questions. The career studies field remains, at least for now, what Whitley (1984) calls a "fragmented adhocracy." This kind of field of enquiry is

> characterised by a low degree of interdependency between researchers, . . . a relatively fragmented knowledge structure and the existence of much disagreement about the relative importance of different problems to be solved by the field. As a result, the problem-solving activity within the field takes place in a rather arbitrary and ad hoc manner, with limited attempts to integrate new solutions with the existing structure of knowledge. (Knudsen, 2003, p. 278)

It is not difficult to see how career studies could be described like this. For example, Moore, Gunz, and Hall (Chapter 2) paint a picture of a field with at least three strikingly different "tributaries" in the literature, which they label sociological, vocational, and developmental, each with quite distinct historical origins. Arthur et al. (1989b, chap. 1) similarly make it clear that careers have been approached from the perspective of pretty much any social science. Others have made the same point. If the field is being studied by many different people, from many different intellectual traditions, and still working within them, it is only to be expected that there should be little interdependency between approaches, yielding a fragmented knowledge structure and little consensus about what really matters.

This is why we want this *Handbook* to provide a focus and a reference point. We hope that it will help reduce the fragmentation of the field's knowledge structure and help those working in it to move toward a consensus about what really matters. Whether, as a result, greater interdependencies among research streams are created, only time will tell.

This characterization also speaks to our attempt to structure this book. Because there is little consensus about what the field "really" consists of and what matters most, nobody has any greater claim to be more authoritative on this point than anybody else. So although we believe that we have achieved reasonably good coverage of the field of career studies, we do so with humility, in no expectation that everyone will agree with us. We only hope that we have satisfied a reasonable proportion of readers with our choices.

To bring the number of themes down to something that would fit within one volume, we combined several from our list and deleted one or two others. Then we invited a leader (or leaders) in the study of each scholarly theme to write a chapter on it, asking them to do two things: first, summarize the state of scholarship on the theme and, second, give their view on what they believed should be happening, or was likely to happen, to research in that area in the future. In subsequent rounds of editing, we then asked most of these authors to include in their chapters cross-citations to other thematic chapters in the volume that were most closely linked with their own.

Those chapters constitute Parts I and II of the book. As a final step, we invited a further group of distinguished careers scholars from a variety of backgrounds to read the drafts of the earlier chapters and to write shorter essays in which they were to reflect on the connections between the various threads described in Parts I and II, suggest new directions for careers research and scholarship, and draw out the implications of the foregoing chapters for practice, both for individuals on their own personal journeys and for those responsible for managing the careers of others. Many of the essayists for what would become Part III of this volume met at IMD in Lausanne, Switzerland, in March 2006, to compare notes and learn from one another before revising their essays for publication.

CONTENT OVERVIEW

This volume, then, is organized in three parts. The first focuses on the origins of the field and its structure, the second on its content, and the third on ways of bringing its disparate threads together. We give a brief overview of each here and introduce them in greater depth at the beginning of each part or section.

Part I is relatively short. It addresses the historical origins (Celia Moore, Hugh Gunz, and Tim Hall) and current structure of the field (Maury Peiperl and Hugh Gunz), fleshing out many of the points made earlier in this introduction.

Part II is the "meat" of the enterprise. It addresses what we defined as the main currents in the study of career under three main section headings: (1) careers and the individual, (2) careers in context, and (3) careers and institutions.*

Section 1 examines careers and the individual: the impact of personality on career outcomes

---

*To some extent, our allocation of chapters among these three headings is arbitrary. For example, is what matters about social marginalization (Chapter 10) its effect on the individual, putting it in Section 1, or the social context that brings it about, putting it in Section 2? Are developmental processes (Chapter 15) important because of their individual focus (Section 1) or because they are at least in part socially determined (Section 2)? Are the institutions of outside hiring (Chapter 17) the institutions within which careers are made (Section 3) or institutions that facilitate careers and, therefore, part of their context (Section 2)? The answer to these questions, of course, is "both." So rather than get caught in an endless debate about the best home for each chapter, we made the judgment calls required of editors, aware as we did so that, often, we could have placed a given chapter elsewhere with almost equal justification.

(Timothy Judge and John Kammeyer-Mueller), occupational choice (Mark Savickas), career counseling (Jenny Kidd), the subjective career (Svetlana Khapova, Michael Arthur, and Celeste Wilderom), work and family life (Jeffrey Greenhaus and Sharon Foley), late career and retirement (Daniel Feldman), careers of the socially marginalized (Pushkala Prasad, Caroline D'Abate, and Anshuman Prasad), and customized careers (Monique Valcour, Lotte Bailyn, and Maria Alejandra Quijada).

But careers are not lived in isolation: Context matters every bit as much as content, and Section 2 addresses this. Wolfgang Mayrhofer, Michael Meyer, and Johannes Steyrer introduce the section by developing a framework for classifying context. Next, there are chapters on mentoring and developmental networks (Dawn Chandler and Kathy Kram), networks and identities (Herminia Ibarra and Prashant Deshpande), stage and process theories of career (Sherry Sullivan and Madeline Crocitto), living to work and working to live (David Guest and Jane Sturges), the institutions of outside hiring (Peter Cappelli and Monika Hamori), and the global career (Maury Peiperl and Karsten Jonsen).

In Section 3 of Part II, we focus on the social institutions within and between which (and, arguably, from which) careers are made. The chapters review career systems and the psychological contracts that bind people to organizations (Holly Slay and Susan Taylor), organizational demography and internal labor markets (Barbara Lawrence and Pamela Tolbert), the relationship between career patterns and organizational performance (Monica Higgins and James Dillon), careers and their role in building and changing institutions (Candace Jones and Mary Dunn), careers across cultures (David Thomas and Kerr Inkson), and boundaries in the study of career (Hugh Gunz, Maury Peiperl, and Daniel Tzabbar).

Part III draws the volume together. It comprises nine essays by Silvia Bagdadli, Yoav Vardi and Sharon Kim, Maria Kraimer and Scott Seibert, Richard Boyatzis, Brooklyn Derr and Jon Briscoe, Philip Mirvis, Wayne Cascio, Audrey Collin, and Nigel Nicholson, who, as explained above, were invited to reflect on the material in Parts I and II. They shared their essays with one another, many coming together at the memorable meeting already noted above.

Their revised essays constitute the conclusion to the *Handbook,* providing a set of personal views of the field based not only on how it is treated in Parts I and II but also on where they themselves believe it has been and, in particular, where it should be going.

Finally, we invited the distinguished careers scholar Edgar Schein, from whose work so much has descended, to contribute a Foreword. But what emerged was so much more than a Foreword that we suggested he split it into a Foreword and an Afterword, the latter a commentary on his view of the state of the field in the light of his reading of the *Handbook.* It is with that Afterword that the volume closes.

NOTES

1. Michael Arthur, personal communication.
2. The figures are approximate, since probable errors in double-counting and misclassification make greater precision impossible.

REFERENCES

Arthur, M. B., Hall, D. T., & Lawrence, B. S. (1989a). Generating new directions in career theory: The case for a transdisciplinary approach. In M. B. Arthur, D. T. Hall, & B. S. Lawrence (Eds.), *Handbook of career theory* (pp. 7–25). Cambridge, UK: Cambridge University Press.

Arthur, M. B., Hall, D. T., & Lawrence, B. S. (Eds.). (1989b). *Handbook of career theory.* Cambridge, UK: Cambridge University Press.

Barley, S. R. (1989). Careers, identities, and institutions: The legacy of the Chicago School of Sociology. In M. B. Arthur, D. T. Hall, & B. S. Lawrence (Eds.), *Handbook of career theory* (pp. 41–65). Cambridge, UK: Cambridge University Press.

Becker, H. S. (2003). *The Chicago School, so-called.* Retrieved December 17, 2003, from http://home.earthlink.net/~hsbecker/chicago.html.

Bray, D. W., Campbell, R. J., & Grant, D. L. (1974). *Formative years in business: A long-term AT&T study of managerial lives.* New York: Wiley.

Dyer, L. (Ed.). (1976). *Careers in organizations: Individual planning and organizational development.* Ithaca: New York School of Industrial Relations, Cornell University.

Freidson, E. (1986). *Professional powers: A study in the institutionalization of formal knowledge.* Chicago: University of Chicago Press.

Hall, D. T. (1976). *Careers in organizations.* Santa Monica, CA: Goodyear.

Hughes, E. C. (1937). Institutional office and the person. *American Journal of Sociology, 43,* 404–413.

Knudsen, C. (2003). *Pluralism, scientific progress and the structure of organization studies.* Oxford: Oxford University Press.

Oxford English dictionary (2nd ed.). (1989). Oxford: Oxford University Press.

Schein, E. H. (1978). *Career dynamics: Matching individual and organizational needs.* Reading, MA: Addison-Wesley.

Van Maanen, J. (1977a). Introduction: The promise of career studies. In J. Van Maanen (Ed.), *Organizational careers: Some new perspectives* (pp. 1–12). London: Wiley.

Van Maanen, J. (Ed.). (1977b). *Organizational careers: Some new perspectives.* London: Wiley.

Whitley, R. D. (1984). The development of management studies as a fragmented adhocracy. *Social Science Information (Information sur les Sciences Sociales), 23*(4–5), 775–818.

Wilensky, H. L. (1960). Work, careers, and social integration. *International Social Science Journal, 12*(4), 543–560.

Wilensky, H. L. (1964). The professionalization of everyone? *American Journal of Sociology, 70*(2), 137–158.

Zerubavel, E. (1995). The rigid, the fuzzy, and the flexible: Notes on the mental sculpting of academic identity. *Social Research, 62*(4), 1093–1106.

PART I

THE HISTORICAL ORIGINS AND CURRENT STRUCTURE OF THE CAREERS FIELD

I n Part I we look at the background to, and structure of, the field of career studies.

The origins of career studies, as we noted in Chapter 1, are often traced to the mid-1970s. In Chapter 2, Moore, Gunz, and Hall search considerably further back than this. The authors identify three main "tributaries" in the literature, which they label sociological, vocational, and developmental. They trace the *sociological* tributary to the work of, among others, Durkheim, Weber, the Chicago school (Hughes, Goffman, Becker, and others), and Schein. The origins of the *vocational* tributary can be seen in the writings of Plato and Cicero, but it was the work of 19th century psychologists such as Galton, Cattell, and Spearman that began to provide a scientific basis to vocational psychology. In a parallel development, Parsons in essence defined the field of vocational choice, and Holland and others provided theoretical and practical guidance to the field. The *developmental* perspective can be traced back at least to Freud and Jung, and the chapter shows how writers such as Maslow, Erikson, Alderfer, Vaillant, Levinson, and Schein built on these early ideas. The chapter concludes by identifying five "tensions" in the history of the field: dialectic metathemes that pervade the study of career. They are (1) individual agency versus social determinism

in the shaping of career, (2) career as process versus career as achieving "fit," (3) fit for the benefit of the individual versus fit for the benefit of the collectivity, (4) career as a social phenomenon versus career as an individual life story, and (5) career scholarship as theoretical prediction versus career scholarship that provides help for individuals living their careers.

Chapter 3 reviews the structure of the field of career studies. Most commentators on career scholarship have remarked on the lack of cohesion of the field; Peiperl and Gunz review a number of attempts that have been made to identify its structure. They organize these contributions under two main headings, which they call topological and taxonomic. Topological approaches identify an underlying dimensionality to the field and then place the work of career scholars on the map defined by these dimensions. Taxonomic approaches, in contrast, organize subfields and sub-subfields of career scholarship under headings organized hierarchically. Within each of these two main headings, there has been little overlap in the classifications that different writers have produced. The chapter concludes by explaining the logic behind the authors' own taxonomy of the field, which underpins the structure of the present volume.

2

TRACING THE HISTORICAL ROOTS OF CAREER THEORY IN MANAGEMENT AND ORGANIZATION STUDIES

CELIA MOORE

HUGH GUNZ

DOUGLAS T. HALL

Contemporary career theory, from within organization studies and management, is commonly traced back to the late 1970s (Arthur, Hall, & Lawrence, 1989b). These years saw not only the publication of three seminal books on career (Hall, 1976; Schein, 1978; Van Maanen, 1977) but also an abundance of discussion and collaboration among organizational scholars. A series of informal seminars and meetings—one a "Mobile Career Seminar" (in which the third author participated) organized and led by Donald E. Super in the early 1970s, others held by academics in the Boston area[1]—as well as some informal exploratory sessions at Academy of Management meetings later led to the formation of an interest group at the Academy in the late 1970s. The group became a full-fledged division in the early 1980s. However, this inaugural phase says very little about the long intellectual history that informs that seminal 1970s work. In addition, although there have been a number of review pieces on the state of career theory in the past 25 years (Arthur, Hall, & Lawrence, 1989a; Savickas, 2000; Schein, 1989;

Sonnenfeld & Kotter, 1982) as well as histories of its various strains (Betz, Fitzgerald, & Hill, 1989; Dalton, 1989; Hall, 2004; Maranda & Comeau, 2000; Super, 1983), career theory, like most organizational scholarship, tends toward ahistoricism (Weiss, 1990). This is an exaggeration, of course, but the core of the criticism remains true. People have been thinking and theorizing about the purpose of work in their lives since long before the inauguration of the informal group organized by Donald Super in the 1970s.

With constant impatience to be moving on to the next, new, "cutting-edge" theory, it can become easy not only to forget (or ignore) the past but also to reinvent the wheel. Certainly, it is true that the contemporary careers field within organization studies did find its feet as a result of that group of researchers collectively defining the field 30 years ago.[2] However, accepting this birth date as specific rather than as a serendipitous catalyst that allowed the careers field to find a home within managerial theory makes likely the rediscovery and false authorship attribution of old ideas. Though the specific use of the term *career* within the sociological and psychological literatures does seem to have a short history— the word itself did not commonly appear in reference to one's professional life or life course until the early 20th century (*Oxford English Dictionary [OED]*, 1933)—theorists have been investigating the hows and whys of individuals' occupations and life courses for centuries.

This chapter takes an explicitly long-range, historical view of the roots of organizational career theory and attempts to trace back its early influences until that catalytic period of the late 1970s. First, it endeavors to "rediscover" the influences—direct and indirect—of early theorists on the nascent careers literature within the three main tributaries of career theory, which we will identify shortly. Second, it attempts to clarify how those influences speak to the early work in the careers field. At the conclusion of the chapter, we will outline a series of intellectual tensions within the history of career theory highlighted by this long-range overview of the field and comment on how these early works, both within the careers field and prior to its existence, may continue to provide inspiration to contemporary career theorists.

THE TRIBUTARIES OF CAREER THEORY

The relative newness of careers as an identified area of study and the inherently interdisciplinary nature of the field has meant that there is rarely consensus about the main intellectual tributaries that feed into career theory's core writings. That so many fields have the potential to inform career theory works against a coherent history of the area, and dissatisfaction with the current siloed nature of the careers field has been lamented in earlier commentaries (Arthur et al., 1989a; Schein, 1989).

Overviews of the field tend to fall into one of two general trends regarding the main influences on career theory. The first trend is to stick to the disciplines that most directly inform the area: sociology and psychology. Barley writes that a comprehensive history of career theory would require an intellectual history of both sociology and psychology (Barley, 1989), calling both disciplines important branches in career theory's "genealogical tree" (Barley, 1989, p. 60). In a similar vein, an early historic overview of the field identified four main, and predominantly siloed, areas of study within the careers literature: (1) a sociological perspective, focused on the social and class determinants of career; (2) an individual differences perspective, focused on predicting how static dispositional differences influence career choice and success; (3) a developmental perspective, focused on a dynamic understanding of career stages; and (4) a life cycle perspective, focused on the individual psychology behind a dynamic vision of career over the life course (Sonnenfeld & Kotter, 1982). The second trend takes a more expansive view of the historic threads of career theory. An example is a later overview of the field (Arthur et al., 1989a), which invited career theorists to attend to the transdisciplinary influences of anthropology, economics, political science, and history on career studies, as well as the more traditional influences of psychology and sociology.

In an effort to create a manageable scope for this chapter, we have decided to take a longer-range view than the main overviews of the field thus far but to retain the more narrow focus on the psychological and sociological roots of career theory's genealogical tree. Tributaries from philosophy, history, anthropology, and literature are noted as they relate to these psychological and sociological roots, though they deserve a more comprehensive treatment elsewhere. When one looks back on the early theory from these disciplines, which helped inform the genesis of the careers field of study, what does one find? How ought the main areas of influence be categorized, and how can their intellectual histories be traced? Recognizing that all boundaries are by necessity somewhat arbitrary, the chapter is divided into three sections, which, for the most part, conform to the general categories developed in Sonnenfeld and Kotter's (1982) review. A fourth, concluding section develops a series of tensions that we have identified as themes across the disciplinary histories and comments on how they remind current career theory of where it has been and might go.

The first section focuses on career theory from a sociological perspective, discussing the theoretical roots that attend to the structural influences over one's working life and the interplay between individuals and institutions; ethnographic and anthropological influences are also relevant here. The second section focuses on career theory from a vocational perspective and details the early theory around "matching men [*sic*] with jobs"; this section taps into the individual differences tradition in psychology and also dovetails with early educational history in the United States and around the period of the World Wars. The third section focuses on career theory from a developmental perspective and encompasses a wide range of psychological perspectives on human adaptation to work over the life course.

Though both the second and the third sections are predominantly psychological in perspective, early vocational theory tends to have a more static view of human nature, with a view to predicting how well individuals will perform in different occupations or jobs, while developmental career theory maintains an intentionally dynamic view of human nature, with a view to understanding how careers and individuals change and adapt over the life course. Finally, while realizing that true transdisciplinary work remains an important goal for the careers field, we believe that it is justified here to leave the three streams separate, as they each derive from

different intellectual traditions; yet to help, in future, mitigate against the siloed present, we close the chapter with a commentary about how a long-range view across disciplines can reinvigorate career theory in general and transdisciplinary work in particular.

It is important to note that taking a long-range, historic view of career theory necessitates understanding a point that is often missed while glossing over the potential history of this field: The term *career*—as "a course of professional life or employment, which affords opportunity for progress or advancement in the world" (*OED*, 1933)—is relatively recent (Chapter 1). There is evidence that it was beginning to be used in this sense in the 19th century, in Britain at least, but it is likely that this usage did not become common until the 20th century. The original meaning of *career*—a course on which a race is run or the speed or trajectory of the course of the race—was the only definition discussed in Samuel Johnson's early dictionary of the English language (1755/1979). The *OED* (1989) cites a number of 19th-century British sources that pick up a sense of a passage through a working life, while the first major American dictionary (Hunter et al., 1895) echoes Johnson's definitions and only briefly adds "a course or line of life" as a "figurative" definition of *career*.

It is not until the first *OED* (1933) that we begin to see the modern development of *career* to mean one's professional life course. Therefore, understanding the importance of earlier terms used to describe one's professional or occupational choices or path, including having a "calling" or a "vocation" as well as work on moral or religious education on the proper course one ought to take in life, is critical to appreciating the roots of career theory. In tracing back the roots of career theory, it is important to remember that to have contemporary relevance, the use of terms similar to those in common usage is not required (see Giddens, 1971, p. viii).

CAREER THEORY FROM A SOCIOLOGICAL PERSPECTIVE

The sociological perspective on careers is characterized by theory and research that focus on broader levels of analysis: It is concerned with the social structures, cultural norms, and institutions that define, direct, and constrain people's actions at the societal level as well as how those structural forces shape the cultural norms around how individuals are employed and find their course through life and determine and shape individuals' behavior as they navigate through institutions, professions, and occupations. For example, career theories of occupational and professional boundary definition, mobility, status assignment, and constraints on occupational choice all have roots in early sociology. A number of early sociological theorists—most important, Émile Durkheim (1858–1917) and Max Weber (1864–1920) in particular—both directly or indirectly contributed to the early work in the careers field, most notably that of Everett Hughes (1928–1956/1958) and also the work of Erving Goffman (especially Goffman, 1959), Howard Becker (1952; Becker, Geer, Strauss, & Hughes, 1961), and Edgar Schein (1971, 1978), among others.

Durkheim

A number of Durkheim's theories are directly relevant to the study of careers, though the "explicit recognition that career could be fruitfully studied as a formal concept" was not directly made in sociology until Hughes' work almost half a century later (Barley, 1989, p. 44). Indeed, it might seem odd to return to Durkheim as an early inspiration for career theorists, especially since his work never explicitly mentions careers nor has a focus on the individual's navigation through institutions (he is much more a sociologist of the community than of the individual). Instead, Durkheim's contribution to the careers literature focuses on the nature of the relationship between the individual and societal structure, the importance of the division of labor to collective and individual identity, and the importance of occupational identity and association to the organization and integration of society.

Durkheim most directly addressed concerns related to individuals' working lives in *The Division of Labour in Society* (1893/1964), the thesis of which is that individuals tend toward increasing functional specialization as society

becomes increasingly industrialized, and these shifts change the foundation of social solidarity. Where social solidarity used to be rooted in individuals sharing broad and similar functions within a community, in an industrial age, it instead needs to be maintained through individuals' dependence on one another within a highly organized division of labor. This division of labor then strongly determines cultural norms and values as well as individuals' occupational lives and identities.

This preoccupation with the division of labor in industrial society echoed similar preoccupations in the work of both Karl Marx (1834–1894/2000) and Adam Smith (1776/1994) but with a rather different focus from those theorists' more economic frame (Giddens, 1971). Durkheim did not moralize that the effect on workers of the division of labor under capitalism was necessarily degrading or implied class conflict, as Marx did, and his understanding went far beyond applauding its economic efficiency, as Adam Smith had (though Smith was certainly more ambivalent about the societal effects of capitalism than one would assume given his image in contemporary memory).

Durkheim's work on the division of labor informs career theory because his ideas on the subject translate well from the societal to the organizational level. He does focus on the organizational level as well as the societal level (though he terms it the "corporative" rather than the organizational level) and sees it as an important secondary source of social cohesion, which can mediate between the societal level and the individual level. His work reminds organizational theorists to pay attention to how career boundaries and job scope within organizations play an important part in determining the cohesiveness of organizational groups and in developing organizational norms.

Occupational groups play an important role in Durkheim's work; he actually intended to write a book on the topic of occupational associations, though we are left with only the 30 pages of the Preface of *The Division of Labour in Society* (Durkheim, 1893/1964) to explain his thinking on the matter. After industrialization, occupational groups gained in importance not only for their potential economic services but also for their capacity for moral influence: "What we see in the occupational group is a moral power capable of containing individual egos, of maintaining a spirited sentiment of common solidarity" (Durkheim, 1893/1964, p. 14). Durkheim even writes that "the corporation [which can represent occupational groups] has been, in a sense, the heir of the family" (1893/1964, p. 17), as a source of collective morality and group identity and as protection against the alienating aspects of postindustrial life. Unfortunately, at the time of his writing, there had been only "fragmentary and incomplete" attempts to build strong occupational associations (1893/1964, p. 5). However, as professional lives have overtaken so many other sources of individual identity in the last century, his work on occupational groups can be both directly and indirectly reflected in later careers literature on professional identity, occupational attachment, and professional ethics.

A final threat of industrialization noted by Durkheim is excessive specialization, in particular when accompanied by social inequality, because it undermines social cohesion (Durkheim, 1893/1964, p. 301). Division of labor can only encourage social integration when specialization is not accompanied by an unjust hierarchical status, which creates gulfs in individual advantage. This speaks more broadly to the literature on career development and growth by cautioning that overly predetermined and/or limited career paths for individuals within society, or even within organizations, have negative consequences for the collective. By requiring people to narrow the scope of their everyday professional activities to atomistic proportions, individuals begin to suffer from *anomie* (or alienation from one's social collective), which then undermines the stability of those collective wholes.

Durkheim's unacknowledged influence can be seen throughout many of the major strains of career theory. His understanding of how the division of labor shapes cultural norms and individual lives speaks to the literature on the meaning of work and careers to individuals. His recognition of the importance of occupational groups to collective morality speaks to the literature on occupational identity and attachment. By addressing the importance of the relationship between one's professional life and one's place in the community, Durkheim has the capacity to influence the careers literature on boundaries, and by attending to the negative consequences of overspecialization within occupations, Durkheim has the capacity to influence the literature on job scope and career development.

For example, Durkheim's focus on how macro-level structures direct and constrain individual behavior has directly and indirectly influenced the work of both Everett Hughes (1928–1956/1958) and Edgar Schein (1978), as they struggle with the inherent tension that arises between individual agency and social control. Durkheim's influence can be seen throughout their work: in thinking about how occupational status is assigned and differently constrained for different individuals, the relationship between institutions and the individuals navigating them, and how social structures help determine individuals' decisions about their working lives.

Weber

Max Weber, though also rarely mentioned directly in the careers literature, provides what continues to be an enduring portrait of the reasons for, value of, and dangers inherent in bureaucratic organizing (Weber, 1920/1947, 1904–1905/1958a, 1922/1958b). He was also the first to describe the characteristics and stages of the administrative or bureaucratic career, newly emerging within early industrialized commerce and the movement in the 19th century toward a public service. Along with Durkheim, Weber was also concerned with a central tension within society between the need for individual freedom and the need for social control, and their theorizing is remarkably consonant, though they maintain different main foci. Whereas Durkheim was concerned with how to maximize the individual freedoms made possible by industrialization, while simultaneously maintaining social integration and social order, Weber was more concerned with the value of individual freedom and humanity, which could be silenced within the efficient but depersonalized "iron cage" of bureaucratic organization (Tiryakian, 1981). Of course, Durkheim was also interested in the positive aspects of freedom, and Weber in the positive aspects of bureaucracy, but their biases were toward slightly different sides of the individual freedom/social order tension.

There are three main ideas in Weber's work with relevance to early career theory. First are his views on bureaucracy and routinization, which include ideas on the commensurate benefits of these processes to organizations in terms of efficiency and reliability and the simultaneous danger of these processes to individual creativity (Weber, 1922/1958b). Charismatic authority is presented as one natural phenomenon that can provide a partial counterbalance to the dangers of bureaucracy's routinization. The second idea is his understanding of how the joint forces of the Protestant ethic and the spirit of capitalism require this process of bureaucratization (Weber, 1904–1905/1958a). Third are his ideas about class and status, which contribute to understanding how the process of assigning individuals to places within hierarchies helps form and support our social systems (Weber, 1922/1958c).

As is well-known, Weber defined a number of characteristics of modern bureaucracy, including (1) fixed and continuous offices covering different jurisdictions, which are (2) governed by rules and/or laws and operating within an (3) organizational hierarchy, managed by officials with (4) fixed sets of duties and (5) predetermined qualifications for office, including (6) specific training for that office (1922/1958b, pp. 196–244). However, contrary to the popular understanding of Weber, which can confuse his theorizing about bureaucracy with a fondness for it, Weber was in fact profoundly ambivalent about the phenomenon and the rationalization of processes that it requires. It has been claimed that Talcott Parsons tempered this ambivalence in his early translations of Weber's work (Weber, 1920/1947), which stressed the positive aspects of Weberian descriptions of bureaucracy, whereas later translations of Weber's work by Hans Gerth and C. Wright Mills (Weber, 1922/1958b) highlighted this ambivalence (DiPadova, 1996).

Weber's concern about bureaucratic rationalization conjures Durkheim's similar concerns about occupational overspecialization:

Its anonymity compels modern man to become a specialized expert, a "professional" man qualified

for the accomplishment of a special career within pre-scheduled channels . . . Weber "deplored" this type of man as a petty routine creature, lacking in heroism, human spontaneity, and inventiveness. (Gerth & Mills, 1958, p. 50)

This vision describes a very particular type of career, in which office holders are ideally devoid of any personalizing qualities and career becomes a reward of security based on acceptance of the bureaucratic process and seniority but which has the detrimental outcome of decreasing opportunities for the ambitious and rewarding the administrative expert (see Weber, 1922/1958b). The outcome of this new professional ideal is the victory of the "specialist" over the "cultivated man," once the historical ideal of an educated person (see Weber, 1922/1958b, pp. 242–243).

Weber's discussion of the effect and efficiency of bureaucratization in the modern state and corporation speaks to the literature on career paths, job scope, occupational and organizational socialization, and occupational and organizational identification. However, much more interesting and potentially influential to career theory are his thoughts on the tension between the gains to efficiency, stability, and procedural fairness provided by bureaucracy and the dangers to individual freedom and growth extended by the same process. This tension translates into career theory as the relationship between an individual's need for growth and development and the organization's need for stability, reliability, and continuity (see Hackman & Oldham, 1980).

For Weber, the establishment of Calvinism provided a catalyst and turning point far beyond its original intentions. Before the Calvinist turn, it was not possible to have a "career" as we currently understand it, not only because economic systems at the time were not designed for any kind of individual occupational choice or mobility but also because religious systems didn't have room for individual volition in choosing a life course. Calvinism, in its prudish obsession with acting as if one were among the heavenly elect, paved the way for capitalism, because the hard work and self-sacrifice that resulted from acting *as if* one were already "chosen" allowed individuals to accrue capital that had no purpose other than to be reinvested into new business ventures. The early development of the capitalistic requirements of mobile capital and voluntary labor then made the contemporary idea of careers possible: Individuals were no longer tied to the occupation they were born into and began to be employed by organizations that could offer career paths and advancement at the expense of less individual freedom and control. Think of the difference between one's professional life within an artisanal economic structure and a corporative one. The *Protestant Ethic and the Spirit of Capitalism,* therefore, challenges career theorists to look systemically at career and occupational motivation and choice, as well as career mobility and advancement issues (Weber, 1904–1905/1958a).

Finally, Weber has been credited with developing one of the earliest analyses of social hierarchy that could handle the nuances between status based on economic power and status based on other forms of social power by separating out "class" hierarchy, or the classification of individuals based on economic advantage, from "status" hierarchy, or the classification of individuals based on honor or occupation (Weber, 1958c, pp. 180–195). Separating the understanding of status and class allows one to conceptualize occupational attachment from both economic and prestige perspectives. Group identity can serve both to separate one group from another (economically or via prestige) and to help a group cohere internally (through commonalities in economic advantage or prestige). This understanding of the distinction between class and status helps inform career theory on occupational or career identity formation and attachment, echoed in Everett Hughes' understanding of the creation of "professions" (Hughes, 1928–1956/1958).

Hughes

Hughes occupies a unique space in the history of career theory. He is often designated as one of the founders of the field and was writing about the sociology of occupations as early as 1928 (Hughes, 1928). Methodologically, Hughes transformed the study of individuals within organizations. His general theoretical stance is not well defined or posited directly in his work, and students of his work disagree about whether or not he had a general theory (Chapoulie, 1996; Helmes-Hayes, 1998). Helmes-Hayes characterizes Hughes' work as interpretive institutional ecology (1998, p. 633), a description that is useful in that it can help make sense of how sociologists of work became divided between those who studied, from a more macro perspective, situations and generalized cases within contexts, and those who predominantly studied, from a more micro perspective, the movement of and interaction between individuals, secondarily within contexts.

Using the institution as the central level of analysis allowed Hughes to continue to focus (in a Durkheimian sense) on the structural forces that constrain and shape human behavior, while remaining attuned to how individuals continually create the meaning and norms within those institutions. For Hughes, institutions serve both a regulatory and a moral function for individuals, providing a source of collective identity and, therefore, mitigating against the ever-present potential for anomie in postindustrial society, as well as serving a primary function for society, as an efficient way to organize resources in order to get things done.

Hughes takes on directly the division of labor and its importance to social relationships (Hughes, 1928–1956/1958, chap. 2). For example, he writes that occupational mobility "implies a removal from the base of one's morals," which has the danger of undermining social stability (Hughes, 1928–1956/1958, pp. 30–31). Like Durkheim, he was interested in the division of labor as a phenomenon with implications beyond the simple economic ones: "Division of labor is more than a technical phenomenon; there are infinite social-psychological nuances in it" (Hughes, 1928–1956/1958, p. 73). Seeing the division of labor as a social phenomenon allowed Hughes to frame work as a crux between the individual and society, pointing out that the division of labor "implies interaction" and that "no line of work can be fully understood outside the social matrix in which it occurs or the social system of which it is part" (1928–1956/1958, p. 75).

Weber also gets scant mention in Hughes's major papers, but his influence is evident throughout them. For example, the trend toward . . . the bureaucratizing of careers does not do away with the struggle of the individual to find a place and an identity in the world of work or with the collective efforts of occupations to exert control over the terms of their work with and for others. (Hughes, 1928–1956/1958, p. 8)

Hughes was similarly concerned with capitalism's potential for treating labor in a dehumanized way, reaffirming Weber's pessimism about the influence of administrative systems on the individual. He wrote that in mobilizing people and making work the central fact of one's life, capitalism "erase[s] the person's past so that he may be completely mobilized for carrying out his mission" (Hughes, 1928–1956/1958, p. 32).

In "Institutional Office and the Person," first published in 1937 and one of his most famous essays, Hughes writes about the characteristics of formally held offices in much the same way that Weber writes about the characteristics of bureaucracy, including how offices define and prescribe one's role and, in so doing, determine and confer status on an individual. He also echoes Weber's understanding of status assignments by pointing out how offices can be communicated through a ritual, such as taking a vow (like the Hippocratic oath for doctors), that separates and defines office-holders from others (1928–1956/1958, chap. 4). Hughes, too, was interested in how professions of different statuses are defined and circumscribed, repeating concerns with "the impermeability of professions to outside view and intervention" (Hughes, 1928–1956/1958, p. 86). This interest in professional or occupational boundaries created a culture at the University of Chicago, in which Hughes's students conducted some of the most important ethnographic studies of professions and occupations, including *Boys in White,* a classic study of the indoctrination of medical students into the profession of medicine (Becker et al., 1961), as well as studies of the careers of the taxi-hall dancer (Cressy, 1932), professional thieves (Sutherland, 1937), and the tubercular patient (Roth, 1963).

Ethnographic Work on Careers

Strains of this concern for the effect of bureaucratization on individuals can be seen directly in

some of the dystopias described in sociological investigations of the "modern corporation," such as *White Collar* by C. Wright Mills (1951), who also translated *From Max Weber* and focused a large section therein on bureaucracy. Weber's concern about bureaucratization was evident in Mills' concern that the hegemony of large organizations as employers was quickly eroding the possibility of autonomous and self-fulfilling work in the 20th century (Rytina, 2001). Weber's concern with the alienating effects of bureaucracy also foreshadows the corporate environment detailed in William Whyte's *Organization Man* (1956) and recalls Erving Goffman's (1959) work on the practice of impression management and the discrepancy between the individual and the face he presents to the outside world as a requirement of his role(s). This is just a small sample of the many theorists in whose writings one can trace the imprint of the theories of Durkheim and Weber.

Structure Versus Class and Status

There are two main trends in early career theory that grew from the sociological perspective. The first of these tended to focus on the social structural determinants of occupational choice and attainment, and a great deal of empirical work studied the effects of class background and parental occupational attainment on the outcomes for individuals. Classic work in this area includes the industrial sociology of Delbert Miller and William Form (1951) and Peter Blau and Otis Duncan (1967). The second trend draws more heavily on the ethnographic work of the Chicago school of sociologists; methodologically, it draws on the same qualitative techniques used to develop earlier work such as *White Collar* and *Organization Man* rather than depending on the heavily quantitative and survey-based techniques of industrial sociologists such as Miller and Form.

Edgar Schein is the most obvious representative of this second sociological trend. His work on career anchors[3] was developed organically through a series of interviews with executives and drew attention to the nature of the subjective career (Schein, 1978), as opposed to the work of sociological theorists following the first trend, who emphasize objective measures, such as occupational attainment, as dependent variables (Sonnenfeld & Kotter, 1982, p. 23). It would be fruitful for current career theory to return to the undercredited influences of Durkheim and Weber for renewed inspiration on topics ranging from professional status to occupational mobility, to the balance between individual agency and social control, and the nature of subjective (vs. objective) careers.

The vocational perspective, to which we turn next, developed in virtual isolation from the sociological threads we have been tracing. Indeed, Schein notes,

> What is most amazing to me is that when I got into the field in the late 50's there was almost zero overlap between the psychologists (Strong, Super, Osipow, Holland) and the sociologists (Hughes, Becker, Goffman, White) . . . Hughes and the sociologists were working on careers as they are lived and had literally no overlap with Super, Osipow, and others who were completely focused on the Strong Interest Inventory and trying to predict, like good psychologists, who would be suitable for what kind of career and, based on psychometric and interview data who would succeed (usually measured narrowly by income). . . . Not a single reference in either group to the other group. This state of affairs led to my paper, "The Individual, the Organization and the Career," which I believe broke the ice and started some thinking about psychological contracts and how organizations (work) and individuals each have to take the other into account. (E. H. Schein, personal communication, January 13, 17, 2005)

We now turn to the genesis of this perspective.

CAREER THEORY FROM A VOCATIONAL PERSPECTIVE

The Early Philosophers

One of the longest histories in career theory belongs to the vocational perspective (an excellent overview of which is provided by Brewer, 1942). However, how one ought to usefully, and often most morally or virtuously, employ one's time in life has been the subject of ongoing and open discussion since Plato. Plato's *Republic,* in

many ways, can be read as an exposition on what positions or occupations in life are appropriate for different individuals within a nation. Book 1 of Cicero's *On Duties,* an important work of moral education from the 1st century BCE, is significantly about the best way in which individuals should find their way through life. He writes, "We must decide what manner of men we wish to be and what calling in life we would follow; and this is the most difficult problem in the world" (Book I, Section 32). Many centuries later, the idea that finding a vocation was a component of one's moral education continued with John Locke, who wrote in *Some Thoughts Concerning Education* (1695/1989) that "children should well study their Natures and Aptitudes, and see, by often Trials, what Turn they easily take, and what becomes them; observe what their native Stock is, how it may be improved, and what it is fit for" (Section 66).

Often these early vocationally slanted writings took a kindly but prescriptive and paternalistic tone: Cicero wrote *On Duties* as a letter to his son, Marcus; Shakespeare, writing as Polonius to his son, Laertes, counsels "to thine own self be true" (*Hamlet,* Act I, Scene 3). These writings may have stressed the moral aspect in determining one's life course for religious or philosophical reasons; the paternalistic overtones may have been motivated because individuals' actual occupational choices at the time they were written were so limited. In mid-19th century England, for example, half of all men continued in exactly the same occupation as their fathers (Miles, 1999, p. 68). In many ways, the degree to which the sociological strain of career theory has been driven by great theorists such as Durkheim and Weber is matched by the degree to which the vocational strain of career theory has been driven by historical forces.

Industrialization and the Search for Predictors of Fit

Class and occupational mobility increased dramatically over the 19th century in Europe. With it, industrialization undermined the traditional artisan and guild-based organization of labor, and migration to cities and across the Atlantic made the placement of immigrants in productive positions in society more urgent

(Herr, 2001). This led Durkheim and Weber to theorize about the metatheoretical implications of this sea change for society. It also led to two more practical imperatives: how to most effectively place this newly mobile and unemployed labor into productive positions and how to help these new immigrants and displaced workers find gainful employment. For the most part, psychologists worked on the first problem, trying to develop effective ways for organizations to place individuals productively into positions, and civic reformers worked on the second, working with individuals to help them find their way in the world.

Psychologists approached the challenge of finding productive positions for this newly relocated and unemployed labor from a scientific perspective. Their methods focused on testing individuals to rank them according to ability or other relevant individual difference characteristics; these tests could then be used to place individuals in occupations that would prove to be the most productive for society. Alternatively, civic reformers grew out of the social welfare movements that prospered after the social disruption of early industrialization; they were more concerned with the interests and wishes of individuals, working with them to determine what type of career choices would offer them the best fit. Though both strains were concerned with "fitting" men—and it was basically men—to jobs, the psychologists tended to think of individuals in aggregate, taking the perspective of what was best for the organization, while the civic reformers tended to focus on the individuals themselves and take the perspective of what occupations might be most fulfilling for them.

This idea that there existed an occupation that would match or fit any individual man implies a static understanding of human nature: Once a correct choice was discovered, whether by expert testing (advocated by those on the scientific side of the equation) or journeys of self-awareness (advocated by those on the social welfare side of the equation), the correct shaped peg would have found a similarly shaped hole. The "pegs-in-holes" metaphor can be traced back to a moral philosophy lecture delivered by Reverend Sydney Smith between 1804 and 1806 at the Royal Institution in London, in which he claimed,

It is a prodigious point gained if any man can find out where his powers lie, and what are his deficiencies,—if he can contrive to ascertain what Nature intended him for: and such are the changes and chances of the world, and so difficult is it to ascertain our own understandings, or those of others, that most things are done by persons who could have done something else better. If you choose to represent the various parts in life by holes upon a table, of different shapes,—some circular, some triangular, some square, some oblong,—and the persons acting these parts by bits of wood of similar shapes, we shall generally find that the triangular person has got into the square hole, the oblong into the triangular, and a square person has squeezed himself into the round hole. The officer and the office, the doer and the thing done, seldom fit so exactly, that we can say they were almost made for each other. (Smith, 1850, pp. 109–110)

However, the two ways through which the peg could find the appropriately shaped hole developed for some time in parallel rather than in unison.

Psychologists and Individual Differences

Psychology as a scientific discipline was in its nascent stages in the 19th century. Psychologists such as Francis Galton (1822–1911), James McKeen Cattell (1860–1944), and Charles Spearman (1863–1945) were optimistic about the field's ability to empirically measure and quantify individual abilities and potential, avidly devising tests to determine the nature and extent of individual differences and using those differences to predict various outcomes. These early proponents of intelligence testing and of the notion that there is a measurable "general intelligence"—or g—that differentiates individuals paved the way for a number of other psychologists to develop their own vocationally relevant tests, resulting in a long list of tests that were either developed specifically for or became important to vocational guidance (for a detailed history of vocational tests, see Betz et al., 1989).

Historians have noted that the individual differences tradition in psychology intertwine with and have an influence on early vocational guidance (Dawis, 1992); this connection has contributed a focus on the prediction made possible by quantitative measures involving multiple dimensions of a person. The side of vocational guidance that focused on selection and prediction mainly served organizational needs: How could one determine where an individual would be placed most advantageously with respect to the organization? Of the quantitative measures involved in making these decisions, three types were most important to vocational theory: ability or intelligence testing, aptitude or technical competence testing, and interest or personality testing.

Galton in England and Cattell in North America were the provenance of "ability," or IQ, tests. The early tests, devised around the turn of the 20th century, tested what could appear to be a set of arbitrary abilities, from an individual's judgment of 10 seconds of time to an individual's ability to correctly bisect a 50-cm line (Cattell, 1890). Alfred Binet and Theophile Simon advanced intelligence testing by improving on earlier tests and understanding that a wider range of testing improved their ability to predict outcomes (Binet & Simon, 1961). Historically, the advances in these types of tests became useful as military enlistment in World War I ballooned, so that within a very tight timeline the U.S. military needed to figure out how to most effectively place hundreds of thousands of personnel (Brewer, 1942).

The Committee on Classification of Personnel in the U.S. Army, chaired by E. L. Thorndike, embarked on one of the largest applications of intelligence and aptitude testing ever conducted, delivering intelligence tests to 1.7 million men and critically influencing the deployment of those military personnel (Army Psychologists, 1921/1961; Bingham, 1919). Belief in the importance of IQ and aptitude testing continued after the war, and Thorndike, Charles Edward Spearman,[4] and Lewis Terman, in particular, studied gifted children at Stanford for decades (Terman, 1925/1961). However, even though validity generalization studies have demonstrated a connection between intelligence and on-the-job performance (Gottfredson, 1986; Hunter, 1986), many of the potentially testable factors that could help predict later employment success remained unaccounted for.

Another huge realm of testing involved determining individual aptitudes for various forms of employment, with tests specifically developed for unskilled labor, skilled trades, secretarial work, nursing, teaching, and many others (Bingham, 1937). This area of testing progressed especially during the Depression, with large, university-based research centers engaged in the occupational placement of both the unemployed and new immigrants into industrial employment (Super, 1983). At the University of Minnesota, in particular, the Minnesota Mechanical Abilities Project (founded in the 1920s) and the Minnesota Employment Stabilization Research Institute (founded in 1931) employed more than 100 staff who endeavored to place thousands of laid-off workers and new immigrants in jobs, using tests of arithmetic, practical judgment, manual and mechanical dexterity, and vocational interests (Paterson & Darley, 1936). This research project became the Occupational Research Program of the U.S. Employment Service, who were the early developers of the technique of job analysis and the founders of the *Dictionary of Occupational Titles* (Dawis, 1992).

This exhaustive work on defining different occupations through job analysis led to the development of assessment centers, which used a range of techniques for evaluating people in the context of particular jobs or occupations to place them into the right career streams within organizations. Indeed, it was Douglas Bray's fascination with assessment centers, developed in the United States by the CIA's predecessor, the Office of Strategic Services, and in the United Kingdom by the War Office Selection Board (and adapted, ironically, from the Prussian Army), that led to his major study of the predictors of managerial success in AT&T (Bray, Campbell, & Grant, 1974; Howard & Bray, 1988) and similar studies in Exxon and GE by resident and academic psychologists (E. H. Schein, personal communication, October 23, 2003).

In the early years of the scientific approach to vocational guidance, the third major area of testing developed—personality or interest testing. Walter Bingham, while at the Carnegie Institute of Technology, developed an inventory of interests that later became the Strong Vocational Interest Blank, one of the most widely used tests of vocational preference

(Strong, 1943) along with the Kuder Preference Record (Kuder, 1966). The test predicted the occupations at which one would excel, based on the similarity of the individual's preferences to the preferences of individuals in various occupations.[5] The theory behind interest testing was conceptually different from the theory behind intelligence or aptitude testing, because it assumed that individual *volition* would determine performance at least as much as static, inherited ability. Though vocational testing and placement have moved beyond a static understanding of human ability and the idea that scores on ability or psychological tests are sufficient in themselves to understand at what occupations individuals will thrive, these early tests and theories continue to maintain some authority in the field (Gottfredson, 1986).

While theorists of individual differences continued to be interested in how testing could be effectively used by organizations for vocational placement, moral and educational concerns continued to drive the second stream of vocational theorists. Instead of being primarily concerned with how *organizations* could most effectively place and gain productively from their human resources, early vocational guidance theorists coming from the moral or educational perspective were propelled by an interest in understanding the *person* side of the peg-in-hole metaphor: In what type of employment would an individual find the greatest fulfillment? This possibly overstates the difference between the two traditions in vocational psychology: The reformers who helped place individuals in jobs throughout the Depression and the World Wars remained motivated by finding their clients employment rather than self-actualization (we address "psychological" fulfillment more explicitly in the next section). The idea of fulfillment here is limited to a social context within which, though career mobility was greater than it had been historically, most individuals remained uneducated and most jobs remained manual and unskilled. Yet the framing within the moral or educational perspective of vocational theory remained more focused on the individuals making productive career choices for themselves rather than on the organization deciding on the most productive placement for itself.

Parsons

Systematic advice books about how best to choose an occupation for oneself were first published as early as 1747 (Brewer, 1942), mixing Horatio-Alger-myth-driven "How to be a success" advice with more moral tracts about how best to conduct oneself through life (e.g., Smiles, 1859/1958; see also Scharnhorst, 1980). A number of early works in this area follow a similar pattern: One ought to (1) find out about oneself; (2) find out about different jobs; and (3) match the knowledge about oneself with knowledge about professions and, thus, make appropriate vocational choices (see, e.g., Proctor, 1933). These types of books proliferated in the early part of the 20th century, but it was the work of Frank Parsons (1854–1908) that had the most important influence on career theory. Parsons played a catalytic role similar to the one played by Everett Hughes within the sociological tradition of career theory (Davis, 1969), though Parsons' interest in careers started in the very late stages of his own career, and his only published work on the subject, *Choosing a Vocation* (Parsons, 1909), appeared posthumously.

A lawyer by training, Parsons became concerned in the later stages of his career about the effects of industrialization on workers, especially on those most vulnerable from an employability perspective (the young, the poor, and new immigrants). He was critical of a social system that ignored its human capital:

> Society is very short-sighted as yet in its attitude towards the development of human resources. It trains its horses, as a rule, better than its men. It spends unlimited money to perfect the inanimate machinery of production, but pays very little attention to the business of perfecting the human machinery, though it is by far the most important in production. (Parsons, 1909, p. 160)

It is important to remember that his work came before the acknowledgment that an important part of organizations' capital investment resides within their trained and educated workforce—"human capital"—as well as in their factories, real estate, and other tangible investments (Becker, 1975). At the time, more thought was going into locomotives than into human resources.

Parsons began volunteering at Civic Service House in Boston, delivering a set of lectures that highlighted how contemporary youth need better assistance before making lifelong employment decisions. The demand of students for private sessions to help them with their vocational choices encouraged him to establish the Vocation Bureau (later run by Bloomfield; see Bloomfield, 1942), a service to help youth choose, prepare for, and succeed in employment. Following the same three-step model that had proliferated in the early self-help works of vocational guidance, he solidified the model that has been credited to him to this day, though he was possibly only more effective at disseminating it rather than being the first to conceive it:

> In the wise choice of a vocation there are three broad factors: (1) a clear understanding of yourself, your aptitudes, abilities, interests, ambitions, resources, limitations, and their causes; (2) a knowledge of the requirements and conditions of success, advantages and disadvantages, compensation, opportunities, and prospects in different lines of work; (3) true reasoning on the relations of these two groups of facts. (Parsons, 1909, p. 6)

Even though what he started in terms of vocational guidance may have been taken up by the more simplistic and instrumental peg-in-hole administrators who wanted to ensure that immigrants and returning soldiers had jobs to go to, the ideas behind his method were much closer to vocational *discovery* as a process of self-actualization: "A thorough study of oneself is the foundation of a true plan of life" (Parsons, 1909, p. 6).

Though consistently credited as the founder of this area of career theory, Parsons was not a typical theorist and never held a university teaching position. However, he was a true revolutionary in the field, passionate about social justice (O'Brien, 2001) and concerned that workers chose how they labored carefully and with a view to finding their own fulfillment. This is especially relevant given that Parsons' work took place in a context in which the ratios of primary school graduates who went on to high school were as low as 1 in 16 (in Boston) to 1 in 30 (in Philadelphia) (Parsons, 1909).

Holland

It is possible to see the influence of both the individual differences tradition and the vocational education tradition in some of the earliest works on career theory. Thorough overviews of many of these early vocational theories, including Ann Roe's personality theory of career choice (Roe, 1956), the work adjustment theory of Lofquist and Dawis (1969), and John Holland's Career Typology (Holland, 1966, 1973), can be found in the overviews by Samuel Osipow (1968, 1983). The inherent tension in the vocational placement and guidance traditions within career theory involves the twin desire to predict people's "best-fit" profession while acknowledging that prediction is, at best, probabilistic, and the fact that person-environment fit involves many interacting variables, which can all potentially change.

John Holland's theory of vocational choice is perhaps the most representative career theory that explores the tension between the need for individuals to continually develop and the priority within vocational guidance to (statically) "fit" individuals to jobs (Holland, 1966, 1973). The continued popularity of employment testing in the prediction of human resource outcomes speaks more to the current research traditions of human resource management than it does to career theory. A major shift in career theory over the last half of the 20th century was toward the consensus that individuals continue to develop over the course of their careers; the notion that individuals could statically be pegged in a hole had been eclipsed by a more dynamic understanding of individual careers. This is addressed in the next section.

CAREER THEORY FROM A DEVELOPMENTAL PERSPECTIVE

The developmental perspective in career theory encompasses some of the most lyrical writings in the literature on careers. In contrast to most vocational theory, which tended (at least in the early years) to view careers as a static, choice-based, or "fit" phenomenon, the developmental perspective understands career as a dynamic and maturing process that evolves over time. The key theorists usually identified with this perspective traditionally build stage-based models of career. Gene Dalton has provided a good overview of many of these theories (1989), which includes the life-span model provided by Donald Super's work on the self-concept in career development (Super, 1990); the individual differences model provided by Edgar Schein's (1978) work on career anchors, which bridges the sociological and developmental divide; and the career pattern model provided by Michael Driver (1982; see also Sullivan and Crocitto, Chapter 15). However, Dalton's overview explicitly excludes more general theories of human development, such as those of Abraham Maslow (1908–1970) and Erik Erikson (1902–1994), as well as theorists of adult development, such as Daniel Levinson, Paul Baltes, and George Vaillant, on the grounds that the developmental *career* theorist has a specific responsibility to attend to one's work life as well as the unique interplay between individual and organization that career theory implies.

This section extends back to these earlier and not exclusively *career* (in Dalton's terms) theorists, since most of the developmental career theorists were influenced by these earlier and more general theories of individual and adult development. The primary and most obvious sources of early theory that influenced developmental career theory are Sigmund Freud (1856–1939) and Carl Jung (1865–1961); yet they can be traced back much further. In a very detailed and thorough early history of developmental psychology, Guenther Reinert discusses relevant work as far back as Democritus, but stresses the 18th century work of Dietrich Tiedemann (1748–1803) on childhood development and Johann Nicolaus Tetens (1736–1807) on life-span development (Reinert, 1979).

It is important to understand how novel it was at the time to consider childhood, or even the whole life course, as a period over which profound individual change could take place. Tiedemann is considered the founder of child study and wrote one of the first works on childhood development, *Observations on the Development of Mental Capacities in Children,* based on a series of diary studies (Mateer, 1918). Before this time, childhood was not generally considered a rich ground for research. Tetens theorized about the "perfectibility and development of man" (Reinert, 1979, p. 211), becoming one of the first major theorists to understand that adult human development could be considered separately from either religious or secular education, such as in Jean-Jacques Rousseau's (1762/1911) *Emile.* Though these works have mostly disappeared from history, they actually bring us around to Freud and Jung, since Freud focused on childhood development, as Tiedemann did, while Jung represents theorists of adult life development, as did Tetens.

The new contribution to developmental psychology provided by Freud and Jung was the understanding of the implications of the unconscious to human development. Freud focused on the influence of major childhood events on later psychological development, while Jung focused on adult development and had a specific interest in the influence of midlife experiences. Both also built stage-based models, which understood human development to be dynamic and progressing. These stage-based models represent a shift from the early vocational stream of career theory, which tended to view careers as a static phenomenon. Instead, Freud, Jung, Maslow, and Erikson all contributed different visions of dynamic individual change and growth over the life cycle, which helped expand career theory beyond "choice and fit" models. However, Baltes, in a chapter on the history of developmental psychology, has noted the continuing (persistent though restrictive) tendency for developmental models to assume that developmental stages are "sequential, unidirectional, moving towards an end state, irreversible, and universal" (1979, p. 262).

Freud

Freud's legacy is perhaps both underrepresented and diffused in the academic literature on careers. Strains of it can be seen in the work of Clayton Alderfer, who pointed out how Freud's work on transference was relevant to understanding how needs from other realms could be sublimated through work (Alderfer, 1972). It is also woven though the work of George Vaillant, whose *Adaptation to Life* (1977) owes a great deal to Freud's theories on the ego mechanisms of defense as well as Anna Freud's later exploration of these ideas (see A. Freud, 1937). Even when not cited directly, the writings of Freud influence heavily our understanding of the interrelationship between love and work (Hazan & Shaver, 1990). A quote commonly attributed to Freud—"Love and work are the cornerstones of our humanness"—does represent an accurate reflection of a sentiment throughout his work, though the common attribution is likely a paraphrase from Erikson's characterization of Freud rather than a direct quotation (Erikson, 1950, see p. 265).

Freud (1930/1961) did claim that life has a twofold foundation: "the compulsion to work, [and] the power to love" (p. 55). In particular, the key role that work plays in a well-adjusted personality and the unhealthy role it can likewise play in a less well-adjusted personality are ongoing themes throughout his writing. Work can represent the most positive achievement in individual life: "Professional activity is a source of special satisfaction if it is a freely chosen one" (p. 30). It can also represent attempts to avoid negotiating the unconscious: Work offers a major potential to "[displace] a large amount of libidinal components" (p. 30). Unfortunately, not only does the difficulty of subjecting most Freudian theories to empirical testing undermine their influence on organizational theory, but Freud's continued priority of childhood influences over the potential for seminal experiences in adult life leaves him with less to contribute to career theory than other developmental theorists. That Freud's developmental stages begin and end in childhood spoke little, at least directly, to later career theorists, who were more interested in the stages of development among and within adults.

Jung

In contrast, Jung presents himself as one of the first theorists of midlife. An early follower of Freud, his work later developed in many new directions, including integrating the study of comparative religion and mythology with psychology and understanding the unconscious as a collective, shared set of archetypes. Most relevant to the study of careers is his focus on the

important changes that occur in midlife and his late-career interest in alchemy (Storr, 1983). In contrast with Freud, who tended to see all adult transitions as ultimately originating in childhood experiences, Jung's own midlife crisis, in 1913 at the age of 38, triggered a new understanding of the period between 35 and 40, which he termed a "phase of life [during which] an important change in the human psyche is in preparation" (Jung, 1931/1969, p. 395, 1971, p. 72). During this phase, individuals tend to shift from a primary focus on the external world to a more internal, reflective state, opening the possibility for profound change and positive growth as well as for withdrawal from "the second half of life" if the tasks of midlife change prove too "unknown and dangerous" (Jung, 1931/1969, p. 396).

Alchemy, though commonly understood as the process through which base metals might be changed to gold, has a broader meaning: to "perfect everything in its own nature" (Storr, 1983, p. 19). This was Jung's ideal prescription for a well-lived life: Individuals ought to persist in the journey toward individuation, the only route to "synthesis between conscious and unconscious, a sense of calm acceptance and detachment, and a realization of the meaning of life" (p. 19). This form of teleology, with the perfection of one's own nature representing the ultimate goal to which individuals should strive in life, can be seen in much of developmental psychology and can be traced back to Jung.

Career theorists who develop stage models of career progression, however, owe a more direct intellectual debt to Maslow and Erikson—Maslow for helping us understand that individuals have a hierarchy of needs that helps explain the differences in human motivation (1954) and Erikson for helping us understand that, over the life course, individuals generally proceed through a series of developmental stages, which will factor heavily in the progress of any individual's career (1950). Both theorists present hierarchical stage-based models that are highly attractive and transportable to theorizing about careers (though they remain frustratingly uncooperative to empirical testing; see Hall & Nougaim, 1968). In particular, Erikson's eight stages of life extended notions of development from childhood through old age in a very accessible way; his model has been taken up by a number of career theorists, though perhaps more superficially than it should have been (Vondracek, 1992).

Maslow

Maslow's theory of motivation rests on a five-step hierarchy of needs, beginning with physiological needs; progressing through safety needs, affiliation needs, achievement and esteem needs; and finally culminating in the need for self-actualization (Maslow, 1954, chap. 5). Individuals are motivated by whatever set of needs are most personally salient to them and are unmet at the time. Once a set of needs has been met, the next higher level of needs assumes greater salience and acts as an individual motivator. An early review of relevant (though predominantly cross-sectional) studies did generally indicate that individuals with lower-level positions within organizations tended to emphasize security needs, individuals with midlevel positions tended to emphasize affiliation and esteem needs, while individuals in senior-level positions were more concerned with self-actualization needs (Vroom, 1964). Self-actualization has remained a popular goal of career counseling, representing a psychological proxy for career "success" (Sackett, 1998). However, more rigorous empirical analysis has had little luck in confirming that individuals are motivated by a hierarchical series of needs; instead, Maslow's work has been reinterpreted by career theorists as speaking to a series of sequential career stages, representing "regularized status passages [rather] than lower-order need gratification" (Hall & Nougaim, 1968, p. 12).

Erikson

Erikson's eight-staged developmental theory contains a number of progressive tasks that are of direct interest to career theory (Erikson, 1950, chap. 7). The stage of "industry versus inferiority" requires that the school-age child integrates an understanding of the importance of work and accomplishment while mitigating against a sense of inadequacy as he or she grapples with learning new technologies. This stage gives way to the stage of "identity versus role confusion," during which the main task is to ensure the development of a strong sense of self, a key factor in developing a strong vocational identity (Vondracek, 1992). In fact, Erikson claimed that the inability to resolve an occupational identity is a primary cause of disturbance in youth (Erikson, 1959). The "intimacy versus isolation" stage, which occurs in early adulthood, requires individuals to commit both to intimate relationships and to stable employment or career (toward midlife) and builds toward the final two stages of life (both after midlife). During the stage of "generativity versus stagnation," individuals are to guide and teach the next generation, while the final stage, "ego integrity versus despair," represents the culmination of a life's journey toward maturity, during which one has accepted the limitations of one's individual life but remains an enlightened leader and legacy builder. Though Erikson's theory suffers from the same weaknesses as the metatheories of Freud and Jung—that they are overgeneral and difficult to test empirically—the notion of the life cycle as a set of progressive tasks continues to inform the literature on career progression and status passages.

Life Course Psychology

Developmental career theory also owes a debt to the broad field of life course psychology, an extension of the early psychological theories of Freud, Jung, and Maslow, geared specifically toward developing models of change in adulthood. Traditional life-span developmental psychology examines human development throughout life, with the perspective "that developmental processes, whatever their age location, can be better understood if they are seen in the context of the entire lifetime of individuals" (Baltes & Brim, 1979, p. xi). Work, or career, figures in many of these theories, such as Alderfer's existence, relatedness, and growth (ERG) theory (1972), Vaillant's work on adult adaptation (1977), and Levinson's work on midlife (1978), but they remain predominantly theories of adult development rather than career theories per se.

Alderfer's ERG theory represents a fusion of theories from a number of different disciplines, though the work is most seriously indebted to Maslow's theories of motivation (Maslow, 1954). Alderfer posed his theory as a more parsimonious and less rigid alternative to Maslow's, though his work is ambivalent about whether it was intended to be an improvement on Maslow's theory or simply inspired by Maslow but more specifically focused on careers. ERG theory posits that individual needs can be characterized by "existence," or the importance of finding equilibrium in the satisfaction of human needs; "relatedness," or the importance of human interactions in social environments; and "growth," or the need of any system to increase in order and differentiation over time.

Alderfer's influences ranged far beyond Maslow, however. His understanding of existence needs was also inspired by anthropological work on material needs and deprivation, from studies of the Siriono Indians of Eastern Bolivia, and from studies of the conditions of soldiers in Vietnam (Holmberg, 1960; Moskos, 1969). His ideas on relatedness needs drew from psychoanalytic theorists such as Bowlby (1965), and Allport's work on open systems theory influenced his understanding of the individual's continued growth needs (Allport, 1960). Just as Erikson had provided a more accessible model for life stages than either Freud or Jung, Alderfer's ERG theory provided a staged model of motivation that was more accessible and had better potential for empirical tests than that of Maslow.

Vaillant's study of successful adult adaptation also represents a theoretical stepping stone between the work of Freud and Jung and that of the early career theorists. In a 35-year cohort study of "people who are well and do well" (Vaillant, 1977, p. 3), Vaillant took Freud's work on the ego mechanisms of defense and arranged them in an evolutionary process, to range from the least to the most adaptive defense mechanisms, based on Freud's premise that individuals with the most mature defenses are best able to both love and work. His study demonstrated that individuals who are most successful are able to change their needs and priorities as they navigate the life cycle and that they demonstrate growth over time. Vaillant believed his longitudinal study also supported the theories of Erikson, finding that subjects at early midlife were more interested in their own careers (conforming to Erikson's stages of industry and identity), while by their 50s they were more interested in their colleagues and staff (conforming to Erikson's stages of intimacy and generativity). He also noted that individuals could get stuck, never fully completing adolescence, living their adult lives as if they were teenagers, and harkening back to Jung's concerns about unsuccessfully meeting the challenge of complete individuation, which one faces at midlife.

Levinson is a third theorist and represents an intermediate between the psychoanalytic theorists' early developmental career theory and current developmental strains of career theory. Seeing his study, *The Season's of a Man's Life,* as a parallel to *Adaptation to Life,* Levinson focused on this midlife decade, which had caught the imagination, in particular, of Erikson and Jung. This decade has historically been rich for career theorists, since at 40, the individual "must deal with the disparity between what he is and what he dreamed of becoming" (Levinson, 1978, p. 30). Levinson distinguished himself from the more purely intraindividual theorists by stressing the interaction between the individual and his or her environment. This joint interest led to theorizing about occupations, since work, as "a major part of individual life and of the social structure" (Levinson, 1978, p. 45), provides a useful framework through which to view this interaction. Levinson posited the universal stages through which most individuals pass, each of which is connected to either structure-building or structure-changing periods. The midlife transition, the point at which individuals become disillusioned with their current reality, involves confronting and reintegrating the polarities that define their lives and represents the most important structure-changing phase of life. Erikson referred to this as the stage of generativity; Jung first proposed it as the turning point between the first and the second half of life.

The difficulty of developing truly dynamic theory that remains open to empirical testing has meant that much of the developmental theorist's ideas have not been explicitly taken up by traditional career theorists. An exception to this is Donald Super, who, influenced by both life stage theorists and social role theorists, built a staged model of careers that posited that career development occurred along a set of phases during which individuals continually implement and then revise self-concepts (e.g., Super, 1990). Super's life-span, life-space approach to careers charges that individuals' developmental tasks and requirements change over time, as do their social roles, both of which influence career development recursively. Work and life satisfaction depend on the ability of individuals to implement their self-concepts in a fulfilling way, appropriate to their life stage and social role at the time. Like Schein, Super believed that the driving self-concept becomes more stable as individuals mature.

There have been serious criticisms of these life course theorists that highlight the need for any theorist of adult development to attend to both intraindividual processes and processes of individual-society interaction. These criticisms, which reached a pinnacle in the debate between Dale Dannefer on the one side and Paul Baltes and John Nesselroade on the other in the *American Sociological Review,* centered on a tension that returns us again to the concerns of sociology (Baltes & Nesselroade, 1984; Dannefer, 1984a, 1984b). Dannefer accused developmental psychology of "ontogenic reductionism—the practice of treating socially produced and patterned phenomena as rooted in the characteristics of the individual organism" (Dannefer, 1984b, p. 847)—and called on developmental psychology to develop a deeper understanding of the relationship between the individual and his environment, while Baltes and Nesselroade defended life course psychology as adequately accounting for the societal effects on the individual (Baltes & Nesselroade, 1984). The debate highlights, from the outskirts of career theory, the longstanding and continuing need for multiple disciplines to better communicate in the development of new theory, a call that remains ill answered to the present day (see Collin, Chapter 32; Schein, Afterword).

Tensions in the
History of Career Theory

It is hard to find a history of the careers field that does not have a call for greater interdisciplinary integration (Arthur et al., 1989a); however, efforts at either successful integration or successfully attending to the richness of past theories are hindered by both the norms of science within individual disciplines and the

ahistoricism of much of organizational behavior theory in general. How might we use this overview of the roots of career theory to best inform future theoretical efforts and protect ourselves from repeating the past? In an attempt to synthesize the history presented in this chapter, we have identified five metathemes that cut across the disciplinary boundaries that tend to separate career theorists. The metathemes are dialectic, in the sense that they are best described as tensions between two opposing concepts (Astley & Van de Ven, 1983). They are (1) individual agency versus social determinism in the shaping of career, (2) career as process versus career as achieving fit, (3) fit for the benefit of the individual versus fit for the benefit of the collectivity, (4) career as a social phenomenon versus career as an individual life story, and (5) career scholarship as theoretical prediction versus career scholarship that provides help for individuals living their careers. Each theme will be examined in turn.

Individual Agency
Versus Social Determinism

Running through the entire literature on career is the tension between individual agency, the notion that we are what we make of ourselves, and social determinism, in which "individual behavior is seen as determined by and reacting to structural constraints that provide organizational life with an overall stability and control" (Astley & Van de Ven, 1983, p. 245). The former, agency, perspective is most evident in the vocational literature, which, as we argued above, is founded on the precept that the individual should find out about his or her individual capacities and match them to the occupation that best suits those capacities. It emerges most forcefully in the 19th-century self-help literature typified by Horatio Alger (see Scharnhorst, 1980) and Samuel Smiles (1859/1958). But it is arguably also evident in the Weberian concept of the Calvinist struggle to succeed and thereby demonstrate that one is a member of the chosen.

Social determinism is a strong component of the sociological tradition we traced above. In their different ways, the early sociologists described how macrosocial structures constrain and enable life chances, such as Durkheim's division of labor or Weber's bureaucracy and status and class hierarchies. These themes were picked up by Hughes and his colleagues and seen in the dystopian writing of Mills and others. The determinism is of two forms, which might be labeled "benign" and "malign." The benign version points to the way in which social systems structure the opportunities that people are presented with—for example, the precise form that a particular bureaucratic structure might take, which in turn shapes the careers that are possible within that bureaucracy (Gunz, 1989). The consequences are neither necessarily good nor bad for the people making their careers. The malign version, in contrast, worries about the dystopic effects of social structure on people's life chances—for example, in terms of the alienating effects of bureaucracy.

Anthony Giddens takes the dualism of agency and structure an important step further by pointing out that the actions of individual agents create and reproduce the structure within which they act: "Structural properties of social systems are both medium and outcome of the practices they recursively organize" (Giddens, 1984, p. 25; see also Whittington, 1992). This provides a theoretical linkage between the two poles—agency and social determinism—by showing how they are not independent of each other. Horatio Alger's heroes, for example, can only experience the rewards of their hard work in societies in which the rules allow them to own the means of production. But in so doing, they reinforce and reproduce the rules that made their success possible.

Process Versus Fit

The tension between career as a dynamic process and career as a choice or fit phenomenon has been continuously apparent throughout the early history of career theory. Most obviously, vocational psychology has tended to view careers statically, as an issue that can be resolved through proper attention to vocational choice and placement. Much of Holland's work on person-environment congruence (Holland, 1966, 1973), for example, is a legacy from the early vocational work that advised individuals to learn about themselves, learn about different jobs, and make appropriate choices with that

knowledge (Parsons, 1909; Proctor, 1933). Round pegs, in other words, tend to stay round and are best fitted into round holes.

On the other hand, developmental psychology, and theories of adult development in particular, invites theorists to understand careers as a dynamic and changing process, in which different needs, values, and motivators are prioritized at different stages over the life course. Here, the peg changes shape as it ages. The ideas of a number of major career theorists incorporate this perspective: Super (1990) integrates life stages with different developmental tasks into his life-span approach to careers; Driver's (1982) typology of career concepts outlines different ways of navigating through careers; and Hall's (1976) model integrates the developmental tasks of career stages with the stages of traditional family development. The general trend in current career theory is toward dynamic models and away from static models, though staged developmental models remain criticized for overgeneralizing their applicability and often assuming unidirectionality and sequentiality, as well as overemphasizing intraindividual processes to the detriment of attending to individual-environment interaction (Dannefer, 1984a). However, the bulk of the empirical work in career theory remains tied to static models, which are easier to design, operationalize, and model statistically.

The Function of Career: Fit for Whom?

Even though dynamic models have generally replaced static models of career processes, the concept of fit remains central to career theory: It continues to be important that individual decisions about career choices result in effective placement, both for the individuals involved and for the productivity of the organization. This leads to the recurring tension: fit for whom? Sociologists have historically emphasized the importance of large swaths of the population being fit successfully in employment to reproduce the social order in a stable way; later industrial sociologists as well as the civic activists involved in placing the huge waves of new immigrants and workers displaced by the Depression remained concerned about the importance at this societal level of the effective placement of individuals in jobs.

More meso-oriented researchers have emphasized the more individual-level factors of appropriate person-job fit as a mutual goal of both individuals (for job satisfaction, needs fulfillment, and personal growth) and organizations (for work group and organizational productivity). Again, Schein's view of the importance of integrating individual and organizational needs in the career process speaks to this mutual goal as an important outcome of fit (Schein, 1971). Finally, micro-oriented psychologists have shied away from considering the organization's needs and have instead focused sharply on the importance of good person-job fit to meet the goal of personal self-expression and/or growth. Many of the developmental theorists, such as Alderfer or Levinson, represent this side of the tension around "fit for whom?" (Alderfer, 1972; Levinson, 1978).

Interestingly, though there are different priorities and ways of answering this question, each answer essentially revolves around finding order in some way. At the macro-level, fit facilitates the stability of the social structure; at the meso level, fit facilitates both individual satisfaction and organizational effectiveness; at the micro-level, fit facilitates the development and potential self-actualization of the individual.

Social Phenomenon or Individual Life Story?

Another theme running through all three disciplinary perspectives relates to the *function* of the career: Who benefits from the career? In the sociological writings, the beneficiary is the social order. Occupational groups are seen as a source of moral influence, and the work role is a method for integrating the individual into his or her social environment. Having individuals settled into stable jobs is a way of preserving order in a chaotic society (so thought Durkheim and Weber) as opposed to having wandering bands of the unemployed, with much free time and little to occupy their minds except thoughts of mischief. Division of labor and occupational specialization are a way of creating an investment in one's craft, and this provides stability and reward in the person's life. A society made up of people who are so invested in and focused on their work is, in all likelihood, not a restive society.

In the vocational perspective, the order is provided by fit between the person and his or her work role. But in this perspective, there are two beneficiaries: society and the individual. And for society, the goal is not so much security and order as it is efficiency and productivity, the harnessing of its human capital. For the individual, the benefit is being in a position that allows expression of one's individual interests and talents. The work of the early psychologists (e.g., Spearman & Jones, 1950) represented an era of optimism that the principles of science could be as well applied to human nature and behavior as to engineering. Finding good fits for individuals was also a way of helping unemployed people and new immigrants find new work and bright futures. There was a spirit of hopefulness of mutual gain for the individual and society, just as large-scale engineering projects, such as the Hoover Dam, would benefit individuals (workers, customers) as well as society (the country's economy).

In the developmental perspective, the career was seen as providing an avenue for individual self-expression and self-actualization. When a person's job and career experiences were positive, the person would be growing and would be excited about and satisfied with this growth. Although this positive energy in its cumulative effects would presumably provide employing organizations and society with high-performing members, the truly important benefit, as seen by the development theorists, would be the individual's psychological growth. Thus, the value was primarily individual rather than societal.

Theory Versus Practice

The final tension that runs through the three disciplinary branches centers on the goal of theory and how theory is to be generated. In much of the sociological tradition, there seemed to be a focus on theory *qua* theory. For example, Durkheim and Weber generated their theory by observing large-scale social movements at a high level. There were no empirical studies and first-hand observations in their writings. The theory was developed inductively rather than with the use of formal deductive reasoning.

There was a difference within the sociological tradition between these theorists and Hughes. The work of Hughes and his colleagues was highly empirical, and they took pains to stay very close to their data and to develop constructs that could be seen clearly in their observations and interviews.

The approach of the vocational researchers was the exact opposite: They were strongly focused on solving problems, such as developing accurate methods of predicting which "round pegs" would end up in which "round holes" and which "square pegs" would wind up in which "square holes." Most of this development in research and theory was driven by the needs of practice: to predict who would end up where and to assist people in making these vocational choices. Whether it was helping unemployed workers find work in the Great Depression or helping military organizations and their personnel make good staffing decisions, the central focus was on meeting a pressing practical human resource problem, and theory-building was done in the service of improving the success of vocational choices.

As for developmental scholars, their point of departure also tended to be in the realm of practice. In their case, the practical issue was how to help individuals achieve a satisfying adjustment as their career evolved over time. Since the theoretical models had a normative basis (i.e., one direction of development is "good" and the opposite direction is "bad"), the ultimate purpose of the theory was to help the person develop in the valued direction. For example, in the case of Maslow, this would be in the direction of self-actualization and away from concern for physiological and safety needs, whereas for Freud or Jung it would be in the direction of greater psychological health.

CONCLUSION

We began this chapter with the observation that the present-day careers literature typically traces its origins to the U.S.-based group of scholars, largely working in business schools, who convened in the late 1970s, decided that they had identified a field of study, and initiated an impressive stream of research and writing in that field. Yet that group was very clear about the intellectual debt that it owed to its predecessors. Schein, for example, admired Everett Hughes' work greatly and used it as a model for his own approach to research (as did Hall, 2004, who was Schein's student). And it was equally clear to them that there were major areas of careers scholarship and research, for example, in the sociological and vocational literatures that we have briefly examined here, which were parallel streams in the classic sense of never—or rarely—meeting.

The 1970s Mobile Career Seminar left its successors an important set of institutional artifacts: groups such as the Careers Division of the Academy of Management. An unintended side effect of this legacy is the impression it seems to have left with present-day careers scholars that the field began with the contributions of that group. Yet as we have shown in this chapter, and as the members of the 1970s group were well aware, the roots of careers scholarship go very much further back into history than this. This is the first of two major reasons that stimulated us to write the present chapter: To adapt Santayana's aphorism that "those who cannot remember the past are condemned to repeat it" (1905/1936, p. 284), those who are unaware of the historical roots of their discipline risk wasting their, and everyone else's, time reinventing concepts and remaking observations.

But, arguably more seriously, the risks inherent in being unaware of the origins of a field are also that one stays unaware of the many streams in careers writing that also descended from the same historical roots and that thrive within different disciplines and different institutions. There is a great deal that we can learn from each other in complex areas of enquiry such as careers, but only if we know of one another's work. As Zerubavel points out, boundaries are double-edged (1995). No scholarly progress is possible without at least some sense of structure, but there is a point at which the boundaries that emerge from this structuring become defensive barriers to understanding and intellectual growth. We offer this chapter as a contribution to a broadening understanding of the nature of careers scholarship and its contributions to the broader field of organization studies.

NOTES

1. Two examples that stand out in the mind of the third author, who was a participant in the forming of the Careers Division of the Academy of Management, were a Boston Area Careers Group that met at various colleges and universities (Harvard Business School, Boston University, Bentley College, MIT, etc.) and an invited conference organized by Edgar Schein and C. Brooklyn Derr at MIT's Endicott House.

2. Please note that we are talking about the study of careers in management and organization studies, not necessarily the study of careers in disciplines such as psychology or sociology. As we will discuss, career studies go back much farther in those disciplines.

3. E. H. Schein (personal communication, January 17, 2005) adds,

> When I published the research on career anchors I also designed a booklet that would teach managers how to do a better job of analyzing work. Pfeiffer [the publisher] mistitled it *Career Survival: Strategic Job/Role Planning.* It was the job/role planning that was the critical element. The booklet had little to do with careers per se, though one could argue that if career occupants had better information on what a job would actually involve by being given better information by the organization, they could plan their careers better . . . the career anchor concept took hold, but the job/role planning has not caught on, though I think it is as or more important for organizations to understand work requirements as individual motives and competencies.

4. Though a lifelong advocate of intelligence testing, Spearman actually backpedaled his belief in a measurable, causally relevant notion of general intelligence shortly before his death, questioning both whether "ability" could be accurately described as causal and whether it could be accurately measured (Gould, 1981; Spearman & Jones, 1950).

5. Interestingly, he found that predicting who would excel as executives was more challenging than predicting success for engineers, lawyers, ministers of religion, or artists; because executives have a broader and more catholic set of interests, it is more difficult to use the inventory to predict who will be successful (Strong, 1927).

REFERENCES

Alderfer, C. P. (1972). *Existence, relatedness, and growth.* New York: Free Press.

Allport, G. W. (1960). The open system in personality theory. *Journal of Abnormal and Social Psychology, 61,* 301–311.

Army Psychologists. (1961). Group examinations: Alpha and beta. In J. J. Jenkins & D. G. Paterson (Eds.), *Studies in individual differences* (pp. 140–176). New York: Appleton-Century-Crofts. (Original work published 1921)

Arthur, M. B., Hall, D. T., & Lawrence, B. S. (1989a). Generating new directions in career theory: The case for a transdisciplinary approach. In M. B. Arthur, D. T. Hall, & B. S. Lawrence (Eds.), *Handbook of career theory* (pp. 7–25). Cambridge, UK: Cambridge University Press.

Arthur, M. B., Hall, D. T., & Lawrence, B. S. (1989b). Preface. In M. B. Arthur, D. T. Hall, & B. S. Lawrence (Eds.), *Handbook of career theory* (pp. xv–xix). Cambridge, UK: Cambridge University Press.

Astley, W. G., & Van de Ven, A. H. (1983). Central perspectives and debates in organization theory. *Administrative Science Quarterly, 28,* 245–273.

Baltes, P. B., & Brim, O. G. (Eds.). (1979). *Life-span development and behavior* (Vol. 2). New York: Academic Press.

Baltes, P. B., & Nesselroade, J. R. (1984). Paradigm lost and paradigm regained: Critique of Dannefer's portrayal of life-span developmental psychology. *American Sociological Review, 49,* 841–847.

Baltes, P. B. (1979). Life-span developmental psychology: Some converging observations on history and theory. In P. B. Baltes & O. G. Brim (Eds.), *Life-span development and behavior* (Vol. 2, pp. 256–279). New York: Academic Press.

Barley, S. R. (1989). Careers, identities, and institutions: The legacy of the Chicago School of Sociology. In M. B. Arthur, D. T. Hall, & B. S. Lawrence (Eds.), *Handbook of career theory* (pp. 41–65). Cambridge, UK: Cambridge University Press.

Becker, G. S. (1975). *Human capital: A theoretical and empirical analysis* (2nd ed.). Chicago: University of Chicago Press.

Becker, H. S. (1952). The career of the Chicago public schoolteacher. *American Journal of Sociology, 57,* 470–477.

Becker, H., Geer, B., Strauss, A., & Hughes, E. C. (1961). *Boys in white: Student culture in medical school.* Chicago: University of Chicago Press.

Betz, N. E., Fitzgerald, L. F., & Hill, R. E. (1989). Trait-factor theories: Traditional cornerstone of career theory. In M. B. Arthur, D. T. Hall, & B. S. Lawrence (Eds.), *Handbook of career theory* (pp. 26–40). Cambridge, UK: Cambridge University Press.

Binet, A., & Simon, T. (1961). The development of intelligence in children. In J. J. Jenkins & D. G. Paterson (Eds.), *Studies in individual differences* (pp. 81–111). New York: Appleton-Century-Crofts. (Original work published 1905–1908)

Bingham, W. V. (1919). Army personnel work. *Journal of Applied Psychology, 3,* 1–12.

Bingham, W. V. (1937). *Aptitudes and aptitude testing.* New York: Harper & Brothers.

Blau, P. M., & Duncan, O. D. (1967). *The American occupational structure.* New York: Wiley.

Bloomfield, M. (1942). *Readings in vocational guidance.* Boston: Ginn.

Bowlby, J. (1965). *Child care and the growth of love* (2nd ed.). Baltimore: Penguin Books.

Bray, D. W., Campbell, R. J., & Grant, D. (1974). *Formative years in business: A long-term AT&T study of managerial lives.* New York: Wiley.

Brewer, J. M. (1942). *History of vocational guidance.* New York: Harper & Brothers.

Catell, J. M. (1890). Mental tests and measurement. *Mind, 15,* 373–380.

Chapoulie, J.-M. (1996). Everett Hughes and the Chicago tradition. *Sociological Theory, 14,* 3–29.

Cressy, P. G. (1932). *The taxi-dance hall: A sociological study in commercialized recreation and city life.* Chicago: University of Chicago Press.

Dalton, G. W. (1989). Developmental views of careers in organizations. In M. B. Arthur, D. T. Hall, & B. S. Lawrence (Eds.), *Handbook of career theory* (pp. 89–109). Cambridge, UK: Cambridge University Press.

Dannefer, D. (1984a). Adult development and social theory: A paradigmatic reappraisal. *American Sociological Review, 49,* 110–116.

Dannefer, D. (1984b). The role of the social in life-span developmental psychology, past and future: Rejoinder to Baltes and Nesselroade. *American Sociological Review, 49,* 847–850.

Davis, H. V. (1969). *Frank Parsons: Prophet, innovator, counselor.* Carbondale: Southern Illinois University Press.

Dawis, R. V. (1992). The individual differences tradition in counselling psychology. *Journal of Counseling Psychology, 39,* 7–19.

DiPadova, L. N. (1996). Towards a Weberian management theory. *Journal of Management History, 2,* 59–64.

Driver, M. J. (1982). Career concepts: A new approach to career research. In R. Katz (Ed.), *Career issues in human resource management* (pp. 23–32). Englewood Cliffs, NJ: Prentice Hall.

Durkheim, E. (1964). *The division of labour in society* (G. Simpson, Trans.). London: Free Press of Glencoe. (Original work published 1893)

Erikson, E. (1950). *Childhood and society.* New York: W. W. Norton.

Erikson, E. (1959). Identity and the life cycle. *Psychological Issues, 1,* 18–164.

Freud, A. (1937). *Ego and the mechanisms of defense.* London: Hogarth Press.

Freud, S. (1961). *Civilization and its discontents.* New York: W. W. Norton. (Original work published 1930)

Gerth, H. H., & Mills, C. W. (Eds.). (1958). Introduction. In *From Max Weber: Essays in sociology* (pp. 3–74). New York: Oxford University Press.

Giddens, A. (1971). *Capitalism and modern social theory: An analysis of the writings of Marx, Durkheim, and Max Weber.* Cambridge, UK: Cambridge University Press.

Giddens, A. (1984). *The constitution of society: Outline of the theory of structuration.* Cambridge, UK: Polity Press.

Goffman, E. (1959). *Presentation of the self in everyday life.* Garden City, NY: Anchor.

Gottfredson, L. (1986). Special Issue: The *g* factor in employment. *Journal of Vocational Behavior, 29,* 293–450.

Gould, S. J. (1981). *The mismeasure of man.* New York: W. W. Norton.

Gunz, H. P. (1989). *Careers and corporate cultures: Managerial mobility in large corporations.* Oxford: Basil Blackwell.

Hackman, J. R., & Oldham, G. R. (1980). *Work redesign.* Reading, MA: Addison-Wesley.

Hall, D., & Nougaim, K. E. (1968). An examination of Maslow's needs hierarchy in an organizational setting. *Organizational Behavior and Human Performance, 3,* 12–35.

Hall, D. T. (1976). *Careers in organizations.* Santa Monica, CA: Goodyear.

Hall, D. T. (2004). The protean career: A quarter-century journey. *Journal of Vocational Behavior, 65,* 1–13.

Hazan, C., & Shaver, P. (1990). Love and work: An attachment-theoretical perspective. *Journal of Personality and Social Psychology, 59,* 270–280.

Helmes-Hayes, R. C. (1998). Everett Hughes: Theorist of the second Chicago School. *International Journal of Politics, Culture and Society, 11,* 621–673.

Herr, E. L. (2001). Career development and its practice: A historical perspective. *Career Development Quarterly, 49,* 196–211.

Holland, J. L. (1966). *The psychology of vocational choice: A theory of personality types and model environments.* Waltham, MA: Blaisdell.

Holland, J. L. (1973). *Making vocational choices: A theory of careers.* Englewood Cliffs, NJ: Prentice Hall.

Holmberg, A. R. (1960). *Nomads of the long bow: The Siriano of Eastern Bolivia.* Chicago: University of Chicago Press.

Howard, A., & Bray, D. W. (1988). *Managerial lives in transition: Advancing age and changing times.* New York: Guilford Press.

Hughes, E. C. (1928). Personality types and the division of labor. *American Journal of Sociology, 33,* 754–768.

Hughes, E. C. (1958). *Men and their work.* Glencoe, IL: Free Press. (Original work published 1928–1956)

Hunter, J. E. (1986). Cognitive ability, cognitive aptitudes, job knowledge, and job performance. *Journal of Vocational Behavior, 29,* 340–362.

Hunter, R., et al. (Eds.). (1895). *The American encyclopaedic dictionary* (1st ed.). Chicago: W. B. Conkey.

Johnson, S. (1979). *A dictionary of the English language.* London: Times Books. (Original work published 1755)

Jung, C. G. (1969). The stages of life (R. F. C. Hull, Trans.). In H. Read, M. Fordham, G. Adler, & W. McGuire (Eds.), *The collected works of C. G. Jung* (2nd ed., Vol. 8, pp. 397–403). Princeton, NJ: Princeton University Press. (Original work published 1931)

Jung, C. G. (1971). *The portable Jung.* Harmondsworth: Penguin Books.

Kuder, G. F. (1966). The occupational interest survey. *Personnel and Guidance Journal, 45,* 72–77.

Levinson, D. J. (1978). *The seasons of a man's life.* New York: Knopf.

Locke, J. (1989). *Some thoughts concerning education.* (J. W. Yolton & J. S. Yolton, Eds.). New York: Oxford University Press. (Original work published 1695)

Lofquist, L. H., & Dawis, R. V. (1969). *Adjustment to work.* Englewood Cliffs, NJ: Prentice Hall.

Maranda, M.-F., & Comeau, Y. (2000). Some contributions of sociology to the understanding of career. In A. Collin & R. A. Young (Eds.), *The future of career* (pp. 37–52). Cambridge, UK: Cambridge University Press.

Marx, K. (2000). *Selected writings* (2nd ed.). Oxford: Oxford University Press. (Original work published 1834–1894)

Maslow, A. H. (1954). *Motivation and personality.* New York: Harper.

Mateer, F. (1918). Historical survey of child study. In *Child behavior: A critical and experimental study of young children by the method of conditioned reflexes* (pp. 13–31). Boston: Badger.

Miles, A. (1999). *Social mobility in nineteenth- and early twentieth-century England.* New York: St. Martin's Press.

Miller, D., & Form, W. H. (1951). *Industrial sociology.* New York: Harper & Row.

Mills, C. W. (1951). *White collar: The American middle classes.* New York: Oxford University Press.

Moskos, C. C. (1969). Why men fight. *Transaction, 7,* 13–23.

O'Brien, K. M. (2001). The legacy of Parsons: Career counselors and vocational psychologists as agents of social change. *Career Development Quarterly, 50,* 66–76.

Osipow, S. H. (1968). *Theories of career development* (1st ed.). New York: Appleton-Century-Crofts.

Osipow, S. H. (1983). *Theories of career development* (3rd ed.). New York: Appleton-Century-Crofts.

Oxford English dictionary (1st ed.). (1933). Oxford: Clarendon Press.

Oxford English dictionary (2nd ed.). (1989). Oxford: Oxford University Press.

Parsons, F. (1909). *Choosing a vocation.* Boston: Houghton Mifflin.

Paterson, D. G., & Darley, J. G. (1936). *Men, women and jobs: A study in human engineering.* Minneapolis: University of Minnesota Press.

Proctor, W. M. (1933). *Vocations, the world's work and its workers.* Boston: Houghton Mifflin.

Reinert, G. (1979). Prolegomena to a history of life-span developmental psychology. In P. B. Baltes & O. G. Brim (Eds.), *Life-span development and behavior* (Vol. 2, pp. 205–254). New York: Academic Press.

Roe, A. (1956). *The psychology of occupations.* New York: Wiley.

Roth, J. A. (1963). *Timetables: Structuring the passage of time in hospital treatment and other careers.* Indianapolis, IN: Bobbs-Merrill.

Rousseau, J.-J. (1911). *Emile.* (B. Foxley, Trans.). London: Dent. (Original work published 1762)

Rytina, S. (2001). Youthful vision, youthful promise, through midlife bifocals: C. Wright Mills' White Collar turns 50. *Sociological Forum, 16,* 563–574.

Sackett, S. J. (1998). Career counseling as an aid to self-actualization. *Journal of Career Development, 24,* 235–244.

Santayana, G. (1936). *The life of reason; or, the phases of human progress* (2nd ed.). New York: Scribner. (Original work published 1905)

Savickas, M. L. (2000). Renovating the psychology of careers for the twenty-first century. In A. Collin & R. A. Young (Eds.), *The future of career* (pp. 53–68). Cambridge, UK: Cambridge University Press.

Scharnhorst, G. (1980). *Horatio Alger, Jr.* Boston: Twayne.

Schein, E. H. (1971). The individual, the organization, and the career: A conceptual scheme. *Journal of Applied Behavioral Science, 7,* 401–426.

Schein, E. H. (1978). *Career dynamics: Matching individual and organizational needs.* Reading, MA: Addison-Wesley.

Schein, E. H. (1989). A critical look at current career development theory and research. In D. T. Hall (Ed.), *Career development in organizations* (pp. 310–331). San Francisco: Jossey-Bass.

Smiles, S. (1958). *Self-help: With illustrations of conduct and perseverance.* London: John Murray. (Original work published 1859)

Smith, A. (1994). *An inquiry into the nature and causes of the wealth of nations.* New York: Modern Library. (Original work published 1776)

Smith, S. (1850). *Elementary sketches of moral philosophy.* New York: Harper.

Sonnenfeld, J. A., & Kotter, J. P. (1982). The maturation of career theory. *Human Relations, 35,* 19–46.

Spearman, C. E., & Jones, L. W. (1950). *Human ability, a continuation of "The abilities of man."* London: Macmillan.

Storr, A. (1983). Introduction. In A. Storr (Ed.), *The essential Jung* (pp. 13–27). Princeton, NJ: Princeton University Press.

Strong, E. K. (1927). Vocational guidance of executives. *Journal of Applied Psychology, 11,* 331–347.

Strong, E. K. (1943). *Vocational interests of men and women.* Stanford, CA: Stanford University Press.

Super, D. E. (1983). The history and development of vocational psychology: A personal perspective. In W. B. Walsh & S. H. Osipow (Eds.), *Handbook of vocational psychology* (Vol. 1, pp. 5–37). Hillsdale, NJ: Lawrence Erlbaum.

Super, D. E. (1990). A life-span, life-space approach to career development. In D. Brown & L. Brooks (Eds.), *Career choice and development: Applying contemporary theory to practice* (pp. 197–261). San Francisco: Jossey-Bass.

Sutherland, E. H. (1937). *The professional thief.* Chicago: University of Chicago Press.

Terman, L. M. (1961). Mental and physical traits of a thousand gifted children. In J. J. Jenkins & D. G. Paterson (Eds.), *Studies in individual differences* (pp. 219–232). New York: Appleton-Century-Crofts. (Original work published 1925)

Tiryakian, E. (1981). The sociological import of a metaphor: Tracking the source of Max Weber's "iron cage." *Sociological Inquiry, 51,* 27–33.

Vaillant, G. E. (1977). *Adaptation to life.* Boston: Little, Brown.

Van Maanen, J. (Ed.). (1977). *Organizational careers: Some new perspectives.* New York: Wiley.

Vondracek, F. W. (1992). The construct of identity and its use in career theory and research. *Career Development Quarterly, 41,* 130–144.

Vroom, V. H. (1964). *Work and motivation.* New York: Wiley.

Weber, M. (1947). *The theory of social and economic organization* (A. M. Henderson & T. Parsons, Trans.). New York: Oxford University Press. (Original work published 1920)

Weber, M. (1958a). *The protestant ethic and the spirit of capitalism* (T. Parsons, Trans.). New York: Scribner. (Original work published 1904–1905)

Weber, M. (1958b). Bureaucracy (H. H. Gerth & C. W. Mills, Trans.). In H. H. Gerth & C. W. Mills

(Eds.), *From Max Weber: Essays in sociology* (pp. 196–244). New York: Oxford University Press. (Original work published 1922)

Weber, M. (1958c). Class, status, party (H. H. Gerth & C. W. Mills, Trans.). In H. H. Gerth & C. W. Mills (Eds.), *From Max Weber: Essays in sociology* (pp. 180–195). New York: Oxford University Press. (Original work published 1922)

Weiss, H. M. (1990). Learning theory and industrial and organizational psychology. In M. D. Dunnette & L. E. Hough (Eds.), *Handbook of industrial and organizational psychology* (2nd ed., Vol. 1, pp. 171–221). Palo Alto, CA: Consulting Psychologists Press.

Whittington, R. (1992). Putting Giddens into action: Social systems and managerial agency. *Journal of Management Studies, 29,* 693–712.

Whyte, W. H. (1956). *The organization man.* New York: Simon & Schuster.

Zerubavel, E. (1995). The rigid, the fuzzy, and the flexible: Notes on the mental sculpting of academic identity. *Social Research, 62*(4), 1093–1106.

3

TAXONOMY OF CAREER STUDIES

MAURY PEIPERL

HUGH GUNZ

Taxonomy: A classification of anything.

—*Oxford English Dictionary* (1989, 2nd ed.)

After all, the purist urge to compartmentalize reality and avoid "mental promiscuity" . . . at all costs belies some deep awareness that the wide divides we envision separating mental entities from one another are actually figments of our own minds.

—Zerubavel (1995, p. 16)

It is often said that you don't know where you stand until you know where you sit. Being able to relate one's own place in the world to those of others makes it possible to know what one is and is not, with what one should occupy oneself, and what one should leave to others. In this chapter, we explain where we sit, so that the reader can understand why the book has the shape it does. We try to answer the following questions: What was our rationale for choosing the topics we did? How do we see the field of career studies?

We have adopted a very personal style in this narrative because, as we shall see, there is no evidence yet of a single, authoritative, and generally accepted view on what career studies "is." There are a great many scholars who have their own view on what it is, but there is not much consensus (or even, in some cases, much overlap). Whether there ever will be is another matter and not one on which we shall speculate. So we do not claim authority here; we simply explain below how we see the field and why and leave it to the reader to agree or disagree.

Chapters 1 and 2 have begun the task of providing our answer to the question, What is the field of career studies? But we have not yet addressed the related question, which precedes any attempt at organizing a field: How does it relate to other disciplines? In Chapter 1, we made it clear that the field, at least as we deal with it in this book, is anchored by Arthur, Hall, and Lawrence's (1989b) concept of "the evolving sequence of a person's work experiences over time" (p. 8). In Chapter 2, Moore, Gunz, and Hall delved into the origins of the field, showing that it springs from several very different intellectual traditions, which still continue as independent lines of enquiry.

Defined in this way, it is evident that the field of career studies is intimately connected with a great many disciplines (Arthur, Hall et al., 1989b, chap. 1). This is why we suggested in Chapter 1 that it may not be a field at all but a perspective on social enquiry, its central concept being the effect on people of the passage of time. As such, it does not so much *relate* to other disciplines as *pervade* them. It is as possible to be a psychologist interested in careers as it is (to use Arthur, Hall et al.'s [1989a] list) to be a sociologist, a social psychologist, an anthropologist, an economist, a political scientist, a historian, or a geographer.

Rather than dwell on the possibility that career studies is not a field at all, we shall take this concept of pervasiveness to provide a starting point for describing our taxonomy. The notion of career studies as a perspective on social enquiry provides, for us, a rationale for gathering a broad range of forms of scholarship under one roof. For the moment, we shall think of this broad range of forms as a "field" and pose the following questions: What is its present shape? What does career studies look like?

Fortunately, we are not the first to attempt such a classification. First, we examine the nature of the territory that we are mapping: Just how well organized is "career studies" as a field? We look at previous classifications and differentiate between the approaches that have been taken. Next, we describe how we went about the task of mapping career studies and set out the result. Finally, we review briefly what we see as the strengths and limitations of our "map."

VIEWS OF THE CAREERS FIELD

The Territory

As will become evident, it is very hard to discern a core pattern of organization in the field of career studies. This point has been made before by Collin and Young (1986):

> There is no accepted corpus of theory in this area as suggested by Sonnenfeld and Kotter's (1982) use of the [phrase] "career theory." Although there is a considerable body of literature embracing research, theory, and speculation about career, it has no organizing principles, little coherence, and variable quality. It has grown sporadically and adventitiously in response to developments within several academic disciplines and in accord with their epistemological, philosophical, and methodological traditions. . . . it is a hybrid without organizing principles. (p. 838)

Curiously, this statement came at a time when many other authors were commenting on the "maturity" of the field. Hall (1987), for example, talks about the field having "come into maturity" (p. 301), and Arthur, Hall et al. (1989b) say, as we reported in Chapter 1, that "we have become a *field*" (italics in the original, p. xv).

Twenty years later, it is not clear that the picture has changed much. By 2000, Collin and Young were still commenting,

> It would seem that the best way of addressing the complex and multilevel relationships that comprise career has to be multidisciplinary. However, this has been called for previously (Arthur, Hall & Lawrence, 1989[b]), but the field of career remains largely fragmented, with a major division between those concerned with organizational careers (Collin, 1996) and others concerned with individual careers. (p. 293)

Perhaps this criticism is a little unfair. As we reported in Chapter 1, the rate at which research articles, in particular, appear each year keeps going up, as does the number of researchers producing them. It has often been pointed out (e.g., Collin, 1998, 2001; Schein, Afterword) that there is a vast gulf that separates the "management" career researchers from the large and flourishing community of career choice, education, and counseling researchers. If to this we add scholars of organization, who although they certainly do not label themselves as career researchers, nevertheless certainly work with career phenomena (many of these are referenced by Higgins and Dillon, Chapter 21, and Jones and Dunn, Chapter 22), we get a large and growing army of academics, publishing in a broad array of journals, of which any one group of researchers has probably encountered only a subset, or writing books, which again are encountered only by those disciplinarily closest to the author.

So the task of keeping track of research and scholarship on careers becomes increasingly difficult. As Schein points out in the Afterword to this volume, this difficulty is made dramatically manifest in the way the literatures attached to each of the topics covered in this *Handbook* fail to overlap. Nor is there anything new to this. In an introduction to two review articles on career mobility within organizations (Anderson, Milkovich, & Tsui, 1981; Stumpf & London, 1981), Boehm (1981) remarks that although the articles ostensibly are on the same subject, the approaches taken are strikingly different. Furthermore, "each article, before final editing, had close to 100 references, yet there were only 4 that were common to the two" (p. 527). That was more than 25 years ago, and the tree that is the field of career studies has grown incredibly since. Little wonder, then, that its branches grow ever more distant from each other.

This looks, in part, as if it is a problem of too many boundaries separating and isolating scholars, something that has been noted in both earlier and later works. For example,

> traditional convergence both within and between fields has broken down. Schein once warned of the price involved in "members of each subset of (careers) researchers" not building theory "on broad enough bases to be relevant to the academic community at large or to practitioners" (Schein, 1986: 315). . . . What is most important now is to keep the academic community and practitioners in touch with one another, to keep the conversation alive, as we strain to build and share a new appreciation of what is going on. (Peiperl & Arthur, 2000, p. 3)

Yet we should remember that

> any notion of orderliness presupposes at least some element of structure, which inevitably presupposes some boundaries. . . . Without at least some mental horizons that would help scholars curb their curiosity, organize their intellectual attention in a more "focused" manner, and essentially separate the relevant from the irrelevant, for example, it would be absolutely impossible to establish any coherent scholarly agenda at all. (Zerubavel, 1995, p. 17)

So it is entirely reasonable to expect that the field of career scholarship is organized into distinct subfields, each following its own agenda. And because each is doing so, it is not surprising that it loses contact with other subfields. That is why we have invited leaders of each to contribute chapters to this *Handbook,* so that their colleagues across the subfields can look over the boundaries separating them, pause, and consider the scope of the wider project of which they are part. And this is why we have chosen to devote a chapter to mapping the field of career studies. What we are attempting here is to sketch out the shape of the field and its structure and to explain our reasons for organizing this *Handbook* as we did. First, we look at how others have done it.

Looking for Patterns in the Output of a Fragmented Adhocracy

We argued in Chapter 1 that the field of career studies is best seen, in Whitley's (1984) terms, as a fragmented adhocracy. Given the "relatively fragmented knowledge structure and the existence of much disagreement about the relative importance of different problems to be solved by the field" (Knudsen, 2003, p. 278) that are implicit in this type of research, not only can we expect a loose consensus at best about what precisely the field comprises but neither can we (or for that matter, anyone else) claim comprehensiveness in the coverage of its literature. Here, we have tried to be *representative,* aiming to show something of the variety of approaches that have been taken to a very complex topic. Our starting point is the explosion of interest in career studies that happened in the 1970s, sparked by the work of scholars such as Schein, Super, and Hall. Although, as Moore, Gunz, and Hall make clear in Chapter 2, each of these scholars was building on the contributions of others, this period marked the appearance of a kind of explicit awareness that career studies existed as a field of study.

There are many edited books and review articles about career that tackle a specific aspect of the field. They do not aim to be comprehensive but have often emerged as highly influential, containing a lot of thoughtful material about the nature and future of the field (e.g., Arthur & Rousseau, 1996; Osterman, 1996; Peiperl, Arthur, & Anand, 2002). Although often cited in this volume, they will not be referenced further in this chapter because they were not intended by their authors to offer an overview of the field.

One particular subfield of career studies, which could broadly be called career counseling, maintains a very clear sense of itself and its boundaries. It publishes regular reviews of work published in the area (e.g., Bingham & Krantz, 2001; Buboltz & Savickas, 1994; Fitzgerald & Rounds, 1989; Flores, Scott, & Wang, 2003; Greenhaus, Parasuraman, & Wormley, 1990; Herr, 2001; Tinsley & Heesacker, 1984) and of theoretical models (see Chen, 2003, for a recent review), but these reviews do not aim to put a structure on the field of career studies overall.

There have been a number of other books (e.g., Arthur, Hall, & Lawrence, 1989b; Glaser, 1968; Hall, 1976, 2002; Hall & Associates, 1986; Peiperl, Arthur, Goffee, & Morris, 2000; Schein, 1978; Van Maanen, 1977) that have taken a broader view and that clearly do aim to place a structure on the field of career studies. There have also been a number of reviews published in journals, although the authors often were addressing a particular issue that shaped the way the authors framed the field. Sometimes the review is incidental to a different purpose—for example, Sullivan's (1999) review of the literature on developmental stage theories and boundaryless careers, which provides the foundation for a thoughtful commentary on the direction careers are taking in the late 20th and early 21st centuries. It is on these contributions that we draw for what follows.

Mapping the Territory

There is a pattern discernible in the approaches that have been taken to defining the field although little agreement about the contents of the pattern. The pattern involves two approaches, one of which has been handled in two distinctive ways. We call the approaches here *topological* and *taxonomic*.

The *topological* approach examines the literature to see if underlying dimensions can be identified so that the subfields of career studies can be mapped in the space defined by these dimensions.

The *taxonomic* approach identifies and lists the different subfields within career studies.

In principle, either approach could have an equally sound theoretical grounding. But in practice, as we shall see, topological approaches are much more clearly grounded in this respect than are taxonomic ones. Perhaps for this reason, there has been little agreement on the structure of a taxonomy of careers.

Topological Approaches (Table 3.1)

We encountered two attempts at mapping areas of career scholarship along different dimensions: maps of organizational careers (Vardi, 1980) and of sociological approaches that have been used in the study of career (Maranda & Comeau, 2000). The dimensions used in these maps often crop up in discussions of career scholarship as Janus-like dualities that pervade careers (e.g., Moore, Gunz, and Hall, Chapter 2) and are worth examining in more detail. Vardi (1980) distinguishes between individual and organizational levels of analysis and subjective and objective approaches, while Maranda and Comeau (2000) identify dimensions they label as structure versus voluntarism and adaptation versus transformation. We look briefly at each pair of dimensions in Table 3.1.

Level of Analysis. Careers may be variously studied as individual, organizational, or societal phenomena, and each kind of study is quite different from the others. At the *individual* level of analysis, it is the person and his or her work history that are of interest. At the *organizational* level, the researcher focuses on the social systems that shape careers—for example, the career systems that are part of the human resource management practices of a business organization (Slay and Taylor, Chapter 19) or the career streams that

Table 3.1   Examples of Topological Approaches to Organizing the Field of Career Studies

Authors	Domain Mapped	Dimension 1	Dimension 2
Vardi, 1980	Organizational careers	Individual–organizational levels of analysis	Subjective–objective
Maranda & Comeau, 2000	Sociological theories relevant to the study of career	Structure (choices determined by constraints, norms, and sanctions)–voluntarism (individual autonomy and free will)	Adaptation (change people so that they can integrate into society)–transformation (change society to integrate people)

form over time as people flow in and out of occupations. At the *societal* level, a researcher might be interested, for example, in mobility between socioeconomic groups or intergenerational mobility between social classes; alternatively, he or she might study the influence of education on how well people do in life.

Subjective Versus Objective. The *subjective-objective* distinction has been central to the study of career since at least the time of Hughes (1937). The duality it identifies is between career as a subjectively experienced process and as a series of status offices (Hughes, 1937) that the career holder passes through and that are evident to everyone else. To oversimplify somewhat, it distinguishes between the career that can be seen by an observer and that might be recorded in the career owner's resumé (objective) and the career an observer can only guess at (subjective) (Khapova, Arthur, and Wilderom, Chapter 7).

Structure Versus Voluntarism, Adaptation Versus Transformation. Both *structure versus voluntarism* and *adaptation versus transformation* share a focus on the nature of *agency* in careers—in other words, the extent to which the career holder affects his or her career. *Structure* is about the way that individual choices are determined by constraints, norms, and sanctions, while *voluntarism* is about individual autonomy and free will in career. *Adaptation* is about changing people so that they can better integrate into social structures (Maranda & Comeau, 2000, use the term *society*), while *transformation* is about changing social structures to better integrate people. Again, these dualities run throughout the careers literature,

often unacknowledged. For example, career boundaries (Gunz, Peiperl, and Tzabbar, Chapter 24) are constraints on career mobility, which may or may not be acknowledged by the actors experiencing them. On the other hand, the study of personality and career (Judge and Kammeyer-Mueller, Chapter 4) focuses on the role that individual characteristics play in shaping careers despite the boundaries that might be encountered.

Taxonomic Approaches (Tables 3.2–3.4)

Authors seem to have taken one of two approaches (see below) to developing their list of headings under which to define the field of career studies, although the line between the two is occasionally blurred. It is also important to note that the topics themselves are not necessarily clearly defined: One cannot always infer accurately the exact territory covered by a given label just from the label. The only way to be sure that a taxonomy of taxonomies, which is the exercise we are engaged in at the moment, identifies the similarities and differences between various authors' approaches to the task is to examine the literatures covered in each. Even then, there can be no guarantee that any two scholars will agree on what a given study is really about or that the interpretation we place on their categorizations is the same as their own.

The first approach, which we called *"discipline or research topic based"* (henceforth, discipline based), typically starts with a list of disciplines or research topics that defines the authors' interest in career studies. Some follow traditional disciplinary boundaries; Peiperl and Arthur (2000), for

Table 3.2   Examples of Taxonomic Approaches to Organizing the Field of Career Studies: Disciplinary or Research Topic Based

Authors	Discipline or Research Topic
Van Maanen, 1977	• Shape of career: internal and external perspectives (direction, timing, outcomes/shape) • Career phases: temporal perspective • Career cube: interactionist perspective (roles, tasks, settings; individual characteristics; family state; outcomes)
Sonnenfeld & Kotter, 1982	• Social structural • Individual traits and their relationship with career choice • Career stage • Life cycle
Arthur & Lawrence, 1984	• Psychology: observable individual differences (vocational psychology, vocational guidance) • Psychological studies of organizations (careers in organizations, management style, employee assessment) • Life stages (developmental psychology, social psychology and normative career expectations, sociological and anthropological approaches to explaining the external definition of life stages)
Collin & Young, 1986	• Ecological (examining careers as the "continuous set of reciprocal processes at all levels and dimensions of society" [p. 845]) • Biographical • Hermeneutical (interpretive)
Collin, 1998	• Career choice, education, and counseling • Organizational psychological and sociological approaches to studying organizational careers
Peiperl & Arthur, 2000	• Psychology (anchored around personality) • Sociology (anchored around social structure) • Education (convergence around vocation) • Management (convergence around the organization of work)

example, organized the literature under four headings: psychology, sociology, education, and management. Others use research categories more closely aligned with career studies—for instance, Sonnenfeld and Kotter's (1982) categorization of the literature into four main threads: social structural, individual trait, career stage, and life cycle. As is evident from Table 3.2, there is little consistency in the perspectives that were chosen: Each group of authors have their own distinctive selection of disciplines that they believe comprise the career field.

The second approach involves a selection of *career-related issues* about which a literature exists or, in the author's view, should exist (Table 3.3). What distinguishes them from the "disciplines" of the first approach is their focus on substantive career phenomena. In the sense we use it here, a discipline represents a way of approaching an issue. For example—and deliberately to oversimplify—psychologists typically examine career choice by focusing on the personality of the person making the choice and how close a match he or she is to the requirements of an occupation. Sociologists, in contrast, might be more interested in the way the choice is constrained by things like social class, income, education, or ethnicity. So a *discipline-based*

Table 3.3 Examples of Taxonomic Approaches to Organizing the Field of Career Studies: Issue Based

Authors	Issue
Glaser, 1968	• Recruitment to organizational careers • Career motivations within the organization • Loyalty and commitment to the organizational career • Sources and strategies of promotion • Managing demotion • Organizational succession • Moving between organizations • Executive and worker career patterns
Hall, 1976	• Career choice • Career stages • Predicting career outcomes: performance • Predicting career outcomes: identity • Predicting career outcomes: attitudes • Predicting career outcomes: adaptability
Hall & Associates, 1986	• Career planning (for the individual) • Career management (for the organization) • Career spectrum (see Hall, 1987)
Hall, 1987	• Individual career processes (adult development, career decision making and motivation, role transitions, socialization) • Person-environment interaction processes (work and family interactions, dual career processes, career plateauing, mentoring, and developmental relationships) • Institutional processes (career paths and ladders, equal employment opportunity, human resource management systems, occupational communities, national culture)
Arthur, Hall, and Lawrence, 1989b	• Individual differences and career outcomes • Chicago School • Adult development • Gender • Racial diversity • Career and family • Work role transitions • Career systems and organizational strategy • Personal disposition as career influence • Career stress • Feminist perspective (communion vs. agency) • Individual-organization fit • Self-designing careers • Tournament versus human capital approaches • Blue-collar careers • Organizational power and politics • Rites of passage • Human capital investment • Career reputations • National culture

(Continued)

Table 3.3 (Continued)

Sullivan, 1999[a]	• Developmental stage theories • Boundaryless careers
Hall, 2002	• Career choice • Developmental stages • Predicting performance, effectiveness • Protean career identity, attitudes • Career adaptability • Career in the context of other life roles

a. Focuses on the changing nature of careers at the end of the 20th century.

Table 3.4   Mixed Approaches

a. Discipline and Issue Based

Collin & Young, 2000	• Career environment • Sociology and careers • Psychology of careers • Careers and values • Construction of time • Boundaryless careers • Career development • Women's careers • Postmodern perspective on careers • Construction and rhetoric of career • Careers, actions, and projects • Place of work in people's lives • Counseling and multicultural issues • Management of careers in organizations • Education and career • Career and social policy
Feldman, 1989[a]	• Content issues (job stability, job exit, socialization, and resocialization) • Theoretical approaches (adult development, stress paradigm, small group behavior, attribution theory, resource dependency/population ecology) • Research methods issues • Managerial practice (individual perspective, organizational perspective)

b. Topological and Disciplinary and Issue Based

Schein, 1978	• Domain mapped: organizational careers • Basic dimension: level of analysis • Issues in taxonomy: individual (biological life cycles, family stages, career stages); individual-organizational (career entry, socialization, psychological contract, career anchors, mid-career issues); organizational (career system management)

a. Examines trends in the study of careers over the previous 10 years.

approach to making this distinction would call one the psychological and the other the sociological perspective. An *issue-based* approach would simply focus on the issue that is being studied, namely career choice.

Given the myriad possible ways in which the careers field could be divided, any such taxonomy typically has an agenda behind it: It represents those authors' view of what matters in the study of career. But not always: As we have seen (Chapter 1), Arthur, Hall, et al. (1989b) let a thousand flowers bloom by explicitly *not* starting with a preconceived view of the structure of the field. Rather, they allowed it to emerge by inviting "review chapters with a point of view" (p. xvii) from leading scholars in the career field and then inviting writers who were not identified with the field to write forward-looking chapters suggesting ways in which the field could usefully develop.

Perhaps not surprisingly, given the variety of approaches taken, the overlap in coverage between these various approaches is not very strong. There are themes that recur; for example, adult development in one form or another is dealt with in a large proportion of the taxonomies. But many more of the themes occur only two or three times, and often only once. This is the case even for topics that one might expect to be relatively foundational—for example, disposition (the role of personality), work-family, psychological contract, mentoring and developmental issues, occupational choice, and demographic diversity.

Finally, the distinction between discipline-based and issue-based taxonomies is not always clear; some authors have combined both, for example, by examining both certain disciplinary contributions to career and specific career issues (Table 3.4a).

On Classifying Career Studies: Taxonomies Versus Topologies

It is common to think of a taxonomic approach as one that organizes a field hierarchically into headings, subheadings, sub-subheadings, and so on. But it will have become obvious to the reader that the approaches we have described as taxonomic show very little of this hierarchical structure. They tend to be lists rather than hierarchies. This puts them at one extreme of what could be thought of as a "continuum of completeness."

At one end of this continuum are taxonomies that are self-contained and complete: Every possible member of the set of objects being classified, known or as yet undiscovered, has a home. For example, since Mendeleev proposed the periodic table of the elements in 1869 in a presentation to the Russian Chemical Society, this classification has proven completely robust. Not only have all the elements discovered since Mendeleev found their place on the table, but theoretical developments in the decades that followed, that gave us a better understanding of the structure of the atom, provided a robust explanation for why the table works so well.

At an intermediate level, the Linnæan classification of living organisms works well in the sense that biologists can locate all living organisms somewhere within it. But it is not unassociated with controversy. Biologists sometimes disagree about the "true" home of a particular organism in the taxonomy or about the major levels and groupings within it. Because it does not have quite the same robust, encompassing theoretical underpinning of the periodic table, it is by no means inconceivable that it will some day be replaced by another way of organizing living organisms. The rumpus in 2006 concerning how planets should be defined and where Pluto belongs in such a classification provides yet another example of the uncertainties surrounding intermediate classifications.

Arguably, at the other end of the "completeness" continuum is a fragmented adhocracy such as career studies. It consists of many different fields of research, some linked to each other, some not, and some completely unaware of each other (as has often been argued, as we saw above, about the split between counseling research and "managerial" career research). It is hard to see how it could be otherwise. Our definition of career (in Chapter 1) as a perspective on social enquiry whose central concept is the effect on people of the passage of time makes it clear that just about any branch of social enquiry could find itself dealing with career-related phenomena. There is simply no equivalent to the theory that explains why atoms are constructed as they are that could provide the same sense of structure to career studies (or, indeed, to any area of organization studies). There is not even the equivalent of the various morphological and genetic theoretical frameworks that help biologists classify living organisms. So it can be very difficult to decide whether a given topic is "inside" or "outside" the field being mapped (it can be hard enough with the Linnæan taxonomy; witness the ongoing controversies over whether viruses are living or not). Without such a clear criterion, it is always possible to add another topic to the "field," with no clear sense of where this accretion process should end.

This is where topologies can help. Unlike taxonomies, they have an inherently theoretical foundation: Types of research are located on a map defined by a limited number of theoretical dimensions. So whereas a list of topics or disciplines can stretch for as long as you might wish it to, the territory defined by a topology has a shape to it. Both Vardi (1980) and Maranda and Comeau (2000) draw the field on two-dimensional maps, giving a sense of wholeness to what they are describing, a little like the sense of wholeness that comes, for example, from the Linnæan classification.

Indeed, Schein took this as his basic organizing approach for his 1978 book (Table 3.4b). It is primarily organized topologically, along the "level of analysis" dimension. Within each of the three major headings (individual issues, individual-organizational issues, organizational issues), he identified a set of issues relevant to that level of analysis. It is on this approach that the current volume is modeled. Next, we explain how we did it.

Our Taxonomy, Topologically Informed

Devising and Implementing a Topology and Taxonomy

As the heading for this section suggests, the procedure we followed when organizing the

material for this book followed that of Schein (1978), combining both taxonomic and topological approaches. We began topologically by considering, as did Schein, that most pervasive of dimensions, level of analysis. Career studies has two of its deepest roots in psychology and sociology and in some sense "meets in the middle" of these two disciplines, so we decided to begin with a "micro to macro" dimension. This was divided into the realms of the individual at one end and institutions (including work organizations) at the other, with "context" in the middle. By *context,* we meant those aspects of the context within which careers are made that lack the conscious structure of the institutions from which societies are built. Certainly, work organizations are forms of institutions, but one of the more notable themes in the careers literature since the 1980s has been an interest in careers *beyond* such organizations. They go under many names (Khapova, Arthur, and Wilderom, Chapter 7), but they have in common the idea (not without controversy, as we shall see in, for example, Chapters 6, 17, and 24) that careers in the late 20th and early 21st centuries are not as limited to work organizations as they once were.

With this one-dimensional topology in mind, then, we switched to a taxonomic approach, specifically issue based. Our reasoning was that we wanted the chapters of the *Handbook* to address current areas of research. A disciplinary taxonomy, we felt, would have interposed a layer of abstraction between the subject matter and its users; we wanted the volume to speak directly to those interested in each particular subfield, as well as to show them the broader field of which each particular subfield is a part. The risk attendant on this decision, of course, is to encourage fragmentation of the field or, at least, not to discourage it. Still, this is a risk in any topological or taxonomic approach, the only difference being the nature of the fault lines dividing the various contributions.

We compiled as comprehensive a list as we could of the topics that we believed to be active areas of scholarship in the field of career studies (Table 3.5). The reader can compare our list with those of others, which we have shown in the tables in this chapter. At least half are to be found in one or more of the other taxonomies, but a good number appear to be new. That is not to say that they are new to the careers literature but that they seem to be new to attempts to pull the field together. That does not in itself, of course, make this collection more comprehensive than others, because as we have already observed, all collections that we have reviewed have introduced material not found elsewhere. It simply illustrates our basic point—that as a fragmented adhocracy the field of career studies is surrounded by ill-defined boundaries, with no strong consensus about what it comprises. We believe that our taxonomy provides as comprehensive a coverage of the field of career studies as has been put forward, but we are under no illusion that this belief will be universally shared.

Next, we mapped our taxonomy onto our one-dimensional level-of-analysis topology as shown in Table 3.5, combining some, as we explained in Chapter 1, to get a manageable number of chapters. There were a small number of topics for which we did not commission separate chapters, in part because we were fairly certain that they were sufficiently pervasive within the field to be covered in many of the other topics. Mostly, we turned out to be right.

A Retrospective Topological Check: How "Complete" Is Our Coverage?[1]

An implication of our discussion on the nature of taxonomies of the kind that we and others have used to describe the careers field is that they cannot be used to test the completeness of the taxonomy's coverage. If there is no good theoretical foundation to the taxonomy—as there is in the Mendeleevian and Linnæan taxonomies—we have no theoretical grounds for saying where the taxonomy should stop. We can simply look forward to progressively larger taxonomies over time.

We argued above that a topological approach is theoretically more sound than what we labeled taxonomic because it creates a map of a field, the dimensions of which have a theoretical rationale. Although we used only one dimension—level of analysis—to organize the chapters of the book, it is instructive to see how they locate themselves on a more complex map. Clearly, we could only do this in a very approximate way, because the authors of each chapter did not, of course, limit themselves to one-dimensional depictions of their topics.

We chose three dimensions: level of analysis, objectivity, and time (Figure 3.1). The first two we have already described (individual-institutional and subjective-objective). Time is, of course, central to our definition of career studies (the effect on people of the passage of time). Researchers may adopt cross-sectional or longitudinal methodologies; they may be interested in the entire life span or just individual stages or phases; they may be interested in the life cycles of people or of institutions. Clearly, we are using *time* in a very broad sense and not one that can be measured with precision on a single scale. The map we are describing is fuzzy at best.

Still, we felt it a useful exercise to see how the chapters in the volume fit on the three-dimensional map. And, as we reviewed the chapters to see (a) at which level of analysis they operated, (b) how they addressed the question of subjectivity versus objectivity, and (c) what was their perspective on time, it became apparent that there was a very broad coverage of the map within the covers of this book.

Nearly all the chapters have an *individual* perspective. Arguably, the two that do not are Chapter 10, which looks at the issues caused by systemic discrimination, and Chapter 17, which is concerned with the institutions of outside hiring. Nine are interested in network phenomena, 14 in organizational-level phenomena, and at least 10 in societal phenomena. For example, Chapter 7 does not just examine the subjective career from a psychological perspective; it introduces social psychological and grand sociological theory as well. And Chapter 16 approaches the careers of those who are not normally thought of as upwardly mobile both from the perspective of the individual and from that of entire occupational categories.

Next, of the 21 chapters in Part II, at least 13 have a *subjective* focus and 16 an *objective* one. At least 8—over a third—have recognizably both. For example, Chapter 4 (personality and career success) examines career success from both perspectives, as does Chapter 11 (customized careers).

Finally, there is a great range of treatment of *time* in the chapters. Although it is common to think of cross-sectional research methodologies

Table 3.5   Taxonomy and Topology of the *Handbook*

| Initial Topic(s) (Taxonomy) | Chapter | | Position in Topology |
	No.	Title	
History	2	Tracing the Historical Roots of Career Theory in Management and Organization Studies	
Taxonomy, subjects	3	Taxonomy of Career Studies	
Personality in career Career success	4	Personality and Career Success	Individual
Occupational choice	5	Occupational Choice	
Career counseling	6	Career Counseling	
Subjective career (calling) Intelligent career	7	The Subjective Career in the Knowledge Economy	
Life balance	8	The Intersection of Work and Family Lives	
Moving to retirement	9	Late Career and Retirement Issues	
Careers of the socially marginalized	10	Organizational Challenges at the Periphery: Career Issues for the Socially Marginalized	
Nontraditional careers	11	Customized Careers	
Contextual issues (exogenous variables)	12	Contextual Issues in the Study of Career	Contextual
Mentoring	13	Mentoring and Developmental Networks in the New Career Context	
Networks	14	Networks and Identities: Reciprocal Influences on Career Processes and Outcomes	
Stage theories	15	The Developmental Theories: A Critical Examination of Their Continuing Impact on Careers Research	
Living to work versus working to live	16	Living to Work—Working to Live: Conceptualizations of Careers Among Contemporary Workers	
Labor markets; war for talent E-enabled careers	17	The Institutions of Outside Hiring	
The global career	18	Global Careers	
Psychological contracts Career systems	19	Career Systems and Psychological Contracts	Institutional
Organizational demography	20	Organizational Demography and Individual Careers: Structure, Norms, and Outcomes	
Career patterns and organizational performance[a]	21	Career Patterns and Organizational Performance	

Career patterns	22	Careers and Institutions: The Centrality of Careers to Organizational Studies	Institutional (continued)
Comparative career management	23	Careers Across Cultures	
Boundaries in the study of career	24	Boundaries in the Study of Career	
Work role transitions			
Resilience		Not included	
Interventions		Passim	
Socialization		Passim, especially Chapters 10, 12, 13, 14, 19, and 22	
Metaphor		Passim	

a. The concept of "organizational performance" broadened considerably during our initial deliberations, encompassing, by the time the chapters were commissioned, the growth and development of institutions generally.

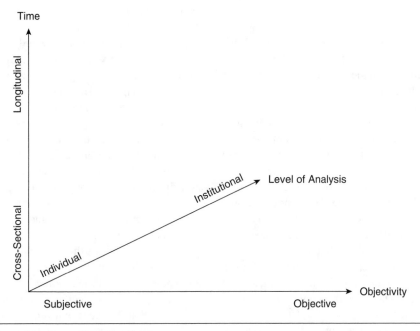

Figure 3.1   Topology of the *Handbook*

as dominant in the field, 13 of the 21 chapters draw on longitudinal studies or explicitly consider longitudinal perspectives. There is, naturally, considerable interest in the life span, either in its entirety or analyzed by stage and phase.

Each chapter covers more than one point on each dimension; it may refer to both individual and organizational perspectives, subjective and objective. So if we were to depict our conclusions graphically in Figure 3.1, we would see not a series of points, but a series of surfaces filling the space pretty much in its entirety. We can conclude from this that although (as we explained above) we can never know whether a taxonomy of career studies provides "complete" coverage of the field, it does seem as though our authors have filled the topological space defined by the dimensions of level of analysis, objectivity, and time. That may not be a complete answer to the question, "How comprehensive is the coverage of this book?" but it goes some of the way toward providing one.

Conclusion: What Might Be Argued to Be Missing From This Taxonomy?

That said, what is missing from our taxonomy (and this book)? Mostly, we shall defer to the authors of Part III, who address this issue directly and who have many suggestions for ways in which the field as represented here could be extended. We can, however, make three brief observations.

First, the taxonomy reflects the national origins of its creators. As Thomas and Inkson point out in Chapter 23 in their discussion of what they call "parochialism in career theory," the concepts with which most authors are working in this book simply do not have much practical meaning to people living in very different kinds of societies. What, they ask, does *career* mean in the sense used in this book (the evolving sequence of a person's work experiences over time) to a young person living in a remote rural area of South Africa in which the concept of "employment" is largely meaningless? Because careers depend on the social forms within which they are made, their meaning must change with the social form. Nowhere is this likely to be more critical than when we are dealing with people's lives in the way that career counselors do. Yet because the book cannot cover everything, its treatment of career is bound firmly to the world of Western-style developed economies. Furthermore, although the contributors to this volume comprise some 15 nationalities, because North Americans have been the most prolific publishers in this particular world, we still see a disproportionately—though far from exclusively—North American perspective on the questions that should be asked and the methodologies that should be used.

A secondary consequence of this perspective is a methodological one. Although qualitative, interpretive research is certainly discussed in the chapters that follow, and there are accounts of interesting and rising methodologies such as narrative analysis (particularly by Kidd in Chapter 6), there is still an emphasis on the kind of work that appears in North American journals. Career is a very rich phenomenon, and it needs rich methodologies to explore it. An exploration of methodology and how it relates to our understanding of career is certainly needed.

Finally, the taxonomy reflects the scholarly origins of its creators. The world of career scholarship from which we come, and from which the authors of this volume are drawn, is dominated by business schools, and to a lesser extent schools in which career counseling is taught. If it had been edited by, for example, sociologists, social anthropologists, or labor economists, it would have been a very different book, even if it had still chosen the focus of work career. Sociologists would almost certainly place more emphasis on major theories such as status attainment (Gunz, Peiperl, and Tzabbar, Chapter 24), intergenerational mobility, or the careers of what Guest and Sturges (Chapter 16) call "those in routine occupations." Social anthropologists would have been drawn, for example, to comparative studies across cultures or to the symbolism and ritual of career transitions. Labor economists (e.g., Osterman, 1996) would have paid much more attention to the structure of internal and external labor markets. And so on.

To tweak slightly the aphorism with which we started this chapter, where we stand depends on where we sit. Our taxonomy is the product of where we sit, and we can claim no more generality than that. We believe it is as comprehensive a taxonomy as has been published in the field of career studies, but—as we said in Chapter 1—we do not expect everyone to agree with us. Part of the great delight and fascination of working with careers, and a direct consequence of the richness of the field, is that everyone has his or her own perspective on what matters in it. As Whitley (1984) points out, to understand the nature of the scholarship going on in a particular discipline, one needs to understand its social organization. While the organization of the field of career studies remains as fragmented and adhocratic as it is, and while we would be happy to be proved wrong on this point, for our part we can do no better by way of organizing its output than what we offer in this volume.

NOTE

1. The analysis underpinning this section was the product of a fascinating discussion involving the authors and Yoav Vardi, to whom we are most grateful.

REFERENCES

Anderson, J. C., Milkovich, G. T., & Tsui, A. (1981). A model of intra-organizational mobility. *Academy of Management Review, 6*(4), 529–538.

Arthur, M. B., Hall, D. T., & Lawrence, B. S. (1989a). Generating new directions in career theory: The case for a transdisciplinary approach. In M. B. Arthur, D. T. Hall, & B. S. Lawrence (Eds.), *Handbook of career theory* (pp. 7–25). Cambridge, UK: Cambridge University Press.

Arthur, M. B., Hall, D. T., & Lawrence, B. S. (Eds.). (1989b). *Handbook of career theory.* Cambridge, UK: Cambridge University Press.

Arthur, M. B., & Lawrence, B. S. (1984). Perspectives on environment and career: An introduction. *Journal of Occupational Behaviour, 5,* 1–8.

Arthur, M. B., & Rousseau, D. M. (Eds.). (1996). *The boundaryless career: A new employment principle for a new organizational era.* New York: Oxford University Press.

Bingham, R. P., & Krantz, J. (2001). Career and vocational assessment 1997–1998: A biennial review. *Journal of Career Assessment, 9*(1), 1–24.

Boehm, V. R. (1981). Scientific parallelism in personnel mobility research: A preview of two approaches. *Academy of Management Review, 6*(4), 527–528.

Buboltz, W. C., & Savickas, M. L. (1994). A 20-year retrospective of *The Career Development Quarterly. The Career Development Quarterly, 42*(4), 367–381.

Chen, C. P. (2003). Integrating perspectives in career development theory and practice. *The Career Development Quarterly, 51*(3), 203–216.

Collin, A. (1996). *Integrating neglected issues into the reconceptualization of career.* Paper presented at the 104th annual convention of the American Psychological Association, Toronto, Ontario.

Collin, A. (1998). New challenges in the study of career. *Personnel Review, 27*(5), 412–425.

Collin, A. (2001). An interview with Mark Savickas: Themes in an eminent career. *British Journal of Guidance and Counselling, 29*(1), 121–136.

Collin, A., & Young, R. A. (1986). New directions for theories of career. *Human Relations, 39*(9), 837–853.

Collin, A., & Young, R. A. (2000). The future of career. In A. Collin & R. A. Young (Eds.), *The future of career* (pp. 276–300). Cambridge, UK: Cambridge University Press.

Feldman, D. C. (1989). Careers in organizations: Recent trends and future directions. *Journal of Management, 15*(June), 135–156.

Fitzgerald, L. F., & Rounds, J. B. (1989). Vocational behavior, 1988: A critical analysis. *Journal of Vocational Behavior, 35*(2), 105–163.

Flores, L. Y., Scott, A. B., & Wang, Y.-W. (2003). Practice and research in career counseling and development: 2002. *The Career Development Quarterly, 52*(2), 98–131.

Glaser, B. G. (1968). *Organizational careers: A sourcebook for theory.* Chicago: Aldine.

Greenhaus, J. H., Parasuraman, S., & Wormley, W. (1990). Effects of race on organizational experiences, job performance evaluations, and career outcomes. *Academy of Management Journal, 33,* 64–86.

Hall, D. T. (1976). *Careers in organizations.* Santa Monica, CA: Goodyear.

Hall, D. T. (1987). Careers and socialization. Special issue: Yearly review of management. *Journal of Management, 13*(2), 301–321.

Hall, D. T. (2002). *Careers in and out of organizations.* Thousand Oaks, CA: Sage.

Hall, D. T., & Associates (1986). *Career development in organizations.* San Francisco: Jossey-Bass.

Herr, E. L. (2001). Career development and its practice: A historical perspective. *The Career Development Quarterly, 49*(3), 196–211.

Hughes, E. C. (1937). Institutional office and the person. *American Journal of Sociology, 43,* 404–413.

Knudsen, C. (2003). *Pluralism, scientific progress and the structure of organization studies.* Oxford: Oxford University Press.

Maranda, M.-F., & Comeau, Y. (2000). Some contributions of sociology to the understanding of career. In A. Collin & R. A. Young (Eds.), *The future of career* (pp. 37–52). Cambridge, UK: Cambridge University Press.

Osterman, P. (Ed.). (1996). *Broken ladders: Managerial careers in the new economy.* New York: Oxford University Press.

Peiperl, M., & Arthur, M. B. (2000). Topics for conversation: Career themes old and new. In M. Peiperl, M. B. Arthur, R. Goffee, & T. Morris (Eds.), *Career frontiers: New conceptions of working lives* (pp. 1–19). Oxford: Oxford University Press.

Peiperl, M. A., Arthur, M. B., & Anand, N. (Eds.). (2002). *Career creativity: Explorations in the remaking of work.* Oxford: Oxford University Press.

Peiperl, M., Arthur, M. B., Goffee, R., & Morris, T. (Eds.). (2000). *Career frontiers: New conceptions of working lives.* Oxford: Oxford University Press.

Schein, E. H. (1978). *Career dynamics: Matching individual and organizational needs.* Reading, MA: Addison-Wesley.

Schein, E. H. (1986). A critical look at current career theory and research. In D. T. Hall & Associates (Eds.), *Career development in organizations* (pp. 310–331). San Francisco: Jossey-Bass.

Sonnenfeld, J. A., & Kotter, J. P. (1982). The maturation of career theory. *Human Relations, 35*(1), 19–46.

Stumpf, S. A., & London, M. (1981). Management promotions: Individual and organizational factors influencing the decision process. *Academy of Management Review, 6*(4), 539–549.

Sullivan, S. E. (1999). The changing nature of careers: A review and research agenda. *Journal of Management, 25*(3), 457–484.

Tinsley, H. E., & Heesacker, M. (1984). Vocational behavior and career development, 1983: A review. *Journal of Vocational Behavior, 25*(2), 139–190.

Van Maanen, J. (Ed.). (1977). *Organizational careers: Some new perspectives.* London: Wiley.

Vardi, Y. (1980). Organizational career mobility: An integrative model. *Academy of Management Review, 5*(3), 341–355.

Whitley, R. D. (1984). The development of management studies as a fragmented adhocracy. *Social Science Information/Information sur les Sciences Sociales, 23*(4–5), 775–818.

Zerubavel, E. (1995). The rigid, the fuzzy, and the flexible: Notes on the mental sculpting of academic identity. *Social Research, 62*(4), 1093–1106.

PART II

Main Currents in the Study of Career

Section 1

Careers and the Individual

I n Part II, we address, as its title suggests, the main currents in career scholarship. As we explained in Chapter 1, it is impossible to claim comprehensiveness in this coverage; nevertheless, each of the topics covered in these 21 chapters has a long history and is the subject of lively scholarly interest. Section 1 looks at research on careers and the individual.

The section begins (Chapter 4) with Judge and Kammeyer-Mueller asking perhaps the most fundamental individual-level career question of all: What is the relationship between personality and career success? After defining career success and its extrinsic and intrinsic components, the authors focus on the five-factor model of personality, perhaps currently the most studied framework for analyzing the relationship between personality and career outcome. They review the research linking each of the five factors—emotional stability, extroversion, openness to experience, agreeableness, and conscientiousness—to career success and then add three other dispositional traits: proactive personality, core self-evaluations, and agentic versus communal orientation. Next, they turn to the question of why these relationships might be observed, organizing their

discussion around a model that proposes that the relationship is mediated by the type of jobs individuals have held over the course of their career, their performance on the job, their social ties, and the features of their job. Next, they consider a number of potential moderators of the relationship, including situational effects and personality (for both situation/career-success and personality/career-success relationships). They conclude by commenting on the modest nature of the personality/career-success effects that have been uncovered thus far, although they note that this does not mean that they are zero. They point to several areas for future study, including improvements in the care taken over study design, the need to include work-family balance as an outcome, and the need for other moderators and traits to be examined.

In Chapter 5, Savickas examines the vast literature on occupational choice. The chapter begins with the observation that the concept only became salient when children no longer took up their parents' occupations as a matter of course ("occupational inheritance"). The forces of industrialization and urbanization led to social reformers, in particular Frank Parsons, focusing on the need to help people find jobs that suited them, which in turn led to vocational guidance as a scientifically based activity. Savickas locates occupational choice under the theoretical rubric of person-environment fit, of which two forms exist: complementary (when an individual and an environment provide what the other wants) and supplementary (when an individual and his or her environment resemble each other). He focuses on Holland's highly influential supplemental theory of vocational personalities and work environments (the famous hexagonal realistic-investigative-artistic-social-enterprising-conventional [RIASEC] model). Four secondary propositions emerge from Holland's work, about the degree of relatedness among types, the fit between personality types and environment types, how closely a person resembles a single type, and the clarity and stability of an individual's self-perceptions and vocational goals. Next, Savickas examines the phases of the decision-making process itself, distinguishing process from content (which occupation the individual chooses). A key attribute that determines the way individuals master the decision-making tasks is career adaptability and its four global dimensions: concern about choices to be made, personal control over the decision-making process, curiosity about possible selves and work scenarios, and confidence in making choices. In his concluding section, Savickas points to new models that are becoming influential and that shift the focus to subjective meaning making and "mattering."

Chapter 6 covers the closely related subject of career counseling. Kidd defines it as "a process that helps individuals not only make career-related decisions but also effectively manage their careers over the life course and develop the emotional resilience to cope with the challenges that arise as their working lives progress." First, she reviews a broad range of theoretical approaches to counseling, starting with the well established person-environment-fit theories and continuing with developmental and cognitive-behavioral theories. Next, she examines some recently emerging approaches, including the narrative approaches referred to at the end of Savickas's chapter, and action theory. Kidd then turns to perspectives on therapeutic counseling that have been applied to career

counseling, the most important of which, she argues, are person-centered and psychodynamic theories. This breadth of theoretical offerings raises important practical and epistemological issues that Kidd discusses before turning to a detailed examination of the counseling process itself. She analyzes it in four stages: building the relationship with the client, enabling the client's understanding, exploring new perspectives, and forming strategies and plans. Finally, she considers how the effectiveness of career counseling might be evaluated.

Chapter 7 moves the focus to the subjective career: the career as it is subjectively experienced by the career owner as opposed to what an observer sees happening. Khapova, Arthur, and Wilderom paint on a broad canvas, exploring the topic from psychological, social psychological, and sociological perspectives. They begin by defining four properties of the subjective career: its duality and its interdependence with the objective career, its perspective on time, and its multidimensionality. Next, they select two authors from each disciplinary tradition—Super and Hall from the psychological, Krumboltz and Bailyn from the social psychological, and Hughes and Giddens from the sociological—and use the four dimensions to examine and contrast each scholar's contribution to our understanding of the subjective career. They then turn to look at theoretical approaches to understanding the subjective career in the self-designing organizations increasingly characterizing the knowledge economy. They describe three: Bandura's social cognitive theory, Arthur and DeFillippi's "intelligent career" theory, and Boyatzis and Kolb's theory of growth and adaptation, showing how each is sensitive to the four dimensions of the subjective career. They conclude the chapter by posing some research challenges for future scholarship on the theme—those posed by the Internet and by globalization. They argue that such challenges need to be tackled by expanding the subjective career agenda and that the three approaches—social cognition, the intelligent career, and growth and adaptation—are exemplars of how this could be done.

The intersection of work and family lives has important implications for understanding the nature of careers. In Chapter 8, Greenhaus and

Foley review the substantial body of research on this topic that has emerged over the past few decades, posing the question, How can individuals derive substantial satisfaction and fulfillment from those roles in life that matter? First, they examine work-family conflict, its antecedents and its consequences. But these two sides of life do not necessarily have to be antithetical; next, they turn the phenomenon on its head by reviewing work-family *enrichment,* its antecedents and consequences. They then review the initiatives that have been used by employers to help employees manage work and the demands of personal life, asking the following questions: Who uses them? Are they useful? What is possible beyond recognizable initiatives (e.g., the family supportiveness of cultures or work environments)? In the latter part of the chapter, the authors widen their enquiry even further, examining two issues that are now increasingly being recognized as highly significant: how work-family issues vary between countries and cultures and how they vary with gender (whether women and men face similar or different experiences in managing work and family responsibilities). They close the chapter by considering the implications of the work-family interface for career studies and propose a rich agenda for future research on this important issue.

Chapter 9 explores several interrelated strands of research surrounding the increasingly important—given the demographic changes that are sweeping the developed world—issues surrounding the late career and retirement stages of career development. Feldman first reviews the research on the work-related attitudes and job performance of older workers. He examines such issues as job attitudes, perceived discrimination, withdrawal behavior, and subjective and objective performance ratings (how older workers' ratings change and how this compares with the extent to which skills actually change). Second, he reviews several of the most frequently discussed phenomena in late career, such as succession into top management, career plateaus, demotions, and downsizing. Third, he examines the broad array of issues related to retirement, including the decision to retire, bridge employment, and adjustment to retirement. The chapter concludes with a discussion of the need for better theory building, of the methodological

issues raised by important questions that still need answering (problems of restriction of range and of the failure to distinguish age from years in an occupation or organization, the overuse of self-report data and underuse of objective measures, and a failure to include forms of support other than salary and to examine the demography of age diversity), and of how both older workers and work organizations can more effectively respond to the challenges associated with this phase of one's career.

Thus far, the chapters have dealt with topics that could be called universalistic, in the sense that the issues they discuss touch everyone, at least potentially. Chapter 10 shifts the focus to an issue that, by definition, does not. Social marginalization can happen in myriad ways. Prasad, D'Abate, and Prasad examine its implications for careers. First, they examine the concept of marginalization itself and its relationship, for example, to stigmatization and otherness, its socially constructed nature, and the way it creates disadvantage and powerlessness. They next identify a number of themes from the literature having to do with gaining entry (recruitment, selection, and hiring of the socially marginalized), getting compensated (wage and salary issues), and career advancement and development. Marginalization has, over the past few decades and in many countries, attracted a major policy focus, and the authors describe the debates over perhaps one of the most contentious and misunderstood of these policies, affirmative action, as well as the impact of such policies and their likely future. But the effects of marginalization cannot be understood fully by concentrating only on formal policies and practices. Culture, ideology, and networking—manifestations of the informal organization—also play key roles. The authors discuss these next, arguing that a major problem faced by the socially marginalized lies precisely in a lack of access to the informal mechanisms that others use to advance their careers. They conclude by reviewing the limitations that they see in the current literature and suggesting directions for future research.

A second nonuniversalistic issue that is gaining in importance is that of what has been called the nontraditional career, defined by Valcour, Bailyn, and Quijada in Chapter 11 as the opposite of Wilensky's "orderly" career. The authors adopt the label "customized" career to bring out the way these careers are the outcome of conscious decisions on the part of those living them—particularly women—to *customize* their careers to their own needs. They begin by describing the pressures that force conformity on traditional careers, setting the scene for juxtaposing them with the customized career, which may differ, they argue, in three possible ways: in terms of time (i.e., work schedules), career timing and continuity, and the nature of the employment relationship (e.g., permanent vs. temporary or employed vs. self-employed). Next, they review the literature to see who customizes their careers in each of the three ways. This, in turn, raises the question, What leads people to customize their careers? Two main categories are suggested: accommodation with family and community and better alignment with personal values and preferences. The authors argue that taking up a customized career is helped by high levels of human capital and plentiful household resources. They examine the role of gender, values, preferences and identity, and the employment context in determining who is more likely to customize. Next, they look at the question, What happens when people customize their careers in terms of career-related outcomes, career success (both subjective and objective), integration of work and personal lives, the way in which these results are moderated by gender, and their impact on identity? The authors conclude with the observation that current forms of customization are, in essence, "Band-Aid" solutions to much more deep-seated societal issues.

4

PERSONALITY AND CAREER SUCCESS

TIMOTHY A. JUDGE

JOHN D. KAMMEYER-MUELLER

Success is relative. It is what we can make of the mess we have made of things.

—T. S. Eliot (1939)

The relationship between personality and career success has provoked a great deal of speculation. It has often been asserted that achievement (especially in capitalist economies) can be explained largely by factors such as individual initiative, effort, and merit. This is the classic "Horatio Alger" story of how one gets ahead in life—through grit, determination, and effort. In this sense, personality is probably a significant determinant of how people will do in their careers. At the same time, luck and institutional factors—such as privilege or inheritance—may influence career success in a way that would attenuate the relationship with personality significantly. Tharenou's (1997) review of the empirical research identified several categories of explanations for career success and found that research has generally favored institutional explanations over individual explanations. Whereas the most commonly investigated influences were demographic (age, sex, marital status, number of children) and human capital (training, work experience, education), researchers have increasingly investigated the possible role of personality in explaining career success. Below, we discuss the dispositional factors that have been related to career success in past research. Before doing so, however, it is important to discuss what we mean by career success and to discuss an organizing framework for our discussion of trait influences on career success (in particular, the five-factor model, FFM).

Definition of Career Success

Career success can be defined as the real or perceived achievements individuals have accumulated as a result of their work experiences (Judge, Cable, Boudreau, & Bretz, 1995). Most research has divided career success into extrinsic and intrinsic components (see also Khapova, Arthur, and Wilderom, Chapter 7; Guest and Sturges, Chapter 16). Extrinsic success is relatively objective and observable and typically consists of highly tangible outcomes such as pay and ascendancy (Jaskolka, Beyer, & Trice, 1985). Conversely, intrinsic success is defined as individuals' subjective appraisal of their success and is most commonly expressed in terms of job, career, or life satisfaction (Gattiker & Larwood, 1988; Judge et al., 1995). Research confirms the idea that extrinsic and intrinsic career success can be assessed as relatively independent outcomes, as they are only moderately correlated (Judge & Bretz, 1994).

The three criteria most commonly used to index extrinsic career success are (a) salary or income, (b) ascendancy or number of promotions, and (c) occupational status. The last factor is perhaps the most intriguing. Occupational status can be viewed as a reflection of societal perceptions of the power and authority afforded by the job (Blaikie, 1977; Schooler & Schoenbach, 1994). Occupational status has long been studied in sociology as a measure of occupational stratification (the sorting of individuals into occupations of differential power and prestige). Sociologists have gone so far as to conclude that occupational status measures "reflect the classical sociological hypothesis that occupational status constitutes the single most important dimension in social interaction" (Ganzeboom & Treiman, 1996, p. 203) and to term occupational status as sociology's "great empirical invariant" (Featherman, Jones, & Hauser, 1975, p. 331). The required educational skills, the potential extrinsic rewards offered by the occupation, and the ability to contribute to society through work performance are the most important contributors to occupational status (Blaikie, 1977). As a result, sociologists often view occupational status as the most important sign of success in contemporary society (Korman, Mahler, & Omran, 1983). Viewed from this perspective, occupational status indicates extrinsic success because of its prestige and because it conveys increased job-related responsibilities and rewards (Poole, Langan-Fox, & Omodei, 1993).

Intrinsic career success is measured in several distinct ways. The most common marker for intrinsic career success is a subjective rating of one's satisfaction with one's career. Items that fit under the career satisfaction umbrella ask respondents to directly indicate how they feel about their careers in general, whether they believe that they have accomplished the things that they want to in their careers or if they believe that their future prospects in their careers are good (e.g., Boudreau, Boswell, & Judge, 2001; Judge, Higgins, Thoresen, & Barrick, 1999; Seibert & Kraimer, 2001). Job satisfaction is often closely related to career satisfaction, but there are some important differences. Particularly, job satisfaction usually is directed around one's immediate emotional reactions to one's current job, whereas career satisfaction is a broader reflection of one's satisfaction with both past and future work history taken as a whole.

Five-Factor Model

Consensus is emerging that an FFM (or the "Big Five") of personality can be used to describe the most salient aspects of personality (Goldberg, 1990). The first researchers to replicate the five-factor structure were Norman (1963) and Tupes and Christal (1961), both of whom are generally credited with founding the FFM. The five-factor structure has been recaptured through analyses of trait adjectives in various languages, factor analytic studies of existing personality inventories, and decisions regarding the dimensionality of existing measures made by expert judges (McCrae & John, 1992). The cross-cultural generalizability of the five-factor structure has been established through research in many countries (McCrae & Costa, 1997). Evidence indicates that the Big Five are substantially heritable (roughly 50% of the variability in the Big Five traits appears to be inherited) and stable over time (Costa & McCrae, 1988; Digman, 1989).

The dimensions comprising the FFM are emotional stability, extroversion, openness to experience, agreeableness, and conscientiousness. Emotional stability represents the tendency to exhibit positive emotional adjustment and seldom experience negative affects (NAs) such as anxiety, insecurity, and hostility. Extroversion represents the tendency to be sociable, assertive, and active and to experience positive affects such as energy and zeal. Openness to experience is the disposition to be imaginative, nonconforming, unconventional, and autonomous. Agreeableness is the tendency to be trusting, compliant, caring, and gentle. Conscientiousness comprises two related facets, achievement and dependability. The Big Five traits have been found to be relevant to many aspects of life, such as interpersonal relations (e.g., Pincus, Gurtman, & Ruiz, 1998) and even longevity (Friedman et al., 1995). As we will see, these traits are also relevant to several aspects of career success. We will also discuss other personality traits that might be relevant for career success where relevant research exists.

WHY DOES PERSONALITY AFFECT CAREER SUCCESS? A PROPOSED MODEL

Starting from the premise that personality can be related to numerous work-relevant outcomes, it is worth considering how personality traits might have an effect on careers. To this end, we propose that Figure 4.1 depicts the most important and empirically supported linkages between personality and career-relevant outcomes that will be reviewed in this chapter. We first propose that personality leads individuals to possess certain jobs both through the process of attraction to the jobs of interest as well as by leading organizations to select certain individuals. Personality also influences individual performance on the job in a way that will lead to higher compensation, new job responsibilities, and promotions into higher organizational ranks. Finally, personality influences the ways in which individuals engage in social interactions at work. Social interactions can lead to any number of outcomes, ranging from improved knowledge of the job and role to more visibility in the organization. These factors combine, in turn, to predict the job features individuals encounter on the job, including both extrinsic

and intrinsic features known to predict job satisfaction. The static nature of this model is a simplification, because it is likely that there would be multiple nonrecursive links (e.g., over time, job features affect social behavior, career success affects job features), but we present this simplified model because there is not sufficient research to discuss these reciprocal relationships at the present time and our model is based on extant empirical results. To demonstrate the relevance of this model, it is first necessary to determine if there is in fact a relationship between personality and career success to explain in the first place. This topic is the subject of the next section.

FIVE-FACTOR MODEL AND CAREER SUCCESS

Below, we review the literature on the relationship of the Big Five to aggregate career success, with our review organized according to each of the Big Five traits. Within each trait, we first discuss the link between the trait and intrinsic success, followed by a discussion of the link between the trait and extrinsic success.

Conscientiousness

In general, conscientiousness is positively correlated with measures of intrinsic career success, though the multivariate evidence is far less consistent. Meta-analytic evidence indicates that conscientiousness is positively associated with job ($\hat{\rho} = .26$; Judge, Heller, & Mount, 2002) and life ($\hat{r}_u = .21$; DeNeve & Cooper, 1998) satisfaction.[1] Judge et al. (1999) found that conscientiousness strongly predicted intrinsic success ($\hat{\beta} = .34$, $p < .01$), even when personality was measured during childhood and the latter variables were measured in midadulthood. On the other hand, several studies have found limited incremental validity of conscientiousness in predicting career success with a multivariate design. Representative findings include nonsignificant relationships of $\hat{\beta} = .06$ (Seibert & Kraimer, 2001) and $\hat{\beta} = .09$ (Bozionelos, 2004) or small but significant effects of $\hat{\beta} = -.05$ among American executives and $\hat{\beta} = .10$ among European executives (Boudreau et al., 2001).

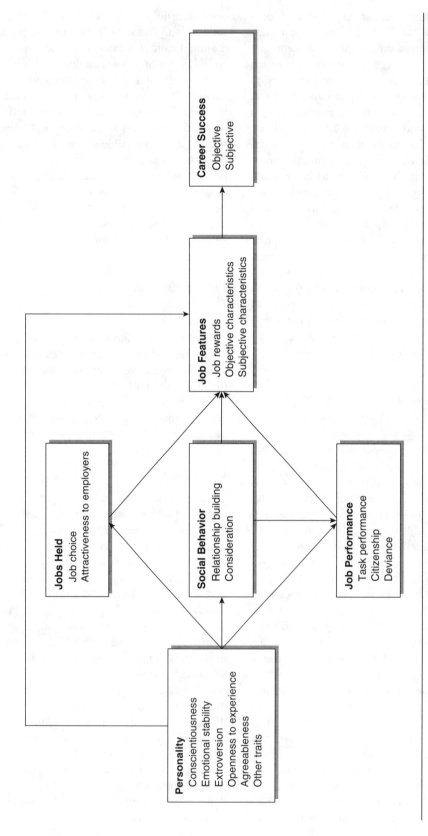

Figure 4.1   Conceptual Model of Personality and Career Success

Thus, though evidence suggests that the bivariate relationship between conscientiousness and indices of intrinsic career success is positive, this relationship tends to deteriorate and becomes less consistent when the influence of the other Big Five traits is taken into account.

Conscientiousness is theoretically linked to extrinsic career success most strongly through the achievement orientation of conscientious persons (McCrae & Costa, 1991). Barrick and Mount (1991) found a small, positive correlation ($\hat{\rho} = .17$) between conscientiousness and salary in five studies. Judge et al. (1999) found that conscientiousness strongly predicted extrinsic success ($\hat{\beta} = .44$, $p < .01$). Conscientiousness also seems to enable persons to obtain promotions into more complex and prestigious jobs. A consistent finding from the assessment center literature is that ratings of achievement orientation effectively predict promotions (e.g., $\hat{r} = .28$, $p < .01$; Howard & Bray, 1994). Orpen (1983) also found that need for achievement predicted 5-year salary growth in a sample of South African managers. Here again, though, there is disconfirmatory evidence. Seibert and Kraimer (2001) found that conscientiousness failed to predict salary ($\hat{\beta} = -.03$, *ns*) and number of promotions ($\hat{\beta} = -.04$, *ns*). Similarly, Bozionelos (2004) found that conscientiousness failed to predict self-reported promotion rate ($\hat{\beta} = -.06$, *ns*). Boudreau et al. (2001) found that conscientiousness was weakly associated with extrinsic career success; across three criteria in two samples, only one coefficient was significant (salary of European executives, $\hat{\beta} = .06$, $p < .05$).

In sum, it appears that the multivariate results on the relationship between conscientiousness and intrinsic and extrinsic success are far from consistent. There is a trend for the relationship to be positive in both cases, but in general, the results vary from moderately strong and positive to quite weak.

Emotional Stability

Evidence generally indicates that emotional stability is positively associated with intrinsic career success or, equivalently, that neuroticism is negatively associated with intrinsic career success. Meta-analytic evidence reliably indicates that those who score high on emotional stability are more satisfied with their jobs ($\hat{\rho} = .29$; Judge et al., 2002) and lives ($\hat{r}_u = .22$; DeNeve & Cooper, 1998). Boudreau et al. (2001) found that emotionally stable individuals were more satisfied with their careers (American, $\hat{\beta}_A = .22$; European, $\hat{\beta}_E = .12$). Seibert and Kraimer (2001) found that emotional stability positively predicted career satisfaction ($\hat{\beta} = .20$, $p < .01$). Judge et al. (1999), however, found that whereas the zero-order correlation between emotional stability and intrinsic career success was significant ($\hat{r} = .22$, $p < .01$), the effect disappeared once the influence of the other Big Five traits was controlled ($\hat{\beta} = .02$, *ns*), and Bozionelos (2004) found that emotional stability failed to predict subjective career success ($\hat{\beta} = .10$, *ns*). Here again, the results are somewhat inconsistent, but in general, emotional stability appears to be positively related to intrinsic career success.

Although not quite as consistent, evidence also indicates a positive relationship between emotional stability and extrinsic career success. Judge et al. (1999) found that emotional stability was positively associated with extrinsic success ($\hat{\beta} = .21$). Boudreau et al. (2001) found that emotional stability was positively associated with extrinsic success (salary, $\hat{\beta} = .15$; promotion, $\hat{\beta} = .15$; and job level, $\hat{\beta} = .06$) among American executives but not among European executives ($\hat{\beta} = .04$, $\hat{\beta} = -.02$, and $\hat{\beta} = -.01$, respectively). Seibert and Kraimer (2001) found that emotional stability did not predict salary ($\hat{\beta} = -.03$, *ns*) or promotions ($\hat{\beta} = .00$, *ns*). Bozionelos (2004) found that emotional stability failed to predict objective career success ($\hat{\beta} = -.04$, *ns*).

In sum, evidence indicates that emotional stability is positively related to intrinsic and extrinsic career success. The former results are more consistent than the latter, though both sets of results show inconsistency when the influence of the other Big Five traits is taken into account.

Extroversion

In general, extroversion is positively associated with intrinsic career success. As Watson and Clark (1997) note, extroversion is closely linked to positive emotionality (also known as positive affectivity), which in turn expresses itself in positive moods, greater social activity, and more rewarding interpersonal experiences. Meta-analytic evidence indicates that extroverts report higher levels of job (Judge et al., 2002: $\hat{\rho} = .25$) and life (DeNeve & Cooper, 1998: $\hat{r}_u = .17$) satisfaction. Boudreau et al. (2001) found that both American and European extroverts reported higher levels of career satisfaction ($\hat{\beta}_A = .10$ and $\hat{\beta}_E = .15$, respectively). Seibert and Kraimer (2001) found that extroversion positively predicted career satisfaction ($\hat{\beta} = .15$, $p < .01$). In Judge et al. (1999), extroversion failed to predict intrinsic career success ($\hat{\beta} = .00$, ns). Bozionelos (2004) found that extroversion failed to predict subjective career success ($\hat{\beta} = .03$, ns). Thus, in general, it appears that extroversion is positively related to intrinsic career success, though the results are not fully consistent.

Extroversion and its facets appear to be positively related to extrinsic career success. Rawls and Rawls (1968) found that measures of dominance and sociability differentiated successful and unsuccessful executives when pay and job title were considered as indices of success. Extroversion was also predictive of salary and job level in two recent studies conducted in the United Kingdom (Melamed, 1996a, 1996b). Well-controlled longitudinal studies also have supported a link between extroversion and extrinsic success. For example, Caspi, Elder, and Bem (1988) found that childhood ratings of shyness were negatively associated with adult occupational status ($\hat{\beta} = -.29$, $p < .01$). Likewise, Howard and Bray (1994) noted that dominance (a characteristic of extroverts, Watson & Clark, 1997) was correlated ($\hat{r} = .28, p < .01$) with managerial advancement. Harrell and Alpert (1989) found that sociability was positively, though not strongly, correlated with earnings 20 years after the trait was measured ($\hat{r} = .14$, $p < .05$). Seibert and Kraimer (2001) found that extroversion positively predicted earnings and promotions ($\hat{\beta} = .13$ in both cases, $p < .01$). Melamed (1996a) found that extroversion was positively correlated with relative wages ($\hat{r} = .25$, $p < .01$) and managerial level ($\hat{r} = .15$ $p < .05$) for men but not for women ($\hat{r} = .07$, ns and $\hat{r} = .09$, ns, respectively). In Bozionelos (2004), extroversion failed to predict objective career success ($\hat{\beta} = .07$, ns).

Thus, extroversion tends to be positively related to intrinsic as well as extrinsic career success. The results are not totally consistent, as one would expect based on data from multiple samples. However, the majority of the evidence suggests that extroverts are more extrinsically successful in their careers and more satisfied with them as well.

Openness to Experience

Openness displays an inconsistent relationship with career success. Judging from the meta-analytic evidence, the association of openness with job satisfaction ($\hat{\rho} = .02$, Judge et al., 2002) is weak and variable. These results are matched by explicit studies of career success. For example, Boudreau et al. (2001) found that openness failed to predict any aspect of intrinsic success, with the exception of a significant but small effect on job satisfaction ($\hat{\beta} = -.07$, $p < .01$) for European executives. Judge et al. (1999) found that childhood openness was positively correlated with adult intrinsic success ($\hat{r} = .21, p < .05$), but that effect became nonsignificant ($\hat{\beta} = .12$, ns) once the influence of the other Big Five traits and intelligence (which correlated $\hat{r} = .51$ with openness) was taken into account. Bozionelos (2004) found that openness failed to predict subjective career success ($\hat{\beta} = .03$, ns). Seibert and Kraimer (2001) found that openness was unrelated to career satisfaction ($\hat{\beta} = .02$, ns).

In terms of extrinsic success, the results are equally inconsistent. Boudreau et al. (2001) found that openness failed to significantly predict any aspect of career success for American or European executives. As with the results for intrinsic career success, Judge et al. (1999) found that childhood openness was positively correlated with adult extrinsic success ($\hat{r} = .26$, $p < .05$), but this effect disappeared ($\hat{\beta} = -.02$, ns) once the influence of the other Big Five traits and intelligence was taken into account. Seibert and Kraimer (2001) found that openness negatively predicted earnings ($\hat{\beta} = -.10, p < .01$) and was unrelated to number of promotions ($\hat{\beta} = -.01$, ns). Bozionelos (2004) found that openness negatively predicted objective career success ($\hat{\beta} = -.15, p < .05$). Thus, it appears that openness bears little consistent relationship with intrinsic or extrinsic career success.

Agreeableness

Evidence tends to indicate a relatively modest but positive relationship between agreeableness and job satisfaction ($\hat{\rho} = .17$, Judge et al., 2002). However, the relationship appears to disappear once adjusted for the influence of the other Big Five traits. Both Judge et al. (1999) and Boudreau et al. (2001) found that agreeableness was unrelated to any measure of intrinsic career success. Seibert and Kraimer (2001) found that agreeableness negatively predicted career satisfaction, though the effect size was rather small ($\hat{\beta} = -.09$ $p < .05$). Conversely, Bozionelos (2004) found that agreeableness positively predicted subjective career success ($\hat{\beta} = .18, p < .05$).

What is more intriguing is that agreeableness appears to be negatively related to extrinsic career success. Judge et al. (1999) found that agreeableness was relatively strongly negatively predictive of extrinsic career success ($\hat{\beta} = -.32, p < .01$), and Boudreau et al. (2001) found that agreeableness negatively predicted all aspects (salary, promotions, job level) for both American and European executives, though the effect sizes were appreciably smaller (e.g., $\hat{\beta} = -.14$, $p < .01$ for American executives' salary). On the other hand, Seibert and Kraimer (2001) found that agreeableness did not predict salary ($\hat{\beta} = -.03$, *ns*) or promotions ($\hat{\beta} = .00$, *ns*). Bozionelos (2004) found that agreeableness negatively predicted objective career success ($\hat{\beta} = -.13$, $p < .05$), which is odd, given that he found agreeable people more intrinsically successful. Thus, it appears that agreeableness is unrelated to intrinsic career success but negatively related to extrinsic career success.

OTHER DISPOSITIONAL TRAITS

The FFM does not exhaust the traits that may be relevant to career success. Below, we review evidence on the relationship of other traits to career success.

Proactive Personality

Two studies have suggested that proactive personality—the tendency to identify and act on opportunities, take the initiative, and persevere—is positively associated with career success.

Seibert, Crant, and Kraimer (1999) found that proactive personality positively predicted earnings ($\hat{\beta} = .11$, $p < .05$), number of promotions ($\hat{\beta} = .12, p < .05$), and career satisfaction ($\hat{\beta} = .30$, $p < .05$). Seibert, Kraimer, and Crant (2001) found that proactive personality was related to career satisfaction ($\hat{r} = .27$, $p < .01$) but was uncorrelated with salary progression ($\hat{r} = .11$, *ns*) or promotions ($\hat{r} = .05$, *ns*). A limitation of these results is that the FFM personality traits were not controlled, which is especially problematic given the existence of studies showing significant relationships between proactivity and both extroversion and conscientiousness (Crant, 1995).

Agentic and Communal Orientation

Abele (2003), studying approximately 800 graduates from a large German university, found that agentic tendencies ("very self-confident," "can make decisions easily," "very active," "very independent") positively predicted objective career success ($\hat{\beta} = .15$, $p < .001$) and subjective career success ($\hat{\beta} = .27$, $p < .001$), which was assessed with a single-item question ("Comparing your occupational development until now with your former student colleagues, how successful do you think you are?"). Abele (2003) further found that communal tendencies ("very kind," "very helpful to others," "very emotional," "able to devote self completely to others," "very warm in relation to others," "very understanding, aware of feelings of others," "very gentle") failed to predict either objective ($\hat{\beta} = -.01$, *ns*) or subjective ($\hat{\beta} = -.01$, *ns*) success. Surprisingly, given the strong conceptual linkages between agentic and communal tendencies and the FFM, Abele did not investigate the incremental validities of these orientations beyond the FFM.

Core Self-Evaluations

Core self-evaluations (CSEs) are a relatively recent addition to the personality literature. CSEs are a set of closely linked traits that include emotional stability, an internal locus of control, self-esteem, and self-efficacy. Those higher in CSEs tend to appraise situations more positively, have higher levels of motivation, and have greater confidence in their ability to positively influence the world around them (Judge, Locke,

& Durham, 1997). We are aware of no research that has explicitly linked CSEs to career success. However, beyond the emotional stability evidence reviewed above, evidence has linked the other core traits to career success. Wallace (2001) found that internal locus of control positively predicted the career satisfaction ($\hat{\beta} = .15$, $p < .01$) and self-reported promotional opportunities ($\hat{\beta} = .17$, $p < .05$) of female lawyers but did not significantly (negatively) predict their earnings ($\hat{\beta} = -.09$, ns). Turban and Dougherty (1994) found that external locus of control was negatively associated with perceived career success ($\hat{r} = .38$, $p < .05$) and self-reported promotions ($\hat{r} = .16$, $p < .05$) but uncorrelated with salary ($\hat{r} = .00$, ns). They also found that self-esteem was uncorrelated with promotions ($\hat{r} = .09$, ns) or salary ($\hat{r} = .10$, ns) but was positively correlated with perceived success ($\hat{r} = .43$, $p < .05$). Melamed (1996a) found that self-confidence negatively predicted job level for women ($\hat{\beta} = -.21$, $p < .05$) but not for men ($\hat{\beta} = .13$, ns); in another sample, self-confidence was positively related to salary and job level for the sample overall ($\hat{r} = .16$, $p < .05$ for both), but the correlations were only significant for men. In interpreting these results, there are causality issues. Because CSEs may be somewhat more malleable than most traits (Bono & Judge, 2003), it is possible that career success causes one to have a positive self-concept.

SUMMARY OF PAST RESEARCH

While reflecting on the results from past research relating personality to career success, several themes emerge. First, the effect sizes are not strong. The modal validities of personality in predicting intrinsic and extrinsic success tend to be in the 20s. In a sense, we have known this for some time (Guion & Gottier, 1965). As Schmitt (2004) recently commented, "The observed validity of personality measures, then and now, is quite low even though they can account for incrementally useful levels of variance in work-related criteria" (p. 348). Mischief is created when we try to make the validities something that they are not. At the same time, thinking in terms of the other dichotomy—that validities are meaningless—is equally misleading.

Second, the results for each trait are not particularly consistent. For every trait, there is more than one weak and/or nonsignificant finding. Clearly, there are studies that would seem to disconfirm the hypothesis that a particular trait is predictive of career success. At the same time, with such qualitative reviews, it is very easy to overinterpret the variability in the estimates (Hunter & Schmidt, 1990). We selected studies that were as representative of the current state of the field as possible, with an emphasis on methodologically rigorous studies conducted with large samples, being careful to represent the diversity of findings currently available. Thus, one should realize that a comprehensive meta-analysis would have illustrated the trend toward results demonstrating fairly weak to moderate, but consistent, relationships between personality and career success. Although this was not the purpose of this chapter, such a review would be worthwhile, indeed necessary, to most properly interpret the findings.

Third, despite the first two points, some trends still emerge. Conscientiousness and extroversion tend to have very weak to positive effects on intrinsic and extrinsic career success. Emotional stability tends to have very weak positive effects on intrinsic and extrinsic success. Agreeableness tends to have very weak to negative effects on extrinsic success and very little effect on intrinsic success. Openness tends to be unrelated to either component of career success. Thus, if one wished to have a career that was deemed successful by conventional standards, one might wish to be conscientious, extroverted, emotionally stable, and perhaps not too agreeable. It would be hard to argue that one would wish to be low in conscientiousness, for example, in order to be successful.

MEDIATORS OF THE PERSONALITY/ CAREER-SUCCESS RELATIONSHIP

Given the evidence that personality is at least sometimes related to career success, it is worth considering why personality traits might lead to superior career outcomes. We proposed earlier that Figure 4.1 depicts the most important and empirically supported linkages between personality and career-relevant outcomes. It will become clear in this section that these relationships are necessarily tenuous because of the conceptual distance from personality as an internal trait to final measures of career success. The stages of the mediating model considered next are as follows: (a) personality leads individuals to possess certain jobs, (b) personality also influences individual performance on the job, and (c) personality influences the ways in which individuals engage in social interactions at work. These factors are proposed to combine to predict the extrinsic and intrinsic features known to predict job and career satisfaction.

Personality and Jobs Held

One mechanism that might lead to a relationship between personality and career success is the effect of personality on the types of jobs that individuals might acquire. These relationships can be broadly divided into the effects of personality on job preferences and the ways in which personality can lead an individual to be considered desirable by employers. In other words, personality can influence what you want as well as what you can get.

The dominant paradigm in the literature on personality and job preferences comes from the long-established program of research on the realistic-investigative-artistic-social-enterprising-conventional (RIASEC) circumplex (see Savickas, Chapter 5; Kidd, Chapter 6; for a review of the research conducted over the past 40 years, see Holland, 1997). The basic proposition of the RIASEC model is that there are stable individual differences in preferences for job characteristics and that individuals who are in jobs that match their preferences will be more satisfied. Although RIASEC types are fairly stable over time (e.g., Lubinski, Benbow, & Ryan, 1995), they are partially distinct from other measures of personality. Openness to experience correlates fairly strongly with the artistic type ($\hat{\rho} = .39$) and the investigative type ($\hat{\rho} = .21$), and extroversion correlates fairly strongly with the enterprising type ($\hat{\rho} = .41$) and the social type ($\hat{\rho} = .25$) (Barrick, Mount, & Gupta, 2003). The relationships between conscientiousness, agreeableness, and emotional stability with any of the RIASEC dimensions are more tenuous. There is also evidence that the RIASEC dimensions add incremental variance in predicting jobs after FFM traits are considered. For example, while RIASEC dimensions rated at graduation were consistently predictive of employment in commensurate jobs (e.g., realistic individuals tend to hold jobs higher in realism) 1 year later, the five-factor personality model provided almost no incremental explanatory power for most job characteristics after RIASEC was considered (De Fruyt & Mervielde, 1999).

The relationship between personality traits and success in the selection process has been explored in several studies. As will be shown later, personality has been related to job performance, so it makes sense that employers might well prefer certain "types" of individuals based on their impressions of who will do best on the job. In a study examining interviewers' perceptions of applicants' "fit" with their organization, the two most predictive variables after general employability was factored out were interpersonal behaviors such as listening and warmth ($\hat{\beta} = .44$) and goal orientation characteristics, such as having goals and plans ($\hat{\beta} = .26$) (Rynes & Gerhart, 1990). Interviewers also perceive that conscientiousness is a significant predictor of hirability across multiple job types ($\hat{\beta} = .40$) and that counterproductive behavior can be predicted by emotional stability ($\hat{\beta} = -.36$), conscientiousness ($\hat{\beta} = -.25$), and agreeableness ($\hat{\beta} = -.24$) (Dunn, Mount, Barrick, & Ones, 1995). Not all interview types are equally affected by personality traits. Some research has suggested that success in situational interviews is less related to extroversion ($\hat{r} = .01$) than success in behavioral interviews ($\hat{r} = .30$) (Huffcutt, Weekley, Wiesner, Degroot, & Jones, 2001).

Another reason why personality might influence interview success is because of the behaviors associated with different personality traits. An increasing number of studies have suggested that impression management is an important component of interview success. Kristof-Brown, Barrick, and Franke (2002) found that extroverts engage in more self-promotion behavior ($\hat{\beta} = .47$) and that self-promotion behavior, in turn, was associated with perceptions of fit between the applicant and the job ($\hat{\beta} = .60$). Agreeableness was associated with nonverbal cues ($\hat{\beta} = .31$), which were related to perceptions of similarity between the interviewer and interviewee ($\hat{\beta} = .37$).

Given the meta-analytic evidence suggesting that impression management is, at best, weakly related to job performance ($\hat{\rho} = .04$), it appears that the tendency for interviewers to favor the extroverted and, in particular, the immodest extrovert is an error in judgment (Viswesvaran, Ones, & Hough, 2001).

The results to date suggest that conscientiousness and extroversion are the dimensions of personality that are most related to success in the screening process. This is interesting in light of the generally positive relationships between these personality traits and career success. Research also suggests that interviewers deliberately try to select conscientious individuals in the hope of obtaining better performance on the job, whereas extroverts are able to improve their success through social influence. As we will see, the linkage of extroversion with social behavior and conscientiousness with performance appears in other areas as well.

Personality and Job Performance

The relationship between personality and job performance has received a huge amount of attention. Seminal meta-analyses demonstrated that there were consistent relationships between the trait of conscientiousness and job performance across a number of jobs, while other personality traits were not associated with performance (Barrick & Mount, 1991). Subsequent studies have generally confirmed this result when more specific measures of the FFM are used (Hurtz & Donovan, 2000); when specific occupations such as sales are examined (Vinchur, Schippmann, Switzer, & Roth, 1998); when data are collected exclusively among the European community (Salgado, 1997); or when specific dimensions of performance, such as citizenship performance (Borman, Penner, Allen, & Motowidlo, 2001), or counterproductivity (Salgado, 2002) are the focus. More recent research has shown that the trait of CSEs is also related to job performance (correlations range from $r = .23$ to $r = .27$) and, moreover, that this trait shows incremental validity in predicting job performance beyond the FFM of personality (Judge, Erez, Bono, & Thoresen, 2003).

A study of 91 sales representatives demonstrated that conscientiousness leads employees to set goals ($\hat{\beta} = .44$) and to be more committed to these goals ($\hat{\beta} = .35$) (Barrick, Mount, & Strauss, 1993). Goal setting was related to sales volume ($\hat{\beta} = .21$) and performance ratings ($\hat{\beta} = .33$), and goal commitment was related to sales volume ($\hat{\beta} = .17$) and performance ratings ($\hat{\beta} = .16$). An alternative, but conceptually related, model of personality and performance was examined in a study of 164 sales agents (Barrick, Stewart, & Piotrowski, 2002). In this study, conscientiousness was related to accomplishment striving ($\hat{\beta} = .48$) and extroversion was related to status striving ($\hat{\beta} = .39$); accomplishment striving was related to status striving ($\hat{\beta} = .45$), which was related to job performance ($\hat{\beta} = .41$). Fewer data directly address the mediating relationship between conscientiousness and other aspects of performance. In a sample of 4,362 soldiers, dependability was related to fewer disciplinary actions ($\hat{\beta} = -.23$), which was in turn related to job performance ($\hat{\beta} = -.27$) (Borman, White, Pulakos, & Oppler, 1991). More research examining other dimensions of personality as predictors of other dimensions of performance is clearly needed.

Research on CSEs has examined mediated models. Evidence, from both lab and field settings further suggests that the effect of CSEs on job performance can be explained by task motivation and goal-setting behavior (Erez & Judge, 2001). In the lab study, the substantial effect of CSEs on task performance ($\hat{\beta} = .35$) dropped considerably ($\hat{\beta} = .18$) after the relationship between CSEs and motivation ($\hat{\beta} = .41$) was taken into account by regressing performance on motivation ($\hat{\beta} = .44$). In the field study, the total effect of CSEs on job performance ($\hat{\beta} = .27$) was 44% mediated by a path from CSEs to goal setting ($\hat{\beta} = .70$) to activity level ($\hat{\beta} = .30$) and from activity level to sales performance ($\hat{\beta} = .57$).

The literature on employee proactivity has also explored mediating models. A longitudinal study of 180 employees involving both self-reports and supervisor reports showed that proactive personality is positively related to innovation ($\hat{\beta} = .18$) and career initiative ($\hat{\beta} = .32$), which in turn were related to salary growth, promotions, and subjective career satisfaction (regression coefficients for the mediators predicting these outcomes were in the range from $\hat{\beta} = .17$ to $\hat{\beta} = .36$) (Seibert, Kraimer, & Crant, 2001).

In light of these results, the effects showing that conscientiousness, CSEs, and proactivity are related to extrinsic and intrinsic career success appear to occur at least partially through the mediating influence of improved motivation and task performance. Conscientiousness also appears to affect career success by producing lower deviance.

Personality and Social Ties

The established paradigms proposing that career success is largely a matter of individual initiative, choice, and effort on the job have been supplemented more recently by research demonstrating that careers are made by social ties as well. Research has shown that individuals with superior positions in social networks are able to achieve superior work outcomes, including access to information, access to resources, and career sponsorship (Seibert, Kraimer, & Liden, 2001). This study showed that career success was greater among individuals who fill a "structural hole," meaning that they were a crucial intermediary between groups of individuals who otherwise have little contact. The core variables that are studied in the social domain of personality at work include measures of relationship building, knowledge of the political domain of the organization, and efforts to actively understand which behaviors are rewarded.

A longitudinal study of the FFM of personality and proactive adjustment among organizational newcomers found that extroversion was significantly related to seeking feedback ($\hat{\beta} = .18$) and building relationships with colleagues ($\hat{\beta} = .23$), while openness to experience was related to feedback seeking ($\hat{\beta} = .16$) (Wanberg & Kammeyer-Mueller, 2000). Relationship building was related, in turn, to social integration ($\hat{\beta} = .20$), role clarity ($\hat{\beta} = .20$), and job satisfaction ($\hat{\beta} = .18$) and negatively related to intention to turnover ($\hat{\beta} = -.24$), while feedback seeking was positively related to job satisfaction ($\hat{\beta} = .20$) and negatively related to turnover (logistic regression coefficient $= -.19$).

Proactive personality has also been investigated in this domain. One study involving 180 employees found that proactive personality was significantly related to political knowledge ($\hat{\beta} = .28$) and career initiative on the job ($\hat{\beta} = .32$), both of which were positively related to subsequent salary progression ($\hat{\beta} = .17$ and $\hat{\beta} = .25$, respectively) and subjective perceptions of career satisfaction ($\hat{\beta} = .25$ and $\hat{\beta} = .36$, respectively) (Seibert, Kraimer, & Crant, 2001). A longitudinal examination involving organizational newcomers found that proactivity was associated with greater role clarity ($\hat{\beta} = .33$), work group integration ($\hat{\beta} = .13$), and political knowledge ($\hat{\beta} = .13$) (Kammeyer-Mueller & Wanberg, 2003). Commitment was found to be higher among those with greater role clarity ($\hat{\beta} = .17$) and work group integration ($\hat{\beta} = .23$), but political knowledge was not significantly related to any markers of newcomer adjustment. A longitudinal study of newcomer adjustment among doctoral students also found that proactivity was positively related to building social relationships with coworkers ($\hat{\beta} = .18$) and positively associated with average levels of role clarity ($\hat{\beta} = .40$) and social integration ($\hat{\beta} = .19$) over the four time periods of the study (Chan & Schmitt, 2000).

The relationship between lower-level employees and more experienced, powerful members of an organization (i.e., mentoring) has been of significant interest in the careers literature. Some research suggests that protégés have an important role in initiating relationships. Initiation of relationships was positively related to internal locus of control ($\hat{\beta} = .37$), self-monitoring ($\hat{\beta} = .43$), and emotional stability ($\hat{\beta} = .26$); initiation was positively related to having mentoring relationships ($\hat{\beta} = .86$), and these mentoring relationships were positively related to career attainment and perceived career success ($\hat{\beta} = .30$) (Turban & Dougherty, 1994). Research in a similar strain involving 184 early-career-stage Hong Kong Chinese has shown that extroversion leads to protégé-initiated mentoring relationships ($\hat{\beta} = .22$) (Aryee, Lo, & Kang, 1999). Unfortunately, because of the correlational nature of these studies, it is difficult to assess causality in any meaningful way. Some studies have suggested, using essentially the same methodology, that having a mentor can increase self-esteem, need for achievement, and need for dominance (Fagenson-Eland & Baugh, 2001).

In sum, the research suggests that individuals who are extroverted are likely to have positive social relationships, which may again serve as a potential mediator of extroversion and career success. Proactivity's effect on career success may also be explained by social relationships. Given the close relationship between extroversion and proactivity, future research should attempt to examine whether one of these variables is the more immediate explanation for career success through social connections.

PERSONALITY AND JOB FEATURES

Researchers have long proposed that there is an important relationship between personality and job features. An obvious area for consideration here is the research on person-environment fit by Holland, described earlier. However, while the RIASEC theory primarily offers propositions regarding how personality might relate to occupational preferences, there are additional reasons why personality might relate to both objective jobs held as well as perceptions of jobs.

One of the most controversial areas for research in the study of personality at work is the role of negative affectivity or neuroticism in perceptions of job characteristics. The arguments boil down to a dispute as to the role of dispositional NA in measures of job characteristics and work reactions. One of the first salvos fired in this battle came when Watson, Pennebaker, and Folger (1986) noted that individuals with high levels of dispositional NA will tend to view their environments in negative terms and also report distress, dissatisfaction, and negative emotions. From the perspective of our model, this implies that personality shapes the subjective perception of job characteristics, which in turn leads to lower career satisfaction. The possibility that dispositional NA can account for both perceptions of a job as well as negative reactions to the job was shown by Brief, Burke, George, Robinson, and Webster (1988), who found that there were significant relationships between NA and job stress ($\hat{r} = .34$) and NA and job strain ($\hat{r} = .57$.) and that the substantial zero-order relationship between stress and strain ($\hat{r} = .37$) was reduced ($\hat{r}_p = .22$) after partialling out NA; relationships between job stress and some other correlates fell even more after accounting for NA. From another angle, research has shown that even after subjectively

rated job characteristics have been partialled out, NA is still negatively related to job satisfaction ($\hat{\beta} = -.18$) (Levin & Stokes, 1989). Another method for factoring out personality as a selection mechanism into certain types of work is by using experiments to randomly assign individuals to working condition. Evidence from laboratory studies generally suggests that individuals high in NA are more likely to see the same tasks more negatively than individuals who are lower in NA (Levin & Stokes, 1989).

An alternative point of view has been proposed by Spector and colleagues, who propose that the relationship between NA and objective job characteristics is a substantial and important one. Burke, Brief, and George (1993) also note that there is a possibility of causal and substantive effects involving dispositional NA, job characteristics, and work attitudes. Evidence from Spector, Jex, and Chen (1995) found that incumbents' self-reported negative affectivity was significantly correlated with expert raters' opinions of these individuals' job autonomy ($\hat{r} = -.14$), variety ($\hat{r} = -.19$), identity ($\hat{r} = -.10$), and complexity ($\hat{r} = .17$). Because the reports of job conditions are taken from significant others, this is fairly good evidence that individuals who are higher in negative affectivity do tend to be in jobs that have worse characteristics. This perspective also serves as a reminder that care must be taken before researchers assume that a relationship between personality and work-related affect necessarily is the result of perceptions being shaped by situations; it is also possible that one of the reasons people higher in negative affectivity are less satisfied at work is because they are in more negative work situations.

Research has also shown that employee perceptions of appropriate emotional displays at work are predicted based on employee extroversion and neuroticism, with extroversion being related to perceptions that jobs demand more positive emotional displays ($\hat{\beta} = .20$) and neuroticism being related to perceptions that jobs demand more suppression of negative emotional displays ($\hat{\beta} = .15$) (Diefendorff & Richard, 2003). The study also showed that perceptions of demands for positive emotional displays were associated with higher job satisfaction ($\hat{\beta} = .39$), while perceptions of demands for suppression of negative emotional displays were associated with lower job satisfaction ($\hat{\beta} = -.22$).

There is evidence beyond simple negative affectivity related to job characteristics. The relationship between CSEs measured in childhood and job satisfaction in adulthood can be explained, in part, by the relationship between CSEs and externally rated job complexity (Judge, Bono, & Locke, 2000). This relationship is at least partially due to the influence of emotional stability described earlier, but it also incorporates the more motivationally loaded traits of self-esteem, self-efficacy, and locus of control. This study also further supports the idea that personality can have a direct effect on objective job characteristics.

To determine if personality characteristics act as a cause or effect of employee reactions, researchers must find ways to move beyond simple correlational designs. One way to approach this problem comes from a two-wave panel study of bank employees and teachers, in which growth needs, strength, NA, and upward striving were measured at multiple points in time (Houkes, Janssen, de Jonge, & Bakker, 2003). Results showed that Time 1 NA was associated with Time 1 emotional exhaustion ($\hat{\beta} = .44$), which in turn led to Time 2 emotional exhaustion ($\hat{\beta} = .64$); Time 1 NA also led to Time 2 NA ($\hat{\beta} = .68$), which in turn was associated with Time 2 emotional exhaustion ($\hat{\beta} = .32$). These results suggest that personality dispositions may build on themselves over time, with initially minor effects becoming greater over time as initial tendencies are exacerbated.

Among the most thorough longitudinal examinations of the relationship between personality and work experiences is the study of a sample of 861 individuals tracked from the beginning of their adult work course at age 18 until the age of 26 (Roberts, Caspi, & Moffitt, 2003). In this study, a combination of objective measures of occupational attainment, resource power, work autonomy, and financial security was taken, along with the subjective measures of satisfaction and involvement. Concentrating only on those results of moderate effect size ($r > .15$), negative emotionality was shown to be especially negatively correlated with occupational attainment ($r = -.27$) and financial security ($r = -.22$). Communal positive emotionality

(similar to agreeableness) was correlated with occupational attainment ($r = .19$), work satisfaction ($r = .15$), and work stimulation ($r = .15$). Agentic positive emotionality (similar to certain aspects of extroversion related to achievement striving) was positively correlated with occupational attainment ($r = .16$) and work stimulation ($r = .17$). Constraint (similar to the dutifulness component of conscientiousness) was positively related to work involvement ($r = .18$) and financial security ($r = .15$). These relationships generally suggest that individual differences measured prior to early work experience do predict objective job characteristics, although the relationships are relatively modest in size. This is especially true in light of the many relationships that were smaller than those reported here. This study should be replicated in future research to see how these results generalize to older populations, given the fact that the adolescent years are a time of considerable variation in personality.

A unique aspect of this study was the explicit examination of how work experiences might affect subsequent personality states. To estimate these effects, personality scores at age 26 were regressed on personality at age 18 and job features. The residual effects found for job features represent changes in the respondents' personality. Again, concentrating on effect sizes over $b = .15$, the results showed that financial security was related to reduced negative emotionality ($\hat{\beta} = -.19$), occupational attainment was associated with increased communion (i.e., positive social relationships) ($\hat{\beta} = .16$), resource power was associated with increased agency (i.e., personal initiative) ($\hat{\beta} = .23$), work involvement was associated with increased agency ($\hat{\beta} = .20$), and work stimulation was associated with increased agency ($\hat{\beta} = .18$). No significant relationships were found for increasing constraint; work satisfaction and work autonomy were not predictive of any changes in personality.

In sum, the research on personality and job characteristics suggests that there is a complex relationship that involves personality shaping selection into certain jobs and certain jobs leading to changes in personality. The evidence generally suggests that neuroticism is likely to result in lower levels of actual and perceived job characteristics, which can explain at least part of the relationship between neuroticism and (lower) career success.

MODERATORS OF THE PERSONALITY/CAREER-SUCCESS RELATIONSHIP

The previous section proposed a theoretical model showing main effects for personality on a variety of mediating mechanisms that might be related to career success. However, there are many contingencies that might alter the relationship between personality and career outcomes. In this section, we consider several potential moderators of the career-success/personality relationship.

One of the most comprehensive efforts to create a theory for incorporating moderators of the relationship between personality and work behavior is associated with the concept of *trait activation* (Tett & Burnett, 2003; Tett & Guterman, 2000). According to the trait activation concept, different situations provide different opportunities for traits to express themselves. For example, a work environment rich in social interactions will be likely to result in bigger differences in behavior between introverts and extroverts. Similarly, a work environment with minimal supervision is likely to result in greater differences in behavior between those high in conscientiousness (who will behave in an organized, goal-directed fashion even without supervision) and those low in conscientiousness (who will take the lack of supervision as an opportunity to relax and reduce work effort). Researchers interested in studying interactions between persons and situations should look most closely at areas where situations open unique opportunities for personality traits to express themselves. The statistical model for trait activation is an interaction between individual dispositions and the relationship between personality and an outcome.

Situations as Moderators of Personality/Career-Success Relationships

One of the historically strongest theoretical explanations for the relationship between

personality and situations is that in weak situations, personality will exert stronger influences on behavior and attitudes. In other words, when there are clear demands on behavior presented by the situation, it is unlikely that personality will matter much. However, when situations don't clearly suggest the correct way to behave, personality tends to have a much stronger effect on how people act.

The personality trait of conscientiousness has been described as involving both an increased personal drive for success as well as greater regulation of one's behavior to meet standards. Both these factors are likely to be especially important in situations where the environment provides minimal direct contingencies for behavior and minimal regulation of behavior. Consistent with this theoretical model, Barrick and Mount (1993) found that the correlation between job performance and conscientiousness was considerably greater in jobs high in autonomy relative to jobs low in autonomy. One study found that extroversion and agreeableness were positively related to contextual performance only when job autonomy was high (Gellatly & Irving, 2001). Similarly, Type A behavior exerted strong effects on performance, job satisfaction, and somatic complaints when perceived control was higher.

As noted earlier, Tett and Burnett (2003) proposed that personality is likely to be most predictive of behavior when there is a correspondence between the trait of interest and situations that might elicit the behavior. A clear example is the relationship between personality traits and socially loaded situations. A meta-analysis of 11 studies found that emotional stability and agreeableness were more strongly related to job performance when individuals had to engage in teamwork as opposed to jobs that required only brief one-on-one interactions with customers (Mount, Barrick, & Stewart, 1998). Evidence suggests that despite the low general correlation found between extroversion and job performance, in a meta-analysis limited to sales jobs, higher levels of achievement striving or "potency" emerged as a significant predictor of supervisor ratings of performance ($r = .28$) and objective measures of sales ($r = .26$) (Vinchur et al., 1998).

A study of a diverse set of 496 individuals found a significant negative relationship between agreeableness and salary among people working in jobs that had a strong people-oriented component, while for those in jobs with a weaker people-oriented component there was no relationship between agreeableness and salary (Seibert & Kraimer, 2001).

Personality as a Moderator of Situation/Career-Success Relationships

An alternative way to think about the interaction between personality and situations is to consider how personality traits may change the relationship between situations and outcomes. In this case, it is possible that some personality traits make it easier for people to take advantage of situations. For example, it is easy to imagine cases in which an opportunity for training or development would lead to career success in general but would be especially useful for individuals who were higher in proactivity, CSEs, or openness to experience.

This area remains relatively speculative because there is not a great deal of research available that examines these possibilities. One study found that requirements for emotional displays at work were more strongly related to poor physical health among those who were low in emotional adaptability (Schaubroeck & Jones, 2000). There is also evidence that openness to experience moderates the relationship between job characteristics and job satisfaction in a manner very similar to the moderating of the relationship between growth need strength and job characteristics (de Jong, van der Velde, & Jansen, 2001). A large-scale longitudinal study, described earlier, showed that negative affectivity moderated the relationship between workload, measured at the same time as NA, and emotional exhaustion, measured 1 year later (Houkes et al., 2003). Further research is clearly needed in this area.

Personality as a Moderator of Personality/Career-Success Relationships

Besides situational moderators of the relationship between personality and work behavior, it is also possible that the constellation of personality traits held by individuals might moderate one another. In other words, it is possible that personality traits operate differently in combination than they do singly.

This is another area where there is not a great deal of research. One study found that for jobs high in interpersonal interactions, the relationship between conscientiousness and job performance ratings was higher for individuals who were highly agreeable (Witt, Burke, & Barrick, 2002). These results suggest that simply being organized, motivated, and dutiful may not be enough to create positive social outcomes; individuals must be sufficiently socially sensitive to make these positive conscientious traits really become evident. Other areas for future research might be to investigate how conscientiousness interacts with openness (open individuals are able to learn more and innovate but only successfully apply this knowledge to the workplace if they have the discipline to see their ideas through) or with emotional stability (emotionally unstable individuals who are not conscientious may be prone to perseverating over their worries and never completing tasks, whereas emotionally unstable individuals who are conscientious will work hard to minimize the reason for their worries).

Another area in which personality might be differentially relevant is the area of creativity. A study conducted by Oldham and Cummings (1996) identified several characteristics, such as insight, curiosity, and originality, that are associated with creativity; it is clear that this study is conceptually close to a measure of openness to experience. These individual differences in dispositional personality were significantly related to obtaining new patents ($R^2 = .07$) but were not significantly related to supervisor ratings of creativity ($R^2 = .01$). However, the interaction between motivating potential score and creative personality was not significant for obtaining new patents ($R^2 = .00$) but was significant for supervisor ratings of creativity ($R^2 = .07$). This suggests that the interactions between personality variables and working conditions may be extremely complex.

CONCLUSION

The literature on personality and career success has received increased attention over the years.

It may be a surprise to many readers that the effect sizes are relatively modest and the results relatively inconsistent. This does not mean, of course, that the effect sizes are zero. Indeed, four of the Big Five traits appear to bear some relation to either extrinsic or intrinsic career success, with conscientiousness and extroversion being associated with slightly higher levels of extrinsic and intrinsic career success and neuroticism and agreeableness being associated with slightly lower levels of career success.

Beyond providing an appraisal of the effects of personality and career success, we sought to review evidence on why personality is related to career success. We reviewed evidence on various mediators of the relationship between personality and career success (personality leads individuals to possess certain jobs, personality also influences individual performance on the job, personality influences the ways in which individuals engage in social interactions at work). We also discussed the linkage between personality and job features, as well as dispositional and situational factors that moderate the personality/career-success relationship.

Although research on personality and career success has come a long way in the past 20 years, there is considerable room for further development. Below, we outline a few areas that especially require further study.

Need for Careful Research Design

Researchers have tended to rely frequently on the use of data gathered at a single point in time to measure the influence of personality on career success. While such designs have shown a considerable correlation between personality traits and career outcomes, several of the studies we reviewed here suggest that conclusions from such studies could be potentially spurious. Moreover, the debate regarding negative affectivity and career outcomes clearly suggests that researchers can be most informative when they make an effort to eliminate alternative explanations for observed correlations.

Inclusion of Work-Family Balance as an Outcome

Because men and women are increasingly occupying the dual roles of breadwinner and homemaker, the issue of work-family conflict has become more prominent (see Greenhaus and Foley, Chapter 8). The issue of work-family balance is conspicuously absent from the literature on personality and career success, however. Do certain personalities emphasize work over family, or the converse? Are some personalities able to better balance work and family demands than others? Is the fit between work and family contingent on personality? Does the balance between work and family demands evolve over time based on personality?

Moderators

Although we reviewed various moderators of the personality/career-success relationship, other moderators need to be investigated. Some areas for future analysis include family status (e.g., spousal concerns, children, or the need to care for other family members), labor market variables (e.g., unemployment rates), and industry characteristics. In the personality/job-performance literature, more systematic progress has been made on the moderator front, including investigations of the situational (Barrick et al., 1993) and dispositional moderators. Some of these moderators should be investigated in the context of career success, and others are undoubtedly worthy of consideration as well.

Other Traits

Although traits beyond the FFM have been investigated (e.g., proactive personality, agentic/communal orientation), we have only scratched the surface of traits that might prove useful. Examination of the lower-order facets of the FFM might prove especially fruitful.

In sum, although considerable advances have been made in our understanding of the dispositional basis of career success, further development is needed. In particular, there is a need to investigate factors that explain the relatively modest and apparently inconsistent results. Process models that investigate mediation will contribute to our understanding of the specific mechanisms by which personality leads to career success; examples of mediators in the current literature include task motivation, social interactions, and goal setting. Studies should also make a greater effort to investigate some of the ways in which personality interacts with the environment to produce career success by studying the ways in which traits moderate the effect of situations and situations moderate the effects of traits.

NOTE

1. Here and throughout the chapter, the following statistical notation will be used: $\hat{\rho}$ = estimated correlation corrected for measurement error, $\hat{r}_u$ = estimated uncorrected correlation, $\hat{\beta}$ = estimated standardized regression coefficient, and $\hat{r}$ = estimated zero-order correlation (uncorrected).

REFERENCES

Abele, A. E. (2003). The dynamics of masculine-agentic and feminine-communal traits: Findings from a prospective study. *Journal of Personality and Social Psychology, 85,* 768–776.

Aryee, S., Lo, S., & Kang, I. (1999). Antecedents of early career stage mentoring among Chinese employees. *Journal of Organizational Behavior, 20,* 563–576.

Barrick, M. R., & Mount, M. K. (1991). The Big Five personality dimensions and job performance: A meta-analysis. *Personnel Psychology, 44,* 1–26.

Barrick, M. R., & Mount, M. K. (1993). Autonomy as a moderator of the relationships between the Big Five personality dimensions and job performance. *Journal of Applied Psychology, 78,* 111–118.

Barrick, M. R., Mount, M. K., & Gupta, R. (2003). Meta-analysis of the relationship between the five-factor model of personality and Holland's occupational types. *Personnel Psychology, 56,* 45–74.

Barrick, M. R., Mount, M. K., & Strauss, J. P. (1993). Conscientiousness and performance of sales representatives: Test of the mediating effects of goal setting. *Journal of Applied Psychology, 78,* 715–722.

Barrick, M. R., Stewart, G. L., & Piotrowski, M. (2002). Personality and job performance: Test of the mediating effects of motivation among sales representatives. *Journal of Applied Psychology, 87,* 43–51.

Blaikie, N. W. (1977). The meaning and measurement of occupational prestige. *Australian and New Zealand Journal of Sociology, 13,* 102–115.

Bono, J. E., & Judge, T. A. (2003). Core self-evaluations: A review of the trait and its role in job satisfaction and job performance. *European Journal of Personality, 17,* S5–S18.

Borman, W. C., Penner, L. A., Allen, T. D., & Motowidlo, S. J. (2001). Personality predictors of citizenship performance. *International Journal of Selection & Assessment, 9,* 52–69.

Borman, W. C., White, L. A., Pulakos, E. D., & Oppler, S. H. (1991). Models of supervisory job performance ratings. *Journal of Applied Psychology, 76,* 863–872.

Boudreau, J. W., Boswell, W. R., & Judge, T. A. (2001). Effects of personality on executive career success in the United States and Europe. *Journal of Vocational Behavior, 58,* 53–81.

Bozionelos, N. (2004). Mentoring provided: Relation to mentor's career success, personality, and mentoring received. *Journal of Vocational Behavior, 64,* 24–46.

Brief, A. P., Burke, M. J., George, J. M., Robinson, B. S., & Webster, J. (1988). Should negative affectivity remain an unmeasured variable in the study of job stress? *Journal of Applied Psychology, 73,* 193–198.

Burke, M. J., Brief, A. P., & George, J. M. (1993). The role of negative affectivity in understanding relations between self-reports of stressors and strains: A comment on the applied psychology literature. *Journal of Applied Psychology, 78,* 402–412.

Caspi, A., Elder, G. H., Jr., & Bem, D. J. (1988). Moving away from the world: Life course patterns of shy children. *Developmental Psychology, 24,* 824–831.

Chan, D., & Schmitt, N. (2000). Interindividual differences in intraindividual changes in proactivity during organizational entry: A latent growth modeling approach to understanding newcomer adaptation. *Journal of Applied Psychology, 85,* 190–210.

Costa, P. T., Jr., & McCrae, R. R. (1988). Personality in adulthood: A six-year longitudinal study of self-reports and spouse ratings on the NEO Personality Inventory. *Journal of Personality and Social Psychology, 54,* 853–863.

Crant, J. M. (1995). The proactive personality scale and objective job performance among real estate agents. *Journal of Applied Psychology, 80,* 532–537.

De Fruyt, F., & Mervielde, I. (1999). RIASEC types and Big Five traits as predictors of employment status and nature of employment. *Personnel Psychology, 52,* 701–727.

de Jong, R. D., van der Velde, M. E. G., & Jansen, P. G. W. (2001). Openness to experience and growth need strength as moderators between job characteristics and satisfaction. *International Journal of Selection & Assessment, 9,* 350–356.

DeNeve, K. M., & Cooper, H. (1998). The happy personality: A meta-analysis of 137 personality traits and subjective well-being. *Psychological Bulletin, 124,* 197–229.

Diefendorff, J. M., & Richard, E. M. (2003). Antecedents and consequences of emotional display rule perceptions. *Journal of Applied Psychology, 88,* 284–294.

Digman, J. M. (1989). Five robust trait dimensions: Development, stability, and utility. *Journal of Personality, 57,* 195–214.

Dunn, W. S., Mount, M. K., Barrick, M. R., & Ones, D. S. (1995). Relative importance of personality and general mental ability in managers' judgments of applicant qualifications. *Journal of Applied Psychology, 80,* 500–509.

Eliot, T. S. (1939). *The family reunion.* New York: Harcourt, Brace.

Erez, A., & Judge, T. A. (2001). Relationship of core self-evaluations to goal setting, motivation, and performance. *Journal of Applied Psychology, 86,* 1270–1279.

Fagenson-Eland, E. A., & Baugh, S. G. (2001). Personality predictors of protégé mentoring history. *Journal of Applied Social Psychology, 31,* 2502–2517.

Featherman, D. L., Jones, F. L., & Hauser, R. M. (1975). Assumptions of social mobility research in the U.S.: The case of occupational status. *Social Science Research, 4,* 329–360.

Friedman, H. S., Tucker, J. S., Schwartz, J. E., Martin, L. R., Tomlinson-Keasey, C., Wingard, D. L., et al. (1995). Childhood conscientiousness and longevity: Health behaviors and cause of death. *Journal of Personality and Social Psychology, 68,* 696–703.

Ganzeboom, H. B. G., & Treiman, D. J. (1996). Internationally comparable measures of occupational status for the 1988 International Standard Classification of Occupations. *Social Science Research, 25,* 201–239.

Gattiker, U. E., & Larwood, L. (1988). Predictors for managers' career mobility, success, and satisfaction. *Human Relations, 41,* 569–591.

Gellatly, I. R., & Irving, P. G. (2001). Personality, autonomy, and contextual performance of managers. *Human Performance, 14,* 231–245.

Goldberg, L. R. (1990). An alternative "description of personality": The Big-Five factor structure. *Journal of Personality and Social Psychology, 59,* 1216–1229.

Guion, R. M., & Gottier, R. F. (1965). Validity of personality measures in personnel selection. *Personnel Psychology, 18,* 135–164.

Harrell, T. W., & Alpert, B. (1989). Attributes of successful MBAs: A 20-year longitudinal study. *Human Performance, 2,* 301–322.

Holland, J. L. (1997). *Making vocational choices: A theory of vocational personalities and work environments* (3rd ed.). Odessa, FL: Psychological Assessment Resources.

Houkes, I., Janssen, P. P. M., de Jonge, J., & Bakker, A. B. (2003). Personality, job features and employee well-being: A longitudinal analysis of additive and moderating effects. *Journal of Occupational Health Psychology, 8,* 20–38.

Howard, A., & Bray, D. W. (1994). Predictions of managerial success over time: Lessons from the Management Progress Study. In K. E. Clark & M. B. Clark (Eds.), *Measures of leadership* (pp. 113–130). West Orange, NJ: Leadership Library of America.

Huffcutt, A. I., Weekley, J. A., Wiesner, W. H., Degroot, T. G., & Jones, C. (2001). Comparison of situational and behavior description interview questions for higher-level positions. *Personnel Psychology, 54,* 619–644.

Hunter, J. E., & Schmidt, F. L. (1990). *Methods of meta-analysis: Correcting error and bias in research findings.* Newbury Park, CA: Sage.

Hurtz, G. M., & Donovan, J. J. (2000). Personality and job performance: The Big Five revisited. *Journal of Applied Psychology, 85,* 869–879.

Jaskolka, G., Beyer, J. M., & Trice, H. M. (1985). Measuring and predicting managerial success. *Journal of Vocational Behavior, 26,* 189–205.

Judge, T. A., Bono, J. E., & Locke, E. A. (2000). Personality and job satisfaction: The mediating role of job characteristics. *Journal of Applied Psychology, 85,* 237–249.

Judge, T. A., & Bretz, R. D. (1994). Political influence behavior and career success. *Journal of Management, 20,* 43–65.

Judge, T. A., Cable, D. M., Boudreau, J. W., & Bretz, R. D. (1995). An empirical investigation of the predictors of executive career success. *Personnel Psychology, 48,* 485–519.

Judge, T. A., Erez, A., Bono, J. E., & Thoresen, C. J. (2003). The core self-evaluations scale:

Development of a measure. *Personnel Psychology, 56,* 303–331.

Judge, T. A., Heller, D., & Mount, M. K. (2002). Five-factor model of personality and job satisfaction: A meta-analysis. *Journal of Applied Psychology, 87,* 530–541.

Judge, T. A., Higgins, C., Thoresen, C. J., & Barrick, M. R. (1999). The Big Five personality traits, general mental ability, and career success across the life span. *Personnel Psychology, 52,* 621–652.

Judge, T. A., Locke, E. A., & Durham, C. C. (1997). The dispositional causes of job satisfaction: A core evaluations approach. *Research in Organizational Behavior, 19,* 151–188.

Kammeyer-Mueller, J. D., & Wanberg, C. R. (2003). Unwrapping the organizational entry process: Disentangling multiple antecedents and their pathways to adjustment. *Journal of Applied Psychology, 88,* 779–794.

Korman, A. K., Mahler, S. R., & Omran, K. A. (1983). Work ethics and satisfaction, alienation, and other reactions. In W. B. Walsh & S. H. Osipow (Eds.), *Handbook of vocational psychology* (Vol. 2, pp. 181–206). Hillsdale, NJ: Lawrence Erlbaum.

Kristof-Brown, A., Barrick, M. R., & Franke, M. (2002). Applicant impression management: Dispositional influences and consequences for recruiter perceptions of fit and similarity. *Journal of Management, 28,* 27–46.

Levin, I., & Stokes, J. P. (1989). Dispositional approach to job satisfaction: Role of negative affectivity. *Journal of Applied Psychology, 74,* 752–758.

Lubinski, D., Benbow, C. P., & Ryan, J. (1995). Stability of vocational interests among the intellectually gifted from adolescence to adulthood: A 15-year longitudinal study. *Journal of Applied Psychology, 80,* 196–200.

McCrae, R. R., & Costa, P. T., Jr. (1991). Adding Liebe und Arbeit: The full five-factor model and well-being. *Personality and Social Psychology Bulletin, 17,* 227–232.

McCrae, R. R., & Costa, P. T., Jr. (1997). Personality trait structure as a human universal. *American Psychologist, 52,* 509–516.

McCrae, R. R., & John, O. P. (1992). An introduction to the five-factor model and its applications. *Journal of Personality, 2,* 175–215.

Melamed, T. (1996a). Career success: An assessment of a gender-specific model. *Journal of Occupational and Organizational Psychology, 69,* 217–242.

Melamed, T. (1996b). Validation of a stage model of career success. *Applied Psychology: An International Review, 45,* 35–65.

Mount, M. K., Barrick, M. R., & Stewart, G. L. (1998). Five-factor model of personality and performance in jobs involving interpersonal interactions. *Human Performance, 11,* 145–165.

Norman, W. T. (1963). Toward an adequate taxonomy of personality attributes: Replicated factor structure in peer nomination personality ratings. *Journal of Abnormal and Social Psychology, 66,* 574–583.

Oldham, G. R., & Cummings, A. (1996). Employee creativity: Personal and contextual factors at work. *Academy of Management Journal, 39,* 607–634.

Orpen, C. (1983). The development and validation of an adjective check-list measure of managerial need for achievement. *Psychology, 20,* 38–42.

Pincus, A. L., Gurtman, M. B., & Ruiz, M. A. (1998). Structural analysis of social behavior (SASB): Circumplex analyses and structural relations with the interpersonal circle and the five-factor model of personality. *Journal of Personality and Social Psychology, 74,* 1629–1645.

Poole, M. E., Langan-Fox, J., & Omodei, M. (1993). Contrasting subjective and objective criteria as determinants of perceived career success: A longitudinal study. *Journal of Occupational and Organizational Psychology, 66,* 39–54.

Rawls, D. J., & Rawls, J. R. (1968). Personality characteristics and personal history data of successful and less successful executives. *Psychological Reports, 23,* 1032–1034.

Roberts, B. W., Caspi, A., & Moffitt, T. E. (2003). Work experiences and personality development in young adulthood. *Journal of Personality & Social Psychology, 84,* 582–593.

Rynes, S., & Gerhart, B. (1990). Interviewer assessments of applicant "fit": An exploratory investigation. *Personnel Psychology, 43,* 15–35.

Salgado, J. F. (1997). The five factor model of personality and job performance in the European Community. *Journal of Applied Psychology, 82,* 30–43.

Salgado, J. F. (2002). The Big Five personality dimensions and counterproductive behaviors. *International Journal of Selection & Assessment, 10,* 117–125.

Schaubroeck, J., & Jones, J. R. (2000). Antecedents of workplace emotional labor dimensions and moderators of their effects on physical symptoms. *Journal of Organizational Behavior, 21,* 163–183.

Schmitt, N. (2004). Beyond the Big Five: Increases in understanding and practical utility. *Human Performance, 17,* 347–357.

Schooler, C., & Schoenbach, C. (1994). Social class, occupational status, occupational self-direction, and job income: A cross-national examination. *Sociological Forum, 9,* 431–458.

Seibert, S. E., Crant, J. M., & Kraimer, M. L. (1999). Proactive personality and career success. *Journal of Applied Psychology, 84,* 416–427.

Seibert, S. E., & Kraimer, M. L. (2001). The five-factor model of personality and career success. *Journal of Vocational Behavior, 58,* 1–21.

Seibert, S. E., Kraimer, M. L., & Crant, J. M. (2001). What do proactive people do? A longitudinal model linking proactive personality and career success. *Personnel Psychology, 54,* 845–874.

Seibert, S. E., Kraimer, M. L., & Liden, R. C. (2001). A social capital theory of career success. *Academy of Management Journal, 44,* 219–248.

Spector, P. E., Jex, S. M., & Chen, P. Y. (1995). Relations of incumbent affect-related personality traits with incumbent and objective measures of characteristics of jobs. *Journal of Organizational Behavior, 16,* 59–65.

Tett, R. P., & Burnett, D. D. (2003). A personality trait-based interactionist model of job performance. *Journal of Applied Psychology, 88,* 500–517.

Tett, R. P., & Guterman, H. A. (2000). Situation trait relevance, trait expression, and cross-situational consistency: Testing a principle of trait activation. *Journal of Research in Personality, 34,* 397–423.

Tharenou, P. (1997). Managerial career advancement. *International Review of Industrial and Organizational Psychology, 12,* 39–93.

Tupes, E. C., & Christal, R. E. (1961). *Recurrent personality factors based on trait ratings* (Technical Report No. 61–97). Wright Patterson AFB, OH: USAF Aeronautical Systems Division.

Turban, D. B., & Dougherty, T. W. (1994). Role of protégé personality in receipt of mentoring and career success. *Academy of Management Journal, 37,* 688–702.

Vinchur, A. J., Schippmann, J. S., Switzer, F. S., & Roth, P. L. (1998). A meta-analytic review of predictors of job performance for salespeople. *Journal of Applied Psychology, 83,* 586–597.

Viswesvaran, C., Ones, D. S., & Hough, L. M. (2001). Do impression management scales in personality inventories predict managerial job performance ratings? *International Journal of Selection & Assessment, 9,* 277–289.

Wallace, J. E. (2001). The benefits of mentoring for female lawyers. *Journal of Vocational Behavior, 58,* 366–391.

Wanberg, C. R., & Kammeyer-Mueller, J. D. (2000). Predictors and outcomes of proactivity in the socialization process. *Journal of Applied Psychology, 85,* 373–385.

Watson, D., & Clark, L. A. (1997). Extraversion and its positive emotional core. In R. Hogan, J. Johnson, & S. Briggs (Eds.), *Handbook of personality psychology* (pp. 767–793). San Diego, CA: Academic Press.

Watson, D., Pennebaker, J. W., & Folger, R. (1986). Beyond negative affectivity: Measuring stress and satisfaction in the work place. *Journal of Organizational Behavior Management, 8,* 141–157.

Witt, L. A., Burke, L. A., & Barrick, M. A. (2002). The interactive effects of conscientiousness and agreeableness on job performance. *Journal of Applied Psychology, 87,* 164–169.

5

OCCUPATIONAL CHOICE

MARK L. SAVICKAS

In considering the psychology of occupational choice, the first third of this chapter
describes the cultural context that moved
industrialized societies from assuming that
youth would inherit their family's occupation
to expecting that adolescents should choose
an occupation that they prefer. The movement
from a model of occupational inheritance to
one of occupational choice leads to a discussion
of Parsons's (1909) matching model and the
superordinate construct of person-environment
(P-E) fit. The middle third of the chapter
describes the individual differences paradigm
for occupational choice as systematized by
John L. Holland (1959, 1997) in his P-E fit
theory of vocational personalities and work
environments. Holland characterizes six types
that form the theory's primary propositions
along with four secondary propositions about
consistency, congruence, differentiation, and
vocational identity. The final third of the
chapter describes the developmental paradigm for occupational choice by explaining
the phases in the decisional process and the
construct of career choice readiness. The
chapter concludes by outlining the decisional
difficulties that individuals may encounter as
they make occupational choices and the career

interventions that counselors use to ease their
clients' vocational decision making.

FROM OCCUPATIONAL
INHERITANCE TO OCCUPATIONAL CHOICE

During the 19th century, children usually shared
in their family's field of work. Accordingly,
many families in Europe and America subscribed to the traditional view that an eldest son
should follow in his father's wake. On the model
of the self-sufficient village, the boy apprenticed
to his father would ensure that whatever service
the family provided would be available to the
next generation of townsfolk, and of course, the
boy's own future would be secure. For a younger
son, there might be several options depending on
which neighbors had no sons of their own to
train, but the eldest was sure to share the father's
occupation. Daughters, of course, faced a different future. These circumstances and the sentiment associated with occupational inheritance
combined to produce railroad, circus, or fishing
families in addition to those families who perpet-
uated their own farm, factory, or business. Today,
living in the 21st century, many parents who
engage in a profession or a family business still

subscribe to the traditional view of occupational inheritance. Furthermore, many of the families who share a collectivist culture believe that parents should choose occupations for their children (Leong, Hardin, & Osipow, 2001). In the cases of both inheritance and assignment, the children do not choose an occupation; instead, they accept the choices conferred on them by their parents.

While some families today continue to prefer occupational inheritance or assignment, as early as 1900, the belief that youth should make their own occupational choices became predominant in industrial societies. Propelled by the forces of industrialization and urbanization from 1890 to 1910, a great number of families moved from farms to cities to find work. Families who lived in cities soon realized that their children would eventually work for an employer rather than in a family business. A corollary development was dissemination of the idea that youth should develop an ambition for work that they would enjoy and, in due course, choose their own occupation.

Concern about how individuals should make occupational choices arose and intensified as the Western world experienced the second wave of the Industrial Revolution. In particular, social workers worried about how they could assist street children, urban migrants from rural towns and villages, and immigrants from other countries make viable and suitable job choices. The old method of having friendly visitors chat with youngsters no longer worked as well as it once had (Baker & Maguire, 2005). As early as 1894, Frank Parsons urged a systematic and scientific approach to matching people and positions when he wrote,

> Men work best when they are doing what nature has especially fitted them for. A sensible industrial system will therefore seek . . . to put men, as well as timber, stone, and iron in the places for which their nature fits them. (Parsons, 1894, p. 16)

In 1908, Parsons organized a bureau in Boston to "give scientific vocational counsel to the young" and a year later published posthumously a book about his new model for vocational guidance. Parsons's (1909) book scientized vocational choice and started the new profession of vocational guidance to replace "friendly visits" in assisting city dwellers make occupational choices.

Scientific vocational guidance, as designed by Parsons, gave order to chaos and generated constructs that made "thinkable" the issues and problems of occupational choice. The model, which career counselors still use today, was first articulated by Parsons (1909) as follows:

> In the wise choice of a vocation, there are three broad factors: (1) a clear understanding of yourself, your aptitudes, abilities, interests, ambitions, resources, limitations, and their causes; (2) a knowledge of the requirements and conditions of success, advantages and disadvantages, compensation, opportunities, and prospects in different lines of work; (3) true reasoning on the relations of these two groups of facts. (p. 5)

Essentially, the matching model states that psychosocial adaptation will be fostered by a good fit between the attributes of the individual and the attributes of the behavioral setting. The degree of fit shapes important outcomes such as occupational success, job satisfaction, and organizational tenure. While Parsons was developing from the perspective of the worker his concept of matching people to positions, Frederic Winslow Taylor (1911) developed from the perspective of the employer his concept of "the first class man," that is, the better, more competent man for doing the job efficiently. This parallel development in scientific management foreshadowed many other parallel developments that were to occur as psychologists worked on the complementary problems of guidance for the individual and selection for the organization (Savickas & Baker, 2005). Today, the parallels between career counseling and human resource management remain; yet the distance between the two lines of development has widened (see Peiperl and Gunz, Chapter 3).

Parsons's matching model solved industrial society's problem of how to assign individuals to work in a manner different from agricultural society's method of occupational inheritance. The matching model provided society with both a public policy and a system of ideas to use in fitting individuals to jobs. In using the model, societies seek four outcomes (Watts, 2005).

First, the model assists individuals to learn about themselves and occupations and how to match the two. Second, the model promotes efficiency in matching individuals to labor market needs. Third, the model contributes to economic development through the effective use of human resources. And fourth, the model encourages social equity and cohesion because individuals are matched to jobs based on abilities, values, and interests rather than based on sex, race, and social class. Because these four important outcomes are attributed to using a "scientific" matching of person to position, psychologists have elaborated and refined the matching model into a superordinate framework called P-E fit (Martin & Swartz-Kulstad, 2000).

PERSON-ENVIRONMENT FIT

While often viewed as a single approach, the broad framework of P-E fit actually consists of a family of matching models. Two major models address two different types of fit—complementary and supplementary (Muchinsky & Monahan, 1987). Complementary fit occurs when an individual and an environment provide what the other wants. Complementary fit produces need fulfillment. Supplementary fit occurs when an individual and the people in an environment possess similar characteristics; that is, they resemble each other. Supplementary fit produces value congruence. The models of complementary fit and supplementary fit are not interchangeable. Accumulated research on each model has found them to be equally, yet differently, predictive of attitudes across work dimensions and outcomes. Cable and Edwards (2004) concluded that "complementary and supplementary fit are interrelated but that both contribute independently to outcomes" (p. 830). Complementary and supplementary fit contribute independently, probably, because they contribute to predicting two independent aspects of establishing oneself in an occupation.

The two distinct aspects of stabilizing in a new job are organizational adaptation and position performance (Savickas, 2004). First, a new employee must fit into the organizational culture that surrounds the job. Organizational adaptation involves participating in the work environment, not performing the job tasks. Organizational adaptation occurs through transactions and negotiations with coworkers in which the new employee engages in efforts to learn about the company of workers, and the veteran workers engage in efforts to socialize with the newcomer. New employees, no matter how experienced in other settings, must first learn how things are done in their new organization; this includes learning about the people, politics, values, language, and history of the organization. There can be some reciprocity in the newcomer changing the company, but this is infrequent and minimal when it does occur. Position performance is the second task of stabilizing in a new job. In addition to organizational adaptation, individuals must demonstrate competence in performing their job duties. They must clearly understand their job tasks, take these responsibilities seriously, and perform the tasks efficiently and effectively.

Organizational adaptation is fostered by supplementary fit, whereas position performance is fostered by complementary fit. These twin models of P-E fit are operationally defined quite differently. The supplementary fit model is implemented by determining the resemblance of an individual to a group of workers who are successful and satisfied in a specific occupation. The complementary fit model is implemented by comparing an individual's knowledge, skills, and abilities with those required to perform the job. For example, an industrial/organizational psychologist must know the principles and procedures for personnel recruitment, selection, training, compensation and benefits, labor relations and negotiation, and personnel information systems.

The need fulfillment model of complementary fit is characterized by a point-to-point matching of an individual's abilities and interests to the job's requirements and rewards. The worker's abilities must complement the job's requirements. When they fit together well, the outcome is occupational success. In parallel fashion, when the job's rewards complement the worker's interests, the outcome is job satisfaction. If complementary fit is poor, then failure and frustration result rather than success and satisfaction. A third outcome of complementary fit arises from success and satisfaction. Workers who are satisfactory and satisfied tend to stabilize in their position, so the third outcome is tenure.

The complementary fit model is popular in personnel selection and military classification because it is easier to select a person for a position than it is to select a position for a person. In both selection and classification, tests are useful for sorting out the most fit candidates by identifying those who possess the needed qualifications for one specific job. Of course, vocational psychologists also use the complementary fit model, a preeminent example being the Minnesota Theory of Work Adjustment or TWA (Lofquist & Dawis, 1961). Proponents of the TWA, along with other vocational psychologists, have developed an extensive repertoire of ability tests and interest inventories to assess clients and then match them to the occupational ability patterns and interest profiles in their databases. It is beyond the scope of this chapter to describe the major programs for appraising vocational fitness for occupational fields and levels. Suffice it to state that career counselors have available numerous tests with which to measure abilities along with many inventories with which to measure interests (Kapes & Whitfield, 2002).

The goal of matching for complementary fit is to use assessment results to help individuals select an occupational level that corresponds to their abilities and an occupational field that corresponds to their interests. For example, in the field of social service, at the highest level one finds the occupation of psychotherapist, while at the lowest level one finds hospital attendant. In the technology field, consulting engineer is at the highest level, whereas laborer is at the lowest level. Of course, the results of such assessment only "guide" individuals to explore certain occupational groups; assessment cannot "select" an occupational goal for any individual. In fact, test scores seem to work better in ruling out options than in identifying possibilities. Picture a 6 × 6 grid with occupational fields across the top and ability levels down the side. Assessment might suggest that occupations contained in the cell at Column 3/Row 3 are a good match for the client. However, the client and counselor cannot easily rule out occupations in the cells that surround Column 3/Row 3. They can be more confident about ruling out the occupations in Rows 1, 5, and 6 and probably all the occupations in Columns 1, 5, and 6.

Guidance work involves helping a person choose an occupation. The guidance problem differs from the selection problem in that it seeks to identify suitable and viable occupations from among the vast number of reasonable alternatives. While the complementary model for P-E is dominant among personnel specialists who do selection and classification, the supplementary model for P-E fit is dominant among guidance specialists. According to Ayres (1913) and later Kitson (1942), vocational tests are useful in selecting persons for positions but not in selecting positions for persons. They reasoned that vocational guidance practitioners need occupational information more than they need personality tests. Ayres (1913) urged practitioners to remember that "people and positions are both plastic, not rigid, and much mutual change of form often takes place without injury to either person or position" (p. 237).

As used in vocational guidance, the supplementary model concentrates on the similarity of an individual to the people who populate an occupation and an organization. The key concept is resemblance. Using the rationale that "birds of a feather flock together," guidance specialists have constructed interest inventories to determine the degree of resemblance between an individual client seeking vocational guidance and a catalog of diverse occupational groups composed of satisfactory, satisfied, and stable workers (Savickas, 1999). In reviewing the results from an interest inventory, a counselor can inform a client about which occupational groups he or she resembles and, by extension, which occupations the client should explore first. Among the first generation of interest inventories, two remain popular today. E. K. Strong published one of the first interest inventories in 1927; today it is known as the *Strong Interest Inventory* (Harmon, Hansen, Borgen, & Hammer, 1994). The second leading interest inventory with a long history was first published by Frederic Kuder in 1939. The current form is the *Kuder Occupational Interest Survey, Form DD* (Kuder & Zytowski, 1991). Strong and Kuder constructed and developed their inventories using strictly empirical methods. Later interest inventories were constructed using a blend of Strong's and Kuder's empirical approach to scale construction with attention to theoretical conceptualizations concerning the structure of interests. Examples of leading interest inventories designed using an explicit conceptual structure include the *Campbell Interest and Skills Survey* (Campbell, Hyne, & Nilsen, 1992), the *UNIACT* (American College Testing Program, 1995), and the *Vocational Preference Inventory* (Holland, 1985). These prominent interest inventories are described, then empirically compared and contrasted, in a monograph by Savickas, Taber, and Spokane (2002) and in an article by Savickas and Taber (2006).

HOLLAND'S THEORY

For Strong and Kuder, the matching model was atheoretical, in that it was not based on an explicit model of vocational behavior. After World War II, the methodology emerged for what was to become known as trait-and-factor psychology, a more sophisticated version of Parsons's matching model. In 1947, Leona Tyler (1947) had complained that the test makers' motto was "If there is a word for it, there's a test for it" (p. 359). So the search began to identify what Tyler called more basic traits. Led by Cattell (1950), Eysenck (1953), and Guilford (1948), psychologists applied factor analysis to identify latent personality traits and ability factors from manifest variables. Then, instead of measuring variables selected individually and intuitively, psychometricians measured latent ability factors and personality traits that have been objectively identified from manifest variables using factor analysis. These personality traits and ability factors were viewed as more basic or fundamental. And, no theory of occupational choice could claim to address more fundamental variables than those conceptualized by John L. Holland (1959, 1997) in his supplemental fit theory of vocational personalities and work environments.

Vocational Personalities

Based on factor analyses of vocational interest inventories conducted by Guilford, Christensen, Bond, and Sutton (1954) and three decades of research on Strong's interest inventory, Holland (1959) formulated a theory of vocational personality types and corresponding work environments. The theory describes and organizes an individual's vocationally relevant experiences into a simplifying taxonomy based on six types: realistic, investigative, artistic, social, enterprising, and conventional (RIASEC). Holland specified each of the six types with a distinct syndrome of interests, competencies, and activities. Thus, each type presents an ideal exemplar characterized by a constellation of personality traits and ability factors, which can be summarized as follows:

1. *Realistic* (R) types report outdoor and mechanical interests, prefer to work with animals and machines, enjoy the role of doer, display physical competencies such as leisure pursuits involving physical skills and challenges, and admire role models such as athletes and adventurers. They often can be heard saying, "Just do it."

2. *Investigative* (I) types report scientific interests, prefer to work with ideas, enjoy the role of thinker, display intellectual competencies such as leisure pursuits involving reading and researching, and admire role models such as scientists, inventors, and detectives. They often can be heard saying, "Let's explore it."

3. *Artistic* (A) types report artistic, literary, and musical interests, prefer to work with feelings, enjoy the role of creator, display aesthetic competencies such as leisure pursuits involving self-expression and appreciation of concerts, theaters, and museums, and admire role models such as artists, composers, writers, and performers. They often can be heard saying, "Let's create it."

4. *Social* (S) types report social interests, prefer to work with people, enjoy the role of helper, display communication competencies such as leisure pursuits involving conversation and social gatherings, and admire role models such as teachers and social workers. They often can be heard saying, "Let's talk about it."

5. *Enterprising* (E) types report sales and managerial interests, prefer to work with opinions, enjoy the role of leader, display persuasive competencies such as leisure pursuits involving

travel and politics, and admire role models such as public officials, military officers, and corporation presidents. They often can be heard saying, "Make it so."

6. *Conventional* (C) types report clerical and business interests, prefer to work with data and records, enjoy the role of member, display organizing competencies such as leisure pursuits involving collecting and genealogy, and admire role models such as teams, altruists, and historians. They often can be heard saying, "God is in the details."

An individual's personality pattern is denoted by listing, in descending order, the three types that the individual most resembles. For example a physics professor (I) who enjoys teaching (S) in a creative way (A) would be coded as ISA. The manager (E) of an accounting department (C) at an automobile manufacturer (R) would be coded ECR. Today, the most popular interest inventories—including the *Campbell Interest and Skills Survey, Kuder Occupational Interest Inventory, Strong Interest Inventory, UNIACT,* and *Vocational Preference Inventory*—each provide scores for the six RIASEC types or some variation on these six themes (Savickas & Taber, 2006). These scores indicate the test taker's degree of resemblance to each of the RIASEC prototypes.

Work Environments

One of Holland's most important contributions was to use commensurate types and terms to characterize six work environments that correspond to each of the six RIASEC personality types. Experiences such as work history, educational achievement, and leisure pursuits can also be coded into one of six types. The rationale is that "birds of a feather flock together," so individuals of like types tend to congregate in a given work environment. As Schneider (1987) explained in his attraction-selection-attrition (ASA) framework for understanding organizations, environments vary in part because of the skills and attitudes of the people in them. According to Schneider's (1987) ASA theory of organizational fit, "since activities in the environment that have an effect on people always

involve people then it is the nature of the people in an environment that make it the way it is" (p. 355). Human beings in an environment create different kinds of behavioral settings by their own behavior. Organizational culture, social climate, and company policies are determined by people who are attracted to the setting, selected to join it, and remain in it. So Holland characterizes an environment based on the people occupied in that work setting.

Holland and his colleagues formulated six prototypical work environments, or ecological niches, that correspond to each of the six personality types. Holland cleverly used this taxonomic approach to construct an occupational classification system as well as to classify other behavioral settings, such as university degree programs, universities, and leisure activities. Researchers are able to "type" a behavioral setting by identifying the most frequently occurring vocational personality types that populate it. For example, the Environmental Assessment Technique (Astin & Holland, 1956) applies this procedure to assign RIASEC types to colleges. Researchers can assign a type to a college by calculating the proportion of professors and students on campus who fall into each of the six RIASEC types. For example, I teach at a university that has a large number of professors and students occupied with the fields of education, sociology, and criminology so it is characterized as a social work environment. In contrast, the university has few technology professors and students and none in agriculture or engineering, so it least resembles a realistic work environment.

Holland's RIASEC vocabulary and typology provide an invaluable resource for articulating accounts of work and workers. It puts words on people's perceptions of the social arrangement of work. These words provide vocational psychologists and occupational sociologists with a concise vocabulary for describing vocational personalities and occupations. The RIASEC vocabulary even strengthens the solidarity of their own subculture by serving as a *sociolect*— that is, a shared language that reflects the group's values, interests, and ideology. Also, the RIASEC vocabulary and typology enable career counselors to teach clients how the work world is organized, compare occupations, and describe what types of work the individual is seeking.

Furthermore, the vocabulary and typology serve career counseling clients by providing a language for articulating who they are as well as for increasing and organizing their self-knowledge. In addition to enabling clients to be more efficient and effective in thinking about themselves and work, the language offers a vocabulary for self-construction. Many counselors report that using Holland's RIASEC language prompts their clients to think heuristically about self and occupations.

The six RIASEC types compose the primary propositions in Holland's theory. The typology has garnered substantial empirical support and constitutes Holland's most important contribution to vocational psychology. Holland supplements the research and reflection on the RIASEC types with four secondary propositions. These propositions address the degree of relatedness among types (consistency), the fit between personality types and environment types (congruence), how closely a person resembles a single type (differentiation), and the clarity and stability of an individual's self-perceptions and vocational goals (vocational identity). Holland (1997) formulated these secondary assumptions about consistency, congruence, differentiation, and identity to refine predictions and expectations derived solely from the six types (p. 4).

Consistency

In the middle of the 1970s, Holland elaborated his RIASEC theory by formulating a simplifying structure that serves as a source of ideas, hypotheses, and possibilities. Holland placed each of the six RIASEC types on a nodal point of a hexagon. The RIASEC types are arranged around the hexagon based on correlation coefficients from inventory scores. The order is R-I-A-S-E-C. This means that the two types most consistent with the artistic type are the type before it (investigative) and the type after it (social). The least consistent type is the furthest away (conventional). At an intermediate degree of consistency are the realistic and enterprising types. Consistency of types within a personality pattern is thought to relate to ease of vocational decision making. Consistent types share many common characteristics. For example, both the realistic type and the investigative type are

viewed as being asocial and interested in things rather than people. Thus, an individual who resembles these two types (i.e., has a code of IR or RI) can search for an occupation that suits these compatible traits, say engineer or mechanic. It is more difficult to find occupations that reward individuals who resemble inconsistent types because their characteristics are more incompatible. For example, individuals who resemble the realistic and social types see themselves as both asocial and social. It is often more difficult for them to identify matching occupations that require a worker to be both reserved and friendly. This does not mean that they cannot find such occupations; it just takes more effort. For example, individuals who see themselves as both asocial and social have found success and satisfaction working as high school physical education teachers because they teach realistic skills to students by doing more than by talking. The teaching role is social yet the content of what they teach is realistic.

The hexagonal compass provides a valuable tool for teaching clients how to organize and store information both about themselves and about the work world. The hexagon is a momentous contribution to vocational psychology because of its utility in teaching individuals how society organizes itself into macro environments such as occupations, school subjects, and leisure activities. In using Holland's hexagon, counselors can teach clients that occupations are socially constructed pathways for contributing to the community. The hexagon can be viewed as a road map that shows where occupational pathways intersect and also as a travelogue that describes the types of people and situations one can meet on the different paths. Birds of a feather do flock together.

Congruence

The same RIASEC hexagon that is used to determine consistency *within* a personality pattern or work environment is also used to determine "goodness-of-fit" *between* a person and an environment. The best or most congruent fit between an individual and an environment has an exact match of personality pattern to occupational pattern. For example, the most congruent fit for an ISA individual would be an ISA environment, as happens when an ISA individual works as a university professor teaching psychology classes in a social science building. The most incongruent fit would have this ISA individual working in an ERC occupation such as selling large stamping machines to automobile manufacturers. Note that the occupation of machine sales is completely incongruent because each letter in the occupational type is opposite on the hexagon of the corresponding letter in the personality type. Of course, there are many degrees of congruence between the extremes of perfect fit and perfect misfit. If needed, researchers and practitioners can calculate precisely the degree of congruence using mathematical formulas (Brown & Gore, 1994).

Differentiation

Differentiation means the degree to which an individual resembles a single RIASEC type. It can be indexed with inventory scores for each of the six types by subtracting the lowest score from the highest score. The larger the difference between these extreme scores, the more the differentiation. High differentiation indicates a specialist with narrow interests and an occupation that is highly focused on one process or product. Low differentiation indicates a generalist with broad interests or that the occupation involves many processes and products. Of course, specialists dislike generalist jobs, even if the jobs are a congruent match to their personality types.

Identity

To help counselors determine a student's readiness for making educational and vocational decisions, Holland added a fourth and final secondary proposition to his theory of occupational choice. In general, identity refers to how an individual thinks about self in relation to society. Vocational identity, in particular, refers to how an individual thinks about his or her own interests and talents relative to occupational goals. Thus, Holland defines vocational identity as the clarity and stability of an individual's self-perceptions and vocational goals. A well-formed vocational identity means that the individual is ready to make decisions that match self-knowledge to educational-vocational information and that result in a fitting occupational choice. An individual with a diffuse vocational identity is more likely to be undecided or indecisive when asked to make an occupational choice.

Clarity of vocational identity can be measured efficiently by using Holland, Daiger, and Power's (1980) *My Vocational Situation* (MVS). The MVS serves as a screening device that intake counselors can use to assign new clients to specific treatments. Two 4-item checklists on the MVS ask respondents to indicate their occupational information needs and identify barriers that block their career decision making. The final portion of the MVS consists of an 18-item Vocational Identity Scale (VIS). Scores on the VIS indicate the degree of readiness to make matching choices. Individuals with high scores usually have already decided or are about to decide, whereas individuals with low scores usually need more time to increase self-knowledge and gather occupational information before attempting to match themselves to fitting occupations and academic degree programs.

Applying Holland's Theory: The Self-Directed Search

A popular instrument for measuring RIASEC type, consistency, congruence, and differentiation is Holland's (1997) *Self-Directed Search* (SDS). While the SDS is often mistaken for being an interest inventory, it is really an intervention presented in the form of two booklets called the *Assessment Booklet: A Guide to Educational and Career Planning* and *The Occupations Finder.* Holland designed the SDS for students who do not have access to a vocational guidance counselor. In taking the SDS, a student simulates the experience of working with a guidance counselor. First, the student taking the SDS lists occupational daydreams or aspirations in the *Assessment Booklet* and then codes each one using a booklet called the *Occupations Finder,* which contains RIASEC types for 1,346 occupations. In this way, the student learns the RIASEC vocabulary and occupational typology. The student then continues to work in the *Assessment Booklet* by responding to a series of short inventories that measure interests and survey activities and estimate competencies. By following the directions at the end of the *Assessment Booklet,* the student scores the inventories and computes total scores for each of the six RIASEC types. This scoring procedure produces a three-letter RIASEC code that indicates the student's degree of resemblance to the types. In the final step, the individual returns to the *Occupations Finder* to identify the occupations that have the same three-letter code. There are also booklets for finding the RIASEC types for college majors (Rosen, Holmberg, & Holland, 1994) and for leisure activities (Holmberg, Rosen, & Holland, 1990). Although the data are old, Astin (1965) determined RIASEC codes for U.S. universities in his book *Who Goes Where to College?*

The Decision-Making Process

The construct of vocational identity and the topic of career choice readiness announce the second grand paradigm in the psychology of occupational choice. Holland's theory of occupational choice is the best contemporary exemplar of the P-E fit framework that Parsons originated when in 1909 he published the first "scientific" book on vocational choice. Because the proponents of P-E fit concentrate on individual differences, their stream of thought is referred to as the *differential* model. As we have already discussed, the P-E fit framework concentrates on differences between individuals and uses these differences to match their abilities and interests to occupational levels and fields.

The second paradigm for research and practice related to occupational choice is called the *developmental paradigm* because it concentrates on differences within an individual across time, not on differences between individuals. The developmental paradigm of occupational choice originated in the middle of the 20th century with the publication of Ginzberg's (1952) developmental theory of occupational choice and Super's (1953) developmental theory of vocational behavior. Because the developmental paradigm concentrates on careers, in contrast to occupations, over time *career counseling* for developing vocational behavior became an intervention to complement *vocational guidance* for matching individuals to fitting occupations. These two types of intervention differ in that career counseling concentrates on developmental processes

(i.e., identity and adaptability), whereas vocational guidance concentrates on adjustment outcomes (i.e., success and satisfaction). The fundamental difference between development and adjustment as counseling outcomes is substantiated in vocational guidance's concentration on the occupational choice itself versus career counseling's concentration on the decision-making process yielding that occupational choice.

Counseling methods that match clients' abilities and interests to occupational requirements and rewards, or identify which occupational groups a client most resembles, work well for clients who are ready to make choices. Decisive clients, those who score high on the VIS, for example, can use the results of interest inventories and aptitude tests to make realistic choices. However, other clients who are not ready to choose encounter difficulties when they try to make occupational choices. In fact, after discussing test results and occupational information, indecisive clients may become even more confused about their occupational options because they have more data than they are ready to use.

Occupational Choice Content and Process

Counselors who are sensitive to variations in clients' readiness to make occupational choices appreciate Crites's (1974) distinction between the *content* of occupational choice and the *process* of vocational decision making. Content refers to which occupation a client should enter and thus concentrates on the client's abilities and interests or resemblances. It asks the question "Which occupation has this client chosen?" Process refers to how a client arrives at an occupational choice and thus concentrates on the client's decisional and developmental concerns. It asks the question "How did the client make this occupational choice?" Crites used the analogy of an assembly line to describe the distinction between occupational choice and vocational decision making. He likened occupational choice to the product and vocational decision making to the production activities.

To more effectively use the matching model and its content-oriented methods, experienced counselors view occupational choice as a process that develops over time, not as an event.

Typically, they conceptualize making educational and vocational choices as an adaptive process through which individuals meet and master social expectations (called developmental tasks) to choose an occupation in which they can fulfill both the job demands and their own needs. The choice process originates when, in early adolescence, individuals encounter the vocational development task and social expectation that they orient themselves to the work world and prepare to enter it. As adolescents become more oriented to the importance of work in their future lives, they find the work role to be increasingly salient. This work role salience produces a "basic readiness" for vocational decision making. Among adults, the readiness to make new occupational choices and career transitions reemerges repeatedly over the life course as individuals consider new opportunities, whether moved by personal pull or employer push.

Regardless of an individual's age, the process model of occupational choice remains basically the same. The decisional process begins when an individual becomes aware of the need to adapt to an imminent or intermediate career change by making an occupational choice. Career changes are considered developmental if they are predictable—such as graduating from high school—and traumatic if they are unpredictable—such as a sudden plant closing. Whether or not the individual foresees the career change, the circumstances require that the individual adapt to the transition by making an occupational choice.

Phases in the Decisional Process

Making occupational choices requires that the individual seek ways to bring psychological needs into balance with social opportunities. To balance inner means and outer ways, the individual must first solve psychosocial problems that are usually unfamiliar, often ill defined, and always complex. Vocational psychologists refer to this problem-solving activity, which in due course leads to an occupational choice, as decision making or the decisional process. The psychosocial problems encountered as part of the decisional process can be conceptualized as a developmental sequence of issues and activities that reoccur during the life course each time an individual faces a career transition and the need to make another occupational choice.

The first phase in the decisional process, *orientation,* begins with awareness of the need to make an occupational choice in the imminent or intermediate future. This need can arise from emergent dissatisfactions or the awareness of either new occupational opportunities or employment threats. Growth in abilities, interests, and values continues throughout life, with certain periods of acceleration prompted by external circumstances and opportunities, including developmental tasks, career transitions, and work traumas. In addition to awareness of the need to eventually make an educational or vocational choice, orientation includes two additional aspects. Awareness should move individuals to become familiar with the timing and tasks of the choice points they will encounter in the near, intermediate, and distant future. Furthermore, after becoming aware of and familiar with the choices to be made, individuals should relate themselves to these choices by becoming actively involved in the decision-making process, starting by exploring possible futures.

Orientation should be followed by *exploration* that enables the individual to make fitting occupational choices based on self-knowledge and occupational information. The exploration phase of vocational decision making has two developmental tasks. The first task involves a broad exploration of self and occupations through which the individual learns about his or her own work values, occupational abilities, and vocational interests as well as about viable occupational fields. The developmental task associated with the first aspect of exploration is to *crystallize vocational preferences* for an occupational group. Occupational group, here, means a set of similar occupations in the same interest field and at the same ability level. For example, the Knowledge of Preferred Occupational Group Test or KPOG (Thompson & Lindeman, 1981; www.vocopher.com) identifies 20 distinct occupational groups that an individual might prefer. To clarify the construct of occupational groups, consider two social type groups that differ in ability level. The social service group includes the occupations of guidance counselor, marriage counselor, school psychologists, school teacher, and social worker.

The personal service group includes the occupations of beautician, hospital attendant, host/hostess, receptionist, and waiter/waitress. The KPOG has a test taker select one of the 20 occupational groups and then measures that individual's fund of information about the occupational group that she or he prefers. This is a useful assessment because it predicts the realism and stability of the individual's eventual occupational choice.

Of course, as a part of in-breadth exploration, an individual can expand her or his preferred occupational group to include occupations from neighboring groups, but eventually, the individual should concentrate on a small group of similar occupations for advanced exploration. The developmental task associated with this second aspect of exploration is to *specify an occupational choice*. The individual should identify and explore in-depth a few occupational alternatives through advanced exploration. This means becoming quite familiar with the requirements, routines, and rewards of a few specific occupations. While in-breadth exploration broadens the horizon, in-depth exploration narrows it. The outcome of in-depth exploration should be a willingness to specify an occupational choice and to commit oneself to implementing that choice.

Following the phases of orientation and exploration, the third phase in developing an occupational choice involves *implementing* the specified choice by entering training for it or by obtaining a trial position in it. At first, the specified choice may be tentative. Initial training may confirm or disconfirm the suitability and viability of the tentative choice. Even after training has been completed, a trial position in the chosen occupation may cause the individual to reconsider the occupational choice. For example, after completing the first 2 years of medical school, students enter clinical clerkships at a hospital. While studying basic science in the medical school, they might have remained committed to their tentative choice of medicine. However, after a month on the hospital wards, a few students become aware of the need to make a different occupational choice. The clerkship as a trial position shows them that the occupation of physician does not suit them. They must now recycle through the tasks of orientation, exploration, and implementation.

In due course, the tentative choices and trial positions of the implementation phase of developing an occupational choice clarify the situation so that the individual is ready to stabilize in a certain occupation and a particular job with a specific employer. Thus, *stabilization* is the fourth and final phase in developing an occupational choice. While stabilizing in a position, as well as consolidating it and advancing in it, the individual experiences a period in his or her work history during which new occupational choices are unnecessary. However, for most individuals, awareness of the need to make new occupational choices will soon enough appear on the horizon because of new occupational opportunities or employment threats.

Most individuals make many important occupational choices throughout their work lives. Each time they make an occupational choice, they recycle through the phases of orientation, exploration, implementation, and stabilization. A small percentage of individuals cycle through the phases of occupational choice only once because after they establish themselves in a position, they remain in that position for the remainder of their work lives. The less stable the economy, the more times a worker is likely to face the need to make an occupational choice. In the current U.S. economy, by age 38, the average person born from 1957 to 1964 had held an average of 10.2 jobs (U.S. Bureau of Labor Statistics, 2004). So it is not unusual for individuals to make a dozen or more occupational choices during their work lives, each time recycling through the four phases of vocational decision making.

Although tautological, it should be noted that "occupational choice" technically refers to choosing an occupation. For example, an individual makes a new occupational choice when moving from the occupation of teaching to the occupation of accounting. However, researchers usually subsume under the broad rubric of occupational choice other types of choices that do not involve a change in occupation. For example, an individual can choose a new job within the same occupation, such as moving from elementary teacher to high school teacher. Or, an individual could change organizations but keep the same job, say when a fifth-grade teacher moves to a position in a different school district. This is really an organizational change, not an occupational change. Each change in position—whether of job, organization, or occupation—involves decision making and choice. For completeness, I should note that individuals do not make career changes. A career is the complete sequence of educational and vocational positions that an individual occupies during his or her life course. Each person has only one career, regardless of the number of positions that person occupies from childhood through retirement.

Individuals who seek career counseling may be concerned about issues in any of the phases of vocational decision making. To be useful to the client, the counselor must provide interventions that directly address the client's concerns. Therefore, when meeting a new client, counselors must assess which phase of developing an occupation choice concerns that individual: orientation, exploration for either crystallization or specification, implementation, or stabilization. Most counselors interview their clients to make this determination; yet there are inventories that can be used for this purpose. For example, the Adult Career Concerns Inventory or ACCI (Super, Thompson, & Lindeman, 1988; www.vocopher.com) includes scales that measure crystallization, specification, implementation, and stabilization. The ACCI can be administered to college students and adults to measure their degree of vocational development and the current focus of their career concerns. The ACCI can also be administered to groups of employees, to conduct a needs analysis for an organization or work group, as well as to graduate students who wish to learn operational definitions of the phases in vocational decision making.

Having determined the client's career concern, the counselor can then provide interventions, such as career education for orienting to the vocational development task, vocational guidance for crystallizing vocational preferences, career counseling for specifying an occupational choice, occupational placement for implementing a tentative choice, and job coaching for stabilizing in a position. Because the developmental model for occupation choice centers on decision making, the remainder of the chapter will concentrate on crystallizing and specifying. The developmental tasks that precede choice (i.e., orientation) and follow choice (i.e., implementation and stabilization) are addressed elsewhere (Savickas, 2004).

Career Adaptability

While the tasks of crystallizing vocational preferences and specifying an occupational choice have been delineated, we have not yet addressed how individuals master these tasks. Development arises from activity and from solving difficulties met in the world. Therefore, developmental tasks are mastered through activities and behaviors, for example, information-seeking behavior and making decisions that solve the problems that the tasks present. While this seems straightforward, numerous individuals encounter difficulty in performing the coping behaviors that master the developmental tasks. Accordingly, vocational psychologists and career counselors have accumulated an impressive literature about the attitudes and competencies that influence when and how an individual engages in the decisional process that leads to an occupational choice (Walsh & Savickas, 2005). Collectively, these critical attitudes and competencies, which shape vocational behavior, are referred to as career adaptability.

Career adaptability is a psychosocial construct that denotes an individual's readiness and resources for coping with imminent, intermediate, and distant vocational development tasks and career transitions (Savickas, 2005). Adaptability for crystallizing vocational preferences and specifying an occupational choice has been the focus of extensive research since the middle of the 20th century. Several researchers have used different variable names to label the same coping attitudes and competencies. In an attempt to unify this research, I examined their linguistic explications, operational definitions, and intercorrelations and then consolidated them into four global strategies for vocational decision making (Savickas, 2002). I referred to these self-regulation strategies as constructs or tools for career building throughout the life course.

The four global dimensions of career adaptability are each named according to their principal functions: concern, control, curiosity, and confidence. The homogeneous variables within each dimension are grouped into attitudes, beliefs, and competencies—the ABCs of career construction—which shape the concrete coping behaviors used to master developmental tasks, negotiate occupational transitions, and resolve work traumas. Attitudes and beliefs are dispositions that prime readiness, whereas competencies are cognitive skills, such as comprehension and problem solving, that condition behavioral responses. So the two key types of variables within each of the four dimensions of adaptability are readiness and resources. While it may sound complicated, career adaptability for making occupational choices can be characterized simply as

1. showing *concern* about choices to be made in the future,

2. increasing personal *control* over the decision-making process,

3. displaying *curiosity* about possible selves and alternative work scenarios, and

4. strengthening the *confidence* needed to make occupational choices.

Career Concern

Concern about the vocational future is the prime dimension in career adaptability. It has been called planfulness, time perspective, anticipation, orientation, and awareness (Savickas, Silling, & Schwartz, 1984). Essentially, concern in all its linguistic forms means an orientation toward the future that disposes an individual to prepare for tomorrow. Concern makes the future feel real as individuals become aware of the vocational development tasks and career transitions to be faced and the choices to be made in the near and distant future. Planful attitudes and a belief in the connection between today's experiences and tomorrow's circumstances incline individuals to engage in activities and experiences that promote competence in planning. A lack of career concern is called *career indifference,* and it reflects a planlessness regarding the future and pessimism about it. Career concern prompts individuals to think about who owns their future and who should make their occupational choices.

Career Control

Possessing a sense of control over one's future is the second most important dimension of career adaptability. The importance of control in the vocational decision-making process is reflected in the large amount of research about variables such as decision making, assertiveness, locus of control, autonomy, self-determination, effort attributions, and agency (Blustein & Flum, 1999). Essentially, control in all its linguistic forms denotes that individuals feel and believe that they are responsible for constructing their own careers. Attitudes of assertiveness and decisiveness incline individuals to make their own choices in a timely manner rather than procrastinate or follow the directions of significant others. Members of the dominant culture in countries such as Denmark, France, the United Kingdom, and the United States, and individuals who have assimilated to these cultures, lean toward independence in balancing self and society (Leong et al., 2001). Of course, many other families prefer interdependence, and their children take pride in their occupational inheritance and assigned choices. Nevertheless, prevalent views about occupation choice and materials for career education both assume that the individual is autonomous in making occupational choices. People living in a more collectivist context do not emphasize their individuality as much, yet they still exercise career control by fine-tuning conferred choices and making those choices personally meaningful by enacting them uniquely. Moreover, counselors recognize that control from either an individualistic or a collectivistic perspective means being intentional about what you do and responsible for how you do it (Spector, Sanchez, Siu, Salgado, & Ma, 2004). In this way, both individualistic and collectivistic approaches to control enable individuals to increase their decision-making competence. A lack of career control is called *career indecision.* A sense of career control prompts curiosity about possible selves and alternative futures.

Career Curiosity

A sense of control increases an individual's initiative to explore the types of work that she or he might prefer as well as the occupational opportunities for performing that work. Career curiosity refers to inquisitiveness about and the exploration of the fit between oneself and the work world. The central role of curiosity in occupational choice and career construction has led to an extensive literature on exploration and information-seeking behavior (Blustein, 2000) and an even larger literature about the outcomes of this behavior—namely, self-knowledge and occupational information. Individuals who have explored both themselves and their situation possess more knowledge about their occupational abilities, vocational interests, and work values as well as about the requirements, routines, and rewards of preferred occupations. In most cases, this increased competence in self-knowledge and occupational information fosters realism and objectivity when the individual makes choices that match self to an occupation. A lack of career curiosity leads to *unrealism* because of naïveté about the work world and inaccurate images of the self. Once an individual has a broad fund of information about self and situation, she or he is able to form realistic occupational daydreams and envision possible selves. These aspirations usually prompt questions concerning one's capacity to convert these ideas into reality.

Career Confidence

The fourth and final dimension of career adaptability is confidence. Self-confidence denotes the anticipation of success in encountering and overcoming obstacles (Rosenberg, 1989). Making and enacting realistic occupational choices involves solving complex problems or at least resolving the problems so that one can move forward. The importance of confidence in solving career problems is reflected in the extensive body of writings about self-esteem, self-efficacy, and encouragement in the literature on educational and vocational decision making (Lent, Brown, & Hackett, 1994). Relative to career adaptability, confidence denotes feelings of self-efficacy concerning one's own ability to successfully execute a course of action needed to make and implement suitable educational and vocational choices.

Individuals build their self-confidence as they solve the problems that they encounter during their exploratory experiences and in the activities of daily living, especially household chores, schoolwork, and hobbies. Success in meeting these challenges increases feelings of self-acceptance and problem-solving competence. In contrast, mistaken beliefs about social roles, gender, and race often produce internal doubts and external barriers that thwart the development of confidence. A lack of career confidence can result in an *inhibition* that thwarts actualizing roles and achieving goals.

Interventions for Decisional Difficulties

The four dimensions of career adaptability enable an individual to approach occupational choices and career transitions with a concern for the future, a sense of control over it, the curiosity to experiment with possible selves and explore opportunities, and the confidence to solve problems in making and implementing occupational choices. Development along these four dimensions of adaptability, however, may not proceed smoothly; there may be fixations and regressions. Delays within or disequilibrium among the four development lines produce problems in specifying occupational choices, which counselors diagnose as indifference, indecision, unrealism, or inhibition. In addition to interviewing clients, counselors may use inventories, such as the Career Development Inventory and the Career Maturity Inventory (www.vocopher.com), to help them make developmental diagnoses of decisional difficulties (Savickas, 2000). Each diagnosis of a specific problem in making an occupational choice leads to a particular career intervention that is formulated to resolve that problem and foster development.

Career counseling directly concentrates on addressing decisional problems as opposed to vocational guidance, which concentrates on matching abilities and interests to occupational levels and fields. The apathy of career indifference is addressed by career counseling interventions designed to foster a forward-looking orientation and awareness of the vocational development tasks and career transitions on the horizon. These interventions assist individuals to formulate occupational daydreams in which they think about their aspirations. The interventions aim to induce a future orientation, foster optimism, make the future feel real, practice planning skills, link present activities to future outcomes, and heighten career awareness. In short, career concern interventions help individuals form positive feelings and beliefs about their vocational future.

Counseling interventions aimed at increasing a sense of career control concentrate on promoting attitudes of decisiveness and competence in decision making. In general, the interventions include assertiveness training, decisional training, attribution training, time management techniques, and self-management strategies. In short, career control interventions help individuals to feel and believe that they own their future.

Counseling interventions that aim at increasing career curiosity concentrate on providing information and teaching information-seeking behavior. These interventions can include interpreting vocational tests that increase self-knowledge and providing occupational information that helps individuals learn about the work world. Other important interventions include clarifying values, discussing intrinsic versus extrinsic rewards, engaging in job simulations, shadowing workers, practicing goal setting, learning how to systematically explore occupations, reading occupational pamphlets, working part-time jobs, and volunteering at community centers. In short, career curiosity interventions help individuals examine what they want to do with their future.

Counseling interventions that aim at increasing career confidence concentrate on building self-efficacy. Career inhibition is reduced by interventions designed to increase feelings of confidence and self-efficacy through role modeling, success acknowledgement, encouragement techniques, anxiety reduction, and problem-solving training. These interventions promote the courage to try when the outcome is in doubt by helping individuals concentrate on *what* they are doing rather than on *how* they are doing. In short, career confidence interventions help individuals gain the assurance that they can achieve their goals. With a sense of concern for the future, a feeling of control over it, curiosity about it, and confidence in it, individuals are ready to engage in vocational decision making and possess the resources with which to make realistic choices in which they match themselves to suitable occupations.

CONCLUSION

The psychology of individual differences that leads to the six types of vocational personalities and work environments along with the psychology of individual development that leads to the four dimensions of adaptability provide two complementary perspectives on occupational choice. The perspective of types concentrates on the content of occupational choice and the personality of the individual who makes them. The perspective of tasks concentrates on the process of occupational choice and problems in decision making. Both perspectives, that of person description and problem diagnosis, should be used to comprehend how individuals make occupational choices as well as to structure career interventions to assist individuals with the decisional process. While career interventions may be conducted from either the vantage point of types or of tasks, intervention produces deeper understanding and broader outcomes when both perspectives are used together. Knowing both what is at stake and how to proceed enhances individuals' abilities to choose and then commit themselves to achieving their goals.

While scholarly research continues to refine the models of individual differences and development, attention has recently turned to building new models for comprehending occupational choice in the postmodern society and global economy (Savickas, 2001). These models have taken the "narrative turn" toward personal constructivism and social constructionism (Cochran, 1997; Savickas, 2006; Young & Collin, 2004). Viewing careers from constructionist and contextual perspectives focuses attention on interpretive processes, social interaction, and the negotiation of meaning. From this standpoint, careers do not unfold; they are constructed as individuals make choices that manifest their identities and substantiate their values in the social reality of work roles. Whereas the positivist approach to occupational choice concentrates on objective facts in matchmaking and congruence, the constructivist approach concentrates on subjective truths in meaning making and mattering (Savickas, 2005). The metaphor of career as story that emerged after the narrative turn has only an inchoate research base at this time—mostly case studies using qualitative methods. Nevertheless, conceptualizing occupational choice as a process of self-construction is gaining adherents because the model fits the 21st-century information era, as the individual differences model fits the machine age (1900–1950) and the individual development model fits the corporate era (1951–2000).

REFERENCES

American College Testing Program. (1995). *Technical manual: Revised unisex edition of the ACT Interest Inventory (UNIACT).* Iowa City, IA: ACT.

Astin, A. W. (1965). *Who goes where to college?* Chicago: Science Research Associates.

Astin, A. W., & Holland, J. L. (1956). The environmental assessment technique: A way to measure college environments. *Journal of Educational Psychology, 52,* 308–316.

Ayres, L. P. (1913). Psychological tests in vocational guidance. *Journal of Educational Psychology, 4,* 231–237.

Baker, D. B., & Maguire, C. P. (2005). Mentoring in historical perspective. In D. L. DuBois & M. J. Karcher (Eds.), *Handbook of youth mentoring* (pp. 14–29). Thousand Oaks, CA: Sage.

Blustein, D. L. (2000). Reinvigorating the study of vocational exploration: A framework for research. *Journal of Vocational Behavior, 56,* 380–404.

Blustein, D. L., & Flum, H. (1999). A self-determination perspective of interests and exploration in career development. In M. L. Savickas & A. R. Spokane (Eds.), *Vocational interests: Meaning, measurement, and counseling use* (pp. 345–368). Palo Alto, CA: Davies-Black.

Brown, S. D., & Gore, P. A. (1994). An evaluation of interest congruence indices: Distribution characteristics and measurement properties. *Journal of Vocational Behavior, 45,* 310–347.

Cable, D. M., & Edwards, J. R. (2004). Complementary and supplementary fit: A theoretical and empirical integration. *Journal of Applied Psychology, 89,* 822–834.

Campbell, D. P., Hyne, S. A., & Nilsen, D. L. (1992). *Manual for the Campbell Interest and Skills Inventory.* Minneapolis, MN: National Computer Systems.

Cattel, R. B. (1950). *Personality: A systematic, theoretical, and factorial study.* New York: McGraw-Hill.

Cochran, L. (1997). *Career counseling: A narrative approach.* Thousand Oaks, CA: Sage.

Crites, J. O. (1974). A reappraisal of vocational appraisal. *Vocational Guidance Quarterly, 22,* 272–279.

Eysenck, H. J. (1953). *The structure of human personality.* New York: Wiley.

Ginzberg, E. (1952). Toward a theory of occupational choice. *Occupations, 30,* 491–434.

Guilford, J. P. (1948). Some lessons from aviation psychology. *American Psychologist, 3,* 3–11.

Guilford, J. P., Christensen, P. R., Bond, N. A., & Sutton, M. A. (1954). A factor analysis of human interests. *Psychological Monographs, 68*(4, Whole No. 375).

Harmon, L. W., Hansen, J. I. C., Borgen, F. H., & Hammer, A. L. (1994). *Strong Interest Inventory: Applications and technical guide.* Palo Alto, CA: Consulting Psychologists Press.

Holland, J. L. (1959). A theory of vocational choice. *Journal of Counseling Psychology, 6,* 35–45.

Holland, J. L. (1985). *Vocational Preference Inventory.* Lutz, FL: Psychological Assessment Resources.

Holland, J. L. (1997). *Making vocational choices: A theory of vocational personalities and work environments* (3rd ed.). Odessa, FL: Psychological Assessment Resources.

Holland, J. L., Daiger, D. C., & Power, P. G. (1980). *My Vocational Situation.* Lutz, FL: Psychological Assessment Resources.

Holmberg, K., Rosen, D., & Holland, J. L. (1990). *Leisure Activities Finder.* Lutz, FL: Psychological Assessment Resources.

Kapes, J. T., & Whitfield, E. A. (2002). *A counselor's guide to career assessment instruments* (4th ed.). Broken Arrow, OK: National Career Development Association.

Kitson, H. D. (1942). Creating vocational interests. *Occupations, 20,* 567–571.

Kuder, G. F., & Zytowski, D. G. (1991). *Kuder Occupational Interest Survey Form DD general manual.* Adel, IA: National Career Assessment Associates.

Lent, R. W., Brown, S. D., & Hackett, G. (1994). Toward a unifying social cognitive theory of career and academic interest, choice, and performance. *Journal of Vocational Behavior, 45,* 79–122

Leong, F. T. L., Hardin, E. E., & Osipow, S. H. (2001). Cultural relativity in the conceptualization of career maturity. *Journal of Vocational Behavior, 58,* 36–52.

Lofquist, L. H., & Dawis, R. V. (1961). *Adjustment to work: A psychological view of man's problems in a work-oriented society.* New York: Appleton-Century-Crofts.

Martin, W. E., & Swartz-Kulstad, J. L. (Eds.). (2000). *Person-environment psychology and mental health: Assessment and intervention.* Mahwah, NJ: Lawrence Erlbaum.

Muchinsky, P. M., & Monahan, C. J. (1987). What is person-environment congruence? Supplementary versus complementary models of fit. *Journal of Vocational Behavior, 31,* 268–277.

Parsons, F. (1894). *Our country's need; or, the development of a scientific industrialism.* Boston: Arena.

Parsons, F. (1909). *Choosing a vocation.* New York: Agathon Press.

Rosen, D., Holmberg, K., & Holland, J. L. (1994). *Educational opportunities finder.* Lutz, FL: Psychological Assessment Resources.

Rosenberg, M. (1989). *Society and the adolescent self-image* (Rev. ed.). Middletown, CT: Wesleyan University Press.

Savickas, M. L. (1999). The psychology of interests. In M. L. Savickas & A. R. Spokane (Eds.), *Vocational interests: Their meaning, measurement, and counseling use* (pp. 19–56). Palo Alto, CA: Davies-Black.

Savickas, M. L. (2000). Assessing career decision making. In E. Watkins & V. Campbell (Eds.), *Testing and assessment in counseling practice* (2nd ed., pp. 429–477). Hillsdale, NJ: Erlbaum.

Savickas, M. L. (Ed.). (2001). The future of vocational psychology [Special issue]. *Journal of Vocational Behavior, 59*(2).

Savickas, M. L. (2002). Career construction: A developmental theory of vocational behavior. In D. Brown & Associates (Eds.), *Career choice and development* (4th ed., pp. 149–205). San Francisco: Jossey-Bass.

Savickas, M. L. (2004). Vocational psychology. In C. Spielberger (Ed.), *Encyclopedia of applied psychology* (pp. 655–667). Amsterdam: Elsevier.

Savickas, M. L. (2005). The theory and practice of career construction. In S. D. Brown & R. W. Lent (Eds.), *Career development and counseling: Putting research and theory to work* (pp. 42–70). Hoboken, NJ: Wiley.

Savickas, M. L. (2006). *Career counseling* (DVD No. 4310737). Washington, DC: American Psychological Association.

Savickas, M. L., & Baker, D. B. (2005). The history of vocational psychology: Antecedents, origin, and early development. In W. B. Walsh & M. L. Savickas (Eds.), *Handbook of vocational psychology* (3rd ed., pp. 15–50). Mahwah, NJ: Lawrence Erlbaum.

Savickas, M. L., Silling, S. M., & Schwartz, S. (1984). Time perspective in career maturity and decision making. *Journal of Vocational Behavior, 25,* 258–269.

Savickas, M. L., & Taber, B. J. (2006). Individual differences in RIASEC profile similarity across five interest inventories. *Measurement and Evaluation in Counseling and Development, 38,* 203–210.

Savickas, M. L., Taber, B. J., & Spokane, A. R. (2002). Convergent and discriminant validity of five interest inventories. *Journal of Vocational Behavior, 61,* 139–184.

Schneider, B. (1987). $E = f(P, B)$: The road to a radical approach to person-environment fit. *Journal of Vocational Behavior, 31,* 353–361.

Spector, P. E., Sanchez, J. I., Siu, O. L., Salgado, J., & Ma, J. (2004). Eastern versus Western control beliefs at work: An investigation of secondary control, socioinstrumental control, and work locus of control in China and the US. *Applied Psychology: An International Review, 53,* 38–60.

Super, D. E. (1953). A theory of vocational development. *American Psychologist, 8,* 185–190.

Super, D. E., Thompson, A. S., & Lindeman, R. H. (1988). *Adult Career Concerns Inventory.* Palo Alto, CA: Consulting Psychologists Press.

Taylor, F. W. (1911). *The principles of scientific management.* New York: Harper.

Thompson, A. S., & Lindeman, R. H. (1981). *Career Development Inventory user's manual.* Palo Alto, CA: Consulting Psychologists Press.

Tyler, L. E. (1947). *The psychology of human differences.* New York: Appleton-Century.

U.S. Bureau of Labor Statistics. (2004, August 25). Number of jobs held, labor market activity, and earnings growth among younger baby boomers: Recent results from a longitudinal survey (USDL 04–1678). *News.* Washington, DC: U.S. Department of Labor.

Walsh, W. B., & Savickas, M. L. (Eds.). (2005). *Handbook of vocational psychology* (3rd ed.). Mahwah, NJ: Lawrence Erlbaum.

Watts, A. G. (2005). Career guidance policy: An international review. *Career Development Quarterly, 54,* 66–76.

Young, R. A., & Collin, A. (2004). Introduction to special issue: Constructivism and social constructionism in the career field. *Journal of Vocational Behavior, 64,* 373–388.

6

CAREER COUNSELING

JENNIFER M. KIDD

As other chapters in this volume show, the study of careers draws on a range of diverse areas of literature. This is also the case with career counseling. One main influence is vocational psychology, which is largely concerned with theory and research relating to occupational choice and early career decision making. Another is therapeutic counseling theory, ideas from which are increasingly informing career-counseling practice. A third area of literature focuses on organizational careers, and this in turn has been influenced by organizational psychology, sociology, and management studies. Unfortunately, there has been little interaction between researchers and writers in these areas, and one purpose of this chapter is to show how theories and concepts from each can inform career-counseling practice.

The first career-counseling services appeared at the turn of the 20th century. Parsons (1909) is generally acknowledged to have been the originator of career counseling (Moore, Gunz, and Hall, Chapter 2), a process that was then called "vocational guidance." His work focused on the early career decision-making process, with the central proposition that individuals should engage in a process of "true reasoning" to achieve a good match between their own characteristics and the

demands of a job. The aim of vocational guidance was to encourage this. Current "person-environment-fit" approaches to career counseling (e.g., Holland, 1997) evolved directly from Parsons' work, and it is remarkable how they have endured over time.

However, in the context of more flexible and diverse career patterns, the view of career counseling as a process of helping people make wise career decisions that set them on a particular career pathway for life is increasingly inappropriate. Career counselors work with clients of any age and at any stage in their careers, helping individuals with a wide range of career-related concerns. Although work and educational choices are likely to be important issues, many clients will also need help in dealing with broader concerns, such as coping with the frustrations of redundancy and unemployment, deciding whether to return to study or work, and finding ways to balance different life roles. In addition, the problems clients voice in the early stages of career counseling may mask deeper emotional issues that will not become apparent until later in the counseling process. Career counseling can therefore be seen as a process that helps individuals not only make career-related decisions but also effectively manage their careers over the life course and develop the emotional resilience to cope with the challenges that arise as their working lives progress. More specifically, the definition of career counseling offered here is as follows:

> A one-to-one interaction between practitioner and client, usually ongoing, involving the application of psychological theory and a recognised set of communication skills. The primary focus is on helping the client make career-related decisions and deal with career-related issues. (Kidd, 2006, p. 1)

A wide range of theoretical perspectives can be drawn on to achieve the aims of career counseling. First, it is useful to distinguish between career theories and career-counseling theories. The former are concerned with how people experience their careers, how they make career decisions, and the environments in which careers are made, while the latter focus on how best to intervene to assist people in their career development. Both are covered in this chapter, but in discussing career theories the emphasis will be on the implications of these for the practice of career counseling. As suggested earlier, a further relevant body of theory is that of therapeutic counseling. Since career and personal concerns are often closely intertwined, it is unhelpful to see career and therapeutic counseling as discrete processes. This chapter will also, therefore, examine briefly some of the major perspectives on therapeutic counseling that have implications for the field of career counseling. This is followed by some observations on eclecticism and integration and on epistemological issues. Later in the chapter, a stage model of the career-counseling process is outlined, followed by discussions of assessment tools and techniques, the provision of career information, and the use of information and communications technology. Last, research on the effectiveness of career counseling is examined.

CAREER AND CAREER-COUNSELING THEORIES

In this section, the career theories and career-counseling theories that have been most influential on practice over the course of the 20th century are discussed. We begin by considering person-environment-fit theories, which were the backbone of career counseling for many years. Developmental and cognitive-behavioral approaches are then discussed. This is followed by a brief review of some of the emerging theories of career development, focusing particularly on postmodern perspectives, embodied by narrative models and action theory. Last, some of the challenges highlighted by these approaches for theory, research, and practice are identified.

Person-Environment-Fit Theories

Person-environment-fit approaches to career counseling emphasize diagnosis and assessment, and a common outcome is a recommendation to the client on an appropriate course of action. The practitioner is likely to use questionnaires and inventories completed before the interview (or a series of interviews) as aids to assessment. Holland's (1997) work has provided one theoretical rationale for this diagnostic approach to career counseling, and this is discussed in detail in Chapter 5 by Savickas in this volume. He proposed that people seek occupations that are congruent with their occupational interests (defined as preferences for particular work activities). His theory states that people and occupational environments can be categorized into six interest types: realistic, investigative, artistic, social, enterprising, and conventional; occupational choice is the result of attempts to achieve congruence between interests and environments; and congruence results in job satisfaction and career stability.

Holland's main proposition, that individuals choose occupations that are congruent with their interests, has generally been supported by research (see, e.g., Spokane, 1985). Holland's assertion that congruence results in satisfaction and stability has found less support, however (Tinsley, 2000; Tranberg, Slane, & Ekeberg, 1993). (For example, the relationship between congruence and job satisfaction is weak, around .20.) This may be because people now tend to think more specifically about the *job* they want rather than what broader *occupation* suits them. Also, occupational titles are inadequate descriptors of work environments (Arnold, 2004).

Furthermore, some writers have questioned the validity of the six-dimensional model of interests. Prediger (2000), for example, has argued that two dimensions of "people" versus "things" and "data" versus "ideas" should be incorporated into the model.

Nevertheless, Holland's model has provided an important theoretical rationale for a person-environment-fit, diagnostic approach to career counseling. According to the theory, the career counselor's primary activity is the assessment of occupational interests and the identification of occupations that match the client's interest profile. A range of instruments is available for assessing interests, including the Strong Interests Inventory (Harmon, Hansen, Borgen, & Hammer, 1994) and the Self-Directed Search (Holland, 1985; available at www.self-directed-search.com).

Until recently, person-environment-fit approaches have given little attention to the role of attributes other than interests in the assessment of fit. Further development of fit models should take account of the links between interests, personality and values (Tinsley, 2000), and abilities. Ackerman and Heggestad (1997), for example, in a review of studies that assessed the relationships between abilities, interests, and personality, found four clusters of traits across these three domains: social, clerical/conventional, science/maths, and intellectual/cultural. Apart from the social cluster, all the clusters included traits across the three domains. Ackerman and Heggestad argue that "abilities, interests and personality develop in tandem, such that ability levels and personal dispositions determine the probability of success in a particular task domain and interests determine the motivation to attempt the task" (p. 239). This suggests that career counselors should use frameworks of fit that integrate various attributes, including abilities, interests, and personality.

The person-environment-fit approach to career counseling has often been characterized as assuming that the career counselor's role is simply to offer "expert" advice based on knowledge of the client and of work opportunities. It has also been criticized for ignoring the processes leading up to a career decision and later career development and focusing too much on initial occupational choices. But person-environment fit is now viewed as more of an ongoing process, where individuals and work environments are in constant reciprocal interaction, and contemporary versions see the client as an active participant in the career-counseling process (Swanson, 1996).

Developmental Theories

Developmental orientations to careers and career counseling have two basic features in common. First, they take the view that choosing a career and managing one's career development involve a continuous process that carries on through life. Second, they use concepts from developmental psychology, such as developmental stages and tasks and career maturity, to describe and explain the process of career development.

The writer most commonly associated with the developmental approach is Donald Super. He proposed that career development proceeds through stages as the individual seeks to "implement a self-concept" in an occupation. Super's original stage theory (1957) portrayed career development as involving five stages: growth, exploration, establishment, maintenance, and decline. In a later formulation (Super, Thompson, Lindeman, Myers, & Jordaan, 1988), four stages were incorporated, and within each, three substages:

1. *Exploration.* Crystallization, specification, implementation

2. *Establishment.* Stabilizing, consolidating, advancing

3. *Maintenance.* Holding, updating, innovating

4. *Disengagement.* Deceleration, retirement planning, retirement living

These stages, as well as research on Super's theory, are discussed in detail in Chapter 15 by Sullivan and Crocitto. It is worth noting here though that in this model, individuals are acknowledged to "recycle": People experiencing mid-career transitions, for example, may need to engage in some of the tasks of early working life.

Career counselors who take a developmental approach attempt to form a comprehensive picture of their clients' career development, encouraging them to move toward a greater awareness of themselves and their situations and to develop decision-making skills. Developmental theorists argue that career-counseling interventions need to be related to the client's developmental stage. For example, during the exploratory stage of career development (around ages 15–24), the focus will be on educational and occupational decision making and the transition to work, while later stages will have a broader emphasis, taking account of other issues, such as work-life balance.

At the time of their introduction, in the 1950s, these ideas signified a sea change in career-counseling practice, based as it was then on a person-environment-fit approach. The view that career development involves developing and implementing a self-concept led career counselors to focus on individuals' views of themselves and their perceptions of opportunities rather than static descriptions of attributes (often derived from testing) and objective descriptions of occupations.

Super's work stimulated a vast amount of research on the exploration stage of development but much less on later stages. One reason for this may be that the processes within later stages are described in only a general way. Because there is little attempt to explain the processes, it is difficult to formulate testable hypotheses, apart from very general ones.

One key concept in developmental models is "career maturity." Career maturity has been defined as an individual's readiness for coping with the tasks of career development as compared with others handling the same tasks. Work has been carried out to assess desirable career attitudes and competencies, and measures of career maturity—for example, The Career Development Inventory (Super, Thompson, Lindeman, Jordaan, & Myers, 1981)—are commonly used to evaluate the effectiveness of career-counseling and other career interventions. Some of these measures are strongly value laden, however, assuming that it is somehow more "mature" to seek intrinsic rather than extrinsic satisfaction from work. Despite calls for alternative constructs to describe the attitudes and skills needed for effective career management in adulthood—for example, "career adaptability" (e.g., Savickas, 2005; Super & Knasel, 1981)—measures of career maturity are still widely used in career counseling.

Cognitive-Behavioral Theories

Cognitive-behavioral career theories arose out of behavioral psychology. As applied to career counseling, they emphasize a change-focused problem-solving approach and the cognitive processes through which people monitor their behavior. Krumboltz's (1983) theory was developed from social learning theory (Bandura, 1977). Krumboltz (1983) argues that people develop beliefs about themselves and work through two kinds of learning experiences: instrumental and associative. Instrumental learning occurs when individuals develop preferences for particular activities when their achievements are rewarded. Associative learning occurs as individuals observe the behavior of significant others and the ways they are rewarded and punished. Individuals form "self-observation generalizations" (beliefs about one's own abilities, interests, values, etc.) as a result of these experiences, and they learn "task-approach skills" (e.g., decision-making skills and orientations toward work). Sequences of these kinds of learning experiences form the basis for career development.

The main task for career counselors using this approach is to assess the "accuracy, completeness and coherence" of clients' beliefs about themselves and the external world (Krumboltz, 1983). Inaccurate beliefs may be linked to various processes, including using a single experience to make inaccurate generalizations about work, comparing oneself with an idealized role model, and emotionally overreacting to negative events. In addition, the career counselor needs to reinforce rational behavior and challenge dysfunctional beliefs by, for example, identifying inconsistencies and confronting illogical systems of beliefs (Mitchell & Krumboltz, 1990).

Emerging Theories of Career Development

More recently developed career theories with clear implications for career counseling include social cognitive career theory—a development of Krumboltz's work (Lent, Brown, & Hackett, 1996); cognitive information processing theory (Peterson, Sampson, Reardon, & Lenz, 1996); Brown's (1996) value-based model of career choice; and Hansen's (1997) integrative life-planning model. Space does not permit coverage of these in this chapter, but good overviews are given in Brown and Associates (2002) and Niles and Harris-Bowlsbey (2002).

It is worth giving more attention to theories that depart from the positivist tradition that has dominated career research, however. The term *postmodern* has been used to describe these approaches, and they emphasize subjective experience and personal agency in career development.

Narrative Approaches

Narrative approaches to career counseling are in line with the postmodern shift away from broad systems of thought, such as Marxism or psychoanalysis, to more "local" truths and knowledge systems. Writers and practitioners taking a narrative approach encourage clients to tell stories about their lives and help them make sense of these and identify key themes within them. Establishing whether the experiences and events described by clients actually occurred is seen as irrelevant; rather, the aim is to help clients understand and explain their experiences in a coherent way and retell or "re-author" their story or stories in a more satisfactory and "agentic" manner. The approach is not entirely new, however. Many commonly accepted counseling techniques and skills are consistent with a narrative approach. For example, empathic reflection of the content and feeling of clients' statements can help them elucidate their stories, and challenging skills can be used to help identify inconsistencies in their narratives.

Cochran (1997) argues that career counseling can be distinguished from other forms of counseling by focusing particularly on narratives that deal with future career development. Cochran also emphasizes the value of helping clients "actualize an ideal narrative," achieving what they would ideally like to do. This involves "wholeness" (constructing a coherent story), "harmony" among values and activities, a "sense of agency" (being proactive and responsible for one's actions), and "fruitfulness" (progress in managing one's career).

Action Theory

Young, Valach, and Collin's (1996) postmodern approach views career development as an "action system" that derives meaning through the social interaction between individuals and others in their social environment. Individuals make sense of their lives and construct their careers through action. Of particular importance are the goal-directed actions that individuals take in career development. These actions are viewed from three perspectives: manifest behavior, conscious cognitions (including thoughts and feelings), and social meaning (the meaning of the action to the self and to others). Career counseling is seen as a project where counselor and client are involved in "joint action." Social meaning is particularly important in career counseling, where language and narrative help people make sense of life events. It is also important to bring contextual information into the career-counseling process—for example, by providing career counseling in settings where "career action" occurs (e.g., the workplace) and by involving significant others in the process.

As some of the emerging theories imply, so as to better inform career-counseling practice over the life span, career theory needs to be more interactive, taking account of relationships between the individual, social environments, and economic institutions. It also needs to be dynamic, attending to how individuals make sense of their unfolding careers over time. Furthermore, career theory needs to encompass not only how decisions are made and how they might be better made but also how people manage progression in their work and in their learning in the context of more diverse and unpredictable career patterns. Coping with this unpredictability requires a degree of emotional resilience. Individuals who cope well are likely to view the future optimistically and welcome frequent changes of job and employer (Watts & Kidd, 2000).

Kidd's (2006) threefold framework of career development incorporates these aspects: career decision making, career management, and career resilience. Stronger theory is needed in all three to provide a sounder theoretical base for career counseling. With regard to *decision making,* we need to know more about how career decisions are typically made, perhaps moving away from the assumption that these decisions are always, or indeed best, made in planful, goal-directed ways. Asking people how they made decisions is fraught with difficulties, and accounts of planful decision making may merely reflect cultural expectations of rational discourse (Moir, 1993). Research that takes account of language and discourse is needed to inform the help that career counselors can provide with career decision making.

We may also need to reconsider the constructs and frameworks of work available to career counselors. Hirsh, Kidd, and Watts (1998) argue that some existing ways of grouping occupations and work roles may be out of date and that skills frameworks rather than occupational classifications may be more robust ways of distinguishing different types of work.

In relation to individual *career management,* theory needs to take account of people's attempts to meet their changing needs within more boundaryless careers. It also needs to take more account of the social context of careers. As Flum (2001) has pointed out, "When boundaries become less visible, interdependence becomes gradually more apparent" (p. 266). There is a growing interest in relational approaches to careers; for example, the work of Higgins and Kram (2001) and Seibert, Kraimer, and Liden (2001) suggests the importance of social relationships in career progression. Furthermore, Kidd, Jackson, and Hirsh (2003) have shown how a diverse range of individuals, using basic helping skills, provide career support to employees.

Career counseling also needs a firmer knowledge base about *career resilience*—how individuals cope with challenges and setbacks in their careers. The role of emotion in career development has received little attention until recently. Feelings like anger, worry, and enthusiasm have rarely been discussed (Kidd, 1998), yet career counselors commonly have clients who are incapable of moving on in their careers because of emotional difficulties. In these situations, the broader theoretical perspectives provided by therapeutic counseling theories have much to offer practitioners.

These observations suggest several challenges for career-counseling theory, research, and practice. First, theories and counseling methods need to take account of the ways careers are constructed, individually and socially. Second, we may need to review the classification systems and descriptors used in career counseling, to reflect changes in the

world of work. Third, we need to recognize that career development is a social process. Career theory should acknowledge the help and support individuals receive from a range of other people. Also, there may be a role for career practitioners in providing training to givers of support. Last, recognizing the emotional aspects of career management acknowledges the important contribution of therapeutic counseling theories.

THERAPEUTIC COUNSELING THEORIES

Several perspectives on therapeutic counseling have been applied to career counseling, the most important of which are the person-centered and psychodynamic approaches. These are discussed in turn.

Person-Centered Theories

The person-centered approach to therapeutic counseling was introduced by Carl Rogers, and it is one of the most commonly practiced. It was originally described by Rogers (1942) as "client-centered," a term that implies that the focus of the counseling session is determined by the client. According to person-centered practitioners, the most important factor affecting the progress made in the counseling session is the relationship between the counselor and the client. Rather than specific interview techniques, it is the attitudes and qualities of the counselor that are the key to success.

These attitudes and qualities are as follows:

- Congruence (or genuineness), which involves being integrated and real in the relationship
- Unconditional positive regard, which requires the counselor to respect the client in a nonjudgmental way
- Empathic understanding, by which the counselor attempts to understand the client from his or her own internal frame of reference and tries to communicate this to the client

Building on Patterson's (1964) work, which was an early attempt to explore how person-centered principles could be applied in career counseling, Bozarth and Fisher (1990) have set out the main characteristics of a person-centered approach to career counseling. They describe them as follows:

Person-centered career counseling is a relationship between a counselor and a client, arising from the client's concerns, which creates a psychological climate in which the client can evolve a personal identity, decide the vocational goal that is fulfilment of that identity, determine a planned route to that goal, and implement the plan. The person-centered career counselor relates with genuineness, unconditional positive regard, and empathy; the locus of control for decisions remains with the client out of the counselor's trust in the self-actualizing tendency of the individual. The focus in person-centered career counseling is that of attitudes and beliefs that foster the natural actualizing process rather than on techniques and goals. (p. 54)

It is surprising that ideas from personal construct psychology (PCP) (Kelly, 1955) have not had more of an influence on person-centered counseling. PCP, a theory of personality that emphasizes the unique ways in which people experience and make sense of the world, contributes to our understanding of individuals' unique experiences of choices and transitions, and one would expect that person-centered career counselors would have incorporated more ideas from this theory.

According to PCP, individuals use bipolar constructs to understand the world. For example, a construct that an individual could use to describe jobs might be "creative/noncreative." Individuals are seen as constantly testing out and elaborating their systems of constructs. The PCP approach to career counseling views the career counselor as attempting to understand how the client construes the world. Techniques include the following:

- Eliciting constructs by asking clients to describe ways in which certain "elements" (which might be jobs) are similar or different
- "Laddering" up the hierarchy of constructs from subordinate constructs (which may be quite concrete) to superordinate constructs, which have a wider application (e.g., by probing *why* certain things are important to the client)

- Moving down the hierarchy of constructs from superordinate ones to subordinate ones (e.g., by asking *how* things differ)
- Asking clients to complete a "grid" comparing elements (e.g., jobs) along certain constructs

As applied to career counseling, PCP could be criticized for its lack of attention to objective reality. For example, it is unclear how concrete data about work are incorporated into the process.

Psychodynamic Theories

Two main assumptions of the psychodynamic approach to psychotherapy and counseling are, first, that individuals' difficulties have their origins in early experiences and, second, that individuals may not be consciously aware of their motives.

Several concepts derived from psychodynamic theories can be helpful in understanding career development. These include defense mechanisms, such as denial (e.g., where a person is unwilling to accept that he or she has been made redundant) and repression (where a threatening memory of an event becomes unavailable to the conscious mind). Psychodynamic approaches also recognize various processes that occur in the interaction between the counselor and the client. Transference is the best-known example, where the client relates to the counselor as if the counselor was an important person in the client's development, such as the client's mother.

Watkins and Savickas (1990), discussing the relevance of psychodynamic theory to career counseling, have outlined some techniques derived from this approach. They argue that career counselors using psychodynamic approaches need to develop skills in assessing life themes and sensing patterns in the life course. A key activity will be "making intelligible interconnections among the episodes of the client's life" (p. 108). Structured interviews, projective techniques, autobiographies, and card sorts are examples of some of the tools that can be used.

Watkins and Savickas (1990) have also identified several types of clients who seem to benefit particularly from a psychodynamic approach. These include those who are indecisive and those who have misconceptions about themselves.

ECLECTIC AND INTEGRATIVE APPROACHES

The orientations described above may give the reader the impression that career counseling operates from a range of clear theoretical principles. However, the flow of knowledge between theory and practice appears to be limited. The career-counseling literature is more prescriptive than analytic (Watts & Kidd, 2000), and career-counseling practice is "often based on a loosely defined set of common practices. . . . without a theoretical foundation" (Whiston, 2003, p. 37). Furthermore, unlike therapeutic counselors, career practitioners rarely adhere to one coherent theoretical orientation, using particular methods and techniques that suit their personal beliefs, their clients, and the issues they bring to the session (Kidd, Killeen, Jarvis, & Offer, 1997; Watson, 1994). Many describe themselves as eclectic, but this seems often to happen by default rather than being a deliberate way of working. One reason for the limited relationship between theory and practice is that the positivist assumptions of much career research conflict with career counselors' concern with encouraging their clients to understand the subjective meanings of their career experiences through the therapeutic relationship (Collin & Young, 1992).

In contrast, the relative merits of approaches that draw on a range of models and techniques versus those that rely on theoretical purity are vigorously debated in the fields of therapeutic counseling and psychotherapy. In particular, there has been much discussion of "technical eclecticism" and "theoretical integration" (Norcross & Grencavage, 1989). Technical eclecticism uses methods and techniques drawn from different sources without necessarily adhering to their parent theories, while theoretical integration involves attempts to synthesize conceptually diverse frameworks. Within therapeutic counseling practice, eclecticism and integrationism are seen as theoretical orientations in their own right, although eclecticism seems to have dropped out of favor recently (McLeod, 2003).

There seems to be a range of options open to career counselors, therefore, who are not satisfied with working within a single theoretical model. First, taking what has been called a "common factors" approach, they might identify the common features from various models that appear to produce gains for the client. Second, they might choose to be eclectic, teasing out specific methods and techniques from the models that appear to be helpful. Third, they might try to develop their own, unique, integrative model.

EPISTEMOLOGICAL ISSUES

Traditional approaches to career counseling—for example, person-environment-fit approaches and developmental approaches—view career planning and career management as ideally rational processes. They are rooted in a positive epistemology, which assumes that objective reality exists and can be assessed through objective observation and measurement. Positivist theories can be criticized for oversimplifying relationships between phenomena, failing to acknowledge the influence of social structure and culture on people's experiences, and assuming that the structure of opportunities is set (Watts & Kidd, 2000).

In contrast, some of the newer orientations to career counseling—for example, narrative approaches—take the view that there are multiple realities, that individuals construct their own reality, and that therefore there are many versions of people's career experiences. Within this perspective, it is possible to distinguish between "constructivist" and "constructionist" paradigms (although the two terms are often used interchangeably). Practitioners and researchers working within a constructivist paradigm emphasize the accounts and descriptions individuals use to construct their worlds, while constructionists are more concerned with the ways these descriptions and accounts are themselves socially constructed (Kidd, 2004; Potter, 1996). As Savickas (1997) argues, the constructivist paradigm, being more concerned with individual psychology, explores the nature of "self-conceiving, self-organizing processes." He suggests that applications of constructivism to career counseling include PCP and narrative approaches. As we have seen, person-centered counseling (Rogers, 1942) is also rooted in constructivism, since it emphasizes the importance of the client's internal frame of reference in the counseling process.

The constructionist paradigm, on the other hand, focuses on how accounts of social phenomena are socially produced (by the culture and by the parties involved in social interactions) and the use of language in this process. Significantly, constructionism shows how the constructs describing individual differences in the careers literature (e.g., work values and occupational interests) are cultural constructions and not necessarily universal (Stead, 2004). An example of a career theory within this perspective is the action theory of Young et al. (1996) (discussed earlier), which proposes that careers are socially constructed through joint action or interactions with significant others.

The important point here is that both approaches assume that in any social interaction, participants "co-create" understandings (Denzin & Lincoln, 2000). Therefore, there are constraints on how far clients' accounts concerning their careers can be seen as reflecting their inner realities and therefore their agency. Edwards and Potter (1992), for example, see conversation as constructed to perform interactional, communicative work, to support or undermine versions of events. If this is so, there are implications for career counseling. Various elements of the career-counseling context could be explored to gain a better understanding of the client-counselor interaction and clients' accounts of their experiences. These include the framing of the situation by both parties, clients' motives and means of impression management, perceptions of power relationships within the interaction, and the use of language and cultural scripts.

Exploring career-counseling interventions in these ways opens up possibilities for multiple interpretations of the career-counseling process and of clients' accounts of their career development. They do not replace understandings based on underlying cognitions and individual agency; rather, they offer additional lenses through which to view the process.

THE CAREER-COUNSELING PROCESS

We discussed earlier some of the basic components of the career-counseling interaction. Many career-counseling texts, irrespective of theoretical orientation, organize their discussion of career-counseling practice within a stage model of career counseling. For example, Kidd's (2003; 2006) model of career-counseling stages and tasks views the career-counseling process as comprising four stages, with associated tasks. These stages are discussed in this section.

In the first stage, building the relationship, the main task is to establish the working alliance. In the second stage, enabling clients' self-understanding, helping clients assess their attributes and their situation is the key task. The third stage, exploring new perspectives, involves challenging and information giving. In the last stage, forming strategies and plans, reviewing progress and goal setting are the main activities. Although the model is oversimplified (usually, sessions move back and forth between stages), it serves to illustrate the key activities.

Stage 1: Building the Relationship

The image of the career counselor as an "expert," offering advice and recommendations on suitable jobs, is an enduring one. Many clients expect career counseling to consist mainly of information about occupations and may be disappointed when they do not receive this. Writers on career-counseling practice tend to take the view, therefore, that it is important to help the client understand that career counseling is a collaborative venture and that they themselves need to be active participants throughout the process. Agreeing on a client-counselor "contract" at an early stage is seen as crucial, and this is asserted in a considerable body of literature. The contract may cover issues of confidentiality; the number, length, and frequency of meetings; and, more generally, the nature of the career-counseling process itself, and it may need to be renegotiated at intervals.

Bordin (1979) used the term *working alliance* to describe the quality of the relationship established early on between the counselor and the client. From a psychoanalytic perspective, he saw the working alliance as arising out of the transference relationship that the client develops with the counselor. Although agreeing and renegotiating a contract may seem fairly straightforward, research with practitioners in the United

Kingdom suggests that there is some confusion about what the contract should consist of and concern that it could come to dominate the career-counseling session (Kidd et al., 1997).

Stage 2: Enabling Clients' Understanding

In the second stage, the main task is seen as helping clients gain a deeper understanding of their situation and the issues that are concerning them. Many clients gain important insights through the counseling process itself, but more structured assessment techniques and tools are often used at this stage.

Assessment Techniques

One of the advantages of using assessment techniques is that they help clients become familiar with conceptual frameworks in order to organize their knowledge of themselves and their situation (Holland, Magoon, & Spokane, 1981). From this point of view, simple self-assessment tools, as well as the knowledge gained through the career-counseling process itself, often produce insights that appear to be as useful as those gained from administering psychometric tests and inventories.

Changes in career-counseling practice have led to a substantial expansion in the purposes and use of assessment techniques. Person-environment-fit approaches to career counseling necessitated robust means of assessing individuals' psychological attributes to recommend career options. While this "test and tell" approach is still prevalent, it is less appropriate where the practitioner works within an orientation in which the client is an equal participant in the career-counseling process. Practitioners using person-centered or narrative approaches, for example, are likely to involve the client in deciding whether assessment tools are needed and, if so, which ones. They are also more likely to use assessment for client self-understanding and exploration rather than make predictions or recommendations. In addition, the information produced from assessment is seen as something to be shared, and clients may be encouraged to express their feelings about its accuracy and usefulness.

Assessment tools used in career counseling may be grouped into two broad categories: informal and formal. Informal tools and techniques include graphic or written portrayals, such as "life lines," or written answers to questions such as "What do you seem to seek out, or avoid, in your life?" and checklists, card sorts, and rating scales relating to work tasks, settings, values, or skills. One problem with the latter is that they may have unknown psychometric properties, and the onus is, therefore, on the practitioner to help the client interpret the results with caution. Structured interviews may also be used involving "systematic reflection on experience" (Kidd, 1988), where clients are encouraged to analyze their past experiences to discover what can be learned from them. Some tools are designed to be used as part of an in-depth process of self-exploration. One example is the Intelligent Career Card Sort (Arthur, Amundson, & Parker, 2002), based on intelligent career theory (Khapova, Arthur, and Wilderom, Chapter 7), which encourages people to consider their values, skills, and relationships and reflect on the implications of these for career development and decision making. Formal tools include psychometric tests and inventories that assess occupational interests, work values, aptitudes, and personality—for example, the Strong Interest Inventory (Harmon et al., 1994) and the Myers-Briggs Type Indicator (Myers & Briggs, 1993), a measure of personality. This category also includes instruments assessing career choice processes, such as decision-making styles and skills, and career maturity (or the psychological readiness for career development tasks). Examples of these types of instruments are the Career Beliefs Inventory (Krumboltz, 1991) and the Career Decision Scale (Osipow, Carney, Winer, Yanico, & Koschier, 1987).

Stage 3: Exploring New Perspectives

Challenging

Mitchell and Krumboltz (1990) see challenging clients' irrational thinking and inaccurate beliefs as key tasks in career counseling. They suggest several guidelines for identifying "problematic" beliefs—for example, "examine the assumptions and presuppositions of the expressed belief" and "confront attempts to build an illogical consistency."

Information Giving

The increasing diversity of careers and the vast amount of information now available on careers means that it is almost impossible for career counselors to keep up-to-date with information about opportunities, even in a limited number of occupational areas. Accordingly, and as Nathan and Hill (2006) suggest, it is more appropriate and realistic for career counselors to view themselves as "general practitioners" with respect to knowledge of occupational and educational opportunities. This stance is more in line with their facilitative role, too.

Different client groups will need different types of labor market information, depending on their age, life stage, and level of qualifications. For example, young people making initial career decisions may value broad frameworks that show how occupations cluster and how they differ, while adults in mid-career may need much more specific information about occupations, employers, and specific jobs. As Hirsh et al. (1998) argue, within the career-counseling literature, the constructs and frameworks used to describe work mainly reflect concern with early choice of occupation and how individuals' interests and values affect that choice. Less attention has been given to other types of decision, for example, choice of type of organization or employer, and decisions about whether to work full- or part-time. Although descriptions and classifications of organizational career systems exist, as do checklists for analyzing other features of organizations, these normally require "insider" knowledge and may be more useful in organizational career interventions.

Another problem with many frameworks is that they are predominantly static, in that they fail to take account of work histories and how careers develop over time. Workers increasingly experience more diverse and flexible career patterns, with certain skills seen as generic (e.g., basic IT skills) and other skills giving them greater ability to move between occupations that were previously viewed as quite different (e.g.,

project management skills). Descriptions of careers need to be updated regularly to accommodate these changes, and new constructs and frameworks of work may be needed.

Niles and Harris-Bowlsbey (2002) set out three responsibilities of counselors in relation to career information. First, they should use only high-quality printed materials, computer-based systems, and Web sites. A comprehensive set of guidelines for selecting sources of information is provided by the American National Career Development Association. These are available at www.ncda.org. Second, they should make these resources known to clients and make them as user-friendly as possible.

Third, it is the counselor's responsibility to help clients process the information. They suggest that the counselor should consider whether the client is ready to receive the information, what are the barriers to the client's use of the information, what kinds of information will be most helpful, what methods of receiving the information will be most effective, and what kind of decision style the client uses.

Stage 4: Forming Strategies and Plans

Most writers see reviewing progress to be an integral part of the career-counseling process at various stages and suggest that it may be necessary to revisit and review the counseling "contract" at certain points. Setting time aside for a review is also seen as useful in assessing the progress made.

Goal Setting

Goal setting theory (e.g., Locke & Latham, 1984) has been applied to the action-planning stage of career counseling, and Miller, Crute, and Hargie (1992) have described what this theory suggests as the main features of effective goals, which are as follows: clear and behaviorally specific, measurable, achievable, owned by the goal setter, congruent with the client's values, and appropriately timescaled (Miller et al., 1992). As we have seen, however, some approaches see the whole intervention largely in terms of goal setting. Mitchell and Krumboltz's (1990) social learning approach and Egan's (2004) model of helping are examples.

The Use of Information and Communications Technology

Computers are potentially a powerful resource in career counseling. They can administer, score, and interpret tests; search databases; teach career-planning concepts; and facilitate interactive dialogue with users. In this section, we discuss some of the issues arising from the introduction of information and communications technology in career counseling.

As Watts (1996) points out, computers offer both opportunities and threats to career counselors. They provide opportunities in that they can improve the career support offered and its accessibility. The main threat, though, is that they can be used to mechanize the human interaction that is at the heart of career counseling. Watts sees the challenge for career services as finding ways to use computer technology in ways that "supplement and extend human potential rather than acting to restrict or replace it" (p. 269).

Computers first began to be used in career education and counseling in the 1960s, with the introduction of computer-aided career guidance systems (CAGS). Three theorists played a key role in their development—Katz, Super, and Tiedeman all designed CAGS—and they saw the computer as a tool through which to teach their theories to users (Niles & Harris-Bowlsbey, 2002). Apart from this objective, CAGS have various specific functions in career counseling. Offer has classified the systems into eight categories:

1. *Self Assessment.* Programs that help individuals assess themselves and which provide a profile in terms that also describe work or educational opportunities. These are commonly based on occupational interests.

2. *Matching Systems.* Programs that match individuals to occupations or courses. These are the most commonly-used applications of computers in career counseling.

3. *Information Retrieval.* Databases of education and training opportunities, or of employers.

4. *Games and Simulations.* Business, training or other career education materials. These enable users to explore occupations in an experiential way.

5. *Decision Aids.* Programs that help individuals analyse the factors they use in decision making, and apply these to a typical decision.

6. *Dedicated Word Processors.* Programs that provide support for CV writing or completing application forms.

7. *Computer-Based Training.* Programs that teach job-seeking skills, for example, handling interviews and making job applications.

8. *Psychometric Tests.* Programs that administer psychological tests and inventories. These are mainly on-line adaptations of pencil-and-paper tests, measuring abilities, aptitudes, personality, etc. (Offer, 1997, cited in Kidd, 2006, p. 122)

Some systems, sometimes described as "mini systems," incorporate only one or two of these functions. Others, often called "maxi systems," include most of the functions and integrate them so that users can move flexibly between tasks. Maxi systems are more useful in modeling the career decision-making process so that individuals can learn decision-making skills.

CAGS vary in their theoretical rationale. For example, some take a person-environment-fit approach, suggesting opportunities that match individual objectively assessed attributes. Others work in a more idiographic way, using the individual's own decision-making constructs.

Although CAGS have transformed career counseling in many ways, they have limitations. For example, it could be argued that they reduce experience, knowledge, and wisdom to data; that they simply manipulate these data according to strict logic; and that this logic is subordinated to set purposes (Watts, 1996). This means that the more emotional and uniquely personal aspects of career development decision making cannot be adequately addressed by a computer. Even the best systems can only *mimic* the core conditions of the counseling relationship. Although CAGS are frequently used on a stand-alone basis, a combination of the computer and face-to-face interaction with a counselor is likely to be more effective than either intervention on its own. In this way, both counselor and computer can be used to play to their distinctive strengths.

There are now a large number of Web sites that offer help with career decision making, and many individuals find using the Internet, either as a stand-alone tool or with the support of a career counselor, helpful in career planning. Many CAGS now offer a parallel version on the Internet. There are hundreds, if not thousands, of other Internet tools that are potentially helpful in career decision making and career management. These differ considerably in their aims, however, as CAGS do. Some focus on assessment, others focus on providing career information (there is now a huge online labor market, for example, as discussed in Chapter 17 by Cappelli and Hamori), and still others concentrate on career planning. With regard to assessing the quality of a site, Offer (2000) suggests a range of questions, as follows:

- Who produced this? What's in it for them? Could there be a conflict of interest? If so, is that openly acknowledged and declared?
- Can I trust them? What are their credentials? Are they relevant to the matter in hand? How else can I contact them if I need to? (or, Why have they not allowed me to do so?)
- Is it up to date? (And how do I tell?) When was it created, and when was it last amended? What does it tell me? (What did I want to know that isn't here? What could they have told me that isn't here? Why didn't they?)
- Is it credible? (If not entirely, why should I believe this over another source that says something different?) Does it fit with what I already know about this subject?
- Can it be corroborated? (Where else can I get information about this? How valid and reliable would that be—more than this?) Does the site itself offer relevant sources and indications as to where its statements can be checked?
- What signs are there, if any, of a lack of quality control on this site? (Any signs of sloppy thinking or practice, even simple misspellings?)
- Who is this aimed at/intended for? Is the agenda persuasion, or a balanced summary of the arguments or available facts? Does it acknowledge any alternative views?
- What other sites does it link to, or what other sources does it suggest—and does that indicate anything about the standpoint of this one?
- What other sources of this information, advice or guidance are there and how might they help me? Would they be better for my purposes than what is offered here? (p. 40)

With access to the Internet, the user may come to career counseling with considerable information about opportunities, just as doctors have "expert patients." Many career counselors will welcome this, because they can spend more time on in-depth issues that require face-to-face discussion, not simply on giving information. However, the lack of control over information on the Internet means that users may be obtaining out-of-date or inaccurate information. Ideally, therefore, users need to be educated through the career-counseling process to be more critical and demanding of Web sites. More general ethical guidelines for "cybercounseling" have been developed by several professional bodies. These are summarized in Niles and Harris-Bowlsbey (2002, pp. 222–223).

THE EVALUATION OF THE EFFECTIVENESS OF CAREER COUNSELING

We turn now to consider how career counseling has been evaluated. First, we discuss the kinds of outcomes that have been assessed in evaluation studies of career counseling, and then we consider the evidence for its effectiveness.

As was shown earlier, the theoretical base for career counseling during the early part of the 20th century was person-environment-fit theory. Career practitioners viewed their main task as assessing individual differences and the characteristics of occupations to make appropriate recommendations about jobs. Accordingly, the earliest studies evaluating career counseling were concerned primarily with establishing how far individuals who entered jobs that were in accord with the recommendations were satisfied and successful in their work (e.g., Hunt & Smith, 1944). However, these studies were essentially assessing the predictive validity of the careers adviser's judgment; they did not directly evaluate the impact of the career advice received. This means that it was impossible to assess whether clients would have been any less likely to enter suitable occupations had they not received career advice (Watts & Kidd, 1978).

These initial studies of effectiveness were not at all concerned with *how* career decisions were made; indeed, clients' job destinations were essentially decided for them by career advisers.

Furthermore, the outcome criteria used were subsequent career states. In contrast, more recent studies have virtually ignored these kinds of "ultimate" outcome criteria, preferring instead to assess what have been called the "learning outcomes" of career interventions. Learning outcomes have been defined by Kidd and Killeen (1992) as "the skills, knowledge and attitudes which facilitate rational occupational and educational decision making and the effective implementation of occupational and educational decisions" (p. 221). Examples of learning outcomes are accuracy of self-knowledge, decision-making skills, career information seeking, and career decidedness.

These kinds of outcome have come to be used in evaluation studies as a result of the shift toward a more developmental orientation to career counseling. Qualitative reviews of studies evaluating the effectiveness of career counseling have generally suggested that career interventions are effective in these terms (e.g., Holland et al., 1981; Swanson, 1995). However, meta-analytic studies of career interventions vary in their conclusions about effectiveness. For example, Oliver and Spokane (1988), in a meta-analysis that analyzed studies published between 1950 and 1982, found an overall average effect size of .82. Whiston, Sexton, and Lasoff (1998), using studies published between 1983 and 1995 and calculating effect size using a weighting procedure to take account of variance, showed a considerably lower average effect size of .30, with individual career counseling producing the greatest effect (.75). The effect size in a third meta-analysis, carried out by Brown and Ryan Krane (2000), was similar (.34). As Whiston, Brecheisen, and Stephens (2003) argue, these varying effect sizes suggest that the career interventions evaluated are, in fact, "a diverse set of interventions with diverse outcomes" (p. 391), since the range of effect sizes may reflect variation in effectiveness, with some interventions being highly effective and others ineffective.

Many of the studies examined in these meta-analyses are investigations into the effectiveness of career interventions in general, not individual career counseling. There have been few investigations into the effectiveness of individual career counseling as compared with other treatment modalities. In an attempt to compare the various treatment modalities used in career interventions, Whiston et al. (2003) carried out a meta-analysis of 57 studies published between 1975 and 2000 and involving 4,732 participants. The most common outcome measures used in the studies were information seeking and career maturity. The results showed that counselor-free interventions (e.g., the use of "stand-alone" CAGS) were less effective than other treatments. The authors concluded that effective career interventions need to include a counseling component.

Evidence exists, therefore, for the effectiveness of career counseling, but our state of knowledge in this area is substantially less than that within psychotherapy outcome research, where there has been a considerable amount of work examining the processes that occur in psychotherapy sessions and assessing the comparative efficacy of different theoretical approaches (Barkham, 2003). This most likely reflects the traditional view of career counseling as a rational approach with an emphasis on testing and information giving, and also the predominantly eclectic methods used by career counselors.

It is worth noting that much research on the effectiveness of career counseling uses students and the unemployed and, to a lesser extent, managers. The reason for this focus is likely to be that students and the unemployed are more accessible than other adults. However, the career-counseling needs of students may differ from those of the general adult population, and samples may be overrepresentative of higher socioeconomic groups.

CONCLUSION

Many of the challenges that career counseling faces in the 21st century are related to meeting the needs of individuals following more diverse and flexible career patterns. It seems that careers are becoming different from the past, but we should not exaggerate the changes that are taking place. Over the last few decades, job tenure in the United Kingdom has been fairly stable. For example, statistics from the Quarterly Labour Force Surveys demonstrate that the number of people who had worked for the same employer for 10 years was very similar in 1986 and in 2004, at around 29% of the workforce. In the United States, there has been only a modest decline in tenure, with a slight increase for those employed in long-term positions in the service industries (Jacoby, 1999).

This chapter has attempted to provide a broad overview of the field of career counseling. Many of the traditional theories, concepts, and techniques reviewed here are still relevant, and the newer perspectives are best seen as adding to the considerable body of knowledge in the field rather than replacing it.

REFERENCES

Ackerman, P. L., & Heggestad, E. D. (1997). Intelligence, personality and interests: Evidence for overlapping traits. *Psychological Bulletin, 121,* 219–245.

Arnold, J. (2004). The congruence problem in John Holland's theory of vocational decisions. *Journal of Occupational and Organizational Psychology, 77,* 95–113.

Arthur, M. B., Amundson, N., & Parker, P. (2002). The development and application of the intelligent career card sort. In *The compass of career.* Copenhagen, Denmark: Civilokonomerne (The Danish Organization for Management and Business Economics). (English translation available at http://www.intelligentcareer.com).

Bandura, A. (1977). *Principles of behavior modification.* New York: Holt, Rinehart & Winston.

Barkham, M. (2003). Quantitative research on psychotherapeutic interventions: Methods and findings across four research generations. In R. Woolfe, W. Dryden, & S. Strawbridge (Eds.), *Handbook of counseling psychology* (pp. 25–73). London: Sage.

Bordin, E. (1979). The generalizability of the psychoanalytic concept of the working alliance. *Psychotherapy: Theory, Research and Practice, 16,* 252–260.

Bozarth, J. D., & Fisher, R. (1990). Person-centered career counseling. In W. B. Walsh & S. H. Osipow (Eds.), *Handbook of vocational psychology* (pp. 45–77). Mahwah, NJ: Erlbaum.

Brown, D. (1996). Brown's value-based, holistic model of career and life-role choices and satisfaction. In D. Brown, L. Brooks, & Associates (Eds.), *Career choice and development* (3rd ed., pp. 337–372). San Francisco: Jossey-Bass.

Brown, D., & Associates (2002). *Career choice and development.* San Francisco: Jossey-Bass.

Brown, S. D., & Ryan Krane, N. E. (2000). Four (or five) sessions and a cloud of dust: Old assumptions and new observations about career counseling. In S. D. Brown & R. W. Lent (Eds.), *Handbook of counseling psychology* (3rd ed., pp. 740–766). New York: Wiley.

Cochran, L. (1997). *Career counseling: A narrative approach.* Thousand Oaks, CA: Sage.

Collin, A., & Young, R. A. (1992). Constructing career through narrative and context: An interpretive perspective. In A. Collin and R. A. Young (Eds.), *Interpreting career: Hermeneutical studies of lives in context* (pp. 1–12). Westport, CT: Praeger.

Denzin, N. K., & Lincoln, Y. S. (2000). The discipline and practice of qualitative research. In N. K. Denzin & Y. S. Lincoln (Eds.), *Handbook of qualitative research* (2nd ed., pp. 1–28). Thousand Oaks, CA: Sage.

Edwards, D., & Potter, J. (1992). *Discursive psychology.* London: Sage.

Egan, G. (2004). *The skilled helper: A problem management and opportunities development approach to helping.* Monterey, CA: Brooks/Cole.

Flum, H. (2001). Dialogues and challenges: The interface between work and relationships in transition. *The Counseling Psychologist, 29,* 261–270.

Hansen, L. S. (1997). *Integrative life planning: Critical tasks for career development and changing life patterns.* San Francisco: Jossey-Bass.

Harmon, L. W., Hansen, J. I. C., Borgen, F. H., & Hammer, A. L. (1994). *Strong interest inventory: Applications and technical guide.* Palo Alto, CA: Consulting Psychologists Press.

Higgins, M. C., & Kram, K. E. (2001). Reconceptualizing mentoring at work: A developmental network perspective. *Academy of Management Review, 26,* 264–288.

Hirsh, W., Kidd, J. M., & Watts, A. G. (1998). *Constructs of work used in career guidance.* Cambridge, UK: CRAC/NICEC.

Holland, J. L. (1985). *The self-directed search: Professional manual.* Odessa, FL: Psychological Assessment Resources.

Holland, J. L. (1997). *Making vocational choices* (3rd ed.). Odessa, FL: Psychological Assessment Resources.

Holland, J. L., Magoon, T. M., & Spokane, A. R. (1981). Counseling psychology: Career interventions, research, and theory. *Annual Review of Psychology, 32,* 279–305.

Hunt, E. P., & Smith, P. (1944). *Scientific vocational guidance and its value to the choice of employment work of a local education authority.* Birmingham: City of Birmingham Education Committee.

Jacoby, S. M. (1999). Are career jobs headed for extinction? *California Management Review, 42,* 123–145.

Kelly, G. A. (1955). *The psychology of personal constructs.* New York: Norton.

Kidd, J. M. (1988). *Assessment in action.* Leicester: NIACE.

Kidd, J. M. (1998). Emotion: An absent presence in career theory. *Journal of Vocational Behavior, 52,* 275–288.

Kidd, J. M. (2003). Career development work with individuals. In R. Woolfe & W. Dryden (Eds.), *Handbook of counseling psychology* (pp. 461–480). London: Sage.

Kidd, J. M. (2004). Emotion in career contexts: Challenges for theory and research. *Journal of Vocational Behavior, 64*(3), 441–454.

Kidd, J. M. (2006). *Understanding career counselling: Theory, research and practice.* London: Sage.

Kidd, J. M., Jackson, C., & Hirsh, W. (2003). The outcomes of effective career discussion at work. *Journal of Vocational Behavior, 62,* 119–133.

Kidd, J. M., & Killeen, J. (1992). Are the effects of careers guidance worth having? Changes in practice and outcomes. *Journal of Occupational and Organizational Psychology, 65,* 219–234.

Kidd, J. M., Killeen, J., Jarvis, J., & Offer, M. (1997). Competing schools or stylistic variation in careers guidance interviewing. *British Journal of Guidance and Counseling, 25,* 47–65.

Krumboltz, J. D. (1983). *Private rules in career decision making.* Columbus: Ohio State University, National Centre for Research in Vocational Education.

Krumboltz, J. D. (1991). *Career beliefs inventory.* Palo Alto, CA: Consulting Psychologists Press.

Lent, R. W., Brown, S. D., & Hackett, G. (1996). Career development from a social cognitive perspective. In D. Brown, L. Brooks, & Associates (Eds.), *Career choice and development* (3rd ed., pp. 373–416). San Francisco: Jossey-Bass.

Locke, E. A., & Latham, G. P. (1984). *Goal setting: A motivational technique that works!* Englewood Cliffs, NJ: Prentice Hall.

McLeod, J. (2003). *An introduction to counseling.* Milton Keynes: Open University Press.

Miller, R., Crute, V., & Hargie, O. (1992). *Professional interviewing.* London: Routledge.

Mitchell, L. K., & Krumboltz, J. D. (1990). Social learning approach to career decision making: Krumboltz's theory. In D. Brown & L. Brooks (Eds.), *Career choice and development: Applying contemporary theories to practice* (pp. 145–196). San Francisco: Jossey Bass.

Moir, J. (1993). Occupational career choice: Accounts and contradictions. In E. Burman & I. Parker (Eds.), *Discourse analytic research* (pp. 17–34). London: Routledge.

Myers, I., & Briggs, K. (1993). *The Myers-Briggs type indicator.* Palo Alto, CA: Consulting Psychologists Press.

Nathan, R., & Hill, L. (2006). *Career counseling* (2nd ed.). London: Sage.

Niles, S. G., & Harris-Bowlsbey, J. (2002). *Career development interventions in the 21st century.* Columbus, OH: Merrill Prentice Hall.

Norcross, J. C., & Grencavage, L. M. (1989). Eclecticism and integration in counseling and psychotherapy: Major themes and obstacles. *British Journal of Guidance and Counseling, 17,* 215–247.

Offer, M. (2000). *Careers professionals' guide to the Internet.* Richmond: Trotman.

Oliver, L. W., & Spokane, A. R. (1988). Career intervention outcome: What contributes to client gain? *Journal of Counseling Psychology, 35,* 447–462.

Osipow, S. H., Carney, C. G., Winer, J. L., Yanico, B., & Koschier, M. (1987). *The career decision scale.* Columbus, OH: Marathon Consulting Press.

Parsons, F. (1909). *Choosing a vocation.* Boston: Houghton Mifflin.

Patterson, P. (1964). Counseling: Self-clarification and the helping relationship. In H. Borow (Ed.), *Man in a world of work* (pp. 434–459). Boston: Houghton Mifflin.

Peterson, G. W., Sampson, J. P., Reardon, R. C., & Lenz, J. G. (1996). A cognitive information processing approach. In D. Brown, L. Brooks, & Associates (Eds.), *Career choice and development* (3rd ed., pp. 423–476). San Francisco: Jossey-Bass.

Potter, J. (1996). *Representing reality: Discourse, rhetoric and social construction.* London: Sage.

Prediger, D. J. (2000). Holland's hexagon is alive and well—though somewhat out of shape: Response to Tinsley. *Journal of Vocational Behavior, 56,* 197–204.

Rogers, C. R. (1942). *Counseling and psychotherapy.* Boston: Houghton Mifflin.

Savickas, M. (1997). Constructivist career counseling: Models and methods. *Advances in Personal Construct Psychology, 4,* 149–182.

Savickas, M. (2005). The theory and practice of career construction. In S. D. Brown & R. W. Lent (Eds.), *Career development and counseling: Putting research and theory to work* (pp. 42–70). Hoboken, NJ: Wiley.

Seibert, S. E., Kraimer, M. L., & Liden, R. C. (2001). A social capital theory of career success. *Academy of Management Journal, 44,* 219–237.

Spokane, A. R. (1985). A review of research on person-environment congruence in Holland's theory of careers. *Journal of Vocational Behavior, 31,* 37–44.

Stead, G. B. (2004). Culture and career psychology: A social constructionist perspective. *Journal of Vocational Behavior, 64,* 389–406.

Super, D. E. (1957). *The psychology of careers.* New York: Harper & Row.

Super, D. E., & Knasel, E. (1981). Career development in adulthood: Some theoretical problems and a possible solution. *British Journal of Guidance and Counseling, 9,* 194–201.

Super, D. E., Thompson, A. S., Lindeman, R. H., Jordaan, J. P., & Myers, R. A. (1981). *Career development inventory.* Palo Alto, CA: Consulting Psychologists Press.

Super, D. E., Thompson, A. S., Lindeman, R. H., Myers, R. A., & Jordaan, J. P. (1988). *Adult career concerns inventory.* Palo Alto, CA: Consulting Psychologists Press.

Swanson, J. L. (1995). The process and outcome of career counseling. In W. B. Walsh & S. H. Osipow (Eds.), *Handbook of vocational psychology* (pp. 217–259). Mahwah, NJ: Erlbaum.

Swanson, J. L. (1996). The theory *is* the practice: Trait-and-factor/person-environment fit counseling. In M. L. Savickas & W. B. Walsh (Eds.), *Handbook of career counseling theory and practice* (pp. 93–108). Palo Alto, CA: Davies-Black.

Tinsley, H. E. A. (2000). The congruence myth: An analysis of the efficacy of the person-environment fit model. *Journal of Vocational Behavior, 56,* 147–179.

Tranberg, M., Slane, S., & Ekeberg, S. E. (1993). The relationship between interest congruence and satisfaction: A meta-analysis. *Journal of Vocational Behavior, 42,* 253–264.

Watkins, C. E., & Savickas, M. L. (1990). Psychodynamic career counseling. In W. B. Walsh & S. H. Osipow (Eds.), *Career counseling: Contemporary topics in vocational psychology* (pp. 79–116). Hillsdale, NJ: Erlbaum.

Watson, C. (1994). Improving the quality of careers guidance: Towards an understanding of the development of personal models. *British Journal of Guidance and Counseling, 22,* 357–372.

Watts, A. G. (1996). Computers in guidance. In A. G. Watts, B. Law, J. Killeen, J. M. Kidd, & R. Hawthorn (Eds.), *Rethinking careers education and guidance: Theory, policy and practice* (pp. 269–283). London: Routledge.

Watts, A. G., & Kidd, J. M. (1978). Evaluating the effectiveness of careers guidance: A review of the British research. *Journal of Occupational Psychology, 51,* 235–248.

Watts, A. G., & Kidd, J. M. (2000). Guidance in the United Kingdom: Past, present and future. *British Journal of Guidance and Counseling, 28,* 485–502.

Whiston, S. C. (2003). Career counseling: 90 years old yet still healthy and vital. *Career Development Quarterly, 52,* 35–42.

Whiston, S. C., Brecheisen, B. K., & Stephens, J. (2003). Does treatment modality affect career counseling effectiveness? *Journal of Vocational Behavior, 62,* 390–410.

Whiston, S. C., Sexton, T. L., & Lasoff, D. L. (1998). Career-intervention outcome: A replication and extension of Oliver and Spokane (1988). *Journal of Counseling Psychology, 45,* 150–165.

Young, R. A., Valach, L., & Collin, A. (1996). A contextual approach to career. In D. Brown, L. Brooks, & Associates (Eds.), *Career choice and development* (3rd ed., pp. 477–512). San Francisco: Jossey-Bass.

7

THE SUBJECTIVE CAREER
IN THE KNOWLEDGE ECONOMY

SVETLANA N. KHAPOVA

MICHAEL B. ARTHUR

CELESTE P. M. WILDEROM

A reexamination of the subjective career concept is timely, given the economy's emergent reliance on knowledge-intensive professional and intellectual capabilities (Powell & Snellman, 2004). In this chapter, we argue that to better understand careers in the knowledge economy, we need to ascribe more importance to the subjective career. This is because in the knowledge economy, in which many of the walls that limited the movement and reach of people are dissolving, people have more power to influence both markets and nation-states than at any time in history (Friedman, 2005; Giddens, 2003). In these circumstances, people's choosing to follow internal, self-generated guidelines for their careers can lead to larger social transformation (Feldman, 2000).

Our purpose here is to seek better understanding of the traditional conception of the subjective career and also of the conception we currently need. For this purpose, we bring together ideas on (a) how fundamental theories have traditionally conceived the subjective career, (b) what the knowledge economy means for the conception of the subjective career, (c) what kind of approaches can help us better understand career dynamics in the knowledge economy, and (d) what issues the knowledge economy raises for future careers research.

As our chapter shows, to focus on the subjective career means to accommodate four basic properties of the subjective career in future research, use interdisciplinary approaches in that research, and focus on careers not only within or between organizations but also in a larger economic context. This context reflects not only the knowledge economy but also the influences of both the Internet and globalization in shaping that economy and reaffirms the importance of interdisciplinary approaches.

THE SUBJECTIVE CAREER IN BEHAVIORAL SCIENCE THEORIES

Let us first examine traditional approaches to the subjective career. This involves reviewing definitions and properties relevant to the subjective career. It also involves examination of how alternative behavioral science approaches have accommodated these properties.

Definitions and Underlying Properties of the Subjective Career

We define *career,* after Arthur, Hall, and Lawrence (1989), as the unfolding sequence of a person's work experiences over time. Careers involve both subjective and objective perspectives. We define the subjective career as the individual's own interpretation of his or her career situation at any given time. We define the objective career as the parallel interpretation of any career provided by society and its institutions (Barley, 1989).

Drawing on our earlier review of contemporary career research (Arthur, Khapova, & Wilderom, 2005), we submit that the subjective career entails four important properties. The first property is concerned with the inherent *duality* between the subjective and objective careers. This means that there are always two sides to a career: a publicly observable (or objective) side and an intrinsic (or subjective) side. Although both sides of the career exist together, they do not necessarily correspond to each other. For example, managers who are successful according to the objective criteria of pay and promotions may report less subjective career satisfaction than objectively less successful colleagues (Judge, Cable, Boudreau, & Bretz, 1995).

The second property concerns *interdependence.* Interdependence means that the two sides of the career not only coexist but also influence one another. That is, the objective career provides the work experiences that a theory may hypothesize to influence the person's subjective view of his or her career situation. Conversely, the attitudes and motivation of the subjective career may be hypothesized to influence a person's objective career as it is seen by others.

The third property of the subjective career concerns a perspective on *time.* Time complicates the nature of the interdependence between the subjective and objective careers and takes us beyond any simple notion of subjective-objective career multicollinearity. Time is intrinsic to, for example, employment stability, skills and experience gained, relationships developed, and opportunities encountered (e.g., Washington & Zajac, 2005).

The fourth property of the subjective career is that we can anticipate that the subjective career involves *multiple dimensions.* These dimensions will reflect different aspects of people's subjective careers—for example, pursuing a professional calling, accumulating new learning, and finding time for families (e.g., Hall, 2002).

Our earlier review showed that contemporary career research often disregarded one or more of these theoretically significant subjective career properties (Arthur et al., 2005). We propose here that examination of the four properties provides a basis for identifying both what is common ground and what is unique to alternative theories. We now turn to examining how six selected behavioral science theories address these four properties.

BEHAVIORAL SCIENCE PERSPECTIVES

Our examination of four subjective career properties intersects three behavioral science disciplines—namely, psychology, social psychology, and sociology. Specifically, we look at six theories that have been influential in contributing to the development of career theory, originating from (a) Super and Hall in psychology, (b) Krumboltz and Bailyn in social psychology, and (c) Hughes and Giddens in sociology.

The choice of these theories may be explained as follows. All of them have been influential within their separate behavioral science disciplines in contributing to the development of career theory. Each of the theories provides insight into the way the subjective career is viewed within its host discipline. Two lines of inquiry per discipline allow us to learn about that discipline's distinct perspective on the subjective career.

Among psychological perspectives, Super's (1980) *theory of career development* extends earlier vocational guidance theories in looking at the interaction of the subjective and the objective careers across the life span (Kidd, Chapter 6; Sullivan and Crocitto, Chapter 15). His work focuses on how subjective and objective careers interact in a person's mind as he or she lives through predictable life stages. A second psychological theory is that of Hall (1976, 2002), whose *protean career theory* suggests that people may no longer see their careers as unfolding in any one organization or in any predictable way. It proposes the notion of a protean career, characterized by adaptation to a shifting environment and by frequent change, self-invention, autonomy, and self-direction (Hall, 2002).

Turning to social psychology, Krumboltz's (1979) *social learning theory* (Kidd, Chapter 6) suggests that "the individual personalities and behavioral repertoires that persons possess arise primarily from their unique learning experiences rather than from innate developmental or psychic processes" (Mitchell & Krumboltz, 1990). Put simply, the theory focuses on how learning from past experiences in the social world influences future career choices. In contrast, Bailyn's (1984) *theory of work and family* (Valcour, Bailyn, and Quijada, Chapter 11) addresses the interplay of work and family systems. The work system represents the arena for a person's contractual relation to the external environment; the family system represents a more internal, self-regulated, and private arena, centered on a primary tie to another person or persons (Bailyn, 1984).

Finally, among sociological perspectives, Hughes's (1937) *theory of social roles* (Moore, Gunz, and Hall, Chapter 2) addresses how individuals experience their work roles within society. The theory represents a larger set of work by the Chicago School of Sociology on the nature and "working constitution" of a society. Of more recent origin is Giddens's (1984) *theory of structuration* (Mayrhofer, Meyer, and

Steyrer, Chapter 12). The theory looks at how people's everyday actions reinforce and reproduce social structures "via the very means whereby they express themselves as actors" (p. 2). The arena for action prominently involves people's careers.

Each of these theories provides insight into the way the subjective career is viewed within its host discipline and illustrates the different focuses that each of the three disciplines provides. The choice of six theories does not, of course, provide a complete review of theories that conceptualize the subjective career. For example, it omits Schein's (1971, 1978) foundational work on organizational careers. However, the choice does allow us to see some overall patterns.

Psychological Perspectives

In Super's (1990) psychological theory of careers, duality refers to "concepts of self and of roles in society" (p. 203). Interdependence between the subjective and objective careers is seen to take place in the mind of the person, "the decision maker in whom all of the personal and social forces are brought together" (p. 203). People are described as mentally filtering objective work experiences into subjective career interpretations and, in turn, projecting these interpretations back onto the world of work. Time is accommodated in the conception of a sequence of career stages—namely, growth, exploration, establishment, maintenance, and decline (Super, 1990). Multiple dimensions come from enacting one or more of the six distinct identities in everyday life—of the child, the student, the leisure seeker, the citizen, the worker, and the homemaker.

In Hall's (2002) psychological approach, the subjective career reflects the changes in values, attitudes, and motivation that occur as a person ages, and the objective career reflects the observable choices made and the activities in which the person engages (p. 11). Hall's approach to interdependence is signaled in his underlying definition of the career as "the individually perceived . . . attitudes and behaviors associated with work-related experiences and activities" (p. 12). The key term *perceived* once more indicates that interdependence is located inside the person's mind. Time organizes the subjective-objective career interaction in a series of learning ministages "of exploration-trail-mastery-exit," through which people adjust to the world and develop their identities (p. 118). Multiple dimensions involve the development of a series of career "sub-identities" that are "aspects of one's self (skills, interests, etc.)" and answer not only to "who I am" but also to "what I do" (p. 73).

Social-Psychological Perspectives

Turning to social-psychological theories, Krumboltz (1979) addresses duality by noting that both internal (subjective) and external (objective) influencers shape the nature and number of career options and the way in which individuals respond. The objective influencers include past learning experiences defined by environmental conditions and events. The subjective influencers incorporate genetic factors and the cognitive and emotional responses (in the form of decisions) to learning experiences. Interdependence is about the interaction between people's learning experiences and people's cognitive responses. That is, people respond to the contingencies that surround them and seek to control their environments to suit their own purposes and needs (Mitchell & Krumboltz, 1990, p. 147). Time organizes this interaction in a sequence of new learning experiences and career behaviors. Multiple dimensions involve variation in the social roles that people experience as well as different responses to those roles.

In Bailyn's (1984) social-psychological theory, duality constitutes the coexistence of the objective career, representing "the arena for a person's contractual relation to the external environment, a place where activities are externally regulated and monitored, and where one is held publicly accountable for one's performance" (p. 89) and the subjective career, which "represents a more internal, more self-regulated, and more private arena, centered on a primary tie to another person or persons." (p. 89) Interdependence between the subjective and objective careers is described in terms of the influence the family or private arena has on the work arena and of the reverse influence that the work arena has on the family or private arena. Time is accommodated in Bailyn's views on how people's career investments vary as time unfolds and as work and family demands change. Multiple dimensions of the person's subjective career involve the experiencing of multiple roles of, for example, a worker and a parent (Bailyn, 1993) and of a representative of the male or female gender (Rapoport, Bailyn, Fletcher, & Pruitt, 2002).

Sociological Perspectives

Turning to sociological theory, Hughes's (1937) *theory of social roles* views the duality of the subjective and objective careers—that is, the career's "two-sidedness"—as a critical property (Barley, 1989, p. 49). The career is seen as a "Janus-like concept," pointing on the one hand to the meanings individuals make of their career situations and on the other hand to institutional forms of career participation (Barley, 1989). Interdependence is underscored in the notion of a series of "status passages," which on the one hand connote a shift from one social role to another and on the other hand involve a change in the person's conception of self. Within each shift, "role look(s) outward toward a pattern of situated activity, whereas identity look(s) inward toward the actor's subjective experience of that situated being" (Barley, 1989, p. 50). Time underlies the unfolding of successive status passages. Multiple dimensions are reflected in the multiple roles through which people exercise influence, take responsibility, and receive recognition in their careers (Hughes, 1937).

In Giddens's (1984) sociological theory, duality stems from the subjective career giving rise to "knowledgeable activities" (activities based on what people know), while the objective career is reflected in the way social roles are performed (p. 2). Interdependence is reflected in the way institutional forms influence how people respond to available social roles in the short term and how people reproduce or modify those social roles in the long term (p. 26). Time is fundamental to Giddens's view of the production, reproduction, and evolution of social life. Time frames both the relatively reversible interactions between the person and society in everyday life as well as the irreversible character of human life over the life course (p. 35). Multiple dimensions of an individual's career reflect the social roles through which individuals produce and reproduce society, which Giddens calls roles of signification, domination, and legitimation (p. 29).

In sum, all six selected behavioral science theories accommodate the four basic properties in their conceptualizations of the subjective career. However, as summarized in Table 7.1, they all offer very distinct perspectives on those properties. The six theories are closest to one another in acknowledging the duality of the subjective and the objective career. Even so, psychologists view subjective-objective career interdependence as occurring in the mind. Meanwhile, social psychologists see this interdependence occurring between the person and his or her everyday work experience. In turn, sociologists see interdependence occurring over the long term as people's career behavior eventually reinforces or modifies the overall social structure. Similar distinctions are evident in the theories' separate approaches to the role of time (as it affects the mind, everyday workplace interaction, or the evolution of society) and to the multiple dimensions of the subjective career (as they also affect the mind, everyday workplace interaction, or the evolution of society).

The separation of career theory into largely disconnected behavioral science disciplines may work well in a relatively stable world. However, in a more dynamic, knowledge-driven world, the utility of such separation raises questions. It is that world to which we now turn.

CAREERS IN THE KNOWLEDGE ECONOMY

Over the past several decades, we have witnessed what has been often referred to as a shift from an industry-based to a knowledge-based economy (Bell, 1973; Block, 1990; Hirschorn, 1984). The knowledge economy may be defined as "production and services based on knowledge-intensive activities that contribute to an accelerated pace of technological and scientific advance as well as equally rapid obsolescence" (Powell & Snellman, 2004, p. 201). The definition points out two important shifts. First, the economy relies heavily on intellectual capabilities rather than on physical inputs or natural resources. Second, a high pace of technological and scientific advancement requires organizations to continually adjust to this advancement. In this section, we briefly outline (a) how the model of more adaptable "self-designing"

organizations, previously seen as an exceptional model, became a mainstream model in the knowledge economy and (b) the greater relevance of interdisciplinary theory in new economic circumstances.

Careers in Self-Designing Organizations

Beginning in the 1960s, scholars began to observe the impact of changing environments on the organizations hosting people's careers. The more dynamic and complex the environment, the more "organic" (rather than "mechanistic") and the more "differentiated" the firm needed to be to succeed. Moreover, the more organic and differentiated the organization, the greater the problems of integration of people's work contributions (Burns & Stalker, 1961; Lawrence & Lorsch, 1967). These observations—which may be seen as early signals of the impending knowledge economy—were picked up by Karl Weick and his colleagues, who were interested in the consequences of the underlying design of organizations. They developed a conception of the "self-designing organization," which they argued was better suited for a changing world. The self-designing organization would maintain itself in a state of frequent, nearly continuous changes in its structures, processes, and goals to optimize the organization's capacity to adapt (Hedberg, Nystrom, & Starbuck, 1976; Nystrom, Hedberg, & Starbuck, 1976; Weick, 1977).

At the most elementary level, "self-design involves generating alternatives and testing them against the requirements and constraints perceived by people in the organization" (Weick, 1977, p. 37). That is, the system may be referred to as self-designing "if it contains the norms, resources, willingness, and mandate to monitor and evaluate its ongoing design, generate alternative designs, and implement the alternatives that are expected to generate a different set of reasonable consequences" (p. 38). Hedberg et al. (1976) argued that operating in this mode was helpful, perhaps necessary, for survival in fast-changing and unpredictable environments. They reasoned that the probable consequences of an ongoing state of experimentation are that organizations learn about a variety of design features and thereby remain flexible (Malhotra, 1996).

Table 7.1 Four Properties of the Subjective Career as Reflected in Six Behavioral Science Theories

Behavioral Science Theories	Duality With Objective Career	Interdependence With Objective Career	Perspective on Time	Multiple Dimensions
Psychology				
Super (1980, 1990)	The subjective career involves concepts of self; the objective career involves concepts of roles in society	Mentally filtered objective work experiences interact with subjective career interpretations	Sequential individual career stages—growth, exploration, establishment, maintenance, and decline	Distinct identities in daily life—child, student, leisure seeker, citizen, worker, and homemaker
Hall (1976, 2002)	The subjective career involves values, attitudes, etc.; the objective career involves observable career choices	Individual perception links between attitudes and behaviors and work-related experiences	A series of learning ministages through which people adjust to the world and develop their identities	Outcomes of the development of career subidentities about both "who I am" and "what I do"
Social Psychology				
Krumboltz (1979)	The objective career reflects past experiences; the subjective career reflects genetic and cognitive factors	The interaction of everyday learning experiences with people's cognitive responses to those experiences	Sequences of successive learning experiences that shape subsequent career behavior	A variety of social roles through which an individual's experiences meet social expectations
Bailyn (1984)	The objective career reflects employment experience; the subjective career reflects personal and family values	Private life and working life coexist and underlie people's choices in acting out those lives	Variation in people's career investments as time unfolds and as work and family demands change	Life and work roles as separately experienced by the individual and by society
Sociology				
Hughes (1937, 1997)	The objective career reflects institutional roles; the subjective career reflects people's adjustment to those roles	The interplay between a person's social roles and conceptions of the self as work experience unfolds	A series of status passages or temporally staged shifts from one social role to another throughout life	Social roles through which people exercise influence, take responsibility, and receive recognition
Giddens (1984)	The subjective career drives how people perform social roles; the objective career reflects those roles	People enact social roles and thereby contribute to reproduction and evolution of society	Underlies both reversible short-term behavior as well as the irreversible character of human life	Social roles through which individuals shape society by signification, domination, and legitimation

According to Weick and Berlinger (1989), the process of self-design is largely dependent on an organization's participants and their ability to continually redesign internal processes. The self-designing organization relies on individuals' willingness to learn and explore and their ability to review their experiences regularly—even to review their ways of reviewing. The design assumption is that people are better at creating new approaches if they perform within relatively underspecified conditions. The self-designing organization, therefore, discourages any long-term commitment to its current structure, tasks, and products, and it prefers local decision making and flat structures in the interest of more rapid adaptation. In self-designing organizations, the "typical markers of the external career such as titles, advancement up a hierarchy, and stable career paths are rare" (Weick & Berlinger, 1989, p. 321). In the absence of these, people need to focus on their subjective careers as a framework for career growth (p. 321). That is, people need to "pursue processes rather than outcomes, competencies rather than titles, fulfillment rather than advancement, and roles rather than positions" (p. 320).

More specifically, Weick and Berlinger (1989) recommend that individuals (a) cultivate "spiral" career concepts that involve changing visions of oneself and of different work and nonwork experiences; (b) decouple identities from jobs and instead emphasize professional identities that transcend any particular job; (c) preserve discretion that enables the recognition of new choices for one's career; (d) identify distinctive competences—abilities and expertise that have the potential to contribute to the self-designing organization's primary goal (namely, its own continuing redesign); and (e) synthesize complex information, since only people able to integrate such information and articulate larger visions can help the self-designing organization succeed. All these recommendations implicate the subjective career, which therefore "assumes special importance" in the self-designing organization (Weick & Berlinger, 1989, p. 321).

The Shift to a Knowledge Economy

By the 1990s, the changes envisaged in the 1960s and 1970s had become commonplace. Open markets and technology had led to a widespread focus on intellectual capabilities rather than on physical inputs or natural resources. The idea of the "boundaryless organization" (Ashkenas, Ulrich, Jick, & Kerr, 1995) emerged, in which

> people do multiple jobs, constantly learn new skills, and frequently shift to new assignments and different locations. Instead of subdividing tasks, such organizations have learned how to pull together diverse activities and people on an as-needed basis, and to focus more on the streamlined process than on the specialized pieces. They champion the new and different, and set up processes and environments that encourage and reward creativity and innovation. (Ashkenas, 1999, p. 6)

The boundaryless organization, as well as other similar contemporary views (Feldman, 2000; Haeckel, 1999; Hedberg, Baumard, & Yakhlef, 2002), reads much like the self-designing organization pioneered by Weick and his colleagues. In these views, individual input assumes higher importance, emphasizing individual influence on the larger institutions of work and society (Peiperl, Arthur, & Anand, 2002). The process of organizations and careers shaping each other is viewed as happening both more broadly and more continuously than in the industrial economy.

Weick's (1996) response to the widespread emergence of the knowledge economy was to ascribe a more generalized importance to the subjective career, to "place more control over the design of the organization in the hands of the people who are building subjective careers" (p. 41). He argued that as organizations become "weaker"—that is, more ambiguous, more unstructured, and with fewer salient guides for action—they dissolve "external guides for sequences of work experience, such as advancement in a hierarchy" (p. 40). The new situation obliges people to begin to rely more "on internal, self-generated guides, such as growth, learning, and integration" (p. 40).

The circumstances described above emphasize a psychological view of the subjective career. However, the enactment of careers leads individuals to contribute to the shaping of social systems. People act as "agents of their own development [and] organize cooperatively in order to learn" (Weick, 1996, p. 45). Weick, therefore, begins with a psychological view—about internally driven career behavior—then transforms it into a social-psychological view—about cooperative organizing—as events unfold.

Weick (1996) further argues that as individuals organize, they organize weak situations into stronger ones. As individuals work, they learn and make sense of uncertainty. They then "enact this sense back into the world to make that world more orderly" (Weick, Sutcliffe, & Obstfeld, 2005, p. 410). Learning processes become turned into scripts that impose structures around previously ambiguous situations. Cooperative behavior over time reshapes a weak situation according to people's career preferences (Weick, 1996, pp. 43–44). This argument transforms a social-psychological argument into a sociological one as we come to face the emergent structure of the organizations that self-designing careers have built.

In sum, Weick calls successively on the three behavioral science disciplines of psychology, social psychology, and sociology in explaining contemporary careers. In doing so, he implicitly challenges the utility to career theory of any one discipline on its own. Rather, he suggests a greater utility for *interdisciplinary* theory in the knowledge economy, where psychological, social-psychological, and sociological perspectives constructively inform one another.

We note that this is not the first appeal for an interdisciplinary approach to the study of careers. In the middle to late 1970s, a seminal body of work was produced by a psychologist (Edgar Schein), a social psychologist (Lotte Bailyn), and a sociologist (John Van Maanen), working out of Massachusetts Institute of Technology (MIT), which made a strong case for such an approach. As one article lamented,

> There exists . . . a curious hiatus between the [psychological and sociological] approaches. On the one hand, we have psychologists saying "people make careers" and, on the other hand, sociologists claiming that "careers make people." . . . Researchers must begin to study both sides of the coin . . . Man is both the creator and the created . . . What is needed is the recognition of the unfolding character of social life viewed from within a framework that explicitly includes the many roles a person can be called on to play . . . Perhaps the best direction in which to proceed is to begin constructing a framework on which an interdisciplinary study of careers and career development can rest. (Van Maanen & Schein, 1976, pp. 44–45)

The emergence of the knowledge economy adds weight to the earlier arguments of the MIT scholars and reinforces the need for new interdisciplinary approaches that would better fit to challenges of the contemporary career theory and research.

APPROACHES TO CAREER RESEARCH IN THE KNOWLEDGE ECONOMY

A number of contemporary career theories have already responded to the calls of the knowledge economy. Among them are new ideas about not only protean careers (Hall, 2002) but also "zigzag" (Bateson, 1994), "boundaryless" (Arthur & Rousseau, 1996), "post-corporate" (Peiperl & Baruch, 1997), "new" (Arthur, Inkson, & Pringle, 1999), and "kaleidoscope" careers (Mainiero & Sullivan, 2005). However, the preceding discussion raises a new question for these theories. Do they respond to Weick's implicit call for an interdisciplinary approach?

In this section, we will pursue the above question by exploring three contemporary theories more deeply. They are the revised social cognitive theory of Bandura (2001), the "intelligent career" conception of Arthur, Claman, and DeFillippi (1995), and the theory of growth and adaptation of Boyatzis and Kolb (2000). Our purpose in doing so is to demonstrate how interdisciplinary approaches can respond to the knowledge economy. For each theory, we describe (a) how it accommodates the basic properties of the subjective career and (b) how it draws on different behavioral science perspectives. We then demonstrate briefly how current career research has used each theory and comment on the opportunities for further research.

Social Cognitive Theory

Bandura's (2001) revised *social cognitive theory* builds on his vision of the individual as an emergent interactive agent. In line with Weick's (1996) ideas, individuals are seen as "agentic operators" or proactive agents that are capable of intentionally organizing their own lives, as well as shaping the character of the social systems around them. Bandura (2001) explains that

> through agentic action, people devise ways of adapting flexibly to remarkably diverse geographic, climatic and social environments; they figure out ways to circumvent physical and environmental constraints, redesign and construct environments to their liking, create styles of behavior that enable them to realize desired outcomes, and pass on the effective ones to others by social modeling and other experiential modes of influence. (p. 22)

The theory takes account of the four basic properties of the subjective career. Duality is reflected in the notions of personal agency and social structure. Interdependence involves their interaction, in which "social structures are created by human activity, and sociostructural practices, in turn, impose constraints and provide enabling resources and opportunity structures for personal development and functioning" (Bandura, 2001, p. 15). Time is accommodated in the theory's core features of human agency (p. 6). These include the individual's capability to orient on the future, present, and past through (a) forethought and intentionality (creating courses of action likely to produce desired outcomes), (b) self-reactiveness (giving shape to appropriate courses of action and their execution), and (c) self-reflectiveness (self-examining one's motivation, values, and life pursuits), correspondingly. Multiple dimensions involve outcomes from the enactment of agency's core features and occur in the form of self-development, adaptation, and self-renewal.

Bandura draws on psychology in his conceptualization of individuals' core features of forethought, intentionality, self-reactiveness, and self-reflectiveness, which enable people to play a part in their self-development, adaptation, and self-renewal. He draws on social psychology in his notion of self-efficacy—whereby people believe in their capabilities to perform in ways that give them some control over events that affect their lives and the lives of others. He relates to sociology in his conceptualization of the ways in which people bring their influence to bear on the social structure and the environment. These ways include the personal mode (which involves direct influence), the proxy mode (which is carried out through others), and—especially relevant to a sociological perspective—the collective mode (which is exercised through socially coordinated and interdependent efforts) (Bandura, 2001).

Bandura's revised social cognitive theory has been already claimed to be one of the three most important approaches to work motivation in the last 30 years (Latham & Pinder, 2005). However, most current career studies draw on a more focused social-psychological adaptation of Bandura's earlier theory by Lent, Brown, and Hackett (1994; see, e.g., Fouad & Guillen, 2006; Gainor, 2006; Lent & Brown, 2006). Among the few exceptions are studies concerned with the examination of self-efficacy and collective-efficacy beliefs as the main determinants of teachers' job satisfaction (Caprara, Barbaranelli, Borgogni, & Steca, 2003) and with the effects of perceived self-efficacy and personal goals on motivation and performance attainments (Bandura & Locke, 2003). A contemporary perspective on the subjective career calls for fresh application of Bandura's (2001) latest rendition of social cognitive theory.

"Intelligent Career" Theory

The "intelligent career" concept (Arthur et al., 1995; DeFillippi & Arthur, 1996) was developed with the emerging knowledge economy in mind. The intelligent career was first proposed as a response to Quinn's (1992) concept of the "intelligent enterprise"—that is, of the knowledge-driven organization. Just as Quinn and subsequent authors saw the knowledge-driven organization developing through its culture, know-how, and networks, so does intelligent career theory see individuals developing through three corresponding "ways of knowing." These are *knowing-why* (reflecting an individual's motivation and identity), *knowing-how* (reflecting an individual's skills and expertise), and *knowing-whom* (reflecting an individual's relationships and networks), respectively. The approach responds to Weick's emphasis on the subjective career in the knowledge economy by placing the subjective career, rather than any one organizational or societal view of the objective career, in charge of the direction and purpose of career development.

Intelligent career theory accommodates the previously described properties of the subjective career. Duality links the objective requirements of the job (the knowing-how skills needed) and the person's subjective response to the job (the knowing-why motivation to perform the job). Interdependence occurs through the interaction among these ways of knowing—for example, knowing-why motivation influences a person's choice of work, the knowing-how experiences that come with the work, and the knowing-whom relationships that grow through the work. It is also fundamental to the intelligent career approach that interdependence among the three ways of knowing occurs over time. In addition, knowing-why involves various dimensions of a person's inner self—such as the person's temperament and values—just as knowing-how and knowing-whom involve various dimensions of the skills and social relationships people develop through their work (Parker, Arthur, & Inkson, 2004).

Through the three ways of knowing and the interaction between them, the intelligent career approach responds to all three behavioral science perspectives previously addressed. From a psychological viewpoint, knowing-why investments reflect the underlying self-concepts, aptitudes, values, and so on that people bring to their work and careers. From a social-psychological viewpoint, individual knowing-why investments interact with both knowing-how and knowing-whom investments, which cover the social role (the job) and social connections a person takes on. From a sociological viewpoint, knowing-whom investments reflect the influence of society on both the person (knowing-why) and his or her work behavior (knowing-how) and also contribute to the further evolution of that society over time.

Since its introduction, the intelligent career model has been successfully used, for example, to examine patterns of career adaptation within a changing national context (Arthur et al., 1999; Cadin, Bender, & Saint-Giniez, 2000), explore gender- and family-related differences in career adaptation (Valcour & Tolbert, 2003), explore the ways in which people can develop more effective mentor networks, and determine predictors of managerial success (Eddleston, Baldridge, &

Veiga, 2004). One study has demonstrated a strong connection between people's investments in all three ways of knowing and subjective career success (Eby, Butts, & Lockwood, 2003). This work points to a range of new research possibilities that link the subjective career to the emerging knowledge economy.

The Theory of Growth and Adaptation

Boyatzis and Kolb's (2000) theory of growth and adaptation is another example that responds to the above ideas about the subjective career. It is concerned with understanding the dynamics of lifelong career development in the contemporary world through three unique modes of individual growth and adaptation. The modes describe growth and adaptation in terms of quests: (a) a quest for mastery in the performance mode (how we perform in the work role), (b) a quest for novelty in the learning mode (what we learn from the work role), and (c) a quest for meaning in the development mode (how we develop as people through the accumulation of work experiences). These modes integrate the authors' earlier conceptualizations of experiential learning as it is applied to lifelong adaptation (Kolb, 1984) and to competency acquisition and development (Boyatzis, 1982).

Like the social cognitive and intelligent career theories, the theory of growth and adaptation takes into account the four basic properties of the subjective career. Duality involves people's subjective adaptation to the objective environment that provides them with work. Interdependence involves interaction between a person's subjective quest (for mastery, novelty, or meaning) and the objective circumstances of his or her employment. For example, a quest for mastery will interact with the time and opportunity that circumstances make available for the quest to be pursued. The notion of time is incorporated in the life span in which the three modes of performance, learning, and development are played out. Multiple dimensions are reflected in, for example, the self-validation that is sought under the performance mode, the self-improvement sought under the learning mode, and the self-fulfillment sought under the development mode.

Each of the theory's three modes may be associated with a particular behavioral science emphasis. The development mode emphasizes a psychological perspective, focusing on a person's fulfillment and personal quest for meaning. The learning mode emphasizes a social-psychological perspective in focusing on a person's learning and the social setting in which learning occurs. Finally, the performance mode brings a sociological perspective by focusing on the social roles that people undertake and on how those roles can influence the larger social environment—for example, when an influential manager leads his or her company along a path of rapid innovation (Boyatzis & Kolb, 2000).

Empirical examination of the theory of growth and adaptation is yet to come. At the time of writing, we have been able to track only one journal publication by Mainemelis, Boyatzis, and Kolb (2002) that reports on the empirical examination of one integral element of their theory—experiential learning theory (Kolb, 1984). However, as Boyatzis and Kolb (2000, p. 90) make clear, there are other elements and implications to consider (for details, see Boyatzis & Kolb, 2000, p. 90). Among them are ideas for helping individuals grow and adapt throughout their careers and life and for addressing the potential conflicts between an individual in each of the modes and the environment through which he or she is pursuing a career.

For all three of the above examples, the interdisciplinary range of the underlying theory appears encouraging, but the empirical evidence behind any theory is still very limited. One problem may be that interdisciplinary research is more difficult to design and conduct. However, it seems important that theory drives research designs rather than the other way around.

A further problem with interdisciplinary approaches may be the question of how to engage more fully with the key challenges of our times. These include two particular challenges associated with the knowledge economy, stemming from the Internet and continuing globalization. We turn to these in the next section.

New Research Challenges

The knowledge economy's use of information technology (IT) is transforming both economic systems and social processes. In particular, the phenomena of (a) the Internet and (b) globalization offer fresh possibilities for individuals and invite more attention from career researchers. We briefly discuss these possibilities according to the overlapping psychological, social-psychological, and sociological perspectives previously discussed.

Careers and the Internet

From a *psychological* standpoint, the Internet offers a new medium for creating and experiencing human identity. Users of the Internet have been described as "dwellers on the threshold between the real and the virtual, unsure of our footing, inventing ourselves as we go along" (Turkle, 1995, p. 10). Moreover, once people have invented their online personae, they can use them to become more aware of how they project themselves; that is, they can "use the virtual to reflect constructively on the real" (Turkle, 2004, p. 22). For example, scientists have been already observed to use the Internet to enhance their identities by defining new research areas and finding opportunities to make unique contributions (Lamb & Davidson, 2005). There are also individuals who use the Internet to "masquerade" in professional roles for which they may not be qualified (Harshman, Gilsinan, Fisher, & Yeager, 2005).

The Internet also offers a wider marketplace for expertise. For example, scientists can now develop and collaborate around more specialized areas of knowledge (Lamb & Davidson, 2005, p. 1). Hackers can trade expertise by collaborating over open-source software (Castells, 2001). The generalized opportunity is one of "becoming your own self-directed and self-empowered researcher, editor, and selector of entertainment" (Friedman, 2005, p. 153)—that is, of exercising your own subjective career. These changes in collaboration, interaction, and data collection challenge, in turn, traditional definitions of expertise and professional identity (Lamb & Davidson, 2005).

From a *social-psychological* perspective, the Internet's ability to connect offers new possibilities for (a) information exchange and (b) further collaboration among participants. For example, one person's online search for help from other programmers led to the rapid growth of an online community to support and develop the Linux operating system (Castells, 2001; DeFillippi & Arthur, 2002). Such virtual communities, organized around common interests and values, take advantage of new forms of virtual communication such as messaging, mailing lists, chat rooms, and so on (Boczkowski, 1999), and increasingly of voice and video communications too (DeFillippi, Arthur, & Lindsay, 2006).

The Internet also provides opportunities for giving and receiving more traditional forms of career support. It fosters the proliferation of weak ties: persons and groups with whom one does not have strong relationships of work, kinship, or sociability but that are useful for information exchange (Wellman & Hampton, 1999). It provides for stronger ties among spatially distant actors too (Wellman & Hampton, 1999) and for the provision of social support in online communities organized around shared values and interests (Castells, 2001). Support is also increasingly available through IT-based career services, such as online counseling and career guidance (Harris-Bowlsbey & Sampson, 2005).

From a *sociological* perspective, the Internet offers new possibilities for institutional initiatives. One such initiative is that of Professions Australia, an umbrella Web-based association of professional associations that seeks to promote new communities of practice both within and across its separate member associations (DeFillippi et al., 2006). In a similar vein, the U.S. National Cancer Institute's "consortia and networks" program seeks to accelerate both performance improvements and learning outcomes in alternative cancer treatments by means of virtual collaboration among specialists from different locations (DeFillippi et al., 2006).

Another sociological phenomenon is the emergence of new frameworks for the integration of work. One such new framework is the open-source approach, associated with the Linux operating system described above, which has been suggested to represent a "new, post-capitalist model of production" (Friedman, 2005, p. 103). Another new framework involves the institutionalization and empowerment of social movements. The Internet is now seen as the "main way" in which social movements "can reach out to those who would adhere to their values, and from there to affect the consciousness of society as a whole" (Castells, 2001, p. 140).

In sum, the emergence of the Internet, and its associated proliferation of information and communication technologies, offers fresh opportunities for the subjective career. Moreover, these opportunities span all three behavioral science perspectives reviewed earlier. The emergence of the Internet also points to the greater significance of virtual space, and therefore of globalization, to which we now turn.

Careers and Globalization

From a *psychological* perspective, globalization (Peiperl and Jonsen, Chapter 18) is diminishing the significance of national identity while adding to the significance of professional identity (Arnett, 2002). The traditional skill-centered basis of professional identity does not follow the old rules of immigration laws, wages, and working conditions (Castells, 2000), and global workers are less frequently citizens of the United States and Western Europe (Harris, Sparrow, & Brewster, 2003). Instead, "anyone with the capacity to generate exceptional value added in any market enjoys the chance to shop around the globe—and to be shopped around, as well" (Castells, 2000, p. 130). New identities are "based less on prescribed social roles and more on individual choices, on decisions that each person makes about what values to embrace and what paths to pursue in love and work" (Arnett, 2002, p. 781).

Globalization also stresses the development of new—global—competencies to be able to collaborate and compete globally. They include (a) developing a "global mindset" to meet the challenges of globalization (Rhinesmith, 1996) and (b) changing from a local to a global identity, or to a successful combination of the two (Kohonen, 2005). "Cosmopolitanism," reflecting a global rather than a local consciousness, is also an increasingly relevant concept (Hannerz, 1996, p. 103). It involves both "a state of readiness" to make one's way in other cultures and "a built-up skill" to behave more or less expertly within a particular system of meaning (Kohonen, 2005).

From a *social-psychological* perspective, globalization stresses new possibilities for global collaboration. Friedman (2005, p. 81) observes "people around the world coming together online to collaborate in writing everything from their own software to their own operating systems to their own dictionary to their own recipe for cola." One prominent group is the scientists mentioned earlier, developing new ideas, reviewing one another's work, and introducing their colleagues to new research partners (Lamb & Davidson, 2005; Sargent & Waters, 2004). The previously mentioned groups of Linux programmers and social activists also communicate across geographically separate locations to develop better software or more powerful collective voices (Castells, 2001).

Businesses benefit from opportunities to bring on board people from anywhere in the world at any time and, thereby, to access the most knowledgeable and competent workers. They also benefit from an opportunity to work on the same product, service, or project up to 24 hours a day using workers from different time zones. Where the economy was once largely limited to local collaboration in physical space, it is now open to, and largely driven by, global collaborations in virtual space (Qureshi, Liu, & Vogel, 2006).

From a *sociological* standpoint, globalization reflects the emergence of fresh institutional arrangements involving outsourcing (of particular parts or services), offshoring (of complete manufacturing or service delivery systems), or interorganizational alliances in research and development (Friedman, 2005). Although there are fresh opportunities for large corporations, globalization also creates possibilities for small companies to offer their products and services in a much larger global marketplace (Friedman, 2005). Scientists, IT professionals, and social activists not only collaborate around the globe, they also build new infrastructures to help them do so (DeFillippi et al., 2006).

In sum, globalization is both a further consequence of the Internet and a catalyst of new opportunities for the subjective career. Also, globalization involves all three of the disciplinary perspectives covered earlier. However, while both the Internet and globalization appear to be major influences over the unfolding of people's subjective careers, they have so far been lightly studied.

Expanding the Subjective Career Agenda

Our story so far is that we need to make greater use of interdisciplinary theories in future work on the subjective career and that such work needs to take into account the emergence of both the Internet and globalization. What are the prospects for this kind of work? One place to begin is with the earlier examples of interdisciplinary theory. How do these stand up to the new research challenges described?

Bandura (2002) suggests that his social cognitive theory may be usefully employed to study the subjective careers of global social activists. Specifically, he suggests that his psychological concepts of forethought, intentionality, self-reactiveness, and self-reflectiveness can help explain the meanings and values that drive these activists. His social-psychological notion of self-efficacy can help explain individuals' beliefs in their ability to influence the world and to reach others who share the same values. It can also help explain how individual self-efficacy contributes to the collective efficacy of a social movement (Bandura, 2002). Finally, the theory suggests how modes of influence (personal, proxy, and collective) may help explain the ways in which social change across the globe can be achieved.

Arthur, Claman, and DeFillippi's (1995) intelligent career theory can be used to explore people's psychological (knowing-why) motivations to join Web-based communities. Preliminary work has already examined how interactions among knowing-why, knowing-how, and knowing-whom investments contribute to the social-psychological exchanges that take place inside these communities (DeFillippi, Arthur, & Parker, 2003). The effects of virtual knowing-whom investments, in particular, have been suggested to underlie the development of new sociological forms of global cooperation and its related institutions (DeFillippi et al., 2006). However, much more research needs to be done on the further implications of these kinds of subjective career investments in the contemporary economy.

Boyatzis and Kolb's (2000) theory of growth and adaptation may be usefully employed to study the subjective career dynamics of participants in global virtual communities. The theory's developmental mode may help explain the cognitions behind workers' motivation for new international projects. The learning mode may help explain the learning dynamics within such cross-cultural collaborations. In turn, the performance mode may help explain the assumption of social roles within the virtual communities (which may be different from roles of physically close cooperation), as well as how these roles affect virtual cooperation and its consequent outcome. However, major research on these kinds of relationships is yet to be undertaken.

In summary, the above three approaches, and prospectively other interdisciplinary approaches to the subjective career, have further potential. They can help us more fully examine the subjective career as it engages with both the Internet and globalization. That examination is urgent if our understanding of the subjective career is to keep pace with the pace of change in the knowledge economy. There is still much work to be done.

CONCLUSION

The emergence of the knowledge economy suggests a range of new challenges for career theory and research. A key challenge is to address the subjective career's increased importance and the related appropriateness of existing theoretical approaches to subjective career research. Our analysis of six major behavioral science theories, across the disciplines of psychology, social psychology, and sociology, has shown that all these remain relevant. However, their separate unidisciplinary orientation is of greater concern in a dynamic, knowledge-driven world. Moreover, our review of the work of Weick and his colleagues confirms the importance of an interdisciplinary perspective.

Alternative theoretical approaches examined in the second part of this chapter—revised social cognitive theory, intelligent career theory, and the theory of growth and adaptation—all demonstrate a capacity for interdisciplinary application. However, new ideas about the subjective career also need to respond to new challenges brought about by both the Internet and globalization. The three approaches examined have only begun to be applied to these critical aspects of the knowledge economy. Further research into the contemporary circumstances of the subjective career is vital for our greater

understanding, as well as for better supporting the people involved.

REFERENCES

Arnett, J. J. (2002). The psychology of globalization. *American Psychologist, 57*(10), 774–783.

Arthur, M. B., Claman, P. H., & DeFillippi, R. J. (1995). Intelligent enterprise, intelligent careers. *Academy of Management Executive, 9*(4), 7–20.

Arthur, M. B., Hall, D. T., & Lawrence, B. S. (1989). *Handbook of career theory.* New York: Cambridge University Press.

Arthur, M. B., Inkson, K., & Pringle, J. K. (1999). *The new careers: Individual action and economic change.* London: Sage.

Arthur, M. B., Khapova, S. N., & Wilderom, C. P. M. (2005). Career success in a boundaryless career world. *Journal of Organizational Behavior, 26*(2), 177–202.

Arthur, M. B., & Rousseau, D. M (1996). *The boundaryless career.* New York: Oxford University Press.

Ashkenas, R. (1999). Creating the boundaryless organization. *Business Horizons, 42*(5), 5–10.

Ashkenas, R., Ulrich, D., Jick, T., & Kerr, S. (1995). *The boundaryless organization: Breaking the chains of organizational structure.* San Francisco: Jossey-Bass.

Bailyn, L. (1984). Issues of work and family in organizations: Responding to social diversity. In M. B. Arthur (Ed.), *Working with careers* (pp. 75–98). New York: Columbia University, Graduate School of Business, Center for Research in Career Development.

Bailyn, L. (1993). *Breaking the mold: Women, men and time in the new corporate world.* New York: Free Press.

Bandura, A. (2001). Social cognitive theory: An agentic perspective. *Annual Review of Psychology, 52,* 1–26.

Bandura, A. (2002). Social cognitive theory in cultural context. *Applied Psychology, 51*(2), 269–290.

Bandura, A., & Locke, E. A. (2003). Negative self-efficacy and goal effects revisited. *Journal of Applied Psychology, 88*(1), 87–99.

Barley, S. R. (1989). Careers, identities, and institutions: The legacy of the Chicago School of Sociology. In M. B. Arthur, D. T. Hall, & B. S. Lawrence (Eds.), *Handbook of career theory* (pp. 41–65). New York: Cambridge University Press.

Bateson, M. C. (1994). *Peripheral visions: Learning along the way.* New York: Harper Collins.

Bell, D. (1973). *The coming of post-industrial society.* New York: Basic Books.

Block, F. (1990). *Postindustrial possibilities: A critique of economic discourse.* Berkeley: University of California Press.

Boczkowski, P. J. (1999). Mutual shaping of users and technologies in a national virtual community. *Journal of Communication, 49*(2), 86–108.

Boyatzis, R. E. (1982). *The competent manager: A model for effective performance.* New York: Wiley.

Boyatzis, R. E., & Kolb, D. A. (2000). Performance, learning, and development as modes of growth and adaptation throughout our lives and careers. In M. A. Peiperl, M. B. Arthur, R. Goffee, & T. Morris (Eds.), *Career frontiers: New conceptions of working lives* (pp. 76–98). Oxford: Oxford University Press.

Burns, T., & Stalker, G. M. (1961). *The management of innovation.* London: Tavistock.

Cadin, L., Bender, A.-F., & Saint-Giniez, V. (2000). *Carrières nomads: Les enseignements d'une comparison internationale.* Paris: Viubert.

Caprara, G. V., Barbaranelli, C., Borgogni, L., & Steca, P. (2003). Efficacy beliefs as determinants of teachers' job satisfaction. *Journal of Educational Psychology, 95*(4), 821–832.

Castells, M. (2000). *The power of identity.* Oxford: Blackwell.

Castells, M. (2001). *The Internet galaxy: Reflections on the Internet, business, and society.* Oxford: Oxford University Press.

DeFillippi, R. J., & Arthur, M. B. (1996). Boundaryless contexts and careers: A competency-based perspective. In M. B. Arthur & D. M. Rousseau (Eds.), *The boundaryless career* (pp. 40–57). New York: Oxford University Press.

DeFillippi, R. J., & Arthur, M. B. (2002). Career creativity to industry influence: A blueprint for the knowledge economy? In M. A. Peiperl, M. B. Arthur, R. Goffee, & N. Anand (Eds.), *Career creativity: Explorations in the remaking of work* (pp. 298–313). Oxford: Oxford University Press.

DeFillippi, R. J., Arthur, M. B., & Lindsay, V. J. (2006). *Knowledge at work: Creative collaboration in the global economy.* Oxford: Blackwell.

DeFillippi, R. J., Arthur, M. B., & Parker, P. (2003). Internet odysseys: Linking Web roles to career and community investments. *International Journal of Human Resource Management, 14*(5), 751–767.

Eby, L. T., Butts, M., & Lockwood, A. (2003). Predictors of success in the era of the boundaryless career. *Journal of Organizational Behavior, 24,* 689–708.

Eddleston, K. A., Baldridge, D. C., & Veiga, J. F. (2004). Toward modeling the predictors of managerial career success: Does gender matter? *Journal of Managerial Psychology, 19*(4), 360–385.

Feldman, M. S. (2000). Organizational routines as a source of continuous change. *Organization Science, 11*(6), 611–629.

Fouad, N. A., & Guillen, A. (2006). Outcome expectations: Looking to the past and potential future. *Journal of Career Assessment, 14*(1), 130–142.

Friedman, T. (2005). *The world is flat.* London: Allen Lane.

Gainor, K. A. (2006). Twenty-five years of self-efficacy in career assessment and practice. *Journal of Career Assessment, 14*(1), 161–178.

Giddens, A. (1984). *The constitution of society.* Berkeley: University of California Press.

Giddens, A. (2003). *Runaway world.* London: Routledge.

Haeckel, S. H. (1999). *Adaptive enterprise: Creating and leading, sense-and-respond organizations.* Boston: Harvard Business School Press.

Hall, D. T. (1976). *Careers in organizations.* Pacific Palisades, CA: Goodyear.

Hall, D. T. (2002). *Careers in and out of organizations.* Thousand Oaks, CA: Sage.

Hannerz, U. (1996). *Transnational connections.* London: Routledge.

Harris, H., Sparrow, P., & Brewster, C. (2003). *International human resource management.* Wimbledon: CIPD.

Harris-Bowlsbey, J., & Sampson, J. P. (2005). Use of technology in delivering career services worldwide. *Career Development Quarterly, 54*(1), 48–55.

Harshman, E. M., Gilsinan, J. F., Fisher, J. E., & Yeager, F. C. (2005). Professional ethics in a virtual world: The impact of the Internet on traditional notions of professionalism. *Journal of Business Ethics, 58*(1), 227–236.

Hedberg, B. L. T., Baumard, P., & Yakhlef, A. (2002). *Managing imaginary organizations: A new perspective on business.* Amsterdam: Pergamon.

Hedberg, B. L. T., Nystrom, P. C., & Starbuck, W. H. (1976). Designing organizations to match tomorrow. In P. C. Nystrom & W. H. Starbuck (Eds.), *Prescriptive models of organizations* (pp. 171–181). Amsterdam: North-Holland.

Hirschorn, L. (1984). *Beyond mechanization: Work and technology in a postindustrial age.* Cambridge: MIT Press.

Hughes, E. C. (1937). Institutional office and the person. *American Journal of Sociology, 1,* 404–413.

Hughes, E. C. (1997). Careers. *Qualitative Sociology, 20*(3), 389–397.

Judge, T. A., Cable, D. M., Boudreau, J. W., & Bretz, R. D. (1995). An empirical investigation of the predictors of executive career success. *Personnel Psychology, 48,* 485–519.

Kohonen, E. (2005). Developing global leaders through international assignments: An identity construction perspective. *Personnel Review, 34*(1), 22–36.

Kolb, D. A. (1984). *Experiential learning: Experience as the source of learning and development.* Englewood Cliffs, NJ: Prentice Hall.

Krumboltz, J. D. (1979). A social learning theory of career decision making. In A. M. Mitchell, G. B. Jones, & J. D. Krumboltz (Eds.), *Social learning and career decision making* (pp. 19–49). Cranston, RI: Carroll Press.

Lamb, R., & Davidson, E. (2005). Information and communication technology challenges to scientific professional identity. *Information Society, 21*(1), 1–24.

Latham, G. P., & Pinder, C. C. (2005). Work motivation theory and research at the dawn of the twenty-first century. *Annual Review of Psychology, 56,* 485–516.

Lawrence, P. R., & Lorsch, J. W. (1967). *Organization and environment: Managing differentiation and integration.* Boston: Harvard University.

Lent, R. W., & Brown, S. D. (2006). On conceptualizing and assessing social cognitive constructs in career research: A measurement guide. *Journal of Career Assessment, 14*(1), 12–35.

Lent, R. W., Brown, S. D., & Hackett, G. (1994). Toward a unifying social cognitive theory of career and academic interest, choice, and performance. *Journal of Vocational Behavior, 45,* 79–122.

Mainemelis, C., Boyatzis, R. E., & Kolb, D. A. (2002). Learning styles and adaptive flexibility: Testing experiential learning theory. *Management Learning, 33*(1), 5–33.

Mainiero, L. A., & Sullivan, S. E. (2005). Kaleidoscope careers: An alternative explanation for the "opt-out" revolution. *Academy of Management Executive, 19*(1), 106–123.

Malhotra, Y. (1996). Organizational learning and learning organizations: An overview. Retrieved June 5, 2005, from http://www.kmbook.com/orglrng.htm.

Mitchell, L. K., & Krumboltz, J. D. (1990). Social learning approach to career decision making: Krumboltz's theory. In D. Brown, L. Brooks, & Associates (Eds.), *Career choice and development* (pp. 145–196). San Francisco: Jossey-Bass.

Nystrom, P. C., Hedberg, B., & Starbuck, W. (1976). Interacting processes as organizational designs. In I. R. H. Kilmann, L. R. Pondy, & D. P. Slevin (Eds.), *The management of organizational design* (pp. 209–230). New York: American Elsevier.

Parker, P., Arthur, M. B., & Inkson, K. (2004). Career communities: A preliminary exploration of member-defined career support structures. *Journal of Organizational Behavior, 25*(4), 489–514.

Peiperl, M. A., Arthur, M. B., & Anand, N. (2002). *Career creativity: Explorations in the remaking of work.* Oxford: Oxford University Press.

Peiperl, M., & Baruch, Y. (1997). Back to square zero: The post-corporate career. *Organization Dynamics, 25*(4), 7–22.

Powell, W. W., & Snellman, K. (2004). The knowledge economy. *Annual Review of Sociology, 30,* 199–220.

Quinn, J. B. (1992). *Intelligent enterprise.* New York: Free Press.

Qureshi, S., Liu, M., & Vogel, D. (2006). The effects of electronic collaboration in distributed project management. *Group Decision and Negotiation, 15*(1), 55–75.

Rapoport, R., Bailyn, L., Fletcher, J. K., & Pruitt, B. H. (2002). Beyond work-family balance: Advancing gender equality and work performance. *Leadership & Organization Development Journal, 23,* 293–299.

Rhinesmith, S. H. (1996). *A manager's guide to globalization.* Chicago: Irwin.

Sargent, L. D., & Waters, L. E. (2004). Careers and academic research collaborations: An inductive process framework for understanding successful collaborations. *Journal of Vocational Behavior, 64,* 308–319.

Schein, E. H. (1971). The individual, the organization, and the career: A conceptual scheme. *Journal of Applied Behavioral Science, 7*(4), 401–426.

Schein, E. H. (1978). *Career dynamics: Matching individual and organizational needs.* Reading, MA: Addison-Wesley.

Super, D. E. (1980). A life-span, life-space approach to career development. *Journal of Vocational Behavior, 16,* 282–298.

Super, D. E. (1990). A life-span, life-space approach to career development. In D. Brown, L. Brooks, & Associates (Eds.), *Career choice and development* (pp. 197–261). San Francisco: Jossey-Bass.

Turkle, S. (1995). *Life on the screen: Identity in the age of the Internet.* New York: Touchstone.

Turkle, S. (2004). Whither psychoanalysis in computer culture? *Psychoanalytic Psychology, 21*(1), 16–30.

Valcour, P. M., & Tolbert, P. S. (2003). Gender, family and career in the era of boundarylessness: Determinants and effects of intra- and inter-organizational mobility. *International Journal of Human Resource Management, 14*(5), 768–787.

Van Maanen, J., & Schein, E. H. (1976). Career development. In J. R. Hackman & J. L. Suttle (Eds.), *Improving life at work: Behavioral science approaches to organizational change* (pp. 30–95). Santa Monica, CA: Goodyear.

Washington, M., & Zajac, E. J. (2005). Status evolution and competition: Theory and evidence. *Academy of Management Journal, 48*(2), 282–296.

Weick, K. E. (1977). Organization design: Organizations as self-designing systems. *Organizational Dynamics, 6,* 31–46.

Weick, K. E. (1996). Enactment and the boundaryless career: Organizing as we work. In M. B. Arthur & D. M. Rousseau (Eds.), *The boundaryless career* (pp. 40–57). New York: Oxford University Press.

Weick, K. E., & Berlinger, L. (1989). Career improvisation in self-designing organizations. In M. B. Arthur, D. T. Hall, & B. S. Lawrence (Eds.), *Handbook of career theory* (pp. 313–328). New York: Cambridge University Press.

Weick, K. E., Sutcliffe, K. M., & Obstfeld, D. (2005). Organizing and the process of sensemaking. *Organization Science, 16*(4), 409–421.

Wellman, B., & Hampton, K. N. (1999). Living networked on and off line. *Contemporary Sociology, 28*(6), 648–654.

8

THE INTERSECTION OF WORK AND FAMILY LIVES

JEFFREY H. GREENHAUS

SHARON FOLEY

Substantial research on the work-family interface has emerged over the past 25 years. An increasing participation of dual-earner partners and single parents in the work force, a blurring of gender roles, and a shift in employee values toward greater life balance have encouraged researchers to examine the many interdependencies between work and family roles (Barling & Sorensen, 1997; Barnett, 1998, 1999; Barnett & Hyde, 2001; Edwards & Rothbard, 2000; Greenhaus & Parasuraman, 1999; Lambert, 1990; Repetti, 1987).

The intersection of work and family lives has important implications for understanding the nature of careers. Not only do career experiences affect individuals' family lives but family life can also have a significant impact on work experiences and career outcomes (Crouter, 1984a, 1984b; Greenhaus & Singh, 2004; Ruderman, Ohlott, Panzer, & King, 2002). Moreover, individuals pursuing boundaryless (Arthur, Inkson, & Pringle, 1999) and protean (Hall, 2002) careers require a keen insight into the work-family

interface to leverage flexibility into a lifestyle that can satisfy a range of work and life values.

Amidst the large array of work-family concepts, we believe that there is an overarching issue that runs through much of the work-family literature: *How can individuals derive substantial satisfaction and fulfillment from those roles in life that matter?* When employees complain about excessive work-family conflict or when they lament the imbalance in their lives, they are reflecting on their inability to be as effective, satisfied, or fulfilled in an important life role as they would like to be. Conversely, when individuals experience work-family enrichment, resources or positive affect acquired in one role enable them to become more effective and more satisfied in the other role (Greenhaus & Powell, 2006).

This concern regarding individuals' achievement of effectiveness, satisfaction, and fulfillment in multiple life roles explicitly or implicitly underlies much of the theory and research on the work-family interface. The aim of this chapter is to examine research on the work-family interface, discuss the implications of the research for the study of careers, and identify future research needs. We limit this chapter to an examination of "work-family" issues rather than "work-life" issues primarily because the vast majority of the research on work-nonwork relationships has been concerned with work and family roles. We also note that most of the research on the work-family interface has been conducted in North American countries among employees who work for organizations. In response to these two restrictions in the literature, we devote a section of the chapter to global and cultural perspectives on the work-family interface, and we identify type of employment (organizational vs. self-employment) as an important area for future research.

First, we discuss work-family conflict, perhaps the most widely studied concept in the work-family literature. The next section focuses on work-family enrichment, an important concept that is not as well established as work-family conflict. In subsequent sections, we examine employer initiatives to ameliorate work-family stress, global and cultural perspectives on work-family issues, and the role of gender in the work-family interface. We attempt to relate each of these discussions to the underlying issue that individuals confront: achieving effectiveness and finding satisfaction and fulfillment in important life roles. The final sections of the chapter present our conclusions, implications of the literature for careers, and suggestions for future research.

WORK-FAMILY CONFLICT

Work-family conflict is produced by simultaneous pressures from work and family roles that are mutually incompatible (Greenhaus & Beutell, 1985). As a result of these incompatible role pressures, participation in one role is more difficult by virtue of participation in the other role. Therefore, individuals who experience extensive work-family conflict compromise their effectiveness or positive affect in one life role because of their experiences in another role.

The dominance of the conflict perspective in the work-family literature has been attributed to the acceptance of a scarcity hypothesis (Marks, 1977; Sieber, 1974). This hypothesis assumes that because time and energy are fixed resources,

individuals who participate in multiple roles experience substantial resource drain (Edwards & Rothbard, 2000) that impairs their effectiveness in other life roles. Despite evidence to the contrary (Baruch & Barnett, 1986), the scarcity hypothesis is apparently held in high enough regard to have generated a substantial amount of research over the past several decades on the measurement, antecedents, and consequences of work-family conflict.

Work-family conflict has generally been measured with self-report scales that assess the perceived interference between the demands of the work role and the family role. Recent refinements to the scales have incorporated the type and the direction of conflict. The type of interference has often been based on the distinction among time-based, strain-based, and behavior-based conflict (Greenhaus & Beutell, 1985). Recent studies (for a comprehensive review, see Frone, 2003) have distinguished the direction of the conflict or interference: Work-to-family conflict (WFC) occurs when work demands interfere with family life and family-to-work conflict (FWC) occurs when family demands interfere with work life. At least one scale includes items that assess both the type and direction of work-family conflict (Carlson, Kacmar, & Williams, 2000).

Antecedents of Work-Family Conflict

Research has often distinguished role characteristics and personal characteristics as antecedents of work-family conflict. In the work domain, role characteristics such as work hours, schedule inflexibility, unsupportive coworkers and supervisors, job constraints, and role stressors have been associated with high levels of work-family conflict. Family role characteristics associated with high work-family conflict include hours spent in family activities, the number and age of children, unsupportive family members, and family-induced stress (Adams, King, & King, 1996; Allen, 2001; Aryee, 1992; Carlson, 1999; Frone, Russell, & Cooper, 1992a; Frone, Yardley, & Markel, 1997; Greenhaus, Parasuraman, Granrose, Rabinowitz, & Beutell, 1989; Parasuraman, Purohit, Godshalk, & Beutell, 1996).

The recent focus on the direction of conflict has produced insight into the differential antecedents of WFC and FWC. In general, the determinants of WFC reside in the work domain, whereas the causes of FWC reside in the family domain (Byron, 2004; Frone, 2003). In other words, work role pressures (such as time involvement at work and job stressors) cause the work role to interfere with family life, and family role pressures (e.g., responsibility for young children, family conflict) cause the family role to interfere with functioning at work.

The belief that work pressures produce WFC and family pressures produce FWC makes intuitive sense and has received empirical support (Frone, 2003). Nevertheless, the arousal of work-family conflict ultimately depends on *simultaneous* pressures from *both* the work and family domains (Greenhaus & Beutell, 1985). For example, for work time commitments to interfere with family life, there must be expectations that the individual participates in the family; otherwise, there's nothing for work to interfere with. In other words, pressure from one role is unlikely to produce conflict in the absence of pressure from the other role. Unfortunately, the majority of the research has not explored interactions between pressures arising simultaneously from the work and family domains.

In addition to role characteristics, recent attention has been paid to the impact of dispositional characteristics on work-family conflict. Positive qualities such as agreeableness, conscientiousness, and a secure relationship style have been associated with low levels of work-family conflict, and negative qualities such as neuroticism, negative affectivity, and a preoccupied relationship style (i.e., a negative self-image and a positive image of others) have been associated with high levels of work-family conflict (Bruck & Allen, 2003; Carlson, 1999; Grzywacz & Marks, 2000; Stoeva, Chiu, & Greenhaus, 2002; Sumer & Knight, 2001; Wayne, Musica, & Fleeson, 2004). It is likely that dispositional characteristics affect work-family conflict indirectly through heightened levels of work stress and family stress (Stoeva et al., 2002).

Consequences of Work-Family Conflict

Extensive conflict has been associated with dissatisfaction, distress, withdrawal, and ineffective performance within the work and family domains (Bruck, Allen, & Spector, 2002; Carlson & Kacmar, 2000; Frone et al., 1997;

Kossek & Ozeki, 1998; MacEwen & Barling, 1994; Netemeyer, Boles, & McMurrian, 1996; Parasuraman et al., 1996). Moreover, excessive work-family conflict can produce destructive parenting tendencies (Stewart & Barling, 1996), heavy alcohol consumption (Frone, Russell, & Barnes, 1996; Frone, Russell, & Cooper, 1993), poor physical and psychological well-being (Frone, 2000; Frone et al., 1996), and a low quality of life (Higgins, Duxbury, & Irving, 1992; Rice, Frone, & McFarlin, 1992).

Although both directions of conflict seem to have equal effects on general health outcomes, the direction of the conflict can determine the specific role outcomes that are affected (Frone, 2003). WFC is associated with family-related distress, withdrawal, and ineffective performance, whereas FWC has its primary impact on distress, withdrawal, and performance in the work domain. In other words, the consequences of work-family conflict are most deeply felt in the role that is the object of the interference, although there are some exceptions to this general principle (Frone, 2003).

It is reasonable to expect that the impact of work-family conflict on negative outcomes is attenuated or buffered by the presence of social support and other coping resources. However, the research on social support has produced mixed findings, sometimes supporting a buffering effect (Stephens & Sommer, 1993; Suchet & Barling, 1986), sometimes not (Parasuraman, Greenhaus, & Granrose, 1992), and at other times revealing a reverse buffering effect in which high support exacerbates the impact of conflict on a negative outcome (MacEwen & Barling, 1988). Evidence regarding the buffering effect of personal coping strategies (time management, informal accommodation of work for family, and role restructuring) on the relationship between work-family conflict and strain outcomes has been promising but somewhat inconsistent (Behson, 2002a; Jex & Elacqua, 1999; Matsui, Ohsawa, & Onglotco, 1995).

It is possible that coping and other behavioral strategies may be more effective at preventing high levels of work-family conflict than attenuating the negative effects of the conflict once it occurs. The impact of proactive coping strategies on reducing work-family conflict is illustrated by the selection, optimization, and compensation (SOC) model of adaptive behavior (Wiese,

Freund, & Baltes, 2002). This model identifies goals (selection), strategies to accomplish goals (optimization), and approaches to overcome obstacles to goal achievement (compensation) as three processes that contribute to successful life management. Baltes and Heydens-Gahir (2003) have demonstrated that individuals who engage extensively in SOC behaviors experience low levels of job and family stressors, which, in turn, produce low levels of WFC and FWC. Time management, another self-management strategy, has also been shown to reduce work-family conflict (Adams & Jex, 1999).

WORK-FAMILY ENRICHMENT

The persistent dominance of the conflict perspective has positioned work and family roles as "enemies" (Friedman & Greenhaus, 2000) that continually interfere with one another. The possibility that work and family can be "allies" has long been recognized (Crouter, 1984a, 1984b; Marks, 1977; Sieber, 1974) and has served as the foundation for research on the virtues of role accumulation (Barnett, 1998, 1999), often referred to as the expansionist hypothesis (Barnett & Baruch, 1985). To the extent that work and family roles are allies, individuals should be able to derive additional effectiveness and satisfaction through their participation in multiple roles.

The notion that work and family roles can benefit one another has been referred to as enrichment (Greenhaus & Powell, 2006; Rothbard, 2001), facilitation (Frone, 2003; Grzywacz, 2002), positive spillover (Crouter, 1984b; Hammer et al., 2002; Hanson, Colton, & Hammer, 2003), and enhancement (Ruderman et al., 2002). Despite the differences in terminology, the concepts refer to very similar phenomena. Greenhaus and Powell (2006) defined work-family enrichment as the extent to which experiences in one role improve the quality of life in the other role, where quality of life includes high performance and positive affect. Grzywacz (2002) views work-family facilitation as the extent to which an individual's active involvement in one domain facilitates enhanced engagement or processes in another domain.

Because enrichment is a bidirectional concept, work can enrich family life (work-to-family enrichment or WFE) and family can enrich work

life (family-to-work enrichment or FWE). Work-family enrichment has been assessed by a variety of self-report scales (Grzywacz, 2000; Kirchmeyer, 1992a, 1992b; Stephens, Franks, & Atienza, 1997; Sumer & Knight, 2001; Tiedje et al., 1990; Tompson & Werner, 1997), and construct validation efforts are underway (Carlson, Kacmar, Grzywacz, & Wayne, 2004; Hanson et al., 2003; Hanson, Hammer, & Colton, 2004).

Understanding how work and family roles strengthen each other requires the development and examination of a theory of work-family enrichment. Greenhaus and Powell's (2006) model proposes that work-family enrichment occurs when resources acquired in the work (family) role are successfully applied to the family (work) role. They identified five types of resources that are most likely to promote work-family enrichment: skills and perspectives, psychological and physical resources (e.g., self-esteem, hardiness), social-capital resources (information and influence), flexibility, and material resources (e.g., money). Greenhaus and Powell specified two mechanisms or paths to enrichment: (1) an instrumental path in which a resource is transferred directly from one role to another role, thereby enhancing performance and positive affect in the second role and (2) an affective path in which positive affect in one role promotes high performance and positive affect in another role (Hanson et al., 2003). Similarly, Grzywacz's (2002) theory of work-family facilitation incorporates "exploitable" or portable resources that can be transferred from one role to another role.

This emphasis on transferable resources is consistent with the early writing of Sieber (1974) and the more recent identification of spillover as the transfer of skills, values, behaviors, and mood from one role to another role (Edwards & Rothbard, 2000). In fact, Voydanoff (2004) has provided support for the notion that the availability of resources within a role enables that role to enrich another role, whereas the presence of stressors in a role causes that role to interfere with another role.

Antecedents of Work-Family Enrichment

Because enrichment results from the direct or indirect transfer of resources from one role to another, any characteristic of the work or family environment that produces resources is capable of generating work-family enrichment. Many studies of situational and personal antecedents of enrichment have produced findings consistent with this view. For example, WFE has been traced to work role quality, job autonomy, learning opportunities, respect at work, meaningful work, and coworker support (Grzywacz & Marks, 2000; Grzywacz, Almeida, & McDonald, 2002; Voydanoff, 2004; Wayne et al., 2004). Moreover, marriage, parenthood, high family involvement, and support from other family members have been associated with high levels of FWE (Grzywacz & Marks, 2000; Grzywacz et al., 2002; Kirchmeyer, 1992b; Wayne et al., 2004).

These findings are consistent with an instrumental path to enrichment. For example, autonomous jobs with substantial learning opportunities can provide employees with new skills, schedule flexibility, and enhanced self-esteem, all of which can be applied fruitfully to the family role. Moreover, being a spouse and parent can present opportunities to develop new skills and perspectives, and receiving support from family members can provide an individual with information and self-confidence. These family-derived skills, perspectives, information, and self-confidence can be transferred to the work domain to enrich one's work life.

In terms of personal characteristics, extroversion, positive affectivity, openness to experience, agreeableness, conscientiousness, and a secure attachment style have been found to be positively related to work-family enrichment (Grzywacz & Marks, 2000; Stephens et al., 1997; Sumer & Knight, 2001; Wayne et al., 2004). We suspect that individuals who possess these positive qualities are capable of acquiring sufficient resources from a role to enrich the quality of another role.

Consequences of Work-Family Enrichment

By definition, work-family enrichment has positive consequences because WFE improves one's family life and FWE improves one's work life. Therefore, it is not surprising that WFE is associated with family satisfaction (Brockwood, Hammer, & Neal, 2003; Hanson et al., 2003; Tiedje et al., 1990), FWE is related to job

satisfaction and organizational commitment (Brockwood et al., 2003; Cohen & Kirchmeyer, 1995; Kirchmeyer, 1992a; Wayne et al., 2004), and both directions of enrichment are related to global outcomes such as life satisfaction, mental health, and physical health (Grzywacz, 2000; Hanson et al., 2003; Hill, 2005).

We should note that participation in work and family roles does not automatically produce work-family enrichment. For one thing, not all individuals acquire substantial resources from role participation, either because the role is not of sufficient quality to provide such resources or because the personality of the individual makes it difficult to extract resources from the role. Moreover, an individual who has acquired a particular resource (e.g., an interpersonal skill) may choose not to apply the resource to the other role or may apply the resource inappropriately (Greenhaus & Powell, 2006).

In sum, excessive work-family conflict limits individuals' capacity to achieve effectiveness and derive satisfaction from multiple life roles, whereas work-family enrichment expands this capacity. Moreover, because conflict and enrichment are independent concepts, they can coexist within the same person. The tendency of individuals to experience a higher level of enrichment than conflict (Greenhaus & Powell, 2006) is a positive sign that reflects a more optimistic view of the work-family interface. Nevertheless, the conflict that many individuals experience as they juggle their work and family responsibilities has prompted employers to initiate programs and policies to alleviate work-family stress.

WORK-FAMILY INITIATIVES

Work-family initiatives are employer-sponsored programs and policies that are designed to help employees manage work and the demands of personal life (Glass & Finley, 2002; Lobel, 1999). Presumably, employees who effectively manage multiple roles hold positive work-related attitudes, are effective at work, improve a firm's bottom line, and, we would add, achieve satisfaction and fulfillment in important life roles.

Researchers have classified initiatives in a variety of ways: formal and informal practices (Anderson, Coffey, & Byerly, 2002), alternative work arrangements and dependent care support (Parker & Allen, 2001), time, information, financial aid, and direct dependent care services (Lobel & Kossek, 1995), segmentative and integrative policies (Grandey, 2001), and flexibility, support, and reduced work hours (Glass & Finley, 2002).

The lack of consistency in the way initiatives are classified extends to the way in which they are assessed. Studies have examined the *introduction* of a work-family initiative (Baltes, Briggs, Huff, Wright, & Neuman, 1999), the *presence* of an initiative (Anderson et al., 2002), the *ability to use* the initiative (Roehling, Roehling, & Moen, 2001), the *intention to use* the initiative (Almer, Cohen, & Single, 2003), the *use* of the initiative (Clark, 2001), the *satisfaction* with the initiative (Aryee, Luk, & Stone, 1998), the *perceived importance* of the initiative (Frone & Yardley, 1996), and the *usability* of the initiative (Eaton, 2003).

As with the type and measure of initiatives, there is extensive variation in the outcomes that have been examined. Although many studies have focused on work-related attitudes such as job satisfaction, organization commitment, and intentions to leave (Allen, 2001; Grover & Crooker, 1995; Kossek & Ozeki, 1998; Scandura & Lankau, 1997), other studies have examined the impact of initiatives on individual or team job performance (Rayman, 1998), work-family conflict (Anderson et al., 2002; Thomas & Ganster, 1995), withdrawal tendencies such as absenteeism, lateness, and turnover (Baltes et al., 1999; Kossek & Nichol, 1992), and organizational performance (Arthur, 2003; Grover & Crooker, 1995; Konrad & Mangel, 2000; Perry-Smith & Blum, 2000).

Who Uses Work-Family Initiatives?

Personal and situational factors have been associated with the utilization of work-family initiatives. Individuals who believe that they can benefit from an initiative are most likely to use it. Therefore, anticipated or actual utilization is high among women (Blair-Loy & Wharton, 2002; Kossek, Barber, & Winters, 1999; Powell, 1997), employees who value family time, and those whose spouse approves of their use of a program or benefit (Almer et al., 2003).

Situational determinants of utilization include work group peer use (Kossek et al., 1999) and the supportiveness of management and the organization (Allen, 2001; Almer et al., 2003; Thompson, Beauvais, & Lyness, 1999).

Inevitably, there are variations in the favorability of employees' attitudes toward work-family initiatives (Frone & Yardley, 1996; Parker & Allen, 2001). Nevertheless, although some individuals may be reluctant to use work-family initiatives if they sense a "backlash" reaction from coworkers who cannot use the initiatives, much of the research discounts the notion of backlash. For example, employees without children do not resent family-friendly policies (Hegtvedt, Clay-Warner, & Ferrigno, 2003), and employees show greater affective commitment and lower turnover intentions in organizations that offer work-family initiatives than in organizations that do not offer them regardless of whether the employees would achieve personal gain from the use of the initiatives (Grover & Crooker, 1995). However, despite the absence of backlash in overall attitudes toward the presence of work-family initiatives, backlash may exist in the form of negative attitudes toward a specific benefit such as an on-site child care center (Rothausen, Gonzalez, Clarke, & O'Dell, 1998).

Are Work-Family Initiatives Useful?

Presumably, organizations provide family-supportive initiatives because they believe that they will experience more successful recruiting, more favorable work attitudes, higher job performance, higher retention, lower absenteeism or lateness, and ultimately greater profitability. Lobel's (1999) review of the research through 1998 was encouraging—largely positive effects of work-life practices on employee attitudes, such as organizational commitment and job satisfaction; generally favorable effects (more often positive or neutral, less often negative) on individual and team performance; and desirable effects on human resource management indicators such as reduced absenteeism, sick days, tardiness, and turnover, and enhanced recruitment.

More recently, Glass and Finley (2002) examined the outcomes related to policy adoption, including increased productivity, reduced worker stress, reduced role conflict, and lower absenteeism and turnover. Their findings suggest that family-responsive policies in the areas of flexible scheduling, employer assistance with child care, and parental leave positively affect both individual and organizational outcomes. Indeed, there is ample evidence that the availability of formal work-family initiatives is associated with low WFC, high job satisfaction, high organizational commitment, and low turnover intentions (Allen, 2001; Anderson et al., 2002; Grover & Crooker, 1995; Kossek & Ozeki, 1998; Scandura & Lankau, 1997).

Although the impact of work-family initiatives is more likely to be positive than negative, the findings have been far from conclusive. Sometimes, their effectiveness depends on a combination of a particular initiative paired with a specific outcome. For example, flextime—but not compressed workweek schedules—affected absenteeism (Baltes et al., 1999), and schedule flexibility—but not dependent care benefits—was negatively related to WFC (Anderson et al., 2002). Moreover, although flexible work schedules have had primarily positive effects on outcomes such as improved job satisfaction and reduced absenteeism, there is also a substantial amount of research that does not support their effectiveness (Bohen & Viveros-Long, 1981; Christensen & Staines, 1990; Clark, 2002). These inconsistent findings demonstrate the need to examine the effects of initiatives across a range of potential outcomes in order to develop detailed initiative profiles (Baltes et al., 1999) and also highlight the need to develop and test theoretical models of work-family initiatives.

Perhaps as a result of the inconsistencies in the literature, researchers have begun to examine potential moderators of the relationships between initiatives and outcomes. Scandura and Lankau (1997) found that positive relationships of a flexible work schedule policy with organizational commitment and job satisfaction were stronger for employees with dependent children than for employees without dependent children. In a similar vein, the relationship between flexible time policies and employee loyalty was amplified for employees of traditional childbearing ages and for parents of school-aged children (Roehling et al., 2001). Moreover, Rau and Hyland (2002) found that workers with high levels of interrole conflict expressed greater attraction to an organization depicted as having a flextime option than those with low levels of conflict.

Lobel (1999) concluded that scant attention had been given to the degree to which work-life initiatives reinforce business strategies. Presumably, organizations adopt work-family initiatives because they meet a strategic need, as suggested by the positive relationship between an organization's proportion of female managers and its propensity to offer a comprehensive work-family program (Ingram & Simons, 1995). The fact that work-family initiatives have been associated with increased perceived organizational performance (Perry-Smith & Blum, 2000), firm productivity (Konrad & Mangel, 2000), and shareholder return (Arthur, 2003) suggest that initiatives can produce outcomes consistent with strategic goals. However, as is the case with individual-level outcomes, not all work-family initiatives have the same impact on profits (Meyer, Mukerjee, & Sestero, 2001).

Beyond Initiatives

Recent research has reflected an increased interest in the family-supportiveness of the culture or work environment (Allen, 2001; Bailyn, 1997; Clark, 2001; Hegtvedt et al., 2003; Kossek, Colquitt, & Noe, 2001; Thomas & Ganster, 1995; Thompson et al., 1999). Family-supportive work environments have two components: family-supportive policies (which we have already discussed) and family-supportive supervisors (Thomas & Ganster, 1995). Family-supportive supervision refers to the sensitivity, empathy, and flexibility provided by a supervisor to assist a subordinate in achieving balance (Parker & Allen, 2002; Thomas & Ganster, 1995). Having a family-supportive supervisor has been associated with employee loyalty and commitment (Aryee et al., 1998; Roehling et al., 2001), citizenship (Clark, 2001), and low levels of WFC, turnover intentions, stress, and absenteeism (Anderson et al., 2002). Supervisors who do not support flexible work options may make it difficult for employees to use the benefits provided by the organization (Allen, 2001; Brewer, 2000; Powell & Mainiero, 1999; Thompson et al., 1999). Therefore, it is not enough to provide family-friendly policies; the implementation of the policies in a supportive environment is crucial to whether they will be used and whether they will promote a loyal workforce (Roehling et al., 2001).

Similar to family-supportive work environments is the construct of family-supportive organization perceptions (FSOP), the "global perceptions that employees form regarding the extent to which the organization is family supportive" (Allen, 2001, p. 414). A supportive culture or strong FSOP perceptions increase the utilization rate of work-family benefits, are positively related to job satisfaction and organizational commitment, and are negatively related to work-family conflict and turnover intentions (Allen, 2001; Thompson et al., 1999). Most important, a supportive work-family culture influences positive work attitudes above and beyond the availability of work-family initiatives (Thompson et al., 1999).

A family-supportive culture is nicely illustrated by Bailyn's (1997) participation in a company's attempt to change its culture by reexamining the way in which work is conducted. An open discussion of work-family issues among teams of employees, an identification of barriers such as face time and close monitoring of employees, and a restructuring of work to meet work goals and family and personal responsibilities characterized this promising approach to creating a truly supportive work environment.

Global and Cultural Perspectives on the Work-Family Interface

The cross-cultural study of work-family issues is still a relatively new area of inquiry (Joplin, Shaffer, Francesco, & Lau, 2003). Because the meaning of work and family varies across countries and cultures (Poelmans, Spector, et al., 2003; Thomas and Inkson, Chapter 23), it is reasonable to expect cultural differences in attitudes and behavior relevant to the work-family interface. Given the prominence of the work-family conflict perspective for the past several decades and the increase in the number of dual-income couples in many countries (Yi & Chien, 2002), it is not surprising that much of the cross-cultural research directly or indirectly examines conflict or interference between work and family roles.

A fundamental question in cross-cultural research is the generalizability of theoretical models of work-family linkages (especially work-family conflict) across cultures and the contingencies that may limit their generalizability (Poelmans, Spector, et al., 2003). In their conceptual paper, Poelmans, Spector, et al. (2003) distinguished "universalistic hypotheses," where the relationships between work-family variables are expected to be similar in all countries from "cross-cultural hypotheses" in which relationships are expected to be different between countries. For example, the universalistic hypotheses focus on a simple dynamic of demands creating more conflict and available resources moderating that relationship. The cross-cultural hypotheses use two basic dimensions expected to be essential in explaining variance between different countries and cultures in work-family conflict: individualism-collectivism and the level of family-supportiveness of the local government and culture. Ling and Powell (2001) developed a conceptual model of work-family conflict in contemporary China that extends the American-based model by incorporating culture-specific factors.

Work-family conflict research has been conducted in many countries, including Israel (Etzion & Bailyn, 1994; Izraeli, 1993), Hong Kong (Fu & Shaffer, 2001; Ngo & Lau, 1988; Stoeva et al., 2002), Singapore (Aryee, 1992; Kim & Ling, 2001), the United Kingdom (Lewis, 1997), and Finland (Kinnunen & Mauno, 1998). Many researchers who use samples in one country comment on whether the findings parallel those found in previous research in the United States. These studies do not provide direct support for cultural influences because there is no comparison sample. However, a small number of researchers have collected comparative data from an American sample and a sample from a country other than the United States (Aryee, Fields, & Luk, 1999; Etzion & Bailyn, 1994; Yang, Chen, Choi, & Zou, 2000). This method allows researchers to identify similarities and differences between cultures and consider contextual cultural influences that may account for observed differences. In one of the few cross-national comparative studies that use more than two countries, Spector and colleagues (2004) collected data from what they refer to as "three culturally distinct regions":

Anglo (e.g., United States and England), China (e.g., Hong Kong and Taiwan), and Latin America (e.g., Argentina and Mexico). Their strategy was to classify the countries into regions based on prior research concerning average country-level individualism-collectivism scores (see below) in order to test their moderator hypotheses and divide the collectivistic countries into two regions because of the considerable cultural differences between China and Latin America.

In a study of the antecedents of work-family conflict, Yang et al. (2000) found that family demand (primarily time pressures associated with tasks such as housekeeping and child care) had greater impact on work-family conflict in the United Stated than in China, whereas work demand (primarily pressures arising from excessive workloads or rush jobs and deadlines) had greater impact on work-family conflict in China than in the United States. On the other hand, Etzion and Bailyn (1994) found a striking similarity between U.S. and Israeli women in the relationship between salary/rank and career-family conflict, and observed no cultural difference in the mean level of career-family conflict. Aryee et al. (1999) found that whereas many of the antecedents and consequences of work-family conflict were similar for the United States and Hong Kong, there were also some interesting cross-country differences (e.g., the life satisfaction of Hong Kong employees was influenced primarily by work-family conflict, whereas that of the American employees was influenced primarily by family-work conflict).

Cross-cultural researchers (e.g., Aryee, 1992; Yang et al., 2000) have relied mainly on differences in national culture as an explanation for differences in work-family conflict across countries. For example, Aryee et al. (1999) noted several distinctive characteristics of Hong Kong culture regarding work and family such as the precedence of family over individual well-being and the primary function of work as a resource for the family's well-being.

The individualistic-collectivistic component of culture is used most frequently to hypothesize or explain cultural differences in work-family conflict. Individualists give priority to their own goals over those of others, whereas collectivists follow the norms and duties imposed by the group to which they belong and put the group's goals ahead of their own (Triandis, 1995). In countries with strong collectivist family units, such as Singapore and Hong Kong, leave benefits tend to be minimal and dependent care is considered the responsibility of the family (Lin & Rantalaiho, 2003). Spector et al. (2004) found a significant relationship between number of hours worked and work/family pressure among individualists (Anglos) but not among collectivists (Chinese and Latin Americans). Yang et al. (2000) attributed different antecedents of work-family conflict partly to cultural differences in individualism-collectivism and partly to different levels of industrial development and material affluence in the two countries. Although rarely applied in international work-family studies to date, Hofstede's (2001) cultural value of masculinity-femininity, which reflects the difference in roles between males and females in a society, may also be a fruitful avenue for further study.

Joplin et al. (2003) identified macro-level conditions (e.g., economic, social, technological, legal, and cultural factors) as potential national-level determinants of work-family conflict. Joplin et al. (2003) contend that it is the (in)compatibility of cultural dimensions with other external influences that leads to differences in the experience of stress and work-family conflict. For example, individuals in societies where macro-level changes run counter to cultural values experience more stress and work-family conflict. Poelmans, Spector, et al. (2003) proposed, but have not tested, that the level of family-supportiveness of the country government will moderate the effect of work and family demands on WFC/FWC with the effect being weaker in highly supportive countries. A high family-supportive government is one that offers nationwide, government-subsidized support in terms of favorable child care and parental leave arrangements (Poelmans, Spector, et al., 2003).

Korabik, Lero, and Ayman (2003) also incorporated sociocultural, contextual, and policy variables into their theoretical framework for conducting cross-cultural work-family research, including the degree of public policy support and service provision available to individuals. A body of research, largely conducted in the European Union, has adopted a macro-level work-family focus that identifies the importance of public policies affecting women's labor force patterns (e.g., Deven & Moss, 2002; Lewis, 1997; Poelmans, Chinchilla, & Cardona, 2003). It is important to understand how these differences in social policies and programs are likely to affect the extent of work-family conflict that individuals experience (Korabik et al., 2003).

The proportion of women in the paid labor force is an important determinant of the existence and extent of family-supportive policies and legislation in various countries. Other factors include a low birthrate, strong economic conditions that require more women to enter the workforce, and political pressures to facilitate work-family balance. An additional determinant is the distribution of the caring responsibility among governments, employers, and families. For example, in countries where extended kinship systems provide dependent care support (e.g., in Spain, Portugal, Greece, and Italy) and caring is treated as a private responsibility, there is little government support (Poelmans, Chinchilla, et al., 2003; Spector et al., 2004). In Europe and the United States, where the proportion of women in the workforce is large, there are legal provisions for parental leave and child care (in the Parental Leave Directive of the European Union and the 1993 Family and Medical Leave Act, respectively) (Asher & Lenhoff, 2001; Lewis, Smithson, & Branner, 1999). Hong Kong and Singapore have similar proportions of women in the workforce as the United States and Europe, yet leave benefits tend to be minimal and dependent care is considered the responsibility of the family (Lin & Rantalaiho, 2003).

In sum, we should not assume that Western findings in work-family research will necessarily generalize to culturally dissimilar countries or regions because there are important cultural differences that can affect relations among variables (Spector et al., 2004). However, future research is required to understand the impact of cultural differences on the level, antecedents, and outcomes of work-family conflict.

GENDER, WORK, AND FAMILY

Juggling work and family roles is no longer considered a "woman's issue" but rather applies to men and women with significant family and work responsibilities. Research indicates that participation in work *and* family life can enhance the well-being of women and men alike (Barnett & Hyde, 2001). Nevertheless, the question remains whether men and women face similar or different experiences in managing work and family responsibilities.

The literature provides little support for the widely held belief that women experience more work-family conflict than men. Frone (2003) observed that men and women generally report similar levels of work-family conflict and that the gender differences that have appeared in some studies are of small magnitude. Research has also not supported Pleck's (1977) plausible prediction—based on a gendered division of labor—that men would experience more WFC and that women would experience more FWC (Eagle, Miles, & Icenogle, 1997; Frone, Russell, & Cooper, 1992b; Gutek, Searle, & Klepa, 1991).

To shed further light on the relationship between gender and work-family conflict, we identified 23 studies that reported gender analyses on WFC and FWC. Our informal survey of the literature provided little support for the contention that work is more likely to interfere with family for men than for women. We found that 44% of the studies revealed no gender differences in WFC, 32% found that women experienced more WFC than men, and 24% observed that men experienced more WFC than women. One would be hard-pressed to conclude anything from these findings other than that the relationship between gender and WFC is not consistent across studies.

The literature on FWC is also equivocal. Consistent with Pleck (1977), there is some evidence that family responsibilities may be more likely to interfere with women's work than with men's work. Women's extensive family or parental responsibilities have been associated with a reduction in work hours or psychological involvement in work (Friedman & Greenhaus, 2000; Galinsky & Bond, 1996; Greenberger & O'Neill, 1993), a restriction of career development opportunities such as mentoring and coaching (Friedman & Greenhaus, 2000), and a tendency to interrupt one's career (Tharenou, 1999). However, these findings are not reflected in the research on gender differences in self-reported FWC. In our informal survey of the literature, we found that 67% of the studies observed no gender differences in FWC, 26% found that women experience more FWC than men, and 7% found that men experienced more FWC than women.

What factors explain the inconsistent presence of gender differences in self-reported work-family conflict? One possibility is that the gendered division of labor at work and home has sufficiently weakened to the point that men and women essentially experience the same level of conflict between work and family roles. Alternatively, it is possible that women have already reduced their work involvement to make it less likely that work would interfere with their family responsibilities. Or perhaps women are more reluctant than men to reveal on a self-report scale that their work interferes with their family role because admitting this interference would be damaging to their self-concept.

Despite admittedly underwhelming evidence for gender differences in work-family conflict, it may be premature to conclude that men and women experience the same type and level of interference between their work and family responsibilities. Instead, it is reasonable to expect within-gender variations in work-family conflict or interference (Parasuraman & Greenhaus, 2002). For example, one study revealed that although women as a group worked the same number of hours as men, mothers worked fewer hours than other groups of women, and substantially fewer hours than fathers, perhaps explaining why women with extensive family commitments experienced relatively low income and career satisfaction (Friedman & Greenhaus, 2000). The presence of young children at home and an unsupportive spouse can also exacerbate gender differences in work-family conflict (Greenhaus, 2004).

When we look at the very few studies that have examined gender differences in self-reported work-family enrichment, an interesting—though tentative—pattern emerges. Our informal review revealed that WFE was stronger for women than men in two thirds of the studies, a trend that seems consistent with the finding that women are more likely than men to use income (Crittenden, 2001) and job-related autonomy and networking (Friedman & Greenhaus, 2000) for

the benefit of their children. Because many women feel more responsible than men for the emotional well-being of their family, women may be more highly motivated to transfer a resource acquired at work to enhance their family's well-being.

The literature also provides suggestions of gender differences in the utilization and effectiveness of work-family initiatives, although the findings are far from conclusive. For example, there is evidence that intentions and actual utilization of work-family programs are stronger for women than men (Almer et al., 2003; Blair-Loy & Wharton, 2002; Kossek et al., 1999; Stroh & Reilly, 1999). In addition, women place more importance than men on initiatives such as job sharing and child care assistance (Frone & Yardley, 1996), view work-family policies more favorably than men (Parker & Allen, 2001), and are less likely than men to anticipate feeling resentment if faced with extra work due to coworkers' family obligations (Hegtvedt et al., 2003). Why women are more likely than men to use formal work-family initiatives can be explained by women's greater need for such support, the tendency of organizations to be more willing to provide formal support to women (Barham, Gottlieb, & Kelloway, 1998), and men's utilization of informal arrangements with their managers (Hall, 1989).

Although women may be more likely to use formal work-family programs, whether they benefit more than men from using the programs is open to question. Several studies have found that relationships of programs or policies with work attitudes and behavior are stronger for women than for men (Chiu & Ng, 1999; Kim, 1998; Scandura & Lankau, 1997), whereas other studies have not found that gender moderates initiative-outcome relationships (Allen, Russell, & Rush, 1994; Anderson et al., 2002; Eaton, 2003). The absence of consistent gender differences may reflect the fact that because men also experience considerable pressure to balance family and work (Behson, 2002b), work-family initiatives are just as relevant for employed fathers as they are for employed mothers. Further complicating the picture is the possibility that men and women may benefit from different types of family-related support (Batt & Valcour, 2003).

THE IMPLICATION OF THE WORK-FAMILY INTERFACE FOR CAREER STUDIES

The interconnections between work and family roles have a number of implications for the study of careers. Career experiences can promote an effective and satisfying family life for individuals who acquire tangible or intangible resources from their work environment (Greenhaus & Powell, 2006). However, overinvolvement in work has a dark side because it can produce conflict, imbalance, and a low quality of life (Greenhaus, Allen, & Foley, 2004; Greenhaus, Collins, & Shaw, 2003).

In a similar vein, skills, self-esteem, and other resources acquired in the family role can promote opportunities and effectiveness in one's career. However, extensive commitment of time and involvement in family life can also restrict opportunities at work, especially for women, either because of conscious decisions to limit career involvement or because of organizations that fail to provide sufficient flexibility to employees with extensive family commitments.

We believe that a "full engagement" in work and family roles, what Marks and MacDermid (1996) call "role balance," has the capacity to enrich experiences in both roles and promote a higher quality of life. However, involvement in family or career, taken to the extreme, inevitably produces interference with the other role. Individuals do experience tradeoffs although it is not currently fashionable to think of work and family roles in a zero-sum manner. An extreme involvement in work—an absorption that passes the threshold of full engagement—is likely to limit opportunities for full participation in family life and, therefore, limit feelings of fulfillment derived from the family role, just as an extreme involvement in family can limit opportunities for full participation in one's career.

Although overinvolvement in one role limits opportunities for effectiveness and fulfillment in the other role, the consequences may be different depending on the role subject to overinvolvement. For example, individuals who are more involved in family than work experience a higher quality of life than those who are more involved in work than family (Greenhaus et al., 2003). Because extreme involvement in either role is likely to require tradeoffs in the form of lower effectiveness and less fulfillment in the other role, it is possible that the alignment of involvement in work and family with one's preferences and life values produces the highest quality of life, not because it eliminates tradeoffs but rather because the tradeoffs are perceived as acceptable.

Issues such as balance, tradeoffs, and fit seem particularly important in light of the expanded meaning of career success that has been observed in recent years (Greenhaus, 2002). No longer bound to define success exclusively in terms of money, status, or advancement, individuals are likely to define career success, at least in part, in terms of achieving balance between career and personal life (Shellenbarger, 1991; Universum Intituted, 1998). Moreover, achieving an appropriate level of balance among life roles is particularly important for individuals pursuing flexible, protean careers (Hall, 2002) because balance and life fulfillment may be crucial ingredients of psychological success.

DIRECTIONS FOR FUTURE RESEARCH

Because of the interconnections between work and family lives, it is virtually impossible to understand career processes without considering the work-family interface. However, additional research is necessary to understand the interdependencies between work and family roles and determine the impact of the interdependencies on career experiences and outcomes.

Although the literature has provided considerable understanding of work-family conflict, future research can be usefully redirected in several ways. As suggested elsewhere (Greenhaus & Parasuraman, 1999; Greenhaus & Powell, 2003), research should focus on specific episodes of potential conflict in addition to the more typically studied ongoing or chronic conflict. Although research on chronic conflict has produced many insights, it is also important to understand how individuals appraise potentially conflictual situations, when and from whom they seek support in specific situations, and ultimately how they resolve—or fail to resolve—the situation.

In studying individuals' reactions to episodes of conflicting role demands, it is important to examine interacting pressures from work and family roles rather than limiting the study to the additive effects of work demands (e.g., job stress) and family demands (e.g., parental responsibilities) on conflict. As noted earlier, it is the coexistence of role pressures from the work and family domains that puts individuals in situations in which conflict is likely to occur.

Those researchers who wish to study chronic work-family conflict should consider alternative research designs that do not involve the use of self-report scales of work-family conflict. Although we have learned a great deal about conflict from the use of these scales, work-family interference can also be inferred from relationships between work-related variables and family-related variables without resorting to self-reports that may be subject to distortion or bias. For example, negative relationships between mothers' family commitments and career involvement (Friedman & Greenhaus, 2000) may capture family's interference with work, and relationships between fathers' job dissatisfaction and their children's dysfunctional behavior (Barling, 1986) may capture work's interference with family.

Because the study of work-family enrichment is so underdeveloped at the present time, there are many fertile research opportunities to increase our understanding of this process. As suggested by Greenhaus and Powell (2006), research should be guided by a comprehensive theory of enrichment, examine how individuals acquire resources from a role and apply them effectively to another role, use multiple methodologies to examine enrichment, and adopt a boundary-crossing perspective (Ashforth, Kreiner, & Fugate, 2000; Nippert-Eng, 1995) to understand how experiences in one role enhance experiences and outcomes in another role.

Moreover, because conflict and enrichment are derived from opposing sets of assumptions— scarcity and expansionist, respectively—it is tempting to view them as antithetical processes that are inversely related to each other such that high conflict implies low enrichment and high enrichment implies low conflict. However, the empirical literature indicates that conflict and enrichment are unrelated and that individuals can simultaneously experience high (or low) levels of both conflict and enrichment. Powell

and Greenhaus (2006) have attempted to distinguish the conditions under which conflict and enrichment are unrelated and the conditions under which they are inversely related. Additional research is necessary to gain further insights into the nature of the relationship between work-family conflict and work-family enrichment.

Work-family conflict and enrichment need to be understood in the context of the larger society in which one lives. Voydanoff's (2001) insightful incorporation of community into the work-family interface presents many opportunities to study how community characteristics affect—and are affected by—work and family lives, as well as how community factors interact with work and family characteristics to predict life outcomes. Moreover, to increase our understanding of the impact of national culture, it is necessary to develop and test theories that specify when universalistic and cross-cultural hypotheses (Poelmans, Spector, et al., 2003) will be supported.

We believe that research should continue to examine the role of gender in the work-family interface. However, it is not enough to determine whether women and men experience similar or different levels of work-family conflict and enrichment. Whatever effects gender may have are likely to be contingent on cultural and subcultural norms, gender-role ideology, spouse attitudes and behaviors, family and career life cycle stages, and other circumstances not yet anticipated. Although these types of variables have been examined to some extent, we are not aware of a theoretical framework that incorporates a wide range of these contingencies into a comprehensive model to guide empirical research on gender, work, and family.

Although useful research on work-family initiatives and supportive work environments has grown considerably in recent years, more attention should be paid to the development of a comprehensive theory to explain why, and under what conditions, different programs, practices, and policies affect individual and organizational outcomes. Understanding why effects occur requires specifying the factors that mediate the impact of programs, practices, and policies on outcomes. One likely mediator is the perception of control (Thomas & Ganster, 1995) that is an outgrowth of supportive and flexible practices and cultures, but there are undoubtedly other variables that explain why particular initiatives are effective. Understanding the conditions under which effects occur requires specifying the factors that moderate the impact of specific initiatives or cultures on particular outcomes. Research has begun to specify such moderators (Roehling et al., 2001; Scandura & Lankau, 1997) but more research is needed. Likely moderators include particular populations of employees (single parents, low-income workers) who may benefit more substantially than other workers or who may benefit more substantially from some practices than from other practices.

Ultimately, it is possible that the "perceived usability" of work-family initiatives is a more important determinant of positive outcomes than the simple presence of initiatives (Eaton, 2003). Perceived usability is an employee's perception of whether he or she is actually free to use existing formal or informal work-family flexibility without jeopardizing his or her career (Eaton, 2003). Additional research is required to understand the factors that contribute to the perceived usability of initiatives and the impact of this perception on individual and organizational outcomes.

As important as family supportive supervisors, practices, and cultures are, they do not relieve employees of the responsibility for taking direct action to enhance individual and family well-being. Research on personal strategies to manage the work-family interface, which has been limited to date (Frone, 2003), needs to be expanded. Several promising lines of research have found that work-family conflict can be reduced through the application of time management activities (Adams & Jex, 1999) and selection-optimization-compensation behaviors (Baltes & Heydens-Gahir, 2003), with perceived control over time mediating the effect of time management and job and family stressors mediating the effect of selection-optimization-compensation behaviors. In a similar vein, Behson (2002a) found that informally adjusting work patterns to accommodate family needs attenuated the relationship between FWC and work stress, was positively related to seeking social support, and was negatively related to emotion-focused coping. Continued research on the effect of proactive strategies on work-family conflict, stress, and well-being would be useful.

Extending the notion of work-family strategies to families, Moen and colleagues (Becker & Moen, 1999; Moen & Yu, 2000) have examined strategies that couples use to manage the work-family interface (Valcour, Bailyn, and Quiyada, Chapter 11). They found that many dual-earner couples scaled back their involvement in work or adopted a gendered "neotraditional" work arrangement in which women work reduced or regular hours at a "job" and men work longer hours in a "career." It is important to extend this research to identify the factors that influence couples to adopt a particular work-family strategy and to examine the impact of different strategies over time.

Finally, we suggest that research examine the impact of self-employment on the intersection of work and family lives. As noted earlier, most of the research to date has been conducted on organizational employees. Although studies of self-employment have emerged in recent years (Loscocco, 1997; Parasuraman et al., 1996), considerably more research is required to understand the extent to which self-employed individuals experience the work-family interface in similar or different ways than organizational employees. For example, Parasuraman and Simmers (2001) found that although self-employed individuals experience greater autonomy and flexibility at work than organizational employees, they also experience more work-family conflict perhaps due to their greater psychological involvement in work. Parasuraman and Simmers's (2001) discussion regarding the tradeoffs of business ownership can serve as a useful guide for future research on self-employment and the work-family interface.

CONCLUSION

It is widely recognized that work and family lives influence each other in numerous ways. Family experiences can restrict or enrich one's career, just as work experiences can restrict or enrich family life. Although there is less agreement regarding the role of gender in the work-family interface, we believe that gender may enter the work-family nexus in complex ways through its interaction with other variables.

Work and family environments have the capacity to trigger work-family conflict and promote work-family enrichment, although we do not necessarily understand the specific element of an environment that has a particular effect for a given group of individuals. Moreover, individual differences, especially in the form of dispositional variables, are increasingly recognized as having potent influences on conflict and enrichment. It is also likely that the effects of environmental and individual characteristics are best understood in the context of the culture in which they are embedded. We believe that future developments in theory and research will provide further insights on how individuals can derive substantial satisfaction and fulfillment from participation in multiple life roles.

REFERENCES

Adams, G. A., & Jex, S. M. (1999). Relationships between time management, control, work-family conflict, and strain. *Journal of Occupational Health Psychology, 4,* 72–77.

Adams, G. A., King, L. A., & King, D. W. (1996). Relationships of job and family involvement, family social support, and work-family conflict with job and life satisfaction. *Journal of Applied Psychology, 81,* 411–420.

Allen, T., Russell, J., & Rush, M. (1994). The effects of gender and leave of absence on attributions for high performance, perceived organizational commitment, and allocation of organizational rewards. *Sex Roles, 31,* 443–465.

Allen, T. D. (2001). Family-supportive work environments: The role of organizational perceptions. *Journal of Vocational Behavior, 58,* 414–435.

Almer, E. D., Cohen, J. R., & Single, L. E. (2003). Factors affecting the choice to participate in flexible work arrangements. *Auditing: A Journal of Practice and Theory, 22,* 1–23.

Anderson, S., Coffey, B. S., & Byerly, R. T. (2002). Formal organizational initiatives and informal workplace practices: Links to work-family conflict and job-related outcomes. *Journal of Management, 28,* 787–810.

Arthur, M. B., Inkson, K., & Pringle, J. K. (1999). *The new careers: Individual action and economic change.* London: Sage.

Arthur, M. M. (2003). Share price reactions to work-family human resource decisions: An institutional perspective. *Academy of Management Journal, 46,* 497–505.

Aryee, S. (1992). Antecedents and outcomes of work-family conflict among married professional women: Evidence from Singapore. *Human Relations, 45,* 813–837.

Aryee, S., Fields, D., & Luk, V. (1999). A cross-cultural test of a model of the work-family interface. *Journal of Management, 25,* 491–511.

Aryee, S., Luk, V., & Stone, R. (1998). Family-responsive variables and retention-relevant outcomes among employed parents. *Human Relations, 51,* 73–87.

Asher, L. J., & Lenhoff, D. R. (2001). Family and medical leave: Making time for family is everyone's business. *Future of Children, 11,* 114–121.

Ashforth, B. E., Kreiner, G. E., & Fugate, M. (2000). All in a day's work: Boundaries and micro role transitions. *Academy of Management Review, 25,* 472–491.

Bailyn, L. (1997). The impact of corporate culture on work-family integration. In S. Parasuraman & J. H. Greenhaus (Eds.), *Integrating work and family: Challenges and choices for a changing world* (pp. 209–219). Westport, CT: Quorum Books.

Baltes, B. B., Briggs, T. E., Huff, J. W., Wright, J. A., & Neuman, G. A. (1999). Flexible and compressed workweek schedules: A meta-analysis of their effects on work-related criteria. *Journal of Applied Psychology, 84,* 496–513.

Baltes, B. B., & Heydens-Gahir, H. A. (2003). Reduction of work-family conflict through the use of selection, optimization, and compensation behaviors. *Journal of Applied Psychology, 88,* 1005–1018.

Barham, E. J., Gottlieb, B. H., & Kelloway, E. K. (1998). Variables affecting managers' willingness to grant alternative work arrangements. *Journal of Social Psychology, 138,* 291–302.

Barling, J. (1986). Fathers' work experience, the father-child relationship and children's behaviour. *Journal of Occupational Behaviour, 7,* 61–66.

Barling, J., & Sorensen, D. (1997). Work and family: In search of a relevant research agenda. In C. L. Cooper & S. E. Jackson (Eds.), *Creating tomorrow's organizations* (pp. 157–169). New York: Wiley.

Barnett, R. C. (1998). Toward a review and reconceptualization of the work/family literature.

Genetic, Social, and General Psychology Monographs, 124, 125–182.

Barnett, R. C. (1999). A new work-life model for the twenty-first century. *Annals of the American Academy of Political and Social Science, 562,* 143–158.

Barnett, R. C., & Baruch, G. K. (1985). Women's involvement in multiple roles and psychological distress. *Journal of Personality and Social Psychology, 49,* 135–145.

Barnett, R. C., & Hyde, J. S. (2001). Women, men, work, and family. *American Psychologist, 56,* 781–796.

Baruch, G. K., & Barnett, R. C. (1986). Consequences of fathers' participation in family work: Parents' role strain and well-being. *Journal of Personality and Social Psychology, 51,* 983–992.

Batt, R., & Valcour, P. M. (2003). Human resource practices as predictors of work-family outcomes and employee turnover. *Industrial Relations, 42,* 189–220.

Becker, P. E., & Moen, P. (1999). Scaling back: Dual-earner couples' work-family strategies. *Journal of Marriage and the Family, 61,* 995–1007.

Behson, S. J. (2002a). Coping with family-to-work conflict: The role of informal work accommodations to family. *Journal of Occupational Health Psychology, 7,* 324–341.

Behson, S. J. (2002b). Which dominates? The relative importance of work-family organizational support and general organizational context on employee outcomes. *Journal of Vocational Behavior, 61,* 53–72.

Blair-Loy, M., & Wharton, A. S. (2002). Employees' use of work-family policies and the workplace social context. *Social Forces, 80,* 813–845.

Bohen, H. H., & Viveros-Long, A. (1981). *Balancing jobs and family life: Do flexible work schedules really help?* Philadelphia: Temple University Press.

Brewer, A. M. (2000). Work design for flexible work scheduling: Barriers and gender implications. *Gender, Work and Organization, 7,* 33–44.

Brockwood, K. J., Hammer, L. B., & Neal, M. B. (2003). *An examination of positive work-family spillover among dual-earner couples in the sandwiched generation.* Paper presented at the annual conference of the Society for Industrial and Organizational Psychology, Orlando, FL.

Bruck, C. S., & Allen, T. D. (2003). The relationship between Big Five personality traits, negative affectivity, type A behavior, and work-family conflict. *Journal of Vocational Behavior, 63,* 457–472.

Bruck, C. S., Allen, T. D., & Spector, P. E. (2002). The relation between work-family conflict and job satisfaction: A finer-grained analysis. *Journal of Vocational Behavior, 60,* 336–353.

Byron, K. (2004). *Antecedents of work-family conflict: A review and meta-analysis.* Paper presented at the 2004 annual meeting of the Society for Industrial and Organizational Psychology, Chicago, IL.

Carlson, D. S. (1999). Personality and role variables as predictors of three forms of work-family conflict. *Journal of Vocational Behavior, 55,* 236–253.

Carlson, D. S., & Kacmar, K. M. (2000). Work-family conflict in the organization: Do life role values make a difference? *Journal of Management, 26,* 1031–1054.

Carlson, D. S., Kacmar, K. M., Grzywacz, J. G., & Wayne, J. H. (2004, August). Measuring work-family facilitation: Development and validation of a multi-dimensional scale. In S. Foley (Chair), *The positive side of the work-family interface: Its meaning, measurement, and relationships with other concepts.* Symposium conducted at the 2004 annual meeting of the Academy of Management, New Orleans, LA.

Carlson, D. S., Kacmar, K. M., & Williams, L. J. (2000). Construction and initial validation of a multidimensional measure of work-family conflict. *Journal of Vocational Behavior, 56,* 249–276.

Chiu, W., & Ng, C. W. (1999). Women-friendly HRM and organizational commitment: A study among women and men of organizations in Hong Kong. *Journal of Occupational and Organizational Psychology, 72,* 485–502.

Christensen, K. E., & Staines, G. L. (1990). Flextime: A viable solution to work-family conflict? *Journal of Family Issues, 11,* 455–476.

Clark, S. C. (2001). Work cultures and work/family balance. *Journal of Vocational Behavior, 58,* 348–365.

Clark, S. C. (2002). Communicating across the work/home border. *Community, Work & Family, 5,* 23–48.

Cohen, A., & Kirchmeyer, C. (1995). A multidimensional approach to the relation between organizational commitment and nonwork participation. *Journal of Vocational Behavior, 46,* 189–202.

Crittenden, A. (2001). *The price of motherhood*. New York: Metropolitan Books.

Crouter, A. (1984a). Participative work as an influence on human development. *Journal of Applied Developmental Psychology, 5,* 71–90.

Crouter, A. (1984b). Spillover from family to work: The neglected side of the work-family interface. *Human Relations, 37,* 425–442.

Deven, F., & Moss, P. (2002). Leave arrangements for parents: Overview and future outlook. *Community, Work & Family, 5,* 237–255.

Eagle, B. W., Miles, E. W., & Icenogle, M. L. (1997). Interrole conflicts and the permeability of work and family domains: Are there gender differences? *Journal of Vocational Behavior, 50,* 168–184.

Eaton, S. C. (2003). If you can use them: Flexibility policies, organizational commitment and perceived performance. *Industrial Relations, 42,* 145–167.

Edwards, J. R., & Rothbard, N. P. (2000). Mechanisms linking work and family: Clarifying the relationship between work and family constructs. *Academy of Management Review, 25,* 178–199.

Etzion, D., & Bailyn, L. (1994). Patterns of adjustment to the career/family conflict of technologically trained women in the U.S. and Israel. *Journal of Applied Social Psychology, 24,* 1520–1549.

Friedman, S. D., & Greenhaus, J. H. (2000). *Work and family: Allies or enemies? What happens when business professionals confront life choices.* New York: Oxford University Press.

Frone, M. R. (2000). Work-family conflict and employee psychiatric disorders: The national comorbidity study. *Journal of Applied Psychology, 85,* 888–895.

Frone, M. R. (2003). Work-family balance. In J. C. Quick & L. E. Tetrick (Eds.), *Handbook of occupational health psychology* (pp. 143–162). Washington, DC: American Psychological Association.

Frone, M. R., Russell, M., & Barnes, G. M. (1996). Work-family conflict, gender, and health-related outcomes: A study of employed parents in two community samples. *Journal of Occupational Health Psychology, 1,* 57–69.

Frone, M. R., Russell, M., & Cooper, M. L. (1992a). Antecedents and outcomes of work-family conflict: Testing a model of the work-family interface. *Journal of Applied Psychology, 77,* 5–78.

Frone, M. R., Russell, M., & Cooper, M. L. (1992b). Prevalence of work-family conflict: Are work and family boundaries asymmetrically permeable? *Journal of Organizational Behavior, 13,* 723–729.

Frone, M. R., Russell, M., & Cooper, M. L. (1993). Relationship of work-family conflict, gender, and alcohol expectancies to alcohol use/abuse. *Journal of Organizational Behavior, 14,* 545–558.

Frone, M. R., & Yardley, J. K. (1996). Workplace family-supportive programmes: Predictors of employed parents' importance ratings. *Journal of Occupational and Organizational Psychology, 69,* 351–366.

Frone, M. R., Yardley, J. K., & Markel, K. S. (1997). Developing and testing an integrative model of the work-family interface. *Journal of Vocational Behavior, 50,* 145–167.

Fu, C. K., & Shaffer, M. A. (2001). The tug of work and family: Direct and indirect domain-specific determinants of work-family conflict. *Personnel Review, 30,* 502–522.

Galinsky, E., & Bond, J. T. (1996). Work and family: The experiences of mothers and fathers in the U.S. labor force. In C. Costello & B. K. Krimgold (Eds.), *The American woman, 1996–1997* (pp. 79–103). New York: Norton.

Glass, J., & Finley, A. (2002). Coverage and effectiveness of family-responsive workplace policies. *Human Resource Management Review, 12,* 313–337.

Grandey, A. A. (2001). Family friendly policies: Organizational justice perceptions of need-based allocations. In R. Cropanzano (Ed.), *Justice in the workplace: From theory to practice* (Vol. 2, pp. 145–173). Mahwah, NJ: Erlbaum.

Greenberger, E., & O'Neil, R. (1993). Spouse, parent, worker: Role commitments and role-related experiences in the construction of adults' well-being. *Developmental Psychology, 29,* 181–197.

Greenhaus, J. H. (2002). Career dynamics. In Borman, W., C., Ilgen, D. R., & Klimoski, R. J. (Eds.), *Comprehensive handbook of psychology, Vol. 12: Industrial and organizational psychology* (pp. 519–540). New York: Wiley.

Greenhaus, J. H. (2004). *Work and family as allies and enemies: Are there gender differences?* Paper presented at the 3rd annual invitational Journalism-Work/Family Conference, May 20, 2004, Boston, MA.

Greenhaus, J. H., Allen, T. D., & Foley, S. (2004, April). Work-family balance: Exploration of a concept. In B. L. Cordeiro & A. A. Grandey

(Chairs), *Holding multiple roles and using family policies: Benefits and costs.* Symposium conducted at the 2004 annual meeting of the Society for Industrial Organizational Psychology, Chicago, IL.

Greenhaus, J. H., & Beutell, N. J. (1985). Sources of conflict between work and family roles. *Academy of Management Review, 10,* 76–88.

Greenhaus, J. H., Collins, K. M., & Shaw, J. D. (2003). The relation between work-family balance and quality of life. *Journal of Vocational Behavior, 63,* 510–531.

Greenhaus, J. H., & Parasuraman, S. (1999). Research on work, family, and gender: Current status and future directions. In G. N. Powell (Ed.), *Handbook of gender and work* (pp. 391–412). Thousand Oaks, CA: Sage.

Greenhaus, J. H., Parasuraman, S., Granrose, C. S., Rabinowitz, S., & Beutell, N. J. (1989). Sources of work-family conflict among two-career couples. *Journal of Vocational Behavior, 34,* 133–153.

Greenhaus, J. H., & Powell, G. N. (2003). When work and family collide: Deciding between competing role demands. *Organizational Behavior and Human Decision Processes, 90,* 291–303.

Greenhaus, J. H., & Powell, G. N. (2006). When work and family are allies: A theory of work-family enrichment. *Academy of Management Review, 31,* 72–92.

Greenhaus, J. H., & Singh, R. (2004). Work-family relationships. In C. D. Spielberger (Ed.), *Encyclopedia of applied psychology* (pp. 687–698). San Diego, CA: Elsevier.

Grover, S. L., & Crooker, K. J. (1995). Who appreciates family-responsive human resource policies: The impact of family-friendly policies on the organizational attachment of parents and non-parents. *Personnel Psychology, 48,* 271–288.

Grzywacz, J. G. (2000). Work-family spillover and health during midlife: Is managing conflict everything? *American Journal of Health Promotion, 14,* 236–243.

Grzywacz, J. G. (2002). *Toward a theory of work-family facilitation.* Paper presented at the 2002 Persons, Processes, and Places: Research on Families, Workplaces and Communities Conference, San Francisco.

Grzywacz, J. G., Almeida, D. M., & McDonald, D. A. (2002). Work-family spillover and daily reports of work and family stress in the adult labor force. *Family Relations, 51,* 28–36.

Grzywacz, J. G., & Marks, N. F. (2000). Reconceptualizing the work-family interface: An ecological perspective on the correlates of positive and negative spillover between work and family. *Journal of Occupational Health Psychology, 5,* 111–126.

Gutek, B. A., Searle, S., & Klepa, L. (1991). Rational versus gender role explanations for work-family conflict. *Journal of Applied Psychology, 76,* 560–568.

Hall, D. T. (1989). Moving beyond the "mommy track:" An organization change approach. *Personnel, December,* 23–29.

Hall, D. T. (2002). *Careers in and out of organizations.* Thousand Oaks, CA: Sage.

Hammer, L. B., Cullen, J. C., Caubet, S., Johnson, J., Neal, M. B., & Sinclair, R. R. (2002). *The effects of work-family fit on depression: A longitudinal study.* Paper presented at the 17th annual meeting of the Society for Industrial Organizational Psychology, Toronto, Ontario.

Hanson, G. C., Colton, C. L., & Hammer, L. B. (2003). *Development and validation of a multidimensional scale of work-family positive spillover.* Paper presented at the 18th annual meeting of the Society for Industrial Organizational Psychology, Orlando, FL.

Hanson, G. C., Hammer, L. B., & Colton, C. L. (2004, August). Work-family positive spillover: Construct definition, measurement development, and validation. In S. Foley (Chair), *The positive side of the work-family interface: Its meaning, measurement, and relationships with other concepts.* Symposium conducted at the 2004 annual meeting of the Academy of Management, New Orleans, LA.

Hegtvedt, K. A., Clay-Warner, W. J., & Ferrigno, E. D. (2003). Factors affecting workers' resentment toward family-friendly policies. *Social Psychology Quarterly, 65,* 386–400.

Higgins, C. A., Duxbury, L. E., & Irving, R. H. (1992). Work-family conflict in the dual-career family. *Organizational Behavior and Human Decision Processes, 51,* 51–75.

Hill, E. J. (2005). Work-family facilitation and conflict, working fathers and mothers, work-family stressors and support. *Journal of Family Issues, 26,* 793–819.

Hofstede, G. (2001). *Culture's consequences: Comparing values, behaviors, institutions and organizations across nations.* Thousand Oaks, CA: Sage.

Ingram, P. L., & Simons, T. (1995). Institutional and resource dependence determinants of responsiveness to work family issues. *Academy of Management Journal, 38,* 1466–1482.

Izraeli, D. N. (1993). Work-family conflict among women and men managers in dual career couples in Israel. *Journal of Social Behavior and Personality, 8,* 371–388.

Jex, S. M., & Elacqua, T. C. (1999). Time management as a moderator of relations between stressors and employee strain. *Work & Stress, 13,* 182–191.

Joplin, J. R. W., Shaffer, M. A., Francesco, A. M., & Lau, T. (2003). The macro-environment and work-family conflict: Development of a cross cultural comparative framework. *International Journal of Cross Cultural Management, 3,* 305–328.

Kim, J. L. S., & Ling, C. S. (2001). Work-family conflict of women entrepreneurs in Singapore. *Women in Management Review, 16,* 204–221.

Kim, S. (1998). Organizational culture and New York State employees' work-family conflict: Gender differences in balancing work and family responsibilities. *Review of Public Personnel Administration, 18,* 57–72.

Kinnunen, U., & Mauno, S. (1998). Antecedents and outcomes of work-family conflict among employed women and men in Finland. *Human Relations, 51,* 157–177.

Kirchmeyer, C. (1992a). Nonwork participation and work attitudes: A test of scarcity vs. expansion models of personal resources. *Human Relations, 45,* 775–795.

Kirchmeyer, C. (1992b). Perceptions of nonwork-to-work spillover: Challenging the common view of conflict-ridden domain relationships. *Basic and Applied Social Psychology, 13,* 231–249.

Konrad, A. M., & Mangel, R. (2000). The impact of work-life programs on firm productivity. *Strategic Management Journal, 21,* 1225–1237.

Korabik, K., Lero, D. S., & Ayman, R. (2003). A multi-level approach to cross cultural work-family research: A micro and macro perspective. *International Journal of Cross Cultural Management, 3,* 289–303.

Kossek, E. E., Barber, A. E., & Winters, D. (1999). Using flexible schedules in the managerial world: The power of peers. *Human Resource Management, 38,* 33–46.

Kossek, E. E., Colquitt, J. A., & Noe, R. A. (2001). Caregiving decisions, well-being, and performance: The effects of place and provider as a function of dependent type and work-family climates. *Academy of Management Journal, 44,* 29–44.

Kossek, E. E., & Nichol, V. (1992). The effects of on-site child care on employee attitudes and performance. *Personnel Psychology, 45,* 485–509.

Kossek, E. E., & Ozeki, C. (1998). Work-family conflict, policies, and the job-life satisfaction relationship: A review and directions for organizational behavior-human resources research. *Journal of Applied Psychology, 83,* 139–149.

Lambert, S. J. (1990). Processes linking work and family: A critical review and research agenda. *Human Relations, 43,* 239–257.

Lewis, S. (1997). International perspectives on work and family. In S. Parasuraman & J. H. Greenhaus (Eds.), *Integrating work and family: Challenges and choices for a changing world.* Westport, CT: Quorum Books.

Lewis, S., Smithson, J., & Branner, J. (1999). Families in transition: Young Europeans' orientations to families and work. *Annals of the American Academy of Political and Social Science, 562,* 83–97.

Lin, K., & Rantalaiho, M. (2003). Family policy and social order: Comparing the dynamics of family policy-making in Scandinavia and Confucian Asia. *International Journal of Social Welfare, 12,* 2–13.

Ling, Y., & Powell, G. N. (2001). Work-family conflict in contemporary China: Beyond an American-based model. *International Journal of Cross Cultural Management, 1*(3), 357–373.

Lobel, S. A. (1999). Impacts of diversity and work-life initiatives in organizations. In G. N. Powell (Ed.), *Handbook of gender and work* (pp. 453–476). Thousand Oaks, CA: Sage.

Lobel, S. A., & Kossek, E. E. (1995). Human resource strategies to support diversity in work and personal lifestyles: Beyond the "family friendly" organization. In E. E. Kossek & S. A. Lobel (Eds.), *Managing diversity: Human resource strategies for transforming the workplace* (pp. 221–243). Cambridge, MA: Blackwell.

Loscocco, K. A. (1997). Work-family linkages among self-employed women and men. *Journal of Vocational Behavior, 50,* 204–226.

MacEwen, K. E., & Barling, J. (1988). Interrole conflict, family support and marital adjustment of employed mothers: A short term, longitudinal study. *Journal of Organizational Behavior, 9,* 241–250.

MacEwen, K. E., & Barling, J. (1994). Daily consequences of work interference with family and family interference with work. *Work & Stress, 8,* 244–254.

Marks, S. R. (1977). Multiple roles and role strain: Some notes on human energy, time and commitment. *American Sociological Review, 42,* 921–936.

Marks, S. R., & MacDermid, S. M. (1996). Multiple roles and the self: A theory of role balance. *Journal of Marriage and the Family, 58,* 417–432.

Matsui, T., Ohsawa, T., & Onglotco, M. (1995). Work-family conflict and the stress-buffering effects of husband support and coping behavior among Japanese married working women. *Journal of Vocational Behavior, 47,* 178–192.

Meyer, C., Mukerjee, S., & Sestero, A. (2001). Work-family benefits: Which ones maximize profits? *Journal of Managerial Issues, 13,* 28–44.

Moen, P., & Yu, Y. (2000). Effective work/life strategies: Working couples, work conditions, gender, and life quality. *Social Problems, 47,* 291–326.

Netemeyer, R. G., Boles, J. S., & McMurrian, R. (1996). Development and validation of work-family conflict and family-work conflict scales. *Journal of Applied Psychology, 81,* 400–410.

Ngo, H. Y., & Lau, C. M. (1988). Interference between work and family among male and female executives in Hong Kong. *Research and Practice in Human Resource Management, 6,* 17–34.

Nippert-Eng, C. E. (1995). *Home and work: Negotiating boundaries through everyday life.* Chicago: University of Chicago Press.

Parasuraman, S., & Greenhaus, J. H. (2002). Toward reducing some critical gaps in work-family research. *Human Resource Management Review, 12,* 299–312.

Parasuraman, S., Greenhaus, J. H., & Granrose, C. S. (1992). Role stressors, social support, and well-being among two-career couples. *Journal of Organizational Behavior, 13,* 339–356.

Parasuraman, S., Purohit, Y. S., Godshalk, V. M., & Beutell, N. J. (1996). Work and family variables, entrepreneurial career success, and psychological well-being. *Journal of Vocational Behavior, 48,* 275–300.

Parasuraman, S., & Simmers, C. A. (2001). Type of employment, work-family conflict and well-being: A comparative study. *Journal of Organizational Behavior, 22,* 551–568.

Parker, L. B., & Allen, T. D. (2001). Work/family benefits: Variables related to employees' fairness perceptions. *Journal of Vocational Behavior, 58,* 453–468.

Parker, L. B., & Allen, T. D. (2002). *Factors related to supervisor work/family sensitivity and flexibility.* Paper presented at the 17th annual meeting of the Society for Industrial Organizational Psychology, Toronto, Ontario.

Perry-Smith, J. E., & Blum, T. C. (2000). Work-family human resource bundles and perceived organizational performance. *Academy of Management Journal, 43,* 1107–1117.

Pleck, J. H. (1977). The work-family role system. *Social Problems, 24,* 417–427.

Poelmans, S. A. Y., Chinchilla, N., & Cardona, P. (2003). The adoption of family-friendly HRM policies: Competing for scarce resources in the labour market. *International Journal of Manpower, 24,* 128–147.

Poelmans, S., Spector, P. E., Cooper, C. L., Allen, T. D., O'Driscoll, M., Sanchez, J. I. (2003). A cross-national comparative study of work/family demands and resources. *International Journal of Cross Cultural Management, 3,* 275–288.

Powell, G. N. (1997). The sex difference in employee inclinations regarding work-family programs: Why does it exist, should we care, and what should be done about it (if anything)? In S. Parasuraman & J. H. Greenhaus (Eds.), *Integrating work and family: Challenges and choices for a changing world* (pp. 167–174). Westport, CT: Quorum Books.

Powell, G. N., & Greenhaus, J. H. (2006). Is the opposite of positive negative? Conceptualizing the relationship between work-family enrichment and work-family conflict. *Career Development International, 11,* 650–659.

Powell, G. N., & Mainiero, L. A. (1999). Managerial decision making regarding alternative work arrangements. *Journal of Occupational and Organizational Psychology, 72,* 41–56.

Rau, B. L., & Hyland, M. A. (2002). Role conflict and flexible work arrangements: The effects on applicant attraction. *Personnel Psychology, 55,* 111–136.

Rayman, P. (1998). *The Radcliffe Fleet work/life integration project.* Cambridge, UK: Radcliffe Public Policy Institute.

Repetti, R. L. (1987). Linkages between work and family roles. In S. Oskamp (Ed.), *Family processes and problems: Social psychological aspects* (pp. 98–127). Newbury Park, CA: Sage.

Rice, R. W., Frone, M. R., & McFarlin, D. B. (1992). Work-nonwork conflict and the perceived quality of life. *Journal of Organizational Behavior, 13,* 155–168.

Roehling, P. V., Roehling, M. V., & Moen, P. (2001). The relationship between work-life policies and practices and employee loyalty: A life course perspective. *Journal of Family and Economic Issues, 21,* 141–171.

Rothausen, T. J., Gonzalez, J. A., Clarke, M. E., & O'Dell, L. L. (1998). Family-friendly backlash-fact or fiction? The justice of organizations' on-site childcare centers. *Personnel Psychology, 51,* 685–706.

Rothbard, N. P. (2001). Enriching or depleting? The dynamics of engagement in work and family roles. *Administrative Science Quarterly, 46,* 655–684.

Ruderman, M. N., Ohlott, P. J., Panzer, K., & King, S. N. (2002). Benefits of multiple roles for managerial women. *Academy of Management Journal, 45,* 369–386.

Scandura, T. A., & Lankau, M. J. (1997). Relationships of gender, family responsibility and flexible work hours to organizational commitment and job satisfaction. *Journal of Organizational Behavior, 18,* 377–391.

Shellenbarger, S. (1991, November 15). More job seekers put family needs first. *The Wall Street Journal,* pp. B1, B12.

Sieber, S. D. (1974). Toward a theory of role accumulation. *American Sociological Review, 39,* 567–578.

Spector, P. E., Cooper, C. L., Poelmans, S., Allen, T. D., O'Driscoll, M., Sanchez, J. I., et al. (2004). A cross-national comparative study of work/family stressors, working hours, and well-being: China and Latin America vs. the Anglo world. *Personnel Psychology, 57,* 119–142.

Stephens, G. K., & Sommer, S. M. (1993). *Work-family conflict, job attitudes, and workplace social support: Investigations of measurement and moderation.* Paper presented at the annual meeting of the Academy of Management, Atlanta, GA.

Stephens, M. A. P., Franks, M. M., & Atienza, A. A. (1997). Where two roles intersect: Spillover between parent care and employment. *Psychology and Aging, 12,* 30–37.

Stewart, W., & Barling, J. (1996). Fathers' work experiences effect children's behaviors via job-related affect and parenting behaviors. *Journal of Organizational Behavior, 17,* 221–232.

Stoeva, A. Z., Chiu, R. K., & Greenhaus, J. H. (2002). Negative affectivity, role stress, and work-family conflict. *Journal of Vocational Behavior, 60,* 1–16.

Stroh, L. K., & Reilly, A. H. (1999). Gender and careers: Present experiences and emerging trends. In G. N. Powell (Ed.), *Handbook of gender and work* (pp. 307–324). Thousand Oaks, CA: Sage.

Suchet, M., & Barling, J. (1986). Interrole conflict, spouse support and marital functioning. *Journal of Occupational Behaviour, 7,* 167–178.

Sumer, H. C., & Knight, P. A. (2001). How do people with different attachment styles balance work and family? A personality perspective on work-family linkage. *Journal of Applied Psychology, 86,* 653–663.

Tharenou, P. (1999). Is there a link between family structures and women's and men's managerial advancement? *Journal of Organizational Behavior, 20,* 837–863.

Thomas, L. T., & Ganster, D. C. (1995). Impact of family-supportive work variables on work-family conflict and strain: A control perspective. *Journal of Applied Psychology, 80,* 6–15.

Thompson, C. A., Beauvais, L. L., & Lyness, K. S. (1999). When work-family benefits are not enough. *Journal of Vocational Behavior, 54,* 392–415.

Tiedje, L. B., Wortman, C. B., Downey, G., Emmons, C., Biernat, M., & Lang, R. (1990). Women with multiple roles: Role-compatibility perceptions, satisfaction, and mental health. *Journal of Marriage and the Family, 52,* 63–72.

Tompson, H. B., & Werner, J. M. (1997). The impact of role conflict/facilitation on core and discretionary behaviors: Testing a mediated model. *Journal of Management, 23,* 583–601.

Triandis, H. C. (1995). *Individualism and collectivism.* Boulder, CO: Westview Press.

Universum Intituted. (1998). *American graduate survey 1988.* Stockholm: Author.

Voydanoff, P. (2001). Incorporating community into work and family research: A review of basic relationships. *Human Relations, 54,* 1609–1637.

Voydanoff, P. (2004). The effects of work demands and resources on work-to-family conflict and facilitation. *Journal of Marriage and Family, 66,* 398–412.

Wayne, J. H., Musisca, N., & Fleeson, W. (2004). Considering the role of personality in the work-family experience: Relationships of the Big Five to work-family conflict and facilitation. *Journal of Vocational Behavior, 64,* 108–130.

Wiese, B. S., Freund, A. M., & Baltes, P. B. (2002). Subjective career success and emotional well-being: Longitudinal predictive power of selection, optimization, and compensation. *Journal of Vocational Behavior, 60,* 321–335.

Yang, N., Chen, C. C., Choi, J., & Zou, Y. (2000). Sources of work-family conflict: A Sino-U.S. comparison of the effects of work and family demands. *Academy of Management Journal, 43,* 113–123.

Yi, C. C., & Chien, W. Y. (2002). The linkage between work and family: Females' employment patterns in three Chinese societies. *Journal of Comparative Family Studies, 33,* 451–474.

9

LATE-CAREER AND RETIREMENT ISSUES

DANIEL C. FELDMAN

A confluence of factors has led to the recent emergence of late-career issues as an important focus of careers research. First and foremost, people are living longer today, with the average life expectancy around 80 years. With longer life spans, many people are staying in the workforce longer or even starting new careers after their "regular" careers come to an end. Second, in several large industrialized countries (such as the United States, Canada, and Australia), the aging of the Baby Boom generation has significantly skewed the mean age of the workforce upward. For instance, the Baby Boomers (considered the generation born between 1945 and 1964) are now the largest age group in the U.S. workforce, and the oldest "boomers" are now in their 60s. Third, age discrimination in hiring, promotion, and termination has become a prominent policy issue in many countries, whether in the form of legislation (e.g., the U.S. Age Discrimination in Employment Act) or not. Finally, changes in governmental pension eligibility requirements as well as rapid increases in health care costs have forced some older employees to stay in the workforce longer simply out of financial necessity (Beehr, Glazer, Nielson, & Farmer, 2000; Feldman, 2003).

Age and career stage are not perfectly synchronous (Sullivan and Crocitto, Chapter 15). There are workers over 50 who are going to graduate school to start new careers, and there are people in their late 40s who are retiring after 30 years of service. Following Greller and Simpson (1999), then, the general boundaries of this chapter are careers issues that typically affect individuals who are over 50 years of age or who have been in the workforce 30 years or longer. As required, we will draw distinctions between career dynamics that are driven by age and those that are driven by extensive years of work experience.

This chapter is organized into four sections. In the first section, we explore the research on the work-related attitudes and job performance of this population and tie together the myriad studies on the feelings and behaviors of late-career employees. Next, we review several of the most frequently discussed phenomena in late career, such as succession into top management, career plateaus, demotions, and downsizing. Then, we examine the broad array of issues relating to retirement, including the decision to retire, bridge employment, and satisfaction with retirement. Finally, we conclude with a discussion of how both older workers and organizations can respond more effectively to the challenges associated with this phase of career development.

WORK-RELATED ATTITUDES AND JOB PERFORMANCE

The job attitudes and job performance of older workers and late-career employees have been studied in a wide variety of organizational settings. However, it is also the case that the age ranges and career-stage boundaries of the samples in these studies have varied widely, as have their job duties and job demands. Below, we highlight the key findings from gerontologists, economists, and organizational behavior and careers scholars on this topic.

Job Attitudes

In terms of job attitudes, the research suggests that both older workers and late-career employees have more positive attitudes toward their jobs (e.g., job satisfaction and job involvement). One explanation for this finding is that late-career workers have more realistic expectations of their jobs than do their younger, less experienced peers. As a result, they experience a smaller discrepancy between what they hope to get from their jobs (both in terms of tangible rewards and intrinsic satisfaction) and what they actually receive from them. They are old enough to have gotten over the "entry shock" of the world of work and senior enough to be less troubled by minor psychological contract violations (Hall & Mirvis, 1995; Lawrence, 1987; Meyer & Allen, 1997).

Another potential explanation of these results is that late-career employees and older workers have jobs that pay more and provide more exciting work duties. Often, as a consequence of increased seniority, older workers accrue jobs that provide greater job security and pay higher fringe benefits (e.g., pension benefits, vacation, and sick leave), particularly since many organizations distribute such benefits on the basis of years of service. Using this rationale, then, older workers are more satisfied with their jobs than younger employees not because of the aging process per se but because older workers have fundamentally more rewarding work situations than their younger colleagues (Arkes & Blumer, 1985; Levinson, 1986; Schwoerer & May, 1996).

Whether late-career employees are happier with their *careers* (as opposed to their *jobs*) is less clear. Certainly, consistent with the logic described above, there are multiple reasons why senior people would have more positive attitudes toward their careers than their younger, less experienced colleagues. Being a partner of a major law firm or accounting firm is typically a more satisfying experience, both in terms of salary and hours worked, than being an associate. In addition, cognitive dissonance may play an important role in the higher career satisfaction of later-career employees. Individuals who have worked 30 years in one career may have internal pressure to self-justify their professional investments as more worthwhile than early-career individuals do.

Nonetheless, there is at least some indirect evidence that satisfaction with one's career tapers off in late career. For example, when older people retire and then come back into the workforce in some type of "bridge employment" (Doeringer, 1990; Feldman & Kim, 2000; Kim & Feldman, 1998, 2000), more than 25% choose a new occupation altogether. What might account for this drop-off in enthusiasm about a particular vocation?

Part of the explanation may rest with the issue of burnout; after 30 years in a vocation, individuals may experience boredom and lack of emotional involvement in their daily activities and psychologically distance themselves from their occupations (Halbesleben & Buckley, 2004). Another potential explanation is that older workers may start devaluing their careers as a means of adjusting to retirement. As workers become more aware of impending retirement, they may start devaluing their vocations to reduce the amount of cognitive dissonance they might experience when they leave them—that is, "I'm not leaving such a great career after all." Third, career paths can change dramatically over the course of a 30-year period, and individuals may look backward and find the changes in their career paths unappealing. For instance, some doctors in their 50s may lose their earlier enthusiasm for medicine because they feel hampered by insurance bureaucracies, health maintenance organizations, and litigation. In retrospect, their (remembered) experiences of their careers when they first entered them are more positive than the careers they experience today (Schacter, 2001).

Perceived Discrimination

A particularly important job attitude to consider here is perceived age discrimination. In trying to explain this phenomenon, Lawrence (1988) draws a distinction between "normative age" and "chronological age." Her research suggests that it is not only chronological age that can create bias but also an individual's age *relative to the expectations of others.* Thus, Lawrence (1988) reports that even within a cohort of individuals at the same chronological age, some can be described as being ahead of schedule, on track, or falling behind, and presumably it is this last group that is most vulnerable to age discrimination.

Along similar lines, the research of organizational demographers (Lawrence and Tolbert, Chapter 20) suggests that the more discrepant an individual's age is with the dominant coalition in a group, the more likely she or he is to be discriminated against. Thus, late-career individuals working primarily with other older employees are less likely to be subjected to bias than late-career individuals working primarily with younger employees (McCain, O'Reilly, & Pfeffer, 1983).

Another job-related attitude that frequently declines with age is organizationally based self-esteem (Pierce & Gardner, 2004). Among the reasons that organizationally based self-esteem may decline later in life are: (1) the increased frequency of negative comments from coworkers and supervisors about the value of older workers (Barnes-Farrell, 2003), and (2) the increased frustration with performance appraisals from supervisors, whose subjective evaluations of older workers tend to be harsher than objective performance indicators might suggest (Rhodes, 1983).

Withdrawal Behavior

In light of the evidence presented above, it is not surprising that older workers, as a group, have lower levels of absenteeism than their younger colleagues (Beehr & Bowling, 2002). While negative stereotypes of older workers suggest that they would have more illnesses that require absences from work, the data indicate that older workers are, in fact, less likely to take days off. One explanation for this finding is that older workers, because they are more highly paid and may have more responsible jobs, are less likely to take days off except when absolutely necessary. Another explanation is that younger workers, particularly those with school-age children, are more susceptible to getting colds and more likely to miss work in order to care for sick children. There is yet another potential explanation for this relationship: namely, that older workers with significant health problems are more likely to exit the workforce altogether via retirement. Consequently, older workers with the worst health problems are less likely to be included in studies of age differences in absenteeism because they are no longer even in the labor market.

Similarly, previous research has found that older workers have lower levels of voluntary turnover (Rhodes, 1983; Warr, 1994). Again, because late-career workers may be more likely to have jobs that pay well and have higher levels of job responsibility, they may be less likely to seek out alternative employment. In addition, many firms distribute benefits such as pension contributions and vacation days on the basis of organizational tenure, further enhancing the financial inducements to stay. Furthermore, many older workers fear age discrimination in the labor market and worry that they wouldn't be able to get good replacement jobs if they quit their current employment. Thus, late-career employees often have fewer "push" factors to get them to leave their present employers and fewer "pull" factors that impel them to enter the open job market.

Job Performance

The topic of job performance of older workers has been attacked from two different perspectives. The first examines whether late-career employees are more likely to receive lower "subjective" performance appraisal ratings from supervisors than their younger colleagues. The second examines whether the "objective" skills of older workers tend to decay over time; here, the research has traditionally examined the degree of decline in "cognitive" skills (such as memory) and "physical" skills (such as gross strength or fine motor control) over time. We discuss each of these issues in more detail below.

Subjective Performance Ratings

In 1983, Rhodes conducted a review of studies that looked at the relationship between age and job performance. She found that there were approximately equal numbers of studies reporting that job performance increases with age, decreases with age, and remains the same. She suggested that the relationship between age and job performance may very well depend on other factors, such as the type of work late-career employees perform and the reliability of performance appraisal instruments. Reexamining the Rhodes findings using statistical meta-analysis, Waldman and Avolio (1986) discovered some interesting patterns of results. When employees are evaluated on objective indices of productivity, older workers actually significantly *outperform* younger workers. However, when older workers are evaluated by supervisors with global rating scales, they receive significantly *lower* evaluations than younger workers.

Thus, rater bias and age discrimination, rather than older workers' productivity levels themselves, seem to account for the widespread belief that job performance declines with age. Older workers whose jobs are primarily managerial in nature, whose job outcomes tend to be less tangible, and whose job duties tend to be less visible may be particularly vulnerable to this kind of age discrimination. In such cases, superiors have more latitude to discriminate against older workers in their evaluations because there are fewer objective, observable data with which to refute superiors' assertions (Feldman, 1988; Perry, Kulik, & Bourhis, 1996; Ryan & Bartlett-Weikel, 1993).

Labor economists such as Lazear (1983) use an "implicit contract model" to explain another potential reason for age bias in subjective performance ratings. Lazear observes that younger workers are paid below their marginal rate of productivity, while older workers are often paid above their marginal productivity. Labor economists hypothesize that this compensation practice evolved to motivate younger workers to put more effort into their jobs and be more loyal organizational citizens with the hope that they, too, would be able to "cash" in when they get older (Hutchens, 1986; Kotlikoff, 1988). However, when faced with the reality of paying older workers wages that are above their marginal productivity, managers want to "change the deal" in order to cut costs (Rousseau, 1995).

In more recent work on the political nature of performance appraisals (see Levy & Williams, 2004; Longenecker, Sims, & Gioia, 1987), several other potential explanations for this divergence in ratings become evident. First, supervisors may be giving late-career employees lower evaluations to give young employees higher pay raises. Thus, the primary motivation for giving late-career employees lower evaluations may not necessarily be discrimination but rather to justify distributing scarce pay raise dollars to younger workers who might otherwise leave the firm. Alternatively, supervisors of late-career employees may give low evaluations to older workers to block potential rivals from being promoted over them or from being promoted into their own jobs.

Objective Performance Indicators

According to Greller and Simpson (1999), there are two ways in which aging can negatively affect the information-processing capabilities of older workers. First, there is some evidence that older workers process new information less speedily than their younger colleagues and, consequently, can't make decisions as quickly (Salthouse, 1996). Second, there is some evidence that older workers have smaller "working memories" than younger people (Just & Carpenter, 1992; Park et al., 1996). That is, older workers cannot keep track of as many variables at the same time and, consequently, have more trouble making complex decisions under time pressure.

While these age-related effects have been found quite consistently, the magnitude and consequences of these deficits may not be as severe as widely believed. Many of the experimental tasks used in these kinds of studies have been rote memory tasks (e.g., recalling paired-word associations). While memorizing rote lists is a common task for younger people, it is a much less frequent activity for older workers, and it may not be the most appropriate way to test their working memories (Schimamura et al., 1995). When the new knowledge to be acquired is linked to existing knowledge, age differences in memory are quite small and frequently inconsequential (Kirasia et al., 1996; Lincourt, Rybash, & Hoyer, 1998).

In terms of physical skills, the literature on gerontology suggests that older workers do experience declines in gross motor strength, fine motor control, visual acuity, and auditory acuity (Greller & Simpson, 1999). However, for most older workers, declines in these capabilities are quite modest (Avolio & Waldman, 1994) and occur after age 70, when most older workers have already left the workforce (Beehr & Bowling, 2002).

What is much harder to get a handle on is how less visible deficits in physical well-being (such as arthritis, diabetes, high blood pressure, chronic pain) affect job performance. Certainly, these physical conditions are both more common and more likely to be severe in older workers, but tightly controlled studies measuring their impact on performance are rare. Research from the retirement literature, though, does suggest that workers with severe health problems are more likely to retire "early" (before reaching 30 years of service), so the main effect of poor physical health may be on workforce exit rather than on workforce performance (Kim & Feldman, 1998).

Another issue that comes into play here is the objective performance criteria on which older workers are being evaluated. The research of Czaja and Sharit (1998), Rao and Rao (1997), and Schwoerer and May (1996) suggests that age-based differences in performance are attenuated when quality is taken into consideration as an outcome variable. Taken collectively, their results indicate that older workers have a propensity to pursue quality in performance tasks and may be more willing to sacrifice quantity to achieve that goal. There is little evidence to date on the relationship between age and extra-role or citizenship behavior (Borman & Motowidlo, 1993), and what evidence does exist

suggests a nonsignificant age effect (Schappe, 1998; Williams & Schiaw, 1999).

In sum, then, the global relationship between age and performance is quite modest in magnitude. Moreover, it is highly dependent on which tasks are being performed, how performance is measured, and who measures it (McEvoy & Cascio, 1989; Warr, 1994).

ASCENDING, PLATEAUING, AND DECLINING CAREER PATHS

While there are numerous career challenges facing older workers, three have received the most attention from researchers. The first is upward career moves, in particular the ability of older workers to move up into senior management and CEO positions. The second is career plateaus, or the leveling off of promotions. This literature explores the causes of older workers being unable to get promoted into positions of greater responsibility and the outcomes of career plateaus for organizations and older workers themselves. The third focus is downward career moves (demotions and downsizing), the advisability of their usage, and the consequences of these staffing decisions. We discuss each of these topics in more detail below.

Executive Succession

Recent research on individual differences in the career patterns of people who successfully reach senior management has primarily focused on demographic variables, management styles, and personality attributes (Judge and Kammeyer-Mueller, Chapter 4) rather than on age per se (McCall & Lombardo, 1983; Peterson, Smith, Martorana, & Owens, 2003; Schneider, Goldstein, & Smith, 1995). One notable exception to this is the sizeable literature on the perceived discrimination that older women and older minorities face in terms of executive succession and their underrepresentation in senior management positions (Judy & D'Amico, 1997; Werner, 2002). Another exception is the research that suggests that older workers accumulate valuable human capital from years (and diversity) of experience (Greller & Simpson, 1999) even if, as noted above, some kinds of intellectual tasks (e.g., memory) become more difficult over time (Greller & Stroh, 2003).

As Beehr and Bowling (2002) note, several researchers have confused the characteristics that cause a person to emerge as a senior executive with the characteristics that make an older worker an effective leader. Some notable exceptions to this trend are Lord, DeVader, and Alliger (1986) and Atwater, Dionne, Avolio, Camobreco, and Lau (1999). Their research suggests that individuals who are more intelligent (have higher cognitive ability), have higher self-esteem, and are more dominant are more likely to emerge as leaders. However, by and large, these traits do not typically change over time and do not typically affect the performance of older workers in senior leadership positions.

Sonnenfeld and Peiperl (1988) investigated the role that career systems (Slay and Taylor, Chapter 19) play in determining whether individuals make it into top management. They suggest that career systems can be arrayed along two dimensions: assignment flow (whether promotion decisions are based on individual performance or the individual's contribution to group performance) and supply flow (whether firms prefer to fill non-entry-level positions with insiders or outsiders). Beehr and Bowling (2002) argue that the supply flow dimension is more strongly related to whether older workers thrive in an organization. In general, they suggest that older managers are more likely to benefit from a promote-from-within policy.

Using more of an organizational demography approach, Pfeffer and his colleagues (Pfeffer, 1982; Pfeffer & Leblebici, 1973; Salancik & Pfeffer, 1974; Wagner, Pfeffer, & O'Reilly, 1984) found that the age and years-of-service distributions of the top executive team have a strong influence on who gets promoted. In organizations where the top executive team has served together a long time, there is a much greater tendency to promote from within. Moreover, they argue that it is not necessarily age per se but rather age relative to other executives that determines ascension into senior management positions (Williams & O'Reilly, 1998).

What is needed next is cross-level research that integrates both the individual- and the organizational-level approaches to investigating the role of age in executive succession (Gunz &

Jalland, 1996). An interesting example of such research is Zajac and Westphal's (1996) article, "Who Shall Succeed? How CEO/Board Preferences and Power Affect the Choice of New CEOs." Using a large longitudinal data set, the authors show that powerful boards of directors are likely to change CEO characteristics to mirror their own demographic profile.

Career Plateaus

While the research on executive succession has taken as its focal point the advancement of older workers into senior management positions, the research on career plateaus has examined the converse question—namely, why are older workers unable to obtain promotions or positions of increasing responsibility? The term *career plateau* was first popularized in the 1970s by Ference, Stoner, and Warren (1977), who conceptualized plateaued managers as those who were unable to advance further up the organizational hierarchy.

Subsequently, Feldman and Weitz (1988) conceptualized the career plateau as the point from which employees are unable to take up or unlikely to be given positions of increased responsibility. They noted that since organizations were continuously eliminating levels of management, operationalizing career plateaus as lack of promotions might lead to erroneous conclusions about the success of executives' career paths. In addition, the 1970s research on career plateaus implicitly or explicitly equated plateaued performance with poor performance. In contrast, Feldman and Weitz (1988) illustrated that some employees who have low needs for career mobility, for instance, are not necessarily poor performers or unhappy in their jobs. They may be simply reordering career aspirations around family needs instead (Judiesch & Lyness, 1999; Schneer & Reitman, 1997).

Over the past 10 years, research on career plateaus has shifted focus to examine how plateaued managers can be helped to be productive and positive contributors to their employing organizations (e.g., Bejian & Salomone, 1995; Hall & Mirvis, 1995). For instance, these authors highlight the need for more comprehensive feedback, greater inclusion of plateaued performers in training programs, the use of challenging project assignments as alternatives to promotions to maintain employee involvement, more lateral and cross-functional moves, and the destigmatization of career paths marked by slow career advancement. What all these approaches have in common is the creation of challenging work assignments in the absence of formal promotions.

Another stream of articles has examined some of the methodological issues involved in studying career plateaus (see Chao, 1990; Stephens, 1994). This research suggests that subjective measures of career plateaus are more significantly and negatively related to work attitudes and behaviors than objective measures are. Nicholson and West (1988) suggest that plateaus should be thought of as deviations from normative expectations about how long individuals should stay in their jobs and how long it should take them to get promoted.

Compared with executive succession, career plateaus have not received as much attention over the past 10 years. However, as organizations' efforts to eliminate levels of management continue and these efforts have a disproportionate effect on older workers in middle-management positions, a resurgence of interest in career plateaus is warranted.

Demotions

Demotions refer to the (typically involuntary) transfer of an employee to a position of lower authority and responsibility (Feldman, 1988). Research on the demotions of older workers has been scarce (for an exception, see Goldner, 1965). In large part, this is due to the fact that demotions are relatively uncommon in English-speaking countries, where it is much more likely that poor-performing older workers will be given early-retirement incentives (ERIs) instead.

Until 1990, most of the research on demotions examined the causes of demotion decisions and whether demotions, despite their negative connotations, could in fact result in positive consequences for workers. Research in the first stream, for instance, looked at the use of demotions to free up advancement opportunities for younger employees (Hall & Isabella, 1985) and to avoid the interpersonal discomfort associated with firing for cause. Examples of the second research stream are Cascio's (1986) work on

Denmark's positive experiences with demotions and Bailyn and Lynch's (1983) examination of the skill-building opportunities that could be made available to employees even within the context of demotions.

Perhaps as a sign of the times, most of the current literature on demotions is devoted to the legal issues surrounding demotions, particularly employers' liabilities for wrongful personnel actions. For instance, Flynn (1996) has explored the ramifications of court decisions for "wrongful demotion" on human resource practices, using *Scott v. Pacific Gas & Electric Company* (California Supreme Court) as its starting point. Similarly, Clark (2003) has written knowledgeably about "constructive demotion" and how it is viewed in the context of adverse action lawsuits under the U.S. Age Discrimination in Employment Act.

Downsizing and Job Loss

While research on career plateaus and demotions has declined over the past 10 years, research on the experiences of older workers who have lost their jobs as a result of downsizing has emerged as a major interest of late-career scholars (Leana & Feldman, 1992). In many ways, the experiences of laid-off older workers are similar to those of their younger colleagues. That is, they typically experience some feelings of depression, anxiety, irritability, and hopelessness. For workers of all ages, layoffs represent not only a loss of income but also the loss of valued work activities, valued friendships, and a coherent structure to the day. Two aspects of the downsizing phenomenon, however, have received particular attention from late-career researchers—namely, vulnerability to layoffs and success in finding satisfactory reemployment.

In general, workers with high seniority tend to be less vulnerable to losing their jobs during downsizing than workers with low organizational tenure, particularly in the case of the blue-collar workforce (Chan & Stevens, 2001; Mazerolle & Singh, 1999). In part, this can be attributed to efforts to avoid litigation surrounding claims of wrongful discharge and age discrimination. Many organizations lack reliable and valid performance appraisal systems that could withstand careful scrutiny from judges and juries. Not wanting to justify their downsizing decisions on such a slender reed, many organizations resort to years of service as an alternative criterion. Organizations can legitimately use years of service as a criterion for downsizing employees, and firms wishing to avoid litigation often do so, thereby granting older workers greater protection from job loss.

The situation is largely opposite in the case of "exempt" white-collar managers. With the push to eliminate whole levels of management to save money, organizations have been disproportionately eliminating middle- and upper-middle-level management positions during downsizing, especially when managers cannot demonstrate direct, tangible value added from their jobs (Addison & Portugal, 1989; Kletzer, 1989). Not surprisingly, the impact of such management thinking negatively affects older workers, who hold the majority of such positions.

Whether they are blue-collar or white-collar workers, though, the evidence is fairly strong that older workers have a more difficult time finding reemployment (Kuhn & Sweetman, 1999). As noted earlier, many supervisors have negative stereotypes of older workers anyway, and hiring older workers who have been let go by another firm is an even less appetizing proposition for them. In some cases, layoffs of older workers occur in industries (such as auto manufacturing) in which employment has been declining nationwide or has been outsourced to other countries, thereby limiting the number of similar jobs available to displaced workers. In still other cases, older workers are so embedded in their communities (by virtue of their home ownership, their family responsibilities for parents, or their spouses' jobs) that geographical relocation to obtain new employment is seen as an unacceptable option (Leana & Feldman, 1992).

Equally troubling, older workers also seem to be more vulnerable to becoming underemployed in their replacement jobs—and for many of the same reasons that make it harder for older workers to get new jobs at all (Feldman, 1996; Turnley & Feldman, 1998). That is, even when older workers get reemployed, they often have to take positions that pay significantly less money than their last jobs paid, that provide substantially poorer benefits, or that entail far less challenging or less responsible job duties. Furthermore, many of the outplacement services that are routinely provided to younger workers (such as assistance in resume writing, interview training, and networking seminars) are too generic in nature to be very helpful to older workers with highly idiosyncratic personal-life and career-stage demands.

Some recent research by Feldman, Leana, and Bolino (2002), though, suggests that individual career-counseling sessions are especially instrumental in sustaining older workers' energy for job hunting and in identifying the most appropriate replacement jobs for them. In addition, recent work on coping strategies of displaced workers suggests that problem-focused coping strategies (such as getting retraining and relocating geographically) are much more helpful in avoiding underemployment than symptom-focused coping strategies (such as seeking out social support from friends, repressing thoughts about the job loss, and increased eating and smoking).

Retirement Issues

The literature on retirement has addressed four questions in substantial detail. First, what factors enter into the decision to retire? Second, when will individuals be most likely to accept organizations' offers of ERIs? Third, when will individuals accept some type of "bridge employment" between leaving their long-term career paths and completely withdrawing from the workforce? Fourth, and finally, what factors determine how well individuals will adjust to retirement and life without work? We consider each of these questions below in more detail.

Before doing so, though, it is important to note that there is wide variance across countries regarding legislation pertaining to retirement. In some countries and in some occupations (e.g., the military and pilots), there are mandatory retirement ages. In other countries (e.g., the United States) and occupations, the retirement age is not mandatory. Here, we will focus most on retirement decisions that take place under *voluntary* conditions.

The Decision to Retire

In general, it appears that the decision to retire is made in two stages. First, workers examine the feasibility of retirement from a financial standpoint: the amount of their monthly pension benefits, the size of their accumulated savings, the income or pension flow expected from a spouse, educated guesses about future rates of inflation and taxation on unearned income, and estimates of ordinary (and extraordinary) expenses in the years ahead (Kim & Feldman, 1998). The smaller the difference in monthly income between working and retirement, the more likely individuals are to exit the workforce.

Then, having established that retirement is financially feasible, individuals assess whether the quality of their current lives would be enhanced or worsened by exit from the workforce. Factors that are frequently considered here are satisfaction with the current job, a strong work ethic, concerns about time hanging heavy on their hands, health concerns, level of involvement in hobbies or outside interests, and spouses' employment status (Barnes-Farrell, 2003). The first three factors (job satisfaction, strong work ethic, and concerns about lack of activity) predispose older workers to remain on their jobs, while the second three factors (poor health, heavy involvement in outside interests, and a spouse who doesn't work or is retired) predispose older workers to take retirement. The results on the effects of (positive) financial well-being and (poor) physical health are particularly strong and consistent across studies (Harpaz, 2002; Talaga & Beehr, 1995).

Early Retirement

The term *early retirement* refers to exit from a long-term job or career path before 65 years of age or before 30 years of service (Feldman, 1994). The same factors discussed above, albeit in a more pronounced fashion, also influence the decision to retire early. For instance, a large inheritance or a sharp decline in physical health may hasten an early retirement decision.

Early retirement can also occur in response to special organizational financial incentives (such as lump-sum payments, increased pension benefits, or extended health care benefits). Such incentives are designed to increase older workers' streams of retirement income and thereby decrease their resistance to leaving the workforce for fear of lack of sufficient income. The use of ERIs is most common in organizations with defined benefit plans. These defined benefit plans guarantee workers an annual pension, generally calculated on the basis of salary and years of service, with penalties for retiring early (before 65 years of age or before 30 years of service). There are several consistent findings in the literature about the effectiveness of ERIs in inducing older workers to retire early.

First, lump-sum bonuses (e.g., one week's extra pay for each year of service) are relatively ineffective in persuading older workers to retire early. Except in cases where older workers are receiving very high payouts (e.g., golden parachutes), the granting of lump-sum bonuses does not appear to change employees' perceptions of their future streams of income.

Second, while the evidence is not completely consistent, the weight of the evidence suggests that poor performers are more likely to accept ERIs than good performers (Kim & Feldman, 1998). Poor performers have low expectations of receiving any large pay raises in the future and so will suffer comparatively smaller losses of income by exiting the workforce early.

Third, it is difficult to predict with precision exactly how many older workers will accept a given ERI. Typically, about one third of those offered ERIs accept them, but there is a lot of variance around that mean (Feldman, 2003). Coupling preretirement counseling with financial incentives tends to increase the acceptance of ERIs. Here, the main reason appears to be that people tend to underestimate the amount of disposable (after tax) income they will receive after they leave the workforce (Hatcher, 2003; Taylor & Doverspike, 2003).

Bridge Employment

By the term *bridge employment*, we mean jobs that older workers take after leaving career-long positions but before exiting the workforce altogether (Doeringer, 1990; Feldman, 1994). In large part, bridge employment has been studied as a means for older workers to adjust more successfully to retirement. The evidence is quite strong that bridge employment does facilitate adjustment to retirement by providing older workers with some structure to their time, supplemental income, and opportunities to develop new interests before finally leaving the work-force (Beehr & Nielson, 1995; Isaksson & Johansson, 2000; Weckerle & Shultz, 1999).

However, bridge employment can also be considered as another type of ERI itself (Feldman & Kim, 2002; Kim & Feldman, 1998, 2000). Guaranteed opportunities to continue working part-time or temporarily after retirement may reduce older workers' anxieties about finances and their reluctance to quit work altogether. Kim and Feldman (1998, 2000) found, in fact, that bridge employment opportunities are quite effective in increasing the acceptance of ERIs; in their research, older workers who were offered opportunities to work on a part-time basis after retirement were 9% more likely to accept ERIs than their counterparts who were not offered bridge employment opportunities. By increasing both financial and psychological well-being, then, bridge employment may tip the balance in getting older workers to accept ERIs.

Many of the same factors that influence retirement decisions in general also play a role in decisions to engage in bridge employment. For example, employees who are highly satisfied with their jobs and are in good health are much more likely to accept bridge employment *with their current employers* than job-dissatisfied older workers in poor health. In contrast, older workers who dislike their present jobs but still need additional income or fear having time hanging on their hands are much more likely to take bridge employment *outside their present organization or career track.* For example, some may start their own businesses or accept jobs in teaching as alternatives to remaining in corporate jobs they no longer enjoy.

Adjustment to Retirement

Finally, there has been a great deal of attention given to how older workers adjust to life without paid employment. While some of this research has been conducted in the organizational sciences literature, much of it has been conducted by gerontology scholars as well.

The primary theoretical perspective used in understanding adjustment to retirement has been Atchley's (1989) "theory of continuity." This theoretical framework suggests that the ability to continue valued activities and routines in retirement is positively associated with adjustment, while disruption of valued activities and routines is negatively associated with adjustment to retirement. Atchley's theory of continuity is also useful in understanding why bridge employment has such a positive influence on adjustment to retirement. It allows older workers to continue with valued activities while they develop new routines and pursuits to replace them in retirement.

Perhaps not surprisingly, many of the variables studied in the context of retirement decisions have also been studied extensively in the context of adjustment to retirement. The three factors that appear to be most critical here are income, health, and social contact (particularly with family members). More specifically, older workers who can continue living with approximately the same standard of living, maintain their health, and have positive relationships with spouses and children tend to adjust to retirement quite well. In contrast, older workers who have to greatly curtail their spending, have declining health, or have lost their spouses to death are much less likely to adjust satisfactorily to retirement (Kim & Feldman, 1998, 2000).

Several researchers have also examined the role that nonwork activities, such as volunteer service and hobbies, play in adjustment to retirement. It has been argued that volunteer service can serve as an opportunity for retirees to feel useful, needed, and productive (Beehr & Bowling, 2002; Omoto, Snyder, & Martino, 2000) and that such service might be an attractive alternative for retirees with a great deal of time on their hands and a great deal of expertise to share. Surprisingly, though, participation in volunteer service is negatively correlated with age (Fischer, Mueller, & Cooper, 1991). Among the proposed explanations given for this relationship are poor health among the elderly, the inability of the elderly to drive or to obtain transportation to volunteer work sites, and the unwillingness of older people to work hard on tasks without being paid (Chambre, 1993).

Another potential explanation is that the rate of participation in volunteer work has skyrocketed among younger adults, who are increasingly turning to these activities as a means of networking for business and professional purposes (Beehr & Bowling, 2002; Omoto et al., 2000). Thus, the amount of participation in volunteer activities may not decline over the life span, but today's young adults are much more active in volunteer work than older adults were at the same age.

The work of Feldman and Kim (2000) suggests another reason for the weak relationships among age, volunteer work, and adjustment to retirement. Their research indicates that there are no differences in adjustment levels across retirees depending on which activity they engage in after they leave the workforce. That is, getting involved in volunteer work does not have a stronger effect on adjustment to retirement than does hanging out with friends and family. What is most critical for a satisfactory adjustment to retirement, though, is that the elderly have definite plans for how they will spend their time. It is the predictability of activity, rather than the activity itself, that may be most essential to a successful adjustment to retirement.

In addition, individuals' enduring personality traits may also play a significant role in determining their adjustment to retirement (Greller & Simpson, 1999). For instance, researchers have found positive correlations between adjustment to retirement and openness to new experience, internal locus of control, a positive problem-solving approach to life, and overall psychological well-being (Reitzes, Mutran, & Fernandez, 1996).

CONCLUSION

Late-career and retirement issues continue to be fertile ground for additional theory building, methodological innovation, and improvements in management practice. Below, we highlight some of the most significant challenges that lie ahead.

Theory Building

In general, empirical research demonstrating differences between older workers and younger workers has far outpaced theoretical explanations for those differences. Some theoretical perspectives have been fruitfully applied to understanding older workers' careers—for example, organizational demography, continuity theory, attribution theory, and relative deprivation theory—but much more research is needed in this area.

Over the past 10 years, in particular, there have been tremendous advances in cognitive neuroscience, and integrating this literature into the study of older workers would give us tremendous insights into their information-processing and decision-making capabilities. Seligman and Csikszentmihalyi's (2000) research on "positive psychology" holds promise for understanding whether, and when, older workers will demonstrate positive self-images and positive attitudes toward others as they age. Earlier research on "career disorderliness" (Kilty & Behling, 1985) might be further used to examine how nonlinear career paths (with multiple exits from the workforce and multiple careers) affect the career motivation, career resilience, and career identity of older workers. While research on the experience of protégés has been very extensive, we do not fully understand when and how mentoring creates a sense of "generativity" for older workers who engage in this activity (Chandler and Kram, Chapter 13; Levinson, 1986). All these approaches, among others, may help us move beyond knowing that age differences do occur to understanding why they occur.

Methodology

On the positive side, research on late-career issues and retirement has increasingly used large data sets and longitudinal data. This has led to some conclusions about older workers that have been quite consistent in magnitude and direction across studies and populations. On the negative side, the construct of "older workers" continues to be somewhat fuzzy. In some cases, there is considerable restriction of range, so that there are very few workers over 50 years of age or very few workers under 65 years of age in the research samples. In other cases, researchers have failed to untangle the effects of chronological age from years in an occupation or years in an organization. Consequently, it is often difficult to determine how many of the differences between older and younger workers are due to age and how many are due to seniority. Clearly, data sets with a greater age range of respondents and finer distinctions drawn between age and years of service are needed to answer some of the most important questions we have about older workers (Zickar & Gibby, 2003).

In addition, there are three research questions, in particular, that really demand more reliable and valid data. First, the role of employee health in retirement decisions and adjustment to retirement has suffered from overuse of global self-report data (e.g., "Overall, how would you rate your health?") and underuse of more objective health indicators (e.g., days hospitalized or number of chronic diseases for which medicine is prescribed). Second, the role of financial wealth in retirement decisions and adjustment to retirement has suffered from overreliance on an employee's own pension benefits to the exclusion of two potentially equally important factors—namely, the spouse's income (or pension) and family savings. Third, while there has been extensive work on gender and race in organizational demography research, there has been considerably less research on age diversity, particularly on the relative age of workers over 50 to that of their colleagues. Obviously, considerations of confidentiality and anonymity make the collection of such data via surveys much more difficult, but better use of archival data (e.g., data on family income) might give researchers some better indirect ways of addressing these questions (Zickar & Gibby, 2003).

Management Practice

By far, the area of research on older workers that has most widely made its way into management practice is retirement planning. Beginning particularly with the research on retirement in the 1970s and continuing on to the present, companies have taken the research on the effectiveness of retirement counseling to heart and implemented it in practice. Companies have also become more sophisticated in how they design ERIs in order to get the right number of employees (and the right employees) to exit at a price the company can afford.

What has not received as much attention, unfortunately, is how to use more effectively those older employees who remain in the workforce. There is still significant age discrimination in the workforce, and faulty stereotypes have limited the opportunities older workers have both with their current employers and in the open labor market. Short of demanding strict adherence to the guidelines of the Age Discrimination in Employment Act, there is little organizations can do by fiat to change employees' attitudes in this regard.

However, there is still much organizations can do to improve the opportunities afforded to older workers. More companies are designing HR systems that provide continuous learning opportunities for workers independent of age. Other organizations are better using older workers to mentor and develop the next generation of employees coming up through the ranks. Still other organizations are improving their performance appraisal and compensation systems to adequately reward older workers for their contributions to the firm even if they are no longer slated for rapid advancement. Some firms are even turning to recent retirees as a source of temporary employees and subcontractors (Greller & Stroh, 2003; London, 2002).

In short, there are a wide variety of ways by which organizations can cultivate and use the talents of older workers. Given the increasing size of the older-worker population, high-quality management of this group is no longer just an option but rather a business necessity.

REFERENCES

Addison, J., & Portugal, P. (1989). Job displacement, relative wage changes, and duration of unemployment. *Journal of Labor Economics, 7,* 281–302.

Arkes, H. R., & Blumer, C. (1985). The psychology of sunk cost. *Organizational Behavior and Human Decision Processes, 35,* 124–140.

Atchley, R. (1989). A continuity theory of aging. *Gerontologist, 29,* 183–190.

Atwater, L. E., Dionne, S. D., Avolio, B., Camobreco, J. F., & Lau, A. W. (1999). A longitudinal study of the leadership development process: Individual differences predicting leader effectiveness. *Human Relations, 52,* 1543–1562.

Avolio, B. J., & Waldman, D. A. (1994). Variations in cognitive, perceptual, and psychomotor abilities across the working life span: Examining the effects of race, sex, experience, education, and occupational type. *Psychology and Aging, 9,* 430–442.

Bailyn, L., & Lynch, J. (1983). Engineering as a life-long career: Its meaning, its satisfaction, and its difficulties. *Journal of Occupational Behavior, 4,* 263–283.

Barnes-Farrell, J. L. (2003). Beyond health and wealth: Attitudinal and other influences on retirement decision-making. In G. A. Adams & T. A. Beehr (Eds.), *Retirement: Reasons, processes, and results* (pp. 159–187). New York: Springer.

Beehr, T. A., & Bowling, N. (2002). Career issues facing older workers. In D. C. Feldman (Ed.), *Work careers: A developmental perspective* (pp. 214–241). San Francisco: Jossey-Bass.

Beehr, T. A., Glazer, S., Nielson, N. L., & Farmer, S. J. (2000). Work and nonwork predictors of employees' retirement ages. *Journal of Vocational Behavior, 57,* 206–225.

Beehr, T. A., & Nielson, N. L. (1995). Descriptions of job characteristics and retirement activities during transition to retirement. *Journal of Organizational Behavior, 14,* 579–594.

Bejian, D. V., & Salomone, P. R. (1995). Understanding midlife career renewal: Implications for counseling. *Career Development Quarterly, 44,* 52–63.

Borman, W. C., & Motowidlo, S. J. (1993). Expanding the criterion domain to include elements of contextual performance. In N. Schmitt & W. C. Borman (Eds.), *Personnel selection in organizations* (pp. 71–98). San Francisco: Jossey-Bass.

Cascio, W. F. (1986). *Managing human resources.* New York: McGraw-Hill.

Chambre, S. M. (1993). Volunteerism by elders: Past trends and future prospects. *Gerontologist, 33,* 221–228.

Chan, S., & Stevens, A. H. (2001). Job loss and employment patterns of older workers. *Journal of Labor Economics, 19,* 484–522.

Chao, G. T. (1990). Exploration of the conceptualization and measurement of career plateau: A comparative analysis. *Journal of Management, 16,* 181–193.

Clark, M. M. (2003). Constructive demotion counts as adverse action under ADA. *HR Magazine,* Vol. 48, pp. 105–106.

Czaja, S. J., & Sharit, J. (1998). Ability-performance relationships as a function of age and task experience for a data entry task. *Journal of Experimental Psychology: Applied, 4,* 332–351.

Doeringer, P. B. (1990). *Bridges to retirement.* Ithaca, NY: Cornell University ILR Press.

Feldman, D. C. (1988). *Managing careers in organizations.* Glenview, IL: Scott Foresman.

Feldman, D. C. (1994). The decision to retire early: A review and reconceptualization. *Academy of Management Review, 19,* 285–311.

Feldman, D. C. (1996). The nature and consequences of underemployment. *Journal of Management, 22,* 385–409.

Feldman, D. C. (2003). Endgame: The design and implementation of early retirement incentive programs. In G. A. Adams & T. A. Beehr (Eds.), *Retirement: Reasons, processes, and results* (pp. 83–114). New York: Springer.

Feldman, D. C., & Kim, S. (2000). Bridge employment during retirement: A field study of individual and organizational experiences with post-retirement employment. *Human Resource Planning, 23,* 14–25.

Feldman, D. C., Leana, C. R., & Bolino, M. C. (2002). Underemployment among downsized executives: Test of a mediated effects model. *Journal of Occupational and Organizational Psychology, 75,* 453–471.

Feldman, D. C., & Weitz, B. A. (1988). Career plateaus reconsidered. *Journal of Management, 14,* 69–80.

Ference, T. P., Stoner, J. A. F., & Warren, E. K. (1977). Managing the career plateau. *Academy of Management Review, 2,* 602–612.

Fischer, L. R., Mueller, D. P., & Cooper, P. W. (1991). Older volunteers: A discussion of the Minnesota Senior Study. *Gerontologist, 31,* 183–194.

Flynn, G. (1996). You demote me and I'll sue you. *Workforce, 75,* 83–87.

Goldner, F. H. (1965). Demotion in industrial management. *American Sociological Review, 30,* 714–724.

Greller, M. M., & Simpson, P. (1999). In search of late career: A review of contemporary social science research applicable to the understanding of late career. *Human Resource Management Review, 9,* 309–347.

Greller, M. M., & Stroh, L. K. (2003). Extending work lives: Are current approaches tools or talismans? In G. A. Adams & T. A. Beehr (Eds.), *Retirement: Reasons, processes, and results* (pp. 115–135). New York: Springer.

Gunz, H. P., & Jalland, R. M. (1996). Managerial careers and business strategies. *Academy of Management Review, 21,* 718–756.

Halbesleben, J. R. B., & Buckley, R. M. (2004). Burnout in organizational life. *Journal of Management, 30,* 859–880.

Hall, D. T., & Isabella, L. A. (1985). Downward movement and career development. *Organizational Dynamics, 14,* 5–23.

Hall, D. T., & Mirvis, P. H. (1995). The new career contract: Developing the whole person at midlife and beyond. *Journal of Vocational Behavior, 47,* 269–289.

Harpaz, I. (2002). Expressing a wish to continue or stop working as related to the meaning of work. *European Journal of Work and Organizational Psychology, 11,* 177–198.

Hatcher, C. B. (2003). The economics of the retirement decision. In G. A. Adams & T. A. Beehr (Eds.), *Retirement: Reasons, processes, and results* (pp. 136–158). New York: Springer.

Hutchens, R. M. (1986). Delayed payment contracts and a firm's propensity to hire older workers. *Journal of Labor Economics, 4,* 439–457.

Isaksson, K., & Johansson, G. (2000). Adaptation to continued work and early retirement following downsizing: Long-term effects and gender differences. *Journal of Occupational and Organizational Psychology, 73,* 241–256.

Judiesch, M. K., & Lyness, K. S. (1999). Left behind? The impact of leaves of absence on managers' career success. *Academy of Management Journal, 42,* 641–651.

Judy, R. W., & D'Amico, C. (1997). *Workforce 2020: Work and workers in the 21st century.* Indianapolis, IN: Hudson Institute.

Just, M. A., & Carpenter, P. A. (1992). A capacity theory of comprehension: Individual differences in working memory. *Psychological Review, 99,* 122–149.

Kilty, K. M., & Behling, J. H. (1985). Predicting the early retirement intentions and attitudes of professional workers. *Journal of Gerontology, 40,* 219–227.

Kim, S., & Feldman, D. C. (1998). Healthy, wealthy, or wise: Predicting actual acceptances of early retirement incentives at three points in time. *Personnel Psychology, 51,* 623–642.

Kim, S., & Feldman, D. C. (2000). Working in retirement: The antecedents and consequences of bridge employment and its consequences for quality of life in retirement. *Academy of Management Journal, 43,* 1195–1210.

Kirasia, K. C., Allen, G. L., Dobson, S. H., & Binder, K. S. (1996). Aging, cognitive resource, and declarative learning. *Psychology and Aging, 11,* 658–670.

Kletzer, L. G. (1989). Returns to seniority after permanent job loss. *American Economic Review, 79,* 536–543.

Kotlikoff, L. J. (1988). The relationship of productivity to age. In R. Ricardo-Campbell & E. P. Lazear (Eds.), *Issues in contemporary retirement* (pp. 100–131). Stanford, CA: Hoover Institute Press.

Kuhn, P., & Sweetman, A. (1999). Vulnerable seniors: Unions, tenure, and wages following permanent job loss. *Journal of Labor Economics, 17,* 671–693.

Lawrence, B. S. (1987). An organizational theory of age effects. *Research in the Sociology of Organizations, 5,* 37–71.

Lawrence, B. S. (1988). New wrinkles on the theory of age: Demography, norms, and performance ratings. *Academy of Management Journal, 31,* 309–337.

Lazear, E. P. (1983). Pensions as severance pay. In Z. Bodie & J. B. Shoven (Eds.), *Financial aspects of the United States pension system* (pp. 57–90). Chicago: University of Chicago Press.

Leana, C. R., & Feldman, D. C. (1992). *Coping with job loss: How individuals, organizations, and communities respond to layoffs.* New York: Macmillan/Lexington Books.

Levinson, D. J. (1986). A conception of adult development. *American Psychologist, 41,* 3–13.

Levy, P. E., & Williams, J. R. (2004). The social context of performance appraisal: A review and framework for the future. *Journal of Management, 30,* 881–906.

Lincourt, A. E., Rybash, J. M., & Hoyer, W. J. (1998). Age, working memory, and the development of instance-based retrieval. *Brain & Cognition, 20,* 100–102.

London, M. (2002). Organizational assistance in career development. In D. C. Feldman (Ed.), *Work careers: A developmental perspective* (pp. 323–345). San Francisco: Jossey-Bass.

Longenecker, C. O., Sims, H. P., & Gioia, D. A. (1987). Behind the mask: The politics of employee appraisal. *Academy of Management Executive, 1,* 183–193.

Lord, R. G., DeVader, C. L., & Alliger, G. M. (1986). A meta-analysis of the relation between personality traits and leadership perceptions: An application of validity generalization procedures. *Journal of Applied Psychology, 71,* 402–410.

Mazerolle, M. J., & Singh, G. (1999). Older workers' adjustments to plant closures. *Relations Industrielles, 54,* 313–337.

McCain, B. E., O'Reilly, C. A., III, & Pfeffer, J. (1983). The effects of departmental demography on turnover: The case of a university. *Academy of Management Journal, 26,* 626–641.

McCall, M. M., & Lombardo, M. M. (1983). What makes a top executive? *Psychology Today, February,* 26–31.

McEvoy, G. M., & Cascio, W. F. (1989). Cumulative evidence of the relationship between employee age and job performance. *Journal of Applied Psychology, 74,* 11–17.

Meyer, J. P., & Allen, N. J. (1997). *Commitment in the workplace: Theory, research, and application.* Thousand Oaks, CA: Sage.

Nicholson, N., & West, M. A. (1988). *Managerial job change: Men and women in transition.* New York: Cambridge University Press.

Omoto, A. M., Snyder, M., & Martino, S. C. (2000). Volunteerism and the life course: Investigating age-related agendas for action. *Basic and Applied Social Psychology, 22,* 181–197.

Park, D. C., Smith, A. D., Lautenschlager, G., Earles, J. L., Frieske, D., Zwahr, M., et al. (1996). Mediators of long-term memory performance across the life span. *Psychology and Aging, 11,* 621–637.

Perry, E. L., Kulik, C. T., & Bourhis, A. C. (1996). Moderating effects of contextual factors in age discrimination. *Journal of Applied Psychology, 81,* 628–647.

Peterson, R. S., Smith, D. B., Martorana, P. V., & Owens, P. D. (2003). The impact of chief executive officer personality on top management team dynamics: One mechanism by which leadership affects organizational performance. *Journal of Applied Psychology, 88,* 795–808.

Pfeffer, J. (1982). *Organizations and organization theory.* Marshfield, MA: Pittman.

Pfeffer, J., & Leblebici, H. (1973). Executive recruitment and the development of interfirm organizations. *Administrative Science Quarterly, 18,* 449–461.

Pierce, J., & Gardner, D. G. (2004). Self-esteem within the work and organizational context: A review of the organization-based self-esteem literature. *Journal of Management, 30,* 591–622.

Rao, G. B., & Rao, S. S. (1997). Sector and age differences in productivity. *Social Science International, 13,* 51–52.

Reitzes, D. C., Mutran, E. J., & Fernandez, M. E. (1996). Does retirement hurt well-being? Factors influencing self-esteem and depression among retirees and workers. *Gerontologist, 36,* 649–656.

Rhodes, S. R. (1983). Age-related differences in work attitudes and behavior: A review and conceptual analysis. *Psychological Bulletin, 93,* 328–367.

Rousseau, D. M. (1995). *Psychological contracts in organizations: Understanding written and unwritten agreements.* Thousand Oaks, CA: Sage.

Ryan, K. M., & Bartlett-Weikel, K. (1993). Open-ended attributions for the performance of the elderly. *International Journal of Aging and Human Development, 37,* 139–152.

Salancik, G. R., & Pfeffer, J. (1974). The bases and uses of power in organizational decision-making: The case of a university. *Administrative Science Quarterly, 19,* 453–473.

Salthouse, T. A. (1996). The processing-speed theory of adult age differences in cognition. *Psychological Review, 103,* 403–428.

Schacter, D. L. (2001). *The seven sins of memory.* New York: Houghton Mifflin.

Schappe, S. P. (1998). The influence of job satisfaction, organizational commitment, and fairness perceptions on organizational citizenship behavior. *Journal of Psychology, 132,* 277–290.

Schimamura, A. P., Berry, J. M., Mangels, J. A., Rusting, C. L., & Jurica, P. J. (1995). Memory and cognitive abilities in university professors: Evidence for successful aging. *Psychological Science, 6,* 271–277.

Schneer, J. A., & Reitman, F. (1997). The interrupted managerial career path: A longitudinal study of MBAs. *Journal of Vocational Behavior, 51,* 411–434.

Schneider, B., Goldstein, H. W., & Smith, D. B. (1995). The ASA framework: An update. *Personnel Psychology, 48,* 747–773.

Schwoerer, C. E., & May, D. R. (1996). Age and work outcomes: The moderating effects of self-efficacy and tool design effectiveness. *Journal of Organizational Behavior, 17,* 469–487.

Seligman, M. E. P., & Csikszentmihalyi, M. (2000). Positive psychology: An introduction. *American Psychologist, 55,* 5–14.

Sonnenfeld, J. A., & Peiperl, M. A. (1988). Staffing policy as a strategic response: A typology of career systems. *Academy of Management Review, 13,* 588–600.

Stephens, G. K. (1994). Crossing internal career boundaries: The state of research on subjective career transitions. *Journal of Management, 20,* 479–501.

Talaga, J., & Beehr, T. A. (1995). Are there gender differences in predicting retirement decisions? *Journal of Applied Psychology, 80,* 16–28.

Taylor, M. A., & Doverspike, D. (2003). Retirement planning and preparation. In G. A. Adams &

T. A. Beehr (Eds.), *Retirement: Reasons, processes, and results* (pp. 53–82). New York: Springer.

Turnley, W. H., & Feldman, D. C. (1998). Psychological contract violations during corporate restructuring. *Human Resource Management, 37*, 71–84.

Wagner, W. G., Pfeffer, J., & O'Reilly, C. A., III. (1984). Organizational demography and turnover in top-management groups. *Administrative Science Quarterly, 29*, 74–92.

Waldman, D. A., & Avolio, B. J. (1986). A meta-analysis of age differences in job performance. *Journal of Applied Psychology, 71*, 33–38.

Warr, P. (1994). Age and employment. In H. C. Triandis, M. D. Dunnette, & L. M. Hough (Eds.), *Handbook of industrial and organizational psychology* (2nd ed., Vol. 4, pp. 485–550). Palo Alto, CA: Consulting Psychologists Press.

Weckerle, J. R., & Schultz, K. S. (1999). Influences on the bridge employment decision among older USA workers. *Journal of Occupational and Organizational Psychology, 72*, 317–329.

Werner, J. M. (2002). Public policy and the changing legal context of career development. In D. C. Feldman (Ed.), *Work careers: A developmental perspective* (pp. 245–273). San Francisco: Jossey-Bass.

Williams, K. Y., & O'Reilly, C. A., III. (1998). Demography and diversity in organizations: A review of 40 years of research. *Research in Organizational Behavior, 20*, 77–140.

Williams, S., & Shiaw, W. T. (1999). Mood and organizational citizenship behavior: The effects of positive affect on employee organizational citizenship behavior intentions. *Journal of Psychology, 133*, 656–668.

Zajac, E. J., & Westphal, J. D. (1996). Who shall succeed? How CEO/board preferences and power affect the choice of new CEOs. *Academy of Management Journal, 39*, 64–90.

Zickar, M. J., & Gibby, R. E. (2003). Data analytic techniques for retirement research. In G. A. Adams & T. A. Beehr (Eds.), *Retirement: Reasons, processes, and results* (pp. 264–292). New York: Springer.

10

ORGANIZATIONAL CHALLENGES AT THE PERIPHERY

Career Issues for the Socially Marginalized

PUSHKALA PRASAD

CAROLINE D'ABATE

ANSHUMAN PRASAD

Throughout history, societies around the world have often marginalized specific social groups by denying them active participation in mainstream life and the rewards that come with it. One of the more salient dimensions of marginalization, arguably, is the exclusion of groups from preferred forms of work and privileged professions. Women, ethnic and religious minorities, the handicapped, and others have endured centuries of such marginalization during different periods of time across the world. Yet it would appear that in the past 100 years or so, the plight of the excluded and the disenfranchised has become much more central to our consciousness.

There seem to be at least two reasons for this. First, during this period, the movement of diverse populations across the world has grown exponentially (Appadurai, 1990), resulting in, among other things, many more visible instances of socioeconomic marginalization that cannot be easily ignored. Second, beginning from the early 20th century, we have also witnessed a growing public discourse around the importance of rights and social justice, a discourse that has largely displaced earlier discourses of sin, virtue, and honor that implicitly and explicitly sanctioned different forms of marginalization (Goldberg, 1993; Taylor, 1994). In part, this changing discourse can be traced to the emergence of modernity, which is more explicitly based on principles of democracy and equality. As a result, challenges facing the socially marginalized in multiple institutional fields, including education, housing, government, corporations, and the media, are very much at the center of public attention today. This chapter, accordingly, looks at social marginalization in the world of work through the prism of career.

The concept of career is a multidimensional one, involving complex questions of acceptance and inclusion in the organizational processes of hiring, recruitment, evaluation, networking, and remuneration. By following the circumstances of the socially marginalized along multiple career dimensions, we can arrive at an informed understanding of the issues they face and the ways in which organizations respond to them. Additionally, our chapter offers a critique of, and commentary on, the literature covering these career issues. We begin by theorizing the concept of social marginality and then reviewing the literature covering the themes relating to career issues of the socially marginalized.

THEORIZING SOCIAL MARGINALITY IN ORGANIZATIONS

Social marginality is a complex multilayered concept that seems to defy easy and straightforward definitions. Marginality conveys a sense of being away from the center or the mainstream and being to various degrees an *outsider* (Becker, 1963; Collins, 1999). Social marginality implies a condition of being deprived of full participation in a society's key institutions, including education, politics, work, the law, entertainment, and the media. Social marginality can occur primarily as a result of individuals' personalities and behaviors, or it can take place on account of individuals' membership in specific social identity groups such as women, blacks, Asians, Hispanics, the aged, and so forth (Thomas & Alderfer, 1989). Our focus in this chapter is on the latter groups, that is, on those who are excluded from society largely because of their *collective identity* rather than because of

individual characteristics or individual acts of deviance.

Social marginality also carries with it elements of *stigmatization.* Crocker and Major (1989) regard stigmatized individuals as visible members of "social categories about which others hold negative attitudes, stereotypes and beliefs, or which on average, received disproportionately poor interpersonal or economic outcomes relative to members of society at large" (p. 609). The notion of social stigma has been most thoroughly articulated by Erving Goffman (1963) in his discussion of how individuals are branded through negative associations with particular "undesirable" groups in society. According to Goffman, a stigma is almost like a blemished identity, which is entirely inescapable and which prevents easy inclusion in key organizations and institutions in society. In many parts of the world, for instance, being gay turns into a stigma that hinders acceptance and advancement in organizations. Stigmas, therefore, marginalize individuals by reducing their entire identity to one-dimensional characteristics or behaviors such as sexual preference, age, religious beliefs, physical handicaps, and so on.

Marginality is also often produced through notions of *otherness.* The "other" is typically characterized as being fundamentally different from oneself and belonging to groups that have either different or unfamiliar attitudes, orientations, and practices (Goldberg, 1994; Prasad & Prasad, 2002). Otherness implies a lack of affinity with the mainstream and engenders a reluctance on the part of dominant groups to interact or mingle with groups considered to be "other." Women, blacks, Hispanics, gays, new immigrants, and many more have all been cast in the role of the other in various societies across the world (Czarniawska & Hopfl, 2002). Otherness is, thus, always predicated on notions of difference. More recent discussions of these themes in postcolonial theory see social marginalization also occurring in conditions of *subalternity* (Guha, 1982). In Guha's terms, the subaltern classes are basically nonelite groups who are subordinated along class, caste, age, gender, office, and numerous other lines of social categorization. Subaltern groups are socially marginalized, in part, through their enforced silence, a silence that is the result of generations of patriarchy and imperialism, among other causes. The concept of the subaltern, thus, widens our understanding of social marginality by contextualizing it in global colonial histories.

Whether groups are cast as alien, outsider, deviant, or other, their marginality is always *socially constructed* and *discursively produced* rather than having a concrete existence on its own that is a product of nature. Marginality is socially constructed through the social categories and labels that attach pejorative and undesirable connotations to specific identity groups (Cavanaugh, 1997). For marginality to become firmly established, however, it also has to be (re-)produced discursively (Foucault, 1973; Mills, 1997) by means of institutional talk, structure, and action. In other words, marginality does not come about only through *individually* held stereotypes and prejudices but through the continual and ongoing circulation of these negative images in textbooks, government and corporate actions and policies, cultural messages and practices, the media, everyday conversations, hiring and promotion guidelines, and so on. In this way, marginality is discursively reproduced, materially and symbolically reinforcing/reinscribing at an everyday institutional level all the negative images that are themselves social constructions. Thus, marginality takes place when discrimination, exclusion, and domination have become matters of habit in thought and practice (Prasad, 1997).

From the foregoing discussion, we can certainly infer that the socially marginalized tend to be somewhat *disadvantaged* and relatively *powerless* members of society (Foucault, 1973; Goffman, 1963; Ragins, 1997). So, who exactly are the socially marginalized? Can we identify them with some measure of confidence? It needs to be noted here that, in addition to its socially constructed and discursive nature, marginality is very much a historically and culturally contingent condition that also has to be understood as a matter of degree. For example, while Jewish people were significantly marginalized in Europe and North America up to the 1960s, their position in the United States and Canada is definitely one of less marginalization today; gay men and lesbians are more marginalized in sections of the United States, the Middle East, and Asia in comparison with certain parts of Western Europe; women tend to be less marginalized in Northern

Europe because of decades of progressive social policies while blacks tend to be marginalized in many different continents. Our point is relatively simple: Social marginality needs to be understood within specific historical contexts and with reference to specific local circumstances. Hence, sweeping universal pronouncements about socially marginalized groups (such as women, ethnic minorities, etc.) are likely to be both hasty and ill-advised.

Looking at legally protected groups who are covered by antidiscrimination legislation can sometimes offer us clues as to who are the socially marginalized in different societies. In the United States, for instance, women, racial and ethnic minorities, and many legal immigrants have some measure of legal protection under Title VII of the Civil Rights Act and the establishment of the Equal Employment Opportunities Commission (EEOC), while older employees are covered under the Age Discrimination Act. Similar pieces of legislation can be found in many other countries, including Canada, the United Kingdom, New Zealand, and the Scandinavian countries, and they give us some idea as to which groups might be socially marginalized within these countries. It is important to note, however, that the laws alone offer us an incomplete picture of who constitutes the socially marginalized. Federal laws in the United States, for example, afford little protection from employment discrimination for gays or individuals with criminal records (no matter how trivial the crime). Moreover, class is rarely singled out for legal protection. Yet it is well established that poor people and individuals from lower class backgrounds are systematically discriminated against in various societies (Marsden, 1997; Scully & Blake-Beard, 2006). More recently, overweight individuals are also claiming a socially marginalized position in a culture that overwhelmingly values slenderness and physical beauty. Research does suggest that the overweight are increasingly stigmatized for their appearance and are being excluded from a range of managerial positions and other attractive career options (Bell & McLaughlin, 2006).

Social marginality, then, must be recognized as a dynamic and shifting phenomenon that is constituted by changing *zeitgeists,* demographic turns, and struggles over economic and symbolic resources (Bourdieu, 1986). Some erstwhile marginalized groups have made great progress in overcoming formal and informal discrimination, while others face renewed cultural and institutional barriers in their fight for inclusion in the workplace. It is important to be conscious of these historical and cultural shifts and variations when commenting on experiences of social marginality at work.

CAREER ISSUES FOR THE SOCIALLY MARGINALIZED: THEMES FROM THE LITERATURE

Looking at the career paths of the socially marginalized provides us with glimpses into their organizational experiences and the obstacles they encounter in the workplace. We can also arrive at some understanding of whether and how these obstacles are overcome, which groups have made greater inroads into organizations, and which have not. We bring these issues to the surface by looking at the more "classic" career themes, viz., gaining employment, remuneration, evaluation and advancement, mentorship and networking, and so on. In addition, we also look at the question of affirmative action because it is explicitly a policy intended to redress centuries of injustice meted out to women, blacks, and other minorities in the United States. We will also be looking at organizational cultures as sites for the informal acceptance or rejection of socially marginalized groups.[1]

Gaining Entry: Recruitment, Selection, and Hiring of the Socially Marginalized

The hiring process is understandably a matter of enormous concern to those who are socially marginalized. It is during recruitment and selection that applicants are faced with maximum prejudice and bias, which in turn can negatively affect their entrance into organizations. At the time of hiring, most applicants are relatively unknown quantities and, therefore, most vulnerable to being stereotyped and stigmatized by organizational decision makers. Certainly, survey research indicates that many socially marginalized groups both anticipate and experience discrimination during the recruitment process. Women anticipate sex discrimination in their careers (McWhirter, 1997) only to have it frequently confirmed. Lyness and Judiesch (1999) found, for instance, that when it comes to external recruitment, male managers are more likely to be hired than female managers, while Dainty et al.'s (1999) ethnographic study of recruitment and selection processes in the construction industry demonstrated that despite recruitment campaigns targeted at women, the male managers who were responsible for hiring preferred to recruit men and used selection processes that lacked formal guidelines and were discriminatory toward women.

Older workers are another group experiencing social marginalization at work. In fact, Hansson, Dekoekkoek, Neece, and Patterson (1997) observed that "the traditional workplace [is] designed for the average 20- to 40-year-old" (p. 226) and requires substantial adjustment to accommodate an aging workforce. Perry, Kulik, and Bourhis (1996) provide empirical support for this in a study that found that lower evaluations were given to older applicants applying for "younger" type jobs (e.g., selling CDs and tapes) than younger applicants despite a similarity of qualifications (Feldman, Chapter 9). Ageism at work is also evidenced in the rising charges of age discrimination as a percentage of total charges of discrimination that were brought before the EEOC over the past few years (U.S. EEOC, n.d.).

Other socially marginalized groups, including racial and ethnic minorities, religious minorities, the physically disadvantaged, and individuals with alternative sexual preferences, also report being victims of hiring discrimination. There is some support for this from survey research as well. Stewart and Perlow (2001) found that evaluators with significant racial biases were likely to engage in occupational segregation by placing blacks in low-status jobs (such as janitors) while placing whites in high-status jobs (such as architects). Hiring discrimination is also reported to be "pervasive" in the workplace experiences of gays, lesbians, and bisexuals (Croteau, 1996), while Jewish Americans are less likely to be selected for managerial and executive positions (Korman, 1989).

The literature is not, however, unanimous in concluding that discrimination is an everyday fact of life for socially marginalized groups. In their study of one-on-one job interviews, Sacco, Scheu, Ryan, and Schmitt (2003) concluded that racial similarity (between applicants and interviewers) was not likely to affect interview outcomes. In another study, Polinko and Popovich (2001) suggested that while obesity often resulted in negative evaluations of work-related characteristics, it did not actually lead to hiring discrimination.

Notwithstanding the occasional study that denies the pervasiveness of sexism, racism, ageism, and other forms of institutional exclusion at work, most scholars are in agreement that socially marginalized groups continue to confront discrimination in organizations. In the United States, the question that continues to get raised is: Why is it that 200 years after the Declaration of Independence and more than 40 years after the passing of the Civil Rights Act, entry into organizations is still fraught with so much difficulty and pain for some social groups? There is an array of plausible explanations for this phenomenon.

First, there is the rather obvious issue of recruiter bias that can work against individuals associated with a spectrum of socially marginalized groups, including, for example, women, racial minorities, and older workers (Finkelstein & Burke, 1998; Shaffer, Joplin, Bell, Lau, & Oguz, 2000; Stewart & Perlow, 2001). Bias typically surfaces in hiring practices through negative images and stereotypes of certain groups. This can include notions such as women being intellectually less capable than men, blacks being lazy, and older workers being incapable of commanding respect on the job. Clearly such biases are likely to influence hiring and selection processes to the detriment of socially marginalized groups. Furthermore, such prejudices tend to intensify and become more influential in hiring decisions when organizational authority figures legitimize discrimination through business justifications such as homogeneity being essential for corporate harmony and teamwork (Brief, Dietz, Cohen, Pugh, & Vaslow, 2000).

Negative images and stereotyping are far from being the only factors behind the continuing lack of adequate representation of socially marginalized groups in mainstream organizations. Decades of sex and race segregation at work and in the professions have resulted in firm convictions about the appropriateness of specific genders and races for specific occupations (Atwater & Van Fleet, 1997; Reskin & Hartman, 1986). Women, for instance, are typically regarded as being more suitable than men for social work positions (Atwater & Van Fleet, 1997), while Asian men are believed to be ideally suited for positions in accounting, finance, and computer servicing, and less suited for positions of executive leadership (Prasad & Prasad, 2003). To compound this problem further, several structural dynamics can keep members of socially marginalized groups from even entering relevant applicant pools. Blacks, for instance, experience a lack of access to several labor markets, less representation in higher education, limited exposure to role models, and overall lower career aspirations (Chung, Baskin, & Case, 1999; McCollum, 1998) that discourage them from planning and preparing for higher-end jobs and careers.

And finally, hiring discrimination can also take place because of dominant groups' preferences for individuals from their own social identity groups (Lawrence and Tolbert, Chapter 20). This can happen even when members of the dominant group harbor few prejudices against other groups. As highlighted by Kanter (1977) in her classic work *Men and Women of the Corporation,* organizational elites show a marked preference for hiring individuals like themselves because difference implies far too much uncertainty, unfamiliarity, and a consequent loss of social comfort.

Getting Compensated: Wage and Salary Issues for the Socially Marginalized

The passing of the Equal Pay Act in America in 1963 signaled an awareness that wage and salary discrimination was present in the country. Most of this discrimination then was believed to be directed against women, and 40 years later, women are still lagging behind men in the salaries they receive. Not only are earning disparities between men and women quite striking, but the wages of non-white women also continue to lag behind their white counterparts (Murrell & James, 2001). While women's wages in the aggregate improved throughout the 1980s, they began to stagnate around 78 cents to a dollar for males in the 1990s (Crampton, Hodge, & Mishra, 1997) and have not made much progress since then. Some estimates even propose that given current trends, the median full-time wage of a woman in the United States will not equal that of a U.S. man until 2050 ("Harper's index," 2005).

Nor is the phenomenon of wage disparity along gender lines restricted to the United States. Similar patterns can be found in Europe and other industrial democracies as well (Allen & Sanders, 2002; England, 1992). In general, it appears that *gender-based wage discrimination* supercedes all other forms of wage discrimination, though non-white women experience even greater wage inequities than white women (U.S. Equal Employment Opportunity Commission, 2004) with black women earning 66 cents to a dollar for males and Hispanic women earning only 59 cents. These are admittedly aggregate figures and do vary according to demographics and occupational choice, but it is still obvious that race and gender clearly produce a *double whammy* effect on the earning capacities of socially marginalized groups.

A complex amalgamation of factors appears to be responsible for the persistence of gender-based wage discrimination even after the introduction of legislation intended to prevent it. First, the laws themselves do not always make it easy for women to prove that they are victims of gender-based discrimination. With respect to the Equal Pay Act, the main problem revolves around establishing definitions of what constitutes "equal" and "unequal" work and skill levels to the satisfaction of the courts. Additionally, many experts argue that the American courts impose a greater burden of proof on women and minorities than on employers in their attempts to prove salary discrimination (Crampton, Hodge, & Mishra, 1997). Federal agencies that investigate wage discrimination complaints are, moreover, increasingly understaffed and take inordinate amounts of time to process these complaints. One result of this is that members of socially marginalized groups are discouraged from bringing their complaints

about wage discrimination to either the EEOC or the courts, and the full effect of the law does not get itself felt at the workplace.

Human capital theorists explain these wage differences mainly in terms of aggregate differences between men and women in terms of education, training, and experience. The argument holds that men tend to invest more in their own education and development and, consequently, reap the rewards of higher salaries (Allen & Saunders, 2002; Lloyd & Niemi, 1979). Others have suggested that the lack of pay parity is partly accounted for by "compensating differentials" such as shorter commuting distances to work, friendly coworkers, and flexible schedules (Gethman, 1987). In other words, women's lower wages are partly judged to be an outcome of their own preferences for congenial and convenient work situations.

Labor economists invariably locate the driving force behind wage inequities in market conditions. Arguing that wages are primarily set by demand-supply conditions, they also highlight the salience of different types of markets (i.e., geographical or occupational) in the wage-setting process (Gethman, 1987). The market argument is entirely exogenous to the organization and absolves the firm from any responsibility in wage discrimination. It also assumes that market forces have a life of their own and should not be tampered with by any governmental intervention.

An institutional perspective recognizes the key role of labor markets *alongside* a tendency of employers to exploit these dynamics in their favor. Institutionalists explain the persistence of earnings discrimination through *sex segregation* at work (Rubery & Fagan, 1995) and more specifically through the creation of *dual labor markets* (Jacobs, 1989), which tend to be more exploitative of women. Segments of the institutional perspective parallel feminist examinations of the origins of sex segregation in the fabric of capitalist patriarchy, which deliberately keeps women in a secondary labor market where wages are lower and working conditions are much poorer (Hartman, 1986). The argument is that women tend to be concentrated in a secondary labor market (comprising schoolteachers, administrative assistants, etc.), which enjoys a relatively low status and is less well paid. Furthermore, recent discussions also suggest that whenever any occupation draws large numbers of women, it is in danger of becoming a low-paying and low-status job (Allen & Saunders, 2002). A number of women are, thus, trapped by institutional barriers in jobs of this nature. While we do not have the space in this chapter to cover the various proposals for reforming this system of dual labor markets, it is worth noting that the idea of *comparable worth* was first floated to redress this problem. The concept of comparable worth (which was advocated by the American women's movement in the 1970s and 1980s) calls for an overall reevaluation of traditional female occupations (such as nursing and schoolteaching) in terms of their *worth* to society and not rely only on market forces to set wages for them. At its core, comparable worth argues that institutional pressures on the labor market keep women's wages at exploitatively low levels and needs to be altered based more on principles of social justice and societal value.

Career Advancement and Development for Socially Marginalized Groups

In the years immediately following the U.S. civil rights and women's movements, the primary concern of socially marginalized groups was to guarantee that they had fair access to employment in all sectors of society. By the 1980s, these concerns had shifted somewhat in focus and began to coalesce around the notion of a "glass ceiling"—a metaphor that refers to the invisible barriers that prevent women and minorities from advancing into senior and executive positions in organizations (Morrison, White, & Van Vilsen, 1987; Murrell & James, 2001). It is important to note that the glass ceiling refers to a very specific form of internal organizational discrimination and not to all forms of race and gender inequality at work.

The 1995 Federal Glass Ceiling Commission described it as "the unseen yet unbreakable barrier that keeps minorities and women from rising to the upper rungs of the corporate ladder regardless of their qualifications and achievements" (p. iii). The glass ceiling concept is, thus, explicitly concerned with systematic organizational discrimination and not with just the prevalence of inequity and marginalization at the workplace. In short, it is concerned with the career stagnation of women and minorities that persists despite their qualifications and ability to perform adequately at senior levels of management (Cotter, Hermsen, Ovadia, & Vanneman, 2001). The notion of the glass ceiling is also more about discrimination at *higher* levels of the organization rather than at entry levels. As Wright, Baxter, and Birkelund (1995) assert, "The glass ceiling hypothesis is not simply a claim about the existence of discrimination within hierarchies; it claims that such discrimination *increases* as one moves up the hierarchy" (p. 428).

While the original discussions of the glass ceiling looked at career blocks for both women and minorities, recent discussions also see sexual preference as creating a "lavender ceiling" that prevents gays and lesbians from moving up organizational ladders (Carr-Ruffino, 1996). Some researchers (Cotter et al., 2001) argue that women experience glass ceiling effects more strongly than minority men, while others (Bell & Nkomo, 1999) insist that black women are even more vulnerable to career stagnation than their female counterparts from other socially marginalized groups. In fact, they argue that the metaphor of a concrete roof (thick and impermeable) is more appropriate in understanding these problems than the glass ceiling. Similar observations are made by Sherman (2002) who sees black women confronting a "rock ceiling" of racism and sexism that prevents them from attaining upward mobility in organizations.

It would be a mistake to think of the glass ceiling as exclusively the product of individual prejudice at higher organizational echelons. Glass ceilings are also produced and maintained by structural organizational characteristics such as existing gender and race imbalances across the organization (Lawrence and Tolbert, Chapter 20), a culture of masculinity, institutional inertia with respect to policy changes, and so on (Dreher, 2003; Goodman, Fields, & Blum, 2003). One major structural factor that is systematically identified as being responsible for glass ceiling effects is the existing sex ratio of the organization as a whole. Research appears to indicate that organizations in which a high number of lower managerial positions are held by women are less likely to suffer from glass ceiling effects (Goodman et al., 2003; Konrad, Winter, & Gutek, 1992). Dreher's (2003) research also suggests that firms with substantial internal work-life programs such as flexitime, elder care, and adoption benefits have thinner glass ceilings that are easier for women to break through. This would tend to imply that glass ceiling dynamics are far more complex than just being offshoots of negative individual attitudes toward women and minorities.

Glass ceilings have a number of consequences for career trajectories of the socially marginalized. They are instrumental in discouraging many members of socially marginalized groups from committing to long-term careers within corporations. Women in particular have displayed a marked tendency to "dodge the glass ceiling" (Weiler & Bernasek, 2001) by quitting their jobs more often than men and launching independent business ventures (Stroh, Brett, & Reilly, 1996) where they have greater control over their own career paths. In addition, glass ceilings have considerable impacts on the identities of the socially marginalized, with long-term implications for their own professional self-confidence and development. Ely's (1995) comprehensive study of women in law firms offers a detailed picture of this phenomenon. Ely compared women lawyers in firms with a high percentage of female partners[2] (no glass ceiling) with their counterparts in firms with a small proportion of female partners (strong glass ceiling) with the intent of exploring the impact of these proportional representations on women's identities.

Ely (1995) found that the women in glass ceiling firms interpreted sex roles in conventional and more stereotypical ways, often also blaming themselves for not advancing in their organizations. Simultaneously, they also internalized their firms' devaluation of women as valid assessments of their own deficiencies. In contrast to this, women in firms with thinner glass ceilings regarded "feminine" attributes as a source of competence and strength, and linked biological sex less closely to a bipolar construction of gender in which masculine traits are reserved for men and feminine traits for women. Ely's study is important because of its findings that the proportional representation of women in *positions of power* affects professional women's

gender identity at work. At an intuitive level, it would also appear that similar dynamics might occur with respect to other socially marginalized groups as well.

Obstacles in the way of career advancement of socially marginalized groups obviously emerge out of a multitude of complex factors. In seeking to overcome these obstacles, the management literature, however, concentrates overwhelmingly on career development programs in general and on *mentorship* in particular (Chandler and Kram, Chapter 13). One reason for this sustained interest in mentoring might lie in the vast amount of research indicating that white men benefit hugely from mentoring relationships in organizations (Ensher & Murphy, 1997). Nevertheless, questions are being increasingly raised about the applicability of this finding for socially marginalized groups, be they women, gays, and lesbians or ethnic and racial minorities.

While mentoring can take different forms (D'Abate, Eddy, & Tannenbaum, 2003), mentors are typically conceptualized as "influential people who significantly help others reach their major life goals" (Lee & Nolan, 1998, p. 4) or as senior organization members who undertake "to provide information, advice, and emotional support to a junior person (the protégé) in a relationship which is set formally by the constraints of the program and lasts for a limited period of time" (Ensher & Murphy, 1997, p. 461). Mentoring (as a formal and semiformal program) has been growing in popularity in a number of organizations (Garvey & Galloway, 2002; MacGregor, 2000) and has been widely linked to a range of positive outcomes, including effective career planning, socialization, and career progression of the protégé.

When it comes to mentoring the socially marginalized, however, a number of complicated dynamics can be at play. Differences and similarities in race, gender, sexual preference, and so on between mentors and their protégés mediate the relationship in complex ways resulting in unexpected tensions and outcomes. Not surprisingly perhaps, researchers searching for clearly identifiable patterns are unable to find them or to reach a consensus about whether race-gender similarities between mentors and protégés are more effective/beneficial than cross-gender and cross-race pairings. Some studies (Lyons & Oppler, 2004; Smith, Smith, & Markham, 2000) have claimed that social identity differences between mentors and protégés have little impact on either the satisfaction with the relationship or the functions provided by it. Others, however, insist that racial similarities in mentoring relationships are much more beneficial in terms of satisfaction and career support (Ensher & Murphy, 1997; Koberg, Boss, & Goodman, 1998). None of these studies, however, seem to recognize the extent to which immediate organizational contexts (in terms of culture, performance pressures, power relationships, etc.) mediate or even override the social identity effects of either mentors or their protégés. Thus, searching for the perfect mentoring relationship in terms of the "right" race or gender of either mentor or protégé is not likely to go very far in actual organizational situations.

More pertinent to the career outcomes of socially marginalized groups is the lack of willingness on the part of senior organizational members to assist minorities with upward mobility (Allen, Poteet, & Burroughs, 1997). There also exists the distinct possibility that minorities fare less well than women in locating mentors (Smith et al., 2000). Many commentators believe that eventually the absence of a strong and supporting mentor can contribute to the formation of glass ceilings for many socially marginalized groups. These concerns over mentorship are mainly expressed with respect to women and racial minorities, but increasingly the career development issues of individuals with alternative sexual preferences (Morrow, Gore, & Campbell, 1996) and older employees (Hall & Mirvis, 1995) are surfacing.

Including Socially Marginalized Groups Through Public Policy: Debates Over Affirmative Action

No discussion of career issues for the socially marginalized would be complete without some consideration of public policies designed to rectify centuries of past discrimination. A number of multiethnic and multiracial countries (such as the United States, Canada, India, and the United Kingdom) have enacted a set of proactive public policy initiatives that augment antidiscrimination legislation with additional measures to enhance equal employment (Skrentny, 1998). In the United States, these efforts—which are broadly termed *affirmative action*—have come under intense public scrutiny and have stirred up an extraordinary level of controversy. Looking closely at some of the prominent debates and discussions around affirmative action helps us gain a better understanding of reactions to the formal inclusion of socially marginalized groups in the workplace.[3]

A succinct definition of affirmative action is provided by the U.S. Civil Rights Commission that defines it as "any measure beyond simple termination of a discriminatory practice, adopted to correct or compensate for past or present discrimination, or to prevent discrimination from recurring in the future" (Bruno, 1995, p. 23). Affirmative action is, thus, a relatively fluid concept that can subsume a wide spectrum of organizational strategies, including outreach efforts, vigilance during selection, and even target quotas (Turner & Pratkanis, 1994). In short (and contrary to much of public perception), in practice, affirmative action can vary from industry to industry and organization to organization.

Two broad and interrelated themes surface in the debates over affirmative action. They are (a) questions around the wider effectiveness of affirmative action (Murrell & James, 1996) and (b) concerns about the supposed unfairness of affirmative action (Crosby, Iyer, Clayton, & Downing, 2003). Needless to say, both themes tend to generate a spectrum of divergent opinions and irreconcilable positions on all sides.

Murrell and James (1996) argue that to assess the efficacy of affirmative action in employment, one should be able to judge if it has resulted in a reduction of discrimination and a firm placement of mechanisms that prevent systematic discrimination from recurring in the future. After examining the so-called gains of affirmative action over the past few decades, they conclude that the achievements of affirmative action in the American workplace are best described as "fragile." In other words, while affirmative action policies and initiatives have certainly opened doors to women in minorities in public and private organizations, these gains are simultaneously very vulnerable to political, cultural, and economic trends all over the country.

In addressing the efficacy of affirmative action, many of its detractors suggest that the gains for women and minorities in employment through affirmative action occur at the expense of organizational performance and productivity. Both the underlying and stated assumptions here are that affirmative action policies encourage the hiring of "unqualified" or "underqualified" individuals with consequences for the eventual performance of organizations. Surprisingly, perhaps, there are not too many studies that look at the performance impacts of affirmative action. Leonard's (1984) field study quite conclusively established that an increase in women and minorities in manufacturing firms following the implementation of affirmative action policies did not have any impacts on productivity. Similar results were obtained by Steel and Lovrich (1987) in their study of police departments after the implementation of affirmative action programs. Despite these relatively conclusive findings, a number of social commentaries and political discussions persist in their insistence that affirmative action policies have detrimental effects on the performance and productivity of organizations.

The second theme taken up by many critics of affirmative action concerns its alleged violations of the principles of justice and fairness. A number of studies document the pervasiveness of such negative attitudes toward affirmative action by majority group members as well as women and minorities who often benefit from them. Based on extensive experimental and field research, Heilman, Block, and Lucas (1992) conclude that a *stigma of incompetence* accompanies affirmative action, burdening its beneficiaries (mainly women and blacks) with negative images of incompetence and underqualification. Such stigmas, moreover, are capable of damaging relationships with coworkers and resulting in long-term career immobilities for women and minorities. Given the ubiquity of these attitudes, it is not surprising that one finds resistance to affirmative action even among socially marginalized groups that are targeted to benefit from it (Northcraft & Martin, 1982). In general, this resistance to affirmative action comes from a tendency to equate it with preferential treatment, which, in turn, raises recipients' doubts about their own ability and competence (Steele, 1990; Turner & Pratkanis, 1994).

Despite their role in advancing career opportunities for some socially marginalized groups (or perhaps because of it), affirmative action programs have been subjected to a strident backlash almost from the moment of their inception. Most of the backlash can be traced to individual white men or ultraconservative institutions such as the Center for Individual Rights and the Federalist Society (Cokorinos, 2003). However, more recently, one can find something of a backlash even among white women who are beginning to express resentment over the "preferential treatment" accorded to blacks at the workplace and in institutions of higher learning (Cokorinos, 2003; Prasad, 2005). In fact, the recent challenges to the University of Michigan's affirmative action policy in college admissions was put forth by white women claiming reverse discrimination in the much celebrated Supreme Court cases *Gratz v. Bollinger* and *Grutter v. Bollinger.* This turn is somewhat ironic because white women have themselves been the major beneficiaries of affirmative action in both higher education and employment in the corporate sector.

The sustained backlash against affirmative action has many different sources. Many affirmative action programs are implemented without adequate communication about the criteria used, leading many employees to believe that unqualified women and minorities are routinely hired to fill affirmative action quotas (Crosby & Cordova, 1996). Such beliefs reinforce existing hostilities toward affirmative action, which is then seen as a scheme of preferential treatment that openly disregards the rights of the dominant group.

Some of the negative sentiment against affirmative action may well be the product of *aversive racism* (Dovidio & Gaertner, 1996, 2000). Aversive racism is generally defined as a more indirect and subtle form of racism that often lies outside the conscious awareness of individuals. Individuals who engage in aversive racism typically pride themselves on their lack of prejudices and support for ideals such as justice and equality. However, in concrete organizational situations, the same individuals are quite quick to derogate and exclude members of many socially marginalized groups without using openly demeaning language (Crosby et al., 2003). Affirmative action frequently serves as an opportunity for aversive racism against blacks to surface under the guise of objections to preferential treatment in their favor (Murrell & James, 1996).

Finally, it is also important to recognize the organized institutional networks of financial and political power that have been actively working since the 1980s to dismantle affirmative action and other programs designed for greater inclusion of socially marginalized groups in the country. As many sociologists and historians have painstakingly revealed, assaults against affirmative action have been systematically orchestrated (Cokorinos, 2003; Stefancic & Delgado, 1996) by a coalition of ultraconservative think tanks and institutions funded by corporate sponsors such as the Coors family (Bellant, 1991) and have been put into action by a number of prominent politicians in office (Saloma, 1984). This body of work underscores the necessity of understanding affirmative action and similar policies as political phenomena that are manipulated by multiple stakeholders with different notions about justice, equality, and democracy in everyday life.

Socially Marginalized Groups and the Informal Organization: Culture, Ideology, and Networking

It would be a mistake to try to understand the career experiences of socially marginalized groups by looking only at formal processes such as recruitment, evaluation, promotion, remuneration, and so on. People's everyday work experiences significantly revolve around the *informal organization* (Perrow, 1986), a relatively less visible organizational domain constituted by a range of varied social interactions, cultural practices, and patterns (such as organizational rites, rituals, myths, etc.), and dominant ideologies and mindsets. Not only is the informal organization the space in which organizational members spend considerable parts of their working lives, but it also significantly shapes and influences (both directly and indirectly) formal organizational structures and processes.

Since the 1980s, cultural analysis has emerged as one of the most popular ways of researching the informal organization. Developed mainly by anthropologists and sociologists, cultural analysis

has been increasingly used by organizational researchers to examine those dimensions of the informal organization that hold relevance for socially marginalized groups. Such cultural studies typically look at dominant ideologies, identity conflicts, and structural forces that influence the inclusion of socially marginalized groups in organizations (Ferguson, 1983; Mighty, 1997; Mills, 2002). A number of these cultural analyses are less interested in uncovering individual biases and prejudices and more concerned with examining the *structuring* of exclusion, discrimination, and marginalization in organizations. Some examples will serve to illustrate this point. Feminists such as Ferguson (1983) and Acker (1990), for instance, argue that organizations themselves are actually *gendered* entities in ways that invariably favor men over women. The point that Acker (1990) makes is that many seemingly gender-neutral organizational processes such as job evaluation are clearly undergirded by images of male employees and masculinity that make genuine inclusion of women something of a problem. Others such as Fletcher (1999) also explore the systematic ways in which female employees' capabilities and competencies are rendered *invisible* to their male colleagues and supervisors. Professional women, thus, have a way of disappearing from the organizational consciousness partly because their managerial styles (even when highly effective) do not fit into the accepted mold of what managers are supposed to be.

Such culturally structured—though often less visible—exclusion is experienced not only by women but also by other socially marginalized groups as well. Creed (2006), for example, points to the prevalence of institutional homophobia, which can take forms such as a generalized discomfort with the very idea of employees having same-sex partners or an organizational unwillingness to accept the alternative sexual preferences of employees. Organizations, thus, turn into "lavender-collar jungles" filled with latent homophobia in which gay, lesbian, and/or bisexual employees are discouraged from coming out of the closet. Mighty's (1997) empirical study of non-white immigrant professional women in Canada, on the other hand, reveals how racial, gender, and immigrant identities intersect to create a number of barriers at the workplace. Mighty (1997) suggests that these women enter a situation of "triple jeopardy" in which they encounter constant marginalization because of their simultaneous membership in three socially marginalized groups, namely, women, non-white, and the immigrant outsider.

The important thing to note here is that a considerable part of the exclusion and marginalization occurring in the contemporary workplace is predominantly a result of culturally structured and institutionalized practices rather than a product of irrational stereotypes and prejudices held only at the individual level. This makes marginalization all the more difficult to overcome. Consider, for instance, the cultural influence that wider myths and legends exert over organizational processes and structures. Prasad (1997) has suggested that enduring social myths such as the Protestant Ethic and the myths of the frontier leave powerful *cultural imprints* on organizations in the form of ideals and expectations that are, by and large, predisposed to favor a particular form of whiteness and masculinity. Heroic archetypes of cowboys invade organizational discourses of leadership, connecting corporate leadership to individualism, self-reliance and ruthlessness, and making it almost entirely the symbolic province of white men (Prasad, 1997).

Focusing on the informal organization, thus, heightens our sensitivity to the important role of *cultural capital* in entering organizations as well as in advancing and succeeding in organizations (Davies-Netzley, 1998). The concept of cultural capital has been developed by Pierre Bourdieu (1986; see also Mayrhofer, Meyer, and Steyrer, Chapter 12), who sees it as comprising those elements of one's formal education, institutional credentials, and informal socialization and training, as well as one's dispositions, habits, mannerisms and etiquette, consumption of specific cultural goods, and so on that help an individual in leveraging socioeconomic advantages for purposes of social, cultural, or professional advancement. With the help of interview data from men and women in senior corporate positions in the United States, Davies-Netzley (1998) concluded that women as well as racio-ethnic minorities are likely to be far shorter on cultural capital than white men, with the result that they either have to make extra efforts to acquire it (e.g., through formal credentialing, adopting new cultural interests, joining relevant

social organizations), or they have to reconcile themselves to losing out to those with greater amounts of cultural capital than themselves. A number of successful female executives in her study, for instance, made concerted efforts to alter their appearance (through desexualization strategies that de-emphasized their femininity) and engaged in conversations about sports and politics that gave them greater standing with their male colleagues and supervisors.

In this regard, moreover, because members of socially marginalized groups lack sufficient cultural capital, they often have inadequate access to professionally useful networks (see Ibarra and Deshpande, Chapter 14; Lawrence and Tolbert, Chapter 20), both within and outside the organizations they work in. Limited access to networking produces multiple disadvantages, including incomplete awareness of important organizational dynamics and difficulties in forming useful coalitions at work (Ibarra, 1993). Ultimately, poor networking contributes to career stagnation through a series of glass ceiling effects.

Contributions and Limitations of Current Literature and Implications for Future Research

The past 30 years or so have witnessed a growing scholarly interest in career issues for the socially marginalized. While this interest has emerged in various academic fields (e.g., organization studies, occupational psychology, labor economics, sociology of work, leadership studies, corporate anthropology), it continues to be largely dominated by the models and methods of social psychology. This has some significant implications for the formulation of the research agenda and the nature of the findings.

First of all, there is a vast emphasis in current research on *individual* expressions of racism, sexism, homophobia, ethnocentrism, ageism, and so on at the level of both cognition and behavior. Innumerable studies seek to establish the existence of rater bias in interviews, attitudes toward mentoring protégés belonging to diverse identity groups, biases in performance evaluation, and so forth. Even though there are minor variations within the literature, the studies mainly confirm the prevalence of prejudice and discrimination toward a number of socially marginalized groups, including women, blacks, non-Christians, gays, lesbians, and bisexuals, Hispanics, and many others as well. Unfortunately, much of the literature rarely goes beyond confirming the presence of bias (e.g., toward understanding its provenance or exploring the complex ways in which it manifests itself in organizations). Goldberg's (1994) critique that "psychologics, while an important dimension in the transformation of political economy, often circumscribes sociologics" (p. 13) can thus be justifiably extended to this genre of research. The influence of psychology can be witnessed, for instance, in the ways in which a host of studies trace social marginality almost exclusively to faulty cognitive processes of individuals, giving rise to a sense that the responsibility for change may also rest solely on individual managers and employees. As Nkomo and Cox (1996) have already warned us, this leaves an entire domain of systematic and structural organizational discrimination relatively underexamined.

While we do not in any way wish to discount the powerful negative impact of irrational prejudices on socially marginalized groups, we would, nevertheless, like to underscore the importance of appreciating the *institutional* (rather than individual) production and reproduction of marginality in organizations and the broader society. Institutional patterns, including organizational rules, procedures, customs, habits, expectations, and images that may not appear to be overtly discriminatory often result (over the long term) in the persistent marginalization of certain disadvantaged groups. While some work has been done in this area (see Collinson, Knights, & Collinson, 1990; Davies-Netzley, 1998; Fletcher, 1999), it remains an area that needs to be more fully investigated.

In addition to mainly focusing on individual attitudes and behaviors, much of the psychologically oriented literature is somewhat *reductionist* in its approach to social marginalization in organizations, primarily concentrating on analyzing relationships between a couple of variables such as social group membership and efficacy or age/sex/race and mentoring relationships, and the like. Moreover, given the positivistic bent of these studies, the researchers also seek to draw highly generalizable (almost universalistic) conclusions from their findings. The

result is a complete de-contextualization of these studies that often offer simplistic (bordering on tautological) descriptions of social marginality. Some of the studies on mentoring relationships, for instance, illustrate this tendency. Innumerable studies in this area seek to establish whether same-sex/race/age mentoring relationships are more effective than cross-sex/age/race ones. Not only are such studies quite inconclusive in the aggregate, they also tell us very little about the complexities of mentoring relationships themselves or the local organizational and societal conditions and contexts in which they are embedded and which undoubtedly influence the dynamics of those relationships.

The literature also seems to be somewhat constrained by its preoccupation with women and blacks as the major victims of marginalization at the workplace. While we do not in any way wish to diminish the significance of the marginalization of either of these groups, we do believe that such an overwhelming focus on these two groups alone may prevent us from developing a fuller understanding of the marginalization of other identity groups, notably Hispanics, Asians, Native Americans, gay men, lesbian women, bisexuals, Muslims, individuals belonging to many non-mainstream minority faiths, overweight employees, and so on. Too often, moreover, the experiences of women and blacks are equated in current literature with those of other groups, giving us a misleading and homogenized picture of the invariant nature of marginalization in organizations. In reality, this is far from being the case as each group experiences marginalization quite differently. Gay men and lesbian women, for instance, are victims of closet dynamics (Creed, 2006) and are stigmatized through images drawn largely from fundamentalist religious doctrines. Hispanics, on the other hand, are often stereotyped as participants of drug cultures and face unique resistance to language use at work, while Muslims in the West are currently excluded mostly because of fears that link them with terrorism. There is also a tendency in sections of the literature to assume that female marginality is, by and large, uniform, despite differences in race, age, ethnicity, and class. Without further belaboring the point, we would advocate keeping in mind that while there are indeed important shared elements in the experience of marginality across different groups, social marginality in organizations is also highly *differentiated and heterogeneous;* the latter point is not sufficiently emphasized in the current literature on the subject.

In brief, we believe that there is a pressing need for more multifaceted research that contextualizes marginalization in both organizations and broader societies and explores its interplay with multiple dynamics, notably identity politics, cultural myths and messages, and institutional pressures (including social movements and regulations). There is a need also for a greater awareness of the variations within experiences of marginalization of different identity groups and the unique historical forces that have shaped those experiences. Many of these concerns, which have been voiced by Nkomo and Cox (1996) in an earlier article on identity in organizations, are yet to be seriously heeded by the discipline of organization studies. The kind of research that we are advocating requires some shifting of methodological gears from a measurement mode to a more *narrative* mode that stresses, among other things, "thick description" (Geertz, 1973) and historical detail while simultaneously paying attention to the power dynamics that invariably underpin questions of social and organizational marginalization. Narrative research would typically include institutional ethnographies (Collinson et al., 1990; Kanter, 1977) and discourse analyses (Litvin, 2002; Mills, 2002) of social marginality within organizations and would offer us insights into the processes (rather than outcomes or predictors) whereby marginalization is produced and sustained in the workplace.

Our foregoing critique might lead some readers to suppose that we are uniformly dismissive of all psychologically based positivist research on career issues for socially marginalized groups. That, however, is not the case. First, we recognize the cumulative contributions that studies in this literature make to the collective understanding of organizational relationships and phenomena. In addition, pieces that are theoretically well grounded and embedded in organizational contexts have much to offer in terms of understanding marginalization of different identity groups in organizations. Konrad

and Linnehan's (1995) study of the complex role played by human resources management structures in alleviating and fostering conditions of social marginality and Brief et al.'s (2000) examination of the relationship between prejudice and resentment toward affirmative action are both cases in point. Both studies go beyond surface interpretations of good intentions and prejudices to uncover the latent dynamics of organizational concealment and elusive racism and, thus, portray social marginalization in much more complex terms.

Indeed, among the more noteworthy contributions of the psychology-based literature to social marginality research is the development and application of a concept that is interchangeably referred to as *symbolic racism* (Kinder & Sears, 1981), *modern racism*, and *aversive racism* (Dovidio & Gaertner, 2000). Symbolic, aversive, or modern racism is a more *indirect* form of racism that gets expressed as hostility to public policies such as affirmative action or as repeated statements about the condition of minority groups that are insidiously demeaning. This would include statements regarding crime rates among blacks or drug usage among Hispanics, which while having a "factual" base, can also have adverse consequences for members of these groups if repeatedly expressed in public and professional settings (without paying sufficient attention to the wider social, political, economic, and other conditions that significantly contribute toward high crime rates among blacks or high drug usage among Hispanics). Aversive/modern/symbolic racism rarely takes the form of crude and open attacks on individuals belonging to socially marginalized groups but, nevertheless, continues to demean and stigmatize them, albeit in subtle and indirect ways. This form of racism is, thus, much harder to identify, especially because individuals who practice it also claim to disapprove of racist attitudes in general.

In general, our understanding of social marginality in organizations would be greatly enhanced by studies and research approaches that are more sensitive to such complexity. For this purpose, our field needs to move away from its overwhelming focus on narrow predictors of possible discrimination (which, in any case, are hard to establish conclusively), and study the dynamics of marginality in organizations as they unfold within broader contexts shaped by wider cultural, historical, political, societal, economic, and other forces. In fields such as anthropology, sociology, communication studies, and cultural studies, investigations of marginality are increasingly being informed by discussions of identity (Goldberg, 1994), institutionalized power (Davies-Netzley, 1998), representation (Said, 1978), and so forth. While such work has begun to have some impact on the examination of career issues of the socially marginalized within organization studies as well (Collinson et al., 1990; Mighty, 1997; Mills, 2002, etc.), there is a clear need for more research that is informed by a range of theoretical perspectives, including feminism, critical race theory, postcolonialism, structuration, queer theory, poststructuralism, and so on, all of which adopt a historical lens and focus on the broader sociocultural dynamics that shape the contours of marginality at work today.

Notes

1. Our discussion of these issues is inevitably restricted by the availability of scholarly work on careers and to works that have been written in or translated into English. Our focus, therefore, tilts toward North America. While much of the literature we discuss may be relevant to other countries and regions, we hesitate to extend many of our conclusions to other parts of the world.

2. Ely herself uses the term *male-dominated* firms to refer to organizations with resilient glass ceilings and *sex-integrated* firms to refer to firms with no or thin glass ceilings.

3. It is important to note that our discussion of affirmative action is of direct relevance mainly to the United States, while simultaneously raising issues that are of importance in other countries as well. However, each nation's public policy is a unique product of historical and cultural circumstances and needs to be understood and evaluated as such.

References

Acker, J. (1990). Hierarchies, bodies, jobs: A theory of gendered organizations. *Gender and Society, 4,* 139–158.

Allen, J., & Sanders, K. (2002). Gender gap in earnings at the industry level. *European Journal of Women's Studies, 9,* 163–186.

Allen, T. J., Poteet, M. L., & Burroughs, S. M. (1997). The mentor's perspective: A qualitative inquiry and future research agenda. *Journal of Vocational Behavior, 51,* 70–89.

Appadurai, A. (1990). Disjuncture and difference in the global cultural economy. *Public Culture, 2,* 15–24.

Atwater, L. E., & Van Fleet, D. D. (1997). Another ceiling? Can males compete for traditionally female jobs? *Journal of Management, 23,* 603–626.

Becker, H. (1963). *Outsiders.* New York: Free Press.

Bell, E. E., & Nkomo, S. M. (1999). Postcards from the borderlands: Building a career from the outside/within. *Journal of Career Development, 26,* 69–84.

Bell, M. P., & McLaughlin, M. E. (2006). Outcomes of appearance and obesity in organizations. In A. Konrad, P. Prasad, & J. K. Pringle (Eds.), *Handbook of workplace diversity* (pp. 455–474). London: Sage.

Bellant, R. (1991). *The Coors connection: How Coors family philanthropy undermines democratic pluralism.* Boston: South End Press.

Bourdieu, P. (1986). The forms of capital. In J. G. Richardson (Ed.), *Handbook of theory and research for the sociology of education* (pp. 241–258). New York: Greenwood.

Brief, A. P., Dietz, J., Cohen, R. R., Pugh, S. D., & Vaslow, J. B. (2000). Just doing business: Modern racism and obedience to authority as explanations for employment discrimination. *Organizational Behavior and Human Decision Processes, 81,* 72–97.

Bruno, A. (1995). *CRS report for congress: Affirmative action in employment.* Washington, DC: Congressional Research Service, Library of Congress.

Carr-Ruffino, N. (1996). *Managing diversity: People skills for a multicultural workplace.* Needham, MA: Pearson.

Cavanaugh, J. M. (1997). (In)corporating the other? Managing the politics of workplace difference. In P. Prasad, A. Mills, M. Elmes, & A. Prasad (Eds.), *Managing the organizational melting pot: Dilemmas of workplace diversity* (pp. 31–53). Thousand Oaks, CA: Sage.

Chung, Y. B., Baskin, M. L., & Case, A. B. (1999). Career development of black males. *Journal of Career Development, 25,* 161–171.

Cokorinos, L. (2003). *The assault on diversity: An organized challenge to racial and gender diversity.* New York: Rowman & Littlefield.

Collins, P. H. (1999). Reflections on the outsider within. *Journal of Career Development, 26,* 85–88.

Collinson, D. L., Knights, D., & Collinson, M. (1990). *Managing to discriminate.* London: Routledge.

Cotter, D. A., Hermsen, J. M., Ovadia, S., & Vanneman, R. (2001). The glass ceiling effect. *Social Forces, 80,* 655–682.

Crampton, S. M., Hodge, J. W., & Mishra, J. M. (1997). The Equal Pay Act: The first thirty years. *Public Personnel Management, 26,* 335–344.

Creed, D. (2006). Seven conversations about the same thing: Homophobia and heterosexism in the workplace. In A. Konrad, P. Prasad, & J. K. Pringle (Eds.), *Handbook of workplace diversity* (pp. 371–400). London: Sage.

Crocker, J., & Major, B. (1989). Social stigma and self-esteem: The self-protective properties of stigma. *Psychological Review, 96,* 608–630.

Crosby, F. J., & Cordova, D. I. (1996). Words worth of wisdom: Toward an understanding of affirmative action. *Journal of Social Issues, 52,* 33–49.

Crosby, F., Iyer, A., Clayton, S., & Downing, R. (2003). Affirmative action: Giving psychology away. *American Psychologist, 58,* 93–115.

Croteau, J. M. (1996). Research on the work experiences of lesbian, gay and bisexual people: An integrative review of methodology and findings. *Journal of Vocational Behavior, 48,* 119–124.

Czarniawska, B., & Hopfl, H. (2002). Introduction. In B. Czarniawska & H. Hopfl (Eds.), *Casting the other: The production and maintenance of inequality in organizations* (pp. 1–6). London: Routledge.

D'Abate, C. P., Eddy, E. R., & Tannenbaum, S. I. (2003). What's in a name? A literature-based approach to understanding mentoring, coaching, and other constructs that describe developmental interactions. *Human Resource Development Review, 2,* 360–384.

Dainty, A. R. H., Neal, R. H., & Bagilhole, B. M. (1999). Women's careers in large construction companies: Expectations unfulfilled. *Career Development International, 4,* 353–371.

Davies-Netzley, S. (1998). Women above the glass ceiling: Perceptions of corporate mobility and strategies for social success. *Gender and Society, 12,* 339–355.

Dovidio, J. F., & Gaertner, S. L. (1996). Affirmative action, unintentional racial biases and intergroup relations. *Journal of Social Issues, 52,* 51–75.

Dovidio, J. F., & Gaertner, S. L. (2000). Aversive racism and selection decisions, 1989 and 1999. *Psychological Science, 11,* 315–319.

Dreher, G. F. (2003). Breaking the glass ceiling: The effect of sex ratios and work life programs on female leadership at the top. *Human Relations, 56,* 541–562.

Ely, R. J. (1995). The power in demography: Women's social constructions of gender at work. *Academy of Management Journal, 38,* 589–634.

England, P. (1992). *Comparable worth: Theories and evidence.* New York: Aldine De Gruyter.

Ensher, E. A., & Murphy, L. (1997). Effects of race, gender, perceived similarity and contact on mentor relationships. *Journal of Vocational Behavior, 50,* 460–481.

Federal Glass Ceiling Commission. (1995). *Good for business: Making full use of the nation's human capital.* Washington, DC: Department of Labor.

Ferguson, K. E. (1983). *The feminist case against bureaucracy.* Philadelphia: Temple University Press.

Finkelstein, L. M., & Burke, M. J. (1998). Age stereotyping at work: The role of rater and contextual factors on evaluations of job applicants. *Journal of General Psychology, 125,* 317–345.

Fletcher, J. K. (1999). *Disappearing acts: Gender, power and relational practice at work.* Cambridge: MIT Press.

Foucault, M. (1973). *Madness and civilization: A history of insanity in the age of reason.* New York: Random House.

Garvey, B., & Galloway, K. (2002). Mentoring at the Halifax plcs (HBOS): A small beginning in a large organization. *Career Development International, 7,* 271–278.

Geertz, C. (1973). *The interpretation of cultures.* New York: Basic Books.

Gethman, B. R. (1987). The job market, sex bias and comparable worth. *Public Personnel Management, 16,* 173–180.

Goffman, E. (1963). *Stigma: Notes on the management of spoiled identity.* Englewood Cliffs, NJ: Prentice Hall.

Goldberg, D. T. (1993). *Racist culture: Philosophy and the politics of meaning.* Oxford: Blackwell.

Goldberg, D. T. (1994). Introduction: Multicultural conditions. In D. T. Goldberg (Ed.), *Multiculturalism: A critical reader* (pp. 1–41). Malden, MA: Malden Press.

Goodman, J. S., Fields, D. L., & Blum, T. C. (2003). Cracks in the glass ceiling: In what kinds of organizations do women make it to the top? *Group and Organization Management, 28,* 475–501.

Guha, R. (1982). On some aspects of historiography of colonial India. In R. Guha (Ed.), *Subaltern studies I: Writings on South Asian history and society* (pp. 1–8). New Delhi: Oxford University Press.

Hall, D. T., & Mirvis, P. H. (1995). The new career contract: Developing the whole person from mid-life and beyond. *Journal of Vocational Behavior, 47,* 269–289.

Hansson, R. O., Dekoekkoek, P. D., Neece, D. M., & Patterson, D. W. (1997). Successful aging at work: Annual review, 1992–1996: The older worker and transitions to retirement. *Journal of Vocational Behavior, 51,* 202–233.

Harper's index (2005, February). *Harper's Magazine,* p. 7.

Hartman, H. (1986). Capitalism, patriarchy and job segregation by sex. In M. Blaxall & B. Reagan (Eds.), *Women in the workplace* (pp. 137–169). Chicago: University of Chicago Press.

Heilman, M. E., Block, C. J., & Lucas, J. A. (1992). Presumed incompetent? Stigmatization and affirmative action efforts. *Journal of Applied Psychology, 77,* 536–544.

Ibarra, H. (1993). Personal networks of women and minorities in management: A conceptual framework. *Academy of Management Review, 18,* 56–87.

Jacobs, J. A. (1989). Long-term trends in occupational segregation by sex. *American Journal of Sociology, 95,* 160–173.

Kanter, R. M. (1977). *Men and women of the corporation.* New York: Basic Books.

Kinder, D. R., & Sears, D. O. (1981). Prejudice and politics: Symbolic racism versus threats to the good life. *Journal of Personality and Social Psychology, 44,* 414–431.

Koberg, C. S., Boss, R. W., & Goodman, E. (1998). Factors and outcomes associated with mentoring among health-care professionals. *Journal of Vocational Behavior, 53,* 58–72.

Konrad, A. M., & Linnehan, F. (1995). Formalized HRM structures: Coordinating equal employment opportunity or concealing organizational practices. *Academy of Management Journal, 38,* 787–820.

Konrad, A. M., Winter, S., & Gutek, B. (1992). Diversity in work group sex composition: Implications for majority and minority members. *Research in the Sociology of Organizations, 10,* 115–140.

Korman, A. K. (1989). The outsiders: On the relationship between Jewish Americans and corporate

America in the problem of work and career. *Man and Work, 2,* 53–58.

Lee, J. H., & Nolan, R. E. (1998). The relationship between mentoring and the career advancement of women administrators in cooperative extension. *Journal of Career Development, 25,* 3–13.

Leonard, J. S. (1984). Anti-discrimination or reverse discrimination? The impact of changing demographics: Title VII and affirmative action or productivity. *Journal of Human Resources, 19,* 145–174.

Litvin, D. R. (2002). The business case for diversity and the "iron cage." In B. Czarniawska & H. Hopfl (Eds.), *Casting the other: The production and maintenance of inequality in organizations* (pp. 160–184). London: Routledge.

Lloyd, C. B., & Niemi, B. T. (1979). *The economics of sex differentials.* New York: Columbia University Press.

Lyness, K. S., & Judiesch, M. K. (1999). Are women likely to be hired and promoted into managerial positions? *Journal of Vocational Behavior, 54,* 158–173.

Lyons, B. D., & Oppler, E. S. (2004). The effects of structural attributes and demographic characteristics on protégé satisfaction in mentoring programs. *Journal of Career Development, 30,* 215–229.

MacGregor, L. (2000). Mentoring: The Australian experience. *Career Development International, 5,* 244–250.

Marsden, R. (1997). Class discipline: IR/HR and the normalization of the workforce. In P. Prasad, A. Mills, M. Elmes, & A. Prasad (Eds.), *Managing the organizational melting pot: Dilemmas of workplace diversity* (pp. 107–128). Thousand Oaks, CA: Sage.

McCollum, V. J. C. (1998). Career development issues and strategies for counseling African Americans. *Journal of Career Development, 25,* 41–52.

McWhirter, E. H. (1997). Perceived barriers to education and career: Ethnic and gender differences. *Journal of Vocational Behavior, 50,* 124–140.

Mighty, J. (1997). Triple jeopardy: Immigrant women of color in the labor force. In P. Prasad, A. Mills, M. Elmes, & A. Prasad (Eds.), *Managing the organizational melting pot: Dilemmas of workplace diversity* (pp. 312–339). Thousand Oaks, CA: Sage.

Mills, A. J. (2002). History/Herstory: An introduction to the problem of studying the gendering of organizations over time. In I. Aaltio & A. J. Mills

(Eds.), *Gender, identity and the culture of organizations* (pp. 115–136). London: Routledge.

Mills, S. (1997). *Discourse.* London: Routledge.

Morrison, A. M., White, R. P., & Van Vilsen, E. (1987). *Breaking the glass ceiling: Can women reach the top of America's largest corporations?* Reading, MA: Addison-Wesley.

Morrow, S. L., Gore, P. A., Jr., & Campbell, B. W. (1996). The application of a socio-cognitive framework to the career development of lesbian women and gay men. *Journal of Vocational Behavior, 48,* 136–148.

Murrell, A. J., & James, E. H. (1996). Assessing affirmative action: Past, present and future. *Journal of Social Issues, 52,* 77–92.

Murrell, A. J., & James, E. H. (2001). Gender and diversity in organizations: Past, present and future directions. *Sex Roles, 45,* 243–257.

Nkomo, S., & Cox, T. (1996). Diverse identities in organizations. In S. Clegg, C. Hardy, & W. Nord (Eds.), *Handbook of organization studies* (pp. 338–356). London: Sage.

Northcraft, G. B., & Martin, J. (1982). Double jeopardy: Resistance to affirmative action from potential beneficiaries. In B. Gutek (Ed.), *Sex-role stereotyping and affirmative action policy* (pp. 32–46). Los Angeles: Institute of Industrial Relations Press.

Perrow, C. (1986). *Complex organizations.* New York: Prentice Hall.

Perry, E. L., Kulik, C. T., & Bourhis, A. C. (1996). Moderating effects of personal and contextual factors in age discrimination. *Journal of Applied Psychology, 81,* 628–647.

Polinko, N. K., & Popovich, P. M. (2001). Evil thoughts but angelic actions: Responses to overweight job applicants. *Journal of Applied Social Psychology, 31,* 905–924.

Prasad, A., & Prasad, P. (2002). Otherness at large: Identity and difference in the new globalized landscape. In I. Aaltio & A. J. Mills (Eds.), *Gender, identity and the culture of organizations* (pp. 57–71). London: Routledge.

Prasad, P. (1997). The protestant ethic and myths of the frontier. In P. Prasad, A. Mills, M. Elmes, & A. Prasad (Eds.), *Managing the organizational melting pot: Dilemmas of workplace diversity* (pp. 129–142). Thousand Oaks, CA: Sage.

Prasad, P., & Prasad, A. (2003). *The rainbow ceiling: Invisible barriers to career advancement.* Paper presented at the annual meetings of the Academy of Management, Seattle, WA.

Prasad, P. (2005). *Colorwashing the corporation: New battles over diversity in the North American workplace.* Manuscript in preparation.

Ragins, B. R. (1997). Antecedents of diversified mentoring behavior. *Journal of Vocational Behavior, 51,* 90–109.

Reskin, B. F., & Hartman, H. I. (1986). *Women's work, men's work: Sex segregation on the job.* Washington, DC: National Academy Press.

Rubery, J., & Fagan, C. (1995). Gender segregation in societal context. *Work, Employment and Society, 9,* 213–240.

Sacco, J. M., Scheu, C. R., Ryan, A. M., & Schmitt, N. (2003). An investigation of race and sex similarity effects in interviews. *Journal of Applied Psychology, 88,* 852–865.

Said, E. (1978). *Orientalism.* New York: Vintage.

Saloma, J., III. (1984). *Ominous politics: The new conservative labyrinth.* New York: Hill & Wang.

Scully, M., & Blake-Beard, S. (2006). Locating class in organizational diversity work: Class as structure, style and process. In A. Konrad, P. Prasad, & J. K. Pringle (Eds.), *Handbook of workplace diversity* (pp. 431–454). London: Sage.

Shaffer, M. A., Joplin, J. R. W., Bell, M. P., Lau, T., & Oguz, C. (2000). Gender discrimination and job-related outcomes: A cross-cultural comparison of working women in the United States and China. *Journal of Vocational Behavior, 57,* 395–427.

Sherman, R. (2002). The subjective experience of race and gender in qualitative research. *American Behavioral Scientist, 45,* 1247–1253.

Skrentny, J. D. (1998). Introduction. In J. D. Skrentny (Ed.), *Color lines: Affirmative action, immigration and civil rights options for America* (pp. 1–28). Chicago: University of Chicago Press.

Smith, J. W., Smith, W. J., & Markham, S. E. (2000). Diversity issues in mentoring academic faculty. *Journal of Career Development, 26,* 251–262.

Steel, B. S., & Lovrich, N. P. (1987). Equality and efficiency trade-offs in affirmative action: Real or imagined? The case of women in policing. *Social Science Journal, 24,* 53–70.

Steele, S. (1990). *The content of our character: A new vision of race in America.* New York: St. Martin's Press.

Stefancic, J., & Delgado, R. (1996). *No mercy: How conservative think tanks and foundations changed America's social agenda.* Philadelphia: Temple University Press.

Stewart, L. D., & Perlow, R. (2001). Applicant race, job status, and racial attitudes as predictors of employment discrimination. *Journal of Business and Psychology, 16,* 259–275.

Stroh, L. K., Brett, J. M., & Reilly, A. H. (1996). Family structure, glass ceilings and traditional explanations for the differential rate of turnover of female and male managers. *Journal of Vocational Behavior, 49,* 99–118.

Taylor, C. (1994). The politics of recognition. In A. Gutman (Ed.), *Multiculturalism* (pp. 25–73). Princeton, NJ: Princeton University Press.

Thomas, D. A., & Alderfer, C. P. (1989). The influence of race on career dynamics: Theory and research on minority career experiences. In M. B. Arthur, D. T. Hall, & B. S. Lawrence (Eds.), *Handbook of career theory* (pp. 133– 158). Cambridge, UK: Cambridge University Press.

Turner, M. E., & Pratkanis, A. R. (1994). Affirmative action as help: A review of recipient reactions to preferential selection. *Basic and Applied Social Psychology, 15,* 43–69.

U.S. Equal Employment Opportunity Commission. (2004). Charge statistics FY 1992 through FY 2003. Retrieved August 23, 2004, from http://www .eeoc.gov/stats/charges.html.

Weiler, S., & Bernasek, A. (2001). Dodging the glass ceiling: Networks and the new wave of women entrepreneurs. *Social Science Journal, 38,* 85–103.

Wright, E. O., Baxter, J., & Birkelund, G. E. (1995). The gender gap in workplace authority: A cross-national study. *American Sociological Review, 60,* 407–435.

11

CUSTOMIZED CAREERS

MONIQUE VALCOUR

LOTTE BAILYN

MARIA ALEJANDRA QUIJADA

W e were asked to write a chapter on nontraditional careers. To do so, we first needed to establish what we mean by career and what a traditional career might look like—only then could we think about the nontraditional career. The definition of "career" in this *Handbook,* as in the previous one (Arthur, Hall, & Lawrence, 1989), is "the evolving sequence of a person's work experiences over time." It is not clear, given this definition, that there is such a thing as a traditional or nontraditional career. Indeed, coming as it does from the Chicago School (see Barley, 1989), this definition is neutral about normative expectations. In *Men and Their Work,* Hughes (1958) writes of the career as "the struggle of the individual to find a place and an identity in the world of work"—or one side of a duality, the other of which is the "organized system" in

which this struggle unfolds (pp. 8–9). There is nothing traditional or nontraditional about this understanding of careers. Rather, careers—in this tradition—are a "perspective . . . a way of looking at things" (Becker, 2004), "a lens with which to view both the dynamic interweave between choice and constraint and the dynamic interplay among society, organizations, and individuals' lives" (Moen & Han, 2001, p. 427). In this sense, careers link individuals to the institutional context in which their lives evolve.

Despite this origin of the definition used in this *Handbook,* the meaning we will use is closer to Wilensky's (1961) "orderly career": a pattern of work involving intense commitment to and continuous engagement with the occupational world, along with a striving for upward mobility and achievement of external markers of success. Careers that would normally be "orderly" in this sense, but are *not*—these are the topics for this chapter. As we will see, such nontraditional careers return us, in some respects, to the more descriptive, less normative view of the Chicago School.

Such "orderly" or "traditional" careers involve full-time, continuous involvement in the workforce, typically starting in one's 20s, following the completion of formal education, and ending with total and permanent withdrawal from the workforce some 40 or 50 years later at retirement. Steady upward advancement within an organization and/or a profession is presumed—or, at the very least, the desire for upward advancement and adherence to norms of behavior typically required for promotion. Put another way, not wanting to get ahead is deviant in Merton's (1968) sense, according to the underlying ideology of the traditional career. Such a career envisions an "ideal worker" for whom employment forms the basis of identity and who grants priority to work over other life domains (Bailyn, 2006; Kanter, 1977; Williams, 2000). Much of the U.S.-based research on careers and career success reflects this view of career. It commonly examines the work histories and experiences of individuals (primarily men) pursuing upward mobility in a managerial or professional field through continuous employment, often with a single employer and typically within a single occupation.

If we compare this ideal career template with the actual careers of a broad sample of people in managerial and professional occupations—and particularly if we pay attention to women's careers—we see different patterns of engagement with the labor force. In this chapter, we review what is known about career paths and patterns that differ in some way from the traditional career template, even though their incumbents are subject to norms that would lead them to follow the traditional career path. We call these nontraditional career paths *customized careers*.[1]

Individuals who craft such careers do so in response to their own and their families' needs, values, and preferences rather than to normative expectations regarding work involvement over the life course. Thus, they may deviate in the amount and scheduling of work hours, or there may be discontinuities in their labor force participation, or

their lives may have more dynamic and transitional employment relationships than is typical in traditional careers. The extent to which people can "choose" to customize varies widely, from situations in which they face few constraints and modify their labor force engagement primarily on the basis of their personal preferences to circumstances where the decision to customize is the only reasonable response to constraints from insupportably high work demands or inadequate child care resources.

Our examination centers on those employees who would ordinarily be expected to work on a full-time, highly involved, continuous basis throughout their working lives. We focus, therefore, on managers and professionals, for whom the traditional career pattern constitutes a powerful cultural schema and places a strong emphasis on significant ongoing work involvement. The career patterns of individuals working in other occupations are equally interesting and important. And people in them face key issues of over- and underemployment, of rigidity of schedules, and of difficulties in managing family responsibilities. But they are not subject to the same cultural expectations of total commitment to career that have traditionally shaped the lives of managers and professionals. They are excluded from this chapter because the possibility to customize is usually not available to them. Indeed, designing a career path that is more influenced by personal values and preferences than by financial exigencies, choosing to withdraw temporarily from the labor force or reducing one's labor force participation during one's "prime" years are options that many workers cannot afford.

By focusing on those workers who do have this option, we emphasize the voluntary customization of labor force engagement patterns. We, therefore, exclude from our discussion individuals who experience unwanted career interruptions or reduce their working hours or engage in nontraditional employment relationships because they are unable to secure traditional career arrangements. We accentuate the roles of *choice* and *control* in making the decision to pursue a customized career, taking into account how the resources and characteristics of individuals, their families, and the organizations and occupations in which they work facilitate or constrain their patterns of involvement in the workforce.

In exploring customized careers, we emphasize the essential *longitudinal* quality of careers. Although career researchers generally agree on this, most research on careers is cross sectional and examines the relationship of some set of work-related characteristics to career-related outcomes at one point in time (for a clear exception to this trend, see work by Moen and colleagues, e.g., Han & Moen, 1999b; Moen, 1985, 2001, 2004). However, we feel that an examination of customized careers must necessarily consider the pattern of people's labor force engagement over time. Indeed, it is hardly possible to identify a customized career without this. Studying customized careers involves examining the interplay between individual actors and institutions over the life course (Blair-Loy, 1999; Elder & Caspi, 1990). We hark back to the Chicago School and view the career concept as providing a "moving perspective" (Hughes, 1958, p. 67) from which we can explore the experience of career customization at multiple points in a person's life.

In addition to the longitudinal quality of careers, we also emphasize the *inseparable connection* between the work domain and other life domains. The traditional career is built on assumptions about the separation between work and nonwork spheres of life, with employment given the highest value and priority (Bailyn, 2006; Larwood & Gattiker, 1987; Williams, 2000). It demands a nearly exclusive focus on work, which is extremely difficult to combine with significant family responsibilities (Greenhaus and Foley, Chapter 8). Indeed, recent media articles about highly educated women opting out completely from such high pressure careers (Belkin, 2003) make this point. The customized career, in contrast, allows people to forge lives between the two extremes of opting out and continuing to meet the normative expectations of traditional careers. The desire to achieve a satisfactory integration of work and "nonwork" is a major factor leading individuals to pursue customized careers (Becker & Moen, 1999; Drobnic, Blossfeld, & Rohwer, 1999; Epstein, Seron, Oglensky, & Sauté, 1999; Meiksins & Whalley, 2002). It is important to note, however, that individual adaptations are constrained by the organization, structures, and culture of work, and by the work practices that reside in these basic taken-for-granted assumptions (Rapoport, Bailyn, Fletcher, & Pruitt, 2002).

Reflecting the theoretical—if not actual—dominance of the traditional career template, career theory still tells us little about "what it means to have a career in a system that does not use traditional external markers to signify progress, advancement, and movement in some consistent direction" (Weick & Berlinger, 1989, p. 313), and even less about how careers are affected as they absorb concerns and values emanating from the personal domain. Weick (1996) notes that a crucial shift in contemporary careers is the replacement of external guides for sequences of work experience by internal, self-generated guides. A growing body of work suggests that the integration of work and family/personal life is a central internal guide for many employees (e.g., Bielby, 1992; Cooper & Lewis, 1999; Friedman & Greenhaus, 2000; Gerson, 1985; Hall, 1986; Mirvis & Hall, 1996; Moen, 1992; Moen & Roehling, 2005). This is consistent with Hall's (1976) notion of the protean career, in which the employee directs his or her own career through a process of self-exploration rather than taking career direction from the organization or occupation (or, for that matter, from societal norms). In the protean career, individuals rely on their own self-defined values and criteria for guides to structure their career paths. Customization, in the way we understand it, is one response to this process of exploration.

In this chapter, we ask what leads people to customize their careers, what forms career customization takes, and what happens when people customize their careers. The chapter is organized as follows: First, we develop a portrait of the traditional career and the forces that shape it. Second, we describe the characteristics of customized careers that differentiate them from the traditional pattern, focusing on three core career elements as useful points of contrast. Third, we ask who pursues customized careers and review what is known about the prevalence and variety of customized career arrangements. Next, we review what is known about the factors associated with customizing. Why do people pursue customized career arrangements, and what are the differences that exist in ratio-nales for customizing? We pay special attention to the individual, family, and organizational fac-tors that influence the pursuit of customized careers for skilled employees. Fourth, we review the effects of customized career arrangements on career outcomes and on the interface between paid work and personal life. We conclude with implications for future research, for career prac-tice, and for the ways in which we think about careers in professional occupations.

We note at the outset that our review is largely limited to the U.S.-based literature on careers and work-life integration. Much of the research in this area is produced in and/or targeted at the United States (Poster, 2005). Although we provide data on national differ-ences in career customization where possible, our review does not explore the factors underly-ing national differences in career patterns, such as differences in public policy, organizational practices, and national cultural values (Lyness & Kropf, 2005). The career "portrait" depicted in this chapter is shaped by factors that are, in some cases, specific to the United States.

THE TRADITIONAL CAREER: INSTITUTIONALIZED RULES AND REGIMES

The traditional career template for managers and professionals developed with the rise of industri-alization and the gendered separation of work from the home that accompanied it. Within the agrarian economy, all members of families engaged in productive labor, a pattern that largely persisted in the early years of industrial-ization (and still persists in much of the develop-ing world today). In Europe, the United States, and other countries, however, men entering industry increasingly sought jobs with wages that would allow them to support a family. Protective legislation and collective bargaining supported this model, eventually "producing a new blueprint, the breadwinner/homemaker model. Thus, industrialization sharpened distinc-tions, dividing activities into gender spheres of paid work and unpaid domestic work . . . [and] led to the development of] identifiable career pathways in particular occupations" (Moen & Roehling, 2005, p. 11). Men, as breadwinners,

followed a lockstep process of first education, then full-time, continuous employment (often involving very long hours) on a track of upward mobility (or at least movement toward seniority associated with particular occupations), and eventually total and irreversible retirement from the workforce (Moen, 2004, p. 232). The model assumed that employees had no outside respon-sibilities and that the home domain was taken care of by someone else—that is, the women of the household. As educated women, and mothers in particular, entered careers in large numbers, they were caught by this "work devotion schema" (Blair-Loy, 2003). Although the tradi-tional career model was strongly influenced by capitalistic pressures, Blair-Loy (2003) notes that it has since become "semi-autonomous from economic factors and has a normative force of its own" (p. 7). As a normative cultural model widely shared among managers and profession-als, it functions to shape both social institutions and personal identities and aspirations.

The identities of those following traditional career patterns are influenced by identification with their employing organizations or their pro-fessional occupations as well as by adherence to and promotion of traditional career norms. Not coincidentally, those individuals who achieve the greatest success within the traditional career pat-tern typically manifest total identification with it through an objective display of intense, single-minded, and sustained focus on and commitment to work, an understanding of this commitment as representing a life meaningfully spent, a strong emotional allegiance to career and employer, and an appreciation of the rewards that accrue from career commitment as representing the righteous fulfillment of the identity enacted.

This career pattern was seen as ideal not only for the purposes of individual accomplishment and socioeconomic advancement but indeed as a cornerstone of social stability (Wilensky, 1961). A wide range of social institutions evolved to support the traditional career. Moen (2004) uses the term "career regime" to refer to the "institu-tionalized rules, routines, and regulations shap-ing occupational trajectories and transitions, as well as the adult life course" (p. 232). Among these are cultural norms and the career-related, institutionalized practices of work organiza-tions, occupations, educational institutions, and government. For example, norms of professional advancement such as partnership and tenure tracks require all-out investment in work during an early period of the career to make partner or tenure, and full-time, long-term continuous involvement thereafter (Williams, 2000). And even where such professional credentialing structures do not exist, as in corporate careers, this pattern of extensive early-career involvement is necessary for subsequent success (Rosenbaum, 1984). In all cases, reducing work time or taking time out of the workforce is seen as deviant and is associated with reduced objective career success (Epstein et al., 1999; Hewlett & Luce, 2005; Judiesch & Lyness, 1999).

The career regime involves an "underlying press toward homogeneity," which, Bailyn (2006) notes, obscures the differences in the goals and orientations among workers (p. 22). Despite the widespread desire of many workers to better integrate their work and personal lives through some form of modified involvement in the workforce (Barnett & Lundgren, 1998; Clarkberg & Moen, 2001), firms as well as government and occupations premise their policies and incentive systems on the assumption that everyone defines success similarly and aspires to traverse a traditional career path, thus reinforcing this modal route (Bailyn, 2006; Kanter, 1977). Employees, in turn, shape their behavior and aspirations in accordance with institutional rewards and patterns of recognition, even if this entails disregard for their work involvement preferences.

With globalization and increased economic competition, the intensity of work demands is increasing (Jacobs & Gerson, 2004; Milliken & Dunn-Jensen, 2005; Valcour & Hunter, 2005), hence seemingly reinforcing these aspects of careers. But there are countervailing forces as well. In the United States, these stem primarily from the increasing participation of mothers in the paid labor force, thus increasing the number of dual-career families and putting great pressure on issues of care—of children, elders, and communities (Harrington, 1999). Additionally, care of children and elders is viewed as the responsibility of individual families in the United States, in contrast to a number of other nations that provide more extensive government support for child and elder care. And unlike countries where households are multigenerational, Americans typically live apart from elderly relatives. Hence the need and impetus for customized careers.

The Customized Career: Alternative Patterns of Occupational Engagement

In developing the idea of the customized career and juxtaposing it with the traditional career pattern, we focus on three core career elements: (1) work time, (2) timing and continuity, and (3) the nature of the employment relationship. Although there is no specific set of criteria that must be met for a career to be considered customized, customized careers differ from traditional careers in relation to at least one—and more frequently more—of these elements. A customized career typically involves a deviation from the norms of *work time* that prevail in the traditional career. Normative career *timing* and *continuity* are also disrupted: Customized careers may have discontinuities uncharacteristic of traditional careers, and individuals following customized careers may find their patterns of labor force engagement out of step with the timing that is associated with the traditional career. Whereas the traditional career is generally characterized by long-term employment as a regular organizational employee with relatively few organizations, the customized career is more likely to include nonstandard *employment relationships,* such as temporary work and independent contracting, as well as greater interorganizational mobility.

Customized careers are less institutionalized than traditional careers. They involve a series of choices and negotiations—with self, family, and organization and/or occupational community. Individuals who customize their careers challenge prevailing traditional career norms; thus, the burden is on them to justify their choices, persuade others as to the feasibility and sensibility of their plans, and negotiate the specific arrangements that will allow them to fit work into their preferred life patterns. Meiksins and Whalley (2002) note that individuals pursuing customized careers must struggle both to construct a new kind of professional identity and to create the arrangements that allow them to live it.

Differentiating Characteristics

As already indicated, we look at three key characteristics that differentiate the customized career from the traditional career. They have to do with the number of hours worked and the schedule that guides them, the timing of paid work throughout the life cycle, and the employment relationship. We look at each of these primarily from the point of view of the person customizing the career, but they also have implications for organizations, as briefly indicated (see Kalleberg, 2000; Kalleberg, Reynolds, & Marsden, 2003, for detailed analyses of these organizational implications).

Time

Customized careers may involve a deviation from standard full-time work schedules. While it is generally expected that managers and professionals will devote at least 40—and frequently, 50 to 60 or more—hours each week to their jobs, week after week and year after year, individuals pursuing customized careers may structure their work time differently. Often this entails some form of reduced hours. This can be accomplished by working fewer hours per day on an ongoing basis, or fewer days per week, or fewer weeks or months in the year. Reduced-hours work may come in the form of part-time work or job sharing. Both have been shown to increase hourly productivity (Harris, 1997; Olmsted & Smith, 1994).

Part-time work is usually associated with "bad" jobs: jobs with low pay, no benefits, and no career progression. Recently, though, there is evidence of reduced-hours arrangements among professionals (Barnett & Gareis, 2002; Briscoe, 2003; Epstein et al., 1999; Lee & Kossek, 2005; More Than Part Time, 2000) that have different characteristics. This "new-concept part-time work" (Barnett & Gareis, 2000; Hill, Martinson, Ferris, & Baker, 2004; Kahne, 1985, 1992) is a "good" part-time job (Tilly, 1992a), which is viewed as relatively permanent with career potential, and has salaries and benefits prorated on the basis of full-time standards.

Job sharing, where two people split the tasks (and job rewards) formerly handled by a single employee, though less frequent and seemingly more difficult to manage, actually has some advantages over part-time work. It allows full time, often even increased coverage of the work, reduces the effects of vacation time and other absences, and offers the possibility of an increased range of abilities and skills for one job (Bahls, 1990; Sheley, 1996). And even though there are some administrative costs associated with job sharing, Harris's (1997) cost-benefit analysis of job sharing in U.K. university settings suggested that a mere 0.35% productivity increase was all that was needed in order to offset the administrative costs. Using the same formula, Harris calculated that a 5% increase in job productivity would result in a ratio of benefits to costs of 14.3 to 1. This study also found that two thirds of personnel directors reported productivity increases, and an even higher percentage reported increased flexibility and continuity of employees in job-sharing arrangements. Job sharing has also been found to be useful in the preretirement period as a way to gradually phase out of work (Graig & Paganelli, 2000; Miyakoshi, 2001).

The customized reduction in work hours is not necessarily permanent, and individuals may modify their work time periodically over the course of their working careers in response to personal preferences and to demands and resources emanating from other areas of their lives. Briscoe (2003), for example, found that 41% of his physician sample in a large medical practice, and 18% of those in small group practices, had at least one period of part-time work in the 10 years preceding his survey. The desire to place some sort of boundary on the often seemingly limitless work time norms of the traditional career is one of the most potent forces leading people to customize their career pattern. Meiksins and Whalley (2002) refer to this as "putting work in its place." Within certain limits, however, it seems as if *control* over work time may be even more important than the actual number of hours worked (Barley & Kunda, 2004; Evans, Kunda, & Barley, 2004; Kalleberg & Epstein, 2001).

Timing

By timing, we mean to look at careers across the life course, which is what Moen and Han (2001) call "biographical pacing." The customized career is often marked by discontinuities.

In contrast to the traditional career pattern of continuous involvement in the workforce from early entry until retirement, customized careers may involve interruptions in labor force engagement. This may take the form of delayed entry into the labor force and/or periods of withdrawal from paid employment (Williams & Han, 2003). An emphasis on timing means looking at careers not only as the evolving sequence of paid work but also including how the employment cycle intersects with the family cycle and, in general, how it fits into a person's life experience (Altucher & Williams, 2003; Bailyn, 2006; Schein, 1978). Timing, in this sense, highlights the longitudinal perspective on careers, as well as the interdependence across different domains of life. Moen and her colleagues (Moen, 2003) give the fullest account of the various patterns that the customization of timing may take.

Women are more likely to participate in alternative timing than men, which reflects the "traditional" division of labor in households (Hewlett & Luce, 2005; Mainiero & Sullivan, 2005). A married woman in her late 30s, for example, may be entering the workforce for the first time after raising children to school age, and thus be in an entry-level career stage when others of her age cohort are in more advanced career stages. Or a woman may leave the workforce to have a child and return initially in a reduced-hours arrangement before resuming full-time employment. Such patterns reflect changes in family structures and lifestyles that are shifting received traditions. At this point in time, however, timing customization still runs against deep-seated cultural and age norms (Lawrence, 1984; Moen, 1985; Schneer & Reitman, 1994). Furthermore, such customization is highly individualized and ignores the possibility that discontinuities and age deviances have organizational as well as personal benefits (Bailyn, 1980, 1982).

Another way in which customized careers may deviate from traditional timing involves preretirement phasedowns and a return to some form of employment after retirement (Graig & Paganelli, 2000; Han & Moen, 1999a). And here, both men and women are involved.

Employment Relationship

Customized careers may involve a variety of employment relationships that differ from the traditional career arrangement of long-term employment with one or a small number of employers (Polivka, 1996). The employment relationships of individuals on customized career paths vary on the following two dimensions: (1) permanent versus temporary, because customized careers are more likely to include work that is performed in the context of a temporary employment relationship, whereas people following traditional careers normally work in permanent employment relationships; (2) organizational employment versus independent contracting or agency employment, because customized careers are more likely to include periods of employment as independent contractors, in contrast to the internal organizational employment in traditional careers. Increasing numbers of professionals are pursuing what have come to be known as "portfolio careers" (Cohen & Mallon, 1999; Gold & Fraser, 2002; Handy, 1994; Mallon, 1999), performing a variety of assignments for different clients rather than working exclusively for a single employer.

Contingency work, that is, temporary work outside of an organizational contract (except perhaps to a temp agency), has usually been seen as a form of exploitation: low-level jobs without benefits or job security (Cooper, 1995). For companies, such arrangements serve as a buffer for traditional employees. Employees working on a part-time or contingent basis are generally the first to go in layoffs. By having a group of employees who can be more easily laid off in the event of a business downturn, firms can protect the employment of the more traditional employees, whose unflagging participation in continuous employment and long work hours are seen as evidence of their superior organizational and career commitment.

There is, however, a form of independent contract work, involving professional or technical work, that fits into our defined domain (e.g., Barley & Kunda, 2004; Meiksins & Whalley, 2002). Such independent contractors are highly skilled workers who have decided to work independently for one or many clients at the same time, none of whom assumes the legal responsibilities of an employer (Allan, 2002; Kalleberg, 2000). They do not have a wage contract and are responsible for their own benefits and tax arrangements (Kalleberg, 2000). They offer firms the opportunity to access specialized skills that might be needed for a short period of time (Davis-Blake & Uzzi, 1993). Even though independent contracting is seen as entailing greater career risk for the individual (due to the relatively lower level of employer commitment they enjoy), there is evidence that this is not always the case. For example, these highly skilled contractors may find it easier to get a job than laid off employees with similar skills (Barley & Kunda, 2004). And one study (Bidwell, 2004) has shown that companies actually keep their employed and contracted workers in almost equal proportions, because the contractors often have more up-to-date skills.

The independent contractor is not usually driven to customize for family reasons. Rather, the decision has more to do with dissatisfaction with being part of an organization and with the politics, incompetence, and inequity they have experienced in their jobs (Kunda, Barley, & Evans, 2002). It is also an option pursued by older workers when faced with retirement. Independent contractors, as opposed to workers who customize by adjusting time or timing, are more often men, older, have more schooling than the average worker, and get higher average salaries than traditional employees (Cohany, 1998; Matusik & Hill, 1998).

In summary, every kind of customization has advantages and disadvantages for the individual and for the employer or client for whom that person is working. In all cases, however, individuals following customized careers typically bear a greater burden for overseeing their own career development than do employees pursuing traditional careers.

Who Customizes?

We have already indicated some distinctions in who customizes, especially as they differ in the particular ways in which the career is customized. It is not easy to obtain good data about the prevalence of any of these customizations. Each form of customization offers answers to different conflicts, preferences, or needs. The adoption of a specific form of customization is also linked to the life stage people find themselves in and the options open to them. Obtaining reliable statistics is difficult given the myriad subtleties involved, but the following give some idea of the extent of different kinds of customization and who is doing which kind of customizing in the United States.

Time

There are many reasons why people might find themselves working part-time. They might not be able to find a full-time job, or illness or injuries might affect their ability to work more. Since our intention is to understand who *chooses* to customize their careers, we would like to know the prevalence of voluntary part-time work. As a primary source for the U.S. labor force, we use data from the Current Population Survey (CPS), available in 2003 on the basis of the 2000 Census (U.S. Census Bureau, 2003b), and focus on their category of part-time work for noneconomic reasons.[2] Part-timers for noneconomic reasons, according to these data, comprise 13.8% of the workforce. Since, however, noneconomic reasons include illness, school, and social security limitations, we also looked at the Survey of Income and Program Participation (SIPP) for 2001 (U.S. Census Bureau, 2001b), which specifically includes a category of "wanted to work part time." Based on these data, 6.9% of the workforce are voluntary part-timers. We suspect that the actual number lies somewhere in between.

There are countries, however, in which part-time work is more prevalent. The Organisation for Economic Co-Operation and Development (OECD) reports that the percentage of workers employed part-time (voluntary and nonvoluntary) is 16.6% for the EU-15 (with country percentages ranging from 5.6% in Greece to 34.5% in the Netherlands, 18.8% for Canada, 27.9% for Australia, 7.7% for Korea, and 26% for Japan) (OECD, 2004). Voluntary part-time in the United Kingdom comprises 19% of the workforce (Office for National Statistics, 2004). In the Netherlands, in particular, both government and unions support part-time jobs that have proportional compensation and benefits.

To obtain more detailed comparisons of American part-time workers, we rely on the CPS material, on the assumption that relative figures are similar in both data sets (CPS and SIPP). Among "management, business, and financial operations" and "professional and related occupations," 10.6% fall into the noneconomic part-time category; in the United Kingdom, 12.3% of the management, business, and professional employees work part-time (voluntary and involuntary) (Equal Opportunities Commission, 2004). Special occupational studies show even smaller numbers: 2.6% in law (Epstein et al., 1999) and < 2% in the finance professions (Wharton & Blair-Loy, 2002). Among the people who have the option to customize their careers—which is our domain—the percentage probably lies somewhere in between.

Most of these part-timers are women. Indeed, in the working population as a whole, only 7.8% of men are noneconomic part-timers, compared with 20.5% of women. More than two thirds (69.3%) of all noneconomic part-timers are female, as are almost three fourths (73.6%) of those in the managerial and professional occupations (U.S. Census Bureau, 2003b).

Finally, returning to the SIPP data, we see that voluntary part-time work is particularly high in the 55 to 64 age group (10.9% as compared with 6.9% for the workforce as a whole), suggesting that it is probably being used as a strategy to ease into retirement. In fact, in the 65+ group, fully 37% of those still working opt for part-time employment. This pattern is also observed in the United Kingdom where 33% of the 55 to 64 age group and 78% of the 65+ age group work part-time (Equal Opportunities Commission, 2004).

Internationally, as in the United States, most part-time workers are women. Keeping in mind that the numbers available are for both voluntary and involuntary part-time, in the EU-15 6.3% of men and 30.1% of women work part-time. The country with the highest percentage of men and women working part-time is the Netherlands (14.8% of men and 59.6% of women); the lowest percentage for women is found in Greece (9.9%) and for men in Spain (2.5%) (OECD, 2004). In Australia, 16.5% of men and 42.2% of women, in Korea, 5.3% of men and 11.2% of women, and in Japan, 14.7% of men and 42.2% of women are part-time workers.

Data on job sharing are even more difficult to find. According to the U.S. SIPP data, only 0.05% of the labor force are in job-sharing positions. Again, though, it is primarily a female choice: 71% of all job sharers are women. It is most prevalent in the 35 to 44 age group and is highest (0.08%) in the "professional specialty"

category (U.S. Census Bureau, 2001b). In contrast, U.K. job sharing represents 1% of the workforce, and 90% of job sharers are women (Equal Opportunities Commission, 2004). Canada's job sharers constitute 1.5% of the workforce, and 84% of them are women (Marshall, 1997).

Timing

To get an idea of the prevalence of noncontinuous career patterns, we turn to the Cornell Couples Study (Moen, 2003). Analyzing the career paths of a group of retirees, Moen and Han (2001) found most in orderly careers, with about two thirds of them being men and one third being women. Two categories, however, deviated from this continuous career path. About 12% of their sample of middle-class working couples delayed entry into the workforce, and 5% followed an intermittent career pattern, that is, alternate periods in and out of the workforce. The story is again a gendered one. All these people were women. Furthermore, the socioeconomic index, which records the prestige of the occupation, was lower for these two groups than for the rest of the sample (Han & Moen, 1999b). Based on these data, all the women who customized by adjusting timing over the life course were responding to the difficulties experienced by working couples with children to manage their three jobs (his paid job, her paid job, and the shared job of raising children and managing a household) and paid a career price. The gender profile of individuals customizing their career timing is changing in younger generations. A more recent study (Hewlett & Luce, 2005) of "highly qualified" Americans (i.e., with graduate, professional, or honors undergraduate degrees) found that 37% of the women and 24% of the men in their sample reported having customized their career timing by leaving work voluntarily at some point during their careers.

Employment Relationship

Approximately 6.4% of the U.S. workforce are independent contractors (U.S. Census Bureau, 2001a). Here, the gender story is very different: Almost two thirds (64.5%) of these are men. They are older and more educated than the average worker: Almost 30% fall into the 35 to 54 age range, with another 16% aged 55 to 64; 27% have associate degrees[3] and 35% have bachelor's degrees. Independent contractors gravitate toward executive and administrative occupations (19.4%) as well as toward occupations having to do with precision production, craft, and repair (19.5%). The industries most highly populated by them are the services and construction industries.

The international picture partially mirrors the U.S. situation. In the European Union, self-employed workers represent 14% of the workforce (ranging from 7.5% in Luxembourg to 32% in Greece), and 73% of them are men. While no educational level dominates, self-employed workers are older, with 24% of them in the 50 to 59 age group and another 12% in the 60+ age group. The largest concentration in an occupational group is for legislators and managers, which represents 23% of self-employed workers, followed by craft-related workers at 18% (Eurostat, 2003).

We see, therefore, that different forms of customizing fit different kinds of people at different periods in their lives. But all allow employees to better integrate their employment with their family and personal interests and responsibilities.

What Leads People to Customize Their Careers?

Our review of the literature indicates that people's reasons for pursuing customized career arrangements can be grouped into two main categories. The first has to do with accommodation to family and community. People who make career adjustments in response to such demands cite reasons such as caring for children or other dependents, easing the burden of dual-career demands, and making time for volunteer work or more extensive community engagement. In general, women are more likely to customize for these reasons and are more likely to do so by shifting the *time* and *timing* of work.

The second set of rationales for customizing centers on the desire to bring the career into better alignment with personal values and preferences. Specific reasons cited include the following: to engage more fully in other life roles, to "get out of the rat race," to gain greater autonomy and control over the nature of work and work time, to achieve more job and work variety, to escape organizational politics and/or

incompetent management, to escape the inequity of the traditional employment relationship (employees are expected to work devotedly for employers who might lay them off at a moment's notice), and to earn more money. These reasons are more often given by men, and they are more likely to become independent contractors. Hence, both the rationales for customizing and the forms it takes vary by gender.

These two sets of reasons are not mutually exclusive. The difficulty in isolating single reasons for customizing reflects the interplay between individual preferences and the institutional contexts that shape career decision making. For example, a professional woman who decides to move from a position that demands very long hours into a job-sharing arrangement may cite her desire to live a more balanced life and make more time for the people and activities she values, but she is also responding to institutionalized structures (e.g., her husband's demanding and inflexible career or the lack of availability of flexible child care) that make her continued adherence to a demanding work schedule unsustainable. In other words, there are a number of factors at the individual, family, and organizational level that are predictive of the decision to customize. We summarize these factors in the following paragraphs.

Individual Resources

High levels of human capital facilitate people's pursuit of customized careers. When workers possess valuable skills that are relatively rare in the labor market, employers will be motivated to provide them with the work arrangements they desire. The most common pattern in customizing work hours is for employees to start in traditional work arrangements, prove their worth to their employer, and then negotiate customized work arrangements. Such situations are often referred to as "retention" jobs (Tilly, 1996) because they reflect employers' desire to retain the employees. A study by Klein, Berman, and Dickson (2000) found that employers were more likely to accommodate requests for part-time arrangements from attorneys with high performance who were seen as difficult to replace. But by demanding traditional top performance before allowing such accommodations, employers miss the opportunity to maximize the potential of all their employees (see Bailyn, 2006).

Besides human capital, social capital is also important. Having marketable skills and relationships with potential clients and other independent workers is key for portfolio careers and to sustain careers as independent contractors (Barley & Kunda, 2004; Batt, Christopherson, Rightor, & Van Jaarsveld, 2001; Kunda et al., 2002; Mallon, 1999; Marler, Barringer, & Milkovich, 2002).

Household-Level Resources

People are more likely to customize when they have resources that facilitate such arrangements. For example, having a spouse whose job provides adequate income and benefits enables the pursuit of a customized career (Hewlett & Luce, 2005). Indeed, one person's opportunity to choose a customized career may depend on a partner's lack of a similar choice.[4] In contrast, employees who are the sole earners in the family unit are less able to risk income, benefits, and job security since they have no one to fall back on financially. Finally, the absolute level of household income is obviously a factor in predicting career customization. Dual-earner couples where both members have relatively low wages are not likely to be able to afford to customize. They do not fall into our domain, since their options are so much more restricted.

Gender

As we have seen, customized careers are heavily gendered, with women being much more likely than men to follow them (Blank, 1990; Epstein et al., 1999; Han & Moen, 1999a; Hewlett & Luce, 2005; Meiksins & Whalley, 2002; Ross & Wright, 1998). Only in independent contracting, a small though growing part of the economy, do we see a preponderance of men (Evans et al., 2004; Meiksins & Whalley, 2002). Men have greater normative demands to pursue full-time, continuous careers, and have less support for deviations from this path. Indeed, not only are women more likely to request to work part-time or take time off, but they are also more likely to be given the opportunity to do so. Reducing work involvement in order to do more child or family care is seen as a legitimate need of women but not of men (Klein et al., 2000). Those few men who opt for reduced work hours are likely not to cite care of children as a reason (Barnett & Lundgren, 1998). They take sick leave or vacation days rather than paternity leave. Traditional gender norms actually restrict men's work choices. Also, since men still tend to earn more than women, it makes more economic sense for women to customize than men (Becker, 1981).

Furthermore, women continue to carry the main responsibility for care giving and maintaining the home (Hochschild & Machung, 1989), even among highly educated professionals. Indeed, a recent study found that wives who earn more than their husbands seem to compensate for this nonnormative circumstance by retaining a traditional gendered division of household labor and doing more of this work than their husbands (Bittman, England, Folbre, Sayer, & Matheson, 2003). The challenge of successfully meeting and integrating the demands of two high-level traditional careers, a household and children is clearly difficult (Barnett & Hall, 2001; Jacobs & Gerson, 2001). The most common response is for wives to customize their career arrangements in order to meet the demands of the nonwork domain (Becker & Moen, 1999; Kossek, Barber, & Winters, 1999). Women's career patterns are much more closely coupled to family and caregiving needs than are men's (Drobnic et al., 1999).

Wives are also more likely than husbands to make career sacrifices to support their spouses' career progress, even among dual-career couples who both start on traditional career paths (Becker & Moen, 1999; Bielby, 1992; Eby, 2001; Pixley & Moen, 2003). In research using data collected during the 1970s, major decisions such as relocation for career opportunities were based almost exclusively on husbands' careers, without regard to wives' employment (e.g., Bielby, 1992; Mincer, 1978). Using a sample of dual-earner couples (primarily managerial, professional, and technical workers) collected in 1999, Pixley and Moen (2003) found that 54% of members of married couples reported that the husband's career had consistently been given priority in making major decisions such as changing jobs, moving, going back to school, or having children, versus only

15% who reported that the wife's career had been given priority. Women continue to be much more likely to reduce their work hours, withdraw from paid employment, or move into self-employment if doing so helps facilitate their husbands' career progress.

The preceding discussion highlights the need to examine career patterns and career decision making within the context of a household rather than examining individual careers in isolation. Our understanding of people's decisions to customize their careers is much richer to the extent that we have awareness of the family context in which such decisions are made (Eaton & Bailyn, 2000; Mainiero & Sullivan, 2005). According to one argument, for example, couple-level career decisions are generally made with the goal of favoring the career advancement of the partner who has greater earning power and career opportunities, typically the husband (Becker, 1981). This argument, however, does not explain why the gendered pattern persists when members of a couple have equivalent levels of human capital. Alternative arguments based on role theory emphasize the pervasiveness of traditional gender-role socialization and the resulting tendency for both men and women to make decisions that reinforce the male-breadwinner model (see Hochschild & Machung, 1989). Barnett and Lundgren (1998) reviewed several studies that lend support to the argument that gender-role ideologies continue to influence women's choices to customize, even when their human capital is equal to or superior to that of their husbands.

Values, Preferences, and Identity

One prominent theme running through contemporary literature on customized career arrangements is that people make decisions to forge their own career paths rather than to conform to expectations because they are better able to honor their own values and preferences by so doing. This theme reflects several, now classic, strands of careers literature that have focused on individuals' search to find their true selves in the midst of career structures that favor homogeneity, including Schein's (1978) work on career anchors, Hall's (1976) work on protean careers, and Arthur and Rousseau's (1996) work on boundaryless careers. Meiksins and Whalley (2002), for instance, found that some of their technical professionals chose to customize their work schedules in order to allow more extensive involvement in hobbies, volunteer work, or religious activities. Other studies have documented both men's and women's choices to reduce work time, temporarily leave the workforce, or change careers to achieve a greater sense of personal authenticity, to be true to themselves, to enable altruistic activity, or to find spiritual fulfillment (Casey & Alach, 2004; Hewlett & Luce, 2005; Ibarra, 2003; Mainiero & Sullivan, 2005). Thus, the salience of individuals' role identities affects the amount of time they devote to each of their roles. People whose identities are centered on work tend to put in longer work hours than people whose identities are centered on family or other nonwork roles (Friedman & Greenhaus, 2000; Hakim, 2002; Major, Klein, & Ehrhart, 2002; Rothbard & Edwards, 2003). Personal values and preferences are also a factor in who leaves traditional careers to pursue independent contracting (Kunda et al., 2002; Mallon, 1999) and in who takes time out of the workforce voluntarily (Blair-Loy, 2003; Kossek et al., 1999).

Employment Context

Past research has identified several features of the employment context that are related to people's opportunity and likelihood to pursue customized careers, including organizational policies, supervisor and coworker supportiveness, an organizational culture that is accepting of diversity, flexible work design, and adequate staffing levels (Epstein et al., 1999; Kossek et al., 1999; Lee, MacDermid, & Buck, 2000; MacDermid, Lee, Buck, & Williams, 2001; Valcour & Tolbert, 2003). Some jobs lend themselves better to customized careers than others. In the legal field, for example, litigators who work on pressing cases have less opportunity to customize than do lawyers who do research-based work with less pressing deadlines (Epstein et al., 1999). Emergency room doctors, who work on scheduled shifts, have more freedom to customize than do surgeons.

Opportunities to customize are also greater when organizations have appropriate staffing levels. When firms are faced with growing demand and/or are "right sizing" in order to be more competitive, managers are less likely to allow employees to customize (Valcour & Tolbert, 2003). Workers' efforts to customize are facilitated by the existence of organizational policies that provide for flexible schedules, part-time work, job sharing, or leaves of absence. The use and benefit of such policies, however, depends on supervisors and coworkers believing that an employee's desire to customize is legitimate.

An organizational culture supportive of diversity in career paths is also important for customized careers. Lee et al.'s (2000) study of organizational approaches to the implementation of reduced-load work arrangements revealed three different paradigms that describe the way in which organizations view and manage this type of customized career arrangement for their managerial and professional employees. The first paradigm, labeled "accommodation," reflects an organization's stance that reduced-load work arrangements are only feasible in a limited range of jobs and are generally disruptive to established organizational routines. The employer's stance is that customizing is likely to be detrimental to employees' careers and that it only makes sense to approve requests for reduced-load work if the organization stands to benefit (e.g., by retaining a valued employee or by getting close to full-time work at a discounted rate of pay). Firms operating under the second paradigm, "elaboration," have more formal policies that support alternative work arrangements and view such arrangements as an important part of attracting and retaining a diverse workforce, but they continue to cling to and uphold traditional career structures for the most part. In these firms, it is still viewed as preferable for workers to follow the traditional career pattern. The third paradigm, "transformation," describes an open and accepting posture wherein "reduced-load work arrangements become a springboard for thinking about new ways of defining and organizing career paths and reward structures for a changing workforce" (Lee et al., 2000, p. 1218). Managers in such firms believe that their organizations need to adapt and change continuously in order to perform well and that they can learn how from the diverse needs of their employees. Rather than being constrained by traditional career structures, they view customized careers as a way for their firms to develop employees for

leadership in the long term. Requests for reduced-load arrangements are not seen as troublesome exceptions, but as normal sources of variability that good managers should be able to respond to effectively.

What Happens When People Customize Their Careers?

Past research examining the effects of customization can be organized around two primary sets of criteria: career-related outcomes and outcomes associated with one's personal life. While the specific effects are often equivocal and related to various personal and organizational factors, we can summarize the literature by saying that customizing a career always involves costs and benefits. People who customize gain more control over their work schedules and conditions of employment but typically give up some control over their career options and future opportunities (Ross & Wright, 1998). In the following paragraphs, we review research that sheds light on how the decision to customize affects career, work-family outcomes, and identity.

Career-Related Outcomes

Research has demonstrated that customizing has a number of positive effects on immediate work-related outcomes such as productivity and satisfaction. People who move from a full-time to a part-time work schedule often report gains in their level of focus and concentration at work and an improved ability to identify priorities and work efficiently (Buck, Lee, & MacDermid, 2002; Epstein et al., 1999; Meiksins & Whalley, 2002). Similarly, individuals who move from traditional employment relationships into independent contracting report greater enjoyment from work because they have more choice about the work they do, greater job variety, a higher level of work challenge, and more direct and immediate responsibility for the results of their work (Barley & Kunda, 2004; Batt et al., 2001; Kunda et al., 2002; Marler et al., 2002; Parker, 2002; Von Hippel, Mangum, Greenberger, Heneman, & Skoglind, 1997). Research on the design of work and intrinsic motivation has established that these qualities (i.e., autonomy, challenge, skill variety, task identity, and feedback) are associated with higher levels of motivation and satisfaction (Hackman & Oldham, 1980).

Objective Career Success

Customized careers are not well institutionalized in organizations and professional occupations, and they tend to put those following them on side tracks (Epstein et al., 1999; Lawrence & Corwin, 2003; Schwartz, 1989). One of the most prevalent themes in the literature is that customized careers require individual negotiation. Whenever an employee who is expected to follow traditional career norms makes the decision to customize, the onus falls on that individual to negotiate for a nonstandard work arrangement.

A second common theme is that customizing has a negative impact on people's objective career success outcomes, as typically measured by earnings and actual or potential promotions. It is well established that people working part-time earn less than people working full time, though not necessarily on an hourly basis (Blank, 1986, as quoted in Tilly, 1992b). Hewlett and Luce (2005) found that even relatively short periods of time out of the workforce (1.2 years on average) are associated with an 18% loss in women's earning power across financial sectors. This figure jumped to 37% for leaves of 3 years or more. Most research also indicates that reduced-hours employment is associated with reduced career opportunity (Blair-Loy & Wharton, 2002; Epstein et al., 1999; MacDermid et al., 2001; Meiksins & Whalley, 2002). In an exception to this trend, a recent study of professional women employed by IBM found that there was no difference in perceived career opportunity reported by part-time and full-time respondents (Hill et al., 2004). This study, however, did not test actual promotion outcomes, only perceptions.

As we have already indicated, the customized career pattern is gendered, and women have greater normative freedom to customize. Consistent with this, women also seem to have less to lose from customizing than men do. Men suffer greater career-related penalties than do women, in terms of both objective and subjective career success outcomes (Han & Moen, 1998, 1999b; Schneer & Reitman, 1990, 1995, 1997; Valcour & Tolbert, 2003). While it is accepted that some women will choose to reduce work involvement in order to meet demands emanating from the nonwork domain, men who make this choice tend to be seen as deviant.

As with reduced-hours work, managers whose work histories include employment gaps pay a penalty both in terms of income and promotions (Judiesch & Lyness, 1999; Ketsche & Branscomb, 2003; Schneer & Reitman, 1990). The evidence on objective career success is less clear with respect to the effects of moving from a traditional employment relationship to independent contracting. While some studies show that independent contractors earn less than their traditionally employed counterparts (Marler et al., 2002), a few have found that people can sometimes earn more as independent contractors (Barley & Kunda, 2004; Batt et al., 2001; Kunda et al., 2002). These studies, however, were conducted in booming high-tech fields in the late 1990s. The differences in the findings of these and other studies suggest that the income of independent contractors is contingent on factors in the external market and is more sensitive to economic fluctuations than is the income of traditional employees. One finding that is not in doubt is that individuals in customized careers must bear more of the burden for managing their own career development than is the case with employees following traditional careers (Batt et al., 2001; Jones, 1996; Valcour & Snell, 2002; Von Hippel et al., 1997).

Employers' decisions not to invest in the career development of their part-time employees are based on stereotypical beliefs that part-time workers have tenuous attachments to the labor force. These assumptions tend to limit the opportunities for training and promotion available to people working reduced hours (Moen, 1985, pp. 114–115). In independent contracting, in contrast, marketable skills drive success, which means that individuals are continuously faced with the challenge of keeping them up to date, particularly in industries characterized by rapidly evolving technology. Such continuous updating requires significant investments of time, energy, and often money on the part of individuals (Batt et al., 2001; Kunda et al., 2002).

Subjective Career Success

A few studies indicate that customizing can have a positive impact on individuals' subjective career success—or at least no negative impact—particularly when the effects of customizing include increasing people's enjoyment of their work and reducing their job-related stress (Gold & Fraser, 2002; Hill et al., 2004; Kunda et al., 2002). More frequently, however, research indicates that customizing a career entails making a career sacrifice on some level. Although customizing is often satisfying, the fact that it goes against prevailing career norms creates a number of problems. Thus, while people relieve themselves of some of the demands of the traditional career, they also give up some of its rewards. In particular, customized careerists struggle with the idea of lost opportunities (Blair-Loy, 2003; Epstein et al., 1999; MacDermid et al., 2001; Mallon, 1999), and the more onerous the perceived trade-offs associated with reduced work involvement the greater the dissatisfaction (Barnett & Gareis, 2000). Research has shown that part-time attorneys often experience diminished professional esteem and morale; some even express feelings of disgrace (Epstein et al., 1999). Anticipation of downtime (time without a current paying project) is something that all contractors experience and that is very stressful for some (Evans et al., 2004).

All in all, the literature suggests that the effects of customizing on subjective career success depend on each individual's career identity and goals. MacDermid and colleagues (2001) identified two groups of people, differentiated on success, in their study of managers and professionals working in reduced-load arrangements. The group who felt that their career arrangements were highly successful were most distinguished from the low success group in terms of their definitions of career success. Members of the low success group defined success in terms of the traditional "objective" career rewards of promotions, raises, and job titles. In contrast, those who felt highly successful held personal definitions of career success that focused more on learning, social relationships, and the content and process of their jobs.

Work/Personal-Life Integration

Customizing the career, which most often means redirecting some time and involvement from the work domain to the personal domain, is usually associated with lower levels of work-family conflict and higher levels of satisfaction with work/personal-life integration (Epstein et al., 1999; Friedman & Greenhaus, 2000; Frone, Yardley, & Markel, 1997; Higgins, Duxbury, & Johnson, 2000; Meiksins & Whalley, 2002; Tolbert, Valcour, & Marler, 2002). As our review to this point indicates, customizing tends to generate positive affect in the work role as well as to help reserve time and energy for other roles. Greenhaus and Powell's (2006) recent review of the literature on work-family enrichment argues that these time-based and psychological resources generated by customizing can, under the right conditions, have positive impacts on work/personal-life integration by stimulating positive affect in work and nonwork roles and/or by facilitating higher performance in both roles, which also tends to produce increased life satisfaction.

Gender Effects

We note two ways in which the effects of customizing on the work/personal-life interface vary by gender. There is evidence that customizing has greater negative effects on the marital and family stability of men than of women (Han & Moen, 1998; Valcour & Tolbert, 2003). Additionally, for women, their reduction of work hours leads to taking on a greater share of the burden of domestic work within the family (Stier & Lewin-Epstein, 2000). Thus, in the face of conventional gender-role norms, it appears that the pattern of women reducing work involvement in response to family demands may reinforce gender inequities within the family. Research that has examined the effects of work hours on life quality at the couple level of analysis has found that life quality indicators (low levels of stress, overload, and work-family conflict, and high levels of coping and mastery) are highest when both spouses work a regular full-time schedule (39–45 hours per week), with neither spouse working either long hours or reduced hours (Moen & Yu, 2000). Customized careers, in contrast, seem to reinforce traditional gender roles, both in the family and at work.

Identity

For professionals, career and identity are tightly entwined. The literature suggests that identity both drives career decision making and is influenced by it in an adaptive-reactive process. The traditional career has a way of forging the identities of those who follow it. As Mary Blair-Loy (2003) elaborates in her book on the careers of executive women in finance, the traditional career is often experienced by its followers as "a calling or vocation that deserves single-minded allegiance and gives meaning and purpose to life" (pp. 1–2). Allegiances to employer, to occupation, and to one's own career success become important elements in the identities of people following traditional career paths. Job loss or perceived lack of career success within the traditional career (e.g., being passed over for a promotion or not attaining the prestige one feels one is entitled to) is often experienced as a real blow to one's sense of self.

For people pursuing customized careers, career identity has a different quality. The literature suggests that the identity of these people is less defined by work, both because of the values that lead them to reject some aspects of the traditional career pattern and the career consequences of these decisions (Epstein et al., 1999). People following customized careers are likely to be more psychologically involved in their families and communities and define success differently than do people pursuing traditional careers, with personal growth and family involvement becoming more important criteria than pay, promotions, or job prestige (Bailyn, 1989; Friedman & Greenhaus, 2000).

Many people pursuing customized careers were solidly on traditional career trajectories at one point in time. For these individuals, identity can be unsettled, with some people reporting that they feel they don't quite "fit" anywhere (Blair-Loy, 2003). Customized careerists, who are often "out of step" with the expected schedule of the traditional career template, frequently suffer some degree of identity ambiguity. For example, Epstein and colleagues (1999) describe the "prestige limbo" of lawyers who have chosen to reduce their work hours and get off the partner track, and consequently end up occupying lower-prestige positions than lawyers who were once junior to them.

In summary, the effects of customization are complex and differ by gender and life stage. Because we have concentrated on individuals, we have seen their customizing in reference to unchanging organizational forms. We have not formulated a set of recommendations for the ways in which organizations might change to accommodate all their employees' needs, interests, and values, but we direct the reader to the following sources for a discussion of these considerations: Bailyn (2006), Barnett and Hall (2001), Friedman, Christensen, and DeGroot (1998), Hewlett and Luce (2005), Kochan (2005), Mainiero and Sullivan (2005), and Rapoport et al. (2002).

IMPLICATIONS AND CONCLUSIONS

Customized careers are clearly not "orderly." But they are becoming more prevalent because the pressures that create the need for them are increasing. There are more families in which all the adults are in the workforce, creating problems of care; employment is becoming less secure, forcing people to adapt in new ways; and lifestyles and values are shifting, leading to multiple ways of forging an identity and multiple definitions of life success. In the face of these pressures, customized careers represent a creative intersection of the changing workforce with its multiple family structures, with the more demanding economic conditions and the resulting new organizational forms.

In general, we can say that there are basically two modal patterns of customization, and they will vary at different points of people's life cycles. One centers on accommodation to family and issues of care. This tends to be a predominantly female pattern during the child-rearing period and often consists of part-time work or job sharing. An exception, here, is that both men and women just prior to or after formal retirement may well customize in this way. The other pattern centers on lifestyle more generally: on having room to encompass, in activities as well as in identity, aspects of life beyond employment. And here we see more of a male pattern and find it personified particularly in contract work. In both cases, though, control over one's time is a key element.

Whether the gendered character of these patterns will lessen as men become more involved in families and women become more entrepreneurial is a key question for all future research in this area. It means that we need to think of work careers in new ways. Not only do they have to be viewed over a life course, but they need to be seen in the context of other aspects of people's lives. What this implies concretely is that careers cannot be studied as if individuals live in isolation; the context of their lives—economically, psychologically, and sociologically—must be considered. In the end, this may require the unit of analysis in careers research to shift from the individual to the household. And it may require different approaches to research design and data collection.

This approach to careers has implications for practice as well. For individuals and those who guide them—career counselors, mentors, and the like—it means an explicit legitimation of all aspects of life when making or advising on choices and decisions about employment. For employers, the issue is more complicated. They too, and their organizations, will have to legitimate the personal lives of their employees. Though counterintuitive, this need not mean turning away from their business goals. Indeed, there are times when business goals are actually better met if workers are supported in customizing their careers to the needs of a given period of their lives. Also, one should not discount the costs of *not* doing so—costs of burnout, stress-related health care needs, turnover, and, in general, loss of motivation and commitment to work. All these can be alleviated by creating an environment where customization is not only permitted on the books but also explicitly accepted and actively supported.

We are aware, of course, that none of this is easy in our individualistic, work-centered society. Individual choices to customize, even though they are important for the individuals who make them, will not be sufficient to deal with the problems that lie behind their need. They serve as important band-aids to growing concerns for working families, but do not touch some of the underlying conditions that create the problems in the first place. To get at these "root causes," we need to study and change current organizational practices and the assumptions about work, commitment, and success that underlie them. Only then will career customization serve both the employee and the employer—as well as society as a whole.

NOTES

1. The phrase "customized careers" draws inspiration from Meiksins and Whalley's (2002) notion of customized work schedules.

2. Part-time work for noneconomic reasons "includes those persons who usually work part time and were at work 1 to 34 hours during the reference week for a noneconomic reason. Noneconomic reasons include: Illness or other medical limitations, childcare problems or other family or personal obligations, school or training, retirement or Social Security limits on earnings, and being in a job in which full-time work is less than 35 hours. This group also includes those who gave an economic reason for usually working 1 to 34 hours but said they do not want to work full time or were unavailable for such work" (U.S. Census Bureau, 2003a).

3. An Associate degree is an academic degree granted by a college or university after the satisfactory completion of a 2-year, full-time program of study or its part-time equivalent. In general, the Associate of Arts (AA) or Associate of Science (AS) degree is granted after completing a program of study similar to the first 2 years of a 4-year college curriculum.

4. The Third Path Institute, founded and run by Jessica DeGroot in Philadelphia, is attempting to teach couples how both can customize so that they can share equally in the joys and responsibilities of both breadwinning and caring.

REFERENCES

Allan, P. (2002, June). The contingent workforce: Challenges and new directions. *American Business Review, 20,* 103–110.

Altucher, K. A., & Williams, L. B. (2003). Family clocks: Timing parenthood. In P. Moen (Ed.), *It's about time: Couples and careers.* Ithaca, NY: Cornell University Press.

Arthur, M. B., Hall, D. T., & Lawrence, B. S. (1989). *Handbook of career theory.* Cambridge, UK: Cambridge University Press.

Arthur, M. B., & Rousseau, D. M. (1996). *The boundaryless career: A new employment principle for a new organizational era.* New York: Oxford University Press.

Bahls, J. E. (1990). Getting full-time work from part-time employees. *Management Review, 79*(2), 50.

Bailyn, L. (1980). The "slow burn" way to the top: Some thoughts on the early years in organizational careers. In C. B. Derr (Ed.), *Work, family, and the career: New frontiers in theory and research.* New York: Praeger.

Bailyn, L. (1982). The apprenticeship model of organizational careers: A response to changes in the relation between work and family. In P. A. Wallace (Ed.), *Women in the work place.* Boston: Auburn House.

Bailyn, L. (1989). Toward the perfect workplace? *Communications of the ACM, 32,* 460–471.

Bailyn, L. (2006). *Breaking the mold: Redesigning work for productive and satisfying lives.* Ithaca, NY: Cornell University Press.

Barley, S. R. (1989). Careers, identities, and institutions: The legacy of the Chicago School of Sociology. In M. B. Arthur, D. T. Hall, & B. S. Lawrence (Eds.), *Handbook of career theory.* Cambridge, UK: Cambridge University Press.

Barley, S. R., & Kunda, G. (2004). *Gurus, hired guns and warm bodies: Itinerant experts in a knowledge economy.* Princeton, NJ: Princeton University Press.

Barnett, R. C., & Gareis, K. (2000). Reduced-hours employment: The relationship between difficulty of trade-offs and quality of life. *Work and Occupations, 27*(2), 168–187.

Barnett, R. C., & Gareis, K. (2002). Full-time and reduced-hours work schedules and marital quality: A study of female physicians with young children. *Work and Occupations, 29*(3), 364–379.

Barnett, R. C., & Hall, D. T. (2001). How to use reduced hours to win the war for talent. *Organizational Dynamics, 29*(3), 192–210.

Barnett, R. C., & Lundgren, L. (1998). Dual-earner couples and the decision to work less: A conceptual model. *Community, Work and Family, 1*(3), 273–295.

Batt, R., Christopherson, S., Rightor, N., & Van Jaarsveld, D. (2001). *Net working: Work patterns and workforce policies for the new media industry.* Washington, DC: Economic Policy Institute.

Becker, G. S. (1981). *A treatise on the family.* Cambridge, MA: Harvard University Press.

Becker, H. (2004, March). *Careers.* Paper presented at the annual meeting of Eastern Sociological Society, New York.

Becker, P. E., & Moen, P. (1999). Scaling back: Dual-earner couples' work-family strategies. *Journal of Marriage and the Family, 61*(4), 995–1007.

Belkin, L. (2003, October 26). The opt-out revolution. *New York Times Magazine,* p. 42ff.

Bidwell, M. (2004). *What do firm boundaries do? Employment relationships and transaction governance in internal and outsourced IT projects.* Unpublished doctoral dissertation, MIT, Cambridge, MA.

Bielby, D. D. (1992). Commitment to work and family. *Annual Review of Sociology, 18,* 281–302.

Bittman, M., England, P., Folbre, N., Sayer, L., & Matheson, G. (2003). When does gender trump money? Bargaining and time in household work. *American Journal of Sociology, 109*(1), 186–214.

Blair-Loy, M. (1999). Career patterns of executive women in finance: An optimal matching analysis. *American Journal of Sociology, 104*(5), 1346–1397.

Blair-Loy, M. (2003). *Competing devotions: Career and family among women executives.* Cambridge, MA: Harvard University Press.

Blair-Loy, M., & Wharton, A. (2002). The overtime culture in a global corporation: A cross-national study of finance professionals' interest in working part-time. *Work and Occupations, 29*(1), 32–64.

Blank, R. M. (1990). Understanding part-time work. *Research in Labor Economics, 11,* 137–158.

Briscoe, F. (2003). *Bureaucratic flexibility: Large organizations and the restructuring of physician careers.* Unpublished doctoral dissertation, MIT, Cambridge, MA.

Buck, M. L., Lee, M. D., & MacDermid, S. M. (2002). Designing creative careers and creative lives through reduced load work arrangements. In M. Peiperl, M. B. Arthur, & N. Anand (Eds.), *Career creativity: Explorations in the remaking of work* (pp. 77–99). Oxford: Oxford University Press.

Casey, C., & Alach, P. (2004). "Just a temp?" Women, temporary employment and lifestyle. *Work, Employment & Society, 18*(3), 459–480.

Clarkberg, M., & Moen, P. (2001). Understanding the time-squeeze: Married couples' preferred and actual work-hour strategies. *American Behavioral Scientist, 44*(7), 1115–1136.

Cohany, S. R. (1998). Workers in alternative employment arrangements: A second look. *Monthly Labor Review, 121,* 3–21.

Cohen, L., & Mallon, M. (1999). The transition from organisational employment to portfolio working: Perceptions of "boundarylessness." *Work, Employment & Society, 13*(2), 329–352.

Cooper, C. L., & Lewis, S. (1999). Gender and the changing nature of work. In G. N. Powell (Ed.), *Handbook of gender and work.* Thousand Oaks, CA: Sage.

Cooper, S. F. (1995). The expanding use of the contingent workforce in the American Economy: New opportunities and dangers for employers. *Employee Relations Law Journal, 20*(4), 525.

Davis-Blake, A., & Uzzi, B. (1993). Determinants of employment externalization: A study of temporary workers and independent contractors. *Administrative Science Quarterly, 38*(2), 195–223.

Drobnic, S., Blossfeld, H. P., & Rohwer, G. (1999). Dynamics of women's employment patterns over the family life course: A comparison of the United States and Germany. *Journal of Marriage and the Family, 61*(1), 133–146.

Eaton, S. C., & Bailyn, L. (2000). Career as life path: Tracing work and life strategies of biotech professionals. In M. Peiperl (Ed.), *Career frontiers: New conceptions of working lives* (pp. 177–198). New York: Oxford University Press.

Eby, L. T. (2001). The boundaryless career experiences of mobile spouses in dual earner marriages. *Group and Organization Management, 61*(1), 133–146.

Elder, G. H., & Caspi, A. (1990). Studying lives in a changing society: Sociological and personological explorations. In A. I. Rabin, S. Zucker, R. A. Emmons, & S. Frank (Eds.), *Studying persons and lives* (pp. 201–247). New York: Springer.

Epstein, C. F., Seron, C., Oglensky, B., & Sauté, R. (1999). *The part-time paradox: Time norms, professional life, family, and gender.* New York: Routledge.

Equal Opportunities Commission. (2004). *Facts about women and men in Great Britain.* UK: Author.

Eurostat. (2003). *European social statistics: Labour force survey results 2002.* Luxembourg: Office for Official Publications of the European Communities.

Evans, J. A., Kunda, G., & Barley, S. R. (2004). Beach time, bridge time, and billable hours: The temporal structure of technical contracting. *Administrative Science Quarterly, 49*(1), 1–38.

Friedman, S. D., Christensen, P., & DeGroot, J. (1998). Work and life: The end of the zero-sum game. *Harvard Business Review, 76*(6), 119–129.

Friedman, S. D., & Greenhaus, J. H. (2000). *Work and family: Allies or enemies?* New York: Oxford University Press.

Frone, M. R., Yardley, J. K., & Markel, K. S. (1997). Developing and testing an integrative model of the work-family interface. *Journal of Vocational Behavior, 50*(2), 145–167.

Gerson, K. (1985). *Hard choices: How women decide about work, career, and motherhood.* Berkeley: University of California Press.

Gold, M., & Fraser, J. (2002). Managing self-management: Successful transitions to portfolio careers. *Work, Employment & Society, 16*(4), 579–598.

Graig, L. A., & Paganelli, V. (2000). Phased retirement: Reshaping the end of work. *Compensation & Benefits Management, 16*(2), 1–9.

Greenhaus, J. H., & Powell, G. N. (2006). When work and family are allies: A theory of work-family enrichment. *Academy of Management Review, 31*(1), 72–92.

Hackman, J. R., & Oldham, G. R. (1980). *Work redesign.* Reading, MA: Addison-Wesley.

Hakim, C. (2002). Lifestyle preferences as determinants of women's differentiated labor market careers. *Work and Occupations, 29*(4), 428–459.

Hall, D. T. (1976). *Careers in organizations.* Pacific Palisades, CA: Goodyear.

Hall, D. T. (1986). Breaking career routines: Midcareer choice and identity development. In D. T. Hall (Ed.), *Career development in organizations* (pp. xxv, 366). San Francisco: Jossey-Bass.

Han, S. K., & Moen, P. (1998, January). *Interlocking careers: Pathways through work and family for men and women.* Paper presented at the IRRA 50th annual conference proceedings, Madison, WI.

Han, S. K., & Moen, P. (1999a). Clocking out: Temporal patterning of retirement. *American Journal of Sociology, 105*(1), 191–236.

Han, S. K., & Moen, P. (1999b). Work and family over time: A life course approach. *Annals of the American Academy of Political and Social Science, 562*(March), 98–110.

Handy, C. (1994). *The empty raincoat: Making sense of the future.* London: Hutchinson.

Harrington, M. (1999). *Care and equality: Inventing a new family politics.* New York: Knopf.

Harris, G. (1997). Is job sharing worthwhile? A cost-benefit analysis in UK universities. *Higher Education, 33,* 29–38.

Hewlett, S. A., & Luce, C. B. (2005). Off-ramps and on-ramps. *Harvard Business Review, 83*(3), 43–54.

Higgins, C., Duxbury, L., & Johnson, K. L. (2000). Part-time work for women: Does it really help balance work and family? *Human Resource Management, 39*(1), 17–32.

Hill, E. J., Martinson, V. K., Ferris, M., & Baker, R. Z. (2004). Beyond the mommy track: The influence of new-concept part-time work for professional women on work and family. *Journal of Family and Economic Issues, 25*(1), 121–136.

Hochschild, A. R., & Machung, A. (1989). *The second shift: Working parents and the revolution at home.* New York: Viking.

Hughes, E. C. (1958). *Men and their work.* Glencoe, IL: Free Press.

Ibarra, H. (2003). *Working identity: Unconventional strategies for reinventing your career.* Boston: Harvard Business School Press.

Jacobs, J. A., & Gerson, K. (2004). *The time divide: Work, family, and gender inequality.* Cambridge, MA: Harvard University Press.

Jacobs, J. A., & Gerson, K. (2001). Overworked individuals or overworked families? Explaining trends in work, leisure and family time. *Work and Occupations, 28*(1), 40–63.

Jones, C. (1996). Careers in project networks: The case of the film industry. In M. B. Arthur & D. M. Rousseau (Eds.), *The boundaryless career* (pp. 58–75). New York: Oxford University Press.

Judiesch, M. K., & Lyness, K. S. (1999). Left behind? The impact of leaves of absence on managers' career success. *Academy of Management Journal, 42*(6), 641–651.

Kahne, H. (1985). *Reconceiving part-time work: New perspectives for older workers and women.* Totowa, NJ: Rowman & Allanheld.

Kahne, H. (1992). Part-time work: A hope and a peril. In D. D. Warme, K. L. P. Lundy, & L. A. Lundy (Eds.), *Working part time: Risks and opportunities.* New York: Praeger.

Kalleberg, A. L. (2000). Nonstandard employment relations: Part-time, temporary and contract work. *Annual Review of Sociology, 26,* 341–365.

Kalleberg, A. L., & Epstein, C. F. (2001). Introduction: Temporal dimensions of employment relations. *American Behavioral Scientist, 44*(7), 1064–1075.

Kalleberg, A. L., Reynolds, J., & Marsden, P. V. (2003). Externalizing employment: Flexible staffing arrangements in U.S. organizations. *Social Science Research, 32*(4), 525–552.

Kanter, R. M. (1977). *Work and family in the United States: A critical review and agenda for research and policy.* New York: Russell Sage Foundation.

Ketsche, P. G., & Branscomb, L. (2003). The long-term costs of career interruptions. *Journal of Healthcare Management, 48*(1), 30–44.

Klein, K. J., Berman, L. M., & Dickson, M. W. (2000). May I work part-time? An exploration of predicted employer responses to employee requests for part-time work. *Journal of Vocational Behavior, 57,* 85–101.

Kochan, T. A. (2005). *Restoring the American dream: A working families' agenda for America.* Cambridge, MA: MIT Press.

Kossek, E. E., Barber, A. E., & Winters, D. (1999). Using flexible schedules in the managerial world: The power of peers. *Human Resource Management, 38*(1), 33–46.

Kunda, G., Barley, S. R., & Evans, J. (2002). Why do contractors contract? The experience of highly skilled technical professionals in a contingent labor market. *Industrial and Labor Relations Review, 55*(2), 234–261.

Larwood, L., & Gattiker, U. E. (1987). A comparison of the career paths used by successful women and men. In B. A. Gutek & L. Larwood (Eds.), *Women's career development* (pp. 129–156). Newbury Park, CA: Sage.

Lawrence, B. S. (1984). Age grading: The implicit organizational timetable. *Journal of Organizational Behaviour, 5*(1), 23–35.

Lawrence, T. B., & Corwin, V. (2003). Being there: The acceptance and marginalization of part-time professional employees. *Journal of Organizational Behavior, 24*(8), 923–943.

Lee, M. D., & Kossek, E. E. (2005). *Crafting lives that work: A six-year retrospective on reduced-load working in the careers and lives of professionals and managers.* Montreal, Quebec: McGill University.

Lee, M. D., MacDermid, S. M., & Buck, M. L. (2000). Organizational paradigms of reduced-load work: Accommodation, elaboration, and transformation. *Academy of Management Journal, 43*(6), 1211–1226.

Lyness, K. S., & Kropf, M. B. (2005). The relationships of national gender equality and organizational support with work-family balance: A study of European managers. *Human Relations, 58*(1), 33–60.

MacDermid, S. M., Lee, M. D., Buck, M. L., & Williams, M. L. (2001). Alternative work arrangements among professionals and managers. *Journal of Management Development, 20*(4), 305–317.

Mainiero, L. A., & Sullivan, S. E. (2005). Kaleidoscope careers: An alternate explanation for the opt-out revolution. *Academy of Management Executive, 19*(1), 106–123.

Major, V. J., Klein, K. J., & Ehrhart, M. G. (2002). Work time, work interference with family and psychological distress. *Journal of Applied Psychology, 87*(3), 427–436.

Mallon, M. (1999). Going "portfolio": Making sense of changing careers. *Career Development International, 4*(7), 358–369.

Marler, J. H., Barringer, M. W., & Milkovich, G. T. (2002). Boundaryless and traditional contingent employees: Worlds apart. *Journal of Organizational Behavior, 23*(4), 425–453.

Marshall, K. (1997). Job sharing. *Perspectives on Labour and Income, 9*(2), 6–10.

Matusik, S. F., & Hill, C. W. L. (1998). The utilization of contingent work, knowledge creation, and competitive advantage. *Academy of Management Review, 23*(4), 680–697.

Meiksins, P., & Whalley, P. (2002). *Putting work in its place: A quiet revolution.* Ithaca, NY: Cornell University Press.

Merton, R. K. (1968). *Social theory and social structure* (enl. ed.). New York: Free Press.

Milliken, F. J., & Dunn-Jensen, L. M. (2005). The changing time demands of managerial and professional work: Implications for managing the work-life boundary. In E. E. Kossek & S. J. Lambert (Eds.), *Work and life integration: Organizational, cultural, and individual perspectives* (pp. 43–59). Mahwah, NJ: Lawrence Erlbaum.

Mincer, J. (1978). Family migration decisions. *Journal of Political Economy, 86*(5), 749–773.

Mirvis, P. H., & Hall, D. T. (1996). Psychological success and the boundaryless career. In M. B. Arthur & D. M. Rousseau (Eds.), *The boundaryless career: A new employment principle for a new organizational era* (pp. 237–255). New York: Oxford University Press.

Miyakoshi, T. (2001). The efficacy of job sharing policy. *Applied Economics Letters, 8,* 437–439.

Moen, P. (1985). Continuities and discontinuities in women's labor force activity. In G. H. Elder (Ed.), *Life course dynamics: Trajectories and transitions, 1968–1980* (pp. 113–155). Ithaca, NY: Cornell University Press.

Moen, P. (1992). *Women's two roles: A contemporary dilemma.* New York: Auburn House.

Moen, P. (2001). *The career quandary* (Vol. 2, No. 1). Washington, DC: Population Reference Bureau.

Moen, P. (2004). Linked lives: Dual careers, gender, and the contingent life course. In W. R. Heinz & V. W. Marshall (Eds.), *Social dynamics of the life course: Transitions, institutions, and interrelations.* Hawthorne, NY: Aldine de Gruyter.

Moen, P. (Ed.). (2003). *It's about time: Couples and careers.* Ithaca, NY: Cornell University Press.

Moen, P., & Han, S. K. (2001). Reframing careers: Work, family, and gender. In V. M. Marshall, W. R. Heinz, H. Krueger, & A. Verma (Eds.), *Restructuring work and the life course.* Toronto, Ontario: University of Toronto Press.

Moen, P., & Roehling, P. (2005). *The career mystique: Cracks in the American dream.* Lanham, MD: Rowman & Littlefield.

Moen, P., & Yu, Y. (2000). Effective work/life strategies: Working couples, work conditions, gender, and life quality. *Social Problems, 47*(3), 291–326.

More than part time. (2000). Boston: Employment Issues Committee of the Women's Bar Association of Massachusetts.

Organisation for Economic Co-Operation and Development. (2004). *OECD Employment Outlook 2004.* Washington, DC: Author

Office for National Statistics. (2004). *Labour market trends October 2004.* Retrieved December 1, 2004, from http://www.statistics.gov.uk/stat base/product.asp?vlnk=550&more=n.

Olmsted, B., & Smith, S. (1994). *Creating a flexible workplace: How to select and manage alternative work options* (2nd ed.). New York: Amacom.

Parker, P. (2002). Creativity in contract workers' careers. In M. Peiperl, M. B. Arthur, & N. Anand (Eds.), *Career creativity: Explorations in the remaking of work* (pp. 123–141). Oxford: Oxford University Press.

Pixley, J. E., & Moen, P. (2003). Prioritizing careers. In P. Moen (Ed.), *It's about time: Couples and careers* (pp. xi, 436). Ithaca, NY: ILR Press.

Polivka, A. E. (1996). Contingent and alternative work arrangements, defined. *Monthly Labor Review, 119*(10), 3–9.

Poster, W. R. (2005). Three reasons for a transnational approach to work-life policy. In E. E. Kossek & S. J. Lambert (Eds.), *Work and life integration: Organizational, cultural, and individual perspectives* (pp. 375–400). Mahwah, NJ: Lawrence Erlbaum.

Rapoport, R., Bailyn, L., Fletcher, J. K., & Pruitt, B. H. (2002). *Beyond work-family balance: Advancing gender equity and workplace performance.* San Francisco: Jossey-Bass.

Rosenbaum, J. E. (1984). *Career mobility in a corporate hierarchy.* Orlando, FL: Academic Press.

Ross, C. E., & Wright, M. P. (1998). Women's work, men's work, and the sense of control. *Work and Occupations, 25*(3), 333–355.

Rothbard, N. P., & Edwards, J. R. (2003). Investment in work and family roles: A test of identity and utilitarian motives. *Personnel Psychology, 56*(3), 699–732.

Schein, E. H. (1978). *Career dynamics.* Reading, MA: Addison-Wesley.

Schneer, J. A., & Reitman, F. (1990). Effects of employment gaps on the careers of M.B.A.'s: More damaging for men than for women? *Academy of Management Journal, 33*(2), 391–406.

Schneer, J. A., & Reitman, F. (1994). The importance of gender in mid-career: A longitudinal study of MBAs. *Journal of Organizational Behavior, 15*(3), 199–207.

Schneer, J. A., & Reitman, F. (1995). The impact of gender as managerial careers unfold. *Journal of Vocational Behavior, 47*(3), 290–315.

Schneer, J. A., & Reitman, F. (1997). The interrupted managerial career path: A longitudinal study of MBAs. *Journal of Vocational Behavior, 51*(3), 411–434.

Schwartz, F. N. (1989). Management women and the new facts of life. *Harvard Business Review, 67,* 65–76.

Sheley, E. (1996, January). Job sharing offers unique challenges. *HR Magazine, 41,* 46.

Stier, H., & Lewin-Epstein, N. (2000). Women's part-time employment and gender inequality in the family. *Journal of Family Issues, 21*(3), 390–410.

Tilly, C. C. (1992a). Dualism in part-time employment. *Industrial Relations, 31*(2), 330–347.

Tilly, C. C. (1992b). Two faces of part time work: Good and bad part-time jobs in U.S. service industries. In D. D. Warme, K. L. P. Lundy, & L. A. Lundy (Eds.), *Working part-time: Risks and opportunities.* New York: Praeger.

Tilly, C. C. (1996). *Half a job: Bad and good part-time jobs in a changing labor market.* Philadelphia: Temple University Press.

Tolbert, P. S., Valcour, P. M., & Marler, J. H. (2002). *Work schedules, work-family balance, and perceived success in work life and in family life* (Working paper #02–09). Ithaca, NY: Bronfenbrenner Life Course Center.

U.S. Census Bureau. (2001a). *Current population survey.* Washington, DC: Author.

U.S. Census Bureau. (2001b). *Survey of income and program participation.* Washington, DC: Author.

U.S. Census Bureau. (2003a). *BLS handbook of methods.* Retrieved May 18, 2004, from http://www.bls.gov/opub/hom/homtoc.htm.

U.S. Census Bureau. (2003b). *Current population survey.* Washington, DC: Author.

Valcour, P. M., & Hunter, L. W. (2005). Technology, organizations, and work-life integration. In E. E. Kossek & S. J. Lambert (Eds.), *Work and life integration: Organizational, cultural, and individual perspectives* (pp. 61–84). Mahwah, NJ: Lawrence Erlbaum.

Valcour, P. M., & Snell, S. A. (2002, August). *The boundaryless career and work force flexibility: Developing human and social capital for organizational and individual advantage.* Paper presented at the annual meeting of the Academy of Management, Denver, CO.

Valcour, P. M., & Tolbert, P. S. (2003). Gender, family, and career in the era of boundarylessness: Determinants and effects of intra- and inter-organizational mobility. *International Journal of Human Resource Management, 14*(5), 768–787.

Von Hippel, C., Mangum, S. L., Greenberger, D. B., Heneman, R. L., & Skoglind, J. D. (1997). Temporary employment: Can organizations and employees both win? *Academy of Management Executive, 11*(1), 93–104.

Weick, K. E. (1996). Enactment and the boundaryless career. In M. B. Arthur & D. M. Rousseau (Eds.), *The boundaryless career: A new employment principle for a new organizational era* (pp. x, 394). New York: Oxford University Press.

Weick, K. E., & Berlinger, L. R. (1989). Career improvisation in self designing organizations. In M. B. Arthur, D. T. Hall, & B. S. Lawrence (Eds.), *Handbook of career theory* (pp. 313–328). Cambridge, UK: Cambridge University Press.

Wharton, A. S., & Blair-Loy, M. (2002). The "overtime culture" in a global corporation: A cross-national study of finance professionals' interest in working part-time. *Work and Occupations, 29*(1), 32–63.

Wilensky, H. L. (1961). Orderly careers and social participation: The impact of work history on social integration in the middle mass. *American Sociological Review, 26,* 521–539.

Williams, J. (2000). *Unbending gender: Why work and family conflict and what to do about it.* New York: Oxford University Press.

Williams, S., & Han, S. K. (2003). Career clocks: Forked roads. In P. Moen (Ed.), *It's about time: Couples and careers.* Ithaca, NY: Cornell University Press.

SECTION 2

CAREERS IN CONTEXT

Careers, as Mayrhofer, Meyer, and Steyrer point out in Chapter 12, are always careers in context. To some extent, we have already explored some aspects of context, if only because it is virtually impossible to separate career from context. But in Section 2, we focus on it explicitly.

We begin with Mayrhofer et al.'s broad introduction to contextual issues in the study of careers. Their aim is "to help the reader to create an image of the exogenous phenomena that shape careers"; they organize this using an "onion skin" model, which places individual career patterns at the center, surrounded successively by contexts of work, origin, society and culture, and the globalizing world. The authors review the literature about research on each of these contextual levels. They analyze the context of work by considering external labor markets, the new forms of working and organizing that have become apparent within the past decade, and social relationships (in particular those resulting from social networks). The context of origin is factored into class and social origin, educational socialization and individual work history, and the current-life context of the individual (e.g., family or marital status). The context of society and culture is examined under the categories of gender, ethnicity, demography, and community factors (the way in which people are integrated into their local communities). Two aspects of the global context are reviewed: internationalization and virtualization. Next, the authors identify four recent developments in career context: a shift in contextual categories, the increasing significance of configurations of variables rather than single variables, the way in which gender has changed from a single variable to an overall perspective, and the intrusion of a pervasive economic logic. Finally, they present what they label a "kaleidoscopic" view of career context, identifying the contributions made by three grand theorists, Bourdieu, Giddens, and Luhmann, to the understanding of career in context.

Chapter 13 addresses a very personal form of context, that of the mentor. Chandler and Kram review the evolution of mentoring in the careers field from a single, long-term, hierarchical relationship to multiple, shorter-term relationships that comprise a developmental network. They examine the construct, the functions and phases of mentoring, and the growing interest in the types of developmental relationships involved in mentoring. Next, they review research on individual and organizational antecedents to and outcomes of mentoring, identifying (as they do throughout the chapter) what, in their words, we don't know (and should). They then turn to examine some of the complexities introduced by diversified relationships and diversity—both gender and race complexities and cross-gender and cross-race challenges and opportunities, as well as age complexities. The authors next turn a developmental lens on mentoring, looking at the contributions of four distinct theoretical perspectives: phase theories, stage theories, relational models, and the recently applied attachment theory. All these raise the critical issue of the strategies that might be applied to foster mentoring—something, it turns out, that still has many unanswered questions associated with it. This leads naturally to a research agenda that the authors propose in the light of the changing context of mentorship.

Sociologists have long viewed the unfolding of a career as intimately tied to a patterned series of relationships that gradually define a person's sense of self. While empirical findings and conceptual developments indicate a strong link between networks and careers, on the one hand, and between career and identity development, on the other, little work thus far has examined the reciprocal relationships between networks and identities as they affect and interact with career phenomena over time. In Chapter 14, Ibarra and Deshpande review what we know to date about how networks affect careers. They report on research examining the effect of networks on objective (jobs, compensation, and promotion) and subjective (satisfaction) career outcomes. They review the mediating effects of networks on careers—in other words, how it is that networks affect career outcomes, arguing that this happens because networks make available a range of instrumental resources (such as information, referrals, assignments) and psychosocial resources (e.g., socialization, mentoring, identity formation). They then examine the factors that moderate these effects—for example, demographic characteristics such as gender and race and certain personality traits. Finally, the authors bring identity into the discussion by reviewing what we know about the reciprocal influence of networks and identity on career dynamics; that is, when careers involve changes of role, identities change with them. Yet we know surprisingly little about these processes, and the chapter concludes with a call for more research in this thematic area.

Sullivan and Crocitto, in Chapter 15, show that context affects not only the development of careers but the development of individuals as well. As the nature of work has changed over the years, so have the career structures associated with it. Models of career development have developed too. The authors begin with Erikson's Freudian model and show how Vaillant's longitudinal study built on it by paying closer attention to the contribution of work and career to adult development, adding inter alia greater understanding of the mid-career phase. Other models reviewed include Super's linear career-stage model, Levinson's life-stage model, Gould's model of adult development, Schein's career dimensions and stages, and Driver's career concepts. The authors show how each reflects the nature of careers at the time the theory was put forward, and how many, too, uncovered different contextual factors affecting the development of their research subjects. They then show how two theories of moral development—those of Kohlberg and Gilligan—have informed the broader issue of career development. Finally, they turn to the so-called sociogenic-ontogenic debate, which addresses directly the question of to what extent career development is influenced by the individual's social environment, and examine attempts to reconcile the two opposing views that frame the debate.

In Chapter 16, Guest and Sturges begin with the proposition that the traditional, upwardly mobile career is not only the creation of a work environment that may no longer be much with us but may also only have ever applied to a minority of "organization men," leaving most people untouched. They review the arguments and evidence for and against the robustness of the traditional career, examining the economic and social changes that have led to this robustness being questioned. They then turn to the second of their two opening propositions, that the traditional career has only ever applied to a minority of the population, and discuss different ways of conceptualizing nonmanagerial careers. In so doing, they challenge a number of assumptions—about, for example, mobility—that have become increasingly common. They draw out three messages: that the study of careers of those who are neither professionals nor managers has indeed been neglected, that there is a need to apply theories that recognize that workers at all levels think in terms of having careers and of managing them, and that there are many assumptions about career preferences and how they might be changing that are not necessarily well-grounded. Drawing on some of their own original research, which provides support for the view that thinking in career terms is much more common than generally supposed, they propose a more encompassing model of career patterns and career choices of those in routine occupations. Their eight-way taxonomy describes career types as different as the traditional constrained career, tourism, disengagement, achievement and service, variety and control, self-employment, opting out, and being locked out.

External labor markets form a critical part of the context in which careers are lived, and in Chapter 17, Cappelli and Hamori provide an account of the origins, the theoretical underpinnings, and the present workings of the external hiring market. They begin with a quick overview of the changes that have swept labor markets in countries such as the United States since World War II. Next, they trace the roots of job search to the early 20th century, showing how the institutions of outside hiring have changed in ways paralleling the economic shifts of the era and providing an interesting counterpoint to the view of search coming from the counseling profession (Savickas, Chapter 5; Kidd, Chapter 6). They then examine the institutions of outside hiring in greater detail, focusing particularly on search firms and retained search firms. They review what they describe as the surprisingly limited research literature on what search firms do and the even more limited literature on their impact. For the latter part of the chapter, the authors turn their attention to the newest institution in the job search field—but now the dominant one—electronic or online recruiting. They look at how it facilitates the first activity to which it was applied—searching for candidates—and, in turn, how it has facilitated applicants' search for jobs. The extraordinary volume of applications generated by online recruiting creates a major problem in matching candidates and employers, and the authors

describe recent approaches to handling this. They conclude with an account of the profound changes sweeping corporations and the commitment of their employees as a result of the rise in online recruiting.

Section 2 concludes with an examination of careers in a global context. In Chapter 18, Peiperl and Jonsen argue that, paradoxically, a sign that the time has finally come for globalization as a concept is that it is now regarded as "old hat"—as a term no longer fashionable. Global careers, they contend, are a basic fact of corporate (and often individual) existence rather than an exciting new idea for pundits to ponder. Defining a global career as one that takes place in more than one region of the world, either sequentially or concurrently, they begin by examining what it is that global career actors actually do. They look at the worldview, tasks, and role of global managers; at what it means to work across cultures; and at the differences between working across national boundaries physically and doing so via communications technology. They then examine global career owners themselves, considering their traits, as well as what the label *global citizen* might mean. Global mobility is clearly key to global careers, and the authors review this under a number of headings. They look at the evidence for global mobility: how much there is, the trends apparent in these numbers, and the extent to which the highly skilled are involved. They consider recent research findings on expatriation and offer some thoughts on the future of global mobility, considering in particular what it is that stimulates people to take the mobility initiative. This discussion leads to the presentation of a model of global careers—their antecedents, drivers, outcomes, and the resulting "career capital." The authors conclude with some thoughts on the future of global careers.

12

Contextual Issues in the Study of Careers

Wolfgang Mayrhofer

Michael Meyer

Johannes Steyrer

Setting the Scene and Choosing the Lens

Careers are always careers in context. Being central to individuals, organizations, and society, they cannot be restricted to the narrow view of individuals moving up corporate or professional hierarchies. Rather, careers are located at the "intersection of societal history and individual biography" (Grandjean, 1981, p. 1057), linking micro and macro frames of reference (Schein, 1978), which traditionally have been regarded as indissoluble (Barley, 1989; Gunz, 1989b; Hughes, 1937). Consequently, the two parts of the picture—individuals on the one hand, context on the other—have received considerable attention. This is true for theorizing about organizations as well as for career research. Under varying labels such as structure versus agency, micro versus macro, or individual versus context, the mutual relationship between the two components in each pairing, as well as their relative importance for explaining individual behavior, is a core theme in theorizing about organizations. The whole continuum of possible viewpoints can be found (for an overview, see, e.g., Staehle, 1999, p. 151ff.). A number of approaches, mainly coming from a psychological angle, emphasize intrapersonal processes and factors, thus focusing on the individual point of view and emphasizing agency. They call attention to factors such as needs and motives, values, or attitudes or more composite concepts such as character or personality. Other concepts underline the importance of contextual factors for behavior of and in organizations. These include organizational structure, culture, or the relevant environment, thus paying attention to the structure argument. Of course, many of the approaches in one way or another recognize the importance of both aspects. However, only a few concepts avoid a theoretical preference for one side or the other. Examples include the very general behavioral formula of Lewin (1936, p. 12) or the elaborated circular relationships between structure and agency in structuration theory (Giddens, 1984).

In career theory, the problem of individual and context is central, too. Both aspects have an established place in theorizing about careers. However, in theoretical as well as empirical research, there is a dominance of models and studies using frameworks that implicitly or explicitly underline an individual-centered perspective. While not equally prominent, the macrosocial context in which careers are made and its influence on the nature of careers across different cultures and countries do have their place. Many studies have taken contextual issues into account. Still, the issues as well as the disciplines that deal with these issues vary widely. As a working definition and point of departure, we view here contextual issues as comprising all those exogenous factors that influence careers of individuals and the organizations and "fields" they are in that hitherto have played a major role in management-related career research.

The purpose of this chapter is to help the reader create an image of the exogenous phenomena that shape careers. The lens used to create such an image seeks topics that emerge when looking for contextual factors in the existing body of career research stemming from the many disciplines that have contributed to the field. Under this heading, we will identify the major issues encountered in describing and explaining the environmental factors influencing careers, thus developing a "history of exogenous topics" as they have come up and been dealt with in career research. They are rooted in a number of well-established as well as comparatively young (sub)disciplines that look at "macro" factors that shape individuals' careers. Among the most important are management, sociology, economics, anthropology, political science, and gender studies. Without elaborating on the core assumptions of each discipline about human behavior and about careers and how to explain (the content aspect) and research (the methodological aspect) them, we will use these disciplines as a source and general background when painting our image of the major exogenous factors influencing careers.

In addition to identifying core topics, this chapter also addresses four major developments in contextual issues over the past two decades: the contexts of work, of origin, and of society and culture and the global context. These developments are at a "metalevel" beyond the single core topics and constitute an integrative perspective on the development of contextual issues over time. The chapter concludes with a look at three major social theories and their potential contributions to the development of the field as well as some considerations about what we shall call a "kaleidoscopic" view of careers.

LOOKING THROUGH ONE LENS: WHAT YOU SEE IS WHAT YOU GET

The discussion that follows is based on a review of the management literature and adjacent fields. In addition, extensive use was made of the historians of the Academy of Management and its Career Division as well as the Academy's electronic archive. This led to material often not easily accessible, such as unpublished conference papers of the 1950s. Out of this, the framework of topics used for this chapter emerged.

The threshold for identifying something as a topic in its own right will be the existence of widely shared labels, such as ethnicity or gender, for an underlying influencing factor, the mutual recognition of the topic in various contributions from a variety of fields, and a substantial number of contributions. Thus, a picture of the "surface issues" of "macro" career research emerges. Relating to different "spheres" of closeness resembling an "onion peel" model with the individuals' career paths in the center, we differentiate between factors related to the origin of the individual, the work context, the national society and culture, and the global context and developments (see Figure 12.1).

The Context of Work

A first "circle of closeness" relates to those contextual factors linked with the work context.

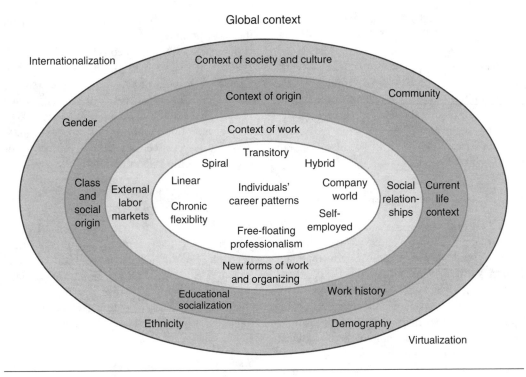

Figure 12.1   Major Contextual Factors in Career Research

Here, the role of the economic and institutional environment, external labor markets, new forms of working and organizing, and work-related social relationships can be identified as major issues.

External Labor Markets

Work careers are embedded in the broader economic and institutional environment. Often, career researchers acknowledge this by using contextual factors such as the economic or legal environment as part of their models (see, e.g., Anderson, Milkovich, & Tsui, 1981; Mihal, Sorce, & Comte, 1984; Rhodes & Doering, 1983). A specific focus has been laid on the external labor market, consisting of the occupational and the secondary labor market (Guest and Sturges, Chapter 16), which structures the career opportunities that individuals encounter. Labor market research is a field of its own and has brought about a vast literature with different aspects. In career terms, contributions from labor economics as well as sociology for a long

time have specifically dealt with issues like labor market segmentation and stratification and dual labor markets (Doeringer & Piore, 1971; Edwards, 1975; Piore, 1975; Tolbert, 1982) and their relationship to various aspects of careers, especially earnings/wages (Theodossiou, 1995) and mobility (Bernhardt, Morris, Handcock, & Scott, 2001). In addition to "mainstream" working and employment relationships, the labor market specifics of such varied groups as artists (Menger, 1999) or prostitutes (Brewis & Linstead, 2000) have been studied.

The career literature in the narrower sense has often provided both a more restricted and a greatly diverse perspective. Beyond a discussion about the specific characteristics of occupations and their labor market consequences (Tolbert, 1996) or the analysis of specific aspects such as the dual labor market hypothesis (Leontaridi, 2002), research includes analyses concerning the type of labor market that IT professionals are in (Boh, Slaughter, & Ang, 2001), the importance of labor market demands and structure for the decision to change careers (Cabral, Rhodes, &

Doering, 1985) and organizational career systems (Sonnenfeld, Peiperl, & Kotter, 1988b), the labor market effects of the status of talent agencies and their consequences for screenwriters' career opportunities (Bielby & Bielby, 1999), and the effects of the labor market or the importance of information about labor market opportunities for subsequent careers during job search (Ullman & Gutteridge, 1974; see also Cappelli and Hamori, Chapter 17).

New Forms of Working and Organizing

In the world of working and organizing, substantial changes can be observed over the past decades. While there is no global uniformity and countries differ to a considerable degree, these drivers push toward a new context of work with a changed consensus on what is regarded as fair, more flexible labor markets; a tendency toward deregulation of national employment systems; and an increasing importance of global markets (Dore, 2004). Hence, the development of new organizational forms such as network or virtual organizations or new ways of working including multiple jobs, precarious working arrangements, or frequent occupational changes is hardly surprising. They are a result as well as a driver of these changes. New forms of working and organizing have been a prominent theme in management research (Ruigrok, Pettigrew, Peck, & Whittington, 1999; Whittington, Pettigrew, Peck, Fenton, & Conyon, 1999) as well as for political decision makers over the past decade (Savage, 2001). To be sure, "new" forms have always been a topic in management literature, indicating that not only truth (*veritas filia temporis,* as Aulus Gellius, the ancient Roman writer and grammarian, wisely remarked in his *Notitiae Atticae*) but also "newness" is the daughter of time in the double sense in which this quote has been interpreted over time: that time will lead truth to the light as well as what is regarded as true depends on time. In its time, Frederick W. Taylor's concept was regarded as new and revolutionary, although today it is used as a symbol for an outdated approach.

Nevertheless, the changes of the past decades have attracted, among others, the interest of career researchers. On the one hand, the new context leads to new forms of careers. A number of labels

have been developed for them; among them, the most prominent are boundaryless (Arthur & Rousseau, 1996), postcorporate (Peiperl & Baruch, 1997), nomad (Cadin, Bender, Saint Giniez, & Pringle, 2000), chaotic (Peterson & Anand, 2002), protean (Hall, 1996), or chronic flexible (Iellatchitch, Mayrhofer, & Meyer, 2003). At the same time, a number of aspects of these new forms are seen in their importance for creating specific opportunities for careers. This includes the changing organizational environment that is constituted by new information technologies (Gattiker & Coe, 1986), the career consequences of project form organizations (Reeser, 1969), the career competition of managers belonging to different strategic business units (Gupta & Seshadri, 1994), or the career opportunities linked with the creation of a new business environment for one's own career through the founding of new firms (Reynolds, 1988).

Social Relationships

Careers are not only or even primarily (as some might argue) determined by individual plans and decisions. The social environment plays a major role, too, for at least two reasons. First, the social environment provides the mirror the individuals need to locate themselves and their efforts in the broader social context. Estimations about one's relative position in a social context are not developed autonomously. They require social comparisons and measures. Second, and partly related, careers are strongly influenced by the social identity of individuals. The image the social environment holds about individuals strongly contributes to what they are entrusted with, which development offers they get, and how they are evaluated. Two elements of the importance of social relationships for careers have received special attention: the networking and mentoring that individuals experience in their work, either within or outside organizations.

Networking (Ibarra and Deshpande, Chapter 14) refers to the process of building up and maintaining a set of informal, cooperative relationships in the social structure of an organization (Burt, 1992). Networks provide opportunities. They offer contacts and supporters that increase effectiveness in negotiations and the number of options and choices available. Studies have analyzed the importance of social networks for the likelihood of promotion, further managerial advancement and higher salaries (Burt, 1992; Orpen, 1996), and career decisions (Higgins, 2001); the role of interpersonal support for management advancement from entry to upper levels (Tharenou, 2001), the influence of various types of social relationships, such as role models, advisors, mentors, and sponsors, on career advancement (Wood & Hertz, 1982); and the effects of social capital on career outcomes such as salary, promotion, and individual satisfaction (Seibert, Kraimer, & Liden, 2001).

The issue of mentoring is linked to the topic of networking (Chandler and Kram, Chapter 13). It is a particular kind of interpersonal relationship in which protégés receive a broad range of career and psychosocial help from a senior manager (Kram, 1988). Conceptually, it has been linked to the networking discussion (Higgins & Kram, 2001) and is seen as a career training and development tool (Hunt & Michael, 1983). Studies analyze, for example, the role of mentoring for various aspects of career, including the link between mentor presence and managers' pay and the frequency of promotions in the early stages of a career (Whitely & Coetsier, 1993), the effects of early-career mentoring for the frequency of promotion (Whitely, Dougherty, & Dreher, 1991) and the development of career attitudes (Ragins, Cotton, & Miller, 2000); and the determinants and career effects of mentoring relationships (Turban & Dougherty, 1994).

The Context of Origin

Within the context of origin, class and social origin, current status, and educational socialization and individual work history are major issues that emerge.

Class and Social Origin

A frequent topic of contextually based career contributions is the role of class and social origin for different aspects of careers. Two major themes can be identified.

First, the influence of different aspects of class and social origin on various facets of career development and success are researched at a macro level. In a landmark study, Blau and Duncan (1967) analyze the effects of the familial socioeconomic background on the career success of individuals in the United States. They find that the socioeconomic background of the family of origin affects the type and length of education that individuals get. In turn, this influences occupational entry and career achievements. However, in later stages of their careers, individuals' socioeconomic background seems to be less important for career outcomes. Previous jobs and work experiences have greater significance during these stages. Focusing on top-level managerial positions in Germany, the United Kingdom, and France, Hartmann (1996, 2000) finds that in all three countries more than three quarters of top managers are of upper-middle-class origin. Furthermore, he shows that in France and Britain selection also works via exclusive education and titles, whereas in Germany personal characteristics associated with the upper middle class are primarily important. Those who grow up in upper-middle-class families therefore know the unwritten habits and rules for elite positions better than those from a different social background.

Beyond such macro studies, the influence of social class on different aspects of work and retirement behavior has been studied (see the overview in Brown, Fukunaga, Umemoto, & Wicker, 1996), also including factors such as family size and parental influence (Kurtz, Boone, & Fleenor, 1987). In addition, a number of studies use socioeconomic background as control and differentiating variables for different facets of careers and career success. Examples include the effects of career mentoring on promotions and compensation received by early-career managers and professionals (Whitely et al., 1991) or career success in early-career stages (Whitely et al., 1991), the differentiating factors between executives and lower managers (O'Donovan, 1962), the development of organizational commitment of medical technologists (Blau, 1999), the influence of social capital on income (Parks-Yancy, 2002), the development of work patterns in different career stages (Raelin, 1984), and the occupational choices of MBA students (Sonnenfeld, Peiperl, & Kotter, 1988a).

A second theme refers, more generally, to inter- and intragenerational mobility. Especially from a sociological viewpoint, this topic has received considerable attention (e.g., Bertaux & Thompson, 1997; Gelles & Levine, 2001; Sorensen, 1975). It is closely linked to the stratification of society according to, for example, economic wealth, gender, or ethnicity. Some authors argue that class is of major importance in industrial societies and derives from inequalities in the possession and control of material resources and access to educational and occupational opportunities. In general, upward mobility entails only small steps and is of limited range. Most people remain close to the level of their family origin. Given the new developments during the past decades—for example, the expansion of white-collar jobs or the opportunities for start-up companies due to new information technologies—the opportunities for short-range upward mobility have increased considerably (Giddens, Duneier, & Appelbaum, 2003). A number of studies cover different aspects of this kind of mobility. These include occupational mobility (Warner & Abegglen, 1955, 1968); upward mobility and the problems linked with it for specific ethnic groups (Cole & Omari, 2003); and the interplay between class, race, and ethnicity in females' working careers (Jones, 2003).

Educational Socialization and Individual Work History

Closely linked to the individual history are aspects dealing with the formal education of individuals and their work history.

The role of education in work careers has many facets that have been dealt with in career research. These include aspects such as the role of education in the entry of minority managers to management positions (Brown & Ford, 1975), career change (Cabral et al., 1985), the learning of new jobs for surface warfare officers in navy ships (Morrison & Brantner, 1991), the gender-related differences in individual career development (Solomon, Bishop, & Bresser, 1985), the differences in managerial career advancement for men and women (Tharenou, 2001), the influence on job rotation and career outcomes (Campion, Cheraskin, & Stevens, 1994), or the differing career orientations of engineers and scientists (Katz & Allen, 1991).

Likewise, the individual work history is seen as an important factor contributing to opportunities within individual career development. Besides the job history within the current organization—an issue that various tournament models (Brüderl, Diekmann, & Preisendörfer, 1991; Rosenbaum, 1979) discuss—this includes the previous personal job history. It is characterized by elements such as the number of employers; the mobility rate; the frequency and pattern of upward mobility; changes in functions, employers and industry; and the relationship between times of employment and unemployment. The importance of work history for career opportunities has been especially researched in connection with the determining factors of managerial career success (Cawsey, Nicholson, & Alban-Metcalfe, 1985; Hambrick & Mason, 1984; Vardi, 1991) as well as the strategic behavior of the companies that are managed (Gunz & Jalland, 1996). In addition, the effects of employment gaps in early and mid-career for career outcomes has also been researched (Schneer & Reitman, 1990).

Current-Life Context

Not only the context of origin but also the current personal context—that is, the personal life situation, including factors such as family situation or marital status (Greenhaus and Foley, Chapter 8)—frame the career-relevant opportunity structure for individuals. Including this factor in research efforts acknowledges that it is not just one's upbringing and socialization that influence career opportunities and decisions. Depending on various characteristics of the current situation, the possibilities for individuals to react to career opportunities differ. At the same time, it is not just the individual decisions that are influenced. The social perception of individuals is shaped, too. For example, whether you are married or not or whether you have children—and if yes, how many—or not influences the image that the social context forms. In turn, this influences decisions about what to expect or demand, what to offer in terms of career opportunities, etc.

Hardly any career studies focus solely on these issues. Notable exceptions are an empirical analysis of the effects of "posttraditional" families, in which both parents are employed on managerial career paths, showing that such a family structure is in various ways related to income and career satisfaction (Schneer & Reitman, 1993), or the role of the family context in career choice (Ferry, Fouad, & Smith, 2000). However, the authors' call for more research in this area has had little response. Nevertheless, a number of studies include elements of the current-life context in their work. Examples include the influence of the family and wage earner status on career change (Cabral et al., 1985). In addition, current-life context issues are used as control variables. Studies exemplifying this include research about the effects of political influencing tactics on career success, with, among others, household responsibilities as a control variable (Judge & Bretz, 1992), or work patterns in different career stages, with number of household members as the control variable (Raelin, 1984).

The Context of Society and Culture

At the national societal and cultural level, four major aspects can be mentioned that constitute important contextual elements for individuals' careers: gender; ethnicity, including the issue of minorities; overall population demography; and communal and societal ties.

Gender

A number of aspects of work-related differences between men and women, such as income differential, participation in the labor market, or promotion patterns, have a long history in research. For example, relating to income, Fuchs (1971), more than 30 years ago, cuttingly pointed out that the "fact that men earn more than women is one of the best established and least satisfactorily explained aspects of American labor market behavior" (p. 9). Not much seems to have changed on both sides of the Atlantic, as some examples for income inequality over the past decades show (Becker, 1985; Christel, 1998; Mincer, 1970; Polachek, 1981; a slightly different notion can be found in Bernhardt, Morris, & Handcock, 1995). However, recent years are characterized by a fundamental research perspective change. For a

long time, sex has been used as one of the many variables differentiating people in the labor market. In what one could justifiably call a paradigm change, a gender perspective has been developed that is used to analyze social phenomena at all types of levels. While it is close to impossible to do justice here to feminist or gender research even in terms of labels, content, and research streams, a number of central assumptions can be observed. Among the most important are the views that gender is regarded as a central category of inequity, that sex/gender still is a blind spot or a hidden category in much of society and research, and that all members of societal structures actively or passively produce and reproduce gender-based inequity. In terms of careers, networks, mentoring, and education are regarded as strategic success factors for females (Hermann, 2003, p. 190).

When discussing gender as a major contextual factor, we can see two types of usages. First, studies involving men and women normally use gender as a control variable (see, e.g., Judiesch & Lyness, 1999; Kilduff & Day, 1994; Turban & Dougherty, 1994). Second, and more in line with the paradigmatic change, are efforts that use the gender perspective or the role of gender as a major variable that matters the most. Such an approach reflects the societal conditions that provide the career opportunity structure in this respect (for an overview of the different types of contributions to career research from a gender perspective, see Hermann, 2003). Specifically, a number of theoretical and empirical studies take such a perspective and analyze the career-oriented or gender-based reasons for the differences in jobs held (Konrad & Cannings, 1990); the specific sources of stress for professional women (Nelson & Quick, 1985); the different career orientations of females (Procter & Padfield, 1999), the link between gender, the broader social context and various career aspects (Jacobson & Aaltio-Marjosola, 2001; Jones, 2003); the entrepreneurial career behavior of women (Bowen & Hisrich, 1986); the effects of gender for managerial promotion and advancement (Cannings, 1988; Tharenou & Conroy, 1994; Tharenou, Latimer, & Conroy, 1994) and performance outcomes (Lobel & St. Clair, 1992); the significance of female role models for the formation of perceptions of justice in promotion decisions (Lemons & Danehower, 1996); the influence of gender on the rating individuals get from their superiors (Tsui & Gutek, 1984); and the importance of an organization's mission for the career advancement of women (Newman, 1994).

Ethnicity

The importance of ethnicity in providing a contextual component of career opportunities is a widely researched topic (see, e.g., the meta-analysis of Fouad & Byars-Winston, 2005; Prasad, D'Abate, and Prasad, Chapter 10). The question of discrimination based on race or membership of an ethnic minority group has received special attention. One crucial reason for such a reduction of opportunities is the tendency toward homophile reproduction. Homophily is the degree of demographic and identity similarity of interaction individuals (Ibarra, 1993). One effect of these homophile reproduction processes is a minority-based (e.g., Pfeffer, Davis-Blake, & Julius, 1995) hierarchy. Studies deal with the significance of race for the rating of managers' promotion potential (Landau, 1995) or career success (Sagas & Cunningham, 2005); organizational experiences, job performance evaluations, and career outcomes (Ibarra, 1995); income differences between black and white individuals (Parks-Yancy, 2002); and the influence of relative demographic position—that is, the degree to which individuals are dissimilar to other members of the work unit in terms of race (Lichtenstein & Alexander, 2000; Lawrence and Tolbert, Chapter 20).

Demography

Demography has received some attention in organizational research using an organizational angle—that is, taking the organization and its demographic composition in terms of age, gender, ethnicity, and the like (for an overview of organizational demography, see, e.g., Lawrence and Tolbert, Chapter 20). Based on this, a number of contributions have analyzed various career-related aspects, such as labor turnover (e.g., McCain, O'Reilly, & Pfeffer, 1983;

Wagner, Pfeffer, & O'Reilly, 1984), internal labor markets (e.g., Stewman & Konda, 1983; Stewman, 1986), career mobility and outcomes (Tepperman, 1975), work processes and outcomes (Chatman, Polzer, Barsade, & Neale, 1998), the composition of corporate elites (Stanworth & Giddens, 1974), the perception and consequences of age (Lawrence, 1988), and organizational manpower-planning processes (Young, 1971), from a demographic angle. In a broader perspective, demography points toward the broader context within which individuals and organizations operate. Most frequently, the demographic make-up of world regions, nation states, or occupations serves as a point of reference when discussing various aspects of vocational behavior (London & Greller, 1991), including aspects such as career success (Lewis & Ha, 1985) and promotion (Barnett, Baron, & Stuart, 2000), organizational career management (Cerdin & Peretti, 2001), emerging career patterns in different countries (Venne, 2001), and class mobility (Gerber & Hout, 2004).

Community Factors

Some studies pay attention to an element of the opportunity structure often overlooked. The role of community factors—that is, the integration of individuals into the local context of the civil, political, and religious community—seems to be relevant for individual careers. These factors have been researched in connection with the willingness to relocate (Shamir, Landau, & Arthur, 1990), training measures for people on welfare (Schneider, 2000), barriers to managerial mobility (Veiga, 1983), or the idea of serving society as a whole and building prestige in the local community (Koch, 1973).

The Global Context

Internationalization

Due to the increasing amount of business done at an international level, career opportunities are enhanced, too, through the need for persons acting at a global level (Mendenhall, Kühlmann, & Stahl, 2000). Global career management covers a number of different aspects, such as the individual characteristics of global managers; global career systems; or the human resource management aspects linked with global careers, such as expatriation and repatriation, compensation, or training and development (for an overview, see Baruch, 2004, p. 210ff.)

A number of studies, especially from the expatriate literature, have dealt with various aspects of opportunity linked with global careers (Peiperl and Jonsen, Chapter 18). This includes the efforts that individuals take to access international labor markets (Vance, 2002) or the consequences that individuals face after repatriation (e.g., Linehan & Scullion, 2002).

Virtualization

Virtualization is one of the recent societal developments that have affected organizations and their processes. Most prominently, virtual teams have received considerable attention (see, e.g., Hertel, Geister, & Konradt, 2005; Maznevski & Chudoba, 2000). For careers, virtualization at different levels of society and organization has various consequences. These include the specifics of careers in virtual organizations and the emergence of new national and international career patterns beyond classical forms of expatriation due to frequent commuting, continuous short-term visits, or enhanced communication opportunities such as videoconferencing (Mayerhofer, Hartmann, Michelitsch-Riedl, & Kollinger, 2004).

While looking at single-contextual factors is important, a more integrative picture yields further insight.

The Context of Contexts: An Integrative View

When looking at the various contextual elements that have been identified above as important for describing and explaining careers over the past two decades, four major developments can be identified. First, a decline in the use of some of the classical core categories of contextual factors and their substitution by new constructs with partly the same labels can be observed. Second, the growing importance of interrelationships between several elements—while none of them as such plays an overriding role in influencing careers—becomes evident.

Third, the rise of gender from a mere variable to an all-encompassing research perspective and methodology changes the notion of contextual factors. Finally, the "great transformation" becomes evident here, too. A more balanced relationship between the economic sphere and the private life is partly replaced by the ever-growing importance of economic categories in all parts of life. This is a noticeable development in career terms—and, to be sure, well beyond that—that influences many contextual factors. All these major developments cut across several of the contextual elements outlined above and constitute components of a more integrative picture that goes beyond the specific issues pointed out in the previous section.

The Rise and Fall of Classical Contextual Categories

Class, social origin, and ethnicity are but the most typical examples of classical contextual categories. They have their established place in social sciences in general and in career research in particular. Yet, from looking at research efforts as well as real life, their meaning has changed. While they still constitute an important part of the picture, their content is different from 20 years ago. True, in some approaches and specific ideological directions, their symbolic and theoretical content and importance remain unchanged. However, avoiding blinders, one can safely argue that their use in the classical sense has decreased. This does not mean that these contextual categories have disappeared altogether. However, they have changed in content and meaning. Two examples—social class and ethnicity—can illustrate this.

Social class still is a concept that works and that can be and is used in theoretical and empirical terms. However, even long-term advocates of the use of social class as a theoretical and empirical category see the need for refining this concept (see, e.g., Grusky & Sørensen, 1998). Given the societal developments of the past decades, this is hardly surprising. While the class concept had its origin and apogee in a situation where society was clearly stratified, the situation of the outgoing 20th century in industrialized countries is clearly different. Instead of identifiable strata—upper versus middle versus lower class or workers versus employers, to mention classical examples, we have a highly fragmented and diverse picture. Social status and income, for example, can no longer clearly be linked to a fixed hierarchy of jobs or societal positions. The examples of (some) high-ranking politicians earning only a small fraction of the income of second-level managers or (some) medical doctors earning clearly less than skilled manual workers, the possibilities linked with the new economy even after the burst of the first bubble at the beginning of the third millennium, or the consequences of far-reaching intergenerational status mobility made possible through increased access to higher education indicate that the concept of social class in theoretical terms has to be more refined. Likewise, it seems arguable that the class concept is less anchored in individuals' self-concept. While the post–World War II generation had parents quite firmly linked to a class-based and largely hierarchical society, they themselves or, at the latest, their children experienced a different societal context. Linked, among others, with the liberation movements of the late 1960s, much of the old bondage of class affiliation was thrown overboard. One can argue—and many might say, rightly so—that this happened primarily at the symbolic and rhetorical level rather than in real life. Still, it is but one further indication that a rather broad and undifferentiated concept has to be refined and adapted to a changing societal structure.

Ethnicity, like social class, is a key variable of the contextual factors influencing careers (Prasad, D'Abate, and Prasad, Chapter 10). The label itself, however, indicates a change. Looking at older studies using this concept, the term *ethnicity* is not found frequently: Race was the appropriate concept and the variable that was used in scientific terms. Likewise, in practical life, race was a crucial issue. The horrible and erroneous assumptions about the importance of race in Hitler's Germany as well as the outrageous second-class citizenship of Afro-Americans in the United States were important roots as well as consequences of such a way of thinking. Again, the situation has changed. In Europe, through the importing of workforce especially from Southern European countries into booming economies like Germany, beginning in the late

1960s, as well as through the deliberate efforts of the European Union to encourage mobility across national boundaries and to remove barriers against such movements, the picture has become more diverse. In the United States, the fiction of the melting pot has been tacitly replaced by the existence of many parallel ethnic universes where the old "black-white" thinking in the double sense of the words has been replaced by a culturally and ethnically highly diverse societal composition. Again, this is not to say that ethnic roots and upbringing have lost their scientific and practical significance. But, just as with social class, the concept has to be more refined. Without looking at other factors in addition to ethnicity, we can make few—or, to be very cautious, less accurate—predictions about the career consequences of ethnic roots.

To be sure, the effects of variables such as social class and ethnicity in "real life" and their effects on careers are quite different cross-culturally. For example, while social classes exist in the United States as well as in France, their effects on upward mobility tend to be different, with France most likely having less social permeability. Likewise, ethnic background takes on a different meaning depending on the concrete life and work context. Ethnic background in a country that has a strong majority group, such as Finland, has different effects than if the population consists of two more or less evenly split groups, such as the Flemings and Walloons in Belgium.

In general, while contextual factors still have their important place in career research, a simple continuation of their use would be dangerous: Today, the significance and meaning of these variables have changed due to changes in society and culture, and they are—and have been—cross-culturally different. Hence, their use in research has to be modified, acknowledging a different meaning for these variables. In turn, in model building, interpreting results, and so on, this has to be acknowledged.

Configurations Instead of Single Variables: The Importance of a Multi-Aspect Focus

Pointing toward the mutual relationship and importance of variables is a truism in social sciences. Yet in the case of contextual career variables in a double sense, this is essential.

First, characteristics of careers require a broad look. Such a complex phenomenon as careers and their determining factors cannot be reduced to one or a few single factors. Assuming that class, ethnicity, educational background, or primary socialization can sufficiently explain individuals' careers would mean overestimating the importance of these factors. While in themselves they constitute important elements, they are only a part of the picture. Only the interplay between several of these factors of the phenomenon of careers can do justice to careers in research terms.

Second, and expanding on this, is the importance of a configuration of contextual factors for an adequate description and explanation of careers. Related to the contextual factors of careers, configuration denotes specific combinations of contextual elements occurring at the same time that have specific consequences for careers. Contextual elements in themselves have little meaning. For example, what do you conclude if you know an individual is a female of Turkish origin living in Germany? True, you can make some assumptions about, for example, career chances since a considerable body of research has dealt with the career prospects of migrants. However, unless you get a fuller picture of the configuration of contextual—and, ideally, individual and institutional—variables, you know comparatively little. Only a look at the specific combination of contextual and other factors allows a more correct deduction of the possible career consequences of such a starting situation. To continue the example, it makes a huge difference for her future career if the female of Turkish origin living in Germany is a secular, Western-looking third-generation German citizen with a university degree seeking a career in public sector organizations having equal-opportunity policies and specific development programs for females than if she is a religiously highly active first-generation immigrant with 8 years of school wearing a Tschador and seeking a career as a clerical assistant. Similar North American examples could be given.

But it is not only the configuration that makes a difference. There is also the case of equifunctional configurations: Different combinations of contextual and other factors lead to a similar result. As we know quite well from personality research, different combinations of personality factors can lead to similar results. The same is true in the contextual realm. It is not a simple "the more, the higher" relationship that characterizes these variables. Through the interplay of several variables, the picture gets more difficult as various effects occur. For example, substitution effects can appear where a disadvantageous social origin is "evened" out by extraordinary parental efforts during education; dynamic circular relationships can lead to a self-reinforcing cycle, as in the case where a specific shortage in the labor market in combination with a political effort in pre-election times to enhance minority employment can turn into a successful political measure that endures as it seems to promise future success in the economic and political system; neutralizing effects between different elements of a configuration of contextual career variables can occur, as is the case if an individual's work history and social origin do not fit.

Neither the call for recognition of the interplay of various factors nor asserting the importance of different configurations to get a fuller picture are brand new in research terms. However, the changes in the career context make this call urgent. While analyses of societal developments differ in all sorts of aspects, many would agree that a higher degree of fragmentation of society, a greater diversity of different life concepts and styles, and a less clear picture of what is generally valued and regarded as legitimate constitute core characteristics of today's industrialized and secular societies. Borrowing metaphorically from economics, instead of one single market with "the" consumer, we face a situation of high market fragmentation with a great variety of consumer preferences looking for a unique mix of goods. Among others, these societal effects lead to the loss of single-contextual elements taking the role of "lead indicators." Being the member of a certain ethnic group or coming from a specific socioeconomic background is no longer—if it ever was—a very strong "stand-alone" predictor for future careers. Only through enlarging and differentiating the view by including configurations of contextual elements can an adequate picture be gained.

Gender: From a Single
Variable to an Overall Perspective

As outlined above in the section on "Gender," gender has had its place in career research for a long time. However, from a more general point of view, gender as a variable has not only undergone a dramatic change in itself, thus illustrating the "rise and fall" of contextual variables mentioned above, it has also provided a new overall perspective on organizational issues.

When looking at influential new developments in organizational research over the past three decades, gender studies inevitably come up. To be sure, there are other important contributions to the theoretical and methodological landscape, such as the increased interest in qualitative studies or the importance of symbolism and postmodernism. Hardly any of them, however, has been as fundamental and encompassing as the development of sex/gender from an important, yet single, variable to an overall ideological, theoretical, and methodological perspective. Going into the merits, problems, and details of this development, which, not surprisingly, is sometimes fiercely debated, would be beyond the scope of this chapter. However, from a descriptive point of view, some typical stages of this development corresponding to core phases in feminist research can be identified (for the following, see Hermann, 2003, p. 106ff.). Until the 1970s, and after the first feminist movement around the turn of the 19th century, microtheoretical approaches—for example, psychological models or socialization approaches—were dominant. From the angle of careers, questions such as the reasons for the different behavior of men and women in work life or the importance of social support for work life were typical. The crisis slowly closing this phase was the disappointing resonance in societal terms and the lack of interest from men and women alike. The next phase from the 1970s onward was characterized by more macro-level conceptualizations. Analyses of power and domination or statistical models of the disadvantages of women were used to deal with questions such as the reasons and consequences of men and women choosing— or finding themselves in—different occupations, the effects of societal structures on

women, and concrete measures to achieve equal opportunities for women. Again, some crisis symptoms announced the transformation of this phase. The political changes in Eastern Europe, the increasing insight into women themselves contributing to the reproduction of a system producing gender-based inequalities, the rejection of the women's movement by some—often successful—women, and the diminishing importance of subject-centered theories led to the increasing significance of alternative theoretical approaches. These explicitly relate to the societal level and combine a micro and a macro perspective. Issues such as the conditions of the production and reproduction of patriarchal structures, the opportunities for changing these structures, and the redefinition of the focal categories—men and women—themselves, as well as the possibilities for political action are typical of this phase starting in the 1990s.

For career research, these developments have several implications. First, as outlined in the previous section, gender now is no longer an isolated and single variable. Rather than continuing the mere comparison between men and women, a gender perspective invites career research to take a broader look at the societal and institutional conditions that produce current career patterns characterized by inequities between men and women. Second, gender-based research proposes theoretical angles that explicitly go beyond the individuals and their intentions and include institutional and contextual elements. Thus, contextual elements regain their importance in explaining individual-level phenomena. Third, some themes are reintroduced or underlined through this type of research. Rather than emphasizing the usefulness of specific competencies for individual career progress, the adequacy of certain career patterns for organizational demands, or the opportunities of choice in today's context, different themes come up. Issues such as inequality, power difference, oppression, unequal opportunity, biases or micro politics become salient. To be sure, none of these provide the whole picture or, in a normative way, should constitute the only or even the main focus. Nevertheless, without these issues, career research is partly blind.

The Great Transformation:
The Intrusion of an Economic Logic

When conceptualizing society as consisting of various subsystems functioning according to unique codes (Luhmann, 1997), the question of the relative importance of these subsystems arises. Given the developments over the past decades, many would support the view that the relationship between different societal subsystems and, hence, different logics and codes has changed. Economic considerations dominate much of the public discussion. There is a growing concern that the political system no longer defines the framework for economic activities. Rather, it seems to be the other way around. Some voices are critical that political decision makers are the appeasers of demands that important economic players insist on. Such claims are examples of a more basic change in the role the economy plays: "The economy no longer is embedded into social relationships, but social relationships are embedded into the economic system" (Polanyi, 1978, p. 88 f.). In any case, one seems to be on safer ground when diagnosing a tendency toward the growing importance of the economic subsystem compared with the other subsystems. Likewise, an integration of the economic logic and its code into other systems can be observed. Two examples can illustrate this. The discussion about the role of costs in the health system makes it clear that there seems to be a swing in many European countries from a client-oriented to a more cost-oriented view. Originally there was—and in some countries such as Austria, still is—the doctrine that you get medical treatment according to your health needs regardless of age and overall health status. In recent times, however, the situation has started to change. In some countries—for example, in the United Kingdom, medical treatment is set in relationship to age, future life expectancy, and so on. This clearly indicates an application of the input-output economic logic: Does the investment in medical treatment pay off, given the conditions of the client? In a similar, though more general, way, Brint (1994) distinguishes between trustee and expert models of professionalism. The former is the notion of professional as trustee of the public good, serving clients on the basis of need.

The latter emphasizes that the professional has an expertise with a market value that is distributed on that basis. Another example from management research shows how the economic logic penetrates private life. A qualitative study found that Austrian managers describe and analyze their family life in economic terms and with an economic framework, liberally using concepts such as efficiency and effectiveness (Kasper, Scheer, & Schmidt, 2002). This seems to be an indicator of the increasing hegemony of the economic logic.

At least two major consequences for the career landscape and contextual factors can be derived from this. First, the dominance of the economic logic changes the relationships of individual life spheres and questions the established division between "life" and "work"[1] (Greenhaus and Foley, Chapter 8). If "economic terms of trade" increasingly become the joint frame of reference for all life, the whole question of spillover effects between various spheres of life has to be discussed in a new light. When boundaries diminish or disappear (Gunz, Peiperl, and Tzabbar, Chapter 24), one can hardly speak about spillover. In addition, developments in one life sphere have more importance for the other spheres as they are closely intertwined. In such a way, the downside of "holistic" lifestyles becomes evident. The protective component of being able to draw a line between work and private life is substituted by a high integration of the various spheres with little privacy (see Fleming & Spicer, 2004, for high-commitment organizations). Second, the new role of the economic logic also changes the characteristics of highly personal activities and instances. Participating in a data-processing or language course is no longer just mere personal development. Instead, it has to be also seen in the light of investment in one's cultural capital and competencies, with positive effects on one's employability. Beyond the individual decision that might still pretend that it happened out of mere interest or fun, the collective definition of such actions is guided by an economic logic: Is this a good investment in personal capital? Can something economically relevant be gained out of it? The revived discussion about intellectual capital, building on the social capital discussion of the 1970s, illustrates this point quite nicely.

These developments lead to the growing importance of contextual factors for career studies. Their influence on individual career behavior is growing. Developments in the career context have a more significant influence on the individual sphere as the logics of these spheres are closely synchronized.

A KALEIDOSCOPIC VIEW: BEAUTY, FORM, AND IMAGE

The final section of this chapter goes beyond the lenses chosen and the "surface views" outlined above. A kaleidoscopic[2] angle seems to be most appropriate. A kaleidoscope, in its basic form an optical instrument in which bits of glass or beads held loosely at the end of a rotating tube are shown in continually changing symmetrical forms by reflection in three mirrors placed at an angle of 60° to each other (more refined versions exist, of course—see, e.g., http://www.brewstersociety.com/images.html), produces highly different results. Yet these results have something in common: Forms and patterns have a strange beauty and are rapidly changing and continually shifting from one set of relations to another while being extremely complex and varied. In this way, new perspectives can be gained; well-known issues look different; and loosely connected, yet isolated, parts are formed into a harmonic overall picture.

While some authors use the metaphor of the kaleidoscope to point out core characteristics of career patterns (see, e.g., Mainiero & Sullivan, 2005; Sullivan and Crocitto, Chapter 15), we use it in a more general epistemological sense to characterize a way of constructing reality. The bits of glass or beads—the "raw materials"—are there and have been laid out in the previous sections. What, then, are the rotating tube with the mirrors and the rotation itself, which are needed to form different pictures of unique beauty, form, and image about careers and their contextual characteristics? We argue that well-elaborated macro theories constitute such a tube and that rotating this tube equals the switch from one theory to another. In each of the cases, given "real" elements are formed into a unique picture by ordering the elements in a specific way. Thus, reality is reconstructed.

Most researchers would agree that to make sense of reality, you need theories—either implicit or explicit ones. To make sense of career reality in general and the contextual issues discussed here in particular, grand social theories that cover various aspects of individual, organizational, and contextual reality seem to be particularly well suited. There are not too many theory candidates of this kind around that have greatly influenced organization theory and found their way into career research. The contributions of the Chicago school of sociology in this respect have been significant and well documented (Barley, 1989). We would like to point toward three grand social theories developed in the past three decades: the social theory of Pierre Bourdieu, the structuration theory of Anthony Giddens, and the theory of autopoietically closed social systems by Niklas Luhmann. All three have been used when theorizing about organizations (see, e.g., Hermann, 2003; Hernes & Bakken, 2003; Sydow & Windeler, 1998). In addition, all three make major promises relevant for career research: They enable multilevel analysis; offer a reflexive relationship between action and structure; go beyond the organization as the main point of reference; avoid the selective bias or one-sided choice of objective versus subjective career or micro- versus macro-level; and include neglected areas such as power distribution, social inequalities, and so on. Each of these theories explicitly deals with contextual factors, assigning them a major role. However, they do not stop at the contextual level. In an effort to provide an integrated "grand" view of social reality, they cut across various levels, providing conceptual linkages. To be sure, these three theories are not the only candidates for an integrated view. Conceptual families such as new institutionalism (Powell & DiMaggio, 1987), variants thereof such as new economic institutionalism (e.g., Ebers & Gotsch, 2001), comparable developments in sociology such as new economic sociology (e.g., Swedberg, 1997), or combinations of approaches (e.g., Velthuis, 1999) could also be used. However, the three approaches chosen—unlike the often scattered and eclectic contributions in the conceptual families mentioned—each constitute a coherent and well-developed theory. Thus, they seem especially suitable for further research on careers. We will briefly present them and their relevance in turn.

Grand Social Theories: Bourdieu, Giddens, and Luhmann

For each of the chosen theories, we will point out their main contribution to organization theory and career research.

Pierre Bourdieu: Field, Habitus, and Capital

Field, habitus, and capital are major elements in the theory of Bourdieu. They also can be used and applied to the area of career.

Fields. For Bourdieu, a social field is a patterned set of practices that suggests competent action in conformity with rules and roles as well as a playground or battlefield in which actors, endowed with a certain field-relevant capital, try to advance their position. As such, fields constitute a network of positions, a playground where actors try to follow individual strategies. Playing according to the rules of the game, as defined by the specific set of capital most valuable for holding power within the field, contributes to the reproduction of the fields (Bourdieu, 1977, 1986).

Habitus. Bourdieu conceptualizes habitus as an ensemble of schemata of perception, thinking, feeling, evaluating, speaking, and acting that preformats all the expressive, verbal, and practical manifestations and utterances of an actor (Krais, 1988). It definitely has a corporal dimension, being the embodied history, the active presence of the whole past of which it is the product (Bourdieu, 1990). Through habitus, regular action patterns over time that are the product neither of external structures nor of mere subjective intention can be explained. The habitus is continually adjusted to the current context. Although primary socialization is of great importance, the development of habitus cannot be restricted to that period. Habitus is constantly reinforced or modified by further experience— that is, by positive and negative sanctions during a whole life. Habitus and field are linked in a circular relationship. Involvement in a field shapes the habitus, which, in turn, shapes the

actions that reproduce the field (Crossley, 2001). To understand and explain the action of players in the field, one needs information about their dispositions and competence—their habitus—and about the state of play in the game as well as the players' individual locations in the field. The actors' logic is shaped both by their habitus and by the requirements and logic of the game as it unfolds.

Capital. Bourdieu differentiates between three basic types of capital: economic, social, and cultural (Bourdieu, 1986). Economic capital appears, above all, in the form of general, anonymous, all-purpose convertible money from one generation to the next. It can be more easily and efficiently converted into cultural, social, and symbolic capital than vice versa (Postone, LiPuma, & Calhoun, 1993). Social capital involves relationships of mutual recognition and acquaintance, resources based on social connections and group or class membership. Cultural or informational capital appears in three forms: (1) incorporated—that is, durable dispositions of habitus; (2) objectivized through cultural products such as books, paintings, machines, and so on; and (3) institutionalized through academic titles and degrees, which are relatively independent of the actually incorporated cultural capital. A fourth type of capital, symbolic capital, is closely related to the respective fields. The rules of a particular social field specify which combination of the basic forms of capital will be authorized as symbolic capital, thus becoming socially recognized as legitimate.

Relevance for Career Research. Bourdieu's concept has been applied at the theoretical as well as empirical level to various aspects of careers (see, e.g., Lindh & Dahlin, 2000). It draws on a number of contextual factors that have been outlined in this chapter. Most notably, this includes all those factors mentioned under the labels of context of origin and context of work. For career research, a number of potential contributions can be identified. First, this concept explicitly addresses the structure-agency problem. The concept of career habitus (Mayrhofer et al., 2004) provides a conceptual link between the different perspectives of contextual and individual influences on career behavior. Second, fields allow a conceptualization of the "arena" of careers without using sectoral, organizational, or occupational categories. Career fields try to cut across these areas and offer a framework for getting a great variety of different career arenas into view (Iellatchitch et al., 2003). Third, the concept of career capitals allows a link between existing approaches (e.g., the debate about competencies, in general, or existing career capital approaches as outlined in DeFillippi & Arthur, 1996) and the greater theoretical context of this approach. A Bourdieuan perspective has been used, for example, to analyze the glass ceiling for women and minorities (Corsun & Costen, 2001).

Anthony Giddens: Duality and the Importance of Rules

Giddens's structuration theory (see also Khapova, Arthur, and Wilderom, Chapter 7) deals with the issue of production and reproduction of social life. For careers, this has important implications.

Agency and Structure. Structuration theory conceptualizes agency and structure as mutually dependent: "Social structures are both constituted by human agency and are the very medium of this constitution" (Giddens, 1976, p. 121). It tries to transcend the often found dualism between structure, perceived as deterministic, static, and objective, and individual agency, perceived as voluntaristic, dynamic, and subjective (Barley & Tolbert, 1997). The context or contextualities of interaction provide the condition and background for individual action, the latter being seen not so much as a series of acts as a "continuous flow of conduct." Structuration theory has its own conceptualization of structure. While it is often seen as independent of human action, structuration theory closely links it in a recursive way to action. It speaks of structure as a "property of social systems, 'carried' in reproduced practices embedded in time and space" (Giddens, 1984, p. 170). Rules as structuring properties play a major role in the reproduction of social systems.

Rules. In the structuration process, rules as "procedures of action" (Giddens, 1984, p. 21)

are central. Generating social practices, they need a link to their historical context to be adequately understood. In the eyes of structuration theory, individuals are not passive as mere recipients and followers of such rules. On the contrary, although they are subject to these rules, they actively create, cocreate, and re-create the rules. Although distinguishing between different types of consciousness, structuration theory emphasizes the importance of seemingly trivial rules. Compared with objective laws, rules, and regulations, the rules "only tacitly grasped by actors" (Giddens, 1984, p. 22) have the greater effect on the structuration process. Thus, they deserve a central place in research activities.

Relevance for Career Research. Structuration theory has been used in career research (e.g., El-Sawad, 2004). Its contributions focus on the following points. First, the issue of rules guiding careers is widespread and has been used extensively in career research (for a career-related view on rules, see, e.g., Van Maanen, 1980). Examples include socialization of newcomers, career logics at the national (Gunz, 1989a) and international (Mayrhofer, 1996) levels, or the importance of rules for career success (Kotter, 1995) and self-fulfillment (Yankelovich, 1982). Applying structuration theory can widen the scope and link the discussion of career rules to a well-developed theory, thus allowing for a broader and more in-depth insight. Second, the concept explicitly focuses on the interplay between agency and structure. It addresses a crucial element of career research, offering a conceptual link between contextual and individual factors. It is not confined to one of the contextual factors mentioned in the previous sections. All of them are potential elements of structure. Even if the degree to which they are created and re-created clearly differs, structuration theory potentially can include them. Third, this view has a strong dynamic component. The processes by which structure and agency are linked constitute a key element. Thus, it allows for constant change and development. For career research, focusing on the dynamic elements of creating/re-creating relevant career structures and linking them to individual behavior, the concept offers fertile ground.

Niklas Luhmann: Autopoietic Closure

Luhmann's theory of social systems proposes a radical view of social systems in general and organizations in particular (see the contributions in Seidl & Becker, 2005, for its importance for organizational theory). Career research can profit from this.

Autopoietic Closure. Organizations and organizational processes are often viewed from an open sociotechnical systems point of view (e.g., Scott, 1981). Social systems theory departs from this route. Based on the notion of autopoiesis as developed in biology (Maturana & Varela, 1980), it develops this idea further and sees organizations as autopoietically closed and consisting of communications or—in the case of formalized organizations—decisions, that is, actions under the pressure of expectations. At the basal level, they are not open to their environment but autopoietically closed: They reproduce the elements they consist of out of the elements they consist of. Social systems are nontrivial machines that constantly alter their internal states and relationships (von Foerster, 1985). From the outside—and all observers are outsiders belonging to the internal or external environment—it is impossible to diagnose their functioning exactly. As indicated, the constituents of social systems are communications, actions, and decisions (these three differ mainly with respect to the observers' position). Persons—more exactly, psychic systems—belong to the internal environment of social systems. They are a *conditio sine qua non* for social systems and stimulate communications. Conceptually, they reside outside the organization as the latter consists only of communications and not of persons. (Luhmann, 1984, 1988, 1989).

Self-Organization. Social systems theory is skeptical about achieving calculable effects in a system since the latter is not fully transparent and manageable. Attempts to push the system in a certain direction—in other words, management efforts—cannot rely on an adequate understanding of the system due to its autopoietic closure. Social systems are not transparent; there are no fully adequate reconstructions of its internal functioning. At the most, "as-if"

assumptions from the outside can be made. Interventions through other psychic or social systems that necessarily come from the outside follow a different logic of intervention than the logic of processes within the social system. Thus, an unbridgeable gap between intervening systems and the organization exists (Willke, 1987). This does not imply that management is impossible. However, the conception of organizations as autopoietically closed social systems has significant consequences for management efforts. Management of such systems can only be self-management. Interventions—that is, management efforts from the outside of the system, for example, by managers—are initially sheer environmental noise. Only after the system reacts to this noise—that is, after the noise stimulates internal operations that, in turn, trigger further operations (communications, actions, decisions)—can one talk about a successful intervention. If and how the social system reacts to intervention noise and further proceeds internally does not depend on the intervening systems—for example, managers—but solely on the system intervened in. Managerial efforts may or may not be taken up by the intervened system and be further processed (Kasper et al., 1999).

Relation to the Environment. For social systems, autopoietic closure is essential for survival in a complex environment. The relationship between system and environment is characterized by a difference in complexity. This difference is the constituting force behind the existence of social systems. If there were no difference, there would be no system but only environment. The question emerging is, How do social systems relate themselves vis-à-vis the environment? Which part of the environment do they (re-)construct within the system and translate into the internal process logic of the system (Luhmann, 1990, p. 32ff., 1992, p. 38ff.)? From a systems theoretical point of view, the answer is clear: via structural coupling. Structural coupling addresses the relationship of social systems to their environment, most notably other social systems. It enables social systems to react to developments in their environment. For example, organizations as social systems are structurally coupled to their environment through psychic systems ("individuals"). The latter sensitize them for specific sections of the organizations' environment. At the same time, structural coupling allows social systems to disregard many parts of the environment. Given the enormous number of possibilities, they are impressed only by very few "instances." Indifference is the standard reaction to most environmental incidents. It is very sharply selective toward the environment as well as toward its own possibilities of "reaction" (Luhmann, 1988, p. 35). Thus, on the one hand, structural coupling implies mutual dependency and selectivity. On the other hand, this also means an enhancement of the system's potential. Through structural coupling, people (psychic systems) or groups (interaction systems) can provide organizations with complexity, and vice versa. In the language of social systems theory, the mutual provision of *eigencomplexity*—that is, the system's own complexity—to enhance the complexity of the other system is called interpenetration (Luhmann, 1984, p. 286ff.).

Relevance for Career Research. Social systems theory has been used to analyze different aspects of careers (see, e.g., Becker & Haunschild, 2003; Mayrhofer & Meyer, 2002). Major themes for career research coming from this theoretical concept include the following. First, social systems theory offers new basic building blocks for career analysis: communications, actions, and decisions, each of them clearly conceptualized. Thus, this theory helps transcend traditional categories in career research and allows a theoretically coherent look across a great variety of career phenomena. If careers are understood as unique sequences of communications/actions/decisions, then they can be theoretically dealt with in line with social systems theory. Second, the autopoietic closure of social systems sheds new light not only on career management (which is not the focus of this chapter) but also on the relevance of contextual factors. From a social systems theory perspective, there is no determining power of contextual factors. Rather than "directly" influencing system internal processes, it is the social system—often, the organization— and its internal schemata that decide on their relevance. For career research, this requires a look at intrasystemic issues even in the case of

research focusing on contextual factors. Third, this concept explicitly takes into account three levels: individuals, more precisely, psychic systems; organizations as social systems of a specific kind; and the environment. Thus, it allows addressing of a key issue in career research— that is, the interplay between these three levels.

Contributing to a Kaleidoscopic Perspective of Careers

After characterizing the chosen grand social theories and linking them to career research, we will outline the major issues that emerge from these three kaleidoscopic views and point toward their relevance for career.

First, and most obviously, the theories mentioned call for an important place for contextual variables in career research. All the theories have a unique conceptualization of context and their specific view of what matters most and propose that without an adequate understanding of contextual factors and the integration of context into the picture, the latter remains incomplete. This creates two demands. Given their focus, the easy part is bringing specific segments of the context to the attention of career research. What is definitely more demanding is the call for a coherent theoretical framework within which the various contextual elements can be anchored. This becomes essential when the single-contextual elements are linked to other elements of career research. Without a coherent theoretical framework, the relative significance and relationship among the contextual variables as well as between them and other variables remains unclear.

Second, changing between various theoretical perspectives increases our understanding of careers. Every theory necessarily has its blind spots and excludes aspects and relationships. A playful "twist of the tube of the kaleidoscope"— that is, the use of various theoretical angles combining the contextual elements mentioned in the following chapters in their specific ways—will produce different pictures of career reality. To be sure, this cannot be done simultaneously. Very much so as the classic kaleidoscope allows different pictures only sequentially, it would be epistemological and theoretical folly to "combine," "unite," or "reconcile" the grand social theories mentioned above or similar approaches: They are too different in their basic assumptions, conceptualizations, and core processes. However, if career research or researchers choose to work with such theories, the field as a whole will profit from the insight gained from these varying perspectives.

Third, grand social theories definitely call for a balanced approach between contextual and individual/organizational variables. While they clearly emphasize contextuality, they are not one-sided or context deterministic. All of them acknowledge the important and integral role of other factors "beyond" context. Thus, they advocate the interplay between factors at various levels, starting from the individual and continuing up to societal factors. For career research, in general, and analyses of the role of contextual factors, in particular, this turns the focus onto multilevel analyses and identifying mechanisms that link these levels. In turn, this requires theoretical (ground) work: It is not enough to acknowledge and empirically research the influence of contextual factors on individuals' careers. Beyond that, theoretically sound explanations of how the link and, possibly, mutual influences work are needed.

Fourth, looking at the scope and content of the perspective of these theories, a call for topics currently in the shadow of much of career research can be identified. These topics include a more constructivist view of contextual factors—that is, how they are construed by various individual and collective actors and integrated into individual patterns of action (Kidd, Chapter 6; Savickas, Chapter 5), the constraining effects of the context as a counterpoint to the sometimes euphoric accounts of context providing only opportunities and (nearly) no threats, the inclusion of conflict, the striving for domination and micropolitical power games, or a "de-individualized" approach to careers that can be conceptualized as a specific pattern of communication.

Concluding Remarks

Careers are always careers in context—this was the starting point of this chapter. Context is, as with careers, not easy to decipher. Depending on one's basic theoretical and/or disciplinary view, it is open to many interpretations and conceptualizations. This chapter opted for a "literature-grounded" approach within the realm of management research and related disciplines. By developing a simple framework allowing a view through various lenses, the chapter has linked existing context-related career research on major contextual factors, thus, it is hoped, providing orientation in the "contextual jungle." Combining these pieces of research into a more integrative view led to the identification of major developments in context-related career research. Pointing toward the future, the potential for well-elaborated social macro theories to develop further context-related career research was analyzed, using the kaleidoscope metaphor as an illustration of these theories' potential.

Of course, our own limitations and biases from factors such as cultural heritage, theoretical preferences, or age have contributed to the current form of this chapter and ruled out alternative setups. In the light of the kaleidoscope metaphor, however, we are relaxed about this: Each approach has its own beauty, form, and image.

Notes

1. That the labeling of this division or the use of the term *work-life* balance is interesting in its own right as it indicates intriguing basic assumptions about life and work—for example, that work does not belong to life—is just mentioned and not commented on further.

2. In Greek, *kalos:* beauty, *eidos:* form, and *scope:* image.

References

Anderson, J. C., Milkovich, G. T., & Tsui, A. (1981). A model of intra-organizational mobility. *Academy of Management Review, 6*(4), 529–538.

Arthur, M. B., & Rousseau, D. M. (Eds.). (1996). *The boundaryless career. A new employment for a new organizational era.* New York: Oxford University Press.

Barley, S. R. (1989). Careers, identities, and institutions: The legacy of the Chicago school of sociology. In M. B. Arthur, D. T. Hall, &

B. S. Lawrence (Eds.), *Handbook of career theory* (pp. 41–65). Cambridge, UK: Cambridge University Press.

Barley, S. R., & Tolbert, P. S. (1997). Institutionalization and structuration: Studying the links between institutions and actions. *Organization Studies, 18,* 93–117.

Barnett, W. P., Baron, J. N., & Stuart, T. E. (2000). Avenues of attainment: Occupational demography and organizational careers in the California Civil Service. *American Journal of Sociology, 106*(1), 88–144.

Baruch, Y. (2004). *Managing careers: Theory and practice.* Harlow: Pearson Education.

Becker, G. S. (1985). Human capital, effort, and the sexual division of labor. *Journal of Labor Economics, 3*(1, Pt. 2), S33–S59.

Becker, K. H., & Haunschild, A. (2003). The impact of boundaryless career on organizational decision making: An analysis from the perspective of Luhmann's theory of social systems. *International Journal of Human Resource Management, 14*(5), 713–727.

Bernhardt, A., Morris, M., & Handcock, M. S. (1995). Women's gains or men's losses? A closer look at the Shrining Gender Gap in earnings. *American Journal of Sociology, 101*(2), 302–328.

Bernhardt, A., Morris, M., Handcock, M. S., & Scott, M. A. (2001). *Divergent paths: Economic mobility in the new American labor market.* New York: Russell Sage Foundation.

Bertaux, D., & Thompson, P. (Eds.). (1997). *Pathways to social class: A qualitative approach to social mobility.* Oxford: Clarendon Press.

Bielby, W. T., & Bielby, D. D. (1999). Organizational mediation of project-based labor markets: Talent agencies and the careers of screenwriters. *American Sociological Review, 64*(1), 64–85.

Blau, G. (1999). Early-career job factors influencing the professional commitment of medical technologies. *Academy of Management Journal, 42*(6), 687–695.

Blau, P. M., & Duncan, O. D. (1967). *The American occupational structure.* New York: Wiley.

Boh, W. F., Slaughter, S., & Ang, S. (2001). Is information technology a "boundaryless" profession? A sequence analysis of the career histories of IT professionals from 1979–1998. *Academy of Management Proceedings,* A1–A6.

Bourdieu, P. (1977). *Outline of a theory of practice.* Cambridge, MA: Cambridge University Press.

Bourdieu, P. (1986). The forms of capital. In J. G. Richardson (Ed.), *Handbook of theory and research for the sociology of education* (pp. 241–258). New York: Greenwood.

Bourdieu, P. (1990). *The logic of practice.* Stanford, CA: Stanford University Press.

Bowen, D. E., & Hisrich, R. D. (1986). The female entrepreneur: A career development perspective. *Academy of Management Review, 11*(2), 393–407.

Brewis, J., & Linstead, S. (2000). "The worst thing is the screwing" (2): Context and career in sex work. *Gender, Work and Organization, 7*(3), 168–180.

Brint, S. (1994). *In an age of experts: The changing role of professionals in politics and public life.* Princeton, NJ: Princeton University Press.

Brown, H. A., & Ford, D. L., Jr. (1975). Minorities in the management profession: The recent MBA graduate. *Academy of Management Proceedings,* 448–450.

Brown, M. T., Fukunaga, C., Umemoto, D., & Wicker, L. (1996). Annual review, 1990–1996: Social class, work, and retirement behavior. *Journal of Vocational Behavior, 49,* 159–189.

Brüderl, J., Diekmann, A., & Preisendörfer, P. (1991). Patterns of intraorganizational mobility: Tournament models, path dependency, and early promotion effects. *Social Science Research, 20,* 197–216.

Burt, R. S. (1992). *Structural holes: The social structure of competition.* Cambridge, MA: Harvard University Press.

Cabral, A. C., Rhodes, S. R., & Doering, M. (1985). Determinants of career change: A path analysis. *Academy of Management Proceedings,* 46–50.

Cadin, L., Bender, A.-F., Saint Giniez, V., & Pringle, J. K. (2000). Carrières nomades et contextes nationaux. *Revue de Gestion des Ressources Humaines, 37,* 76–96.

Campion, M. A., Cheraskin, L., & Stevens, M. J. (1994). Career-related antecedents and outcomes of job rotation. *Academy of Management Journal, 37*(6), 1518–1543.

Cannings, K. (1988). Managerial promotion: The effects of socialization, specialization, and gender. *Industrial and Labor Relations Review, 42*(1), 77–88.

Cawsey, T. F., Nicholson, N., & Alban-Metcalfe, B. (1985). Who's on the fast track? The relationship between career mobility, individual and task characteristics. *Academy of Management Proceedings,* 51–55.

Cerdin, J.-L., & Peretti, J.-M. (2001). Trends and emerging values in human resource management in France. *International Journal of Manpower, 22*(3), 216–229.

Chatman, J. A., Polzer, J. T., Barsade, S. G., & Neale, M. A. (1998). Being different yet feeling similar: The influence of demographic composition and organizational culture on work processes and outcomes. *Administrative Science Quarterly, 43,* 749–780.

Christel, C. (1998). The impact of education and labour market experience on earnings: What is the difference between men and women? *Statistical Journal of the UN Economic Commission for Europe, 15*(2), 137–148.

Cole, E. R., & Omari, S. R. (2003). Race, class and the dilemmas of upward mobility for African Americans. *Journal of Social Issues, 59*(4), 785–802.

Corsun, D. L., & Costen, W. M. (2001). Is the glass ceiling unbreakable?: Habitus, fields, and the stalling of women and minorities in management. *Journal of Management Inquiry, 10*(1), 16–25.

Crossley, N. (2001). The phenomenological habitus and its construction. *Theory and Society,* (30), 81–120.

DeFillippi, R. J., & Arthur, M. B. (1996). Boundaryless contexts and careers: A competency-based perspective. In D. T. Hall & D. M. Rousseau (Eds.), *The boundaryless career* (pp. 116–131). New York: Oxford University Press.

Doeringer, P. B., & Piore, M. J. (1971). *Internal labor markets and manpower analysis.* London: D. C. Heath.

Dore, R. (2004). *New forms and meanings of work in an increasingly globalized world.* Geneva: International Institute for Labour Studies.

Ebers, M., & Gotsch, W. (2001). Institutionenökonomische theorie der organisation. In A. Kieser (Ed.), *Organisationstheorien* (4th ed., pp. 199–251). Stuttgart: Kohlhammer.

Edwards, R. C. (Ed.). (1975). *Labor market segmentation.* Lexington, MA: Lexington Books.

El-Sawad, A. (2004, July 1–3). *Playing the game: Rules and "re-creational careers."* Paper presented at the European Group of Organisation Studies 2004, Sub-Theme 9: Careers—relating the individual to the context, Ljubljana, Slovenia.

Ferry, T. R., Fouad, N. A., & Smith, P. L. (2000). The role of family context in a social cognitive model for career-related choice behavior: A math and science perspective. *Journal of Vocational Behavior, 57,* 348–364.

Fleming, P., & Spicer, A. (2004). "You can checkout anytime, but you can never leave": Spatial boundaries in a high commitment organization. *Human Relations, 57*(1), 75–94.

Fouad, N. A., & Byars-Winston, A. M. (2005). Cultural context of career choice: Meta-analysis of race/ethnicity differences. *Career Development Quarterly, 53*(3), 223–233.

Fuchs, V. R. (1971). Differences in hourly earnings between men and women. *Monthly Labor Review, 94*(5), 9–16.

Gattiker, U. E., & Coe, L. (1986). Relationship of computer attitudes with perception of career success. *Academy of Management Proceedings,* 294–298.

Gelles, R. J., & Levine, A. (2001). *Sociology: An introduction* (6th ed.). New York: McGraw-Hill.

Gerber, T. P., & Hout, M. (2004). Tightening up: Declining class mobility during Russia's market transition. *American Sociological Review, 69*(5), 677–693.

Giddens, A. (1976). *New rules of sociological method: A positive critique of interpretative sociologies.* New York: Basic Books.

Giddens, A. (1984). *The constitution of society. Outline of the theory of structuration.* Cambridge, UK: Polity Press.

Giddens, A., Duneier, M., & Appelbaum, R. P. (2003). *Introduction to sociology* (4th ed.). New York: W. W. Norton.

Grandjean, B. D. (1981). History and career in a bureaucratic labor market. *American Journal of Sociology, 86*(5), 1057–1092.

Grusky, D. B., & Sørensen, J. B. (1998). Can class analysis be salvaged? *American Journal of Sociology, 103,* 1187–1234.

Gunz, H. (1989a). *Careers and corporate cultures. Managerial mobility in large corporations.* Oxford: Basil Blackwell.

Gunz, H. (1989b). The dual meaning of managerial careers: Organizational and individual levels of analysis. *Journal of Management Studies, 26*(3), 225–250.

Gunz, H. P., & Jalland, R. M. (1996). Managerial careers and business strategies. *Academy of Management Review, 21*(3), 718–756.

Gupta, A. K., & Seshadri, S. (1994). Horizontal resource sharing: A principal-agent approach. *Academy of Management Proceedings,* 37–41.

Hall, D. T. (1996). Protean careers of the 21st century. *Academy of Management Executive, 10*(4), 8–16.

Hambrick, D. C., & Mason, P. A. (1984). Upper echelons: The organization as a reflection of its top managers. *Academy of Management Review, 9*(2), 193–206.

Hartmann, M. (1996). *Topmanager: Die Rekrutierung einer Elite.* Campus Verlag: Frankfurt/New York.

Hartmann, M. (2000). Class-specific habitus and the social reproduction of the business elite in Germany and France. *Sociological Review, 48*(2), 262–282.

Hermann, A. (2003). *Karrieremuster im Management als ergebnis geschlechtlich gesteuerter Austausch-prozesse: Die Sozialtheorie Pierre Bourdieus als Ausgangspunkt für eine geschlechterbasierte Karrierebetrachtung.* Unpublished doctoral thesis, Wirtschaftsuniversität Wien, Vienna.

Hernes, T., & Bakken, T. (2003). Implications of self-reference: Niklas Luhmann's autopoiesis and organization theory. *Organization Studies, 24*(9), 1511–1535.

Hertel, G., Geister, S., & Konradt, U. (2005). Managing virtual teams: A review of current empirical research. *Human Resource Management Review, 15,* 69–95.

Higgins, M. C. (2001). Changing careers: The effects of social context. *Journal of Organizational Behavior, 22*(6), 595–618.

Higgins, M. C., & Kram, K. E. (2001). Reconceptualizing mentoring at work: A developmental network perspective. *Academy of Management Review, 26*(2), 264–288.

Hughes, E. C. (1937). Institutional office and the person. In *Men and their work* (pp. 57–67). Glencoe, IL: Free Press.

Hunt, D. M., & Michael, C. (1983). Mentorship: A career training and development tool. *Academy of Management Review, 8*(3), 475–485.

Ibarra, H. (1993). Personal networks of women and minorities in management. A conceptual framework. *Academy of Management Review, 18*(1), 57–87.

Ibarra, H. (1995). Race, opportunity, and diversity of social circles in managerial networks. *Academy of Management Journal, 38*(3), 673–703.

Iellatchitch, A., Mayrhofer, W., & Meyer, M. (2003). Career fields: A small step towards a grand career theory? *International Journal of Human Resource Management, 14*(5), 728–750.

Jacobson, S. W., & Aaltio-Marjosola, I. (2001). "Strong" objectivity and the use of Q-methodology in cross-cultural research: Contextualizing the experience of women managers and their scripts of career. *Journal of Management Inquiry, 10*(3), 228.

Jones, S. J. (2003). Complex subjectivities: Class, ethnicity, and race in women's narratives of upward mobility. *Journal of Social Issues, 59*(4), 803–820.

Judge, T. A., & Bretz, R. D., Jr. (1992). Political influence behavior and career success. *Academy of Management Proceedings,* 58–62.

Judiesch, M. K., & Lyness, K. S. (1999). Left behind? The impact of leaves of absence on managers' career success. *Academy of Management Journal, 42*(6), 641–651.

Kasper, H., Mayrhofer, W., & Meyer, M. (1999). Management aus systemtheoretischer Perspektive: eine Standortbestimmung. In D. V. Eckardstein, H. Kasper, & W. Mayrhofer (Eds.), *Management* (pp. 161–210). Stuttgart: Schäffer-Poeschel.

Kasper, H., Scheer, P. J., & Schmidt, A. (2002). *Managen und lieben. Führungskräfte im Spannungsfeld von Familie und Beruf.* Wien: Ueberreuter.

Katz, R., & Allen, T. J. (1991). Age, education and the technical ladder. *Academy of Management Proceedings,* 352–356.

Kilduff, M., & Day, D. V. (1994). Do chameleons get ahead? The effects of self-monitoring on managerial careers. *Academy of Management Journal, 37*(4), 1047–1060.

Koch, J. L. (1973). Fitting job and career patterns to the technician's expectations. *Academy of Management Proceedings,* 359–365.

Konrad, A. M., & Cannings, K. (1990). Sex segregation in the workplace and the mommy track: Sex differences in work commitment or statistical discrimination? *Academy of Management Proceedings,* 369–373.

Kotter, J. P. (1995). *The new rules. How to succeed in today's post-corporate world.* New York: Free Press.

Krais, B. (1988). Der Begiff des Habitus bei Bourdieu und seine Bedeutung für die Bildungstheorie. In B. Dewe, G. Frank, & W. Huge (Eds.), *Theorien der Erwachsenenbildung.* Munich: Hueber.

Kram, K. E. (1988). *Mentoring at work: Developmental relationships in organizational life.* Lanham, MD: University Press of America.

Kurtz, D. L., Boone, L. E., & Fleenor, C. P. (1987). Parental influence and family size as variables shaping CEO careers. *Review of Business, 9*(1), 9–12.

Landau, J. (1995). The relationship of race and gender to managers' ratings of promotion potential. *Journal of Organizational Behavior, 16,* 391–400.

Lawrence, B. S. (1988). New wrinkles in the theory of age: Demography, norms, and performance ratings. *Academy of Management Journal, 31*(2), 309–337.

Lemons, M. A., & Danehower, V. C. (1996). Organizational justice and the glass ceiling: The moderating role of gender schemas. *Academy of Management Proceedings,* 398–402.

Leontaridi, R. M. (2002). Career, experience and returns to human capital: Is the dual labour market hypothesis relevant for the UK? *Research in Economics, 56*(4), 399–426.

Lewin, K. (1936). *Principles of topological psychology.* New York: McGraw-Hill.

Lewis, G. B., & Ha, M. (1985). Impact of the Baby Boom on career success in Federal Civil Service. *Public Administration Review, 11–12,* 951–956.

Lichtenstein, R., & Alexander, J. A. (2000). Perceived promotional opportunities in veterans affairs hospitals: A reexamination of relational demography theory. *The Journal of Applied Behavioral Science, 36*(3), 269–296.

Lindh, G., & Dahlin, E. (2000). A Swedish perspective on the importance of Bourdieu's theories for career counseling. *Journal of Employment Counseling, 37,* 194–203.

Linehan, M., & Scullion, H. (2002). Repatriation of European female corporate executives: An empirical study. *The International Journal of Human Resource Management, 13*(2), 254–267.

Lobel, S. A., & St. Clair, L. (1992). Effects of family responsibilities, gender, and career identity salience on performance outcomes. *Academy of Management Journal, 35*(5), 1057–1069.

London, M., & Greller, M. M. (1991). Demographic trends and vocational behavior: A twenty year retrospective and agenda for the 1990s. *Journal of Vocational Behavior, 38,* 125–164.

Luhmann, N. (1984). *Soziale systeme. Grundriß einer allgemeinen theorie.* Frankfurt: Suhrkamp.

Luhmann, N. (1988). Organisation. In W. Küpper & G. Ortmann (Eds.), *Mikropolitik* (pp. 165–186). Opladen: Westdeutscher.

Luhmann, N. (1989). *Die Wirtschaft der Gesellschaft* (2nd ed.). Frankfurt: Suhrkamp.

Luhmann, N. (1990). *Ökologische Kommunikation* (3rd ed.). Opladen: Westdeutscher.

Luhmann, N. (1992). *Die Wissenschaft der Gesellschaft.* Frankfurt: Suhrkamp.

Luhmann, N. (1997). *Die Gesellschaft der Gesellschaft.* Frankfurt: Suhrkamp.

Mainiero, L. A., & Sullivan, S. E. (2005). Kaleidoscope careers: An alternate explanation for the opt-out revolution. *Academy of Management Executive, 19*(1), 106–123.

Maturana, H. R., & Varela, F. J. (1980). *Autopoiesis and cognition.* Dordrecht: D. Reidel.

Mayerhofer, H., Hartmann, L. C., Michelitsch-Riedl, G., & Kollinger, I. (2004). Flexpatriate assignments: A neglected issue in global staffing. *International Journal of Human Resource Management, 15*(8), 1371–1389.

Mayrhofer, W. (1996). *Mobilität und Steuerung in international tätigen Unternehmen.* Stuttgart: Schäffer-Poeschel.

Mayrhofer, W., Iellatchitch, A., Meyer, M., Steyrer, J., Schiffinger, M., & Strunk, G. (2004). Going beyond the individual. Some potential contributions from a career field and habitus perspective for global career research and practice. *Journal of Management Development, 23*(9), 870–884.

Mayrhofer, W., & Meyer, M. (2002). "No more shall we part?" Neue Selbständige und neue Formen der Kopplung zwischen Organisation und ihrem personal. *Zeitschrift für Personalforschung, 16*(4), 599–614.

Maznevski, M. L., & Chudoba, K. M. (2000). Bridging space over time: Global virtual team dynamics and effectiveness. *Organization Science, 11,* 473–492.

McCain, B. E., O'Reilly, C., & Pfeffer, J. (1983). The effects of departmental demography on turnover: The case of a university. *Academy of Management Journal, 26*(4), 626–641.

Mendenhall, M. E., Kühlmann, T. M., & Stahl, G. (2000). *Developing global business leaders: Policies, processes, and innovations.* New York: Quorum Books.

Menger, P.-M. (1999). Artistic labor markets and careers. *Annual Review of Sociology, 25,* 541–574.

Mihal, W. L., Sorce, P. A., & Comte, T. E. (1984). A process model of individual career decision making. *Academy of Management Review, 9*(1), 95–103.

Mincer, J. (1970). The distribution of labor incomes: A survey with special reference to the human capital approach. *Journal of Economic Literature, 8*(1), 1–26.

Morrison, R., & Brantner, T. M. (1991). What affects how quickly a new job is learned? *Academy of Management Proceedings,* 52–56.

Nelson, D. L., & Quick, J. C. (1985). Professional women: Are distress and disease inevitable? *Academy of Management Review, 10*(2), 206–218.

Newman, M. A. (1994). Gender and Lowi's thesis: Implications for career advancement. *Public Administration Review, 54*(3), 277–284.

O'Donovan, T. R. (1962). Differential extent of opportunity among executives and lower managers. *Academy of Management Journal, August,* 139–149.

Orpen, C. (1996). Dependency as moderator of the effects of networking behavior on managerial career success. *Journal of Psychology, 130,* 245–248.

Parks-Yancy, R. (2002). Antecedents of managerial and professional career trajectories and their differential effects on blacks and whites: Gaining parity through human and social capital. *Academy of Management Proceedings,* A1–A6.

Peiperl, M., & Baruch, Y. (1997). Back to square zero: The post-corporate career. *Organizational Dynamics, Spring,* 7–22.

Peterson, R. A., & Anand, N. (2002). How chaotic careers create orderly fields. In M. A. Peiperl, M. Arthur, R. Goffee, & N. Anand (Eds.), *Career creativity.* Oxford: Oxford University Press.

Pfeffer, J., Davis-Blake, A., & Julius, D. J. (1995). The effects of affirmative action officer salary changes on managerial diversity. *Industrial Relations, 34,* 73–94.

Piore, M. J. (1975). Notes for a theory of labor market stratification. In R. C. Edwards, M. Reich, & D. M. Gordon (Eds.), *Labor market segmentation* (pp. 125–150). Lexington, MA: Heath.

Polachek, S. W. (1981). Occupational self-selection: A human capital approach to sex differences in occupational structure. *Review of Economics and Statistics, 63*(1), 60–69.

Polanyi, K. (1978). *The great transformation. Politische und ökonomische Ursprünge von Gesellschaften und Wirtschaftssystemen.* Frankfurt: Suhrkamp.

Postone, M., LiPuma, E., & Calhoun, C. (1993). Introduction: Bourdieu and social theory. In C. Calhoun, E. LiPuma, & M. Postone (Eds.), *Bourdieu. Critical perspectives* (pp. 1–13). Cambridge, MA: Polity.

Powell, W., & DiMaggio, P. J. (Eds.). (1987). *The new institutionalism in organizational analysis.* Chicago: University of Chicago Press.

Procter, I., & Padfield, M. (1999). Work orientations and women's work: A critique of Hakim's theory of the heterogeneity of women. *Gender, Work and Organization, 6*(3), 152–162.

Raelin, J. A. (1984). An analysis of the work patterns of salaried professionals over three career stages. *Academy of Management Proceedings,* 58–62.

Ragins, B. R., Cotton, J. L., & Miller, J. S. (2000). Marginal mentoring: The effects of type of mentor, quality of relationship, and program designing on work and career attitudes. *Academy of Management Journal, 43*(6), 1177–1194.

Reeser, C. (1969). Some potential human problems of the project form of organization. *Academy of Management Proceedings, August,* 111–113.

Reynolds, P. D. (1988). Organizational births: Perspectives on the emergence of new firms. *Academy of Management Proceedings,* 69–73.

Rhodes, S. R., & Doering, M. (1983). An integrated model of career change. *Academy of Management Review, 8*(4), 631–639.

Rosenbaum, J. E. (1979). Tournament mobility: Career patterns in a corporation. *Administrative Science Quarterly, 24,* 220–241.

Ruigrok, W., Pettigrew, A., Peck, S. I., & Whittington, R. (1999). Corporate restructuring and new forms of organizing: Evidence from Europe [Special issue]. *Management International Review, 39*(2), 41–64.

Sagas, M., & Cunningham, G. B. (2005). Racial differences in the career success of assistant football coaches: The role of discrimination, human capital, and social capital. *Journal of Applied Social Psychology, 35*(4), 773–797.

Savage, P. (2001). *New forms of work organization: The benefits and impact on performance.* European Work Organisation Network. (Report presented to DG Employment & Social Affairs, European Union)

Schein, E. H. (1978). *Career dynamics: Matching individual and organizational needs.* Reading, MA: Addison-Wesley.

Schneer, J. A., & Reitman, F. (1990). Effects of employment gaps on the careers of M.B.A.'s: More damaging for men than for women?

Academy of Management Journal, 33(2), 391–406.

Schneer, J. A., & Reitman, F. (1993). Effects of alternative family structures on managerial careers. *Academy of Management Journal, 38*(4), 830–843.

Schneider, J. A. (2000). Pathways to opportunity: The role of race, social networks, institutions, and neighborhood in career and educational paths for people on welfare. *Human Organization, 59*(1), 72–85.

Scott, W. R. (1981). *Organizations: Rational, natural, and open systems.* Englewood Cliffs, NJ: Prentice Hall.

Seibert, S. E., Kraimer, M. L., & Liden, R. C. (2001). A social capital theory of career success. *Academy of Management Journal, 44*(2), 219–237.

Seidl, D., & Becker, K. H. (Eds.). (2005). *Niklas Luhmann and organization studies.* Malmö: Liber.

Shamir, B., Landau, J., & Arthur, M. B. (1990). Factors related to managers' and professionals' willingness to relocate. *Academy of Management Proceedings,* 48–52.

Solomon, E. E., Bishop, R. C., & Bresser, R. K. (1985). Moderators of gender differences in career development: A facet classification. *Academy of Management Proceedings,* 56–60.

Sonnenfeld, J. A., Peiperl, M. A., & Kotter, J. P. (1988a). Corporate career systems and individual career profiles: A longitudinal analysis. *Academy of Management Proceedings,* 53–57.

Sonnenfeld, J. A., Peiperl, M. A., & Kotter, J. P. (1988b). Strategic determinants of managerial labor markets: A career systems view. *Human Resource Management, 27*(4), 369–388.

Sorensen, A. B. (1975). The structure of intragenerational mobility. *American Sociological Review, 40,* 456–471.

Staehle, W. H. (1999). *Management* (8th ed.). Munich: Vahlen.

Stanworth, P., & Giddens, A. (1974). An economic elite. A demographic profile of company chairmen. In A. Giddens & P. Stanworth (Eds.), *Elites and power in British society* (pp. 81–101). Cambridge, UK: Cambridge University Press.

Stewman, S. (1986). Demographic models of internal labor markets. *Administrative Science Quarterly, 31,* 212–247.

Stewman, S., & Konda, S. (1983). Careers and organizational labor markets: Demographic models of organizational behavior. *American Journal of Sociology, 88*(4), 637–685.

Swedberg, R. (1997). New economic sociology: What has been accomplished. What is ahead. *Acta Sociologica, 40,* 161–182.

Sydow, J., & Windeler, A. (1998). Organizing and evaluating interfirm networks: A structurationist perspective on network processes and effectiveness. *Organization Science, 9*(3), 265–284.

Tepperman, L. (1975). Demographic aspects of career mobility. *Canadian Review of Sociology and Anthropology, 12,* 136–177.

Tharenou, P. (2001). Going up? Do traits and informal social processes predict advancing in management? *Academy of Management Journal, 44*(5), 1005–1017.

Tharenou, P., & Conroy, D. (1994). Men and women managers' advancement: Personal or situational determinants. *Applied Psychology, 43*(1), 5–31.

Tharenou, P., Latimer, S., & Conroy, D. (1994). How do you make it to the top? An examination of influences on women's and men's managerial advancement. *Academy of Management Journal, 37*(4), 899–931.

Theodossiou, I. (1995). Wage determination for career and non-career workers in the UK: Is there labour market segmentation? *Economica, 62*(246), 195–211.

Tolbert, C. M. I. (1982). Industrial segmentation and men's career mobility. *American Sociological Review, 47,* 457–477.

Tolbert, P. S. (1996). Occupations, organizations, and boundaryless careers. In M. B. Arthur & D. M. Rousseau (Eds.), *The boundaryless career: A new employment principle for a new organizational era* (pp. 331–349). New York: Oxford University Press.

Tsui, A. S., & Gutek, B. A. (1984). A role set analysis of gender differences in performance, affective relationships, and career success of industrial middle managers. *Academy of Management Journal, 27*(3), 619–635.

Turban, D. B., & Dougherty, T. W. (1994). Role of protégé personality in receipt of mentoring and career success. *Academy of Management Journal, 37*(3), 688–702.

Ullman, J. C., & Gutteridge, T. G. (1974). Job search in the labor market for college graduates: A case study of MBAs. *Academy of Management Journal, 17*(2), 381–386.

Vance, C. M. (2002). The personal quest for building global competence: A taxonomy of self-initiating career path strategies for gaining business experience abroad. *Academy of Management Proceedings,* B1–B6.

Van Maanen, J. (1980). Career games: Organizational rules of play. In C. B. Derr (Ed.), *Work, family, and the career* (pp. 111–143). New York: Praeger.

Vardi, Y. (1991). Military and field experience as enhancers of managerial promotions in a governmental agency: Implications for second careers. *Academy of Management Proceedings,* 62–66.

Veiga, J. F. (1983). Mobility influences during managerial career stages. *Academy of Management Journal, 26*(1), 64–85.

Velthuis, O. (1999). The changing relationship between economic sociology and institutional economics: From Talcott Parsons to Mark Granovetter. *American Journal of Economics and Sociology, 58*(4), 629–649.

Venne, R. A. (2001). Population aging in Canada and Japan: Implications for labour force and career patterns. *Canadian Journal of Administrative Sciences, 18*(1), 40–49.

von Foerster, H. (1985). *Sicht und Einsicht: Versuche zu einer operativen Erkenntnistheorie.* Braunschweig: Vieweg.

Wagner, W. G., Pfeffer, J., & O'Reilly, C. (1984). Organizational demography and turnover in top-management groups. *Administrative Science Quarterly, 29,* 74–92.

Warner, W. L., & Abegglen, J. C. (1955). *Occupational mobility in American business and industry.* Minneapolis: University of Minnesota Press.

Warner, W. L., & Abegglen, J. C. (1968). Organizational career patterns of business leaders. In B. Glaser (Ed.), *Organizational careers: A sourcebook for theory* (pp. S441–S445). Chicago: Aldine.

Whitely, W., Dougherty, T. W., & Dreher, G. F. (1991). Relationship of career mentoring and socioeconomic origin to managers' and professionals' early career progress. *Academy of Management Journal, 34*(2), 331–351.

Whitely, W. T., & Coetsier, P. (1993). The relationship of career mentoring to early career outcomes. *Organization Studies, 14*(3), 419–441.

Whittington, R., Pettigrew, A., Peck, S., Fenton, E., & Conyon, M. (1999). Change and complementarities in the new competitive landscape: A European panel study. *Organization Science, 10*(5), 583–600.

Willke, H. (1987). Strategien der intervention in autonome systeme. In D. Baecker, J. Markowitz, R. Stichweh, H. Tyrell, & H. Willke (Eds.), *Theorie als passion* (pp. 333–361). Frankfurt: Suhrkamp.

Wood, F. R., & Hertz, R. (1982). Influential associations in organizations. *Academy of Management Proceedings,* 399–402.

Yankelovich, D. (1982). *New rules: Searching for self-fulfillment in a world turned upside down.* New York: Bantam Books.

Young, A. (1971). Demographic and ecological models for manpower planning. In D. J. Bertholomew & B. R. Morris (Eds.), *Aspects of manpower planning* (pp. 75–97). London: English Universities Press.

13

Mentoring and Developmental Networks in the New Career Context

Dawn E. Chandler

Kathy E. Kram

After over 30 years of research on mentoring, changes in the career context at the end of the 20th century have necessitated a significant reconceptualization of this phenomenon (Arthur & Rousseau, 1996; Hall, 1996; Higgins & Kram, 2001; Peiperl & Arthur, 2000; Peiperl & Baruch, 1997). Whereas the career of the past was characterized by linear, upward mobility within one organization over the duration of an individual's "working" life span, today's "post-corporate" career (Peiperl & Baruch, 1997) is becoming increasingly "boundaryless," marked by more transitions across as well as within organizations (Arthur & Rousseau, 1996). This shift in the ways careers are enacted has profound implications both for individuals who must build relationships to learn, develop, and grow and for organizations

that strive to enable relational learning and collaboration.

This chapter reviews the field of mentoring and its transformation concomitant to changes in the structure of careers. Researchers have made tremendous strides in understanding key facets of mentoring and other developmental relationships. We will overview contributions using four primary themes: (1) the nature of mentoring, including types of mentoring and other developmental relationships, as well as relationship functions, phases, and processes; (2) relevant individual and organizational antecedents and outcomes; (3) complexities of cross-gender, cross-race, and cross-cultural relationships; and (4) interventions designed to foster mentoring and other developmental relationships. As the chapter unfolds, the reader will note that within each of these themes, we will highlight how mentoring has *transformed,* both in theory and in practice, from a single, long-term, hierarchical relationship to include multiple, shorter-term relationships that make up a *developmental network* (Higgins & Kram, 2001).

After an overview of research to date, we will offer insight as to gaps in the literature and questions and concepts that warrant future investigation. One area that we believe shows great promise in aiding our understanding of mentoring is the intersection of career theory and adult development theory. We have dedicated a section of the chapter to exploring how an individual's phase and stage affect his or her developmental network and the process of relational learning in general.

Two other recent mentoring literature reviews will be insightful for any reader interested in the topic (Noe, Greenberger, & Wang, 2002; Wanberg, Welsh, & Hezlett, 2003).[1] Our chapter can be distinguished from, and complements, these reviews—both of which are excellent contributions to the extant literature—by providing an in-depth historical account of the evolution of the field from a focus on a single, stable, mentor dyad to the consideration of a developmental network comprising multiple dyadic alliances that vary in strength of tie and intimacy. We strongly believe that for mentoring research to be relevant to practitioners, we must develop a research agenda that is closely aligned with the current realities of the work context.

Furthermore, we seek to provide a research agenda that features questions and develops concepts that are most pressing, given the reconceptualization of mentoring we highlighted above from a dyadic to a network phenomenon and the increasingly complex and turbulent environment within which mentoring relationships now exist. Before we start our account, we want to point out to the reader that this chapter necessarily adopts an American focus—this perspective is taken because the mentoring research to date is overwhelmingly empirically based on American participant experiences. The reader is, therefore, encouraged to consider the discussion as representing one national setting rather than being generalizable across all points of the globe. Also, this statement highlights that one of the most fruitful areas for future research is an examination of mentoring across cultural and national contexts.

We start by describing the mentoring phenomenon and depicting the new career context and how it has reshaped mentoring, thus necessitating further development of this field of study.

THE NATURE OF MENTORING AND THE NEW CAREER CONTEXT: CONSTRUCT, FUNCTIONS, PHASES, TYPES OF RELATIONSHIPS

The traditional notion of mentoring relationships—and the one most closely examined by academics—was first identified by Levinson, Darrow, Klein, Levinson, and McKee (1978), who systematically studied men as they progressed through adulthood. Levinson et al. (1978) found that the mentor represented one of the most important relationships in a young adult man's life as he "pursued his dream" and "became his own man." The original conception of a mentor can actually be traced back to Greek roots; Odysseus secured the aid of his friend, Mentor, to counsel and guide his son, Telemachus (Hamilton, 1999).

Shortly after Levinson et al.'s (1978) seminal work on adult development, the work of several researchers (e.g., Dalton, 1989; Dalton & Thompson, 1986; Dalton, Thompson, & Price, 1977; Kram, 1983, 1985a, 1985b) firmly placed mentoring in the contemporary literature by establishing the functions and phases of relationships, affirming the value of mentoring, and outlining an agenda for future examination. In particular, early studies showed that mentoring advanced the protégé's career and enhanced the senior's sense of worth and self-esteem (e.g., Dalton, 1989; Dalton et al., 1977; Dalton & Thompson, 1986).

Kram's (1985a,) early research on mentoring dyads ended with the implication that individuals may, in fact, receive support from a set or "constellation" of developmental relationships that include a mentoring relationship as well as other developmental relationships including peer relationships. In short, Kram's work suggested that individuals typically have more than one mentor and that not all of the individual's mentors reside within the context of his or her job. Despite her assertion of the importance of mentoring and other developmental relationships (Kram, 1985a; Kram & Hall, 1996), most of the empirical studies through the late 1980s and early 1990s focused on single or primary relationships. This work defined a mentor as an individual who holds a more senior position within the same organization (Hunt & Michael, 1983; Noe, 1988a, 1988b).

Construct

To date, multiple definitions of a mentor have been advanced, but researchers in the field have not unconditionally accepted any specific one. In general, mentors are defined "as individuals with advanced experience and knowledge who are committed to providing support and upward mobility to their protégés' careers" (Ragins, 1999, p. 349). This general definition emphasizes "complementarity" (Kram, 1988; Kram & Isabella, 1985) as it conveys the sense that the mentor supports the growth of skills, knowledge, and career support that the protégé lacks at the relationship's inception. More recent conceptualizations (e.g., Kram & Hall, 1996) offer insight into the potential mutuality between the mentor and protégé in that the mentor may receive career and personal benefits, making them "co-learners." Despite the lack of consistency in the field related to a precise mentoring definition, there is strong agreement as to the general notion of a mentor (Wanberg et al., 2003).

Mentoring Functions and Phases

Early scholarly interest in mentoring aimed at delineating key characteristics of the dyadic relationship, including the *functions* served and relational *phases* (e.g., Kram, 1983, 1985a). Kram (1983, 1985a) identified (1) career functions, which include sponsorship, coaching, protection, and providing exposure, visibility, and challenging assignments, and (2) psychosocial functions, which include role modeling, acceptance and confirmation, counseling, and friendship. Over time, studies have provided strong support for the existence of these functions[2] (e.g., Noe, 1988a, 1988b; Ragins & McFarlin, 1990; Scandura, 1992; Scandura & Ragins, 1993).

Importantly, later research (e.g., Ragins, 1997a, 1997b; Thomas, 1993b) would underscore the nuances associated with the functions served by mentors. More specifically, men and women, on average, offer different types of functional support to protégés: men tend to offer more career or instrumental support, whereas women tend to offer relational, psychosocial support (Miller, 1976, 1991). Furthermore, some studies suggest that non-Caucasians receive different types or levels of functional support from Caucasians (Cox & Nkomo, 1991; Koberg, Boss, Chappell, & Ringer, 1994; Viator, 2001b).

Moreover, studies in the 1980s indicated that mentors offer different levels and types of support based on their respective career stage; for example, individuals at later career stages are more likely to offer support than are individuals at an early career stage (Levinson et al., 1978; Kram, 1985a). Likewise, the type of functional support that protégés need tends to vary on the same three dimensions of gender, race, and career stage. For example, a study of black executives demonstrated that the dual support provided by both white and black mentors resulted in greater career and psychosocial support than did one-mentor relationships (regardless of mentor demographics: Thomas & Gabarro, 1999). In addition, studies of women indicate similar benefits (Kram & Hall, 1996; Ragins, 1997a, 1997b). Thus, partnering with only one individual appears to present certain challenges—due to individual limitations—that are overcome or mitigated by engaging support from several individuals, thus creating a developmental network.

Researchers also began examining relationships for the existence of phases (e.g., Kram, 1985a; Missirian, 1982; Phillips, 1978; Pollock, 1995). Kram's (1985a) work, for example, identified the phases—initiation, cultivation, separation, and redefinition—of mentoring relationships and the processes governing each phase. Her research further highlighted how relationships and their content vary according to the protégé's life stage. Numerous studies have substantiated the existence of these phases (e.g., Higgins, 2000; Kram & Isabella, 1985; Missirian, 1982; Noe, 1988b; Phillips-Jones, 1983; Zey, 1984). Recent changes in the career context, however, suggest that the phases asserted in Kram's work may be truncated as individuals transition in and out of organizations with more frequency. For example, relationships may be compressed or curtailed when a mentor or protégé leaves the employing organization prior to the completion of the relational cycle.

Developmental Relationships

Over time, researchers (e.g., Eby, 1997; Hall & Kahn, 2001; Kram & Isabella, 1985; Thomas, 1993a) elaborated on types of developmental relationships because they recognized that individuals draw support from numerous people who may offer different types or varying levels of career and psychosocial support.

Essentially, although not all developmental relationships are of the true "mentor" quality—characterized by high amounts of both career and psychosocial support—the reality of people's experience is that they gain mentoring support from a broad range of "developers" (Allen, Russell, & Maetzke, 1997; Higgins, 2001; Kram, 1985a). For example, a protégé may have three types of peer "developer" relationships at work—informational, collegial, and special (Kram & Isabella, 1985)—each representing varying levels of support. Hall and Kahn (2001) identified different kinds of naturally occurring work relationships that can be used to foster development: (1) mentor/protégé, (2) coach/sponsor, (3) support group/network, (4) supervisor/coworker, (5) project team/task force, (6) training workshop/ program, and (7) role model. There are now a number of typologies available that delineate a variety of relationships that can be developmental (e.g., Eby, 1997; Kram & Cherniss, 2001).

Higgins and Kram's (2001) work asserted the need for a reconceptualization of mentoring. As we shall see, it described how, over the course of their careers, individuals draw support from a network of "developers," thus creating different types of relationships within the "boundary" of an evolving network. Their contribution to the literature was very timely given the altered career context. The more fluid the career, the harder it becomes to draw support from one individual exclusively. Rather, an individual's network would consist of developers from various social systems, including work, family, community organizations, and peer groups.

Drawing from social network theory (e.g., Burt, 1992; Granovetter, 1983; see also Ibarra and Deshpande, Chapter 14), Higgins and Kram (2001) developed a typology of developmental networks based on two primary dimensions: (1) strength of developmental tie and (2) diversity of network, which included range (the number of social systems from which relationships stem) and density (the degree of connectedness of developers). The utilization of these dimensions enabled the encompassment of prior work on varying levels of functional support (indicative of strength of tie between the protégé and developer) and on types of relationships (indicative not only of varying support but also of diversity of social systems).[3]

This reconceptualization was largely the result of changes in the career environment (Arthur & Rousseau, 1996; Mirvis & Hall, 1996). Today's career context has been referred to as the "post-corporate career" (Peiperl & Baruch, 1997), the "boundaryless" career (Arthur & Rousseau, 1996; Mirvis & Hall, 1996), and the protean career (Hall, 1996), all of which suggest that careers cross formal organizational boundaries more frequently than in the traditional career context. The protean career highlights how individuals must constantly change—in the spirit of the Greek god Proteus who "morphed" at will—in tandem with an environment in flux. While the degree of "boundarylessness" varies according to industry and geographic location, the evidence suggests that the traditional career context is gradually shifting toward a new career context (Peiperl & Arthur, 2000; Peiperl & Baruch, 1997).

Given outsourcing, downsizing, and other changes, individuals are likely to build their careers in multiple organizations, occupations, and industries and hence cannot rely on one single mentor but rather must consider a network of "developers" (Higgins, 2001; Higgins & Kram, 2001; Higgins & Thomas, 2001) to aid their careers. Furthermore, the turbulence of the new career context underscores the importance of relationships as a source of learning, social support, and other resources (Fletcher, 1994; Hall, Briscoe, & Kram, 1997; Hall & Kahn, 2001; Kram, 1996; Kram & Hall, 1991). Individuals in today's context must learn more quickly and engage in more mini learning cycles throughout their lives than did individuals in past decades (Hall, 1996).

The reconceptualization of mentoring relationships from a single dyadic relationship to a network of developmental relationships reveals several areas for inquiry, including how the new career context influences the texture and duration of the *phases* of developmental relationships and how those *phases* may vary based on the type of relationship, how the *functional* support provided by developers may vary based on whether they are inside or outside an individual's employing organization, and how *developmental networks* vary in composition based on demographic factors such as age, gender, and nationality.

INDIVIDUAL AND ORGANIZATIONAL ANTECEDENTS AND OUTCOMES

As researchers made progress in the exploration of salient characteristics of mentoring and other developmental relationships, they began broadening their examination to include antecedents and consequences, at both the individual—mentor and protégé—and the organizational levels. In particular, individual-career and organizational-level outcomes were of interest due to (1) the proliferation of formal mentoring programs in organizations by the mid-1980s and (2) the expansion of research on adult development that highlighted the role of relationships in driving growth (e.g., Gilligan, 1982; Kegan, 1982; Levinson et al., 1978; Miller, 1976, 1991).

Antecedents

In general, antecedents are either *individual* or *organizational* factors that affect the formation of developmental relationships and networks. While much empirical work has been dedicated to understanding these antecedents, we believe that much more needs to be understood, particularly in light of career context changes that have altered the way in which careers are enacted.

Individual career antecedents include both *mentor* and *protégé* factors. Among the factors related to the protégé are personality traits, demographics, individual career stage characteristics, individual needs, characteristics desired by mentors, and gender attributes (masculinity and femininity gender characteristics). It has been postulated that protégé factors influence both the initiation of relationships and the kind of mentoring received.[4]

One of the first antecedents to be systematically studied is that of career stage (Sullivan and Crocitto, Chapter 15). First, it was noted that individuals who assumed the mentoring responsibility had already passed through earlier career stages (Dalton & Thompson, 1986; Kram, 1985a). Later, studies of relationship dyads illuminated how the career stage of the protégé was what solidified relationships with mentors as the two individuals' career stage needs were complementary (Kram, 1985a; Thomas, 1993b). Over time, it became evident that relationships that did not evolve into positive mentoring alliances frequently involved individuals who had conflicting career stage needs (e.g., the protégé was ready to move on to greater responsibility and autonomy, while the mentor persisted in needing the same individual to take direction from him: Kram, 1985a; Scandura, 1992).

Since early studies on the impact of career stage on mentoring, myriad antecedents have been examined. With respect to personality factors, individuals with greater self-esteem, lower negative affectivity, higher self-monitoring, a Type A personality, and greater extroversion are more inclined to initiate relationships and receive mentoring (Aryee, Lo, & Kang, 1999; Turban & Dougherty, 1994). Demographic factors include age, gender, race (all of which will be discussed in the section "Complexities of Diversified Relationships and Diversity"), education, and marital status. An individual's level of education has shown mixed results on initiation of relationships—one study showing that better-educated individuals are more likely to initiate a relationship (Aryee et al., 1999) and another finding no relationship (Turban & Dougherty, 1994)—and little impact on mentoring received (e.g., Aryee, Wyatt & Stone, 1996; Lankau & Scandura, 2002). It appears that unmarried individuals may be more likely to initiate a mentoring relationship (Turban & Dougherty, 1994), but the research is inconclusive regarding mentoring received (e.g., Dreher & Ash, 1990; Seibert, Kraimer, & Liden, 2001).

Organizational tenure and rank have been explored as precursors to relationships and to mentoring received; most of the studies showed either no relationship between the factors and mentoring or provided mixed results (e.g., Burke & McKeen, 1997; Cox & Nkomo, 1991; Fagenson, 1989, 1992; Lankau & Scandura, 2002). Studies on protégé characteristics that are desired by mentors include protégés with a strong learning orientation, who are competent and motivated, and who remind mentors of themselves (Allen, Poteet, & Burroughs, 1997; Allen, Poteet, & Russell, 2000).

Other studies have examined whether certain job or career history characteristics are related to whether an individual has a mentor. For example, studies have shown that there is no relationship between academic performance in postsecondary school (e.g., Judge & Bretz, 1994) or law school admission test scores (Laband & Lentz, 1995) and the report of having a mentor. Most of the variables examined—e.g., education (Colarelli & Bishop, 1990), work history (Kirchmeyer, 1998), hours worked per week (Judge & Bretz, 1994)— have yielded mixed results.

Much less research has examined antecedents related to the mentor. Studies have examined desired mentor characteristics as perceived by protégés (e.g., Gaskill, 1991; Olian, Carroll, Giannantonio, & Feren, 1988) and factors that suggest what motivates individuals to mentor others (e.g., Allen et al., 2000; Aryee, Chay, & Chew, 1996), including demographic variables such as age and educational level, career experiences, personality attributes, and competence. Protégés seek mentors who are capable of developing others, who have knowledge of both their roles and the political nuances within an organization, and who are in positions of respect and high rank (Gaskill, 1991). Protégés are interested in maintaining relationships with mentors who have solid interpersonal skills (Olian et al., 1988).

Better-educated individuals seem more likely to be comfortable in a mentoring role (Allen, Poteet, Russell, & Dobbins, 1997). According to Levinson's seminal work on male adult development, mentors are likely to be midlevel career individuals who desire to aid the career development of a younger protégé (Levinson et al., 1978). Individuals who have more tenure in an organization or fill a high-ranking organizational role may feel more comfortable serving as mentors (Ragins & Cotton, 1993).

Personality traits such as positive affectivity (Aryee, Chay, et al., 1996), high self-monitoring (Mullen & Noe, 1999), altruism (Aryee, Chay, et al., 1996), higher self-esteem (Aryee, Chay, et al., 1996; Kram, 1988), and high learning goal orientation (Godshalk & Sosik, 2003) seem more likely to be characteristic of individuals who are motivated to mentor others.

Organizational-level (also described as "situational") factors, such as the composition of an organization's workforce, can affect interaction patterns (Kanter, 1977; see Higgins & Kram, 2001, for an overview of these factors) and, hence, an individual's opportunities and constraints when forming relationships. Very little empirical research has formally explored the organizational antecedents that affect the formation, or lack thereof, of mentoring and other developmental relationships. Below are factors suggested by Higgins and Kram (2001) that potentially affect the formation of relationships.

Research on temporal and physical proximity, for instance, demonstrates that spatial proximity facilitates the initiation of ties (Festinger, Schachter, & Back, 1950). Furthermore, aspects of the industry or task can shape the cultivation of ties (Baker, 1992). Since developmental networks span organizational boundaries, these considerations are important. For instance, working in certain industries—for example, entertainment—can enhance the likelihood of forming multiple extra-organizational ties (Ensher, Murphy, & Sullivan, 2000).

An organization's formal structure affects the degree to which certain individuals interact with one another, thus influencing network choices (Burkhardt & Brass, 1990). Changes in organizational technology—for example, the availability of information technology, such as electronic mail—affects the probability of interaction (Fulk, Steinfield, Schmitz, & Power, 1987).

Finally, an organization's culture (Hall, 1996; Kram & Bragar, 1992) can facilitate or hinder learning within developmental relationships; socially accepted norms prescribe behavior related to assisting others and, more generally, to growing employees' skills and competencies.

Much of the research to date on protégé and mentor antecedents has been on relatively immutable characteristics such as personality traits and demographic variables. Moreover, some of the inconclusive findings suggest *moderating* variables that are yet to be explored. For example, it may be that certain competencies such as emotional intelligence affect both the initiation and the ability to foster strong mentoring relationships. Certain individuals may have a "developmental intelligence" (Chandler, 2007) that allows them to effectively assess their developmental needs and enables them to seek out mentors who can aid them in meeting those needs. Similarly, Kram's (1988) work suggested that attitudes toward authority, conflict, intimacy, values, and self-competence perceptions affect the kind of developmental relationships sought. As we will describe in more detail later, adult development theories posit that individuals at higher stages of growth may be more effective mentors and protégés. Finally, more work should elucidate how "developmental cultures" (Hall, 1996) affect the formation of informal relationships.

Outcomes

From the onset, academic researchers were keenly interested in the individual career and organizational consequences of mentoring relationships. Given the organizational investment in mentoring programs, it was clear that a research agenda should include the impact of relationships on *individual*—both *mentor* and *protégé*—outcomes and produce an understanding of whether programs enhance *organizational* effectiveness.

One of the most substantiated areas of mentoring research relates to mentoring and positive *protégé* career outcomes. Mentoring has been associated with subjective outcomes such as career (Fagenson, 1989) and job satisfaction (Bahniuk, Dobos, & Hill, 1990), expectations for advancement, job commitment (e.g., Laband & Lentz, 1995), clarity of professional identity, and sense of competence (Kram, 1985a) and objective outcomes such as higher rates of promotion and total compensation (Whitely, Dougherty, & Dreher, 1991), career progress (Walsh & Borkowski, 1999; Zey, 1984), and protégé change (Lankau & Scandura, 2002).

Although the benefits of mentoring are well documented, studies have also shown that negative protégé experience may result from dissimilar beliefs and attitudes (Eby, McManus, Simon, & Russell, 2000). Scandura (1998), in an exploration of the "dark side" of mentoring, modeled the processes and outcomes associated with dysfunctional relationships. Drawing on literature from social psychology, Scandura described negative behaviors such as harassment, deception, and sabotage. Of critical importance in the new career context is an understanding of whether, and under what conditions, having multiple mentors produces positive protégé outcomes. More recent studies have suggested that having more than one mentor is associated with positive career expectations (Baugh & Scandura, 1999), work satisfaction, and the intention to stay with an organization (e.g., Higgins, 2000; Higgins & Thomas, 2001). In contrast, having multiple mentors may result in role conflict and higher job burnout (Baugh & Scandura, 1999; Fagan & Walter, 1982).

Research on mentor outcomes has produced similar positive results. Mentors receive myriad potential benefits, including access to information, social feedback, job performance (Mullen & Noe, 1999), greater support networks (Allen, Poteet, & Burroughs, 1997), fulfillment from teaching a protégé (Busch, 1985), personal satisfaction and an increase in power (e.g., Burke & McKeen, 1997; Kram, 1985a), career satisfaction (e.g., Johnson, Yust, & Fritchie, 2001), and recognition and respect from others (Kram, 1985b).

Similar to protégé outcomes, potentially negative aspects of mentoring include fear of favoritism, potentially time-consuming interactions, destructive relationships, vulnerability through exposure of one's career trials and errors, and negative effects associated with unsuccessful relationships (Allen, Poteet, & Burroughs, 1997; Zey, 1984).

There is a paucity of research related to the organizational outcomes of mentoring. Wilson and Elmann (1990) suggested that mentoring can enhance organizational retention and job performance, foster a strong corporate culture, and implicitly convey expectations of behavior to employees. One qualitative study, which involved in-depth interviews with over 100 executives, suggested positive organizational outcomes of mentor and protégé interactions, including enhanced organizational communication, enhanced productivity, more effective employee socialization, and employee integration (Zey, 1984).

What We Don't Know About Individual and Organizational Outcomes (and Should)

Understanding the conditions that lead to positive and negative individual and organizational outcomes is of utmost importance. One key issue associated with outcomes relates to the need for more controlled studies that can effectively rule out other correlational factors that may lead to success. For example, protégé characteristics such as ability or emotional intelligence may cause individuals to be more desirable protégé candidates or more likely to initiate a developmental relationship. Second, the new career context is characterized by more individual career transitions and a need to learn quickly. More emphasis should be placed on exploration of how mentoring influences career changes and personal learning. Finally, further identification of organizational outcomes is needed.

COMPLEXITIES OF DIVERSIFIED RELATIONSHIPS AND DIVERSITY

After, and partially as a result of, the U.S. civil rights movement in the 1960s and affirmative action laws passed in the 1970s, formal mentoring programs abounded in organizations. Attention to diversity also came as a result of women and people of color leaving organizations at higher rates than their white male counterparts or plateauing at higher rates (Morrison, White, & Van Velsor, 1994).

Initially, researchers examined how mentoring programs affected gender equality—more specifically, whether programs allowed women to "break the glass ceiling." Over time, researchers also began exploring the impact of race on the formation of relationships, processes, and subsequent mentoring outcomes.

More recently, Ragins (1997a, 1997b) defined diversified (diverse) mentoring relationships as "comprising mentors and protégés who differ on the basis of race, ethnicity, gender, sexual orientation, class, religion, disability, or other group memberships associated with power in organizations" (p. 24). Noe et al. (2002) noted that "most research has been focused on the impact of demographic diversity between mentor and protégé on the mentoring relationship" (p. 143). Specifically, most of the recent research conducted throughout the 1980s to the present day has fallen into three categories—gender, race, and age.

Gender and Race Complexities

Despite the importance of mentoring for all individuals, regardless of gender, race, organizational rank, or otherwise, it has been asserted that mentoring can be particularly important for women and ethnic minorities as they attempt to overcome barriers to advancement (e.g., Kram, 1985a, 1985b; Ragins, 1999; Thomas, 1993a, 1993b; Thomas & Gabarro, 1999; see also Prasad, D'Abate, and Prasad, Chapter 10). Both women and minorities hold few senior positions in organizations; those who do "break through" (Thomas & Gabarro, 1999) to the more senior ranks—e.g., executive level—of organizations face different obstacles and challenges and typically face a different and distinct path from their white, male counterparts (e.g., Thomas & Gabarro, 1999).

It has been asserted, for example, that mentors can aid female and ethnic minority protégés in several ways, including offering insight into corporate politics (Ragins, 1989), providing "reflected power" that diminishes the power disadvantage of being an outsider in an "old boy's network" (Kanter, 1977), and sharing information that otherwise would not be accessible (Ragins, 1989, 1997a, 1997b).

Research on both gender and race has focused on (1) relationship initiation, (2) mentoring received, or (3) relationship outcomes.[5] Although researchers have made great strides since the impact of gender and race became of interest to academics, more research is needed due to equivocal and mixed findings. With respect to the former two themes—relationship initiation and mentoring received, some research reports parity between women and men (e.g., Burke, McKeen, & McKenna, 1990; Dreher & Ash, 1990; Fagenson, 1989; Hubbard & Robinson, 1998; Noe, 1988a; Ragins & McFarlin, 1990; Scandura & Ragins, 1993; Scandura & Williams, 2001; Turban & Dougherty, 1994) and minorities and Caucasians (e.g., Dreher & Cox, 1996; Greenhaus, Parasuraman, & Wormley, 1990; McGuire, 1999; Thomas, 1990; Viator, 2001a), whereas other studies suggest that women and minorities are at a disadvantage (Bahniuk, Dobos, & Hill, 1990; Cox & Nkomo, 1991; McGuire, 1999; Ragins & Cotton, 1991), both in initiating and in receiving mentoring.

With respect to mentoring outcomes, research is somewhat more conclusive. Studies suggest that women and men both receive career benefits—e.g., job satisfaction, compensation, and career mobility—associated with mentoring (e.g., Baugh, Lankau, & Scandura, 1996; Dreher & Ash, 1990; Fagenson, 1989). Of the few studies that have been conducted related to race, it appears that ethnic minorities do gain career satisfaction from having a mentor (Friedman, Kane, & Cornfield, 1998) and that under certain conditions, minorities experience equal benefits relative to their Caucasian counterparts (Blake-Beard, 1999).

Cross-Gender and Cross-Race Challenges and Opportunities

Mentoring research has provided interesting and valuable insight related to cross-gender and cross-race relationships. Studies (e.g., Bowen, 1985; Burke & McKeen, 1997) suggest particular benefits associated with heterogeneous pairings that cannot be conferred by homogeneous relationships, because heterogeneous pairings allow participants to gain knowledge of the diverse styles and perspectives. Other studies have posited that women and ethnic minorities who receive greater career outcomes—such as compensation and career attainment—relative to their peers reported currently having male mentors or having prior male mentors (e.g., Bahniuk, Hill, & Darus, 1996; Dreher & Cox, 1996; Ragins & Cotton, 1999; Wallace, 2001).[6] However, heterogeneous relationships have also presented particular challenges not faced by homogeneous

pairings. For instance, cross-gender relationships have also been associated with difficulties related to the possibility of romantic involvement (Hurley & Fagenson-Eland, 1996), fear of sexual harassment (Bowen, 1985; Ragins & Cotton, 1991), stereotyping (Tajfel & Turner, 1986), the "developmental dilemma" of having either an "unproductive closeness" or an "unproductive distance" (Clawson & Kram, 1984), and different expectations or miscommunication (Kram, 1988; Kram & Hall, 1996) due to gender perceptions.

Gender and racial stereotypes, in particular, can be powerful impediments to effective cross-gender and cross-race relationships (Kram, 1985a; Thomas, 1999). If individuals are unaware of their untested assumptions regarding members of another race or opposite gender, they are likely to behave in ways that undermine the relationship's potential. Thomas (1999), for instance, describes how historical relational patterns between blacks and whites are brought into current workplace relationships as "racial taboos." Similarly, Clawson and Kram's (1984) research suggests how negative stereotyping hinders relational processes and subsequent outcomes.

Research on cross-gender and cross-race relationships suggests that women and ethnic minorities may benefit from dual support systems (e.g., Kram, 1985a, 1985b; Thomas, 1990), which means that they seek assistance from two individuals (who differ in gender or racial identity, depending on the protégé's salient characteristics) rather than relying on a supervisor or single mentor. For example, research that has examined cross-gender and same-gender relationships (e.g., Ragins, 1989; Ragins & Cotton, 1999; Sosik & Godshalk, 2000) has shown that the nature of the relationship—whether it is heterogeneous or homogeneous—affects the types and amount of mentoring received. Because individuals may experience mentoring differences based on whether the mentor is a male or female, they may optimize benefits by receiving dual support by having relationships with both a man and a woman.

Research on the impact of race offers a similar conclusion. Thomas's (1990) study found that blacks reported a larger percentage of same-race dyads that were not supervisory or outside their departments than did Caucasians, who reported same-race dyads that were supervisory. This study suggests that African Americans (and other ethnic minorities) might benefit from dual support systems. Moreover, one study (Dansky, 1996) suggests that professional associations and other group organizations may serve important mentoring functions to women and ethnic minorities, who may be disadvantaged within their organization. The notion that women and ethnic minorities may benefit from more than one individual is consistent with the reconceptualization of mentoring as a developmental network.

Age Complexities

Since the 1990s, age has come under scrutiny by academic mentoring researchers. Studies on how absolute age—or age discrepancies between the mentor and the protégé—affects mentoring relationships and outcomes parallel demographic shifts in the workplace.

For instance, although age does not seem to determine whether an individual will initiate a mentoring relationship (Aryee et al., 1999; Burke & McKeen, 1997; Ragins & Cotton, 1991), studies have suggested that as individuals get older, they receive less career mentoring (Whitely et al., 1991). One study (Feldman, Folks, & Turnley, 1999) showed that receipt of mentoring was not affected by the age discrepancy between mentor and protégé.

The implication of the foregoing discussion is that age may be an important factor in determining individuals' network composition and relational content. Older individuals, although equally likely to initiate a mentoring relationship, seem to receive less career support than their junior counterparts. Age differences between mentor and protégé do not seem to influence the amount of mentoring a protégé receives.

As we will elaborate in the next section, while the few studies mentioned above are helpful in understanding how age influences mentoring, much more research is needed, particularly in light of the aging populations in a number of countries.

What We Don't Know About Diversified Relationships and Diversity (and Need To)

Although much research has been dedicated to understanding the complexities and challenges of diversified relationships, more is needed, particularly in light of an increasingly global and turbulent career environment. First, we believe that using in-depth interviews to closely scrutinize the *process* of mentoring will yield important insight into the conflicting findings summarized above and the challenges posed in cross-race and cross-gender relationships. Although some studies to date indicate no differences between women and minorities and groups with greater power in organizations, other research suggests that these groups do face barriers that impede relational processes and positive outcomes. We believe that a reliance on survey methodologies quite possibly obscures the differences between white, Caucasian males and women and minorities in obtaining mentoring support and securing subsequent benefits.

Understanding the conditions that cause positive relational outcomes is critical to mounting strategies (see Ragins, 1997a, 1997b; Thomas, 1993a, 1993b, for strategies for overcoming the challenges of diversified relationships) to alleviate relational challenges. Furthermore, the foregoing discussion suggests that more studies are needed to disentangle the moderating factors that complicate clearer findings. Unclear findings related to cross-gender studies, for example, suggest the presence of moderating factors—e.g., the length of the relationship (Turban, Dougherty, & Lee, 2002), the emotional competence of both parties (Goleman, 1995), and the developmental stage of both parties (e.g., Kegan, 1982, 1994)—that confound results.

As baby boomers, the largest group as a percentage of the workforce in countries such as the United States, Australia, New Zealand, and Canada, approach retirement, age presents an increasingly important individual-level factor to be explored. We believe that the new career context may have important implications for this generation of individuals, as they serve both as mentors and as protégés seeking knowledge to adapt to a turbulent, demanding environment.

Younger individuals, who entered the workforce during the new career period, may feel comfortable with uncertainty, the need for continuous learning, and the need to rely more on technology. Baby boomers, in contrast, have been more accustomed to the security and certainty of the traditional career context. As mentors, they may feel overwhelmed by the requirement of having to constantly learn while continuing to offer protégés adequate time, empathy, and patience for providing support. As protégés, they may feel unaccustomed to securing support from several individuals, both inside and outside an employing organization, as well as continuously learning at the pace required to succeed.

More studies on whether and why older individuals receive less career support, particularly given that they seem equally likely to initiate a relationship, should be explored. Studies should examine under what conditions older individuals seek out developmental relationships. For example, are older individuals who populate senior positions in organizations less likely to cultivate developmental relationships than those at more junior positions? Are older individuals more likely to seek out relationships during a career change than when they have been in an existing position for a period of time? Finally, as countries' populaces age, it is important to understand the challenges and opportunities older individuals face in cultivating and nurturing developmental relationships.

Additionally, given the increasing demographic diversity in the global workforce and with organizations increasing multinational activities, more research should be conducted on other types of diversity—for example, sexual orientation or religion. With respect to studies on race, most participants have been African American, or research designs have lumped minorities into one group (e.g., McGuire, 1999; Mobley, Jaret, Marsh, & Lim, 1994); research using other ethnic minorities should be conducted (as an exception, Goto, 1999, examined Asian individuals). One noteworthy point related to the foregoing discussion is that most of the research on diversified relationships has focused on traditional mentoring relationships rather than other kinds of developmental relationships. Future research should address the challenges and opportunities related to diversity in other developmental relationships—for example, peers and network groups.

Shifts in the underlying career context suggest that greater research emphasis should be placed on diversity that results from cross-functional teams in flatter organizations and from multinational corporations (MNCs) operating in a global environment (e.g., see Noe et al., 2002, for an elaboration on this point; see also Peiperl and Jonsen, Chapter 18). For organizations to be most efficient in today's environment, they must nurture advanced communication systems such as cross-functional teams designed to foster timely information from diverse vantage points within an organization. This area focuses on diversity of perceptions and information diversity, which result from being located in different functional areas of organizations.

Moreover, MNCs that operate in a global environment will fashion teams of nationally diverse members as well as formal mentoring programs involving cross-national mentor-protégé pairings. Given this global trend, research should be conducted that emphasizes how nationality, culture, and other cross-border variables affect developmental networks.

Finally, to date, an important unanswered question is, What are the unique benefits of cross-race relationships? We can speculate that these relationships benefit both parties—instrumental support opens doors for minority protégés and both learn about how to build effective alliances with people of different backgrounds.

The nature of mentoring, associated antecedents and outcomes, and complexities of diversified relationships have, in general, received close academic scrutiny.

A DEVELOPMENTAL LENS ON MENTORING

We now examine mentoring from a developmental perspective. We have argued that mentoring and mentoring scholarship are moving toward viewing the phenomenon in terms of developmental relationships, which suggests that it would be fruitful to examine theories of adult development to see if they can suggest new lines of research. In this section, we elaborate on the value of using an adult developmental perspective to provide a unique and uncharted analysis of mentoring. Our discussion will be aimed at describing linkages between mentoring and four areas of adult development—phase theories, stage theories, relational theories, and attachment theory. We want to stress that we realize that this "tour" of adult developmental theories is necessarily brief (see Sullivan and Crocitto, Chapter 15). However, we believe the discussion is important as it is intended to offer creative, valuable lines of future research (also, see Chapter 15 by Sullivan and Crocitto).

Phase Theories

Since Levinson et al. (1978) first wrote about the importance of mentoring for men in early adulthood, this relationship has been defined as one that enables a young adult to "realize his dream." In the context of careers, the dream included goals for establishing and advancing in a career with the coaching and guidance of a more senior adult. As research on mentoring has progressed, it has become clearer that one important reason why mentoring alliances have the potential to be strong, enduring, and powerful in their impact is the complementarity in developmental needs that is brought to these relationships (Kram, 1988). This developmental perspective has the potential to help us understand why some alliances (formal and informal) never realize their potential to foster development and learning, why others become dissatisfying after a period of mutual learning, and why some individuals are more inclined to seek or provide mentoring assistance at various points in a career than others.

Levinson et al.'s (1978) model is an example of adult developmental *phase* theories, which describe how individuals face unique developmental tasks at different periods or ages during their lives and careers (Dalton, 1989; Dalton et al., 1977; Dalton & Thompson, 1986; Gould, 1978; Hall, 1996; Levinson, 1996; Schein, 1978; Super, 1957, 1986; Sullivan and Crocitto, Chapter 15). These tasks reflect the challenges that individuals must address if they are to experience personal efficacy and move into subsequent stages. Each model emphasizes a particular aspect of growth and development.

With this perspective at the forefront, we can predict that individuals bring a certain willingness and capacity to each relational opportunity that is shaped and limited by developmental position. In the new career context, there are already many examples of individuals for whom life phase and career stage are out of sync. For

example, an individual who is enacting a protean career is likely to experience numerous career transitions and mini learning cycles rather than a linear unfolding of one career that is correlated with the unfolding of adulthood (Hall, 2002).

Young individuals in the early phase of their careers face the principal challenge of developing a viable professional identity in their chosen occupation. In all likelihood, their commitment to the organization is provisional, and they are motivated to learn the skills that will enable them to meet performance expectations and prepare for advancement. Although individuals may receive support from peers, their networks are likely to be dominated by older or senior organizational members who can be responsive to their developmental needs. Individuals at an early career phase may not yet sense that they have something to offer a peer in exchange for their support and coaching.

Similarly, individuals at midlife and mid-career face a different set of developmental tasks generally characterized by reassessment and redirection, often motivated by an internal desire to modify and/or amplify the life structure that has been built in the first half of adulthood (Levinson et al., 1978; Schein, 1978). Often, individuals at this life and/or career stage will find new satisfaction in facilitating growth in younger adults (Kram, 1988; Levinson et al., 1978). Indeed, mentoring alliances are often quite engaging and rewarding for senior members of the pairs precisely because these relational opportunities become sites for addressing the developmental tasks of this period. In addition, these individuals may receive valuable information and psychosocial support from their junior protégés.

Stage Theories

Stage theories can offer further insight into the mentoring phenomenon (e.g., Kegan, 1982, 1994; Loevinger, 1978; Torbert, 1991). Stage theories can be considered hierarchical in that one stage is more advanced than its predecessor and each successive stage incorporates the "know-how" from earlier stages. More specifically, individuals do not lose the insight they gained at earlier stages but rather move into a broader, integrative stage. In contrast to phase theories (e.g., Dalton et al., 1977; Levinson,

1996; Levinson et al., 1978), stage theories posit that developmental position is not strictly aligned with age or career stage, though they may be correlated.

Kegan (1982, 1994), for example, offers a "constructive-developmental," six-stage theory, which suggests that throughout the life course individuals are engaged in a process of meaning making. This process leads them from being embedded in their own subjectivity to an increasingly stronger ability to take the world, including themselves, as object. This "subject/object dialectic" manifests itself by the degree to which individuals can balance the opposite yearnings for inclusion and for independence. Development is depicted over time as a helix with movement back and forth between strong desires for inclusion and separation; managing these opposing needs occurs mostly at the subconscious level, though very much affecting how individuals approach relationships. At the most advanced stage, the *interindividual,* individuals are perhaps most able to engage in intimate growth-enhancing connections with others.

Thus, how individuals manage the continuous tension between autonomy and connection will influence their willingness and ability to engage in growth-enhancing relationships at work. Kegan's (1982, 1994) helix suggests that at earlier positions, individuals may be too embedded in relationships (or, alternatively, too detached from relationships) to objectively reflect and absorb the lessons that are offered. For example, the theory suggests that the individual at the *interpersonal* stage has not sufficiently differentiated himself or herself from his or her significant others. An individual at this stage has not yet sufficiently achieved a meaningful sense of professional identity. In contrast, the individual who has progressed to the "autonomous, self-regulating" *institutional* stage, where the desire and capacity for autonomy and distinctiveness dominate, may distance himself or herself from the mentor and seek out peer relationships that are more mutual, in which each individual fosters the learning of the other.

The foregoing discussion implies a certain complexity regarding how phase and stage may interact. For example, although two individuals may be at the same phase (e.g., early adulthood), their developmental networks may vary if they are at different stages, or "levels of mind."

Relational Models

Relational models of growth—which are considered neither phase nor stage—similarly identify the importance of interdependence in building relationships that facilitate growth and personal learning (Fletcher, 1996, 1999; Jordan, Kaplan, Miller, Stiver, Surrey, 1991; Miller, 1976). This new perspective on growth and development reinforces the hypothesis that individuals who reach Kegan's (1982, 1994) developmental positions of *institutional* or *interindividual* (Kegan's highest stage) can enact a stance of interdependence toward relationships; have a baseline of emotional competencies, including empathy, self-reflection, the flexibility to move in and out of novice and expert roles, collaboration, and trust; and are most likely to experience a rich array of developmental alliances.

Attachment Theory

Recently, Noe and his colleagues (2002) added to this line of inquiry by noting that attachment theory may further our understanding of why some individuals seek out developmental relationships and others refrain from doing so. First defined by Bowlby (1969) (see Noe et al., 2002, for original mentoring application), attachment theory suggests that early parent-child relationships result in one of three attachment styles that are brought to relationships later in life—secure base, avoidant, and ambivalent. Individuals with secure base attachment styles are more likely to embrace opportunities to be mentored and are more likely to do so informally or in the context of a formal program than those with either avoidant or ambivalent styles.

The impact of historical attachments on current developmental relationships is likely to be moderated by the individual's level of self-awareness (Hall, 1996). Greater self-awareness, for example, allows the individual to choose to either replicate or dramatically alter historical relational patterns in new relationships. In either case, this individual difference may account for the mixed results in mentoring program outcomes and in the dearth or richness of developmental networks.

STRATEGIES TO FOSTER MENTORING

Long before there was adequate understanding of mentoring and its various forms, organizations began to consider how to foster mentoring for various employee populations. The earliest application was for young, high-potential individuals who were perceived to be on a fast track to significant managerial positions (Roche, 1979; Shapiro, Haseltine, & Rowe, 1978; Spiezer, 1981). In these instances, senior executives were generally assigned to mentor specific high-potential candidates (generally, white males) to help them learn the ropes of management and prepare for promotion. Little structure or guidance was provided to these pairs, yet the outcomes were generally positive since senior executives intuitively knew what had helped them earlier in their careers. A small number of fortunate individuals benefited from these alliances. Presumably, the high-potential system worked, too, because sponsorship from a senior executive gave candidates the right connections and pushed opportunities their way that were denied to other juniors.

As concerns for equal opportunity began to surface in the late 1970s, organizations became more interested in how to make mentoring available to a wider range of employee groups. Thus began a proliferation of programmatic initiatives to foster mentoring between juniors and seniors (Chao, Walz, & Gardner, 1992; Douglas & McCauley, 1997). Those programs that targeted specific employee groups (e.g., high-potential managers, high-potential women, high-potential people of color, organizational newcomers) seemed to be more effective than those that did not specify the particular target population and their development needs (Gaskill, 1991; Single & Muller, 2001; Tyler, 1998). Within a decade, there had been enough experimentation with formal mentoring programs for a number of conditions to surface as being essential to positive individual and organizational outcomes. These included specific objectives linked to business and human resources (HR) strategy, relevant orientation and

training, planned follow-up monitoring and evaluation, voluntary participation, active sponsorship from senior management, and a skilled program coordinator (Kram & Bragar, 1992).

As research on mentoring progressed, it became apparent that mentoring occurs informally, or it can be engineered (formally assigned), and in all likelihood there are differences in process and outcomes between the two (Noe et al., 2002; Ragins & Cotton, 1999; Wanberg et al., 2003). In addition, research on the complexities of cross-gender, cross-race, and cross-cultural alliances strongly suggested that if a diverse workforce was to benefit from mentoring, assistance on these matters would be necessary (Ragins, 1999; Scandura & Ragins, 1993; Thomas, 1993a, 1993b). As a consequence, strategies to promote mentoring began to routinely include education and training that would equip both parties to address such complexities when necessary. Finally, as it became apparent that both seniors and juniors can derive multiple benefits from mentoring alliances, seniors' developmental goals were taken into account in the design of formal programs (Kram & Hall, 1996).

Systematic attempts to evaluate the effectiveness of formal mentoring programs have had mixed results (Chao et al., 1992; Noe, 1988a, 1988b; Ragins & Cotton, 1999; Seibert, 1999). Some of these differences can be explained by the distinctive underlying assumptions and infrastructure that surround the formal programs (Noe et al., 2002; Wanberg et al., 2003). Several studies that compared formal and informal mentoring relations have also reported mixed results (Allen, Eby, Poteet, Lentz, & Lima, 2004; Fagenson-Eland, Marks, & Amendola, 1977; Ragins, Cotton, & Miller, 2000; Viator, 2001a, 2001b). The one conclusion that we can draw is that formal programs have the potential to foster effective mentoring alliances but that additional research is needed to determine more precisely under what conditions such initiatives will warrant the investment required to make them worthwhile.

For example, when formal programs are aligned with the business and HR strategy of the organization, and the surrounding organizational culture and reward system are equally aligned, positive individual and organizational outcomes are more likely than when such programs are created in isolation and/or in a context characterized by low trust and an absence of concern for learning and development (Kram & Bragar, 1992; Noe et al., 2002). Wanberg et al. (2003) urge researchers to consider both the proximal outcomes—such as satisfaction with the relationship, skill building, and affective learning—as well as a number of distal outcomes—including promotions, increased compensation, increased life satisfaction, retention, and organizational commitment—that are designed and achieved.

As research on mentoring has progressed, so has our understanding of careers and career development in an increasingly turbulent and complex global environment (Arthur & Rousseau, 1996; Hall, 2002; Hall & Mirvis, 1995). The trends of multiple careers in a lifetime, as well as flatter, team-based, and rapidly changing work environments, call for a reevaluation of how mentoring can be facilitated. Now that researchers have reconceptualized mentoring as a developmental network, the one-on-one formally assigned relationships seem too narrowly focused; this is, in part, because evaluations of these programs have reported mixed results. More important, perhaps, there are other relationships that clearly provide good alternatives to the traditional, long-term, and exclusive hierarchical relationships (Higgins, 2000; Higgins & Thomas, 2001).

In recent years, efforts to foster mentoring through professional networks of like groups (e.g., women's networks, black professional networks, Latino groups), peer coaching, and mentoring circles have proliferated (e.g., Kram & Hall, 1996). These approaches have in common organizationally sanctioned structures designed to increase the likelihood that individuals who can mutually benefit from one another get connected. These interventions are based on the premise that individuals who strengthen their developmental networks to include multiple relationships of strong and diverse ties are more likely to continually learn, develop, and achieve personal and professional goals through the developmental assistance that is offered by an enriched network (Higgins, 2000; Higgins & Kram, 2001; Higgins & Thomas, 2001).

Finally, there is a growing consensus that self-awareness, empathy, and various social skills are prerequisites for building "learningful"

relationships (Goleman, 1998; Cherniss & Goleman, 2001) and that these personal and social competencies can be developed, given the desire to learn as well as the opportunities to practice new skills and get relevant feedback (Cherniss & Adler, 2000; Kram & Cherniss, 2001; Kram, Ting, & Bunker, 2002). Thus, making such educational and training opportunities available to individuals is an important alternative and/or complement to formal mentoring programs. It is already known from a variety of studies that such educational interventions are more likely to have a lasting impact if the context to which individuals return from such experiences has an infrastructure in place that encourages, reinforces, and supports the interpersonal skills that have been acquired (Cherniss & Adler, 2000; Douglas & McCauley, 1997; Kram et al., 2002).

Clearly, there are many unanswered questions about how to foster mentoring in organizations. While we have some examples of formal programs that have produced positive results for both individuals and organizations, we have yet to delineate what preconditions will ensure that the positive outcomes of formally arranged relationships outweigh the potentially negative consequences—including a narrow focus on one mentorship rather than a developmental network of relationships, discouragement among those who were not chosen to participate, and the disillusionment of those who participated and experienced only modest benefits. In addition, further research is needed to better understand how the size of an organization, the developmental stage and the emotional competence of targeted populations, and related HR practices influence the appropriate intervention strategy. Future work in this area should evaluate approaches that combine the various strategies outlined here.

A RESEARCH AGENDA

Throughout this chapter, we have emphasized a historical perspective of mentoring that highlights an initial research focus on the traditional mentoring relationship that has segued to a new focus on developmental networks. This new emphasis on developmental networks is consistent with a turbulent environment characterized by more frequent career transitions in flatter organizations. We have asserted that individuals draw support—both career and psychosocial—from a number of developers throughout their careers. Each of the four primary themes—the nature of mentoring, antecedents and consequences, the complexities of diversified relationships, and intervention strategies—reflects the evolution toward developmental networks comprising multiple, shorter-term relationships.

Going forward, research should seek to scrutinize mentoring with an acknowledgement of the career context and developmental network reality. We are not suggesting that the traditional mentoring relationship is obsolete, because it is a critical vehicle of learning and overall support for individuals and organizations, and many important questions relate to the traditional relationship. We

do assert, however, that it is of utmost importance that academic researchers begin to explore developmental networks as they reflect significant changes in how individuals experience career growth and learning.

We will first describe the general challenges for future research on mentoring themes and then delve more deeply into concepts that are consistent with the current career reality. Next, we will describe important questions aimed at understanding developmental networks and pertinent concepts. Table 13.1 compares concepts that were most salient and important for traditional, hierarchical careers with those that should be more closely scrutinized in the new career context. In Box 13.1 we give a number of questions related to the developmental network that are quite relevant to a responsive research agenda.

Table 13.1 Evolution of Salient Mentoring Concepts

	Traditional Career Context	*New Career Context*
Individual-Level Factors	• Willingness to mentor • Career stage • Complexities of gender and race (demographic variables)	• Developmental intelligence • Emotional intelligence • Developmental stage/phase • Developmental culture • Complexities of cross-cultural • relationships • Self-awareness • Identity
Relational Processes and Characteristics	• Dyads • Relationship functions • Long-term, stable relationships • Relationship phases	• Developmental networks • Relational learning • Multiple, dynamic relationships • Relationship formation • Relationship management
Outcomes	• Turnover • Professional development • Career advancement • Job satisfaction • Commitment	• Personal learning • Career change/transitions • Perceived justice • Unique benefits of diverse relationships

NOTE: Concepts are italicized in the text to aid the exposition.

Box 13.1 Sample Questions for Future Research

Individual- and Organizational-Level Antecedents

1. What characteristics (e.g., developmental intelligence, stance toward authority, emotional competence) enable the individual to initiate and build relationships that are responsive to current developmental needs?

2. What role does the protégé play in the formation of the developmental network?

3. What role does developmental stage play in relational learning?
   a. How does developmental stage influence an individual's mentoring capacity?

4. How do cultural differences influence the types of, and composition of, networks?
   a. How does cultural background shape an individual's expectations of developmental relationships?
   b. How does culture influence how individuals view relational learning?

5. How do organizations create conditions that foster developmental networks?
   a. How do organizations influence an individual's willingness to be a developer?
   b. How do organizations ensure that protégés' expectations are consistent with what developers can offer?
   c. How does an organization's "developmental culture" influence the formation of developmental relationships?

Relational Processes and Characteristics

1. How are the relationships within the developmental network formed?

2. How does geographical distance influence the formation of developmental relationships?

3. How do developmental networks vary with respect to composition?

4. What types of developmental networks exist?

5. How do developmental networks vary over time?

6. How has the new career context influenced mentoring and developmental relationship phases?

7. What functional support do "outside" developers play in career development?

Individual and Organizational Outcomes

1. How should organizations assess the impact of interventions on individual and organizational outcomes?

2. How do developmental networks facilitate or hinder career transitions?

3. How do diversified mentoring relationships contribute to perceived organizational justice?

4. What are the individual and organizational benefits of diversified relationships?

5. How do developmental networks influence personal learning?

NOTE: The dashed lines indicate that some questions fall into two categories.

Challenges for Future Research

The foregoing discussion suggests a number of areas that can strengthen mentoring and developmental network studies. First, qualitative research, primarily longitudinal, in-depth interviews and ethnographies, can yield a better understanding of the *processes* of mentoring. To date, much research is limited by methodologies—for example, self-reported surveys—that cannot capture the nuances of mentor/developer and protégé interaction. We believe, for example, that a grounded theory (Glaser & Strauss, 1967) approach to the study of dyadic processes related to diversified relationships will uncover the challenges and disadvantages faced by minorities, women, and other groups with relatively less power (Ragins, 1997a, 1997b, 1999). Also, relatively little attention has been given to how relationships are formed; phase models describe relationship evolution after the relationship has been established, however tentatively. Research on the process of relationship formation is critical to a comprehensive understanding of mentoring.

Second, conflicting and inconclusive findings in certain areas—for example, antecedents and diversified relationships—suggest moderating variables that convolute explanatory relationships. Both qualitative research and controlled studies will aid in unearthing moderators and, subsequently, testing for more substantive, comprehensive findings. Third, researchers should continue to refine definitions of mentoring and other developmental relationships. For example, researchers should seek clear construct definitions and operationalizations of "developmental networks" and "developers," as well as discriminate between mentoring and other similar constructs—for example, leadership. Fourth, social network methodologies (e.g., UCINET: Borgatti, Everett, & Freeman, 1998) will be useful in examining the strength and diversity of ties, as well as the overall composition of developmental networks.

Fifth, as suggested earlier, the adult development perspective has much to offer in efforts designed to answer some critical questions. This developmental lens can help us understand why some individuals find developmental relationships more easily than others. In addition, it can help us delineate variations of relationship dynamics that are observable across relationships and across organizations. The nuances of mentoring relationships and developmental networks are likely to be better understood as we take the developmental tasks and attachment patterns of all participants into account. Indeed, the learning that occurs in the context of relationships at work will change over the life course as individuals move from one stage or developmental position to the next. And, given the dramatic shifts in the career context, changes in phases, stages, and position are likely to happen more quickly and more often than the original models suggest.

Finally, as we advised the reader to note at the onset of the chapter, a research agenda must include more empirical research on mentoring and developmental networks in a global context. By examining mentoring in other national settings or developmental networks that include members from different countries, we can begin to understand how these relationships are similar and dissimilar as well as provide practitioners with practical advice on managing their individual networks.

The Evolution of Salient Mentoring Concepts

As shown in Table 13.1, the evolution from the traditional to the new career context has been accompanied by a concomitant shift in salient mentoring variables. As the career context changed, the way in which individuals experience the mentoring phenomenon was indelibly altered, thus necessitating a revision of focal concepts related to individual and organizational antecedents, relational processes and characteristics, and outcomes (see Table 13.1).

The salient mentoring concepts in the *traditional career context* (Arthur, Inkson, & Pringle, 1999; Mirvis & Hall, 1996) reflected the mentoring phenomenon as it existed during that historical time frame. As explained earlier in the chapter, individuals enacted their careers within comparatively more hierarchical organizations over longer durations of time; the notion of "lifetime employment" existed for some individuals. These key features of traditional careers allowed individuals—both mentors and protégés—to interact over longer periods with more frequency and with a sense of security that enabled *stable, dyadic relationships* between seniors and juniors as vehicles for career development. Relationships, because of their duration—typically 3 to 8 years (Kram, 1983, 1985a; Kram & Isabella, 1985)—went through relatively predictable *phases.*

Organizations sought to find willing, capable mentors who could be incentivized to teach juniors to excel and advance up the corporate ladder. Researchers, therefore, were keen to examine factors that influenced *a willingness to mentor.* One factor in particular, *career stage* (Dalton & Thompson, 1986; Hall, 2002; Sullivan and Crocitto, Chapter 15), affected this willingness; middle-career individuals who had sufficiently learned their respective roles and perceived having job security were more likely to want to be "generative" (Erikson, 1982) by training others. This factor, however, is not as likely to have the same explanatory power in today's career context since individuals now cycle through mini career cycles quite frequently as a result of the turbulent environment they are in. As a consequence, we can speculate that fewer will have the luxury of job security, and therefore, other antecedent factors that shape willingness to mentor will be more important.

Furthermore, as noted, organizations implemented formal programs, in part to redress unequal opportunities for women and ethnic minorities; thus, researchers explored how *demographic variables* such as gender and race complicated an individual's ability to foster and maintain mentoring relationships as well as reap positive benefits. Moreover, since individuals stayed in organizations over relatively long periods of time, mentoring programs were assessed, in part, by how they influenced *job commitment, intentions to stay, job satisfaction,* and *turnover,* in addition to *career development.* During the traditional career era, organizations focused more on formal programs and less on relational learning through naturally occurring, informal relationships.

The *new career context,* which is a vastly different landscape, requires examining mentoring using new constructs. Marked by turbulence, more frequent career transitions, and the need for continual learning both by individuals and

by organizational teams, individuals enacting "protean" careers can no longer expect to have a single mentor but rather should maintain a *network of "developers"* who can provide various opportunities for *relational learning.* Individuals must strive to become "perfect protégés" (Hill, 1991), who proactively form and maintain a portfolio of developers who meet their career and personal needs. Because of the need for individuals to take a very active role in shaping their own development, scholars should more closely scrutinize the role that personal competencies such as *identity, self-awareness,* and *emotional* and *developmental intelligences* play in aiding some individuals to better steer their career journeys. As described in the section "A Developmental Lens on Mentoring," individuals' *developmental stage* and *phase* will affect their interest in maintaining, and their ability to manage, relationships as well.

Organizations should not only rely on formal mentoring programs, but they should also seek to foster *developmental cultures* that enhance the likelihood of positive mentoring and developmental relationship experiences. As organizations cross national borders, they must consider how developmental relationships are affected both by the complexities associated with *cultural differences* and vast spatial distances as well as by the *unique opportunities offered by diversity.* Similarly, organizations should consider how the aging workforce to be found in a great many countries might have an impact on mentoring relationships and build strategies to ensure continual learning for all employees. Whereas formal mentoring in the traditional career context was driven, in part, by a social need to create equal opportunity for all employees, mentoring in the new career context is driven primarily by a business need to create a high-performing global workforce.

In contrast to the traditional career context, individuals will more likely experience numerous career transitions across organizations throughout their careers. Organizations, armed with this knowledge, should seek to develop programs and foster cultures that facilitate accelerated *personal learning.* Individuals' developmental networks will influence *career changes* and *transitions;* for instance, different network types will more likely emphasize more or less knowledge of career opportunities outside individuals' employing organizations, while other networks may allow for greater intra-organizational mobility and transmission of organizational knowledge (Higgins, 2000).

Relevant Questions for Future Research

The sample research questions in Box 13.1 are aimed at both individual and organizational variables and at single developmental relationships as well as networks. Furthermore, the questions are intended to enhance our understanding of mentoring in the new career context. For example, within the section Individual- and Organizational-Level Antecedents, questions include those that address mentor and protégé competencies and characteristics such as an individual's developmental stage, cultural variables, and organizational conditions that influence both relationship formation and effective interaction.

The section Relational Processes and Characteristics includes questions about how relationships are formed, how networks evolve over time, what types of networks exist, and the role played by developers outside an employing organization. Finally, the Individual and Organizational Outcomes include much needed research of the impact of mentoring—both formal and informal—on organizational-level outcomes, on the benefits of diverse relationships and on how diversified mentoring relationships affect protégées' perceptions of organizational justice (e.g., Greenberg, 1986), on personal learning, and on career change.

Mentoring research has been valuable both to managers and HR practitioners as they contemplate how to enhance employees' career development and to individuals as they navigate their careers. Although researchers have made great strides toward a comprehensive understanding of the mentoring phenomenon, much more is needed, particularly in light of the new career context. Our purposes have been to provide a literature overview of the primary mentoring themes and to detail the evolution of mentoring from an emphasis on career growth through dyadic, long-term, stable relationships to growth through multiple, tumultuous, shorter-term

relationships that form developmental networks. We believe that an emphasis on new salient concepts and questions given the new career context will guide a fruitful, relevant agenda going forward.

NOTES

1. Wanberg et al. (2003) focus on a broad survey of empirical research conducted to date, provide a conceptual model of formal mentoring programs, develop propositions consistent with the model, and outline a future research agenda related to the primary mentoring themes. The formal mentoring program model—and the accompanying propositions—is aimed at (1) program outcomes, (2) the nature of mentoring within the context of a formal relationship, (3) the antecedents of positive formal program outcomes, and (4) the process through which formal programs lead to positive outcomes.

Noe et al. (2002) briefly describe the evolution of mentoring to its current conceptualization of a developmental network, review the mentoring literature (in slightly less detail than Wanberg et al., 2003), explain four theoretical perspectives that have been used to study mentoring relationships, and also provide a research agenda. Their discussion of the theoretical lenses through which mentoring relationships have been viewed is useful in highlighting underexamined aspects of mentoring and in underscoring constructs (e.g., leadership and organizational citizenship) that need to be better distinguished from mentoring. The authors' research agenda includes the following: (1) methodological issues that need to be addressed—including construct definition consistency and an overreliance on self-report data; (2) whether mentoring relationships are best developed at early- or later-career stages; (3) the interplay between contextual factors—such as organizational culture, structure, and reward systems—and mentoring relationships; and (4) how attachment theory (Bowlby, 1969)—which stresses how early-childhood relationships affect adult relationships—might inform our understanding of mentoring, such as who is likely to be drawn to a mentoring relationship, either as a mentor or as a protégé.

2. Three instruments designed to measure mentoring functions are (1) Mentoring Functions Scale (Noe, 1988a, 1988b), (2) Mentoring Functions Questionnaire (Scandura, 1992), and (3) Mentoring Role Instrument (Ragins & McFarlin, 1990).

3. We would like to note the concomitant development of the social network literature over the past two decades and to discern the conceptual distinction between a developmental network and the broader social network. Another chapter in this book is dedicated to the impact of social networks on career theories. We believe that it is important for readers to note the concurrent growth of both fields as well as the distinction between the two.

Simultaneous to the evolution in the field of mentoring is the growth of academic interest in networks within and between organizations (e.g., Burt, 1992; Ibarra, 1993; Granovetter, 1973, 1983; Ibarra, 1992, 1993; Jones, Hesterly, & Borgatti, 1997; Uzzi, 1997). Underlying the network literature is the notion that economic transacting and individual choices in organizational life are, in part, affected by, and embedded in, the social context. More specifically, interfirm activity and individual decisions are either facilitated or hindered by the network of firms and individuals, respectively, within which they reside. This fact of organizational and career life further substantiates the transformation of mentoring as it highlights the reality that individuals will learn and grow from, or be hindered by, constraints associated with the larger social context and/or personal networks.

The key distinction demarcating mentoring and developmental relationships from those in an individual's larger social network is the quality or strength of the tie that a protégé has with a "developer." In essence, developmental relationships are those that involve a more frequent and/or higher-quality transmission of information, greater career enhancement, and more psychosocial and other types of support than the remainder of an individual's network.

To better envision the difference between a developmental network and a social network, one can imagine that a social network comprises all of an individual's contacts, which vary in terms of frequency of contact and strength of the relationship; a developmental network is a smaller network within the entire network and is composed of those relationships that offer the functional support of mentoring.

4. See Wanberg et al. (2003) for a detailed empirical overview of protégé factors.

5. See Wanberg et al. (2003) and Noe et al. (2002) for detailed empirical overviews of these studies; see Ragins (1999, 2002) for detailed summaries of research on gender and descriptions of diversified relationships and challenges.

6. It has been suggested that the mentor's rank may be confounding results as men still traditionally hold higher positions than women in corporate hierarchies (e.g., Ragins, 1999; Wanberg et al., 2003).

REFERENCES

Allen, T. D., Eby, L. T., Poteet, M. L., Lentz, E., & Lima, L. (2004). Career benefits associated with mentoring for protégés: A meta-analysis. *Journal of Applied Psychology, 89*(1), 127–136.

Allen, T. D., Poteet, M. L., & Burroughs, S. M. (1997). The mentor's perspective: A qualitative inquiry and future research agenda. *Journal of Vocational Behavior, 51,* 70–89.

Allen, T. D., Poteet, M. L., & Russell. J. E. A. (2000). Protégé selection by mentors: What makes a difference? *Journal of Organizational Behavior, 21,* 271–282.

Allen, T. D., Poteet, M. L., Russell. J. E. A., & Dobbins, G. H. (1997). A field study of factors related to supervisors' willingness to mentor others. *Journal of Vocational Behavior, 50,* 1–22.

Allen, T. D., Russell, J. E. A., & Maetzke, S. B. (1997). Formal peer mentoring: Factors related to protégés satisfaction and willingness to mentor others. *Group & Organization Management, 22*(4), 488–507.

Arthur, M. B., Inkson, K., & Pringle, J. K. (1999). *The new careers: Individual action and economic change.* Thousand Oaks, CA: Sage.

Arthur, M. B., & Rousseau, D. M. (Eds.). (1996). *The boundaryless career: A new employment principle for a new organizational era.* New York: Oxford University Press.

Aryee, S., Chay, Y. W., & Chew, J. (1996). The motivation to mentor among managerial employees: An interactionist approach. *Group & Organization Management, 21,* 261–277.

Aryee, S., Lo, S., & Kang, I.-L. (1999). Antecedents of early career stage mentoring among Chinese employees. *Journal of Organizational Behavior, 20,* 563–576.

Aryee, S., Wyatt, T., & Stone, R. (1996). Early career outcomes of graduate employees: The effect of mentoring and ingratiation. *Journal of Management Studies, 33,* 95–118.

Bahniuk, M. H., Dobos, J., & Hill, S. E. K. (1990). The impact of mentoring, collegial support, and information adequacy on career success:

A replication. *Journal of Social Behavior and Personality, 5,* 431–451.

Bahniuk, M. H., Hill, S. E. K., & Darus, H. J. (1996). The relationship of power-gaining communication strategies to career success. *Western Journal of Communication, 60,* 358–378.

Baker, W. (1992). The network organization in theory and practice. In N. Nohria & R. G. Eccles (Eds.), *Networks and organizations: Structure, form and action* (pp. 396–429). Boston: Harvard Business School Press.

Baugh, S. G., Lankau, M. J., & Scandura, T. A. (1996). An investigation of the effects of protege gender on responses to mentoring. *Journal of Vocational Behavior, 49,* 309–323.

Baugh, S. G., & Scandura, T. A. (1999). The effects of multiple mentors on protégé attitudes toward the work setting. *Journal of Social Behavior and Personality, 14,* 503–521.

Blake-Beard, S. D. (1999). The cost of living as an outsider within: An analysis of the mentoring relationships and career success of black and white women in the corporate sector. *Journal of Career Development, 26,* 21–36.

Borgatti, S. P., Everett, M. G., & Freeman, L. C. (1998). *UCINET 5.0 for Windows 95/NT.* Columbia: Analytic Technologies.

Bowen, D. D. (1985). Were men meant to mentor women? *Training and Development Journal, 39*(2), 31–34.

Bowlby, J. (1969). *Attachment and loss: Attachment* (Vol. 1). New York: Basic Books.

Burke, R. J., & McKeen, C. A. (1997). Benefits of mentoring relationships among managerial and professional women: A cautionary tale. *Journal of Vocational Behavior, 51,* 43–57.

Burke, R. J., McKeen, C. A., & McKenna, C. S. (1990). Sex differences and cross-sex effects on mentoring: Some preliminary data. *Psychological Reports, 67,* 1011–1023.

Burkhardt, M. E., & Brass, D. J. (1990). Changing patterns or patterns of change: The effects of a change in technology on social network structure and power. *Administrative Science Quarterly, 35,* 104–127.

Burt, R. S. (1992). *Structural holes.* Cambridge, MA: Harvard University Press.

Busch, J. W. (1985). Mentoring among graduate schools of education: Mentor's perceptions. *American Educational Research Journal, 22,* 257–265.

Chandler, D. E. (2007). *Developmental intelligence. The role of the protégé in the formation and maintenance of the developmental network.* Manuscript in preparation.

Chao, G. T.; Walz, P. M., & Gardner, P. D. (1992). Formal and informal mentorships: A comparison on mentoring functions and contrast with non-mentored counterparts. *Personnel Psychology, 45*(3), 619.

Cherniss, C., & Adler, M. (2000). Promoting emotional intelligence in organizations. Alexandria, VA: American Society for Training and Development.

Cherniss, C., & Goleman, D. (Eds.). (2001). *The emotionally intelligent workplace: How to select for, measure, and improve emotional intelligence in individuals, groups, and organizations.* San Francisco: Jossey-Bass.

Clawson, J. G., & Kram, K. E. (1984, March). Managing cross gender relationships. *Business Horizons, 23*(3), 22–32.

Colarelli, S. M., & Bishop, R. C. (1990). Career commitment: Functions, correlates, and management. *Group & Organization Studies, 15,* 158–176.

Cox, T. H., & Nkomo, S. M. (1991). A race and gender-group analysis of the early career experience of MBAs. *Work & Occupations, 18,* 431–446.

Dalton, G. W. (1989). Developmental views of careers in organizations. In M. B. Arthur, D. T. Hall, & B. S. Lawrence (Eds). *Handbook of career theory* (pp. 89–109). New York: Cambridge University Press.

Dalton, G. W., & Thompson, P. (1986). *Novations: Strategies for career development.* Glenview, IL: Scott, Foresman.

Dalton, G. W., Thompson, P., & Price, R. (1977). The four stages of professional careers. *Organizational Dynamics, Summer,* 19–42.

Dansky, K. H. (1996). The effect of group mentoring on career outcomes. *Group & Organization Management, 13*(1), 5–21.

Douglas, C. A., & McCauley, C. D. (1997). A survey on the use of formal developmental relationships in organizations. *Issues & Observations, 17,* 6–9.

Dreher, G. F., & Ash, R. A. (1990). A comparative study of mentoring among men and women in managerial, professional, and technical positions. *Journal of Applied Psychology, 75,* 539–546.

Dreher, G. F., & Cox, T. H., Jr. (1996). Race, gender, and opportunity: A study of compensation attainment and the establishment of mentoring relationships. *Journal of Applied Psychology, 81,* 297–308.

Eby, L. T. (1997). Alternative forms of mentoring in changing organizational environments: A conceptual extension of the mentoring literature. *Journal of Vocational Behavior, 51,* 125–144.

Eby, L. T., McManus, S. E., Simon, S. A., & Russell, J. E. A. (2000). The protégé's perspective regarding negative mentoring experiences: The development of a taxonomy. *Journal of Vocational Behavior, 57,* 1–21.

Ensher, E. A., Murphy, S. E., & Sullivan, S. E. (2000, Spring). *The boundaryless career in the entertainment industry: Examining the employment experiences of executive women.* Paper presented at the Creative Careers Conference, London Business School, London.

Erikson, E. H. (1982). *The life cycle completed: A review.* New York: W. W. Norton.

Fagan, M. M., & Walter, B. (1982). Mentoring among teachers. *Journal of Educational Research, 76,* 113–118.

Fagenson, E. A. (1989). The mentor advantage: Perceived career/job experiences of protégés versus non-protégés needs. *Journal of Vocational Behavior, 45,* 55–78.

Fagenson, E. A. (1992). Mentoring: Who needs it? A comparison of protégés and non-protégés needs for power, achievement, affiliation, and autonomy. *Journal of Vocational Behavior, 41,* 48–60.

Fagenson-Eland, E. A., Marks, M. A., & Amendola, K. L. (1977). Perceptions of mentoring relationships. *Journal of Vocational Behavior, 51,* 29–42.

Feldman, D. C., Folks, W. R., & Turnley, W. H. (1999). Mentor-protégé diversity and its impact on international internship experiences. *Journal of Organizational Behavior, 20,* 597–611.

Festinger, L., Schatcher, S., & Back, K. (1950). *Social pressures in informal groups: A study of human factors in housing.* Palo Alto, CA: Stanford University Press.

Fletcher, J. K. (1994). *Toward a theory of relational practice in organizations: A feminist reconstruction of "real" work.* Unpublished doctoral dissertation, Boston University, Boston.

Fletcher, J. K. (1996). A relational approach to the protean worker. In D. T. Hall (Ed.), *The career is dead—long live the career: A relational approach to careers* (pp. 101–131). San Francisco: Jossey-Bass.

Fletcher, J. K. (1999). *Disappearing acts: Gender, power, and relational practice at work.* Cambridge: MIT Press.

Friedman, R., Kane, M., & Cornfield, D. B. (1998). Social support and career optimism: Examining the effectiveness of network groups among black managers. *Human Relations, 51,* 1155–1177.

Fulk, J., Steinfield, C., Schmitz, J., & Power, G. (1987). A social information processing model of media use in organizations. *Communication Research, 14,* 529–552.

Gaskill, L. R. (1991). Same-sex versus cross-sex mentoring of female protégés: A comparative analysis. *Career Development Quarterly, 40,* 48–63.

Gilligan, C. (1982). In a different voice: Psychological theory and women's development. Cambridge, MA: Harvard University Press.

Glaser, B. G., & Strauss, A. L. (1967). *The discovery of grounded theory: Strategies for qualitative research.* Chicago: Aldine.

Godshalk, V. M., & Sosik, J. J. (2003). Aiming for career success: The role of learning goal orientation in mentoring relationships. *Journal of Vocational Behavior, 63,* 417–437.

Goleman, D. (1995). *Emotional intelligence.* New York: Bantam Books.

Goleman, D. (1998). *Working with emotional intelligence.* New York: Bantam Books.

Goto, S. (1999). Asian Americans and developmental relationships. In A. J. Murell, F. J. Crosby, & R. J. Ely (Eds.), *Mentoring dilemmas: Developmental relationships within a multicultural organizations. Applied social research* (pp. 47–62). Mahwah, NJ: Lawrence Erlbaum.

Gould, R. (1978). *Transformations: Growth and change in adult life.* New York: Simon & Schuster.

Granovetter, M. S. (1973). The strength of weak ties. *American Journal of Sociology, 6,* 1360–1380.

Granovetter, M. S. (1983). The strength of weak ties: A network theory revisited. *Sociological Theory, 1,* 201–233.

Greenberg, J. (1986). Determinants of perceived fairness of performance evaluations. *Journal of Applied Psychology, 71,* 340–342.

Greenhaus, J. H., Parasuraman, S., & Wormley, W. M. (1990). Effects of race on organizational experiences, job performance evaluations and career outcomes. *Academy of Management Journal, 33,* 64–86.

Hall, D. T. (1996). Protean careers in the 21st century. *Academy of Management Executive, 10*(4), 8–16.

Hall, D. T. (2002). *Careers in and out of organiza-tions.* Thousand Oaks, CA: Sage.

Hall, D. T., Briscoe, J. P., & Kram, K. E. (1997). Identity, values, and learning in the protean career. In C. L. Cooper & S. E. Jackson (Eds.), *Creating tomorrow's organizations: A handbook for future research in organizational behavior* (pp. 321–337). London: Wiley.

Hall, D. T., & Kahn, W. A. (2001). Developmental relationships at work: A learning perspective. In C. Cooper & R. J. Burke (Eds.), *The new world of work* (pp. 49–74). London: Blackwell.

Hall, D. T., & Mirvis, P. H. (1995). The new career contract: Developing the whole person at midlife and beyond. *Journal of Vocational Behavior, 47,* 269–289.

Hamilton, E. (1999). *Mythology.* New York: Warner Books.

Higgins, M. C. (2000). The more, the merrier? Multiple developmental relationships and work satisfaction. *Journal of Management Develop-ment, 19,* 277–296.

Higgins, M. C. (2001). Career change: a social influ-ence perspective. *Journal of Organizational Behavior, 22,* 595–618.

Higgins, M. C., & Kram, K. E. (2001). Recon-ceptualizing mentoring at work: A developmental network perspective. *Academy of Management Review, 26*(2), 264–288.

Higgins, M. C., & Thomas, D. A. (2001). Constel-lations and careers: Toward understanding the effects of multiple developmental relation-ships. *Journal of Organizational Behavior, 22,* 223–247.

Hill, L. (1991). *Beyond the myth of the perfect mentor: Building a network of developmental relationships* (Case No. 9–491–096). Boston: Harvard Business School.

Hubbard, S. S., & Robinson, J. P. (1998). Mentoring: A catalyst for advancement in administration. *Journal of Career Development, 24,* 289–299.

Hunt, D. M., & Michael, C. (1983). Mentorship: A career training and development tool. *Academy of Management Review, 8*(3), 475–485.

Hurley, A. E., & Fagenson-Eland, E. A. (1996). Challenges in cross-gender mentoring relation-ships: Psychological intimacy, myths, rumours, innuendoes and sexual harassment. *Leadership and Organization Development Journal, 17*(3), 42–49.

Ibarra, H. (1992). Homophily and differential returns: Sex differences in network structure and access in an advertising firm. *Administrative Science Quarterly, 37,* 422–447.

Ibarra, H. (1993). Personal networks of women and minorities in management: A conceptual framework. *Academy of Management Review, 18,* 56–87.

Johnson, K. K. P., Yust, B. L., & Fritchie, L. L. (2001). Views on mentoring by clothes and tex-tiles faculty. *Clothing and Textiles Research Journal, 19*(1), 31–40.

Jones, C., Hesterly, W. S., & Borgatti, S. P. (1997). A general theory of network governance: Exchange conditions and social mechanisms. *Academy of Management Journal, 22*(4), 911–945.

Jordan, J. V., Kaplan, A. G., Miller, J. B., Stiver, I. P., & Surrey, J. L. (1991). *Women's growth in con-nection: Writings from the Stone Center.* New York: Guilford Press.

Judge, T. A., & Bretz, R. D., Jr. (1994). Political influence behavior and career success. *Journal of Management, 20,* 43–65.

Kanter, R. M. (1977). *Men and women of the corpo-ration.* New York: Basic Books.

Kegan, R. (1982). *The evolving self: Problem and process in human adult development.* Cambridge, MA: Harvard University Press.

Kegan, R. (1994). *In over our heads: The mental demands of modern life.* Cambridge, MA: Harvard University Press.

Kirchmeyer, C. (1998). Determinants of managerial career success: Evidence and explanation of male/female differences. *Journal of Management, 24,* 673–692.

Koberg, C. S., Boss, R. W., Chappell, D., & Ringer, R. C. (1994). Correlates and consequences of protégé mentoring in a large hospital. *Group & Organization Management, 19,* 219–239.

Kram, K. E., Ting, S., & Bunker, K. (2002). On-the-job training for emotional competence. *Leadership in Action, 22*(3), 3–7.

Kram, K. E. (1983). Phases of the mentoring relationship. *Academy of Management Journal, 26*(4), 608–625.

Kram, K. E. (1985a). *Mentoring at work: Developmental relationships in organizational life.* Glenview, IL: Scott, Foresman.

Kram, K. E. (1985b). Improving the mentoring process. *Training and Development Journal, 39*(4), 40–43.

Kram, K. E. (1988). Mentoring in the workplace. In D. T. Hall (Ed.), *Career development in organizations* (pp. 160–201). San Francisco: Jossey-Bass.

Kram, K. E. (1996). A relational approach to career development. In D. Hall & Associates (Eds.), *The career is dead: Long live the career* (pp. 132–157). San Francisco: Jossey-Bass.

Kram, K. E., & Bragar, M. C. (1992). Development through mentoring: A strategic approach. In: D. H. Montross & C. J. Shinkman (Eds.), *Career development: Theory and practice* (pp. 221–254). Springfield, IL: Charles C. Thomas.

Kram, K. E., & Cherniss, C. (2001). Developing emotional competence through relationships at work. In C. Cherniss & D. Goleman (Eds.), *The emotionally intelligent workplace* (pp. 254–285). San Francisco: Jossey-Bass.

Kram, K. E., & Hall, D. T. (1991). Mentoring as an antidote to stress during corporate trauma. *Human Resource Management, 28*(4), 493–510.

Kram, K. E., & Hall, D. T. (1996). Mentoring in a context of diversity and turbulence. In E. E. Kossek & S. A. Lobel (Eds.), *Managing diversity: Human resource strategies for transforming the workplace*. Oxford: Blackwell.

Kram, K. E., & Isabella, L. A. (1985). Mentoring alternatives: The role of peer relationships in career development. *Academy of Management Journal, 28*(1), 110–132.

Laband, D. N., & Lentz, B. F. (1995). Workplace mentoring in the legal profession. *Southern Economic Journal, 61,* 783–802.

Lankau, M. J., & Scandura, T. A. (2002). An investigation of personal learning in mentoring relationships: Content, antecedents, and consequences. *Academy of Management Journal, 45,* 779–790.

Levinson, D. J. (with Levinson, J.). (1996). *Seasons of a woman's life*. New York: Knopf.

Levinson, D. J., Darrow, D., & Klein, E., Levinson, M., & McKee, B. (1978). *Seasons of a man's life*. New York: Knopf.

Loevinger, J. (1978). *Ego development*. San Francisco: Jossey-Bass.

McGuire, G. M. (1999). Do race and sex affect employees' access to help from mentors? Insights from the study of a large corporation. In: A. J. Murrell, F. J. Crosby, & R. J. Ely (Eds.), *Mentoring dilemmas: Developmental relationships within multicultural organizations. Applied Social Research* (pp. 105–120). Mahwah, NJ: Lawrence Erlbaum.

McManus, S. E., & Russell, J. E. A. (1997). New directions of mentoring research: An examination of related constructs. *Journal of Vocational Behavior, 51,* 145–161.

Miller, J. B. (1976). *Towards a new psychology for women*. Boston: Beacon Press.

Miller, J. B. (1991). The development of women's sense of self. In J. V. Jordan, A. G. Kaplan, J. B. Miller, I. P. Stiver, & J. L. Surrey (Eds.), *Women's growth in connection*. New York: Guilford Press.

Mirvis, P. H., & Hall, D. T. (1996). Psychological success and the boundaryless career. In M. B. Arthur & D. M. Rousseau (Eds.)., *The boundaryless career* (pp. 237–255). New York: Oxford University Press.

Missirian, A. K. (1982). *The corporate connection. Why executive women need mentors to reach the top*. Englewood Cliffs, NJ: Prentice Hall.

Mobley, G. M., Jaret, C., Marsh, K., & Lim, Y. Y. (1994). Mentoring, job satisfaction, gender, and the legal profession. *Sex Roles, 31,* 79–98.

Morrison, A. M., White, R. P., & Van Velsor, E. (1994). *Breaking the glass ceiling: Can women reach the top of America's largest corporations?* Reading, MA: Addison-Wesley.

Mullen, E. J., & Noe, R. A. (1999). The mentoring information exchange: When do mentors seek information from their protégés? *Journal of Organizational Behavior, 20,* 233–242.

Noe, R. A. (1988a). Women and mentoring: A review and research agenda. *Academy of Management Review, 13,* 65–78.

Noe, R. A. (1988b). An investigation of the determinants of successful assigned mentoring relationships. *Personnel Psychology, 41,* 457–479.

Noe, R. A., Greenberger, D. B., & Wang, S. (2002). Mentoring: What we know and where we might go. In: G. R. Ferris & J. J. Martoccio (Eds), *Research in personnel and human resources management* (Vol. 21, pp. 129–174). Oxford: Elsevier Science.

Olian, J. D., Carroll, S. J., Giannantonio, C. M., & Feren, D. B. (1988). What do protégés look for in a mentor? Results of three experimental studies. *Journal of Vocational Behavior, 33,* 15–37.

Peiperl, M. A., & Arthur, M. B. (2000). Topics for conversation: Career themes old and new. In M. A. Peiperl, M. B. Arthur, R. Goffee, & T. Morris (Eds.), *Career frontiers: New conceptions of working lives* (pp. 1–20). Oxford: Oxford University Press.

Peiperl, M. A., & Baruch, Y. (1997). Back to square zero: The post-corporate career. *Organizational Dynamics, Spring,* 7–22.

Phillips, L. (1978). Mentors and protégés: A study of the career development of women managers and executives in business and industry (Doctoral dissertation, University of California at Los Angeles, 1977). *Dissertation Abstracts International, 38*(11), 6414A.

Phillips-Jones, L. (1983, February). Establishing a formalized mentoring program. *Training and Development Journal, 37,* 38–42.

Pollock, R. (1995). A test of conceptual models depicting the developmental course of informal mentor-protégé relationships in the workplace. *Journal of Vocational Behavior, 46,* 144–162.

Ragins, B. R. (1989). Barriers to mentoring: The female manager's dilemma. *Human Relations, 42,* 1–22.

Ragins, B. R. (1997a). Diversified mentoring relationships in organizations: A power perspective. *Academy of Management Review, 22,* 482–521.

Ragins, B. R. (1997b). Antecedents of diversified mentoring relationships. *Journal of Vocational Behavior, 51,* 90–109.

Ragins, B. R. (1999). Gender and mentoring relationships: Definitions, challenges, and strategies. In: G. N. Powell (Ed.), *Handbook of gender and work* (pp. 347–370). Thousand Oaks, CA: Sage.

Ragins, B. R. (2002). Understanding diversified mentoring relationships: Definitions, challenges, and strategies. In D. Clutterbuck & B. R. Ragins (Eds.), *Mentoring and diversity: An international perspective* (pp. 23–53). Woburn, MA: Butterworth Heinemann.

Ragins, B. R., & Cotton, J. L. (1991). Easier said than done: Gender differences in perceived barriers to gaining a mentor. *Academy of Management Journal, 34,* 939–951.

Ragins, B. R., & Cotton, J. L. (1993). Gender and willingness to mentor in organizations. *Journal of Management, 19,* 97–111.

Ragins, B. R., & Cotton, J. L. (1999). Mentor functions and outcomes: A comparison of men and women in formal and informal mentoring relationships. *Journal of Applied Psychology, 84,* 529–550.

Ragins, B. R., Cotton, J. L., & Miller, J. S. (2000). Marginal mentoring: The effects of type of mentor, quality of relationship, and program design on work and career attitudes. *Academy of Management Journal, 43,* 1177–1194.

Ragins, B. R., & McFarlin, D. B. (1990). Perceptions of mentor roles in cross-gender mentoring relationships. *Journal of Vocational Behavior, 37,* 321–339.

Roche, G. R. (1979). Much ado about mentors. *Harvard Business Review,* 14–28.

Scandura, T. A. (1992). Mentorship and career mobility: An empirical investigation. *Journal of Organizational Behavior, 13,* 169–174.

Scandura, T. A. (1998). Dysfunctional mentoring relationships and outcomes. *Journal of Management, 24,* 449–467.

Scandura, T. A., & Ragins, B. R. (1993). The effects of sex and gender role orientation on mentorship in male-dominated occupations. *Journal of Vocational Behavior, 43,* 251–265.

Scandura, T. A., & Williams, E. A. (2001). An investigation of the moderating effects of gender on the relationships between mentor initiation and protégé perceptions of mentoring functions. *Journal of Vocational Behavior, 59,* 342–363.

Schein, E. H. (1978). *Career dynamics: Matching individual and organizational needs.* Reading, MA: Addison-Wesley.

Seibert, S. E. (1999). The effectiveness of facilitated mentoring: A longitudinal quasi-experiment. *Journal of Vocational Behavior, 54,* 483–502.

Seibert, S. E., Kraimer, M. L., & Liden, R. C. (2001). A social capital of career success. *Academy of Management Journal, 44,* 219–237.

Shapiro, E., Haseltine, F., & Rowe, M. (1978). Moving up: Role models, mentors, and the "patron system." *Sloan Management Review, Spring,* 51–58.

Single, P. B., & Muller, C. B. (2001). When email and mentoring unite: The implementation of a nationwide electronic mentoring program. In: J. J. Phillips & L. K. Stromei (Eds.), *Creating mentoring and coaching programs* (pp. 107–122). Alexandria, VA: ASTD.

Sosik, J. J., & Godshalk, V. M. (2000). The role of gender in mentoring: Implications for diversified and homogenous mentoring relationships. *Journal of Vocational Behavior, 57,* 102–122.

Speizer, J. J. (1981). Role models, mentors and sponsors: The elusive concepts. *Signs: Journal of Women in Culture and Society, 6,* 692–712.

Super, D. E. (1957). *The psychology of careers.* New York: Harper & Row.

Super, D. E. (1986). Life career roles: self-realization in work and leisure. In D. T. Hall (Ed.), *Career development in organizations.* San Francisco: Jossey-Bass.

Tajfel, H., & Turner, J. C. (1986). The social identity theory of intergroup behavior. In S. Worchel & W. G. Austin (Eds.), *Psychology of intergroup relations* (2nd ed., pp. 7–24). Chicago: Nelson-Hall.

Thomas, D. A. (1990). The impact of race on managers' experiences of developmental relationships. *Journal of Organizational Behavior, 2*(4), 479–492.

Thomas, D. A. (1993a). Mentoring and irrationality: The role of racial taboos. In L. Hirschhorn & C. K. Barnett (Eds.), *The psychodynamics of organizations.* Philadelphia: Temple University Press.

Thomas, D. A. (1993b). Racial dynamics in cross-race developmental relationships. *Administrative Science Quarterly, 38*(2), 169.

Thomas, D. A. (1999). Mentoring and diversity in organizations: The importance of race and gender in work relationships. In A. Daly (Ed.), *Diversity in the workplace: Issues and perspectives.* Washington, DC: National Association of Social Workers Press.

Thomas, D. A., & Gabarro, J. J. (1999). *Breaking through: The making of minority executives in corporate America.* Boston: Harvard Business School Press.

Torbert, W. (1991). *The power of balance: Transforming self, society and scientific inquiry.* Newbury Park, CA: Sage.

Turban, D. B., & Dougherty, T. W. (1994). Role of protégé personality in receipt of mentoring and career success. *Academy of Management Journal, 34,* 331–351.

Turban, D. B., Dougherty, T. W., & Lee, F. K. (2002). Gender, race and perceived similarity effects in developmental relationships: The moderating role of relationship duration. *Journal of Vocational Behavior, 61,* 240–262.

Tyler, K. (1998, April). Mentoring programs link employees and experienced execs. *HR Magazine* (Vol. 43, pp. 98–103).

Uzzi, B. (1997). Social structure and competition in interfirm networks: The paradox of embeddedness. *Administrative Science Quarterly, 42,* 35–67.

Viator, R. E. (2001a). An examination of African-Americans' access to public accounting mentors: Perceived barriers and intentions to leave. *Accounting, Organizations & Society, 26,* 541–561.

Viator, R. E. (2001b). The association of formal and informal public accounting mentoring with role stress and related job outcomes. *Accounting, Organizations & Society, 26,* 73–93.

Wallace, J. E. (2001). The benefits of mentoring for female lawyers. *Journal of Vocational Behavior, 58,* 366–391.

Walsh, A. M., & Borkowski, S. C. (1999). Cross-gender mentoring and career development in the health care industry. *Health Care Management Review, 24*(3), 7–17.

Wanberg, C. R., Welsh, E. T., & Hezlett, S. A. (2003). Mentoring research: A review and dynamic process model. *Research in Personnel and Human Resources Management, 22,* 39–124.

Whitely, W. T., Dougherty, T. W., & Dreher, G. F. (1991). Relationship of career mentoring and socioeconomic origin to managers' and professionals' early career progress. *Academy of Management Journal, 34,* 331–351.

Wilson, J. A., & Elmann, N. S. (1990). Organizational benefits of mentoring. *Academy of Management Executive, 4,* 88–94.

Zey, M. (1984). *The mentor connection.* Homewood, IL: Dow-Jones-Irwin.

14

NETWORKS AND IDENTITIES

Reciprocal Influences on Career Processes and Outcomes

HERMINIA IBARRA

PRASHANT H. DESHPANDE

Networks of relationships are the social resources as well as social contexts in which careers take shape. A large body of empirical research provides evidence of the central role networks play in the career development process. Networks directly shape career outcomes by regulating access to jobs, providing mentoring and sponsorship, channeling the flow of information and referrals, augmenting power and reputations, and increasing the likelihood and speed of promotion (e.g., Brass, 1984; Burt, 1992; Granovetter, 1973; Higgins & Kram, 2001; Podolny & Baron, 1997). Social networks also affect careers indirectly as settings in which processes such as socialization and identity development unfold (Barley, 1990; Van Maanen & Schein, 1979). Career decisions are socially embedded and, thus, influenced by the social networks that affect referrals and opportunities as well as the development and change in people's identities over time.

While the past decades of research have yielded a great deal of knowledge about the kinds of networks that produce desirable career outcomes and the situational characteristics that shape the possibilities within which people construct their social networks, we know much less about what leads people to form networks with particular characteristics, nor do we understand well what factors produce significant changes in people's networks over the course of their careers. In this chapter, we develop the view that an important motive for network interaction is the construction, maintenance, and alteration of valued social identities. This perspective departs from a view of the formation of network ties in organizational settings that is premised exclusively on conceptions of economic and social exchange (DiMaggio, 1992). Instead of acting only to maximize, or to trade off, instrumental and expressive resources, individuals and organizations, by forging, maintaining, and dissolving network links, develop, manage, and change their identities (Ibarra, Kilduff, & Tsai, 2005).

A focus on identity, as well as current career trends, necessarily brings into focus the need for paying greater attention to network dynamics. Understanding what leads people to form relationships, in turn, sheds light on what leads them to alter fundamentally their patterns of interaction with others. We argue that an identity perspective on the relationship between networks and careers is especially relevant in a world in which, increasingly, career changes are self-initiated rather than imposed as part of formal organizational socialization or career-planning processes and in which the experience of role transition and career change has also become more frequent (e.g., Arthur & Rousseau, 1996). There is a debate among scholars about whether career jobs in a single organization have become less common, making career transitions more prevalent. For example, Cappelli (1999) pronounced the demise of "career jobs," while Jacoby (1999) claimed that this pronouncement was premature. To settle such competing claims, more empirical research is needed on how the frequency of career transitions has changed historically in the modern workplace. If careers appear, nevertheless, to be more fluid and self-designing, the context in which they unfold has certainly changed. Organizational trends such as restructuring, alliance formation, globalization, and the externalization of work, as well as the rise of freelance careers and the increasing use of Internet-based job boards (Cappelli and Hamori, Chapter 17) and professional communities, suggest a work environment in which multiple, sometimes competing, groups, rather than a single firm, provide potential anchors for a person's professional identity. In this chapter, we encourage research on the interactions among multiple identities and networks that integrate or segment those identities, as well as speculate about the dynamic processes that lead to career development and change.

This chapter is organized in two sections. In the first section, we review what we know about how networks affect careers. Our understanding about the current state of the field is summarized in Figure 14.1. We review evidence of direct effects on career outcomes, as well as the large body of conceptual and empirical work on mediators of the relationship between networks and careers, in particular access to resources and identity development. While empirical findings and conceptual developments suggests a strong link between networks and career outcomes, on the one hand, and between networks and identity construction processes, on the other, little work thus far has examined the reciprocal relationships between networks and identities as they affect and interact with career phenomena over time. The second section argues that future studies must investigate the social processes by which networks and identities coevolve with career experiences and transitions and suggests directions for research on how people adjust, adapt, and change the relationships that form such a critical part of their work lives.

With a plethora of research findings comes a plethora of books and articles that provide overviews of basic network terms, methods, and controversies. Our objective in this chapter is neither to attempt a comprehensive review of the relevant dimensions of networks nor to catalog the current debates in the field on the advantages and disadvantages of closure versus structural holes, or strong versus weak ties. Rather, we refer the reader to excellent reviews that already exist (see Kilduff & Tsai, 2003; Perry-Smith & Shalley, 2003; Seibert, Kraimer, & Liden, 2001).

RESEARCH TO DATE ON NETWORKS AND CAREERS

This section focuses on the current state of research on career outcomes of networks as well as the processes by which networks shape professional and managerial careers. Career is "the evolving sequence of an individual's work experiences over time" (Arthur, Hall, & Lawrence, 1989). Networks directly shape career outcomes by influencing job attainment, promotion, and income (Belliveau, O'Reilly, & Wade, 1996; Boxman, De Graaf, & Flap, 1991; Brass, 1984;

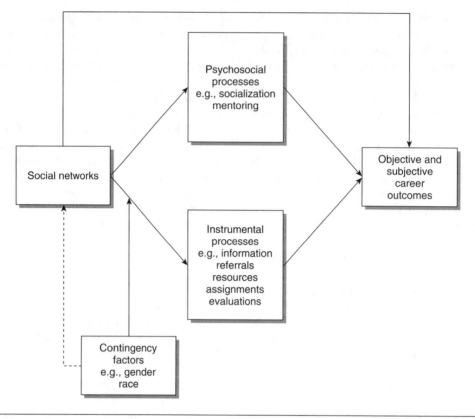

Figure 14.1 The Landscape of Research on Networks and Careers

Burt, 1992; Granovetter, 1985; Podolny & Baron, 1997; Seidel, Polzer, & Stewart, 2000). They also directly affect a variety of processes that mediate the relationship between networks and careers, including channeling flows of information, resources, and sponsorship; regulating influence and reputation; providing socialization; mentoring; and providing models for constructing identities (Brass, 1981; Granovetter, 1973, 1985; Higgins & Kram, 2001; Ibarra, 1999; Morrison, 2002; Westphal & Milton, 2000; Zuckerman, Kim, Ukanwa, & von Rittmann, 2003).

We rely on some basic career concepts to organize current findings and identify promising areas for future work, notably objective and subjective career (Hughes, 1937) and the distinction between instrumental and psychosocial resources (Kram, 1985). The objective career is manifested in extrinsic measures of career success, objectively observable achievements such as salary and promotions; the subjective career

refers to the individual's subjective feelings, inter alia, of satisfaction, accomplishment, and passion with respect to their careers (Khapova, Arthur, and Wilderom, Chapter 7). Instrumental career resources include information, influence, and sponsorship; psychosocial resources include socialization, mentoring, friendship, and identity formation (Kram, 1985).

As illustrated in Figure 14.1, we attempt to capture the current state of knowledge on the relation between networks and careers in three parts. First, we summarize the research demonstrating direct social network effects on objective career outcomes such as job attainment, promotions, and salary, on the one hand, and subjective career outcomes such as satisfaction, on the other. This essentially correlational body of empirical evidence has relied on many of the mediating mechanisms outlined in Figure 14.1 as theoretical explanations for the effects of networks on career; but empirical evidence on the actual causal mechanisms linking network characteristics to career outcomes is scant. Second, we provide an overview of research delineating the two primary mediating mechanisms—instrumental and psychosocial processes—that explain how networks shape careers. Third, we summarize network research on contingency factors moderating the effect of networks on career outcomes and mediating variables, in particular gender and race. Finally, we conclude with an assessment of key gaps in this tradition. We note that the bulk of network research on career outcomes has favored the objective career to the detriment of the subjective career, as well as examining instrumental rather than psychosocial mediators. We note as well that the feedback arrows and dynamic processes that shape both networks and careers are often mentioned but infrequently investigated.

Effects of Networks on Objective and Subjective Career Outcomes

A wealth of empirical studies has established direct linkages between network characteristics and career outcomes. Social networks affect objective career outcomes, including promotion and advancement to senior ranks (Brass, 1984; Burt, 1992; Podolny & Baron, 1997), compensation (Belliveau et al., 1996; Boxman et al., 1991; Burt, 1997; Seidel et al., 2000), entry into the organization (Bridges & Villemez, 1986; Granovetter, 1973, 1995; Montgomery, 1992; Petersen, Saporta, & Seidel, 2000), access to occupations (Lin & Dumin, 1996; Lin, Ensel, & Vaughn, 1981), and performance (Sparrowe, Liden, Wayne, & Kraimer, 2001). Networks also affect subjective career outcomes, notably people's own subjective experience and satisfaction with their work life and role (Gersick, Bartunek, & Dutton, 2000).

Objective Career: Jobs, Compensation, and Promotion

Job attainment was one of the earliest career outcomes studied by network researchers. Granovetter's (1973) seminal findings on the strength of weak ties inspired a large number of empirical studies; these generally support his claim that individuals with many weak ties are

at an advantageous position in the job market compared with those with redundant ties. A strong tie between two individuals is characterized by more time spent together and greater intimacy and emotional intensity, whereas a weak tie is characterized by occasional contact. Weak ties are argued to be more valuable since they act as bridges among diverse networks and bring new information not available through redundant ties in close cohesive networks (for a review, see Granovetter, 1982). Empirical support for the strength of weak ties argument, however, is strongest for finding a job, in comparison with other outcomes such as promotion and salary (Boxman et al., 1991; Granovetter, 1982; Lin et al., 1981).

As network research shifted attention from career outcomes to processes, recent research on job attainment has accordingly recognized the multistage nature of processes and explored network effects at the various stages of the recruitment and hiring processes. Fernandez and Weinberg (1997) attempted to sort out the mechanisms by which ties lead to job offers. They found that job applicants who were referred by a current employee of the bank that they were studying had more appropriate résumés and better-timed applications and were more likely to be interviewed and ultimately receive a job offer than applicants who were not referred by a current employee. The authors postulate that two mechanisms may account for these differences: information and influence. In terms of information, social ties communicate otherwise unobtainable information about the job and employer, on the one hand, and about the applicant, on the other. For example, employee referrals increase the likelihood of a job offer by obtaining a better match between the new hire and the job requirements (Fernandez, Castilla, & Moore, 2000). Social ties are also multiple sources of influence, including a "reflected basking" effect that favorably influences the employer's view of the candidate (Seidel et al., 2000).

The role of referrals appears to be particularly important in explaining how network ties affect the job attainment prospects of women and minorities. Petersen et al. (2000) observed that most of the effects of race on hiring outcomes are explained by network disadvantages at the referral stage, before the organization comes into contact with the potential candidates. Similarly, Fernandez and Sosa (2003) found that most gender bias creeps into the hiring process via network processes associated with referral. This recent body of work indicates that job attainment is a multistage process that may be affected by different network characteristics at different stages and, as we discuss further below, begins to deepen our understanding about the interplay between networks and job attainment by pointing to mediating effects.

A more limited body of empirical evidence indicates that networks also affect compensation (Belliveau et al., 1996; Boxman et al., 1991; Burt, 1997). While the social network literature on compensation is much smaller than the compensation literature within the economics tradition, it has revealed some unique insights about the managerial wage-setting process. Jobs found through weak social ties and work-related informal contacts lead to higher income (Bridges & Villemez, 1986). However, these effects greatly diminish when controls are added for worker productivity. Consistent with Fernandez et al.'s (2000) findings, network ties appear to enhance income primarily through better job matching rather than through unfair advantage.

Network ties to insiders also appear to yield advantages when it comes to salary negotiation (Seidel et al., 2000). This mechanism explained the salary differentials between racial majorities and minorities: Members of demographic minorities, who were less likely to have existing ties to insiders, lacked negotiation power on starting salary.

The effect of networks on compensation is not restricted to the focal individual's network; relative differences in social capital between the focal individual and key decision makers appear also to have an effect. Belliveau et al. (1996) found that CEO compensation depends not only on the CEO's social network but also on the network of the compensation committee chair. Compensation committee chairs with higher absolute social capital were able to set lower CEO pay, while CEOs with relatively higher social capital than their committee chairs garnered higher compensation.

Networks also increase the likelihood and speed of promotion (Brass, 1984; Boxman et al.,

1991; Burt, 1992; Podolny & Baron, 1997). In a study of managerial careers, Burt (1992) found that managers with nonredundant networks advanced more quickly in their careers. These ties provide information and resources that actors can access in competitive situations, including mobility contests. Following Burt, Podolny and Baron (1997) argued that different networks provide different resources or benefits associated with mobility. They found that mobility is indeed enhanced by having a large, sparse network of informal ties for acquiring information and resources. But consistent role expectations are also important for performance and mobility, and these arise from a small, dense network of individuals (Podolny & Baron, 1997). As discussed further below, although these authors make theoretical arguments about mediating mechanisms, their empirical evidence concerns exclusively the direct effects of networks on promotion.

Subjective Career: Satisfaction

Networks have powerful effects on attitudes and perceptions and thus may predict a range of subjective career phenomena, including job satisfaction, perceptions of ability to take risks, feelings of belonging or acceptance, and organizational commitment (see Ibarra & Andrews, 1993; Rice, 1993, for reviews). Although empirical work on the direct link between network characteristics and career satisfaction has been scarce, recent qualitative studies (Gersick et al., 2000) and conceptual treatments (Stephens, 1994) have renewed interest in this connection.

Gersick et al. (2000) point out that valuable relationships are important in their own right as career outcomes. Their empirical study was carried out in academia where formal structures are more diffuse and career outcomes such as job attainment and tenure decisions are very closely linked to networks of relations. It would be worthwhile to explore whether certain professional contexts make subjective career outcomes more salient than objective career outcomes— for example, whether a banker values subjective career outcomes as strongly as a research scientist or musician. Similarly, it would be interesting to examine if prior attainment of objective outcomes changes the importance attached to subjective career outcomes by individuals. It is plausible that the attainment of objective career outcomes yields diminishing returns for the individual, and after attaining a certain threshold level of objective outcomes, the valence for subjective career outcomes increases as a potential path for career growth. Alternatively, a prior lack of objective career attainment might increase the valence for subjective outcomes, since subjective outcomes can serve as resources for coping with the situation of failure to attain objective career outcomes. Although arguments can be made in both directions, there is no denial of a need to explore the linkage between objective and subjective career outcomes (Khapova, Arthur, and Wilderom, Chapter 7).

Mediating Effects of Networks on Career Outcomes

As noted above, although most researchers who have studied the direct effects of networks on career outcomes have inferred mediating mechanisms, few have provided direct evidence of these effects (Seibert et al., 2001, are a notable exception); at the same time, many studies about proposed mediators, as summarized below, fail to measure career outcomes. Following evidence provided by Seibert et al. (2001) that the effects of social networks on career success are fully mediated by access to information, access to resources, and career sponsorship, we use these categories to review the literature on how networks affect career outcomes through instrumental processes and how these, in turn, affect both concrete job prospects and satisfaction with one's career. Subsequently, we review the literature on how networks affect career outcomes through psychosocial processes including socialization, mentoring and role modeling, and identity formation. In this domain, empirical evidence linking mediating processes to objective and subjective career outcomes is scarce.

Instrumental Processes

Network ties are conduits of valuable information for career success (Fernandez et al., 2000; Morrison, 2002; Podolny & Baron, 1997; Seibert et al., 2001). The literature on egocentric networks emphasizes the information benefits of personal networks characterized by weak ties, nonredundant relationships, and high range of diversity. Weak ties serve as bridges through which socially distant ideas, influences, or information reach the individual (Granovetter, 1973) and as a means for contact with people of higher status (Lin, 1982). Strong ties, in contrast, tend to connect people to similar others, and thus, a network high in strong ties is more likely to link the individual to interconnected parties and redundant resources and to confine interaction to people of similar social and occupational status. More recent work reveals, however, that in work organizations, people use strong and weak ties to access different kinds of valuable information (Shah, 1998).

People who are centrally located within organization-wide webs of interaction also have greater control over scarce resources and enjoy a broad array of benefits and opportunities unavailable to those on the periphery of the network (Brass, 1992; Burt, 1982; Ibarra, 1993). Network centrality is correlated with perceived power, promotion (Brass, 1984), and the ability to diagnose the "political landscape" (Krackhardt, 1992). Networks not only provide direct and indirect access to resources, they also serve as signals of the current or likely future status of an individual. Being perceived to have connections to the "right people," for example, has a positive effect on individuals' reputations as effective performers (Kilduff & Krackhardt, 1994). Network structure shapes career outcomes by influencing reputation in the organization (Brass, 1984) and evaluations of a person's potential (Ibarra, 1995, 1997). Social networks also affect the extent to which individuals learn, comply with, and internalize organizational and occupational norms regarding the presentation of self (Ibarra, 1999).

Kram (1985) defined sponsorship as connections that support a junior person's career advancement by opening doors and providing exposure, protection, and challenging assignments. Although the terms *mentor* and *sponsor* are often used interchangeably, we will limit our discussion here to these instrumental roles and treat mentoring relationships below under our discussion of psychosocial support (Kram, 1985). A broad literature documents the positive effects of sponsorship relationships on promotion (Dreher & Ash, 1990) and job satisfaction (Chao, Walz, & Gardner, 1992). But although scholars have begun to integrate research on social networks with work on mentoring and careers (Higgins & Kram, 2001; Seibert et al., 2001), empirical work on how networks influence sponsorship dynamics remains scarce.

Psychosocial Processes

Early socialization in the organization has a significant effect on the careers of individuals. Morrison (2002) found that the characteristics of newcomers' networks, in particular size, density, strength, range, and status, related to three different indications of learning: organizational knowledge, task mastery, and rule clarity. The characteristics of their friendship networks, in turn, affected their social integration and organizational commitment.

Social networks enable career development by providing sources of mentoring and role-modeling relationships (Higgins & Kram, 2001; Ibarra, 1999). Mentors (see also Chandler and Kram, Chapter 13) provide counseling with respect to personal and professional dilemmas; ongoing support, acceptance, and confirmation; and, eventually, mutual caring that extends beyond the requirement of the job (Kram, 1985). By modeling valued behaviors, attitudes, and skills, they help the junior person achieve competence and a clear professional identity (Morrison, 2002; Sparrowe et al., 2001). Although mentors have been identified as a critical part of a broader, career-related network, little empirical work to date has investigated what kinds of networks facilitate the formation of mentoring relationships; the link between mentoring and both objective and subjective career outcomes, however, is better established (Higgins & Kram, 2001).

The development of a professional identity has been a central theme in the careers literature (Schein, 1978). Although identity development occurs in the context of a network of relationships, little empirical research has investigated the relationship between identity and networks. Networks are not only sources of information and support, they are also the contexts in which individuals discover, construct, and transmit their identities (Coleman, 1988; Foreman & Whetten, 2002). Following Coleman (1988), a recent stream of network theory and research

considers networks as providers of social identity, conveying a sense of personal belonging within a collectivity and clear normative expectations associated with one's role (Podolny & Baron, 1997). Network ties enable individuals to improvise their identities and undergo career transitions successfully (Ibarra, 1999). Recent research has begun to study networks not as instruments for achieving preconceived career ends but as career-defining ends in and of themselves (Gersick et al., 2000).

An interesting avenue for exploring the effects of networks on careers as mediated through their effect on identity arises from recent work suggesting that different identities are advantageous at different stages in the career (Zuckerman et al., 2003). Complex, multivalent identities are advantageous because they afford greater flexibility, while simple, focused identities are advantageous because they facilitate evaluation. Focused identity is helpful in gaining entry into an arena but, subsequently, leads to increasing limitations (Zuckerman et al., 2003). In the following section, we will further examine the potential consequences of such interactions for career outcomes.

Moderators of the Effects of Networks on Careers

Among the various contingency factors that appear to moderate the effect of networks and careers, most empirical work has focused on gender and race. Studies involving the moderating effects of personality characteristics are rare, although certain psychological variables such as self-monitoring appear to influence career success through their effects on networks (Mehra, Kilduff, & Brass, 2001). Mehra et al. (2001) demonstrate that chameleon-like self-monitors are more likely to occupy central positions in a network, build strategically advantageous network positions over time, and exhibit better workplace performance. As discussed in more detail below, these studies raise important questions about how different people and groups create and benefit from social networks as their careers unfold.

Demographic variables such as gender, race, religion, occupation, and age shape the network structure and composition through availability, exclusion, and identity dynamics (Ibarra, 1992, 1995; McPherson, Smith-Lovin, & Cook, 2001; Mehra, Kilduff, & Brass, 1998; Mollica, Gray, & Trevino, 2003). In skewed organizational settings, in which white men dominate in positions of power and authority, women and minorities tend to experience both exclusionary pressures from the dominant group and heightened preferences for same-race or -gender ties as a basis for shared identity (Lawrence and Tolbert, Chapter 20; Mehra et al., 1998). Identity confirmation, however, is a network formation mechanism that operates independently of membership in a similar social category (Milton & Westphal, 2005; Mollica et al., 2003). But although homophilous (i.e., within group) ties provide access to valuable psychosocial support, they also limit access to instrumental resources (Ibarra, 1993; Mollica et al., 2003). Empirical evidence on the disadvantages of homophily is ample in studies of the career disadvantages faced by ethnic minorities (Prasad, D'Abate, and Prasad, Chapter 10). However, marked disadvantages in recruitment (Petersen et al., 2000) and salary negotiations (Seidel et al., 2000) disappear once network composition is accounted for. This means that if individuals from ethnic majorities and minorities have identical networks of personal ties, there is no further discrimination in recruitment or salary negotiations. The discrimination in recruitment and salary negotiation arises due to the differences between networks of individuals belonging to majority and minority ethnic communities.

A combination of exclusion and identity dynamics appears to lead women and minorities to develop "functionally differentiated" informal networks: one for access to task-oriented networks and resources through internal ties to the mostly white, male coworkers who populate the power structure and the other through external ties to same-gender or -race contacts that can provide both psychosocial support and nonredundant information or resources (Ibarra, 1993, 1995, 1997). They also explain findings that members of underrepresented groups particularly benefit from cosmopolitan networks. Westphal and Milton (2000) found that minority directors tend to be more influential if they have direct or indirect social network ties to majority directors through common memberships on other boards (Westphal & Milton, 2000).

Identity concerns also explain the finding that successful women and ethnic minorities tend to be well connected to both minority and majority circles and have wide-ranging networks that extend outside focal work units and firms (Ibarra, 1995; Thomas & Higgins, 1996). The pertinence of male colleagues as role models can be limited since ways of conveying competence and confidence are often gender typed (Ibarra, 1999). More generally, networks have a significant role in shaping professional identity, cultural beliefs about race and gender, and, consequently, self-perceptions that affect career-relevant decisions (Correll, 2001). However, the bulk of empirical studies have concerned themselves with the effect of demographic characteristics in regulating the relationships among networks, instrumental resources, and the objective career.

Summary of Current Research

Empirical findings have converged on several principles, including the value of diverse networks, weak and strong ties, and structural holes or bridging positions (Burt, 1992; Granovetter, 1985; Higgins & Kram, 2001). Contingency approaches followed, delineating the characteristics of people and situations that make being connected in one way or another more or less useful (Burt, 1997). These studies generally conclude that strong, redundant and weak, nonredundant ties serve different purposes (Higgins & Kram, 2001; Podolny & Baron, 1997). The former are more closely associated with the objective career and instrumental resources, while the latter enhance the subjective career and access to psychosocial resources. This picture is complicated when the moderating effects of industry or organizational demography are considered: Strong and weak, redundant and nonredundant ties appear to be differentially useful for members of minority and majority communities (Burt, 1992; Ibarra, 1995, 1997), but the effects of numerical representation (the social environment) still need to be untangled from the effects of identity (individual motives and preferences in building networks).

Among the mediating variables, the relationship between social identity and social networks has been remarkably underinvestigated. Yet social-psychological processes such as social comparison (Taylor, 1998, chap. 2, pp. 62–63), categorization (Fiske, 1998, chap. 25, pp. 364–375), and attraction (Berscheid & Reis, 1998, chap. 22), which shape social identity, provide the conceptual underpinning for prevalent network theories. Similarly, while the social networks within which individuals are embedded have effects on their social identity development, identity also affects social networks, specifically those aspects of identity that are ascribed rather than achieved. Demographic characteristics such as gender and ethnicity are particularly salient aspects of individuals' identities and can have strong effects on network ties and, through these ties, on career outcomes. The effects of career outcomes may also be indirect: Career changes, for example, can trigger identity changes that lead the focal person to seek out and build a different network configuration.

Furthermore, no empirical research has tested a dynamic model. While networks affect careers, it is also likely that career outcomes affect a person's network position and characteristics, as well as the instrumental and psychosocial mediating processes. In comparison with studies on network consequences, there are few studies on the formation of networks. In addition, studies that examine career outcomes as antecedents to the network structure are virtually absent. However, we can conjecture about certain mechanisms that might possibly mediate the effect of career outcomes on network formation and evolution. Changes in technology leading to material role changes bring about changes in interpersonal roles and, in turn, change the network structure (Barley, 1990). Organizational members who adapt faster to environmental changes such as the introduction of new technology establish more ties and attain central positions in their network (Burkhardt & Brass, 1990). The number and strength of previous ties in a group affects the probability that members will enter or leave a group (McPherson, Popielarz, & Drobnic, 1992). It is plausible that the ability to adapt to new technology and the number and strength of a person's existing ties are evolutionary outcomes of the career path the person has followed.

Also, status and reputation may mediate the link between previous career outcomes and network formation by reducing the uncertainty perceived by other actors about the focal actor's potential output quality (Podolny, 2001). Prestige, status, and visibility are, in turn, influenced by previous career success (Kotter, 1982). Thus, individuals with successful careers may enjoy high status, drawing network members toward them and leading to their further inclusion and the demand for their information and advice. However, this is an inferred mechanism based on two distinct studies (Kotter, 1982; Podolny, 2001) and can at best serve as a starting point for a much needed empirical investigation into the link from career outcomes to network formation.

In sum, we know little about how networks emerge and about the processes that produce significant changes in networks over the course of an organization's life cycle or a person's career. We suggest two reasons why the dynamic study of networks is essential to understanding the complex relationships among networks, identity, and careers. First, careers develop as people pass through transitions. Although career transitions have been conceptualized as requiring major changes in role relationships and networks, they typically have not been studied with network methods. Second, the pace of change in careers and in the organizations in which they unfold has increased such that a network perspective premised on assumptions of stability rather than change runs the risk of distracting researchers from the most promising questions.

RECIPROCAL INFLUENCES OF NETWORKS AND IDENTITY ON CAREER DYNAMICS

Although networks have been thoroughly studied as conduits for information and resources, we still know little about the role they play in creating and shaping identities. Social networks socialize aspiring members, regulate inclusion, and convey normative expectations concerning roles. As such, they confer social identity (Podolny & Baron, 1997). Furthermore, people adapt to new professional roles by experimenting with provisional selves that represent trials for possible, but not yet fully elaborated, professional identities (Ibarra, 1999). Network characteristics potentially affect the creation, selection, and retention of these possible selves because the essential processes—selective observation and imitation—are highly dependent on incumbent professional networks, from which are selected more or less adequate models for identity trials. Network characteristics such as the number and diversity of models, the emotional closeness of relationships, and the extent to which models share with the focal individual salient social and personal characteristics are likely to affect what possible selves people try and test. These networks, however, are not static inputs to the adaptation process. Rather, they evolve in concert with people's identity experiments. As new role aspirants seek more suitable models, they alter their networks and forge new relationships premised on new possible selves.

We take as given, therefore, that social identity emerges through network processes: The people around us are active players in the cocreation of who we are at work. Work identities are created, deployed, and altered in social interactions with others. Identities, therefore, change as people change roles, jobs, and organizations (e.g., Becker & Carper, 1956; Hill, 1990; Ibarra, 1999). How people negotiate, with themselves and with others, what identities they craft as they assume a new work role, and what "raw material" serves as input to that crafting process provide a promising new direction for empirical attention (Ibarra, 2003). Exploring the reciprocal interaction between networks and identities is particularly pertinent in a world in which individuals enjoy considerable choice regarding occupations, employers, and career paths (Albert, Ashforth, & Dutton, 2000).

Identity and Network Change in Career Transition

Just as few studies have examined networks over time, few attempts have been made to explore the role of networks of relationships in transporting an individual from one role to the next. Career transitions not only require the learning of new skills and competencies but also the development of new or the altering of old relationships. Thus, career transitions (Ibarra, 2006a, 2006b) are facilitated or hindered by the relational context—the set of relationships with peers, seniors, and juniors inside and outside the

firm—in which they take place (Hall, 1996; Kram, 1988).

Moving into a new career or learning a new line of work is a social learning process in which people become active participants in the practices of a social community, constructing new identities in relation to this community and its members by participating in initially peripheral yet legitimate ways (Lave & Wenger, 1991). Every entry into a new community or network of relationships represents a departure from a previous set of contacts. In career change, therefore, the process of assuming a new professional identity unfolds in parallel with a process of "becoming an ex" and is rarely a simple matter of adaptation to an existing and easily observable role but rather a process of identifying or creating one's own possibilities (Ebaugh, 1988; Ibarra, 2003). Our current theories, fashioned by empirical work on early-career socialization, well-institutionalized status passages, and easily identifiable role incumbents, are not well equipped to explain the dynamics of changing well-entrenched professional identities and making work role transitions in which both the destination (i.e., What career do I want next?) and the processes for getting there are relatively undefined at the outset.

Network studies can clarify influences on the necessary transition period that lies between role endings and beginnings, a time when identity is multiple, ill-defined, and provisional (Bridges, 1980; Turner, 1969). This transition period appears to be shaped by cumulative changes in a person's work activities, social networks, and the narratives constructed to explain these changes (Ibarra, 2006b). Ibarra (2006b) argues that career transitions are facilitated by dual network tasks—forging new connections with people and groups who can help a person in transition explore possible selves and at the same time ending or diluting the strong ties within which outdated identities had been previously negotiated. Encounters with people in alternative careers provide validation for the changes a person may be contemplating and knowledge about the feasibility and attractiveness of new options, such as freelance work (Ailon-Souday & Kunda, 2003).

Furthermore, in the process of becoming an "ex," people establish ties that are compatible with the desired future "self"; these ties precede the actual change, "pulling" the individual into the new role informally rather than being formed later as a function of the new role requirements (Ebaugh, 1988). Commitment to a new career escalates as the salience and intensity of relationships premised on that career increase; at the same time, an eroding commitment to the old career, its professional norms and referents, unfolds with decreased social contact in that sphere (Hoang & Gimeno, 2003; Ibarra, 2006a, 2006b; Stuart & Ding, 2003).

Diluting the strength of old ties and networks is as important as creating new connections. Old identities are the result of earlier identity negotiations (Swann, 1987), in which the interaction partners form images of the focal individual that are consonant with those identities and, therefore, come to expect a particular set of behaviors. With public, repeated interaction, the focal person becomes more committed, even locked in, to that identity (Schlenker, Dlugolecki, & Doherty, 1994; Swann, 1987). New or distant acquaintances, in contrast, not only provide models and safety but also form a substitute normative community within which new identities can be negotiated without sanction (Ibarra, 2003). Stuart and Ding (2003), for example, found that university scientists who were socially connected to ex-colleagues who had left academics to work in biotech firms were more likely to leave academia for biotech themselves. These extra-university ties, they argue, facilitate the formation of a reference group that condones what the scientific community sanctions (Stuart & Ding, 2003).

CONCLUSION

This chapter reviews the development of research on networks and careers to date. The field has come a long way from the simple correlational studies between network characteristics and career outcomes such as job attainment or hierarchical position. A broad range of recent research has untangled a variety of mechanisms and contingency factors that regulate the effects of networks on careers. However, there remain many riddles in the field that are yet to be resolved and many important emerging questions to be addressed. In particular, we focused

on two areas for further research and theory development. First, we argued that future network research should focus on subjective career processes and outcomes, including the development of social identity and satisfaction with one's subjective career. Second, we argued that future research is needed to explore processes of self-reinvention and examine transitional states between clearly articulated identities and well-established network roles. We suggest that social identity theory provides a fruitful foundation from which to consider the dynamics by which networks change over time. Of critical importance for further theoretical development and empirical testing are questions concerning the sequencing of identity and network changes at critical life junctures and status passages.

While these remain key questions for the future, there is a need for greater theoretical clarity in specifying the dynamics of network emergence and change. We note how punctuated equilibrium, complexity, and evolutionary theories are already informing network scholars and suggest that these theories can further inform our work (Perry-Smith & Shalley, 2003).

These promising new directions require new conceptions of networks and, potentially, new methods. Conceptually, we advocate a view of network behavior that extends beyond the currently dominant instrumental or exchange perspective. An identity perspective provides a theory of motives for this new view: Instead of acting only to maximize, or trade off, instrumental and expressive resources by forging, maintaining, and dissolving network links, people develop, manage, and change their identities. Methodologically, traditional approaches within the social sciences have tended to neglect processes of reciprocal causation and coevolution concerning individuals and the networks within which they are embedded. But these reciprocal and coevolutionary processes underlie many of the important mediating processes that determine the shape and course of careers. We conclude by suggesting that future research should shift focus from how networks provide advantage in a fixed or stable environment to how networks help people or organizations learn and change.

The networks within which people are embedded have important consequences for the success and failure of their careers, whether objectively or subjectively defined. Over the past decades we have learned a great deal about what kinds of networks produce desirable career outcomes and what situational characteristics shape the possibilities within which people and organizations construct their social networks. Future theory and research stand to benefit from a more complex, dynamic, and interactive view of how careers unfold alongside a shifting array of personal and professional relationships.

REFERENCES

Ailon-Souday, G., & Kunda, G. (2003). The local selves of global workers: The social construction of national identity in the face of organizational globalization. *Organization Studies, 24*(7), 1073–1096.

Albert, S., Ashforth, B. E., & Dutton, J. E. (2000). Organizational identity and identification: Charting new waters and building new bridges. *Academy of Management Review, 25,* 13–17.

Arthur, M. B., Hall, D. T., & Lawrence, B. S. (1989). *Handbook of career theory.* New York: Cambridge University Press.

Arthur, M. B., & Rousseau, D. M. (1996). *The boundaryless career: A new employment principal for a new organizational era.* New York: Oxford University Press.

Barley, S. R. (1990). The alignment of technology and structure through roles and networks. *Administrative Science Quarterly, 35,* 61–103.

Becker, H. S., & Carper, J. (1956). The elements of identification with an occupation. *American Sociological Review, 21,* 341–348.

Belliveau, M. A., O'Reilly, C. A., & Wade, J. (1996). Social capital at the top: Effects of social similarity and status on CEO compensation. *Academy of Management Journal, 39*(6), 1568.

Berscheid, E., & Reis, H. (1998). Attraction and close relationships. In D. Gilbert, S. Fiske, & G. Lindzey (Eds.), *The handbook of social psychology* (Vol. 2, pp. 193–281). New York: Oxford University Press.

Boxman, E. A. W., De Graaf, P. A., & Flap, H. E. (1991). The impact of social and human capital on the income attainment of Dutch managers. *Social Networks, 13,* 51–73.

Brass, D. J. (1981). Structural relationships, job characteristics, and worker satisfaction and performance. *Administrative Science Quarterly, 26,* 331–348.

Brass, D. J. (1984). Being in the right place: A structural analysis of individual influence in an organization. *Administrative Science Quarterly, 29*(4), 518–539.

Brass, D. J. (1992). Power in organizations: A social network perspective. In G. Moore & J. A. Whitt (Eds.), *Research in politics and society* (pp. 295–323). Greenwich, CT: JAI Press.

Bridges, W. (1980). *Transitions: Making sense of life's changes.* Cambridge, MA: Perseus.

Bridges, W., & Villemez, W. (1986). Informal hiring and income in the labor market. *American Sociological Review, 51,* 574–582.

Burkhardt, M. E., & Brass, D. J. (1990). Changing patterns or patterns of change: The effects of a change in technology on social network structure and power. *Administrative Science Quarterly, 35*(1), 104–127.

Burt, R. S. (1992). *Structural holes.* Cambridge, MA: Harvard University Press.

Burt, R. S. (1997). The contingent value of social capital. *Administrative Science Quarterly, 42,* 339–365.

Burt, R. S. (1982). *Toward a structural theory of action.* New York: Academic Press.

Cappelli, P. (1999). Career jobs are dead. *California Management Review, 42*(1), 146–167.

Chao, G. T., Walz, P. M., & Gardner, P. D. (1992). Formal and informal mentorships: A comparison on mentoring functions and contrast with non-mentored counterparts. *Personnel Psychology, 45*(3), 619–636.

Coleman, J. S. (1988). Social capital in the creation of human capital. *American Journal of Sociology, 94*(Suppl.), S95–S120.

Correll, S. J. (2001). Gender and the career choice process: The role of biased self-assessments. *American Journal of Sociology, 106*(6), 1691–1730.

DiMaggio, P. (1992). Political networks: The structural perspective by David Knoke. *Administrative Science Quarterly, 37*(1), 172–174.

Dreher, G. F., & Ash, R. A. (1990). A comparative study of mentoring among men and women in managerial, professional, and technical positions. *Journal of Applied Psychology, 75*(5), 539–546.

Ebaugh, H. R. F. (1988). *Becoming an ex: The process of role exit.* Chicago: University of Chicago Press.

Fernandez, R. M., Castilla, E. J., & Moore, P. (2000). Social capital at work: Networks and employment at a phone center. *American Journal of Sociology, 105*(5), 1288–1356.

Fernandez, R. M., & Sosa, L. (2003, August 16). *Gendering the job: Networks and recruitment at a call centre.* Paper presented at the annual meeting of the American Sociological Association, Atlanta, GA.

Fernandez, R. M., & Weinberg, N. (1997). Sifting and sorting: Personal contacts and hiring in a retail bank. *American Sociological Review, 62*(6), 883–899.

Fiske, S. (1998). Stereotyping, prejudice and discrimination. In D. Gilbert, S. Fiske, & G. Lindzey (Eds.), *The handbook of social psychology* (Vol. 2, pp. 357–414). New York: Oxford University Press.

Foreman, P., & Whetten, D. A. (2002). Members' identification with multiple-identity organizations. *Organization Science, 13*(6), 618–635.

Gersick, C. J. G., Bartunek, J. M., & Dutton, J. E. (2000). Learning from academia: The importance of relationships in professional life. *Academy of Management Journal, 43*(6), 1026–1044.

Granovetter, M. S. (1973). The strength of weak ties. *American Journal of Sociology, 6,* 1360.

Granovetter, M. S. (1982). The strength of weak ties: A network theory revisited. In P. V. Marsden & N. Lin (Eds.), *Social structure and network analysis* (pp. 105–130). Beverly Hills, CA: Sage.

Granovetter, M. S. (1985). Economic action and social structure: The problem of embeddedness. *American Journal of Sociology, 91,* 481–510.

Granovetter, M. S. (1995). *Getting a job: A study of contacts and careers* (2nd ed.). Chicago: University of Chicago Press.

Hall, D. T. (1996). *The career is dead: Long live the career.* San Francisco: Jossey Bass.

Higgins, M. C., & Kram, K. E. (2001). Reconceptualizing mentoring at work: A developmental network perspective. *Academy of Management Review, 26*(2), 264–298.

Hill, L. A. (1990). *Becoming a manager: Mastery of a new identity.* Boston: Harvard Business School Press.

Hoang, H., & Gimeno, J. (2003, August 1–6). *Becoming an entrepreneur.* Paper presented at the 63rd annual meeting of the Academy of Management, Seattle, WA.

Hughes, E. C. (1937). Institutional office and the person. *American Journal of Sociology, 43,* 404–413.

Ibarra, H. (1992). Homophily and differential returns: Sex differences in network structure and access in an advertising firm. *Administrative Science Quarterly, 37,* 422–447.

Ibarra, H. (1993). Network centrality, power, and innovation involvement: Determinants of technical and administrative roles. *Academy of Management Journal, 36,* 471–501.

Ibarra, H. (1995). Race, opportunity, and diversity of social circles in managerial networks. *Academy of Management Journal, 38*(3), 673–703.

Ibarra, H. (1997). Paving an alternate route: Gender differences in network strategies for career development. *Social Psychology Quarterly, 60,* 91–102.

Ibarra, H. (1999). Provisional selves: Experimenting with image and identity in professional adaptation. *Administrative Science Quarterly, 44*(4), 764–791.

Ibarra, H. (2003). *Working identity: Unconventional strategies for reinventing your career.* Boston: Harvard Business School Press.

Ibarra, H. (2006a). Career change. In J. H. Greenhaus & G. A. Callanan (Eds.), *Encyclopedia of career development* (pp. 77–82). Thousand Oaks, CA: Sage.

Ibarra, H. (2006b). *Identity transitions: Possible selves, liminality and the dynamics of career change.* Manuscript in preparation.

Ibarra, H., & Andrews, S. (1993). Power, social influence and sense making: Effects of network centrality and proximity on employee perceptions. *Administrative Science Quarterly, 38,* 277–303.

Ibarra, H., Kilduff, M., & Tsai, W. (2005). Zooming in and out: Connecting individuals and collectivities at the frontiers of organizational network research. *Organization Science, 16*(4), 359–371.

Jacoby, S. M. (1999). Premature reports of demise. *California Management Review, 42*(1), 168–179.

Kilduff, M., & Krackhardt, D. (1994). Bringing the individual back in: A structural analysis of internal market for reputation in organizations. *Academy of Management Journal, 37,* 87–108.

Kilduff, M., & Tsai, W. (2003). *Social networks and organizations.* London: Sage.

Kotter, J. P. (1982). What effective general managers really do. *Harvard Business Review, 60*(6), 156–167.

Krackhardt, D. (1992). The strength of strong ties: The importance of philos in organizations. In N. Nohria & R. G. Eccles (Eds.), *Networks and organizations: Structure form and action* (pp. 216–239). Cambridge, MA: Harvard Business School Press.

Kram, K. E. (1985). *Mentoring at work: Developmental relationships in organizational life.* Glenview, IL: Scott, Foresman.

Kram, K. E. (1988). *Mentoring at work: Developmental relationships in organizational life.* New York: University Press of America.

Lave, J., & Wenger, E. (1991). *Situated learning. Legitimate peripheral participation.* Cambridge, UK: University of Cambridge Press.

Lin, N. (1982). Social resources and instrumental action. In P. V. Marsden & N. Lin (Eds.), *Social structure and network analysis* (pp. 131–145). Beverly Hills, CA: Sage.

Lin, N., & Dumin, M. (1996). Access to occupations through social ties. *Social Networks, 8,* 365–385.

Lin, N., Ensel, W., & Vaughn, J. (1981). Social resources and the strength of ties. *American Sociological Review, 46,* 393–405.

McPherson, J. M., Popielarz, P. A., & Drobnic, S. (1992). Social networks and organizational dynamics. *American Sociological Review, 57*(2), 153–170.

McPherson, J. M., Smith-Lovin, L., & Cook, J. (2001). Birds of a feather: Homophily in social networks. *Annual Review of Sociology, 27*(1), 415.

Mehra, A., Kilduff, M., & Brass, D. J. (1998). At the margins: A distinctiveness approach to the social identity and social networks of underrepresented groups. *Academy of Management Journal, 41*(4), 441–452.

Mehra, A., Kilduff, M., & Brass, D. J. (2001). The social networks of high and low self-monitors: Implications for workplace performance. *Administrative Science Quarterly, 46*(1), 121–146.

Milton, L. P., & Westphal, J. D. (2005). Identity confirmation networks and cooperation in workgroups. *Academy of Management Journal, 48,* 191–212.

Mollica, K. A., Gray, B., & Trevino, L. (2003). Racial homophily and its persistence in newcomers' social networks. *Organization Science, 14*(2), 123–146.

Montgomery, J. (1992). Job search and network composition: Implications of the strength-of-weak-ties hypothesis. *American Sociological Review, 51,* 586–596.

Morrison, E. W. (2002). Newcomers' relationships: The role of social network ties during socialization. *Academy of Management Journal, 45*(6), 1149–1160.

Perry-Smith, J. E., & Shalley, C. E. (2003). The social side of creativity: A static and dynamic social network perspective. *Academy of Management Review, 28*(1), 89–106.

Petersen, T., Saporta, I., & Seidel, M. (2000). Offering a job: Meritocracy and social networks. *American Journal of Sociology, 106*(3), 763–816.

Podolny, J. M. (2001). Networks as pipes and prisms of the market. *American Journal of Sociology, 107,* 33–60.

Podolny, J. M., & Baron, J. N. (1997). Resources and relationships: Social networks and mobility in the workplace. *American Sociological Review, 62*(5), 673–693.

Rice, R. E. (1993). Using network concepts to clarify sources and mechanisms of social influence. In G. Barnett & W. Richards, Jr. (Eds.), *Advances in communication network analysis* (pp. 43–52). Norwood, NJ: Ablex.

Schein, E. H. (1978). *Career dynamics: Matching individual and organizational needs.* Reading, MA: Addison-Wesley.

Schlenker, B. R., Dlugolecki, D. W., & Doherty, K. (1994). The impact of self-presentations on self-appraisals and behavior: The roles of commitment and biased scanning. *Personality and Social Psychology Bulletin, 20,* 20–33.

Seibert, S. E., Kraimer, M. L., & Liden, R. (2001). A social capital theory of career success. *Academy of Management Journal, 44*(2), 219–237.

Seidel, M.-D. L., Polzer, J. T., & Stewart, K. (2000). Friends in high places: The effects of social networks on discrimination in salary negotiations. *Administrative Science Quarterly, 45*(1), 1–24.

Shah, P. P. (1998). Who are employees' social referents? Using a network perspective to determine referent others. *Academy of Management Journal, 41*(3), 249.

Sparrowe, R. T., Liden, R. C., Wayne, S., & Kraimer, M. (2001). Social networks and the performance of individuals and groups. *Academy of Management Journal, 44*(2), 316–325.

Stephens, G. K. (1994). Crossing internal career boundaries: The state of research on subjective career transitions. *Journal of Management, 20*(2), 479–501.

Stuart, T. E., & Ding, W. (2003, August). *The social structural determinants of academic entrepreneurship: An analysis of university scientists' participation in commercial ventures.* Paper presented at the Academy of Management Conference, Seattle, WA.

Swann, W. B., Jr. (1987). Identity negotiation: Where two roads meet. *Journal of Personality and Social Psychology, 53,* 1038–1051.

Taylor, S. (1998). The social being in social psychology. In D. Gilbert, S. Fiske, & G. Lindzey (Eds.), *The handbook of social psychology* (Vol. 1, pp. 58–98). New York: Oxford University Press.

Thomas, D. A., & Higgins, M. C. (1996). Mentoring and the boundaryless career: Lessons from the minority experience. In M. B. Arthur & D. M. Rousseau (Eds.), *The boundaryless career: A new employment principle for a new organizational era* (pp. 268–281). New York: Oxford University Press.

Turner, J. C. (1969). *From ritual to theatre: The human seriousness of play.* Chicago: Aldione.

Van Maanen, J., & Schein, E. H. (1979). Toward a theory of organizational socialization. In B. M. Staw & L. L. Cummings (Eds.), *Research in organizational behavior* (Vol. 1, pp. 209–264). Greenwich, CT: JAI Press.

Westphal, J. D., & Milton, L. P. (2000). How experience and network ties affect the influence of demographic minorities on corporate boards. *Administrative Science Quarterly, 45*(2), 366–398.

Zuckerman, E. W., Kim, T.-Y., Ukanwa, K., & von Rittmann, J. (2003). Robust identities or nonentities? Typecasting in the feature-film labor market. *American Journal of Sociology, 108*(5), 1018–1074.

15

The Developmental Theories

A Critical Examination of Their Continuing Impact on Careers Research

SHERRY E. SULLIVAN

MADELINE CROCITTO

C areers are embedded in the social landscape of a particular place and time. The intent of the early developmental career theories, as detailed in this chapter, was to describe the work life of the typical post–World War II professional. At that time, the average employee was a man who worked for one or two organizations until retirement, while his wife was at home caring for their children. These linear stage models, typified by the theories of Donald Super (1957) and Daniel Levinson (1978), were rooted in theories of psychological life development, such as those delineated by Freud (Solnit, 1992) and Erikson (1968).

Despite recent environmental changes and academic criticisms questioning the validity of these models (Baruch, 2004), the traditional linear career stage models still dominate much of the empirical research on careers (Arthur &

Rousseau, 1996; Feldman, 1989; Sullivan, 1999). In a review of 58 articles in five journals, Arthur and Rousseau (1996) found that 74% of the articles on careers assumed environmental stability, 76% had an intrafirm focus, and 81% had hierarchical assumptions. Similarly, Arthur, Khapova, and Wilderom's (2002) 11-year review of the career success research reported that few of the 80 articles examined, conceptualized, or operationalized success in ways meaningful to understanding nontraditional careers. For instance, only one third of the articles recognized any two-way interdependence between objective and subjective career success, with few acknowledging the influence of either career mobility or extraorganizational support on career success.

As times changed, organizational forms in most Western countries evolved from tall and multilayer to flat and lean as firms downsized to become more flexible in response to rapid technological advancements and increased global competition. In the 1970s and 1980s, managers, older workers, and the more educated—those previously less affected by downsizing—experienced the highest job loss rates (Cappelli et al., 1997). Newer career models arose, such as Michael Driver's (1979, 1982) spiral and transitory career patterns, which described nonlinear career paths. Established models also evolved and began to recognize nonlinear patterns, such as Super's addition of the recycling process whereby individuals revisited concerns of earlier career stages (Super, Zelkowitz, & Thompson, 1981). Likewise, the linear models changed in response to increasing workforce diversity, as was the case when Levinson (1978) expanded his original study of men to also study the seasons of a woman's life (Levinson, 1996). The study of careers became mainstream when best-seller lists began to include titles such as Gail Sheehy's books *Passages* (1976) and *Pathfinders* (1981), which focused on how people adapt to career and life transitions. Similarly, Carol Gilligan's (1982) controversial book *In a Different Voice* sparked increased interest in gender differences in adult development (for a review, see Gallos, 1989).

In the 1990s, high-level executives joined the ranks of the under- and unemployed while many, such as physicians, faced serious threats (e.g., managed care, rising insurance rates) to their professional independence (Crocitto, Sullivan, & Carraher, 2004). The psychological employment contract had changed from one in which workers exchanged loyalty for job security to a new contract in which workers exchanged performance for continuous learning and marketability (Altman & Post, 1996; Hall & Mirvis, 1996; Rousseau, 1989; Rousseau & Wade-Benzoni, 1995). In response to these changing workplace dynamics, scholars (Hall & Mirvis, 1996; Sullivan, 1999; Sullivan, Carden, & Martin, 1998) sought ways to reconcile the developmental models with newer, nontraditional models such as the boundaryless (Arthur & Rousseau, 1996) and protean (Hall, 1996a, 2004) models (see Valcour, Bailyn, and Quijada, Chapter 11).

The purpose of this chapter is to trace the history of these fundamental theories in order to provide a greater understanding of how the study of careers has evolved—and continues to evolve—as workplace realities have changed. We hope this chapter provides not only a review of these theories but also suggests avenues for future research into the changing nature of careers and the context in which they occur.

THEORIES OF CAREER DEVELOPMENT

There have been a large number of conceptual and empirical articles as well as books on the theories of career development. For purposes of this chapter, we have chosen to focus on the most influential writings. We begin this chapter by detailing the early theories of psychologists Erik Erikson (1968) and George Vaillant (1977). Next, we explore the theories of career and life development (Driver, 1982; Gould, 1978; Levinson, 1978; Schein, 1978; Super, 1957) as well as the models of moral development as they influence career decision making (Gilligan, 1982; Kohlberg, 1969). We close the chapter by examining the debate among scholars regarding the psychological and sociological approaches to development. This debate highlights the fact that developmental theories often consider the interplay between psychological development and the context in which the development occurs.

Historical Roots: The Psychoanalytical Approaches

We begin this chapter by examining the psychoanalytical approaches that provide the historical roots for many career theories. First, the ideas of Erik Erikson (1968) are discussed. Erikson's conceptualizations were influenced by Freud's beliefs about the effect of work on psychological growth and development (Solnit, 1992). Then, the ideas of George E. Vaillant (1977) are presented. Vaillant's work extended Erikson's thinking by using a longitudinal empirical approach to study personal development.

Erikson's Eight Stages of Psychosocial Development

One of the most enduring and influential models of adult growth is Erik Erikson's (1968) model of psychosocial development. Erikson drew on the writings of Sigmund Freud and Freud's contention that an individual's unconscious and past experiences influence choices about work, values, and other life areas (Solnit, 1992). Work, especially that which produces success as measured by hierarchical rank and income, is one of the major ways in which people attain adulthood. It is the means through which individuals become productive members of society, gain independence, develop their identity, and come to respect themselves (Moen & Wethington, 1999).

During this process of adult development, Erikson (1968, 1980) proposed that individuals must pass through eight stages, each with its attendant requirements or "dilemmas" determined by age and social demands. In each stage, the individual must balance the possible positive or negative outcomes while addressing stage-specific developmental tasks. The eight stages of Erikson's model are as follows: Stage 1, trust versus mistrust; Stage 2, autonomy versus shame and doubt; Stage 3, initiative versus guilt; Stage 4, industry versus inferiority; Stage 5, identity versus role confusion; Stage 6, intimacy versus isolation; Stage 7, generativity versus stagnation; and Stage 8, ego integrity versus despair.

Erikson anticipated that problems in each of these stages hamper a person's movement toward mental health in adulthood. Thus, we think that his ideas may be useful in understanding career outcomes such as job satisfaction, self-efficacy, and performance, as well as negative work behaviors. For example, individuals who do not develop trust in Stage 1 are less confident and are more likely to make career choices that do not match their capabilities. They may be mistrustful of authority as well as of attempts to improve their work life through human resource interventions such as training and development. Individuals who do not develop autonomy in Stage 2 may simply accept the first job offer they receive, without pursuing alternative, perhaps better, opportunities. For the child, problems in this stage often result in wrongdoing and shame; for the adult, unresolved issues associated with Stage 2 could result in insubordination, antisocial authority relationships, and sabotage. In Stage 3, individuals identify with role models and become aware of gender identification.

Gender affects career interests, often causing women to choose occupations that result in less pay, less power, and fewer avenues for advancement (Bell, 2005). Those who have unresolved issues from Stages 4 and 5 may feel inferior and have learning problems.

The stages most relevant to studying careers start at Stage 4. During Stage 4 (from age 6 to puberty), children start school with a sense of whether adults can or cannot be trusted. The children also determine to what extent they may rely on themselves. Over time and through exploration, children attain levels of autonomy and capability which may range from low to high. It is at Stage 5, identity versus role confusion, when individuals begin to focus on career concerns. In this stage, young adults (approximately ages 19 to 25) begin to think about what occupations to prepare for while creating sexual, religious, and political identities. Children are especially concerned with learning about work and play, division of labor, and opportunity. Thus, problems that occur in Stages 4 and 5 may cause individuals to experience difficulties in developing a clear occupational identity. If an individual forms a clear identity in this stage, then rich relationships, including those with work colleagues, are developed. This formation of an adult identity along with separation from one's parents is associated with career decidedness, exploration, confident decision making, and the ability to engage in career-related decisions and tasks.

Erikson identified Stages 6 to 8 as the stages of adulthood. Although in Stage 6 he focused his discussion on interpersonal love, the search for intimacy could also include the deepening of work relationships, especially in light of the increasing number of hours many employees devote to their work as well as the frequency of office romances and friendships. His later work (Erikson, 1980) addressed this stage in terms of developing relationships with others, which is crucial to becoming an effective leader and team player, as well as building the networks necessary for career success. The emphasis on relationships, teamwork, and networking are themes highlighted in many of the more recent career theories (Arthur & Rousseau, 1996; Hall, 1996b; Mainerio & Sullivan, 2006; Ibarra and Deshpande, Chapter 14).

In Stage 7, generativity versus stagnation (approximately ages 25 to 50), individuals develop integrity, take their place in the world, and become outwardly focused on contributing to society. If earlier stages have been successfully navigated, during Stage 7, individuals develop ego integrity and wisdom while learning to accept themselves and others. These individuals often become mentors and respected keepers of organizational, industry, or occupational knowledge. Successful transition through Stages 6 and 7 may explain why some individuals become leaders and make a good match between occupational choice and personal abilities and preferences, while others falter and have unhappy work lives. Individuals who effectively reach this point of personal development may be better able to handle and make choices about career events such as career transitions and reinventions triggered by downsizing, outsourcing, or other environmental factors. In Stage 8, individuals accept responsibility for their lives and acknowledge having passed through the previous stages. Failing successful passage through these stages, individuals may despair and be unable to develop new lives. In this stage, individuals will not tolerate work environments incongruent with their personal ethical codes. They may leave their employer, change occupations, or try to lead change efforts within the organization. People in Stage 8 wish to leave a legacy and may engage in volunteer activities that could dovetail nicely with corporate social responsibility efforts.[1]

Overall, Erikson is recognized for offering a useful framework of development activities necessary for a person to grow into—and throughout—adulthood. His theory is supported by subsequent research (i.e., Gould, 1978; Vaillant, 1977) and may also be useful for understanding the role of careers in personal development (Greenhaus, Callanan, & Godshalk, 2000). Like current thinking on life-long learning (e.g., Hall, 1996a; Mallon & Walton, 2005), Erikson envisioned continual adult development after middle age in the form of reaching out to others as a mentor or sage and/or assuming a position of leadership. He also acknowledged the role of society and in a democratic society the freedom of self-determination in developing a healthy personality. However, despite the many positive aspects of his theory, Erikson neither addressed

how problems in early developmental stages may be overcome later in life nor entertained the idea that some stages might be passed over.

In the next section, we examine the ideas of George E. Vaillant (1977). Like Erikson, Vaillant accepts Freud's concept of mental health as the ability to work and love. In contrast to Erikson, Vaillant focused more directly on careers and offered an empirical examination of how personal development is or is not accomplished.

Vaillant's Theory of Adaptation to Life

Building on Erikson's (1968) ideas, Vaillant (1977) proposed that men with good mental health, successful relationships, and flourishing careers make use of mature adaptation psychological mechanisms and personal relationships to continue to develop throughout their lives. To test his ideas, Vaillant (1977, 2002) used the longitudinal Grant Study database to study male Harvard University alumni as they moved through a modified version of Erikson's stage model. Noting that there was as much as a two-decade gap between Erikson's Stage 6 Intimacy and Stage 7 Generativity, Vaillant added the stage of "Career Consolidation" (starting at approximately age 30) between these two stages to better describe what occurs in male development from the second decade through the fourth decade of life. During the Career Consolidation stage, men replace their parents with other role models who can contribute to their career success. Material success becomes a driving factor.

According to Vaillant, in the Career Consolidation stage, men experience two conflicts: (1) the conflict between upward mobility and settling down and (2) the conflict between conformity and the creation of career identification. Having formed close personal relationships beyond the immediate family through marriage or via participation in a group such as a religious group or the military, men devote themselves to their careers. The emphasis is on getting ahead, with men concentrating on finding a mentor, building work competencies, conforming to job expectations such as climbing the organizational ladder, setting goals, and being competitive. Although there is little questioning of personal or career choices, there is a conflict, however, between decisions such as relocating for a promotion or better job and settling down. Men make the choice to sacrifice adolescent ideas and further self-exploration and instead choose to play by "the rules of the game" in an effort to attain career success, money, and possessions. The overriding goal is to conform to societal expectations of what successful men are supposed to do and be while forming an identity of who they are and what path they take. For example, one of the men in Vaillant's study was an artist/painter who as an adolescent didn't know what he wished to paint. Using his skills for commercial purposes such as advertising was an anathema to him. Therefore, he chose to become an editor and journalist. Only when he reached age 50 did he recognize what he wanted to paint and redirected his energies toward his earlier interests, to public acclaim (Vaillant, 1977, p. 214). Thus, the preferred career identification was subsumed in the need to earn a living and learn more about oneself while meeting social expectations. Only with self-knowledge, personal growth, and the use of mature coping mechanisms that occur with life development will the preferred and perhaps "true" career identity of an individual finally emerge.

Vaillant (2002) also considered later-stage adult development beyond what is commonly accepted as midlife, as well as the joys of active engagement through work or other activities. He argued that adult development involves being a "Keeper of the Meaning"—that is, remembering one's culture and involvement in the community. We think that Vaillant's ideas on later-stage development are applicable to the growing number of professionals seeking career change in today's work environment, opting out of corporate life (see Mainiero & Sullivan, 2006), as well as those individuals retiring from work but continuing to contribute their talent to community service.

In sum, while Vaillant acknowledged that adult development may not be orderly, he subscribed to the idea that personal development comes from successful use of the adaptive mature coping mechanisms of altruism (empathy), creative sublimation, suppression (patience), and humor. Although his work builds on, and supports, the scholarship of Erikson, Vaillant placed greater emphasis on the contribution of work and careers to adult development. He observed that one must have good

social skills in order to have a career and suggested that the four career criteria of contentment, compensation, competence, and commitment be used to evaluate successful adult development. He also argued that individuals are capable of overcoming difficulties, such as a difficult childhood, to attain career success through the personal and social development gained from work experiences.

Unlike Erikson, Vaillant (1977, 2002) also included women in his later studies.[2] He proposed that although there were gender differences in development (e.g., in retirement, women were better able to develop their creativity than men), for the most part, men and women followed the same stages. He also examined the potential role of social factors in explaining life events (e.g., comparison of male Harvard graduates with Inner City men) and observed that few of the men who were mentally healthy were sidetracked by physical health problems or happenstance such as an accident. Furthermore, he ascertained that a person could overcome social factors and also integrate career and family responsibilities.

Vaillant (1977, 2002) further acknowledged how the environment influences a person's life path and described incorporating Clausen's (1972) four life-course factors to examine the men in his initial study (p. 462). The first life factor comprises the benefits afforded by social class, age, gender, and other demographics along with major social events such as an economic depression. The second life factor is personal effort. The third life factor comprises the types of guidance and social support offered by mentors, parents, and role models. The fourth life factor combines personal resources such as health and natural abilities; Vaillant included defense mechanisms in this fourth category. Vaillant admitted choosing a sample that was similar in terms of the first two factors (i.e., they were white, males, U.S. born and educated at a renowned institution, and with an analogous commitment to personal effort and achievement). He was also able to examine childhood psychological problems, health, the climate in the household, relationships with parents and siblings, and high school achievements. Those men who had difficult childhoods, strained relationships with parents, and few relationships with others were unhappy, anxious, in poorer health, and in later years, they had unsuccessful work lives and marriages (if indeed they ever did marry). Simply, those without love and guidance had fewer personal resources to help them, which was evident in their careers and personal life. Furthermore, both Erikson and Vaillant in their later work credited the role of creativity and social support in longevity and life satisfaction, which is consistent with contemporary thoughts about relational careers (for a description of relational careers, see Schultheiss, 2003).

Identity Formation and Career Development

Both Erikson and Vaillant recognized the importance of work in identity formation. For example, Erikson (1968) suggested that career development is one of the central challenges to the process of identity formation. Furthermore, both identity and career development are influenced by psychological and sociological factors, including personality, behavior, learning, expectancies, communication, coping, interpersonal relationships, technology (Miller, 1988), cohort effects, and individual differences (Baltes & Nesselroade, 1984). Given this interplay between psychological and sociological factors, measures designed to assess vocational choices and chart a career course may support psychological development and provide information about potential careers (Crocitto & Sullivan, 2005), especially to individuals without knowledge of the full range of occupational and educational opportunities and those with few economic resources (Bell, 2005).

One of the most recognized theories of career decision making is Holland's model of vocational choice (1973, 1985). Holland's theory and its related measure, the Holland Vocational Preference Inventory, are well-known to scholars and practitioners alike. Because the Vocational Preference Inventory has logical and measurement functionality, it has been used by career counselors in a variety of settings and has been the subject of much research scrutiny (Sharf, 1997).

Similar to Erikson and Vaillant, Holland suggested that traits, parental preferences, and childhood experiences create natural preferences, which, over time, lead to the development of interests and coping styles as well as occupational preferences (Savickas, Chapter 5; Kidd, Chapter 6; Baruch, 2006). Holland (1973, 1985, 1997) predicted that individuals will seek out work environments that match with the six personality types he identified (Realistic, Investigative, Artistic, Social, Enterprising, and Conventional). Failure to work in a situation with good personality-environment fit results in role conflict (Latack, 1981), whereas a good fit generates satisfaction and performance (Holland, 1985, 1997). Holland's six types have been incorporated into the Strong-Campbell Interest Inventory (Hansen & Campbell, 1985), which is often used in the college setting (Tomlinson & Evans-Hughes, 1991), the time at which most individuals are developing their self-identification and evaluating their career options. The assistance of career counselors using these measures is likely most useful in Erikson's Stage 5, the life point at which an individual considers how a career contributes to personal identity.

In addition to Holland's measure, career counselors have used a number of other tools to assist individuals with their career development. For instance, the Myers-Briggs Type Indicator (MBTI), which also links personality to occupational choice, is one such widely used instrument. The MBTI classifies personality types based on a four-letter code that describes preferences by which people receive information and evaluate their environment. Combinations of these "types" (extrovert-introvert, sensitive-intuitive, thinker-feeler, judger-perceiver) result in a set of personality traits, interests, values, needs, and "habits of mind" (Myers, 1980). Research has found that these personality types are related to occupational preferences (Kroeger, 2002) as well as other career outcomes (e.g., Amundson, Borgen, & Tench, 1995; Seibert, Kraimer, & Crant, 2001). Career counselors regularly employ the MBTI in combination with the Strong Vocational Interest Inventory to help clients connect their personalities (as measured by the MBTI) with their interests (as measured by the Strong inventory) as well as to help clients gain better information about themselves and appropriate labor markets (Healy, 2000). Counselors are also beginning to use newer measures, such as the Intelligent Career

Card Sort (ICCS), to assist in career development. The ICCS taps personality traits and characteristics that individuals employ to gain self-knowledge. This self-knowledge is used in developing the goals and action steps to create a successful career strategy (Wnuk, Amundson, Arthur, & Parker, 2003). Certainly, the type of information and the social support provided by career counseling and coaching is useful at the start of one's career (Erikson's Stage 5) and through the formation of a career identity and work relationships (Erikson's Stage 6). Likewise, an individual who has difficulty in the Career Consolidation stage (Vaillant, 1977) and has taken a step back to rethink earlier decisions may find these instruments useful. These tools may assist the individual in decision making and, if necessary, reorienting a career choice and strategy, especially if he or she realizes that a career choice is inconsistent with a preferred career identity.

Developmental scholars, such as Erikson and Vaillant, have acknowledged the importance of career decisions on the identity formation of young adults. It is of continuing importance for scholars to examine the effects of personality and individual differences on career choices and how such choices are constrained by sociological factors. Moreover, because of the widespread use of many of these theory-based counseling tools, researchers may find that career counselors are a rich source of information and ideas about developmental processes. For instance, the assistance of career counselors using these theories and measures may mitigate sociological constraints (e.g., little education, lack of role models, limited opportunities) by exposing individuals to a broader range of career possibilities and encouraging greater personal growth.

In the next section, we review the stage theories of career development. These theories discuss how individuals move through predictable stages across the life span.

STAGE THEORIES OF CAREERS

There are a number of well-known stage theories, including the works of Super (1957), Levinson (1978), Gould (1978), and Schein (1978). We begin by examining Donald Super's

(1957) theory of career stages. Super moves beyond the earlier psychological perspectives of Erikson and Vaillant to a more focused study of personal development through career decisions across one's life.

Super's Linear Career Stage Model

Donald Super's (1957) theory of career stages used a life-span approach to describe how individuals implement their self-concept through vocational choices. Super suggested that the process of choosing an occupation that permits maximum self-expression occurs over time and can be summarized in four career stages:

1. *Exploration,* a period of engaging in self-examination, schooling, and the study of different career options

2. *Establishment,* a period of becoming employed and finding a niche

3. *Maintenance,* a period of holding on to one's position and updating skills

4. *Disengagement,* a period of phasing into retirement

Research on Super's theory supports the idea of implementing the self-concept through one's career (Osipow, 1983) and differences in attitudes and behaviors across the career stages (e.g., Cohen, 1991; Lynn, Cao, & Horn, 1996; Pogson, Cober, Doverspike, & Rogers, 2003; Stumpf & Rabinowitz, 1981; Weeks, Moore, McKinney, & Longnecker, 1999). Much of this research, however, has been cross-sectional (Hackett, Lent, & Greenhaus, 1991), used age as a proxy for psychological career stage (Chao, 1986; Ornstein & Isabella, 1990), or employed inconsistent measures of the stages across studies (Cooke, 1994; Greenhaus & Parasuraman, 1986; Hackett et al., 1991). Researchers have often drawn on Super's theory as a post hoc explanation for their findings rather than for hypothesis testing (Hackett et al., 1991).

Because of the problems inherent in conducting longitudinal research, adequate tests of Super's suggested linear pattern have not been performed, causing many to question whether an uninterrupted progression depicts reality (Mainiero & Sullivan, 2006; Reitman &

Schneer, 2005; Schneer & Reitman, 1993) and whether cultural norms affect how careers unfold (Sullivan, 1999). In Western societies, for example, a growing number of individuals—both men and women—are taking themselves off the fast track (Ibarra, 2003), de-emphasizing the linear upward movement that was prized at the time Super conducted his research. Moreover, recent research suggests that while a modified linear career path may hold for most men of the Baby Boom generation, thus providing support for Super's theory, alternative career paths may be more likely for women and men of the X and Y Generations (Mainiero & Sullivan, 2005, 2006). Super himself was aware that some individuals will have nonlinear, interrupted career paths, and that these individuals would, in his term, *recycle*—that is, return to the issues of early career stages (Super et al., 1981).

Although Super's addition of the recycling process incorporated more flexibility into his original linear model, relatively little empirical or conceptual work has been published on it (Bejian & Salomone, 1995; Morrison, 1977; Smart & Peterson, 1997). Super wrote very little about the process (Sullivan, 1999); thus, there was little to guide future research on career recycling. To help further define the concept and establish a research agenda, Sullivan, Martin, Carden, and Mainiero (2003) conducted an exploratory, in-depth study of 15 recyclers. Unlike some previous research (Morrison, 1977), they did not view recycling as a maladaptive process but instead saw it as one way to explain interruptions in linear career paths. These researchers detailed the likely causes of recycling (organizational changes, personal plateaus, and personal crises) and common characteristics of those who recycle (low risk aversion, optimism), suggesting future avenues of study. They refined Super's description by implicitly stating that recycling is most likely to occur with mature individuals, especially those in mid-career, and that it is highly unlikely that younger individuals, especially those in the early stages of their careers, will recycle.

Although Super (1957) contended that his theory was applicable to both genders, studies have not supported its generalizability to women (Ornstein & Isabella, 1990). Super (1987, 1992) updated his ideas with the development of the "Life-Career Rainbow" model, which describes how individuals differ in the amount of commitment and participation they devote to six major roles (child, student, leisurite, citizen, worker, and homemaker) across the career stages. For example, at the peak of their careers, some individuals may engage in only two roles (e.g., homemaker and worker), while others at the same age and stage may engage in many roles. Choices regarding commitment to these roles cause various levels of role conflict, stress, and self-fulfillment. Super's Life-Career Rainbow model better captures the experiences of individuals with discontinuous careers, especially women, and better recognizes work and non-work roles—and the potential conflict among them—than his original model. His revisions are similar to Powell and Mainiero's (1992, 1993) "River of Time" model, which describes how women place themselves somewhere on a continuum where at different times they emphasize their career, their relationships, or balance both.

Besides concerns regarding the generalizability of Super's model to women, its applicability to the contemporary workplace has also been questioned (Hall, 1996b; Ornstein & Isabella, 1993; Osterman, 1996; Weick, 1996). Although Super's model implies long-term employment with one or two firms, evidence suggests that workers in industrialized countries change their jobs much more frequently (Arthur & Rousseau, 1996). Similarly, Super's (1957) theory emphasized success as defined by hierarchical rank and financial gains, but individuals may actually measure success using more subjective measures. The number of individuals focusing on subjective rather than objective success may be increasing, as more people choose careers outside the borders of traditional organizations (Gunz & Heslin, 2005) or search for the work they were destined to do—that is, their true calling (Hall & Chandler, 2005). For example, in a qualitative study of 18 male and 18 female managers, Sturges (1999) reported that individuals, especially women and older managers, used a range of internal and intangible criteria (e.g., personal achievement and recognition) to define success. Given the changes in the work landscape, especially the increase in nonlinear career patterns, scholars have called for a more detailed study of career success, suggesting that because success is a multifaceted concept (Gunz & Heslin, 2005), the interplay between objective and subjective success needs to be examined more closely (Arthur et al., 2002; Nicholson & De Waal-Andrews, 2005; for a detailed discussion of career success, see also Judge and Kammeyer-Mueller, Chapter 4; for a recent meta-analysis of objective and subjective career success, see Ng, Eby, Sorensen, & Feldman, 2005).

There have been dramatic changes in the workplace since Super's theory originated in 1957, and Super and various associates have revised his earlier work to incorporate some of these changes. A more recent conceptualization of his approach (1) accepts that people change over time as individuals learn about occupations and themselves; (2) acknowledges the role of social factors such as socioeconomic background, education, social issues (e.g., gender and race stereotypes and bias), and opportunities in career development; (3) describes career development as an assemblage of learning experiences and social interactions across time; and (4) accommodates individual differences in work and life satisfaction, even considering that work may be a peripheral means to implement one's self-concept (Super, Savickas, & Super, 1996).

Like Super, other scholars have also suggested alterations to Super's theory in order to account for changes in the work environment. For example, instead of one set of career stages as depicted by Super, Hall, and Mirvis (1996) proposed multiple, shorter learning cycles over the life span, which are driven by constant learning and mastery rather than by chronological age.[3] Thus, an individual's career will be characterized by a series of mini-stages of exploration-trial-mastery-exit across functions, organizations, and other work boundaries. Likewise, Sullivan et al. (1998) developed "The Career Grid," which differentiates career types along two continua: transferability of competencies (i.e., how portable or organization specific an individual's knowledge, skills, and abilities are) and internal work values (i.e., the relatively stable goals individuals attempt to achieve through their careers). The Career Grid integrates Super's theory with the boundaryless careers literature (Arthur & Rousseau, 1996) by acknowledging that some individuals may still have traditional careers as delineated by Super, while others may have more discontinuous careers.

Super's research has had a great impact on the field of careers and personal development. His work continues to influence scholars as indicated by Power and Rothausen's (2003) mid-career development model, which is based on Super's maintenance stage (see also Power, 2006). In addition to Super's contributions to the field, his research provided interesting insights into the evolution of theory development and how an individual's own life experiences affect research interests and ideas. For example, as a young man, Donald Super characterized the last stage of the career as decline, a time when a worker's productivity and contributions decreased. As did Erikson (1997) and Valliant (2002), Super in his later years reflected on his own life journey and revisited his earlier work. He renamed the career stage of decline "disengagement." His viewpoint changed; he recognized that some individuals might decline but that others, like himself, maintained their level of performance or increased their contributions to society.

Another scholar whose impact on the study of career development rivaled that of Donald Super was psychologist Daniel Levinson (1978). Like Super, Levinson proposed a stage model to describe how men develop over the course of their life spans. Unlike Super, however, Levinson (1996) expanded his work to include the examination of women's life stage development. In the next section, we detail Levinson's research.

Levinson's Life Stage Model

In his book *Seasons of a Man's Life,* Daniel Levinson (1978, 1986) featured a model of life development based on chronological age. Using in-depth interviews of 40 men aged 35 to 45, he maintained that life structures were defined by alternating periods of stability—in which individuals pursue goals, values, and related activities—and periods of transition—in which the goals and activities of the previous period are reappraised. The typical transition period lasted about 5 years, and periods of stability lasted about 5 to 7 years. These periods of stability permitted individuals to focus on non-work issues, develop work skills, and mentally prepare themselves for the next transition period. Levinson outlined three life eras:

1. *Preadulthood* (birth to age 22), which established the foundation for responsible adulthood

2. *Early adulthood* (ages 22 to 45), which is characterized by significant decisions regarding marriage, occupation, and lifestyles as well as a focus on achieving career goals, establishing mentor relationships, and managing the stress of the midlife transition

3. *Middle adulthood* (ages 40 to 65), which is characterized by a reduction in career investments, changes related to retirement and family roles as well as a focus on evaluating one's life while confronting one's own death

A fourth and fifth life era, late adulthood (ages 65 to 80) and late late adulthood (age 80+), were recognized by Levinson but not detailed.

Levinson reported that as men progress through these life stages, they typically have the assistance of two important individuals: the mentor and the "special woman." The mentor, usually an older, more established member of the work organization, takes the young man under his wing, provides career advice, and protects him from political harm. This mentoring relationship is often very intense, much like a master-apprentice relationship whereby a young man learns the craft at the feet of a maestro. In addition to the mentor, the man also has the help of the special woman, his stay-at-home wife. His wife cares for him and their children, creating a safe haven for him to return to at the end of his long workday. The special woman supports his climb up the corporate ladder in many ways, perhaps by hosting dinner parties for his bosses, participating in charity activities with the other company wives, or by placing few demands on her husband so he can focus his energy on his work.

The mentor and the special woman may be of particular assistance to the man as he experiences the uncertainties of the midlife crisis. Of all the transitions described by Levinson (1978), his ideas on the midlife crisis have garnered the greatest interest, especially in the popular press. Levinson characterized the midlife crisis as a time in which a man experiences crisis because he has realized that his career dreams may not be realized and that his life is half over. Unfortunately, the midlife crisis has become negatively stereotyped as a time in which men behave erratically and try to recapture their youth, as depicted in popular movies such as *10* and *The First Wives Club*. Although some men may have difficulties with midlife issues, others may view it as an opportunity to reevaluate their careers and switch to a different line of work (see Crocitto, 2006; Power, 2006). The midlife crisis, as well as other parts of Levinson's theory, have been widely criticized and challenged (Cytrynbaum & Crites, 1989; Dannefer, 1984). For example, Lawrence (1980) found that relatively few individuals actually experience a midlife crisis. Personal discomfort at this point in one's life may also be attributed to work-related factors such as increased competition from younger workers and organizational circumstances (Nickle & Maddox, 1988).

Like Super's (1957) theory, another major challenge to Levinson's theory is its applicability to women (Cytrynbaum & Crites, 1989). In one of the earliest tests of its generalizability to women, Roberts and Newton (1987) reported that although women progressed through similar periods of stability and transitions as men, they tended to have "split dreams." Unlike men who had "the dream" that focused on the career and was supported by relationships with the mentor and the special woman, women, by age 30, changed their focus from either career to family or vice versa. Similarly, in a much anticipated follow-up to his book on men's development, Levinson (1996) conducted in-depth interviews with 45 female academics, homemakers, and business professionals between the ages of 35 and 45.[4] He found that women progress through the same age-related stages as men but face "gender splitting" (i.e., cultural, social stereotypes, and sexism). Thus, while the men Levinson studied focused on their career goals and developed relationships that complemented these goals (e.g., the special woman and mentor who supported the career), the women often had to struggle with marriages or other relationships that were obstacles to their development.

Levinson's life structure approach provides a useful framework for studying the career processes of executive women, because it examines the impact of social change on women's developmental tasks and career development (e.g., Gersick & Kram, 2002). We suggest that future examinations and revisions of Levinson's model recognize key gender differences in career experiences, including time expectations related to child rearing (Heckert et al., 2002) and household duties (Coltrane, 2000); the importance of organizational support systems (Forret & de Janasz, 2005) and job characteristics (Heckert et al., 2002) as they relate to work/family balance; the relative influence of a partner on career saliency (Moya, Exposito, & Ruiz, 2000) and financial rewards (Schneer & Reitman, 2002); and the impact of organizational cultures, which discourage work/family balance (Van Vianen & Fischer, 2002) and impede the career advance of women through discriminatory practices (Murrell & James, 2001; see also Prasad, D'Abate, and Prasad, Chapter 10). Likewise, given that Levinson's model assumed that the man will have a stay-at-home wife, further investigation of the applicability of Levinson's model to men in dual-career marriages, who are stay-at-home fathers, as well as men who are single parents, is needed.

On the whole, there has been relatively little empirical research on Levinson's theory (Swanson, 1992), with little support for the link between specific age groups and attitudes (Ornstein & Isabella, 1990; Smart & Peterson, 1994). In addition to potential differences due to gender, a number of factors may influence the link between age and proposed stage-related attitudes and behaviors, including individuals who are atypical in their procession through the stages due to increased time pursuing advanced education and professional training; individuals who start their careers later than their peers or experience career interruptions due to family demands, including downshifting or opting out of the workforce (Mainiero & Sullivan, 2005, 2006); and individuals who match their attitudes and behaviors to those of their older or younger work group (Cleveland & Shore, 1992).

Additional research on Levinson's, as well as other stage theories, using multiple measures of age (e.g., chronological age, professional tenure, age relative to other members of work group or profession) is needed. Similarly, rather than focusing on Levinson's theory as a stage model, it has been suggested that the theory be viewed as one of individual accommodation, with emphasis placed on how identity changes instead of how age transitions occur (e.g., Greller & Simpson, 1999).

Unlike some previous theories of development, Levinson's research suggested differences in the life development of men and women. In a similar vein, Roger Gould (1978) examined the adult development of both men and women and also identified important gender differences in how careers are perceived. Gould's ideas are described in the next section.

Gould's Views on Adult Stage Development

Roger L. Gould (1978), an academic psychiatrist and psychoanalyst, examined the place of work and career in adult development. Similar to Levinson, he grouped attitudes toward work by age, with developmental tasks varying by decade. During their 20s, men use work as the major way to differentiate themselves from their parents and become an adult. During their 30s, men seek career success. Analogous to Vaillant's (1977) phase of Career Consolidation and Levinson's (1978) "Becoming One's Own Man," Gould noted that the 30s are the time of career commitment or change, with some men believing that work will somehow protect them from misfortune and maladies. In their 40s, men realize that the belief they held in their 30s that "work success will make me happy" is a false assumption. Men become more in tune with their inner selves, are more likely to engage in mentoring, feel rejuvenated about work or—failing that—realize that they need to change careers. Gould found that men lacking a connection between their inner selves and work are more likely to have low levels of performance and exhibit other negative work behaviors, thus supporting Vaillant's (1977) findings.

Women, in contrast, had different career experiences. Gould argued that childhood socialization results in women wishing to maintain a traditional family role. Some women may fear career success because they believe it will lead to isolation. Women who choose careers in their 20s may forgo having children until later in life when they feel the pressure of their biological clock. Others without children face the quandary of being unable to fully commit to their careers because they feel they should have children. Some women in dual-career situations may hire assistance with household tasks or may temporarily leave the workplace. They may feel pressure about their workforce participation or attribute their internal conflict to their husbands.

In addition to gender differences in adult development, Gould also recognized class differences by distinguishing between the jobs of the working class and the careers of the middle class. For example, working-class women must be employed in order to financially support their families. These women may feel overburdened by trying to simultaneously work and rear children or may view their children as the highlight of their lives. Working-class men may turn to hobbies to replace the challenge and achievement no longer available to them through their jobs. In comparison with the jobs of the working class, those in the middle class talk of "a career" and view it as a means of improving their quality of life; these individuals never completely scale their self-imposed ladder of upward mobility. Social events, such as golf and attending country club events, become opportunities for career advancement. The meaning of work, especially for men, is a recognition of how the self is transformed through work-related choices. These work-related decisions convey inner motivations and make use of the individual's talents and capabilities. Career choices are a means of life development, with individuals finding self-fulfillment through their careers (Gould, 1978).

In general, both Gould and Super viewed career progression as a result of expressing one's self-concept through a series of career choices. Although Super, Levinson, and others focused on the careers of professionals, Gould differentiated between the experiences of the working class and those of the middle class—a distinction that many believe is even greater today as the labor force becomes polarized between highly technically skilled professionals and those with lower skill levels. As the study of careers evolved, Gould, Levinson, Super, and others recognized the impact of contextual factors (e.g., childhood experiences, societal norms) on an individual's progression through life/career stages. Edgar Schein (1978) extended the work of these previous researchers by introducing an organizational element to the study of adult development. His focus on the effect of the individual's movement within organizations on the individual's career stage progression is presented in the next section.

Schein's Career Dimensions and Stages

Edgar Schein (1978) postulated that individuals move through three career dimensions: (1) the hierarchical dimension of upward movements within the organization; (2) the functional or technical dimension, which follows the development of additional capabilities and knowledge; and (3) the inner circle dimension in which individuals move toward the center as they become trusted members of a profession, occupation, or organization. Individuals move through these dimensions in a series of stages and related tasks. Schein (1978) identified the following stages:[5]

- *Stage 1* consists of childhood, adolescence, and early adulthood (birth to age 21). Activities in this stage involve seeking role models, knowing one's needs, interests, capabilities, values, and goals, and finding opportunities to use and develop them.
- *Stage 2* consists of entry into the work environment (ages 16 to 25). Appropriate activities include locating, applying, and negotiating the job search process to successfully make a realistic job choice.
- *Stage 3* is composed of basic training (same as Stage 2, ages 16 to 25). The individual becomes regulated to the work world, learns how to work with coworkers and a boss, and adapts to the norms of a given culture.
- *Stage 4* consists of full membership in early career (ages 17 to 30). The individual pursues development of expertise and responsibility to improve performance and working relationships with colleagues and a mentor as well as the reconciliation of the desire for independence with the demands of organizations.
- *Stage 5* includes the mid-career transition and focuses on full career membership (age 25+). It involves making decisions about becoming a specialist or generalist, continuous learning, attaining visibility and responsibility, and arranging for long-range career goals.

- *Stage 6* includes the mid-career crisis (ages 35 to 45). It is a period of reassessment of where one stands in a career and the place of a career in one's life space.
- *Stage 7* considers two possible avenues: (1) becoming a leader or (2) assuming the role of a nonleader (age 40 to retirement). Those who assume the role of a leader become responsible for long-range planning and developing future leaders (age is less relevant to this avenue). Those who assume the role of a nonleader become mentors, build interests and skills, and assume more responsibility while accepting a lesser role at work to seek personal development elsewhere.
- *Stage 8* consists of decline and disengagement (age 40 to retirement; age varies with individual differences and circumstances). It involves acclimating to a diminished role and the lessening impact of work on one's life.
- *Stage 9* includes the last phase of retirement (may start at age 50 or 60). It involves a greater adjustment to a self-identity derived from activities and learning beyond work and the use of knowledge and experience to benefit others.

According to Schein (1978), as individuals navigate through these stages, career anchors internal to the person act as both driving and constraining forces on career decisions. Schein believed that if individuals are placed in situations that are incongruent with their values, which fail to meet their needs or in which they are unlikely to triumph, then they will be "pulled back" by their anchor to a situation in which they are more likely to meet success. Schein defined a career anchor as the pattern of an individual's self-perceived talents, values, and motives. Relying on interviews of 44 male alumni of Massachusetts Institute of Technology, he delineated eight such career anchors: technical, managerial, security/employment stability, creativity/ entrepreneurship, autonomy/independence, service/ dedication to a cause, challenge, and lifestyle (Schein, 1978, 1985). Other scholars have suggested additional career anchors (e.g., employability, work/family balance, and spirituality/ purposeful work; see Baruch, 2004).

In particular, Schein's complex model involved not only the recognition of career movement through three dimensions but also progression through a series of nine career stages that are guided by an individual's career anchor or anchors. His theory took into account how biological and social aging processes, family relationships, and the career operate as interdependent cycles, each with its own milestones, choices, goals, and end points. He differentiated between the external career markers of hierarchical progression up organizational levels and the internal career markers of career achievement, which are largely based on the individual's subjective judgment. Schein's (1978) conceptualization of careers is well cited in the literature, and empirical research has supported his career anchors across time - and culture (Marshall & Bonner, 2003). Similar to Schein's conceptualization, the well-known theory of Michael Driver (1979) moved career theory beyond linear, age-, or stage-related patterns. Instead of focusing on stages, he examined how personal characteristics as well as the organizational environment influence developmental career patterns.

Driver's Developmental Career Concepts

Michael Driver (1979, 1982) was among the first to delineate patterns of career development beyond the traditional ontogenic, biological linear models. He identified four career concepts that are differentiated by a preferred career pattern and work motives. Driver suggested that the preferred career pattern reflects three factors, which he defines as (1) time of career choice (i.e., at the time of youth, at cyclical time intervals, or constantly throughout the career), (2) permanence of career choice (i.e., whether a choice made in youth is followed for life or whether changes occur annually or within time frames of several years), and (3) direction of career change (i.e., vertical, lateral, or no evident pattern). Work motives reflect important differences in reward preferences that drive individuals' careers and influence career decisions and the career concept (Driver & Brousseau, 1992). Driver (1979, 1982; Brousseau & Driver, 1994; Driver & Brousseau, 1992) identified four career concepts:

1. *The linear career concept* is similar to Super's model in that it represents patterns of

upward movement within the organizational ranks and a desire for power and achievement. Career choices are made early in life and rarely altered.

2. *The steady-state/expert career concept* depicts those who choose their careers fairly early and tend to stay with their chosen career. These individuals are motivated by job security and stability, or opportunities to enhance competence and expertise.

3. *The spiral career concept* describes those who are motivated by self-development, creativity, and the desire to help develop others. These individuals continually evaluate career choices, making career changes taking place within 5- to 7-year cycles.

4. *The transitory career concept* is typified by those who engage in continuous career choice and frequent changes, usually every 1 to 4 years. These individuals tend to make lateral career moves as they strive for independence and autonomy.

Driver further expanded his model to link career patterns to preferred organizational cultures, arguing that firms have linear, steady state, spiral, or transitory career cultures (Driver & Coombs, 1983). For instance, to work in an organization congruent with their career concept, those with linear career patterns would seek organizations offering opportunities for upward movement, whereas those with spiral career patterns would choose organizations known for offering cross-functional development and other opportunities for personal development. Those with a steady-state career pattern would seek stable organizations with good benefits packages. Those with a transitory career pattern would prefer organizations offering special assignments or opportunities for rotating jobs. An individual who is able to match his or her career pattern with an organizational culture that can best meet the needs of that pattern should have more positive work outcomes. For example, Driver and Coombs (1983) found morale and self-perceived productivity to be higher for those with a steady-state career pattern in an organization with a perceived steady-state career culture.

All in all, Driver's model took the developmental career stage models in a new direction by moving beyond a stage-based approach to career development and by suggesting the nontraditional spiral and transitory career patterns. Unfortunately, relatively little empirical research has been completed on Driver's theory and the research that has been completed tends to be cross-sectional.[6]

In the next section, we examine stage-based theories of moral development. Like Driver's model, these theories have enhanced our understanding of nontraditional careers. Moreover, whereas past theories have been criticized for their lack of recognition of gender differences, the theories of moral development bring gender to the foreground. They suggest a theory-based framework by which to study how men and women enact their careers.

THEORIES OF MORAL DEVELOPMENT

While at first blush it may appear that the theories of moral development have little relation to the study of how careers unfold, these theories have been integrated into newer models of career development, providing an intriguing dimension that goes beyond the popular boundaryless career model. To better comprehend the contribution of these theories to the careers literature, we present a brief review and critique of the two most prominent theories of moral development. Next, we discuss how these ideas have been integrated into current career models, introducing a new and exciting dimension to the study of careers.

The Perspectives of Kohlberg and Gilligan

The two best-known—and controversial (e.g., Vreeke, 1991)—theories of moral development are those of Lawrence Kohlberg and Carol Gilligan. Kohlberg (1969, 1976) put forth cognitive differences in moral development as an explanation for why individuals faced with similar ethical circumstances make different decisions. He proposed that individuals progress through six universal stages of moral reasoning. These six stages are grouped into three levels (preconventional, conventional, and postconventional), with each level representing an advancement of the person's ability to understand and integrate diverse viewpoints. Kohlberg suggested that individuals make moral decisions using a justice orientation according to the rule of law.

Despite research that supports the idea that men and women are equally able to decide moral issues using the rule of law, and the prominence of the theory (Hurd & Brabeck, 1997; Simola, 2003), Kohlberg's ideas have been criticized for two major reasons. First, the Moral Judgment Interview used to test his ideas was originally validated only with men, leading to questions of generalizability to women. Second, the scoring of the Moral Judgment Interview rated the desire to maintain relationships and meet the expectations of others as a less advanced stage in moral development than the desire for justice and fairness. Research in the late 1960s and early 1970s found that men tended to exhibit a justice orientation, whereas women tended to exhibit a care orientation (see below), leading some to question whether the theory and the related instrument were gender biased (Jaffee & Hyde, 2000).

The most widely read criticisms of Kohlberg's work came from his student, Carol Gilligan (1982). She suggested that gender differences in moral reasoning were due to gender stereotypes rather than biological reasons, with no one type of moral reasoning superior to another (Gilligan & Wiggins, 1987). For women, connecting and taking care of others is reinforced by society. For men, separating from others and becoming an individual is reinforced.

Gilligan (1982) proposed a three-stage model of moral development. In the first stage, women are focused on themselves to ensure survival. In the next stage, women shift from caring for themselves to caring for others. In the third stage, women realize their own power and that others have a responsibility for their own lives. Women's moral development is the reverse of men's; men start with the assumption that individuality is important, emphasize workplace accomplishments, and then eventually explore intimacy and connections with others. Thus, Gilligan suggests that while men use a justice orientation, women use a care orientation when making moral decisions.

Like Kohlberg's model, Gilligan's model has also been criticized. One major concern is that although several methods, including the Ethic of Care Interview, were developed to help test the three stages of moral development, empirical tests have not been completed. Advances in moral thought may occur through the process of questioning old beliefs and forming new ones rather than through a developmental sequence of increased moral maturity as detailed by Gilligan. Second, Gilligan suggested that individuals prefer one mode of reasoning over the other, but there are mixed results about the intraindividual consistency over time and situations. Third, some have criticized Gilligan's work, maintaining that it is unclear what the relationship is between the justice and care orientations (e.g., incompatible alternatives, complements to each other), what constitutes moral maturity, whether a justice or care orientation should be used to solve moral dilemmas, and just how the theory can be tested. Fourth, while most scholars agree there is more than one mode of moral reasoning, many still question the existence and relative importance of gender differences (Jaffee & Hyde, 2000), with some research (e.g., Karniol, Grosz, & Schnorr, 2003) suggesting that gender role orientation accounts for more of the differences than does gender. Jaffee and Hyde's (2000) meta-analysis of 113 empirical studies found that 73% of the studies that measured the care orientation and 72% of the studies that measured the justice orientation did not find any significant gender differences. The effect sizes for gender differences in the care orientation and the justice orientation were small.[7]

The issue of gender differences in moral development has been a lingering controversy. We suggest that continuing to test exclusionary hypotheses and viewing the justice and care orientations as either/or choices will not end this debate. Instead, we recommend that scholars examine both orientations simultaneously, measuring both the degree of caring orientation and the degree of justice orientation exhibited by an individual.

Moral Development and the Enactment of Careers

Recently, careers scholars have begun to explore how these theories of moral development can help us better understand career decisions and career patterns. For example, using a multimethod approach and a sample of more than 1,700 men and women, Mainiero and Sullivan (2005) found distinct differences in how men and women enact their careers. These differences were in line with proposed gender differences in moral orientations—that is, women were more care oriented, men were more justice oriented. Women's careers were relational, with their career decisions being part of a larger, interconnected web of people, issues, and different life aspects that had to come together into a carefully balanced package. When women make career decisions, they factor in the needs of others (e.g., children, spouses, aging parents). Women were significantly more likely than men (41.1% women, 24.4% men) to report, "I made changes in my career due to family demands," while more men than women reported family demands were "not a factor" (40.2% men, 30.1% women). More women than men (42.7% women, 15.0% men) reported, "My spouse moved to another geographical location and I followed." These findings are clearly in line with Gilligan's idea that women focus on connections and relationships more than men.

Similarly, in line with Gilligan's idea that men are more focused on justice, rules, and agency, Mainiero and Sullivan (2006) found that men make career decisions from a goal orientation, focusing on independent action. Unlike women, the men they studied usually kept their career and family issues separated. Significantly more men than women reported making career transitions because "An opportunity presented itself for more money, greater security" (30.7% men, 24.4% women) and "A risky opportunity presented greater long term payoff" (18.1% men, 11.8% women).

To help explain the differences in how women and men enact careers, Mainiero and Sullivan (2005, 2006; Sullivan, Martin, & Carden, 1996) coined the term *kaleidoscope career*. Using the metaphor of the kaleidoscope, they suggested that men and women alter the patterns of their careers by rotating the varied aspects of their lives to arrange their relationships and roles in new ways. Because women's careers are relational, each decision and action a woman takes is evaluated in terms of the lasting impact it will have on others around her. They

discovered that while women tend to have discontinuous career patterns, men of the Baby Boomer generation, including those in dual-career marriages, had more uninterrupted career patterns focused on achievement. So despite recent conceptualizations that people, in general, are moving toward more nontraditional, boundaryless careers, many of the men studied had career paths similar to the linear career patterns detailed by Super (1957; Powell & Mainiero, 1992; see Mainiero & Sullivan, 2006 for more details of their 5-year research project that examined the Kaleidoscope Careers of more than 3,000 individuals; see also Cabrera, 2007). Moreover, unlike most previous studies, Mainiero and Sullivan's (2005, 2006) research took a broader perspective by examining work/nonwork issues rather than work/family issues so that relationships with friends, elderly relatives, community members as well as oneself (e.g., personal development and needs) were also factored into career choices. Similarly, they also considered how societal factors (e.g., discrimination, stereotyping, government policies) and environmental influences (e.g., organizational culture, workplace policies, supervisor attitudes and behaviors) influence the career choices of men and women.[8]

In sum, the stage-based theories of moral development provide fascinating insights into how careers unfold. These ideas can be readily extended beyond the discussion of ethics because research suggests that career decisions are also guided by the care and justice orientations. And some newer theories have integrated ideas from moral development into models of career development. Despite the promise of this line of research, more empirical study is needed. With the exception of Mainiero and Sullivan (2005, 2006), no published studies have directly applied Gilligan's ideas to the study of career development. Early research (see Mainiero & Sullivan, 2006) suggests that extending these theories to career decision making could provide additional insights into career patterns, especially potential gender differences in how careers unfold (see also Gallos, 1989).

Just as gender differences explain variations in ethical thinking and decision making, other demographic variables may influence career thinking and decision making. The stage theorists were primarily influenced by the biology and psychology of human development as manifested in careers. Even so, they often acknowledged the influence of family and social culture on personal development. In the next section, we examine how theories progressed beyond a biological, age-related view of careers to consider the social context in which they emerge and flourish.[9] We examine the views of career development and decisions which also encompass social factors.

The Context of Career Development

One major criticism of the stage theories of career development is that many of them do not fully explore the implications of the context in which careers are enacted (Dannefer, 1984; Savickas, 2002). However, more recent research integrates the heavily developmental approach to understanding careers with the inclusion of environmental and social variables. For example, Savickas (2002) analyzed Super's well-known model using a multilevel context to devise a theory of career construction. He portrayed a career as engendered within a social enterprise in which a person is connected to the larger group, including parents and peers. Members of the group serve as both role models and centers of work knowledge and help the person fashion an occupation. Savickas (2002) contended that because individuals and circumstances are in constant motion, the individual-occupational match is always evolving. So while Savickas (2002) discussed Super's stages as an ontogenic (i.e., age-based) series, he extends Super's work by including external environmental (i.e., sociogenic) forces as a part of each stage of adult career development as follows:

1. *Exploration.* The person explores career options and makes an occupational choice that fits within the relevant sociocultural environment. Through this exploration, the person gains not only self-knowledge but also information about society and how to cope with work issues.

2. *Establishment.* The person finds his or her occupational niche and has become a part of a work organization and the larger community.

3. *Maintenance.* The person reassesses himself or herself with the help of his or her social group. The person compares himself or herself with other workers, considers family issues, and notes changes in the work environment to maintain his or her occupational choice and self-concept.

4. *Disengagement.* The person may again reflect on his or her life and forges a new life structure outside an occupation and work organization.

Savickas (2002) further noted the cultural context of Super's model, recognizing that it reflected the society and organizations of the mid-20th century. Savickas explained, for example, that in the Maintenance stage, individuals who do not work in large, bureaucratic organizations may need to recycle into new positions. These individuals will need the flexibility to start over again in various jobs given today's economy and the boundaryless work landscape.

While Savickas (2002) looked at a specific developmental theory and revised it to include aspects of the social environment, sociologists have examined the effects of a host of variables on career choices. Research has found that the context of career choices and progress is often related to the socioeconomic background of a person's family, race, and gender, as well as early work experiences such as adolescent employment and internships (Fouad & Byars-Winston, 2005; Greenhaus, Parasuraman, & Wormley, 1990; Johnson & Mortimer, 2002; Miller, 1988). Sociologists offer a rich analysis of how parental occupations, race, ethnicity, community characteristics, family structure, education, and work organization experiences can influence occupational choices and mobility (Johnson & Mortimer, 2002; Guest and Sturges, Chapter 16). For example, Trusty, Ng, and Plata (2000) studied a large sample of diverse post–secondary school students and found differences in career choices based on gender, race, and socioeconomic level. Moreover, they reported a three-way interaction among these variables and underscored the complexity and interplay of contextual factors that influenced career choices.

Similarly, the work of Shore, Cleveland, and Goldberg (2003) illustrated the importance of contextual variables by examining the relationship between a manager's age and the age of his or her subordinates. Shore and colleagues (2003) found that younger manager/older employee dyads resulted in lower performance ratings and fewer promotions, as well as lower levels of training and development for the older subordinate worker. Additionally, older managers were more likely to rate older employers lower than did younger managers. These researchers also found that employees themselves perceived their career future as dimmer when there was a dissimilarity between the employees' and manager's ages. Dyad age mismatches were also related to job performance and organizational commitment. These findings indicate that relational demography is an important factor in the study of career outcomes.

Besides differences based on socioeconomic background, race (Trusty et al., 2000), gender (Gilligan, 1982; Gould, 1978; Levinson, 1996), and age (Shore et al., 2003), researchers have also studied how organizational context influences careers. For instance, Moen and Sweet (2002) explored the intersection of life stage and organizational context when investigating couples working for the same employer (i.e., coworking). Women who cowork are at an earlier life stage, as are coworking couples who have no or young children. In these cases, both the husband's and wife's career are equally considered. Coworker professional men have higher job prestige in comparison with men who are not part of coworking couples, with prestige levels being higher in companies that had greater percentages of coworking partners. Coworking men with no children worked longer hours and were less likely to turnover than coworking men at a later life stage, whether or not they had older children. Professional women with nonprofessional husbands benefited from coworking, earning more than their spouses but also believing that spillover effects to home life were more likely. In general, Moen and Sweet (2002) reported that coworking men benefited the most from the arrangement and that coworking had the greatest impact on couples without children. This study clearly illustrated how the interaction of working conditions, gender, occupational level, life stage, and organizational practices and policies influence career outcomes. It demonstrated the intersection of the personal and organizational, with work and organizational experiences potentially encroaching into the time that might be devoted to family for those coworking couples without children. Thus, organizational polices that allow for coworking benefit the organization in terms of lower turnover, job prestige, and employees working more hours and at the same time also helping individuals keep prestigious, good-paying jobs while managing work/nonwork spillover.

Given the number of variables that influence career development, it should not be surprising that there has been great debate over how to best study careers. The most well-known debate on this issue has taken place between those who advocate the ontogenic (e.g., age-based stages) approach and those who support the sociogenic (i.e., social environment) approach. The next section summarizes these deliberations.

The Ontogenic/Sociogenic Debate

Dannefer (1984) provided one of the most comprehensive analyses of the shortcomings of the stage-based developmental theories. In the article that triggered a now-classic debate, Dannefer claimed that the stage development theories that had set forth age-determined universal stages (i.e., ontogenic) did not consider the influence of the social environment on the individual. In support of his position, he argued that the logic of stage theorists is flawed; it is incorrect to study the life cycle of an individual and then aggregate the results. He suggested that if we assume that careers typically progress through stages, then there is an existing argument for these theories without the appropriate empirical evidence. Using Levinson's (1978) research on men's life stage development as a case in point, Dannefer (1984) illustrated two major deficiencies with these approaches. First, because there were no specific methods to classify and measure each life history, there was no way to replicate the major life events and transitions Levinson specifies. Second, there was the problem of the omnibus variable in terms of one primary predictor (e.g., biological age) and one outcome variable (e.g., stage). Thus, Dannefer argued that age and other variables that may be related to work and nonwork were viewed outside the context of the culture in which they were embedded. Because age is correlated with many other historically and culturally specific factors, there are numerous confounding variables that Levinson's approach did not take into account. While Dannefer (1984) acknowledged that some of the developmental theories do mention the environment, he contended that they still gave short shrift to the essential and major role of environmental factors and that the environment was often only considered when explaining failure to advance through stages or nonnormative/abnormal career behaviors. Acceptance of the developmental theories was so pervasive in sociology that Dannefer alleged an "ontogenetic fallacy" existed in the field (Dannefer, 1984, p. 109).

In rebuttal, Baltes and Nesselroade (1984) countered that Dannefer overemphasized sociogenic factors to the neglect of ontogenic ones and that some developmental theories, such as Baltes's (1979) model, had evolved to include individual differences and adaptations. They also explained that the term *nonnormative* referred to similarity in a descriptive or empirical view and was not a value judgment against those who failed to progress through the prescribed age stages, as Dannefer (1984) asserted. Baltes and Nesselroade (1984), for example, distinguished between normative and nonnormative life experiences but did not evaluate these life experiences. Instead, they further explained the sociogenic model of development proposed earlier by Baltes and his colleagues (see Baltes & Brim, 1979; Baltes, Cornelius, & Nesselroade, 1979). The model explains three features of human development: (1) age-graded influences, including biological markers and environmental issues associated with age (e.g., age-appropriate forms of interaction such as peer pressure and cliques in adolescence; Gleitman, Fridlund, & Reisberg, 1999); (2) history-graded influences, including biological and social features that are related to what is occurring historically (e.g., generations/cohorts of individuals who experience the same event at the same age such as a period of economic depression or recession, living under an unpopular political regime, or a war); and (3) nonnormative influences or unpatterned events that may affect an individual regardless of age or environment (e.g., the impact of a sudden business downturn that

results in a job loss or the effect of a personal health problem on career outcomes). These three influences may vary at different points across the life span (Baltes & Nesselroade, 1984), with individuals demonstrating "intellectual plasticity" in that they continually adapt to their environment and continue to develop (see Baltes, Staudiner, & Lindenberger, 1999).

In addition to the work of Baltes and his colleagues, developments in career theory since the publication of Dannefer's (1984) criticisms have also addressed some of these issues. For instance, Super, Thompson, and Lindeman (1988) developed the Career Concerns Inventory (CCI) to measure career stage, independent of age. Other scholars, besides Super and his colleagues, have also successfully tested Super's theory by examining the independent variables of psychological career stages, as measured by the CCI, as well as the effects of biological age, on numerous work-related dependent variables (Sullivan, 1999). Similarly, Driver and his colleagues' (Brousseau & Driver, 1994; Driver, 1982; Driver & Brousseau, 1992) work on career concepts acknowledged the effects of both personal development and the environment on career patterns. His first two career concepts, linear and steady-state/expert, are related to the ontogenic theories in terms of a continuous movement of time and personal growth through career advancement. His second two concepts, spiral and transitory, reflect more recent changes in the landscape of work expectations that require people to continually build their skills and knowledge (Hall, 1996a) in order to adapt to organizational changes and employment circumstances such as layoffs due to mergers. These concepts also identified nontraditional, nonlinear careers, including the understudied occupations of entrepreneurs (who build, fail, rebuild, and sell businesses) and professionals, such as physicians (who move from research to private practice to international pro bono work) and lawyers (who move from private practice to public service).

The debate prompted Baltes and Nesselroade (1984) to call on scholars to agree on the same interpretation of concepts. For example, while a cohort is a basic unit of analysis and a process in sociology, psychologists are more likely to use the same concept to explain an aberration or a distinct historical event. Likewise, both sides agree that there is a lack of empirical research and acknowledge the difficulties of conducting longitudinal research. To fully test the validity of developmental theories, however, longitudinal studies must be completed in order to understand the interchange of psychological and sociological events—between self-identity and social identity—as well as how such events affect the cumulative set of experiences that constitute a career. Scholars on both sides of this debate do underscore interdisciplinary differences in approaching human development in general, and careers in particular, highlighting the real need to reconcile psychological and sociological views of adult development.

Reconciling the Ontogenic and Sociogenic Views

Calls for reconciling the ontogenic and sociogenic views on adult career development have prompted new careers frameworks. One such context for dealing with the psychological and sociological features of careers was proposed by Levenson and Crumpler (1996). They suggested a liberative framework that integrates the ontological/stage approach as well as the sociogenic influences of education, role models, and other cultural issues. They posited that as individuals progress through stages and life experiences, they become liberated; they are able to move to a greater level of freedom beyond biological and social expectations. In terms of careers, such liberation could be found in cases of career change and creative endeavors that supersede social pressures toward conformity. In terms of contemporary career theory, such enlightened individuals meet Arthur and Rousseau's (1996) sixth meaning of boundaryless—that is, the recognition of a boundaryless future regardless of structural constraints. Support for this perspective can also be found in Gilligan's (1982) focus on relationships, which is more typical of women's ways of knowing, as well as the literature on cultural groups—for example, collectivistic versus individualistic (Schultheiss, 2003), and identity formation and career decision making (Holland, 1973, 1985).

An extension to the liberation approach was offered by Avolio and Sosik (1999), who proposed the use of different levels of analysis

in understanding the impact of work on individuals and vice versa. Specifically, they offer five levels as follows:

Level 1: the individual
Level 2: the individual and work environment
Level 3: the accumulation of work and life events
Level 4: the cohort
Level 5: the use of Levels 1 to 4 while projecting into the future

This approach recognizes that while the ontogenic theories describe the passages of adult development (Level 1), it is also possible that education, social level, work, and home circumstances may influence an individual's cognitive abilities (Levels 2 and 3). In addition to individual differences in handling the demands of different life stages, cohorts influence attitudes toward work and nonwork life (Level 4), with overall life structure rendering career stages as relative (Level 5). This framework integrated the reciprocal impact of the situations studied by the ontogenic and sociogenic views.

While Avolio and Sosik's (1999) approach was consistent with the sociogenic triple-model factors of development—which include age-related events such as entering school, normative history-related events such as being in college during the time of a controversial war, and other random events (Baltes et al., 1999), it suggested other layers of analysis and another means for understanding the complexities of careers. For example, while intellect may be biologically determined, research has shown an increase in test scores, which may be attributed to better health, education, and work conditions for a present-day cohort (Baltes et al., 1999). Because biology, psychology, social psychology, behavior, psychosocial relationships, socioeconomic status, and racio-ethnic group affiliation influence adult development (Von Dras & Blumenthal, 2000), it makes sense to examine personal and situational factors as well as age and stages when developing models of careers.

Another framework that may be useful in reconciling the psychological and sociological views is Social Learning Theory (SLT). SLT considers traits as well as the context or environment in which careers or other events take place, underscoring the holistic nature of career choice, human development, and decision making. SLT assumes that people are aware of their environment and try to control it. Social learning can take place through vicarious learning and the influence of role models and can also be affected by macro-level variables such as social policy (Osipow, 1983). The manner in which the individual understands the environment and demonstrates adaptive behavior as well as expectancies and subjective values are major components of SLT (Gleitman et al., 1999). Learning through direct experience or vicariously reinforces an individual's skills, and self-learning as positive or negative emotions are attached to the learning experiences. Beliefs about (1) one's talents, abilities, and skills; (2) the environment; and (3) learning lead an individual to select certain tasks, using all three of these beliefs to discover their interests and choose a career path. The SLT framework suggests that people must be alert to their environment. People must have situational awareness to realize that job elements change, that life-long learning is necessary and shouldn't stop after initial occupational choice, and that actions must be taken in response to environmental changes (Mitchell & Krumboltz, 1996).

The liberative approach and SLT offer frameworks by which the ontogenic and sociogenic views can be reconciled so that a better understanding of career development can be achieved. The debate among scholars regarding the best approaches to studying careers highlights the importance of considering the complexities of individuals as well as their interaction with significant social groups, careers, and other relevant environmental factors. An increased dialogue between scholars on both sides of the debate as well as with career counselors (Brown, 2002; Hartung, 2002) may encourage the development and testing of existing and new theories that accurately capture the complexities of careers while recommending ways to improve the quality of individuals' work and lives.

Conclusion

Because both work and careers are cognitive and socially constructed (Barley, 1989; Hughes,

1958), factors such as technology, learning, expectancies, communication, coping, interpersonal relationships (Miller, 1988), cohort effects (Baltes et al., 1999; Sheehy, 1981), individual differences (Baltes & Nesselroade, 1984), and the demographic variables of race, gender, and age (for a review, see Whitson & Keller, 2004) influence them. Due to these numerous often interconnected variables, the complexities of careers are difficult to conceptually and empirically capture. It is perhaps inevitable that no one theory or schema can fully address the psychological, social, and cultural aspects of careers. Rather, each theorist exposes his or her training and predilection for focusing on specific aspects of a life span.

The purpose of this chapter was to review and critically evaluate the key developmental theories that provide major insights into how careers unfold.[10] We have reviewed the basic tenets of these theories while recognizing points of agreement and disagreement among them as well as flaws and controversies (e.g., the sociogenic and ontogenic debate) associated with them. Despite the rise of newer theories of careers, such as the protean, boundaryless, and kaleidoscope models, the developmental career theories continue to provide a rich theoretical foundation for research and practice.

Notes

1. During his later years, Erikson reflected on his stages, suggesting a ninth stage of gerotranscendance in which the elder struggles to transcend the infirmities of aging to attain a level of satisfaction beyond our physical world (Erikson, 1997).

2. Vaillant's 1977 book was reprinted in 1995 by Harvard University Press.

3. Although ages associated with each stage were delineated by Super, he noted that these ages were not ironclad rules.

4. Levinson conducted the interviews during the 1980s, and the final version of the book was completed after his death (Newton, 1994).

5. Schein noted that the ages assigned to each stage were approximate. Some of his stages have similar or overlapping age ranges.

6. We were saddened by the recent death of Michael Driver. He was mentor to current career

scholars such as Suzanne C. de Janasz, a major contributor to the literature on careers, and one of the founders of the Careers Division of the Academy of Management. The field is indebted to him for his many contributions.

7. In response to critics, Gilligan argues that the construct of moral orientation cannot be adequately captured by quantitative means, but instead qualitative research, which cannot be examined by the meta-analysis process, must be used. Men and women may use both modes of reasoning, with men favoring the justice and women favoring care, but these differences cannot be captured by cross-sectional designs used in much of the research (Jaffee & Hyde, 2000).

8. Thanks to Yehuda Baruch, Monica Forret, and Gayle Baugh for their comments and insights into gender differences in career management and development.

9. See also Kanter (2001) for a more recent analysis of environmental context.

10. Our thanks to John R. Gavencak and Lisa Mainiero for their helpful comments on earlier versions of this manuscript and to Carole Ottenheimer for her research assistance. Portions of this chapter are based on a paper that won the 2005 Michael Driver Best Regional Paper Award, Careers Division at the annual meeting of the Academy of Management.

REFERENCES

Altman, B. W., & Post, J. E. (1996). Beyond the social contract: An analysis of the executive view at twenty-five larger companies. In D. T. Hall (Ed.), *The career is dead: Long live the career* (pp. 46–71). San Francisco: Jossey-Bass.

Amundson, N. E., Borgen, W. A., & Tench, E. (1995). Counseling and the role of personality and intelligence. In D. H. Saklofske & M. Zeidner (Eds.), *International handbook of personality and intelligence* (pp. 603–619). New York: Plenum Press.

Arthur, M. B., Khapova, S. N., & Wilderom, C. P. M. (2002, August). *Career success in a boundaryless career world.* Paper presented at the National Academy of Management Meetings in Denver, CO.

Arthur, M. B., & Rousseau, D. M. (1996). The boundaryless career as a new employment principle. In M. B. Arthur & D. M. Rousseau (Eds.), *The boundaryless career* (pp. 3–20). New York: Oxford University Press.

Avolio, B. J., & Sosik, J. J. (1999). A life-span framework for assessing the impact of work on white-collar workers. In S. L. Willis & J. D. Reid (Eds.), *Life in the middle* (pp. 249–271). San Diego, CA: Academic Press.

Baltes, P. B. (1979). Life-span developmental psychology: Some converging observations on history and theory. In P. B. Baltes & O. G. Brim, Jr. (Eds.), *Life-span development and behavior* (Vol. 2, pp. 255–279). New York: Academic Press.

Baltes, P. B., & Brim, O. G., Jr. (Eds.). (1979). *Life-span development and behavior* (Vol. 2). New York: Academic Press.

Baltes, P. B., Cornelius, S. W., & Nesselroade, J. R. (1979). Cohort effects in developmental psychology. In J. R. Nesselroade & P. B. Baltes (Eds.), *Longitudinal research in the study of behavior and development* (pp. 61–87). New York: Academic Press.

Baltes, P. B., & Nesselroade, J. R. (1984). Paradigm lost and paradigm regained: Critique of Dannefer's portrayal of life-span developmental psychology. *American Sociological Review, 49*(6), 841–847.

Baltes, P. B., Staudinger, U. M., & Lindenberger, U. (1999). Lifespan psychology: Theory and application to intellectual functioning. *Annual Review of Psychology, 50,* 471–507.

Barley, B. R. (1989). Careers, identities, and institutions: The legacy of the Chicago School of Sociology. In M. B. Arthur, D. T. Hall, & B. S. Lawrence (Eds.), *Handbook of career theory* (pp. 41–65). New York: Cambridge University Press.

Baruch, Y. (2004). Transforming careers from linear to multidirectional career paths: Organizational and individual perspectives. *Career Development International, 9*(1), 58–73.

Baruch, Y. (2006). Organizational career management. In J. Greenhaus & G. A. Callanan (Eds.), *Encyclopedia of career development* (pp. 572–580). London: Sage.

Bejian, D. V., & Salomone, P. R. (1995). Understanding midlife career renewal: Implications for counseling. *Career Development Quarterly, 44,* 52–63.

Bell, M. (2005). A new vision of management in the 21st century: Diversity and career choice issues for young workers. Paper presented at the annual meeting of the Academy of Management, Honolulu, HI.

Brousseau, K. R., & Driver, M. J. (1994). Enhancing informed choice: A career-concepts approach to career advisement. *Selections, 10*(3), 24–31.

Brousseau, K. R., Driver, M. J., Eneroth, K., & Larsson, R. (1996). Career pandemonium: Realigning organizations and individuals. *Academy of Management Executive, 19*(4), 52–56.

Brown, C. (2002). Career counseling practitioners: Reflections on theory, research, and practice. *Journal of Career Development, 29*(2), 109–127.

Cabrera, E. F. (2007). Opting out and opting in: Understanding the complexities of women's career transitions. *Career Development International, 12*(2), 218–237.

Cappelli, P., Bassi, L., Katz, H., Knoke, D., Osterman, P., & Useem, M. (1997). *Change at work.* New York: Oxford University Press.

Chao, G. (1986). *An empirical exploration of career stages.* Paper presented at the meetings of the National Academy of Management, Chicago, IL.

Clausen, J. A. (1972). The life course of individuals. In M. W. Riley, M. Johnson, & A. Foner (Eds.), *Aging and society: Vol. 3. A sociology of age stratification* (pp. 457–514). New York: Russell Sage.

Cleveland, J. N., & Shore, L. M. (1992). Self-and supervisory perspectives on age and work attitudes and performance. *Journal of Applied Psychology, 77,* 469–484.

Cohen, A. (1991). Career stage as a moderator of the relationships between organizational commitment and its outcomes: A meta-analysis. *Journal of Occupational Psychology, 64,* 253–268.

Coltrane, S. (2000). Research on household labor: Modeling and measuring the social embeddedness of routine family work. *Journal of Marriage and Family, 62,* 1208–1233.

Cooke, D. K. (1994). Measuring career stage. *Human Resource Management Review, 4*(4), 383–398.

Crocitto, M. (2006). Middle career stage. In J. H. Greenhaus & G. A. Callanan (Eds.), *Encyclopedia of career development.* Thousand Oaks, CA: Sage.

Crocitto, M., & Sullivan, S. E. (2005). *A review of the developmental theories of careers.* Paper presented at the annual meeting of the Southwest Academy of Management, Dallas, TX.

Crocitto, M., Sullivan, S. E., & Carraher, S. M. (2004). Private practice physicians: The case of healthcare entrepreneurs. In *Entrepreneurs in the health professions: The special case of physicians.* Symposium conducted at the annual meeting of the Southwest Academy of Management, Dallas, TX.

Cytrynbaum, S., & Crites, J. O. (1989). The utility of adult development theory in understanding career adjustment process. In M. B. Arthur, D. T. Hall, & B. S. Lawrence (Eds.), *Handbook of career theory* (pp. 66–88). New York: Cambridge University Press.

Dannefer, D. (1984). Adult development and social theory: A paradigmatic reappraisal. *American Sociological Review, 49*(1), 100–166.

Driver, M. J. (1979). Career concepts and career management in organizations. In C. L. Cooper (Ed.), *Behavioral problems in organizations* (pp. 79–139). Englewood Cliffs, NJ: Prentice Hall.

Driver, M. J. (1982). Career concepts: A new approach to career research. In R. Katz (Ed.), *Career issues in human resource management* (pp. 23–32). Englewood Cliffs, NJ: Prentice Hall.

Driver, M. J., & Brousseau, K. R. (1992). *The Driver-Brousseau career concept model.* Los Angeles, CA: Decision Dynamics.

Driver, M. J., & Coombs, M. W. (1983, October). *Fit between career concepts, corporate culture, and engineering productivity and morale.* Paper presented at the IEEE Conference on Enhancing Engineering Careers, Palo Alto, CA.

Erikson, E. H. (1968). *Identity, youth, and crisis.* New York: W. W. Norton.

Erikson, E. H. (1980). *Identity and the life cycle.* New York: W. W. Norton.

Erikson, J. M. (1997). *The life cycle completed.* New York: W. W. Norton.

Feldman, D. C. (1989). Careers in organizations: Recent trends and future directions. *Journal of Management, 15*(2), 135–156.

Forret, M. L., & de Janasz, S. (2005). Perceptions of an organization's culture for work and family: Do mentors make a difference? *Career Development International, 10,* 478–492.

Fouad, N. A., & Byars-Winston, A. M. (2005). Cultural context of career choice: Meta-analysis of race/ethnicity differences. *Career Development Quarterly, 53*(3), 223–234.

Gallos, J. V. (1989). Exploring women's development: Implications for career theory, practice, and research. In M. B. Arthur, D. T. Hall, & B. S. Lawrence (Eds.), *Handbook of career theory* (pp. 110–132). New York: Cambridge University Press.

Gersick, C., & Kram, K. E. (2002). High-achieving women at midlife: An exploratory study. *Journal of Management Inquiry, 11*(2), 104–127.

Gilligan, C. (1982). *In a different voice.* Cambridge, MA: Harvard University Press.

Gilligan, C., & Wiggins, G. (1987). The origins of morality in early childhood relationships. In J. Kagan & S. Lamb (Eds.), *The emergence of morality in young children* (pp. 277–305). Chicago: University of Chicago Press.

Gleitman, H., Fridlund, A. J., & Reisberg, D. (1999). *Psychology* (5th ed.). New York: W. W. Norton.

Gould, R. L. (1978). *Transformations: Growth and change in adult life.* New York: Simon & Schuster.

Greenhaus, J. H., Callanan, G. A., & Godshalk, V. M. (2000). *Career management* (3rd ed.). Fort Worth, TX: Dryden Press.

Greenhaus, J. H., & Parasuraman, S. (1986). Vocational and organizational behavior, 1985: A review. *Journal of Vocational Behavior, 29,* 115–176.

Greenhaus, J. H., Parasuraman, S., & Wormley, W. M. (1990). Effects of race on organizational experiences, job performance evaluations, and career outcomes. *Academy of Management Journal, 33*(1), 64–86.

Greller, M. M., & Simpson, P. (1999). In search of late career: A review of contemporary social science research applicable to the understanding of later career. *Human Resource Management Review, 9*(3), 309–347.

Gunz, H. P., & Heslin, P. A. (2005). Reconceptualizing career success. *Journal of Organizational Behavior, 26,* 105–111.

Hackett, G., Lent, R. W., & Greenhaus, J. H. (1991). Advances in vocational theory and research: A 20-year retrospective. *Journal of Vocational Behavior, 38,* 3–38.

Hall, D. T. (1996a). Protean careers of the 21st century. *Academy of Management Executive, 10*(4), 8–16.

Hall, D. T. (1996b). Long live the career. In D. T. Hall (Ed.), *The career is dead: Long live the career* (pp. 1–12). San Francisco: Jossey-Bass.

Hall, D. T. (2004). The protean career: A quarter-century journey. *Journal of Vocational Behavior, 65,* 1–13.

Hall, D. T., & Chandler, D. E. (2005). Psychological success: When the career is a calling. *Journal of Organizational Behavior, 26,* 155–176.

Hall, D. T., & Mirvis, P. H. (1996). The new protean career: Psychological success and the path with a heart. In D. T. Hall (Ed.), *The career is dead: Long live the career* (pp. 15–45). San Francisco: Jossey-Bass.

Hansen, J. I. C., & Campbell, D. P. (1985). *Manual for the SVIB-SCII* (4th ed.). Palo Alto, CA: Consulting Psychologists Press.

Hartung, P. J. (2002). Cultural context in career theory and practice: Role salience and values. *Career Development Quarterly, 51*(1), 12–25.

Healy, C. C. (2000). Interpreting the Myers-Briggs Type Indicator to help clients in understanding their Strong Interest Inventory. *Journal of Career Development, 26*(4), 295–308.

Heckert, T. M., Droste, H. E., Adams, P. J., Griffin, C. M., Roberts, L. L., Mueller, M. A., et al. (2002). Gender differences in anticipated salary: Role of salary estimates for others, job characteristics, career paths, and job inputs. *Sex Roles, 47*(3/4), 139–151.

Holland, J. L. (1973). *Making vocational choices: A theory of careers.* Englewood Cliffs, NJ: Prentice Hall.

Holland, J. L. (1985). *Making vocational choices: A theory of vocational personalities and work environment* (2nd ed.). Odessa, FL: Psychological Assessment Resources.

Holland, J. L. (1997). *Making vocational choices: A theory of vocational personalities and work environments* (3rd ed.). Odessa, FL: Psychological Assessment Resources.

Hughes, E. C. (1958). *Men and their work.* Glencoe, IL: Free Press.

Hurd, T. L., & Brabeck, M. (1997). Presentation of women and Gilligan's ethic of care in college textbooks, 1970–1990: An examination of bias. *Teaching of Psychology, 24*(3), 159–167.

Ibarra, H. (2003). *Working identity: Unconventional strategies for reinventing your career.* Boston: Harvard Business School Press.

Jaffee, S., & Hyde, J. S. (2000). Gender differences in moral orientation: A meta-analysis. *Psychological Bulletin, 126*(5), 703–726.

Johnson, M. K., & Mortimer, J. T. (2002). Career choice and development from a sociological perspective. In D. Brown & Associates (Eds.), *Career choice and development* (pp. 37–81). New York: Wiley.

Kanter, R. M. (2001). *Evolve! Succeeding in the digital culture of tomorrow.* Boston: Harvard School Press.

Karniol, R., Grosz, E., & Schnorr, I. (2003). Caring, gender role orientation and volunteering. *Sex Roles, 49*(1/2), 11–19.

Kohlberg, L. (1969). Stage and sequence: The cognitive developmental approach to socialization. In D. A. Goslin (Ed.), *Handbook of socialization theory and research* (pp. 348–480). Chicago: Rand McNally.

Kohlberg, L. (1976). Moral stages and moralization: The cognitive-development approach. In T. Lickona (Ed.), *Moral development and behavior: Theory, research and social issues* (pp. 31–53). New York: Holt, Reinehart, & Winston.

Kroeger, O. (with Thuesen, J. M., & Rutledge, H.). (2002). *Type talk at work.* New York: Dell.

Latack, J. C. (1981). Person/role conflict: Holland's model extended to role-stress research, street management, and career development. *Academy of Management Review, 6,* 89–103.

Lawrence, B. S. (1980). The myth of the midlife crisis. *Sloan Management Review, 4*(21), 35–49.

Levenson, M. R., & Crumpler, C. A. (1996). Three models of adult development. *Human Development, 39,* 135–149.

Levinson, D. J. (1978). *The seasons of a man's life.* New York: Knopf.

Levinson, D. J. (1986). A conception of adult development. *American Psychologist, 41,* 3–13.

Levinson, D. J. (1996). *The seasons of a woman's life.* New York: Knopf.

Lynn, S. A., Cao, L. T., & Horn, B. C. (1996). The influence of career stage on the work attitudes of male and female accounting professionals. *Journal of Organizational Behavior, 17,* 135–149.

Mainiero, L. A., & Sullivan, S. E. (2005). Kaleidoscope careers: An alternative explanation for the "opt-out generation." *Academy of Management Executive, 19*(1), 106–123.

Mainiero, L. A., & Sullivan, S. E. (2006). *The opt-out revolt: How people are creating kaleidoscope careers outside of companies.* New York: Davies-Black.

Mallon, M., & Walton, S. (2005). Career and learning: The ins and the outs of it. *Career Development International, 34*(4), 468–487.

Marshall, V., & Bonner, D. (2003). Career anchors and the effects of downsizing: Implications for generations and cultures at work. A preliminary investigation. *Journal of European Industrial Training, 27*(6/7), 281–291.

Miller, J. (1988). Jobs and work. In N. J. Smelser (Ed.), *Handbook of sociology* (pp. 327–360). Newbury Park, CA: Sage.

Mitchell, L. K., & Krumboltz, J. D. (1996). Krumboltz's learning theory of career choice and counseling. In D. Brown & Associates (Eds.), *Career choice and development* (3rd ed., pp. 233–280). San Francisco: Jossey Bass.

Moen, P., & Sweet, S. (2002). Two careers, one employer: Couples working for the same corporation. *Journal of Vocational Behavior, 61,* 466–483.

Moen, P., & Wethington, E. (1999). Midlife development in a life course context. In S. L. Willis & J. D. Reid (Eds.), *Life in the middle: Psychological and social development in middle age.* San Diego, CA: Academic Press.

Morrison, R. (1977). Career adaptivity: The effective adaptation of managers to changing role demands. *Journal of Applied Psychology, 62*(5), 549–558.

Moya, M., Exposito, F., & Ruiz, J. (2000). Close relationships, gender, and career salience. *Sex Roles, 42*(9/10), 825–846.

Murrell, A. J., & James, E. H. (2001). Gender and diversity in organizations: Past, present, and future directions. *Sex Roles, 45*(5–6), 243–257.

Myers, I. B. (1980). *Gifts differing.* Palo Alto, CA: Consulting Psychologists Press.

Newton, P. M. (1994). Daniel Levinson and his theory of adult development: reminiscence and some clarifications. *Journal of Adult Development, 1*(3), 135–147.

Ng, T. W. H., Eby, L. T., Sorensen, K. L., & Feldman, D. C. (2005). Predictors of objective and subjective career success: A meta-analysis. *Personnel Psychology, 58,* 367–408.

Nicholson, N., & De Waal-Andrews, W. (2005). Playing to win: Biological imperatives self-regulation, and trade-offs in the game of career success. *Journal of Organizational Behavior, 26,* 137–154.

Nickle, B. W., & Maddox, R. C. (1988). Fortysomething: Helping employees through the midlife crisis. *Training and Development Journal, 42*(12), 49–51.

Ornstein, S., & Isabella, L. A. (1990). Age vs. stage models of career attitudes of women: A partial replication and extension. *Journal of Vocational Behavior, 36,* 1–19.

Ornstein, S., & Isabella, L. A. (1993). Making sense of careers: A review 1989–1992. *Journal of Management, 19*(2), 243–267.

Osipow, S. H. (1983). *Theories of career development.* Englewood Cliffs, NJ: Prentice Hall.

Osterman, P. (1996). *Broken ladders.* New York: Oxford University Press.

Pogson, C. E., Cober, A. B., Doverspike, D., & Rogers, J. R. (2003). Differences in self-reported work ethic across three career stages. *Journal of Vocational Behavior, 62,* 189–201.

Powell, G. N., & Mainiero, L. A. (1992). Cross-currents in the river of time: Conceptualizing the complexities of women's careers. *Journal of Management, 18,* 215–237.

Powell, G. N., & Mainiero, L. A. (1993). Getting ahead: In career and life. In G. N. Powell (Ed.), *Women and men in management* (pp. 186–224). Newbury Park, CA: Sage.

Power, S. J. (2006). *The midcareer success guide, planning the second half of your working life.* Westport, CT: Greenwood.

Power, S. J., & Rothausen, T. J. (2003). The work-oriented midcareer development model: An extension of Super's maintenance stage. *The Counseling Psychologist, 31*(2), 157–197.

Reitman, F., & Schneer, J. A. (2005). The long term impacts of managerial career interruptions: A longitudinal study of men and women MBAs. *Group and Organization Management, 30*(3), 243–262.

Roberts, P., & Newton, P. (1987). Levinsonian studies of women's adult development. *Psychology and Aging, 2*(2), 154–163.

Rousseau, D. M. (1989). Psychological and implied contracts in organizations. *Employee Responsibilities and Rights Journal, 2*(2), 121–139.

Rousseau, D. M., & Wade-Benzoni, K. A. (1995). Changing individual-organization attachments: A two-way street. In A. Howard (Ed.), *Changing nature of work* (pp. 290–321). San Francisco: Jossey-Bass.

Savickas, M. L. (2002). Career construction: A developmental theory of vocational behavior. In D. Brown & Associates (Eds.), *Career choice and development* (4th ed., pp. 149–205). San Francisco: Jossey-Bass.

Schein, E. H. (1978). *Career dynamics: Matching individual and organizational needs.* Reading, MA: Addison-Wesley.

Schein, E. H. (1985). *Career anchors: Discovering your real values.* San Diego, CA: University Associates.

Schneer, J. A., & Reitman, F. (2002). Managerial life without a wife: Family structure and managerial career success. *Journal of Business Ethics, 37,* 25–38.

Schneer, J. A., & Reitman, F. (1993). Effects of alternative family structures on managerial career paths. *Academy of Management Journal, 36,* 830–843.

Schultheiss, D. E. P. (2003). A relational approach to career counseling: Theoretical integration and practical application. *Journal of Counseling and Development, 81*(3), 301–310.

Seibert, S. E., Kraimer, M. L., & Crant, J. M. (2001). What do proactive people do? A longitudinal model linking proactive personality and career success. *Personnel Psychology, 54*(4), 845–874.

Sheehy, G. (1976). *Passages.* New York: E. P. Dutton.

Sheehy, G. (1981). *Pathfinders.* New York: Bantam Books.

Sharf, R. S. (1997). *Applying career development theory to counseling* (2nd ed.). Pacific Grove, CA: Brooks.

Shore, L. M., Cleveland, J. N., & Goldberg, C. B. (2003). Work attitudes and decisions as a function of manager age and employee age. *Journal of Applied Psychology, 88*(3), 529–537.

Simola, S. (2003). Ethics of justice and care in corporate crisis management. *Journal of Business Ethics, 46,* 351–361.

Smart, R., & Peterson, C. (1994). Stability versus transition in women's career development: A test of Levinson's theory. *Journal of Vocational Behavior, 45,* 241–260.

Smart, R., & Peterson, C. (1997). Super's career stages and the decision to change careers. *Journal of Vocational Behavior, 51,* 358–374.

Solnit, A. J. (1992). Fate, choice, and retribution in Freud's psychoanalysis. In Garcia, E. E. (Ed.), *Understanding Freud: The man and his ideas* (pp. 101–122). New York: New York University Press.

Stumpf, S. A., & Rabinowitz, S. (1981). Career stage as a moderator of performance relationships with facets of job satisfaction and role perceptions. *Journal of Vocational Behavior, 18,* 202–218.

Sturges, J. (1999). What it means to succeed: Personal conceptions of career success held by male and female managers at different ages. *British Journal of Management, 10,* 239–252.

Sullivan, S. E. (1999). The changing nature of careers: A review and research agenda. *Journal of Management, 25,* 457–484.

Sullivan, S. E., Carden, W. A., & Martin, D. F. (1998). Careers in the next millennium: A reconceptualization of traditional career theory. *Human Resource Management Review, 8,* 165–185.

Sullivan, S. E., Martin, D. F., & Carden, W. A. (1996). Kaleidoscope careers: A new direction in career theory. Paper presented at the Southern Management Association meetings.

Sullivan, S. E., Martin, D. F., Carden, W. A., & Mainiero, L. A. (2003). The road less traveled: How to manage the recycling career stage. *Journal of Leadership and Organizational Studies, 10*(2), 34–42.

Super, D. (1957). *Psychology of careers.* New York: Harper.

Super, D. E. (1987). Life career roles: Self-realization in work and leisure. In D. T. Hall & Associates (Eds.), *Career development in organizations* (pp. 95–119). San Francisco: Jossey-Bass.

Super, D. E. (1992). Toward a comprehensive theory of career development. In D. H. Montross & C. J. Shinkman (Eds.), *Career development: Theory and practice* (pp. 35–64). Springfield, IL: Charles C Thomas.

Super, D., Savickas, M. L., & Super, C. M. (1996). The life-span, life-space approach to careers. In D. Brown & Associates (Eds.), *Career choice and development* (3rd ed., pp. 121–178). San Francisco: Jossey-Bass.

Super, D., Thompson, A., & Lindeman, R. (1988). *Adult career concerns inventory: Manual for research and exploratory use in counseling.* Palo Alto, CA: Consulting Psychologists Press.

Super, D. E., Zelkowitz, R. S., & Thompson, A. S. (1981). *Career development inventory: Adult form I.* New York: Columbia University.

Swanson, J. L. (1992). Vocational behavior, 1989–1991: Life span career development and reciprocal interaction of work and nonwork. *Journal of Vocational Behavior, 41,* 101–161.

Tomlinson, S. M., & Evans-Hughes, G. (1991). Gender, ethnicity, and college students' responses to the Strong-Campbell Interest Inventory. *Journal of Counseling and Development, 70*(1), 151–155.

Trusty, J., Ng, K., & Plata, M. (2000). Interaction effects of gender, SES, and race-ethnicity on postsecondary educational choices of U.S. students. *Career Development Quarterly, 49*(1), 45–60.

Vaillant, G. E. (1977). *Adaptation to life.* Boston: Little, Brown.

Vaillant, G. E. (2002). *Aging well: Surprising guideposts to a happier life from the landmark Harvard study of adult development.* Boston: Little, Brown.

Van Vianen, A. E. M., & Fischer, A. (2002). Illuminating the glass ceiling: The role of organizational culture preferences. *Journal of Occupational and Organizational Psychology, 75,* 315–337.

Von Dras, D. D., & Blumenthal, H. T. (2000). Biological, social-environmental, and psychological dialecticism: An integrated model of aging. *Basic & Applied Social Psychology, 22*(3), 199–213.

Vreeke, G. J. (1991). Gilligan on justice and care: Two interpretations. *Journal of Moral Education, 20*(1), 33–47.

Weeks, W. A., Moore, C. W., McKinney, J. A., & Longenecker, J. G. (1999). The effects of gender and career stage on ethical judgment. *Journal of Business Ethics, 20,* 301–313.

Weick, K. (1996). Enactment and the boundaryless career: Organizing as we work. In M. B. Arthur & D. M. Rousseau (Eds.), *The boundaryless career* (pp. 40–57). New York: Oxford University Press.

Whitson, S. C., & Keller, B. K. (2004). The influence of the family of origin on career development: A review and analysis. *The Counseling Psychologist, 32*(4), 493–521.

Wnuk, S., Amundson, N. E., Arthur, M. B., & Parker, P. (2003). Intelligent Career Card Sort (ICCS)®. Career exploration system: Guide for licensed consultants. Andover, MA: ICCS Developers.

16

LIVING TO WORK—
WORKING TO LIVE

Conceptualizations of Careers Among Contemporary Workers

DAVID E. GUEST

JANE STURGES

The traditional model of the career as a series of upwardly mobile steps toward some pinnacle of life-time achievement is deeply embedded in the Western industrial psyche. It reflects modernist ideas of progress, with progress for the individual and society manifested as growth and as movement onward and upward. At the same time, it is highly individualistic, as captured in the notion of competing against rivals in a career tournament (Rosenbaum, 1979). The career concept, therefore, fits well with the American Dream. Yet the reality has invariably been rather different. Throughout the 20th century, the upwardly mobile career was always the preserve of a minority of "organization men" (Whyte, 1956), out of the reach of the majority of workers (Barley, 1989). Contemporary debates suggest that this traditional model of the career may be even less applicable in the 21st century.

There have been many attempts to provide a more encompassing definition of a career (Gunz and Peiperl, Chapter 1). A typical broader definition, offered by Arthur, Hall, and Lawrence (1989), is "the evolving sequence of a person's work experiences over time" (p. 8). The Chicago School, to which we shall return later, takes an even broader view, embracing the development of individual identities within their social context. Despite a recognition that many careers are nonhierarchical and that it is important to study the range of career patterns and experiences, most academic research has focused on the traditional hierarchical career. Indeed, as Zabusky and Barley (1996) note, "Equating career success with vertical mobility has become so entrenched that most popular and academic discourse on career would be incomprehensible without assuming a hierarchy" (p. 187). The aim of this chapter is to broaden the discourse to consider the range of careers that lie beyond the traditional hierarchical model.

The chapter starts with an analysis of the changes that are affecting traditional hierarchical careers and argues that changes that appear to threaten the traditional hierarchical career provide an opportunity to raise the profile and salience of alternative career patterns. It then presents alternative perspectives on the career, drawing mainly on sociological literature and focusing on the careers of those at lower levels in organizations. Building on this and on debates about the centrality of work, we present a classification of nonhierarchical careers, drawing on some contemporary U.K. survey evidence to illustrate the career types in the classification.

THE TRADITIONAL CAREER: ROBUST OR IN RETREAT?

The traditional career, where the individual moves onward and upward within a stable organizational hierarchy, has always been a comforting ideal. For those who progress in their careers in the large corporations, the rewards today are better than ever before. The pay gap between the top industrial leaders and those at the bottom of the workforce has expanded dramatically in both the United States (Freeman, 2000) and the United Kingdom (Machin, 1999), and the gap is widening in other industrialized countries. Yet the nature of the organizational hierarchy means that not everyone can progress and very few can make it to the top.

The traditional career is now widely considered to be under threat. Two major types of challenges have been identified. One concerns structural changes, while the other is associated with a change in values among those who might be expected to seek an upwardly mobile career. The structural changes—highlighted, for example, by Osterman (1996) and Cappelli (1999)—essentially argue that organizations have become leaner, flatter, and, with respect to internal career opportunities, meaner. These changes are a product of external competitive

pressures. They are manifested first in general organizational restructuring to become more responsive to dynamic markets—as described, for example, by Kanter (1989)—but are also reflected in the increasingly unpredictable life cycles of many organizations as their fortunes ebb and flow. Second, they can be seen in the process reengineering of the 1990s, which sought to cut costs by focusing on core activities. Third, they are manifested in the outsourcing of both noncore activities and activities that can be done more cheaply offshore or elsewhere. The logical outcome is that leaner, fitter, and flatter structures contain fewer steps in the organizational hierarchy and provide fewer rungs on a thinner career ladder. There is, therefore, less space and less scope for progress. Furthermore, the traditional organizational career is predicated on organizational stability and survival. Where this cannot be guaranteed, it becomes necessary to look beyond the boundaries of the organization in pursuit of career progress (Arthur & Rousseau, 1996).

Earlier in this chapter, reference was made to growing income inequality. In a context where there are opportunities for career mobility, this may be less of a concern. However, the changes outlined above imply that opportunities may be declining. A careful analysis by Dickens (1999) confirms that in the last two decades of the 20th century, wage mobility, which can serve as a powerful proxy for career mobility, has steadily fallen in the United Kingdom. Those on low earnings generally remained on low earnings, while the earnings of those who were already better off continued to increase. This evidence indicates that despite claims about an increasingly flexible labor market, in practice, opportunities to progress within it are declining.

The extensive academic discourse about the loss of the traditional career is almost exclusively concerned with one relatively small section of the working population—namely, those whom we might expect to find in managerial and executive grades in medium and large organizations. Much less consideration is given to how structural changes might affect the careers of those in lower grades. This may reflect a view that they are essentially disposable costs, to be outsourced or offshored, rather than assets to be fought over in the "war for talent." Alternatively, for those who have an interest in traditional careers, they may appear less affected by career-related changes and therefore provide a less interesting research focus. Yet in any discussion of careers, they remain a silent majority, whose concerns and experiences deserve a higher priority.

The structural changes are likely to have implications for the job security and income of those employed in sections of the organization that lack any significant hierarchical labor market. Job security is self-evidently threatened by the downsizing, outsourcing, and offshoring that has accompanied organizational change. Cost cutting will affect pay. This is most apparent in the United States, where real wages fell in the 1980s among those in the lower levels of organizations, only recovering under the Clinton presidency (Freeman, 2000). A further consequence may be work intensification and longer hours as organizations seek to ratchet up efficiency. Since it is unlikely that values and work or career preferences will change swiftly to come in line with these structural changes, it is possible to predict from this a decline in job satisfaction. The available evidence for the United Kingdom appears to support this (Green, 2006; Layard, 2005).

Some authors have argued that the emerging picture is more complex. Batt (1996), for example, claims that there are competing trends associated with structural change. On the one hand, there has been the cost cutting and centralization of control, which reflects a traditional response to external threats. On the other hand, some organizations have adopted the more novel response of decentralization and empowerment. In a number of European countries, this has been overlaid by legislation creating opportunities for greater flexibility of employment arrangements—for example, with respect to part-time working and parental leave. This second strategy will have a distinctly different impact on those who work at lower levels in organizations. It implies that some organizations will seek to involve people more fully in their work, offering more responsibility and autonomy and at the same time seeking to enhance their commitment to the organization so that they use their autonomy for the benefit of the organization. This strategy also implies that development is experienced within the job and

within the same organization. Much has been written about the human resource practices associated with this approach (Appelbaum, Bailey, Berg, & Kalleberg, 2000; Ichniowski, Kochan, Levine, Olson, & Strauss, 1996). Nevertheless, it is unclear how far it fits with the career preferences of those on the receiving end of such practices. To explore this more fully, we need to consider these preferences among nonmanagerial workers.

First, however, we need to explore the challenges to the traditional career presented by changes in values among those embarking on careers and particularly those entering managerial and professional jobs. For some time, it has been argued that achieving a balance between home life and work life is becoming a higher priority for many people (Greenhaus and Foley, Chapter 8). As long ago as the late 1980s, it was suggested that U.K. managers were becoming less interested in career success as it has been traditionally understood and more in the career as a means of enhancing personal lifestyles, which are separate from, rather than subordinated to, work roles. They were more drawn to their families as a source of satisfaction and less prepared to sacrifice their lifestyles for their careers (Scase & Goffee, 1989). This conclusion is supported by Schein's research findings in the United States, which show that growing numbers of people are endorsing a "lifestyle" career anchor where the individual's career is seen as an integral part of his or her total lifestyle (Schein, 1996).

Two main factors have been identified as contributing to this apparent shift in values, which has led to a growing interest in work-life balance. First, the entry of women into the workforce has made issues concerning balancing home and work more relevant for more people. The United Kingdom, for example, is typical of Western countries in that women now comprise nearly 50% of those at work. This puts employers under pressure to recognize the importance of families and out-of-work responsibilities to individuals by offering benefits such as parental leave and part-time working, as increasing numbers of women work and more men are willing to play a greater role in bringing up their children. However, the increased participation of women in the workforce additionally appears to engineer a more basic shift in values. There is evidence that women's work values tend to differ from those espoused by their male colleagues, focusing on achievement in terms of factors such as accomplishment (Beutell & Brenner, 1986) and respect (Mason, 1994), with the result that they are less likely to endorse traditional, hierarchical models of career progression. This difference in values is supported by more recent research in the United Kingdom, which showed that women's conceptions of what career success meant to them were based more on personal recognition and achievement than objective measures of pay and hierarchical position (Sturges, 1999).

Second, it is argued that the younger generation at work today hold different values from those of their older colleagues, because of formative influences in their youth, such as media technology, globalization, economic instability, and AIDs (Tulgan, 1996). In particular, it is suggested that they wish to develop and manage their careers on their own terms, as opposed to traditional hierarchical career norms (Cannon, 1995). An important part of this career individualism is said to be an aspiration to achieve balance between the work and nonwork aspects of their lives. Recent research supports these conclusions. Following a comparative generational study, Smola and Sutton (2002) concluded that today's younger cohort hold different values from those held by individuals of the same age a generation earlier in that they are less likely to feel that work should be an important part of life. This conclusion is supported by the findings of a study exploring young peoples' values across four European countries, which again found strong evidence of a desire to lead a balanced lifestyle (Lewis, Smithson, & Kugelberg, 2002). Despite these claims, it is unclear how far young workers choose in practice to act on these values, and there is some evidence that they may get drawn into more traditional work patterns (Sturges & Guest, 2004).

While the idea of work-life balance is a relatively new theme in the research on managerial and professional workers, there is a well established, largely sociological tradition of research and analysis on the meaning of work among nonmanagerial workers (see, e.g., Meaning of Work Team, 1987). In some cases, this has involved studies of communities (see, e.g., Young &

Willmott, 1973). In others, it involves accounts of working lives such as those famously presented by Terkel (1977). In the context of contemporary debates about work-life balance, there is the long-standing stream of work initiated by writers such as Dubin (see, e.g., Dubin, Champoux, & Porter, 1975) arguing that work was not a central life interest among many nonmanagerial workers. Others, such as Parker and Smith (1976), subsequently refined the analysis to distinguish more clearly the range of relationships between work and leisure. One implication of this research is that large swathes of the workforce have never sought to engage in the pursuit of a hierarchical career, and their work derives meaning partly through its relation to their lives outside work rather than from the experience of work itself. The contemporary arguments about changes in values, admittedly not always well supported by empirical evidence, would suggest that this tendency is spreading to other sections of the working population. Issues of values and how they might be changing, therefore, form part of the context within which to explore conceptualizations of nonmanagerial careers.

CONCEPTUALIZING NONMANAGERIAL CAREERS

Barley (1989) has noted that if we accept the dominant model of the career as a pattern of progress onward and upward, then it probably excludes the working lives of about 80% of Americans. Among those excluded will be many professional workers who have opted for a nonhierarchical career. They will include family doctors and dentists, solicitors, accountants, and others whose working lives are spent in small, local partnerships. In many cases, these professionals will have nonhierarchical careers by choice rather than as a result of labor market constraints. What this means is that we need a classification of nonhierarchical careers that is broad enough both to encompass this type of professional worker, who chooses to work in a setting where there is little or no opportunity for upward mobility, as well as those with few qualifications, who are forced into roles without opportunities for mobility as a result of their marginal position in the labor market.

One response to the problem of identifying and classifying nonhierarchical careers is simply to accept the broad definition of career offered by Arthur and colleagues (1989) and consider career as an evolving sequence of work experiences. However, this is unsatisfactory in two respects. The first is that, as Zabusky and Barley (1996), quoted earlier, note, the idea of career as involving hierarchical movement is deeply embedded in the academic discourse, and this almost certainly reflects the typical layperson's view of career as well. The second is that such a broad definition lacks analytic rigor and hides the possible range of career experiences and career perceptions among those who do pursue or do not have access to a hierarchical career. We, therefore, need to develop an analytic framework within which to consider those careers that can begin to capture some of the varieties of experience and their implications.

An essential starting point for the analysis is the work of the Chicago School of sociologists, who from early in the 20th century have had a long-standing interest in working-class careers. They developed the distinction, since adopted by many others, between the objective structural definition of a career, embedded in organizations and open to external observation, and the subjective career, reflecting the ways in which individuals make sense of their career experiences. Hughes (1937) defined the subjective career as "the moving perspective in which the person sees his life as a whole and interprets the meaning of his various attributes, actions and things that happen to him" (p. 413). Crucially, Hughes and others in the Chicago School argue that social structures both shape and help make sense of careers and can, in turn, be partly shaped by careers. One of the key institutions that has received considerable attention in the context of careers is the labor market, particularly the concept of the dual labor market (Piore & Sabel, 1984). Those who by virtue of their education and background find themselves in the secondary labor market may also find that their opportunities for the traditional hierarchical career are strictly limited.

Subjective definitions of career are inevitably bound up in a social context and in experience. As Zabusky and Barley (1996) note, "The social context in which the career takes place . . . serves as both a blueprint and a filter. It directs the paths that people forge through their lives while providing symbols and interpretations for separating meaningful from meaningless identities and activities" (p. 187). This social context may lie both inside and outside work. It is therefore essential to understand the social context as a basis for understanding how all careers are construed.

The acceptance of the importance of context that has been a hallmark of the Chicago School in its perspective on careers overlaps in important ways with the sociological research on orientations to work conducted in the United Kingdom in the 1960s and 1970s. Goldthorpe, Lockwood, Bechhofer, and Platt (1968) reported the orientations of workers in three factories in Luton, a new town to which many of these workers had been recently attracted. Their core argument was that workers developed orientations based on their experiences outside work that affected their attitudes and behavior at work. More specifically, many of these workers, particularly those doing semiskilled assembly line work, had developed what they termed an instrumental orientation whereby work was viewed primarily as a means to an end. That end was to maximize earnings to permit the achievement of family goals outside work. Primacy was therefore given to high earnings and job security, with little interest either in the intrinsic content of the job or the social context at work. Furthermore, like the technicians described by Zabusky and Barley (1996), they expressed little interest in the idea of promotion. The authors recognized but paid less attention to the different orientations, including those of craft workers, whom they described as solidaristic, reflected in giving primacy to the craft and to fellow craft workers, and a bureaucratic orientation, representing the priorities of clerical workers, who sought long-term employment and, within the constraints of the internal labor market, some sense of progress within the firm.

The work of Goldthorpe et al. (1968) has been extensively criticized (see, e.g., Hill, 1981). Blackburn and Mann (1979) replicated the work among a larger sample of workers in generally low-skill jobs in the town of Peterborough in England. They found a wide range of orientations and, often, combinations of priorities.

There was little basis on which to award primacy to the instrumental worker or indeed to the three types identified by Goldthorpe et al. (1968). Nor was there much evidence that a high priority was attached to the traditional hierarchical and promotion-based career. Prandy, Stewart, and Blackburn (1982) then conducted a somewhat similar study with a large sample of U.K. white-collar workers and found that promotion continued to be important both in itself and through its influence on other aspects of work.

Despite some limitations, these studies are important in drawing attention to workers' as opposed to managers' careers and to the idea that the social context and experiences help shape the meaning of a career. This context includes both social upbringing and subsequent experiences. For example, most of the affluent workers studied by Goldthorpe et al. (1968) were selected from the age group where they had young families and a strong need to maximize their earnings. As they grew older, it is possible that their priorities might have changed. The set of studies also highlight the diversity of orientations or career preferences among the nonmanagerial working population. The evidence shows that it is misleading to offer a general characterization of blue-collar workers as instrumental or as having any other single dominant orientation or career preference. Another of the findings to emerge from the series of studies of orientations was that, as Hill (1981) has emphasized, experiences at work could have an important influence on what workers valued and sought from work. We should, therefore, consider work experiences alongside external influences in seeking to understand work preferences.

A further key feature of the British sociological studies of orientations to work was their adoption of an action frame of reference. The instrumental workers were managing their own careers rather than letting management take charge or accepting the traditional passivity of some working-class communities. In doing so, they were implementing a "life project" that often included a geographical move away from their family roots. There are similarities in this perspective to Weick and Berlinger's (1989) notion of a form of active subjectivity whereby workers impose sense on careers in increasingly ambiguous contexts.

One feature of all the studies of orientations is that they were conducted with samples of men. As indicated earlier, as women assume a much more central role in the workforce, women's orientations and definitions of careers and success in careers become important issues. Hakim (1996) has argued that women increasingly fall into two categories with respect to their employment choices. A growing group selects a conventional career and in many respects follows the traditional path pursued by men, while another group gives priority to life at home and chooses routine work or part-time work. This analysis has been criticized for its lack of attention to institutional constraints on those in routine jobs in the secondary labor market. On the other hand, Belt (2005) finds a range of career orientations among women doing the same jobs in call centers. There are some for whom the job is a stepping stone to advancement or better work elsewhere and who will not stay for long, some who seek a career within the organization while recognizing that the scope for advancement is limited, and others who are content to stay in the job for a long period and who clock up long years of service. In other words, within the same job there are women who could fit into both of Hakim's categories.

The concept of orientations that has provided a focus for the analysis of the careers of those in mainly routine occupations has a number of similarities to Schein's concept of "career anchors," which has been more explicitly applied to the study of managerial careers. Schein (1993) views a career anchor as a product of values, motives, talents, and skills that form a self-concept, which in turn shapes the kind of career a person wishes to pursue. Career anchors emerge out of experiences both outside work, as part of the socialization process, and inside work. They may take time to establish and may modify somewhat as a person passes through career and life stages, but Schein sees them as essentially stable over the long term. As a way of establishing real priorities, he defines the anchor as what you would not give up. Schein has developed a list of eight career anchors, based on research with MIT MSc graduates. While he argues that they can be applied across the workforce, this remains open to question. It would therefore be interesting to explore how far these orientations or anchors can be identified within a contemporary working population that extends beyond a managerial sample. Relevant work has been reported from within a qualitative perspective using Weick's concept of enactment by Arthur, Inkson, and Pringle (1999) among 75 New Zealanders and by Cadin, Bailly-Bender, and Saint-Giniez (2000) among 75 French workers. Both are particularly concerned with the way in which people from a range of backgrounds enact their careers, and both emphasize the greater scope for choice and variety in the contemporary organizational world with its more permeable boundaries. Both also imply that distinctions of all types affecting careers are becoming more blurred, and as a result, they themselves do not seek systematically to differentiate between the career patterns and preferences of those working at different levels in organizations. This brief analysis of how we might begin to conceptualize workers' careers has highlighted the importance of the subjective and socially constructed career alongside the more traditional focus on the objective characteristics of career progress (Judge and Kammeyer-Mueller, Chapter 4). It has also emphasized the importance of economic and social structures in shaping opportunities, aspirations, and perceptions. This context serves potentially as both a constraint and an opportunity. It is a constraint in the sense that those without the appropriate education, qualifications, and early opportunities may be excluded from traditional hierarchical careers. But it is an opportunity in so far as it can shape perceptions of alternatives, albeit within a more limited range. Therefore, for example, even in a quite tightly constrained internal labor market, if the opportunity to move through successive job gradings to many workers looks like a career and in terms of increases in income and possibly in some aspects of status it subjectively feels like a career, then perhaps we should accept that it is a career. This fits with the broad definition of a career; but it is only one kind of nonhierarchical career experience, and we need to consider the alternatives alongside it.

In beginning to consider alternative models of workers' careers, we should recognize that while managers may wish to control them, workers should be seen as the key actors, shaping and making sense of their careers, although within constraints imposed by the labor market. We should also recognize that there are many assumptions about contemporary career preferences and how they may be changing and that we need to be cautious about uncritically accepting these assumptions. There is a long stream of research on work as a central life interest, which contends that for many lower-grade workers it is not central to their lives (Dubin, Champoux, & Porter, 1975). This blends into the wider debate about structural and value-based changes, allied to the growing concern for work-life balance, a debate that is being strongly influenced by the feminization of the workforce. In an attempt to progress the analysis of workers' careers, the next section outlines and illustrates a framework within which to consider the varieties of career experience.

CAREER PATTERNS AND CAREER CHOICES OF THOSE IN ROUTINE OCCUPATIONS: TOWARD A NEW CONCEPTUAL FRAMEWORK

For those in routine occupations, particularly if they have low skills and limited educational qualifications, objective career opportunities can be limited. Nevertheless, aspirations for career advancement may remain quite strong among many in these occupations. Human resource practitioners have been skilled in creating the impression of career paths and selling this to such workers (Scott, 1994). There may be good reason to do this, building on the arguments presented by Batt (1996), outlined earlier, as a means of retaining the commitment of valued workers. In such cases, the traditional concept of a career as "an evolving sequence of a person's work experiences over time" (Arthur et al. 1989) may be relevant, but we need to incorporate a sense of subjectively perceived upward progression even if it may not fit with the traditional definition of upward career mobility and even when it does not appear as such to an outsider. In other words, among some of the 80% of the American population that, according to Barley (1989), are excluded from the possibility of vertical career mobility, there may be a genuine perception that such mobility exists for them, even if the scale of such mobility falls far short of what the executive might classify as vertical mobility.

However, this does not cover the range of career possibilities for those engaged in occupations that do not offer the traditional vertical mobility. We need to develop a framework within which to analyze the range of alternatives that they face. There are a number of existing classifications that might provide useful pointers. Driver (1982) outlined four possibilities, albeit using the traditional hierarchical career as the main point of reference: (1) the steady-state career, where a person stays in the same job or professional role for most of his or her career; (2) the traditional linear career, in which a person moves onward and upward within an organization; (3) the spiral career, consisting of several different careers; and (4) the transitory career, in which there is a great deal of job change and no identifiable career pattern. Cadin et al. (2000) offer a five-point continuum from what they describe as a sedentary career, reflecting a long period in the same position in the same organization, to a nomadic career, which involves frequent job change. The typology is based on two main dimensions of job/occupation stability or change and organizational stability/change, with a variant to incorporate "borderers," who move in or out of self-employment. Although useful in capturing the dimensions of more traditional and contemporary career patterns, neither classification encompasses the range of possibilities within nonhierarchical careers.

Probably the most useful existing framework has been developed by Thomas (1989), who focuses explicitly on workers' careers. In his analysis of blue-collar careers, Thomas argues that structures associated with class and education, the organizational arrangement of occupations, including division of labor, and the segmentation of labor markets all in turn structure and constrain blue-collar careers. Thomas posits a range of responses, rejecting at the outset the case made by those, such as Blauner (1964), Braverman (1975), and Edwards (1979), who have argued that resistance or alienation are the most likely responses. Instead, he identifies a range of possible alternatives. The first is the opportunity to structure a career by moving from the periphery to the center of an occupation. One

illustration of this is the scope to become more central to an organization or professional or occupational group through the acquisition and utilization of knowledge, experience, and social capital. The second, and closely related, response suggested by Thomas (1989) is to construct and compete for more subtle status differences within an occupation or even a small cluster of similar jobs. The third is to become instrumental and view work more as a means to an end. The fourth is to engage in what he terms tourism or job mobility as a basis for variety, experience, and, possibly, some forms of advancement. Finally, he highlights the importance of cycles and games, by which he means constructing variety and control within the job.

Thomas (1989) was particularly interested in blue-collar workers. Over the past two decades, the restructuring of employment has meant that routine white-collar jobs and, in particular, service jobs have expanded at the expense of blue-collar work and deserve to be given some primacy. Also, as noted in the examples provided, many professional and technical jobs lack hierarchy and may most appropriately be analyzed in terms of achievement rather than advancement. In this context, the growing dominance of corporate bureaucracies at the expense of professional bureaucracies in much of the public sector, at least in the United Kingdom, has placed constraints on the exercise of professional autonomy. This can limit the scope for an achievement-oriented career or a career moving from the periphery to the center of a professional group and block off other "escape routes" for those seeking variety.

What follows is an attempt to build on and extend existing analytic frameworks, and more particularly that of Thomas (1989), taking into account some of the contemporary developments in and debates on working life. In attempting any classification, it is necessary to bear in mind both the objective and the subjective dimensions of the career. We offer a classification below that builds on the elements contained in the typologies listed above. However, they need to be nuanced to reflect the scope within an apparently constrained career to identify certain opportunities. We focus mainly on the "careers" of those in routine occupations where labor market constraints limit the scope for hierarchical progression. However, in the context of debates about the changing nature of careers, it has the potential to be used as a framework within which to analyze most types of career, including those of professional workers and others who may not work within any identifiable career hierarchies. Its distinguishing feature is that it starts out from the perspective of those engaged in the more routine types of occupation.

There appear to be two important dimensions around which an analysis might be based. The first of these addresses the extent to which the experience of work is mainly based within an organization or is predominantly external to a specific organization, whether by choice or necessity. The second dimension concerns the extent to which work forms a central life interest and is a major part of life or whether it is more of a means to an end, to be tolerated rather than enjoyed. This second dimension has added relevance in the context of debates about work-life balance and arguments that both work and organizational life are becoming less of a priority for many people. Table 16.1 illustrates how within this simple framework, we can identify a range of types of career. In the following section, we elaborate on each of the types we have identified and illustrate them using a variety of sources, including, in particular, two recent research studies.

The two recent studies, both U.K. based, were designed to explore career orientations and career anchors across different sectors of the workforce in the light of debates about changing career preferences and opportunities.

The first study is based on a stratified random sample of 1,000 workers in Great Britain in 2004 (Guest & Conway, 2004). They were stratified to be representative of broad occupational status, age, gender, and region, based on the

authoritative U.K. Labour Force Survey. However, the survey included only those who were employees and only those working in organizations employing 10 or more people. In the event, using the National Statistics Socio-Economic Classification, 50% of the sample fell into the higher or lower managerial and professional categories; 23% were in lower intermediate, supervisory, and technical occupations; and 25% were in semiroutine and routine occupations. Two percent did not answer the relevant question. By taking a broad sample of the working population, it should be possible to compare the career aspirations and values of those at different levels within the working population and, in particular, to compare those in lower-level blue- and white-collar jobs with those in managerial and professional jobs.

The second study used the career anchors developed by Schein (1993) to explore the career preferences of pharmacists and pharmacy technicians (Guest, Battersby, & Oakley, 2007). The interest in the comparison lies in the different labor markets in which they operate. Pharmacists have 4 years of academic training, while technicians take lower-level technician courses. At present, there is no scope for transfer from technician to pharmacist, and as a result, the scope for career progression among pharmacy technicians is significantly constrained. Yet the two occupations work closely alongside each other with some scope for sharing and transfer of activities. Building on the work of Zabusky and Barley (1996), the career orientations of technicians are of particular interest, especially with respect to the priority given to achievement and advancement.

The data were collected as part of a larger study of the backgrounds, career aspirations, and work attitudes of pharmacists and pharmacy technicians. The sample of pharmacists is a

Table 16.1   A Classification of Careers That Includes Those in Routine Occupations

	Intra-Organizational	*Extra-Organizational*
Work as Central	Traditional-constrained career Achievement	Tourism Self-employment
Work as Marginal	Variety and control Disengagement	Opted out Locked out

stratified random sample of the U.K. population of registered pharmacists, collected through the Royal Pharmaceutical Society of Great Britain, to which all practicing pharmacists must be affiliated, while the technician sample included all members of the Pharmacy Technicians Society and a cross-section of technicians working for the largest pharmacy retail chains. Responses were received from 1,293 pharmacists and 594 pharmacy technicians, in both cases a response rate of close to 60%.

The Traditional Constrained Career

There is good evidence that even within an objectively constrained set of external and internal labor market circumstances, a sizeable minority of workers aspire to an upwardly mobile career and, more important, perceive that opportunities for this type of career exist within their current work settings.

Despite claims that structural changes have reduced promotion opportunities and many blue-collar workers have limited promotion aspirations, allied to Barley's (1989) contention that objective vertical career mobility is closed to many Americans and the U.K. evidence about the lack of wage mobility, subjective perceptions of opportunities may be rather different. Although self-report is subject to distortion, surveys reported by Gallie, White, Cheng, and Tomlinson (1998) show that in 1994, 40% of workers in the United Kingdom believed that they had a 50–50 or better chance of getting promoted in their present job, up from 36% in 1984. The increase had been mainly among women, particularly those working part-time. Even among those on temporary contracts, 21% thought they had a 50–50 or better chance of getting promoted with their current employer, and perhaps reverting to a more subjective definition of a career but still retaining the notion of upward mobility, 49% thought that they were in an occupation with a career ladder.

Scott (1994) has illustrated how perceptions of promotion opportunities can arise, even in a context where hierarchy is apparently being flattened. He describes how in a chocolate factory, the four manual grades were each divided into five subcategories, resulting in 20 levels of manual employee. It was possible to progress

through these grades by demonstrating proficiency and effectiveness, partly through training. In practice, the requirement to pass an aptitude test meant that some workers had better opportunities to progress than others. As a result, 59% of those who had passed the test and already progressed to the second main grade perceived promotion as probable, but 67% of those in the lower grade, mainly those who had not passed the aptitude test, did not consider it possible. In short, approaches, such as job evaluation, to create a hierarchy of job grades can create the appearance of a promotion ladder, even for workers who remain in much the same job.

Along similar lines, Belt (2005), in her study of a number of call centers, found that even within a very flat organizational hierarchy, where the only realistic moves, and then only for a minority, are to assistant team leader and team leader, most workers could see career opportunities. As Belt notes, "There was evidence of a strong belief among interviewees that call centres provide positive contexts in which women are able to build careers" (p. 186). Yet in the same paper, Belt describes how call centers have been characterized as the new employment ghettoes for women, replacing the old typing pools in the provision of dead-end jobs.

There is, then, evidence that promotion opportunities may be perceived to exist in a wide variety of settings, even among those for whom objective career opportunities may appear to be limited and among workers who may not attach a high priority to career mobility.

The comparison between pharmacists and pharmacy technicians helps illustrate the importance of the different priorities attached to the traditional career and to the way in which opportunities can be perceived. The first point of interest is that the pharmacy technicians have a strong career orientation. The study used Schein's (1993) career anchors. Asked about the priority given to "having a progressive career, climbing to a senior position in an organization with broad accountability," the pharmacy technicians gave it a significantly higher priority than the pharmacists. In other words, pharmacy technicians, despite their objective restrictions, retain a traditional career orientation. Pharmacists have considerable career choices across a variety of settings, ranging from a lifetime of self-employment in a single chemist shop to a hierarchical career in a large organization. In contrast, pharmacy technicians experience more objective constraint but express stronger aspirations for a traditional career and on the whole are more satisfied with their career choice and career progress. They reflect the desire for, and broad satisfaction with, a traditional but constrained career. Comparing pharmacists and pharmacy technicians, there appears to be a large difference between their career opportunities and their subjective perception of both these opportunities and their experience of progress. Despite the combination of greater constraint and a stronger career orientation, the pharmacy technicians are more satisfied with their career progress.

Achievement and Service

As Zabusky and Barley (1996) note, there is the opportunity to develop a career by moving from the periphery to the center of an occupation, usually within a given organizational context, and therefore to have a career based on achievement rather than advancement. They argued that "technicians measured career success in terms of accumulated expertise, accomplishment in the face of a new challenge, and the gradual acquisition of a reputation for skill" (p. 202). However, they also noted the importance attached to a discourse of "respect," with lack of respect constantly reflected in terms of low pay. In this case, therefore, while achievement may reflect the primary career orientation, secondary orientations were concerned with respect and recognition of respect through pay.

For both pharmacists and pharmacy technicians, career progress based on achievement is an option, and there was evidence that for both, this was an attractive option. While there may be some limited opportunity for promotion among pharmacy technicians within the hierarchy of a large hospital, university department, or retail chemist, there was also scope to move to a central role by virtue of tenure, experience, and citizenship behavior. The same opportunity exists for those who spend long periods with an organization such as the police and prison services and thereby develop considerable local expertise and move to the center by virtue of a form

of social capital and knowledge of organizational history and procedures (Van Maanen, 1975). Not only is this form of "career" pursued by many in professional and technical occupations, either because of limited opportunities for advancement or in preference to advancement, but it is also common in sectors such as the broadly defined entertainment industry. Musicians and actors, for example, can move from a peripheral role as they seek to establish themselves to a much more central role as they acquire "star" status.

Variety and Control

As Thomas (1989) notes, for those who have no opportunity for upward mobility and occupy a role with little intrinsic interest, one response may be to "construct" a career by creating variety and interest within the role. This might take a variety of forms. In the days when workplace trade unionism was a powerful force, one escape route lay in becoming a shop steward. This provides a form of control within a pluralist context. Workers may seek other forms of control. There is the long-standing literature from the Hawthorne studies (Roethlisberger & Dickson, 1939) through the classic accounts by Whyte (1955) and Roy (1958) on "banana time" to more recent illustrations of various activities ranging from pilfering to minor confrontations with management (see, e.g., Ackroyd & Thompson, 1999), which illustrate the ways in which workers seek control and variety in work.

One of the criticisms of contemporary employment is that more effective surveillance mechanisms have reduced the opportunity to engage in what the organization would define as counterproductive behavior. Green (2006) has noted some general reduction in autonomy and has linked this to a more general decline in job satisfaction. It may, therefore, be the case that the scope to develop a "career" based on seeking to extend the frontier of control (Goodrich, 1920) is becoming less feasible. However, this may underestimate the ingenuity of workers who regard work as a necessity but who feel little loyalty to the organization in constructing a form of control and viewing the expansion of the sphere of control as a kind of success. For example, those with experience learn how to use bureaucracy and rules as a source of power and influence, often to the considerable frustration of management (Crozier, 1964).

Disengagement

Disengagement can appear under several guises. Its major feature is that work is not a central life interest. A worker may therefore adopt an instrumental attitude where income assumes priority. In some dual-career families with dependents, flexibility, perhaps in the form of complementary shift patterns, may be a priority. There was strong evidence of disengagement among a proportion of the sample in the U.K. national study. At least 23% expressed a preference for a disengaged career. Among this group, 91% agreed that a career was not important to them, 88% said they would prefer a series of jobs at the same level rather than striving for promotion, 76% preferred to live for the present rather than plan for the future, and 74% agreed that work was marginal to their life. It was notable that they tended to be older, in lower-level jobs, and on lower incomes. This suggests that, whether by choice or constraint, they are giving greater priority to life outside work rather than adopting a primarily instrumental view of work. This goes further than work-life balance in that the balance leans toward life outside work.

Tourism

Among those who believe that they are in an occupation with a career ladder but for whom promotion appears blocked, an alternative route to career progression is to change employers and engage in what Thomas (1989) terms *tourism*. Tourism also offers a form of mobility, variety, and escape for workers who do not seek advancement. The growing literature on boundaryless careers (Arthur & Rousseau, 1996) indicates that the concept of mobility across organizations has acquired as much salience in the analysis of managerial and professional workers as it has for those at lower levels in organizations. The rapid changes alluded to earlier may force mobility on many people. A key question is therefore how far mobility across jobs and employers is a matter of choice. Thomas identified this as a career strategy for low-skill workers.

The analysis of the national U.K. sample indicated that about 20% displayed values that fitted with this strategy. They displayed low commitment to their current organization, preferred a short time with a lot of organizations to a long time with one, wanted to manage their own careers, and preferred employability to job security. Interestingly, they tended to be young graduates rather than the less well qualified. For those in routine occupations, tourism may provide an opportunity for some limited upward progression. However, it is more likely to offer variety in a context where routine work may become very boring or unduly intensive. It seems likely, although we need more evidence, that this may be particularly appealing as a form of career management for those in routine white-collar jobs such as call centers and retail stores (Belt, 2005).

The evidence suggests that we must be careful not to overstate the amount of change in mobility. In the United Kingdom, which falls around the middle of Organisation for Economic Co-Operation and Development (OECD) countries in terms of average job tenure, it has been argued (Burgess & Rees, 1997) that there has been little change in job tenure and therefore little increase in mobility between 1975 and 1998. Since this appears to conflict with popular assumptions as well as with some other data, Gregg and Wadsworth (1999) tried to reconcile the different sources of evidence. They conclude that, overall, there has been little change in average job tenure but that this hides some reduction in tenure among men, particularly older men, and a growth in tenure among women, particularly women with dependent children.[1] There is no evidence that those in the lower-grade jobs are particularly prone to job change. Across the working population the proportion of graduates with a tenure of 10 years or more had fallen from 34.3% in 1985 to 32.9% in 1998, while for those with no educational qualifications it had only reduced from 40.5% to 38.7% and for those with intermediate level qualifications, from 31.2% to 30.3%. By implication, "tourism" is not a growing career strategy for many of those in lower-level blue- and white-collar jobs. Indeed, it is more likely to be found among those pursuing managerial and professional careers. There is also evidence that the second form of mobility—across hierarchies and, by implication, the class divide—has been static or declining in a country such as the United Kingdom, despite attempts to broaden the education base.

The Self-Employed Career

A further type of career for those at all levels but perhaps particularly for those with low skills and in routine roles is self-employment. This may appear high risk, but it provides a form of variety and offers a career through effective networking to establish contacts and connections. Examples range from those working in the construction industry to craft workers, gardeners, and window cleaners. Through their networks and friendship ties, they may from time to time broaden their activities to help friends who have a particular contract and perhaps a deadline. This career route is also followed by increasing numbers of workers in managerial and professional roles who want to escape the controls of conventional organizational life. For some, it provides an opportunity to build an organization. They may not move within a hierarchy, but they can create hierarchical careers for others.

The national U.K. sample excluded the self-employed. However, in the pharmacists' study, it is notable that a significant number of pharmacists opted for self-employment status and worked within a variety of employment contracts, including temporary contracts, while some simultaneously held two, three, or even four part-time jobs. The evidence indicates that they are at least as satisfied as those in permanent jobs and on career ladders, and in some respects they report higher levels of quality of working life, including better work-life balance and less work-related stress (Guest, Oakley, Clinton, & Budjanovcanin, 2006).

Opting Out

The final group consists of those who, for a variety of reasons, have opted out of employment. Some may belong to the "black" or "informal" economy, but most will be economically inactive. In the current context, where about 75% of those of working age in the United Kingdom

are economically active, a record high level, it might seem strange to focus on this group. However, there are two reasons to do so. One relates to age, the other to social disadvantage.

A notable feature of employment patterns in recent years has been the decline in the proportion of men aged 50 years and above who are economically active. As Disney (1999) has shown, the proportion of men aged 60 to 65 in employment fell from about 80% to less than 50% over two decades from 1980. Among those aged 50 to 59, the proportion has fallen from over 90% to 75%. A somewhat similar pattern, albeit less marked, has been occurring in many other European countries. A key issue is whether this fall in employment among older men is a result of their choice or a process of exclusion (see also Feldman, Chapter 9). We cited evidence earlier that older workers were more inclined to seek work-life balance. But they were also more inclined to want to work for as long as possible rather than retire early. This suggests that the fall in employment of older workers is a product of exclusion by employers. Disney reaches the same conclusion. He notes that occupational pension schemes helped ease the passage among those for whom they were available, while invalidity allowances provided a mechanism for maintaining an income among those in lower-skill occupations, more particularly in areas of depressed employment. According to survey evidence, among those who retired early without an occupational pension, 32% cited their own ill health and 21%, involuntary redundancy. Only 10% cited factors such as being "fed up with work," "want[ing] to spend more time with the family," or "wanting to enjoy life while young and fit" (Disney, 1999). In short, the working lives of many low-skill workers are shortened against their wishes, and invalidity benefit has provided a major legitimate means of funding this process. They have not retired; instead, they have adjusted to a career stage in which they have opted out of work.

A final feature of opting out is the growing tendency of people at various stages of their career, but notably those at the early-career stage, to take a "gap year" or a career break. It is possible that the example of the growing number of women who have successfully resumed careers after a short break for child-bearing has resulted in greater confidence that this is feasible. It is also possible that the high demands of many jobs make this more desirable. There appears to be a greater willingness to trust to employability to ensure job opportunities, and this makes temporary opting out a more attractive option.

Locked Out

Gregg, Hansen, and Wadsworth (1999) note that in 1999, 18% of households with people of working age in them had no one in work. OECD figures suggest that the level is even higher—somewhere above 20%. Only Finland, Belgium, and France have a higher proportion. When we look just at households with children, then the United Kingdom is clearly out in front, and 90% of workless families with children are defined as poor. The point that Gregg and colleagues make is that the rising levels of employment and arguments about growing flexibility in employment and career choices have hidden a divide between families in which all adults of employment age work and those in which none work. This has implications for poverty, but it also means that when we consider the careers of those in routine and low-skill occupations, we must recognize that for a sizeable minority, their "career" is long-term unemployment or disability. The structural features of this are highlighted in the link between education and opportunity. In 43% of workless households, the occupiers have no educational qualifications of any kind, and a further 44% have only a basic school-leaving qualification. Gregg and colleagues suggest that the growth of workless households can be attributed to a combination of limited employment opportunities in certain regions and the low pay in jobs that are available failing to compensate sufficiently for the loss of unemployment and other benefits. Factors such as education and occupation contribute some small additional explanation. For a significant minority of those who might find themselves in the lower-grade occupations, the choice of career strategy is ruled out by long-term absence from the active labor force. In considering the choices available and the constraints in place, we would do well to bear in mind this neglected but sizeable minority.

CONCLUSION

A key conclusion emerging from this analysis is that for those in routine occupations or in technician-type roles, it is not a matter of working to live or living to work. Both are valid descriptions of the experiences of some workers some of the time. No evidence emerges from the data presented here of widespread disaffection with, or withdrawal from, work, although for some, work is not a central life interest and others, for a variety of reasons, find themselves excluded from conventional employment.

This chapter has explored perspectives on the careers of those in routine occupations requiring relatively low skills. It has presented evidence to suggest that many, at least in the United Kingdom, retain fairly conventional hierarchical career aspirations. However, labor market factors mean that their career opportunities are seriously constrained. Nevertheless, through a variety of mechanisms, and with the increasing help of contemporary human resource policies, many believe that they can see possibilities for and experience a hierarchical career. The availability of the opportunity to move through grades in an apparently progressive upward career does not necessarily mean that this is an appealing option, and there are also many alternatives that can be attractive to workers in these lower-level occupations. They include what we have termed tourism, disengagement, achievement, and variety. We have also drawn attention to the sizeable proportion of low-skill workers who constitute the long-term unemployed. The choices of career for these low-skill occupational groups are determined by a combination of education and qualifications, the state of the labor market, particularly in their region, and their own preferences, which will be shaped by the social context and their life experiences both outside and inside the world of work. In these respects, these workers are no different from those in higher-level occupations. It appears that many of those in employment in routine jobs retain an interest in some form of traditional hierarchical career and are often able to construct for themselves the perception of career opportunities and even career progress. However, the reality is that key features of the labor market and their position in it are serious constraints on any realistic hierarchical career progress. As a result, alternative conceptions of a career and of career advancement need to be considered, and this chapter has attempted to outline what some of these alternatives might be.

NOTE

1. Cf. Cappelli and Hamori (Chapter 17), who note that voluntary turnover and involuntary turnover move in opposite directions over the business cycle and therefore mask each others' effects.

REFERENCES

Ackroyd, S., & Thompson, P. (1999). *Organizational misbehaviour.* Thousand Oaks, CA: Sage.

Appelbaum, E., Bailey, T., Berg, P., & Kalleberg, A. (2000). *Manufacturing advantage.* Ithaca, NY: ILR Press.

Arthur, M. B., Hall, D. T., & Lawrence, B. S. (1989). *Handbook of career theory.* Cambridge, UK: Cambridge University Press.

Arthur, M. B., Inkson, K., & Pringle, J. K. (1999). *The new careers.* Thousand Oaks, CA: Sage.

Arthur, M. B., & Rousseau, D. M. (Eds.). (1996). *The boundaryless career.* Oxford: Oxford University Press.

Barley, S. (1989). Careers, identities, and institutions: The legacy of the Chicago school of sociology. In M. B. Arthur, D. T. Hall, & B. S. Lawrence (Eds.), *Handbook of career theory* (pp. 41–65). Cambridge, UK: Cambridge University Press.

Batt, R. (1996). From bureaucracy to enterprise? The changing jobs and careers of managers in telecommunications service. In P. Osterman (Ed.), *Broken ladders: Managerial careers in the new economy* (pp. 55–80). Oxford: Oxford University Press.

Belt, V. (2005). A female ghetto? Women's careers in telephone call centres. In S. Deery & N. Kinnie (Eds.), *Call centres and human resource management* (pp. 174–197). Basingstoke: Palgrave.

Beutell, N. J., & Brenner, O. C. (1986). Sex differences in work values. *Journal of Vocational Behavior, 28,* 29–41.

Blackburn, R., & Mann, M. (1979). *The working class in the labour market.* London: Macmillan.

Blauner, R. (1964). *Alienation and freedom.* Chicago: Chicago University Press.

Braverman, H. (1975). *Labor and monopoly capital.* New York: Monthly Review Press.

Burgess, S., & Rees, H. (1997). Job tenure in Britain, 1975–92. *Economic Journal, March,* 334–344.

Cadin, L., Bailly-Bender, A.-F., & Saint-Giniez, V. (2000). Exploring boundaryless careers in the French context. In M. A. Peiperl, M. B. Arthur, R. Goffee, & T. Morris (Eds.), *Career frontiers: New conceptions of working lives* (pp. 228–255). Oxford: Oxford University Press.

Cannon, D. (1995). *Generation X and the new work ethic.* London: Demos.

Cappelli, P. (1999). *The new deal at work.* Boston: Harvard Business School Press.

Crozier, M. (1964). *The bureaucratic phenomenon.* Chicago: University of Chicago Press.

Dickens, R. (1999). Wage mobility in Great Britain. In P. Gregg & J. Wadsworth (Eds.), *The state of working Britain* (pp. 206–224). Manchester: Manchester University Press.

Disney, R. (1999). Why have older men stopped working? In P. Gregg & J. Wadsworth (Eds.), *The state of working Britain* (pp. 58–74). Manchester: Manchester University Press.

Driver, M. (1982). Career concepts—a new approach to career research. In R. Katz (Ed.), *Career issues in human resource management* (pp. 23–32). Englewood Cliffs, NJ: Prentice Hall.

Dubin, R., Champoux, J., & Porter, L. (1975). Central life interests and organizational commitment of blue-collar and clerical workers. *Administrative Science Quarterly, 20,* 411–421.

Edwards, R. (1979). *Contested terrain.* New York: Basic Books.

Freeman, R. (2000). The curative powers of full employment: The American experience. In N. Burkitt (Ed.), *A life's work: Achieving full and fulfilling employment* (pp. 15–23). London: IPPR.

Gallie, D., White, M., Cheng, Y., & Tomlinson, M. (1998). *Restructuring the employment relationship.* Oxford: Oxford University Press.

Goldthorpe, J., Lockwood, D., Bechhofer, F., & Platt, J. (1968). *The affluent worker: Industrial attitudes and behaviour.* Cambridge, UK: Cambridge University Press.

Goodrich, C. (1920). *The frontier of control.* London: Bell.

Green, F. (2006). *Demanding work.* Princeton, NJ: Princeton University Press.

Gregg, P., Hansen, K., & Wadsworth, J. (1999). The rise of the workless household. In P. Gregg & J. Wadsworth (Eds.), *The state of working Britain* (pp. 75–89). Manchester: Manchester University Press.

Gregg, P., & Wadsworth, J. (1999). Job tenure, 1975–1998. In P. Gregg & J. Wadsworth (Eds.), *The state of working Britain* (pp. 109–126). Manchester: Manchester University Press.

Guest, D., Battersby, S., & Oakley, P. (2007). *Future pharmacy workforce requirements.* London: Royal Pharmaceutical Society of Great Britain.

Guest, D., & Conway, N. (2004). *Employee well-being and the psychological contract.* London: CIPD.

Guest, D., Oakley, P., Clinton, M., & Budjanovcanin, A. (2006). Free or precarious? A comparison of the attitudes of workers in flexible and traditional employment contracts. *Human Resource Management Review, 16,* 107–124.

Hakim, K. (1996). *Key issues in women's work: Female heterogeneity and the polarisation of women's employment.* London: Athlone Press.

Hill, S. (1981). *Competition and control at work.* London: Heinemann.

Hughes, E. C. (1937). Institutional office and the person. *American Journal of Sociology, 43,* 404–443.

Ichniowski, C., Kochan, T., Levine, D., Olson, C., & Strauss, G. (1996). What works at work: Overview and assessment. *Industrial Relations, 35,* 299–333.

Kanter, R. (1989). *When giants learn to dance: Mastering the challenge of strategy, management, and careers in the 1990s.* New York: Simon & Schuster.

Layard, R. (2005). *Happiness.* New York: Penguin Press.

Lewis, S., Smithson, J., & Kugelberg, C. (2002). Into work: Job insecurity and changing psychological contracts. In J. Brannen, S. Lewis, A. Nilsen, & J. Smithson (Eds.), *Young Europeans, work and family* (pp. 69–88). London: Routledge.

Machin, S. (1999). Wage inequality in the 1970s, 1980s and 1990s. In P. Gregg and J. Wadsworth (Eds.), *The state of working Britain* (pp. 185–205). Manchester: Manchester University Press.

Mason, E. S. (1994). Work values: A gender comparison and implications for practice. *Psychological Reports, 74,* 415–418.

Meaning of Work Team (MoW). (1987). *Meaning of work.* London: Academic Press.

Osterman, P. (Ed.). (1996). *Broken ladders: Managerial careers in the New Economy.* Oxford: Oxford University Press.

Parker, S., & Smith, M. (1976). Work and leisure. In R. Dubin (Ed.), *Handbook of work, organization and society* (pp. 37–64). Chicago: Rand McNally.

Piore, M., & Sabel, C. (1984). *The second industrial divide.* New York: Basic Books.

Prandy, K., Stewart, A., & Blackburn, R. (1982). *White-collar work.* London: Macmillan.

Roethlisberger, F., & Dickson, W. (1939). *Management and the worker.* Boston: Harvard University Press.

Rosenbaum, J. E. (1979). Tournament mobility: Career patterns in organizations. *Administrative Science Quarterly, 24,* 220–241.

Roy, D. (1958). Banana time: Job satisfaction and informal interaction. *Human Organization, 18,* 158–168.

Scase, R., & Goffee, R. (1989). *Reluctant managers: Their work and lifestyles.* London: Routledge.

Schein, E. H. (1993). *Career anchors* (Rev. ed.). San Diego, CA: Pfeiffer.

Schein, E. H. (1996). Career anchors revisited: Implications for career development in the 21st century. *Academy of Management Executive, 10*(4), 80–88.

Scott, A. (1994). *Willing slaves?* Cambridge, UK: Cambridge University Press.

Smola, K. W., & Sutton, C. (2002). Generational differences: Revisiting generational work values for the new millennium. *Journal of Organizational Behavior, 23,* 363–382.

Sturges, J. (1999). What it means to succeed: Personal conceptions of career success held by male and female managers at different ages. *British Journal of Management, 10,* 239–252.

Sturges, J., & Guest, D. (2004). Living to work or working to live? Work-life balance early in the career. *Human Resource Management Journal, 14*(4), 5–20.

Terkel, S. (1977). *Working.* New York: Pantheon.

Thomas, R. (1989). Blue-collar careers: Meaning and choice in a world of constraints. In M. B. Arthur, D. T. Hall, & B. S. Lawrence (Eds.), *Handbook of career theory* (pp. 354–379). Cambridge, UK: Cambridge University Press.

Tulgan, B. (1996). *Managing Generation X: How to bring out the best in young talent.* Oxford: Capstone.

Van Maanen, J. (1975). Police socialization: A longitudinal examination of job attitudes in an urban police department. *Administrative Science Quarterly, 20,* 207–228.

Weick, K., & Berlinger, L. (1989). Career improvisation in self-designing organizations. In M. B. Arthur, D. T. Hall, & B. S. Lawrence (Eds.), *Handbook of career theory* (pp. 313–328). Cambridge, UK: Cambridge University Press.

Whyte, W. H. (1955). *Money and motivation.* New York: Harper & Row.

Whyte, W. H. (1956). *The organization man.* New York: Simon & Schuster.

Young, M., & Willmott, P. (1973). *The symmetrical family.* London: Routledge.

Zabusky, S., & Barley, S. (1996). Redefining success: Ethnographic observation on the careers of technicians. In P. Osterman (Ed.), *Broken ladders: Managerial careers in the new economy* (pp. 185–214). Oxford: Oxford University Press.

17

THE INSTITUTIONS OF OUTSIDE HIRING

PETER CAPPELLI

MONIKA HAMORI

For much of the period following World War II, the reality of careers for most people in the United States and in other industrialized countries was reasonably straightforward. First, they were likely to be employees, increasingly so as compared with earlier generations as people moved from farms and individual proprietary enterprises into larger and larger enterprises. Second, they chose an employer soon after leaving school and spent their entire working life with that employer. Despite the belief that the United States was a wide-open economy where people picked up and moved, the average employee tenure in the United States as late as the 1970s equaled that of Japan, a country where the stereotype was the reverse (Hall, 1982). The idea that one could experience a succession of jobs that represented advancement in status and rewards had real relevance for blue-collar workers where job ladders, typically based on seniority, allowed at least some

advancement up a hierarchy based on skill. For white-collar and management jobs, career prospects were much richer and more complex, offering the possibility of considerable upward mobility that was driven by a range of factors, including the characteristics of the organizations in which one worked, an individual's own interests and attributes, and the intersections between these two.

Research on careers reflected this reality. One school, arguably the dominant approach in terms of the volume of work produced, took a sociological approach. This stream examined career paths within occupational professions on the one hand (Becker, 1952; Rosenbaum, 1979) and focused on the characteristics of organizations that affected the careers of individuals on the other (e.g., Doeringer & Piore, 1971; Stewman & Konda, 1983; White, 1970). It also examined how a few predictors (such as social class or institutional prestige) are related to career success or status attainment (Blau & Duncan, 1967). An extensive review of this stream of literature is given by Blair-Loy (1999). The other school took a psychological perspective and focused on the attributes of individuals (e.g., the Big Five personality traits— Boudreau, Boswell, Judge, & Bretz, 2001; Judge, Higgins, Thoresen, & Barrick, 1999), their needs and interests, as the drivers of career outcomes (Schein, 1985; Schneider, 1987). A frequently examined outcome in this stream is "intrinsic" (or "subjective") career success (e.g., Erdogan, Kraimer, & Liden, 2004; Judge, Kammeyer-Mueller, & Bretz, 2004; Judge and Kammeyer-Mueller, Chapter 4). Most of the researchers who describe their field as "careers" have roots in vocational or other subfields of psychology. For the most part, these two traditions did not intersect. But they shared the common notion that careers operated inside an organization, and both focused on the richer career patterns of managers and executives.

The reality of careers in the new millennium is quite different. In the United States, for example, jobs are increasingly at risk over time. The earnings loss that displaced workers experience when they move on to an alternative employer has also been growing, and managers are now at as great a (or greater) risk of job loss as production workers (Farber, 2003). Those who lose their jobs now stay unemployed longer, reflecting the fact that they are no longer

rehired when business improves as was the case in earlier generations. In Europe, the trend toward longer-term unemployment began even earlier (Blanchard, 2004). Consequently, attachment to an individual employer has fallen sharply, as indicated clearly by the U.S. data shown in Figure 17.1.

More people are independent contractors— just less than 7% of the U.S. workforce—and as much as 30% are in "nonstandard" jobs, such as part-time employment, temporary help, and contract work (see DiNatale, 2001). Similarly, in many European countries such as the Netherlands and Spain, a quarter of the workforce was involved as temporary help or in leased employment (see Connelly & Gallagher, 2004; de Ruyter & Burgess, 2000, for surveys of research across countries).

Careers are no longer necessarily inside the organization phenomena (Cappelli, 1999; Jacoby, 1999). They are now much more likely to involve movement between employers and, in many cases, movement from employment to self-employment and vice versa. In 1999, 22% of *Fortune* 100 CEOs had been with their companies for more than 35 years as compared with just 10% in 2004, and the average tenure for *Fortune* 100 CEOs has decreased from 7 to 6 years since 1998 (Spencer Stuart, 2004). Expectations have also changed. A survey of 455 senior executives revealed that in 1990, 74% expected to work for four or fewer companies

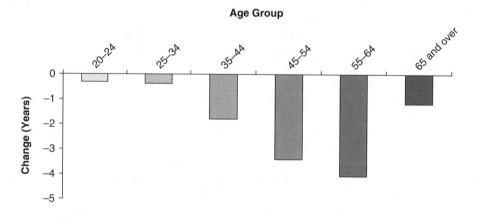

Figure 17.1   Change in Median Years of Tenure, 1983 to 1998, Adult Men by Age

SOURCE: Bureau of Labor Statistics. Median tenure declines among older men, 1983–2000. http://www.bls.gov/opub/ted/2000/aug/wk4/art05.htm.

over the course of their career. Today, 53% of those executives expect to work for seven or more companies before their career ends (Association of Executive Search Consultants [AESC], 2004). In addition, most executives think that their most attractive career opportunity would come up by changing the organization that they work for (AESC, 2004).

The earlier research traditions that examined the individual and organizational attributes that affect careers are, of course, still relevant, but there are important limits to both. The contemporary notion of a "boundaryless career" has identified the fact that individuals move across organizations, but exactly how that movement takes place is not so obvious. The research under that heading (e.g., Arthur & Rousseau, 1996) sees careers as progressing based on the personal interests and agendas of the individual, but the reality of modern careers is that the amount of control that individuals have in shaping their careers is both limited and strongly conditioned by the opportunities available to them (Slay and Taylor, Chapter 19).

In an environment where careers no longer operate entirely within organizations, a new set of factors becomes important: labor markets and the institutions that operate within them to match individuals to jobs. In the arguments that follow, we focus on managerial jobs because they have been the focus of most of the attention and research on careers. We consider first the history of the role of labor markets in managerial careers. We then discuss search theory, the theoretical framework that is most relevant for understanding the matching of individuals with jobs in labor markets. Finally, we examine the labor market institutions that are particularly important for shaping managerial careers. These include search firms and, most recently, the arrangements that have been made possible by the Internet. These topics have been largely ignored by the previous research on careers and are the focus of this chapter.

THE RISE, DECLINE, AND REBIRTH OF OUTSIDE SEARCH

In the early days of U.S. corporations, there were few management jobs and even fewer executive positions. Most companies were "virtual" in the sense that a great many operations were outsourced. Executive positions were held by owners and a handful of close associates, typically family members. The need for middle management came when corporations began to vertically integrate and the need for coordination and standardization rose. The need for executives came later, with the rise of the multidivisional firm and the requirements of managing middle managers.

In those early days of management, and especially executive, careers, positions were filled largely through outside hiring. Large corporations such as General Motors and DuPont grew by acquisition, hiring in the founders of the acquired firms as executives in the new, larger corporation. After World War I, many companies were concerned about their ability to staff the growing number of management and executive positions and began experimenting with programs to develop "talent" (qualified managers) internally and promote from within. But most of those experiments died with the Great Depression.

The economic boom following World War II, combined with the fact that most companies did no hiring in the decade of the Great Depression that preceded the war, created a serious talent shortfall in most companies. The immediate response of employers to this shortfall of talent, as in previous generations, was to raid competitors for talent. One consequence of this interest in poaching talent from competitors was the rise of the modern recruiting industry. A survey by the New York Association of Private Office Personnel Agencies, which were essentially "staffing" companies that found candidates for employers, indicated that only 2% of employers used them in 1940, but by 1948, 28% of employers used them consistently and 68% used them occasionally. These agencies were not like contemporary search firms. They based their business on lists of individuals who identified themselves as wanting to change jobs and essentially rented that list to employers who had jobs to fill. They were not good at helping employers find executive talent, perhaps because few executives were willing to identify themselves as wanting to move. Frank Zintl, Head of the Executive Employment Service in Philadelphia, noted that "there is definitely a shortage of men in the $25,000 bracket," what would have been the executive rank ("Can Job Agencies Find Your Man," 1949, p. 21). The inability to find senior management and executive talent through agencies led companies to turn to existing management consulting firms for help. These firms took a different approach and would search for executive talent among employed executives for a daily fee of $50 to $300 per day, a significant fee at that time. Booz Allen Hamilton was one of the early leaders in executive search, and as one of their leaders described the challenge, "The man we are looking for is usually employed at the present" ("Can Job Agencies Find Your Man," 1949, p. 21). From this process, the modern industry of executive search was born.

The management consulting firms got into the search business as an extension of their general interest in helping existing clients solve their problems. But the business of executive search was seen as slightly unsavory (Byrne, 1986) in that talking to a headhunter was evidence of a lack of loyalty to one's current employer. There was also the sense that the consulting firms engaged in headhunting had something of a conflict of interest as they could learn about their client's executives during their consulting assignments and then recruit those executives away for business elsewhere. Several important firms spun off their talent search businesses as a result—Korn/Ferry was created from Booz Allen Hamilton and Heidrick and Struggles from McKinsey & Company. AT Kearney was the only one to retain its executive search business (Byrne, 1986).

Given the overall shortage of managerial talent in the economy, however, employers soon found that they could not meet their human resource needs by hiring from outside, and they shifted their attention toward the internal development of talent. Outside hiring was an exception, especially in large organizations where spending one's entire career in the same organization was the rule rather than the exception. What governed careers in this period were, for the most part, the rules and verities associated with organizational life, especially those that described bureaucracies. The academic study of careers was essentially built around advancement within a bureaucratic framework. The term *internal labor markets,* which was used to understand the principles governing careers inside organizations (Doeringer & Piore, 1971), was a misnomer in the sense that they were not markets at all but instead were bureaucratic practices that served some of the functions of markets. Outside markets and search generally played a minor role, except at the entry level, for careers, especially those for managers and executives.

In the 1980s, things began to change with the waves of corporate restructuring that led to relentless downsizing of jobs, efforts that were increasingly directed at the management ranks. The task of organizations shifted from developing talent to shedding talent—"delayering" organizations and reengineering to reduce management content. Internal development of managerial talent proved unnecessary in this environment. At the very top ranks, however, the demand for outside hires actually increased (see below). The rising demands on corporations to improve financial performance and respond more quickly to changing markets led to more frequent restructuring and faster, more radical changes in business strategies. That demand, in turn, created pressure for companies to look outside for executives with different experiences and skill sets to run companies. It would not be far wrong to see at least some of this development as less about searching for better executives in some absolute sense and more about a "churning" of talent, rearranging executives across firms as the needs of those companies changed.

Along with more outside hiring of CEOs came an extension of search to other positions in the executive ranks. To change organizations more quickly, outside CEOs began to hire outside executives to fill new roles. Changes in business strategy and corporate restructuring became synonymous with changing executives. The search business expanded down the organizational chart as each functional area, in turn, began to see outside hires as a means of allowing them to change more quickly.

The economic expansion of the 1990s, the longest in U.S. history, certainly contributed to the search business as sustained growth meant that companies soon exhausted their internal talent pools. The most important development within that period of expansion was the rise of information technology (IT) and its labor force.

IT work is defined by standards that are created by vendors (e.g., "Cisco-certified" technicians) or by other organizations (e.g., COBOL programming) and that cut across organizations. IT work, therefore, is reasonably similar across companies. The workers who perform IT tasks also have skill sets that translate across organizations: A Java programmer can do similar work in reasonably similar ways across companies. When the demand for IT services began to explode in the mid-1990s, companies looked outside to find people who could do this work. Because the demand for these workers was so hot, virtually all of them had jobs already. When they were hired, then, they left a vacancy in their previous organization that had to be filled from the outside, what White (1970) first described as a "vacancy chain" problem. Even a small number of IT vacancies could generate a huge amount of IT hiring in this manner. And outside search expanded enormously to meet that demand. What is important about these developments is that outside search became an option—in many cases the preferred option—for providing not just the rare skills and experience sets associated with idiosyncratic executive positions but also the routine and commodity-like skills associated with lower-level, nonmanagement jobs. The rise of outside hiring for lower-level and nonexecutive positions helped create a new set of labor market institutions to match people with jobs.

An important development accelerating this outside hiring for lower-level and more traditional positions has been the rise of nondegree credentials that certify skills and proficiency in various technical areas. These credentials are typically issued by independent organizations outside the educational community and are mostly associated with IT, where companies such as Microsoft and Cisco issue certifications for individuals who have completed training and demonstrated proficiency in the use of those systems. Literally millions of these credentials have been issued, and unlike academic degrees, they are highly focused on actual job tasks (see Clifford Adelman, 1997, on the rise of certifications and credentialing in the labor market). The consequence of these credentials is to increase the ease with which individuals can move across organizations by certifying that they can perform

tasks central to reasonably standard jobs with a high level of proficiency. Together, these developments have accelerated the movement toward something like professional labor markets for jobs that were previously seen as internal, technical functions (see Leicht & Fennell, 1997).

There has been a long debate in the economics literature as to whether the above trends have actually changed average job turnover. Unfortunately, these studies tend to combine involuntary turnover with voluntary turnover, while the concern above is mainly with the former. Furthermore, the two types of turnover move in opposite directions over the business cycle, tending to reproduce stability in the summary number.[1] While the studies have long shown rising overall turnover for some groups in the labor force (e.g., for men), only more recent data have begun to show increased turnover in the overall labor force (Neumark, 2002).

Studies of turnover in the executive labor markets are less ambiguous. As compared with 1980, the turnover rates of top executives in *Fortune* 100 companies were sharply higher in 2001; employer tenure was significantly lower as was the percentage of lifetime employees (Cappelli & Hamori, 2004). Other studies also show an increase in turnover. In 2001, annual CEO turnover amounted to 9.2%, a 53% increase from 1995, while the average CEO tenure declined from 9.5 years to 7.3 years (Lucier, Spiegel, & Schuyt, 2002). A growing number of companies now rely on outsider successors.[2] In a sample of 120 U.S. industrial corporations that are reasonably representative of publicly held companies (Ocasio, 1999), the prevalence of outsider selection, a rarity in earlier generations, was approximately 25%. Murphy and Zabojnik (2004) report that outsider CEOs represented 30% of all CEOs in the late 1990s.

Unlike internal succession, which appears to be largely insulated from the outside market, executive search and outside hiring appear to be very sensitive to the level of demand in the economy. Demand for outside candidates plummeted by double-digit levels between 2000 and 2002 (ExecuNet Executive Talent Demand Index, 2004).[3]

The growth of outside hiring is a significant development for a number of reasons. Given that human capital is increasingly seen as the most fundamental aspect of organizations, the decision to hire from the outside market represents an important change in the boundary of firms. Outside hiring represents the "buy" side of the basic "make versus buy" choice, and the outside acquisition of human capital implies that the firm is more open in a fundamental way to outside markets. Hiring on the outside market means that the most important factors determining how positions are filled in organizations are no longer shaped by the bureaucratic principles that were the mainstay of research about careers from the 1950s on. Similarly, these bureaucratic principles are no longer the fundamental determinants of individual career patterns. Markets and the principles for understanding them are what matter now. Arguably, the most important of these market-based principles is search, and the institutions that shape market search—search firms and arrangements such as job boards that facilitate search—become crucial.

THEORETICAL MODELS OF JOB SEARCH

As noted above, research and academic models of careers have been focused almost entirely on an inside-the-organization approach. There is relatively little aimed at understanding movement and advancement across organizations. One important exception concerns job search. Search theory developed within economics to model the supply side of the labor market. It characterizes the behavior of individuals who are looking for employment under conditions of imperfect information, and it is designed to help explain the spells of employment and unemployment that can be related to an individual's job search behavior (Zanchi, 2000).

Early job search models focused on the behavior of employed and unemployed workers searching for jobs without modeling the behavior of employers. In these models, job seekers are seen as trying to decide how much time and energy to invest in looking for a job—or a new one if they are already employed. The conceptual problem arises when they are presented with offers: How do they know when to accept a job and when to keep searching to see if an alternative is available? The models turn on their individual circumstances—specifically, their "reservation wage," or the minimum they are willing to accept, and the factors that determine it—and on the pattern of information they are receiving about opportunities from their search.

Equilibrium search models, on the other hand, model both the supply and the demand side of the labor market (Zanchi, 2000). Their goal is to describe employers' optimal wage-setting strategy: In these models, the wage being offered is typically the only information that a job seeker gets from the search. Wage-setting strategies are seen as a function of employer characteristics, the search behavior of job seekers, and the wage strategies of other employers. In addition to these search models, there is also a literature on bilateral matching that contrasts direct interaction with intermediated interaction, as illustrated in arrangements ranging from marriage to real estate to labor markets. Intermediaries come to play a role in these search-theoretic models due to the frictions in the search market.

The intermediated models are perhaps closest to managerial and, particularly, executive search labor markets. They see two "agents" seeking to be matched with each other, such as an employer and a job seeker (Van Raalte & Webers, 1998). Their search is often inefficient: First, the agents are often unable to interact with each other (Van Raalte & Webers, 1998). Second, there is uncertainty as to whether the agent will meet another agent who matches his or her criteria (Van Raalte & Webers, 1998). Third, much of the information that is required to ensure a successful match between two agents is unknown or only observed with uncertainty (Saloner, 1985). In the labor market, for example, information about job candidates, such as years of schooling and experience, academic grades, and letters of recommendation, convey less than complete information to employers (Simon & Warner, 1992). To reduce uncertainty in such an environment, the opinion of expert third parties becomes important. Saloner (1985), for example, showed how employers relied on old boys' networks to screen out low-quality applicants. Fourth, since agents cannot identify the true quality of a good agent without a substantial investment of time and energy, the search process takes a long time to complete in the absence of expert intermediaries (Biglaiser, 1993; Rubinstein & Wolinsky,

1987). This helps explain why there are search firms and search consultants and why they tend to specialize by occupation or, for general management, by industry, where expert knowledge is required to assess performance.

An interesting question, underexplored in this literature, is why employers cannot or do not develop the infrastructure to address this lack of information themselves and why they rely on intermediaries to do it for them. Certainly, one explanation is simply that most employers do not do enough hiring within specific labor markets to make the investment worthwhile. Anecdotal evidence suggests that larger employers are more likely to develop internal search capacity for lower-level jobs. They still use search firms for more senior positions, however.

The process of thinking about labor market intermediaries begins with considering the general characteristics of all intermediaries, not just those in employment. Middlemen are agents who trade but do not own or physically alter the "good" they are trading. They make a profit by buying a good and selling it to someone else at a higher price (Biglaiser, 1993). One type of middleman, the *market maker,* sets an ask price and a bid price and sells and buys on his or her own account, while *match makers* simply establish matches between parties (van Raalte & Webers, 1998; Yavas, 1992). The labor market intermediaries described in this chapter fit the matchmaker model, although it is worth noting that other parts of the human capital industry, such as temporary help agencies, fit the description of market makers. Presumably, the explanation for the differences is that market makers operate where there are enough similar jobs and vacancies to have something like a real market price. Matchmakers operate where the jobs and executives are more idiosyncratic.

Three main roles that have been identified for middlemen can be generalized to labor market intermediaries in the managerial/executive marketplace as well: First, because of the volume of exchanges with which they are involved, middlemen can make the investments in information that, in turn, make search efficient by decreasing the uncertainty of completing a match (Yavas, 1994) and shortening the time period that agents have to wait to complete a

transaction. For example, they are able to judge an applicant's credentials, experience, and true intentions (e.g., Are they serious about changing jobs?) more accurately than the less experienced employer, and they may also be able to judge whether the stated job requirements are truly accurate (e.g., Is this a "wish list"—will the employer settle for less?). As a result, they reduce overall search costs (Rubinstein & Wolinsky, 1987). Benner (2003) argues that the reduction of these transaction costs is one of the most important roles for labor market intermediaries. Second, the intermediaries are something of a guarantor of quality, because they will stay in the market longer than either the buyer or the seller and, thus, have an incentive to report the true quality of the goods in order to preserve their reputation (Biglaiser & Friedman, 1994). Some executive search firms, for example, guarantee their placement for a year. That is, they will undertake to replace at their cost an executive who has been dismissed because of poor performance or behavior (e.g., sexual harassment) that one might have expected a good search to have uncovered.

In the absence of intermediaries, empirical research has shown that agents form clusters—classes or groups based on some important common attribute or background—and find their matches within these clusters (Bloch & Ryder, 2000; MacNamara & Collins, 1990). Again, there is some anecdotal evidence for such behavior in the labor market. Networking studies, for example, find that individuals often find jobs through social contacts, clubs, or other arrangements that are not based on the labor market per se (e.g., Granovetter, 1973). Studies of middlemen also found that those who charged a uniform participation fee—for example, marriage brokers or travel agents—only serviced the upper part of the market. Lower-quality agents were left to search on their own in the market (Bloch & Ryder, 2000). Middlemen charging different commissions to different agents (such as real estate agents or headhunters), in contrast, only attracted agents of lower quality (Bloch & Ryder, 2000), because agents of higher quality ended up paying a higher price for the matching services and, thus, preferred to search in the decentralized market. Anecdotal evidence suggests an analogy to executive search in the sense that the best candidates clearly operate through the leading search firms, while lower-quality candidates seem to hunt for jobs on their own.

Only a few papers have addressed the impact of market intermediaries on individuals in the context of labor markets. Kahn and Low (1990), for example, find that both unemployed and employed job searchers were more likely to use labor market intermediaries when they had a shorter tenure on the job, were on unemployment insurance coverage, and expected greater variability in their wage offer distribution.

This line of research has had some difficulty when examined empirically within economics. The important aspects of this approach, in fact, operate inside an individual's head, whereas the data typically used in the studies are quite different and come from labor market outcomes. It might be a promising approach for career researchers interested in understanding who decides to look for an alternative job and why some search longer than others before accepting one. The typical approach to this question in organizational behavior and industrial psychology is to model it as being driven by dissatisfaction with one's current job, which is an inside-the-organization problem. It may be just as promising to focus on opportunities in the labor market and the characteristics of an individual's search behavior. Career researchers can also make use of individual survey-based data to measure more directly attributes such as individuals' perception of their value or "price" in the labor market in order to test some of these search models.

DESCRIBING THE INSTITUTIONS OF SEARCH AND OUTSIDE HIRING

The organizations involved in helping match individuals to employers constitute a vast human capital industry. The descriptions below focus on the most central tasks in outside search: finding candidates and jobs and facilitating matches between them. It is important to note that this simple taxonomy leaves out an array of businesses that facilitate this process by handling the separate tasks that support outside hiring, such as selection testing, verifying credentials, relocation services, and so on.

Overall, one can think of an "employment services industry" that puts workers and employers together as including temporary help, professional employer organizations (which take on the legal obligations of an employer but not their day-to-day management), and employment placement agencies of various kinds.[4] This industry employed 3.6 million people in the United States in April 2004 (Staffing Industry Analysts, 2004). The Staffing Industry Report forecasts that the total industry revenue will exceed $100 billion in 2004. The biggest industry segment, temporary help, is forecast to grow to nearly $81 billion. In the human resource consulting service category, which includes executive search services, employment was at 95,300 in April 2004.

Search Firms

Search firms that act as intermediaries between job seekers and employers remain important players in the recruiting process. One type of these firms is "contingency" recruiters, who are paid a fee only if they successfully place a candidate with an employer. The typical salary range of positions filled by contingency recruiters was below $100,000 in 2004 and was associated with mid- and lower-managerial and professional jobs. These positions are seen more or less as commodities, jobs that are reasonably standard in terms of skill requirements, so the key issue is more finding a body to fill them than finding a perfect match. Contingency recruiters make up 85% of all recruiters and handle 90% of all executive placements (Finlay & Coverdill, 2002). According to another estimate, contingent fee recruiters account for approximately half the revenues within the $16.1 billion "place and search industry" (Staffing Industry Analysts, Inc., 2001, www.staffingindustry.com, quoted in Burton, 2003).

Contingency recruiters are in competition with each other to make a placement and have no assurance that they will be paid. Therefore, they cannot invest many resources into a search assignment. Contingency search firms work with a large number of openings. They learn the basic facts about a job vacancy and, using a large database of potential candidates drawn in part from those actively seeking jobs, they look for apparent matches and send information about applicants to their client firms in the hope that the candidates will be interviewed. Their operational objective is to get as many résumés in front of the client as possible in order to facilitate a hire rather than investing the time and energy to identify the perfect match. References are not checked carefully, and the guarantee to replace poor-performing hires is typically limited to 30 days. Contingency recruiters provide candidates with a great deal of exposure since they send many résumés to their clients, something that can be especially useful to individuals early in their career (Kennedy Information, 2003).

One way to think about contingency search is that it is a way of outsourcing the process of gathering applicants—that is, the recruiting function. An interesting issue that concerns the future of contingency search is that online recruiting now provides a cheaper and arguably easier way to gather information (see below).

Retained Search Firms

Most of the recruiting at the executive level is done by retained search firms. Retained executive search firms place senior-level executives and work under an exclusive contract with the client organization; that is, only one firm is searching for candidates. They are paid a retainer fee irrespective of whether they make a placement. When the search firm signs the contract, it also undertakes that it will not recruit from the client company within 2 years following the assignment. These "nonpoaching" agreements can create some interesting strategy dynamics: A client firm may decide to retain a retained search company for a job at least in part to keep that company from trying to hire away any of its other employees; similarly, the retained search firm may turn down a job from a particular company precisely because it wants to hire executives away from them.

Partly because they are paid whether or not a search is successful, retained search firms have no need to fill a vacancy with just any candidate and have a clearer incentive to identify the best candidate for a particular job. Retained search firms effectively serve as a management consultant on these assignments, helping clients understand what the open position really

requires and what kind of candidate would truly be of use to them.

The most important players in retained executive search are large, multioffice, multinational search firms, such as Korn/Ferry, Heidrick & Struggles, Russell Reynolds, Spencer Stuart, and Egon Zehnder, or small, boutique search firms that target certain specialized markets, such as Cromwell Partners or Jay Gaines & Co. in the financial services industry. Recruiting firms may be generalists, covering multiple management functions or industries, or specialists, concentrating on filling vacancies in a specific function or industry. While focusing on a single function or industry makes search very effective, generalist firms have the distinction of handling the most senior of the executive positions (e.g., CEOs) because they require general management skills (Kennedy Information, 2003). Retained executive search firms may also be "pure" search firms that only do executive placement, or they can be firms that offer ancillary services, such as organizational development or relocation.

The total revenues of the executive search industry are very hard to estimate because there are many small and privately held companies. The best estimates suggest that revenues are about $11.5 billion worldwide, with more than half of that generated in the United States (*Executive Recruiter News,* in Khurana, 2002). Hunt-Scanlon consultants report that in 2003, the combined revenue of the 25 largest U.S. search firms was $1.2 billion. In the United States, 54% of the companies relied on executive search firms to fill executive-level jobs paying above $150,000 between 2001 and 2003 (International Association of Corporate and Professional Recruiters, 2003).

As outside hiring became more the norm, the search industry became more sensitive to economic conditions and has experienced something of a boom and bust cycle. During the period 1989–1995, the executive search industry experienced a decline, because of the 1991 recession in the United States and related international declines. But the boom years from 1995 to 2000 more than made up for that decline, with the double-digit growth in each year linked to the boom in the Internet and telecommunications sectors. The 2001 recession saw another sharp reversal resulting from the end of the Internet bubble in the United States, the telecommunications industry downturn in Europe, and the crash of the Japanese financial system, with widespread layoffs in the industry.

IT has also affected the process of executive search, as described in more detail below. This is especially so in the process of "candidate identification," where information is gathered on executives from millions of Web sites on the Internet, extracted, and combined into a searchable database. As the process of identifying candidates gets easier and becomes more of a commodity, the value proposition of retained search firms will have to shift as well, from the identification of executives to assessment and consulting.

Research on Executive Search

Despite the important role that executive search firms play in the human capital management of corporations, relatively few academic papers have addressed what they do. One set of papers describes how the search industry is structured (Britton & Ball, 1994; Britton, Clark, & Ball, 1992a, 1992b; Feldman, Sapienza, & Bolino, 1997), and another explores the roles that they play (Ammons & Glass, 1988; Britton & Ball, 1999; Clark, 1995; Clark & Salaman, 1998; Khurana, 2002). The papers by Britton and colleagues (Britton et al., 1992a, 1992b; Britton & Ball, 1994) use the structure-conduct-performance paradigm to provide an analysis of the characteristics of the executive search industry. The authors focus on the factors that contribute to the industry's low entry barriers: the industry's low market concentration, almost no evidence of economies of scope and scale, and the small size of the firms in the market. In another industry-level analysis, Feldman et al. (1997) show how the growth of executive search firms has affected their specialization. Older firms are more likely to function on a retainer basis and serve more functions and industries. The findings suggest that executive search firms aim to build an image that signals their differentiating expertise and know-how. They do not necessarily compete on size.

The stream of papers on the role that search firms perform identifies them as having two major roles, as expert and mediator. The "expert" view is essentially an applied version of the roles for intermediaries in the search literature in economics. Ammons and Glass (1988) for example, look at the context of local government and contrast the arguments of government officials for and against the use of executive search firms. They find that the factor responsible for local governments' increased reliance on search firms is the perception of increased complexity (the job of managing a local government is more difficult, and finding a suitable candidate is more difficult today than in the past) and the assumption that search firms have more expertise and are capable of understanding and managing that complexity.

Another expertise-based argument comes from Britton and Ball (1999), who rely on the agency theory framework to portray the opportunistic behavior of executive search consultants and clients in the search process. Because search firms have information advantages over their clients, they may engage in opportunistic behavior with respect to them—for example, overcharging the client and not expending enough effort during the search assignment.

The second set of papers sees the role of search firms as mediators between client firms and potential employees. Clark (1995) and Clark and Salaman (1998) use the dramaturgical metaphor to examine the roles of executive search consultants. Executive search consultants are "impresarios" to the key event and provide the backstage support for the relationship between the client and the candidate.

Khurana (2002) looks at the unique context of CEO searches, which are structurally different from those for nonmanagerial employees and managers due to the small number of buyers and sellers, the great risk presented to both parties, and the large gap of geographical distance and network contacts that often exists between CEO candidates and companies. Khurana identifies three roles of search firms: They act as coordinators and as mediators between two parties, and they also play a legitimating role—that is, they constitute an objective third party to the selection process and signal to the stakeholders of the recruiting organization that the client is dedicated to recruiting a CEO. Khurana's account goes beyond both the traditional roles described by practitioners (e.g., Conarroe, 1976) and those described in the economic literature on matchmakers.

Finlay and Coverdill (2002), in an ethnographic study of contingency fee recruiters, identify both an expertise-based and a mediating role. As noted above, contingency recruiters are less involved in making matches than are retained recruiters and play more the role of candidate identification. The authors argue that these recruiters provide key economic and political advantages over an employer's own human resource professionals in the recruiting and selection process. As noted earlier, they are more adept at searching other companies for candidates by cultivating networks and by mining companies for information. They produce candidates more quickly because they specialize in narrow segments of the labor market, which enables them to use the same candidates for subsequent searches and accelerates the search process. Because they are not members of the organization and are not being influenced by organizational interests, they act as a candid, objective third party to the client.

The special mediating role of contingency recruiters comes from their unique situation of only being paid if a match is made between a job and a candidate. They, therefore, need to persuade clients to give a job order and accept the candidate, while candidates need to be persuaded to consider and accept the offer. While contingency recruiters are weaker agents than retained recruiters because their clients neither depend on them nor are socially tied to them, they have an incentive to persuade them to make a deal so that the recruiters get paid. With clients, the recruiters may try to build long-term relationships. With candidates, the recruiters have even less leverage and have to manage this relationship in ingenious ways—for example, through identifying candidates' special psychological needs that may attract them to a new opportunity.

Research on the Impact of Search Firms

Research on the effects associated with organizations' reliance on search firms is more limited. Finlay and Coverdill (2002) argue that the higher a manager rises in an organization, the more his or her advancement depends on social skills. Fit (an employer's sense of comfort with and trust in an employee) matters most for higher-level positions, in which evaluation is the most uncertain. Finlay and Coverdill argue that contingency recruiters rely heavily on "chemistry," the highly subjective evaluation of the quality and ease of interaction with a candidate. And by doing so, they also perpetuate patterns of inequality and opportunity because employers tend to feel most comfortable with candidates who are like themselves. The most discriminatory criteria used, they argue, are age, appearance, gender, and race. Recruiters devalue older workers, females, minorities, and those who are overweight and unattractive.

Khurana (2002) argues that search consultants tend to target a highly visible, narrow group of executives. He claims that this selection process is not aligned with the technical or efficiency goals of the CEO search. The recruiting organization's perception of a CEO candidate is largely determined by the CEO's previous employer. The most demanded CEOs come from employers who show an above-average financial performance and have a status that is higher than that of the recruiting organization. Boards most commonly obtain status-related judgments from rankings such as those produced by *Fortune* magazine or *Business Week*. The executive's actual performance in a prestigious organization matters less for these recruiting decisions, perhaps in part because it is so difficult to assess. Khurana labels the mechanism that governs executive selection "social matching," a filtering process where directors seize on readily identifiable characteristics such as previous position (high, such as CEO or president) and previous employer (a high-performing and highly reputable company). Recruiting organizations (and search consultants) resort to social matching because it is difficult to obtain relevant information on the CEO candidate's performance from other sources. Social matching also serves as a legitimating mechanism, because it produces "defensible" candidates. Because of social matching, the external CEO search has created a closed ecosystem of top-tier executives.

Descriptive analysis of the proprietary search data set of an executive search firm that contains career-related information on 14,000 executives in the financial services sector confirms

Khurana's claims in the broader executive labor market. The executives who were selected into the database are affiliated with disproportionately large companies that are, on average, in the top 5% of their industries in sales and in the top 6% in total assets. The average company has more than 33,000 employees. Thirty-six percent of the employers are either on the *Fortune* or on the *Forbes* 500 largest companies lists. Furthermore, 34% are on *Fortune*'s most admired companies list, and 32% are included either in the Dow Jones or in the S&P 500 stock indexes. The data suggest that executives from publicly traded, large-sized corporations that are visible have a much higher chance of being contacted for an executive position opening (Hamori, 2004).

Interestingly, the client companies (the companies for which the search firms take on the assignment) have a lower market value and lower sales and net income figures than the companies that are targeted by the search firm. The percentage of publicly held and "most admired" companies among clients is also significantly lower than among the database companies (41% vs. 54% and 26% vs. 33%, respectively) (Hamori, 2004).

Other analyses find that the executives who leave reputable organizations receive larger promotions when they join a new firm than the executives of organizations with little reputation capital. As a consequence, executives are more inclined to move to large-sized organizations and organizations on "*Fortune*'s Most Admired" rankings, other things being equal, and they are willing to accept smaller promotions to do so (Hamori, 2004).

Interview evidence with 45 search consultants adds additional insights as to how executive search firms mediate and alter the process of executive selection (Hamori, 2004). The type of executive that is ultimately selected for an open executive position is partly a function of executive attributes or the needs of the recruiting organization and partly a function of the experience and biases of the search consultant. Search consultants influence the placement in many ways: The executive-organization fit that is established with a placement depends on how well the search consultant is capable of assessing the organization initially, how critical he or she can be toward the top management team in identifying the competencies that the organization needs, and how well he or she can represent the organization to the executives in the marketplace.

The size and quality of the executive pool that is contacted during the search can be as much a function of the industry-specific experience of the search consultant and his or her ties to the "discussion networks" in an industry as that of the attractiveness of the recruiting organization. The prestige of an executive search firm, the quality of the selling pitch, the persistence of the search consultant, and the trust that he or she manages to establish with targeted candidates all determine the quality of the executives placed. The search consultant is the first screen to executive candidates and ends up presenting only a small fraction of the executives who were contacted for the search to the client. Because the recruiting organization has very little control over this phase of the search, the "short list" of executives is a reflection of the preferences and biases of the search consultant rather than those of the recruiting organization. Future research needs to address these aspects of the search process and their implications in greater detail.

ONLINE RECRUITMENT[5]

The newest institutions in the area of job search are the companies that provide support for electronic or online recruiting. These companies began with the Internet boom and, in particular, with the explosion of personal, career-related information that is available on the World Wide Web. There are at least three important innovations in job search associated with online recruiting, and all flow from its ability to offer vast amounts of information cheaply. The first is to extend the candidate identification noted above that executive search firms do—hunting down the best individuals for job vacancies—into the low-cost, mass market. The second is to allow individuals to gain unprecedented amounts of information about job opportunities and potential employers, shifting the balance of power in the recruiting process. The third is to open up the possibility for cheaper and more effective matching processes between employers and employees in the mass market. Although none of these developments are new conceptually, the ability to execute these tasks differently does change the practice of job search and recruiting and selection in important ways.

Facilitating Candidate Search

The first use of the Internet in hiring was simply to facilitate the collection of the kind of information about candidates that search firms and individual employers interested in outside hiring sought. Because so much information about individuals became available on the Web, it was possible to learn much more about potential candidates and to do so incredibly more cheaply than ever before. This information solved what had been the fundamental problem of outside hiring from the days of the first search firms, the issue of adverse selection. Like the Groucho Marx joke about not wanting to join any club that would have him as a member, recruiters only want the best candidates, and those tend to be the ones who have no reason to move because their employers appreciate how good they are. Those who are actively looking and applying for jobs, on the other hand, may be problem workers who need to find a new job. Relying on applicants for outside hires created adverse selection problems. Relying on search firms could solve that problem but was such an expensive path that its usefulness was limited only to the highest-paying jobs. Online search, in contrast, made it possible to do what search firms were good at, find good candidates who were not necessarily looking to move, but do so cheaply.

Online job search from the recruiter side relies on searching the World Wide Web to find information about potential candidates, what have come to be known as "passive applicants" in the recruiting business. Many people have their résumés posted on their personal Web pages, but more important for recruiters are more objective Web pages, such as industry associations or—better yet—those associated with individual employers that report information about workplace achievements. Some of these search techniques can be reasonably sinister, such as

"flipping the URL," which means getting inside a company's internal Web pages to look for information such as "employee of the month" awards or other indications of competence.

In the search for these passive applicants, Internet recruiters during the tight labor market of the late 1990s were aided by a slew of new resources, such as sites that pay participants for confidential leads and references about fellow workers who might be interested in moving. Some companies were very creative in finding ways to get potential applicants to reveal their abilities. Cisco Systems, for example, was well-known for techniques such as holding contests online with prizes oriented for Internet engineers in part as a way of identifying creative, potential employees.

The most important new source of information about potential applicants, however, and the icons of online recruiting are the job boards, such as www.monster.com, the first job board and in many ways the most important player in online recruiting, where potential candidates can post their résumés and potential employers can post job advertisements. Job boards take the traditional classified advertisements a step further by providing information about jobs and candidates and allowing both recruiters and potential candidates to search and find each other. Perhaps because job boards got started when labor markets were tight, their economic model has been to require employers to pay for job ads while potential applicants post their information for free. Monster reports that there were more than 40 million individuals in some way affiliated with its site in 2004, although most were not actively looking for a new job. The recent acquisition of the HotJobs job board by Yahoo! is an important innovation in the industry as the Yahoo! connection provides a potentially huge audience for the HotJobs site, and audience equals market in the world of recruiting. The downside of job boards for employers is that, unlike Internet-based job search, job boards still raise the adverse selection issue: Because individuals must decide to post their information, it is not clear whether those who are seeking jobs are "problem" applicants who want out of their current jobs. But as the posting of résumés becomes more and more routine, the adverse selection issue becomes less and less relevant.

Facilitating Applicant Search

Online resources have also changed the process for individuals seeking jobs. Job boards are perhaps the most important manifestation because they make it possible for job seekers to get detailed information quickly and cheaply on thousands of jobs. As early as 1998, data from the U.S. Bureau of the Census found that 15% of job seekers were using the Internet and that the biggest constraint to its use, one that was rapidly being overcome, was simply gaining access to the Internet (Kuhn & Skuterud, 2000).

On a typical Monday in 2004, the peak time for job searches, about 20 million people searched for jobs at monster.com alone, and there were thousands of job boards where résumés and job openings were posted. More than two thirds of the people searching job boards are passive candidates, currently employed and not immediately looking for another job (Kuhn & Skuterud, 2004). Some estimates suggest that as much as 10% of the time individuals spend on the Internet is spent searching for jobs.

New Web sites provide a vast array of job information directly to job seekers, effectively eliminating what had been the employer's monopoly on information about jobs and careers. Sites such as www.vault.com or www.wetfeet.com offer information about what jobs are really like in specific companies as well as insights into what specific companies ask in job interviews. These sites have grown increasingly sophisticated, selling applicants advice and information that comes from in-depth reporting and from interviews with the employees of prospective companies. Other sites such as www.salarysource.com offer customized data on compensation by job and location. The hiring frenzy in the late 1990s spawned a cat-and-mouse game between employers, who searched the job boards to see if any of their employees were looking for jobs, and online services such as www.hotjobs.com, which allowed applicants to block their current employer from seeing their résumés on those sites. In the past, job applicants could only rely on an employer's own description of what their jobs were like and word of mouth to check on its accuracy. Now, these online resources give individuals a great deal of cheap and valuable information about jobs. By doing so, they have shifted a great deal of power to individuals in the job search process. Many third-party Web sites now offer job seekers premium services such as résumé writing, résumé distribution, interview skills, networking parties, and relocation tools.

Online recruiting is now the most important source of job search information for both applicants and employers. It has made information about jobs and applicants incredibly more available. But has it changed the process of employment or even job search in any fundamental way?

Arguably, the biggest change brought on by online recruiting for employers is that it has facilitated the move for recruiting to become more like marketing. Surveys during the tight labor market in the late 1990s found that 20% of employees applied for a job at a company in response to seeing the company's *product* ads. Much of the information that applicants use to form their impressions of companies as a place to work comes from general advertising, and companies such as Accenture and GE Power Systems have explicitly attempted to tie positive company images into hiring. Sophisticated companies built a human resources "brand" by tying all their recruiting ads in with their product ads—similar formats, similar colors and styles—so that applicants immediately recognize the company. Booz Allen Hamilton, for example, lets applicants see what a consulting engagement is like, in this case a pro bono engagement to help the Special Olympics, which also demonstrates the company's community-oriented values. Applicants are increasingly pushed to Web sites where their online recruiting systems operate. Software on search engines allows recruiters to target banner job ads to individuals based on the topic they are searching.

During the tight labor market of the late 1990s, online recruiting helped companies move toward relationship marketing for recruiting. Vendors such as www.selectminds.com create alumni networks of former employees through company portals on their corporate Web sites, which can be used to find and hire back employees as well as distribute marketing information about the company. The option of e-mailing a job ad to a friend is perhaps the most common relational recruiting technique.

More and more corporations now do their own online recruiting: A survey by iLogos (2003) found that 94% of Global 500 companies used their corporate Web sites for recruiting in 2003 (only 29% in 1998). These companies found that they can cut recruiting costs by relying more on their own Web sites instead of outside job boards. Sprint, for example, claims to have cut Internet spending by 40% by handling its own online recruiting. In a quest to save money, companies will be making less use of job boards and relying more on the employment sections of their own Web sites for hiring.

Making Matches Between Candidates and Employers

One of the challenges raised by the marketing-meets-recruiting aspects of online recruiting is that it generates so many applicants that sorting them out is difficult. Companies that use job boards especially complain that job boards make it so easy for candidates to apply for jobs that many unqualified applicants do so. The avalanche of applicant information raises the problem of screening. Traditional methods of sorting out applicants, such as having human resources staff review them, become prohibitively expensive when the numbers of applicants go up by 100 times or more, as they have with online recruiting. Most companies and job boards now ask simple screening questions, such as "Are you willing to move?" or "When are you prepared to start work?," as a way to get down to a more serious set of applicants, but even then, the numbers are still daunting.

The most common solutions to the screening problem are to use various kinds of applicant tracking systems, software that organizes and classifies applicants. More sophisticated systems, known as hiring management systems (HMSs), do more, such as analyzing the success of various recruitment channels. Virtually all large companies use these systems. Systems such as the one at Union Pacific allow applicants to check on the status of their application at any point in the process; Humana's HMS automatically asks applicants in their database to update their résumés every 6 months.

Companies such as Pricewaterhousecoopers go much further, with online applications that contain sophisticated psychometric instruments that evaluate the suitability of individuals for relevant jobs. In 2000, JPMorgan's Web site contained a particularly clever online application for college students. It appeared to be a computer game based on job hunting and investment decisions, one that revealed information about the interests, attitudes, and abilities of applicants. Allstate Insurance has taken the process one step further when signing up independent agents. It begins with an online application that the company scores against a profile of successful agents. If the score meets a certain threshold, the applicant is then asked to complete a more detailed questionnaire. And if the score on that questionnaire meets a target, then a face-to-face interview is scheduled. The applicants hear back almost instantly about whether they have moved on to the next step. An iLogos/Recruitsoft survey of employers in 2000 found that 12% test applicants online, although many more may rely on a vendor, such as a job board, to do it for them. A vast array of vendors offer help in this area, such as www.brainbench.com, which provides a wide range of tests to certify the skills of individual applicants, or www.hirecheck.com, which does background checks on applicants.

Another implication of HMSs is to change the way career information is organized. Typically, employees are no longer allowed to submit résumés, a process that in the past gave them control and discretion over how they reported their career information. Now, the hiring systems require applicants to essentially complete applications that organize that information in ways that suit the particular employer. The traditional process of laboring over the construction of one's résumé is becoming less important now that employers are structuring their request for information differently. A second, and more important, implication is that these systems change the criteria that determine who gets through the application process. Most job hunters are familiar with simple screening systems that hunt for key words in job applications, such as "COBOL programmer," and this leads to another cat-and-mouse game between applicants and employers: Employers try to find cheap ways to screen applicants, the applicants in turn load up their applications with key words to get through the screens, the employers move on to more sophisticated techniques, and so on. It is not clear what the net outcome of this process is. It is true that applicants have access to more potential employers, and employers can screen more candidates. Presumably, this makes for better matches and a more efficient labor market. On the other hand, the screening of candidates is more mechanical and, arguably, less accurate, reducing somewhat the value of all the additional information and the quality of the matches.

More sophisticated versions of HMS software may have important implications for streamlining and aligning the recruiting and staffing function. They can operate essentially like enterprise resource planning systems, in this case making it possible to track candidates from their recruitment source through the hiring process into employment, connecting with training and performance data to identify, for example, which recruitment sources provide the best-quality hires. These processes increase the speed of hiring dramatically. They also make it easier to outsource aspects of the recruiting process. Many vendors such as Manpower, Bernard Hodos, and Exult will take over any or all parts of new employee acquisition, from identifying candidates to screening to making offers. HMS programs can make it relatively easy to integrate the functions of unrelated vendors.

The speed of hiring issue has important implications for public policy. The fact that potential applicants can find information about jobs more quickly, that potential employers can find similar information about applicants quickly, and that HMSs make it possible to make matches more quickly can actually reduce unemployment, at least that aspect of it, known as "frictional" unemployment, that is associated with the time required to find new jobs. And there is evidence that online recruiting has had this effect (Kuhn & Skuterud, 2004).

Changes in the Recruiting Function

At least during the tight labor market of the late 1990s, employers responded to this shift in power by making recruiting much more like a sales function, in contrast to the rest of human resources, which tends to be a more deliberative and reactive function. The much faster pace of recruiting requires a different personality style to deal with tasks where quick results are critical, outcomes are easily and constantly measured, and failure is a common outcome. Some companies moved the recruiting function into its own area. The recruiting function at Cabletron's Global Technology Services, for example, reports to the business development area, where the culture and pace of work are more similar and entrepreneurial.

The most important long-term change driven by online recruiting may be the continued merging of marketing and recruiting. The ability of companies to leverage recruiting off of general marketing is continuing in interesting ways. Technology companies such as Cisco are developing increasingly sophisticated online libraries of information to help engineers and other customers solve technical problems. These companies track the use of their libraries for a variety of purposes, including identifying users to recruit. Even more innovative is the reverse process, using online recruiting to help market company products and services. For example, investment companies such as Fidelity Investments realized that the applicant databases that they maintain are an excellent source of information for marketing purposes. After all, the applications contain a wealth of details about life interests and attitudes in addition to more typical demographic information. And if the companies can maintain a relationship with applicants whom they do not hire, perhaps they can sell them things. HMSs can help in this regard, although most are not yet set up to do so. Cisco routinely meets requests from other companies to learn about its online recruiting prowess and, in the process, helps generate demand for the Cisco equipment and services that make those operations possible.

Online recruiting also raises new challenges for employers, the first of which is retention. If it is easier for your company to hire experienced workers, it is also much easier for your competitors to hire away your workers. Voluntary turnover may also be higher because employees can now find new jobs more quickly. In the past, employees who got angry with their boss or company might feel like quitting but would calm down before they could begin to look for another job. Now, they can post their résumé on a job board in minutes and be contacted by potential employers within 24 hours. One implication is that employers need to be much more active in heading off the issues that push employees to think about moving because once employees start looking, there is no time to respond. Even if employees do not leave, receiving all this information about job opportunities is likely to change them in a variety of ways. Research on organizational commitment (Bateman & Strausser, 1984) has demonstrated that having more job choices reduces the commitment that employees have to their current job, and online recruiting makes it much easier to get many job offers quickly.

When online recruiting began, some companies searched job boards for their employees' résumés and effectively punished them for shopping around. When labor markets tightened, employers used the same information to target those employees for retention bonuses. Some software can check to make sure that there are no unauthorized links from employee home pages or other sites back into the company intranet, behind its firewall. Cigna, for example, changed the e-mail addresses of its IT employees to make it harder for recruiters to get to them.

Another approach to retention, especially for larger firms that have more openings, is to preempt outside hiring by building an internal online job network to facilitate job changes inside the organization. Building an internal online system may be the best way to counter the increasingly common situation where it is easier to find a new job with a different company than to get a different job in your own organization. As of 2005, roughly one third of large employers in the United States have online, internal job boards that automate traditional job posting arrangements.

Similarly, companies have a choice as to how to respond to the avalanche of information comparing jobs and wages across companies. The online industry also provides many alternative sources of information about what jobs are like in a company. In addition to objective sites such as wetfeet.com or vault.com, there are others that specialize in derogatory material. Monitoring of these sites by organizations may help provide some insight as to what one's employees are

saying and provide the opportunity to correct information from other sources. Some companies have been known to "bait" chat room discussions by having their managers counter criticisms of the company or post positive comments without identifying themselves. More generally, companies can try to fight access to this information, an approach that is quite likely to backfire, or they can preempt the comparisons by monitoring the information themselves and providing their own data about issues such as their position in the market.

Online search also facilitates the possibility of essentially outsourcing at least part of the recruiting process to vendors. But employers may be liable for the mistakes that their vendors make on their behalf. HMSs can be used to validate more easily the selection criteria that employers use, although whether they will take advantage of that ability is not yet obvious. Outside the Unites States, legal issues concerning online recruiting may be more complex. In the European Union (EU), for example, there are enormous restrictions on the use of electronic data collected about individuals. Directives from the EU prohibit employers from moving data from online job applications across national boundaries as multinational companies with a centralized database would otherwise do. ("Safe harbor" provisions permit U.S. companies that register with the EU and U.S. governments and that agree to certain privacy guarantees to move data within their companies.) Nor can such data be used for anything other than the explicit purpose for which the candidate submitted the data. Even the common practice of holding the application in a database and considering it later for a job other than the one for which it was originally submitted may violate these directives (Hogler, Henle, & Bemus, 1998).

Online recruiting has also had some influence at the executive level and on the executive search industry. As noted earlier, the ability to find potential applicants through online sources mimicked what at least contingency search did and, therefore, offered some potential challenge to it. Heidrich & Struggles and Korn/Ferry created online subsidiaries to handle their lower-level executive positions, and job boards also have begun including higher-level, managerial positions. For more senior positions, a 2003 survey of executive recruiters found that virtually all use the Internet for the search process; 67% posted the majority of their jobs online, and all do research online. Forty percent of candidates were identified via the Internet. Most recruiters also have moved parts of their hiring processes to the Web, creating confidential Web sites for each position, so that potential candidates and employers can communicate instantly through their recruiter (ExecuNet Report: Hype vs. Reality, 2003).

More revealing is the finding that the number of executives who say that they have their résumés posted online has jumped from 52% in 2000 to 75% in 2002. A comparison of more than 2,500 users in 2003 and 2004 of BlueSteps, a career management service for senior executives on the AESC Web page, showed that the salary bracket between $200,000 and $300,000 had the greatest number of executives who had posted their résumés (29%). Compared with 2003, this is also the salary bracket that expanded the most rapidly. The $150,000 to $200,000 bracket (28%) and the $100,000 to $150,000 bracket (26%) are the two next most populous categories (AESC, 2004). The ExecuNet Executive Job Market Intelligence Report (2004) concluded that next to networking with personal and business contacts, searching and responding to Internet ads was seen by executives as the most important strategy for advancing their career.

Online recruiting may also have effects on other areas of employment. In terms of career advancement, the popular advice, namely, that individual employees needed to market themselves aggressively through networking and other strategies to enhance their visibility may be less necessary now given the ease with which individuals can be identified online, at least when labor markets are tight. The notion that teamwork, project-based work, and more flexible assignments are eroding the notion of standardized and clearly defined jobs is also being influenced by the online world. The HR-XML Consortium, made up of online recruiting and human capital companies, has been working to standardize descriptions of jobs and applicant credentials.

Whether job boards and other online recruiting providers will become important intermediaries between employers and employees, as opposed to simply facilitating the exchange of information between them, is an open question. Sites such as Opus360 and Freeagent.com were working to organize the market for independent contractors, estimated at 8% to 16% of the U.S. workforce. These sites put contractors and customers together and even provide office support for independent contractors. Individuals may also develop some attachment to the job boards and other employment sites, especially those that have helped them find jobs, and may come to trust the information they provide on issues such as career management as being more objective and independent than what is provided by their employer. Job boards such as monster.com are big enough now to sell information to large employers about what their average employee is looking for in terms of jobs and where they are looking. They could also provide employees with information about how careers progress.

Monster and HotJobs have full-service job sites that offer marketing alliances, database access, and career services for users (Li, 2002). Job seekers are more likely to visit these sites due to the wide range of job opportunities and employers and the robust career content offerings. Small- to midsized employers who cannot invest sufficiently in their own corporate Web sites may opt for the full-service capabilities of a commercial job board vendor.

Overall, the U.S. online recruiting industry is projected to be a 2.6-billion industry by 2007, representing 29% of all recruitment ad revenues (Li, 2002). Even in the economic recession of 2000 and 2001, online recruitment continued to grow, and job boards such as Monster and HotJobs reported annual revenue increases of 47% and 22% (Li, 2002).

Overall, then, online search has changed the practice of job search in important ways, for both employers and employees. In terms of conceptual issues, the institutions and practices associated with online search have made it significantly easier to move across organizations. They have increased radically the amount of information that individuals have about jobs, and they have also increased sharply the number of applicants to which individual employers have access. All these developments can be seen as making labor markets more efficient. In the long term, such changes per se are better for the economy. How exactly they change other things, such as employment relationships; how individuals advance in careers; and how employers meet their needs for labor, are open questions.

CONCLUSION

Research about careers in recent decades has focused on managerial positions in large part because the pattern of jobs that managers held was both the most elaborate and potentially the most important for society, as they culminated in executive roles of running large corporations. No doubt because the pattern of managerial careers was so strongly oriented inside individual firms, research has also focused inside firms.

The factors that have helped move managerial careers away from an inside-the-firm view are both powerful and varied, but there is little doubt that movement across employers now represents an important part of the careers of virtually all managers. Careers now take individuals both within firms and their internal labor markets and across employers. The factors that had been seen as crucial to understanding career advancement within firms are still relevant, but so are the much less understood factors that influence the movement of individuals across organizations.

Among the most central issues in career research is understanding the pattern of jobs that make up individual careers. This includes the pace at which individuals advance in responsibility and achievement associated with their jobs, the fundamental aspect of economic mobility, and the path through different jobs that such advancement takes. Explanations for these aspects of careers change quite fundamentally when movement across employers becomes important. For example, how does movement across employers affect one's subsequent career path? While it might seem reasonable to assume that such movement is desirable for employees because they choose it, we know almost nothing about the effects on the specifics of career outcomes. Voluntary turnover and employee retention also become a more central part of career research given that individuals can now easily change employers.

Economics has a great deal to say about markets in general and labor markets in particular. The conceptual arguments from economics about job search are particularly important in helping us understand the movement of individuals across employers. These arguments fit in well with traditional research on careers because the focus of both is on individuals and on their decision-making process. Expanding career research to include how individuals decide when and how to hunt for alternative jobs would be a logical extension of the existing paradigm.

The more challenging development concerns the institutions that govern movement in the labor market across organizations. There is no doubt that online job search is changing in fundamental ways how individuals think about their careers as well as how they move across jobs. The expanding role of recruiters is equally important for managerial employees. Because that expansion has been more gradual, however, it has been less noticed. The problem for career research is that understanding institutions does not fit neatly inside its existing paradigm. Behavioral research more generally has tended toward methodological individualism and explanations for behavior that do not rely on contextual factors such as institutions (e.g., Cappelli & Sherer, 1991). While questions such as the role of recruiters and online search in career outcomes are clearly within the domain of career studies, it is hard to approach them with any of the dominant theoretical paradigms. To illustrate the problem, suppose one conducted a study of the role of search consultants based on theoretical frameworks at the organizational level, for example, from sociology. That study would be seen as closer to organizational sociology, because of the alignment with theory, than to career research, despite the alignment with topic.

The downside of this mismatch for research is the nontrivial risk that understanding the institutions of job search and labor market mobility will simply fall through the cracks, despite its importance, because it does not fit the paradigm of those who are interested in the topic of careers. The antidote is to recognize that these institutions are so fundamental to understanding how modern careers function and operate that the paradigm at least should flex to take them in.

Labor markets and the institutions that move individuals around the managerial labor market—search firms and online recruiting in particular—have become an increasingly important and under-researched component of managerial careers as outside hiring has become more significant. The attributes and characteristics of these institutions affect the process of job search and, more fundamentally, who gets which job. At the same time, the expanding nature of search firm activity and online recruiting has facilitated the move toward outside hiring and careers that take individuals across organizations. This process has its own important implications. Among them is the declining loyalty to employers.

NOTES

1. Cf. Guest and Sturges (Chapter 16), who note that in the United Kingdom an overall stability in job tenure has been masked by a reduction among men and an increase among women.

2. Outsider CEOs are most commonly defined as CEOs who have been with the organization for less than 1 year.

3. Executives who have changed employers since the stock market boom years of the late 1990s found, for example, that employers provide less unearned bonuses and stock options than they did around 2000 and slightly less generous compensation offerings overall (ExecuNet Executive Job Market Intelligence Report, 2004). Of the positions recruiters filled in 2003, 32% included a sign-on bonus, down from 36% reported for 2002 and 43% for 2001. Employers continue to temper their use of stock options, with 47% of jobs filled, including an options offer, compared with 53% in 2002. When asked how executive job offers were affected by the state of the economy in 2003, 78% of search professionals agreed or strongly agreed that job specifications had become more demanding and 74% said that employers were less flexible with their offers. Sixty-seven percent said that candidates are more willing to negotiate (ExecuNet Executive Job Market Intelligence Report, 2004).

4. Benner (2003), who describes Silicon Valley intermediaries, provides a good typology of labor market intermediaries. He distinguishes between private-sector, membership-based, and public-sector intermediaries. Private-sector intermediaries are of four types: temporary help firms, consultant brokerage firms (which recruit professional contractors for temporary positions), Web-based job sites, and professional employer organizations (which provide human resource administrative services to firms and are the legal employer of record for employees working for the client firm). Membership-based intermediaries, such as guild-like and professional associations, place employees who form their membership. Public-sector intermediaries include (1) the range of institutions that make up the workforce development system and aim to connect disadvantaged workers with jobs, (2) education-based institutions that provide adult education and job-related training to employees and have increasingly become market intermediaries, and (3) community and nonprofit organizations that engage in job training and placement services.

5. Much of the material in this section is drawn from Peter Cappelli (2001). Similar ideas about how online recruiting might affect the labor market generally can be found in David H. Autor (2001).

REFERENCES

Adelman, C. (1997). *Leading, concurrent, or lagging? The knowledge content of computer science in higher education and the labor market.* Washington, DC: U.S. Department of Education.

Ammons, D. N., & Glass, J. J. (1988). Headhunters in local government: Use of executive search firms in managerial selection. *Public Administration Review, 48*(3), 687–693.

Arthur, M. B., & Rousseau, D. M. (1996). The boundaryless career as a new employment principle. In M. B. Arthur & D. M. Rousseau (Eds.), *The boundaryless career* (pp. 132–149). New York: Oxford University Press.

Association of Executive Search Consultants. (2004). *Industry trends.* Retrieved May 31, 2004, from http://www.aesc.org/announcements/trends.html.

Autor, D. H. (2001). Wiring the labor market. *Journal of Economic Perspectives, 15*(1), 25–40.

Bateman, T. S., & Strasser, S. (1984). A longitudinal analysis of the antecedents of organizational commitment. *Academy of Management Journal, 27*, 95–112.

Becker, H. (1952). The career of the Chicago public school teacher. *American Journal of Sociology, 57*, 470–477.

Benner, C. (2003). Labor flexibility and regional development: The role of labor market intermediaries. *Regional Studies, 36*(6–7), 621–633.

Biglaiser, G. (1993). Middlemen as experts. *Rand Journal of Economics, 24*(2), 212–223.

Biglaiser, G., & Friedman, J. W. (1994). Middlemen as guarantors of quality. *International Journal of Industrial Organization, 12,* 509–531.

Blair-Loy, M. (1999). Career patterns of executive women in finance: An optimal matching analysis. *American Journal of Sociology, 104*(5), 1346–1397.

Blanchard, O. J. (2004). *Explaining European unemployment.* NBER Reporter, Summer 2004. Cambridge, MA: National Bureau of Economic Research.

Blau, P. M., & Duncan, O. D. (1967). *The American occupational structure.* New York: Free Press.

Bloch, F. & Ryder H. (2000). Two-sided search, marriages and matchmakers. *International Economic Review, 41*(1), 93–115.

Boudreau, J. W., Boswell, W. R., Judge, T. A., & Bretz, R. D., Jr. (2001). Personality and cognitive ability as predictors of job search among employed managers. *Personnel Psychology, 54,* 25–50.

Britton, L. C., & Ball, D. F. (1994). Executive search and selection consultancies in France. *European Business Review, 94*(1), 24–29.

Britton, L. C., & Ball, D. F. (1999). Trust versus opportunism: Striking the balance in executive search. *Service Industries Journal, 19*(2), 132–149.

Britton, L. C., Clark, T. A. R., & Ball, D. F. (1992a). Executive search and selection: Imperfect theory or intractable industry? *Service Industries Journal, 12*(2), 238–250.

Britton, L. C., Clark, T. A. R., & Ball, D. F. (1992b). Modify or extend? The application of the structure conduct performance approach to service industries. *Service Industries Journal, 12*(1), 34–43.

Burton, M. D. (2003). Headhunters by Coverdill and Finlay. [Review]. *Industrial & Labor Relations Review, 56*(3), 555–556.

Byrne, J. (1986). *Headhunters.* New York: Macmillan.

Can job agencies find your man? (1949, January 1). *Business Week,* p. 21.

Cappelli, P. (1999). Career jobs are dead. *California Management Review, 42*(1), 146–165.

Cappelli, P. (2001). Making the most of online recruiting. *Harvard Business Review, 79*(3), 139–146.

Cappelli, P., & Hamori, M. (2004). The new road to the top. *Harvard Business Review, 83*(1), 24–32.

Cappelli, P., & Sherer, P. D. (1991). The missing role of context in OB: The need for a meso approach. In L. L. Cummings & B. M. Staw (Eds.), *Research in organizational behavior* (pp. 55–110). Greenwich, CT: JAI Press.

Clark, T. (1995). *Managing consultants: Consultancy as the management of Impressions.* Buckingham, PA: Open University Press.

Clark, T., & Salaman, G. (1998). Creating the "right" impression: Towards a dramaturgy of management consultancy. *Service Industries Journal, 18*(1), 18–38.

Conarroe, R. R. (Ed.). (1976). *Executive search: A guide for hiring outstanding executives.* New York: Van Nostrand Reinhold.

Connelly, C. E., & Gallagher, D. G. (2004). Emerging trends in contingent work research. *Journal of Management 30*(6), 959–983.

de Ruyter, A., & Burgess, J. (2000). Part-time employment in Australia: Evidence for globalization? *International Journal of Manpower, 21*(6), 452–463.

DiNatale, M. (2001). Characteristics and preference for alternative work arrangements, 1999. *Monthly Labor Review, 124*(3), 28–49.

Doeringer, P. B., & Piore, M. J. (1971). *Internal labor markets and manpower analysis.* Lexington, MA: D. C. Heath.

Erdogan, B., Kraimer, M. L., & Liden, R. C. (2004). Work value congruence and intrinsic career success. The compensatory roles of leader-member exchange and perceived organizational support. *Personnel Psychology, 57*(2), 305–332.

ExecuNet executive talent demand index. Retrieved May 31, 2004, from http://www.execunet.com/talentdemand.cfm?cfid=2151574&cftoken=765397.

ExecuNet executive job market intelligence report. (2004). Retrieved May 31, 2004, from http://www.execunet.com/e_trends_survey.cfm?pid=ASUV04.

ExecuNet report: Hype vs. reality: The state of executive Internet recruiting in 2003. (2003). Retrieved May 31, 2004, from http://www.execunet.com/r_download_internet_reality.cfm.

Farber, H. S. (2003). Job loss in the United States, 1981–2003. *Journal of Labor Economics, 17*(4), S142–S169.

Feldman, D. C., Sapienza, H. J., & Bolino, M. C. (1997). Patterns of growth and specialization in the executive search industry. *Journal of Managerial Issues, 9*(2), 176–186.

Finlay, W., & Coverdill, J. E. (2002). *Headhunters. Matchmaking in the labor market.* Ithaca, NY: ILR Press.

Granovetter, M. S. (1973). The strength of weak ties. *American Journal of Sociology, 78*(6), 1360–1380.

Hall, R. E. (1982). The importance of lifetime jobs in the U.S. economy. *American Economic Review, 72*(4), 716–724.

Hamori, M. (2004). *Executive search and selection with mediation: The role of search firms in executive succession.* Unpublished doctoral dissertation, University of Pennsylvania, Philadelphia.

Hogler, R. L., Henle, C., & Bemus, C. (1998). Internet hiring and employee discrimination: A legal perspective. *Management Review, 8*(2), 149–165.

iLogos. (2003). *Global 500 Web site recruiting survey.* Retrieved May 31, 2004, from http://www.taleo.com/en/company/overview/ilogos.html.

International Association of Corporate and Professional Recruiters. (2003). *IACPR 2003 survey.* Retrieved May 31, 2004, from http://www.iacpr.org.

Jacoby, S. M. (1999). Are career jobs headed for extinction? *California Management Review, 42*(1), 123–145.

Judge, T. A., Higgins, C. A., Thoresen, C. J., & Barrick, M. R. (1999). The Big Five personality traits, general mental ability and career success across the life span. *Personnel Psychology, 52*(3), 621–652.

Judge, T. A., Kammeyer-Mueller, J., & Bretz, R. D. (2004). A longitudinal model of sponsorship and career success: A study of industrial-organizational psychologists. *Personnel Psychology, 57*(2), 271–303.

Kahn, L. M., & Low, S. A. (1990). The demand for labor market information. *Southern Economic Journal, 56*(4), 1044–1058.

Kennedy Information. (2003). *Kennedy's pocket guide to working with executive recruiters.* New York: Author.

Khurana, R. (2002). *Searching for a corporate savior: The irrational quest for charismatic CEOs.* Princeton, NJ: Princeton University Press.

Kuhn, P., & Skuterud, M. (2000). Job search methods: Internet versus traditional. *Monthly Labor Report, 123*(10), 3–11.

Kuhn, P., & Skuterud, M. (2004). Internet job search and unemployment durations. *American Economic Review, 94*(1), 218–232.

Leicht, K., & Fennell, M. L. (1997). The changing organizational context of professional work. *Annual Review of Sociology, 23*, 219–231.

Li, C. (2002, April 8). *Online recruitment grows up* (Business View Report). Cambridge, MA: Forrester Research.

Lucier, C., Spiegel, E., & Schuyt, R. (2002). Why CEOs fall. *Strategy + Business, 28*(3), 35–47.

MacNamara, J., & Collins, E. (1990). The job search problem as an employer-candidate game. *Journal of Applied Probability, 28*, 815–827.

Murphy, K. J., & Zabojnik, J. (2004). CEO pay and appointments: A market-based explanation for recent trends. *American Economic Review, 94*(2), 192–196.

Neumark, D. (Ed.). (2002). *On the job: Is long-term employment a thing of the past?* New York: Russell Sage.

Ocasio, W. (1999). Institutionalized action and corporate governance: The reliance on rules of CEO succession. *Administrative Science Quarterly, 44*(2), 384–417.

Rosenbaum, J. E. (1979). Tournament mobility: Career patterns in a corporation. *Administrative Science Quarterly, 24*, 220–241.

Rubinstein, A., & Wolinsky, A. (1987). Middlemen. *Quarterly Journal of Economics, 102*(3), 581–594.

Saloner, G. (1985). Old boy networks as screening mechanisms. *Journal of Labor Economics, 3*(3), 255–267.

Schein, E. H. (1985). *Career anchors: Discovering your real values.* San Diego, CA: Pfeiffer.

Schneider, B. (1987). The people make the place. *Personnel Psychology, 40*(3), 437–453.

Simon, C. J., & Warner, J. T. (1992). Matchmaker, matchmaker: The effect of old boy networks on job match quality, earnings, and tenure. *Journal of Labor Economics, 10*(3), 306–330.

Spencer Stuart. (2004). *"Route to the Top" survey of Fortune 700 CEOs.* Retrieved May 31, 2004, from http://www.spencerstuart.com.

Staffing Industry Analysts. (2004). *Staffing industry report.* Retrieved May 31, 2004, from http://www.staffingindustry.com/issues/sireport.

Stewman, S., & Konda, S. L. (1983). Careers and organizational labor markets: Demographic models of organizational behavior. *American Journal of Sociology, 88*, 637–685.

Van Raalte, C., & Webers, H. (1998). Spatial competition with intermediated matching. *Journal of Economic Behavior and Organization, 34,* 477–488.

White, H. C. (1970). *Chains of opportunity.* Cambridge, MA: Harvard University Press.

Yavas, A. (1992). Marketmakers vs. matchmakers. *Journal of Financial Intermediation, 2,* 33–58.

Yavas, A. (1994). Middlemen in bilateral search markets. *Journal of Labor Economics, 12*(3), 406–429.

Zanchi, L. (2000). Recent contributions to the search theory of the labour market: Introduction. *Bulletin of Economic Research, 52*(4), 257–260.

18

GLOBAL CAREERS

MAURY PEIPERL

KARSTEN JONSEN

It often seems to happen that when some word or phrase referring to the future has become so clichéd that people stop using it, its time has finally come. *Globalization* was a very popular business term in the late 1980s, at a time when most business really was not yet global (although capital markets then began to be); it grew in use throughout the 1990s to become probably the most published topic in business (e.g., Bartlett & Ghoshal, 1989; Giddens, 2000a, 2000b; Klein, 2001; Moran & Riesenberger, 1994; Wolf, 2004), mirroring a steady increase in global business activity and giving rise to a whole raft of theory, field research, commentary, and reactions (see, e.g., Friedman, 1999, 2005; Stiglitz, 2002). Now, it is old hat—a senior editor at *Harvard Business Review* recently commented that, in essence, the readers of that illustrious journal have little further interest in articles with the term *global* in the title.[1] Managers and management scholars alike seem to be looking for something new to think about.

But the decrease in the popularity of the buzzword as a business term has paralleled an increase in the actual phenomenon itself. In the same way in which the Internet has continued to grow and become part of the everyday lives of people across the planet (and for some of the same reasons), the globalization of business has become not so much news[2] as a fundamental fact of life. And from a careers perspective, we will argue, globalization seems, at the time of this writing, just to be taking off.

Of course, there have always been those few whose careers unfolded on a global stage, or at least across a number of countries, and history charts countless examples of population migrations for reasons of basic need. But recent research suggests that just as goods and natural resources began to move across borders in large volumes at the time of the industrial revolution, just as financial capital began to flow freely across borders with the deregulation and computerization of the 1980s,[3] and just as information of all kinds began to flow across borders in vast quantities with the advent of the Internet in the early 1990s, managers and professionals now appear to be crossing borders to work and working across borders in greater numbers than ever before (Özden & Schiff, 2006; see below). The presence of this new critical mass of global professionals means (among other things) that the global career needs to be better studied and better understood if the field of career studies is to remain current.

We take as a working definition the following: *A global career is a career[4] that takes place in more than one region of the world, either sequentially or concurrently.[5]*

We do not yet know much about global careers by this definition, except as they may fit under the more restrictive heading of "expatriation," a topic of some research interest since about 1980. Most of the research published on careers across borders falls into one of three categories: (1) comparative studies looking at the differences in careers between or among nations (see Thomas and Inkson, Chapter 23), (2) the above-mentioned studies of expatriation (see below), and (3) profiles of successful global leaders (Green, Hassan, Immelt, Marks, & Meiland, 2003; Kets de Vries, 2004; Kets de Vries & Florent-Treacy, 1999, among others) (and occasionally, unsuccessful ones—see, e.g., Adler et al., 1995). But although there is no shortage of books and articles on, for example, how to staff effectively in a global firm or what kind of characteristics are required of leaders in a global environment, there is relatively little research describing the career development of professionals whose working lives unfold in an arena not limited by national borders.

The main aim of this chapter is to take a global view of a nominally individual-level phenomenon—that is, to consider the careers of the increasing number of people who work across national borders, and in particular across regions of the world. If, as often appears to be the case, such borders are more permeable than ever before (Ohmae, 1990; see also Gunz, Peiperl, and Tzabbar, Chapter 24), then such careers, and the limited research evidence so far describing them, must assume a more important role in our field. We will attempt here to draw together that research and to present a model for the antecedents, characteristics, and consequences of the global career.

We consider the phenomenon of the global career from three perspectives. First, what is the span of activity of global career actors? What does it mean to do global work? A number of researchers have treated this subject, both from the point of view of the firm and from that of the individual actor, and our review will consider both institutional and individual approaches. Second, what are the characteristics and what is the orientation of people with global careers? How do such people think, feel, and act? Are their global attributes inborn or developed later? A fair amount of research has begun to address these questions, though not often specifically from the point of view of careers, and we will summarize its findings on several levels. Finally, how does international career movement take place? When, where, and why do individuals decide to cross borders, and what is the role of institutions, societies, and other forces in bringing this about? Here, we will review some of the literature on migration (though we will not focus on immigration per se) and expatriation and also present additional data from several primary sources, finishing with our own model of global careers.

ACTING GLOBAL: WHAT TRANSNATIONAL PEOPLE AND INSTITUTIONS DO

Global Firms

Between the late 1960s and the end of the 20th century, the number of multinational companies (MNCs) in 15 of the world's largest developed economies rose from 7,000 to 40,000 (United Nations Conference on Trade and Development, UNCTAD, 2000). With the sharp increase in cross-border flows of goods and capital, especially in the late 1980s, researchers began to focus in earnest on the phenomenon of the global firm (e.g., Doz & Hedlund, 1990; Spivey & Thomas, 1990; Tichy, 1988). This continued throughout the 1990s (e.g., Bryan, Fraser, Oppenheim, & Rall, 1999; Ohmae, 1995; see Birkinshaw, 1999, for a review) and into this millennium (e.g., Doz, Santos, & Williamson, 2001; Oppenheim, 2004). In perhaps the best known of many such efforts, Bartlett and Ghoshal (1989) identified a new ideal type of organizational model they referred to as "the transnational." They defined the three key activities of the transnational firm as follows:

1. Building competitiveness through an integrated network

2. Developing flexibility to allow needed differentiation in different parts of that network (such as different national markets)

3. Facilitating learning through multiple innovation processes

These activities are necessary, the authors argued, for any company to operate competitively in an open, global economy.

Ohmae (1987, 1990) was one of the first to describe the new global system in which such firms operated. But in considering the response of business enterprises to globalization, Ohmae (1990) observed,

> The changes have been so rapid that they have outrun the ability of managers to make needed institutional adjustments—companies have been slow to break up nearsighted headquarters and spread their staff more broadly. More important, changes have far outrun companies' ability to make more difficult, because less visible, adjustments in underlying assumptions and points of view. Most companies are still nationalistic deep down and see only local customers' needs as well as they need to.
>
> But sooner than most people think, our belief in the "nationality" of most corporations will seem quaint. It is already out of date. (pp. 9–10)

Ohmae (1990) went on to describe, in contrast, how some firms succeed in the global economy by developing "equidistant managers" (chap. 2)—those who consider all customers, and by extension all markets and all employees, as being "equidistant" from the corporate center and therefore able to decide without asymmetry or bias how to serve, supply, or support them to the greatest good of the whole enterprise.

Global Managers: Worldview

Clearly, then, one aim of managers in transnational firms should be to take a "world" view of business, not restricted to the culture in which they grew up or in which the headquarters of their employing firm is located. At a strategic level, they need to develop systemic views of all the major flows (supply resources, information, finished goods and services, capital, people) in their area of responsibility, in order to optimize, where appropriate, over a global playing field.

A systemic view in a world economy is, of course, more complex than in a regional or local one; however, it may present more opportunities. Thus, a global professional may, for example, have to understand at least the basics of how the currency futures markets can allow the business to hedge risk, even if he or she is not a finance specialist. At a personal level, he or she may work to balance several retirement plans or other investments across a set of different markets, each with different rules.

Global Managers: Tasks and Roles

Although the kinds of activities we are discussing are most prominent at senior levels, they, and other tasks like them, are more and more present in the middle layers of work organizations. So much globally interdependent work now takes place at nearly all professional levels that many companies, including small- to medium-sized enterprises, struggle to find enough mid-level people with the skills to handle it (Anderson & Boocock, 2002; Bikson, Treverton, Moini, & Lindstrom, 2003).

Of course, no one person can or should try to do every kind of task that might fall within the global manager's realm. Extending their model of the transnational to the level of the individual, Bartlett and Ghoshal (1992) identified three different kinds of middle-level global managers, along with their key roles: (1) the business manager (strategist, architect, and coordinator), (2) the country manager (sensor, builder, and contributor), and (3) the functional manager (scanner, cross-pollinator, and champion). Beyond these, the authors also identified the more senior corporate manager (leader, talent scout, and developer), whose job is primarily to source and support managers in the other three roles. They concluded that all these roles were necessary in global firms and largely mutually exclusive, representing complementary skill sets that no one person was ever likely to have.

The activities of global career owners also need to be considered outside, or at least beyond, any single work organization. Kotter, who in earlier work (1982) had profiled the activities of (primarily) American managers working in American companies in the United States, in 1995 published the results of a 20-year study of the careers of 115 MBAs, titled *The New Rules: How to Succeed in Today's Post-Corporate World.* He found, among other things, that successful managers were charting their own career paths, taking into account both the potential benefits and the hazards of an increasing number of global opportunities; moving toward smaller, more flexible organizations where they could stay fast and flexible; and increasingly dedicating themselves to continuous learning because of a clear business need to do so in order to compete on a global stage. This last point has also been stressed by McCall and Hollenbeck (2002), who make the point that "people learn to be global by doing global work." Although this may happen within one firm, increasingly it seems to happen across firms and through nontraditional work arrangements (Arthur, Inkson, & Pringle, 1999; Valcour, Bailyn, and Quijada, Chapter 11).

Working Across Cultures

Much of what is meant by "doing global work" must be included in the category of crossing cultural boundaries, a key activity for global managers. A long stream of research exists on the dimensions of difference between cultures (Gannon, 2001; Hofstede, 1980, 2001; House, Gupta, Dorfman, Javidan, & Hanges, 2004; Schwartz, 1992, 1994a, 1994b; Trompenaars, 1993; see also Thomas & Inkson, 2004; Thomas and Inkson, Chapter 23). Although not directly related to the present discussion, this research is significant for defining the dimensions across which transnational institutions, and those who work in them, must operate. Probably the most comprehensive study in this stream is that produced by House and colleagues (2004), who collected comprehensive data from 62 countries (the "GLOBE" project) to explicate seven dimensions, drawn in part from those of Hofstede (1980, 2001). These were

1. Performance orientation

2. Gender egalitarianism

3. Assertiveness

4. Individualism/collectivism

5. Power distance

6. Humane orientation

7. Uncertainty avoidance

Although the findings of this research are beyond the scope of this chapter, the list (and the hundreds of dimensions in the many earlier studies from which it in part is derived) serves to illustrate the sheer number and complexity of the basic cultural differences across which global professionals may have to navigate.

Global Activity: Physical and Intermediated

It is worth noting the difference between crossing borders physically and crossing them in terms of culture and markets—that is, via work interactions that demand a change in one's frame of reference. Figure 18.1, based on two continua from none to a great deal, depicts four different combinations of global activity, with characterizations of each.[7] Traditionally, we have considered global activity to be about traveling (see the section on expatriation, below), and this is still important, as there is no substitute for direct human interaction. Still, "doing global work," as McCall and Hollenbeck (and others) describe it may more correctly be characterized as interacting across different cultures and markets, whether or not in person. Therefore, it is important to note the contrast (shown in the lower-right and upper-left quadrants of the figure) between those who travel a great deal but interact only within one culture (normally, the headquarters culture of the firm) or who live and work as expatriates in enclaves detached from the local environment (*global travelers*) and those who stay physically in one country but interact virtually with people from many others, changing frames of reference as required (*virtual global citizens*). The latter may, in fact, be more "global" than the former.

On the other diagonal of Figure 18.1, those who cross both physical and cultural borders may be considered "truly" global (*"real" global citizens*), while those who cross neither may be considered local. For the purpose of this discussion, however, we take the liberty of labeling the

Figure 18.1   Different Combinations of Global Movement and Global Interaction

latter professionals *potential global citizens.* This is not merely wishful thinking; it also takes into account the continuing globalization of management and the professions, as well as workers generally, across the majority of industries[8] and the likelihood that, sooner or later, these individuals will start to move, albeit slowly, further along at least one of the two dimensions of the figure.

Global Citizens

The "real global citizens" quadrant in Figure 18.1 perhaps merits a bit more discussion. The term *global citizen* has been used many times, over many years, to very different purposes. From its Greek origin of somebody belonging to a city, "citizen" became increasingly associated with the nation-state. However, in the context of globalization and increasing interconnectedness, the state-centered notion has come under some "postnational" pressure (e.g., Wagner, 2004), and for our purposes a global citizen is someone whose main affiliation is not with any one country or countries but with the world as a whole. For "affiliation," we refer to how the individual sees himself or herself, rather than to objective measures such as nationality or origin.

For an example, let us look at three Canadian-born children of the same Pakistani parents. The first child might never have been to Pakistan and might hold a Canadian passport, but might nonetheless consider himself a Pakistani in that he views his main loyalty as being to that country. The second child might hold both Canadian and Pakistani passports and might consider herself a Pakistani Canadian, with split loyalties. The third child might, like his older brother, hold only a Canadian passport; but having gone first to boarding school in the United Kingdom and then to university in France and since then having held jobs in Abu Dhabi, Kenya, Germany, and Malaysia, he considers himself not to have any particular national affiliation but to be a "citizen" of the world at large.

"Global citizenship," then, derives more from experience and attitude than from origins. Still, the key element of the global career—working across regions of the world—must surely be a driver that makes some individuals embrace a global affiliation above and beyond any national ones. So, too, must be demographic factors such as being the child of immigrants—beginning with a two-country orientation and expanding, perhaps, from there—or the child of expatriates, a growing population sometimes referred to as "third-culture kids," who may feel at home both anywhere and nowhere (Pollock & Van Reken, 2001).

Working Concurrently in Different Countries

Figure 18.1 does not adequately address the activity set when one has substantial responsibilities in more than one place at the same time (like one of our colleagues who has offices in both Switzerland and China). In such cases, it is also necessary, as a next—but hardly a final—step, to consider differences in language, time zone, and the shape and accessibility of the individual's network in each location. These logistical aspects of multi-location jobs are, of course, additions to, rather than merely modifications of, the fundamental cross-cultural aspects.

Cross-Cultural Tasks

There exists a stream of research on the key tasks involved in working across cultures (see, e.g., Adler, 2002; Earley & Erez, 1997; Schneider & Barsoux, 2003; Ting-Toomey, 1999). According to Lane, DiStefano, and Maznevski (2006), the task of creating value while crossing cultures has three elements: mapping, bridging, and integrating.

Mapping means analyzing and setting out the differences between people according to their underlying attributes, particularly cultural ones. In a multinational team it may seem obvious that members will have different perspectives, but deliberately mapping these differences develops an appreciation of how they affect teamwork. There are three steps to the mapping principle: (1) selecting which characteristics to map, (2) describing members' characteristics, and (3) identifying their impact.

Bridging is communicating effectively across differences to bring people and ideas together. Effective communication is "sending and receiving meaning as it was intended." Especially in situations marked by diversity, the key to bridging is to prevent miscommunication.

Although good bridging is critical, understanding one another's perspectives does not guarantee that a group can bring everything together and come up with good decisions. For that, a team needs to integrate. Integrating is where understanding (from mapping) and communicating (from bridging) get converted into productive results. There are three important steps to integrating: (1) managing participation, (2) resolving disagreements, and (3) building on ideas. All three require good mapping and bridging.

With the discussion of research that describes not only the characteristics of the field on which global careers are played out but also some of the skills necessary to play on that field, we have already begun the consideration of the attributes of global career owners. This is the subject of the next section.

GLOBAL CAREER OWNERS: CHARACTERISTICS AND ORIENTATION

The vast majority of the literature relating to global careers is about attributes—the characteristics, mindsets, and skills associated, in various forms and in widely varying degrees, with success at working across cultures—and often includes valuable advice on how to develop these (e.g., Adler, 2002; Dalton, Deal, Ernst, & Leslie, 2000; Dalton, Ernst, Deal, & Leslie, 2002; Gregersen, Morrison, & Black, 1998; Mendenhall & Oddou, 1985; Oddou, Mendenhall, & Ritchie, 2000; Schneider & Barsoux, 2003; Thomas & Inkson, 2004). We will not attempt to survey this literature here but will rather describe one recent synthesis of it.

As part of a broader project on global management (Lane, Maznevski, Mendenhall, & McNett, 2004), Bird and Osland (2004) reviewed both existing research and management practice on "global competencies," drawing in particular on an earlier study (Mendenhall & Osland, 2002; see Cullen, 2000) that identified over 200 different characteristics identified by researchers and corporations as important for effective global leaders. Rejecting the idea that effective action will flow from the content of such competencies, Bird and Osland adopted a process view, considering what characteristics would promote three key activities of intercultural communication: (1) decoding the situation, (2) identifying what action would be most effective, and (3) taking the appropriate action with behavioral skill (see also Thomas & Inkson, 2004; Thomas & Osland, 2004).

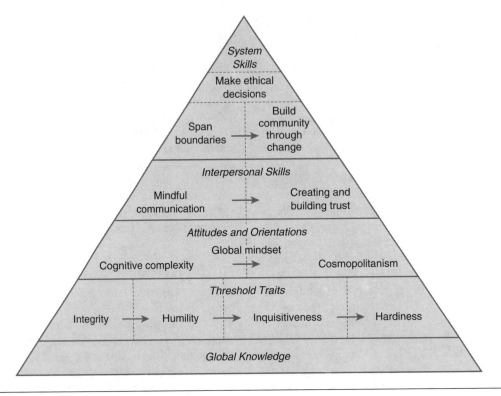

Figure 18.2   The Building Blocks of Global Competencies

SOURCE: From Bird, A., & Osland, J. S., "Global Competencies: An Introduction," in Lane, H., Maznevski, M., Mendenhall, M., and McNett, J., *Handbook of Global Management,* copyright © 2004. Reprinted with permission of Blackwell Publishing.

Bird and Osland distilled these attributes into a pyramid-shaped model (Figure 18.2). Beginning with an underpinning of global knowledge—the basic facts relevant either to the whole world or to the particular part of it concerning the career step in question—the authors move up through four more levels of personal attributes.

Threshold traits include four key attributes, related in part to elements of personality (see Judge and Kammeyer-Muller, Chapter 4):

1. *Integrity,* the existence of a clear personal ethical code combined with consistency and completeness of character and behavior

2. *Humility,* the showing of deferential respect reflecting openness to other points of view and lines of action

3. *Inquisitiveness,* the propensity toward questioning and finding things out—the active side of openness

4. *Hardiness,* the ability to cope well physically and emotionally with stress in new situations—that is, resilience

Distilled from all the leadership attributes explored in dozens of studies, these fundamental elements, say the authors, are the ones that best distinguish potentially successful global leaders from others who, while perhaps already successful leaders in a local situation, are not likely to succeed on a global stage.

Attitudes and orientations include cognitive complexity—the ability to hold conflicting ideas without rejecting any as wrong, and still to function—and cosmopolitanism—a positive approach to the multicultural world, a belief that it is a good thing. The combination of these two attitudes the authors call the *global mindset.* It is elaborated by Boyacigiller, Beechler, Taylor, and Levy (2004). Global mindset has also been defined as "the ability to develop and interpret criteria for personal and business performance that are independent from the assumptions of a single country, culture, or context" (Maznevski and Lane, 2003, p. 172).

Interpersonal skills include mindful communication and creating and building trust. These are elaborated by Thomas and Osland (2004) and Whitener and Stahl (2004), respectively. It is noteworthy that these are high-level skills, encompassing a range of other, simpler abilities, many of which are important in all leadership situations but which aggregated in this way are particularly applicable to global work.

System skills at the top of the pyramid include the ability to span boundaries of all kinds; to manage change at both individual and organizational levels and sometimes beyond, including the creation of communities for change; and to see things from a large enough perspective to make ethical decisions taking into account the implications of individual and collective actions on all who may be affected. These are elaborated by Beechler, Søndergaard, Miller, and Bird (2004), Osland (2004), and McNett and Søndergaard (2004), respectively.

Research cited by Lane et al. (2004), as well as that carried out by Dalton et al. (2000) and McCall and Hollenbeck (2002), suggests that most of the attributes listed here can be learned and/or improved. Possible exceptions are the basic personality-linked characteristics of inquisitiveness and, to a lesser extent, integrity and hardiness. This is on the whole good news for those who would develop their global skills: Global managers are clearly not born, but made. After all, what is there about the human animal that would make it naturally prepared to work across cultures? We evolved in small clan groups of about 150, in which everyone knew one another, spoke the same rudimentary language, and only rarely traveled far enough to encounter other groups or cultures (for more background and the implications of evolutionary psychology for management, see Nicholson, 2000). Global management and global careers are very recent phenomena in human history.

How many "globally competent" professionals there are and how many the world may need are questions largely beyond the scope of this chapter. But the mobility aspect of global careers and the traits and skills of global career owners, discussed above, that enable them to be

successful in a mobile career environment lead us to the third section of this chapter, the subject of international career movement.

GLOBAL MOBILITY: CAUSES, COMPONENTS, AND CONSEQUENCES

A man is of all sorts of luggage the most difficult to be transported.

—Adam Smith (1776)

The most essential element in our definition of a global career is the crossing of national and regional boundaries in the course of one's work or, more broadly speaking, of one's life. Thus, we consider geographic mobility as central to the global career concept. It is often claimed that "success has never been so closely associated with mobility" (see, e.g., Lasch, 1995).

In the same vein as we explored above in Figure 18.1, however, it is worth asking whether the phenomenon of globalization actually *requires* increases in the movement of people. The public perception of globalization and the convergence of shopping malls and main streets in cities across the globe easily lead to generalizations such as the "breakdown of geography" or the "fall of the sovereign state." *Globalization* thus refers to the compression of the world and the intensification of people's *consciousness* of the world as a whole (Robertson, 1992).[9] This is partially triggered, of course, by increasing access to information, especially via technologies such as television, the Internet, and other global media that are the leading edge of globalization and, for some, identity creation (Arnett, 2002); it is underpinned by the constant increase in the world trade of goods since World War II;[10] and it is perhaps most clearly manifested by the growing power and market value of multinational corporations—a fact that also looms large in the public consciousness worldwide.

Still, few if any of these factors lead unambiguously to the conclusion that career owners are—or should be—increasingly changing countries. In fact, it stands to reason that activity in many workplaces is increasingly global without those doing the work having to move at all (the "virtual global citizens" of Figure 18.1).

But while there may be more and more need for awareness of global forces—supply chains, consumer preferences, currency markets, language differences—in any given workplace or job, having to deal with information and people from outside one's native environment while still living within it is not comparable with leaving that environment altogether. As we stated above, it is the latter experience that forms the essential foundation for the global career, and we thus consider it as a phenomenon on its own merits, whether or not it is a natural outcome of the globalization of the world economy.

How Much Global Mobility Is There?

What, then, has been the pattern of movement of professionals across borders? Relatively little research has directly addressed this question. To have any kind of picture, it is necessary to piece together fragments of data from a variety of sources.

The literature and statistics on labor migration suffer from a lack of clarity on how to define "immigrants," "emigrants," "skills level," and the like (Dumont & Lemaître, 2005). For example, some countries count only people who are foreign-born in the various migrant categories, while others count people of foreign nationality or citizenship (United Nations, UN, 2005). In trying to determine who might be counted as professional labor (itself a rather fuzzy term; see Friedson, 1986), we must attempt to interpret terms such as "highly skilled" (restricted to managers or scientists in some reports), "level of manpower" (from the lowest to highest), and "people with university degrees." Although there must be substantial overlap between these categories, any totals arrived at by summing across the countries using them must be considered at best vague approximations.

Looking at "skilled labor movement" and, in particular, the permanent movement of professionals, the centrally held and publicly available databases hold very little data, especially when it comes to differentiation between categories of labor, such as skilled versus unskilled and permanent versus temporary. It is clear, however, that most migrant workers in the world can be categorized as unskilled labor and that the "unregistered" or illegal movement of people

consists almost exclusively of unskilled labor. For convenience purposes, "skilled migrants" in this chapter are defined as those who have at least a tertiary education, irrespective of where they have completed their schooling (at least 4 years of education after primary and secondary school). This is consistent with most of the institutional reports covering the subject (e.g., Lowell & Findlay, 2001; UN, 2005).

Trends in the Movement of People

As we argued above, the mobility of people is often not part of the *measurement* of globalization, but it can nevertheless be considered a key component thereof (Lowell & Findlay, 2001), and it can be argued that there is a certain correlation between industrialization and the movement of people (especially leading to increasing urbanization). To what extent increased trade leads to increased migration is debatable; in neoclassical trade theory, countries produce and export goods in areas where they have competitive advantages and, hence, have no reason to move people around. But of course there are a variety of opposite forces in play, particularly when we move the unit of analysis from the country to the transnational enterprise: The coordination and ongoing development of such entities require at least some movement of people across borders, and the borders themselves have less significance for the entity than they do, of course, for countries.

Depending on the period of comparison, it can be concluded that worldwide migration of labor, generally speaking, is *not increasing* as part of the globalization picture. Thus, the big surge in the international flow of goods and capital has *not* been matched by an equivalent flow of migrants in the post–World War II era (Özden & Schiff, 2006). Certain regions (e.g., the United States) had relatively much higher migration at the beginning of the 20th century than they have today. What have changed dramatically are the origins of immigrants, from developed countries (Western Europe in particular) to developing countries.

The period between 1975 and 2005 shows a pattern with wide variety across nations and regions but with a relatively stable, slightly increasing long-term migrant level, corresponding to 2.3% to 2.9% of the total world population (World Migration, 2005: see in particular chap. 23; Zlotnik, 1998)—depending on how this is measured.[11] In essence, the number of immigrants has increased everywhere (doubled over 30 years), but so has the world population. In Europe, however, the net migration was responsible for some 80% of the overall population growth during the second half of the 1990s (Thorogood & Winqyist, 2003).

Although there is only scarce evidence for the latest trends, the limited global increase of immigrants during the 1990s has seemed to flatten out, perhaps due to more restrictive policies by many of the major receiving countries. The period between 2003 and 2004 even saw a reverse trend from the latter half of the 1990s, with a *decrease* of people immigrating to some major Organisation for Economic Co-Operation and Development (OECD) countries (OECD, 2005).

Only Europe seems to have experienced an increase in permanent immigrants since the late 1990s (OECD, 2005). Intra-EU mobility has remained rather modest, and the immigration to the old EU countries from the 12 newer EU countries is expected to be moderate even after full onset of labor mobility, with the balance in favor of young, well-educated people in transitory rather than permanent posts. The main "target" countries for immigrants in Europe are Germany, Austria, Italy, and the United Kingdom (Chammartin & Cantú-Bazaldúa, 2004).[12]

There have been a few noticeable and consistent trends *across* regions. First, the number of female immigrants has increased to approximately 49% (OECD, 2001; UN, 2004). Second, there has been a sharp increase in the number of international students, leading to a level higher than 10% in some European countries (United Nations Educational, Scientific, and Cultural Organization, UNESCO, 2004). Third, there has been a rise in the migration of workers from developing countries to industrial countries during the past few decades. Migrants represented approximately 4% of the industrialized countries' total workforce in 1998 (International Labour Organization, ILO, 2004). More than 60% of immigrants now live in the so-called developed world, and immigration to the developed world far exceeds its natural population growth. In contrast, the population growth in the so-called developing world far exceeds the slight increase of immigrants (Global Commission on International Migration, GCIM, 2005).

Of course, any increase in migrants generally does not necessarily mean an increase in professionals crossing borders for career reasons. The predominating motivation for most of the world's migrants remains "family reasons" (OECD, 2001); that is, they are migrating to join their spouses and family members (either leaving simultaneously or later). However, the overarching explanation for migration as a phenomenon is the opportunity to gain more money and an expected higher standard of living,[13] which can be driven by wage disparity (pull effect) or untenable conditions (push effect). Thus, it is still the minority of the world's migrants who are driven by adventure or career advances.

The Highly Skilled

There are strong macro forces pushing migrations of certain parts of the workforce, in particular the highly skilled. These include growing urbanization, civil conflicts, increasing transactional employment, free-movement policies, globalization and standardization of education, cultural factors, entrepreneurial opportunities, labor shortages, political uncertainty, wars, wage disparity, and differences in standards of living (e.g., see ILO, 2004; Wickramasekera, 2002, for overviews). This has led to the so-called brain drain (see, e.g., Stalker, 2000, chap. 8), which could potentially have detrimental effects for developing countries, which lost 10% to 30% of their highly educated workforce throughout the 1990s (Lowell & Findlay, 2001), with very little corresponding inflow. North America also suffered from a high outflow of highly skilled people (approximately 15% over the same period) but benefited from a very high inflow: Foreign-born persons, for example, accounted for approximately 25% of the total number of PhDs (Dumont & Lemaître, 2005).[14]

It is estimated that 90% of highly skilled migrants live inside the 30-state OECD area (Özden & Schiff, 2006).[15] The highly skilled workforce represents approximately one third of all labor migrants in the OECD area, with wide variation across countries (Table 18.1).

Table 18.1 Highly Skilled Workers as a Percentage of Immigrant Labor, 2005

Country	Percentage
Australia	34
Canada	51
France	9
Germany	17
Italy	15
Japan	31
Scandinavia	25
United Kingdom	21
United States	40

SOURCE: World Bank (2006).

The 1990s showed an increase in labor migration at the professional level, due in part to the booming information technology (IT) sector escalating the need to send experts around the globe. Such specialized needs, as well as more general opportunities for experts to obtain higher incomes and more interesting experiences, led to a steady worldwide increase in the proportion of immigrants with a tertiary education, from 30% in 1990 to 35% (of all immigrants) in 2000 (Özden & Schiff, 2006).

Expatriation

> Expatriates feel more alive overseas because of the adventure, the challenge, and the learning inherent in the experience. This is why so many of them describe it as the most significant experience of their lives. They are challenged to learn and master new skills and settings in a way that has never been necessary in their own culture. (Osland, 1995, p. 16)

Studies of expatriation proliferated throughout the 1990s, as part of the increase in cross-cultural studies detailed above and in Thomas and Inkson (Chapter 23). Two particularly comprehensive syntheses are the volumes by Black, Gregersen, & Mendenhall (1992) and Stroh, Black, Mendenhall, and Gregersen (2005), both of which describe the process of expatriation from a company's strategic need, through the process of selection of candidates, preparation for and execution of the overseas assignment,

and repatriation/reintegration (often a key failure of company-managed expatriation efforts). Two more personal depictions are Osland's (1995) depiction of working abroad as a classical hero's adventure and Oddou and Derr's (1999) text comprising a set of individual journeys in various geographic and cultural environments.

There is still some disagreement about the use of the term *expatriate*. From Latin, it literally means "one who, or that which, is out of the country." Some writers use the term as broadly as this etymology implies, to mean anyone living away from their home country for any period. Others focus only on those living abroad on work assignments, often with some minimum time criterion. Taking the more restrictive view, we use *expatriate* to refer to skilled professionals who move across borders at the behest of their employers for a minimum of 1 year. Typically, these people are sent from headquarters to a field location to take care of a specific task that the firm believes cannot be handled locally. Tungli and Peiperl (2007) reported that companies from the four countries with the largest share of global firm headquarters (the United States, the United Kingdom, Germany, and Japan) indicated that the majority of their expatriates were still those sent out from headquarters to a foreign location rather than "inpatriates" (those brought from overseas for an assignment in the headquarters country) or "third-country nationals" (those moved from one non-headquarters country to another). For a transnational company that takes a truly global approach in developing and managing its professional workforce, the latter group might be expected to be the largest; however, there are still relatively few such companies. The main reasons for an expatriate assignment were to set up a new operation or to fill a skill gap (though individual development was also an important reason).

From the available labor data, within the classification of expatriation there has been a shift away from "rich to poor," so that three out of every four transferees now move from one developed country to another (ILO, 2004; Morley & Heraty, 2004). In contrast to the data collected by Tungli and Peiperl (2007), Harris, Brewster, and Sparrow (2003) suggest that this may be partially explained by the trend of employing third-country nationals rather than assignees from headquarters.

In more and more companies, it is a widespread, well-documented belief that an overseas assignment helps one's professional career advancement, as well as bringing opportunity for personal development and enrichment. Global competencies are well recognized, and "internationalism" is considered a major career anchor by global leaders (Suutari & Taka, 2004). Some studies, however, have shown a growing disconnection between expatriate assignments and long-term career plans and a discontent with the way companies are managing international assignments and repatriation (see, e.g., Stahl & Cerdin, 2004). Others have found that companies are doing a rather poor job in helping employees develop important global competencies (Black, Morrison, & Gregersen, 1999).

The sharp rise in the number of dual-career couples (see, e.g., Valcour & Tolbert, 2003) and the spouse's high influence on one's willingness to relocate (Konopaske, Robie, & Ivancevich, 2005) are some reasons to believe that the supply of potential candidates for traditional expatriate postings is declining. Family, health, stress, and safety considerations often hinder one's willingness to move (Forster, 2000; Welch & Worm, 2006), and when they are combined with the often diminishing expatriate remuneration packages being offered by corporations,[16] many candidates who are offered the possibility of an overseas move turn it down.

The expatriate lifestyle may have more attractions for either early- or late-career employees, who are likely to have fewer family responsibilities (Forster, 2000) but often may not have the profile required for the post in question. Even looking beyond traditional family situations, it can be difficult to find much support for a growing willingness to move abroad. Women, for example, constitute a growing proportion of the workforce at the managerial levels that are often expatriated. Yet women are less likely to be sent abroad for various reasons. These include widely held perceptions that dual-career issues hinder women's ability to relocate internationally (Moore, 2002); their unwillingness to accept overseas assignments (van der Velde, Bossink, & Jansen, 2005); companies' reluctance to send them (Adler, 1984); and what Fischlmayr (2002) termed their "own faults" for not being selected, such as lack of self-confidence and stereotypical, traditional role behavior.

Although the evidence varies, on the corporate side the number of intracompany moves of workers with families seems no longer to be increasing and is probably decreasing when compared with the rate of expansion of global business (Harris & Brewster, 1999). Several studies pointed to country-specific declines in the number of expatriates even in the 1990s (e.g., Beamish & Inkpen, 1998; Salt & Clarke, 1998). They are supported by a low anticipated acceptance of further international assignments by individuals (Forster, 1996), for the reasons discussed above as well as due to anticipated disappointment with repatriation. There is no shortage of studies measuring the negative net effects on returning expatriates (e.g., Black, Mendenhall, & Oddou, 1991; Johnson, Lenartowicz, & Apud, 2006; Tung, 1982), many of whom come home prematurely (Napier & Peterson, 1991). Although some reports are more optimistic when it comes to the future of expatriation and the role it plays in multinational organizations (e.g., Stahl, Miller, & Tung, 2002; Windham International, 2001), there has been a widely acknowledged concern about how the demand for globally competent staff will be met (e.g., Mayerhofer, Hartmann, & Herbert, 2004; Mayerhofer, Hartmann, Michelitsch-Riedl, et al., 2004).

The Future of Global Mobility

The strong stream of literature focusing on expatriation is perhaps witness to an *expected* increase in the mobility of the highly skilled (e.g., Mendenhall, 2001). Certainly, the need for international *availability* of the highly skilled— professional executives or technical specialists—is strong and probably growing. Yet as we have seen, the *mobility* of many candidates for traditional moves may not be as high as needed. Traditional expatriation of professionals with families seems not to be on the increase, and expatriate remuneration packages are probably on the decline. How, then, do we reach a balance of supply and demand when it comes to international labor? What other categories of highly skilled workers will fill the growing need for global professionals?

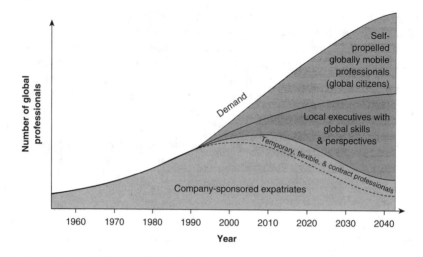

Figure 18.3   A View of the Future Global Professional Workforce

Figure 18.3 depicts what is, in our view, a likely evolution of the global professional workforce. It depicts the demand for global professionals as sharply increasing and continuing to do so in the foreseeable future (though not as sharply by the middle of the 21st century as today, since by then we expect most of the global networks that companies were only beginning to build at the turn of the millennium to be well established). It suggests that the number of company-sponsored expatriates, as discussed above, is peaking at about the time of this writing and will decline (but not disappear) over the coming few decades.

Local Talent

By far the most important source for full-time, global, professional labor to substitute for roles formerly filled by expatriates are professionals from the local areas themselves, where expertise may formerly have been lacking. Increasingly, companies are looking to local labor markets to fill roles once thought (by the companies at least) to be locally unfillable. Given the extreme emphasis placed on higher education in recent decades in markets once considered lacking in professional skills (notably India and China, but many others as well), companies looking for talented professionals are doing more and more of their hiring in nonheadquarters markets.

Such an approach to professional staffing also redresses the long-standing concern of local executives that they were undervalued and underutilized by their companies, which had continually sent armies of headquarters executives out to run their local operations. On the part of transnational companies, in which the headquarters-local distinction is less applicable, the idea that only headquarters culture or Western-trained executives were globally oriented or globally mobile is fast falling by the wayside, and third-country nationals from all parts of the globe are being given the chance—based largely on merit but also on cost—to pursue global careers.

Individuals Taking the Mobility Initiative

There is a third category of global professional, however, that we see as also supplying a substantial portion of the demand shown in the figure. These are the people who move globally, not at the request of their companies but on their own initiative. They are often highly educated and constitute a ready-made (if not a large) labor market in many important business locations around the globe. They come from all parts of the world, and their numbers are increasing. Many of them fit the description we gave above of the "global citizen." One of their key attributes is that they have elected to actively manage their own careers.

An individual's career typically includes more than one company, since lifelong commitments are becoming rare and most firms, since at least the late 1980s, have not shown an inclination, or an ability, to reciprocate them. We are indeed seeing a shift from organization-based careers to careers managed by individuals as active agents (Arthur & Rousseau, 1996; Hall, 2002; Peiperl & Baruch, 1997; see also Khapova, Arthur, and Wilderom, Chapter 7), asserting themselves in developing and utilizing their global competencies.

Self-initiated foreign work experience (Suutrari & Brewster, 2000) does imply more international mobility—a mobility that comes through intrinsically initiated journeys (including, often, changing employers) rather than through more traditional expatriation (see Vance, 2005, for further elaboration). This phenomenon was first described by Inkson, Arthur, Pringle, & Barry (1997) as overseas experience (OE). Yet there is still a lack of data behind this postulated trend. OE is described as "a personal odyssey, initiated and resourced by the self"— often with diffuse goals including career development, seeing the world, trying something different, and finding oneself. (See Table 18.2 for a description.)

Self-initiated cross-border moves are an integral part of the changes associated with the notion of "boundaryless careers" (Arthur & Rousseau, 1996; Peiperl & Baruch, 1997; Stahl et al., 2002), which suggests a freedom to change one's employment to whatever may be a better fit to one's broader life, constraints (such as health or family), and preferences—for example, deciding to return home after an international assignment, even if that option is not offered by the present employer.

Table 18.2   Characteristics of the Overseas Experience (OE)

1. Cultural experiences as important as work
2. Geographical mobility
3. Curiosity driven
4. Personal learning agendas
5. Individual is self-supporting
6. Weak company attachments

SOURCE: Inkson, Arthur, Pringle, and Barry (1997).

Although there are few data available on the number of self-driven globally mobile professionals, we would predict that their numbers are increasing—not least because of the increasing numbers of international students (referred to earlier) as well as highly skilled migrants and expatriates in recent decades. We see those international students and the children of those migrants and expatriates as the main populations constituting this cadre of self-driven global professionals. The ways in which they actively develop their own careers will shape the way we view the global career for years to come.

Temporary or Flexible Assignments and Contract Employees

Within any of the categories in Figure 18.3, we can also find temporary, flexible, or contract labor (they are shown in the figure as taking a slice out of "company-sponsored expatriates" because this is the group we see them most directly replacing). These are, of course, important and growing parts of many companies' workforces (see Handy, 1990, for a model and discussion). For example, companies are increasingly using "nonstandard" arrangements in their expatriate assignments (Tahvanainen, Welch, & Worm, 2005). Typical of these arrangements are assignments of shorter time periods—crucially, without moving the person's family. In some cases, these may be filled by "commuters," who shuttle between home and (overseas) work, and in others, by "globetrotters," international business travelers who are continually on the move and who return "home" only periodically (Welch, Welch, & Worm, 2007). Such "flexpatriates" (Mayerhofer, Hartmann, & Herbert, 2004) cross cultural and national boundaries on short notice and often in project-related tasks, maintaining their family and home base. The flexpatriates are, like the (often young) people on an OE, more proactively in charge of their own career and the assignments that are involved.

In many areas, the increasing use of contingent or contract labor (see Valcour, Bailyn, and Quijada, Chapter 11) has meant that even very highly skilled people are sometimes hired on short-term contracts. Where this applies to global work—for example, in IT, international law, or cross-border finance—contracting or outsourcing may substitute for having full-time employees on the ground in various locations. This kind of work has received quite a lot of attention because it suits the needs of corporations as well as the increasing class of men and women with a strong interest in "freedom" and home-based work (see Barley & Kunda, 2006, for further discussion on this subject).

A MODEL FOR THE GLOBAL CAREER

Based on the activities, attributes, and mobility characteristics of global professionals that emerge from existing research, as well as on our own recent experience working with global firms and global career owners, to aid our understanding of what might be called "global career dynamics," we assembled a dynamic process model for global careers. Figure 18.4 depicts the model which is centered on one key event—the decision to make a cross-border move for work or other career-related reasons.[17]

Antecedents

Demographic and personality factors, as well as social background and early experience, affect both the kinds of opportunities an individual has as well as the way he or she looks for and evaluates those opportunities. Although this list is not comprehensive, it encompasses the four basic areas of (1) *family background* (nationality/nationalities, language/s spoken from birth, family relationships, values espoused in the family, and ethnicity—racial and cultural), which helps shape one's world and worldview; (2) *early experience* (in particular cross-cultural experience), which can prime one for further such ventures; (3) *personality* factors (in particular those elements identified by Bird & Osland, 2004, and discussed above) related to successful global working; and (4) the elements of *social background* (values espoused in society/societies and orientation toward the world) that further shape one's approach to the world. These factors, we posit, mediate the way in which individuals seek opportunities and make choices as their careers unfold (see the career habitus of Mayrhofer, Meyer, and Steyrer, Chapter 12).

Drivers

The immediate causes for global moves include being told to move by an employer (with no choice other than to quit) or other powerful entity (e.g., a parent or the head of a family, or a government or military authority); being asked to move by an employer (with various potential consequences of saying no), a potential employer (to take a new opportunity somewhere else), or a significant other (often the subject of protracted negotiation and stress, though not always; for further references, see Valcour, Bailyn, and Quijada, Chapter 11); perceiving a specific opportunity that includes a move (perhaps after a targeted search); or being driven to move on one's own, without any stimulus or motivation connected to a particular job. The latter driver may occur for a variety of reasons—anything from basic economic need to the desire to get away from a former partner; it is, however, an often neglected area of career studies (see also Prasad, D'Abate, and Prasad, Chapter 10). Still, as more and more opportunities to cross borders come about, it is important to remember that many people choose to move (or for that matter, not to move) not because of a job but for their own, unrelated needs.

Outcomes

When a career owner moves to a new part of the world, two key metrics for success may be applied to that move and its after-effects: objective career success (how well the person has done in terms of rewards, promotions, recognition, and other such visible indicators) and subjective career success (satisfaction, sense of accomplishment, and sense of self-worth, to name a few). (Judge and Kammeyer-Mueller, Chapter 4 and Khapova, Arthur, and Wilderom, Chapter 7 treat the objective/subjective dichotomy in some depth.) It may be, of course, that in a new setting and culture, the way in which the objective career is judged is different from the way it was in the person's last job, and it may also be true that the person's own subjective criteria evolve and change with the experience of the new situation. Thus, it may make the most sense to look at the global career not as a

ANTECEDENTS

- **Family background**
  Nationality
  Language
  Relationships
  Values
  Ethnicity
- **Early experience**
  Countries lived in
  Cultures studied or
  experienced
- **Personality**
  Integrity
  Humility
  Inquisitiveness
  Hardiness
- **Social background**
  Values
  Local/global orientation

DRIVERS

- **Told to move**
  By employer
  By other agent
- **Asked to move**
  By employer
  By potential employer
  By significant other
- **Perceives a specific
  opportunity**
- **Driven to move on own**
  By basic economics
  By political necessity
  For adventure
  By cultural/religious interest
  To learn/develop skills
  To develop a strong c.v.
  To get away from
  something/someone
  For family reasons

**DECISION TO MOVE TO
COUNTRY/REGION**

CAREER CAPITAL

- Global knowledge
- Cultural breadth
- Language skills
- Interpersonal skills
- Cognitive complexity
- Cosmopolitanism
- System skills
- Global network
- Global track record

OUTCOMES

- **Objective career success**
  Tangible rewards
  Promotions
  Recognition
- **Subjective career success**
  Satisfaction
  Sense of accomplishment
  Sense of self-worth

Figure 18.4   A Model for the Global Career

365

series of moves, jobs, and results but rather as a long-term accumulation of assets.

Career Capital

Career capital (Arthur, Claman, & DeFillippi, 1995; see also Bourdieu's concept of social capital as described by Mayrhofer, Meyer, and Steyrer, Chapter 12) is the term we apply to the set of assets accumulated over time as the global career unfolds. Within the limits of practicality and time (frequent moves often suggest superficiality and lack of trustworthiness), the more regions and cultures in which a person learns to work effectively, the more global career capital he or she accumulates. Global career capital includes the kinds of assets and abilities shown in Figure 18.2, discussed above, in particular *global knowledge, cultural breadth, language skills, interpersonal skills, cognitive complexity, cosmopolitanism,* and *system skills.* It also includes, of course, a *global network* and *global track record.*

The Global Mobility Cycle

The model implies that global careers are only built over many cross-regional or cross-national moves. While this may be an overstatement, it is difficult to overemphasize how much each repetition of the global mobility cycle (the loop constituting the right side of Figure 18.4) augments an individual's career capital. A study of European CEOs and COOs (Peiperl & Estrin, 2000) found that they had each lived and worked in an average of four countries, about half inside and half outside Europe (although, interestingly, the majority had found their top-level jobs back in their country of origin). Practically all global companies now require that anyone hired or promoted into top management ranks have experience working in multiple countries.

It might be said, then, that the global career is really an accumulation of capital based on experience across countries, and especially across regions (where differences are often greater than between countries in the same area), based on a cycle of moving, working, and learning. Still, referring again back to Figure 18.1, it should always be noted that merely traveling does not always convey global knowledge

and that working across cultures does not always take place across great distances. It is, rather, the maximization of both countries/regions worked in and cross-cultural work accomplished that accumulates the most global career capital and makes one most likely to be able to claim the title of global citizen.

WHITHER GLOBAL CAREERS?

To ask, "Where are global careers going?" one might just as well ask where work is going. More and more, we see the extent to which national boundaries matter less and less to business, as goods and capital flow freely and as many people, visa restrictions notwithstanding, are ready to move across those borders when the circumstances are right. Of course, this boundarylessness and readiness to move vary with the geographic, industry, cultural, and professional lenses one applies, but even so, we believe that there is an overall trend toward the globalization not just of business but of work itself—one that is not likely to go away, though it certainly has faced (and will continue to face) setbacks from time to time.

Research on global careers is still in its infancy. We cannot even say with any certainty how many people are engaged in cross-border work, let alone succeeding at it. Gathering this kind of data from the businesses and associations with a clear interest in it seems an obvious place to begin. A second step would be to gather data enabling the mapping of work across the quadrants in Figure 18.1, both retrospectively and prospectively, to see how much change is really occurring toward the globalization of work and careers.

Further work also needs to be carried out on the cultural and individual characteristics that enable cross-cultural working and global mobility, not only to further test the work already done but also to profile how many people have such characteristics, how they are developed, how they are changing, and whether they continue to lead to success as global careers expand.

At the institutional level, it is important to ask what kind of role global organizations, in particular multinational corporations, are playing in the evolution of global social structures and what this means for career opportunities for those within, as well as those outside, these entities. Conversely, work on how individual careers shape institutions (see Higgins and Dillon, Chapter 21; Jones and Dunn, Chapter 22) should be expanded to the global arena, so that we can better understand the individual and network dynamics that bring such potentially powerful entities into being.

Finally, it should be emphasized that, in large measure, what it takes to understand global careers is to live them. Many of the best research insights into global careers have come from researchers who themselves have pursued such paths. To live a global career is to accept more (or at least, more constant) uncertainty than has typically been the case and to embrace lifelong learning to a degree heretofore unnecessary in most work occupations. Such an approach to life and work is potentially as important to those who study careers as it is to those who pursue them. In short, as we look around at the changing nature of work and careers generally, there is no escaping the conclusion that, at least for professionals, making one's place in the world of work often also means making one's way across the places of the working world.

NOTES

1. M. Peiperl, personal communication, May 22, 2006.

2. A recent count of articles with "globalization" in the title supported this view, showing a peak around the period between 2003 and 2004 and then beginning to decline (as a percentage of all articles published).

3. It has been claimed that in the global economy, money has lost its link to nationality (Lasch, 1995).

4. "[T]he evolving sequence of an individual's work experiences over time"; see Chapter 1 and also Arthur, Hall, and Lawrence, 1989.

5. Most existing research considers moves across countries, not regions. In order not to eliminate consideration of this research in our discussion, we will not enforce the cross-region limitation but will comment on its implications where appropriate.

6. We consider, in particular, the careers of professionals (see Freidson, 1986, for a discussion of the term) as such persons are likely to have more choice

in their career movements, although this is far from certain in any particular case.

7. In the figure, *home* refers only to one place, but determining which place fits this reference may be complicated in some cases. We propose that where the individual in question has more than one permanent home or native culture, the first (or in fact, any) of these be used for purposes of counting the time spent "away."

8. See Stalker (2000) for further discussion.

9. See Arnett (2002) for a discussion of contemporary terms relating to globalization.

10. The following table shows the global merchandise trade export figures in millions of U.S. dollars (USD):

Year	USD in Millions
1948	58,000
1958	110,000
1968	242,000
1978	1,307,000
1988	2,869,000
1998	5,499,000
2005	10,393,000

SOURCE: WTO online statistics.

International trade has also risen significantly in proportion to GDP—for Europe since the late 1930s and for the United States since 1970 (Stalker, 2000).

11. In addition to varying definitions of *migrant*, the disintegration of states represents an important proportion of the total stock of international migrants. For example, out of a total of some 175 million migrants in the year 2000, the disintegration of the former Soviet Union accounted for approximately 27 million (World Migration, 2005), more or less equivalent to the relative rise in the postulated global migration. Although professionals clearly represent only a small fraction of those counted in these statistics, the same phenomenon has affected them as well.

12. It may not be an exaggeration to say that labor mobility, much heralded with the advent of the EU, is the least-used freedom in the Union.

13. At many points in history, this has been driven largely by industrialization in the destination country, which provided for higher earning potential than in the country of birth (Stalker, 2000).

14. It is argued by some that the brain drain has been overestimated and is balanced to a certain extent

by "brain gain" due to high return rates and transfer of knowledge (OECD, 2002). There is a stream of additional terms related to the movement of especially highly skilled labor, including optimal brain gain, brain waste, brain circulation, brain exchange, brain globalization, brain export, and so on (Lowell & Findlay, 2001).

15. It is worth noting, however, that India and China are the two primary emerging destinations.

16. Estimates of the annual cost of an expatriate have ranged from three to five times that of a local hire (see, e.g., Baker & Roberts, 2006; Forster, 2000). In an increasingly global market, such rates cannot be sustainable in the long term. It is perhaps not surprising, then, that in a seminar on global mobility in June 2006, comprising 70 senior executives from over 50 global companies, the authors found that fully one third of those in attendance reported that their company's expatriate remuneration packages were decreasing.

17. As is the custom in the expatriation literature, we here consider only moves intended to last at least 1 year. We also consider cross-regional moves more significant than cross-country moves within one region.

References

Adler, G., Ready, D. A., Schneider, S. C., Johansson, B., Trompenaars, F., & Borboa, R. (1995). The case of the floundering expatriate. *Harvard Business Review, 73,* 4.

Adler, N. J. (1984). Women do not want international careers: And other myths about international management. *Organizational Dynamics, 13*(2), 66–79.

Adler, N. J. (2002). *International dimensions of organizational behavior* (4th ed.). Cincinnati, OH: South-Western.

Anderson, V., & Boocock, G. (2002). Small firms and internationalisation: Learning to manage and managing to learn. *Human Resource Management Journal, 12*(3), 5–24.

Arnett, J. J. (2002). The psychology of globalization. *American Psychologist, 57*(10), 774–783.

Arthur, M. B., Claman, P. H., & DeFillippi, R. J. (1995). Intelligent enterprise, intelligent careers. *Academy of Management Executive, 9*(1), 7–20.

Arthur, M. B., Hall, D. T., & Lawrence, B. S. (1989). *Handbook of career theory.* New York: Cambridge University Press.

Arthur, M. B., Inkson, K., & Pringle, J. K. (1999). *The new careers.* London: Sage.

Arthur, M. B., & Rousseau, D. M. (1996). *The boundaryless career: A new employment principle for a new organizational era.* New York: Oxford University Press.

Baker, W. M., & Roberts, F. D. (2006). Managing the cost of expatriation. *Strategic Finance, May,* 35–41.

Barley, S. R., & Kunda, G. (2006, February). Contracting: A new form of professional practice. *Academy of Management Perspectives, 21*(1), 45–66.

Bartlett, C., & Ghoshal, S. (1989). *Managing across borders: The transnational solution.* Boston: Harvard Business School Press.

Bartlett, C., & Ghoshal, S. (1992). What is a global manager? *Harvard Business Review, 70,* 5.

Beamish, P. W., & Inkpen, A. (1998). Japanese firms and the decline of the Japanese expatriate. *Journal of World Business, 33*(1), 35–50.

Beechler, S., Søndergaard, M., Miller, E. L., & Bird, A. (2004). Boundary spanning. In H. W. Lane, M. L. Masnevski, M. E. Mendenhall, & J. McNett (Eds.), *The Blackwell handbook of global management: A guide to managing complexity* (pp. 121–133). London: Blackwell.

Bikson, T. K., Treverton, G. F., Moini, J., & Lindstrom, G. (2003). *New challenges for international leadership.* Santa Monica, CA: RAND, National Security Research Division.

Bird, A., & Osland, J. (2004). Global competencies: An introduction. In H. W. Lane, M. L. Masnevski, M. E. Mendenhall, & J. McNett (Eds.), *The Blackwell handbook of global management: A guide to managing complexity* (pp. 57–80). London: Blackwell.

Birkinshaw, J. M. (1999). Globalization and multinational corporate strategy: An internal market perspective. In N. Hood & S. Young (Eds.), *The globalization of multinational enterprise activity and economic development* (pp. 55–79). London: Macmillan.

Black, J. S., Gregersen, H. B., & Mendenhall, M. E. (1992). *Global assignments: Successfully expatriating and repatriating international managers.* San Francisco: Jossey-Bass.

Black, J. S., Mendenhall, M., & Oddou, G. (1991). Toward a comprehensive model of international adjustment: An integration of multiple theoretical perspectives. *Academy of Management Review, 16*(2), 291–317.

Black, J. S., Morrison, A., & Gregersen, H. B. (1999). *Global explorers: The next generation of leaders.* New York: Routledge.

Boyacigiller, N., Beechler, S., Taylor, S., & Levy, O. (2004). The crucial yet elusive global mindset. In H. W. Lane, M. L. Masnevski, M. E. Mendenhall, & J. McNett (Eds.), *The Blackwell handbook of global management: A guide to managing complexity* (pp. 81–93). London: Blackwell.

Bryan, L., Fraser, J., Oppenheim, J., & Rall, W. (1999). *Race for the world: Strategies to build a great global firm.* Boston: Harvard Business School Press.

Chammartin, G. M. F., & Cantú-Bazaldúa, F. (2004). *Migration prospect after the 2004 enlargement of the European Union.* Geneva: ILO.

Cullen, J. B. (2000). *Multinational management: A strategic approach.* Cincinnati, OH: South-Western.

Dalton, M. A., Deal, J., Ernst, C. T., & Leslie, J. B. (2000). For global managers, a world of difference. *Leadership in Action, 20*(4), 5–9.

Dalton, M. A., Ernst, C. T., Deal, J., & Leslie, J. B. (2002). *Success for the global manager: How to work across distances, countries and cultures.* San Francisco: Jossey-Bass.

Doz, Y., & Hedlund, G. (1990). *Managing the global firm.* London: Routledge.

Doz, Y., Santos, J., & Williamson, P. (2001). *From global to metanational: How companies win the knowledge economy.* Boston: Harvard Business School Press.

Dumont, J.-C., & Lemaître, G. (2005). *Counting immigrants and expatriates in OECD countries: A new perspective* (OECD Social, Employment and Migration Working Papers No. 25). Paris: OECD.

Earley, P. C., & Erez, M. (1997). *The transplanted executive.* New York: Oxford University Press.

Fischlmayr, I. C. (2002). Female self-perception as barrier to international careers? *International Journal of Human Resource Management, 13*(5), 773–783.

Forster, N. (1996). *A report on the management of expatriates in 36 U.K. Companies* (Cardiff Business School Report). Cardiff: Cardiff Business School.

Forster, N. (2000). The myth of the "international manager." *International Journal of Human Resource Management, 11,* 1.

Freidson, E. (1986). *Professional powers: A study of the institutionalization of formal knowledge.* Chicago: University of Chicago Press.

Friedman, T. (1999). *The Lexus and the olive tree.* New York: Farrar, Straus & Giroux.

Friedman, T. (2005). *The world is flat.* London: Allen Lane.

Gannon, M. (2001). *Understanding global cultures: Metaphorical journeys through 23 nations* (2nd ed.). Thousand Oaks, CA: Sage.

Giddens, A. (2000a). *Runaway world.* London: Routledge.

Giddens, A. (2000b). *The third way and its critics.* Cambridge, UK: Polity Press.

Global Commission on International Migration. (2005). *Migration in an interconnected world: New directions for action.* Switzerland: Author.

Green, S., Hassan, F., Immelt, J., Marks, M., & Meiland, D. (2003). In search of global leaders. *Harvard Business Review, 81*(8), 38–44.

Gregersen, H. B., Morrison, A. J., & Black, J. S. (1998). Developing leaders for the global frontier. *Sloan Management Review, 40*(1), 21–32.

Hall, D. T. (2002). *Careers in and out of organizations.* Thousand Oaks, CA: Sage.

Handy, C. (1990). *The age of unreason.* Boston: Harvard Business School Press.

Harris, H., & Brewster, C. (1999). The coffee machine system: How international selection really works. *International Journal of Human Management, 10,* 488–500.

Harris, H., Brewster, C., & Sparrow, P. (2003). *International human resource management.* London: Chartered Institute of Personnel & Development.

Hofstede, G. (1980). *Culture's consequences: International differences in work-related values.* Beverly Hills, CA: Sage.

Hofstede, G. (2001). *Culture's consequences* (2nd ed.). Thousand Oaks: Sage.

House, R. J., Gupta, V., Dorfman, P. W., Javidan, M., & Hanges, P. J. (Eds.). (2004). *Culture, leadership, and organizations: The GLOBE study of 62 societies.* Thousand Oaks: Sage.

Inkson, K., Arthur, M. B., Pringle, J. K., & Barry, S. (1997). Expatriate assignment versus overseas experience: Contrasting models of international human resource development. *Journal of World Business, 32*(4), 351–368.

International Labour Organization. (2004). *Towards a fair deal for migrant workers in the global economy.* Paper presented at the 92nd session of the International Labour Conference, Geneva.

Johnson, J. P., Lenartowicz, T., & Apud, S. (2006). Cross-cultural competence in international business: Toward a definition and a model. *Journal of International Business Studies, 37,* 525–543.

Kets de Vries, M. F. R. (2004). Putting leaders on the couch. A conversation with Manfred F. R. Kets de Vries [Interview by Diane L. Coutu]. *Harvard Business Review, 82*(1), 64–71.

Kets de Vries, M. F. R., & Florent-Treacy, E. (1999). *The new global leaders: Richard Branson, Percy Barnevik, David Simon and the remaking of international business.* San Francisco: Jossey-Bass.

Klein, N. (2001). *No logo: No space, no choice, no jobs.* London: Flamingo.

Konopaske, R., Robie, C., & Ivancevich, J. M. (2005). A preliminary model of spouse influence on managerial global assignment willingness. *International Journal of Human Resource Management, 16,* 405–426.

Kotter, J. P. (1982). *The general managers.* New York: Free Press.

Kotter, J. P. (1995). *The new rules: How to succeed in today's post-corporate world.* New York: Free Press.

Lane, H., DiStefano, J. J., & Maznevski, M. L. (2006). *International management behavior: Text, readings, and cases* (5th ed.). Oxford: Blackwell.

Lane, H. W, Maznevski, M. L., Mendenhall, M. E., & McNett, J. (Eds.). (2004). *The Blackwell handbook of global management: A guide to managing complexity.* London: Blackwell.

Lasch, C. (1995). *The revolt of the elites.* New York: W. W. Norton.

Lowell, B. L., & Findlay, A. (2001). *Migration of highly skilled persons from developing countries: Impact and policy responses* (International Migration Papers, 44, Synthesis Report). Geneva: ILO.

Mayerhofer, H., Hartmann, L. C., & Herbert, A. (2004). Career management issues for flexpatriate international staff. *Thunderbird International Business Review, 46*(6), 647–666.

Mayerhofer, H., Hartmann, L. C., Michelitsch-Riedl, G., & Kollinger, I. (2004). Flexpatriate assignments: A neglected issue in global staffing. *International Journal of Human Resource Management, 15*(8), 1371–1389.

Maznevski, M. L., & Lane, H. W. (2003). Shaping the global mind-set: Designing educational experiences for effective global thinking and action. In N. Boyacigiller, R. Goodman, & M. Philips (Eds.), *Teaching and experiencing cross-cultural management: Lessons from master teachers* (pp. 171–184). London: Routledge.

McCall, M., & Hollenbeck, G. (2002). *Developing global executives.* Boston: Harvard Business School Press.

Mendenhall, M. (2001). New perspectives on expatriate adjustment and its relationship to global leadership development. In M. Mendenhall, T. Kuhlmann, & G. Stahl. (Eds.), *Developing global business leaders: Policies, processes, and innovation.* Westport, CT: Quorum.

Mendenhall, M. E., & Oddou, G. R. (1985). The dimensions of expatriate acculturation: A review. *Academy of Management Review, 10,* 39–47.

Mendenhall, M. E., & Osland, J. S. (2002, June). *An overview of the extant global leadership research.* Symposium presentation at Academy of International Business, Puerto Rico.

McNett, J., & Søndergaard, M. (2004). Making ethical decisions. In H. W. Lane, M. L. Masnevski, M. E., Mendenhall, & J. McNett (Eds.), *The Blackwell handbook of global management: A guide to managing complexity* (pp. 152–169). London: Blackwell.

Moore, M. J. (2002). Same ticket, different trip: Supporting dual-career couples on global assignments. *Women in Management, 17*(2), 61–67.

Moran, R. T., & Riesenberger, J. R. (1994). *The global challenge: Building the new worldwide enterprise.* London: McGraw-Hill.

Morley, M., & Heraty, N. (2004). International assignments and global careers. *Thunderbird International Business Review, 46*(6), 633–646.

Napier, N. K., & Peterson, R. B. (1991). Expatriate re-entry: What do repatriates have to say? *Human Resource Planning, 14,* 1.

Nicholson, N. (2000). *Managing the human animal.* London: Thomson Learning. (Published in the United States as *Executive instinct: Managing the human animal in the information age.* New York: Crown.)

Oddou, G., & Derr, C. B. (1999). *Managing internationally: A personal journey.* Orlando, FL: Dryden Press.

Oddou, G., Mendenhall, M., & Ritchie, J. B. (2000). Leveraging travel as a tool for global leadership development. *Human Resource Management, 39*(2/3), 159–172.

Ohmae, K. (1987). *Beyond national borders.* Homewood, IL: Dow Jones-Irwin.

Ohmae, K. (1990). *The borderless world: Power and strategy in the interlinked economy.* New York: Harper Business.

Ohmae, K. (1995). *The end of the nation state.* London: HarperCollins.

Oppenheim, J. (2004). Corporations as global citizens. *McKinsey Quarterly, 1,* 4–5.

Organisation for Economic Co-Operation and Development. (2001). *Trends in international migration* (Annual Report). Paris: Author.

Organisation for Economic Co-Operation and Development. (2002, July). International mobility of the highly skilled. *OECD Observer, 232,* 1–7.

Organisation for Economic Co-Operation and Development. (2005). *Trends in international migration and in migration policies.* Paris: Directorate for Employment, Labour and Social Affairs.

Osland, J. S. (1995). *The adventure of working abroad: Hero tales from the global frontier.* San Francisco: Jossey-Bass.

Osland, J. S. (2004). Building community through change. In H. W. Lane, M. L. Masnevski, M. E. Mendenhall, & J. McNett (Eds.), *The Blackwell handbook of global management: A guide to managing complexity* (pp. 134–151). London: Blackwell.

Özden, C., & Schiff, M. (Eds). (2006). *International migration, remittances and the brain drain.* Washington, DC: World Bank.

Peiperl, M., & Baruch, Y. (1997). Back to square zero: The post-corporate career. *Organizational Dynamics, Spring,* 7–22.

Peiperl, M., & Estrin, S. (2000). *Chief executives in the New Europe: Challenges, shortages, and an agenda for change.* Brussels: Association for Executive Search Consultants (AESC) Europe.

Pollock, D. C., & Van Reken, R. (2001). *Third culture kids.* Yarmouth, MN: Nicholas Brealey.

Robertson, R. (1992). *Globalization.* London: Sage.

Salt, J., & Clarke, J. (1998). Flows and stocks of foreign labour in the UK. *Labour Market Trends, 106*(7), 371–386.

Schneider, S. C., & Barsoux, J.-L. (2003). *Managing across cultures* (2nd ed.). Harlow: Financial Times Prentice Hall.

Schwartz, S. H. (1992). Universals in the content and structure of values: Theoretical advances and empirical tests in 20 countries. In M. P. Zanna (Ed.), *Advances in experimental social psychology* (pp. 1–65). San Diego, CA: Academic Press.

Schwartz, S. H. (1994a). Beyond individualism/collectivism: New dimensions of values. In U. Kim, H. C. Triandis, C. Kagitçibasi, S. C. Choi, & G. Yoon (Eds.), *Individualism and collectivism: Theory, applications, and methods* (pp. 85–119). Thousand Oaks, CA: Sage.

Schwartz, S. H. (1994b). Beyond individualism-collectivism: New cultural dimensions of values. In R. Goodwin (Ed.), *Personal relationships across cultures* (pp. 22–36). London: Routledge.

Spivey, W. A., & Thomas, L. D. (1990). Global management: Concepts, themes, problems, and research issues. *Human Resource Management, 29*(1), 85–97.

Stahl, G. K., & Cerdin, J.-L. (2004). Global careers in French and German multinational corporations. *Journal of Management Development, 23,* 9.

Stahl, G. K., Miller, E. L. & Tung, R. L. (2002). Toward the boundaryless career: A closer look at the expatriate career concept and the perceived implications of an international assignment. *Journal of World Business, 37*(3), 216–227.

Stalker, P. (2000). *Workers without frontiers.* Geneva, Switzerland: ILO.

Stiglitz, J. (2002). *Globalisation and its discontents.* London: Penguin.

Stroh, L. K., Black, J. S., Mendenhall, M. E., & Gregersen, H. B. (2005). *International assignments: An integration of strategy, research, and practice.* Mahwah, NJ: Lawrence Erlbaum.

Suutari, V., & Brewster, C. (2000). Making their own way: International experience through self-initiated foreign assignments. *Journal of World Business, 35,* 4.

Suutari, V., & Taka, M. (2004). Career anchors of managers with global careers. *Journal of Management Development, 23,* 9.

Tahvanainen, M., Welch, D., & Worm, V. (2005). Implications of short-term international assignments. *European Management Journal, 23,* 6.

Thomas, D. C., & Inkson, K. (2004). *Cultural intelligence.* San Francisco: Berrett-Koehler.

Thomas, D. C., & Osland, J. S. (2004). Mindful communication. In H. W. Lane, M. L. Masnevski, M. E. Mendenhall, & J. McNett (Eds.), *The Blackwell handbook of global management: A guide to managing complexity* (pp. 94–108). London: Blackwell.

Thorogood, D., & Winqyist, K. (2003). Women and men migrating to and from the European Union. In *Eurostat—Statistics in focus* (Theme 3, pp. 1–7). Luxembourg: Office for Official Publications of the European Communities.

Tichy, N. (1988). Setting the global human resource management agenda for the 1990's. *Human Resource Management, 27*(1), 1–18.

Ting-Toomey, S. (1999). *Communicating across cultures.* New York: Guilford Press.

Trompenaars, F. (1993). *Riding the waves of culture: Understanding cultural diversity in business.* London: Nicholas Brealey.

Tung, R. L. (1982). Selection and training procedures of U.S., European, and Japanese multinationals. *California Management Review, 25*(1), 57–71.

Tungli, Z., & Peiperl, M. (2007). Expatriate practices in German, Japanese, UK and US multinational companies: A comparative study. Paper revised and resubmitted to *Human Resource Management.*

United Nations. (2005, October). *Counting immigrants and expatriates in OECD countries: A new perspective.* Paper presented at the fourth coordination meeting on international migration. New York: United Nations Secretariat.

United Nations Conference on Trade and Development. (2000). *World investment report 2000.* New York: Author.

United Nations Educational, Scientific, and Cultural Organization. (2004). *International flows of selected cultural goods and services, 1994–2003.* Montreal, Canada: UNESCO Institute for Statistics.

van der Velde, M. E. G., Bossink, C. J. H., & Jansen, P. G. W. (2005). Gender differences in the determinants of the willingness to accept an international assignment. *Journal of Vocational Behavior, 66,* 81–103.

Valcour, P. M., & Tolbert, P. S. (2003). Gender, family and career in the era of boundarylessness: Determinants and effects of intra- and inter-organizational mobility. *International Journal of Human Resource Management, 14*(5), 768–787.

Vance, C. M. (2005). The personal quest for building global competence: A taxonomy of self-initiating career path strategies for gaining business experience abroad. *Journal of World Business, 40,* 374–385.

Wagner, A. (2004). Redefining citizenship for the 21st century: From the national welfare state to the UN global compact. *International Journal of Social Welfare, 13,* 278–286.

Welch, D., Welch, L., & Worm, V. (2007). The international business traveller: A neglected but strategic human resource. *International Journal of Human Resource Management, 18*(2), 173–183.

Welch, D. E., & Worm, V. (2006). International business travellers: A challenge for IHRM. In G. K. Stahl & I. Björkman (Eds.), *Handbook of research in international human resource management* (pp. 283–301). Northampton, NH: Edward Elgar.

Whitener, E., & Stahl, G. K. (2004). Creating and building trust. In H. W. Lane, M. L. Masnevski, M. E. Mendenhall, & J. McNett (Eds.), *The Blackwell handbook of global management: A guide to managing complexity* (pp. 109–120). London: Blackwell.

Wickramasekara, P. (2002). *Asian labour migration: Issues and challenges in an era of globalization.* Geneva: ILO.

Windham International. (2001). Global relocation trends 2001 survey report. National Foreign Trade Council, SHRM Global Forum, and GMAC Global Relocation Services. New York: Windham International.

Wolf, M. (2004). *Why globalization works.* New Haven, CT: Yale University Press.

World Migration. (2005). *Cost and benefits of international migration* (Vol. 3). Switzerland: IOM.

Zlotnik, H. (1998). International migration 1965–96: An overview. *Population and Development Review, 24*(3), 429–468.

SECTION 3

CAREERS AND INSTITUTIONS

Section 2 of Part II reviewed contextual issues in career scholarship. In Section 3, we focus on a specific form of context—namely, the institutions within and among which careers are made and which, in turn, careers shape.

We begin the section with a chapter linking the contextual material in Section 2 with the institutional material in Section 3. Slay and Taylor, in Chapter 19, show how career systems provide structure to careers within institutions and how psychological contracts provide the necessary linkages to make them work. First, they provide a brief review of the literature on psychological contracts: what types exist, how they have changed, and what issues surround psychological contract violation and fulfillment. Next, they examine two models of career systems—one linked to the business strategy followed by a firm and the other to the firm's need for particular human capital characteristics—and look at the empirical support for each. With these two conceptual building blocks in place, the authors start constructing a prescriptive model for enhancing psychological contract fulfillment by effectively managing career systems. They begin by showing how career mobility plays a key role in developing the psychological contract. They then show how three different types of mobility (hierarchical, radial, and functional/technical) affect psychological contract fulfillment. The links between mobility and contract fulfillment are mediated by four

different forms of "employment modes" defined by human capital career system theory and moderated by features of the system, including non-task-related interactions and three features of the organization's climate: people's perception of the relevance of the human resource system to achieving important goals and the consistency and fairness in its application.

In Chapter 20, Lawrence and Tolbert discuss a critical institutional property: demographic structure. Demographic influences on careers operate, as they point out, at many levels of analysis, from the individual to the organization. Quite a lot is known about the impact of demographic variables on career outcomes; what is missing is an understanding of the connecting mechanisms. There is a paucity of theory connecting these different levels of analysis—a frequent criticism of career theory—and in this chapter, the authors organize their review of the literature around a model that fills this gap. They begin by considering what determines the distribution of demographic attributes: for example, the impact of birth cohort sizes on the demographic composition of organizations or the influence of technological change on the distribution of occupations. Also influential, they argue, are attribute-linked organizational norms (what people regard as "typical" of a job or a career path), and the authors next review what might influence these. Attribute distributions and norms, in turn, affect the opportunity structure of an organization, but these effects are also partially mediated by interpersonal and intergroup relations; for example, in a society in which tensions surround race, the racial composition of a workforce will affect working relationships, which in turn affect opportunities facing individuals. The authors show how these organizational and group-level phenomena affect individuals' career-related decisions and behaviors. Finally, the authors close the loop by considering the impact that career-related outcomes have on organizational demography.

A contextual approach to understanding careers typically examines the impact of context on career. But, as Lawrence and Tolbert point out in Chapter 20, the direction of causality needs to be reversed too: Careers affect context. In Chapter 21, Higgins and Dillon examine the relationship between career patterns and organizational performance. A major contribution to our understanding of this relationship comes from upper echelon theory. The authors review this large body of research, showing that there are three kinds of mechanisms that connect senior executives' careers to organizational outcomes. First, there is a process effect: The backgrounds of members of the upper echelon affect the kind of decisions they take. Second, a resource effect is at work: Careers confer both human capital (people learn over the course of their careers) and social capital (they acquire connections over the course of their careers). Both affect the performance of the corporations they manage. Third, careers send signals; that is, they have symbolic value. The career backgrounds of members of executive teams, for example, send signals to the markets about the quality of the teams. The authors then turn to other streams of the literature that contribute to our understanding of the impact of careers on organizational performance, most notably that on executive succession. Finally, they identify a number of emerging lines of research that have the potential to move the field forward, highlighting the work of Gunz, Jones, and Higgins. They draw the threads together with some thoughts on the future direction of research on this topic.

In Chapter 22, Jones and Dunn examine the relationship between careers and institutions. Higgins and Dillon closed their chapter with an observation similar to that of Lawrence and

Tolbert: Careers are not just the product of organization: They shape it. Jones and Dunn take this as a point of departure: "Careers and institutions," they say, "are intimately connected and mutually reinforcing." They, too, identify the duality of careers as property and careers as process. Careers as property imprint social practices and understandings in the way that dominant groups maintain their dominance by blocking access to influential positions to those in other groups. Careers as process work by altering or standardizing role sequences; this perspective examines the sequence of roles that people experience to see how changes in these sequences are related to changes in institutions. By the same token, standardizing these role sequences results in institutional stability. But institutional properties and processes matter equally, as well. Institutional properties shape roles and role relations, and institutional processes encode or disassociate social knowledge from roles and role relationships. So, by bringing careers and institutions together, the authors argue, "we illuminate the role that individuals play in institutional processes and how institutional properties and processes shape individual actions through how knowledge is socially constructed and encoded into individuals through career systems." Finally, the authors look at the role of career in three key institutional processes: creation, reproduction, and transformation. They conclude by returning to Hughes' famous call to study career as a central concept, linking micro- and macro-levels of analysis and anchoring the study of many central institutional problems.

Chapter 23 broadens the institutional perspective yet further. Thomas and Inkson examine careers across national cultures, opening with a vivid illustration of the nature of the phenomenon: What relevance does the concept "career" have to a South African community in which unemployment is 98%, and nobody in most families has held a job for generations? Pointing to what they label as the "parochialism" of career theory as it exists today—its exclusive focus on the institutions of Western societies—they show how basic concepts such as bureaucracy, meritocracy, individual, and freedom of choice simply do not translate across many national boundaries; the embeddedness of career in national culture-bound institutions is too great. They examine the economic, political, and cultural influences that are relevant to the question, before reporting on the types of cross-cultural career research reported in the literature, which they classify under four headings: indigenous, replication, comparative, and intercultural research. Next, the authors examine a number of methods issues. They argue that because the field is still relatively underdeveloped it has the chance of avoiding methodological problems that have plagued other areas of cross-cultural research—problems of equivalence, sampling, data collection and measurement, and data analysis. Finally, they offer a framework for comparative career studies based on five career processes that are affected by cultural context—namely, the perceptions of career, career decision making, career development, career mobility, and career management.

The section concludes with an examination of career boundaries. Boundaries define institutions, but, argue Gunz, Peiperl, and Tzabbar in Chapter 24, they are also central to the study of career and a unifying thread that runs throughout the volume. They give careers their shape and provide a language by means of which we can describe and discuss careers. The authors begin with the question, "What do career boundaries separate and surround?" arguing that they delineate what the individual crosses when making a work role transition and that their socially constructed nature is central to understanding them. The authors conceive of boundaries initially taking shape in the minds of the actors involved—the career owner (ego) and the many people with whom he or she interacts at each stage of his or her career (alters)—as a *subjectively* perceived set of differences between the role currently occupied and those that might be occupied. The beginning of a career boundary, in other words, is a set of perceptions about a given work role transition. Over time, a consensus may develop among an influential group of social actors that a pattern of some kind can be discerned in these transitions. If this happens, we see the beginnings of what the authors call an *objective* career boundary. This may take on the properties of a social fact and a life of its own, as an important shaper of labor markets and careers. A central property of career boundaries is their permeability, which the authors argue is a consequence of two things—a reluctance to move on the part of the career owner and a reluctance to select on the part of those with whom the career owner interacts. These "reluctances" spring from *awareness* that a work role transition is possible, an assessment of its *achievability,* and its *attractiveness.* Taken together, these provide the basis of a model for understanding the phenomenon of career boundary permeability.

19

CAREER SYSTEMS AND PSYCHOLOGICAL CONTRACTS

HOLLY S. SLAY

M. SUSAN TAYLOR

The nature of the employment relationship and the shape of organizational career paths have undergone significant change during the past two decades, not only in America but also in Asia, Western Europe, and many other parts of the world (Cappelli, 1999; Osterman, 1996; Peiperl, Arthur, Goffee, & Morris, 2000). For example, Cappelli (1999) comments,

> What ended the traditional employment relationship is a variety of new management practices, driven by a changing environment, that essentially brings the market—both the market for a company's products and the labor market for its employees—directly inside the firms. And once inside, the market's logic quickly becomes dominant, pushing out of its way the behavioral principles of reciprocity and long-term commitment, the

internal promotion and development practices and the concerns about equity that underlie the more traditional employment contract. (p. 1)

Similarly, Batt (1996) writes about changes in managers' career paths in the AT&T system beginning in the late 1980s and early 1990s and notes that not only has career movement changed, but it has become much less common within that organization:

> Downsizing [at AT&T] has also, at least during this period of transition, reduced overall mobility throughout management. Although job ladders on paper have not changed, movement has halted. In 1990, for example, approximately 5% of managers were promoted to higher pay grade, a fraction of what existed in the 1950s through 1970s. (p. 72)

AUTHORS' NOTE: The authors contributed equally to the development of this chapter; therefore, the names are listed alphabetically rather than in order of contribution.

Batt's observations about decreasing levels of career movement within AT&T are echoed by other researchers studying organizations as well as authors in the popular press (Koudsi, 2001; Morin, 1996).

These changes raise questions about linkages between organizational career systems, that is, the collections of policies, priorities, and actions that organizations use to manage the flow of their members into, through, and out of the organization over time (Sonnenfeld & Peiperl, 1988), and the nature of the exchange between the organization and individual employees. These questions include the following: (1) How do career systems affect the nature of employees' psychological contracts, that is, their perceptions of the exchange relationship that exists with their employing organization? (2) What are the resulting outcomes of these effects in terms of employee perceptions of contract fulfillment, employee work attitudes and behaviors, and organizational performance and success? (3) How might career systems be managed more effectively to ensure employee perceptions of psychological contract fulfillment and favorable outcomes for both the employee and the organization?

In this chapter, we seek to answer the first two questions through reviews of the research literature on psychological contracts and career systems and then develop and present an integrated prescriptive model that proposes answers to the third question about more effective management of career systems. To accomplish this objective within the space available, however, we constrain our prescriptive focus on career system activities to those dealing with career movement or mobility in vertical, lateral, and radial directions within the organization (Schein, 1978; Sonnenfeld, 1989).

Yet we argue that this limited focus is sufficiently powerful to account for much of the impact that career systems have on employees' psychological contracts because critical knowledge and skill development, individual feelings of trust, inclusion, and commitment, and ultimately, future employability are all nested in thoughtfully selected intraorganizational mobility or movement. Thus, although a growing global competitiveness in the marketplace during the late 1980s clearly forced many organizations to restructure their workforce and their organizational design in order to achieve greater flexibility, efficiency, speed, and agility, and thus to limit vertical career movement (as the AT&T quote by Batt [1996] above illustrates), we believe that many firms also overreacted by unnecessarily restricting other types of intraorganizational career movement that many individuals view as important inducements. Our intention is to show how returning to a thoughtfully and selectively applied program of career movement, well fitted to the needs and job demands of different employee groups, will result in greater perceptions of contract fulfillment for employees as well as greater flexibility and performance for their organizations. Toward this end, our chapter begins with a selective review of psychological contract concepts that reflect the nature of different employment relationships and provides evidence of the relationship between career development activities and the nature of the psychological contract.

PSYCHOLOGICAL CONTRACTS

Psychological contracts are defined by Conway and Briner (2005) as "an employee's subjective understanding of promissory-based reciprocal exchanges between him and herself and the organization" (p. 35), and thus, psychological contracts are based in an employee's perceived reality, whether or not shared by the employing organization, and concerns the promises that each party is believed to have made to the other about the nature of their exchange relationship during employment. The psychological contract literature has increased dramatically in the past 20 years (Tekleab & Taylor, 2003), making this one of the most popular conceptualizations of the employee-organization relationship.

The foundation for the development of psychological contracts is organizations' recognition that their human resources are critical assets that offer opportunities for sustained competitive advantage (Barney, 1991). Thus, individuals and the organization engage in a series of ongoing negotiations, whereby the firm may offer developmental and career management activities in exchange for the use of individuals' capabilities, which further contribute to the organization's competitive advantage in at least two ways: (1) by enhancing its own set of capabilities (Coff, 1997), and thereby its competitive advantage, and (2) by relying on loyal and committed employees to enhance its flexibility to change strategic direction quickly or by benefiting from high work quality and innovation (Rousseau, 1995; Sonnenfeld, 1989).

Herriot and Pemberton (1996) propose that psychological contracts originate from an ongoing four-stage process whereby (1) parties *inform* one another of their needs and what they are prepared to offer in return, (2) *negotiations* take place and continue until parties agree on what they promise and are prepared to accept, (3) parties *monitor* one another's activities to ascertain whether or not they live up to their promises, and (4) *renegotiations* occur over time as parties' needs and desires change or until one party decides to *exit* the relationship. However, the types of contracts that can result from this contracting process are far from being all the same.

Types of Psychological Contracts

Prior research has identified four types of psychological contracts. Beginning in the late 1980s, Rousseau drew on work from the legal arena by MacNeil (1985) to propose and empirically support two kinds of contracts. *Transactional* contracts are relatively short term in nature and involve a "fee-for-service" kind of exchange whereby specific, primarily short-term duties are exchanged by the employee for payment or monetary inducements from the organization. *Relational* contracts are likely to include a wider range of inputs, some of which are relational in nature and fairly abstract, such as loyalty, commitment, hard work, and value for the person; to be stated in more general, rather than specific, terms; and to last for a longer period of time. In addition to transactional and relational contracts, two other types of contracts have appeared in the literature. First, Rousseau (1995) cited former General Electric CEO Jack Welch as the originator of the hybrid (part transactional, part relational) "balanced contract," combining a mix of shorter-term transactional features with an emphasis on internalized values and the importance of longer-term values over making the numbers in the short term. Dabos and Rousseau (2004) further refined the nature of balanced contracts by stating that they include expectations of shared risk between the employee and the firm such that employers promise to develop employees, and employees understand that changing economic conditions may alter what the organization can promise and deliver. Moreover, in balanced contracts, employees are obligated to take greater personal responsibility for development and career management. Finally, the terms of balanced psychological contracts are continually renegotiated as the needs of the organization and the individual change over time.

Second, Greenberg, Roberge, Ho, and Rousseau (2004) proposed the concept of idiosyncratic contracts or "deals" (I-deals). I-deals result when employers and employees voluntarily enter into highly customized agreements regarding nonstandard employment terms in response to tight labor markets and critical organizational demands for particular skill sets. Examples might include employees who are paid more than others for a given job due to their unique skill set or employees who are rewarded for their creativity by being given substantially more flexibility in work hours to deal with personal life issues. I-deals are marked by (1) being negotiated individually based on an employee's market value, (2) introducing a degree of within-group heterogeneity of benefits or inducements among coworkers, (3) serving the interests of both employer and employees, (4) varying in form and scope, and (5) being available (as appropriate) to either prospective or current employees. Rousseau (2004) argues that I-deals are growing rapidly in popularity; yet she also recognizes that they have a propensity to be perceived as unfair by other employees unless care is taken when creating them.

Recent Changes in Psychological Contracts

Regardless of the type of contract, however, as implied by Cappelli's (1999) quote at the beginning of this chapter, the increasingly market-driven focus that has dominated employment relationships during the past 25 years has resulted in many changes in the developmental and career management aspects of organizations' career systems, which in turn have affected employees' perceptions of their psychological contracts (Robinson & Rousseau, 1994). For example, many organizations have flattened their structures and reduced levels in the management hierarchy to decentralize decisions and allow employees more discretion to use their skills, thus increasing the organization's speed and agility in ways that enhance its competitive advantage (O'Reilly & Pfeffer, 1995). However, flatter organizational structures have brought fewer opportunities for upward mobility; so "working hard" is simply not enough to guarantee continuing promotions over one's career within a work organization. Furthermore, the promise of long-term job security is something few organizational leaders can or will make in today's digital and global economy. As former CEO Jack Welch stated, "Companies cannot promise their people lifetime employment. Global competition is too fierce and economic cycles too frequent for any such guarantees. But they can promise their people every chance for employability—skills that will make them more attractive if they are forced to part ways" (Welch & Welch, 2005, p. 109). Like Welch and GE, many organizations and their leaders have substituted continuing training and development for long-term employment security and regular hierarchical advancement with a given firm. Interestingly, however, despite the noted reductions in employment security and career advancement opportunities, many firms continue to seek loyalty, commitment, and identification from their employees. For example, Ho, Ang, and Straub (2003) found that even when IT employees were moved to contract status, managers continued to have expectations that they would act as subordinates, accepting additional tasks rather than those explicitly contracted.

Developmental opportunities and career development activities in an organization's career system exert a significant effect on employees' perceptions of their psychological contracts. This is consistent with Conway and Briner's (2005) arguments that several *organizational factors* are important in shaping individual contract perceptions, including the information gleaned from HRM policies and practices (career systems), and that the sheer number of HRM practices enacted by an organization is positively related to employees' perceptions of promises made by the organization. Furthermore, Sturges, Conway, Guest, and Liefooghe (2005) found that organizational development and career management activities were positively related to perceptions of psychological contract fulfillment, which in turn mediated the relationships between organizations' developmental and career management activities and employees' affective organizational commitment (the degree of attachment to and identification with the employer; see Meyer & Allen, 1997) as well as their job performance. Finally, these researchers reported that continuance organizational commitment (an individual's sense that leaving the organization will result in personal losses; see Meyer & Allen, 1997) mediated the relationship between psychological contract fulfillment and voluntary turnover. Thus, it appears that developmental and career management activities resulting from organizations' career systems may have an impact on employees' perceptions of contract fulfillment, which in turn mediates important job attitudes and employee performance. Because of the growing role that perceptions of contract fulfillment and what has been traditionally viewed as its opposite, contract violation, play in determining the impact of career mobility on individuals' perceptions of their psychological contract, we briefly review what is currently known about these concepts.

PSYCHOLOGICAL CONTRACT VIOLATION AND FULFILLMENT[1]

Contract Breach or Violation

Morrison and Robinson (1997) define breach as a party's emotional reaction to a violation and violation as the cognitive recognition of unmet promises. Contract violation/breach may occur as one result of the subjective nature of the psychological contract, since the employee and the organization do not necessarily share the same perception of what has been promised. As a result, one party may perceive violations that are not even recognized by the other party (called "inadvertent violations" by Rousseau, 1995). Of course, violations may also occur when parties intentionally choose not to live up to their promises ("reneging," Rousseau, 1995), often because one party feels the other has reneged on its promises, or when a party is no longer able to meet promised commitments due to changes in its circumstances ("contract disruption," Rousseau, 1995).

Several studies find that employees tend to perceive violations fairly frequently. For example, Robinson and Rousseau (1994) found that 55% of an MBA graduate sample reported experiencing contract violation within the first 2 years on the job. Similarly, in a diary-keeping study of 45 individuals who were either part-time MBA students or bank employees, Conway and Briner (2002) reported that 69% of their sample identified at least one broken promise over the 10-day research period. Finally, Lester, Turnley, Bloodgood, and Bolino (2002) investigated a combined sample of part-time working MBA students and telecommunications employees and found that 65% of their sample reported that employer contributions failed to meet the level promised to them.

Both Rousseau (1995) and Morrison and Robinson (1997) have developed conceptual models of the contract breach or violation process. The models differ in that Morrison and Robinson, given their distinction between contract breach and violation, devote greater attention to developing the process whereby employees perceive contract breach, whereas only Rousseau's model discusses the consequences of perceived contract violation. Rousseau and McLean Parks (1993, p. 36) note that contract violations erode trust, undermine the employment relationship, lower employee contributions, such as performance and attendance, and lower employer investments, such as retention and promotion. They also posit that once relational contracts are violated, they become more transactional in nature. Later studies have confirmed virtually all the above propositions (Lester et al., 2002; Robinson, 1996; Robinson & Morrison, 2000; Robinson & Rousseau, 1994; Turnley & Feldman, 1999). While much of the research on psychological contracts in the mid- to late 1990s looked at various aspects of contract violation or breach, a smaller group of studies have instead examined contract fulfillment, arguably the opposite of contract breach or violation.

Contract Fulfillment

Several studies have found that the perception of contract fulfillment, like that of contract breach/violation, is a significant predictor of employee attitudes and behaviors. Nevertheless, as we illustrate below, findings across studies tend to differ on (1) whether contract breach/violation or fulfillment is a stronger predictor of individual reactions and (2) whether the two occupy opposite ends of the same continuum or are actually two separate dimensions.

Research by Coyle-Shapiro and Kessler (2000) on a sample of British public sector employees found that contract fulfillment, the extent to which the other party has met promises of inducements made within one's psychological contract, was positively related to employees' affective organizational commitment and self-reported organizational citizenship behavior. Conway and Briner (2002) used a diary-keeping methodology to investigate the frequency of perceived contract breaches, fulfillment, and—one step higher than fulfillment—incidences of exceeding promises as well as employees' emotional reactions to these states. Their findings revealed that contract breaches and exceeded promises both occurred frequently, with some 69% of their 45-person sample reporting at least one breach over the 10-day study period and 62% reporting at least one case where the inducements received from the organization exceeded what had been promised. Breaches were more likely to evoke feelings of betrayal than hurt from contract holders, while exceeded promises were more likely to yield feelings of self-worth than surprise. Breaches had a stronger effect on participants' moods than did exceeded promises. Additionally, Lester et al. (2002) compared supervisor and employee perceptions of contract breach, contract fulfillment, and exceeded promises. Somewhat surprisingly, given Conway and Briner's (2002) findings with respect to mood, Lester et al. (2002) found that fulfilled and exceeded promises led to higher levels of employee performance and affective commitment than did contract breach.

Conway and Briner's (2005) book on the psychological contract further reviews existing research on contract breach or violation and contract fulfillment and reaches a different conclusion about the nature of their relationship. The authors take issue with the traditional view that contract fulfillment is a single continuum running from break through fulfillment to overfulfillment and has a linear effect on outcomes such as organizational commitment and performance. They note that their own findings showing contract breach had a stronger effect on employee mood than did exceeded promises. Conway and Briner (2002) are not supportive of a single linear function and also cite another empirical study reporting discrepant results. For example, Lambert, Edwards, and Cable (2003) found that while exceeded promises in some contract areas (pay) led to higher levels of job satisfaction, exceeded promises in other areas (job or task variety) subsequently led to job dissatisfaction. Thus, Conway and Briner (2005) conclude that three possible relationships may exist between contract fulfillment and contract outcomes: (1) there is a linear relationship that goes from broken to kept promises but levels off as contract fulfillment goes beyond "meeting" what the other party promised; (2) there are a number of different relationships depending on which "promise" is being examined (e.g., pay vs. task variety), as in the case of the Lambert et al. (2003) study; and (3) breaking and exceeding promises for the same contract item are independent dimensions, much as Herzberg (Herzberg, Mausner, & Snyderman, 1959) proposed many years ago with his hygiene and motivator factors of job satisfaction. As will be evident from our model discussed below, we advocate Position 2—that the nature of the function between contract violation and fulfillment and various individual reactions depends on what is being promised and that fulfillment of perceived career mobility promises is very important for employee satisfaction, commitment, performance, and continued employment. Nevertheless, we concur with Conway and Briner (2005) that the traditional view of breach and fulfillment lying on a single continuum and having a linear relationship with these outcomes is far too simplistic and that, ultimately, only further empirical work will answer the question of which of the three possibilities offers the best explanation.

Summary

In this section, we introduced four different types of psychological contracts and also provided evidence that career systems affect individuals' perceptions of the nature of their

psychological contracts as well as their perceived level of contract fulfillment, both of which affect employee attitudes and behaviors, such as job satisfaction, organizational commitment, performance, and turnover. In the next section, we review two popular career system models that extend the career system/psychological contract linkage to different employee groups and posit that different career systems tend to generate different types of psychological contracts.

CAREER SYSTEM THEORIES AND THE PSYCHOLOGICAL CONTRACT

Defining Career Systems

A career system is the set of human resource management (HRM) policies and practices as well as management actions that serve to direct employees during their tenure with an organization (Sonnenfeld & Peiperl, 1988). As in the extant HRM literature, generally, much of the theorizing around career systems has focused primarily on *content* or the practices contained within organizational career systems (Bowen & Ostroff, 2004). However, as suggested in the opening quote from Cappelli, changes in the external environment and the corresponding firm strategy cause firms to alter the objective nature of the employment exchange and, subsequently, the composition of career systems. Therefore, our review of the literature in this section examines two conceptual models: (1) Sonnenfeld and Peiperl's (1988) strategic response typology and (2) Lepak and Snell's (1999) HR architecture. In the following paragraphs, we describe each model, note its basic components and the purpose it seems to serve for organizations, review recent research testing model validity, and where possible, propose its effect on employees' psychological contracts.

Career System Models

Although many career system models appear in the research literature (e.g., Gunz, 1989; Von Glinow, Driver, Brousseau, & Prince, 1983), mindful of space limitations we chose to focus on two that best reflect the current marketplace for labor.

Strategic Response Typology: Strategy as a Driver of Career Systems

The strategic response typology of career systems (Sonnenfeld & Peiperl, 1988; Sonnenfeld, Peiperl, & Kotter, 1988) reflects an organization's beliefs, policies, and plans concerning two important HRM processes: supply flow and assignment flow. Supply flow describes the extent to which firms hire new employees at levels above entry level or rely on internal development and succession. Assignment flow describes the extent to which the organization focuses on individual versus team/group contributions. The combination of these two processes yields four different types of career systems that

are aligned with firms' larger competitive strategy to survive and thrive in the existing marketplace (Figure 19.1). Below, we provide a brief explanation of each quadrant in the typology.

External Supply Flow, Group Contribution Assignment Flow: The Fortress

The fortress career system is used by firms whose strategy is to react to their external environment rather than control it. Adoption of this system is stimulated by crisis and the "struggle for survival" (Sonnenfeld & Peiperl, 1988, p. 593), and as a result, such organizations are primarily focused on retrenchment as a means to cut costs through layoffs. Therefore, the

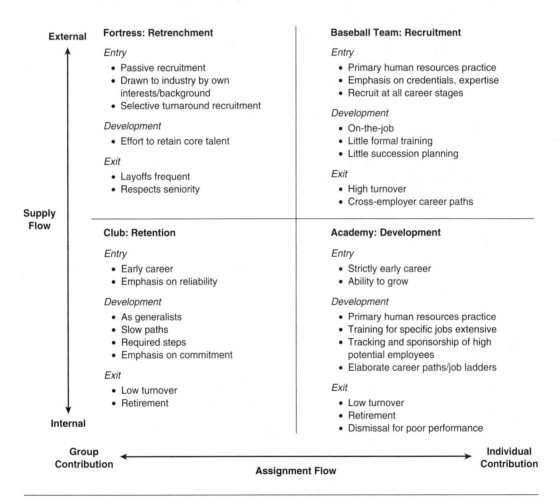

Figure 19.1 Sonnenfeld and Peiperl's (1988) Strategic Response Typology

SOURCE: Sonnenfeld, J. A., & Peiperl, M. A., "Staffing policy as a strategic response: A typology of career systems," in *Academy of Management Review,* copyright © 1988. Reprinted with permission.

content of the career system includes severely limited training and development. Staffing actions are undertaken only to acquire turn-around expertise and inexpensive replacements for exiting organizational members.

Internal Supply Flow, Group
Contribution Assignment Flow: The Club

Club career systems are found in organizations that are striving to defend their market positions rather than to enhance them. Such firms are often protected by legislation or favorable monopolistic conditions, and as a result, clubs stress job security and their employees often see themselves as pursuing a mission that contributes to the greater public good, believing that fulfilling the firm's mission is more important than market concerns. There is often upward career mobility based on seniority and organizational contributions rather than individual job achievement. Because clubs rely extensively on staffing from within, employees tend to enter in early career and remain throughout their work life. Learning and development occur primarily on the job, and employees become generalists who move slowly upward along a structured path. Thus, employees develop firm-specific knowledge and intense loyalty to their organization, and many HRM practices support the internal flow of people. An excellent example of this career system type is provided by United Parcel Service in the 1980s, as seen from this quote from its employee handbook cited in Sonnenfeld et al. (1988):

> We Promote From Within. Whenever possible, we fill managerial positions from our ranks . . . We fill a vacancy from the outside only when we cannot locate one of our own people who has the capacity or . . . skills . . . which may be required. (p. 370)

External Supply Flow, Individual Contribution
Assignment Flow: The Baseball Team

Organizations relying on a strategy of continuous innovation often use baseball team career systems that are not based on employment security but rather on a permanent openness to extra-ordinary external talent at all career stages. This enables them to fuel continuing innovation. Baseball teams rely heavily on recruitment and selection HRM practices in order to hire "stars": talented and proven individuals who can contribute immediately to firms' strategic goals without the need for training and development. Relatively few career system practices are devoted to employee development. Many advertising and broadcasting firms, among others, exemplify baseball team career systems.

Internal Supply Flow and Individual
Contribution Assignment Flow: The Academy

Firms that strive for continuing dominance in established markets and consciously choose to respond more slowly than organizations competing on continuous product and service innovations typically adopt academy career systems. Academies "take care of their people" by promising and providing job security, developmental opportunities, and career advancement. These career system characteristics motivate continuing skill development and stimulate organizational commitment and immense loyalty in their typically long-term and highly capable employees. The academy career system model sets the standard for career systems in the 1950s throughout the late 1980s, at least within the United States, and was found in organizations such as AT&T and IBM.

Empirical Tests of the Model and
Relationships to the Psychological Contract

Our literature review identified only one direct and one indirect empirical test of the Sonnenfeld and Peiperl (1988) typology. Baruch and Peiperl (2003) conducted the direct test that examined the level of support for the two dimensions of supply flow and assignment flow, while also attempting to verify the four proposed quadrant archetypes—namely, academy, baseball team, club, and fortress. Their research results supported the validity of a supply flow dimension but failed to confirm the assignment flow dimension. Not surprisingly, then, they found mixed evidence for the four types of organizational career systems proposed. For example, they found some support for the proposed fortress versus club distinctions; however, fortresses did not report generally being in a retrenchment mode, and clubs did not generally provide long-term employment. Little support was found for the club versus academy or baseball team distinctions. An important implication of this research is that the relationship between organizational strategies and career systems may be best reflected in whether they follow a "make" or "buy" strategy. Make strategy firms rely on internal labor markets for the development of human capital, investing heavily in HRM and career systems. Academies and clubs thus employ a make strategy. In contrast, buy strategy firms are characterized by a reliance on the external labor market to provide needed knowledge and skills. Fortresses and Baseball Teams thus employ a buy strategy (Peck, 1994).

Our literature review identified one indirect test of the Sonnenfeld and Peiperl (1988) career system model that explicitly examines the question of make versus buy. Peck (1994) indirectly tested a simplified version of the Sonnenfeld and Peiperl model by examining the HRM characteristics associated with firms pursuing a make or buy orientation, based on their strategic goals. However, she found that organizations focusing on the pursuit of new products and markets used staffing, development, and internal labor markets (while Sonnenfeld and Peiperl would have predicted such firms would have baseball team career systems that rely extensively on the external labor markets). Additionally, Peck (1994) found that the more the firms strived to defend their market positions (a strategy associated with club career systems in Sonnenfeld and Peiperl's model), the *lower* their dependence on internal labor markets for the development of human capital. However, Peck's conclusion is that the relationship between strategy and career system practices is complex because HRM practices are multifaceted and include not only training and development but also compensation and retention practices (such as rewarding longevity and avoiding downsizing). Therefore, the relationship between firm strategy and the actual content of career systems requires further elucidation.

Peck's (1994) study also examined the proposed chain of relationships between organizational strategy, HRM practices, and the employment relationship, as assessed by the psychological contract (relational vs. transactional).

Specifically, Peck hypothesized an association between career-related (HRM) policies and practices and psychological contracts: A make orientation would be associated with relational contracts and a buy orientation with transactional contracts. There was limited support for this hypothesis, with only retention practices showing a significant relationship to transactional contracts, while staffing and development practices as well as compensation practices were not significantly associated with the relational psychological contract.

In summary, the relatively small amount of research (two studies) examining the Sonnenfeld and Peiperl (1988) career system model provides very limited support for proposed linkages between business strategy and the four career archetypes (academy, baseball team, club, and fortress), between predicted differences in career system characteristics and archetypes, or between systems and psychological contracts. In part, the weak support found for the model may have resulted from the cross-sectional nature of the data and the tendency of HRM practices to lag changes in business strategy (Baird & Meshoulam, 1988; Peck, 1994), but it is also clear that the assignment flow dimension provides a shaky foundation for the model and that the strategy→HRM philosophy→HRM practice characteristics chain of relationships is more complex than model propositions would suggest. Finally, this research provided little insight into the relationship between the configuration of HRM practices associated with the four career system archetypes and the various forms of psychological contracts identified earlier.

Human Resource Architecture: Human Capital Characteristics as Drivers of Career Systems

Lepak and Snell (1999) also developed a model proposing four employment modes that shed light on the nature of career systems (Figure 19.2). Their unique contribution is the introduction of the idea that the competencies and contributions desired by an organization from its employees drive its choice of HRM practices, including those concerning employee development and career management.

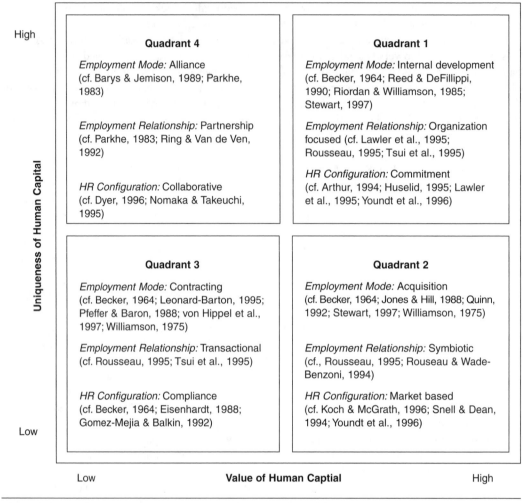

Figure 19.2   Lepak and Snell's (1999) Human Resource Architecture Model

SOURCE: Lepak, D. P., & Snell, S. A., "The human resource architecture: Toward a theory of human capital allocation and development," in *Academy of Management Review*, copyright © 1999. Reprinted with permission.

Fundamentally, Lepak and Snell (1999) propose that the decision to invoke a particular set of career practices is a function of value, defined "as the ratio of strategic benefits to customers derived from skills relative to the costs incurred" (p. 35), and uniqueness, that is, the degree to which an individual has firm-specific skills that are not widely available in the external market of human capital. Employees are valuable to the extent that their skills contribute to the amount a customer is willing to pay for the organization's products or services, whereas employees are unique if their skills are useful to the employer but not widely available in the external labor market.

The HR architecture typology builds on the work of Sonnenfeld and Peiperl by replacing their assignment flow dimension with the value of human capital, while retaining and explicating the supply flow dimension's distinction between reliance on external versus internal labor markets. Using the dimensions of value and uniqueness, Lepak and Snell (1999) develop four employment modes. The first is *internal development,* where individuals possess skills of high value and high uniqueness, and contribute to the firm's strategic objectives and help establish competitive advantage. In this case, Lepak and Snell argue that the firm will seek to develop an *organization-based* relationship (Tsui, Pearce, Porter,

& Hite, 1995) with these employees by applying commitment-based HRM practices (Arthur, 1994) that provide for enhanced employee skills, motivation, and autonomy in decision making. Developmental and career management practices are also used within the organization's fostering of an organization-based relationship. As Lepak and Snell (1999) note, "Human capital theorists suggest that firms . . . invest significantly to develop unique skills through extensive training initiatives. To complement training, organizations might sponsor career development and mentoring programs to encourage employees to build idio-syncratic knowledge" (p. 37).

Thus, in the internal development mode of employment, the firm uses HRM practices, such as training, development, and career pathing, which build and maintain human capital skills that are both valuable and unique, in exchange for employees' organizational commitment, loyalty, and flexibility in performing work assignments as needed by the firm. The type of psychological contract closest to this mode is *relational.*

The second employment mode, termed *acquisition,* consists of employees who are high in strategic value but low in uniqueness, which means that they are widely available throughout the labor market. This mode strives for the creation of *symbiotic employment relationships* that are characterized by both parties' recognition of mutual benefits and a relationship duration that lasts as long as the mutual benefit continues. In this case, however, while expecting a certain amount of loyalty from employees, organizations also recognize that like the relationship itself, this loyalty is temporary and will last only as long as the relationship delivers mutual benefits. Thus, employees are less committed to the organization and more focused on their career than are those in the internal development mode and are willing to move to wherever they can gain the greatest return on their skills, experience, and abilities. Similarly, organizations using the acquisition mode tend to hire employees who already possess the skills necessary to make an immediate contribution and, thus, sponsor minimal developmental or career advancement opportunities as this investment will be lost, or worse transferred to competitors, when employees exit the firm to move to other employers. Firms using the acquisition mode may, however, invest heavily in entry-level

career activities such as employee orientation (Sonnenfeld & Peiperl, 1988) to ensure that employees are able to make immediate contributions to the firm. We propose that the nature of the psychological contract with these employees is closest to the *balanced* contract, whereby the organization's limited investment in the employee's long-term job security is offset by the employee's short-term loyalty and commitment.

The third employment mode, *alliance,* is used with employees who are high in uniqueness but low in value. Alliance relationships are formed so that both the employee and the organization can gain the benefits associated with the specialized knowledge of the other party "without incurring the entire costs of internal employment" (Lepak & Snell, 1999, p. 41). For example, a highly specialized process engineer may form an ongoing consulting relationship with a pharmaceutical company to work on specific processes. As the engineer's specialized knowledge is useful for only some of the manufacturing processes, the firm will not try to hire the individual full time but is willing to sponsor the engineer's attendance at training and development programs that enable more effective knowledge sharing and team building. The engineer may also desire the flexibility of a consulting relationship with several different companies to work on several developing technologies within his or her area of expertise and garner higher pay. Therefore, the relationship is a collaborative one of mutual benefit that offers some investment in the employee's future.

The alliance mode is similar to the contracting mode (discussed below) in that organizational flexibility is the primary benefit for the organization. However, alliance employment provides unique, rather than commodity, resources and dictates the use of more collaborative HRM practices, which provide for the development of participating employees and makes some level of commitment to the firm desirable. We propose that the psychological contract type most closely linked to the alliance mode will be the *I-deal,* whereby the inducements an employee receives from the organization depend on the attributes and contributions the individual brings to the negotiation table.

The final employment mode, *contracting,* is used with employees who have skills that are low on value and uniqueness. Firms will tend to engage in contractual relationships with such employees through either outsourcing or the hiring of temporary workers and will try to manage these workers through compliance, using HRM systems that closely monitor employee performance to make certain that clearly established standards are met. Compliance systems ensure that employees have the minimum training required to conform to organizational rules, but as in the acquisition mode, there is little career development. Rather, the organization retains the flexibility to hire and fire employees as dictated by market demands, keeping labor costs low in order to match fluctuations in demand for goods or services. Clearly, the psychological contract linked most closely to the contracting mode is the short-term, highly specific, limited-inducement *transactional* type.

In summary, Lepak and Snell's model (1999) extends prior theoretical work by specifying the characteristics of employees that cause firms to differentially value and manage them and, as a result, to form qualitatively different kinds of employment relationships with them. It also introduces employment modes that include two used with external employees, while developing the nature of these modes and explaining why they are necessary. This model has already generated a slight theoretical revision (the internal development mode is now referred to as knowledge based in order to separate the nature of HRM practices from the modes themselves) and two empirical studies by Lepak and his associates, which we review below.

Empirical Tests of the Model and Relationships to the Psychological Contract

Lepak and his colleagues have conducted two direct tests of the HR architecture model. The first study by Lepak and Snell (2002) examined the value and the uniqueness of human capital for the four proposed employment modes and also attempted to validate the nature of HRM practices within these modes. It did not examine predictions of differential relationships across modes or consider the psychological contract. The research used a survey-based methodology, a cross-sectional design, and a sample of 148 firms (response rate of 6.5%). Respondents

included senior executives, senior HR managers, and line managers.

Results supported model predictions that human capital value is higher in knowledge-based and job-based employment than in contract work and alliances. However, there was mixed support for uniqueness predictions since the researchers found that alliance workers were less unique than knowledge-based workers and not significantly different in uniqueness from job-based workers. Also, contrary to hypotheses, firms used three different types of HRM practice configurations (commitment-based, productivity-based, and collaborative-based) for knowledge workers rather than just the predicted commitment-based configuration. However, the other employment modes matched the hypothesized HRM configurations (job-based employment used productivity-based HRM, contractual work arrangements used compliance-based HRM, alliances used collaborative-based HRM).

Overall, the study provided moderate to strong support for the HR architecture model. Implications of the research suggest that firms see knowledge-based workers as the most unique and valuable human capital and as a result exhibit a high level of flexibility in managing these workers through a variety of HRM practices.

A study by Lepak, Takeuchi, and Snell (2003) further tested the HR architecture model by examining the impact of the employment modes on firm performance. Additionally, the authors further refined the definition of employment modes by incorporating the constructs of coordination and resource flexibility (Sanchez, 1995; Tsui et al., 1995). Coordination flexibility ensures that a firm can adjust the numbers of individuals employed within the firm in response to environmental dynamism. Resource flexibility, in contrast, is attained when individuals within the firm are able to perform a variety of tasks, using abilities often gained through job rotation and other career development practices.

The study found that firm performance was positively related to the use of contract and knowledge-based workers. Indeed, the combination of both modes of employment was found to result in higher firm performance than the use of either in isolation. This result supports Lepak and Snell's arguments that firms must use a number of different employment modes to maximize performance. Additionally, results supported the hypotheses that knowledge-based employment (resource flexibility) and contract employment (coordination flexibility) are both positively related to firm performance. Moreover, the study results show that combinations of employment modes have important implications for firm performance. For example, return on equity was higher for firms that relied on knowledge-based and contract employees than for those that did not use either mode or used one but not the other.

In summary, a growing base of research has examined the HR architecture model proposed by Lepak and Snell (1999), including the validity of the four employment modes (alliance, contract, knowledge-based, and job-based) and their corresponding HRM configurations (collaboration, compliance, commitment, and productivity). Thus far, findings provide moderately strong support for the model's prediction of a direct linkage between the use of multiple employment modes and higher levels of firm performance. However, to date, no research has examined whether different types of psychological contracts characterize each employment mode.

Looking across the two career system models, Lepak and Snell's HR architecture clearly represents a refinement and extension of the original Sonnenfeld and Peiperl (1988) typology. Since empirical research to date provides moderate to strong support for its predictions, we use the Lepak and Snell (1999) model as a foundation for our integrative prescriptive model of effective career system management.

Toward a Prescriptive Model: Enhancing Psychological Contract Fulfillment Through Effective Management of Career Systems

One important aspect of the real new deal [management changes based in economic and market forces] is that it has eliminated many of the human resource practices, based on internal, administrative principles, that essentially buffered both employers and employees from the pressures of the outside labor market. Practices like predictable promotion and career paths . . . (Cappelli, 1999, p. 37)

To date, the research in the organizational sciences does not offer a comprehensive career system model that explains how the negative effects of decreased job security on individual commitment and loyalty across the employment modes may be offset through the thoughtful application of enhanced career mobility. In the first part of this section, we review and extend earlier research by Schein (1978) to suggest how different forms of career movement may be used to enhance perceived psychological contract fulfillment within all four employment modes.

The Importance of Career Mobility

According to Schein, careers represent the mutual influence of the individual on the organization and the organization on the individual (Hall, 2002). Thus, when organizations provide employees with valued career mobility, the employees, in turn, are motivated to work hard and innovate in ways that benefit the organization (Schein, 1978). Career systems that include thoughtfully selected types of career mobility also provide employees with opportunities to develop new skills, knowledge, and relationships that can positively benefit the organization and meet employee needs and desires (Schein, 1978). Therefore, in the following section, we explore Schein's research on career mobility.

Schein: The Career Cycle

According to Schein (1978), intraorganizational career movement in all organizations occurs along three basic dimensions—hierarchical, functional/technical, and radial (Gunz, Peiperl, and Tzabbar, Chapter 24). Movement along the hierarchical dimension is primarily vertical as individuals move from an entry-level position within the organization to a middle position and finally, in many cases, to a senior or executive level. These moves are accompanied by commensurate increases in pay and status. Finally, in line with job characteristics theory, which posits that the design of work motivates employees and produces desired outcomes such as satisfaction, hierarchical movement provides individuals with increased autonomy and variety (Hackman & Oldham, 1976).

Career movement also occurs along a second, functional/technical dimension in two ways: (1) An individual may enter a functional specialty, such as engineering, and continue in that specialty throughout his or her entire career but developing his or her technical expertise within this area or (2) an individual may move *across* functional specialties. For example, an individual might begin his or her career in one function, engineering, subsequently move in 3 to 5 years into research and development, move on to a HR staff position, and eventually wind up in a general management position. Additionally, functional/technical movement provides individuals with increased variety and identity as individuals come to see organizational processes and functions more holistically rather than in a "silo" manner (Hackman & Oldham, 1976).

The final type of career mobility in Schein's cycle is "movement toward the inner circle of the organization" (p. 38) or radial mobility. As individuals become more trusted and valued by the organization, they are consequently given greater access to its inner core. In Schein's words, "movement toward the core of the organization is most clearly signaled by being given access to special privileges and special categories of information—the "secrets" of the organization" (p. 38). While hierarchical movement *may* accompany movement toward the inner circle, it is not automatic but is dependent on the level of trust that other key players in the organization have for a particular individual.

Mobility and the Psychological Contract

A psychological contract is formed which defines what the employee will give in the way of effort and contribution in exchange for challenging or rewarding work, acceptable working conditions, organizational rewards in the form of pay and benefits, and an *organizational future in the form of a promise of promotion or other forms of career advancement* [italics added]. (Schein, 1978, p. 112)

While the career systems literature reviewed in the previous section discusses the kinds of work, working conditions, pay, and benefits that might be used with different employee populations, it sheds little light on the practical challenge of how employees can experience career mobility they will value in a way that is feasible and beneficial for their organization. It is noteworthy that Schein suggested the need for organizations to be flexible and creative in their use of mobility events to help shape employees' psychological contracts. Thus, Schein hypothesized a scenario such as this: Employees who desire and expect vertical movement (upward mobility) are highly motivated by promotional opportunities that the organization promises in exchange for hard work and significant contributions. As a result, an employee works hard to meet performance requirements for his or her entry-level position. Once the employee's achievements are noticed by the organization, it promotes the individual to a middle-level position when one becomes available. Subsequently, the employee sees that the organization delivers on its promise of *valued* mobility and will then develop greater psychological attachment to the firm in the form of organizational commitment. Thus, vertical movement can not only be rewarding but also facilitate psychological contract fulfillment for employees who are highly motivated by upward mobility (and who are able, eventually, to achieve it).

In addition, Schein's model suggests that enhanced radial mobility will be related to the relational nature of psychological contracts between employees and their organizations. As an employee acts to satisfy a promise of capable performance to the organization, the employer, in turn, perceives the individual as loyal and trustworthy and gives him or her enhanced radial mobility, that is, greater closeness, trust, and attachment to others located at the organization's core. Over time, the employee's psychological contract slowly becomes more relational in nature, emphasizing relational outcomes such as trust, support, and stewardship. Thus radial career movement may provide an employee with feelings of psychological contract fulfillment even in the absence of vertical mobility.

Moreover, work by Taylor, Audia, and Gupta (1996) indirectly supports the idea that hierarchical and functional/technical movement may positively influence employees' psychological contracts and, subsequently, reactions such as affective commitment and lower turnover. Taylor and her colleagues posit that frequent mobility is valued because it is a signal of career progression and provides a source of challenge. Their findings indicate that managers who stay in the same job for extended periods of time report lower levels of affective commitment and higher levels of turnover. This relationship was even more pronounced for successful managers than for those with low levels of success. Therefore, functional/technical movement also may facilitate the contract fulfillment of employees valuing mobility.

Empirical Tests of the Model and Relationships to the Psychological Contract

While our literature review revealed no direct empirical tests of Schein's career cycle model, research on organizational insider status (Stamper & Masterson, 2002) provides some indirect evidence supporting it.

Perceived organizational insider status (PIS) is "the extent to which an individual perceives him or herself as an insider within a particular organization" (Stamper & Masterson, 2002, p. 876). This status is posited to mediate the relationship between employees' objective level of organizational inclusion (assessed by tenure and average hour per week worked) and their level of perceived organizational support (POS)—that is, their global belief concerning the extent to which the organization values their contributions and cares about their well-being (Eisenberger, Huntington, Hutchinson, & Sowa, 1986). PIS is also posited to mediate the relationship between organizational inclusion and behavioral consequences such as level of altruistic organizational citizenship behavior (positive relationship) and production deviance work behaviors such as exaggerating to get out of work or intentionally working slower (negative relationship). The Stamper and Masterson (2002) study provides support for Schein's predictions that radial movement, presumably reflected in increasing levels of perceived insider status, does influence both positive and negative behavior toward the organization in predicted ways.

Further indirect support for Schein's three modes of career mobility may be found in theories that have been tested and that have found widespread acceptance, such as job characteristics theory (Hackman & Oldham, 1976), as well as recent empirical work, which indirectly demonstrate that radial and lateral (functional/technical) movement positively affects proxies for psychological contract fulfillment, such as satisfaction and turnover (Stamper & Masterson, 2002; Taylor et al., 1996). In the next section, we integrate Schein's career cycle model with employment modes to develop a career system framework aimed at maximizing employee psychological contract fulfillment.

Development of an Integrative Model

Our proposed model integrates career mobility as discussed in Schein's career cycle and both career system practices and psychological contract types associated with the four employment modes discussed in Lepak and Snell's HR architecture. In addition, we integrate work by Bowen and Ostroff (2004) identifying overarching features of career systems such as consistency, validity, and relevance that positively moderate the relationship between system HRM practices and organizational outcomes. The model depicted in Figure 19.3 and discussed in this section was designed to integrate aspects of the career systems, psychological contract, and HR literatures to outline the components necessary for building career systems that maximize employee contract fulfillment.

Overview

The model proposes that selected types of career movement, along with the practices of particular career system types, together enhance individuals' perceptions of contract fulfillment for the type of psychological contract associated with their given employment mode. As noted earlier, the model assumes that organizations' delivery of more (upward vertical, lateral, and radial) career movement than promised to employees is expected to yield contract fulfillment and favorable attitudinal and behavioral reactions, such as job satisfaction, organizational commitment, performance, and citizenship behavior. Furthermore, the strength of the positive effect of career movement and other system activities on contract fulfillment will be positively moderated by overarching system features such as the amount of non-task-related social interaction between individuals in different employment modes, the consistency with which the organization delivers on its promises, the relevance of the career activities,

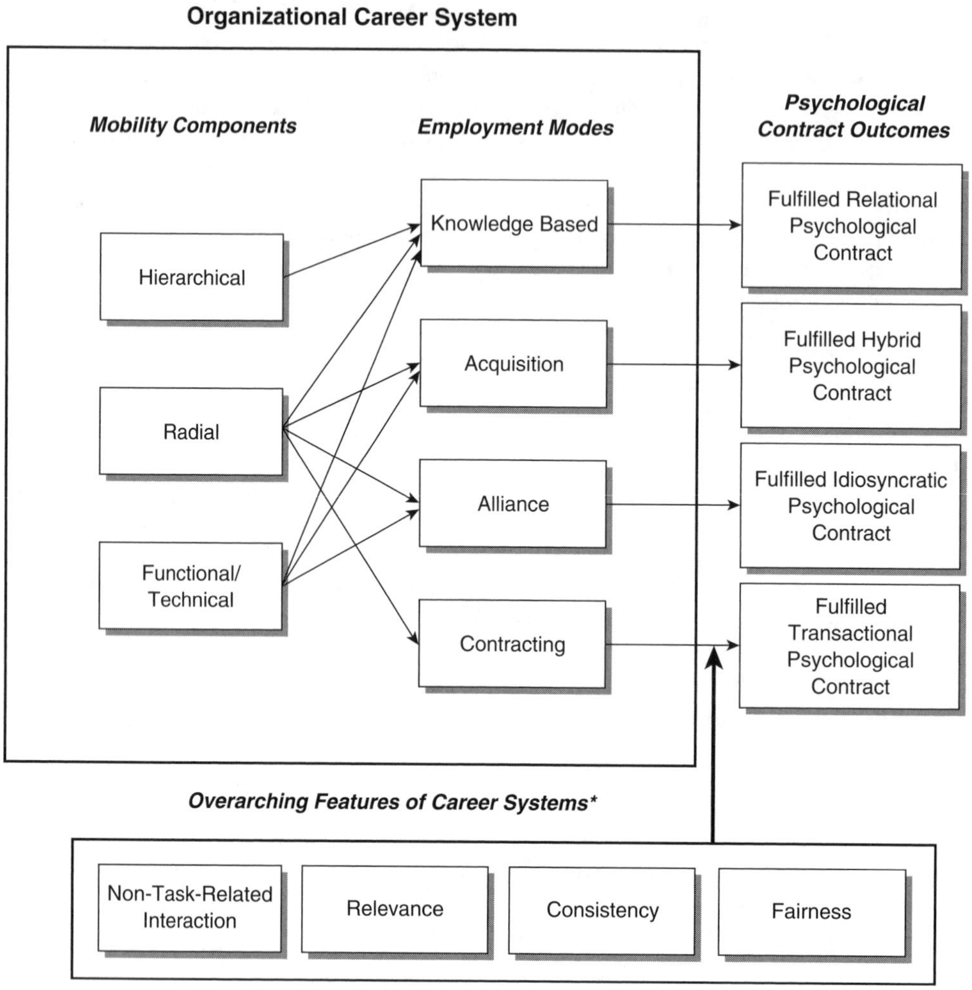

Organizational Career System

Figure 19.3   Slay and Taylor Model of Career Systems and Employee Psychological Contracts

*Overarching features of career systems moderate the relationships between all employment modes and psychological contracts.

and the fairness with which career movement and system activities are provided to employees. The selected career movement and system activities proposed for each employment mode are discussed below.

Knowledge Based

Recall from prior career system discussions that the knowledge-based category comprises human capital that is considered both highly valuable and unique and that is acquired (after entry-level positions) mostly from internal labor markets. Organizations focus on the development of these employees to create firm-specific assets that have the potential to create competitive advantage (Lepak & Snell, 1999; Reed & DeFillippi, 1990). Lepak and Snell (1999) describe the employment relationship as "encouraging significant mutual investment on the part of employers and employees" (p. 36), and firms use a commitment-based HRM system that typically includes mentoring programs, pay focused on the development of skills, and knowledge sharing as well as developmental performance appraisals.

Additionally, within the knowledge-based employment mode, job design provides a means of employee development. Therefore, we propose that integrating all three types of career movement—hierarchical, functional/technical, and radial mobility—is a useful way to enhance the psychological contract fulfillment because employees in this mode will tend to value career movement highly and will respond positively to the receipt of levels of career mobility that exceed that promised by the organization (Conway & Briner, 2005). Thus, when organizations add types of mobility to the contract outcomes of knowledge-based employees that exceed prior mobility promises, we propose that a strong sense of contract fulfillment will result and will subsequently lead to higher levels of job satisfaction, organizational commitment, and positive work behavior.

More specifically, the organization's provision of hierarchical advancement will become a way of rewarding knowledge acquisition, developing skill sets at a higher level, and recognizing the potential of the employee. However, as hierarchical movement will be constrained by flatter organizational structures, the addition of functional/technical mobility will enable employees to learn the operational idiosyncrasies of the firm by working in a variety of functional positions, accruing a broad range of skills and knowledge, and will signal the employee that while vertical movement is not possible, they are valued and not experiencing "arrested mobility" (Veiga, 1981). Finally, the use of radial movement will make employees privy to closely held information in the firm, including financial goals, forecasts, competitive challenges, and a wide range of information that had been previously reserved for organizational elites (Case, 1997). Therefore, we predict that the addition of all three types of career movement to the existing career system attributes proposed by Lepak and Snell (1999) will lead to fulfilled relational psychological contracts for employees within the knowledge-based mode.

Acquisition

Like employees in the knowledge-based employment modes, acquisition-mode human capital is internal and highly valuable although not unique in the external labor market.

Organizations typically do not invest in the development of employees in acquisition mode but are instead seeking to capitalize on the investment of others by buying ready-made talent. The resulting employment relationship is symbiotic and will endure as long as both parties (employee and employer) find it mutually beneficial. Therefore, employees expect attractive benefits but not necessarily promises of development or lifelong employment, while firms "expect a certain degree of loyalty to the firm while the relationship exists" (Lepak & Snell, 1999, p. 39), realizing that these employees may ultimately join other firms that they find can better meet their needs. On this basis, firms implement market-based HRM systems where the primary emphasis is on staffing rather than on training and development.

After hire, employees are empowered to use the skills they have acquired to benefit the firm and gain monetary rewards based on their contribution (Lepak & Snell, 1999). Thus, we argue that firms will benefit from adding radial and functional/technical mobility beyond those levels initially promised to employees. Greater use of functional/technical mobility will provide employees with a stronger understanding of how the firm creates value as a whole and enable them to form broader social networks that enable the achievement of work goals in the absence of formal authority. Radial mobility will enhance employees' sense of being trusted and valued by the organization, a meaningful benefit in and of itself, while also providing them with financial and strategic information that shows how to increase their contributions to organizational goals (Case, 1997). Because skill development is also likely to occur as a result of learning the relationship between operations, their decisions, and the bottom line, acquisition employees will also see the benefits of their loyalty to the firm as their external employability is being developed. Thus, we predict that acquisition-mode employees will express higher levels of balanced contract fulfillment followed by higher levels of job satisfaction, continuance organizational commitment and citizenship behavior, and performance.

Alliance

In the alliance mode, employees are recruited from sources external to the firm, and provide human capital that is unique, although not strategically valuable. The employment relationship is best described as a partnership (Lepak & Snell, 1999) with an emphasis on "mutual investment in the relationship and . . . trust . . . while still protecting their investments and gaining access to each other's talents" (p. 41). Therefore, the HRM system used with alliance employees is collaborative and contains training, job rotations, and other investments that allow for knowledge sharing between these workers and the firm.

The organizational objectives for the alliance worker are similar to those for acquisition workers; that is, there is a need for loyalty, knowledge exchanges, and the employee's interest in advancing organizational goals. However, the alliance employee is employed in a nonpermanent status to allow firms enhanced flexibility, to gain the benefit of the unique skill as needed without the expense of internalizing human capital that does not provide a sustained competitive advantage. Therefore, our proposals for career mobility are similar to those for the acquisition worker. We argue that the integration of this employment mode with radial and functional/technical mobility will enable psychological contract fulfillment. Galunic and Anderson (2000) found that insurance agents were more committed to an insurer when they felt that their human capital (knowledge and practices) was specific to that insurer. Independent insurance agents, who often represent more than one insurer, may be thought of as alliance workers. Galunic and Anderson posited that these agents have a great concern for remaining mobile and marketable in a manner similar to alliance workers in the HR architecture typology. The researchers found that insurance agents indicated a greater degree of emotional attachment and sense of relationship signified by expecting a long-term relationship and expressing loyalty when firms invested in the agents. Thus, we posit that functional/technical mobility allows an opportunity for development of firm-specific assets leading to greater commitment. We propose that providing both radial and functional/technical mobility beyond the level promised to alliance employees will result in the fulfillment of their psychological contracts as well as enhanced job satisfaction, affective commitment, and performance, enabling the firm to enhance its flexibility while also enhancing the employees' external employability.

Contracting

Employees in the contracting mode are typically externalized and hired through an agency. The human capital in this mode is neither valuable nor unique, neither enhancing competitive advantage nor providing skills that cannot be readily found in the external labor market. Lepak and Snell (1999) describe the employment relationship as transactional and focused on the "economic nature of the contract" (p. 40). The HRM system associated with this mode ensures that workers comply with firm rules and policies while also providing little training, few rewards, and virtually no emphasis on career development.

Yet Lepak and Snell suggest that failing to invest in HRs at the organizational margins is a mistake (p. 42), and we concur, pointing out that contract employees must be able to perform well enough not to pose a burden on acquisition and knowledge-based employees. Therefore, we suggest two ways to enhance the effectiveness of contract employees. First, employers should invest in providing adequate training for the employees to perform satisfactorily the jobs to which they are assigned. Broschak and Davis-Blake (2006) state that because of inadequate contract employee training "standard workers often must take on additional uncompensated training and supervision of temporary workers" (p. 378). They find that a lack of training is positively associated with poor coworker relations. Second, contract employees who demonstrate knowledge and skills that can add strategic value to the firm should be exposed to radial mobility and drawn in along the radial dimension, so that they are given information appropriate to respected external team members. This radial movement will serve to recognize the worth of the contract employee. Because research by Lambert et al. (2003) found that satisfaction increases where delivered levels of recognition and relationships exceed promised levels, we propose that contract employees whose exposure to radial mobility exceeds the level promised to them will experience a sense of transactional contract fulfillment and, subsequently, display higher levels of job satisfaction, normative commitment, and performance.

In conclusion, our integrated, prescriptive model of effective career system management argues for the matching of each employment mode and its corresponding career system HRM practices with a particular type of intraorganizational career mobility (hierarchical, functional/technical, radial) to achieve employee psychological contract fulfillment.

Yet the success of the proposed career systems depends not only on the integration of mobility and practices but also on holistic, overarching features of the career system that are present in the organization regardless of the employment mode. The second part of our model addresses these elements.

The Moderating Effects of Overarching Features of Career Systems on Career Movement: Psychological Contract Relationship

We posit that two overarching features of career systems have a moderating influence on the success of those career systems in minimizing employee psychological contract violations: effectively managing nonstandard work arrangements and developing a strong climate for psychological contract fulfillment. In the discussion above, we described each type of employment mode and how mobility constructs should be integrated. However, in this section, we suggest features that must be common to *all* the modes and, indeed, the entire career system to ensure that psychological contracts are fulfilled. To develop the case for the inclusion of these features, we review here research on HRM and the linkage between HRM systems and important organizational outcomes such as satisfaction.

Managing Heterogeneous Employment Modes

Recently, research by Broschak and Davis-Blake (2006) demonstrated that diversity in employee modes leads to heightened turnover intentions due to tensions between those in different employment modes. However, their research suggests that increasing non-task-related interactions such as eating in the firm cafeteria or participation in other activities where external and internal employees may share personal information will attenuate the effect of nonstandard work arrangements on dissatisfaction and turnover. Therefore, while the use of multiple employment modes may result in dissatisfaction signified by heightened turnover, we posit that building non-task-related interactions into organizational systems will enable the integrated career system described in Figure 19.3 to achieve greater fulfillment of psychological contracts.

Climate Strength

Bowen and Ostroff (2004) have observed that HRM systems (including career systems) provide signals to employees about desired responses and that a strong climate enables the transmission of messages to employees and the development of a "collective sense" of firm expectations (p. 204). Career systems, then, may better support the fulfillment of psychological contracts when a strong climate supporting psychological contract fulfillment is present. Psychological climate is defined as a "shared perception of what the organization is like in terms of practices, policies, procedures, routines, and rewards—what is important and what behaviors are expected and rewarded" (p. 205). Thus, while we have described how both content and the selected use of different types of mobility may positively influence perceptions of psychological contract fulfillment, it is also important that we consider the conditions under which those career systems will influence employee perceptions of what is expected and rewarded. Bowen and Ostroff (2004) posit that relevance, consistency, and fairness aid in establishing strong climates. We suggest that these three elements of climate enhance the ability of a career system to result in fulfilled psychological contract outcomes for workers within different employment modes (see Figure 19.3).

Relevance. Relevance means that individuals see that the system enables the achievement of important goals. In each of the employment mode descriptions above, we suggested ways in which the individual's and the organization's goals may be aligned. For example, using functional/technical mobility allows alliance, contract, acquisition, and knowledge-based employees to gain skills that ensure employability while also enabling them to be productive and achieve monetary rewards. Similarly, radial mobility gives individuals access to firm-specific information that may be used to achieve organizational goals.

Consistency. Organizations must do what they claim they will do if their messages concerning career management are to be taken as valid. Organizations that promise career mobility to their employees must consistently display the kind of movement promised to show employees that such movement is indeed possible.

Fairness. Finally, Bowen and Ostroff (2004) state that fairness aids in agreement between firms and employees about the messages sent by the career system. They maintain that all the dimensions of fairness are important—distributive, procedural, and interactional (Folger & Cropanzano, 1998). This should be especially important when the firm is using a diversity of employment modes. Employees should believe that while there are different systems for different kinds of employees, these systems (1) are just in their distribution of outcomes, (2) provide individuals with voice, and (3) treat all employees, regardless of employment mode, with respect.

Thus, consistent with the proposals of Bowen and Ostroff (2004), we argue that career systems that operate in a climate reinforced by relevance, consistency, and fairness are likely to be more effective in fulfilling employees' psychological contracts, with resulting benefits for their job attitudes and work behaviors.

CONCLUSION

In this chapter, we sought to answer three questions concerning the relationship between organizations' career systems and the psychological contracts of their employees: (1) How do career systems affect the nature of employees' psychological contracts, that is, their perceptions of the exchange relationship that exists with their employing organization? (2) What are the resulting outcomes of these effects in terms of employee work attitudes and behaviors and, subsequently, organizational performance and success? (3) How might career systems be used to manage the employment exchange relationship more effectively for both individuals and organizations? We addressed Questions 1 and 2 through selective reviews of the psychological contract and career system literatures, while Question 3 was examined through an integrative, prescriptive model of career systems. We argue that such an integrated model is valuable both for managers, in managing career systems to maximize employee contract fulfillment and its value-creating consequences, and for academics, in better understanding the relationship between career systems and psychological contracts and in shaping a future research agenda.

As the economic landscape continues to change, it is increasingly important that those who manage work organizations understand how to manage career systems to garner the flexibility needed to survive and be successful and how to use heterogeneous employment modes and not sacrifice performance through psychological contract violations. In the applied tradition of much of the careers research summarized in this chapter, we offer the integrative model developed here as a further step in helping organizations better navigate these waters.

NOTE

1. Much of this section is taken from Tekleab and Taylor (2003).

REFERENCES

Arthur, J. B. (1994). Effects of human resource systems on manufacturing performance and turnover. *Academy of Management Journal, 37,* 670–687.

Baird, L., & Meshoulam, I. (1988). Managing two fits of strategic human resource management. *Academy of Management Review, 13,* 116–128.

Barney, J. B. (1991). Firm resources and sustained competitive advantage. *Journal of Management, 17,* 99–120.

Baruch, Y., & Peiperl, M. (2003). An empirical assessment of Sonnenfeld's career systems typology. *International Journal of Human Resource Management, 14,* 1267–1283.

Batt, R. (1996). From bureaucracy to enterprise? The changing jobs and careers of managers in telecommunications service. In P. Osterman (Ed.), *Broken ladders: Managerial careers in the new economy* (pp. 55–80). Oxford: Oxford University Press.

Bowen, D. E., & Ostroff, C. (2004). Understanding HRM-firm performance linkages: The role of the "strength" of the HRM system. *Academy of Management Review, 29,* 203–221.

Broschak, J. P., & Davis-Blake, A. (2006). Mixing standard work and nonstandard deals: The consequences of heterogeneity in employment arrangements. *Academy of Management Journal, 49,* 371–393.

Cappelli, P. (1999). *The new deal at work.* Boston: Harvard University School Press.

Case, J. (1997). Opening the books. *Harvard Business Review, March–April,* 118–127.

Coff, R. W. (1997). Human assets and management dilemmas: Coping with hazards on the road to resource based theory. *Academy of Management Review, 22,* 374–403.

Conway, N., & Briner, R. B. (2002). A daily diary study of affective responses to psychological contract breach and exceeded promises. *Journal of Organizational Behavior, 23,* 287–302.

Conway, N., & Briner, R. B. (2005). *Psychological contracts at work: A Critical evaluation of theory and research.* Oxford: Oxford University Press.

Coyle-Shapiro, J., & Kessler, J. (2000). Consequences of the psychological contract for the employment relationship: A large scale survey. *Journal of Management Studies, 37,* 908–930.

Dabos, G. E., & Rousseau, D. M. (2004). Mutuality and reciprocity in the psychological contracts of employees and employers. *Journal of Applied Psychology, 89,* 52–72.

Eisenberger, R., Huntington, R., Hutchinson, S., & Sowa, D. (1986). Perceived organizational support. *Journal of Applied Psychology, 71,* 500–507.

Folger, R., & Cropanzano, R. (1998). *Organizational justice and human resource management.* Thousand Oaks, CA: Sage.

Galunic, D. C., & Anderson, E. (2000). From security to mobility: Investments in human capital and agent commitment. *Organization Science, 11,* 1–20.

Greenberg, J., Roberge, M.-E., Ho, V. T., & Rousseau, D. M. (2004). Fairness in idiosyncratic work arrangements: Justice as an I-deal.

Research in Personnel and Human Resource Management, 23, 1–34.

Gunz, H. P. (1989). *Careers and corporate cultures: Managerial mobility in large corporations.* Oxford: Basil Blackwell.

Hackman, J. R., & Oldham, G. R. (1976). Motivation through the design of work. *Organizational Behavior and Human Decision Processes, 16,* 250–279.

Hall, D. T. (2002). *Careers in and out of organizations.* Thousand Oaks, CA: Sage.

Herriot, P., & Pemberton, C. (1996). Contracting careers. *Human Relations, 49,* 757–790.

Herzberg, F., Mausner, B., & Snyderman, B. (1959). *The motivation to work.* New York: Wiley.

Ho, V. T., Ang, S., & Straub, D. (2003). When subordinates become IT contractors: Persistent managerial expectations in IT outsourcing. *Information Systems Research, 14,* 66–86.

Koudsi, S. (2001). You're stuck. *Fortune, 144,* 111–113.

Lambert, L. S., Edwards, J. R., & Cable, D. M. (2003). Breach and fulfillment of the psychological contract: A comparison of traditional and expanded views. *Personnel Psychology, 56,* 895–934.

Lepak, D. P., & Snell, S. A. (1999). The human resource architecture: Toward a theory of human capital allocation and development. *Academy of Management Review, 24,* 31–48.

Lepak, D. P., & Snell, S. A. (2002). Examining the human resource architecture: The relationships among human capital, employment and human resource configurations. *Journal of Management, 28,* 517–543.

Lepak, D. P., Takeuchi, R., & Snell, S. A. (2003). Employment flexibility and firm performance: Examining the interaction effects of employment mode, environmental dynamism, and technological intensity. *Journal of Management, 29,* 681–703.

Lester, S. W., Turnley, W. H., Bloodgood, J. M., & Bolino, M. C. (2002). Not seeing eye to eye: Difference in supervisor and subordinate perceptions of and attributions for psychological contract breach. *Journal of Organizational Behavior, 23,* 39–56.

MacNeil, I. R. (1985). Relational contract: What we do and do not know. *Wisconsin Law Review, 3,* 483–525.

Meyer, J. & Allen, N. (1997). *Commitment in the workplace: Theory, research, and application.* Thousand Oaks, CA: Sage.

Morin, W. J. (1996). You are absolutely, positively on your own. *Fortune, 134,* 222.

Morrison, E. W., & Robinson, S. L. (1997). When employees feel betrayed: A model of how psychological contract violation develops. *Academy of Management Review, 22,* 226–256.

O'Reilly, C., III, & Pfeffer, J. (1995). *Southwest Airlines: Using human resources for competitive advantage (#HR1A).* Boston: Harvard Business School.

Osterman, P. (Ed.). (1996). *Broken ladders.* New York: Oxford University Press.

Peck, S. (1994). Exploring the link between organizational strategy and the employment relationship: The role of human resources policies. *Journal of Management Studies, 31,* 715–736.

Peiperl, M. A., Arthur, M. B., Goffee, R., & Morris, T. (Eds.). (2000). *Career Frontiers: New conceptions of working lives.* Oxford: Oxford University Press.

Reed, R., & DeFillippi, R. (1990). Causal ambiguity, barriers to imitation and sustainable competitive advantage. *Academy of Management Review, 15,* 88–102.

Robinson, S. L. (1996). Trust and breach of the psychological contract. *Administrative Science Quarterly, 41,* 574–599.

Robinson, S. L., & Morrison, E. W. (2000). The development of psychological contract breach and violation: A longitudinal study. *Journal of Organizational Behavior, 21,* 525–546.

Robinson, S. L., & Rousseau, D. M. (1994). Violating the psychological contract: Not the exception but the norm. *Journal of Organizational Behavior, 15,* 245–259.

Rousseau, D. M. (1995). *Psychological contracts in organizations.* Thousand Oaks, CA: Sage.

Rousseau, D. M. (2004). Psychological contracts in the workplace: Understanding the ties that motivate. *Academy of Management Executive, 18,* 120–127.

Rousseau, D. M., & McLean Parks, J. (1993). The contracts of individuals and organizations. *Research in Organizational Behavior, 15,* 1–44.

Sanchez, R. (1995). Strategic flexibility in product competition. *Strategic Management Journal, 16,* 135–159.

Schein, E. H. (1978). *Career dynamics: Matching individual and organizational needs.* Reading, MA: Addison-Wesley.

Sonnenfeld, J. A. (1989). Career system profiles and strategic staffing. In M. B. Arthur, D. T. Hall, & B. S. Lawrence (Eds.), *Handbook of career theory* (pp. 202–224). Cambridge, UK: Cambridge University Press.

Sonnenfeld, J. A., & Peiperl, M. A. (1988). Staffing policy as a strategic response: A typology of career systems. *Academy of Management Review, 13,* 588–600.

Sonnenfeld, J. A., Peiperl, M. A., & Kotter, J. P. (1988). Strategic determinants of managerial labor markets: A career systems view. *Human Resource Management, 27,* 369–388.

Stamper, C. L., & Masterson, S. S. (2002). Insider or outsider? How employee perceptions of insider status affect their work behavior. *Journal of Organizational Behavior, 23,* 875–894.

Sturges, J., Conway, N., Guest, D., & Liefooghe, A. (2005). Managing the career deal: The psychological contract as a framework for understanding career management, organizational commitment and work behavior. *Journal of Organizational Behavior, 26,* 812–838.

Taylor, M. S., Audia, G., & Gupta, A. K. (1996). The effect of lengthening job tenure on managers' organizational commitment and turnover. *Organizational Science, 7,* 632–648.

Tekleab, A. G., & Taylor, M. S. (2003). Aren't there two parties in an employment relationship? Antecedents and consequences of organization-employee agreement on contract obligations and violations. *Journal of Organizational Behavior, 24,* 585–609.

Tsui, A. S., Pearce, J. L., Porter, L. W., & Hite, J. P. (1995). Choice of employee-organization relationship: Influence of external and internal organizational factors. In G. R. Ferris (Ed.), *Research in personnel and human resource management* (Vol. 13, pp. 117–151). Greenwich, CT: JAI Press.

Turnley, W. H., & Feldman, D. C. (1999). The impact of psychological contract violations on exit, voice, loyalty, and neglect. *Human Relations, 52,* 895–922.

Veiga, J. F. (1981). Do managers on the move get anywhere? *Harvard Business Review, 59,* 20–38.

Von Glinow, M. A., Driver, M. J., Brousseau, K., & Prince, J. B. (1983). The design of a career oriented human resource system. *Academy of Management Review, 8,* 23–32.

Welch, J., & Welch, S. (2005). *Winning.* New York, NY: HarperCollins.

20

ORGANIZATIONAL DEMOGRAPHY AND INDIVIDUAL CAREERS

Structure, Norms, and Outcomes

BARBARA S. LAWRENCE

PAMELA S. TOLBERT

Careers, the evolving sequences of individuals' work experiences over time, and the factors that shape them, have long fascinated both popular and academic audiences (Arthur, Hall, & Lawrence, 1989). Individuals want to know how their personal attributes, perhaps their intelligence, gender, or experience, propel them along the pathways they desire. They are curious about what sorts of organizational conditions facilitate mobility or create barriers along the way. Organizations want to discern the conditions that allow them to attract and retain the best employees and comprehend how internal and external labor markets affect the desirability of the career inducements they offer. Understanding the impact of organizational demography on individuals' career choices and on the opportunity structure that confronts them is relevant to both of these perspectives.

As the terms *career choices* and *opportunity structure* suggest, demographic influences on careers operate at multiple levels of analysis: at the individual level, on individuals' perceptions of work environments and career decisions, and at the organization level, on group dynamics and organizational selection processes. However, there are few theories that explicate the processes that bridge these levels (Arthur, Khapova, & Wilderom, 2005; Khapova, Arthur, and Wilderom, Chapter 7). What are the dynamics by which demographic patterns influence an individual's career choices? Similarly, how do individual actions shape the processes of demographic change within organizations? This chapter presents one approach to exploring such questions.

The argument we develop involves different literatures and concepts at different levels of analysis. Although we offer several propositions about the causal relationships between the demographic composition of organizations and individual careers, we do this with two understandings. The first is that these relationships are often, in fact, reciprocal. In other words, demographic distributions influence the norms that evolve in organizations, but norms also influence demographic distributions. Similarly, norms influence intergroup relations, but the latter also influence norms. This conception of reciprocal relationships is consistent with Giddens's (1976, 1984) notion of the "duality of structure." The second understanding is that a construct's relative fixity or permanence influences the primary direction of its effect (Rosenberg, 1968). For any one individual, for example, an organization's demography is likely to exert a stronger and more immediate influence on his or her career expectations or outcomes than the other way around. Thus, while we assume reciprocity among all the constructs discussed, we use relative fixity to assign an initial direction of causality in developing our arguments.

STRUCTURE, NORMS, AND CAREER OUTCOMES: CONCEPTS AND RELATIONS

Research focusing on the distribution of attributes, such as age, gender, and race, among the members of an organization or organizational unit (Pfeffer, 1983, p. 303) has linked the demographic composition of organizations to an array of career-related outcomes.[1] For example, studies have shown that men express more dissatisfaction with their jobs and a greater willingness to quit when they are in work groups with a larger proportion of women (Tsui, Egan, & O'Reilly, 1992); that individuals rely on age-graded timetables that reflect the age distribution of organizational members at various ranks in evaluating their own career performance (Lawrence, 1984b); and that organizational compensation practices are significantly influenced by the distribution of women and minorities in various positions (Tolbert, 1986).

Despite considerable interest in organizational demography over the past three decades

(Dionne, Randel, Jaussi, & Chun, 2004; Williams & O'Reilly, 1998), the nature of the interdependencies between individual-level perceptions, career outcomes, and organization-level compositional patterns and norms has received little attention. We build on a conceptual model proposed by Lawrence (1988, 1996) and apply it to the study of organizational demography with a specific emphasis on career-related outcomes (see Figure 20.1). Based on our review of demographic research and this model, we offer multilevel propositions for future research on careers. Given the potential scope of this topic, we cover only a few of the many areas in which additional research is warranted. The following discussion provides working definitions for the individual-, group-, organization-, and high-level concepts used in the model.

A *demographic attribute* is any relatively stable characteristic of individuals that can be used to categorize them. Demographic attributes acquire salience for individuals' career-related decisions, behaviors, and actions because people use them as a basis for social comparison (McPherson & Smith-Lovin, 2001; Tajfel & Turner, 1979). When individuals try to figure out, "What happens to someone like me in this organization?" they often look to others with similar demographic attributes. Do other women hold positions of responsibility in this group? Do people who attended my college have a good chance of receiving promotions? Do others with job experiences like mine hold high-level management positions? Although many demographic attributes, such as functional area (Bantel, 1994), organizational tenure (Wagner, Pfeffer, & O'Reilly, 1984), education (Sobel, 1982), and occupation (Avolio, Waldman, & McDaniel, 1990), can be used as a basis for such comparisons, our discussion highlights gender, race, and age. These attributes have been termed *diffuse status characteristics* (Berger, Fisek, Norman, & Zelditch, 1977; Ridgeway & Erickson, 2000) because they are associated with society-wide, shared evaluations of social status. Gender and age have long been identified as critical social categories (Linton, 1942), and race and ethnicity have become increasingly important with the growing diversity of organizations.[2]

The *distribution of an attribute* within an organization thus refers to the proportion of

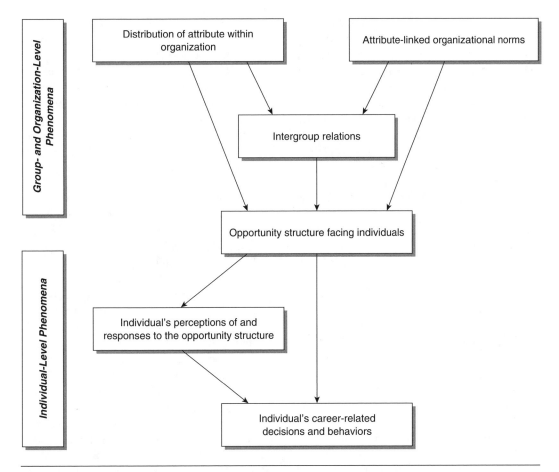

Figure 20.1 A Multilevel Model of the Connections Between Organizational Demography and Individual Careers

individuals that fall within different categories of a given attribute, either generally throughout the organization or specifically within a career-relevant segment.[3] Examples include the distribution of individuals' ages within a business unit, the proportion of men among the faculty of a university, and the relative number of members from a particular racial minority in high-level technical positions. *Attribute-linked organizational norms* are shared judgments among organizational members about the typical behaviors, actions, or occurrences that connect individuals' attributes to careers. For instance, if employees believe that most supervisors are men between the ages of 25 and 35, a 50-year-old woman may have difficulty becoming a supervisor. Such norms both affect and are affected by the distribution of attributes in the organization. As we will discuss, norms can

be modified as the distribution changes, but they may also affect the likelihood that a change will occur, through influencing personnel and personal decisions within the organization.

Both the distribution of attributes and attribute-linked norms shape *intergroup relations*, how individuals with a particular attribute respond to and interact with others who differ on that attribute. Insofar as norms define certain attributes as more or less "typical," the entry of individuals with nonconforming attributes into an organization may give rise to conflictual intergroup relations. Research suggests that such relations are conditioned by the relative sizes of groups defined by a given attribute. In this context, the term *majority or minority group* refers to the relative size of such attribute-defined groups rather than to their relative status or power.

The *opportunity structure* refers to the set of probabilities that individuals with given attributes will gain access to career-related rewards. Career-related rewards include formal recognition, such as promotions, salary, and benefits, as well as less formal rewards, such as public acknowledgement, selection for important committees, or assignment to critical tasks and responsibilities. The literature suggests that opportunity structures are contingent on individual attributes. Thus, all else being equal, women typically receive lower wages than do their male counterparts (Blau, Ferber, & Winkler, 1997); racial minorities are less likely to be promoted than members of dominant groups (Zatzick, Elvira, & Cohen, 2003; Prasad, D'Abate, and Prasad, Chapter 10); and older workers are less likely to be recognized as having management potential than younger workers (Rosen & Jerdee, 1976, 1977). An opportunity structure that is unfavorable to individuals with particular attributes, by definition, means that their chances of being promoted, receiving increased compensation, or receiving other forms of organizational recognition and rewards are, on average, comparatively low.

The model suggests that the opportunity structure exerts a direct effect on a wide range of individuals' *career-related decisions and behaviors*. These may involve actions that affect the careers of others, as well as individuals' own careers. For instance, an individual who perceives the opportunity structure as unfavorable may decide to leave the organization, give up on trying to positively influence supervisors' assessments of his or her work, or bring a lawsuit against the organization. A manager may write performance evaluations based on the criteria that he or she perceives as valued by the organization, perhaps including the individual's age or functional area. Most work to date on organizational demography, however, has focused on individuals' job satisfaction, organizational commitment, promotions, and turnover as key career outcomes.

Career-related decisions and behaviors are conditioned by individuals' *perceptions of the opportunity structure* or their estimates of the probability that an employee with specific demographic attributes will receive career-related rewards. Objective indicators of the opportunity structure of an organization—for example,

actual rates of promotion for individuals with particular attributes—may be only loosely related to individuals' perceptions of the opportunity structure. Research shows that people often misperceive demographic phenomena, such as attribute distributions or norms (Lawrence, 1988; Rosenbaum, 1989), and sometimes respond in unexpected ways to variations in opportunities. For example, many studies document that women are less dissatisfied with their jobs than men, despite the fact that they have lower promotion rates. One explanation for this is that they compare themselves with other women rather than with men (Crosby, 1982; Tomaskovic-Devey, 1993). Thus, variations in individuals' perceptions of the opportunity structure determine how they respond to it.

The model involves two types of connecting relationships: direct and indirect (Lawrence, 1997, p. 7). A direct relationship is deterministic in the sense that the result can be predicted without knowledge of other factors. For instance, assuming no changes in the labor force, no intra-organizational mobility, and a standard retirement age, the age distribution of an organization's employees in Year 1 predicts its age distribution in Year 10 and thus projects the opportunity structure facing individuals at that time. In contrast, an indirect relationship is one whose effect is conditioned by a third variable. In our model, the impact of attribute distributions on the opportunity structure operates, in part, through its effects on intergroup relations. In another example, the opportunity structure reflects probabilities, but its effect on career outcomes depends on how individuals perceive those probabilities and how they interpret what they observe.

As noted, we view the relationships among components of the model as being reciprocal. However, for ease of discussion, we begin by considering the exogenous forces that initially shape the demographic composition of an organization and then consider the dynamics implied by the model.

What Determines the Distribution of Attributes?

The representation of individuals with particular attributes in an organization reflects the influence of larger social institutions, particularly work and family arrangements, that exist at the time organizations and occupations are created. These institutions, in turn, are influenced by changes in population, world events, the economy, and technology. Easterlin's (1987) analysis of variations in the size of U.S. birth cohorts—variations that reflect responses to natural catastrophes, wars, and other historical conditions—shows how such variations affect a generation's marital and employment opportunities.

Easterlin (1987) argues that small birth cohorts enjoy greater employment opportunities than large birth cohorts. For instance, the population cohort born in the United States during the Great Depression of the 1930s was relatively small. The birth rate declined from around 26 per 1,000 in the 1920s to around 17 per 1,000 in the 1930s. When members of this cohort entered the labor market in the post–World War II years, they faced little competition for jobs and thus experienced relatively high advancement opportunities and earning power. In a context where social norms strongly supported the traditional patriarchal, single-earner family, this contributed to a decline in the representation of women in the paid labor force. Relatively high wages made it feasible for families to exist with a sole breadwinner. Although Easterlin does not discuss it specifically, this had implications for changes in the demographic composition of organizations, many of which had relied heavily on women to constitute their workforce during the war years (Kessler-Harris, 2003).

It also contributed to the production of a relatively large birth cohort, the Baby Boom, born between 1946 and 1964. With most mothers staying at home during this time, couples could afford to care for larger families. The Baby Boom thus reflected a return to higher birth rates, which increased from 17 per 1,000 during the 1930s to 25 per 1,000 in the 1950s. Unlike their parents, members of this cohort experienced stiff competition from peers for stable jobs that paid well. It became more difficult to support a family on a single income and this, in conjunction with the greater economic independence for women promoted by the Women's Movement, led to a major increase in the proportion of women in the labor force (Blau et al., 1997). Increased economic competition for jobs led to increases in the ages

of those who started families as well as increases in their rates of marital stress and divorce. Moreover, it altered the age distribution of working men and women, transforming the career norms and timetables that evolved.

Such generational swings in birth rates thus play a major role in fashioning the social and economic environment in which organizations and occupations evolve. Evidence suggests that social conditions at the time organizations are founded leave an enduring impact on their structure (Stinchcombe, 1965). As employees tend to hire others similar to themselves, variations in attribute distributions are likely to reflect, to some extent, differences in organizational age and founding dates.

Proposition 1: The distribution of a given attribute within an organization is a function of the distribution of individuals with that attribute in the workforce at the time of the organization's founding.

Likewise, technological changes that lead to the growth of new occupations or to the decline of older ones also affect the demographic composition of organizations as organizations incorporate these occupations as part of their structure (Abbott, 1988; Barley & Tolbert, 1991). The forces that shape the demography of occupations are beyond the scope of this chapter (but see also Correll, 2004; Reskin & Ross, 1990; Wright & Jacobs, 1994); however, since occupations often acquire distinct gender, age, and racial identities, changes in occupationally based specializations are likely to alter the demography of organizations. Thus, for example, changes in office technology around the turn of the century resulted in the addition of typists and stenographers to many businesses; because these occupations were female dominated, the additions produced a substantial increase in the proportion of women in employing organizations (Davies, 1982; DeVault, 1990). In contrast, changes in the switching technologies used in communications organizations, making operator-assisted phone calls the exception rather than the rule, have led to a substantial decline in this female-dominated occupation. Systematic instruction in and use of computer technology began in the 1970s. Consequently, individuals who became familiar with this technology first were primarily those still in school when the technology began to spread. This affected the age distribution of individuals who had the skills needed to enter computer-based occupations in organizations.

Proposition 2: The distribution of attributes in an organization is a function of the demographic composition of occupations that are represented within the organization.

General social norms that define individuals with certain attributes as typical employees also serve to shape the demography of organizations. Until the past few decades of the 20th century, women in most Western countries were discouraged from participating in paid work (Kessler-Harris, 2003).[4] Consequently, most work organizations were male dominated. Shifts in the normative environment that began in the 1960s, supporting the employment of women and racial and ethnic minorities, led to major changes in the composition of the labor force in many countries and, hence, in the demography of many organizations. As age discrimination became less politically acceptable in the United States, it was codified into law, and many organizations removed age-based retirement provisions. This contributed to a significant increase in the average age of employees in some organizations, such as universities, during the past few decades (see also Porter, 2004).

Proposition 3: Changes in general social and occupational norms lead to changes in the distribution of demographic attributes in organizations.

WHAT DETERMINES ATTRIBUTE-LINKED ORGANIZATIONAL NORMS?

Norms are shared beliefs about typical behaviors, actions, or occurrences in a given social situation.[5] When many individuals traverse the same sequence of jobs in an organization, the path comes to be viewed as a typical career. People want to make sense out of those who traverse these typical paths. Independent of any formal explanation, such as "She was the best person for the job," individuals create their own

sense and nonsense of who and what the organization values. The observable attributes of successful individuals play a large role in this process. They act as signals (Spence, 1973), providing important information about what kind of person is esteemed.

During the Silicon Valley dot.com revolution in the 1990s, the generational distribution of computer skills produced entrepreneurs who were in their 20s. This age-based norm acquired a meaning among venture capitalists that founders of computer companies should be young, and with this interpretation came age-linked explanations for success. Young founders were seen as being more up-to-date technically, less risk averse, and more willing to work hard than older founders. As a result, venture capitalists were unlikely to fund older entrepreneurs, which, in turn, increased the number of young entrepreneurs and reinforced this age norm. Interestingly, on the other side of the ocean, entrepreneurs in Britain faced a very different situation. Here, venture capitalists viewed young people as lacking the requisite management experience and as being too inclined to take risks. Hence, in direct contrast to those in Silicon Valley, British entrepreneurs found it very difficult to get funding unless they were more than 30 years of age (Lawrence, 2004).

Proposition 4: The higher the proportion of individuals who follow the same career path and share a particular demographic attribute, the greater the likelihood that the attribute will become normatively identified with the career.[6]

The development of attribute-linked norms also depends on the general social significance attached to the attribute, and this may differ across groups, organizations, or societies. The higher the salience of an attribute, the more likely it is for people to use it in defining careers. For instance, Earley (1999) found that an individual's education and the prestige of the institution that provided it are critical to his or her status in France, whereas in the United States, gender and race are more important. In Thailand, age and education top the list of status determinants. Thus, career norms in these different societies may be differentially shaped by attribute-linked status norms.

Proposition 5: The greater the cultural salience of a given attribute, the greater the probability that career-related norms involving the attribute will develop.

Given Proposition 4, that norms evolve when many individuals follow similar career paths, attribute-linked norms should change with changes in the distribution of attributes in an organization. However, it takes time for people to observe and make sense of change. Thus, it seems likely that changes in norms will lag behind changes in distributions. This process is reflected, for instance, in the experience of one utility company, in which a gradual shift occurred in the selection of people for top management positions. While field engineers were once the dominant group in these positions, over time, people from marketing became more heavily represented. This shift required repeated decisions before employees began to perceive the pattern. The first marketing promotions were treated as deviants, with reactions such as "That promotion was a fluke" or "The person who got the job was very good, so it didn't matter where she came from." However, over time, the pattern became more pronounced, and the norm changed (interviews by the first author).

Proposition 6: Attribute-linked norms change when individuals perceive a systematic shift in the attributes of those rewarded by the opportunity structure.

Change also depends on how salient individuals feel the attribute is to successful organizational careers. In the case of the utility company described above, employees saw functional background as an important selection criterion for positions at the highest levels of the company. As a result, they paid attention when the functional background of newly selected top managers changed from operations to marketing. In general, the attributes of employees hired or selected for important positions and the attributes of employees who are fired or demoted from important positions are likely to be observed more quickly and by more observers than the attributes of people hired for or fired from unimportant positions. Consequently, the norms linked to such achievement-relevant

attributes may change more rapidly than those linked to less salient attributes.

Proposition 7: The speed with which attribute-linked norms change increases with the increasing salience of a demographic attribute for successful careers within the organization.

The pace of change in attribute-linked norms is apt to decline as an organization gets larger or more geographically dispersed. The difficulty of observing change in such settings attenuates the impact of distributional change on norms. For instance, in a 20-person organization, one new employee is scrutinized by everyone, whereas in a 100-person organization, one new employee may or may not be noticed depending on which office he or she works in and what job he or she assumes.

Proposition 8: The larger or more dispersed the organization, the longer the lag between changes in demographic distributions and changes in attribute-linked norms.

The pace of change in attribute-linked norms is also slowed down by selection processes, which both reflect and reinforce existing attribute distributions. One of the most consistent results in social network research is that individuals prefer demographically similar others (McPherson & Smith-Lovin, 2001). Appold, Siengthai, and Kasarda (1998), using data from 114 multinational firms in Japan and the United States and 40 domestic firms in Thailand, found that preferences for similar others were more important than either market incentives or national culture as predictors of the inequitable distribution of women in high-skill jobs. People frequently use demographic attributes such as age, gender, race, organizational tenure, and educational background to define salient similarity categories. Thus, an Intel engineer who graduated from Arizona State may be more likely to hire other engineers from Arizona State than equally qualified engineers from Ohio State. This process, called attraction, selection, and attrition by psychologists (Schneider, 1987) and homosocial reproduction by sociologists (Kanter, 1977), means that over time and if other factors are held constant, attribute distributions in careers tend to become more pronounced. As individuals whose attributes vary from the majority leave (O'Reilly, Caldwell, & Barnett, 1989), similar-attribute others are apt to be selected to take their places, and the diversity of the population decreases.

> *Proposition 9:* The longer an attribute-linked norm has been linked to a career outcome, the more entrenched that norm becomes and the more difficult it is to change.

This raises the question of whether attribute-linked norms are more resistant to change in situations where the proportion of minority members is small or in situations where the proportion is more balanced. For example, if the proportion of men and women is equal, is it easier or more difficult to change the norms than if the proportion is skewed—that is, when the proportion of the minority group is small relative to the majority group? One perspective suggests that it is easier. In a study of part-time local union officers, Izraeli (1983) found that women were perceived as having more influence in a balanced group than in a skewed group and that "promale" stereotypes were stronger in skewed groups than in balanced groups. One interpretation of this finding is that as the proportions of minority and majority members become more balanced, it is easier to change norms because there is more support for women playing important roles than in skewed groups. However, it is also possible that changing norms in a balanced group is more difficult. Individuals in balanced groups are more likely than those in skewed groups to be conscious of norms and to actively question or enforce them. Some research suggests that it is only when the proportion of minority members reaches some threshold level that majority members engage in norm-enforcing activities (e.g., Blalock, 1967; Reskin & Ross, 1990; Wharton & Baron, 1987). This increased sensitivity makes majority members more likely to block further changes in the norms. Thus, the direction of the relationship between the proportion of members with a given demographic attribute and the relative resistance of the group to changing its attribute-linked norms is uncertain. Two competing propositions are suggested.

> *Proposition 10:* The larger the proportion of minority members with a given attribute, the less resistance there is to these members and, thus, the easier it is to change attribute-linked norms.

> *Proposition 11:* The larger the proportion of minority members with a given attribute, the more resistance there is to these members and, thus, the more difficult it is to change attribute-linked norms.

Change propositions involve complex relationships with time, and there are many questions here that we do not address. For instance, change in attribute-linked norms likely depends on the speed with which distributions change. A dramatic increase in the minority proportion may produce faster change in attribute-linked norms than a slower increase because it operates as an "unfreezing" event and facilitates a move to new norms. However, it might also engender strong conflict and resistance from the majority group, making change in attribute-linked norms more difficult. Similarly, a slow increase in the minority proportion may be more effective because the gradual change is easier for individuals to accommodate. Alternatively, it may make it easier for individuals to ignore the changes, and attribute-linked norms may remain resistant to change.

HOW DO ATTRIBUTE DISTRIBUTIONS AND ATTRIBUTE-LINKED NORMS AFFECT THE OPPORTUNITY STRUCTURE?

Both the distribution of attributes within an organization and attribute-linked norms shape an opportunity structure—the probabilities that individuals will receive recognition, mobility, and increased compensation. For example, the distribution of attributes, in conjunction with processes of organizational growth and decline, exerts a direct influence on mobility opportunities. Stewman (1986) describes "Venturi effects" in organizations, similar to those in fluid mechanics, in which mobility is constrained by bottlenecks in personnel flows.[7] An example of such effects is illustrated by the case of an organization with a large cohort of employees at Level 1, originally hired during a period of organizational expansion. These employees are apt to find themselves competing for a relatively small number of available jobs at Level 2. There are few winners for the Level 2 competition and, consequently, the percentage of Level 1 employees who get to Level 2 is low. However, if Level 3 has a larger number of job openings, the percentage of those who achieved Level 2 who then move on to Level 3 will be high. Thus, the relative size of a cohort compared with the number of job openings affects the occurrence of bottlenecks or cascades in promotion chances.

The U.S. defense industry provides an example of such vacancy chains. When government defense spending declined in the 1970s, the number of young engineers hired by aerospace firms declined, producing a bimodal age distribution that was common throughout the industry. During the 1990s, the older engineers in this distribution began to retire, and there were insufficient numbers of mid-career engineers to replace them. Organizations had to reexamine employees of all ages to find the best replacements from the available pool. This created advancement opportunities for young, experienced engineers that had not existed previously. It also created fresh opportunities for older engineers who had been passed over earlier as "too old." Finally, it created a new career entry port. When qualified, internal candidates could not be found, many firms rehired older employees as consultants (Lawrence, 2004). Thus, demographic patterns may undermine the operation of internal labor markets—that is, systems of organizational advancement that are based on strong norms about appropriate points of entry and job ladder connections (Hollister, 2004; Osterman, 1984; Osterman & Burton, 2006).

Proposition 12: When an attribute is closely connected to career success, gaps in the attribute distribution produce greater opportunities for others without that attribute than they would otherwise experience.

The distribution of attributes also affects an organization's opportunity structure through its influence on social network connections, which serve as sources of information about career opportunities, social support, and social capital

(Brass, 1985; Burt, 1992; Cleveland & Hollmann, 1990; Ibarra, 1992, 1995). Because individuals prefer interacting with similar others (Mollica, Gray, & Trevino, 2003), the social networks of organizational members whose attributes fall in the demographic majority are likely to be larger than those of individuals who are members of demographic minorities (Ibarra and Deshpande, Chapter 14). The latter are thus less likely to gain access to the career-related information (Friedman, Kane, & Cornfield, 1998) or social capital that flows through networks (Burt, 1992). Moreover, fewer minority group members than majority group members are apt to be in positions of power. As a result, network access to people who can serve as career mentors and sponsors is apt to be more restricted for individuals who belong to demographic minorities. The more skewed the attribute distribution, the more unfavorable the opportunity structure will be for minority members.

Proposition 13: The less common the representation of a minority attribute among individuals occupying higher-status positions in an organization, the less access minority members have to social capital, and thus the less favorable the opportunity structure is for them.

The opportunity structure is also shaped by attribute-linked norms. An array of studies provides evidence that the opportunity structure is more favorable for individuals whose attributes are consistent with attribute-linked norms (Smith, 2002; Tomaskovic-Devey, 1993). The reason for this, in part, is that people tend to perceive others with the typical attributes of successful employees as performing better than those who lack such characteristics (Carli, 2001; Cohen & Roper, 1972; Pugh & Wahrman, 1983). For example, in a study of mobility in a large corporation, Rosenbaum (1984) found that employees who were not initially successful in getting promoted faced declining chances of promotion. This decline reflected the perception that these individuals had been passed over and were too old to be "rising stars," a definition that affected their performance evaluations. Such perceptions may be more likely to operate in organizations characterized by well-defined internal labor markets

(Osterman, 1984). Likewise, Eagly and Karau's (2002) review of research on women as leaders concluded that because men are generally expected to hold leadership roles, women in these roles are often evaluated as performing worse than their male counterparts, even when they exhibit the same behaviors.

Lawrence (1988, 1990) found that the age distribution of individuals in an organization created an age-based opportunity structure for managerial careers. This structure defined which ages were seen as typical for a given career level. Individuals who were younger than what was typical for their level were seen as ahead of schedule, and individuals who were seen as older than what was typical were viewed as behind schedule. This perceived timetable appeared to be based on the distribution of ages within the organization; however, there were also interesting differences. Individuals seemed to overestimate the ages of the youngest employees and underestimate the ages of the oldest employees in a given career level. Moreover, they created age differences between levels that did not exist in reality. Thus, being ahead of, on, or behind schedule appeared to influence individuals' perceptions of work and the probability that they would receive high performance evaluations.

The stronger an attribute-linked norm, the greater and more consistent is its impact on the opportunity structure. The strength of an attribute-linked norm refers to the extent to which organizational members accept or agree with the norm. Using the example above, if all managers agree that entry-level applicants are typically 20 to 23 years old, then this age bracket will exert a greater impact on the opportunity structure than if only half of them agree. The probability that a 30-year-old applicant will be hired is lower when agreement is high than when it is low. The strength of this norm also depends on the status of the agreeing managers. If the 50% who think 20 to 23 years is the right age include most of the highest-status managers, this attribute-linked norm is likely to exert a larger impact on the opportunity structure than if the 50% include no high-status managers.

Proposition 14: As agreement on an attribute-linked norm increases, its impact on the opportunity structure increases.

Proposition 15: As the status of those who agree on an attribute-linked norm increases, its impact on the opportunity structure increases.[8]

Individuals in an organization or work group may not be conscious of how demographic norms shape the opportunity structure until changing conditions require a shift in established personnel practices. For instance, Sea World in California faced a dilemma in the 1990s. They were used to hiring young people of college age to host their "guests" at the park. No one questioned this age norm until they began experiencing difficulties finding enough young people to fill the positions. When this occurred, they had to rethink their hiring criteria. The theme park ended up realizing that their criteria—friendly, helpful, and able to work part-time—could be filled equally well by another employment group: retirees. These new employees more than adequately met the park's performance criteria: They had lower absence rates and were more likely to remain at the park than college students (Lawrence, 2004).

How Do Intergroup Relations Affect the Opportunity Structure?

In addition to their direct effects on the opportunity structure, attribute distributions and attribute-linked norms also have indirect effects through their impact on interpersonal and intergroup relations. Members of formal organizational units, such as teams, departments, or divisions, frequently divide themselves informally into groups based on attribute-linked norms. For instance, a person belonging to a racial minority hired into a task force composed primarily of members from a majority group may feel more comfortable discussing his or her questions with other minority members, and majority task force members may avoid talking with the minorities because they find it uncomfortable. This creates two informal groups within the task force.

Intergroup relations, thus, refers to the interactions among such informal groups. The ease of intergroup interactions depends on the attribute-linked norms that evolve. When demographically different members join a work group or organization, existing members may react positively through support and acceptance or negatively by engaging in overt or covert discrimination. If attribute-linked norms increase the conflict between minority and majority group members, or even the resistance of majority group members to the minority, this is likely to create an opportunity structure that is disadvantageous for minorities. The processes that connect attribute distributions, attribute-linked norms, and intergroup relations are difficult and perhaps not possible to separate. Thus, some of the empirical evidence in this section builds on ideas developed previously. However, rather than focusing on how this literature connects the distribution of attributes to the development, strength, and change of attribute-linked norms, we use it to explore how intergroup relations produce conflicts that shape the opportunity structure.

Exactly how the proportion of minority members—that is, individuals whose characteristics don't conform to the norms—affects group dynamics is the subject of some debate in organizational demography (Tolbert, Graham, & Andrews, 1999). Some research suggests that conflictual group relations are most likely to ensue when there is only a small shift in the demography of a previously homogeneous group. Members react negatively to initial violations of demographic norms, but as the demographic pattern continues to change, so do the norms, thus leading to less conflict. Other studies suggest that reactions to initial, small changes in demographic patterns are likely to be minimal and that conflict is more likely to occur when the number of "violations" of a demographic norm reaches some threshold level.

A Social Contact Approach: Small Minority Groups Produce Conflict

Kanter's (1977) analysis of the entry of women into a traditionally male work group supports the first view. She noted that men responded to their new female colleagues in a number of ways: They exhibited acute awareness of the women's actions and behaviors, increased solidarity with other men, and a propensity to cast women in more traditional, "female" roles when interacting with them. Whether intended or not, such reactions created

a relatively uncomfortable work environment for the women, affecting their perceived (and probably actual) opportunities for advancement. Kanter predicted that as the proportion of women in the group increased, men's negative reactions to women's presence would decrease, presumably as the demographic norms changed. This prediction is consistent with the general logic of social contact theory (Brown, 2000), which suggests that stereotypes and negative perceptions of members of other social groups flourish under conditions of limited social interaction between group members. Increased intergroup contact, resulting from the expansion in the number of minority members in a group, is expected to result in the reduction of such prejudices (Blau, 1977; Brown, 2000).

Several empirical studies favor this general argument. For example, a study of officers in the Israeli army (Pazy & Oron, 2001) found that women officers were evaluated more negatively than their male counterparts when there were few women in the unit. Women's performance evaluations improved, however, as the proportion of women in the unit increased. Similarly, studies of business firms by Blum, Fields, and Goodman (1994) and Huffman (1999) indicated that organizations with a higher proportion of women overall had a higher proportion of women in management positions. Likewise, another result from the Izraeli (1983) study cited earlier found that women on committees with relatively few women were significantly more likely to feel constrained by gendered role expectations than women on committees with better gender balance. And Konrad, Winter, and Gutek's (1992) study of white-collar work groups showed that women's sense of social isolation decreased and their job satisfaction increased as the proportion of women in their work group increased.

Research by Chatman and Flynn (2001), suggesting that demographic heterogeneity affects the development of norms that help regulate intergroup relations, is also consistent with a social contact approach. In two studies, one with MBAs and the other with financial services officers, groups that were demographically heterogeneous on a composite relational measure of sex, race, and citizenship were less likely than demographically homogeneous groups to form cooperative norms in the early stages of the groups' existence. Their explanation is that initially, people respond to visible, status-linked differences by assuming that those who are different are not going to be as cooperative as those who are similar. However, their findings also indicate that over time, as relationships become based in experience, the impact of such differences decline. This would suggest that the impact of intergroup relations on the opportunity structure declines as interactions among minority and majority members accrue over time.

A Social Competition Approach: Larger Minority Groups Produce Conflict

Other work, however, indicates that negative reactions by majority members to minority members are most likely when the proportional representation of the minority in the organization becomes relatively large. That is, reactions to violations of demographic norms may not occur until a certain threshold representation of minority members is reached, and this may exacerbate, rather than reduce, these reactions. Initial studies supporting this argument focused on the indices of racial conflict and discrimination in U.S. communities (Blalock, 1967), but it has also received support in research on gender inequality and discrimination in organizations. For example, a study of the Israeli civilian labor force by Kraus and Yonay (2000) found that women were less likely to rise to positions of authority when they were in occupations with a large proportion of women than when they were in male-dominated occupations; they argue that increases in the proportion of women in an occupation lead to increased competition between men and women and to discrimination against women.

Likewise, a study of a federal agency found that women who worked in departments with higher proportions of women reported that they received less support, on average, from their male colleagues than women in departments with fewer women (South, Bonjean, Markham, & Corder, 1987). Tsui et al. (1992) found that increasing the proportion of women and minorities exerted little impact on their own experiences, but white men experienced decreasing psychological commitment, increasing

frequency of absences, and decreasing intent to stay. More indirect evidence of a relationship between the size of a minority group and discrimination is provided by a number of studies that show that women in organizations with a higher proportion of women at a given job level are likely to receive lower levels of compensation than men at those levels (Martin & Harkreader, 1993; Pfeffer & Davis-Blake, 1987; Tolbert, 1986).

Although there is little agreement on the sources of inconsistent evidence on the question of how the relative size of a minority group influences conflict, there is agreement that changes in the proportion of individuals who hold a given demographic attribute do produce changes in the frequency of such a conflict. Thus, the two literatures suggest competing arguments about how attribute distributions influence intergroup relations and, in particular, how they affect the propensity of members of dominant groups to discriminate against members of minority groups.[9] This, in turn, affects the kinds of opportunity structures that minority members face. The first literature suggests the following:

> *Proposition 16:* The more skewed the attribute distribution in an organization, the greater the level of conflict among attribute-defined groups and the more likely that the opportunity structure will reflect discrimination against members of a minority group.

In contrast, the second literature suggests the following:

> *Proposition 17:* The less skewed the attribute distribution in an organization, the greater the level of conflict among groups and the more likely that that the opportunity structure will reflect discrimination against members of a minority group.

One explanation for this controversy may be that attribute-linked norms vary across organizations in ways that mediate the impact of group proportions on intergroup conflict. For example, Ely and Thomas (2001) found three distinctive perspectives on diversity that appear to operate as norms in a bank that they studied. In branches with an integration-and-learning perspective, employees perceived diversity as an indicator of the group's potential for new insights and skills required for business performance. In branches with an access-and-legitimacy perspective, employees valued diversity as a mechanism for the organization to gain access and legitimacy in culturally diverse markets. Finally, in branches with a discrimination-and-fairness perspective, employees viewed diversity as demonstrating the morally correct stance of providing equal opportunities to all employees. While all three perspectives motivated managers to increase the diversity of their employees, only the first produced attribute-linked norms that used an individual's minority background as a positive evaluation criterion.

Unfortunately, with few exceptions (e.g., Chatman & Flynn, 2001; Cohen, Broschak, & Haveman, 1998), studies of demographic composition and group relations have relied on cross-sectional data. More research using longitudinal data might help us better understand the processes through which demographic changes lead to or reduce the intergroup conflict that leads to discriminatory behavior in the opportunity structure. In addition, comparative research on the impact of different attributes is needed to determine whether, as seems likely, the strength of reactions to violations of demographic norms is affected by the cultural salience of the attribute. For example, based on the Earley (1999) study cited earlier, changes in age-based patterns in organizations may generate less resistance than changes in gender or race, at least in the United States, whereas they may generate more resistance in Thailand.

How Does the Opportunity Structure Affect Career-Related Decisions and Behaviors?

Our model suggests that the relationship between organizational demography and individuals' career-related decisions and behaviors is complex. To the extent that the opportunity structure that individuals face is contingent on their demographic attributes, individuals with the same apparent qualifications do not have equal access to organizational rewards. Logically, this influences individuals' work within the organization.

Those who make decisions about the careers of others use the opportunity structure as an indicator of the organization's values and use these values for evaluation and promotion decisions. Those who then face less favorable opportunities than others are probably less willing to invest time and energy in their careers and perhaps more inclined to leave the organization.

Perceptions of the Opportunity Structure

The relationship between the opportunity structure and career-related decisions and behaviors is mediated in large part by individuals' perceptions. Research shows that individuals rely on their perceptions of the opportunity structure, even when those perceptions are inaccurate. Lawrence (1984a) found that managers who saw themselves as behind schedule held more negative attitudes toward work than those who saw themselves as on schedule—even when their behind-schedule perceptions were wrong. Several studies suggest that inaccurate perceptions of organizational opportunity structures are the norm, not the exception. In an automobile factory, Chinoy (1955) found that recently hired workers expected rapid promotions and that they continued to hold this faulty belief for some time afterward. Goldner (1970) found that only half of all the managers in a manufacturing firm who expected promotions actually received them. Similarly, Rosenbaum (1989) found that foremen's and managers' expectations for promotion were considerably inflated over reality. Because such perceptions influence behavior, it is important to consider what factors tend to make individuals' perceptions of the opportunity structure more or less accurate.

The literature suggests several explanations for perceptual accuracy. One is that accuracy depends on an individual's social context. In small organizations, everyone knows everyone else. Consequently, to the extent that the opportunity structure can be inferred from observation, the same information is available to all. In large organizations, the situation differs. Research in one large organization suggests that employees do not populate their social context with randomly selected others (Lawrence, 2006). When asked to identify everyone they knew, employees showed systematic, attribute-based selection patterns. This suggests that individuals in large organizations may not observe representative examples of the opportunity structure. For instance, it would not be surprising if a manager from a female-dominated marketing department had a very different view of the opportunity structure than a manager from a male-dominated R&D department. Even though both may then compete for the same position in the corporate office, their perceptions of opportunity emanate from their observations, and these may not be representative of the position to which they aspire.

This suggests that individuals' organizational experiences, represented by attributes such as their organizational tenure or the number of departments in which they have worked, also influence perceptual accuracy. New employees know few others; thus, their perceptions of the opportunity structure depend on what they have been told or read. Such initial information may or may not be representative of reality. Although many employers value realistic job previews, many want new employees to believe that there is room for growth and may present overly positive possibilities. Moreover, some employers may be unaware of the actual opportunity structure themselves and, thus, may be overly positive because they share their own inaccurate perceptions. Over time, as individuals meet more people and learn more about the organization, the information they receive is likely to become more representative of the opportunity structure, and thus, the accuracy of their perceptions should increase.

Proposition 18: The accuracy of an individual's perceptions of the organization's opportunity structure increases with the increasing representativeness of the other employees he or she knows.

A second possibility is that individuals' motives or needs influence their perceptual accuracy. Social psychologists find that people are motivated to be hopeful and, thus, to see situations as more encouraging than they actually are (Taylor & Brown, 1988). Such unrealistically positive self-evaluations and optimism are essential components of normal mental health and well-being. Studies show that people with falsely positive views of their health, such as those who believe that they will survive AIDS, live longer than those with a more realistic perspective (Taylor, Lerner, Sherman, Sage, & McDowell, 2003). Thus, individuals may misperceive the opportunity structure because it is in their best interests to do so. Such positive illusions are consistent with individuals' tendency to make upward social comparisons with high-achieving others (Arrowood & Friend, 1969; Festinger, 1954; Gruder, 1971). In the Chinoy (1955), Goldner (1970), and Rosenbaum (1984) studies cited above, employees perceived more favorable opportunities than actually existed. When asked to select others who are the most similar to them in their careers, individuals tend to select others who are at higher hierarchical levels in the organization (Gibson & Lawrence, 2006). As a result, individuals may show a persistent, positive bias in their observations of the opportunity structure.

Proposition 19: The accuracy of an individual's perceptions of the organization's opportunity structure decreases with his or her increasing propensity to view the probabilities of opportunity with a positive bias.

A third possibility is that social encoding influences perceptual accuracy (Fiske & Taylor, 1991). Individuals are more likely to observe the career successes and failures that embody the opportunity structure if the people who experience them, the values they represent, or the decision makers and decision processes they use are salient, vivid, and accessible. These three processes are related, and there is insufficient evidence to detail their independent effects on perceptual accuracy. However, the following discussion presents several examples of how these processes may work.

The salience of events depends on, among other things, status and social identity. When individuals are given a list of women and men, they are likely to overestimate the proportion of women on the list if the women's names are more well-known than the men's names (Kahneman & Tversky, 1972). Thus, we might expect that the higher the status of a job, the more likely individuals will be to observe the attributes of those who hold, are selected for, or select the person who gets the job. University faculty, for instance, are more likely to remember the attributes of both the applicants and the selection committee for chaired full professor jobs than for assistant professor jobs. The attributes of employees who get selected for key task forces are more likely to be remembered than the attributes of others selected for less prestigious work.

Social identity influences the salience of remembered others because individuals consistently pay more attention to others with similar attributes than to others with different attributes (McPherson & Smith-Lovin, 2001). Thus, an employee is more likely to observe and remember the career successes and failures of others with similar traits and in similar jobs than those of others. This process becomes more complex when individuals are making observations using more than one attribute. Distinctiveness theory (McGuire, McGuire, Child, & Fujioka, 1978; McGuire, McGuire, & Winton, 1979; McGuire & Pawawer-Singer, 1976; Mehra, Kilduff, & Brass, 1998) suggests that when an individual holds two minority identities, he or she will identify with the group that is least well represented. Thus, for example, if there are more women than African Americans in an organization in the United States, a woman will identify with African Americans, whereas if there are more African Americans than women, she will identify with women. The more salient identity should exert a stronger impact on her perceptions of the opportunity structure. In other words, she may pay more attention to the career successes and failures of other women than of other African Americans.

The accessibility of information about the opportunity structure also influences the accuracy of individuals' perceptions. For example, if only 22- to 24-year olds are hired for an associate job in an investment bank, it is likely that individuals' perceptions of their ages will be more accurate than if the range is 22 to 44 years of age. The larger range presents a more uncertain distribution, and this increases the likelihood of regression biases. Similarly, the smaller the number of individuals holding a given position, the more accurate individuals' perceptions are likely to be. It is not surprising that estimates of the ages of high-level managers in an organization are more

accurate than estimates of the ages of lower- and middle-level managers (Lawrence, 1988). In addition to differences in job status, there are much fewer individuals holding the high-level than the low-level jobs; thus, perceptions of the former are likely to be more accurate. Overall, these examples lead to the following propositions:

Proposition 20: The positive association between the accuracy of an individual's perceptions of the organization's opportunity structure and the representativeness of the employees he or she knows is moderated by the salience, vividness, and accessibility of those employees to the individual.

Proposition 21: From the sample of all known individuals, the more salient, vivid, and accessible others are to the individual, the greater the influence of their attributes on his or her perceptions of the opportunity structure.

The Impact of Perceptions on Career-Related Decisions and Behaviors

Inaccurate perceptions may influence career-related outcomes in several ways. First, it seems likely that individuals regard the distribution of attributes as an index, or signal (Spence, 1973), of the opportunity structure in organizations. The second author recalls being strongly impressed by the absence of senior women faculty members in some academic departments when she was interviewing for faculty positions; rightly or wrongly, she interpreted this as a negative sign of her own career prospects in those departments. That organizations take these observations seriously is evident in the careful selection of individuals with diverse demographic attributes for marketing documents, such as annual reports and university admission brochures.

Several studies suggest that people do make career-related decisions based on such observations. Research by Zatzick et al. (2003) found that individuals with a higher proportion of their own racial group in the level above them were less likely to leave the organization than those with a lower proportion. Similarly, Ely (1995) found a negative relationship between the proportion of women partners in a law firm and women associates' tendency to perceive differences between the attributes of successful lawyers and their own attributes. Geraci and Tolbert (2002) found that universities with a higher proportion of women faculty are more likely than those with a lower proportion to hire additional women. Although this hiring pattern may result, in part, from a university's willingness to make offers to women, it may also result from a greater propensity by women to accept offers from these universities, because they view them as having more promising career opportunities. These studies support the argument that individuals do take the distribution of demographic attributes in organizations as signals of their own opportunities for career advancement (see also Thomas, 1990). If their perceptions of these distributions are wrong, their perceptions of the opportunity structure will also be inaccurate.

> *Proposition 22:* Individuals who perceive themselves as demographically similar to others with successful careers will have more favorable perceptions of the organization's opportunity structure and are more likely to accept job offers than individuals who perceive themselves as demographically different.

Second, individuals' perceptions of the opportunity structure may predict the conditions under which they experience violations of their psychological contract with the organization (Slay and Taylor, Chapter 19). Granrose and Portwood (1987) found that when individuals perceive that their own career plans match those of their organization's, their satisfaction with the organization and intent to stay increase. When this psychological contract is violated, it exerts a negative impact on those career-related decisions and behaviors. Research suggests that managers connect career success with the frequency of job mobility (Herriot, Gibson, Pemberton, & Pinder, 1993; Lawrence, 1984b). Taylor, Audia, and Gupta (1996) found that lengthening job tenure increased the probability that successful managers with high-responsibility jobs decreased their commitment to the organization and increased their probability of leaving it. These managers appeared to base their perceptions of the opportunity structure on continued job mobility. When the frequency of their own job moves declined, they perceived this as a violation of their psychological contract with the organization regarding their promised rewards for high performance.

> *Proposition 23:* As an individual's perception of his or her probability of success within the opportunity structure increases, his or her commitment to and satisfaction with the organization increases.

Regardless of the accuracy of their perceptions, when individuals perceive the opportunity structure to be unfavorable, their career-related decisions and behaviors may be affected in different ways. One response entails lowering aspirations—not applying for promotions and not being as concerned about performance. As a result, demographic patterns become self-perpetuating. This has been one of the primary explanations for why women consistently exhibit lower pay expectations than men. Women are more likely to compare themselves with other women, and because other women earn less than men, women develop lower pay expectations (Major & Konar, 1984).[10]

Alternatively, individuals may respond to perceptions of limited opportunities by changing employers. This may account, in part, for the finding that women have much higher rates of interorganizational mobility than men and for the negative relationship between individuals' rates of inter- and intraorganizational mobility (Felmlee, 1982; Valcour & Tolbert, 2003). A number of studies suggest that turnover decisions are associated with the higher levels of intergroup conflict that accompany demographic change. It seems possible that in addition to or in combination with the conflict, these changes produce unfavorable perceptions of the opportunity structure, which increase the probability of turnover.

Several studies show that men's dissatisfaction with their work and expressed intentions to change jobs increased as the proportion of women in their organizational group increased (Tsui et al., 1992; Wharton & Baron, 1987). Likewise, a study of academic departments by Tolbert, Simons, Andrews, and Rhee (1995) showed that the rates of turnover among women faculty increased as the proportion of women in the department increased; this was attributed to the higher levels of intergroup conflict associated with changes in the attribute distribution. In the same vein, a study of the relationship between the size of tenure cohorts and turnover behavior by McCain, O'Reilly, and Pfeffer (1983) found that faculty turnover increased in departments with either one particularly large tenure cohort or substantial gaps between tenure cohorts. They suggested that this occurs because such gaps make communication across cohorts problematic, which increases conflict and power struggles.

Proposition 24: The less favorable individuals' perceptions of the opportunity structure are, the lower their job satisfaction and organizational commitment and the greater their probability of turnover.

A third response to perceptions of an unfavorable opportunity structure is to try to *change* the structure, either through bringing legal action or by mobilizing other employees to lobby for changes within the organization. Little is known about the conditions that encourage such proactive responses (but see also Balser, 2002) or, specifically, how organizational demography may influence different responses to lower expectations of obtaining career-related rewards. This represents a promising avenue for further research on demography and careers.

How Do Individual Career-Related Outcomes Shape Organizational Demography?

We've now come full circle, and although we have focused on one direction in the relationships among organizational demography and individual career-related decisions and behaviors, we would be remiss if we didn't mention what may happen in the opposite direction. The career choices that individuals make can also result in reshaping existing attribute-linked norms and distributions within an organization. Individuals who apply for positions that have traditionally been held by employees with other attributes may make existing norms more transparent, which may, in turn, lead those norms to be questioned and, ultimately, to change. Similarly, organizations that suffer high rates of turnover in segments of their workforce and have problems attracting new employees may be motivated or required to reexamine existing personnel practices. For example, research by Ingram and

Simons (1995) showed that organizations facing tighter labor markets for female employees were more likely to establish "family-friendly" policies. A large number of organizations have established a variety of structural arrangements, including mentoring programs, networking programs, and other "diversity management" programs, all of which have the explicit goals of reducing turnover and promoting demographic diversity in the workforce. While the impact of such policies on organizational norms and actual attribute distributions to date is still unclear (Glass & Estes, 1997), it *is* clear that individual career choices are taken into account by organizational decision makers in efforts to fashion a more attractive workplace, and in the long run, this is likely to affect demographic outcomes.

It is also worth noting that concerns with issues of attracting and retaining employees have been given added force in the past half-century by the threat of lawsuits and general legal pressures to demonstrate nondiscriminatory practices. In this context, individuals who perceive the opportunity structure in an organization to be inequitable may choose not to leave it but to try to change it through legal action. Work by a variety of researchers (Kelly & Dobbin, 1998, 1999; Leonard, 1990) suggests that legal forces are often key factors in producing change in the attribute distribution and organizational policies (and thus, presumably, in organizational norms).

Thus, there are a variety of ways in which individual actions can, in the long run, produce significant changes in organizational patterns, including demographic patterns (Barley & Tolbert, 1997). The relation between individual actions and changes in organizational demography is likely to be much more difficult to map than the reverse relationship because of the relative fixity of the constructs. Nonetheless, a full understanding of the relation between organizational demography and individual careers requires recognition of their mutual influences.

A Few Summary Thoughts

Our purpose in this chapter was to sketch a broad outline of multilevel questions that research on organizational demography suggests for the study of careers. In some cases, we have sufficient empirical evidence to be specific about proposed relationships. In others, our contribution is to identify relevant variables, posit alternate explanations, and puzzle about possible outcomes. One variable that emerged in our conversations as a significant, relatively unexplored feature in these hypotheses is time. Although time is always lurking in the background of career studies, it became particularly relevant in exploring these multilevel connections, perhaps because the scale of change for individuals differs so much from that for organizations. Certainly, as we discussed these ideas and others, it became increasingly clear that the relationships we propose merely skim the surface of potential complexities.

Much intriguing territory lies within the processes that connect careers as individual phenomena with careers as social or structural phenomena. Topics such as career success, for instance, are typically studied from either subjective or objective perspectives. Yet it seems likely that they are not independent (Arthur et al., 2005). Attribute distributions are frequently studied as direct predictors of career-related outcomes. Yet including attribute-linked norms and intergroup relations seems likely to offer a more nuanced understanding of this relationship. Individuals base their career decisions on their perceptions of reality, so exploring what happens when perceptions and reality differ may help explain the variability in employees' responses to the opportunity structure. Until we explore these relationships and others like them, we will never really comprehend careers as individual phenomena that are inextricably embedded within social contexts. There is clearly a great deal of work to be done to understand the processes that connect demographic structure, attribute-linked norms, and career outcomes in organizational settings. We hope this chapter encourages additional steps in that direction.

NOTES

1. Studies of organizational demography tend to differ from studies of the relationship between individual demographic attributes and career-related outcomes. The former focus on the compositional effects of demographic distributions, whereas the latter focus on the individual effects of demographic attributes. Examples of organizational demography studies include McCain et al. (1983), showing that gaps in tenure cohorts are associated with higher turnover, and Tsui et al. (1992), showing that increasing work group diversity is associated with lower levels of psychological attachment. Examples of individual demographic attribute studies include McNeely's (1988) research on human service workers, showing a positive relationship between job satisfaction and age, and Loscocco and Kalleberg's (1988) study, comparing American and Japanese employees in terms of the effects of age on job commitment.

2. We recognize that interactions among demographic attributes also influence careers, but these interactions are beyond the scope of this chapter; hence, our discussion is limited to the effects of single demographic attributes.

3. The term *organizational demography* has been used broadly to refer to the representation of particular attributes in a variety of organizational groupings, including work groups or departments, given levels of management, and whole organizations. To our knowledge, no work to date has focused on the problem of what the relevant unit of analysis is in understanding the influence of demography on any particular outcome.

4. It is worth noting that these norms were briefly redefined during the years of the first and second world wars, when the employment of women was encouraged as an act of patriotism; however, once the labor crises created by the wars were over, the norms constraining women from paid employment were reestablished with amazing rapidity.

5. This definition follows in the tradition of others who define norms as frames of reference or regularities (Newcomb, Turner, & Converse, 1965). It does not include either behavioral expectations or sanctions for deviance. Our interest in how attribute-based norms emerge within organizations suggests that demographic patterns exist before behavioral expectations become attached to them. It is likely that the opposite also occurs: Behavioral expectations associated with demographic patterns outside the organization influence the likelihood that these attributes will become salient inside the organization. However, we treat the two concepts as independent effects and thus consider them separately. We exclude sanctions from our definition because norms defined by sanctioning behaviors cannot be separated from their effects (Cancian, 1975).

6. In these propositions, we discuss the proportion of individuals holding a given attribute rather than the number of individuals. Thus, these propositions examine what happens when the number of women increases *relative* to the total number of employees or when the number of old employees increases *relative* to the number of young and middle-aged employees. However, it is possible that an increase in numbers without an increase in proportions might produce the same response. An influx of new minority hires might be quite visible and salient to everyone, even though a company hires other employees as well. Moreover, there is evidence that the impact of proportions on individual outcomes is not linear (Gibson & Cordova, 1999; Izraeli, 1983). Thus, these propositions should be taken as general directions for exploring these topics.

7. The authors thank Hugh Gunz for his helpful elaboration describing this concept.

8. These propositions do not explore intriguing questions about how the interaction between the numbers and status of those who agree influences the opportunity structure and under what conditions agreement is more important than status and vice versa.

9. Another possibility not explored here is that the skewness of the attribute distribution is not the critical factor. It may be that the change from one proportion of a minority to another is what increases or decreases the conflict. Thus, conflict ensues because majority members see the change in the attribute distribution and are uncomfortable with it.

10. Gibson and Lawrence (2006) found that this explanation may be incomplete. In their study, no gender differences in career expectations appeared for employees at low career levels after controlling for the gender and career level of comparison others. In contrast, significant gender differences appeared at high career levels: Women at these levels showed lower career expectations than men, even when controls were added.

REFERENCES

Abbott, A. (1988). *The system of professions.* Chicago: University of Chicago Press.

Appold, S. J., Siengthai, S., & Kasarda, J. D. (1998). The employment of women managers and professionals in an emerging economy: Gender inequality as organizational practice. *Administrative Science Quarterly, 43*(3), 538–565.

Arrowood, A. J., & Friend, R. (1969). Other factors determining the choice of a comparison other. *Journal of Experimental Social Psychology, 5,* 233–239.

Arthur, M. B., Hall, D. T., & Lawrence, B. S. (1989). *The handbook of career theory.* Cambridge, UK: Cambridge University Press.

Arthur, M. B., Khapova, S. N., & Wilderom, C. P. M. (2005). Career success in a boundaryless career world. *Journal of Organizational Behavior, 26*(2), 177–202.

Avolio, B. J., Waldman, D. A., & McDaniel, M. A. (1990). Age and work performance in nonmanagerial jobs: The effects of experience and occupational type. *Academy of Management Journal, 33*(2), 407–422.

Balser, D. B. (2002). Agency in organizational inequality: Organizational behavior and individual perceptions of discrimination. *Work and Occupations, 29,* 137–165.

Bantel, K. A. (1994). Strategic planning openness: The role of top team demography. *Group and Organization Management, 19*(4), 406–424.

Barley, S. R., & Tolbert, P. S. (1991). At the intersection of organizations and occupations. In S. R. Barley & P. S. Tolbert (Eds.), *Research in the sociology of organizations* (pp. 1–23). Greenwich, CT: JAI Press.

Barley, S. R., & Tolbert, P. S. (1997). Institutionalization and structuration: Studying the links between action and institution. *Organization Studies, 18*(1), 93–117.

Berger, J., Fisek, H., Norman, R., & Zelditch, M. (1977). *Status characteristics and social interaction.* New York: Elsevier.

Blalock, H. M. (1967). *Toward a theory of minority-group relations.* New York: Wiley.

Blau, F. D., Ferber, M. A., & Winkler, A. E. (1997). *The economics of women, men and work.* Upper Saddle River, NJ: Prentice Hall.

Blau, P. M. (1977). A macrosociological theory of social structure. *American Journal of Sociology, 83,* 26–54.

Blum, T. C., Fields, D. L., & Goodman, J. S. (1994). Organization-level determinants of women in management. *Academy of Management Journal, 37*(2), 241–268.

Brass, D. J. (1985). Men's and women's networks: A study of interaction patterns and influence in an organization. *Academy of Management Journal, 28,* 327–343.

Brown, R. (2000). *Group processes: Dynamics within and between groups.* Malden, MA: Blackwell.

Burt, R. S. (1992). *Structural holes: The social structure of competition.* Cambridge, MA: Harvard University Press.

Cancian, F. M. (1975). *What are norms? A study of beliefs and action in a Maya community.* London: Cambridge University Press.

Carli, L. L. (2001). Gender and social influence. *Journal of Social Issues, 57,* 725–741.

Chatman, J. A., & Flynn, F. J. (2001). The influence of demographic heterogeneity on the emergence and consequences of cooperative norms in work teams. *Academy of Management Journal, 44*(5), 956–974.

Chinoy, E. (1955). *Automobile workers and the American dream.* New York: Random House.

Cleveland, J. N., & Hollmann, G. (1990). The effects of the age-type of tasks and incumbent age composition on job perceptions. *Journal of Vocational Behavior, 36,* 181–194.

Cohen, E. G., & Roper, S. S. (1972). Modification of interracial interaction disability: An application of status characteristic theory. *American Sociological Review, 37*(6), 643–657.

Cohen, L. E., Broschak, J. P., & Haveman, H. A. (1998). And then there were more? The effect of organizational sex composition on the hiring and promotion of managers. *American Sociological Review, 63*(5), 711–727.

Correll, S. J. (2004). Constraints into preferences: Gender, status, and emerging career aspirations. *American Sociological Review, 69,* 93–113.

Crosby, F. J. (1982). *Relative deprivation and working women.* New York: Oxford University Press.

Davies, M. (1982). *Woman's place is at the typewriter: Office work and office workers, 1879–1930.* Philadelphia: Temple University Press.

DeVault, I. A. (1990). *Sons and daughters of labor: Class and clerical work in turn-of-the-century Pittsburgh.* Ithaca, NY: Cornell University Press.

Dionne, S. D., Randel, A. E., Jaussi, K. S., & Chun, J. U. (2004). Diversity and demography in organizations: A levels of analysis review of the literature. *Multi-Level Issues in Organizational Behavior and Processes, 3,* 181–229.

Eagly, A. H., & Karau, S. J. (2002). Role congruity theory of prejudice toward female leaders. *Psychological Review, 109,* 573–598.

Earley, P. C. (1999). Playing follow the leader: Status-determining traits in relation to collective efficacy across cultures. *Organizational Behavior and Human Decision Processes, 80*(3), 192–212.

Easterlin, R. A. (1987). *Birth and fortune: The impact of numbers on personal welfare* (2nd ed.). Chicago: University of Chicago Press.

Ely, R. J. (1995). The power in demography: Women's social constructions of gender identity at work. *Academy of Management Journal, 38,* 589–634.

Ely, R. J., & Thomas, D. A. (2001). Cultural diversity at work: The effects of diversity perspectives on work group processes and outcomes. *Administrative Science Quarterly, 46*(2), 229–273.

Felmlee, D. H. (1982). Women's job mobility patterns within and between employers. *American Sociological Review, 47,* 142–151.

Festinger, L. (1954). A theory of social comparison processes. *Human Relations, 7,* 117–140.

Fiske, S. T., & Taylor, S. E. (1991). *Social cognition* (2nd ed.). New York: McGraw-Hill.

Friedman, R., Kane, M., & Cornfield, D. B. (1998). Social support and career optimism: Examining the effectiveness of network groups among black managers. *Human Relations, 61,* 1155–1176.

Geraci, H. A., & Tolbert, P. S. (2002, August). *More or less: Gender composition of universities and the hiring of women faculty.* Paper presented at the Academy of Management Conference, Denver, CO.

Gibson, D. E., & Cordova, D. I. (1999). Women's and men's role models: The importance of exemplars. In A. Murrell, F. Crosby, & R. Ely (Eds.), *Mentoring dilemmas: Developmental relationships within multicultural organizations* (pp. 121–142). Mahwah, NJ: Lawrence Erlbaum.

Gibson, D. E., & Lawrence, B. S. (2006). *Social comparison and gender: The relative effect of similar-gender referents and standard setters on expected achievement.* Working paper, The Anderson School at UCLA.

Giddens, A. (1976). *New rules of sociological method.* London: Hutchinson.

Giddens, A. (1984). *The constitution of society.* Berkeley: University of California Press.

Glass, J. L., & Estes, S. B. (1997). The family responsive workplace. *Annual Review of Sociology, 23,* 289–314.

Goldner, F. H. (1970). Success vs. failure: Prior managerial perspectives. *Industrial Relations, 9,* 453–474.

Granrose, C. S., & Portwood, J. D. (1987). Matching individual career plans and organizational career management. *Academy of Management Journal, 30*(4), 699–720.

Gruder, C. L. (1971). Determinants of social comparison choice. *Journal of Experimental Social Psychology, 7,* 473–489.

Herriot, P., Gibson, G., Pemberton, C., & Pinder, R. (1993). Dashed hopes: Organizational determinants and personal perceptions of managerial careers. *Journal of Occupational and Organizational Psychology, 66,* 115–123.

Hollister, M. N. (2004). Does firm size matter anymore? The new economy and firm size wage effects. *American Sociological Review, 69,* 659–676.

Huffman, M. L. (1999). Who's in charge? Organizational influence on women's representation in managerial positions. *Social Science Quarterly, 80,* 738–756.

Ibarra, H. (1992). Homophily and differential returns: Sex differences in network structure and access in an advertising firm. *Administrative Science Quarterly, 37*(3), 422–447.

Ibarra, H. (1995). Race, opportunity, and diversity of social circles in managerial networks. *Academy of Management Journal, 38,* 673–703.

Ingram, P. L., & Simons, T. (1995). Institutional and resource dependence determinants of responsiveness to work family issues. *Academy of Management Journal, 38,* 1466–1482.

Izraeli, D. N. (1983). Sex effects or structural effects? An empirical test of Kanter's theory of proportions. *Social Forces, 62,* 153–165.

Kahneman, D., & Tversky, A. (1972). Subjective probability: A judgment of representativeness. *Cognitive Psychology, 3*(3), 430–454.

Kanter, R. M. (1977). *Men and women of the corporation.* New York: Basic Books.

Kelly, E., & Dobbin, F. (1998). How affirmative action became diversity management: Employer response to antidiscrimination law, 1961–1996. *American Behavioral Scientist, 41,* 960–984.

Kelly, E., & Dobbin, F. (1999). Civil rights law at work: Sex discrimination and the rise of maternity leave policies. *American Journal of Sociology, 105,* 455–492.

Kessler-Harris, A. (2003). *Out to work: A history of wage-earning women in the United States* (2nd ed.). New York: Oxford University Press.

Konrad, A. M., Winter, S., & Gutek, B. A. (1992). Diversity in work group sex composition: Implications for majority and minority members.

Research in the Sociology of Organizations, 10, 115–140.

Kraus, V., & Yonay, Y. P. (2000). The effect of occupational sex composition on the gender gap in workplace authority. *Social Science Research, 29,* 583–605.

Lawrence, B. S. (1984a). Historical perspective: Using the past to study the present. *Academy of Management Review, 9,* 307–312.

Lawrence, B. S. (1984b). Age grading: The implicit organizational timetable. *Journal of Organizational Behavior, 5,* 23–35.

Lawrence, B. S. (1988). New wrinkles in the theory of age: Demography, norms and performance ratings. *Academy of Management Journal, 31,* 309–337.

Lawrence, B. S. (1990). At the crossroads: A multiple-level explanation of individual attainment. *Organization Science, 1,* 65–86.

Lawrence, B. S. (1996). Interest and indifference: The role of age in the organizational sciences. *Research in Personnel and Human Resources Management, 14,* 1–59.

Lawrence, B. S. (1997). The black box of organizational demography. *Organization Science, 8*(1), 1–22.

Lawrence, B. S. (2004). How old you are may depend on where you work. In S. Chowdhury (Ed.), *Next generation business handbook* (pp. 986–1006). Hoboken, NJ: Wiley.

Lawrence, B. S. (2006). Organizational reference groups: A missing perspective on social context. *Organization Science, 17,* 80–100.

Leonard, J. S. (1990). The impact of affirmative-action regulation and equal-employment law on black employment. *Journal of Economic Perspectives, 4,* 47–63.

Linton, R. (1942). Age and sex categories. *American Sociological Review, 7,* 589–603.

Loscocco, K. A., & Kalleberg, A. L. (1988). Age and the meaning of work in the United States and Japan. *Social Forces, 67*(2), 337–356.

Major, B., & Konar, E. (1984). An investigation of sex differences in pay expectations and their possible causes. *Academy of Management Journal, 27*(4), 777–792.

Martin, P. Y., & Harkreader, S. (1993). Multiple gender contexts and employee rewards. *Work and Occupations, 20,* 296–336.

McCain, B. E., O'Reilly, C., & Pfeffer, J. (1983). The effects of departmental demography on turnover: The case of a university. *Academy of Management Journal, 26,* 626–641.

McGuire, W. J., McGuire, C. V., Child, P., & Fujioka, T. (1978). Salience of ethnicity in the spontaneous self-concept as a function of one's ethnic distinctiveness in the social environment. *Journal of Personality and Social Psychology, 36,* 511–520.

McGuire, W. J., McGuire, C. V., & Winton, W. (1979). Effects of household sex composition on the salience of one's gender in the spontaneous self-concept. *Journal of Experimental Social Psychology, 15,* 77–90.

McGuire, W. J., & Pawawer-Singer, A. (1976). Trait salience in the spontaneous self-concept. *Journal of Personality and Social Psychology, 33,* 743–754.

McNeely, R. L. (1988). Age and job-satisfaction in human-service employment. *Gerontologist, 28*(2), 163–168.

McPherson, J. M., & Smith-Lovin, L. (2001). Birds of a feather: Homophily in social networks. *Annual Review of Sociology, 27,* 415–444.

Mehra, A., Kilduff, M., & Brass, D. J. (1998). At the margins: A distinctiveness approach to the social identity and social networks of underrepresented groups. *Academy of Management Journal, 41,* 441–452.

Mollica, K. A., Gray, B., & Trevino, L. K. (2003). Racial homophily and its persistence in newcomers' social networks. *Organization Science, 14,* 123–136.

Newcomb, T. M., Turner, R. H., & Converse, P. E. (1965). *Social psychology: The study of human interaction.* London: Routledge & Kegan Paul.

O'Reilly, C. A., Caldwell, D. F. & Barnett, W. P. (1989). Work group demography, social integration and turnover. *Administrative Science Quarterly, 34,* 21–37.

Osterman, P. (1984). *Internal labor markets.* Cambridge: MIT Press.

Osterman, P., & Burton, M. D. (2006). Ports and ladders: The nature and relevance of internal labor markets in a changing world. In S. Ackroyd, R. Batt, P. Thompson, & P. S. Tolbert (Eds.), *The Oxford handbook of work and organizations* (pp. 425–448). Oxford: Oxford University Press.

Pazy, A., & Oron, I. (2001). Sex proportion and performance evaluation among high-ranking military officers. *Journal of Organizational Behavior, 22*(6), 689–702.

Pfeffer, J. (1983). Organizational demography. In L. L. Cummings & B. M. Staw (Eds.), *Research in organizational behavior* (Vol. 5, pp. 299–357). Greenwich, CT: JAI Press.

Pfeffer, J., & Davis-Blake, A. (1987). The effects of the proportion of women on salaries: The case of college administrators. *Administrative Science Quarterly, 32,* 1–24.

Porter, E. (2004, August 29). Coming soon: The vanishing work force. *New York Times,* p. 1.

Pugh, M. D., & Wahrman, R. (1983). Neutralizing sexism in mixed-sex groups: Do women have to be better than men? *American Journal of Sociology, 88*(4), 746–762.

Reskin, B., & Ross, P. A. (1990). *Job queues, gender queues: Explaining women's inroads into male occupations.* Philadelphia: Temple University Press.

Ridgeway, C. L., & Erickson, K. G. (2000). Creating and spreading status beliefs. *American Journal of Sociology, 106*(3), 579–615.

Rosen, B., & Jerdee, T. H. (1976). The influence of age stereotypes on managerial decisions. *Journal of Applied Psychology, 61,* 428–432.

Rosen, B., & Jerdee, T. H. (1977). Too old or not too old. *Harvard Business Review, 55*(6), 97–107.

Rosenbaum, J. E. (1984). *Career mobility in a corporate hierarchy.* San Francisco: Academic Press.

Rosenbaum, J. E. (1989). Organizational career systems and employee misperceptions. In M. B. Arthur, D. T. Hall, & B. S. Lawrence (Eds.), *The handbook of career theory* (pp. 329–353). Cambridge, UK: Cambridge University Press.

Rosenberg, M. (1968). *The logic of survey analysis.* New York: Basic Books.

Schneider, B. (1987). The people make the place. *Personnel Psychology, 40,* 437–453.

Smith, R. A. (2002). Race, gender and authority in the workplace: Theory and research. *Annual Review of Sociology, 28,* 509–542.

Sobel, I. (1982). Human capital and institutional theories of the labor market: Rivals or complements? *Journal of Economic Issues, 16,* 255–272.

South, S. J., Bonjean, C. M., Markham, W. T., & Corder, J. (1987). Sex differences in support for organizational advancement. *Work and Occupations, 14,* 261–285.

Spence, A. M. (1973). Job market signaling. *Quarterly Journal of Economics, 87*(3), 355–374.

Stewman, S. (1986). Demographic models of internal labor markets. *Administrative Science Quarterly, 31*(2), 212–247.

Stinchcombe, A. L. (1965). Social structure and organizations. In J. G. March (Ed.), *Handbook of organizations* (pp. 142–193). Chicago: Rand-McNally.

Tajfel, H., & Turner, J. C. (1979). An integrative theory of intergroup conflict. In W. G. Austin & S. Worchel (Eds.), *The social psychology of intergroup relations* (pp. 33–48). Monterey, CA: Brooks/Cole.

Taylor, M. S., Audia, G., & Gupta, A. K. (1996). The effect of lengthening job tenure on managers' organizational commitment and turnover. *Organization Science, 7*(6), 632–648.

Taylor, S. E., & Brown, J. D. (1988). Illusion and well-being: A social psychological perspective on mental health. *Psychological Bulletin, 103,* 193–210.

Taylor, S. E., Lerner, J. S., Sherman, D. K., Sage, R. M., & McDowell, N. K. (2003). Are self-enhancing cognitions associated with healthy or unhealthy biological profiles? *Journal of Personality and Social Psychology, 85*(4), 605–615.

Thomas, D. S. (1990). The impact of race on managers' experiences of developmental relationships: An intra-organizational study. *Journal of Organizational Behavior, 11,* 479–492.

Tolbert, P. S. (1986). Organizations and inequality: Sources of earnings differences between male and female faculty. *Sociology of Education, 59*(4), 227–236.

Tolbert, P. S., Graham, M. E., & Andrews, A. A. (1999). Group gender composition and work group relations. In G. N. Powell (Ed.), *Handbook of gender and work* (pp. 179–202). Thousand Oaks, CA: Sage.

Tolbert, P. S., Simons, T., Andrews, A. A., & Rhee, J. (1995). The effects of gender composition in academic department on faculty turnover. *Industrial and Labor Relations Review, 48,* 562–579.

Tomaskovic-Devey, D. (1993). *Gender and race inequality at work: The sources and consequences of job segregation.* Ithaca, NY: Cornell University Press.

Tsui, A. S., Egan, T. D., & O'Reilly, C. A. (1992). Being different: Relational demography and organizational attachment. *Administrative Science Quarterly, 37,* 549–579.

Valcour, P. M., & Tolbert, P. S. (2003). Gender, family and career in the era of boundarylessness: Determinants and effects of intra- and inter-organizational mobility. *International Journal of Human Resource Management, 14*(5), 768–787.

Wagner, W. G., Pfeffer, J., & O'Reilly, C. A. (1984). Organizational demography and turnover in top-management groups. *Administrative Science Quarterly, 29,* 74–92.

Wharton, A. S., & Baron, J. N. (1987). So happy together? The impact of gender segregation on men at work. *American Sociological Review, 52*(5), 574–587.

Williams, K. Y., & O'Reilly, C. A. (1998). Demography and diversity in organizations: A review of 40 years of research. *Research in Organizational Behavior, 20,* 77–140.

Wright, R., & Jacobs, J. A. (1994). Male flight from computer work: A new look at occupational resegregation and ghettoization. *American Sociological Review, 59,* 511–536.

Zatzick, C. D., Elvira, M. M., & Cohen, L. E. (2003). When is more better? The effects of racial composition on voluntary turnover. *Organization Science, 14*(5), 483–496.

21

CAREER PATTERNS AND ORGANIZATIONAL PERFORMANCE

MONICA C. HIGGINS

JAMES R. DILLON

This chapter examines the question of how career patterns influence organizational performance. Much of the traditional research on careers in the 1970s and early 1980s viewed career streams as results of organizational and other macro-level influences and viewed career success as the product of matching individual traits with organizational needs (e.g., Holland, 1973). For example, studies of careers focused on career management from the perspective of the organization (e.g., Hall, 1976; Sonnenfeld & Peiperl, 1988) or as an intersection where both individual and organizational needs were met (e.g., Schein, 1978). At the time of publication of the *Handbook of Career Theory* (Arthur, Hall, & Lawrence, 1989), most of the research continued in this vein with articles on topics such as rites of passage at work and strategic staffing, but also expanded into then-emerging ideas about minority careers, work/life issues, the individual's perceptions/experience of a career, and individual career development. There was also an emerging theme at that time

that advocated the need for people to take charge of directing their own careers—that rather than be shaped by external forces, careers might be shaped by individuals themselves (e.g., Bell & Staw, 1989; see Hall & Mirvis, 1996).

Adding back this notion of agency to the study of careers also laid the foundation for scholars to examine how the career patterns and choices of individuals might ultimately affect the performance of firms rather than simply the career consequences for individuals. Still, the notion of turning tradition on its head and studying how individuals' careers might shape organizations was quite a novel idea—an idea identified in a synthesis chapter of the Handbook (Nystrom & McArthur, 1989) but only barely discernable in the original Handbook chapters themselves. At the time, there was in fact little theoretical or empirical work linking careers to organizational outcomes.

One theory that would eventually lead the investigation into how career patterns influence organizational performance is upper-echelons theory. An upper echelon refers to the top management team (TMT) and/or board members of a focal firm.[1] Upper-echelon theory was emerging in organizational theory in the mid-1980s, and throughout the past two decades it has focused on how the composition of a firm's senior-most executive ranks affects a variety of organizational outcomes (e.g., Hambrick & Mason, 1984; Useem, 1979).

This body of research began with theoretical work by Hambrick and Mason (1984) and grew rapidly with empirical work centered on examining the many ways in which top executives' backgrounds may affect organizational outcomes, including, but not limited to, the performance of firms (for a review, see Finklestein & Hambrick, 1996). Some of these effects were closely linked to specific aspects of executives' career histories. In early research, scholars proposed that the set of "givens" that executives bring to their work in an organization is influenced by certain aspects of their prior career paths, such as "tenure in the organization" and "functional background" (Hambrick & Mason, 1984, p. 196). As the empirical work in this area expanded in the 1990s, the career histories of executives and their influence in organizations were examined in several ways that have established important theoretical links between career histories and organizational outcomes.

In this chapter, we will focus on several specific ways that upper-echelon researchers have investigated how executive career histories may influence organizational outcomes. While we draw primarily on upper-echelons research, we also bring insights from other streams of research that bear on senior executive mobility, such as studies of insider versus outsider selection. At the end of the chapter, we will consider emerging research and future directions for the study of career patterns and their effects on organizational outcomes that include, but are not limited to, research on upper echelons.

THE UPPER-ECHELON LENS: SENIOR EXECUTIVE CAREERS AND ORGANIZATIONAL PERFORMANCE

If we consider the body of upper-echelon research that emerged during the 1980s and 1990s, three patterns or categories of mechanisms can be identified that link senior executive career histories to organizational outcomes: (a) how the strategic decision-making *process* of members of a firm's upper echelon affects firm outcomes, (b) how the *substance* or resources that executives carry with them influence firm outcomes, (c) and how *signals* that derive from executives' career histories can affect firm outcomes.

Process: The Effects of Senior Executive Careers on Strategic Decision Making

The first mechanism that scholars have focused on that links career histories and organizational outcomes is group process—specifically, the decision-making processes of top executive teams. Here, scholars tend to study various facets of background diversity within a team, such as functional diversity among TMT members, and the ways in which such diversity affects TMT decision making. This has been the dominant perspective taken over the past two decades in upper-echelon research and has dovetailed nicely with parallel research in organizational behavior that has focused on the impact of various forms of group diversity and resultant processes on team outcomes.

Early contributors to the field of upper-echelon research, who proposed that executives have a strong influence on the direction and performance of firms, emphasized leader decision making as the main vehicle by which executives' careers make a difference in the performance of firms (e.g., Gupta & Govindarajan, 1984; Hambrick & Mason, 1984; Useem, 1979). This senior-level decision making was called "strategic leadership" (Finklestein & Hambrick, 1996; Hambrick, 1989; Phillips & Hunt, 1992). The fact that most upper-echelon decisions are group-level decisions rather than individual-level decisions presented an important opportunity for scholars to apply methods and theory from the literature on small group processes to empirically examine such a mechanism linking executive careers to strategic leadership processes.

TMT researchers thus drew on central tenets and research on groups to build their arguments, including in particular the research on small group diversity. Early work on group decision making in the 1970s suggested that the degree of diversity among team members can have a strong influence on the effectiveness of the decisions made (e.g., Hoffman, 1978; Janis, 1972; Steiner, 1972). Some of this research emphasized the benefits of diversity (Hoffman, 1978)—for example, with respect to producing creative or innovative solutions (e.g., Bantel & Jackson, 1989)—whereas other studies emphasized negative consequences of group diversity, such as conflict (e.g., Janis, 1972). In the groups literature, diversity measures often included demographic characteristics such as age and sex (e.g., Cady & Valentine, 1999; Hoffman & Maier, 1961; see also Lawrence and Tolbert, Chapter 20). In much of this research, snapshots were taken of a group's diversity at a particular point in time and then empirically linked to group outcomes.

TMT researchers have employed similar methods to measure the diversity of career backgrounds in groups of senior managers, under the hypothesis that upper-echelon team member diversity should generate differences in strategic leadership outcomes. Included in these measures were some career-history-related measures such as tenure at the firm, tenure on the TMT, inside versus outside succession, and functional background. The manner of measuring tenure and functional diversity has varied across studies, and the results have been mixed—much as findings from the research on groups have been mixed and depend, for example, on the nature of the task or the outcome of interest.

A number of studies have found that diverse TMT functional backgrounds are beneficial for firm performance. One organizational outcome of interest in these studies is the resolution of complex, nonroutine problems, and the generation of creative solutions (McLeod, Lobel, & Cox, 1996; Wanous & Youtz, 1986). For example, Bantel and Jackson (1989) found that TMT functional diversity in the banking industry enhanced organizational innovation, and Wiersema and Bantel (1992) found that a TMT's educational-specialization diversity (i.e., the diversity of their educational majors) was associated with greater levels of strategic change in a firm.

In contrast, other studies have found TMT heterogeneity to be negatively associated with certain group outcomes that are hypothesized to affect firm outcomes. For example, researchers have found evidence that diverse executive teams are less aware of resource levels and trends in their environments (Sutcliffe, 1994) and less able to achieve strategic consensus because of poorer team process (Knight et al., 1999; Miller, Burke, & Glick, 1998). More commonly, however, researchers have found evidence to support the proposition that TMT diversity does positively influence aspects of firm performance (e.g., Murray, 1989; Wiersema & Bantel, 1992).

Throughout this research on TMT group process, the differing cognitive frames that executives bring from earlier career experiences—whether labeled as values, beliefs, or perspectives—have been the primary explanatory mechanism assumed to be producing these group outcomes that are of significance to organizations. But variation in the empirical findings leaves substantial opportunity for future research in this area. For example, researchers could incorporate cognitive research that examines how individual executives' career histories affect their orientations and perspectives on strategic problems. In research on the effects of specific individual members of upper echelons, for example, researchers have studied how functional-assignment experience may be associated (Dearborn & Simon, 1958; Hitt & Tyler, 1991) or unassociated (Beyer et al., 1997; Walsh, 1988) with managerial perceptions of and approaches to solving strategic problems (see also Bunderson & Sutcliffe, 2002). In addition, research on the effects of executive careers on subsequent belief structures has emphasized the role of social influence of peers (Chattopadhyay, Glick, Miller, & Huber, 1999). This recent work points out the difficulty of identifying specific or detailed causal mechanisms between career histories and organizational outcomes using functional background alone and suggests that future research on TMT career histories and subsequent decision making might incorporate process variables and mechanisms that are behavioral (e.g., information sharing) as well as cognitive (beliefs, perspectives).

It is also important to acknowledge that, in this stream of research, there are issues of measurement that probably confound the collective findings of these studies and so make it difficult to discern what are and are not useful ways to think about and study "career patterns" in TMTs. For example, functional diversity has been conceptualized in different ways in different studies, ranging from measuring dominant functional background (the most common measure) to measuring a manager's entire functional background or only the functional nature of the current assignment (for a review, see Bunderson & Sutcliffe, 2002). This diversity of diversities has produced conflicting results sometimes. In a recent study designed to resolve these issues, Bunderson and Sutcliffe (2002) examined both dominant function diversity within a TMT and intraindividual functional diversity (i.e., the functional breadth of individual members, aggregated across the team); the latter measure captures a more nuanced view of executive career patterns and, indeed, was found to have a stronger influence on two organizational outcomes, information-sharing and unit performance.

What is perhaps most important to keep in mind then is, just as the small groups research has found, outcomes are most affected by group characteristics and diversity that are relevant to the problem at hand. Therefore, rather than continue to broaden our conceptualizations of TMT diversity and to test for an increasing array of relationships with organizational performance, future upper-echelons research would benefit greatly from a tighter alignment between specific mechanisms proposed and, hence, group characteristics studied, and specific facets of organizational performance.

Resources: Career Histories as a Source of Resources for the Firm

A second kind of argument that scholars have made regarding the link between top executive careers and firm outcomes is that executive careers are a source of resources for a firm. There are two types of resources that stem from career histories and that are hypothesized to be carried with individuals as they traverse organizations and, in turn, affect organizational performance: human capital and social capital. The concepts of human capital (see Becker, 1964) and social capital (see Coleman, 1988; Granovetter, 1973) are seminal theories that have been employed in organizational and sociological

research for decades. In recent years, however, scholars have begun to use these constructs to inform our understanding of how senior executive careers affect organizations.

This trend in research interests may be tied to macro-level changes occurring in our economy and work environment—specifically, the increasing mobility of workers (see Cappelli, 1999) as well as the rise in salience of entrepreneurship in our economy during the 1990s. Some career scholars began writing about these changes in the 1980s and 1990s (e.g., Daft & Lewin, 1993; Kanter, 1989; for a brief review, see Arthur & Rousseau, 1996a, pp. 5–9). In particular, career scholars focused on the decline of the "organization man" (Whyte, 1956) and the rise of the boundaryless career (Arthur & Rousseau, 1996b)—that is, the shift from the employer to the employee in the ownership of the management of one's career. As a direct consequence, scholars began to study career streams that stretch beyond a single employer and, importantly, what it is that individuals who make such transitions bring to their new posts. Hall termed this new kind of career "the protean career" (1976, p. 201; Hall & Mirvis, 1996). Career research on this topic led to a focus on career decisions that include a change in employer (Higgins, 2001) and that emphasize a new psychological contract between employer and employee (Rousseau, 1989). In tandem, upper-echelon researchers similarly turned their prism to focus on factors associated with career moves that might affect firms and, in particular, on the resources that managers bring with them as they traverse organizations.

Human Capital

As individuals engage in their careers, they learn and develop, and in that process, they acquire skills and knowledge that can be valuable to the firms they are later employed by. Such acquired skills and knowledge are aspects of "human capital." Work experience is one source of human capital (Bird, 1996), educational experience is another (Coleman, 1988). These resources may be considered assets that can benefit firms. Furthermore, such assets may become especially salient when executives cross organizational boundaries to a new company, since during such times a firm "acquires" assets, such as knowledge and skill sets, stemming from a senior executive's career history.

Research in this area includes studies of the effects of the international experience of chief executive officers (CEOs) and TMT members on firm performance (e.g., Carpenter, Sanders, & Gregersen, 2000, 2001) and the effects of executives' industry experience on success of new venture (e.g., Kor, 2003). Here, scholars generally argue that the experience set of an executive can be a "valuable, rare, and inimitable resource" (Carpenter et al., 2001, p. 494) for a focal firm that employs the executive. The empirical results of studies of TMTs whose members have international or industry experience generally show that firms employing such executives perform better financially than their peers (e.g., Carpenter et al., 2001), especially when the nature of the human capital (e.g., international experience) corresponds to the needs of the firm (e.g., significant multinational operations). Furthermore, executives with international experience are also more likely to stretch their firm to take reasonable international risks when the executives themselves have international experience (Carpenter, Pollock, & Leary, 2003).

In other empirical work, variables such as an executive's prior position level in a previous job are frequently used as indicators of not just the type but also the depth or level of experience that executives have attained in their careers and so, the value to the firm of that "resource." Upper-echelon scholars have employed such measures to examine firm outcomes such as a firm's ability to garner the support of alliance partners. For example, Eisenhardt and Schoonhoven's (1996) research suggests that TMT members' prior high-level management experience can endow firms with the skills necessary to identify and assess potential alliances and negotiate favorable partnership arrangements.

In a similar line of work, Kor's (2003) longitudinal study showed that the level of previous industry experience of managers of entrepreneurial firms is an important determinant of the rate of growth the firm experiences. Such studies have demonstrated a link between executives' career experience and organizational performance and suggest that executives can bring critical industry knowledge and capabilities that can

positively influence firm performance. Related research on new venture growth finds that executives' combined career experience in a focal industry is positively related to the growth rate of a young firm (Eisenhardt & Schoonhoven, 1990). These studies suggest that executives have skills and abilities that are unique and valuable to that industry and so can affect not just individuals and how their careers progress (as traditional career research has examined) but how firms perform as well. More generally, the basic argument is that an upper echelon's experience base—which derives from the cumulative effects of top executives' career backgrounds—can yield valuable human capital that can positively affect a firm's performance.

Social Capital

In addition to human capital, senior executives also bring with them, by virtue of their previous career experiences, resources in the form of connections that they have accumulated. When these social resources are tapped to meet the needs of a focal firm, they may benefit that firm's performance as well. Research in this area includes studies of the extraorganizational affiliations of board members and management teams and their effects on organizational outcomes such as access to financing, revenue generation, and firm survival (e.g., Higgins & Gulati, 2003; Pennings, Lee, & Witteloostuijn, 1998). Scholars argue that when its executives have worked at a certain kind of firm or within a certain sector or industry, a focal organization benefits from the ties that were built there. Thus, for example, the social capital of partners in professional services firms, who are responsible for generating new business for the company, has a direct impact on the ability of the firm to generate revenue and hence survive; research shows that the number of ties carried from the prior work experience of partners in accounting firms, for example, is an important predictor of a firm's continued survival, because such ties represent relationships with potential clients (Pennings et al., 1998).

Research on the career-based affiliations of upper-echelon members of young firms has also suggested that different kinds of career experiences may yield different kinds of connections and, thus, enhance a firm's social resources in the form of network ties to specific industries or sectors (Higgins & Gulati, 2003). Scholars have also examined how the breadth of connections stemming from prior career experiences affects firm outcomes. For example, in their study of how upper echelons can enhance a firm's abilities to form strategic alliances, Eisenhardt and Schoonhoven (1996) demonstrated that the social capital of TMT members—measured as the breadth of companies with which they had previous employment connections—helps predict the formation of strategic alliances beyond explanations centered on human capital or transaction-cost economics theories alone.

Although human capital is the primary mechanism emphasized in the vast majority of research about the resources that TMTs carry with them during career transitions, research on boards of directors, in contrast, has tended to emphasize the importance of social capital. For example, in their role as advisors to executives, boards are more effective in providing strategic counsel to top management when they have ties to strategically related organizations (Carpenter & Westphal, 2001). In other research on boards, scholars have found that joint ventures are more likely to form when firms have board interlocks (mutual ties via board seats; Gulati & Westphal, 1999). And research on the relationship between board composition and firm bankruptcy found that boards with a larger number of external directors—individuals holding posts in other firms and industries—were less likely to go bankrupt when facing financial trouble, a result the authors attribute to the external directors' ability to provide access to valuable external social resources (Daily & Dalton, 1994, p. 1606).

Most recently, research on TMTs has similarly begun to focus on the mechanism of social capital. TMT scholars have begun to examine how different kinds of career histories yield different kinds of employment-based ties, which affect the kinds of endorsements that firms receive in very specific ways (e.g., Higgins & Gulati, 2006). For example, research suggests that the greater the match between a firm's top executives' employment affiliations and the kind of alliance partner a firm is trying to attract, the greater the likelihood that a partnership will indeed form (Kim & Higgins, 2005). Underlying this work is the basic argument that social capital or ties with other organizations is a product of the career paths of executives whose career experiences span different firms, giving an executive's current employer advantageous access to resources, opportunities, and partners at critical junctures.

Signal

A third way that scholars have examined how career histories affect organizational performance is through the signaling of status or legitimacy that may be associated with executives' prior roles, positions, or employment affiliations. When certain career experiences confer greater prestige on an executive, that executive's career carries a symbolic value that affects external judgments about the firm. One of the underlying arguments in this body of research is that, simply put, status begets status—what has often been dubbed the "Matthew effect" (Merton, 1973) after the biblical maxim, "To him that hath shall be given [more]" (Matthew 25:29). Thus, firms whose senior executives have high-status or prestigious-looking résumés are more likely to attract the attention of prestigious partners, who interpret the decision of high-status executives to affiliate themselves with the firm (thus risking their own careers on the firms' good fortunes) as a reliable endorsement of the quality of the firm. Upper-echelon studies that emphasize the symbolic value of the prestige of top executive's careers, thus, do so in the context of studying the effects of senior executive career histories on appraisals of the firm by external constituencies such as prestigious investment banks (Higgins & Gulati, 2003), high-quality investors (Higgins & Gulati, 2006), or desired alliance partners (Eisenhardt & Schoonhoven, 1996).

In a related fashion, and drawing on the seminal work of Spence (1974), who argued that status can serve as a proxy for quality, upper-echelon scholars have similarly argued that the status of an upper echelon can serve as a proxy of firm quality. Along this line of reasoning, the status of upper-echelon members' careers can translate to affect the perceived quality of a firm. These arguments regarding executives' status and its impact on external evaluations of firm quality are especially salient in highly uncertain contexts, such as when young firms seek capital or when troubled firms attempt to avoid bankruptcy. At such times, firms are trying to *acquire* or *repair* organizational legitimacy and rely on signals associated with executive's careers to do so (for a review of organizational legitimacy, see Suchman, 1995).

A series of studies by D'Aveni and colleagues focused on the legitimacy-enhancing effects of firms led by top executives with certain kinds of backgrounds. These studies examined linkages between TMT career histories and outcomes related to firm bankruptcy. For example, this research has shown that senior executives who had graduated from top business and law programs or had previously worked in prestigious business, government, or legal positions were better able to garner lenience from creditors when the firms they led were in default (D'Aveni, 1989, 1990).

At the other end of a firm's life cycle, scholars have demonstrated that investors in the initial public offerings (IPOs) of young firms (typically with no history of products or profits) look to the career histories of the firm's executives for signals of the young firm's legitimacy (e.g., Eisenhardt & Schoonhoven, 1996). For example, a study of new ventures in Silicon Valley showed that career histories can play an important role in the formation of start-ups; founders of new ventures who have worked at prominent employers in the industry are more apt to take risks and at the same time are more effective at securing funding for their young firms (Burton, Sørensen, & Beckman, 2002). In recent research, Higgins and Gulati (2006) distinguished between different kinds of organizational legitimacy that are signaled by the career histories of a firm's top management team; they examine what they term *resource legitimacy*, which stems from upper-echelon members' employment affiliations, and *role legitimacy*, which stems from the positions held by certain top managers. These two facets of upper-echelon career histories were found to have significant and positive effects on the quantity and quality of institutional investors that invest in a young firm.

Other Perspectives

Outside the upper-echelons umbrella, certain other streams of organizational research also lend insight into the relationship between career patterns and organizational performance. The literature that focuses on executive succession, for example, has examined questions regarding the impact of the career backgrounds of incoming CEOs on firm outcomes. For example, scholars have asked whether it is more advantageous for a firm to hire a chief executive from inside or outside the firm. Put differently, do career experiences inside or outside the firm give CEOs any distinct advantages in leading the firm? This question of whether to develop leaders internally or acquire them from outside the organization is analogous to the cost accountant's "build versus buy" decision—and the research addressing this question has produced mixed results. For example, researchers have found that outsider CEO successions are often associated with higher firm profitability or more favorable market reactions (Lubatkin, Chung, Rogers, & Owens, 1986; Reinganum, 1985; Warner, Watts, & Wruck, 1988). At the same time, others have found insider successions to be associated with the same positive outcomes (Beatty & Zajac, 1987; Furtado & Rozeff, 1987; Worrell & Davidson, 1987; Zajac, 1990). These results were sometimes moderated by the firm's presuccession performance, but still with inconclusive results.

Part of the challenge in identifying the relationship between successor origin and firm performance could be that both insiders and outsiders are hypothesized to bring different kinds of beneficial resources to a firm. For insiders, this often includes familiarity with an organization, its culture and processes; while for outsiders, it includes a potentially fresh or unique outside perspective. These different research results could be attributable to the different needs of firms at a given time. Indeed, organizational scholars have examined several contingencies that could explain the mixed insider/outsider results.

Arguing for a contingent theory of executive succession, Kerr and Jackofsky (1989), for example, argued that the value of insider versus outsider CEOs depends on two factors: (a) the nature of the organization, where more stable and hierarchical organizations do better developing their own CEOs and (b) the environment, where more predictable environments amenable to steady growth favor internal candidates. Such contingency theories have become more common as researchers try to make sense of the large body of insider/outsider succession research (for reviews and examples of contingent theories, see Kesner & Sebora, 1994; Lin & Li, 2004). Thus, much like the upper-echelons research, the CEO succession literature suggests that senior executives develop specific abilities, such as human capital, and also acquire certain resources, such as social capital, that they carry with them through their career paths. Studies of successor origin also extend our purview of the value of executives' careers to firms by considering factors such as knowledge of and familiarity with the culture, systems, and politics of a particular organization that may be carried by an insider and the fresher perspective on these same matters that may be carried by an outsider. Both of these are aspects of career experience that may also affect important organizational outcomes.

Beyond the traditional organizational behavior and careers literatures, scholars in other fields have also begun to view career histories as a lens for understanding organizational performance, particularly in the context of young firms. During such times, a firm has no previously established track record and, therefore, concerns regarding organizational legitimacy are especially salient. For example, in the entrepreneurship literature, research by scholars such as Deeds, DeCarolis, and Coombs (1997) have examined how board career history and focal top managers' career histories affect the financial performance of young firms. In the finance literature, for example, a study investigating factors that affect entrepreneurs' level of equity ownership in their own firms has included measures of the amount of work experience that entrepreneurs have, both in total and as owners of previous businesses (Bitler, Moskowitz, & Vissing-Jørgensen, 2005). In another study, finance scholars investigated whether new ventures were more likely to be founded by individuals with career backgrounds in large corporations or in other start-ups (Gompers, Lerner, & Scharfstein, 2005). In the organizational strategy literature, for example, scholars have examined how higher levels of industry experience and senior-management experience decrease IPO underpricing and, hence, increase the amount of value that a firm is able to capture

from its IPO (Cohen & Dean, 2005). Thus, in many respects, this perspective of senior executive careers as conduits of both resources and signals of legitimacy, credibility, or reputation (depending on the terminology and research audience) has gained substantial momentum, even beyond the field of careers.

EMERGING RESEARCH AND FUTURE DIRECTIONS

As the foregoing review shows, prior research has emphasized the effects of career histories on interactions among upper-echelon members within an organization or across organizations as individuals move from one to another. These studies tend to treat an executive's career background as a current trait brought with them from some previous experience—whether it is knowledge, contacts, or status. However, the vast majority of prior studies have not sufficiently examined how such career-generated characteristics are formed—that is, career *patterns* beyond a particular snapshot in time are often ignored. Still, several important pieces of research have begun to emerge that do examine career effects across individuals from a single organization (including the pattern of career experiences that produce substantial and signal effects) and even within individuals (patterns in the evolution of individual careers). Such research has examined the dynamic career processes that shape managers over the course of their careers and that, in turn, affect organizational outcomes.

Emerging Research

Work by Gunz (1989) was one of the first pieces of research to propose a theoretical framework for examining the influence of career patterns on organizations. His research suggested that the dominant career patterns (organizational career logics) in a firm are mutually reinforcing with the firm's strategy and structure. Gunz compared these underlying, inferred patterns or "logics" with jungle gyms in which different rungs represent different job positions. Although the career pathways or streams within an organization are not directly visible to an outside observer, they are inferentially discernable by studying the movement of individuals on the "jungle gyms" over the course of their careers.

As part of that research, Gunz (1989) investigated the career streams of several large manufacturing companies. He found that the sequences of career moves within a firm formed patterns that played out in an organizational career logic that was characteristic of that firm—a result that provided preliminary support for his theoretical framework. For example, companies characterized by steady growth in a familiar domain where many similar jobs could be found tended to have career logics in which managers advanced to positions of greater and greater responsibility (more subordinates, larger budgets) within similar positions; in contrast, firms that grew through internal entrepreneurship in new, unfamiliar domains tended to have career logics focused around a particular business or venture within the larger firm.

Gunz's (1989) focus on the actual pattern or "logic" of careers within an organization—rather than just a static (e.g., functional) measure of careers—remains one of the most important and interesting contributions of his study. In the future, research that empirically examines the relationships he proposed between career patterns and a firm's strategy and structure would be useful to the study of how career patterns affect organizational outcomes. Along those lines, the more recent studies we discuss below have built on this seminal theoretical and methodological groundwork in their investigation of career patterns in and across firms.

A second major study of career patterns was work done by Jones (2001), which examined the career histories of major entrepreneurs within a single industry over a 25-year period. In her in-depth research drawing on both historical and archival data sources, Jones analyzed the history of the American film industry and showed how entrepreneurs from different career backgrounds played different roles in the industry. By carefully tracking the full professional biographies of individuals who eventually started or managed movie production and distribution companies, Jones demonstrated that successful entrepreneurs were able to lead change in periods that better suited their particular knowledge and networks, as embodied in their career histories, whereas less successful entrepreneurs lacked the

career-based experience and, hence, the contacts and skills that were relevant in the changing environment. In its beginnings, the film companies focused on developing and standardizing film *technology*, and the most successful entrepreneurs in this era had technological backgrounds in manufacturing and invention and were seasoned at working within the legal and regulatory environment of this field. As the film industry evolved to its later emphasis on movie *content*, successful entrepreneurs were those with backgrounds in theater, retail, and distribution—with the accompanying business contacts and knowledge of consumer entertainment markets and talent management that turned out to be vital for success. Jones highlights the coevolution of individual career, firm, and industry histories by looking at each of these different levels of analysis. She also observes changes in entrepreneurs' skills sets after launching a new venture in response to industry and competitive changes, which in turn enabled some of their firms to survive and enact strategic change. The entrepreneurs, in turn, exerted great effort in shaping the film industry and their firms to suit their particular strengths and career backgrounds (e.g., expertise with certain technologies or deep experience with certain distribution channels). This iterative, interactive exchange between executives, firms, and industries is another example of how the career histories of individuals can have a formative and lasting influence on companies and even entire industries.

Most recently, Higgins (2005) studied the career patterns of executives both within and across organizations in the health care and life sciences sectors. Combining analyses of a large archival data set of more than 3,200 career histories of biotechnology executives with 78 detailed career-history interviews of executives in the health care industry, Higgins identified the process of "career imprinting," a mechanism by which a unique set of capabilities, connections, cognition, and confidence is cultivated by employees who are all working at a particular firm at a particular period of time. This research found that organizations produce a different "imprint" on their employees who extend beyond a particular functional or role background. Instead, an "organizational career imprint" is associated with a specific organization and derives from the pattern of career experiences that are shared by employees of that firm. Thus, a career imprint comprises not only skills or capabilities but also certain kinds of connections, confidence, and cognition that are unique to having worked at a particular parent organization during a specific period of time.

Higgins (2005) also found that when managers leave an organization, they carry with them that organization's career imprint, which can have significant consequences for their own performance as well as that of their future employers. Specifically, her study of biotechnology executives showed that Baxter International, a health care company in the midwestern United States, produced managers who picked up an entrepreneurial career imprint from their careers at Baxter. This entrepreneurial career imprint grew out of Baxter's global growth strategy, its decentralized structure, and its selection, socialization, and management development practices and the career experiences that resulted from these factors. In comparison, Merck's managers cultivated a scientific career imprint as a result of its product development strategy and science-driven culture that influenced the kinds of career experiences people had at work. The dynamic career patterns embodied in a career imprint may have consequences that extend beyond firms and to entire industries. In the 1970s and 1980s, for example, former Baxter managers—with their entrepreneurial career imprint—were more likely to serve in chief executive roles in the emerging biotechnology industry, whereas former Merck employees were more likely to serve as scientific advisors. Thus, Higgins (2005, p. 277) concludes that not only are careers embedded in organizations, but organizations are also embedded in careers.

Future Directions

These examples of emerging trends and studies in careers research call attention to three directions for future study that promise to advance our understanding of the relationships between career patterns and organizational outcomes.

First, careers represent a rich portrait of the past that can have multifarious effects on the future of firms. Understanding those effects will require measuring more than just a slice in time of career history. Theory and empirical results in upper-echelons research help demonstrate that when employees cross organizational boundaries, they carry some of their career experiences with them, affecting certain organizational outcomes. Complementing this conclusion, the emerging research that we have discussed here provides a way for scholars to step deeper into organizational processes and understand *how* employees take their experiences with them while at the same time promising to provide a richer picture of the dynamics over the course of a career and their subsequent effects on organizations.

From a theoretical standpoint, these emerging studies examine sequences rather than snapshots of careers—patterns rather than silhouettes—an approach that opens the way for a more comprehensive understanding of the mutually recursive effects of careers and organizations on one another. Such research focuses on "career patterns" in a dynamic sense and so provides a richer portrayal of how careers can influence organizations and even industries. This approach stands in contrast to the majority of studies reviewed in this chapter, which look at career histories as snapshots in time, informed by an individual's career history only as a present-day characteristic of who they are. In the future, research that truly examines career *patterns* can lend insight into how not only career characteristics but also career and leader development patterns influence individuals and the firms they lead and manage.

On a related point, when such career patterns are mapped onto their effects on organizations, the resulting models can become very complex. It is no coincidence that the methods of measuring career patterns in these emerging studies are primarily qualitative, as this approach permits the exploration of new, intricate patterns in the sequence of career experiences across organizations and is well suited to the inductive phase of building theory about career effects on organizations. Perhaps with the exception of Abbott's algorithmic analysis (e.g., Abbott & Hrycak, 1990), the complexity of the patterns in the emerging work reviewed here lend themselves to a qualitative approach rather than the quantitative one used in most upper-echelon research.

Over time, however, and as constructs that capture career patterns become better specified and measures validated, career theory would benefit from a hybrid of complementary methodological approaches. Indeed, although the aforementioned studies by Gunz (1989), Jones (2001), and Higgins (2005) do employ qualitative analyses to analyze career patterns, they also draw from quantitative data in varying degrees to bolster their findings. Using statistical analyses and tests of archival data, both Jones and Higgins provided additional support for the relationships they discovered between entrepreneurs' early career histories and later business outcomes, and Gunz examined the statistical distributions of different types of career transitions in his subject companies.

Second, nearly all the studies reviewed here connecting career patterns with organizational outcomes have focused on the careers of senior executives and board members in the upper echelons of a firm, what Gunz (1989) called the *dominant* or *modal* career logic in an organization. But careers influence organizations through the initiative and leadership of many individuals and not just a few at the very top of an organization. Therefore, moving forward, it is important also to understand the effects of career patterns of other members of a firm. It is reasonable to think that other key members of a firm who collectively have a very significant impact on organizational performance, such as star performers (Groysberg, Nanda, & Nohria, 2004), would also find their current performance to be influenced by their career histories, including the human and social capital they bring individually as well as in their collective contributions to group process.

Finally, all the emerging studies we have discussed lend insight into the mutually recursive influences of careers and organizations on one another (Jones and Dunn, Chapter 22). We note that Jones (2001) looked at "coevolution" of careers and organizations; Higgins (2005) observed organizations producing career imprints, which in turn affected other organizations; and Gunz (1989) highlighted career-organization interactions that were mutually reinforcing. Even some of the upper-echelons research has demonstrated a two-way causal effect—a double feedback loop—between organizations and careers (e.g., D'Aveni,

1990; Hambrick & D'Aveni, 1992; Sutton & Callahan, 1987). Although the vast majority of careers research examines the unidirectional effects of organization or environment on careers, in fact they both exist in a symbiotic relationship as part of an integrated system, a reality seldom recognized in career theory (for an exception, see Gunz & Jalland's, 1996, "integrated model" of how careers and organizations interrelate). Future contributions to career theory should take this relationship into account.

These three levers for future research—studying dynamic career patterns, key organization members outside a firm's upper echelon, and the symbiotic relationship between careers and organizations—all appear to be fruitful paths for future career research and promise to strengthen our collective understanding of careers and the ways in which they influence organizational performance.

NOTE

1. We note that research on boards (e.g., Pfeffer, 1972; Westphal & Zajac, 1997) and top managers (e.g., Eisenhardt, & Bourgeois, 1988; Finkelstein, 1992) has often proceeded in parallel and that definitions of what constitutes the team of people who sit at the "top" of a firm has caused some debate in the literature (see Finkelstein & Hambrick, 1996). Here, we will use either "upper echelon" or "TMT," since it is in the latter instance that the bulk of the work on career histories (rather than simply board seats) has occurred.

REFERENCES

Abbott, A., & Hrycak, A. (1990). Measuring resemblance in sequence data: An optimal matching analysis of musicians' careers. *American Journal of Sociology, 96*(1), 144–185.

Arthur, M. B., Hall, D. T., & Lawrence, B. S. (1989). *The handbook of career theory.* Cambridge, UK: Cambridge University Press.

Arthur, M. B., & Rousseau, D. M. (1996a). The boundaryless career as a new employment principle. In M. B. Arthur & D. M. Rousseau (Eds.), *The boundaryless career: A new employment principle for a new organizational era* (pp. 3–20). New York: Oxford University Press.

Arthur, M. B., & Rousseau, D. M. (Eds.). (1996b). *The boundaryless career: A new employment principle for a new organizational era.* New York: Oxford University Press.

Bantel, K. A., & Jackson, S. E. (1989). Top management and innovations in banking: Does the composition of the top team make a difference? *Strategic Management Journal, 10,* 107–124.

Beatty, R. P., & Zajac, E. J. (1987). CEO change and firm performance in large corporations: Succession effects and manager shifts. *Strategic Management Journal, 8,* 305–317.

Becker, G. S. (1964). *Human capital: A theoretical and empirical analysis, with special reference to education* (Vol. 80). New York: National Bureau of Economic Research (distributed by Columbia University Press).

Bell, N. E., & Staw, B. M. (1989). People as sculptors versus sculpture: The roles of personality and personal control in organizations. In M. B. Arthur, D. T. Hall, & B. S. Lawrence (Eds.), *The handbook of career theory* (pp. 227–231). Cambridge, UK: Cambridge University Press.

Beyer, J. M., Chattopadhyay, P., George, E., Glick, W. H., Ogilvie, D., & Pugliese, D. (1997). The selective perception of managers revisited. *Academy of Management Journal, 40*(3), 716–737.

Bird, A. (1996). Careers as repositories of knowledge: Considerations for boundaryless careers. In M. B. Arthur & D. M. Rousseau (Eds.), *The boundaryless career: A new employment principle for a new organizational era* (pp. 150–170). New York: Oxford University Press.

Bitler, M. P., Moskowitz, T. J., & Vissing-Jørgensen, A. (2005). Testing agency theory with entrepreneur effort and wealth. *Journal of Finance, 60*(2), 539–576.

Bunderson, J. S., & Sutcliffe, K. M. (2002). Comparing alternative conceptualizations of functional diversity in management teams: Process and performance effects. *Academy of Management Journal, 45*(5), 875–893.

Burton, M. D., Sørensen, J. B., & Beckman, C. (2002). Coming from good stock: Career histories and new venture formation. In M. Lounsbury & M. Ventresca (Eds.), *Research in the sociology of organizations* (Vol. 19, pp. 229–262). New York: Elsevier.

Cady, S., & Valentine, J. (1999). Team innovation and perceptions of consideration: What difference does diversity make? *Small Group Research, 30*(6), 730–751.

Cappelli, P. (1999). *The new deal at work: Managing the market-driven workforce.* Boston: Harvard Business School Press.

Carpenter, M. A., Pollock, T. G., & Leary, M. M. (2003). Testing a model of reasoned risk-taking: Governance, the experience of principals and agents, and global strategy in high-technology IPO firms. *Strategic Management Journal, 24,* 803–820.

Carpenter, M. A., Sanders, W. G., & Gregersen, H. B. (2000). International assignment experience at the top can make a bottom line difference. *Human Resource Management, 39*(2/3), 277–285.

Carpenter, M. A., Sanders, W. G., & Gregersen, H. B. (2001). Bundling human capital with organizational context: The impact of international assignment experience on multinational firm performance and CEO pay. *Academy of Management Journal, 44*(3), 493–511.

Carpenter, M. A., & Westphal, J. D. (2001). The strategic context of external network ties: Examining the impact of director appointments on board involvement in strategic decision making. *Academy of Management Journal, 44,* 639–660.

Chattopadhyay, P., Glick, W. H., Miller, C., & Huber, G. P. (1999). Determinants of executive beliefs: Comparing functional conditioning and social influence. *Strategic Management Journal, 20*(8), 763–789.

Cohen, O. D., & Dean, T. J. (2005). Information asymmetry and investor valuation of IPOs: Top management team legitimacy as a capital market signal. *Strategic Management Journal, 26,* 683–690.

Coleman, J. S. (1988). Social capital in the creation of human capital. *American Journal of Sociology, 94,* S95–S120.

Daft, R. L., & Lewin, A. Y. (1993). Where are the theories for the "new" organizational forms? An editorial essay. *Organization Science, 4*(4), i–vi.

Daily, C., & Dalton, D. R. (1994). Bankruptcy and corporate governance: The impact of board composition and structure. *Academy of Management Journal, 37*(6), 1603–1617.

D'Aveni, R. (1989). Dependability and organization bankruptcy: An application of agency and prospect theory. *Management Science, 35*(9), 1120–1138.

D'Aveni, R. (1990). Top managerial prestige and organizational bankruptcy. *Organization Science, 1*(2), 121–142.

Dearborn, D. C., & Simon, H. A. (1958). Selective perception: A note on the departmental identifications of executives. *Sociometry, 21,* 140–144.

Deeds, D. L., DeCarolis, D. M., & Coombs, J. E. (1997). The impact of firm-specific capabilities on the amount of capital raised in an initial public offering: Evidence from the biotechnology industry. *Journal of Business Venturing, 12,* 31–46.

Eisenhardt, K. M., & Bourgeois, L. J. (1988). Politics of strategic decision making in high-velocity environments: Toward a midrange theory. *Academy of Management Journal, 31*(4), 737–770.

Eisenhardt, K. M., & Schoonhoven, C. B. (1990). Organizational growth: Linking founding team, strategy, environment, and growth among U.S. semiconductor ventures, 1978–1988. *Administrative Science Quarterly, 35,* 504–529.

Eisenhardt, K. M., & Schoonhoven, C. B. (1996). Resource-based view of strategic alliance formation: Strategic and social effects in entrepreneurial firms. *Organization Science, 7,* 136–150.

Finkelstein, S. (1992). Power in top management teams: Dimensions, measurement, and validation. *Academy of Management Journal, 35*(3), 505–538.

Finkelstein, S., & Hambrick, D. C. (1996). *Strategic leadership: Top executives and their effects on organizations.* St. Paul, MN: West Publishing.

Furtado, E., & Rozeff, M. (1987). The wealth effects of company initiated management changes. *Journal of Financial Economics, 18,* 147–160.

Gompers, P., Lerner, J., & Scharfstein, D. (2005). Entrepreneurial spawning: Public corporations and the genesis of new ventures, 1986 to 1999. *Journal of Finance, 60*(2), 577–614.

Granovetter, M. S. (1973). The strength of weak ties. *American Journal of Sociology, 78*(6), 1360–1380.

Groysberg, B., Nanda, A., & Nohria, N. (2004). The risky business of hiring stars. *Harvard Business Review, May,* 92–100.

Gulati, R., & Westphal, J. D. (1999). Cooperative or controlling? The effects of CEO-board relations and the content of interlocks on the formation of joint ventures. *Administrative Science Quarterly, 44,* 473–506.

Gunz, H. P. (1989). *Careers and corporate cultures: Managerial mobility in large corporations.* Oxford: Basil Blackwell.

Gunz, H. P., & Jalland, R. M. (1996). Managerial careers and business strategies. *Academy of Management Review, 21*(3), 718–756.

Gupta, A. K., & Govindarajan, V. (1984). Business unit strategy, managerial characteristics, and business unit effectiveness at strategy implementation. *Academy of Management Journal, 27*(1), 25–41.

Hall, D. T. (1976). *Careers in organizations.* Glenview, IL: Scott, Foreman.

Hall, D. T., & Mirvis, P. H. (1996). The new protean career: Psychological success and the path with a heart. In D. T. Hall (Ed.), *The career is dead— Long live the career: A relational approach to careers* (pp. 15–45). San Francisco: Jossey-Bass.

Hambrick, D. C. (1989). Guest editor's introduction: Putting top managers back in the strategy picture. *Strategic Management Journal, 10,* 5–15.

Hambrick, D., & D'Aveni, R. (1992). Top team deterioration as part of the downward spiral of large corporate bankruptcies. *Management Science, 38*(10), 1445–1466.

Hambrick, D., & Mason, P. (1984). Upper echelons: The organization as a reflection of its top managers. *Academy of Management Review, 9,* 193–206.

Higgins, M. C. (2001). Changing careers: The effects of social context. *Journal of Organizational Behavior, 22*(6), 595–618.

Higgins, M. C. (2005). *Career imprints: Creating leaders across an industry.* San Francisco: Jossey-Bass.

Higgins, M. C., & Gulati, R. (2003). Getting off to a good start: The effects of upper echelon affiliations on underwriter prestige. *Organization Science, 14*(3), 244–263.

Higgins, M. C., & Gulati, R. (2006). Stacking the deck: The effects of top management backgrounds on investor decisions. *Strategic Management Journal, 27,* 1–25.

Hitt, M. A., & Tyler, B. B. (1991). Strategic decision models: Integrating different perspectives. *Strategic Management Journal, 12*(5), 327–351.

Hoffman, L. R. (1978). The group problem-solving process. In L. Berkowitz (Ed.), *Group processes* (pp. 101–114). New York: Academic Press.

Hoffman, L. R., & Maier, N. R. F. (1961). Quality and acceptance of problem solutions by members of homogeneous and heterogeneous groups. *Journal of Abnormal and Social Psychology, 62,* 401–407.

Holland, J. L. (1973). *Making vocational choices.* Englewood Cliffs, NJ: Prentice Hall.

Janis, I. L. (1972). *Victims of groupthink.* Boston: Houghton Mifflin.

Jones, C. (2001). Co-evolution of entrepreneurial careers, institutional rules and competitive dynamics in American film, 1895–1920. *Organization Studies, 22*(6), 911–944.

Kanter, R. M. (1989). *When giants learn to dance: Mastering the challenge of strategy, management, and careers in the 1990s.* New York: Simon & Schuster.

Kerr, J., & Jackofsky, E. (1989). Aligning manager with strategies: Management development versus selection. *Strategic Management Journal, 10,* 157–170.

Kesner, I. F., & Sebora, T. C. (1994). Executive succession: Past, present and future. *Journal of Management, 20*(2), 327–372.

Kim, J. W., & Higgins, M. C. (2005). Where do alliances come from? The effects of upper echelons on alliance formation. In K. M. Weaver (Ed.), *Proceedings of the 65th annual meeting of the Academy of Management* [CD]. Academy of Management (ISSN 1543–8643).

Knight, D., Pearce, C. L., Smith, K. G., Olian, J. D., Sims, H. P., & Smith, K. A., et al. (1999). Top management team diversity, group process, and strategic consensus. *Strategic Management Journal, 20*(5), 445–465.

Kor, Y. Y. (2003). Experience-based top management team competence and sustained growth. *Organization Science, 14*(6), 707–719.

Lin, Z., & Li, D. (2004). The performance consequences of top management successions: The roles of organizational and environmental contexts. *Group & Organization Management, 29*(1), 32–66.

Lubatkin, M., Chung, K., Rogers, R., & Owens, J. (1986). The effect of executive succession on stockholder wealth of large corporations. *Academy of Management Review, 11,* 497–512.

McLeod, P. L., Lobel, S. A., & Cox, T. H. (1996). Ethnic diversity and creativity in small groups. *Small Group Research, 27,* 248–264.

Merton, R. K. (1973). *The sociology of science.* Chicago: University of Chicago Press.

Miller, C. C., Burke, L. M., & Glick, W. H. (1998). Cognitive diversity among upper-echelon executives: Implications for strategic decision processes. *Strategic Management Journal, 19*(1), 39–58.

Murray, A. I. (1989). Top management group heterogeneity and firm performance. *Strategic Management Journal, 10,* 125–141.

Nystrom, P. C., & McArthur, A. W. (1989). Propositions linking organizations and careers. In M. B. Arthur, D. T. Hall, & B. S. Lawrence (Eds.), *The handbook of career theory* (pp. 490–505). Cambridge, UK: Cambridge University Press.

Pennings, J. M., Lee, K., & Witteloostuijn, A. V. (1998). Human capital, social capital, and firm dissolution. *Academy of Management Journal, 41*(4), 425–440.

Pfeffer, J. (1972). Size and composition of corporate boards of directors: The organization and its environment. *Administrative Science Quarterly, 17*(2), 218–228.

Phillips, R. L., & Hunt, J. G. (Eds.). (1992). *Strategic leadership: A multiorganizational-level perspective.* Westport, CT: Quorum Books.

Reinganum, M. (1985). The effects of executive succession on stockholder wealth: A reply. *Administrative Science Quarterly, 30,* 375–376.

Rousseau, D. M. (1989). Psychological and implied contracts in organizations. *Employee Rights and Responsibilities Journal, 2,* 121–139.

Schein, E. H. (1978). *Career dynamics: Matching individual and organizational needs.* Reading, MA: Addison-Wesley.

Sonnenfeld, J. A., & Peiperl, M. A. (1988). Staffing policy as a strategic response: A typology of career systems. *Academy of Management Review, 13,* 588–600.

Spence, A. M. (1974). *Market signaling: Informational transfer in hiring and related screening processes.* Cambridge, MA: Harvard University Press.

Steiner, I. D. (1972). *Group process and productivity.* San Diego, CA: Academic Press.

Suchman, M. C. (1995). Managing legitimacy: Strategic and institutional approaches. *Academy of Management Review, 20*(3), 571–610.

Sutcliffe, K. M. (1994). What executives notice: Accurate perception in top management teams. *Academy of Management Journal, 37*(5), 1360–1378.

Sutton, R., & Callahan, A. (1987). The stigma of bankruptcy: Spoiled organizational image and its management. *Academy of Management Journal, 30*(3), 405–436.

Useem, M. (1979). The social organization of the American business elite and participation of corporation directors in the governance of American institutions. *American Sociological Review, 44*(4), 553–572.

Walsh, J. P. (1988). Selectivity and selective perception: An investigation of managers' belief structures and information processing. *Academy of Management Journal, 31*(4), 873–896.

Wanous, J. P., & Youtz, M. A. (1986). Solution diversity and the quality of group decisions. *Academy of Management Journal, 29,* 149–158.

Warner, R., Watts, R., & Wruck, K. H. (1988). Stock prices and top management changes. *Journal of Financial Economics, 20,* 461–492.

Westphal, J. D., & Zajac, E. J. (1997). Defections from the inner circle: Social exchange, reciprocity, and the diffusion of board independence in U.S. corporations. *Administrative Science Quarterly, 42,* 161–183.

Wiersema, M. F., & Bantel, K. A. (1992). Top management team demography and corporate strategic change. *Academy of Management Journal, 35,* 91–121.

Whyte, W. H. (1956). *The organization man.* New York: Simon & Schuster.

Worrell, D., & Davidson, W. (1987). The effect of CEO succession on stockholder wealth in large firms following the deaths of the predecessor. *Journal of Management, 13,* 509–515.

Zajac, E. J. (1990). CEO selection, succession, compensation and firm performance: A theoretical integration and empirical analysis. *Strategic Management Journal, 11,* 217–230.

22

CAREERS AND INSTITUTIONS

The Centrality of Careers to Organizational Studies

CANDACE JONES

MARY B. DUNN

areers scholars, through linking persons to institutions, have the potential to contribute important insights to a wide range of organizational issues such as innovation, entrepreneurship, strategy, field formation, the evolution of occupations and professions, and new industry creation to name but a few. More than 15 years ago, Barley (1989) noted the potential for career theory to be at the "vanguard of organization studies" (p. 60). Careers scholars, however, are yet to claim their role as a conceptual bridge and intellectual anchor in these exciting areas. Barley's call to focus on careers as the mechanism linking persons and institutions has gone virtually unheeded by all but a handful of scholars during the past 15 years (for exceptions, see Burton, Sørensen, & Beckman, 2002; Gunz, 1989; Higgins, 2002; Jones, 2001, 2002; Peterson & Anand, 2002; Whitley, 2003).

Because careers link persons to institutions through organizations and occupations, careers provide insight into how stability and change occur within institutions. For example, when organizations and occupations socialize new members into existing roles (e.g., Van Maanen & Barley, 1984; Van Maanen & Schein, 1979) or when leaders imprint established social understandings and templates into organizational structures and strategies (Boeker, 1997; Burton et al., 2002; Gunz & Jalland, 1996; Jones, 2001), institutions are reproduced through careers. Careers may also change institutions when individuals leave one institutional context for another, diffusing their understandings of structures, strategies, and social relationships. For example, entrepreneurs who came from a retail background transformed the understanding of the film industry from one of technology driven by control over patents to content driven by control over narrative stories and stars (Jones, 2001, 2005). Individuals may also transform existing institutions through altering occupational roles and career lines within organizations (Lounsbury & Kaghan, 2001).

Although the intimate relationship between careers and institutions was described by Everett Hughes, only a few institutional scholars use careers as a lens to illuminate institutional change and stability. As Hughes (1936) states so succinctly, "The movements of people and the bearing of such movements . . . are to institutions as both cause and effect" (pp. 182–183). We extend Hughes's insight into the relationship between careers and institutions by examining the properties and processes of both careers and institutions. Tolbert and Zucker (1996) note that institutional scholars have given little attention to the processes of institutions but instead have mainly focused on the properties that affect a qualitative state of institutionalization, treating structures as simply institutionalized or not and missing considerable insights about the process by which institutionalization occurs. By better understanding the properties and process of careers and institutions, we showcase the central role of careers on institutional change and stability.

We begin by identifying the relationship between careers and institutions and how, because of this relationship, careers may provide important insights into stability and change in institutions. Next, we review the literature, identifying two prevalent ways in which scholars have conceptualized the relationship between careers and institutions—as property and as process—and how these conceptions of careers inform our understanding of change and stability in institutions. We also describe the interaction of careers and institutions, both of which are properties and processes. Finally, we identify three moments where we can see most clearly the relationship between careers and institutions: when institutions are being created, reproduced, and transformed. We do not develop a process model of how these institutional moments may be related to one another, but instead we review how researchers have conceptualized the relationship between careers and institutions.

CAREERS AND INSTITUTIONS

An individual's career, objectively, involves a series of roles or offices with associated statuses (Hughes, 1937), which are typically revealed through a sequence of jobs or work experiences (Arthur, Hall, & Lawrence, 1989). Institutions are "establishments of relative permanence of a distinctly social sort" (Hughes, 1936, p. 180). Hughes (1939) explains that this includes "a set of mores or formal rules fulfilled by people acting collectively in complementary capacities or offices" (p. 297). This calls attention to the role that people play in shaping institutions while simultaneously being shaped by them (Higgins and Dillon, Chapter 21).

A key insight of Hughes was that careers and institutions are intimately connected and mutually reinforcing. Careers show the movement of people across offices and statuses, while institutions reveal how individuals in various roles, statuses, and offices are interdependent in their actions. For example, an aspiring architect must attend architectural school, where he or she is trained by professors, processed by administrators, and further socialized by participating in charrettes with fellow students whose designs are judged by established architects. On graduation, this aspiring architect apprentices for 3 years in an architectural firm working on projects with principal architects, project architects, CAD operators, and a variety of other specialists such as engineers, interior designers, and building contractors. To practice, the architect must pass a licensing exam developed and evaluated by a select committee of established architects and regulatory board members. In pursuing this career, an architect is shaped by institutional demands such as licensing, apprenticeship, and building codes, but may also, under the right environmental conditions, alter the institution of architecture by forging new kinds of roles and sequences of roles such as architect-engineers who possessed the requisite knowledge and skills to invent and build modern skyscrapers (Thornton, Jones, & Kury, 2005).

To understand how careers link individuals and institutions through organizations and occupations, we need to examine the "ecology of institutions" (Hughes, 1936), anchoring careers and institutions in both time and space (Abbott,

1997). A person's career unfolds in sequences of roles in occupations and organizations, placing the individual in temporal and spatial context. To locate organizations and occupations within their spatial context, institutional scholars focus on interdependence and mutual influence among organizations, occupations, and professions (DiMaggio, 1991). While scholars have examined careers using both the individual and institutional levels of analysis, they have not attended to the important role of careers as the mechanisms that link persons to institutions.

CAREERS AS PROPERTY AND AS PROCESS

Careers have been conceived of in the literature as either property or process, but rarely have both conceptions been used together. Careers as property capture the prevailing roles—their relationships and understandings—of a time period. Scholars who focus on careers as property treat career histories as a repository of individual experiences and knowledge (Bird, 1994) or of a social era's prevalent structures, relations, and practices that become encoded into the person (e.g., Fligstein, 1991; Thornton & Ocasio, 1999). Careers as process reveal how the sequences of roles may reinforce or alter prevailing roles, relationships, and understandings. Scholars who view careers as processes focus on uncovering how the sequences of roles are shaped by or reshape an organization, occupation, or field (e.g., Abbott & Tsay, 2000). In fact, career and institutional scholars often use structuration to examine how careers unfold within organizations (e.g., Gunz, 1989; Whitley, 2003), occupations (Barley, 1989; Barley & Tolbert, 1997; Lounsbury & Kaghan 2001), and institutional fields (DiMaggio, 1991). By combining these two perspectives—career as property and as process—we illuminate how and when institutions change or remain stable.

Careers as Property: Imprinting Social Practices and Understandings

Scholars who view careers as property of individuals, organizations, and occupations often draw on Stinchcombe's (1965) famous "imprinting" thesis, which suggests that entrepreneurs and leaders encode the dominant practices and mental models of an era into their organizational structures and strategies (Gunz & Jalland, 1996). When careers encode and replicate existing social practices and understandings within an institution, stability results. For example, in the U.K. Civil Service, the administrative class kept the specialists under their thumb by ensuring that their career structure never included access to the top positions (e.g., Ridley, 1968). Thus, the career system replicated and reinforced existing social practices and understandings of who should have access to influential positions in the organization, creating what Kanter (1977) referred to as the "homosocial reproduction of managers."

Institutional change occurs when individuals migrate from one institutional context to another, diffusing social practices and understandings. These individuals act as "Johnny Appleseeds," planting new understandings, relations, and practices (DiMaggio & Powell, 1983). For example, scholars have examined how executive or entrepreneurial migration is related to new strategies or high rates of innovation when migration crosses organizational or institutional boundaries (Boeker, 1997; Kraatz & Moore, 2002; Pfeffer & Leblebici, 1973). They have also studied how shifts in institutional environments, which obsolete some and value more highly other logics and skills, are reflected in executive succession in organizations within a field (Fligstein, 1991; Thornton & Ocasio, 1999). Careers are also a property when they act as signals of competencies or status that facilitate access to critical resources such as funding for movie projects (Faulkner, 1987; Jones, 2002), new high-technology firms (Burton et al., 2002), or initial public offer success for biotechnology firms (Higgins, 2002; Higgins & Gulati, 2003).

Scholars who view careers as property employ cross-sectional or a series of static comparisons of specific time periods. Institutional stability is driven by control over the career system, which reproduces similar individuals into established roles within occupations and organizations. Institutional change is also seen in the career system, when leaders with different understandings, training, and relations are selected and when they bring these new understandings and practices into their roles in organizations and occupations (Fligstein, 1991; Thornton & Ocasio, 1999). In contrast to this focus on comparing the content of roles, occupations, or organizations at points in time, scholars who view careers as process focus on how standardizing or altering the sequences of roles that individuals experience over time shape institutions.

Careers as Process: Altering or Standardizing Role Sequences

Scholars who view careers as a process focus on the sequences of roles with their associated offices and statuses experienced by individuals, capturing temporal dynamics and locating individuals within a particular institutional context (Abbott, 1997; Hughes, 1936; for review, see Abbott & Tsay, 2000). Institutional stability results when careers socialize individuals by standardizing a particular sequence of roles and experiences across generations of individuals, which reproduces social knowledge attached to a role in a more reliable way. For example, the professions typically follow a lock step format of training. To become a physician, one must attend medical school, do a 2-year residency, move onto an area of specialization in a fellowship, pass board certification exams, and then finally join a practice or gain a hospital appointment.

When careers are processes, institutional change becomes encoded in and enacted by different roles and sequences of these roles. For example, the rise of centralized capital in the early to mid-1900s, and its associated need for regional rather than local banks, transformed banking careers at Lloyd's Bank from immobility based on local identity and ascription to mobility based on social class and achievement (Stovel, Savage, & Bearman, 1996). The creation of art museums as a field with a shared ideology of accessible works and educating the public was intimately related to the rise of new occupational careers (professionally trained and accredited art staff for museums), a related knowledge base (e.g., exhibits and conservation), professional associations, and expert staff roles (DiMaggio, 1991).

Careers as process examine the order of role sequences that individuals experience to capture how changes in sequences are related to changes in institutions (Abbott & Hrycak, 1990). This approach is similar to institutional scholars who examine how changes in sequences of events alter understandings and practices (Sewell, 1996;

Thornton et al., 2005). Sewell (1996) describes how the storming of the Bastille altered French citizens' understanding of their role as citizens and their relationship with the French Monarchy, triggering the French Revolution.

Institutional stability is driven by standardizing the sequence and content of roles and by controlling who may enter what roles within an occupation or organization, reinforcing existing social knowledge. Institutional change occurs when either the sequence of roles or the entrants who play these roles are altered within an organization or occupation. When individuals experience different sequences of roles or succession routes, it exposes occupations and organizations to new understandings, practices, and relations (Fligstein, 1991; Thornton & Ocasio, 1999), thereby increasing the likelihood that roles, and corresponding institutions, will be reinterpreted and potentially changed. By examining careers as processes—changes in sequences of roles and who occupies these roles—scholars avoid reification in how careers are conceptualized and researched (Evetts, 1992).

Next, we describe institutional properties and processes, which capture the content and construction of social knowledge, and suggest that careers, which socialize individuals into occupations and organizations, are a primary vehicle for social knowledge to become attached to the roles that populate our organizations and occupations within institutions.

Careers and Institutional Properties and Processes

Institutional properties capture the social knowledge of how things work, or should work, that is attached to roles and role relations. Properties are seen in the division of labor (Hughes, 1937) or in institutional logics, whereby understandings of identities, governance mechanisms, mission and values, and forms of capital, guide behavior within a particular institutional context (Friedland & Alford, 1991; Thornton, 2004; Weber, 1947). This social knowledge is encapsulated in roles and role relations (Berger & Luckmann, 1967). A career focuses our attention on how individuals enact their roles and role relations in organizations and occupations that make up institutions.

Tolbert and Zucker (1996) take a phenomenological approach to build a theoretical model of institutional processes. Institutional processes encode or disassociate social knowledge from roles and role relationships through habitualization, objectification, sedimentation, and deinstitutionalization (Berger & Luckmann, 1967; Oliver, 1992; Tolbert & Zucker, 1996; Zucker, 1977). In habitualization, new roles and relationships among roles are created in response to a specific need or problem (Tolbert & Zucker, 1996). In addition, individuals will create new roles and role relations when they move from one institutional context to another and import their previous knowledge to the new situation. In the early stages of creation, a new role or career path may not make sense to others so it may have a variety of names, signaling this confusion. For example, in the early days of film narratives, screenwriters were called scenarist (after those who painted scenes) rather than playwrights because of differences between film and theater. In contrast, actors' roles were quite similar so the role and name transferred easily from theater to film. This exemplifies that objectification, where social knowledge of roles and role relationships become social facts because they are collectively shared, which facilitates their transfer across generations of role occupants (Zucker, 1977) and industries. In sedimentation, roles and role relationships are taken for granted by individuals. For example, screenwriters have had a guild for more than 70 years and membership in the industry is defined by belonging to a guild. Film schools, not culinary schools, teach the craft of screenwriting and this is seen as obvious and taken for granted by individuals. In deinstitutionalization, individuals question their assumptions about particular roles and role relations that were previously taken for granted. For example, film animation is increasingly done on computers by programmers rather than by artists. Animators come from different backgrounds and use distinct skills. Sequences of events may trigger deinstitutionalization of how roles and role relationships are understood, accumulating into new understandings and perceptions. For example, the rise of computer video games means that audiences see and understand animation differently than earlier generations. Disney is in the

process of retraining its animators to understand and enact their roles differently with one another and with directors to tap into and meet these new understandings by audiences. The social knowledge of the artist has become increasingly disassociated from animated movies being replaced by computer programming, deinstitutionalizing the grip artists held over animation, and requiring a new knowledge base for the role and altering their role relations with directors and other movie personnel.

Careers and institutions are ends and means—both have properties and processes. A career highlights the relationship between persons and institutions, whereas institutions highlight how knowledge is socially constructed but locally enacted through individuals. By marrying institutions and careers, we illuminate the role that individuals play in institutional processes and how institutional properties and processes shape individual actions through how knowledge is socially constructed and encoded into individuals through career systems. Table 22.1 provides a summary of the properties and processes of institutions and careers and how they influence one another.

Next, we examine how careers as processes and properties link individuals to institutional moments of creation, reproduction, and transformation (DiMaggio, 1988) to provide a fuller understanding of how careers illuminate institutional change and stability.

CAREERS AND INSTITUTIONS: CREATION, REPRODUCTION, AND TRANSFORMATION

We review relevant literature to show how career properties and processes link individuals to institutions during creation, reproduction, and transformation (see Table 22.2). Since the processes and properties of institutions and careers are most easily seen during formation and transformation, we focus more on institutional creation and transformation.

Institutional Creation

Institutional creation occurs when entrepreneurs enter into new arenas, launching new careers and new industries as first steps in field

Table 22.1   Properties and Processes of Careers and Institutions

		Institutions	
		Property	*Process*
Careers	*Property*	Social understandings and relations are encoded into individuals Empirical exemplars: Fligstein's (1991) comparison of careers that occupied organizations during different decades; Thornton's (2002) comparison of publishing executives editorial versus market logics	Institutional events alter understandings of roles, role relations, and who can enter roles Empirical exemplars: Jones (2001) demonstrated a rise in immigration and a shift in film audiences altered understanding of film from technology to content. This triggered a shift in entrepreneurs who have distinct career backgrounds; Barley (1986) described how new imaging technologies changed the roles and relationships between radiologists and radiological technologists
	Process	Standardizing the sequences by which individuals experience roles creates reproduction of these roles Empirical exemplar: Reed (1978) showed that standardizing sequences excludes specialists from high-level foreign service positions. Altering the sequences of roles also can change the content of the institution Empirical exemplar: Stovel et al. (1996) showed that the centralization of capital shifted careers from local identity and immobility to social class and mobility	New roles are created and new sequences of work roles evolve with the creation of new fields and institutions Empirical exemplar: Smith-Doerr (1999) depicted how the new biotechnology industry created new roles and unclear career sequences for participants. For instance, it is possible for PhD-level life scientists to move between academia and industry. It is possible for new PhD graduates to do a postdoc in a biotech firm before attaining an academic position

formation. This entrepreneurial activity is often sparked by changes in regulations, technologies, or immigration and enacted by entrepreneurs who are optimally positioned structurally and personally motivated to see and take advantage of these opportunities and realize their interests (Hargadon & Douglass, 2001; Jones, 2001; Peterson & Berger, 1971).

When individuals shape institutions through careers, entrepreneurs import specific beliefs, skills, models, and practices, in other words a set of institutional building blocks (DiMaggio & Powell, 1983), acquired from previous experience into a new context. These building blocks serve to guide action and relationships and are often reframings of existing beliefs and organizational models for a new audience (Burton, 2001; Hargadon & Sutton, 1997; Jones, 2001). For instance, early founders in the biotechnology industry were elite academic scientists who

Table 22.2   Careers and Institutions: Creation, Reproduction, and Transformation

	Creation	*Reproduction*	*Transformation*
Career Properties of Institutions Flow of individuals through the social order	Individuals experience roles and role sequences as evolving and ambiguous

Example: Individual careers move between industry and academia rather than strict separation in the biotechnology industry | Individuals experience key roles and role sequences that constitute a career as clearly defined

Example: Medical students at most medical schools are put into the clinic sooner to increase motivation and quality of patient care | Individuals have the opportunity to combine roles and/ or role sequences to initiate and reflect change in social order

Example: Medical students at HST experience alternative course sequences and also combined roles— PhD-MD—to train and enhance their ability to invent new medical technologies |
| *Institutional Properties of Careers* Design, reproduction, and change of social order by powerful actors through key events | Institutional event creates new roles and role relations

Example: NIH's active support and creation of the Medical Science Training Program (MSTP) to preserve scientific rigor of medical training | Institutional events reenact role relations and sequences

Example: Yearly matching of medical students to hospital residencies | Institutional events combine existing roles and role sequences

Example: Government adopts design-build process that integrates roles and alters sequence of roles. Architect is no longer the lead firm in a sequential process. Architects, engineers, and contractors form team that jointly enacts their roles |
| *Career Processes* How individuals' careers influence institutions | Entrepreneurs migrate to new field or industry, importing career structures and organizing templates | Incumbents select, socialize, and promote newcomers into existing roles and role sequences, reproducing structure | Boundary spanners who are exposed to alternative practices and models hybridize them by combining existing roles and altering role sequences |
| *Institutional Processes* How institutions shape individuals' careers | Habitualization of roles in new industry or occupation to form field | Objectification and sedimentation of established roles, role sequences, and role relations | Deinstitutionalization of existing roles and role sequences and reinstitutionalization of new roles and role sequences |

SOURCE: HST, Health Sciences and Technology; NIH, National Institutes of Health.

imported beliefs and practices from academe to their new biotechnology firms, including the values of scientific research, publishing, and interorganizational collaboration (Kenney, 1986; Powell, Koput, & Smith-Doerr, 1996; Smith-Doerr, 1999; Zucker & Darby, 1996; Zuker, Darby, & Brewer, 1994). When taking biotechnology firms public, executives who came from the pharmaceutical industry imported different models of business practices that were shaped by their previous experiences in the other context (Higgins & Gulati, 2003; Higgins, 2002). Jones's (2001) study of the origins of the film industry highlights how early film founders imported mental models from manufacturing careers, bringing an economizing logic of action to film and emphasizing technical skills and careers within their firms. In this way, entrepreneurs' previous career experiences, which tap into specific social practices and mental models, can profoundly shape how work is conducted in new organizations and industries, influencing field formation.

During institutional creation, roles are emerging, which makes for unclear understandings of a role and ambiguous boundaries in the role relations needed to carry out work. For individuals, career experiences are likely to involve multiple and unfamiliar roles (Eisenhardt & Schoonhoven, 1990), creating liabilities of newness as participants seek to work out their understandings of roles and role relations (Stinchcombe, 1965). New roles and role relations also lack legitimacy, which depends on understandings that were taken for granted and acceptance of mental models by internal participants and critical external parties or sponsors (Aldrich & Fiol, 1994). For instance, Smith-Doerr (1999) argues that respected academic founders helped biotechnology quickly become a legitimate avenue for cutting-edge science and research career paths when industry science was typically viewed as "not real science." Since respected academic scientists endorsed biotechnology from the very beginning, they were able to establish career paths and practices that helped biotechnology careers to be seen as analogous to academe and became a legitimate career option for PhDs in life sciences.

One of the primary tasks of entrepreneurs is to habitualize roles and role relations—that is,

to create commonly shared perceptions and understandings for action and interaction. One way in which entrepreneurs habitualize the roles and role sequences defining a career is to import legitimate models from one context into the new context or have legitimate actors sponsor these models, as described above in biotechnology. In addition, the use of formal roles and models increases common perceptions among participants and eases the transfer of these perceptions from one generation to the next (Zucker, 1977). In this way, entrepreneurs have considerable influence over the way roles and careers will be enacted, and this influence can be strongest in new contexts where no dominant model of career path exists. Saxenian's (1994) work demonstrates the profound influence that career sequences can have in organizations and between regions in the same industry. For instance, careers in Silicon Valley were enacted across firms, enhancing rates of firm foundings, whereas along Route 128 in Massachusetts, careers occurred within firms, dampening new firm-founding rates. There is much to be gained by studying career histories as sequences as well as property to illuminate the dynamics of organizations, occupations, and fields.

Institutional Reproduction

Institutional reproduction occurs when incumbents select and socialize newcomers into established roles and promote those who adhere to expected role behaviors, ensuring the stability of organizational, occupational, or professional roles over generations (e.g., Van Maanen & Barley, 1984; Van Maanen & Schein, 1979). For instance, "The scientific apprentice is physics' way of ensuring the survival of physics" (Van Maanen & Schein, 1979, p. 211). Once selected, socialization is the process by which people enter the social structure (Hall, 1987) and learn how to act, think, and see the world through the eyes of more experienced colleagues (Van Maanen & Schein, 1979). The passing of positions or knowledge from generation to generation increases predictability (Van Maanen & Schein, 1979) and transmits shared culture across participants over time (Selznick, 1957; Van Maanen & Barley, 1984). Institutional researchers have focused on how institutions persist when leaders are socialized in a similar way and are relatively homogeneous (Selznick, 1957). Together, selection and socialization create a system for reproducing roles, either within an organization or across occupational communities of individuals who share professional identities, knowledge, and values, and see themselves as engaged in similar work.

Institutions shape individuals when the content of roles, role relations, and the typical role sequence for a career are widely understood by participants. When this happens, careers are a means of replicating social understandings and structures (Abbott, 1997; Gunz, 1989; Hughes, 1958). Through this process of reproduction over time, careers enact and reinforce existing social institutions because stable roles and role sequences guide and shape individuals' movement through an organization or occupation. For example, longitudinal data on the careers of elites in metropolitan police departments from 1870 through 1947 showed that career sequences and backgrounds of police became less diverse and more standardized over time, which reduced disruption due to turnover (Maniha, 1974). In Hollywood, studio musicians moved from routinized work in television series and movies to creative work on theatrical films with larger budgets and bigger stars (Faulkner, 1987). This standardization of career sequences restricted interaction to a small set of freelancers of similar status and experience who worked repeatedly with one another (Faulkner & Anderson, 1987). Because insiders tend to select those who are similar to them, they reproduce organizational and occupational roles. In this way, leaders may become a "pool of almost interchangeable individuals" (DiMaggio & Powell, 1983, p. 152) where the movement of executives among firms stabilizes and coordinates interorganizational behavior (Pfeffer & Leblebici, 1973) and diffuses practices among organizations in a field (DiMaggio & Powell, 1983). This system of selection and socialization is associated with established occupations in relatively stable organizations and occupations as it tends to reinforce existing roles and provides few opportunities for change to occur to the dominant models.

Institutions shape individuals when roles and role sequences are standardized. In this case, career structures are perceived as objective and less likely to be questioned, inhibiting change (Berger & Luckmann, 1967; Zucker, 1977). Research on women's careers in finance, after the enforcement of women's employment rights in the 1970s, showed that women experienced more freedom in pursuing finance careers but also greater rigidity in their career trajectories, effectively inhibiting change by restricting where women could move (Blair-Loy, 1999). Organizations, through their formal career systems, may buffer themselves from external demands for change. For example, after World War II, key stakeholders in the United States, such as the Congress, the press, and other agencies, demanded that the Foreign Service Office (FSO) move into more specialized areas and open up alternative career paths for specialists (Reed, 1978). However, the Foreign Service was able to resist these demands and buffer itself from changes in its environment by making "seniority the most important determination of promotion from one personal rank or grade to the next" (Reed, 1978, p. 408). In essence, the alternative career path of specialist, which housed the newest and most different FSO members, was decoupled from the rest of the organization, allowing the FSO to neutralize demands for change. In this way, stability was created, inhibiting transformation either by allowing little room for deviance from legitimate standards or by curtailing the movement of "deviants" through the system.

Institutional Transformation

Institutional transformation occurs when one set of goals, values, and guiding principles is supplanted by another among organizations in an industry or field. For example, chief executive officers with career backgrounds first from manufacturing, next sales and marketing, and then finance supplanted one another and dominated Fortune 100 firms during different eras (Fligstein, 1991), executives in higher education publishing shifted from publishing to business backgrounds (Thornton & Ocasio, 1999), and entrepreneurs with backgrounds in retail and marketing usurped those with manufacturing and technology backgrounds in the film industry (Jones, 2001). However, the change process need not always reflect total replacement of one set of values for another; in fact, change can involve the hybridization or blending of existing values and guiding principles with those from alternative arenas (Sewell, 1992). Thus, change involves the dual processes of replacing or altering old practices with the adoption or creation of new practices. The extent of change, whether total replacement or some level of hybridization occurs, may be a matter of degree and is an empirical question.

New roles and role sequences are important for understanding how institutions may be transformed. New roles herald the importance of new knowledge or skill sets needed in organizations and occupations (e.g., chief information officer with the rise of information technology and chief medical officer with rise of medical technology). New role sequences allow occupants to bring new knowledge and understandings to enacting their roles. New sequences may also create competing understandings of the appropriate way to enact a role. For instance, the roles of clinical physician and physician-scientists came to light in the late 1960s and early 1970s. Kimberly (1981) chronicled the creation of a new medical school in 1970 that broke with tradition and placed students in the clinic sooner. Instead of waiting until the conclusion of the second year of medical school, students interacted with patients from the start. During the same time period, the National Institutes of Health (NIH) actively supported increasing the scientific rigor of medical programs by creating the Medical Science Training Program in 1964 to support research training for medical students that leads to a combined MD/PhD degree. The NIH also encouraged and provided funding for programs such as the Health Science and Technology Program at Harvard Medical School and Massachusetts Institute of Technology to train medical students to bridge the gap between basic science, engineering, and clinical research. In these programs, students typically do not interact with patients until the third year when they have a solid scientific foundation. Career sequences, including educational and professional training, can make a critical difference in understanding the knowledge that leaders will bring to bear in solving problems. For example, publishing executives with backgrounds in editing saw networks as solutions to organizational problems of resource competition, whereas executives with business backgrounds saw marketing and finance as solutions to problems of resource competition (Thornton, 2002).

When participants are exposed to new roles and role sequences, this undermines their taken-for-granted assumptions, which is a key step in deinstitutionalizing standard practices (Oliver, 1992). In fact, both Scott (1995) and Powell (1991) propose that the competing claims of professionals can introduce change within a field. When professionals have competing understandings of appropriate roles and sequences, it can introduce change by creating ambiguity over taken-for-granted practices. Recent research examines how leaders, who migrate to organizations along less typical career paths, are more likely to create institutional transformation. Kraatz and Moore (2002) in their study examining U.S. liberal arts colleges' adoption of vocationally oriented programs, which was considered antithetical to the goals and values of liberal arts, found that schools that adopted such programs were more likely to have had college presidents who migrated from less prestigious schools and schools already possessing these programs. They also found that the liberal arts colleges preserved their core curriculum or "technical core" while ushering in the professional courses, reflecting hybridization rather than total replacement of practices and logics. These findings suggest that different career sequences, reflected in distinct migration patterns, may speed or impede change. Thus, although rarely studied, career sequences can provide important insights into institutional transformation by elucidating how competencies are developed, where new knowledge comes from, and when exposure to alternative understandings is likely to provoke questions about taken-for-granted practices, setting deinstitutionalization processes in motion.

DIRECTIONS FOR RESEARCH: CHALLENGES AND OPPORTUNITIES

A key challenge in reviewing research on the relationship between careers and institutions is that careers researchers rarely connect their studies on individuals' careers to their effects on organizations, occupations, or fields. By doing so, careers researchers have difficulty showing how individual careers may drive larger social forces and institutions rather than being the victim of such forces. In contrast, institutional scholars focus on the relationships between organizations, occupations, and fields, rarely including individuals. Thus, some scholars argue that they "eviscerate—literally 'remove the guts from'—institutions, and thus often result in 'hollowed-out' explanations of institutional change and persistence" (quoting Stinchcombe in Kraatz & Moore, 2002, p. 139). Clearly, the relationship between individuals and institutions is critical for understanding key phenomena of interest to organizational scholars and practitioners. Careers, as the mechanism that links individuals to institutions, provide a lens for understanding and illuminating these phenomena.

A careers lens has the potential to contribute to institutional perspectives by serving as a bridge between the old institutional theorists who focused on leadership and change within organizations and neoinstitutional theorists who focused on diffusion processes of practices within a field of organizations. In addition, by examining career as processes—specifically the sequence of career roles—we may gain insight into when and how change is possible. To date, no research that we are aware of has examined how career processes—different sequences of work experiences—rather than career properties captured by career backgrounds may generate or transform new industries, occupations, or institutions, providing an area ripe for future research.

Careers research has the potential to provide a conceptual bridge between micro- and macro-levels of analysis and an intellectual anchor to phenomena of keen interest to organizational scholars such as new industry creation, entrepreneurship, occupational change, and field formation. When careers are the means for understanding complex and important social phenomena, then careers research will move to the vanguard of organization studies.

REFERENCES

Abbott, A. (1997). Of time and space: The contemporary relevance of the Chicago School. *Social Forces, 75,* 1149–1182.

Abbott, A., & Hrycak, A. (1990). Measuring resemblance in sequence data: An optimal matching analysis of musicians' careers. *American Journal of Sociology, 96,* 144–185.

Abbott, A., & Tsay, A. (2000). Sequence analysis and optimal matching methods in sociology: Review and prospect. *Sociological Methods and Research, 29*(1), 3–33.

Aldrich, H. E., & Fiol, C. M. (1994). When fools rush in? The institutional context of industry creation. *Academy of Management Review, 19*(4), 645–670.

Arthur, M. B., Hall, D. T., & Lawrence, B. S. (1989). Generating new directions in career theory: The case for a transdisciplinary approach. In M. B. Arthur, D. T. Hall, & B. S. Lawrence (Eds.), *The handbook of career theory* (pp. 7–25). Cambridge, UK: Cambridge University Press.

Barley, S. R. (1986). Technology as an occasion for structuring: Evidence from observations of CT scanners and the social order of radiology departments. *Administrative Science Quarterly, 31*(1), 78–108.

Barley, S. R. (1989). Careers, identities, and institutions: The legacy of the Chicago school of sociology. In D. T. Hall, B. S. Lawrence, & M. B. Arthur (Eds.), *The handbook of career theory* (pp. 41–60). Cambridge, UK: Cambridge University Press.

Barley, S. R., & Tolbert, P. S. (1997). Institutionalization and structuration: Studying the links between action and institution. *Organization Studies, 18*(1), 93–117.

Berger, P., & Luckmann, T. (1967). *The social construction of reality.* New York: Doubleday.

Bird, A. (1994). Careers as repositories of knowledge: A new perspective on boundaryless careers. *Journal of Organizational Behavior, 15*(4), 325–344.

Blair-Loy, M. (1999). Career patterns of executive women in finance: An optimal matching analysis. *American Journal of Sociology, 105*(5), 1346–1397.

Boeker, W. (1997). Executive migration and strategic change: The effect of top manager movement on product-market entry. *Administrative Science Quarterly, 42*(2), 213–236.

Burton, M. D. (2001). The company they keep: Founders' models for organizing new firms. In C. B. Schoonhoven & E. Romanelli (Eds.), *The entrepreneurship dynamic: Origins of entrepreneurship and the evolution of industries* (pp. 13–39). Stanford, CA: Stanford University Press.

Burton, M. D., Sørensen, J. B., & Beckman, C. M. (2002). Coming from good stock: Career histories and new venture formation. *Research in the Sociology of Organizations, 19,* 229–262.

DiMaggio, P. (1988). Interest and agency in institutional theory. In L. G. Zucker (Ed.), *Institutional patterns and organizations* (pp. 3–21). Cambridge, MA: Ballinger.

DiMaggio, P. (1991). Constructing an organizational field as a professional project: U.S. art museums, 1920–1940. In W. W. Powell & P. J. DiMaggio (Eds.), *The new institutionalism in organizational analysis* (pp. 267–292). Chicago: University of Chicago Press.

DiMaggio, P., & Powell, W. (1983). The iron cage revisited: Institutional isomorphism and collective rationality in organizational fields. *American Sociological Review, 48,* 147–160.

Eisenhardt, K. M., & Schoonhoven, C. B. (1990). Organizational growth: Linking founding team, strategy, environment, and growth among U.S. semiconductor ventures, 1978–1988. *Administrative Science Quarterly, 35*(3), 504–529.

Evetts, J. (1992). Dimensions of career: Avoiding reification in the analysis of change. *Sociology, 26*(1), 1–21.

Faulkner, R. R. (1987). *Music on demand: Composers and careers in the Hollywood film industry.* New Brunswick, NJ: Transaction Books.

Faulkner, R. R., & Anderson, A. B. (1987). Short-term projects and emergent careers: Evidence from Hollywood. *American Journal of Sociology, 92,* 879–909.

Fligstein, N. (1991). The structural transformation of American industry: An institutional account of the causes and consequences of diversification in the largest firms, 1919–1979. In W. W. Powell & P. J. DiMaggio (Eds.), *The new institutionalism in organizational analysis* (pp. 311–336). Chicago: University of Chicago Press.

Friedland, R., & Alford, R. (1991). Bringing society back in: Symbols, practices, and institutional contradictions. In W. W. Powell & P. J. DiMaggio (Eds.), *The new institutionalism in organizational analysis* (pp. 232–263). Chicago: University of Chicago Press.

Gunz, H. (1989). The dual meaning of managerial careers: Organizational and individual levels of analysis. *Journal of Management Studies, 26,* 225–250.

Gunz, H. P., & Jalland, R. M. (1996). Managerial careers and business strategies. *Academy of Management Review, 21*(3), 718–756.

Hall, D. T. (1987). Careers and socialization. *Journal of Management, 13*(2), 301–321.

Hargadon, A., & Sutton, R. (1997). Technology brokering and innovation in a product development firm. *Administrative Science Quarterly, 42,* 716–749.

Hargadon, A. B., & Douglass, Y. (2001). When innovations meet institutions: Edison and the design of the electric light. *Administrative Science Quarterly, 46*(3), 476–501.

Higgins, M. C. (2002). Careers creating industries: Some early evidence from the biotechnology industry. In M. A. Peiperl, M. B. Arthur, & N. Anand (Eds.), *Career creativity: Explorations in the remaking of work* (pp. 280–297). Oxford: Oxford University Press.

Higgins, M. C., & Gulati, R. (2003). Stacking the deck: The effects of upper echelon affiliations for entrepreneurial firms. *Organization Science, 14*(3), 244–263.

Hughes, E. C. (1936). The ecological aspect of institutions. *American Sociological Review, 1,* 180–189.

Hughes, E. C. (1937). Institutional office and the person. *American Journal of Sociology, 43*(3), 404–413.

Hughes, E. C. (1939). Institutions. In R. E. Park & E. Reuter (Eds.), *An outline of the principles of sociology* (p. 281–330). New York: Barnes & Nobles.

Hughes, E. C. (1958). *Men and their work.* New York: Free Press.

Jones, C. (2001). Coevolution of entrepreneurial careers, institutional rules and competitive dynamics in American film, 1895–1920. *Organization Studies, 22*(6), 911–945.

Jones, C. (2002). Signaling expertise: How signals shape careers in creative industries. In M. A. Peiperl, M. B. Arthur, & N. Anand (Eds.), *Career creativity: Explorations in the remaking of work* (pp. 209–228). Oxford: Oxford University Press.

Jones, C. (2005). From technology to content: The shift in dominant logic in the early American film industry. In T. Lant, J. Lampel, & J. Shamsie (Eds.), *The business of culture: Strategic perspectives on entertainment and media* (pp. 195–204). Mahwah, NJ: Lawrence Erlbaum.

Kanter, R. M. (1977). *Men and women of the corporation.* New York: Basic Books.

Kenney, M. (1986). *Biotechnology: The university-industrial complex.* New Haven, CT: Yale University Press.

Kimberly, J. (1981). Managerial innovation. In P. Nystrom & W. Starbuck (Eds.), *Handbook of organizational design* (pp. 84–104). New York: Oxford University Press.

Kraatz, M. S., & Moore, J. H. (2002). Executive migration and institutional change. *Academy of Management Journal, 45,* 120–143.

Lounsbury, M., & Kaghan, W. N. (2001). Organizations, occupations and the structuration of work. In R. Hodson (Series Ed.) & S. Vallas (Vol. Ed.), *Research in the sociology of work: Vol. 10. The transformation of work* (pp. 25–50). Amsterdam: Elsevier.

Maniha, J. K. (1974). The standardization of elite careers in bureaucratizing organizations. *Social Forces, 53*(2), 282–288.

Oliver, C. (1992). The antecedents of deinstitutionalization. *Organization Studies, 13*(4), 563–588.

Peterson, R. A., & Anand, N. (2002). How chaotic careers create orderly fields. In M. A. Peiperl, M. B. Arthur, & N. Anand (Eds.), *Career creativity: Explorations in the remaking of work* (pp. 257–279). Oxford: Oxford University Press.

Peterson, R. A., & Berger, D. G. (1971). Entrepreneurship in organizations: Evidence from the popular music industry. *Administrative Science Quarterly, 10,* 97–106.

Pfeffer, J., & Leblebici, H. (1973). Executive recruitment and the development of interfirm organizations. *Administrative Science Quarterly, 18*(4), 449–461.

Powell, W. W. (1991). Expanding the scope of institutional analysis. In W. W. Powell & P. J. DiMaggio (Eds.), *The new institutionalism in organizational analysis* (pp. 183–203). Chicago: University of Chicago Press.

Powell, W., Koput, K., & Smith-Doerr, L. (1996). Interorganizational collaboration and the locus of innovation: Networks of learning in biotechnology. *Administrative Science Quarterly, 41,* 116–145.

Reed, T. L. (1978). Organizational change in the American Foreign Service, 1925–1965: The utility of cohort analysis. *American Sociological Review, 43,* 404–421.

Ridley, F. F. (Ed.). (1968). *Specialists and generalists: A comparative study of the professional civil servant at home and abroad.* London: Allen & Unwin.

Saxenian, A. (1994). *Regional advantage: Culture and competition in Silicon Valley and Route 128.* Cambridge, MA: Harvard University Press.

Scott, W. R. (1995). *Institutions and organizations.* Thousand Oaks, CA: Sage.

Selznick, P. (1957). *Leadership in administration: A sociological interpretation.* Berkeley: University of California Press.

Sewell, W. H., Jr. (1992). A theory of structure: Duality, agency, and transformation. *American Journal of Sociology, 98,* 1–29.

Sewell, W. H., Jr. (1996). Historical events as transformations of structures: Inventing revolution at the Bastille. *Theory and Society, 25,* 841–881.

Smith-Doerr, L. (1999). *Career paths in the life sciences: Processes and outcomes of organizational change.* PhD dissertation, University of Arizona, Tuscon.

Stinchcombe, A. (1965). Social structure and organizations. In J. G. March (Ed.), *Handbook of organizations* (pp. 142–169). Chicago: Rand McNally.

Stovel, K., Savage, M., & Bearman, P. (1996). Ascription into achievement: Models of career systems at Lloyds Bank, 1890–1970. *American Journal of Sociology, 102,* 358–399.

Thornton, P. H. (2002). The rise of the corporation in a craft industry: Conflict and conformity in institutional logics. *Academy of Management Journal, 45,* 81–101.

Thornton, P. H. (2004). *Markets from culture: Institutional logics and organizational decisions in higher education publishing.* Stanford, CA: Stanford University Press.

Thornton, P., Jones, C., & Kury, K. (2005). Institutional logics and institutional change in organizations: Transformation in accounting, architecture, and publishing. *Research in the Sociology of Organizations, 23,* 127–172.

Thornton, P., & Ocasio, W. (1999). Institutional logics and the historical contingency of power in organizations: Executive succession in the higher education publishing industry, 1958–1990. *American Journal of Sociology, 105*(3), 801–843.

Tolbert, P. S., & Zucker, L. G. (Eds.). (1996). *The institutionalization of institutional theory.* London: Sage.

Van Maanen, J., & Barley, S. R. (1984). Occupational communities: Culture and control in organizations. *Research in organizational behavior, 6,* 287–365.

Van Maanen, J., & Schein, E. (1979). Toward a theory of organizational socialization. *Research in organizational behavior, 1,* 209–264.

Weber, M. (1947). *A theory of social and economic organization.* New York: Free Press.

Whitley, R. (2003). The institutional structuring of organizational capabilities: The role of authority sharing and organizational careers. *Organization Studies, 24*(5), 667–695.

Zucker, L. G. (1977). Role of institutionalization in cultural persistence. *American Sociological Review, 42*(5), 726–743.

Zucker, L. G., Darby, M. R. (1996). Star scientists and institutional transformation: Patterns of invention and innovation in the formation of the biotechnology industry. *Proceedings of the National Academy of Sciences, 93*(23), 12709–12716.

Zucker, L. G., Darby, M. R., & Brewer, M. B. (1994). *Intellectual capital and the birth of U.S. biotechnology enterprises* (Working Paper No. 4653). Cambridge, MA: National Bureau of Economic Research.

23

Careers Across Cultures

David C. Thomas

Kerr Inkson

The study of career management has long recognized the existence of international differences in career patterns and practice (Osipow, 1983) and also the need to culturally adapt career counseling practice (Sue & Sue, 1990). However, the systematic study of careers from a cross-cultural or comparative perspective is still in its infancy. The literature in this area is fragmented and lacks a coherent framework to guide inquiry. We suggest that it is possible and desirable to examine cultural differences in careers by considering both the ways in which culture legitimizes career patterns and practices through the institutions of society and how it determines the culturally based attitudes, beliefs, perceptions, and expectations that individuals have about careers.

Modern industrial societies, the source of most career theory, are also the home of individualistic values and high levels of achievement motivation (Yang, 1988). They encourage career ambition, hierarchical organizations and bureaucracy supporting status advancement, and division of labor and professionalization promoting career specialization. Yet even in these societies specific groups have their own quite different, socially sanctioned modes and models for understanding and acting out their careers (e.g., Juntunen et al., 2001). When we cross international borders and look at the sequences of work experiences of people from very different societies, and their interpretation of these experiences, we should expect to find even greater differences.

In a recent conference for career counselors attended by one of the authors, a careers expert working in the remote rural areas of South Africa showed photographs of the conditions of career protagonists (Maree, 2004). Over a hundred black children, all perfectly dressed in starched school uniforms, crowded into a shack-like classroom with rickety furniture and an almost defunct blackboard. Other children were shown walking around the countryside hunting for scraps of food during school hours. In some areas, the unemployment rate was as high as 98%, and no one in most families had had a job for generations. How would they understand the term *career* or even the term *employment?* Of what value to them was the consideration of vocational interests or career maturity or boundaryless career? In an article on black South African careers, Watson and Stead (2001) criticize the indiscriminate application of the assumptions of "free choice" in careers and the conventional focus in South African career studies on individual psychological variances without consideration of environmental factors that render this focus irrelevant. While this may be an extreme case, most societies vary to a greater or lesser extent from the utopian world of talent, individuality, prosperity, and choice in which most of the career theory developed elsewhere in this book has been generated.

In this chapter, we first examine the need for a cross-cultural perspective and outline some of the important limitations of current careers research. Second, we examine the types of cross-cultural career studies that have been or can be conducted and the questions that they address. Third, we outline some of the methodological issues associated with the study of comparative career management. And, finally, we propose a framework for the study of careers from a comparative perspective.

Parochialism in Career Theory

The study of careers, like its sibling management studies, is the product of a particular perspective, in a particular set of cultures, at a particular point in time (see Boyacigiller & Adler, 1991). Cultural differences, therefore, pose important issues for career theory and research. The systematic study of careers is a relatively recent phenomenon (Boerlijst, 1998; Moore, Gunz, and Hall, Chapter 2), with, as noted previously, an indelible imprint of the societal context in which it developed.

One example of the issues posed by cross-cultural difference is the literature on the *boundaryless career* (Arthur & Rousseau, 1996)—a concept that has become popular in recent years. Boundaryless career theory is based on the notion that society progresses from a structured industrial state to a relatively flexible new economy in which boundaries—for example, those between organizations—have become

more permeable. The boundaryless careerist implicitly admired in this literature is the highly qualified mobile professional who builds his or her career competencies and economic value through transfer across boundaries. He or she is explicitly and implicitly contrasted with more staid careerists pursuing traditional or organizational careers, who, it is implied, are at risk in a rapidly changing society because their career-relevant skills and networks are associated with single organizations vulnerable to unexpected change. Though not stated explicitly, the implication is that everyone should seek to become more boundaryless through the acquisition of relevant, portable career competencies (DeFillippi & Arthur, 1996). Boundaryless career theory may make good sense in the world in which it was developed—the fracturing corporate world of the United States in the 1990s, but how well does it transcend cultural boundaries?

Pringle and Mallon (2003) set out to show the limitations of this very Western theory and point out the difficulties for ethnic minorities in building the self-confidence, career skills, and individualism required to easily take advantage of boundaryless conditions. They note that "the experiences of those whose world-view is framed through collective responsibilities accentuate the individualistic assumptions of boundaryless careers" (p. 846) (see also Gunz, Peiperl, and Tzabbar, Chapter 24). In a related critique, Dany (2003) notes the continuing influence in France of external structures and cues marking and restricting individuals' careers. She concludes that "a firm's career management practices still mark the careers of its employees. . . . They serve as benchmarks for making sense of the world and limit the career strategies of individuals" (p. 835).

Granrose and Chua (1996) provide a nice example of the principle of boundarylessness being used on a collective basis. In Chinese family businesses, it is the collective—the extended family—that uses principles of networking and the development of trust in reciprocal relationships to place family members into ever-growing businesses as a means of extending family influence and wealth. Individual family members are constrained in what career moves they make. The family makes decisions in the interest of the family as a whole, yet entrepreneurial careers are fostered in the family interest. Chinese family business careers also offer a contrast to Western models, showing that the use of collectivist nepotism rather than individualist merit as a means of determining career advancement provides a level of trust that may be of benefit to both sides of the exchange.

The account above draws attention to the parochialism in which much conventional career theory and practice is embedded and gives rise to questions about the appropriateness of common career concepts and issues. For example, in command economies (or even transition economies), is occupational choice—implying individual autonomy—an issue? Or is the counterpart concept personnel selection and allocation the only truth? What of dual-career couples in societies where wives are regarded as chattels or where people identify as members of the extended rather than the nuclear family? Is ethnicity not a major determinant of inequality of career opportunity for women (Kamenou, & Fearfull, 2006)? How can careers be directed toward work-life balance in societies where unremitting dawn-to-dusk toil is necessary just for survival? In many societies, conventional concepts of career may be incomprehensible or may be understood as ideals that accrue to the privileged elite. Counsell (1999) expresses such views in his review of career strategies in Ethiopia, showing that national politics and local (collectivist) tribal traditions frame careers in ways not seen in Western contexts.

THE NEED FOR A CROSS-NATIONAL PERSPECTIVE

Conventional (often U.S. based) career theory (e.g., Brown & Associates, 2002) tends to focus on the psychological processes of individual decision making, particularly in relation to occupational choice. But even basic notions such as individual decision making and choice may be problematic, for example, in collectively oriented totalitarian states, where people are allocated to jobs or gain them through family connections rather than choosing occupations and gaining jobs on an open labor market.

For example, Skorikov and Vondracek (1993) offer a commentary on the dissolution of the old Communist-controlled U.S.S.R. and its transfiguration into a set of independent, democratic nations and the immediate effects of such changes on careers. According to these authors, in the communist system, which controlled the country prior to the late 1980s, work was considered important not in terms of individual achievement or self-fulfillment but only insofar as work performance assisted the collective good. Official systems of advancement were hierarchy based, while actual systems of advancement were political, nepotistic, and corrupt. Those advancing in their careers were therefore objects of contempt. Career decisions were not so much chosen by individuals as allocated by central authorities and organizations, leading to a high external locus of control in career behavior. Even when, with the advance of *perestroika* and the dissolution of the U.S.S.R. in the late 1980s and early 1990s, the authorities attempted to liberalize management practices and encourage Western-style individualism and proactive career behavior, they found that individuals were unable or unwilling to change their entrenched negative attitudes to career. Skokirov and Vondracek (1993) criticize the error of "a personological focus that neglects social and cultural factors in career development" (p. 315).

Much of conventional career studies may legitimately be criticized for building theories of career around postindustrial free-market democratic institutions and values such as *bureaucracy, meritocracy, individual, freedom of choice, free enterprise, open labor market, peace, occupation, profession, occupational choice, hierarchy, progress, work ethic,* and *socioeconomic status.* Nearly all the research has been conducted in societies where such institutions and predominant values could be assumed. Authors such as Vondracek, Lerner, and Schulenberg (1986) (see also Patton & McMahon, 1999) rightly advocate consideration of contextual variables such as sociocultural context, economic conditions, and labor laws in terms of whether they provide contextual explanations of individual career behavior. The importance of such contextualism increases rapidly when we cross national boundaries.

Research on careers gets much of its dynamic from the interest of policymakers and practitioners in different societies in providing educational and vocational processes that will assist individuals in making good career decisions, particularly occupational choice. For example, Arthur and McMahon (2005) argue for the cross-cultural contextualization of career counseling.

Law (1993) provides an interesting perspective on the development of careers work (e.g., counseling and guidance) in different societies:

> Careers work appears first in societies where informal and traditional means of assigning life roles seem both ineffective and inequitable. Significant features of that change are the following: (a) economy becomes science and technology dependent; (b) families become less extended, more nuclear, and (c) population becomes more mobile, less rooted in contained communities. Relatives—important sources of informal and traditional "guidance"—are therefore less able to help . . . These conditions were quintessentially met at the turn of the (20th) century on the East Coast of the United States. Here Frank Parsons formulated some of the first ideas about career guidance. (p. 298)

Law (1993) goes on to describe how theories of differential psychology and occupational matching were subsequently exported from the United States to the United Kingdom. In both countries, powerful career guidance movements developed, simultaneously reflecting the economic conditions and institutions of their societies and shaping a conventional wisdom about the functioning of *ideal* careers. The ideology of such guidance has come less to present people with solutions to their career decisions and more to enable them to develop their information-gathering and problem-solving skills and, thereby, to make good decisions for themselves. That reflects a Western view of individual inner-directedness (Riesman, 1961), which may be at odds with the traditional other-directedness of less developed economies but is critical when societies are in rapid economic expansion. The historical perspective enables us to understand something of the evolutionary nature of careers and career studies and the fact that this evolution takes place at a different rate in different national contexts.

Economic and Political Forces

The issue has been given added urgency in recent years by two related processes, globalization and the economic development of non-Western cultures. These have given non-Western cultures more of a Western *face,* thrusting the economic and business institutions of liberal Western capitalism in head-to-head interaction with the mores of less developed societies. Globalization has been described as the absence of borders and barriers to trade (Ohmae, 1995; Peiperl and Jonsen, Chapter 18), the "crystallization of the world as a single place" (Robertson, 1995, p. 38.) A useful general definition describes globalization as an increase in the permeability of traditional boundaries, including physical borders such as nation-states and economies, industries and organizations and less tangible borders such as cultural norms or assumptions (Parker, 1998, pp. 6–7). This increase in permeability is the result of shifts in technological, political, and economic spheres. With the advent of free-trade areas, traditional economic boundaries between countries have been dramatically reduced, and global careers have become more prevalent.

Organizational boundaries are also affected by globalization. In modern multinational corporations, production, sales and marketing, and distribution might all be located in different countries to capitalize on certain location-specific advantages. Additionally, conventional organizational forms are giving way to networks of less hierarchical relationships (Kogut, 1989) and cooperative strategic alliances with other firms (Jarillo, 1988). These changes mean that the opportunity structures around which careers are based may be altered in one country as a result of decisions made in another. Also, in many countries demographic shifts are occurring in the workforce. These demographic changes include the increased cultural diversity of workforces, both through temporary assignment and through international migration. The globalization of product and service markets is thus paralleled by a globalization of the labor market, meaning that careers are increasingly played out in contexts whose institutions and cultures change dramatically around the career actor.

Another factor differentially influencing the career contexts of some countries is privatization. Governments in both developed and developing countries are selling state-owned business to private investors at an increasing rate. Because these enterprises have often been noncompetitive, privatization has had a dramatic effect on the work life and career perspectives of employees. The privatization of government-run enterprise in the former Soviet Union, where some 12,000 state-owned companies were sold ("Russia's State Sell-Off," 1994), is the most obvious example of this worldwide trend (e.g., Sanderson, Walsh, & Hayes, 1990). However, the exact nature of reform varies. For example, in China and Vietnam, which are still governed by the Communist Party, vestiges of state socialism continue to have influence.

A key goal of the socialist system was economic security for the masses, including a fundamental belief that labor is not a commodity to be bought and sold but a resource to be employed. To support growth, the labor surplus (unemployment) was to be absorbed by the public sector. But the majority of surplus labor was unskilled; while the growing economy required high skills, most surplus labor was in villages while the need was in cities; and uneven regional development created a high demand in some areas but not in others (Kornai, 1992). These factors created a chronic shortage of labor. The bureaucratic control of employment, and therefore of careers, began with education, where choices open to individuals were severely limited and/or were channeled toward a particular type of work. In China, for example (prior to reforms), lifetime employment by state-owned enterprises was much sought after. The contrast with conventional concepts of careers being based on free individual choice is stark and the problems of adjustment acute. Having previously acquired patterns of career behavior that worked in the socialist system, individuals are unwilling to change their attitudes and behavior in the face of the new realities (Skorikov & Vondracek, 1993).

Thus, changes resulting from globalization and from the transition of former communist societies toward free-market systems reinforce the importance of considering national context in the study of careers. But while the societal context of careers is embodied in the economic, political, and technological conditions mentioned here, our primary target is the more fundamental concept of culture.

CULTURE

Culture is singled out as uniquely important to career theory and practice for three reasons. First, the economic, legal, and political characteristics of a society are inexorably linked to its culture. Even where systems are dictated by a single person or clique and maintained through force, history and culture contribute to their development. Culture stems from the fundamental ways in which a society learns to interact with its environment. The economic, legal, and political systems that develop over time are the visible elements of a more fundamental set of shared cultural meanings (Thomas, 2002). Culture affects the institutions of society in their goals, the way they operate, and the attributions people make for policies and behavior (Schwartz, 1992). Second, unlike economic, legal, and political institutions, culture is largely invisible; its influence is therefore difficult to detect and often—for example, in the context of careers—overlooked. Finally, as noted at the outset of the chapter, culture operates both through the legitimization in the institutions of society of career practices and patterns and through the different attitudes, beliefs, perceptions, and expectations that it gives individuals about careers.

Culture is a societal-level construct, but it exists within the knowledge systems of individuals. Therefore, like all knowledge systems, it is formed during childhood and reinforced throughout life (Triandis, 1995). Much of our understanding of cultural variation has developed through our study of values (e.g., Kim, Triandis, Kagitcibasi, Choi, & Yoon, 1994). Value orientations are the shared assumptions about how things ought to be or how one should behave (Rokeach, 1973). They result from solutions that social groups have devised for dealing with the problems that all people confront. Because there are limited ways in which societies can deal with these problems (Kluckhohn & Strodtbeck, 1961), it is possible to develop a system that categorizes and compares societies on the basis of their values. This value system has a profound influence on attitudes and behavioral assumptions, including those that relate to career.

Consider, for example, the way in which Hofstede's (1980)[1] classic description of variation in cultural values across 52 countries intersects with conventional career theory and research. Hofstede used comparable samples of employees of a major multinational from nations around the world to characterize these nations in terms of four major value dimensions. These dimensions have major potential effects on both culturally based career-affecting institutions and the individual enactment of careers:

• *Individualism and collectivism* denote the extent to which one's self-identity is defined according to individual characteristics or by the characteristics of the groups to which one belongs and the extent to which individual or group interests dominate one's decision making. They influence the degree to which people feel responsible for their own actions and strive for independence and individual rewards as against feeling loyalty to the extended family and/or community and subjection to group norms. The United States and many European countries are high on individualism. Theories of career typically characterize the career as a long-term individual project, one of personal agency through which each person seeks individual career success, which is judged purely by individual achievement, rewards, and satisfaction. The notion of collective experience of careers, or collective criteria for career success, appears little in the literature. Parker, Arthur, and Inkson (2004) report a study of Pacific Island professionals, in which career success was defined in terms of providing assistance to the ethnic community. Can "a theory with individualism at its heart be generalized beyond the industrialized West?" (Pringle & Mallon, 2003, p. 846).

• *Power distance* refers to the extent to which power differences—for example, between a boss and a subordinate or between a higher-status and a lower-status person—are expected and tolerated. The United States and Western European countries tend to be low on power distance, and on this basis, career

theories and advocacy emphasize the democratic notion that "Jack's as good as his Master" and that anyone can get to the top. Societies where power distances are maintained by traditional norms, status, and practices may develop career principles and understandings that are quite different.

• *Uncertainty avoidance* is the extent to which the culture emphasizes ways to reduce uncertainty and create stability—for example, having clear written rules and procedures or strong norms to guide action. Formal procedures and norms governing matters such as work allocation and succession may be much more necessary in a country with high uncertainty avoidance. In the West, where uncertainty avoidance is relatively low, it is fashionable in times of substantial economic and organizational change to stress tolerance of uncertainty; career resilience and career improvisation (Waterman, Waterman, & Collard, 1994) are seen as cardinal career virtues. The problems of boundaryless careers and the virtues of stability and structure in careers are likely to be more apparent in societies with high uncertainty avoidance.

• *Masculinity and femininity* reflect the differences between the traditional male goals of ambition and achievement and the female orientations of nurturance and interpersonal harmony—for example, the balance between seeking promotion at work and having good relationships with others. The United States and Western Europe tend to be above average on masculinity, and career theories, which have often been developed largely with reference to economically active male employees, have a distinctly masculine bias in their concepts of career goals and the means of achieving them—for example, through striving for success and through competitive tournaments (Rosenbaum, 1984). Heslin (2005) draws attention to cultural differences in masculine/doing-oriented and feminine/being-oriented definitions of career success. The corrective literature on women's careers as examples of communion rather than agency (Marshall, 1989, 1995) may have its counterpart in the career behavior of people in feminine cultures, such as those in Scandinavia.

TYPES OF CROSS-CULTURAL CAREER RESEARCH

In researching this review, we were limited to English-language accounts in mainstream literatures. Even so, in related areas of organizational behavior, such as communication, groups, and leadership, there are detailed accounts of the main aspects of cross-cultural difference and studies of phenomena conducted both with mixed culture groups and other culture groups in other environments (e.g., Adler, 2002; Thomas 2002). However, we were struck by the relative paucity of material on comparative or cross-cultural career issues. In a somewhat more limited review of multicultural career development studies in three leading career journals, Koegal and Donin (1995) report similar findings not only with regard to the number of articles but also as to their focus. Specifically, only 14% of the articles they reviewed emphasized multicultural concerns in the broadest sense, including studies of career counseling in foreign (non-U.S.) cultures and with American minority groups. In fact only four studies considered more than one country. The majority (50%) of these studies involved the assessment of high school or university students with regard to work values and preferences, self-concept, occupational perceptions, expectations, and interests.

The limited amount and narrow focus of cross-cultural careers research presented a challenge with regard to a useful structure for this chapter. To provide a forward-looking perspective as opposed to a mere review of past work we have organized the following discussion around types of cross-cultural career studies, in which we identify their characteristics and the types of questions they can answer. Then we have provided representative examples of each type. The research types are indigenous, replication, comparative, and intercultural.

Indigenous Research

This type of research focuses on the different ways in which career actors behave and careers are managed in specific cultural settings. These studies are conducted within a single country or culture. However, they assume cultural differences—and in extreme cases they assume that cultures are unique (Berry, 1969)—and employ locally generated theory to explain and predict behavior. For example, employment practices in Japan are described as being open-ended, with an expectation of a long-term relationship in which contributions and rewards balance over time (Morishima, 1995)—the archetype of the organizational career. Another contemporary example is provided by Counsell and Popova (2000) in a description of career perceptions and strategies in Bulgaria, while Metcalfe (2006) explores the obvious question of the influence of Islamic culture on the careers of women in the Middle East. Interestingly, the results suggested that the majority of respondents were unsure of, or pessimistic about, career prospects and tended to advocate strategies that the authors labeled corruption. Again, the contrast with mainstream career studies is sharp. Finally, in an interesting and well-designed qualitative study, Juntunen et al. (2001, p. 282) examined the meaning of career and related concepts for adult American Indians. A key finding was that "career was generally considered to be a long term or life long activity with strong links to one's contribution to the world," suggesting the need to consider community context when counseling American Indians.

Replication Research

These studies are conceived and managed by a researcher in one country and then repeated in other countries by the originator or by local collaborators. These attempts at replication typically assume that the concepts being measured and the relationships being studied have the same meaning to the participants in the new culture as they did in the original culture and that the responses in the two cultures can be compared directly. Sometimes concepts can be applied successfully within another culture, such as in Wakabayashi and Graen's (1984) application of vertical dyad linkages to career progress in Japan. However, the assumption of equivalence where it may not exist is potentially a reason why studies often fail to replicate across cultures (Smith & Bond, 1999). In their review of career development research, Koegel and Donin (1995) registered their surprise at the failure of researchers to state whether or not their instruments were validated for the multicultural populations being studied.

An example of replication research is Fouad and Arbona's (1994) examination of the cross-cultural validity of Super's (1957, 1990) theory of vocational development. This theory suggests a common career progression through successive stages of career development. The theory and the concepts and measurement instruments associated with it have been internationally influential, so there is a substantial set of studies to draw from. Fouad and Arbona (1994) concluded that most of the cross-cultural work on career maturity shows that individuals seem to progress through developmental stages and accomplish vocational tasks appropriate to these stages.

The replication of a study of the recent careers of a representative sample of New Zealanders (Arthur, Inkson, & Pringle, 1999) in France (Cadin, Bailly-Bender, & Saint-Giniez, 2000) is an additional example of how this research type can be productively employed. The French study suggested that in comparison with the relatively boundaryless careers practiced by New Zealanders in a recently deregulated economic and business environment, French careers are more stable, more predictable, and more influenced by dominating bureaucratic institutions.

The validation of both the Strong-Campbell Interest Inventory in Hispanic populations (Hansen & Fouad, 1984) and the application of Holland's realistic-investigative-artistic-social-enterprising-conventional (RIASEC) theory in African American culture (Swanson, 1992), in Pakistan (Khan, Alvi, Shaukat, Hussain, & Baig, 1990), with Mexicans (Flores, Spanierman, Armstrong, & Velez, 2006), and with native Americans (Hansen, Scullard, & Haviland, 2000) are additional examples of this type of research. Some support for the cross-cultural use of inventories, such as the most recent update of the Strong Interest Inventory (Day & Rounds, 1998; Strong, Hansen, & Campbell, 1994), has been presented. However, the extent to which the construct validity of such instruments has been adequately established, which we will discuss in more detail ahead, is

questionable. For example, in some cases, instruments have not even been translated into the native language (e.g., Khan et al. 1990).

Koegel and Donin (1995) report that the most popular foreign locations for the career development research they reviewed, accounting for more than 50% of the studies, were, in order, Israel, Japan, and Canada. While they did not distinguish between indigenous and replication research, the need to broaden sample locations is nevertheless obvious.

Comparative Research

Comparative studies seek to find the similarities and differences that exist across cultures with regard to a particular career issue. *Descriptive* comparative studies document the similarities and differences, while *predictive* studies test the relationships suggested by theory, including theories predicting the cross-cultural differences that will be found.

The vast majority of cross-cultural studies we reviewed fell into the descriptive comparative category. For example, the original Meaning of Work (MOW) studies (MOW International Research Team, 1987) fall into this category, as does a subsequent study of career patterns across seven European countries (Claes & Antonio Ruiz Quintanilla, 1994). In the latter study, both similar and culture-specific career patterns were found.

Comparative studies of the management of expatriates (e.g., Kopp, 1994; Peterson, Napier, & Shul-Shim 2000; Tung, 1982; Tungli & Peiperl, 2004) also fall into the descriptive comparative category. Another example of this category is a study of the career paths of the CEOs of the top 200 companies in France and Germany (Bauer & Bertin-Mourot, 1997), in which performance within the company was shown to be three times as important to attaining the CEO job in Germany as it was in France, where advancement is derived from the reputation of one's educational institution.

Fouad (1995) reviewed a number of studies that report differences between Hispanics and other groups on several career variables, including interests, vocational aspirations, and educational experiences. These investigations indicated little difference in the interest patterns of

Hispanics and other groups. However, the studies raised questions as to the extent to which the measures of interests used were universal (see Fouad & Dancer, 1992). Vocational aspirations of Hispanics were found to be as high or higher than those of whites or African Americans; however, their career expectations were lower than their aspirations (Fouad, 1995). In hiring for jobs, Hispanics have been found to attach higher importance to subjective traits but lower importance to objective traits than non-Hispanics (Pappas, 2006).

A number of other comparative studies of vocational interest in different cultural groups have been conducted. For example, Carter and Swanson (1990) found that African Americans tended to have more social-enterprising-conventional (see Holland, 1985) interests than white Americans. Sue and Kirk (1972) compared the vocational interests of Chinese and American women and those of Japanese and Anglo-Americans. Meir, Melamed, and Abu-Freha (1990) examined differences in the relationship of vocational, avocational, and skill utilization congruence to well-being in Jews and Bedouins in Israel.

Fouad (1988) administered the Career Maturity Inventory (Crites, 1978) to Israeli and U.S. students. On every scale, except the decisiveness subscale, a significant effect for culture was found, with Israelis scoring lower. This result echoed comparative findings between American students living in Lebanon and Arab students (Morocco, 1976).

Descriptive comparative research has also addressed the effects of cultural differences on both career-decision-making styles and types of career paths. Mau (2000) found consistency between Taiwanese and American students in the use of a rational career-decision-making style. However, a smaller percentage of Taiwanese students endorsed this style, and American students were less likely to endorse a dependent decision-making style. Kelly, Brannick, Hulpke, Levine, and To (2003) described the career paths of employees in Hong Kong, Singapore, Mainland China, and Ireland. They found distinctly different career patterns on certain career dimensions, with Mainland Chinese participants describing the most traditional career path, Singaporean and Irish participants having the least traditional, and those from Hong Kong a

dual approach. These studies appear to show the relative influence of (Western) individualism versus (Asian) collectivism in determining the processes of career decision making.

In an interesting qualitative study, Hansen and Wilcox (1997) compare German and American career ideologies and structures. They suggest that conformity, stability, formal hierarchy, rapport building, and high regard for technical and scientific skills are more representative of German career perceptions than American.

While descriptive comparative studies give information about the *what* aspects of cultural comparison, predictive studies include an emphasis on the *how* of cultural influence. For example, Lauver and Jones (1991) present some intriguing results regarding differential effects of gender on career self-efficacy in white, Hispanic, and American Indian samples but fail to define the mechanisms through which culture might be operating. An example of a predictive comparative approach is presented in an article by Derr and Laurent (1989), in which research involving perceptions of career success factors across five cultures (France, Britain, United States, Germany, and the Netherlands) were examined (Laurent, 1986). The significant cross-cultural differences among the five groups caused the authors to suggest that the very concept of career has different meanings across cultures.

In an attempt to establish cultural values as a mechanism of cultural influence Hartung, Speight, and Lewis (1996) assessed the effect of individualism and collectivism on the career-related variables of occupational choice, career plans, and work values. The failure to find significant relationships in this study may be related to sample selection (all Americans, though of different cultural origin) and construct measurement, as discussed in more detail later in this chapter.

Intercultural Research

Intercultural research seeks to understand the interactions between culturally different actors and considers the culture of all parties in the interaction as well as contextual explanations for observed similarities and differences. Our review of comparative career research failed to reveal any studies that clearly fell into this category of research. The absence of research in this category results largely from the failure of studies to specify the mechanisms of cultural influence. Our finding here is consistent with a more general finding by Koegel and Donin (1995) that multicultural careers research often lacks a conceptual or theoretical basis. One recent study that approximated our definition of an intercultural study is Pang's (2003) application of the boundaryless career concept to nonindividualistic cultures by examining the career patterns of first- and second-generation Chinese in Britain and Hong Kong. Using secondary data, she showed how a common cultural heritage interacts with different cultural contexts to result in differing career patterns. The framework we present ahead will, we hope, lead to more research of this type.

In summary, all four types of cross-cultural research, indigenous, replication, comparative, and intercultural, have their place in describing, explaining, and predicting career concepts across cultures. And some interesting comparative results have been presented. However, many more cross-cultural studies, particularly those in the more sophisticated predictive comparative and intercultural categories, are needed. Additionally, the loci of this research need to be broadened to account for a much greater degree of cultural variation.

METHODS ISSUES IN CROSS-CULTURAL CAREERS RESEARCH

Because of its stage of development, careers research has the opportunity to avoid the methodological problems that have plagued other areas of cross-cultural research. In the following section, we discuss some of the most prominent of these issues.

Studies that involve two or more cultures share common methodological issues that are not present in domestic research. These come under the broad headings of equivalence, sampling, data collection, and measurement and data analysis.

Equivalence

Perhaps the most important issue in cross-cultural research is the idea of equivalence.

There is a strong likelihood of bias because of cultural differences in values, attitudes, and normative behavior. Equivalence cannot be assumed and must be established at three key points: conceptualization of theoretical constructs, study design, and data analysis (van de Vijver & Leung, 1997).

Construct equivalence is the extent to which the concepts examined have the same meaning in different cultures. Without construct equivalence, comparisons are impossible. The involvement of researchers from different cultures helps in achieving construct equivalence.

Method equivalence is the extent to which the measurement unit is the same in all groups. Threats to method equivalence include acquiescence and extremity bias. Acquiescence is the tendency for some cultural groups to agree (or disagree) with most of the questions asked. Extremity bias involves the way different cultures use particular response scale formats—for example, systematically choosing extreme points on rating scales (e.g., Hui & Triandis, 1989). Also, different levels of familiarity with the construct being studied and communication between researcher and participants can contribute to nonequivalence.

Finally, *metric* equivalence is the extent to which survey items have similar measurement properties across different groups. Nonequivalence can result from poor item translation, complex item wording, and culture-specific issues with regard to item content. For example, in their Pakistan study, Khan et al. (1990) found it necessary to modify numerous items of Holland's (1977, 1985) Self-Directed Search and Career Readiness questionnaires because of educational and cultural differences.

Equivalence means that culturally different participants understand concepts in the same way. Unmodified instruments will rarely be equivalent across cultures. Therefore, instrument development and data collection strategies must play a much larger role in cross-cultural studies.

Sampling

Several unique sampling problems present themselves in cross-cultural research. First, because of subcultural variation within countries, any sample selected from a specific geographic region does not necessarily represent the country (Brislin, Lonner, & Thorndike, 1973). Second, inconsistencies between countries in the availability of sampling frames (lists of possible participants) can affect the sample—for example, the lack of phone books or business directories in developing countries.

Where random samples are not possible, researchers can use systematic sampling where selection of participants is based on theoretical considerations. In these cases, the max/min/con principle, that an efficient research design *maximizes* variance on key research variables, *minimizes* random variance, and *con*trols extraneous variance, applies (Kerlinger, 1986). Thus, for cross-national comparisons, countries should be selected on dimensions that are as far apart as possible (e.g., the United States and China on the individualism-collectivism dimension). The problem is that countries that vary on one dimension may also differ on other dimensions (e.g., economic, political, legal). One way to deal with this problem is to test propositions with samples in different countries matched according to key dimensions.

Data Collection

The most common methods of data collection in cross-cultural careers research are questionnaires and interviews (Koegel & Donin, 1995; Peng, Peterson, & Shyi, 1991). This is not surprising because it is Western-trained researchers who conduct most international research. The "have questionnaire, will travel" approach can have unanticipated negative consequences. Cultures differ in people's familiarity with particular research methods and their readiness to participate. Such differences particularly affect the self-administered questionnaires so popular in careers research. Factors such as language differences and variation in literacy rates are obvious. But in addition, the level of familiarity with or attitude toward specific research methods can dramatically influence responses. For example, Shenkar and Von Glinow (1994) found that the unfamiliarity of Chinese with multiple-choice questionnaires was a significant source of bias. Also, in many countries, a researcher's purpose is suspect (Napier & Thomas, 2001).

Participants may view the researcher as an agent of management or government—a perception that may be hard to prevent if those groups control access to participants. Using standard research instruments worldwide may raise sensitive issues. For example, questions related to time off for family activities attracted a particularly emotive response from Pacific Islanders in New Zealand (Napier & Thomas, 2001).

Respondents may not have a frame of reference with which to respond to questions. For example, North Americans are used to responding to hypothetical questions. However, in many cultures, to provide a meaningful answer, respondents require a concrete example or a detailed explanation of the context (Shenkar & Von Glinow, 1994). The most common qualitative method is the interview. The advantages of interviews include the ability to deal with complex topics, probe for clearer answers, and give feedback to respondents. However, a key disadvantage is the interaction between interviewer and respondent. For example, the characteristics of the interviewer (age, gender, personal appearance, tone of voice) can influence respondent answers, and the interviewer can selectively perceive or anticipate the respondent's answers. When the interviewer and respondent are culturally different, the opportunity for error is heightened. A considerable literature exists with regard to improving interview techniques in international settings (e.g., Brislin, Lonner, & Thorndike, 1973; Pareek & Rao, 1980).

Measurement and Data Analysis

Particularly relevant to cross-cultural research are two measurement and data-handling issues. These are the coding of qualitative data and the comparability of multi-item scales.

Often, in careers research, rich descriptions or observations are content analyzed and thereby reduced for further empirical analysis or simply (in ethnographic work) interpreted by the researcher in terms of his or her theory. A problem arises in establishing the categories into which the researcher tabulates observations or his/her interpretation, for these will likely reflect cultural orientation (Usunier, 1998). These difficulties can be reduced if researchers take the trouble to embed themselves in the culture in depth prior to conducting the interviews, maximize their awareness of their own biases, and involve researchers from the host culture where possible (see Juntunen et al., 2001, for an example of this approach).

The second issue involves the comparability of measures of career constructs using multiple-item rating scales. As noted previously, it is important that the underlying construct is understood in the same way in different cultures. The extent to which this has been accomplished can be assessed after data are collected. First, the basic psychometric properties of the instrument, such as its internal consistency, reliability, or item to total correlations, are assessed. Differences in these properties between cultures can be closely examined. Second, the structures of the multiple-item scales can be evaluated across cultures. Similar structures indicate comparability of measurement. Sophisticated statistical techniques are available to conduct these analyses, as are methods for controlling for any cross-cultural dissimilarity discovered (van de Vijver & Leung, 1997). However, with a few exceptions such as Fouad's (1993) work on vocational assessment, research done on career variables in this regard is limited.

Our overall impression is that the lack of more sophisticated cross-cultural research is a result of both the stage of development of the field of study and the lack of a framework to guide inquiry. Our desire to see the field advance beyond the descriptive-comparative stage of inquiry causes us to propose the following framework.

FRAMEWORK FOR COMPARATIVE CAREER STUDIES

Our review of the literature suggests that there are at least five career processes that are affected by cultural context. These are the perceptions of career, career choice, career development, career mobility, and career management.

Career Perception

Is the term *career* functional in contrasting cultural contexts? Richardson (2000) argues that even in Western societies, the term carries ideological loadings, such as the focus on only paid work, which makes it inappropriate and disempowering in counseling situations with certain groups. Notwithstanding the apparently universal experience of "unfolding sequences of work experiences over time," nevertheless we may have to recognize that in some cultural and economic settings—for example, those characterized by high unemployment, subsistence conditions, low labor mobility, and submergence of individual effort in a collective will, the concept of career may have limited value and may even be dysfunctional, and other concepts with less connotation of continuity and cumulativeness—*work, employment, fulfillment*—may have to have priority.

Career Choice

Much of the focus in career studies is on career choice, particularly occupational choice. Theory and practice implicitly assume a rational decision-making or problem-solving model to choose from a wide range of alternatives (e.g., Peterson, Lumsden, Sampson, Reardan, & Lenz, 2002). Here, it needs to be recognized that many individuals from other cultures have little, if any, discretion to make their own career decisions, though Western research and practice on vocational fit and the like may have something to offer those who make decisions for others.

Career Development

Career development theories are concerned with the construction and change in the career over time, with a specific recognition of the cumulative impact of ageing, learning, and life cycle on the career. Theorists such as Gottfredson (2002), Savickas (2002), and Super (1990) focus on internal psychological variables, self-concept development, adjustment of aspirations, and the like in the career conceptualization, attitudes, and decision making of individuals. Contextual variables such as social class and gender are recognized (e.g., Johnson & Mortimer, 2002) but not necessarily integrated with theory and practice. For example, Dawis and Lofquist (1984, see also Dawis, 2002) posit a "person-environment-correspondence theory" of career development but focus largely on person variables, with environment variables confined apparently to those of job and occupation. However, in recognizing the effects of cultural variability on the theory, Dawis (2002, p. 458) states that the "the problem may lie not so much in the theory as in the (measurement) instruments used to operationalize the theory." Career development theorists need to recognize that to understand the influence of culture, they need to go far beyond the creation of occupational interest inventories and other instruments adjusted for cultural bias. They must engage in the development of new models of career development that are radically altered to account for major context differences from the U.S. environment in which most current theories have been developed. The ideas of Vondracek et al. (1986) for appropriate emphasis in career theory on contextual variables badly need to be extended. More recently, Young, Valach, and Collin (2002) have proposed a *contextualist* theory of career that specifically recognizes cultural variances.

Career Mobility

In a globalizing world, researchers interested in careers as resources for international organizations, high-tech industries, and fast-growth economies seek new models of career emphasizing mobility—between jobs, occupations, organizations, industries, and, of course, cultural and geographical settings. The *new careers* (Arthur et al., 1999) are arguably more mobile than ever before. In their career behavior, individuals migrate more and more into new subcultural and cultural settings, sometimes in their home country and at other times in new countries. Even when they stay where they are, migration brings culturally different people to *them,* again requiring new career-relevant attitudes and behavior. While the literature in this area recognizes the underlying nature of careers as constantly changing repositories of learning and knowledge (Bird, 1996), theory and practice need to recognize the importance of cultural career adaptation and learning through the explicit acquisition of *cultural intelligence* (Earley & Ang, 2003; Thomas & Inkson, 2004).

Career Management

Career management refers to the stimulation and control of career behavior by organizations, mainly through practices of human resource management relating to the selection, allocation, development, education, promotion, evaluation, and remuneration of staff. Organizations have a responsibility to provide a supportive environment for the career of their culturally diverse and, often nowadays, international workforces, and the uniform imposition of U.S.-developed international human resource systems across culturally diverse subsidiaries may be counterproductive (Dowling, Welch, & Schuler, 1999). The preoccupation with the problems of expatriate assignment should be extended to consideration of the culturally appropriate career management of all employees in foreign settings and the longer-term global careers of corporate employees. Organizations should seek to learn new models of career management through their own diversities in international practices. For example, a recent study by Bozionelos (2006) raises issues about the appropriateness of conventional mentoring practices developed in Anglo contexts for the career support of employees in Greece. Okurame and Balogun (2005) raise similar questions for African nations.

Influencing these career outcomes is a fundamental tension between structure and agency (Peiperl & Arthur, 2000). Structures are the institutional frameworks of society: class, ethnicity, gender, as well as government, education systems, professional structures, and employing organizations. These frameworks allow, attract, constrain, or direct career behavior. Agency in this context is proactive individual or collective career behavior, the exertion of personal will over social structure in the creation of careers.

Our approach to understanding the influence of culture on careers accommodates both of these avenues of influence. Figure 23.1 presents a graphic of this process.

Are careers primarily a reflection of institutions, or is it open to individuals to transcend and even create institutions through their own career behavior? As shown in Figure 23.1, cultural factors affect careers through both mechanisms.

First, cultural forces shape the institutions of society that provide the formal direction and restrictions, legitimization, and institutional values and norms—the structures of opportunity and incentive—within which individuals must pursue their careers. Culture and these institutions

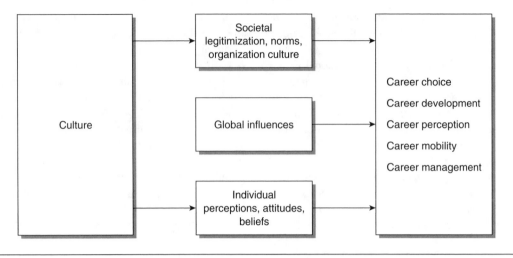

Figure 23.1   Framework for Cross-Cultural Careers Analysis

are inevitably linked as they have evolved together. A study by Schmitt-Rodermund and Silbereisen (1998) demonstrates this mechanism of influence. They found significant differences between East and West Germany shortly after unification. However, during the following years, similarity between the two Germanys with regard to the process of career development increased. Specifically, as differences in social context diminished, so did measures of career variables such as career maturity. This caused these authors to conclude that career development is culture specific.

Second, culture acts directly on individuals, influencing their work values, perceptions, beliefs, and personal attitudes to careers. The result is individual career behavior—for example, in occupational choice; career self-development; and mobility between jobs, occupations, and organizations. Individuals are not necessarily aware of these influences and simply make choices about career that feel correct.

A key issue is the balance of influence, as between societal structures and individual proactivity, in determining these career outcomes. Weick (1996), for example, notes the contribution of "weak" situations, with few salient structural cues to the encouragement of mobile boundaryless careers that can be powerfully enacted by their career holders in an environment relatively free of constraints, such as a deregulated economy. In contrast, centralized

societies with state allocation of labor and poverty-stricken societies where career action is limited by economic succession are examples of "strong" situations where perspectives encouraging individual enactment may be limited.

Our approach to the influence of culture on career theory and practice is consistent with the kinds of intermediate mechanisms identified by Hartung (2002). He suggests that culture can be seen to operate though both social roles and individuals' work values. This is the kind of thinking about *how* culture operates on specific career variables that is needed.

A final variable in Figure 23.1 is global influences—those factors that have a universal effect on careers. While truly pan-cultural effects need to be empirically verified, it is possible, based on the discussion of globalization presented previously, to identify some likely candidates. For example, the explosion in information technology is likely to have similar effects across cultures on factors such as career perception and choice. Also, with the fall of communism, Western-style capitalist economic systems seem increasingly the preferred context for careers. Therefore, many of the assumptions about careers that have their foundation in this system will become more valid in the future as economies around the world change. However, we must keep in mind that the rapid adoption of capitalism does not mean that cultural values will change at the same rate. And, alternatives to

Western-style capitalism are influenced by forces such as the rapid growth of Islam. Therefore, we need to be much more sensitive to the economic, political, and cultural differences that, despite globalization, continue to make for huge differences in people's career experiences.

Conclusion

In career studies, there appears to be a massive *lacuna* in cross-cultural theory and research. This may well be because of a well-intentioned recognition that the provision of adequate understanding of careers and career services is a problem in *all* cultures (Feller, Russell, & Whichard, 2005; Goodman & Hansen, 2005). But it is also because of a difference in the clientele for research and for practice in culturally sensitive management. In areas such as leadership and groups, the client is recognizably the manager or the business company, seeking to improve organizational performance and eager for expertise that will enable it to better manage overseas subsidiaries or multicultural workforces. While career studies contribute to international human resource management, their main potential beneficiaries are individual career actors. The members of minority cultures and immigrant cultures in the developed world, or of exotic cultures elsewhere, may have too little labor market power to shape the concepts and research of career scholars.

However, as globalization shapes the world of work, the need for scholars and managers equally to understand the cultural influence on careers has never been greater. These economic, political, and technological changes present challenging contextual variation around the career actor that must be considered. Culture, a fundamental set of values, attitudes, and behavioral assumptions, influences careers both by legitimizing and determining the career patterns and practices in society and through individuals' culturally based attitudes to and perceptions of career. The resulting diversity of alternative ways of understanding human working behavior as it evolves over time has much to offer career theorists and researchers. We hope that the framework presented here serves to encourage development in this area.

Note

1. We rely on Hofstede's conceptualization of culture as a finite number of dimensions because it makes sense, because it has been validated in subsequent work, and because of its simplicity in explaining the possible career effects of cultural values. However, it is not without critics (e.g., Dorfman & Howell, 1988; Roberts & Boyacigiller, 1984), and a number of subsequent studies of cultural variation have been conducted (see, e.g., Chinese Culture Connection, 1987; House, Hanges, Javidan, Doerfman, & Gupta, 2004; Trompenaars, 1993.) A recent, and perhaps the most sophisticated to date, mapping of cultural values that can be properly applied to the individual level of analysis can be found in the work of Shalom Schwartz and his colleagues (Sagiv & Schwartz, 1995, 2000; Schwartz, 1992, 1994; Schwartz & Bilsky, 1990), and in a departure from value orientations, the mapping of social axioms across cultures has recently been proffered (Bond et al., 2004).

References

Adler, N. J. (2002). *International dimensions of organizational behavior.* Boston: Wadsworth.

Arthur, M. B., Inkson, K., & Pringle, J. K. (1999). *The new careers: Individual action and economic change.* London: Sage.

Arthur, M. B., & Rousseau, D. M. (Eds.). (1996). *The boundaryless career: A new employment principle of a new organizational era.* New York: Oxford University Press.

Arthur, N., & McMahon, M. (2005). Multicultural career counseling: Theoretical applications of the systems theory framework. *Career Development Quarterly, 53*(3), 208–222.

Bauer, M., & Bertin-Mourot, B. (1997). *Radiographie des grands patrons Franccaise: Les conditions d'acces au pouvoir.* Paris: L'Harmattan.

Berry, J. W. (1969). On cross-cultural comparability. *International Journal of Psychology, 4,* 119–128.

Bird, A. (1996). Careers as repositories of knowledge: Considerations for boundaryless careers. In M. B. Arthur & D. M. Rousseau (Eds.), *The boundaryless career: A new employment principle of a new organizational era* (pp. 150–168). New York: Oxford University Press.

Boerlijst, J. G. (1998). Career development and career guidance. In J. D. Pieter Drenth & T. Henk (Eds.), *Handbook of work and organizational psychology: Vol. 3. Personnel psychology* (2nd ed.). Hove: Psychology Press.

Bond, M. H., Leung, K., Au, A., Tong, K-K., de Carrasquel, S. R., Murakami, F., et al. (2004). Culture-level dimensions of social axioms and their correlates across 41 cultures. *Journal of Cross-Cultural Psychology, 35,* 548–570.

Boyacigiller, N. A., & Adler, N. J. (1991). The parochial dinosaur: Organizational science in a global context. *Academy of Management Review, 16*(2), 262–290.

Bozionelos, N. (2006). Mentoring and expressive network resources: Their relationship with career success and emotional exhaustion among Hellenes employees involved in emotion work. *International Journal of Human Resource Management, 17*(2), 362–378.

Brislin, R. W., Lonner, W. J., & Thorndike, R. M. (1973). *Cross-cultural research methods.* New York: Wiley.

Brown, D., & Associates. (2002). *Career choice and development* (4th ed.). San Francisco: Jossey-Bass.

Cadin, L., Bailly-Bender, A.-F., & Saint-Giniez, V. (2000). Exploring boundaryless careers in the French context and national contexts. In M. Peiperl, M. B. Arthur, R. Goffee, & T. Morris (Eds.), *Career frontiers: New conceptions of working lives.* Oxford: Oxford University Press.

Carter, R. T., & Swanson, J. L. (1990). The validity of the Strong Interest Inventory with black Americans: A review of the literature. *Journal of Vocational Behavior, 36,* 195–209.

Chinese Culture Connection. (1987). Chinese values and the search for culture-free dimensions of culture. *Journal of Cross-Cultural Psychology, 18*(2), 143–164.

Claes, R., & Antonio Ruiz Quintanilla, S. (1994). Initial career and work meanings in seven European countries. *Career Development Quarterly, 42*(4), 337–352.

Counsell, D. (1999). Careers in Ethiopia: An exploration of careerists' perceptions and strategies. *Career Development International, 4*(1), 46–52.

Counsell, D., & Popova, J. (2000). Career perceptions and strategies in the new market-orientated Bulgaria: An exploratory study. *Career Development International, 5*(7), 360–368.

Crites, J. O. (1978). *Administration and use manual for the Career Maturity Inventory.* Monterey, CA: CTB/McGraw-Hill.

Dany, F. (2003). "Free actors" and organisations: Critical remarks about the new careers literature. *International Journal of Human Resource Management, 14*(5), 821–839.

Dawis, R. V. (2002). Person-environment-correspondence theory. In D. Brown & Associates (Eds.), *Career choice and development* (4th ed., pp. 427–464). San Francisco: Jossey-Bass.

Dawis, R. V., & Lofquist, L. H. (1984). *A psychological theory of work and adjustment.* Minneapolis, MN: University of Minneapolis Press.

Day, S. X., & Rounds, J. (1998). Universality of vocational interest structures among racial and ethnic minorities. *American Psychologist, 53,* 728–736.

DeFillippi, R. J., & Arthur, M. B. (1996). Boundaryless contexts and careers: A competency-based perspective. In M. B. Arthur & D. M. Rousseau (Eds.), *The boundaryless career: A new employment principle of a new organizational era* (pp. 116–131). New York: Oxford University Press.

Derr, C. B., & Laurent, A. (1989). The internal and external career: A theoretical and cross-cultural perspective. In M. B. Arthur, D. T. Hall, & B. S. Lawrence (Eds.), *Handbook of career theory* (pp. 454–471). Cambridge, UK: Cambridge University Press.

Dorfman, P. W., & Howell, J. P. (1988). Dimensions of national culture and effective leadership patterns: Hofstede revisited. *Advances in International Comparative Management, 3,* 127–150.

Dowling, P. J., Welch, D. E., & Schuler, R. S. (1999). *International human resource management: Managing people in a multinational context* (3rd ed.). Cincinnati, OH: South-Western College.

Earley, P. C., & Ang, S. (2003). *Cultural intelligence: Individual interactions across cultures.* Stanford, CA: Stanford University Press.

Feller, R. W., Russell, M., & Whichard, J. A. (2005). Career techniques and interventions: Themes from an international conversation. *Career Development Quarterly, 54*(1), 36–47.

Flores, L. Y., Spanierman, L. B., Armstrong, P. I., & Velez, A. D. (2006). Validity of the Strong Interest Inventory with Mexican American high school students. *Journal of Career Assessment, 14*(2), 183–202.

Fouad, N. A. (1988). The construct of career maturity in the United States and Israel. *Journal of Vocational Behavior, 32,* 49–59.

Fouad, N. A. (1993). Cross-cultural vocational assessment. *Career Development Quarterly, 42*(1), 4–13.

Fouad, N. A. (1995). Cross-cultural vocational assessment of Hispanics: Assessment and career intervention. In F. L. Long (Ed.), *Career development and vocational behaviour* (pp. 165–191). Hillsdale, NJ: Lawrence Erlbaum.

Fouad, N. A., & Arbona, C. (1994). Careers in a cultural context. *Career Development Quarterly, 43*(1), 96–104.

Fouad, N. A., & Dancer, L. S. (1992). Cross-cultural structure of interests. *Journal of Vocational Behavior, 40,* 129–143.

Goodman, J., & Hansen, L. S. (2005). Career development and guidance systems across cultures: The gap between policies and practices. *Career Development Quarterly, 54*(1), 57–65.

Gottfredson, L. S. (2002). Gottfredson's theory of circumscription, compromise and self-creation. In D. Brown & Associates (Eds.), *Career choice and development* (4th ed., pp. 37–81). San Francisco: Jossey-Bass.

Granrose, C. S., & Chua, B. L. (1996). Global boundaryless careers: Lessons from Chinese family businesses. In M. B. Arthur & D. M. Rousseau (Eds.), *The boundaryless career: A new employment principle for a new organizational era* (pp. 201–217). Oxford: Oxford University Press.

Hansen, C. D., & Wilcox, M. K. (1997). Cultural assumptions in career management: Practice implications in Germany. *Career Development International, 2*(4), 195–202.

Hansen, J. I. C., & Fouad, N. A. (1984). Translation and validation of the Spanish form of the Strong-Campbell Interest Inventory. *Measurement and Evaluation in Counseling and Performance, 20,* 3–10.

Hansen, J. I. C., Scullard, M. G., & Haviland, M. G. (2000). The interest structures of Native American college students. *Journal of Career Assessment, 8*(2), 159–172.

Hartung, P. J. (2002). Cultural context in career theory and practice: Role salience and values. *Career Development Quarterly, 51*(1), 12–25.

Hartung, P. J., Speight, J. D., & Lewis, D. M. (1996). Individualism-collectivism and the vocational behavior of majority culture college students. *Career Development Quarterly, 45,* 87–96.

Heslin, P. A. (2005). Conceptualizing and evaluating career success. *Journal of Organizational Behavior, 26,* 113–136.

Hofstede, G. (1980). *Culture's consequences: International differences in work related values.* Beverly Hills, CA: Sage.

Holland, J. L. (1977). *The self-directed search.* Palo Alto, CA: Consulting Psychologists Press.

Holland, J. L. (1985). *Making vocational choices* (2nd ed.). Englewood Cliffs, NJ: Prentice Hall.

House, R. J., Hanges, P. J., Javidan, M., Doerfman, P. W., & Gupta, V. (Eds.). (2004). *Culture, leadership, and organizations: The GLOBE study of 62 societies.* Thousand Oaks, CA: Sage.

Hui, C. H., & Triandis, H. C. (1989). Effects of culture and response format on extreme response styles. *Journal of Cross-Cultural Psychology, 20,* 296–309.

Jarillo, J. (1988). On strategic networks. *Strategic Management Journal, 9,* 31–41.

Johnson, M. K., & Mortimer, J. T. (2002). Career choice and development from a sociological perspective. In D. Brown & Associates (Eds.), *Career choice and development* (4th ed., pp. 39–81). San Francisco: Jossey-Bass.

Juntunen, C. L., Barraclough, D. J., Broneck, C. L., Seibel, G. A., Winrow, S. A., & Morin, P. M. (2001). American Indian perspectives on the career journey. *Journal of Counseling Psychology, 48*(3), 274–285.

Kamenou, A., & Fearfull, A. (2006). Ethnic minority women: A lost voice in HRM. *Human Resource Management Journal, 16*(2), 154–172.

Kelly, A., Brannick, T., Hulpke, J., Levine, J., & To, M. (2003). Linking organisational training and development practices with new forms of career structures: A cross-national exploration. *Journal of European Industrial Training, 27*(2), 160–168.

Kerlinger, F. N. (1986). *Foundations of behavioral research* (3rd ed.). Chicago: Holt, Rinehart & Winston.

Khan, S. B., Alvi, S. A., Shaukat, N., Hussain, M. A., & Baig, T. (1990). A study of the validity of Holland's theory in a non-Western culture. *Journal of Vocational Behavior, 36,* 132–146.

Kim, U., Triandis, H. C., Kagitcibasi, C., Choi, S. C., & Yoon, G. (Eds.). (1994). *Individualism and collectivism: Theory, applications, and methods.* Thousand Oaks, CA: Sage.

Kluckhohn, C., & Strodtbeck, K. (1961). *Variations in value orientations.* Westport, CT: Greenwood.

Koegel, H. M., & Donin, I. (1995). Multicultural career development: A methodological critique of 8 years of research in three leading career journals. *Journal of Vocational Behavior, 32*(2), 50–62.

Kogut, B. (1989). A note on global strategy. *Strategic Management Journal, 10,* 383–389.

Kopp, R. (1994). International human resource policies and practices in Japanese, European, and United States multinationals. *Human Resources Management, 33,* 581–599.

Kornai, J. (1992). *The socialist system: The political economy of communism.* Princeton, NJ: Princeton University Press.

Laurent, A. (1986). The cross-cultural puzzle of international human resource management. *Human Resource Management, 25*(1), 91–102.

Lauver, P. J., & Jones, R. M. (1991). Factors associated with perceived career options in American Indian, white, and Hispanic rural high schools students. *Journal of Counseling Psychology, 38*(2), 159–168.

Law, B. (1993). Understanding careers work. *Career Development Quarterly, 41*(4), 297–313.

London, M. E., & Stumpf, S. A. (1982). *Managing careers.* Reading, MA: Addison-Wesley.

Maree, K. (2004). *Facilitating (post) postmodern/ narrative/brief career counselling in South Africa: Classic dream or traditional nightmare.* Paper presented at the Research Roundtable, Australian Association of Career Counsellors Conference, Coolangatta, Queensland.

Marshall, J. (1995). *Women managers moving on: Exploring career and life choices.* London: Thomson.

Marshall, J. C. (1989). Re-visioning career concepts: A feminist invitation. In M. B. Arthur, D. T. Hall, & B. S. Lawrence (Eds.), *Handbook of career theory* (pp. 275–291). Cambridge, UK: Cambridge University Press.

Mau, W. C. (2000). Cultural differences in career decision making styles and self-efficacy. *Journal of Vocational Behavior, 57*(3), 365–378.

Meaning of Work International Research Team. (1987). *The meaning of working: An international view.* New York: Academic Press.

Meir, E., Melamed, T., & Abu Freha, A. (1990). Vocational, avocational and skill utilization congruences and their relationship with well-being in two cultures. *Journal of Vocational Behavior, 36,* 153–165.

Metcalfe, B. D. (2006). Exploring cultural dimensions of gender and management in the Middle East. *Thunderbird International Business Review, 48*(1), 93–107.

Morishima, M. (1995). The Japanese human resource management system. In J. D. Jennings & L. Moore (Eds.), *HRM in the Pacific Rim: Institutions, practices and values* (pp. 119–150). New York: Walter de Gruyter.

Morocco, J. C. (1976). Vocational maturity of Arab and American high school students. *Journal of Vocational Behavior, 8,* 367–373.

Napier, N. K., & Thomas, D. C. (2001). Some things you may not have learned in graduate school: A rough guide to collecting primary data overseas. In B. Toyne, Z. Martinez, & R. Menger (Eds.), *International business scholarship: Mastering intellectual, institutional, and research design challenges.* Westport, CT: Quorum Books.

Ohmae, K. (1995). *The end of the nation state.* Cambridge, MA: Free Press.

Okurame, D. E., & Balogun, S. K. (2005). Role of informal mentoring in the career success of first-line bank managers: A Nigerian case study. *Career Development International, 10*(6), 512–521.

Osipow, S. H. (1983). *Theories of career development* (3rd ed.). Englewood Cliffs, NJ: Prentice Hall.

Pang, M. (2003). Boundaryless careers: The (in-)voluntary (re-)actions of some Chinese in Hong Kong and Britain. *International Journal of Human Resource Management, 14*(5), 809–820.

Pappas, S. C. (2006). Diversity in the workplace. *Employee Relations, 28*(2), 119–129.

Pareek, U., & Rao, T. V. (1980). Cross-cultural survey and interviewing. In H. C. Triandis & W. W. Lambert (Eds.), *Handbook of cross-cultural psychology.* Boston: Allyn & Bacon.

Parker, B. (1998). *Globalization: Managing across boundaries.* London: Sage.

Parker, P., Arthur, M. B., & Inkson, K. (2004). Career communities: A preliminary exploration of member-defined career support structures. *Journal of Organizational Behavior, 27,* 489–514.

Patton, W., & McMahon, M. (1999). *Career development and systems theory: A new relationship.* Pacific Grove, CA: Brooks/Cole.

Peiperl, M. A., & Arthur, M. B. (2000). Topics for conversation: Career themes old and new. In M. A. Peiperl, M. B. Arthur, R. Goffee, & T. Morris (Eds.), *Career frontiers: New conceptions of working lives.* Oxford: Oxford University Press.

Peng, T. K., Peterson, M. F., & Shyi, Y. P. (1991). Quantitative methods in cross national management research: Trends and equivalence issues. *Journal of Organizational Behavior, 12,* 87–107.

Peterson, G. W., Lumsden, J. A., Sampson, J. P., Reardon, R. C., & Lenz, J. G. (2002). Using a cognitive information processing approach in career counseling with adults. In S. G. Niles (Ed.), *Adult career development: Concepts, issues and practices.* Tulsa, OK: National Career Development Association.

Peterson, R. B., Napier, N. K., & Shul-Shim, W. (2000). Expatriate management: A comparison of MNCs across four parent countries. *Thunderbird International Business Review, 2,* 145–166.

Pringle, J. K., & Mallon, M. (2003). Challenges for the boundaryless career odyssey. *International Journal of Human Resource Management, 14*(5), 839–853.

Reisman, D. (1961). *The lonely crowd: A study of the changing American character.* New Haven, CT: Yale University Press.

Richardson, M. S. (2000). A new perspective for counsellors: From career ideologies to empowerment through work and relationship practices. In A. Collin & R. A. Young (Eds.), *The future of career* (pp. 197–211). Cambridge, UK: Cambridge University Press.

Roberts, K. H., & Boyacigiller, N. A. (1984). Cross-national organizational research: The grasp of the blind men. In B. M. Staw & L. L. Cummings (Eds.), *Research in organizational behavior* (Vol. 6, pp. 423–475). Greeenwich, CT: JAI Press.

Robertson, R. (1995). Glocalization: Time-space and homogeneity-heterogeneity. In M. Featherstone, S. Lash, & R. Robertson (Eds.), *Global modernities* (pp. 25–44). London: Sage.

Rokeach, M. (1973). *The nature of human values.* New York: Free Press.

Rosenbaum, J. E. (1984). *Career mobility in a corporate hierarchy.* New York: Academic Press.

Russia's State Sell-Off. (1994, July 7). It's sink or swim time. *Business Week,* p. 46.

Sagiv, L., & Schwartz, S. H. (1995). Value priorities and readiness for outgroup social contact. *Journal of Personality and Social Psychology, 69,* 437–448.

Sagiv, L., & Schwartz, S. H. (2000). A new look at national culture: Illustrative applications to role stress and managerial behavior. In N. N. Ashkanasy, C. Wilderom, & M. F. Peterson (Eds.), *The handbook of organizational culture and climate.* Thousand Oaks, CA: Sage.

Sanderson, S. W., Walsh, S., & Hayes, R. H. (1990). Mexico: Opening ahead of Eastern Europe. *Harvard Business Review, 68,* 32–38.

Savickas, M. (2002). Career construction: A developmental theory of vocational behavior. In D. Brown & Associates (Eds.), *Career choice and development* (4th ed., pp. 149–205). San Francisco: Jossey-Bass.

Schmitt-Rodermund, E., & Silbereisen, R. K. (1998). Career maturity determinants: Individual development, social context, and historical time. *Career Development Quarterly, 47*(1), 16–31.

Schwartz, S. H. (1992). Universals in the content and structure of values: Theoretical advances and empirical tests in 20 countries. In M. P. Zanna (Ed.), *Advances in experimental social psychology* (pp. 1–65). San Diego, CA: Academic Press.

Schwartz, S. H. (1994). Beyond individualism/collectivism: New dimensions of values. In U. Kim, H. C. Triandis, C. Kagitçibasi, S. C. Choi, & G. Yoon (Eds.), *Individualism and collectivism: Theory, applications, and methods* (pp. 85–119). Thousand Oaks, CA: Sage.

Schwartz, S. H., & Bilsky, W. (1990). Toward a universal psychological structure of human values. *Journal of Personality and Social Psychology, 53,* 550–562.

Shenkar, O., & Von Glinow, M. (1994). Paradoxes of organizational theory and research: Using the case of China to illustrate national contingency. *Management Science, 40*(1), 56–71.

Skorikov, F. W., & Vondracek, F. W. (1993). Career development in the Commonwealth of Independent States. *Career Development Quarterly, 41*(4), 314–329.

Smith, P. B., & Bond, M. H. (1999). *Social psychology across cultures.* Boston: Allyn & Bacon.

Strong, E. K., Hansen, J. I. C., & Campbell, D. (1994). *Strong Interest Inventory.* Palo Alto, CA: Consulting Psychologists Press.

Sue, D. W., & Kirk, B. A. (1972). Psychological characteristics of Chinese-American students. *Journal of Counseling Psychology, 6,* 471–478.

Sue, D. W., & Sue, D. (1990). *Counselling the culturally different: Theory and practice.* Cambridge, UK: Cambridge University Press.

Super, D. E. (1957). *The psychology of careers.* New York: Harper & Row.

Super, D. E. (1990). A life-span, life-space approach to career development. In D. Brown & L. Brooks (Eds.), *Career choice and development* (pp. 197–261). San Francisco CA: Jossey-Bass.

Swanson, J. L. (1992). The structure of vocational interests for African-American college students. *Journal of Vocational Behavior, 40,* 144–157.

Thomas, D. C. (2002). *International management: A cross-cultural perspective.* Thousand Oaks, CA: Sage.

Thomas, D. C., & Inkson, K. (2004). *Cultural intelligence: People skills for global business.* San Francisco: Berrett-Koehler.

Triandis, H. C. (1995). *Individualism and collectivism.* Boulder, CO: Westview.

Trompenaars, F. (1993). *Riding the waves of culture.* Burr Ridge, IL: Irwin.

Tung, R. L. (1982). Selection and training of U.S., European, and Japanese multinationals. *California Management Review, 25,* 57–71.

Tungli, Z., & Peiperl, M. A. (2004). *Expatriate practices in German, Japanese, U.K. and U.S. multinational companies: A comparative study.* Unpublished manuscript, London Business School, London.

Usunier, J. C. (1998). *International and cross-cultural management research.* London: Sage.

van de Vijver, F., & Leung, K. (1997). *Methods and data analysis for cross-cultural research.* Thousand Oaks, CA: Sage.

Vondracek, F. W., Lerner, R. M., & Schulenberg, J. E. (1986). *Career development: A life-span developmental approach.* Hillsdale, NJ: Erlbaum.

Wakabayahsi, M., & Graen, G. B. (1984). The Japanese career progress study. A 7-year follow-up. *Journal of Applied Psychology, 69,* 603–614.

Waterman, R. H., Waterman, J. A., & Collard, B. A. (1994). Toward a career resilient workforce. *Harvard Business Review, 72*(4), 87–95.

Watson, M. B., & Stead, G. B. (2001). Contextual transformation and the career development of South African youth. In C. R. Stones (Ed.), *Socio-political and psychological perspectives on South Africa* (pp. 173–195). New York: Nova Science.

Weick, K. (1996). Enactment and the boundaryless career: Organizing as we work. In M. B. Arthur & D. M. Rousseau (Eds.), *The boundaryless career: A new employment principle of a new organizational era* (pp. 40–57). New York: Oxford University Press.

Yang, K. S. (1988). Will societal modernization eventually eliminate cross-cultural psychological difference? In M. H. Bond (Ed.), *The cross-cultural challenge to social psychology.* Newbury Park, CA: Sage.

Young, R. A., Valach, L., & Collin, A. (2002). A contextualist explanation of career. In D. Brown & Associates (Eds.), *Career choice and development* (4th ed., pp. 206–252).

24

Boundaries in the Study of Career

Hugh Gunz

Maury Peiperl

Daniel Tzabbar

Before I built a wall I'd ask to know
What I was walling in or walling out

—Robert Frost, *Mending Wall*

In a world imagined by apostles of self-help such as Horatio Alger, Samuel Smiles (Smiles, 1958), or Hollywood, anyone can do anything; there are no limits to the life that can be led. Yet casual empiricism shows that if there is any truth in this assertion, it applies to a remarkable few. We watch the careers of those who start from humble beginnings and rise to dizzy heights with a mixture of awe and suspicion, perhaps animated by a tinge of jealousy. Awe, because the achievements are so remarkable; suspicion, just *because* the achievements are so remarkable. It might be that if we can attribute these paragons' rise to anything other than ability and hard work—for example, to a wise choice of parent or good social connections—we have found a way

AUTHORS' NOTE: We are most grateful to Celia Moore for her help in reviewing the literature for this chapter. It has also greatly benefited from the suggestions of Martin Evans and Michael Jalland.

of excusing ourselves from our own relative failure. But to observers and students of social phenomena, the suspicion (probably) has a different genesis: our interest in explaining the way societies work. There is no more central and fascinating aspect of society that needs explaining than the way its members live their lives and what this means for the institutions that comprise that society (Hughes, 1937).

Lives without limits don't, of course, have to involve climbing to the commanding heights. In a boundaryless world, I can become pretty much anything I want, provided I think I can do it and the people (if any) who are needed to make it possible do too. But the caveats that we are introducing here—the "ifs" that surround life chances—are, for most of us, very real and indicate the presence of what we shall call in this chapter *career boundaries*. If work careers are patterns of movement across a social landscape formed by the complex networks of economic society, then career boundaries are the lines on that social landscape that mark discontinuities in the patterns, points at which there are constraints on these movements. Some boundaries create only minor interruptions to the flow, while others are major blockages, allowing only a very few people to pass them. It is these discontinuities that give form to careers; their nature and origins are the subject of this chapter.

Indeed, the theme of boundaries is a unifying thread that runs throughout this volume; there is not a chapter in which they are not an important underlying—and sometimes overarching—concept.[1] In this chapter, we put the spotlight on them, asking, "What do they enclose? Where do they come from?" and, most important, "What is it that makes some career boundaries permeable and others impermeable?" Impermeable boundaries are barriers to mobility; permeable boundaries are ones people cross with relative ease. Boundary permeability (Schein, 1971), therefore, plays a central role in determining the overall shape of people's careers.[2]

Permeability is a property of boundaries that is more complex than it first appears. Why might this be? If a boundary separates two jobs that are, for instance, very different from each other, need radically different kinds of training, or are a very long way apart geographically, surely it will be impermeable—the kind of impassable boundary that Gunz, Evans, and Jalland (2002) call "frontiers"? The professions provide many examples of such boundaries: A nurse's chance of becoming a physician, without abandoning his or her training as a nurse and beginning again at medical school, is zero; and Guest and Sturges (Chapter 16) describe an impermeable boundary between pharmacy technicians and pharmacists. By the same token, it should be easy to move between jobs that are very similar to each other and close geographically, as do technical professionals in Silicon Valley (Saxenian, 1996).

But if that is so, why is it the case, as Saxenian reports, that jobs on Route 128 outside Boston, ostensibly very similar to Silicon Valley jobs, were not as amenable to this kind of mobility? Why might a senior management job in, for instance, the United Kingdom, be accessible to someone with working class origins but the French equivalent be quite inaccessible to the son of a French worker? And why should one professional find it easier than another, equally well-qualified person, to win competitive contracts? The answer, of course is that there are a great many things that go into the mix that determines career boundary permeability. In our examples here, these include the differing cultures of the electronics industries in Silicon Valley and Route 128, the way the social class systems work in the United Kingdom and France, and the varying individual ability of professionals to network, to learn about contracts, and to win the confidence of their potential clients. Our aim in this chapter is to try to put some structure on this mix, so that permeability can be better understood and predicted.

Boundaries are things that separate and surround other things. We begin by asking the following question: What is it that career boundaries separate and surround? Next, we remind ourselves that social boundaries are social constructs, often playing roles well beyond simply separating A from B. One implication of this is that it is boundaries that *define* the things they enclose; in other words, the boundary comes first, followed by the entity it surrounds. We draw on Abbott's model of social boundary formation to suggest a way of conceptualizing career boundaries in which they start forming in the minds of people as a set of beliefs about given kinds of work role transitions (subjective boundaries). If many people come to agree on the nature of these subjective boundaries, they start to become objective social facts. Finally, we show how this way of conceptualizing career boundaries allows us to explore the many influences that affect the permeability of career boundaries.

WHAT DO CAREER BOUNDARIES SEPARATE AND SURROUND?

Political boundaries separate and surround jurisdictions, organizational boundaries do the same for organizations, and occupational boundaries for occupations (Abbott, 1995). What is it that career boundaries separate? The use of spatial metaphors is widespread in the sociological literature (Silber, 1995), but as Silber points out, they are used in many different ways, with varying degrees of "strength." To say, analogously, that career boundaries surround and delimit careers is to beg the question of what is meant by "career": What is the "space" that is being delimited?

The focus in this volume is on work careers, so the landscape on which the boundaries are "drawn" is the set of networks of economic social organization to which we refer above. Many would argue, as does Savickas in Chapter 5, that "each person has only one career, regardless of the number of positions that person occupies from childhood through retirement," and that is certainly the implication of Arthur, Hall, and Lawrence's (1989, p. 8) definition adopted for this volume ("the evolving sequence of a person's work experiences over time"). But the term *career* is also very commonly used in the sense of a *fragment* or stage of a working life. For example, a professional hockey player may say that an injury means that "his career is over," meaning his career as a professional hockey player; there is no implication that he does not intend ever to work again. Again, Chandler and Kram (Chapter 13) refer to recent "trends of multiple careers in a lifetime." To continue with sporting examples, professional sportspeople, such as soccer or baseball players, may spend their playing lives out of choice with one team; others move from team to team as their teams' owners do deals of various kinds. For the non-moving player, a career boundary surrounds their

team. For the mobile player, the team boundary is relatively permeable and a more salient one surrounds, for example, the role of striker (football) or hitter (baseball). In both cases, the boundary is eventually crossed when their playing days are over, and the interesting question concerns the destination chosen. Do they, for example, leave their sport entirely, move to another "career" in the sport as coach or manager, or become an expert sports commentator?

In this chapter, as with the *Handbook* overall, we shall continue to use "career" to mean the entire "evolving sequence of a person's work experiences over time." So it is evident that career boundaries as we have described them in the previous paragraph do not "enclose" entire *careers*. In that sense, they differ from, for example, boundaries surrounding a profession (with certain qualifications to which we return below). Instead, they "surround" *career stages*. Hence, an entire work career, that is, a sequence of career stages, involves crossing any number of career boundaries.

For example, a family doctor may cross none, and retire from the practice that she joined (or set up) when she became fully qualified. In contrast, it is by no means uncommon for senior executives to have crossed a good many boundaries between business functions (as they gain experience of different kinds), corporations, and perhaps, as they get more senior, industries. Indeed, Schein's (1971; see also Slay and Taylor, Chapter 19) conical model sets the scene for many such transitions. He describes three forms of transitions within a given organization: between levels in the hierarchy, between functions, or toward greater centrality of power (*inclusion*). It is not difficult to generalize these three types beyond the hierarchical work organization that Schein was describing. A professional engineer or architect, for example, might gain higher levels of qualification or certification (*hierarchical*), join a different kind of practice (*functional*), or become influential as an officer in or a member of an important committee of his or her professional body (*inclusional*).

So for any one individual, although his or her work career can be viewed as a sequence of roles, in many respects it is the *sequence of work role transitions* that give it its distinctiveness. Gunz (1989), for example, shows how organizational career logics (dominant career patterns; see Higgins and Dillon, Chapter 21) are distinguished between organizations by the patterns of transition distinctive of each kind of organizational career logic. A key dimension in Sonnenfeld and Peiperl's (1988) typology of career systems concerns the nature of the boundary people cross as they join companies (is there a single port of entry at junior levels or can people join at any hierarchical level?). Career boundaries, then, do not enclose entire careers, but rather *a career, at the individual level of analysis* (Peiperl and Gunz, Chapter 3)*, becomes a sequence of boundary-crossings that are largely responsible for giving it its form.*

Is it possible to conceive of an alternative form of career boundary that surrounds an entire career (which could, perhaps, be called a "total career boundary")? At the individual level of analysis, probably not; it is likely that the concept only takes on meaning at a higher level of aggregation. We define below things we shall call "objective" career boundaries, those which have been commonly enough observed to take on an objective reality for the people involved in crossing or managing them. If enough people can be seen crossing a given sequence of objective career boundaries, this allows us to identify a career "stream" (Gunz & Jalland, 1996)—namely, a pattern in the flow of people across the social landscape. There are limited circumstances under which a total career boundary can be identified between those who are in the stream and those who are not, although it may be very fuzzy.

For example, despite what we said above about career boundaries differing from occupational boundaries, there are certainly some occupations in some jurisdictions for which a total career boundary surrounds the occupation. Careers in professions such as medicine typically comprise a sequence of work role transitions between jobs, none of which can be held without a professional qualification; thus, a total career boundary can be said to surround them. This boundary is fuzzy because, even in very closed professions such as medicine, people may join in mid-career or leave to do something else before their work lives are over. Another example is provided by Unilever's (2003) long-established U.K.-based management development scheme (UCMDS),[3] which explicitly

recruits a small group of trainees who go through a 2-year program and who, it is implied, are then identified for senior positions within Unilever. As of 2003, the past three Unilever Chairmen had started as UCMDS trainees (Unilever, 2003). Such so-called fast track schemes for management appear to be somewhat under strain (Baruch & Peiperl, 1997; Viney, Adamson, & Doherty, 1997), with considerable ambiguity surrounding the nature of the psychological contract between employer and employee, as careers have become less organizationally bound than they were in the middle to late decades of the 20th century. Nevertheless, to the extent that an elite cadre of executives is identified (perhaps covertly) by an organization, a career stream can be said to exist with an almost impermeable boundary surrounding it. Such examples, however, are likely to be rare.

THE SOCIALLY CONSTRUCTED NATURE OF BOUNDARIES

At first sight, career boundaries may seem to be objective, unproblematic phenomena. In most developed countries, for example, one cannot just hang up a sign saying "physician" and expect to be allowed to treat patients. There are usually laws preventing anyone doing this who has not gone to medical school, served their time as a trainee of various kinds, and passed the necessary qualifying exams administered by the body that the state authorizes to do such things. In other words, there is a strong, impermeable boundary around the medical profession, which is controlled by the designated authority. It does not stop there, either: Different medical specialties will typically have their own barriers to entry, creating career boundaries within the general territory of medicine. Similarly, any employer who requires a particular set of qualifications or experience when recruiting is putting up a career boundary in the sense that it is not possible for just anyone to apply to join the organization and be accepted simply on the basis that there is a vacancy to be filled.

Yet it is not as simple as this. Anyone who has been unfortunate enough to lose their job after the age of 50 is highly likely to have encountered impermeable organizational career boundaries, which are not experienced by potential recruits with lesser qualifications and experience but who are 25 years younger. All manner of reasons are given for age discrimination of this kind, some good and some not so good (Kanfer & Ackerman, 2004), but the upshot is the same: Organizations often surround themselves with career boundaries whose permeability varies with the age (or other attributes) of the potential boundary-crosser, but the fact of this differential permeability may not be made public in, for example, the way the position is advertised. There may be an asymmetry, in other words, in the way in which a career boundary is seen by different actors: The information that "insiders" have about the nature of the boundary is different from what "outsiders" have.

The implication of these examples—and the idea underpinning concepts such as the "protean" (Hall, 1976), "boundaryless" (Arthur & Rousseau, 1996), or "post-corporate" (Peiperl & Baruch, 1997) career—is that career boundaries are more than just simple objective social facts. An organizational career boundary may, by common consent, be seen to surround a particular organization; but to someone who views their career as boundaryless, in other words who sees their career not in the context of that organization but of, perhaps, a community of practice (Mutch, 2003), the organizational career boundary is not particularly salient. Similarly, "protean-ness" involves a state of mind in which career boundaries are dissolved by a process of personal transformation: One crosses boundaries by changing one or more important attributes of one's identity.

Career boundaries, in other words, are as real as the actors experiencing or managing them make them. In this, they resemble other forms of social boundaries, which are, of course, imaginary creations. As Fiol (1989, citing Wilden) says of organizational boundaries,

> Organizational boundaries are imagined lines drawn to separate the organization from its surrounding environment and to specify how internal roles and functions are related but also separated from one another. . . . Corporate boundaries thus define and delimit corporate relationships, delineating areas of autonomy and self-control as well as areas of interdependence. (p. 277)

Indeed organizational boundaries can be viewed as instruments of social control rather than as simple objective facts. Fleming and Spicer (2004) argue that during the industrial revolution, employers drew a boundary around the work organization "that, although by no means impermeable or impervious, formed a line of division between the organization and the outside world" (pp. 78–79). This gave the organization more control over employees at work but no responsibility for what happened to them outside work. Fleming and Spicer show how modern, so-called high-commitment organizations blur this boundary to increase their control over their workforce, so that work is taken home and home is brought to work.

Next, we consider a key implication of boundaries as social constructs: that it is boundaries that create the things that they demarcate.

BOUNDARIES COME BEFORE THE ENTITIES THEY ENCLOSE

The view of boundaries as social constructs has led many authors to argue that organizational boundaries come before the organizations they define (e.g., Heracleous, 2004; Lamont & Molnar, 2002):

> Instead of viewing the boundary as analytically drawn, or as Etzioni suggests, as incidental to an organization (Goffman, 1961), boundary setting is intrinsic to the very process of organizing. Boundaries are not "by-products" of organization, but rather organization (defined broadly, ranging from informal groups to formal organizations) evolves through the processes of boundary setting. Like any social system, an organization emerges through the processes of drawing distinctions, and it persists through the reproduction of boundaries. The focus is moved from what goes on inside the organization to its margins, where it is produced and reproduced. (Hernes, 2004, pp. 10–11)

Indeed Abbott (1995) argues that this observation—that boundaries come before the entities that they enclose—may be true of social boundaries more generally. He shows how it is the emergence of boundaries between different kinds of practitioners that can give rise to occupational groups rather than the other way round. In other words, it is the formation of the boundary that defines the group (see, for example, Diamond, Allcorn, & Stein, 2004). He uses the example of how, in the early days of computing, two distinct ways of working with computers developed. The first involved designing systems and the second, coding the software that would make the systems work. Gradually, it became apparent that this distinction was to be found in many different organizations, which Abbott calls "sites of difference." In other words, people realized that the distinction between analyzing systems and programming was a common one, to be found in many different "sites of difference" (Figure 24.1). In due course, this led to what Abbott calls a social "hooking up" process, as the occupations of "systems analyst" and "programmer" were created. Or to use another of Abbott's examples,

Social work as an entity came into existence [in the U.S.] when various social agents—the leaders of the settlement and charities organization movements, the heads of state boards, the superintendents of institutions—began to hook up these sites of difference into larger proto-boundaries and then into larger units. . . . That is, social work emerged when actors began to hook up the women from psychiatric work with the scientifically trained workers from the kindergartens with the non-church group

in friendly visiting and the child workers in probation. All those people were placed "within" social work, and the others ruled outside it. An image was then developed to rationalize this emerging reality as a single thing. Unfortunately, in the process of making such a hook-up, certain areas (like probation) may have ultimately proven too distant, in some sense, to have one of their parties included in the emerging thing called social work. (p. 869)

Abbott's argument, then, is that social "things" (as he calls them) such as professions are the *consequence* rather than the *cause* of social boundaries; in other words, the boundaries form first and the institutions take shape within the boundaries. The model links micro- to macro-levels of analysis in a very useful way because it provides an explanation for the way in which boundaries and institutions develop at the macro-level through micro-level processes.[4] It is also a theory that explains change: It focuses on developmental and change processes rather than taking the existence of a profession, for example, for granted. This, we shall argue, provides a most useful starting point for an examination of career boundaries.[5] It is not the nature of a particular "career" that needs explaining, but the way in which that career pattern is maintained distinct from other career patterns, changes over time perhaps by combining

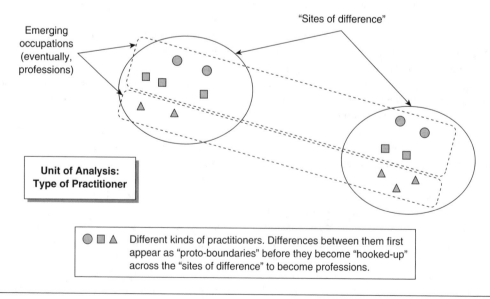

Figure 24.1   Abbott's (1995) Theory of Occupational Emergence

with others, or disappears. For example, it is currently commonplace to argue that the "organizational" career is disappearing in favor of something more boundaryless. But the evidence seems to be that it is not so much a *disappearance* as a *reconstruction* of boundaries that happens in these circumstances (Bagdadli, Solari, Usai, & Grandori, 2003) and sometimes not as much of a reconstruction as one might expect (Pringle & Mallon, 2003):

> The stories we heard were less about breaking free than about reconstructing the boundaries: both structural and ideological. Seeking long-term contracts with organisations, they hoped to re-embed themselves within organisational worlds. On an ideological level, the participants struggled to rewrite their views about work. Most still judged themselves by the codes of employment. It appeared that participants were attempting to establish new employment contexts which in some ways approximated those that they had only recently left. (Cohen & Mallon, 1999, p. 346)

Our interest, then, is in the way career boundaries are constructed so as to give shape and form to careers. So, for example, to the extent that we observe an interruption in the flow of people across the boundary surrounding Organization A, in the sense that a large proportion of its employees spend a good part of their work career on the "inside" of the boundary even though they may often change jobs within the organization, we can talk about an organizational career boundary defining an organizational career. But if we observe many of Organization B's employees leaving for other employers or becoming self-employed contractors and being replaced by others from outside the organization (perhaps as contractors rather than employees), we conclude that Organization B's career boundary is more permeable than that of Organization A and that the careers of the people in question are (to some extent at least) boundaryless.

THE GENESIS OF CAREER BOUNDARIES

We take the following approach to describing the genesis of career boundaries as social artifacts. First, we distinguish between subjective and objective boundaries; next, we explain the unit of analysis that we adopt, that is, the work role transition; and finally, we use an example from practice to show how subjective boundaries can form and be transformed into objective boundaries.

Subjective and Objective Career Boundaries

The examples we have given above, both concrete (e.g., the baseball or football players) and theoretical (e.g., Schein's conical model), hint at the great complexity of career boundaries. It is not just that a single occupation can be surrounded by multiple boundaries, but each boundary is also multifaceted, in the sense that it marks the transition to many different kinds of roles. To gain some conceptual traction in such a slippery area, we start from a subjectivist position: We view career boundaries as initially taking shape as ideas in the heads of the actors—career owners and those with whom they interact. These ideas, which can be anything from inchoate to well developed, are about what the focal person might be able to do next. We refer to them as *subjective* career boundaries, because they are essentially held privately by each individual. They become *objective* when a hooking-up process (to use Abbott's [1995] term) begins, and at least some of the ideas are shared by enough actors for a macro-level pattern to become apparent. So in our professional baseball player example, there is a relatively well-established boundary between player and coach, emerging from a relatively well-developed set of shared expectations about what it takes to be able to cross it, simply because it is in the nature of the coaching role that it is very difficult for anyone to do the job without first having been a player. In other words, the career of coach is defined by the boundary surrounding it, and this is well-enough understood by enough people for the term to have a generally understood meaning. In our terms, then, the shared understanding of how the boundary works means that we can talk about it as having an objective ontology (Figure 24.2). The process we are describing can be seen as a special case of the more general institutional processes discussed by Jones and Dunn (Chapter 22), in which social knowledge is encoded or dissociated

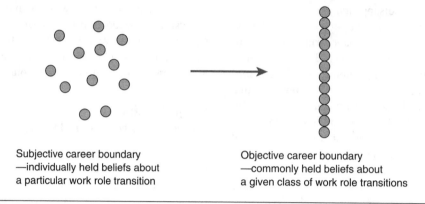

Subjective career boundary
—individually held beliefs about
a particular work role transition

Objective career boundary
—commonly held beliefs about
a given class of work role transitions

Figure 24.2   Subjective and Objective Career Boundaries

"from roles and role relationships through habitualization, objectification, sedimentation and de-institutionalization."

We have made it sound as if consensus always emerges. But this is by no means necessarily the case, of course. We defined career boundaries above as social constructs, implying that the way the consensus comes about, if indeed it does, is entirely contingent on what may be very complex social processes. So, for example, the boundary surrounding a company may be clearly defined in everyone's minds: This is what you have to do in order to get a job at the X Corporation. But it may not be anything as uncontroversial as this. The HR Department of X may be absolutely clear about what they do to hire people. But the word on the street could just as easily be, "Never mind what X says, the reality is that it only takes people who come from Ivy League schools, who have connections with the family owning the company, or who belong to a particular ethnic or religious group, or who are Freemasons," and so on.

We cannot generalize here about the ease with which a consensus may develop, turning a set of subjective boundaries into a recognizable objective boundary. How, or even whether, it happens depends on the ability of some of the actors involved to impose their views on everyone else and on the different ways in which the rest of the actors interpret what is going on. But for simplicity of presentation, we shall assume that it *is* possible for objective boundaries to emerge in the way we describe, if only because it is self-evidently the case that they do. While it is always

possible to find controversial boundaries like the kind we described above, it is equally true that good working consensuses emerge about many, if not most, of the boundaries that we encounter in life. The ones for which this fails to happen are the ones that keep the lawyers busy.

This distinction between subjective and objective boundaries draws on an established tradition in the careers literature (Derr & Laurent, 1989; Hughes, 1937; Khapova, Arthur, and Wilderom, Chapter 7), although with an important difference. The subjective and objective *careers* are both properties of the individual: the same career, but seen from radically different perspectives. However, *career boundaries* are only properties of the individual at the *subjective* level.

Subjective career boundaries are those that are constructed in the heads of the people experiencing them. Just as social networks can be analyzed in terms of a focal person (*ego*) and everyone who can be connected with the focal person by means of the network (*alter*), there are two broad classes of actors who matter in the construction of subjective career boundaries: (a) the career owner (ego) and (b) everyone else who affects the career of the career owner (alter). Alter can take many forms depending on the situation of ego. For example, a new graduate looking for her first job will, like it or not, get advice from many directions, including parents, teachers, friends, and relations (as in the wonderful scene from the movie *The Graduate* in which the hero is told, at the graduation party thrown by his parents, "Plastics!").

When she applies for jobs, she encounters yet more alters: the gatekeepers (King, 2004)[6] to each employer who manage or are involved in the personnel selection process. But if ego is a mid-career manager who has just lost his job, the set comprising alter will differ in many respects: outplacement consultants (if the manager is lucky), the network of contacts that he has built up over his career (Granovetter, 1973), family and friends, and, of course, the gatekeepers to the occupation(s) that he is currently examining. In each of these two cases, the alters with whom the focal person interacts are shaping, to a greater or lesser extent, ego's view of what he or she can do next.

Since objective career boundaries emerge from a consensus of these actors, in which powerful figures decide how proto-boundaries should be hooked up to define the career stage that emerges, they are properties of a *social entity* such as an organization, an industry, an occupation, or a community. So while subjective career boundaries are properties of *individuals*, objective boundaries are properties of *social entities*. The two kinds of boundaries, therefore, exist at distinctly different levels of analysis.

The Work Role Transition as the Unit of Analysis

If the unit of analysis for Abbott's model of the emergence of professions is the *type of practitioner*, the corresponding unit for our model of the emergence of objective career boundaries is the *work role transition* (Nicholson, 1984). Such transitions are by no means confined to organizational models of work roles. Interpreting the term in its broadest sense, it is simply the transition from one work role to another. Either or both of the roles might be organizational (e.g., market research assistant or vice president of operations) or occupational (e.g., physician, software engineer, HR consultant); they could differ in being full- or part-time, employee or contingent worker, and so on. They may, in other words, have everything or nothing to do with formal organization, and the full characterization of a work role transition can involve a great many dimensions. As we have seen, Schein's (1971) conical model of

career boundaries describes three kinds of transitions within a given organization: between levels in the hierarchy, functions, or centrality to power (*inclusion*). But a transition might also involve a change of location (e.g., moving to another plant or office that might or might not be in the same geographical area or jurisdiction), product or process, employer, status as employee or contractor, industry, intensity of employment (i.e., full- or part-time), and so on. Finding a pattern within the maze of possible work role transitions is a challenge:

> Organizations are not pyramids, they are scattered encampments on a wide terrain of hills and valleys, and careers are not ladders, but stories about journeys and routes through and between these encampments. Some of these paths and stories are well trodden and well known, others are improvised and haphazard. Many have unclear beginnings and no obvious endings: they just peter out. Careers, as stories of these journeys, often get better with the telling. Logic, consistency and meaning are reassuringly accessible when one analyses the past, but become strangely elusive when one dispassionately appraises the present. Careers can be viewed as fictions about the past to help us feel good about the future. (Nicholson & West, 1988, p. 94)

Origins of Career Boundaries: An Example From Practice

We depict a highly simplified model of the emergence of career boundaries in Figure 24.3, using the example of lawyers, who have a number of typical career options open to them. A few typical of the U.S. or Canadian context are detailed in what follows. Lawyers may stay in private practice—working as sole practitioners—or join a law firm. Often, they become corporate (sometimes called "in-house") counsel in industry or commerce (Gunz, 1991)—employees in the normal sense of the term as opposed to autonomous professionals (for an early analysis of this phenomenon, see Daniels, 1975). In the United States, furthermore, there is a well-trodden path from the law office to the CEO office (Priest & Krol, 1986). Finally, it is quite common for lawyers to enter politics and to return to practicing law if they lose office. We show this schematically in Figure 24.3 (for simplicity, we

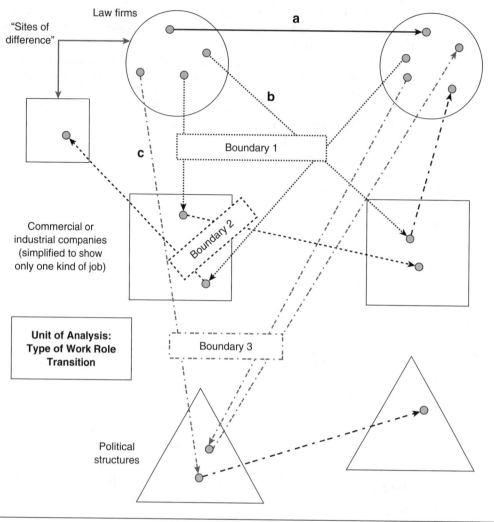

Figure 24.3   Work Role Transitions and Career Boundaries: An Example From Legal Practice

identify only one kind of position in business; let us assume that it is that of corporate counsel).

The figure shows most of these possible work role transitions in a highly idealized world, each type of arrow showing a different type of transition. The "sites of difference" are the firms—the law firms, corporations, or political structures (e.g., the British Parliament, the German Bundestag, a town council)—within which lawyers operate, and the differences here are the different work role transitions that can be made within or between these sites of difference. The transitions are differentiated from each other on the basis of the differences between the roles on either side of the transition.

So, for example, the topmost transition, Arrow a, is between two law firms; Arrow b is between a law firm and a corporate counsel position, and Arrow c takes the lawyer into politics.

Each individual's perspective on each work role transition is a subjective boundary—in Abbott's terms a proto-boundary—because the individual ideas have not yet been hooked up into externally visible patterns of movement. So a subjective boundary is no more than a set of ideas that a lawyer has about what it is like, for example, to move from one law firm to another, or to move from private practice to corporate counsel, or to move from either into politics. One subjective boundary could be ideas about how impossible and undesirable it is to move to corporate work; another could be about how good and easy it would be to move to a larger and more prestigious firm as partner. An objective boundary starts becoming apparent when patterns in the way in which people actually make work role transitions become sufficiently evident to enough participants in the process (the career owners themselves and the people involved in selecting them for the roles to which they move) for the boundary to become an objective social fact. In other words, *an objective boundary appears when a critical mass of people—that is, enough people who are in a position such that they can impose their views about the boundary on most other people—agree that it exists.*

The figure shows three objective boundaries. Let us assume that it becomes apparent that an increasing number of lawyers are making b-type transitions, from private practice to corporate counsel. When enough do, the move ceases to be an occasional, idiosyncratic, and perhaps unnoticed work role transition and is instead seen as a "normal career move" undertaken by lawyers with any of a number of recognizable interests, for example, wanting to specialize in commercial practice, desiring eventually to move into corporate management, or looking for a job with regular hours that do not involve being called at 11:30 p.m. on Saturday nights by clients arrested for being drunk and disorderly (Gunz, 1991). Boundary 1 thus emerges.

Similarly, Boundary 2 is between corporate counsel roles in different corporations and Boundary 3 is between private law practice and politics. The analogy of Abbott's "hooking-up" process in which agents, typically quite deliberately, identify commonalities across practitioners of different kinds and exploit the differences between these commonalities and other practitioners to establish, for example, a profession, is the gradual general recognition that many people do indeed move from private practice to corporate counsel, from one corporate counsel role to another, or from private practice to politics and back.

At this stage, we can refer to the career boundaries as "objective" because the consensus that they represent begins to affect the behavior of whole groups of people. For example, if it becomes evident that a lot of

lawyers become politicians, then people might choose law school as a good way to get into politics. Again, if it becomes known that CEOs often have legal training, this encourages corporate search committees to go out of their way to canvass lawyers when seeking their new leaders, even though the lawyers may know little, if anything, about the industry or firm in question. The process of boundary-crossing becomes institutionalized as conventions develop around it. To take another example, university business schools are mostly relatively recent creations. In many countries, their initial faculty were drawn from many sources: those parts of the academic world in which subjects such as commerce or accounting were taught, or disciplines that seemed to be related to managerial and organizational processes such as psychology and sociology, and the industrial and commercial worlds in which management was practiced. Faculty who came from the academic world and understood its norms about scholarship fitted in better with the rest of the university (although they were often dismissed by their practitioner colleagues and executive students as unworldly), so a pattern became increasingly evident of sourcing new faculty from doctoral programs rather than from business. Now, in North America, and increasingly elsewhere, the career boundary surrounding business school faculty is highly structured with its timetable, procedures, conventions, and rituals. It has taken on the full guise of an objective career boundary.

The emergence of the boundaryless career as a concept owes much to this phenomenon. As moves between companies became more common in many economies (e.g., Arthur, Inkson, & Pringle, 1999; Nicholson & West, 1988, p. 94), it became possible to label (or as Cohen and Mallon [1999] implicitly argue, mislabel) the careers of these organizational boundary-crossers as boundaryless. The hooking-up process here was being conducted by scholars (most notably Arthur & Rousseau, 1996) identifying the phenomenon, giving it a label, and writing extensively about it. A literature developed around the concept, and although vigorous debate continues about its pervasiveness in the world of work (e.g., Cappelli, 1999; Jacoby, 1999a, 1999b; Pringle & Mallon, 2003), even skeptics accept that organizational boundaries are more permeable than they used to be (Scott, 2004).

BOUNDARY PERMEABILITY

We can now come to the central concern of this chapter—namely, a consideration of what affects the permeability of career boundaries. We use the term in a sense somewhat different from that of Schein (1971, p. 405), who distinguishes between the *degree of permeability* and the *filtering properties* of boundaries. The filters, for Schein, are "the process or set of rules by which one passes through the boundary" (p. 406). Here, we combine the two under the "permeability" label, looking at the filtering processes and rules as part of what goes into defining the permeability of a given boundary.

As we signaled in the introduction to this chapter, many factors can come into play in deciding how permeable a given boundary might be. DiPrete (1987, p. 424), for example, clearly identifies some of these complexities, arguing that four factors specifically control the permeability of organizational career boundaries:

1. skills-based contingencies

2. information-based contingencies

3. contingencies due to the particular configuration of positions in an organization (institutional)

4. contingencies arising from the institutionalization of formal structure (institutional)

To provide a language for our discussion of permeability, we next introduce two underpinning concepts: reluctance to move and reluctance to select.

The Permeability of Subjective Boundaries: Reluctance to Move and to Select

To get a clearer understanding of how permeable a given career boundary might be, we need to return to the subjective level of analysis. What does it mean to say that a subjective boundary is impermeable?

We defined a subjective career boundary as a set of ideas that the focal person (ego) has about a given work role transition. The more reluctant ego is to examine a particular transition or, having examined it, to make the move, the more impermeable is the subjective boundary in the mind of ego. Following Gunz, Evans, and Jalland (2000, pp. 28–29), we shall call this kind of boundary a *reluctance to move,* in the sense that it is a reluctance on the part of ego to consider a given option, perhaps because she or he is unaware that it exists, views it as unattractive for some reason, or sees it as unattainable. A reluctance to move

> refers to the boundaries that career-owners construct in their minds, which constrain careers: the limits we place on ourselves when we wonder what we could possibly do. Someone's despair at being laid off may be explained in part in terms of the boundaries she has in her mind which make it hard for her to see who else might value her services. Someone else's confidence in a similar situation may spring from the ease with which she believes she can move into a new job or occupation, in other words, from the absence of mental barriers. (Gunz et al., 2000, p. 29)

We have seen how alters play an important role in affecting ego's reluctance to move. They can be gatekeepers, advisors, role senders, opinion leaders, or any of the myriad people who might influence ego's decision process one way or the other. But any alters who are gatekeepers to a career stage (in the sense that we are using it here, that is, a career fragment) have an additional role: They can choose not to select ego. This is what Gunz et al. (2000, pp. 28–29) refer to as a *reluctance to select.* It can have an entirely rational basis: Hospitals, for example, are hardly likely to hire medical staff who are not medically qualified, and a cancer hospital is going to need a lot of oncologists. But because the proto-boundary is subjective, its basis can be murkier. We referred above to the reluctance of recruiters to hire the middle-aged, which may be based on rational considerations of ability but may also be less than rational (Kanfer & Ackerman, 2004). In the worst cases, such as those involving racial prejudice, the proto-boundary may be entirely irrationally based

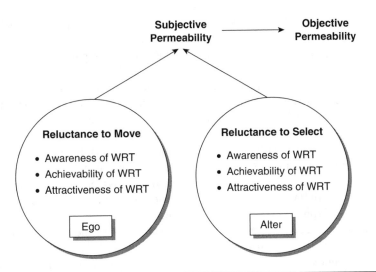

Figure 24.4   Antecedents of Career Boundary Permeability

NOTE: WRT = work role transition

(Prasad, D'Abate, and Prasad, Chapter 10), but whatever the form it takes, it is real. A selector who is reluctant to select a particular person creates a barrier for that person, which, if the proto-boundary is hooked up across many like selectors, becomes an objectively observable boundary. In a community dominated by racists, for example, everybody knows that it is virtually impossible for members of the oppressed racial group to get the jobs that the bigots deny them.

The remaining alters—those not directly involved in the selection process—may nevertheless influence both a reluctance to move or to select. Mentors might advise their protégés (or friends and family their friends or relatives) to either make the move or not, advisors or opinion leaders may encourage or discourage recruiters to hire a particular individual, and so on. Our point is simply that the "reluctances" can be complex in origin, and their sources highly contingent on the situation in which ego finds himself or herself. We explore the implications of this complexity in the next section.

Determinants of Boundary Permeability

By focusing on reluctance to move and to select, we adopt a subjective starting point. This allows us to explore permeability by drawing on explanations that may have psychological roots but that, in turn, may well be the outcome of social forces. We shall draw on a range of literature because the origins of these "reluctances" can be complex, and as we shall see, they can be viewed from both psychological and sociological perspectives.

Reluctances to move and to select depend on three facets of the situation (Figure 24.4): (1) an *awareness* that a given work role transition actually exists as a possibility, (2) an assessment of the *achievability* of making the work role transition, and (3) the *attractiveness* of the work role transition. In each case, the facet can be approached from the perspective of the career owner (ego) or those with whom the career owner interacts (alter). For the remainder of the chapter, we look at each of these three facets. First, we examine their influence on subjective permeability; we turn to the objective in the following section. We can do no more than touch on the vast literature underpinning each facet, and our examples are intended to be purely illustrative.

1. Awareness

An awareness that a given work role transition actually exists as a possibility (cf. DiPrete's, 1987, p. 424, "information-based contingencies") is the first facet of permeability. It points to a pervasive barrier to mobility, namely simply not knowing that a job or a contract exists or not being known about by people looking for someone to fill a role. Even within an organization, selectors can be quite unaware of potential recruits if the organization is big enough and they are organizationally distant enough. This is even more the case for the adverse selection problem, when mistrust of the motives of managers whom the selector does not know figures into the mix. DiPrete (1987) quotes an old saying in government: "'they pass the queen of spades'—the worst card in the game of hearts—underlin[ing] the danger of recruiting an unknown" (pp. 424–425).

This phenomenon is easily recognized as a case of bounded rationality (March & Simon, 1958)—the limits to human intellectual capacities by comparison with the complexities of the problems and situations that we face. We therefore adopt simplified models that capture what we hope are the main features of a problem, without capturing all its complexities. Moving and selecting are both, then, characterized by "satisficing": searching for satisfactory, rather than optimal, outcomes. Satisficing involves considering only a limited number of options, typically closely related to ego's experience and that of alters close to ego, manifested as March and Simon's (1958) so-called local search.

The hazards of local search are well recognized in the practitioner literature. Job seekers have a rich set of offerings to call on (perhaps most notably Bolles's long-running series, for example, Bolles, 2007), replete with advice on how to find out about possibilities that you might never have thought of and also how to make sure that people who might offer you a position get to know of you. Similarly, the recruitment literature (e.g., Hall & Goodale, 1986) emphasizes the need to cast as wide a net as possible when searching for candidates. Of course, it is not as if this advice is always heeded: Large firms, for example, seem to have much broader and more systematic search processes than small ones, are more likely to rely on objective qualifications, such as academic record and extracurricular activities, and use a greater number of selection procedures in making hiring decisions (Barber, Wesson, Roberson, & Taylor, 1999).

Sociologists have long been interested in the way in which life chances are affected by social forces. In its most parsimonious form, the status attainment model postulates that the social status of one's parents affects one's opportunity structure via the level of schooling one achieves, which in turn affects occupational level (Duncan, Featherman, & Duncan, 1972; Rubin, 1976). Ethnographic studies reveal how this is not necessarily a matter of educational level imposing limits based on technical qualification. For example, Willis's (1977) study of "how working class kids get working class jobs" illustrates graphically how children move into working class or middle-class occupations simply because that is the way things happen in their social group: It is as if an incongruent occupation is invisible to them. Vermeulen and Minor (1998) provide a fascinating account of how the circumstances of rural life and gender limited the career possibilities seen by a group of women and how "most of the information and advice these women received about occupations and colleges came from their parents" (p. 243). Most of them, for example, did not realize that scholarships were available to them that might have enabled them to go to college.

2. Achievability

The second facet, achievability, depends on a subjective assessment of one's capabilities (or those of a candidate) vis-à-vis a given position, occupation, way of life (e.g., full-time vs. part-time work, employee vs. contracting), organizational or national culture, and so on. The difference between this and awareness is that the decision maker is aware of the work role transition; he or she must then come to a view on whether or not the transition is possible. For ego, the question is, "Can I do it?" For alter, it is, "Can she or he do it?" We tend to write off countless possible roles in life, simply because we do not think that we are capable of them.

One obvious driver of achievability is the *contrast* of the boundary in question. This is "the number of core and peripheral features that differ between a pair of role identities and the extent of the differences, where core features are weighted more heavily" (Ashforth, Kreiner, & Fugate, 2000, p. 475)—that is, the difference in the nature of the roles at either side of the boundary or the magnitude of the change experienced by someone making a work role transition across the boundary. Contrast, in the terms of Ashforth et al., is an amalgam of Louis's (1980) "change," the objective differences between the two situations, and "contrast," the subjectively experienced differences. It resembles Nicholson's (1984) "novelty," "the degree to which the role permits the exercise of prior knowledge, practiced skills, and established habits" (p. 178). The higher the contrast of a boundary, the less permeable it is likely to be, other things being equal.

But other things here are far from equal, for many reasons. For example,

> The impermeability of group boundaries may refer to an objective impossibility of changing group affiliations, but it may also only be experienced as such because values that are central to their self-concept prevent people from freely moving from one group to another. (Ellemers, 1993, p. 32).

We consider some of these reasons here, under the headings of (a) ability and self-efficacy, (b) circumstances, and (c) path dependency.

a. Ability and Self-Efficacy. The question of how suitable an individual is for a position is, of course, from the perspective of ego, central to the occupational choice literature (Savickas, Chapter 5). From the perspective of a selector (alter), it is the selection literature—the art and science of matching candidate to role—that is relevant. Much of it comes down to abilities, those special skills, talents, and aptitudes that allow a person to perform in some areas better than in others (Jones, 1992).

People's abilities limit their choices and influence their decision to consider certain options (Dawis & Lofquist, 1984). Moreover, people's judgment about their capabilities to organize and execute courses of actions explains why they tend to explore a narrow set of career opportunities over the course of their life. Lent and colleagues' (Lent, Brown, & Hackett, 1994; Lent, Hackett, & Brown, 1999; Lent, Lopez, Brown, & Gore, 1996; see also Kidd, Chapter 6; Khapova, Arthur, and Wilderom, Chapter 7) social cognitive career theory (SCCT), grounded in Bandura's (1986) social cognitive theory, argues that

some persons may prematurely eliminate potentially rewarding occupational pursuits because of inaccurate self-efficacy, outcome expectations, or both. . . . [E]ven persons with well-developed and differentiated interests in a particular career path will be unlikely to pursue that path if they perceive (accurately or inaccurately) substantial barriers to entering or advancing in that career. (Brown & Lent, 1996, p. 355)

In the view of Brown and Lent (1996), people often experience narrowed interests either because they have been exposed to a restricted range of efficacy-building experiences or because they have developed inaccurate occupational self-efficacy or outcome expectations. Lowered perceived efficacy along important career-related dimensions could, in turn, unduly restrict the types of occupations considered and affect performance and persistence in the pursuit of a chosen occupation (Betz & Hackett, 1981). Coping efficacy, the degree to which individuals possess confidence in their ability to cope with or manage complex and difficult situations, may also influence the perception of barriers or obstacles to certain career options (Bandura, 1997). People who possess relatively high levels of coping efficacy are more likely than those with low coping efficacy to engage in efforts to overcome perceived barriers associated with particular goals or objectives (Hackett & Byars, 1996).

b. Circumstances. The question of why some people feel able to tackle a particular role and others do not can depend as much on a person's circumstances as it can on his or her abilities. Gunz et al. (2002, pp. 64ff), building on work such as that of Gunz (1989), argue that contrast—the difference between roles—is not the sole explanation for impermeability, because there are situations in which people cross high-contrast boundaries with ease. In constructional organizational career logics (Gunz, 1989; see also Higgins and Dillon, Chapter 21), people do just this. For example, an IT professional in one of the companies Gunz studied moved abruptly within the firm to become a chemical plant maintenance manager.

A second, institutional, set of forces is also at work (cf. DiPrete, 1987, p. 424), emerging from many sources—for example,

- contracts of employment (employers will sometimes impose contracts on valuable employees that prevent them from moving to competitors for a given time),
- external jurisdictions (e.g., immigrant professionals often find major obstacles placed in their way, ostensibly to check their expertise but frequently to keep them from competing with home-trained professionals),
- social attitudes such as the glass ceiling (Hultin, 2003; Lyness & Thompson, 1997; Van Vianen & Fischer, 2002) faced by many women,
- labor organization, and
- boundaries of inclusion (it can be very hard to join the "in" group).

Economic need, lack of family support, or various other considerations (e.g., gender or ethnic discrimination) may inhibit the pursuit of primary interests or preferred career goals. Simply put, some—perhaps most—people are not granted the opportunity to make career choices under optimal conditions. For example, someone from an ethnic minority group may realize that there are few representatives in a certain career field from their ethnic group and prematurely foreclose on a potentially rewarding career only because their environment has offered limited efficacy-building opportunities or because a lack of ethnic minority representation in that career has led to an inaccurate set of self-efficacy beliefs or occupational outcome expectations (Prasad, D'Abate, and Prasad, Chapter 10). In other words, particular circumstances can make almost any given career option seem out of reach. Vermeulen and Minor (1998) provide a familiar example of how the women in their study felt their career choices to be constrained by circumstances such as marriage and motherhood, themes readily recognizable by most women in contemporary societies around the world. Indeed, the so-called glass ceiling is the result of a generally irrelevant characteristic—a candidate's sex—being used to downgrade that candidate's suitability for a position.

c. Path Dependency. The standard selection model is essentially path independent in its thinking: Candidates are assessed on their suitability for the role in question. But Rosenbaum's (1984) study of job-advancement

mechanisms in a large firm over a 10-year period demonstrated a path dependence to careers that meant that "by at least the third year of employment, an employee's eventual career chances ha[d] been fundamentally affected" (Rosenbaum, 1979, p. 238). Particular individuals, identified early for advancement, quickly became "stars." Attendance at particular colleges had an important impact on advancement; often, individuals were earmarked for advancement before they had been with the firm long enough to permit sufficient observation of their performance or accurate judgments.

In other words, achievability in the view of someone selecting ego for a role is not necessarily just a matter of "measuring up" the candidate for his or her current capabilities. We carry labels with us that we acquire early in life and that mark us down for success or otherwise in at least some, but certainly not all (Forbes, 1987), forms of organization, regardless of how well we might be performing now. For example, a youth who has not taken the toughest courses early in his or her schooling encounters many barriers against taking higher-level mathematics and science courses in secondary school. University entrance and completion then become only remote possibilities. Similarly, it is difficult if not altogether impossible for a young high school dropout to return to school and eventually become a physician. In later life, it is difficult for a 55-year-old displaced autoworker to find another job with pay and benefits comparable to those in his or her old job. The processes that determine which individuals win and lose in the tournament of life are composed of a complex interaction of individual actions and "rules of the game."

This path dependency reflects a well-established sociological theme—namely, that life chances can be set very early in life, however supposedly egalitarian the society (e.g., Duncan, Yeung, Brooks-Gunn, & Smith, 1998). Hollingshead's (1965) study of Elmtown's youth is a classic investigation of the role social class plays in human development in general: Social class influenced student career aspirations, with individuals coming from a higher class aspiring to professional or business careers, while individuals coming from lower classes aspired primarily to service trades. In a similar vein, Osipow (1997) found that children generally follow careers that resemble those of their fathers.

If the achievability of making a work role transition is about the question, "Can I or he or she do it?" the third feature, attractiveness, is about the question, "How much does he or she want to do it?"

3. Attractiveness

The third facet of a reluctance to move or to select, attractiveness, again depends on a subjective assessment, but now of the valence of the work role transition rather than its achievability. How much is the career owner drawn to the new role, and to what extent is alter drawn to ego for reasons other than the technical "fit" arguments implicit in the "achievability" facet?

This question, too, leads to a vast literature on occupational choice (see Kidd, Chapter 6; Savickas, Chapter 5). Much of the "vocational" thread in career scholarship (Moore, Gunz, and Hall, Chapter 2) has addressed the question, "To what kind of job is a given individual drawn?" To crudely summarize the answer, people are believed to gravitate toward environments congruent with their personality (e.g., Holland, 1997).

The attractiveness of occupations has fascinated psychologists not working in the vocational field too. Those who have focused on the characteristics of the individual have typically concentrated on values (which are also of interest to vocational psychologists, of course). Values significantly affect career decisions (Bailyn & Schein, 1976; Schein, 1978); people seem to choose jobs (Feather, 1995; Judge & Bretz, 1992) or organizations (Chatman, 1989; Oldham, 1976) that match their values. Schein's richer metaphor of "career anchors" is consistent with the value theorist's perception of values (e.g., England, 1967; Rokeach, 1973). Like values, career anchors are viewed as a criterion for career-related decisions. According to Schein (1978),

> Career anchors . . . are "inside" the person, functioning as a set of driving and constraining forces of career decisions and choices. . . . The career anchor functions in the person's work life as a way of organizing experience, identifying one's area of contribution in the long run, generating criteria for

kinds of work settings in which one wants to function, and identifying patterns of ambitions and criteria for success by which one will measure oneself. (pp. 125–127)

Hence, when an individual is forced to make a decision, the career anchor will serve as a criterion that guides him or her to choose from among several options, and this criterion will stay relatively constant across all of his or her career decisions.

In a completely separate stream of literature from vocational psychology, cognitive psychologists draw on expectancy theory (Vroom, 1964) to examine what drives both the attractiveness of career alternatives (Brooks & Betz, 1990; Vroom, 1966; Wanous, 1972) and the choices made (Connolly & Vines, 1977; Greenhaus, Sugalski, & Crispin, 1978; Vroom, 1966). A recent meta-analysis of the literature (Chapman, Uggerslev, Carroll, Piasentin, & Jones, 2005) organizes applicants' attraction under six categories: (a) job and organizational characteristics, the attractiveness of objective features of the job; (b) recruiter characteristics, given that, when (as is often the case) a candidate may not know much about the position, he or she may be more influenced by the person doing the hiring (Harris & Fink, 1987); (c) perceptions of the recruiting process; (d) perceived fit, either with the organization (person-organization fit) or with the job (person-job fit); (e) perceived alternatives (sometimes called "perceived marketability," which interestingly, turned out not to affect attractiveness); and (f) hiring expectancies, as defined by expectancy theory.

Many of the sociological studies to which we have referred above implicitly or explicitly direct attention to how groups from different social strata are differentially drawn to different occupations. Willis's (1977) working-class kids, for example, were either unaware of or, if they were aware, unattracted to middle-class jobs (an example of how the different determinants of boundary permeability may work together). Guest and Sturges (Chapter 16) describe factory workers and technicians who have little interest in promotion, the route to supervisory or managerial jobs. Occupation and social class, in other words, can have a profound influence on the attractiveness of other occupations.

Finally, reluctance to select may also be affected by attractiveness, for reasons both defensible and less so. The reason may be defensible, for example, when one candidate is preferred over another because it is seen to be in their or the organization's better, longer-run interests to make this move (perhaps the preferred candidate needs this position to prepare them for more senior roles). It may be less defensible if the recruiter is personally attracted more to one candidate than to another. The attraction may be on the basis of similarity (Giberson, Resick, & Dickson, 2005; Turban & Jones, 1988) in terms of personality, social class, or some other kind of ascriptive characteristic such as ethnicity; or it may be pretty much at the end of the indefensibility scale, on the basis of sexual attraction.

The Permeability of Objective Boundaries

In the previous sections, we have been exploring what might affect the permeability of subjective career boundaries, the perceptions people have about given work role transitions. This permeability is a function, we argued, of awareness on the part of the actors (ego and alters) that the work role transition exists, its achievability, and its attractiveness, emerging as either or both of a reluctance to move and/or to select (Figure 24.4). Because these perceptions are subjectively held and because, as we have seen, they can be influenced by a very wide range of factors, the outcome—whether or not ego makes the move—may well vary from one person to another, even when they are in similar situations. That is in the nature of subjective processes.

If, however, a "hooking-up" process should happen, so that an objective boundary starts appearing, then the situation in principle becomes somewhat more predictable. We described the hooking-up process above as one in which a consensus starts forming around the nature of a particular class of work role transition, and it is likely that this consensus will include ideas about the emergent objective boundary's permeability. For example, the consensus makers might find themselves agreeing on the need for a particular qualification or designation, as North American university business

schools did when they began to require PhDs of their entering faculty or as many occupations do as they strive for professional status. Or they might come to a view on the kind of experience that is needed, as the film industry did (Jones, 2001; Jones and Dunn, Chapter 22), making it difficult if not impossible for anyone without that specific experience to gain entry.

How might the three facets—awareness, achievability, and attractiveness—influence this process? There is clearly a considerable element of unpredictability to it. For example, the bounded rationality that causes some people to be aware of a particular potential work role transition while others are not is likely to depend to a great extent on luck. Similarly, a sense of inability, or lack of self-efficacy, is essentially idiosyncratic to ego. And attractiveness is perhaps the least likely of the three to affect the permeability of objective career boundaries, simply because its origins are, in the main, personal to ego or alter.

But we also identified structural elements to each of the three facets. Awareness, or lack of it, can originate as well, we argued, from more complex social phenomena springing from ego's place in society. Circumstantial reasons for achievability typically draw on structural phenomena, as do many of the path-dependent processes we listed. Attractiveness can also have structural origins, as for example with Willis's working-class kids or the attraction of selectors to members of their own social class. And because structural phenomena affect *categories* of people in systematic ways, they increase the likelihood that the facet will affect the permeability of an emergent objective boundary. So, for example, social class, mediated by the three subjective facets of awareness, achievability, and attractiveness, has systematic and predictable effects on the permeability of objective boundaries.

Interestingly, we can expect that as a consensus develops around the work role transition and an objective boundary emerges, it is likely to be *less* permeable than the aggregate of the subjective boundaries from which it formed. While the boundary is subjective, there is room for disagreement about how permeable it is. In other words, people may have differing levels of awareness that the work role transition is a possibility, differing views on what is required to make it achievable, and differing views on its attractiveness. So it is likely that for some groups of actors, the boundary may be relatively permeable even though it is not at all for many others. But as the consensus develops and an objective boundary begins to emerge, the divergence of views diminishes, and the "holes" that resulted from some people thinking of the boundary as permeable become plugged. In other words, as objective boundaries emerge as social facts—to the extent that they do, as we discussed above—the variety of life chances diminishes.

CONCLUSION

Our starting point for this chapter was the assertion that career boundaries are central to the nature of careers. They give careers their shape and provide us with a language by means of which to describe and discuss careers. When we talk about careers that are boundaryless, organizational, professional, customized, or ending, we are using the language of boundaries, because each implies a relationship between a life course and one or more boundaries. Boundaries are implicated in every chapter in this volume; they are a unifying thread that runs through the field of career studies.

In this chapter, we explored the nature, genesis, and permeability of career boundaries. We conceived of boundaries initially taking shape in the minds of the actors involved—the career owner (ego) and the many people with whom he or she interacts at each stage of his or her career (alters)—as a *subjectively* perceived set of differences between the role he or she currently occupies and those that might be occupied. The beginning of a career boundary, in other words, is a set of perceptions about a given work role transition. Over time, a consensus may develop among an influential group of social actors that a pattern of some kind can be discerned in these transitions. If this happens, we see the beginnings of what we called here an *objective* career boundary. This may take on the properties of a social fact and a life of its own, as an important shaper of labor markets and careers.

We then delved into the minds of ego and alter to suggest that subjective boundaries are

the consequence of two things: a reluctance to move on the part of ego and a reluctance to select on the part of those alters with whom ego interacts. Each could well be influenced by many other alters. These "reluctances," we argued, spring from *awareness* that a work role transition is possible, an assessment of its *achievability*, and its *attractiveness*. Taken together, these provide the basis of a model by means of which we can understand the phenomenon of career boundary *permeability*.

We have only been able to scratch the surface of the scholarship that relates to each of these three facets (awareness, achievability, and attractiveness). Yet it is evident that the number of factors that could be at play whenever anyone contemplates making a transition between work roles is potentially massive. It is also evident that contemplating these factors draws one into many, if not most, areas of career scholarship, which should come as no surprise if our starting point in this chapter holds true—namely, that boundaries are a central concept to the understanding of careers. But why is it important to go into such depth to understand the reasons for the permeability—or otherwise—of subjective career boundaries?

Subjective career boundaries are essentially idiosyncratic; they are an expression of the reluctance to move of a specific person (ego) and the reluctances to select of a specific set of alters. But the more that these reluctances have systematic origins—the life circumstances that flow from membership of a given social class, the prejudices surrounding membership of a given ethnic group, the legal restrictions on practicing certain occupations—the more likely it is that a consensus will build up across the "sites of difference" (Figure 24.3) about the permeability of that subjective career boundary, making it, in turn, more likely that objective career boundaries will become apparent and that these boundaries will become less permeable overall (as we argued at the end of the previous section). And the more systematic their origins, the better our chances of predicting whether objective boundaries will appear and how permeable they are likely to be.

In other words, the better our understanding of the influences that might be at work in the minds of people living their careers in any given setting, the more likely it is that we can predict the nature of the objective career boundaries that might emerge. And it is the objective boundaries, as we have seen, that give form and shape to careers at the collective level, allowing us to make generalizations about careers and their patterns. So to career researchers, we offer the model described in this chapter as a source of ideas for exploring career boundaries. Studies drawing on it could range from positivist (e.g., testing hypotheses concerning the awareness, achievability, and attractiveness of specific boundaries) to hermeneutic (e.g., interpreting ethnographic studies of careers in terms of those three facets). There are other twists to the model that could also be examined. For example, because it defines subjective career permeability as emerging from two sources—ego and alter— the possibility arises that many different combinations of "reluctance" are possible, each with its own implications for the actors. Examples include an ego who is keen to move but an alter who does not want to select, an ego who does not want to move but an alter who wants him or her to, or both agreeing either that the move should happen or that it should not.

Boundaries, in general, are fundamental to the process by which order is generated in intellectual enquiry: "Any notion of orderliness presupposes at least some element of structure, which inevitably presupposes some boundaries" (Zerubavel, 1995, p. 17). Career boundaries are a special case of this general organizing principle, and the orderliness that they create is that which is necessary to make sense of the structure of our working lives. From time to time, the nature of this structure may be challenged, as it was from the early 1990s as careers in many societies became less dominated by single work organizations. But there is no evidence thus far that its absence, for most people, is accompanied by anything other than a sense of dislocation, to which the response is to seek a new kind of structure and a re-creation or reorganization of career boundaries.

NOTES

1. Durkheim (Moore, Gunz, and Hall, Chapter 2) was perhaps the earliest sociologist to argue that career boundaries are deeply implicated in the structure and

functioning of societies. Social marginalization on the basis of race or sex is about boundaries that vary in permeability depending on race or sex, while examining personality helps us understand how personal characteristics help or hinder boundary-crossing; networks and identities are intimately connected with the boundaries that are crossed to attain given career outcomes; occupational choice and counseling address the boundary between nonwork and work (or one kind of work and another kind), while retirement issues are about crossing the boundary between work and nonwork; work/family issues are about the boundaries we cross every day between different partitions in our lives; mentoring is to do with more experienced people helping those less so across critical boundaries in life; stage and life course theories are about the boundaries we cross as we age and become more experienced, and how predictable they are; living to work and working to live is about the different structure of boundaries faced by people in different occupations and social classes; global careers address the disappearance of national boundaries, while cross-cultural scholarship examines them; the subjective career is about the way in which we perceive and reconstruct boundaries in our minds; customized careers are those in which people reconstruct time boundaries in order to fit their careers better to their lives; external labor markets and career systems are defined by boundaries separating occupations, employers, and jobs; organizational demography depends on boundaries defining the categories about which demographic statements can be made; career patterns—whether linked to institutions or organizational performance—must be described in terms of the boundaries that constrain and enable the careers; and the differing levels of analysis in the study of the macrosocial context of careers are distinguished by the boundaries that separate them.

2. It can have secondary effects, too. In an interesting set of studies, Ellemers (1993) shows that for people in low-status groups, the more permeable the boundary, the lower their loyalty to their group. Social change, therefore, is less likely in groups surrounded by permeable boundaries; their members opt for social competition with each other, escaping the group to better themselves instead.

3. Unilever Companies Management Development Scheme (UCMDS) has been re-launched as the Unilever Graduate Leadership Programme (UGLP).

4. Abbott is anxious to avoid positioning his model as a straightforward micro- to macro-translation framework because, he contends, he could easily

have inverted the story to show how macro-level entities, by playing the role of sites of difference, could affect micro-level entities such as personality (Abbott, 1995, p. 864).

5. Indeed Abbott argues that one of the metrics that may be used to measure propinquity in the social space under examination "might be professional mobility between areas, or career structure linkages between areas" (Abbott, 1995, p. 867).

6. King (2004) uses the term in a more general sense: "individuals who influence the progress of a career" (p. 118).

REFERENCES

Abbott, A. (1995). Things of boundaries. *Social Research, 62*(4), 857–882.

Arthur, M. B., Hall, D. T., & Lawrence, B. S. (1989). Generating new directions in career theory: The case for a transdisciplinary approach. In M. B. Arthur, D. T. Hall, & B. S. Lawrence (Eds.), *Handbook of career theory* (pp. 7–25). Cambridge, UK: Cambridge University Press.

Arthur, M. B., Inkson, K., & Pringle, J. K. (1999). *The new careers: Individual action and economic change.* Thousand Oaks, CA: Sage.

Arthur, M. B., & Rousseau, D. M. (Eds.). (1996). *The boundaryless career: A new employment principle for a new organizational era.* New York: Oxford University Press.

Ashforth, B. E., Kreiner, G. E., & Fugate, M. (2000). All in a day's work: Boundaries and micro role transitions. *Academy of Management Review, 25*(3), 472–491.

Bagdadli, S., Solari, L., Usai, A., & Grandori, A. (2003). The emergence of career boundaries in unbounded industries: Career odysseys in the Italian New Economy. *International Journal of Human Resource Management, 14*(5), 788–808.

Bailyn, L., & Schein, E. H. (1976). Life/career considerations as indicators of quality of employment. In A. Biderman & T. Drury (Eds.), *Measuring work quality for social reporting.* Beverly Hills, CA: Sage.

Bandura, A. (1986). *Social foundations of thought and action.* Englewood Cliffs, NJ: Prentice Hall.

Bandura, A. (1997). *Self efficacy: The exercise of control.* New York: Freeman Press.

Barber, A. E., Wesson, M. J., Roberson, Q. M., & Taylor, M. S. (1999). A tale of two job markets:

Organizational size and its effects on hiring practices and job search behavior. *Personnel Psychology, 52*(4), 841–867.

Baruch, Y., & Peiperl, M. (1997). High flyers: Glorious past, gloomy present, any future? *Career Development International, 2*(7), 354.

Betz, N. E., & Hackett, G. (1981). The relationship of career-related self-efficacy expectations to perceived career options in college women and men. *Journal of Counseling Psychology, 28,* 329–345.

Bolles, R. N. (2007). *What color is your parachute? 2007: A practical manual for job-hunters and career changers* (2007 ed.). Berkeley, CA: Ten Speed Press.

Brooks, L., & Betz, N. E. (1990). Utility of expectancy theory in predicting occupational choices in college students. *Journal of Counseling Psychology, 37,* 57–64.

Brown, S. D., & Lent, R. W. (1996). A social cognitive framework for career choice counseling. *Career Development Quarterly, 44*(4), 354–366.

Cappelli, P. (1999). Career jobs are dead. *California Management Review, 42*(1), 146–167.

Chapman, D. S., Uggerslev, K. L., Carroll, S. A., Piasentin, K. A., & Jones, D. A. (2005). Applicant attraction to organizations and job choice: A meta-analytic review of the correlates of recruiting outcomes. *Journal of Applied Psychology, 90*(5), 928–944.

Chatman, J. A. (1989). Improving interactional organizational research: A model of person-organization fit. *Academy of Management Review, 14*(3), 333–349.

Cohen, L., & Mallon, M. (1999). The transition from organisational employment to portfolio working: Perceptions of "boundarylessness." *Work, Employment & Society, 13*(2), 329–352.

Connolly, T., & Vines, C. V. (1977). Some instrumentality—Valence models of undergraduate college choice. *Decision Sciences, 8,* 311–317.

Daniels, A. K. (1975). Professionalism in formal organizations. In J. B. McKinlay (Ed.), *Processing people* (pp. 303–338). New York: Holt, Rinehart & Winston.

Dawis, R. V., & Lofquist, L. (1984). *A psychological theory of work adjustment.* Minneapolis: University of Minnesota Press.

Derr, C. B., & Laurent, A. (1989). The internal and external career: A theoretical and cross-cultural perspective. In M. B. Arthur, D. T. Hall, & B. S. Lawrence (Eds.), *Handbook of career theory* (pp. 454–471). Cambridge, UK: Cambridge University Press.

Diamond, M., Allcorn, S., & Stein, H. (2004). The surface of organizational boundaries: A view from psychoanalytic object relations theory. *Human Relations, 57*(1), 31–53.

DiPrete, T. A. (1987). Horizontal and vertical mobility in organizations. *Administrative Science Quarterly, 32*(3), 422–444.

Duncan, G. J., Yeung, W. J., Brooks-Gunn, J., & Smith, J. R. (1998). How much does childhood poverty affect the life chances of children? *American Sociological Review, 63*(3), 406–423.

Duncan, O. D., Featherman, D. L., & Duncan, B. (1972). *Socioeconomic background and achievement.* New York: Seminar Press.

Ellemers, N. (1993). The influence of social structural variables on identity management strategies. *European Review of Social Psychology, 4,* 27–57.

England, G. W. (1967). Personal values systems of American managers. *Academy of Management Journal, 10,* 107–117.

Feather, N. T. (1995). Values, valences and choice: The influence of values on the perceived attractiveness and choice of alternatives. *Journal of Personality and Social Psychology, 68,* 1135–1151.

Fiol, C. M. (1989). A semiotic analysis of corporate language: Organizational boundaries and joint venturing. *Administrative Science Quarterly, 34,* 277–303.

Fleming, P., & Spicer, A. (2004). "You can checkout anytime, but you can never leave": Spatial boundaries in a high commitment organization. *Human Relations, 57*(1), 75–94.

Forbes, J. B. (1987). Early intraorganizational mobility: Patterns and influences. *Academy of Management Journal, 30*(1), 110–125.

Giberson, T. R., Resick, C. J., & Dickson, M. W. (2005). Embedding leader characteristics: An examination of homogeneity of personality and values in organizations. *Journal of Applied Psychology, 90*(5), 1002–1010.

Goffman, E. (1961). *Asylums.* New York: Doubleday.

Granovetter, M. (1973). The strength of weak ties. *American Journal of Sociology, 78*(6), 1360–1380.

Greenhaus, J. H., Sugalski, T., & Crispin, G. (1978). Relationships between perceptions of organizational size and the organizational choice process. *Journal of Vocational Behavior, 13*(1), 116–125.

Gunz, H. P. (1989). *Careers and corporate cultures: Managerial mobility in large corporations.* Oxford: Basil Blackwell.

Gunz, H. P., Evans, M. G., & Jalland, R. M. (2000). Career boundaries in a "boundaryless" world. In M. A. Peiperl, M. B. Arthur, R. Goffee, & T. Morris (Eds.), *Career frontiers: New conceptions of working lives* (pp. 24–53). Oxford: Oxford University Press.

Gunz, H. P., Evans, M. G., & Jalland, R. M. (2002). Chalk lines, open borders, glass walls and frontiers: Careers and creativity. In M. A. Peiperl, M. B. Arthur, & N. Anand (Eds.), *Career creativity: Explorations in the remaking of work* (pp. 58–76). Oxford: Oxford University Press.

Gunz, H. P., & Jalland, R. M. (1996). Managerial careers and business strategies. *Academy of Management Review, 21*(3), 718–756.

Gunz, S. P. (1991). *The new corporate counsel.* Toronto: Carswell.

Hackett, G., & Byars, A. M. (1996). Social cognitive theory and the career development of African American women. *Career Development Quarterly, 44,* 322–340.

Hall, D. T. (1976). *Careers in organizations.* Santa Monica, CA: Goodyear.

Hall, D. T., & Goodale, J. G. (1986). *Human resource management: Strategy, design and implementation.* Glenview, IL: Scott Foresman.

Harris, M. M., & Fink, L. S. (1987). A field study of employment opportunities: Does the recruiter make a difference? *Personnel Psychology, 40,* 765–784.

Heracleous, L. (2004). Boundaries in the study of organization. *Human Relations, 57*(1), 95–103.

Hernes, T. (2004). Studying composite boundaries: A framework of analysis. *Human Relations, 57*(1), 9–29.

Holland, J. L. (1997). *Making vocational choices: A theory of careers.* Odessa, FL: Psychological Assessment Resources.

Hollingshead, A. B. (1965). *Elmtown's youth: The impact of social classes on adolescents.* New York: Wiley.

Hughes, E. C. (1937). Institutional office and the person. *American Journal of Sociology, 43,* 404–413.

Hultin, M. (2003). Some take the glass escalator, some hit the glass ceiling? Career consequences of occupational sex segregation. *Work & Occupations, 30*(1), 30–61.

Jacoby, S. M. (1999a). Are career jobs headed for extinction? *California Management Review, 42*(1), 123–145.

Jacoby, S. M. (1999b). Premature reports of demise. *California Management Review, 42*(1), 168–179.

Jones, C. (2001). Coevolution of entrepreneurial careers, institutional rules and competitive dynamics in American film, 1895–1920. *Organization Studies, 22*(6), 911–944.

Jones, L. K. (Ed.). (1992). *The encyclopedia of career change and work issues.* Phoenix, AZ: Oryx Press.

Judge, T. A., & Bretz, R. D., Jr. (1992). Effects of work values on job choice decisions. *Journal of Applied Psychology, 77,* 261–271.

Kanfer, R., & Ackerman, P. L. (2004). Aging, adult development and work motivation. *Academy of Management Review, 29*(3), 440–458.

King, Z. (2004). Career self-management: Its nature, causes and consequences. *Journal of Vocational Behavior, 65*(1), 112–133.

Lamont, M., & Molnar, V. (2002). The study of boundaries in the social sciences. *Annual Review of Sociology, 28,* 167–195.

Lent, R. W., Brown, S. D., & Hackett, G. (1994). Toward a unifying social cognitive theory of career and academic interest, choice and performance. *Journal of Vocational Behavior, 45,* 79–122.

Lent, R. W., Hackett, G., & Brown, S. D. (1999). A social cognitive view of school-to-work transition. *Career Development Quarterly, 47,* 297–311.

Lent, R. W., Lopez, F. G., Brown, S. D., & Gore, P. A., Jr. (1996). Latent structure of the sources of mathematics self-efficacy. *Journal of Vocational Behavior*, 49(3), 292–308.

Louis, M. R. (1980). Career transitions: Varieties and commonalities. *Academy of Management Review, 5*(3), 329–340.

Lyness, K. S., & Thompson, D. E. (1997). Above the glass ceiling? A comparison of matched samples of female and male executives. *Journal of Applied Psychology, 82*(3), 359–375.

March, J. G., & Simon, H. A. (1958). *Organizations.* New York: Wiley.

Mutch, A. (2003). Communities of practice and habitus: A critique. *Organization Studies, 24*(3), 383–401.

Nicholson, N. (1984). A theory of work role transitions. *Administrative Science Quarterly, 29*(2), 172–191.

Nicholson, N., & West, M. (1988). *Managerial job change: Men and women in transition.* Cambridge, UK: Cambridge University Press.

Oldham, G. R. (1976). The motivational strategies used by supervisors: Relationships to effectiveness indicators. *Organizational Behavior and Human Performance, 15,* 66–86.

Osipow, S. H. (1997). *Theories of career development* (3rd ed.). New York: Prentice Hall.

Peiperl, M. A., & Baruch, Y. (1997). Back to square zero: The post-corporate career. *Organizational Dynamics, 25*(4), 7–22.

Priest, T., & Krol, J. (1986). Lawyers in corporate chief executive positions: Career characteristics and "inner group" membership. *International Journal of the Sociology of Law, 14*(1), 33–46.

Pringle, J. K., & Mallon, M. (2003). Challenges for the boundaryless career odyssey. *International Journal of Human Resource Management, 14*(5), 839–853.

Rokeach, M. (1973). *The nature of human values.* New York: Free Press.

Rosenbaum, J. E. (1979). Tournament mobility: Career patterns in a corporation. *Administrative Science Quarterly, 24*(2), 220–241.

Rosenbaum, J. E. (1984). *Career mobility in a corporate hierarchy.* London: Academic Press.

Rubin, L. B. (1976). *Worlds of pain: Life in the working-class family.* New York: Harper & Row.

Saxenian, A. (1996). Beyond boundaries: Open labor markets and learning in Silicon Valley. In M. B. Arthur & D. M. Rousseau (Eds.), *Boundaryless careers: A new employment principle for a new organizational era.* New York: Oxford University Press.

Schein, E. H. (1971). The individual, the organization and the career: A conceptual scheme. *Journal of Applied Behavioral Science, 7,* 401–426.

Schein, E. H. (1978). *Career dynamics: Matching individual and organizational needs.* Reading, MA: Addison-Wesley.

Scott, W. R. (2004). Reflections on a half-century of organizational sociology. *Annual Review of Sociology, 30,* 1–21.

Silber, I. F. (1995). Space, fields, boundaries: The rise of spatial metaphors in contemporary sociological theory. *Social Research, 62*(2), 323–355.

Smiles, S. (1958). *Self-help* (centenary ed.). London: J. Murray.

Sonnenfeld, J. A., & Peiperl, M. A. (1988). Staffing policy as a strategic response: A typology of career systems. *Academy of Management Review, 13*(4), 588–600.

Turban, D. B., & Jones, A. P. (1988). Supervisor-subordinate similarity: Types, effects, and mechanisms. *Journal of Applied Psychology, 73*(2), 228–234.

Unilever. (2003). *UCMDS*. Retrieved June 2, 2005, from http://www.ucmds.com/index.cfm.

Van Vianen, A. E. M., & Fischer, A. H. (2002). Illuminating the glass ceiling: The role of organizational culture preference. *Journal of Occupational & Organizational Psychology, 75*(3), 315–337.

Vermeulen, M. E., & Minor, C. W. (1998). Context of career decisions: Women reared in a rural community. *Career Development Quarterly, 46,* 230–245.

Viney, C., Adamson, S., & Doherty, N. (1997). Paradoxes of fast track management. *Personnel Review, 26*(3), 174–186.

Vroom, V. H. (1964). *Work and motivation.* New York: Wiley.

Vroom, V. H. (1966). Organizational choice: A study of pre- and post-decision processes. *Organizational Behavior and Human Performance, 1*(2), 212–225.

Wanous, J. P. (1972). Occupational preferences: Perceptions of valence and instrumentality and objective data. *Journal of Applied Psychology, 56,* 152–155.

Willis, P. (1977). *Learning to labour: How working class kids get working class jobs.* Westmead: Saxon House.

Zerubavel, E. (1995). The rigid, the fuzzy, and the flexible: Notes on the mental sculpting of academic identity. *Social Research, 62*(4), 1093–1106.

PART III

SYNTHESIS

Part III draws the volume together. Its authors constitute a distinguished group of careers scholars whom the editors invited to reflect on the material in Parts I and II, to explore connections between the different threads described, and to establish new directions for careers research and scholarship. Additionally, they were invited to draw out the implications of the foregoing chapters for practice, both for individuals on their personal journeys and for those responsible for shaping—or helping shape—the careers of others (line managers, HR managers, and career counselors).

Specifically, we invited each of these scholars to write an essay setting out where they think the field of career studies is going. We made some suggestions, although we were at pains to add that we did not want the essayists to feel restricted by them. We asked them which theoretical frameworks, lines of research, or areas of scholarship

- look promising?
- might emerge, or are becoming more important?
- are missing (but shouldn't be)?
- could build on each other?
- need more development?
- could be given a graceful funeral?
- have implications for practitioners (and if so, what kind of practitioners, and what are the implications)?

Once the drafts were ready, they were circulated among the group of essayists. Many of the writers met at IMD in Lausanne, Switzerland, in early 2006 to compare notes and discuss one another's essays. The essays were then revised, and the results comprise Part III.

Each essayist approached the task from their own very personal perspective, so that the collection emerging from the process is extremely varied. Bagdadli (Chapter 25) begins by focusing on the design of career systems, pointing firmly to the need to study career systems in the way they are understood by HR professionals. Vardi and Kim (Chapter 26) identify what they refer to as the "dark" side of careers, arguing that in the literature in general and the *Handbook* in particular this is a much-neglected perspective. Kraimer and Seibert (Chapter 27) focus on how people build external (to organizations) labor markets into their views of opportunity structures. Boyatzis (Chapter 28) addresses the question of how to "conceptualize a person's quest for an ideal future and turn that into a desired career path." Derr and Briscoe (Chapter 29) take a retrospective look at what they describe as the "catalytic" period of the 1970s, identifying themes that are still significant today as well as themes that are not but fruitfully could be.

The final essays take a more eclectic route. Mirvis (Chapter 30) is inspired by the "tour guides," as he describes the authors of Parts I and II, to take some side trips of his own in the field of careers. Cascio (Chapter 31) introduces some emerging trends and paradoxes and identifies avenues for future research. Collin (Chapter 32) examines the many meanings of career, contrasting the richness of the concept with the poverty of thought about it to be found in the literature. Finally, Nicholson (Chapter 33) contrasts early writings on careers with those in the *Handbook* and asks, "How much better off are we [now]? Where are the big ideas, or is that an immature longing for a field where a thousand flowers are blooming?"

25

DESIGNING CAREER SYSTEMS

Are We Ready for It?

SILVIA BAGDADLI

The 2007 *Handbook of Career Studies* represents a marvelous opportunity to confirm the fascination of career research that originates from the possibility of working at the crossroads of several disciplines and across the individual and organizational perspectives. The latter, however, seems still less developed than the former, much as it was in the 1989 *Handbook of Career Theory.*

What seems particularly undeveloped is an organizational design (OD) perspective of career systems, which is still in its infancy if compared with the design of organizational forms developed since the mid-1950s and more recently, roughly 20 years ago, with the design of human resource management (HRM) systems that attracted HRM researchers and a few career scholars *strictu sensu* under the theoretical frame of strategic human resource management (SHRM; Huselid, Jackson, & Schuler, 1997; Schuler, 1987). It is amazingly underdeveloped if we consider the importance of HRM systems, and in particular of career systems, for achieving a competitive advantage; practitioners who are now, thanks to theoretical approaches

such as the resource-based view (RBV) of the firm (Kamoche, 1996; Wernerfelt, 1984), more aware that the development of human capital (Becker, 1964), which is the core of career systems, is one of the most critical actions in attaining organizational success and performance.

"Career systems are the collections of policies, priorities, and actions that organizations use to manage the flow of their members into, through, and out the organizations over time" (Sonnenfeld & Peiperl, 1988, p. 588). Career systems include entry, development, and exit systems. Career development systems include socialization, career planning, succession planning, training, and promotion. Promotion systems require the definition of criteria for advancement, and this implies the existence and use of performance, potential, and skill evaluation systems. Career systems, in this broad definition, encompass the larger part of HRM systems and hence represent, or should represent, one of the most critical areas of research for academics and of interest to HR managers.

Chapter 19 of the *Handbook* by Slay and Taylor awakens interest in the topic. Their detailed review on the one side reveals the weakness of existing theoretical models and empirical findings, and on the other signals the promising road opened by the most recent models.

The authors' review includes few models of career systems: the Sonnenfeld and Peiperl (1988) model and the Lepak and Snell (1999) model, two typical contingent designing models. Empirical research based on these models is insufficient, and only the latter received moderately strong empirical support. Each model considers different contingencies: strategy, and value and uniqueness of skills, respectively.

Are these the only or the right contingencies that we should consider in proposing a model for designing career systems? We know by reading several chapters of this *Handbook*, especially those in Sections 2 and 3 of Part II, that there are many variables internal and external to organizations that can affect the design and the effectiveness of career systems. "Careers are always careers in context," observe Mayrhofer, Meyer, and Steyrer in their opening to Chapter 12. Overall, the *Handbook* contains a review of most of the variables that can affect the design and effectiveness of career systems. Should we account for those variables in proposing a model for designing career systems? Do national, cultural, or institutional diversity or differences in the educational systems count, as for example, Thomas and Inkson suggest in the *Handbook* (Chapter 23)? Or should we propose a global and universalistic model for designing career systems?

In a different research field, the OD field, contingent models rose in the late 1950s and developed as the structural contingency school throughout the 1960s and 1970s, thereby drawing to the attention of researchers many external contingencies, such as environmental dynamism and uncertainty (Lawrence & Lorsch, 1967; March & Simon, 1958), or internal contingencies, such as size (Pugh, Hickson, Hinings, & Turner, 1969), technology (Woodward, 1965), interdependence (Thompson, 1967), and, of course, strategy (Chandler, 1962), to cite just a few. As far as the design of career systems is concerned, do contingencies matter? Do strategy, industry, technology, size, or other internal variables matter? Do organizational structure, job content, or individual demographics (age,

tenure, sex, etc.) matter? Which of these variables should be included in a model for designing career systems?

These are very difficult questions. HR managers ask these questions and want to know which contingencies matter in order to design career systems in different contexts and different organizations. Are we ready to answer them?

So far, we know that a good designing model includes a few variables only, as the disadvantages deriving from reducing the complexity of reality are balanced and surmounted by the advantages of a powerful prescription. Moreover, Slay and Taylor (Chapter 19) show that the line of research on career systems looks promising, although it needs more development, and can offer a preliminary answer to these questions.

Reading Chapter 19 and the literature in the SHRM area (Bowen & Ostroff, 2004; Delery & Doty, 1996), we can tell that there is room to doubt that any external or internal contingency can influence the relationship between career systems and performance, that there are ideal types that an organization's systems should resemble, or that there are "best practices" that fit all contexts and all organizations. All findings are dubious and the universalistic-contingent-configurational debate (Delery & Doty, 1996) is still a hot topic among SHRM scholars and is far from resolved.

In the OD field, more than 40 years have passed since the first propositions of contingent models for OD took shape. These models replaced the universalistic propositions à la McGregor (1960). The traditional contingent approach envisaged organizational forms as a set of consistent traits often theoretically conceived as ideal type: the "organic" versus the "mechanistic" form (Burns & Stalker, 1961), to cite a common one. Ideal types had to be consistent with the contingent variable(s) in order to be effective; for example, organic forms were better suited in dynamic environments and mechanistic forms in stable ones.

More recently, the contingency school has been criticized and different modes of theorizing are emerging in the OD field. The frontier of the OD research area makes claims for combinative models based on mechanism complementarities and substitutability more than consistency (Child, 2002; Grandori, 2004; Zenger & Hesterly,

1997). Organizational forms can be more effective combining in an innovative way attributes and traits that are not necessarily consistent according to the traditional contingent approach. To give an example, "high powered incentives," usually considered typical of market type organizations, "can be infused into large hierarchical firms" (Zenger & Hesterly, 1997, p. 211).

It is time career researchers, and in particular those scholars more oriented toward the organizational perspective and OD and willing to orient practitioners' actions, enter the debate with strength and take advantage of previous research both in the SHRM area and in the OD area, which should not be perceived as two separate areas. Slay and Taylor show the way. They acknowledge the potential of the results of the Lepak and Snell model and its empirical testing as a foundation for proposing their "integrative prescriptive model" (Slay and Taylor, Chapter 19).

We can add further observations and stimuli for future research based on the Lepak and Snell (1999) model. We observe that the typology is built using one contingency: the value and uniqueness of human resources. This frame integrates the typical organizational economic reasoning (Doeringer & Piore, 1971; Williamson, Wachter, & Harris, 1975) with the resource-based view of the firm and allows career scholars to enter SHRM by proposing a model for designing career systems that could contribute to enhancing organizational performance. The model proposed by Lepak and Snell (1999) adopts a "contingent configurational view" (p. 42), but it includes a sort of universalistic reasoning as it is claiming that all companies with certain kinds of skills should adopt a certain type of HR configuration, regardless of industry, strategy, or other external or internal contingencies. It is a contingent model, but not a typical one, since the contingent variable is the value and uniqueness of human resources and not the most commonly used company's strategy that, ultimately, produces results irrelevant to design HR configurations. Taking a closer look, the model and the results from its empirical tests (Lepak & Snell, 2002; Lepak, Takeuchi, & Snell, 2003) resemble the combinative models proposed by the vanguard of OD theory. The results from empirical tests of the model show that not only do the best companies have a multiplicity of arrangements at the

company level (Lepak et al., 2003) but also there is a stronger link with superior performance for organizations that use a mix or combination of practices, not the ideal typical ones, with the most important type of human resources—the knowledge-based workers, characterized by high value and high uniqueness. These empirical results seem to confirm the combinative models set forth by OD scholars who are proposing and preliminarily testing the superior validity of the complementarity of arrangements more than their internal consistency. Under this frame, not only the traditional external or vertical fit of the contingent reasoning (Schuler & Jackson, 1987) but also the internal or horizontal fit (Delery & Doty, 1996) of configurational and universalistic reasoning, namely, the consistency of policies and practices used in an organization, seem in crisis. What appears to emerge from tests of the last model is a different fit, the fit between the type of career system desired by employees and those offered by the organization. This fit is rising as a universalistic principle in contemporary organizations together with principles of fair treatment, democratic participation in organizations, and the need for not breaching psychological contracts (Rousseau, 1995), no matter how transactional or relational (Rousseau, 1995) they are. This reasoning resembles that of Bowen and Ostroff (2004) on the *strength* of HRM systems, claimed as more important than the specific type of HRM systems and practices for explaining organizational success and superior performance. The new integrative model proposed by Slay and Taylor includes both dimensions: the relevance of career systems for psychological contracts and the importance of a strong climate for organizational performance.

Although theoretical reasoning and empirical testing of career-system-designing models need further improvement, the way opened by Sonnenfeld and Peiperl and developed by Lepak and Snell seems promising. We now have something to say to those responsible for managing flows in organizations: Superior performance comes from the use of a mix of career systems combined with the fit between career systems offered and desired. The task of contemporary HR managers is likely to be about "crafting new solutions rather than comparatively assessing few established solutions" (Grandori, 2004, p. 58).

Moreover, we can tell HR managers that good solutions, or, in other words, good career systems, allow organizations to bring to the top echelons people able to craft new strategies as rapidly as needed by changing environments—people capable of driving organizational change imposed by strategic change, a change supported by career systems designed to enhance organizational flexibility. There is no superior performance coming from the fit between the strategy and the career system or HR architecture but coming from the use of a mix of career systems that enable valuable resources to climb to the top and design winning strategies and organizational forms (Weick & Berlinger, 1989). Higgins and Dillon in Chapter 21 of the *Handbook* offer us a key to understanding the power of the individual perspective brought into the organizational perspective and relieve HR professionals from the heavy burden of designing. Organizations design career systems and patterns, and career systems and patterns in turn design organizations in a mutually reinforcing cycle (Gunz & Jalland, 1996).

To conclude, we must answer the unanswered questions we raised. What should we say to HR managers about the need for considering external (culture, educational systems, legislation, labor market, unions, etc.) contingencies? What do we learn from the wealth of information the *Handbook* offers?

We suggested that a good model economizes variables and we supported Slay and Taylor's enthusiasm for the Lepak and Snell model saying that the road opened looks promising. This implies the suggestion not to burden models with external variables. But as many European academics know, not only are Eastern and Western countries different, but Western countries are very different from one another, too, and what could work in America might be different in Germany or France.

Therefore, we suggest using the wealth of information found in the *Handbook* to identify variables that practitioners should consider as potential limits to action or obstacles to the effectiveness of enacted career systems. Two examples will help clarify this:

1. We know that educational systems at the undergraduate and graduate levels can vary across nations. There are countries with very specialized undergraduate courses and others with more generalist courses. The effectiveness of different types of socialization and training programs will vary according to the degree of specialization and professionalism of undergraduate courses. This is what we call an obstacle to the effectiveness of career systems, and HR managers will have to decide, first, to whom to address developmental investments and, second, which type of training will be more effective with respect to the specific national educational systems.

2. The degree of freedom in choosing contractual arrangements can be limited by national labor legislation that can reduce the flexibility of organizations. Overall, the *Handbook* constitutes an important review of variables that might influence the effectiveness of implemented career systems or limit the organization's freedom in adopting any mix of practices or any career system.

A different approach would be to specify the conditions (external and internal to organizations) under which a proposed career system model or a certain typology might hold (Grandori, 2001). One could, for example, specify that the recourse to contractual work (Lepak & Snell, 1999) will be higher in those countries that allow temporary employment or have allowed it for a longer time.

In sum, we do not have all the answers and we surely need more research on career-system-designing models, but the road is open and seems promising.

REFERENCES

Becker, G. (1964). *Human capital.* New York: Columbia University Press.

Bowen, D. E., & Ostroff, C. (2004). Understanding HRM-firm performance linkages: The role of the "strength" of the HRM system. *Academy of Management Review, 29*(2), 203–221.

Burns, T., & Stalker, G. M. (1961). *Management of innovation.* London: Tavistock.

Chandler, A. D. (1962). *Strategy and structure.* Boston: MIT Press.

Child, J. (2002). A configurational analysis of international joint ventures. *Organization Sciences, 23*(5), 781–815.

Delery, J. E., & Doty, D. H. (1996). Modes of theorizing in strategic human resource management: Tests of universalistic, contingency and configurational performance predictions. *Academy of Management Journal, 39,* 802–835.

Doeringer, P., & Piore, M. (1971). *Internal labor markets and manpower analysis.* Lexington, MA: Heath.

Grandori, A. (2001). Methodological options for an integrated perspective on organizations. *Human Relations, 54*(1), 37–47.

Grandori, A. (2004). The changing core of organization and organization theory: From contingency to combinative. *Rivista di Politica Economica* [Special International Issue], *January/February,* 49–62.

Gunz, H. P., & Jalland, R. M. (1996). Managerial careers and business strategy. *Academy of Management Review, 21,* 718–756.

Huselid, M., Jackson, S. E., & Schuler, R. S. (1997). Technical and strategic human resource management effectiveness as determinants of firm performance. *Academy of Management Journal, 40*(1), 171–188.

Kamoche, K. (1996). Strategic human resource management within a resource: Capability view of the firm. *Journal of Management Studies, 33*(2), 213–233.

Lawrence, P., & Lorsch, J. (1967). *Organizations and environment.* Boston: HBS Press.

Lepak, D. P., & Snell, S. A. (1999). The human resource architecture: Toward a theory of human capital allocation and development. *Academy of Management Review, 24*(1), 31–48.

Lepak, D. P., & Snell, S. A. (2002). Examining the human resource architecture: The relationships among human capital, employment, and human resource configurations. *Journal of Management, 28*(4), 517–543.

Lepak, D. P., Takeuchi, R., & Snell, S. A. (2003). Employment flexibility and firm performance: Examining the interaction effects of employment mode, environmental dynamism, and technological intensity. *Journal of Management, 29*(5), 681–704.

March, J. G., & Simon, H. A. (1958). *Organizations.* New York: Wiley.

McGregor, D. (1960). *The human side of enterprise.* New York: McGraw-Hill.

Pugh, D. S., Hickson, D. J., Hinings, C. R., & Turner, C. (1969). The context of organizational structure. *Administrative Science Quarterly, 14,* 91–114.

Rousseau, D. M. (1995). *Psychological contracts in organizations: Understanding written and unwritten agreements.* Thousand Oaks, CA: Sage.

Schuler, R. S. (1987). Personnel and human resource management choices and organizational strategy. *Human Resource Planning, 10*(1), 1–17.

Schuler, R. S., & Jackson, S. E. (1987). Linking competitive strategies with human resource management practices. *Academy of Management Executive, 1*(3), 207–219.

Sonnenfeld, J. A., & Peiperl, M. A. (1988). Staffing policy as a strategic response: A typology of career systems. *Academy of Management Review, 13,* 588–600.

Thompson, J. D. (1967). *Organization in action.* New York: McGraw-Hill.

Wernerfelt, B. (1984). A resource-based view of the firm. *Strategic Management Journal, 5*(2), 171–180.

Weick, K., & Berlinger, L. (1989). Career improvisation in self-designing organizations. In M. B. Arthur, D. T. Hall, & B. S. Lawrence (Eds.), *Handbook of career theory* (pp. 313–329). Cambridge, MA: Cambridge University Press.

Williamson, O. E., Wachter, M. L., & Harris, J. E. (1975). Understanding the employment relation: The analysis of idiosyncratic exchange. *Bell Journal of Economics, 6*(1), 250–278.

Woodward, J. (1965). *Industrial organization: Theory and practice.* London: Oxford University Press.

Zenger, T. R., & Hesterly, W. S. (1997). The disaggregation of corporations: Selective intervention, high powered incentives and molecular units. *Organization Sciences, 8*(3), 209–222.

26

CONSIDERING THE DARKER SIDE OF CAREERS

Toward a More Balanced Perspective

YOAV VARDI

SHARON H. KIM

The *Handbook of Career Studies* offers a collection of insightful chapters that address pertinent research topics on work careers. A wide range of topics, including themes from personality and career (Chapter 4) and careers of the socially marginalized (Chapter 10) to boundaries (Chapter 24) and contextual issues in the study of careers (Chapter 13), provides readers with vital insights into these subject matters, as well as some significant directions for future research. Nevertheless, after thoroughly reviewing the chapters and analyzing their contents, we concluded that certain directions and linkages are conspicuously still missing in career research. The review actually revealed that there is a definite emphasis on positive aspects of careers; only a handful of papers allude to negative issues.

We propose that as much as careers in general, and organizational careers in particular, are considered an attractive personal and social endeavor, as much as we are socialized to adhere to career rules and timetables, and as much as we prefer to study career success and achievement, we must also recognize and study the less proclaimed facets of careers. In particular, we refer to those aspects of careers that may be conceptually and empirically related to organizational phenomena described by such constructs as unethical behavior, political behavior, unconventional conduct, deviance, counterproductive behavior, misbehavior, and the like (for extensive reviews, see Griffin & O'Leary-Kelley, 2004; Vardi & Weitz, 2004). Thus, our objective in this commentary is to advocate a more balanced view of careers, focusing on the inevitable relationship between the career experience and various forms of organizational misbehavior.

In essence, given that careers are broadly conceptualized as time- and work-related experiences, to promote a more realistic understanding of careers, all facets of these experiences must be explored, including their "darker," less-visited, sides. Consider a hypothetical case: In a company, several hopefuls submit their candidacy for several vacant section-head jobs. The company decides to hire outsiders rather than to promote from within. While we prefer to study how the newcomers do, we tend to ignore the subsequent heartache and frustration felt by the losers and the deep hostility they now harbor against their employer, let alone the retributive acts they may engage in for vengeance. Such an approach may represent a common bias. Below, we discuss what we believe is missing from the general body of careers research, the potential that exists, our proposed framework for studying careers and organizational misbehavior, and finally our conclusions and directions for future research.

ARE WE MISSING SOMETHING?

Students of organizations frequently invoke the "tip of the iceberg" metaphor to illustrate the argument that a considerable part of any organization is difficult to observe and understand. Following this metaphor, the visible portion of the organization (e.g., location, form, measurable patterns) is approximately 10% of the entire mass, while the vast majority of the organization (e.g., values, motives, and preferences) remains "under water." We believe that this descriptive imagery is also applicable to the career phenomenon. Thus, current and previous research notwithstanding, there still remains much to be discovered. Undoubtedly, further advancement of knowledge about careers, both within and outside organizations, can illuminate many dimensions of life in general, and work life in particular, that have become essential to individuals, families, professions, and organizations. For example, Higgins and Dillon (Chapter 21) discuss how signals associated with executive careers, regarding career histories, can help struggling organizations rebuild legitimacy.

They posit that the individual executive career can be endowed with symbolic value that affects external judgment of the firm to which the individual belongs based on associations with the executives' prior roles, positions, or employment affiliations. This assertion emphasizes how much influence the career holds and continues to gain in both business and in society. In this particular example, the individual executive career potentially carries enough influence to repair broken confidence and rebuild fallen organizational reputations.

Though occupational and organizational careers have become a definitive temporal aspect of individual and organizational lives, we must avoid focusing on those aspects of career phenomena that are readily accessible or that are in the mainstream discourse at the expense of other aspects that are hidden, obscure, difficult to measure, or controversial. Is it possible that we are indeed biased in our treatment of careers, perhaps reflecting our own career successes and triumphs? Are we perhaps influenced by the very biases we teach about such as social desirability and political correctness? Are we subconsciously bound by our inclination to use positive and optimistic language? Thus, while reading the chapters, we kept asking ourselves questions such as the following: Are careers portrayed as mostly positive experiences? Can careers be fully examined without the consideration of failure, loss, and disappointment? Can personality factors in careers be examined without considering egoism, aggressiveness, and dishonesty? Can mentorship be fully understood without the consideration of ingratiation and exploitation? Can we discuss career outcomes mostly in terms of success and achievement while ignoring dishonesty, resentment, or betrayal?

As career scholars we must ask ourselves whether we accurately portray a "complete" career picture. Are negative traits, attitudes, emotions, intentions, and behaviors not part and parcel of people's career experiences? Undoubtedly, we bring our own (largely positive) career experiences to our science, which may partially explain our myopic perspective. Sullivan and Crocitto (Chapter 15), for example, reference the potential influence of personal experiences on careers research with their account of Donald Super and his modified perspective on the experiences of aging workers. They write that as Super aged and reflected on his own life journey and continued his contributions to the [careers] literature, he renamed the career stage of decline. Instead of decline he used the term: "disengagement."

THE POTENTIAL EXISTS

As Moore, Gunz, and Hall (Chapter 2) observe, career theory has prominent roots in early psychology and sociology. Though contemporary organizational careers research is thought to have begun in the mid-1970s, theoretical contributions by such founding fathers of social and behavioral sciences as Durkheim, Weber, Freud, Jung, and Erikson cannot be overlooked. To these theorists of human behavior, the idea of a career was a somewhat ambiguous concept, though not lacking complexity, consequences, and disadvantages.

For example, on the societal level, Weber's ideas about the potentially conflicting needs of organizations and individuals had anticipated the frustration experienced by many career men and women working in large formal organizations decades after his death. Indeed, Weber's theories on the effects of bureaucracy have left a considerable imprint on academic theory in multiple disciplines, including organizational science. It is quite logical to relate phenomena such as incivility or white-collar crime to the grinding and alienating career realities of apersonal bureaucratic systems that still employ large portions of the workforce. At the individual level, Erikson clearly delineated developmental dynamics that included both adjustment and maladjustment. Moore et al. write, "Erikson claimed that the inability to resolve an occupational identity is a primary cause of disturbance in youth." This statement is significant and demonstrates that many career experiences can indeed be negative right from the start.

Unquestionably, many individuals are maladjusted in their careers, yet we tend to focus on those that are resilient, successful, and able to overcome such developmental obstacles. An excellent example of a common negative career experience is Savickas's description of the concept of "career indifference," or the lack of concern for the career that reflects a "planlessness

regarding the future and pessimism about it" (Chapter 5). Despite the prevalence of such experiences, contemporary research consistently addresses career congruence, adjustment, and fit (e.g., Holland's model) and de-emphasizes career maladjustment and mismatch.

Many contributors to this volume have portrayed the contemporary "postmodern" career as a variable, multifaceted experience that requires a flexible framework in which it can be adequately captured. Dealing with contemporary career variety, Mayrhofer, Meyer, and Steyrer's (Chapter 12) contribution on contextual issues on the study of careers describes some of the pivotal macrocontextual factors in careers research, including origin, society, and culture. Similarly, Khapova, Arthur, and Wilderom's chapter "The Subjective Career in the Knowledge Economy" also addresses the postmodern career with their attention to subjective career properties and contemporary circumstances and challenges (Chapter 7). In view of such complexity, from both macro and micro perspectives, it is apparent that we may no longer assess careers against normative benchmarks. They must be investigated in context and processed with enough realism to encompass the desirable benefits to the individual and the organization, *and* the costs and disadvantages that may result.

Indeed, as evidenced in this volume, career scholars do consider an impressive range of topics such as the career effects of personality, age, race, gender, sexual orientation, disabilities, and social marginalization. For example, Judge and Kammeyer-Mueller's chapter on personality and career success explores the relationship between the Big Five personality traits and career success (Chapter 4), and Ibarra and Deshpande explore the influence of networks and identities on career processes and outcomes (Chapter 14). Others concern themselves with important research topics such as family issues, alternative employment, mentoring interactions, and retirement dilemmas. Still, we maintain that researchers must go beyond those mainstream career subjects if we are to achieve a better understanding of their intricacies and effects. We should explore, for instance, how personality traits may breed career failures, how an individual's successes influence his or her colleagues' career demeanor and behaviors, why for many individuals organizational careers are unrewarding and stressful experiences, and why certain individuals risk their careers to "blow the whistle" on their employer, while others prefer not to.

We should perhaps go back to some of our conceptual roots to study causes and outcomes of psychological failure, "plateauing" and "deadwooding," radial movement politics, chronic career mismatches, negative socialization, dual-career conflicts, protean career despair, and so on. This knowledge should allow us to map a different realm of careers, and may help develop a richer topography of this important research field. For example, in this volume, Jones and Dunn (Chapter 22) discuss how the migration of individuals from organization to organization can result in the diffusion of positive social practices and understandings. Undoubtedly, the diffusion of such elements can produce beneficial outcomes; however, we must also consider what may be the result of the migration of individuals with negative intentions or unethical social practices and understandings. What are the implications for the organizations that house these careers? How might these "imported" misbehaviors affect the progress of such organizations?

It seems to us that although researchers clearly strive to further explain careers both "above and below water," certain dimensions continue to remain generally overlooked. While some of the more strikingly negative aspects of careers (e.g., built-in conflicts, marginality, and discrimination) are featured, much of the omnipresent negative experiences associated with day-to-day career management remain largely unaddressed. We know that both working and nonworking (e.g., laid-off, unemployed) individuals experience stress, anxiety, anger, disappointment, frustration, and similar feelings throughout their careers for a multitude of reasons. For some individuals, these experiences may even become triggers of aggression and retaliatory behavior (see Skarlicki & Folger, 2004). Slay and Taylor touch on this in their chapter on career systems and psychological contracts (Chapter 19). They posit that employees who perceive violations of promises of "valued career mobility" will experience a significant decrease in organizational commitment. Our question is whether such a reaction may lead

them to engage in counterproductive conduct as a form of reprisal, and how such conduct might affect their future careers.

As reflected in this *Handbook,* contemporary careers research uses a wide-angle lens to capture a panoramic view of the career field and is progressively becoming more inclusive of different circumstances and individuals observed in a diversified workforce. For example, Feldman's contribution on late career and retirement issues outlines very relevant topics for the changing age demographic of the workplace and the career phases of the Baby Boomer (Chapter 9). Prasad, D'Abate, and Prasad reference similar subjects in their chapter. They posit that the inclusion of "Hispanics, Asians, Native Americans, gay men, lesbian women, bisexuals, Muslims, and individuals belonging to many non-mainstream minority faiths, overweight employees, and so on," can indeed widen the range of understanding regarding the careers of the socially marginalized (Chapter 10). We certainly agree. Still, continuing with our photography metaphor, we should prefer to take the more unusual pictures that may require kneeling, climbing, or digging to explore those less-visited aspects of the career experience that are not as obvious, are more problematic, but yet, no less prevalent and consequential.

CAREERS AND ORGANIZATIONAL MISBEHAVIOR

Similar critical observations have been made about the shortcomings of management studies, organizational sociology, and organizational behavior (e.g., Analoui & Kakabadse, 1992; Vardi & Wiener, 1996; Vaughn, 1999). Their common assertion was that by emphasizing normative rather than controversial approaches and constructs, these fields of study have become positively skewed in the way they portray organizations and organizational life. During the past 15 years, a more balanced view of organizations has been sustained by a surge of interest in "deviant" yet prevalent forms of work-related behavior (e.g., Griffin & O'Leary-Kelly, 2004). For example, the term *organizational misbehavior* (OMB) defined as any *intentional action* by members of organizations that violates core organizational and/or societal norms (Vardi & Wiener, 1996), encompasses a full spectrum of phenomena of work-related misconduct present in *every* organization and experienced by most members during their careers.

A general framework recently proposed by Vardi and Weitz (2004) outlines the concept in terms of OMB manifestations, antecedents, and mediators (i.e., intentions to misbehave). The categories of OMB manifestations include intrapersonal misbehavior, interpersonal misbehavior, production misbehavior, property misbehavior, and political misbehavior. OMB antecedents are classified into the following levels: individual, position, group, and organization. Applying such a framework to careers can produce interesting research propositions. For example, at the individual level, frustration regarding the inability to receive a promotion may affect the intention to misbehave and subsequently lead to production misbehavior in the form of rule breaking or sabotaging work processes. At the organizational level, a strong culture that "forces" careerist employees to work long hours may affect the intention to misbehave and lead to political misbehavior such as deception, where employees manipulate office technology (e.g., time-stamped e-mail) to create the false impression that work is being done when it actually is not. Figure 26.1 presents the typological framework. This model also provides ideas for actions that organizations may take in managing members' behavior over time (i.e., points of HR intervention A, B, C, and D). Hence, it could pertain directly to career management systems as well (see Chapter 19) by addressing the organization's ability to monitor and cope with managers' and employees' inclination to engage in various forms of misbehavior. It proposes points of possible intervention commensurate with "career stages": preemployment selection, socialization processes, performance and conduct monitoring, employment maintenance and prevention practices, and exit. Thus, even from a practical perspective, the connection between learning about career dynamics in relation to patterns of misconduct at work seems to be a worthwhile endeavor.

As highlighted by a number of the contributors to the *Handbook,* people face a great deal of economic competition for jobs. Lawrence and Tolbert discuss the effect competition has on career

demographics such as increased age of those who start families (Chapter 20). Certainly, employers are also facing new challenges as their workforce alters its composition and character. Cappelli and Hamori in their chapter on the institutions of outside hiring describe how online recruiting is raising new problems for employers, including increased turnover and the threat of poaching (Chapter 17). Such intense competition surrounding recruitment and retention may provide just the "right" impetus for career-related OMB. According to Cappelli and Hamori, some employers monitor Web sites such as WetFeet.com and Vault.com that provide job seekers with alternative sources of information about companies in the marketplace. They anonymously counter negative remarks about their companies in chat rooms or post positive comments to bulletins, producing their own aggressive form of impression management (Chapter 17).

These examples represent the stressful career circumstances that should be recognized as realities of careers in the postmodern context. The effect of these situations on individuals, individual careers, organizations, and organizational careers is likely to be significant, especially with regard to the growing incidence of misconduct at work such as employee theft and various forms of harassment and substance abuse. We would propose, for example, that intense career competition, discrimination, and burnout could potentially lead to many manifestations of OMB such as production, property, and political acts of defiance. For example, Bratton and Kacmar (2004) explored the dark side of impression management in relationship to extreme careerism, defined as the propensity to pursue career advancement, power, or prestige through any positive or negative non-performance-based activity that is deemed necessary. In their study, they consider such (mis)behaviors as blaming, intimidation, and taking credit for someone else's work. Without a doubt, the costs and consequences of OMB can affect many parties, including individual employees, organizations, consumers, the general public, and governmental agencies, among others. Yet again, despite the potentially significant consequences to individuals (e.g., workaholism, substance abuse, and health problems) and organizations (e.g., whistle blowing, retaliation, fraud, and

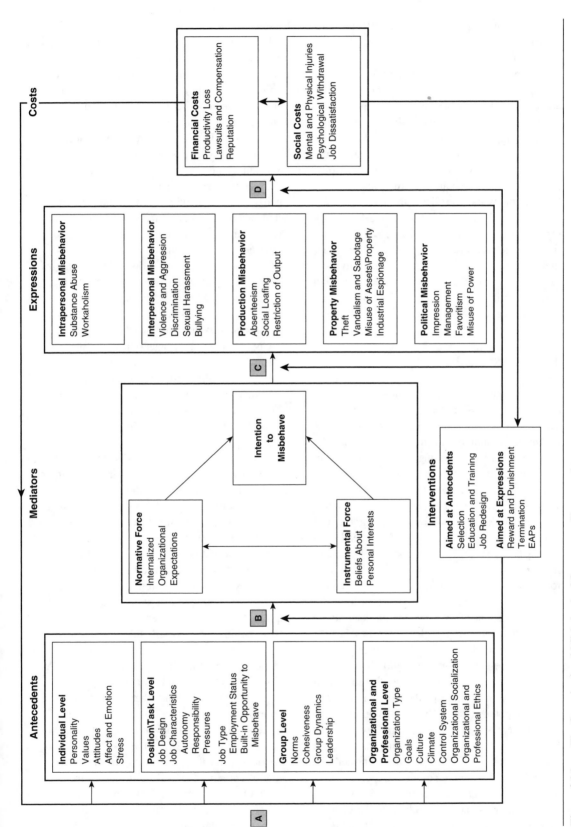

Figure 26.1   The Organizational Misbehavior Management Framework

SOURCE: From Vardi, Y., & Weitz, E. *Misbehavior in Organizations: Theory, Research, and Management,* copyright 2004. Reprinted with permission of Lawrence Erlbaum.

sabotage), the pervasive nature of OMB remains inadequately addressed in career research.

It is important to reemphasize that OMB can affect both careers and organizations. Typical examples of OMB include a wide range of job- and career-related behaviors from incivility and minor vandalism to sabotage, theft, and harassment, to major fraud, insider trading, aggressive headhunting, and spying. Growing empirical research, the business press, and our own professional experiences attest to the prevalence of OMB in the workplace. Though much of it may inflict tolerable harm and is often overlooked by organizations, we have also witnessed and continue to observe, certain incidents of misconduct that can result in the demise of individual careers, and in extreme cases, the demise of an entire organization (e.g., Enron Corporation and its indicted executives).

THE BALANCING ACT

Exploring the links between these phenomena and careers may significantly enrich our understanding of how the careers of individuals and of organizations unfold and interact over time. For students of careers, including elements of OMB in research and literature would serve an important role. First, it would encourage a more balanced view of careers, one that includes both benefits and drawbacks. Second, by reflecting the full range of career behavior, we may further lessen the gap between career theory and career management practices. Indeed, several contributors to this *Handbook* (e.g., Kidd, Chapter 6 on career counseling) expressed concern regarding the problems associated with this type of disparity.

Traditionally, the joy of careers has been a strong theme underlying much of existing career theory and research. But we should also consider their downside. For example, Chandler and Kram suggest that in this age of the protean career (a source of potential stress and confusion in and of itself!), the best way to approach mentorship may be to have multiple developers rather than a single mentor (Chapter 13). Yet we must consider that multiple and potentially conflicting loyalties may affect an individual's career in negative ways as well. Greenhaus and Foley advocate the concept of work-family enrichment, the extent to which

experiences in one role improve the quality of life in the other role, where quality of life includes high performance and positive affect (Chapter 8). However, the diminishing boundary between family and work (especially for dual-career families where conflict may become acute) bears a significant psychological toll on the modern career person. This idea was recently explored by Hammer, Saksvik, Nytrø, Torvatn, and Bayazit (2004) in a study of workplace norms and work-family conflict as correlates of stress and health. Their examination of job stress and the subsequent health problems related to work-family conflict expands on some of the more serious consequences of working people with families.

Kidd's poignant observation of the struggles of career counseling also illustrates the "darker" side of careers. She aptly states,

> Although work and educational choices are likely to be important issues, many clients will also need help in dealing with broader concerns, such as coping with the frustrations of redundancy and unemployment, deciding *whether* [italics added] to return to study or work, and finding ways to balance different life roles. (Chapter 6)

Thomas and Inkson also discuss potential sources of negative affect in careers in their chapter on careers across cultures (Chapter 23). They explore limitations of current careers research citing that "most societies vary to a greater or lesser extent from the utopian world of talent, individuality, prosperity, and choice." We agree with their assertion that the world of mediocrity, sameness, scarcity, and constraint is a reality for many, and it should be adequately represented in careers research.

Identifying the "darker" side of careers logically covers a much larger segment of working individuals and their real life experiences. As referenced by Guest and Sturges in Chapter 16, "Barley (1989) has noted that if we accept the dominant model of the career as a pattern of progress onward and upward, then it probably excludes the working lives of about 80 per cent of Americans." By the same token, the current concepts of careers may still be irrelevant to many forms of work experiences across the world. Guest and Sturges further reiterate how the nature of organizational hierarchies signifies that "not everyone can progress, and very few can make it to the top." Yet we (both academics and practitioners) continue to be fascinated by those few. First, we should pay more attention to the majority of people who never reach that pinnacle. How do they feel about their inability to succeed? Does losing the competition actually affect their work? Do they become more inclined to engage in unconventional forms of work behavior? Second, how does the success of the few influence their conduct when they reach the top? Are they now more inclined to engage in misbehavior intended to benefit the organization (OMB Type O) as an expression of gratitude? Our point is that such questions are significant and should be addressed by mainstream careers research.

Conclusions and Directions for Future Research

On the whole, it appears that researchers still expound on the positive aspects of careers and on available opportunities at the expense of their potential downsides and threats. But organizational and occupational realities have changed dramatically and so has our understanding of them. We agree with Sullivan and Crocitto who suggest in their chapter on stage and process theories of careers that changing workplace realities provide the backdrop for the evolving study of careers (Chapter 15). Hence, the direction of future careers research can be very exciting if we expand our exploration of both affective and behavioral components of careers. For instance, Prasad, D'Abate, and Prasad point out that according to research, many socially marginalized groups both anticipate and experience discrimination during the recruitment process (Chapter 10). The next step may be to research how these individuals fare once they succeed in being hired. Do they feel triumphant, or have they become chronically embittered? Are they likely to overperform or underperform? Behave or misbehave? What effect does this experience have on their lifetime career?

As we continue to make progress in this field, we should remember those prevalent work-related experiences that do not fit the "ideal career." As such, researching a link between career failure and the incidence of particular manifestations of OMB (e.g., continuous interpersonal

misbehavior in the form of retaliation) may be one direction to take. Alternatively, studying highly competitive work processes (e.g., commissioned sales or recruiting) could shed light on the effects of "shady" undermining behaviors on such careers. A rich field of investigation can be the long term effects of OMB on individual careers. Some individuals who are, for example, victims of interpersonal OMB (e.g., sexual harassment, supervisory bullying) may become "organizational pariahs" after reporting incidents or "blowing the whistle." Studying these dynamics could provide a great deal of information not only to researchers, but to those HR practitioners who manage career systems.

Moreover, almost every contribution to the *Handbook* made reference to the growing complexity in the workplace, at home, and in the world. For instance, Valcour, Bailyn, and Quijada discuss the customized career as a way to "forge lives between the two extremes of opting out and continuing to meet the normative expectations of traditional careers" (Chapter 11). Such circumstances have a powerful impact on the career and can be expected to persist as the work environment faces the challenges of a global boundaryless society and economy. Competition, transition, an aging and diverse workforce, downsizing, restructuring, and even corporate and governmental scandals are very real conditions for today's working population. Such complexities undoubtedly require multifocal as well as unbiased and flexible observations.

In conclusion, incorporating the negative aspects of careers and accepting misbehavior as a significant and salient component of organizations can serve to encourage a balanced perspective for studying the temporal interaction between person and organization. To that effect, we again assert our initial premise: Without exploring the darker side of careers, a well-rounded, balanced, and comprehensive understanding of careers cannot be successfully attained.

References

Analoui, F., & Kakabadse, A. (1992). Unconventional practices at work: Insight and analysis through participant observation. *Journal of Managerial Psychology, 7,* 1–31.

Barley, S. (1989). Careers, identities, and institutions: The legacy of the Chicago School of Sociology. In M. B. Arthur, D. T. Hall, & B. S. Lawrence (Eds.), *Handbook of career theory* (pp. 41–60). Cambridge, UK: Cambridge University Press.

Bratton, V., & Kacmar, K. M. (2004). Extreme careerism: The dark side of impression management. In R. Griffin & A. O'Leary-Kelly (Eds.), *The dark side of organizational behavior* (pp. 291–308). San Francisco: Jossey-Bass.

Griffin, R. W., & O'Leary-Kelly, A. M. (Eds.). (2004). *The dark side of organizational behavior.* San Francisco: Jossey-Bass.

Hammer, T. H., Saksvik, P. Ø., Nytrø, K., Torvatn, H., & Bayazit, M. (2004). Expanding the psychosocial work environment: Workplace norms and work-family conflict as correlates of stress and health. *Journal of Occupational Health Psychology, 9,* 83–97.

Skarlicki, D., & Folger, R. (2004). Broadening our understanding of organizational retaliatory behavior. In R. Griffin & A. O'Leary-Kelly (Eds.), *The dark side of organizational behavior* (pp. 373–402). San Francisco: Jossey-Bass.

Vardi, Y., & Wiener, Y. (1996). Misbehavior in organizations: A motivational framework. *Organization Science, 7,* 151–165.

Vardi, Y., & Weitz, E. (2004). *Misbehavior in organizations: Theory, research, and management.* Mahwah, NJ: Lawrence Erlbaum.

Vaughn, D. (1999). The dark side of organizations: Mistake, misconduct, and disaster. *Annual Review of Sociology, 25,* 271–305.

27

CONTINUITY, EMERGENCE, AND OPPORTUNITIES FOR CONVERGENCE

MARIA L. KRAIMER

SCOTT E. SEIBERT

andbooks not only map what we know about a given area, but they often serve to mark the issues and preoccupations of a given period and provide direction toward future research. One major milestone marking the progress of career studies was the *Handbook of Career Theory* (Arthur, Hall, & Lawrence, 1989). While the current *Handbook* is a distinctly different effort, it may be instructive to think about our own current preoccupations by examining some of the important issues of that period. The *Handbook of Career Theory* was structured without regard to disciplinary boundaries in that it was divided into sections regarding current approaches, new ideas, and future directions. One of the stated goals of that earlier *Handbook* was to stimulate a multidisciplinary approach to the study of careers (Arthur et al., 1989), and it did indeed reflect a broad set of disciplinary perspectives on career issues, including anthropology, economics, and political science. The structure and content of the current *Handbook of Career Studies* reflects the

level of success resulting from that previous effort. Rather than reflecting disciplines, the current *Handbook* is organized around levels of analysis: individual, contextual, and institutional aspects of career studies. Each of these areas reflects a considerable accumulation of research knowledge and insights drawn from multiple disciplinary perspectives.

Yet ironically, some of the most notable contributions, in our judgment, from the 1989 *Handbook* (Arthur et al., 1989) were not from previously underexplored social science disciplines, but from the traditional disciplinary mainstays of career research: psychology, social psychology, and sociology. For example, Bell and Staw drew attention to the dynamic role personality might play in shaping characteristics of the setting in which the person operates, characteristics that in turn can lead to individual satisfaction and success. Weick and Berlinger examined the intersection of self-designing organizations and subjective careers. Barley's chapter reconnected career studies with one of

511

the traditional roots of sociology. Pfeffer highlighted the important role interests, power, and organizational politics play in achieving career outcomes. Each of these contributions, although well-grounded in their respective disciplines, continues to inform work that is being done today, including many chapters of the current *Handbook.* We believe that this will also be the case with a number of chapters in the current *Handbook,* as the authors find important new insights drawn from recent developments in the traditional source disciplines of career studies.

The individual level of analysis continues to be well represented in research and theorizing in the area of career studies. Themes carried over from the previous book include the role of personality in careers, occupational choice, and career counseling as well as issues regarding the careers of women and minorities. Not only is a great deal of previous research summarized, but important insights and directions for future work are offered. Judge and Kammeyer-Mueller (Chapter 4), for example, develop a conceptual model designed to explain *why* or *how* personality relates to career success. This chapter strongly suggests that we need more sophisticated models of personality effects in the career area—the era of the "laundry list" approach has ended. The theme of the subjective career, just beginning to emerge in 1989, has fully blossomed. The subjective perspective has essentially legitimized a broad range of issues and working populations that now merit full chapters, including issues related to marginalized populations, work-family dynamics, and late career issues. Subjectivity remains an important theme underlying the boundaryless, self-directed, or customized career. Perhaps, we are at a point where this area would benefit from greater integration. For example, Khapova, Arthur, and Wilderom (Chapter 7) explore the theories that might help us understand the largely developmental challenges of enacting a boundaryless career. Valcour, Bailyn, and Quijada (Chapter 11), on the other hand, review empirical evidence regarding the nature and forms of customized careers, the factors driving the adoption of customized careers, and the prevalence of such careers. While the subjective career perspective is theoretically explicit regarding the interdependence of objective and subjective careers, the customized career focuses most explicitly on the externally visible aspects of careers—such as time devoted to work, timing of major career milestones, and the legal nature of the employment relationship—that may have been shaped by subjective requirements. While the career field was well ahead of practice when it first began to consider the implications of the self-directed career (e.g., Hall, 1976), we think that we are entering a period in which the greatest gains will come from examining more and more explicit empirical models informed by developed theoretical perspectives. Overall, we feel that the individual level of analysis has demonstrated considerable progress and yet still exhibits a number of promising avenues for further development.

New themes also emerge from the traditional disciplines when contextual aspects of careers are considered. Mentoring, social identity, and developmental networks (Chapters 13 and 14) form an interesting cluster of issues that alone justify the importance of this level of analysis. Chandler and Kram (Chapter 13) provide both a summary of important findings and an agenda for future research that suggests that scholarship on this topic can and should continue for some time. Industrial relations and labor economics, on the other hand, are not disciplines normally associated with careers research. Chapter 17 (Cappelli and Hamori) demonstrates that this has been an important oversight. It describes the important role of search processes and institutional arrangements in external labor markets. Lawrence and Tolbert (Chapter 20), on the other hand, focus on determinants, especially demographic determinants, of the internal opportunity structure of the organization. We suggest that this internal versus external orientation can and essentially must be integrated from the subjective perspective of the individual. We believe that this is another important opportunity for convergence in the new themes explored in this *Handbook* and provides some preliminary suggestion for such an integration below. Again, we find a great deal of continuity with previous career preoccupations. These are embodied by the impressive collection of relevant studies and findings summarized in these sections of the *Handbook.* Yet we find a number of interesting and promising new directions emerging since the snapshot provided by the 1989 *Handbook.* Above, we have suggested some areas where the way forward might involve convergence among these multiple themes. We take the remainder of this essay to highlight two sets of converging themes that we think can be profitably explored.

POWER IN THE NEW EMPLOYMENT RELATIONSHIP

Almost two decades ago, Pfeffer (1989) laid out a number of career-related processes and outcomes in organizations affected by political dynamics, including hiring, internal mobility, and wage determination. A number of researchers have examined issues of politics and impression management in the context of career-related issues (e.g., Seibert, Kraimer, & Crant, 2001; Wayne, Liden, Graf, & Ferris, 1997); however, a view of career dynamics that encompasses a power-based view has never been fully developed. This is particularly relevant given the recent history of changes in organizing strategies and the nature of the employment relationship (e.g., Chapter 19 by Taylor and Slay). A brief review of these changes will help set the context for what follows.

Beginning in the late 1980s, about the time the last *Handbook* was published, a new set of organizing strategies were beginning to emerge, especially but not exclusively in the United States. Major components of this strategy, including workforce reductions or downsizing, flattening of organizational structures, outsourcing work previously done in-house, the use of contingent labor, and increased use of strategic alliances, characterized the changes in organizing that had major implications for the careers of managerial, technical, and professional workers. Although these incipient changes were not well reflected in the 1989 *Handbook,* throughout the 1990s, an awareness of the extent of the changes reached the academic literature on careers (e.g., see Cappelli and Hamori, Chapter 17; Guest and Sturges, Chapter 16; Jones and Dunn, Chapter 22; Sullivan and Crocitto, Chapter 15; Taylor and Slay, Chapter 19).

Starting in the 1990s, Rousseau and her colleagues began a research program on the nature of the psychological contracts between employers and employees (see Chapter 19 by Taylor and Slay). Much of the early research was concerned with unilateral violations of the psychological contract by employing organizations (e.g., Rousseau, 1990; Rousseau & Aquino, 1993). Robinson and Rousseau (1994) found that two of the three most frequent violations concerned career issues such as failure to provide the level of training and development promised or the speed of the promotion schedule. Osterman (1996) observed that career ladders for managers in a range of industries were "broken." Hall (1996) declared that "the career is dead," at least in the traditional sense of a steady upward move in terms of income, status, power, and security. The single phrase that best seemed to capture these changes in career dynamics was "the boundaryless career" (Arthur & Rousseau, 1996). The boundaryless career was one that might unfold across multiple organizations, jobs, and skill sets. It meant that workers would need to be more proactive in managing their own careers and career development.

But a funny thing happened on the way to the new organization. Just as companies were becoming adept at increasing their flexibility and decreasing their commitments and obligations to employees, researchers and consultants began to focus on the critical strategic role of human capital assets and human resource (HR) systems for organizational effectiveness. Scholars began to recognize that the ability of a company to attract and retain critical human resources could be seen as a source of sustained competitive advantage because such competencies are rare, valuable, and not easily copied (Barney & Wright, 1998). Empirically, a body of work was beginning to show that constellations of sophisticated HR practices were associated with bottom-line measures of firm performance (e.g., Huselid, 1995). Perhaps more important, rapid economic growth and a high demand for particular types of employees had changed the relative bargaining leverage of these high-demand employees. While companies continued to be interested in lean and flexible operations, they began to realize the importance of an aggressive stance toward recruiting and retaining the best employees. Perhaps the culminating phrase for this period was coined by McKinsey consultants: "the war for talent" (Michaels, Handfield-Jones, & Axelrod, 2001). These HR consultants were recommending that employers do whatever it takes to recruit talented employees. Employee development was seen as one of the most important inducements for attracting top talent. The confluence of the boundaryless career mind-set of employees and the strategic HR perspective in organizations has several implications for individuals' negotiations with organizations and their careers.

One implication of the changes in the nature of the employment relationship is that ambiguity has been introduced as to the relative bargaining power of individuals versus employers with regard to either formal contract negotiations or less formally defined employment terms and conditions. This ambiguity in the power balance stems from the fact that while organizations no longer offer employment security and offer fewer opportunities for upward mobility, they recognize that to attract key human resources they need to offer employees benefits such as career development and valuable work experiences that enhance their employability. This has implications for individuals negotiating new employment contracts and continued employment contracts. With regard to new hires, the increased prevalence of idiosyncratic deals, as Rousseau (2005) has recently termed the arrangements organizations make to accommodate critical employees, suggests that new hires may potentially have more negotiating power when establishing the terms and conditions of their individual employment. Individuals with a boundaryless mind-set may be especially good at negotiating idiosyncratic deals for themselves that provide short-term benefits with less interest in long-term promises. The short-term focus of individuals may take many employers by surprise. How organizational managers learn to negotiate with and meet expectations of the boundaryless career individual is still open to investigation.

When considering that employees increasingly evaluate external career opportunities in conjunction with the nature of new psychological contracts, even greater ambiguity regarding the power balance that employees hold relative to organizations when negotiating continued employment terms has been introduced. Our own research (Kraimer, Seibert, Wayne, Liden, & Bravo, 2006) has shown that organizations can no longer expect even traditional markers of high employee investment and a relational employment contract—such

as investments in employee development—to be reciprocated with employee loyalty and effort. Rather, employees may be more or less permanently engaged in a relatively calculative assessment of their future career opportunities within the current organization relative to those available on the external labor market. From a psychological contract perspective, careers researchers have noted that employees today expect employability rather than job security. Employability means that employees are interested in developing general, marketable skills and knowledge and that they are less interested in developing firm-specific skills (Pearce & Randel, 2004). This means that organizations have put themselves in a position in which they are investing in their employees in such a way that it makes their employees more marketable on the external labor market. Furthermore, as Cappelli and Hamori (Chapter 17) discussed, the innovations in Internet technology (e.g., online recruiting) have made it easier for employees to evaluate their relative market value or "price." Thus, an important and interesting question is whether employability training increases employees' market value and, thus, power in negotiating continued contracts and employment terms. To help answer this question, we concur with Cappelli and Hamori that theoretical and empirical research should examine how employees develop perceptions of their own value in the labor market.

A second implication of the new organizational strategies is with respect to employees' power and influence within their employing organization. As reviewed by Taylor and Slay (Chapter 19), one of the dimensions of career movements within organizations according to Schein's (1978) career cone model is radial movements. Radial movements are those toward the "inner circle." From a power perspective, one would expect that employees in the inner circle will have more power than employees in the periphery, all else being equal (Brass & Burkhardt, 1993). As Taylor and Slay (Chapter 19) note, radial mobility is more likely to occur within relational psychological contracts than in transactional psychological contracts. Yet the mobile, short-tenured worker is more likely to have a transactional mind-set (Rousseau, 1990). That highly mobile workers may be less likely to be part of the inner core is further supported by the fact that strong, trusting relationships take time to develop (Coleman, 1990). Whether mobile workers are able to develop relationships with employees in the "inner circle" and achieve the power that may come with radial career movements toward the inner core is an empirical question that needs to be addressed in research. If mobile workers are less likely to be part of the inner core, what effect does this have on these workers' relative power in negotiating continuing contracts within their current organization, and might a lack of power perpetuate their interorganizational movements as they seek greater returns externally? Such a power perspective allows careers researchers to contribute to research on turnover, the employment relationship, and negotiations.

The development of personal power within organizations is not only an issue for highly mobile workers but also for workers striving to achieve work-life balance (Greenhaus and Foley, Chapter 8). One way workers may achieve work-life balance is through disengagement from the workplace. In particular, these workers may prefer not to be heavily embedded within the "politics" of their employing organization (Barley & Kunda, 2004). This raises several questions. Does work-life balance come at the expense of not only lack of upward mobility but also lack of radial mobility? Perhaps the apparent "glass ceiling" that women face may partly result from their desire to achieve work-life balance and do so through disengagement in organizational politics.

In sum, the new organizational strategies that created the boundaryless career mind-set of workers and the externalization of workers has several implications for individual's power vis-à-vis their employing organizations. Above, we highlighted two general topics for future research to consider: the power balance between individuals and organizations in negotiating new and continuing contracts and the impact mobility (and perhaps the desire for work-life balance) might have on individual's power within organizations.

ALTERNATIVE EMPLOYMENT MODES

The second topic that was not fully explored in this *Handbook* was new employment modes.

This was surprising because the external orientation of workers may imply, as Cappelli and Hamori noted in Chapter 17, that the rules and principles of classical bureaucratic theory will play a diminished role in shaping future career patterns. Instead, individuals may increasingly turn to alternative employment modes for the kinds of income stability, procedural regularities, and other psychic and material outcomes previously delivered by the internal labor market in organizations. The boundaryless perspective has acknowledged that individuals increasingly look toward the external labor market for opportunities and financial gains, but it hasn't offered a fully articulated alternative view of employment. The basic view is that employees are aware of the fluid or transient nature of their employment relationship with any one organization. We suggest, however, that this is merely one end of a range of employment modes that can be arrayed along a dimension of increasingly external or transient inclusion in the organization.

At the low end of externalization are temporary workers. Temporary workers are explicitly hired for a limited length of time, although the specific term of employment may be quite open ended and the possibility of permanent employment ever present. At an increasing level of externalization are contract workers. Contracting often involves project work that is of a fixed duration as well as the establishment of relatively explicit responsibilities and rates of pay. The worker is presumably hired for specific skills and expertise and does not necessarily become a full member of the organization in terms of responsibilities, relationships, and commitments. Consulting is another mode of externalized employment that is project based. Consulting projects often involve a specific organizational problem, issue, or change initiative with an explicit compensation contract, a relatively fixed time frame, and measurable outcomes. Consultants may be self-employed or working within a professional practice. They may also be engaged with more than one client at the same time. If contracting can be considered contingent labor for technical workers, then perhaps consulting should be considered contingent labor for managerial workers. At the furthest extreme is complete self-employment in the form of entrepreneurship, where the individual founds and/or runs his or her own organization. An entrepreneur may build on previous experience with an existing organization and supply goods or services to that organization or may actually enter into competition with existing firms (e.g., Higgins and Dillon, Chapter 21). Each of these forms or modes of employment involves engagement with an employing organization that is limited in duration and may be partial in terms of time commitment, responsibilities, and psychological engagement.

One can have an entire career within one of these modes of employment, but it is more likely that one will transition through these modes of employment throughout one's working life. In fact, transitioning across these modes may be a more common career path or career strategy than the traditional career ladder. For example, many technical workers may plan to gain work experience within a firm directly after completing their formal education, plan to become contract workers for the greater financial rewards in mid-career, but finally hope to move into permanent employment during later career stages. At the other end of one's career, senior managerial and technical workers may view contract or consulting work as a natural transition stage between permanent full-time employment and full retirement. Research is needed to examine what prompts individuals to choose traditional employment versus one of the above alternative employment modes. Where explicit attention is devoted to such topics as external labor markets or work externalization, further implications for individual career perceptions or decision making can be drawn out. For example, various models of career choice or career stage development (see Sullivan and Crocitto, Chapter 15) might consider explicitly incorporating the possibility of the various employment modes in meeting employees' needs and goals. New conceptualizations of career choices may also be necessary to accommodate the fact that the organization itself and its structures and policies play a diminished role in individual's career choices. For example, entrepreneurs are more concerned with designing, staffing, and leading organizations of their own making. Topics that might have a bearing on the choice of an alternative career mode include Chapter 5 (Savickas) on occupational choice,

Chapter 11 (Valcour, Bailyn, and Quijada) on customized careers, and Chapter 14 (Ibarra and Deshpande), which discusses social networks and identities.

CONCLUSION

Throughout the above discussion, we argued that the boundaryless mind-set of employees, in conjunction with the changes in the employment relationship, affect individuals' career outcomes and career decisions in fundamental ways. One final thought is that perhaps the definition that employees ascribe to "opportunity structure" is also worthy of additional consideration. Schein's (1978) cone model of career movements suggested three types of opportunities—hierarchical, functional, and radial. Have the changes in organizational design and operation diminished the validity of this way of looking at career progress? Are these three types of career movements relevant today? Are there other types of career movements that individuals would define as opportunities? This latter question is especially worthy of reconsideration in light of the demographic changes that many developed countries are experiencing. Clearly, the perspectives presented throughout the *Handbook* offer many promising directions for careers research.

REFERENCES

Arthur, M. B., Hall, D. T., & Lawrence, B. S. (1989). *Handbook of career theory.* Cambridge, UK: Cambridge University Press.

Arthur, M. B., & Rousseau, D. M. (1996). The boundaryless career as a new employment principle. In M. G. Arthur & D. M. Rousseau (Eds.), *The boundaryless career: A new employment principle for a new organizational era* (pp. 3–20). New York: Oxford University Press.

Barley, S. R., & Kunda, G. (2004). *Gurus, hired guns, and warm bodies: Itinerant experts in a knowledge economy.* Princeton, NJ: Princeton University Press.

Barney, J., & Wright, P. (1998). On becoming a strategic partner: The role of human resources in gaining a competitive advantage. *Human Resource Management, 37*(1), 31–46.

Brass, D. J., & Burkhardt, M. E. (1993). Potential power and power use: An investigation of structure and behavior. *Academy of Management Journal, 36,* 441–470.

Coleman, J. S. (1990). *Foundations of social theory.* Cambridge, MA: Harvard University Press.

Hall, D. T. (1976). *Careers in organizations.* Pacific Palisades, CA: Goodyear.

Hall, D. T. (1996). *The career is dead—long live the career: A relational approach to careers.* San Francisco: Jossey-Bass.

Huselid, M. (1995). The impact of human resource management practices on turnover, productivity, and corporate financial performance. *Academy of Management Journal, 38*(3), 635–672.

Kraimer, M. L., Seibert, S. E., Wayne, S., Liden, R., & Bravo, J. (2006, August). *Career management and employee performance and retention: Making career investments pay off.* Paper presented at the Academy of Management annual meetings, Atlanta, GA.

Michaels, E., Handfield-Jones, H., & Axelrod, B. (2001). *The war for talent.* Boston: Harvard Business School Press.

Osterman, P. (1996). *Broken ladders: Managerial careers in the new economy.* New York: Oxford University Press.

Pearce, J. L., & Randel, A. E. (2004). Expectations of organizational mobility, workplace social inclusion, and employee job performance. *Journal of Organizational Behavior, 25,* 81–98.

Pfeffer, J. (1989). A political perspective on careers: Interests, networks, and environments. In M. B. Arthur, D. T. Hall, & B. S. Lawrence (Eds.), *Handbook of career theory* (pp. 380–396). Cambridge, UK: Cambridge University Press.

Robinson, S., & Rousseau, D. M. (1994). Violating the psychological contract: Not the exception but the norm. *Journal of Organizational Behavior, 15*(3), 245–259.

Rousseau, D. M. (1990). New hire perceptions of their own and their employer's obligations: A study of psychological contracts. *Journal of Organizational Behavior, 11,* 389–400.

Rousseau, D. M. (2005). *I-deals: Idiosyncratic deals employees bargain for themselves.* Armonk, NY: M. E. Sharpe.

Rousseau, D. M., & Aquino, K. (1993). Fairness and implied contract obligations in job terminations: The role of remedies, social accounts, and procedural justice. *Human Performance, 62*(2), 135–149.

Schein, E. H. (1978). *Career dynamics: Matching individual and organizational needs.* Reading, MA: Addison-Wesley.

Seibert, S. E., Kraimer, M. L., & Crant, J. M. (2001). What do proactive people do: A longitudinal model linking personality and career outcomes. *Personnel Psychology, 54,* 845–874.

Wayne, S. J., Liden, R. C., Graf, I. K., & Ferris, G. R. (1997). The role of upward influence tactics in human resource decisions. *Personnel Psychology, 50*(4), 979–1006.

28

A COMPLEXITY PERSPECTIVE ON INTENTIONAL CHANGE IN CAREERS

RICHARD E. BOYATZIS

This volume has compiled a robust array of research, theory, and thoughts about careers. The chapters help us understand what we know, what we believe, and what we hope to discover about the shape and structure of careers. And yet, the one theme notably absent is how the human spirit, one's dreams and aspirations, drives careers. David Thomas and Kerr Inkson's Chapter 23 helps us appreciate that not everyone has the same capability to affect the future of their lives and careers. Many of us who are professionals and managers, however, do have the opportunity to reach for our dreams and make life and work closer to our desires in the future. Not only do those of us with higher education have this capability but also the millions of immigrants and refugees who risk their lives to move to places where they, or more likely, their children, can have opportunities for a better life—which involves a chance at better careers.

This chapter will attempt to explain how we can conceptualize a person's quest for an ideal future and turn that into a desired career path. It not only involves the development of career options but also includes the development of abilities, talent, and networks.

To understand this, we must embrace both complexity theory and intentional change theory (Boyatzis, 2006). Career development theories, such as those so well reviewed in Sherry Sullivan and Madeline Crocitto's Chapter 15, often describe the process. The career development theories they reviewed are often descriptions (e.g., Driver's, Dalton and Thompson's, Schein's, or Super's models), and post hoc descriptions at that, of what occurred. They are not a theoretical model of how and why it occurred. Theories of how adults change their behavior and abilities are not much better.

To begin our intellectual journey, let us review what we know about adult behavior change, and in particular desired or intentional change. For all the time, effort, and money invested in attempts to help individuals develop through education, training, and coaching, there are few theories that help us understand the change process. Other than in Prochaska, DiClemente, and Norcross (1992) and McClelland (1965), the actual process of change is left like a mysterious black box.

One of the reasons for this paucity of good theory is that the underlying paradigm on which the change process is conceptualized is lacking in credibility. The idea of smooth, continuous change does not fit with the reality most of us experience. Three features of complex systems and complexity theory that are needed for this exploration are (1) nonlinear and discontinuous dynamical systems, including tipping points and catastrophic change; (2) self-organizing into patterns of equilibrium or disequilibrium in which emergent events start a new dynamic process through the pull of specific attractors; and (3) fractals or multileveledness (the application of a theory at all levels of social organization) and the interaction among these levels through leadership and reference groups.

To review, a complex system is a multilevel combination of systems that may behave in a way independent of any one of the component systems (Complexity Forum, 2001).[1] It is more than a simple system (at a single level) or a complicated system, such as nonlinear dynamics within a simple system (Complexity Forum, 2003). When different simple systems are combined or integrated, the result is typically a large and complicated system. But to be a complex system, it must have (1) overall output that interacts with (e.g., is emergent) or is caused by a coordinator or agent between the levels and (2) output that is different from the output at other levels (Complexity Forum, 2002).

Specifically, to be a complex system, it must have (1) structure and (2) function (Complexity Forum, 2001). The structure includes, at the minimum, scale, architecture, and interaction. Scale or fractals refer to the multiple level of systems that are mirror images of or comparable with each other. The "architecture" is a model or description of how the components affect each other. Interaction is the process of merging, integrating, coordinating, or emerging that occurs between the levels of the complex system. Function includes, at the minimum, dynamics as described by differential equations, chaotic or periodic relationships, and so on; the possible existence of various types of attractors; and the possible ways the inputs relate to the outputs. Now, let us turn to how people change themselves and their careers.

INTENTIONAL CHANGE

Intentional change theory (ICT) describes the complex system involved in intentional change.

At the individual level, ICT[2] describes the essential components and process of desirable, sustainable change in one's behavior, thoughts, feelings, and perceptions. The "change" may be in a person's actions, habits, or competencies. It may be in their dreams or aspirations. It may be in the way they feel in certain situations or around certain people. It may be a change in how they look at events at work or in life. It is "desired" in that the person wishes it so or would like it to occur. It is "sustainable" in that it endures—lasts a relatively long time.

A "desirable, sustainable change" may also include the desire to maintain a current desirable state, relationship, or habit. For example, a person may have his or her ideal career but may seek a change in work-life balance, as Greenhaus and Foley (Chapter 8) explained, as a path to increased life satisfaction. But knowing that things can atrophy or drift into a less desired state, the desire to maintain the current state requires investment of energy in this maintenance, while external (or internal) forces may naturally provoke a change. The same applies to careers. Careers can be vehicles with which a person can make a contribution, achieve desired accomplishments or have desired impact, get ahead or be successful and happy.

Desired sustainable changes in an individual's behavior, thoughts, feelings or perceptions are, on the whole, discontinuous. Changes in a person's career, even those desired, will often be discontinuous. So whether we are describing the career itself or the changes a person makes to enable a development of his/her career, the change process is not smooth. The changes appear as emergent or catastrophic changes over time and effort, which is an essential component of complex systems (Casti, 1994). The experience is one of an epiphany or discovery (Boyatzis, 2006). Self-awareness or mindfulness (of self and context, both social and natural) (Boyatzis & McKee, 2005) is inversely proportionate to the degree of surprise or discovery. When one is highly self-aware, he or she will experience the change process as more of a set of smooth transitions.

The same forces result in the changes often being nonlinear. So this brings us to the first feature of ICT as a complex system. *The change process is often nonlinear and discontinuous, appearing or being experienced as a set of discoveries or epiphanies.*

For example, in trying to understand career or job choice, many authors have overlooked the tipping point concept (Holland, 1995). Gladwell (2000) popularized the idea. This idea, taken from complexity theory, is that up to a certain point, a person's choice of jobs may seem linear—moving up within an organization. But at a specific moment, a person may meet someone at a dinner party who is looking for someone like him or her. If this seemingly surprise event turns into a new job, a discontinuity occurs, and the effect of a small incremental increase in the person's behavior produces a dramatic increase in effectiveness (Boyatzis, 2006). This relationship has also been referred to as "the butterfly effect" or trigger point. We believe that an analogous dynamic affects the process of change, which is why its documentation may not have appeared in research using continuous statistical methods or without sufficiently frequent measurement of effects to note a point of discontinuity or tipping point. In this age of Protean careers (Hall, 1996) or portfolio careers, tipping points may occur at periodic intervals.

The process of intentional change is graphically shown in Figure 28.1 (Boyatzis, 1999, 2001; Goleman, Boyatzis, & McKee, 2002).

It is important to note that often an intentional change process must begin with a person wanting to change. This desire may not be in their consciousness or even within the scope of their self-awareness. Wake-up calls, or moments and events that awaken the person to the need for consideration of a change, may be required to bring the person to the process of desired, intentional change (Boyatzis, McKee, & Goleman, 2002.

THE FIVE DISCOVERIES OF INTENTIONAL CHANGE THEORY

This brings us to the next feature of ICT as a complex system. *The change process actually involves a sequence of discontinuities, called discoveries, which function as an iterative cycle in producing the sustainable change at the individual level. These are (1) the Ideal Self and a Personal Vision; (2) the Real Self and its comparison with the Ideal Self, resulting in an assessment of one's strengths and weaknesses, in a sense a Personal Balance Sheet; (3) a Learning Agenda and Plan; (4) Experimentation and practice with the new behavior, thoughts, feelings, or perceptions; and (5) Trusting, or Resonant Relationships that enable a person to experience and process each discovery in the process.*

The First Discovery: Catching Your Dreams, Engaging Your Passion

The first discontinuity and potential starting point for the process of intentional change is the discovery of who you want to be. Our Ideal Self is an image of the person we want to be. It appears to have three major components, which drive the development of this image of the Ideal Self, as shown in Figure 28. 2: (1) an image of a desired future; (2) hope that one can attain it; and (3) aspects of one's core identity, which includes enduring strengths, on which one builds for this desired future. This is explained in detail in Boyatzis and Akrivou (2006). It emerges from our ego ideal, dreams, and aspirations. The past 20 years have revealed literature supporting the power of positive imaging or visioning in sports psychology, meditation and biofeedback research, and other psychophysiological research. It is believed that the potency of focusing one's thoughts on the desired end state of condition is driven by the emotional components of the brain (Goleman, 1995).

This research indicates that we can access and engage deep emotional commitment and psychic energy if we engage our passions and conceptually catch our dreams in our Ideal Self-image. It is an anomaly that we know the importance of consideration of the Ideal Self, and yet often, when engaged in a change or learning process, we skip over the clear formulation or articulation of our Ideal Self-image. If a parent, spouse, boss, or teacher tells us something that should be different, they are telling us about the person *they* want us to be. As adults, we often allow ourselves to be anesthetized to our dreams and lose sight of our deeply felt Ideal Self. This is also true about the specific jobs and career that are constituents of our Ideal Self and Personal Vision. This is exactly what happens to those who find themselves in marginal careers, as described by Pushkala Prasad, Caroline D'Abate, and

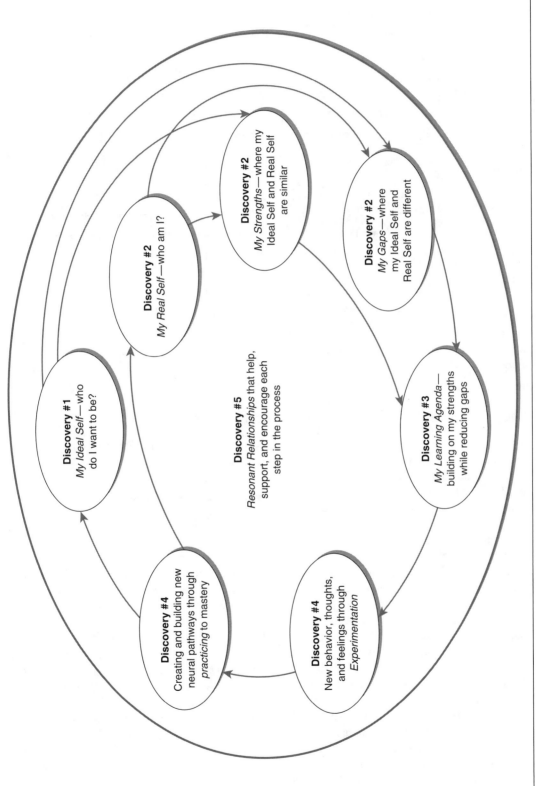

Figure 28.1 Boyatzis's Theory of Self-Directed Learning

521

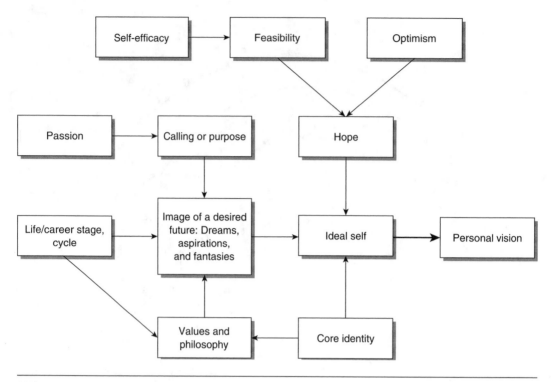

Figure 28.2 Components of the Ideal Self

SOURCE: Boyatzis and Akrivou (2006). Reprinted with permission.

Anshuman Prasad (Chapter 10), and those with nontraditional careers, as discussed by Monique Valcour, Lotte Bailyn, and Maria Alejandra Quijada (Chapter 11). Expectations of friends and family, as well as those in work organizations and society at large, force people into typical careers and career paths, leaving little room for them to pursue their dreams.

It is also clear from this framework that "strengths-based" approaches to development will probably work better than current methods but will fall short of what the person can achieve (Roberts, Dutton, Spreitzer, Heaphy, & Quinn, 2005). They are essentially a "best-fit" approach: Find your strengths, then fit them into a job/career, as described by Jennifer Kidd (Chapter 6). In focusing on the person's established strengths and the resulting "best fit," these models fail to capture the energy inherent in dreams of the future and new possibilities as well as the emotional driver of hope. Because they are based on what the person has done in the past, they do not adequately engage a

person's dreams of the future or consideration of possibilities.

The Second Discovery: Am I a Boiling Frog?

For normal reasons, the human psyche protects itself from the automatic "intake" and conscious realization of all information about oneself. These ego-defense mechanisms serve to protect us. They also conspire to delude us into an image of who we are that feeds on itself, becomes self-perpetuating, and eventually may become dysfunctional (Goleman, 1985). This affects careers by causing people to slip into comfortable patterns and beliefs about themselves. Sometimes these are affected by others' expectation about their careers or attitudes as to their capabilities—strengths or lack thereof.

The greatest challenge to an accurate current self-image (seeing yourself as others see you and consistent with other internal states, beliefs, emotions, etc.) is the boiling frog syndrome. It is said that dropping a frog into a pot of boiling water will result in its immediately jumping out. But place a frog in a pot of cool water, and gradually raise the temperature to boiling, and the frog will remain in the water until it is cooked. Many people drift along in their careers like boiling frogs, unaware of the loss of excitement, creativity, and eventually performance.

For you to truly consider changing a part of yourself, you must have a sense of what you value and want to keep. Those areas in which your Real Self and Ideal Self are consistent or congruent can be considered Strengths. Likewise, to consider what you want to preserve about yourself involves admitting aspects of yourself that you wish to change or adapt in some manner. Areas where your Real Self and Ideal Self are not consistent can be considered Gaps, or weaknesses.

The Third Discovery: Mindfulness Through a Learning Agenda

The third discontinuity in intentional change is development of an agenda and focusing on the desired future. While performance at work or happiness in life may be the eventual consequence of our efforts, a Learning Agenda focuses on development. A learning orientation arouses a positive belief in one's capability and the hope of improvement. This results in people setting personal standards of performance rather than "normative" standards that merely mimic what others have done (Beaubien & Payne, 1999). Meanwhile, a performance orientation evokes anxiety and doubts about whether or not we can change (Chen, Gully, Whiteman, & Kilcullen, 2000). This Learning Agenda can help persons develop a new career, revitalize their current one, or explore possibilities.

Self-Organizing and the Pull of Two Attractors

Intentional change produces sustainable, desirable changes as an iterative, cyclical process. *As a complex system, it engages the cycle again through the self-organizing properties of the human organism. Two attractors, the Positive Emotional and Negative Emotional Attractors (PEA and NEA), determine the context of the self-organizing process and whether it is an adaptation*

to existing conditions or an adaptation to new, emergent conditions. A self-organizing system is inherently homeostatic, with the possibility of some form of deterioration if it is not perfectly efficient (which human organisms do not appear to be). Just as the properties in a closed system move toward maximum entropy over time, as predicted from the second law of thermodynamics, dissonance occurs in the human and in our social organizations unless there is intentional investment. Another way to say this is that adaptations and adjustments based on Argyris's (1985) concept of single loop learning will result in a self-sustaining system of a person, his or her life and performance. But over time, even with these properties of self-organization, deterioration will occur.

This is because the human organism is not a fully closed system. Among other things, we need social interaction to allow our "open-loop" emotional system to function (Goleman et al., 2002). Even more dramatic in its destabilizing effect is the advent of one's life and career cycles. Whether these are the traditional 7-year "itch" cycles or those of varying periodicity described by Erikson, Sheehy, and Levinson, as discussed by Sherry Sullivan and Madeline Crocitto (Chapter 15), a person occasionally looks for a change. These are moments of invitation for what Argyris (1985) called "double loop learning." This helps explain why double loop learning is so difficult and so relatively infrequent. It is inherently destabilizing and must fight against the self-organizing property inherent in a person.

Intentional change theory offers an explanation as to how the disequilibrium occurs and then the force that drives a new self-organizing system. An attractor becomes the destabilizing force. We call this the PEA. It pulls people toward their Ideal Self. In the process of focusing them on future possibilities and filling them with hope, it arouses the parasympathetic nervous system (PSNS) (Boyatzis, Smith, and Blaize, 2006). Once the PSNS is aroused, they have access to more of their neural circuits and find themselves in a calmer, if not elated, state in which their immune system is functioning well and their body is sustained. They are able, in this state, to experience neurogenesis (i.e., the conversion of hippocampal stem cells into new neurons) and the new degrees and extent of learning that become possible. It is even suggested that formation of learning goals or learning-oriented goals builds from this attractor and results in more successful change.

But another attractor is also at play in the system—the NEA. In an analogous manner, it arouses the sympathetic nervous system, which helps humans deal with the stress and threat and protect themselves. Within the threatened environment and state, the NEA pulls a person toward defensive protection. In this arousal, the body shunts blood to the large muscle groups, closes down nonessential neural circuits, suspends the immune system, and produces cortisol— important for protection under threat (Sapolsky, 2004). But cortisol inhibits or even stops neurogenesis and overexcites older neurons, rendering them useless (Boyatzis, Smith, & Blaize, 2006).

If a person's adaptation is self-organizing, then desired change not already part of this system is only possible when it is intentional—just like careers fulfilling others' expectations, as Mark Savickas discussed in Chapter 5, contrasting inherited and legacy jobs and careers with what the person might want to do. We could add that because of the difficulty in sustaining the effort, it also must be driven by a powerful force. This is where the Ideal Self activates the energy of the PEA and the two attractors become "a limit cycle" for the person (Casti, 1994). This also helps us understand why there is a need for more positivity than negativity in change efforts, but there are upper limits to the effectiveness of positivity as well (Losada & Heaphy, 2004). So others' expectations, social and cultural beliefs about the good life, and other factors conspire to keep people locked into a career path that might be increasingly boring every year. Many of these come from exogenous factors, as discussed by Wolfgang Mayrhofer, Michael Meyer, and Johannes Steyrer (Chapter 12).

The process of desired, sustainable change requires behavioral freedom and permission to try something new and see what happens. This "permission" comes from interaction with others, as we will see in the fourth and fifth discoveries in the process.

The Fourth Discovery: Metamorphosis

The fourth discovery is to experiment and practice desired changes. Acting on the plan and toward the goals involves numerous activities. These are often made in the context of experimenting with new behavior. Typically, following a period of experimentation, the person practices the new behaviors in the actual settings within which they wish to use them, such as at work or at home. During this part of the process, intentional change looks like a "continuous improvement" process.

To develop or learn new behavior, the person must find ways to learn more from current or ongoing experiences. To experiment by taking a new job is high risk and involves too much disruption of a person's life. That is, the experimentation and practice do not always require attending "courses," a new activity, or a new job. It may involve trying something different in a current setting, reflecting on what occurs, and experimenting further in this setting. Sometimes, this part of the process requires finding and using opportunities to learn and change.

Dreyfus (1990) studied managers of scientists and engineers who were considered superior performers. Once she documented that they used considerably more of certain abilities than their less effective counterparts, she studied how they had developed some of those abilities. One of the distinguishing abilities was group management, also called team building. She found that many of these middle-aged managers had first experimented with team-building skills in high school and college, in sports, clubs, and living groups. Later, when they became "bench scientists and engineers," working on problems in relative isolation, they still continued using and practicing this ability in activities outside work. They practiced team building and group management in social and community organizations, such as 4-H Clubs, professional associations in planning conferences, and so on. These activities set the stage for the "nerds" to become effective managers—a career path that they might never have considered when they were in college or working at research studies.

The Fifth Discovery: Relationships That Enable Us to Learn

Our relationships are an essential part of our environment. The most crucial relationships are often a part of groups that have particular importance to us. These relationships and groups give us a sense of identity, guide us as to what is appropriate and "good" behavior, and provide feedback on our behavior. In sociology, they are called reference groups. These relationships create a "context" within which we interpret our progress on desired changes and the utility of new learning, and they even contribute significant input to formulation of the Ideal (Chandler and Kram, Chapter 13; Herminia Ibarra and Prashant Deshpande, Chapter 14; Kram, 1996).

In this sense, our relationships are mediators, moderators, interpreters, sources of feedback, and sources of support and permission of change and learning. They may also be the most important source of protection from relapses or returning to our earlier forms of behavior. Wheeler (1999) analyzed the extent to which MBA graduates worked on their goals in multiple "life spheres" (i.e., work, family, recreational groups). In a 2-year follow-up study of two of the graduating classes of part-time MBA students, she found that those who worked on their goals and plans in multiple sets of relationships improved the most, more than those working on goals in only one setting, such as work or within one relationship. Such development also opens one's eyes and imagination to other possibilities for their next job or career.

In a study of the impact of the yearlong executive development program for doctors, lawyers, professors, engineers, and other professionals, Ballou, Bowers, Boyatzis, and Kolb (1999) found that participants gained self-confidence during the program. Even at the beginning of the program, others would say that these participants were very high in self-confidence. It was a curious finding. The best explanation came from follow-up questions to the graduates of the program. They explained the evident increase in self-confidence as an increase in the confidence to change. Their existing reference groups (i.e., family, groups at work, professional groups, community groups) all had an investment in their staying the same; meanwhile the person wanted to change. The Professional Fellows Program allowed them to develop a new reference group that encouraged change. As Dawn Chandler and Kathy Kram (Chapter 13) have discussed, these development relationships can help people see new aspirations.

Daniel Feldman (Chapter 9) described the possibilities of late-career revival and the changing concepts of retirement. In this way, others can help revitalize a person or keep people from giving up too early in their lives and careers.

Based on social identity, reference group, and now relational theories, our relationships both mediate and moderate our sense of who we are and who we want to be. We develop or elaborate our Ideal Self from these contexts. We label and interpret our Real Self from these contexts. We interpret and value Strengths (i.e., aspects considered our core that we wish to preserve) from these contexts. We interpret and value Gaps (i.e., aspects considered weaknesses or things that we wish to change) from these contexts. So these relations not only help us develop but also provide a basis for our identity and hope for the future, as described by Herminia Ibarra and Prashant Deshpande (Chapter 14).

FRACTALS AND INTERACTION AMONG THE LEVELS

Now, we come to the aspect of ICT that makes it a truly complex system—its multileveledness. *According to the theory, sustainable change occurs at any level of human and social organization through the same ICT. In this sense, these other levels are fractals of ICT at the individual level.* In other words, desired, sustainable change within a family, team, or small group occurs through the cyclical iteration of the group through what can be called the "group-level definition" of the five discoveries. In this case, the Ideal Self becomes a shared vision of the future of the group. What does the group want to be, what can it be in the future? Similarly, desired, sustainable organizational change occurs through ICT's five discoveries at the organizational level, and so on at the community, country, and global levels. These other levels are listed in order of increasing social size: individual; dyad or couple; team, group, family, coalition; organization; community; country/culture; and global.

The fractals have an impact on the organization's response to a person's desired changes. But it also helps us understand how an organization might resist helping people reach for their dreams and energize themselves. As Peter Cappelli and Monika Hamori (Chapter 17) described, organizations will resist people acting like independent contractors—even though they often are. In this sense, families, teams, communities, or organizations might treat people and their careers as property, as described by Candace Jones and Mary Dunn (Chapter 22).

But a primary feature of a complex system is that there is an interaction among the levels and that interaction produces adaptive or emergent behavior. *The first degree of interaction between and among the individual, small group, and organization levels of ICT is leadership. The second degree of interaction, which in addition to leadership, allows interaction among all levels of ICT, is through the formation and use of reference groups.*

CONCLUDING THOUGHT

People change. People change themselves, their jobs, and careers. People change in desired ways but not without intentional efforts. But again, without intentional efforts, the changes are slow, result in worse unintentional consequences to the original desire, and arouse a shared hopelessness about the future and diminish the human spirit. In this chapter, an attempt has been made to complement the other chapters in this volume by looking at how people change intentionally. Using concepts from complexity theory and intentional change theory, it is hoped that we can conceptualize and study yet another dimension of people's careers—how they reach for their dreams.

NOTES

1. Complexity Forum is the faculty seminar held at Case Western Reserve University in 2001, 2002, and 2003. It was chaired by Professor Mihajlo D. Mesarovic, with Professors James Alexander, David Aron, Eric Baer, Robert Barmish, Randolph Beer, Richard Boyatzis, Bo Carlsson, Meil Greenspan, Max Hutton, Eva Kahana, Joseph Koonce, Kenneth Loparo, Vincent McHale, Shiva Satry, Kenneth Singer, Daniel Solow, Sree Sreenath, Kurt Strange, Masood Tabib-Asar, Phillip Taylor, and Donal Voltz.

2. The name of the theory was Self-Directed Learning for many years (Boyatzis, 1999, 2001; Goleman, Boyatzis, & McKee, 2002).

REFERENCES

Argyris, C. (1985). *Strategy, change, and defensive routines.* Boston: Pitman.

Ballou, R., Bowers, D., Boyatzis, R. E., & Kolb, D. A. (1999). Fellowship in lifelong learning: An executive development program for advanced professionals. *Journal of Management Education, 23*(4), 338–354.

Beaubien, J. M., & Payne, S. C. (1999, April). *Individual goal orientation as a predictor of job and academic performance: A meta-analytic review and integration.* Paper presented at the meeting of the Society for Industrial and Organizational Psychology, Atlanta, GA.

Boyatzis, R. E. (1999). Self-directed change and learning as a necessary meta-competency for success and effectiveness in the 21st century. In R. Sims & J. G. Veres (Eds.), *Keys to employee success in the coming decades* (pp. 15–32). Westport, CN: Greenwood.

Boyatzis, R. E. (2001). How and why individuals are able to develop emotional intelligence. In C. Cherniss & D. Goleman (Eds.), *The emotionally intelligent workplace: How to select for, measure, and improve emotional intelligence in individuals, groups, and organizations* (pp. 234–253). San Francisco: Jossey-Bass.

Boyatzis, R. E. (2006). Intentional change theory from a complexity perspective. *Journal of Management Development, 25*(7), 607–623.

Boyatzis, R. E., & Akrivou, K. (2006). The ideal self as a driver of change. *Journal of Management Development, 25*(7), 624–642.

Boyatzis, R. E., & McKee, A. (2005). *Resonant leadership: Renewing yourself and connecting with others through mindfulness, hope, and compassion.* Boston: Harvard Business School Press.

Boyatzis, R., McKee, A., & Goleman, D. (2002). Reawakening your passion for Work. *Harvard Business Review, 80*(4), 86–94.

Boyatzis, R. E., Smith, M., & Blaize, N. (2006). Sustaining leadership effectiveness through coaching and compassion: It's not what you think. *Academy of Management Journal on Learning and Education, 5*(1), 8–24.

Casti, J. L. (1994). *Complexification: Explaining a paradoxical world through the science of surprise.* New York: Harper Collins.

Chen, G., Gully, S. M., Whiteman, J. A., & Kilcullen, R. N. (2000). Examination of relationships among trait-like individual differences, state-like individual differences, and learning performance. *Journal of Applied Psychology, 85*(6), 835–847.

Dreyfus, C. (1990). *The characteristics of high performing managers of scientists and engineers.* Unpublished doctoral dissertation, Case Western Reserve University, Cleveland, OH.

Gladwell, M. (2000). *The tipping point: How little things can make a big difference.* New York: Little, Brown.

Goleman, D. (1985). *Vital lies, simple truths: The psychology of self-deception.* New York: Simon & Schuster.

Goleman, D. (1995). *Emotional intelligence.* New York: Bantam Books.

Goleman, D., Boyatzis, R. E., & McKee, A. (2002). *Primal leadership: Realizing the power of emotional intelligence.* Boston: Harvard Business School Press.

Hall, D. T. (Ed.). (1996). *The career is dead—long live the career.* San Francisco: Jossey-Bass.

Holland, J. (1995). *Hidden order: How adaptation builds complexity.* Reading, MA: Helix Books.

Kram, K. E. (1996). A relational approach to careers. In D. T. Hall (Ed.), *The career is dead: Long live the career* (pp.132–157). San Francisco: Jossey-Bass.

Losada, M., & Heaphy, E. (2004). The role of positivity and connectivity in the performance of business teams: A nonlinear dynamics model. *American Behavioral Scientist, 47*(6), 740–765.

McClelland, D. C. (1965). Toward a theory of motive acquisition. *American Psychologist, 20*(5), 321–333.

Prochaska, J. O., DiClemente, C. C., & Norcross, J. C. (1992). In search of how people change: Applications to addictive behaviors. *American Psychologist, 47*(9), 1102–1114.

Roberts, L., Dutton, J. E., Spreitzer, G., Heaphy, E., & Quinn, R. E. (2005). Composing the reflected best-self portrait: Pathways for becoming extraordinary in work organizations. *Academy of Management Review, 30*(4), 712–736.

Sapolsky, R. M. (2004). *Why zebras don't get ulcers* (3rd ed.). New York: Harper Collins.

Wheeler, J. V. (1999). *The impact of social environments on self-directed change and learning.* Unpublished doctoral dissertation, Case Western Reserve University, Cleveland, OH.

29

THE CATALYTIC 1970S

Lessons for the 2000s

C. BROOKLYN DERR

JON P. BRISCOE

I
n Chapter 2 of this *Handbook,* Moore, Gunz, and Hall cover vast territory to trace the intellectual roots of career studies. By focusing on the work of great foundational thinkers such as Durkheim, Weber, Hughes, Mills, Freud, Jung, and Maslow, they help us understand career studies before the 1970s, a *catalytic* period when the field emerged in its current form.

The reason the scholars writing Chapter 2 give for differentiating the underlying theory from the 1970s work is that they would like to demonstrate that the field has substantial theoretical roots. Looking forward, however, we maintain that the 1970s were different from the 1980s and 1990s in career studies. The 1970s were catalytic in that they represented the renewal of the field. They can be conceived as innovative, theory producing, and full of collegial dialogue. Some of the best minds in the United States and Europe came together at this exciting moment to reinvent the career studies

field and to establish it in professional societies. In the later periods, researchers sought to more systematically study specific dimensions of 1970s theories and to further institutionalize the field (e.g., by forming the Careers Interest Group and, later, the Careers Division in the Academy of Management [AOM]).

Moore, Gunz, and Hall (Chapter 2) recognize, however, that "all boundaries are by necessity somewhat arbitrary" and that "career theory . . . tends toward ahistoricism." The popularity of social history over the past 40 years can be attributed, in large measure, to looking close-up at social movements and focusing on a variety of actors and "common" persons as opposed to "great" persons. It is by studying in-depth the lives of ordinary people that we better understand the historical context (Ulrich, 1991).

This chapter looks at the catalytic 1970s period of career theory, its actors, and writings in more depth and delineates several significant themes that remain important today. It also discusses how the nature of the generative work was of a kind that allowed rich ideas to be exchanged. It is suggested that the themes, and especially the nature of epistemology from this crucial period, could be fruitfully used to our advantage today.

THE IMPORTANCE OF THE MIT SCHOOL AND EARLY BEGINNINGS

Many of the 1970s career theorists trace their mentoring roots to Edgar Schein at the Sloan School of Management at the Massachusetts Institute of Technology (MIT). MIT scholars who pioneered the field, many of whom remain important today, include (Douglas) Tim Hall, Lotte Bailyn, Dave Kolb, John Van Maanen, Barbara Lawrence, John Kotter, and Ralph Katz.

Other important early theorists outside MIT were in the Boston area at the time when cross-university seminars and other interactions were commonplace and may have influenced their thinking. Gene Dalton, Paul Thompson, Jim Clawson, Jeff Sonnenfeld, and Brooke Derr were at Harvard. As the name suggests, the "Mobile Career Seminar" organized by Donald Super (Moore, Gunz, and Hall, Chapter 2) traveled to include a variety of scholars. Katz (1982b, pp. xiii–xiv) also describes a seminar on careers presented in Los Angeles in 1976 by the Organizational Studies Faculty at MIT.

THE GENESIS AND REARING OF A NEW SCHOLARLY COMMUNITY

The career studies movement took an important step forward when a small group of scholars met in Gene Dalton's hotel room at the 1977 Western AOM Meeting in Sun Valley, Idaho. Dalton and Thompson (then at Brigham Young University [BYU]), Schein (MIT), Driver and several of his students (University of South California [USC]), and Derr (then at the Naval Post Graduate School) were present. The discussion centered on whether or not the interest in career studies was sufficient to constitute a new subfield, and if so, what were some of its

dimensions. Those present decided to assemble a larger group and spend several days discussing career studies as a possible new field. Derr had access to Office of Naval Research (ONR) funds, and Schein's early research on career anchors was funded by ONR; so it was agreed to convince ONR to fund such a meeting.

Schein and Derr cohosted a retreat at the MIT Endicott House in 1978. Working to sketch the dimensions of the new career studies field were about 15 scholars, including Lotte Bailyn and John Van Maanen (MIT), Hall (Northwestern University), Paul Evans and Fernando Bartolomé (Institut Européen d'Administration des Affaires [INSEAD]), Gene Dalton and Paul Thompson (BYU), Michael Driver and Dianne Sundby (USC), Robert and Rona Rapoport (Institute of Family and Environmental Research in London), Bob Morrison (Navy Personnel Research & Development Center), and Carol Weiss and Anne Harlan (Wellesley College). One conclusion of this first meeting of the nascent "careers group" was that "career" included long-term work history and encompassed those aspects of personal life that have an impact on work life.

A follow-up meeting, also funded by ONR, convened 2 years later in 1980 at the Asilomar Conference Center near Monterey, California. Many from the 1978 meeting attended, as well as new invitees such as David Kolb (Case Western Reserve University) and doctoral students Meryl Louis (UCLA) and Barbara Lawrence (MIT). The focus of this meeting was on new career theories and ways to research them.

THE ACADEMY OF MANAGEMENT

At the AOM Annual Meeting in Atlanta in 1979, the informal careers group debated whether to form an official AOM interest group. Dalton, Derr, and others worried that the size and formality of the Academy (formal papers, presentation mentality, AOM rules) might inhibit the free-flowing discussions and intellectual output of the informal meetings. Driver, joined by Tom Gutteridge (Southern Illinois University), pushed hard to formalize and legitimize the new field via recognition in the Academy. Hall served on the AOM Board of Governors and reported a favorable reaction from the governors on the possibility of forming a Careers Interest Group. The group was formally accepted and began operating in 1980 with Driver as its first chair.

After the Detroit AOM meeting in 1980, Jeffrey Sonnenfeld, Sam Rabinowitz, Joe Raelin, Michael Arthur, Barbara Lawrence, Kathy Kram, and others quickly joined the new Careers Interest Group and helped provide leadership. Professional Development Workshops (PDWs) continued the rich informal and personal discussions of the earlier group. Dan Levinson led a PDW, for example, on adult life stage development and its impact on career stages. Several other PDW sessions focused on work-life issues and women and careers. The new phenomenon of two-career couples, some of them entering academe, was of particular interest.

A Historiographical Analysis of the 1970s Literature

As scholars rushed to make their ideas public and define this reinvented field, books were the quickest way to get ideas to market. This was also a period when writing a chapter in or editing a scholarly volume was career enhancing. Hall's *Careers in Organizations* (1976) was one of the first volumes to appear, followed by Schein's *Career Dynamics* (1978). Books on adult life stages, such as Levinson's *The Seasons of a Man's Life* (1978), were also du jour (e.g., Evans & Bartolomé, 1980a; Hall & Hall, 1979; Kanter, 1977; Rapoport & Rapoport, 1975, 1978).

Several edited volumes from this period included important theoretical essays and research-based chapters. Van Maanen (1977a) edited a volume representing the thinking of the Organizational Studies Faculty at MIT. The lead author's book contained chapters by attendees of the early careers group meetings (Derr, 1980a). Katz (1982b) published essays plus chapters by participants of the 1976 Los Angeles MIT symposium. Readers edited by Jelinek (1979b) and Morgan (1980) assembled collections of already published and some new work on careers.

Several journal articles were also seminal. Schein's articles on the individual, the organization, and the career (1971), and on career anchors (1975) received much attention. Dalton

and Thompson's research on career obsolescence (1971) and career stages of professionals (Dalton, Thompson, & Price, 1977) generated considerable buzz. Scholars also took note of Evans and Bartolomé's (1979) work on personal versus professional life. The 1980 AOM paper by Sonnenfeld and Kotter (published in 1982) provided an important conceptual overview of the field.

Reviewing significant articles and chapters of the catalytic 1970s reveals the major themes under exploration. While many of these concepts did not pass the later scrutiny of hard empirical analysis, they are nevertheless important in understanding the parameters of the field during this creative period.

Theme 1: Internal Career Orientations

Some careers literature from the 1970s questioned the definition of career success (Kaye, 1982; Lorsch & Barnes, 1972; Steiner, 1980; Tarnowieski, 1980). Hall (1976) posited a subjective inner career that was as important as or more important than the more objective, organizationally defined career. In this "new career ethic," he cited "a decrease in concern for loyalty to one's employer. This also implies less organizational control over the employee, or put more positively, more freedom for the individual" (p. 200). Van Maanen (1977b) and Schein (1977, 1978, 1996) further elaborated the internal-external concept. The internal career is a self-definition of career success; it is more subjective, long-term, and stable and represents life goals as well as work goals. The external career is an organizational or professional definition of career success; it is more short term and fast changing and is more objective, or outside the person's control (Derr & Laurent, 1989).

Building on Hall and Schein, 1970s researchers explored the internal career paradigm. Driver (1980, 1982) conceived of four "career concepts" that constitute the way a person thinks about the career. These, like other cognitive phenomena, were to identify the differences between talented individuals and help organizations design accordingly. Schein's five "career anchors" (1975, 1977, 1978) serve as a "master motive," or the thing a person would give up last (Schein, 1977, p. 53). They require organizations to offer multiple rewards and career paths to win full participation (Schein, 1977, pp. 63–64). DeLong (1982) added empirical evidence to support Schein, fleshed out the anchors concept, and developed a career anchors research questionnaire. Derr built on Schein's concepts to uncover a new career anchor called the warrior or the adventurer (1980b, 1982b). His later "career success maps" theory (1986) identified five basic career success orientations that can change over time and require various strategies for achieving them in organizations and occupations.

More recently, Hall, Briscoe, and Kram (1997) and Hall (2002, 2004) maintain that "the career as we have known it is dead," but the protean career, in which the criterion for success is internal or psychological, is very much alive. The "boundaryless career" was developed by Arthur and his colleagues (Arthur & Rousseau, 1996; Arthur, Khapova & Widerom, 2005; DeFillippi & Arthur, 1994); it also includes an internal career dimension.

After brief reference to Schein and Driver, Moore, Gunz, and Hall (Chapter 2), true to their commitment to unveil the long-term roots of the field, go on to elaborate the more foundational work of Freud, Jung, Maslow, Erickson, and modern life stage theorists. In discussing the 1970s theorists, Moore, Gunz, and Hall maintain, "Dalton [1989] has provided a good overview of many of these [other developmental] theories."

A closer look at the Dalton essay, however, uncovers that he may have been retrofitting internal career theorists to update his own earlier conceptual work (1972). For example, while Dalton categorizes Schein as developmental, he considers Driver as providing only a typology of career patterns and Derr's model as not developmental (Dalton, 1989, p. 94). In reality, Driver (1980) addresses how career concepts interact with decision-making styles and how this has an impact on organization development, and Derr (1986) considers how to design reward systems and career opportunities to best use the talents of diverse internal careerists, and how various career success maps evolve over time. All three of these internal career frameworks and the ways of measuring them have been used extensively for career development purposes in industry for 35 years.

In Sullivan and Crocitto's Chapter 15 in this *Handbook,* more attention is given to the developmental theorists. Schein and Driver are treated in some detail, but much more homage is paid to the adult life stage theorists, who are important to the developmental perspective.

The dynamics of the internal career remain an important dimension of contemporary career studies. In addition to the career counseling tools discussed by Kidd in Chapter 6, the tools developed by Schein (2006) and Derr (Novations, 2007) are still used by career counselors and by corporations, such as General Mills and DuPont. Ibarra and Deshpande use the external/internal career concept in Chapter 14. Briscoe, Hall, and DeMuth (2006) have developed measures for certain protean and boundaryless career attitudes, and this is a step forward. In a similar fashion, we need to encourage young scholars to build on the instruments of Schein, DeLong, Driver, and Derr and find ways to measure internal career orientations in scientifically acceptable ways.

The very concept of the career as both organizational and personal, internal and external, was a significant contribution of the catalytic 1970s. This may have falsely bifurcated the field and separated scholars working in the organizational dimensions of career studies from those examining the personal dimensions. By putting forward such an inclusive definition of career studies, however, researchers can now more accurately reflect on why and how individuals make career choices, the dimensions of career success and satisfaction, and what happens to the idea of a career during moments of extreme changes in the nature of work (e.g., the movement from the industrial economy to the new information economy in the 1990s and early 2000s).

Theme 2: Careers and Personal Life Issues

Because the career was redefined in the 1970s to include those aspects of personal life that interact with work, information about adult life stage development was of keen interest. Levinson's

(1978) book is mentioned above. The adult life stage theme was also well represented in chapters in the edited volumes (Hall, 1976, 1980b; D. J. Levinson, 1979, 1980; H. Levinson, 1980; Orth, 1979; Wolfe & Kolb, 1980). Managing midlife crises and retirement were part of this literature.

Expanding the definition of career to include both work and life made work-life balance an important 1970s issue (Bailyn, 1977, 1980; Evans & Bartolomé, 1979, 1980a, 1980b). Closely connected to this was an attempt to understand how the "new" dual-career couples functioned (Hall & Hall, 1980; Sundby, 1980). Some integrative work explored how family, career, and adult life stages intersect (Rapoport & Rapoport, 1980).

Work-life conflict (Greenhaus & Beutell, 1985; Parasuraman & Greenhaus, 1997) later emerged as a key issue as workplace demands grew more and more intense (Milliken & Dunn-Jensen, 2005). Lobel (1991) explored how balance may be achieved through a values and social-identity perspective. Some researchers focused on special work-life issues for dual-paycheck couples (Bumpus, Crouter, & McHale, 1999; Payden & Buehler, 1995). Research in this vein continues today with an emphasis on family-to-work conflict (Kossek & Ozeki, 1998), how companies might adapt (Bailyn, Fletcher, & Kolb, 1997; Powell & Mainiero, 1999), and special issues for males and females (Judge, Boudreau, & Bretz, 1994; Pleck, 1999).

Spillover between work and family is a typical focus (Friedman, Christensen, & DeGroot, 1998; Kirchmeyer, 1992) with work often viewed as corrupting or compromising family roles. However, work can also be seen as enriching nonwork roles (Rothbard, 2001). The issue of work and life balance remains on the forefront of concern for both individuals and the companies who hope to retain them in most advanced economies, but special issues exist within the United States (Derr & Sandholtz, 2002; Sandholtz, Derr, Buckner, & Carlson, 2002). Greenhaus and Foley's Chapter 8 discusses work-life issues.

Theme 3: Careers in Their Social Context

Careers work in the 1970s was influenced by the dominant American social issue of the period: women's rights in the workplace. Careers and affirmative action and women's careers were popular themes (Epstein, 1980; Harlan & Weiss, 1980; Jelinek, 1979a, 1979b; Kanter, 1980; Reif, Newstrom, & Monczka, 1979). Van Maanen (1977b, 1982) and others were interested in the career as a metaphor for understanding broader work culture and social identity. Women's careers, and the great pressure women face, is still a hot topic as the basic obstacles to equality and balance remain (Allen, Herst, Bruck, & Sutton, 2000; Eby, Casper, Lockwood, Bordeaux, & Brinley, 2005; Mainiero & Sullivan, 2005).

Various interests still drive a focus on the social context of careers. The broad work of the boundaryless career can be considered to be a virtual redefining and widening of the social context (Arthur, Inkson, & Pringle, 1999). The emphasis on a changing psychological contract (Rousseau, 1995) and the way organizations shape individual perceptions of their career in times of rapid change has also emerged as an extremely active area of interest (Hall & Moss, 1998).

In the "new career," can we assume that everyone has similar perceptions and opportunities? Research in the United States suggests that race plays a big role, and this is a continuing thematic area of social context and careers in recent years. Minority managers have been shown to sense lower opportunities in their careers (Greenhaus, Parasuraman, & Wormley, 1990) and favorably rated, minority, "high-potential" candidates are found to have more extensive networks (Ibarra, 1995). The reality of race and identity has been shown to have implications for assessment and intervention (Betz & Gwilliam, 2002).

Sonnenfeld and Kotter (1982) called this dimension of career research the "social class determinants." In fact, this *Handbook* has a number of chapters addressing current burning issues that fall into this category. The chapters on the socially marginalized (Chapter 10), customized careers (Chapter 11), the macrosocial context in which careers are made (Chapter 12), and the meaning of the career to those who work only to live (Chapter 16)—all these relate to this broader social context theme. Without such a category, it is also difficult to place the important, new cross-cultural work in an ongoing historical typology (see Chapter 23).

THEME 4: CAREERS AND ORGANIZATIONS

Some 1970s work on careers and organizations focused on career planning and staffing issues (Burack, 1979; Burack & Gutteridge, 1979; Hall & Hall, 1980; Hall & Morgan, 1979; Wellbank, Hall, Morgan, & Hammer, 1980), including how to best manage the careers of valuable employees. Schein and others focused on careers' implications for person/organizational fit and human resource management (Schein, 1971, 1978, 1982; Van Maanen, Schein, & Bailyn, 1980).

Dalton and Thompson (Graves, Dalton, & Thompson, 1980; Dalton, Thompson, & Price, 1977) wrote from the perspective of helping professional employees work more effectively in organizations across the four stages of the career. Transitions between jobs, stages, and occupations (Beckhard, 1977; Derr, 1982a; Graves, 1982; Louis, 1980; Morrison & Holzback, 1980) were also a concern, as was the general focus on the careers of technical and professional workers (Bailyn, 1982).

Mentoring in organizations was an important topic for both individuals and organizations and was tied into organizational socialization (Berlew & Hall, 1979; Clawson, 1980; H. Levinson, 1980). Career management from the perspective of effective organizational indoctrination, psychological contracts, and avoiding career obsolescence and plateauing was part of this overall socialization concern (Bailyn, 1980; Feldman, 1980; Ferrence, 1979; Hall, 1980a; Kotter, 1980; D. J. Levinson, 1980; Sonnenfeld, 1980; Van Maanen, 1982; Warren, Ferrence, & Stoner, 1979; Webber, 1980).

Katz (1977, 1982a), Seybolt (1980), and others linked careers to job enrichment. Van Maanen (1980) and Derr (1982a) explored how to study politics in organizations using the careers approach. Jennings (1971), Korda (1975), Lee (1980), Josefowitz (1980), and Zaleznick and Kets de Vries (1975) all wrote about the strategies and tactics powerful careerists use to achieve their career agendas. Several of these books became primers for women managers.

In more recent years, career development has focused on self-preparation for a "war for talent" in which one continuously prepares for new job opportunities in the labor market (Cappelli, 1999; Reich, 2001). In addition to buying talent from the marketplace, companies also focus on managing talent and high-potential employees (Conger & Fulmer, 2003; Derr, Briscoe, & Buckner, 2002). Succession planning in a world of exiting baby boomers and scarce young talent is also an increasingly important topic. Chapters 19 to 22 of the *Handbook* also address the relationship between careers and organizations.

LESSONS FROM THE 1970S

One main catalyst of the prolific work of the 1970s was the nature of intellectual endeavor during that period. It was a generative period wherein defining the field was a product of intellectual curiosity, the desire to build a new community, and an emphasis on producing innovative new theories.

We believe that rich and participative dialogue was one key to the catalytic 1970s. Technology played a role in this, by omission. It was important to meet face-to-face, and this was the most practical way to collaborate in many cases. Without large data sets readily available on the computer, face-to-face discussions and theory building were also emphasized, and qualitative research methods were more common. Such endeavors sometimes resulted in publishing chapters in scholarly books, which was at that time seen as respectable.

Career studies in the 1970s were also a very human activity. Scholars could easily discuss the interface between work, relationships, and self-development in their own lives. Ample attention was given to work-life balance and to accepting those who had made life decisions that were not career enhancing. The result was that something meaningful, scholarly, and lasting emerged from informal interactions.

We think that another key to the 1970s being so generative was the sense of building a scholarly community. There seemed to be great concern about "getting it right" in terms of defining the new field. The very process of participative dialogue reflected values of tolerance and innovation. Cultures can be "strong" as their values are widely and deeply shared, but they cannot be adaptive if those values do not allow introspection, adaptation, and change. We view the communities that formed in the 1970s as building a strong and adaptive culture where two values drove people's energies: (1) the effort to be inclusive, that is, to include traditional career perspectives plus related issues and anything personal that overlapped into work from private life (and to include all kinds of scholars), and (2) the effort to gain legitimacy for the field and make it academically respected. Substantial time was given to collaborating in order to define the field as broadly as possible.

LOOKING FORWARD: THE CATALYTIC 2000S

Because there is currently so much pressure to publish in a narrow range of journals in order to survive and thrive in today's academic world, it might be difficult to relive the kind of movement experienced in the 1970s. Publishing in highly competitive journals is both difficult and time-consuming. While this has raised the quality of one kind of scholarship, it may have reduced the quality of the scholarly conversation as scholars' freedom to actively participate in informal meetings or write thought pieces has been curtailed. Career studies today remain central to organizational studies, but they seem to lack the excitement of the 1970s era.

How can the 2000s become a catalytic chapter for careers scholarship? Building on the experience of the 1970s and reflecting on challenges that present themselves now unrelated to the 1970s, we have some propositions.

AN AGE-OLD PROBLEM: ADAPTATION AND INTEGRATION

As Schein (1992) points out, organizational culture is essentially a pattern of basic assumptions that a group develops and legitimizes in learning to deal with problems of "external adaptation" and "internal integration." In contrast to the 1970s, the scholarly careers community may be well established in organizational scholarship and in the major academic professional societies. Its survival and recognition may depend to a significant degree on producing scholarship that is seen as legitimate in the larger context of current organizational studies. Thus, pressure to publish in certain journals, and emphasize quantitative methods and empirical data, are forces that shape us. This is the age-old issue of gaining legitimacy via engaging in respected ongoing scholarly activities.

We have the opportunity, pressure, and responsibility to prove our relevance and worth to the larger community of management scholars and practitioners, some of whom do not recognize the primacy of career theory and scholarship to the key questions facing management today. This is a legitimate and important endeavor if we are to adapt to our external environment. However, we must also carefully manage the internal integration of our community in a way that extends its unique spirit and helps it remain innovative and passionate, so that we do not just follow and evaluate key ideas generated elsewhere.

BUILDING DIALOGUE AND COMMUNITY IN A GLOBAL CONTEXT

The careers community is much larger and more diverse than in the 1970s. Its members exist all around the world. In addition to the challenge of dialogue across global cultures, the content and context of what we study has also been extended. To some degree, the 1970s (and we would argue that this has still not changed substantially) was myopically focused on career assumptions in Anglo societies (Inkson, 2006; Thomas and Inkson, Chapter 23). Thus, we face a challenge now of not only more diversity among career scholars but also myriad career contexts around the world in which to create and focus the dialogue we see as crucial.

While the careers community may not have the same fervor of the 1970s, it still retains many of the values that made it unique, such as open-mindedness, inclusivity, a developmental perspective, and a recognition of the whole person (for scholars and research populations alike). Thus, we are well positioned to recycle the generative era of the 1970s from a values perspective. The challenge in many ways is one of reflection, concentration, and discipline as we engage in dialogue that may not at first come easily in a more complex internal and external environment.

The careers community needs to seek ways to make sure that new and different voices are heard. Some of the maverick theories of yesteryear have become today's status quo and now need freshening themselves. Thus, it is critical that a plethora of scholars representing many cultures can be heard. One way of doing this is to create several smaller communities that interact with the larger global careers community. Just as groups formed at MIT, Harvard, BYU, and USC, newer groups are building critical mass in careers research at places such as the University of Toronto, London Business School, IMD, INSEAD, Boston University, EM Lyon, the University of Melbourne, and the Vienna University of Economics and Business Management. Many of these groups enjoy substantial diversity in doctoral students who come from all corners of the world. A priority may be that existing faculty who do not represent Western perspectives make sure to learn from and incorporate cross-cultural perspectives as much as they inculcate their own.

Note that while many centers of excellence extend beyond the United States in careers, they all have what would be considered to be a Western perspective. This is reflected with few exceptions in careers scholarship as well. For example, when boundaryless careers have been tested, they have been tested against the context of France (Cadin, Bailly-Bender, & de Saint-Giniez, 2000), the United Kingdom (Gratton, Zaleska, & de Menezes, 2002), and New Zealand (Arthur et al., 1999). All these countries are individualistic in Hofstede's (1980) framework, and all would fall among Western Europe or English-speaking regions in Schwartz's (2004) seven world regions. Thus, even when Western notions of career success and self-directed career behavior are verified or dismissed, they are usually done so within a relatively narrow cultural context. It should be noted, however, that the U.S. version of the boundaryless career concept does not completely transfer over to even a Western country such as France (Dany, 2003).

Similar to the 1970s, it seems to us that the time is ripe for more theory-generating work that better understands what makes careers unique within cultures and common and/or distinct across cultures.

Thus, it behooves us to build critical masses of careers scholars in more countries around the world and to strengthen those communities that already exist. The Careers Division of the AOM may consider becoming more established around the globe, for example. The Asian AOM should also feature a careers group. This is one challenge; another of course is to strengthen and facilitate those communities' connections to one another and to the larger careers community.

The most obvious way to build both communities and connections is to purposefully seek out working relationships with our scholarly counterparts across the globe. This is a win-win for both sides of the scholarly relationship (or beyond) as well as the careers community itself. A great example of this is Michael Arthur, whose own curiosity and interest helped invigorate careers research in various countries such as New Zealand and Norway and went on to produce synergistic relationships and some excellent scholarly contributions (e.g., Arthur et al., 1999, 2005). Chompookum and Derr's (2004) work in Thailand is also notable. We advocate more such relationships, in ever more diverse cultures.

This will involve taking risks with scholars and would-be scholars who may lack the uniform training that is taken for granted in the developed West. But the rewards will be manifold as we engage in mutual learning. There is probably a place for socialization and for inculcating the basic assumptions of the careers community that have allowed it to thrive these many years: values around process and around the ultimate meaning and usefulness of career theory for individuals and organizations, more than around any particular approach or theory. There is also room to question some of our basic assumptions that were premised on work done in the United States.

Beyond vertical and horizontal developmental relationships across cultures, it may be useful for geographical, cultural, and even ideological subgroups to form their own communities around the world with a great sense of purpose. A major element from the 1970s seems to us now to be missing: the sense of presence and intimacy that characterized the 1970s meetings. Perhaps this can occur in smaller venues, especially as research is conducted across borders.

To give voice to smaller communities, larger communities and organizations such as the Careers Division of the AOM and key journals in the field must continually define themselves in inclusive ways that broaden the conversation and beckon new theories and the innovative testing of established theory.

CONCLUSION

This chapter has been devoted primarily to endeavors within academia, but many of the same premises used for expanding careers dialogue, community, and theory across cultures can be applied to vocational contexts that focus on careers: from guidance counselors, to coaching, to career development within organizations, and to university education (e.g., see Chapters 5 and 6 by Savickas and by Kidd, respectively).

This brings us back to the dilemma of internal integration and external adaptation. How do we remain a robust community while adapting to the substantially complex external environment? We believe that this tension can be managed in part by maintaining an active and sensitive dialogue within the boundaries of the field. In many ways, the directions defined in the 1970s still remain: long-term work history along with conceptualizations encompassing those aspects of personal life that have an impact on work life. There is still a focus on the internal and external careers, but the context in which they play out has dramatically changed for many in terms of time, space, and complexity. We believe that the global environment beckons us to act as true scholars who are open to new perspectives on both the world of work and work-life issues. This prospect is truly exciting and dynamic, and can reinfuse our scholarship in the 2000s with the passion and excitement that marked the catalytic 1970s.

In a sense, we must be exemplars of what we teach: boundaryless and values driven (Briscoe & Hall, 2006) in our approach to our careers and our communities. This involves seeing opportunities (Sullivan & Arthur, 2006) and taking risks. Our own and our colleagues' careers will be enhanced as we seek the larger good so that our careers community may survive, prosper, and sustain the values that generated it nearly four decades ago.

REFERENCES

Allen, T., Herst, D. E., Bruck, C. S., & Sutton, M. (2000). Consequences associated with work-to-family conflict: A review and agenda for future research. *Journal of Occupational Health Psychology, 5*(2), 278–308.

Arthur, M. B., Inkson, K., & Pringle, J. K. (1999). *The new careers: Individual action and economic change.* Thousand Oaks, CA: Sage.

Arthur, M. B., Khapova, S. N., & Wilderom, C. P. M. (2005). Career success in a boundaryless career world. *Journal of Organizational Behavior, 26*(2), 177–202.

Arthur, M. B., & Rousseau, D. M. (1996). *The boundaryless career: A new employment principle for a new organizational era.* Oxford: Oxford University Press.

Bailyn, L. (1977). Involvement and accommodation in technical careers: An inquiry into the relation to work at mid-career. In J. Van Maanen (Ed.), *Organizational careers: Some new perspectives* (pp. 109–132). New York: Wiley.

Bailyn, L. (1980). The slow-burn way to the top: Some thoughts on the early years of organizational careers. In C. B. Derr (Ed.), *Work, family and the career* (pp. 94–105). New York: Praeger.

Bailyn, L. (1982). Trained as engineers: Issues for the management of technical personnel in mid-career. In R. Katz (Ed.), *Career issues in human resource management* (pp. 35–49). Englewood Cliffs, NJ: Prentice Hall.

Bailyn, L., Fletcher, J. K., & Kolb, D. (1997). Unexpected connections: Considering employees' personal lives can revitalize your business. *Sloan Management Review, 38*(4), 11–19.

Beckhard, R. (1977). Managerial careers in transition: Dilemmas and directions. In J. Van Maanen (Ed.), *Organizational careers: Some new perspectives* (pp. 149–160). New York: Wiley.

Berlew, D. E., & Hall, D. T. (1979). The socialization of managers: Effects of expectations on performance. In M. Jelinek (Ed.), *Career management for the individual and the organization* (pp. 73–84). Chicago: St. Clair Press.

Betz, N. E., & Gwilliam, L. R. (2002). The utility measures of self-efficacy for the Holland themes in African American and European American college students. *Journal of Career Assessment, 10*(3), 283–300.

Briscoe, J. P., & Hall, D. T. (2006). The interplay of boundaryless and protean careers: Combinations and implications. *Journal of Vocational Behavior, 69*(1), 4–18.

Briscoe, J. P., Hall, D. T., & DeMuth, R. L. F. (2006). Protean and boundaryless careers: An empirical exploration. *Journal of Vocational Behavior, 69*(1), 30–47.

Bumpus, M. F., Crouter, A. C., & McHale, S. M. (1999). Work demands of dual-earner couples: Implications for parents' knowledge about children's daily lives in middle childhood. *Journal of Marriage and Family, 61,* 465–475.

Burack, E. H. (1979). Why all the confusion about career planning? In M. Jelinek (Ed.), *Career management for the individual and the organization* (pp. 319–324). Chicago: St. Clair Press.

Burack, E. H., & Gutteridge, T. G. (1979). Institutional manpower planning: Rhetoric v. reality. In M. Jelinek (Ed.), *Career management for the individual and the organization* (pp. 369–382). Chicago: St. Clair Press.

Cadin, L., Bailly-Bender, A.-F., & Saint-Giniez, V. (2000). Exploring boundaryless careers in the French context. In M. Peiperl, M. B. Arthur, R. Goffee, & T. Morris (Eds.), *Career frontiers: New conceptions of working lives* (pp. 228–255). Oxford: Oxford University Press.

Cappelli, P. (1999). *The new deal at work: Managing the market-driven work force.* Boston: Harvard Business School Press.

Chompookum, D., & Derr, C. B. (2004). The effects of internal career orientations on organizational citizenship behavior in Thailand. *Career Development International, 9*(4–5), 406–423.

Clawson, J. G. (1980). Mentoring in managerial careers. In C. B. Derr (Ed.), *Work, family, and the career* (pp. 144–165). New York: Praeger.

Conger, J. A., & Fulmer, R. M. (2003). Developing your leadership pipeline. *Harvard Business Review, 81*(12), 76–85.

Dalton, G. W. (1972). A review of concepts on careers. In J. Lorsch & L. B. Barnes (Eds.), *Managers and their careers: Cases and readings* (pp. 59–84). Homewood, IL: Richard D. Irwin.

Dalton, G. W. (1989). Developmental views of careers in organizations. In M. B. Arthur, D. T. Hall, & B. S. Lawrence (Eds.), *Handbook of career theory* (pp. 89–109). New York: Cambridge University Press.

Dalton, G. W., & Thompson, P. H. (1971). Accelerating obsolescence of older engineers. *Harvard Business Review, September/October,* 57–67.

Dalton, G. W., Thompson, P. H., & Price, R. L. (1977). The four stages of professional careers: A new look at performance by professionals. *Organizational Dynamics, Summer,* 19–42.

Dany, F. (2003). "Free actors" and organizations: Critical remarks about the new career literature, based on French insights. *International Journal of Human Resource Management, 14*(5), 821–838.

DeFillippi, R. J., & Arthur, M. B. (1994). The boundaryless career: A competency-based perspective. *Journal of Organizational Behavior, 15*(4), 307–324.

DeLong, T. J. (1982). The career orientations of MBA alumni: A multidimensional model. In R. Katz (Ed.), *Career issues in human resource management* (pp. 50–64). Englewood Cliffs, NJ: Prentice Hall.

Derr, C. B. (Ed.). (1980a). *Work, family, and the career.* New York: Praeger.

Derr, C. B. (1980b). More about career anchors. In C. B. Derr (Ed.), *Work, family, and the career* (pp. 166–187). New York: Praeger.

Derr, C. B. (1982a). Career switching and organizational politics: The case of naval officers. In R. Katz (Ed.), *Career issues in human resource management* (pp. 65–81). Englewood Cliffs, NJ: Prentice Hall.

Derr, C. B. (1982b). Living on adrenalin: The adventurer-entrepreneur. *Human Resource Management, 21*(2–3), 6–12.

Derr, C. B. (1986). *Managing the new careerists: The diverse career success orientations of today's workers.* San Francisco: Jossey-Bass.

Derr, C. B., Briscoe, J. P., & Buckner, K. (2002). Managing leadership in the United States. In C. B. Derr, S. Roussillon, & F. Bournois (Eds.), *Cross-cultural approaches to leadership development.* Westport, CT: Quorum Books.

Derr, C. B., & Laurent, A. (1989). The internal and external careers: Theoretical and cross-cultural perspectives. In M. B. Arthur, D. T. Hall, &

B. S. Lawrence (Eds.), *Handbook of career theory* (pp. 454–471). New York: Cambridge University Press.

Derr, C. B., & Sandholtz, K. (2002). Beyond juggling: Cross-cultural issues in work-life balance. *Management et Conjoncture Sociale, 616,* 102–106.

Driver, M. J. (1980). Career concepts and organizational change. In C. B. Derr (Ed.), *Work, family, and the career* (pp. 18–37). New York: Praeger.

Driver, M. J. (1982). Career concepts: A new approach to career research. In R. Katz (Ed.), *Career issues in human resource management* (pp. 23–32). Englewood Cliffs, NJ: Prentice Hall.

Eby, L. T., Casper, W. J., Lockwood, A., Bordeaux, C., & Brinley, A. (2005). Work and family research in IO/OB: Content analysis and review of the literature. *Journal of Vocational Behavior, 66,* 124–197.

Epstein, C. F. (1980). Institutional barriers: What keeps women out of the executive suite? In M. A. Morgan (Ed.), *Managing career development* (pp. 187–194). New York: D. Van Nostrand.

Evans, P. A. L., & Bartolomé, F. (1979). Professional and private life: Three stages in the life of managers. *Organizational Dynamics, Spring.*

Evans, P. A. L., & Bartolomé, F. (1980a). *Must success cost so much?* New York: Basic Books.

Evans, P. A. L., & Bartolomé, F. (1980b). The relationship between professional life and private life. In C. B. Derr (Ed.), *Work, family, and the career* (pp. 281–317). New York: Praeger.

Feldman, D. C. (1980). A practical program for employee socialization. In M. A. Morgan (Ed.), *Managing career development* (pp. 73–86). New York: D. Van Nostrand.

Ferrence, T. P. (1979). The career plateau: Facing up to life at the middle. In M. Jelinek (Ed.), *Career management for the individual and the organization* (pp. 175–179). Chicago: St. Clair Press.

Friedman, S. D., Christensen, P., & DeGroot, J. (1998). Work and life: The end of the zero-sum game. *Harvard Business Review, November/December,* 119–129.

Gratton, L., Zaleska, K. J., & de Menezes, L. M. (2002, June). *The rhetoric and reality of the "new careers."* Paper presented at the Harvard Business School Conference on Career Evolution, London.

Graves, J. P. (1982). Successful management and organizational mugging. In R. Katz (Ed.), *Career issues in human resource management*

(pp. 116–125). Englewood Cliffs, NJ: Prentice Hall.

Graves, J. P., Dalton, G. W., & Thompson, P. H. (1980). Career stages in organizations. In C. B. Derr (Ed.), *Work, family, and the career* (pp. 18–37). New York: Praeger.

Greenhaus, J. H., & Beutell, N. J. (1985). Sources of conflict between work and family roles. *Academy of Management Review, 10*(1), 76–88.

Greenhaus, J. H., Parasuraman, S., & Wormley, W. M. (1990). Effects of race on organizational experiences, job performance evaluations, and career outcomes. *Academy of Management Review, 33*(1), 64–86.

Hall, D. T. (1976). *Careers in organizations.* New York: Scott Foresman Series.

Hall, D. T. (1980a). Socialization processes in later career years: Can there be growth at the terminal level? In C. B. Derr (Ed.), *Work, family, and the career* (pp. 219–233). New York: Praeger.

Hall, D. T. (1980b). Potential for career growth. In M. A. Morgan. (Ed.), *Managing career development* (pp. 87–99). New York: D. Van Nostrand.

Hall, D. T. (2002). *Protean careers in and out of organizations.* Thousand Oaks, CA: Sage.

Hall, D. T. (2004). The protean career: A quarter-century journey. *Journal of Vocational Behavior, 65*(1), 1–13.

Hall, D. T., Briscoe, J. P., & Kram, K. E. (1997). Identity, values, and learning in the protean career. In C. L. Cooper & S. E. Jackson (Eds.), *Creating tomorrow's organizations* (pp. 321–335). London: Wiley.

Hall, F. S., & Hall, D. T. (1979). *The two-career couple.* Reading, MA: Addison-Wesley.

Hall, F. S., & Hall, D. T. (1980). Dual-career couples. In M. A. Morgan (Ed.), *Managing career development* (pp. 217–232). New York: D. Van Nostrand.

Hall, D. T., & Morgan, M. A. (1979). Career development and planning. In M. Jelinek (Ed.), *Career management for the individual and the organization* (pp. 325–348). Chicago: St. Clair Press.

Hall, D. T., & Moss, J. E. (1998). The new protean career contract: Helping organizations and employees adapt. *Organizational Dynamics, Winter,* 22–37.

Harlan, A., & Weiss, C. L. (1980). Career opportunities for women managers. In C. B. Derr (Ed.), *Work, family, and the career* (pp. 188–199). New York: Praeger.

Hofstede, G. (1980). *Culture's consequences: International differences in work-related values.* Beverly Hills, CA: Sage.

Ibarra, H. (1995). Race, opportunity, and diversity of social circles in managerial networks. *Academy of Management Journal, 38*(3), 673–703.

Inkson, K. (2006). Protean and boundaryless careers as metaphors. *Journal of Vocational Behavior, 69*(1), 48–63.

Jelinek, M. (1979a). Career management and women. In M. Jelinek (Ed.), *Career management for the individual and the organization* (pp. 277–284). Chicago: St. Clair Press.

Jelinek, M. (Ed.). (1979b). *Career management for the individual and the organization.* Chicago: St. Clair Press.

Jennings, E. E. (1971). *Routes to the executive suite.* New York: McGraw-Hill.

Josefowitz, N. (1980). *Paths to power.* Reading, MA: Addison-Wesley.

Judge, T. A., Boudreau, J. W., & Bretz, R. D. (1994). Job and life attitudes of male executives. *Journal of Applied Psychology, 79*(5), 767–782.

Kanter, R. M. (1977). *Work and family in the United States.* New York: Russell Sage.

Kanter, R. M. (1980). Climbing the pyramid alone. In M. A. Morgan (Ed.), *Managing career development* (pp. 195–201). New York: D. Van Nostrand.

Katz, R. (1977). Job enrichment: Some career considerations. In J. Van Maanen (Ed.), *Organizational careers: Some new perspectives* (pp. 133–148). New York: Wiley.

Katz, R. (1982a). Managing careers: The influence of job and group longevities. In R. Katz (Ed.), *Career issues in human resource management* (pp. 154–181). Englewood Cliffs, NJ: Prentice Hall.

Katz, R. (Ed.). (1982b). *Career issues in human resource management.* Englewood Cliffs, NJ: Prentice Hall.

Kaye, B. L. (1982). *Up is not the only way.* Englewood Cliffs, NJ: Prentice Hall.

Kirchmeyer, C. (1992). Perceptions of nonwork-to-work spillover: Challenging the common view of conflict-ridden domain relationships. *Basic and Applied Social Psychology, 13,* 231.

Korda, M. (1975). *Power: How to get it, how to use it.* New York: Random House.

Kossek, E. E., & Ozeki, C. (1998). Work-family conflict, policies, and the job-life satisfaction relationship: A review and directions for organizational behavior-human resources research. *Journal of Applied Psychology, 83,* 139–149.

Kotter, J. P. (1980). The psychological contract: Managing the joining up process. In M. A. Morgan (Ed.), *Managing career development* (pp. 63–72). New York: D. Van Nostrand.

Lee, N. (1980). *Targeting the top.* New York: Doubleday.

Levinson, D. J. (1978). *The seasons of a man's life.* New York: Ballantine.

Levinson, D. J. (1979). The midlife transition: A period in adult psychological development. In M. Jelinek (Ed.), *Career management for the individual and the organization* (pp. 218–233). Chicago: St. Clair Press.

Levinson, D. J. (1980). The mid-life transition. In M. A. Morgan (Ed.), *Managing career development* (pp. 133–139). New York: D. Van Nostrand.

Levinson, H. (1980). On being a middle-aged manager. In M. A. Morgan (Ed.), *Managing career development* (pp. 123–132). New York: D. Van Nostrand.

Lobel, S. A. (1991). Allocation of investment in work and family roles: Alternative theories and implications for research. *Academy of Management Review, 16*(3), 507–521.

Lorsch, J., & Barnes, L. B. (Eds.). (1972). *Managers and their careers: Cases and readings.* Homewood, IL: Richard D. Irwin.

Louis, M. R. (1980). Toward an understanding of career transitions. In C. B. Derr (Ed.), *Work, family, and the career* (pp. 200–218). New York: Praeger.

Mainiero, L. A., & Sullivan, S. E. (2005). Kaleidoscope careers: An alternative explanation for the opt-out revolution. *Academy of Management Executive, 19*(1), 106–123.

Milliken, F. J., & Dunn-Jensen, L. M. (2005). The changing time demands of managerial and professional work: Implications for managing the work-life boundary. In E. E. Kossek & S. J. Lambert (Eds.), *Work and life integration.* Mahwah, NJ: Lawrence Erlbaum.

Morgan, M. A. (Ed.). (1980). *Managing career development.* New York: D. Van Nostrand.

Morrison, R. F., & Holzback, R. L. (1980). The career manager role. In C. B. Derr (Ed.), *Work, family, and the career* (pp. 75–93). New York: Praeger.

Novations. (2007). *Talent development program workbook.* Boston, MA: The Novations Group, www.novations.com.

Orth, C. D. (1979). How to survive the mid-career crisis. In M. Jelinek (Ed.), *Career management for the individual and the organization* (pp. 239–248). Chicago: St. Clair Press.

Parasuraman, S., & Greenhaus, J. H. (1997). *Integrating work and family: Challenges and choices for a changing world.* Westport, CT: Quorum Books.

Payden, S. L., & Buehler, C. (1995). Coping with the dual-income lifestyle. *Journal of Marriage and Family, 57,* 101–110.

Pleck, J. H. (1999). Balancing work and family. *Scientific American, 10,* 38–43.

Powell, G. N., & Mainiero, L. A. (1999). Managerial decision making regarding alternative work arrangements. *Journal of Occupational and Organizational Psychology, 72,* 41–56.

Rapoport, R., & Rapoport, R. N. (1975). *Leisure and the family life cycle.* London: Routledge & Kegan Paul.

Rapoport, R., & Rapoport, R. N. (1978). *Working couples.* New York: Harper & Row.

Rapoport, R., & Rapoport, R. N. (1980). Balancing work, family and leisure: A triple helix model. In C. B. Derr (Ed.), *Work, family, and the career* (pp. 318–328). New York: Praeger.

Reich, R. (2001). *The future of success.* New York: Alfred Knopf.

Reif, W. E., Newstrom, J. W., & Monczka, R. M. (1979). Exploding some myths about women managers. In M. Jelinek (Ed.), *Career management for the individual and the organization* (pp. 266–276). Chicago: St. Clair Press.

Rothbard, N. P. (2001). Enriching or depleting? The dynamics of engagement in work and family roles. *Administrative Science Quarterly, 46,* 655.

Rousseau, D. M. (1995). *Psychological contracts in organizations.* Thousand Oaks, CA: Sage.

Sandholtz, K., Derr, C. B., Buckner, K., & Carlson, D. (2002). *Beyond juggling: Rebalancing your busy life.* San Francisco: Berrett Koehler.

Schein, E. H. (1971). The individual, the organization and the career. *Journal of Applied Behavior Science, 7,* 401–426.

Schein, E. H. (1975). How career anchors hold executives to their career paths. *Personnel, 52,* 11–24.

Schein, E. H. (1977). Career anchors and career paths: A panel study of management school graduates. In J. Van Maanen (Ed.), *Organizational careers: Some new perspectives* (pp. 49–64). New York: Wiley.

Schein, E. H. (1978). *Career dynamics: Matching individual and organizational needs.* Reading, MA: Addison-Wesley.

Schein, E. H. (1982). Increasing organizational effectiveness through better human resource planning and development. In R. Katz (Ed.), *Career issues in human resource management* (pp. 3–22). Englewood Cliffs, NJ: Prentice Hall.

Schein, E. H. (1992). *Organizational culture and leadership* (2nd ed.). San Francisco: Jossey-Bass.

Schein, E. H. (1996). Career anchors revisited: Implications for career development in the 21st century. *Academy of Management Executive, 10,* 80–88.

Schein, E. H. (2006). *Career anchors: Participant workbook.* San Francisco: Pfeiffer.

Schwartz, S. H. (2004). Mapping and interpreting cultural differences around the world. In H. Vinken, J. Soeters, & P. Ester (Eds.), *Comparing cultures: Dimensions of culture in a comparative perspective* (pp. 43–73). Leiden: Brill.

Seybolt, J. W. (1980). The impact of work-role design on career satisfaction. In C. B. Derr (Ed.), *Work, family, and the career* (pp. 51–74). New York: Praeger.

Sonnenfeld, J. A. (1980). Dealing with the aging workforce. In M. A. Morgan (Ed.), *Managing career development* (pp. 158–170). New York: D. Van Nostrand.

Sonnenfeld, J. A., & Kotter, J. P. (1982). The maturation of career theory. *Human Relations, 35,* 19–46.

Steiner, J. (1980). What price success? In M. A. Morgan (Ed.), *Managing career development* (pp. 178–184). New York: D. Van Nostrand.

Sullivan, S. E., & Arthur, M. B. (2006). The evolution of the boundaryless career concept: Examining physical and psychological mobility. *Journal of Vocational Behavior, 69*(1), 19–29.

Sundby, D. Y. (1980). The career quad: A psychological look at some divergent dual-career families. In C. B. Derr (Ed.), *Work, family, and the career* (pp. 329–353). New York: Praeger.

Tarnowieski, D. (1980). Toward a new definition of success. In M. A. Morgan (Ed.), *Managing career development* (pp. 173–177). New York: D. Van Nostrand.

Ulrich, L. T. (1991). *A midwife's tale: The life of Martha Ballard, based on her diary, 1785–1812.* New York: Alfred A. Knopf.

Van Maanen, J. (Ed.). (1977a). *Organizational careers: Some new perspectives.* New York: Wiley.

Van Maanen, J. (1977b). Summary: Towards a theory of the career. In J. Van Maanen (Ed.), *Organizational careers: Some new perspectives* (pp. 161–180). New York: Wiley.

Van Maanen, J. (1980). Career games: Organizational rules of play. In C. B. Derr (Ed.), *Work, family, and the career* (pp. 111–143). New York: Praeger.

Van Maanen, J. (1982). Boundary crossings: Major strategies of organizational socialization and their consequences. In R. Katz (Ed.), *Career issues in human resource management* (pp. 85–115). Englewood Cliffs, NJ: Prentice Hall.

Van Maanen, J., Schein, E., & Bailyn, L. (1980). The shape of things to come: A new look at organizational careers. In M. A. Morgan (Ed.), *Managing career development* (pp. 3–12). New York: D. Van Nostrand.

Warren, E. K., Ferrence, T. P., & Stoner, J. A. F. (1979). The case of the plateaued performer. In M. Jelinek (Ed.), *Career management for the individual and the organization* (pp. 180–185). Chicago: St. Clair Press.

Webber, R. A. (1980). Career problems of young managers. In M. A. Morgan (Ed.), *Managing career development* (pp. 100–116). New York: D. Van Nostrand.

Wellbank, H. L., Hall, D. T., Morgan, M. A., & Hammer, W. C. (1980). Planning job progression for effective career development. In M. A. Morgan (Ed.), *Managing career development* (pp. 271–278). New York: D. Van Nostrand.

Wolfe, D. M., & Kolb, D. A. (1980). Beyond specialization: The quest for integration in mid-career. In C. B. Derr (Ed.), *Work, family, and the career* (pp. 239–280). New York: Praeger.

Zaleznik, A., & Kets de Vries, M. F. R. (1975). *Power and the corporate mind.* Boston: Houghton-Mifflin.

30

CAREER STUDIES

Personal "Side Trips"

PHILIP H. MIRVIS

The many contributors to this volume on careers traverse multiple levels of analysis and frames of reference to trace thematic lines through the vast terra covered by career studies. These are seasoned navigators who know their stuff and more than they can say in the brief confines of time/space allotted to them. Unhampered on these counts, my intent is to report on personal side trips that zigzag across their routings and highlight some of the ideas and questions that arise.

To begin, let's take up the line explored by Jones and Dunn (Chapter 22) that careers and institutions coevolve and influence one another. This parallels Greenhaus and Foley's Chapter 8, which shows the bidirectional interplay of work-family and family-work conflicts, as well as the potential for mutual enrichment across these spheres. When considering family-friendly "initiatives," however, our work-family guides speak mostly to how organizational policies, programs, and work environments affect working parents and their performance on the job. My side trip heads in the other direction: to look into how these initiatives

came about and coevolve with organizations and societies.

WHAT'S BEHIND WORK-FAMILY ACTIVITY IN COMPANIES?

The presenting reasons why companies care about working parents are familiar: on the demand side, increases in women in the paid labor force, and thus in two-career couples and working single mothers, chiefly in the United States, the United Kingdom, and northern Europe, make up the main vector. Concurrent changes in family structures and roles and in the careers and financial aspirations of working women in these areas, as well as in southern Europe, northern Asia, Brazil, and most segments of the urban, industrialized, modernizing world, have created widespread and vocal pressure that employers and host governments do something to aid working parents.

On the supply side, these sociodemographic trends are coincident with changes in occupational profiles, wage structures, and job stresses in industry that have added to the strain on working people and their families. Accordingly, a combination of family-friendly legislation, in Scandinavia foremost but increasingly everywhere, along with industry peer-group pressure and enlightened self-interest have led organizations to adopt ameliorative work-life initiatives.

The Labor Force 2000 Survey, a study of human resource investments and practices in a sample of over 400 private and public sector organizations in North America by me and several colleagues (Mirvis, 1993), gives at least a glimpse of which organizations are most apt to have family-friendly practices and why: firms that employ a *larger proportion* of women and those that believe such efforts contribute to the recruitment and retention of employees—classic "HR drivers," to adopt the lingo. A deeper cut into the data finds, however, that an even stronger predictor is the number of women in an organization's *professional* and *managerial ranks*.

This means that it is about numbers as Rosabeth Moss Kanter (1977) opined but that it may be more specifically about (a) the pressure generated by a growing, comparatively high-power minority group in organizations (professional women) and (b) the attendant comfort level of an even higher power group of men (chiefly executives) who know and work with these women, increasingly have spouses in similar circumstances, have work-family conflicts of their own to deal with, and simply cannot deny or "pooh-pooh" the work-family issues that they encounter so regularly and in so many forms.[1]

On the latter point, it would be useful to understand better how senior managers think about work-family matters, not to mention the fuller panoply of life and lifestyle concerns of working people, when they think about career development, mentor peers and subordinates, and consider company policies in this arena. Lew Platt, the former CEO of Hewlett Packard, was a strong proponent of work-family balance based on firsthand experience: His wife died young, and he took an active role raising his children. What other factors besides personal experience—for example, age, generation, empathy, developmental stage, not to mention strategic necessity—make executives more thoughtful about and socially sensitive to the especially human side of careers?

A closer look at the process by which companies adopt work-family initiatives, however, suggests that top executive attitudes may not be as important as once thought. My time spent as a fellow with the Work-Family Roundtable of the Center for Work and Family, Boston College, a body composed of corporate work-family representatives, put a human face to numbers and power politics. In many instances, forum members, mostly midlevel professional women, lacked strong executive buy-in and backing and began their efforts as the solo "champion" for work-family innovation in their companies.

Interestingly, by self-report they operate like "tempered radicals"—a term coined by Deborah Meyerson (2001) in her studies of how professionals advance social issues in organizations. These champions built coalitions of support, first among women and then among men, achieved "small wins," and made progress from the middle, up and down. In so doing, they leveraged external influences, such as cover stories in magazines on the work-family "issue" and corporate rankings of family friendliness prepared by *Working Mother* magazine, and drew on the example and support of forum members. Query for theorists and researchers: Is this comparatively quiet and incremental strategy a function of the following:

1. the champions' personal and countercultural "differentness" (Meyerson, 2001),

2. their relative influence and status as midmanagers (a hierarchical explanation),

3. the kind of social issue they are pressing (stereotyped as a woman's concern),

4. all of the above, and/or

5. something else?

FROM CAREERS TO EMERGENT ORGANIZATION

One possible "something else" is hinted at in the chapter on networks and identities by Ibarra and Deshpande (Chapter 14). In the case of work-family, a vast and multilayered network of analysts, advocates, academics, and journalists, from think-tanks, consulting firms, universities, and the media, has taken shape to study work-family matters, convene informative and influential gatherings, develop and document best practices, honor innovative companies, and define new expectations for both employers and working people. As an example, the Sloan Foundation, host of an academic network, funds a variety of studies in this area, maintains an extensive library of research and working papers, and features bios of "work-family leaders" on its Web site. And the practice-oriented Work-Family Roundtable has spun off three additional networks: U.S. regional groups that engage smaller businesses, a global forum, and a pan-corporate lobby group that aims to affect public policy.

This is a classic example of emergent organization: In this case, a big, diffuse interorganizational network has emerged around career-related phenomena. There are other academic- and service-oriented examples in the career orbit, including networks formed around issues such as workforce diversity, employee health and wellness, and training and development; practical concerns such as the inplacement of young people and outplacement of mature workers; plus broad-based subjects such as the link between business and education or the transition from welfare to work.

What is the institutional identity of these kinds of networks? Are they about human service—as Sarason (1977) views them, social innovation; broader-based sociopolitical change; or, as some might contend, pacification and maintenance of the power structure? And what about the identities of the many career scholars who populate them: dispassionate observers; evidence-based advocates; scholarly champions; or, as sometimes happens, bystanders, dupes, or servants to power? A profile of these kinds of emergent organizations, in their many configurations, might help illuminate member's motives and aims, their point of entry and influence in organizations, and their possible and probable roles. It is noteworthy, in any case, how such broad-based interest in and attention to careers seem to generate careers for so many different kinds of people.

RECONFIGURING THE STUDY OF WORK-LIFE

The chapter by Mayrhofer, Meyer, and Steyrer (Chapter 12) presents an appealing figure that arrays in a series of concentric circles the many contextual forces impinging on the study of careers. Wend your way through each of the layers, and a "configuration" emerges that helps explain some career-related phenomena—rather like a route through a circular maze. Work-life is one of those multilevel, multiframe phenomena that can be reconfigured to carry career scholars into organization theory and societal history. Another side trip concerns the reconfiguration of work-life in these areas of inquiry.

Studies find, for example, that firms that are human resource leaders invest more time and money not only in work-family initiatives but also in diversity programs, employee training and development, workplace innovation, and the like (Mirvis, 1997). Parker and Hall (1993), hewing to the humanistic, person-centered history of career studies, trace this employee responsiveness to seeing the "whole person" at work. My own view is that the company investment across these fronts comes from seeing all this connected to being what leading business theorists and strategists idealize as a more flexible and responsive company (Mirvis & Hall, 1996).[2] What do you theorize?

As for social history, work-family can be conceptualized as a social movement, connected to some extent to the women's and civil rights movement, and as a "social issue" addressed in the corporate and public sectors as well as in civil society. But does the study of work-and-family, as a subject linking career and organization studies, take a different shape when considered as part of the corporate responsibility movement that addresses broadly matters of employee welfare and the impact of business on society (see Pitt-Catsouphes & Googins, 2005)? This side trip might turn scholars' attentions from the mainline focus on the careers and needs for "balance" of professional and managerial women to the plight of low-wage women workers and contingent labor.

Along this detour, one encounters another constellation of interests and actors: the Hitachi and Ford Foundations that fund studies of the family problems of the working poor; scholars located in departments of social work rather than the business school; a few companies, including hoteliers, microlenders, and some grocers, that are making a difference in this employment arena; and some labor unions that are finally on this job. Look, too, at the interesting new forms of association among poor women—such as SEWA, the Self-Employed Women's Association in India—that promote self-employment and enable villagers to organize into a communal workforce. This sort of emergent organizing is taking shape in many developing and emerging markets.

While on this side trip to distant lands, also take a look at careers across cultures, as the chapter by Thomas and Inkson (Chapter 23) has done. Then, consider how corporate career plans and employee choices should be framed in light of the complex stresses faced by Asian women, who often must, as mothers, balance personal, organizational, and modernist pressures to continue in their paid work career against cultural imperatives to return to a homemaker role. Also ask, How should we frame work-family issues in Japan, where national policies aim to reduce the amount of time men are away from home and increase the caché of their becoming fathers—all in service to a society suffering from a fractional birth-to-death ratio?

Surely the scope of such subjects beckons business school faculty to join with economists, social workers, psychologists, sociologists, and anthropologists, not to mention myriad business people and others in the work-family network, to understand better what's going on and try to make things better. Several years ago, the best measure of a firm's family friendliness was its policies and profile of programs. Now, the better measure is its climate and culture—Can people talk openly about family conflicts at work and get "informal" help dealing with them? But shouldn't business scholars ask, as Ellen Galinsky (1999) has done, How are the children doing? Shouldn't this be a key measure of family friendliness? Don't we need help to do this kind of research?

OLDER WORKERS

Another chapter by Feldman (Chapter 9), on late-career and retirement issues, raises the same general class of questions across multiple strata but yields some different answers. Here, studies of North American companies have found no

significant predictors of initiatives aimed at older workers, largely because there are so few, even in otherwise progressive firms. The press in the United States, Europe, and Japan has awakened to the "demographic time bomb" posed by an aging society, and the issue is being talked about extensively in academic conferences and business and public policy circles. But insofar as I can tell, there is no "aging worker" forum of company representatives; no ranking of how friendly companies are to their older employees; and no substantial network of scholars, advisors, and helpers to advance attention to the issue in industry. Are these in the offing?

Feldman does a thoughtful job of debunking myths about older workers and marshalling evidence of their value to an enterprise. A side trip to the chapter on the psychological contract, by Slay and Taylor (Chapter 19), would also call attention to how the fracture of the traditional contract has been particularly hard on today's older workers. Wandering into the chapter by Prasad, D'Abate, and Prasad (Chapter 10) would, in turn, lead one to wonder, To what extent are older workers a socially marginalized group? This reminds me of the classic sociological distinction between an "issue" and a "problem." A subject such as an aging workforce is an issue so long as it involves someone "out there." It becomes a "problem" when it comes closer home. Career scholars are not immune to this phenomenon. Downsizing among blue-collar workers, for instance, has been more or less commonplace for over a century. Career scholars, myself included, picked up on it when it spread to white-collar and professional jobs in the 1980s and affected, to put it bluntly, "folks like us." In my view, the aging of the workforce in industrialized countries is a "problem." You figure out why.

CROSS-GENERATION CONFLICT

These side trips raise worries about impending tensions between generations in the Western workforce. It seems likely, for example, that the retirement age in the United States and Europe will be extended. This could stall advancement aspirations for younger workers and likely complicate performance appraisals and pay decisions in companies, with litigation to follow.

And the competing claims of young and old to public monies and services are sure to have an impact on employment policies and practices in the private sector, not to mention definitions and perceptions of a career. Again, business scholars will need to work with peers from other disciplines to get their minds and research arms around the fuller range of late-career and retirement issues that lie ahead.

Early in my career, the generational issue of greatest interest to me concerned what was behind the frustrations of younger people entering the workforce in the 1970s. They were what Daniel Yankelovich (1981) called the "new-breed" worker with higher education levels than their predecessors and more "anti-authority" attitudes. And they were not well suited to the routinized industrial and service job designs of that era or to the conformist, strictly hierarchical business cultures of the time. As a result, the 1970s was an era of the "blue-collar blues" and "white-collar woes" and when the quality of American-made goods began to decline and then pale versus imports from Japan.

The sociodemographic configuration suggested that these problems stemmed in part from a "generation gap" between the incoming *M*A*S*H* generation of baby boomers and the "organization men" running enterprise. This kind of configuration has such high face validity that it continues to be applied to cross-generational differences in work attitudes attendant on the arrival of Gen X and Y workers and on conflicts experienced between, say, "geeks and geezers." Spin the circles a different way, however, and a different explanatory configuration emerges.

On a side trip into attitudes of sociodemographic groups, for instance, it turns out that age, more so than generation, is a stronger predictor of cynicism about business and (political) leadership (Kanter & Mirvis, 1989). While some contend, and persuasively, that the pendulum swings from generation to generation in American society and that Gen Xers are less anti-authority and more conformist than boomers (Howe & Strauss, 1993; Strauss & Howe, 1992), they are nonetheless less trusting of their leaders and less sanguine about what motivates their fellow man. Interestingly, income and education level are far better than either age or generation in predicting cynicism about

work. This reminds one of the importance of generating alternative and competing hypotheses when framing career studies.

Travel over to process-and-stage theories, in the chapter by Sullivan and Crocitto (Chapter 15), and a clean, competing alternative to the generational hypothesis does emerge. Rosabeth Moss Kanter, as one example, never fully embraced the uniqueness of baby boomers and argued that boomers' nonconformist, anti-authority outlooks would temper considerably on reaching the middle life and career age. In essence, she argued that age and stage trump generation as an explanatory concept.

Frankly, there is evidence on both sides when it comes to the U.S. population. Career scholars who want to track this cross-culturally would be well-advised to survey young workers in China and India—labeled the "ultra new human" and the "new tech breed," respectively—to see how their outlooks develop over time and test alternative configurations of the import of sociodemography on work and career attitudes versus national and business culture.

It would also be useful to study what's behind the formation of work "character types" across the globe. Michael Maccoby (1977), for instance, located the "gamesman" at a time when baby boomers were moving up in industry and the hypercompetitive U.S. firm was emerging that would both take on Japan Inc. and meet the profit aspirations of shareholders. Questions: Should the gamesman be considered a work and career archetype or more a product of its time? Are any such career types of global relevance, or in an era of global connectivity, is this question even worth raising?

CAREER STUDIES AS A BOUNDARYLESS CAREER

Mayrhofer, Meyer, and Steyrer (Chapter 12) contend that careers intersect "societal history and individual biography." A foray into the customized career, covered in the chapter by Valcour, Bailyn, and Quijada (Chapter 11), brings this closer to home—mine. Mirvis and Hall (1994), referencing one of our mentors, Henry Morgan, have made the point that careers in the not too distant past stretched across multiple generations, then more recently to one lifetime, and nowadays to episodes in one's life. Henry had such a life— as a founding HR director of Polaroid, the owner of/investor in one of the first minority-owned television stations, the dean of a management school, and otherwise a social entrepreneur but mostly working in organizations. His life course is emblematic of what most career scholars mean by the boundaryless career.

From my mid-career onward, by comparison, I've been essentially a freelancer: self- and singly employed, working through networks to offer my wares. This course has maximized my personal freedom but has often left me asking, like many freelancers, Where is my kingdom? The side trips I've described coincide with my own journey: Self-employment affords more free time to spend with children and recreating, if you so choose and can afford it. There are loose informal networks of, say, househusbands, road warriors, and free agents that you can connect to at the playground, the airport, or midday at the gym; and surely on their laptops at Starbucks. But these don't lend much to one's personal identity or provide much social support. Hence, my institutional work identity and reference group concerns the hybrid academic-consultant industry where I occupy the self-styled and largely illusory niche of scholarly practitioner (Mirvis, 1996).

At my age and stage, however, I've noticed myself and peers in this network feeling a combination of anxiety and activism as we consider our "next" and perhaps last career stage. Our numbers have expanded significantly to include many who have retired early, willingly or not, from organizational and academic careers who nonetheless aspire to and thirst for continued learning, an opportunity to serve society broadly more so than business specifically, as well as a sense of community and common cause. This is a bunch that has resisted emergent organization, in practice and principle, and that now seemingly seeks a kingdom to populate and serve.

I wonder to what extent career studies will reconfigure "retirement" as a minicareer with its own multiple stages, anchor points, and institutional intersections; and I wonder, too, what its psychosocial meaning will be to a generation of baby boomers who, though healthier and perhaps more service minded than their predecessors, will not in large numbers have sufficient savings and pensions to cease working for money and will likely be pressed by the young to "give back" some of their entitlements. How will we draw boundaries around this boundaryless career? That is my next side trip.

NOTES

1. To complicate this a bit, it is notable that corporate investments in and programs geared to employee diversity initiatives are not predictable based on the proportion of nonwhite males in the upper echelons; rather, it is the proportion of women and even more so of racial/ethnic minorities in a firm's workforce overall. Is the driver here numbers? To what extent do power, paternalism, opportunity, or threat factor in? What else?

2. Not too long ago, observers spoke of the emerging trend toward flexible schedules in industry. Later, they termed it flexi-time. Now, it's flextime (without the hyphen). Such "languaging" is one indicator of the institutionalization of a social phenomenon in its time. What other language is worth noticing? It is worth mentioning, tangentially, that the term *flexfirm,* my moniker for the flexible and responsive company, still has a limited following.

REFERENCES

Galinsky, E. (1999). *Ask the children: What America's children really think about working parents.* New York: William Morrow.

Howe, N., & Strauss, W. (1993). *13th Gen: Abort, retry, ignore, fail?* New York: Vintage Press.

Kanter, D. L., & Mirvis, P. H. (1989). *The cynical Americans: Living and working in an age of discontent and disillusion.* San Francisco: Jossey-Bass.

Kanter, R. M. (1977). *Work and family in the United States: A critical review and agenda for research and policy.* New York: Russell Sage.

Maccoby, M. (1977). *The gamesman.* New York: Simon & Schuster.

Mirvis, P. H. (Ed.). (1993). *Building the competitive workforce: Investing in human capital for corporate success.* New York: Wiley.

Mirvis. P. H. (1996). Midlife as a consultant. In P. J. Frost & M. S. Taylor (Eds.), *Rhythms of academic life.* Thousand Oaks, CA: Sage.

Mirvis, P. H. (1997). Human resource management: Leaders, followers and laggards. *Academy of Management Executive, 11*(2), 43–56.

Mirvis, P. H., & Hall, D. T. (1994). Psychological success and the boundaryless career. *Journal of Organizational Behavior, 15,* 365–380.

Mirvis, P. H., & Hall, D. T. (1996). New organizational forms and the new career. In D. T. Hall & Associates (Eds.), *The career is dead: Long live the career.* San Francisco: Jossey-Bass.

Meyerson, D. (2001). *Tempered radicals: How people use difference to inspire change at work.* Boston: Harvard Business School Press.

Parker, V., & Hall, D. T. (1993). Workplace flexibility: Faddish or fundamental. In P. H. Mirvis (Ed.), *Building the competitive workforce: Investing in human capital for corporate success.* New York: Wiley.

Pitt-Catsouphes, M., & Googins, B. (2005). Recasting the work-family agenda as a corporate responsibility. In Kossek & Lambert (Eds.), *Managing work-life integration in organizations: Future directions for research and practice.* Boston: Erlbaum.

Sarason, S. (1977). *Human services and resource networks: Theory and practice.* San Francisco: Jossey-Bass.

Strauss, W., & Howe, N. (1992). *Generations: The history of America's future, 1584 to 2069.* New York: Harper.

Yankelovich, D. (1981). *New rules: Searching for self-fulfillment in a world turned upside down.* New York: Random House.

31

TRENDS, PARADOXES, AND SOME DIRECTIONS FOR RESEARCH IN CAREER STUDIES

WAYNE F. CASCIO

In this short chapter, we will identify some emerging trends, some peculiar paradoxes that confront career-studies researchers, and some promising avenues for future research in this field. We begin by highlighting briefly some emerging trends in careers.

DECLINING FERTILITY RATES AND AGING POPULATIONS

As Feldman discusses in his chapter on late-career and retirement issues (Chapter 9), the career issues facing older workers require greater theoretical and empirical elaboration than has been seen in the literature to date. This stream of research only increases in importance given the global demographic trends of declining fertility rates and rapidly aging populations. In most developed countries around the world, we can expect fewer younger workers and more older workers (Carnell, 2000). Although a fertility rate of 2.1 children per woman is needed just to replace the current population, in Europe the fertility rate has dropped to 1.42, and in Japan to 1.43. Spain has the world's lowest fertility rate, at 1.15 (National Center for Policy Analysis, 2006). In the United States, the Census Bureau predicts that the number of workers aged 20 to 44 will increase by 0.4% between 2000 and 2010 and by 4% between 2010 and 2020 (U.S. Census Bureau, 2004).

Of course, the flip side of low fertility is an aging population. China has the fastest-aging population in the world, largely due to its policy of one child per family. To appreciate this, consider that 35 years ago in China the population proportion of children to the aged (65 years and older) was 6:1. Today, the elderly population is

AUTHOR'S NOTE: I would like to acknowledge the able research assistance of Celia Moore in providing cross-references to other chapters in this volume and helpful suggestions for improving this one.

twice as great as the number of children. In Thailand, the elderly will account for 14% of the population within 20 years, while children will only represent 12% (People's Daily Online, 2004). Among the broad regions of the world, Europe has the highest proportion of the population age 65 years and older, and it should remain the global leader in this category well into the 21st century. However, the most rapid acceleration in aging, especially in the United States, will occur after 2010, when the large, post–World War II Baby Boom cohort begins to reach age 65 (Population Matters, 2006). These trends may not lead to labor shortages (Cappelli, 2005), but they will likely lead to shorter employment relationships, more contingent work, independent contracting, and other free market arrangements.

GROWING INFLUENCE AT WORK OF GENERATIONS X AND Y

Generation X, also known as "baby busters" (born between 1965 and 1980), includes approximately 50 million members in the United States, or about one third of the American workforce. They have grown up in times of rapid change, both social and economic. Hurt more by parental divorce and having witnessed corporate downsizing first hand, they tend to be independent, cynical, and do not expect the security of long-term employment. Note the perspectives on careers demonstrated by younger workers, as discussed in Guest and Sturges on "living to work, working to live" (Chapter 16). On the other hand, they also tend to be practical, focused, and future oriented. They demand interesting work assignments, thrive on open-ended projects that require sophisticated problem solving, and are certainly computer literate.

Generation Y (born after 1980), with more than 80 million members, has grown up amid more sophisticated technologies, and has been exposed to them earlier than members of Generation X ever were. This is a group that grew up with e-mail, not snail mail. Multitasking is easy for them. This implies both good news and bad news for employers. The good news is that Generation Y will be good at engaging in multiple tasks, filtering out distractions, and juggling numerous projects. The bad news? Short attention spans, the constant need for stimulation/entertainment,

and a blurring of the lines between work and leisure time while on the job ("The new workforce," 2001; Tsacoumis, 2002).

NONLINEAR CAREERS

Traditionally, careers were defined in terms of a period of education, then work (typically 20 to 30 years), then retirement. As Valcour, Bailyn, and Quijada's chapter on customized careers points out (Chapter 11), we are only in the early stages of understanding career paths and patterns that differ from the "orderly" careers that constitute the bulk of careers research. Yet such understanding is increasingly important, as today, with longer life spans (77 to 82 years in developed countries), increased affluence among at least some individuals, and the creative destruction of jobs (see below), nonlinear careers are becoming more common, as people move in and out of the workforce for varying periods of time, often changing the type of work they are doing (Berk, 2004; White, 2005). Median years of tenure on the job in the United States (data up to January, 2006) is only 2.9 for workers aged 25 to 34, and 9.3 for those aged 55 to 64 ("Employee tenure in 2006," 2006). The average worker goes through about nine jobs by age 32, and 10% of the American workforce actually switches occupations every year (Daniels & Vinzant, 2000).

To be sure, workers are demanding more flexibility in their work schedules (Conlin, Merritt, & Himelstein, 2002; Corporate Voices for Working Families, 2005). Greenhaus and Foley do a nice job of outlining the importance of flexibility in supporting rewarding work and personal lives among employees, while also demonstrating how work increasingly has encroached on our leisure time (Chapter 8). A less appreciated perspective on the work-life interface, however, is to notice how leisure has crept into the job. As Brady (2002) noted,

> Workers increasingly are Internet shopping, exercising, chatting with friends, or otherwise building breaks into their day. They may work at midnight, but they also feel free to take off at 3 p.m. to see a child's school play. The aging of the workforce, and the need for constant education, are creating a less rigid view of careers—one that lets people dip in and out of the job market, work into their 70s,

or take time off in their 30s to study, travel, or raise children. (p. 142)

In a 2005 poll, 93% of workers reported that they spent an average of 10.5 hours per week on the Internet. They spent an average of 73% of that time on work-related sites, and 27% on nonwork-related sites (Breeden, 2005).

To help explain the "opt-out" or career-interruption phenomenon among women, Mainiero and Sullivan (2005) developed the concept of kaleidoscope careers. Like a kaleidoscope that produces changing patterns when the tube is rotated and its glass chips fall into new arrangements, women tend to shift the patterns of their careers (early, mid, and late) by rotating different aspects of their lives to arrange their roles and relationships in new ways. According to this model, each action taken by a woman during her career has a profound and long-lasting effect on others around her (again, see Chapter 11).

With respect to retirement, most employees will *choose* when they will leave, because mandatory retirement at a specified age can no longer be required legally (in the United States). While many younger employees are leaving the workforce (nearly 2 million aged 25 to 54 from 2001 to 2004), older workers are streaming back in, with labor-force participation among workers aged 55 and older at 36% in 2004. At Procter & Gamble, for example, 18,400 workers left the company with voluntary buyout packages between 2002 and 2003 (Hilsenrath, 2004).

Among baby boomers, 80% say they plan to do at least some work after they "retire," specifically, work part-time for interest or enjoyment (30%), work part-time for income (25%), start their own businesses (15%), work full time in a new job or career (7%), and other (3%) (Farrell, 2004; "Just what kind," 2002). Many want in retirement what they currently don't have: *balance*. They want what aging experts now call a *blended life course*—an ongoing mix of work, leisure, and education (Morris, 1996).

THE MIDLIFE SEARCH
FOR MEANING: AMONG WOMEN

Everyone will experience a midlife transition, typically in their late 40s to early 50s. Such transitions tend to be characterized by symptoms such as an awareness of advancing age and an awareness of death, an awareness of bodily changes related to aging, knowing how many career goals have been or will be attained, and a search for new life goals. This intersection between the life course and careers research is documented comprehensively in the chapter on stage and process theories of careers by Sullivan and Crocitto (Chapter 15). However, greater attention needs to be paid to the differences between men and women as they search for meaning across the courses of their lives. Some men who experience midlife crises acquire expensive toys and second wives. As gender roles change, however, evidence indicates that more women than men now report turbulent midlife transitions, 36.1% versus 34%, respectively (Wethington, cited in Shellenbarger, 2005).

Whereas male midlife crises are more likely to be driven by work or career issues (Helyar, 2005), women's are more likely to begin with family events or problems, such as a divorce, a parent's death, or an extramarital affair. More women are having midlife crises because they can (Shellenbarger, 2005). Their income has posted powerful gains in comparison with men's over the past 15 years; nearly one third of wives now earn more than their husbands, and the proportion of women earning more than $100,000 has tripled in the past decade. A second reason is that women have the skills and resources to make career changes or to start their dream businesses at midlife, if they wish. According to the U.S. Bureau of Labor Statistics, the proportion of professional jobs held by women, including engineering, medicine, law, architecture, teaching, and computer science, has increased to 54.7% from 51.1% in 1990. Women now earn 58% of all college degrees and 59% of master's degrees, according to the National Center for Education Statistics.

The midlife turmoil is manifesting itself in a number of ways. While the number of extramarital affairs among women (nearly one in six) is approaching that of men (about one in five), organized religion is also drawing significant support from midlife women's quest for meaning (Shellenbarger, 2005). Many are changing careers to pursue work that is more altruistic or fulfilling. Others are returning to higher education to pursue new interests, engaging in adventurous sports (e.g., wall climbing, kayaking, wilderness camping). Interviews with older women in their 60s and 70s who had experienced midlife crises more than a decade ago revealed, without exception, that if given the chance to do it all again, they would embrace new undertakings even more wholeheartedly (Shellenbarger, 2005). These priorities are hinted at again in Valcour, Bailyn, and Quijada (Chapter 11).

CREATION AND DESTRUCTION OF JOBS: THE NEED FOR CAREER RESILIENCE

Driven by digitization, the Internet, and high-speed data networks that encircle the globe, knowledge work is migrating to countries where skilled labor and low wages coexist. This is globalization's next wave, and it is helping to reshape the global economy ("The new global job shift," 2003). While 3.3 million white-collar jobs are expected to shift from the United States to low-cost countries by 2015, Europe is joining the trend too. British banks such as HSBC Securities have huge back offices in China and India. French companies are using call centers in Mauritius, and German multinationals such as Siemens and roller-bearings maker INA Schaeffler are hiring in Russia, the Baltics, and Eastern Europe. Thomas and Inkson's chapter on careers across cultures (Chapter 23) reminds us of the continuing hegemony of Western models of careers, even as the globalization of the economy multiplies the types of "careers" individuals hold in different geographies and economies worldwide.

In short, we are witnessing job destruction—and job creation—on a global scale. Consider how it has affected the U.S. economy. During the 10-year period 1993 to 2002, that economy created 318 million new jobs and destroyed 300 million of them for a net gain of 18 million jobs. Considering that there are about 140 million jobs in the entire American economy and that an average of about 30 million jobs are created and destroyed each year, this implies that the United States creates and destroys roughly 20% of its jobs every year (Mayforth, 2005)! So much for job security.

What does this imply for careers? It implies that career resilience is an essential survival skill in the 21st century, an opinion echoed in Kidd's chapter on career counseling (Chapter 6). Employees at all levels cannot afford to be complacent, and they must constantly assess their employability. They must weigh continuously the opportunity costs of staying where they are, all the while staying on the lookout for attractive opportunities elsewhere. This implies that individuals will tend to focus the concept of loyalty inward to take care of their own careers first, a change in psychological contract norms noted by Slay and Taylor (Chapter 19).

REFUSAL OF PROMOTIONS

As they pass up promotions in favor of having a life, growing numbers of employees are bucking a corporate society that rewards unbridled ambition (Hube, 2004). Perhaps the biggest challenge these employees face is convincing their bosses that they are not underachieving slackers. Moreover, if their job titles do not change, and they do not assume more responsibility, there is a good chance that their compensation will not change appreciably either.

On the other hand, some companies have come to recognize that nonclimbers can be good for business—as long as they are productively plateaued, not passively plateaued. Productively plateaued people take affirmative steps to let their bosses know they like where they are, for example, in sales, engineering, or customer service. They constantly seek out professional-development opportunities that will help improve the quality and efficiency of their work. Higher-level executives know they can count on productively plateaued employees to mentor incoming employees and to join cross-departmental committees or project teams. Indeed, the most enlightened organizations recognize that productively plateaued employees are far more valuable than many of those who are promoted beyond their competencies. Individuals can actively aspire to the "productive plateau" as a way to find more balance between their work and personal lives (see Guest and Sturges, Chapter 16).

PERSISTENCE OF AGE-RELATED STEREOTYPES

Age stereotypes are an unfortunate impediment to the continued growth and development of workers more than 50 years of age. A 2004 survey by ExecuNet (www.ExecuNet.com) found that 82% of senior executives consider age bias a serious problem in today's workplace, up from 78% in 2001 (Fisher, 2004). Consider just one common myth about age, namely, that older workers are less productive than younger workers.

Cumulative research evidence on almost 39,000 individuals indicates that in both professional and nonprofessional jobs, age and job performance are generally unrelated (McEvoy & Cascio, 1989). Indeed, the relationship of aging to the ability to function, and the implication of aging for job performance, are complex. Overwhelming evidence contradicts simple notions that rate of decline is tied in some linear or direct fashion to chronological age. Rather, the effects of aging on performance can be characterized by stability and growth, as well as decline, with large individual differences in the timing and amount of change in the ability to function (Czaja, 1995; Landy et al., 1992; Sterns & Miklos, 1995; see also Feldman, Chapter 9).

Some companies are trying to change age-related stereotypes and to encourage older workers to keep working. Thus, Volkswagen instituted a "50-Plus" program that includes features such as the following: modifying job designs to accommodate the needs of older workers, providing employees with more active health promotion, and expanding lifelong learning for all workers. It did that because surveys had shown that older workers tend to receive substantially less corporate training than younger workers (Adler, 2004).

Raising the compulsory retirement age may help, but in and of itself, it may do little to combat "ageism." The United States and Australia have abolished compulsory retirement ages completely but most of the rest of the world has not (Adler, 2004). In the United Kingdom, a new compulsory retirement age of 65 took effect in October, 2006, while Japan only raised its compulsory retirement age—enforced by 90% of Japanese companies—from 60 to 65 in 2004.

FOUR PARADOXES IN CAREER MANAGEMENT

In this section, we will highlight briefly some paradoxes in career management that may

appear glaringly obvious but that continue unabated. Paradox #1 is that *fewer young workers are entering the labor force at the same time as organizations continue to provide incentives for older workers to leave.* Consider these sobering statistics:

- U.S. workers aged 55 to 64 will grow 51% to 25 million from 2005 to 2012.
- By 2012, those aged 35 to 44 will shrink by 7% from the 2005 level.
- Half of America's 400,000 electric-utility workers will be eligible to retire in the next 5 years.
- Half the U.S. government's civilian workforce also will be eligible to retire in the next 5 years.
- Forty percent of the U.S. manufacturing workforce is expected to retire in the next 10 years.
- Result: A possible shortage of 5 million skilled workers between 2010 and 2012.

Certainly in situations characterized by massive overstaffing, as in the United States automobile industry, early-retirement offers for older workers make sense. In many other situations, though, the rationale is less clear. Most people would agree that older workers' experience, wisdom, and institutional memories (memories of traditions, of how and why things are done as they are in an organization) represent important assets to firms. Without systematic efforts to convert this human capital into structural capital (in the form of manuals, databases, or knowledge-management systems), firms may lose not only people to staff their operations but also all the accumulated wisdom and experience as older workers walk out the door. Consider just one example of the consequences of losing these valuable workers, as cited by the *Financial Times.* "When the Russians approached International Harvester to build a factory, there was no one left who knew how it was done" (Adler, 2004, p. 4).

Paradox #2 is that *while technology frees people to work anytime, anywhere, it also shackles them as never before* (Sughrue, 2006). Thus, only about 30% of American workers have a standard workday schedule—40 hours per week, during the day, Monday through Friday (Rivas, 2006). For the remainder, atypical workdays have become the norm, as cell phones and

BlackBerrys become ubiquitous. Many employees also find themselves on call after their conventional day ends. The average employee now spends 3 hours per day responding to voice and electronic mail (Sughrue, 2006). Moreover, in the global marketplace, businesses operate 24 hours to serve overseas clients or to monitor foreign events. Experts expect that nonstandard and weekend work is here to stay because the trends that fuel it, such as advances in technology coupled with a changing economy, show signs of expanding, not shrinking (Rivas, 2006).

Paradox #3 is that *as life spans are increasing, savings rates are not keeping pace.* Human life spans have expanded dramatically, especially during the 20th century. In classical Greece and Rome, for example, typical life expectancy was 28 years. In medieval England it was 33, expanding only to 37 by the end of the 19th century. By the early 20th century it had reached 50, rose to 65 by 1940, and, as noted earlier, in the Western world it currently varies from 77 to 82 (Wikipedia, 2006). There is great variability, however, particularly among the poor and the wealthy. In Zimbabwe, for example, people live an average of 36 years, while in Japan, they live an average of 82 years (World Health Organization, 2006).

Longer life spans mean that once individuals stop working, their savings and pension assets will need to last longer than ever before. Savings, in its simplest form, is what is left behind from income after consumption (Mandel, 2005). At a national level, workers and businesses in countries such as Japan, Germany, Russia, Saudi Arabia, China, Norway, and Switzerland tend to save much, while those in Portugal, Turkey, Italy, Australia, Britain, Spain, and the United States tend to save less ("Too much money," 2005).

We noted earlier that 8 in 10 baby boomers expect to work, at least part-time, after they "retire," but only a third of them expect to scale back their lifestyles during their retirement years (Korczyk, 2001). A thorough review of many studies that have been done on savings rates by generation concluded that boomers can expect to live roughly 2 years longer than their parents. If they retire at roughly the same age as their parents did, then they will need more retirement wealth to provide the same standard of living over a longer period of time. The good news is that the typical baby boomer has more current income and wealth than his or her parents did at the same age, is accumulating wealth at roughly the same rate, and thus is likely to have more income in retirement. A number of uncertainties remain, however, such as the behavior of the stock and housing markets. Baby boomers are more likely than their parents to own stock and tend to be more exposed to stock market risk. While many boomers who own homes have benefited from rising home values, many also have used that rise to take on home-equity-financed debt. This suggests that at least some boomers could end up poorer in retirement than their parents were (Congressional Budget Office, 2003; DeVanney & Chiremba, 2005).

Paradox #4 is *the need for regular feedback among workers from generations X and Y, coupled with patterns of irregular feedback in organizations.* Generations X and Y, the largest generations of young people since the 1960s, are beginning to come of age. They're called "echo boomers" because they are the genetic offspring and demographic echo of their parents, the baby boomers. Born after 1965, there are nearly 80 million of them in the United States, and they're already having a huge impact on entire segments of the economy.

Echo boomers are a reflection of the sweeping changes in the economy over the past 20 years. They are the first to grow up with computers at home, in a 500-channel TV universe. They are multitaskers with cell phones, music downloads, and instant messaging on the Internet. They are totally plugged-in citizens of a worldwide community (Kroft, 2005).

When pediatrician Dr. Mel Levine was asked, "When a young person shows up for work at his or her first job, what do they expect and what are they finding?" he responded,

> They expect to be immediate heroes and heroines. They expect a lot of feedback on a daily basis. They expect grade inflation, they expect to be told what a wonderful job they're doing. [They expect] that they're going to be allowed to rise to the top quickly. That they're going to get all the credit they need for everything they do. And boy, are they naive? Totally naive, in terms of what's really going to happen. (Levine, in Kroft, 2005)

What is likely to happen? A 2004 study by RainmakerThinking of more than 500 managers in 40 different organizations found, unfortunately, that few managers consistently provide their direct reports with what Rainmaker calls the five management basics. These are clear statements of what's expected of each employee, explicit and measurable goals and deadlines, detailed evaluation of each person's work, clear feedback, and rewards distributed fairly. Only 10% of managers provide all five of the basics at least once a week. Only 25% do so once a month. About a third fail to provide them even once a year (Tulgan, 2004)! Clearly, there is much room for improvement in these areas.

SOME DIRECTIONS FOR FUTURE RESEARCH IN CAREER STUDIES

In this final section, we will identify and discuss briefly five promising areas for future research based on the trends and paradoxes we have discussed thus far. The first area is strategies for breaking down age stereotypes. As we noted earlier, the relationship of aging to the ability to function, and the implication of aging for job performance, is complex. Age stereotypes persist, even as the number of older workers increases. The field desperately needs research that will reduce or eliminate such stereotypes, as noted by Feldman in Chapter 9.

The second area that deserves research and further understanding is the meaning of career success in the Internet age. Given the increasingly temporary nature of relationships between employers and employees, coupled with flattened hierarchies in organizations and endless restructuring, it will be important to identify what career success means to individuals at various stages of their careers. Do men and women define it similarly? Do definitions of career success vary across cultures?

The next area that deserves attention is related to the previous one—namely, the implications of career resilience in a dynamic business environment (Waterman, Waterman, & Collard, 2001). Given the pace of change, employees in every country and at all levels will need to reinvent themselves multiple times throughout their careers (see Kidd, Chapter 6).

Career-studies researchers have a great opportunity to provide meaningful insights and advice about career resilience to current and future generations.

The fourth area involves expatriate employees, specifically "globalites" who spend their entire work lives outside their home countries (Peiperl and Jonsen, Chapter 18). What are the distinguishing characteristics of these individuals—that is, their values, goals, personality characteristics, and preferences? Why are some people especially suited for expatriate assignments, moving from one to another, while others are not? To be sure, early identification of such individuals is especially valuable, and career-studies researchers can provide insights into this entire area.

A final area of fruitful research involves the implications for individuals and organizations of a "blended life course" or a "kaleidoscope career," as noted in many of the chapters that discuss the increasingly varied and flexible nature of careers (Chapters 8, 9, 11, and 16). What are the advantages and drawbacks of such career paths? Practically speaking, are there patterns of behavior that might make it possible for organizations to predict periods of engagement and disengagement? What strategies might facilitate reengagement? What is the effect of temporary disengagement on staffing, compensation, performance management, and development? These are all tantalizing questions, and career-studies researchers are well positioned to provide answers. Doing so will broaden the body of knowledge in the career studies field, it will help educate managers about current and emerging issues in this area, and it will also enrich the lives of employees everywhere.

REFERENCES

Adler, R. (2004, December). *Reinventing retirement.* Retrieved May 30, 2006, from http://www .civicventures.org.

Berk, C. C. (2004, March 29). Now for something completely different. *The Wall Street Journal,* p. R5.

Brady, D. (2002, August 26). Rethinking the rat race. *Business Week,* pp. 142, 143.

Breeden, R. (2005, May 10). More employees are using the Web at work. *The Wall Street Journal,* p. B4.

Cappelli, P. (2005). Will there really be a labor shortage? In M. Losey, S. Meisinger, & D. Ulrich (Eds.), *The future of human resource management* (pp. 5–14). Hoboken, NJ: Wiley.

Carnell, B. (2000, May 18). *Total fertility rates.* Retrieved May 30, 2006, from http://www.over population.com.

Congressional Budget Office. (2003, November). *Baby boomers' retirement prospects: An overview.* Retrieved April 14, 2006, from http://www.cbo.gov.

Conlin, M., Merritt, J., & Himelstein, L. (2002, November 25). Mommy is really home from work. *Business Week,* pp. 101–104.

Corporate Voices for Working Families. (2005, November). *Business impacts of flexibility: An imperative for expansion.* Retrieved May 18, 2006, from http://www.cvwf.org.

Czaja, S. J. (1995). Aging and work performance. *Review of Public Personnel Administration, Spring,* 46–61.

Daniels, C., & Vinzant, C. (2000, February 7). The joy of quitting. *Fortune,* pp. 199–202.

DeVanney, S. A., & Chiremba, S. T. (2005, March 16). *Comparing the retirement savings of the baby boomers and other cohorts.* Retrieved April 9, 2006, from U.S. Department of Labor, Bureau of Labor Statistics Web site: http://www .bls.gov/opub/cwc/cm20050114ar01pl.htm.

Employee tenure in 2006. (2006, September). Retrieved March 1, 2007, from ftp://ftp.bls.gov/ pub/news.release/tenure.txt.

Farrell, C. (2004, July 26). No need to hit the panic button. *Business Week,* pp. 77–80.

Fisher, A. (2004, February 9). Older, wiser, job-hunting. *Fortune,* p. 46.

Helyar, J. (2005, May 16). 50 and fired. *Fortune,* pp. 78–90.

Hilsenrath, J. (2004, February 17). More Americans are leaving the workforce. *The Wall Street Journal,* pp. B1, B10.

Hube, K. (2004, March 29). Thanks, but no thanks. *The Wall Street Journal,* pp. R4, R7.

Just what kind of retiree will you be? (2002, June 17). *Business Week,* p. 10.

Korczyk, S. M. (2001). Baby boomers head for retirement. *Journal of Financial Planning, March,* 116–123.

Kroft, S. (Executive Producer). (2005, September 4). The echo boomers. *60 Minutes* [Television broadcast]. New York: Columbia Broadcasting System.

Landy, F. J., Bland, R. E., Buskirk, E. R., Daly, R. E., DeBusk, R. F., Donovan, E. J., et al. (1992). *Alternatives to chronological age in determining standards of suitability for public safety jobs*

(Tech. Rep.). Penn State University, Center for Applied Behavioral Sciences.

Mainiero, L. A., & Sullivan, S. E. (2005). Kaleidoscope careers: An alternate explanation for the "opt-out" revolution. *Academy of Management Executive, 19*(1), 106–123.

Mandel, M. (2005, July 11). Totting up savings. *Business Week.* Retrieved May 30, 2006, from http://www.businessweek.com.

Mayforth, H. (2005, September 12). The myth of job security. *Infoworld,* p. 64.

McEvoy, G. M., & Cascio, W. F. (1989). Cumulative evidence of the relationship between employee age and job performance. *Journal of Applied Psychology, 74,* 11–20.

Morris, B. (1996, August 19). The future of retirement. *Fortune,* pp. 86–94.

National Center for Policy Analysis (2006). The world's declining fertility rate. Retrieved May 30, 2006, from http://www.ncpa.org.

The new global job shift. (2003, February 3). *Business Week.* Retrieved May 30, 2006, from http://www.businessweek.com.

The new workforce: Generation Y. (2001). *Workplace Visions, 2,* 1–7.

People's Daily Online. (2004, October 21). Retrieved May 30, 2006, from http://english.people.com.cn.

Population Matters. (2006). *Preparing for an aging world.* Retrieved May 30, 2006, from http://www .rand.org.

Rivas, T. (2006, April 4). Atypical workdays becoming routine. *The Wall Street Journal,* p. A19.

Shellenbarger, S. (2005). *The breaking point: How female midlife crisis is transforming today's women.* New York: Henry Holt.

Sterns, H. L., & Miklos, S. M. (1995). The aging worker in a changing environment: Organizational and individual issues. *Journal of Vocational Behavior, 47,* 248–268.

Sughrue, K. M. (Executive Producer). (2006, April 2). Working 24/7. *60 Minutes* [Television broadcast]. New York: Columbia Broadcasting System.

Too much money. (2005, July 11). *Business Week.* Retrieved May 30, 2006, from http://www .businessweek.com.

Tsacoumis, S. (2002, April). *Workplace demographics.* Workshop presented to the Society for Industrial and Organizational Psychology, Toronto, Ontario, Canada.

Tulgan, B. (2004, June 28). *The under-management epidemic.* Retrieved September 13, 2004, from http://www.rainmakerthinking.com.

U.S. Census Bureau. (2004). *Projected population change in the United States among persons ages 20 to 44 and 45 to 64, from 2000 to 2010 and 2010 to 2020.* Retrieved September 18, 2005, from http://www.census.gov.

Waterman, R. H., Jr., Waterman, J. A., & Collard, B. A. (2001). *Toward a career-resilient workforce.* Cambridge, MA: Harvard Business Review Enhanced Edition. (Product No. 7206)

White, E. (2005, August 2). I quit! . . . for a while. *The Wall Street Journal,* pp. B1, B8.

Wikipedia. (2006). *Timeline for humans.* Retrieved April 9, 2006, from http://en.wikipedia.org/wiki/Life_expectancy.

World Health Organization. (2006). *World health report, 2006 statistical annex, Table 1.* Retrieved July 6, 2006, from http://www.who.int/whr/2006/annex/en/index.html.

32

THE MEANINGS OF CAREER

The editors invited suggestions on how the field of career studies, as represented by their classification in Chapter 3, could be extended. In response to their invitation, this chapter examines the meaning—or rather meanings—of *career,* first through analysis and then synthesis, and discusses their implications for the field.

THE MEANINGS OF CAREER

Everybody understands what *career* is. The trouble with it, though, is that it is so broad and vague. It is an everyday word used by a variety of people, in a variety of contexts, from a variety of perspectives, for a variety of purposes, and with various levels of specificity or generality, focus or breadth. It is used, for example, in career guidance for youth and adults, government employment schemes, management development, life planning. It is looked at from a variety of perspectives (different disciplines, traditions, and epistemologies). Lay people, academics, practitioners of

various kinds, and policymakers all use it for their own purposes (personal, scholarly, social, managerial, economic, political, etc.). All this suggests that there are myriad ways in which *career* is being used and that hence it has many meanings.

A *Handbook* such as this, written from the perspective of management and organization studies, and constrained by the practicalities of publishing, cannot embrace them all. Nevertheless, like the literature generally, it recognizes their multiplicity and variety: in the wide range of topics covered, the recognition of the coexistence of the objective and subjective career (Arthur, Hall, & Lawrence, 1989; Goffman, 1959; Hughes, 1937; Stebbins, 1970; Young & Collin, 2000; in several chapters in the *Handbook,* most particularly Chapter 7 by Khapova, Arthur, and Wilderom), the call for "interdisciplinary" (this *Handbook*), "transdisciplinary" (Arthur et al., 1989), "multidisciplinary" (Collin & Young, 2000) approaches, and perhaps in the very notion of career studies. However, questions that arise from this multiplicity are not raised. How do these meanings differ from one another? How are

AUTHOR'S NOTE: I am indebted to Dr. Raoul Van Esbroeck, Vrije Universiteit, Brussel, and Dr. James Athanasou, University of Technology, Sydney, for sharing with me their knowledge of career scholars across the world, as I was preparing the ground for this chapter.

they related to one another? Is their range fully and adequately represented?

A Taxonomy of the Meanings of Career

One way of addressing these questions might be to develop a taxonomy and order the meanings hierarchically. Some shared meaning can be inferred in how *career* is used: the movement of a person through both time and social space (see Arthur et al., 1989; Collin, 2000a). Hence, although these uses may be as unlike as apples and oranges, career could still be classifiable at an abstract level as "fruit." This *Handbook* would illustrate that well. Although the contributors were given the same definition (see the Introduction, Chapter 1 by Gunz and Peiperl), they were still able to cover a wide range of topics under that rubric. In other words, career could be regarded as a superordinate concept that subsumes the various meanings for which it is used, suggesting the potential for a hierarchical taxonomy.

However, just as Peiperl and Gunz in Chapter 3 had difficulties in classifying career studies, so there is also a stumbling block here. To order the meanings systematically they have to be defined, and definition is lacking in the literature. It often appears to be taken for granted that the meaning will be obvious from its particular context or to its particular readership, that a definition is not necessary, that it would perhaps be superfluous or overly pedantic. For instance, not all the chapters in the *Handbook* refer to the definition the editors had stipulated, and in some it might be difficult to infer it. This means that systematic relationships between the apples and oranges and fruit cannot be established, rendering career as a superordinate concept relatively sterile and of limited utility. It is, hence, probably more productive to dispense with attempting a taxonomy and to treat career as a construct, a looser form of generalization. From a social constructionist perspective, which will be referred to later, career is an "overarching construct" (Young & Valach, 1996, p. 364) that creates a "canopy of meaning" (Berger, 1967, in Roberts, 1980, pp. 163–164).

Parameters of Career

Another way of addressing the questions asked earlier would be to analyze career in terms of its various parameters (using that term to mean the factors that define it). A number of these are referred to in the literature, for example, its "dualities." The word *career* originally denoted a pathway or movement along it (see also Moore, Gunz, and Hall, Chapter 2), but now it frequently carries the dual meanings of pathway and movement along it: the coexistence of organizational/institutional/ societal reality and the individual's movement through it and experience of it, of both objective and subjective. Furthermore, Chapter 2 identifies five dialectical metathemes in the career field, which are the "tensions between two opposing concepts." Those relevant to the meanings of career (rather than to career studies) are individual agency versus social determinism in the shaping of career; career as process versus career as achieving "fit"; whether the "fit" is for the benefit of the individual or of the collectivity; and whether career is a social phenomenon or an individual life story. Moreover, as well as emphasizing how career relates past, present, and future, Collin & Young (2000) point to its "multiple dualities," including its use as rhetoric and praxis (pp. 295–296).

Analytical categories for the meanings of *career* could be developed from such dualities. For example, it has been analyzed in terms of the perspective from which it is viewed and of what it is used to do (Collin, 1990). The perspective could be that of the person whose career it was (the "actor"), or of someone else observing that career (the "observer"), and its function could be to describe or to interpret. This analysis resulted in a four-cell model: the actor's career as (1) described or (2) interpreted by the actor; another person's career, or career generally, (3) described or (4) interpreted by an observer. Although today I would use different terminology and would want to reinterpret that analysis in light of social constructionism, it did differentiate various meanings. It brought out the point, also noted by Gunz and Heslin (2005), that it was not sufficient to construe the subjective career solely as individual experience, for the actor could regard his or her career both subjectively and objectively, while the observer could be aware of another's external objective and subjective career. (Khapova, Arthur, and Wilderom in Chapter 7 add further to the understanding of the subjective career and Blustein, Schultheiss, and Flum [2004] take a social constructionist approach to it.)

Other parameters of career have been identified in the literature. Schein (1976) uses three dimensions (the stages of life, career, and family; the external factors of occupations, roles, and work settings; and the internal factors of motives, values, and talents) to construct his "career cube." (Given the core meaning identified above, those dimensions could perhaps be fruitfully recast as time, social space, and the individual.) Schein also (1971, 1978; see Slay and Taylor, Chapter 19) looks at the organizational career in terms of a cone. Law (1981), too, builds a three-dimensional model (p. 333)—of career theories—which could also be used to analyze the meanings of career. His dimensions are sociological/psychological theories, differential/developmental theories, and "the progressively more autonomous conceptions of the ways in which people participate in the achievement of their careers." Further parameters can be seen throughout the *Handbook.* For example, Prasad, D'Abate, and Prasad (Chapter 10) write of the "multidimensional concept of career," referring to organizational experiences such as entry and advancement; Chandler and Kram (Chapter 13) allude to the "dimensions" of gender, race, and career stage; Slay and Taylor (Chapter 19) to supply flow and assignment flow. However, their value for the analysis suggested here has to be questioned when they are not clearly defined or when, as with Collin (1990), Law (1981), and Schein (1976) above, the "dimensions" are not continua. Moreover, the parameters are not necessarily compatible with one another, and although together they start to build up an in-depth picture of career, it does not amount to a coherent one. The relationships between the multiple meanings remain unclear.

The Tapestry of Career

Reading about so many different kinds of career in the *Handbook* reawakened my interest in its multiple meanings (Collin, 1990), and I had intended this chapter to examine the relationships between them. However, definitions are needed for systematic study (and especially if career is to be treated as an "interdisciplinary" subject, for its literature would then have to address a multidisciplinary and multiprofessional readership, with its various traditions and expectations), and my attempt soon foundered on the lack of them. There are probably many reasons for their absence, including the difficulty in establishing boundaries noted in Peiperl and Gunz (Chapter 3) and Gunz, Peiperl, and Tzabbar (Chapter 24). It could also be, in part, more pragmatically because definitions add to the length of a piece and might seem to be irritatingly repetitive in any collection of writing about career. For whatever reason, there is this vagueness at the heart of career studies, so that the attempt to analyze the multiple meanings is working against the grain of the material. Hence, I now turn from looking at them analytically to seeing them holistically, recognizing career as a whole, instead of trying to differentiate its parts and examining them separately.

This approach accepts that the multiple meanings of career are fuzzy constructs, not clearly differentiated, not necessarily stable over time, or not universally recognized. From this changed perspective, it can be seen how difficult definition is, and why there were so few attempts at it in the literature. The meanings are very different from the firm, observable categories of apples, oranges, and fruit, and so that analogy has to be abandoned here, along with the traditional mechanicist epistemology of the field, in favor of the contextualist "world hypothesis" (Pepper, 1942). This recognizes the wholeness of phenomena (such as career, Collin, 1997), the interpenetration of their features, and their embeddedness in their context, unlike the traditional approach that breaks phenomena into their component parts for analysis. To illustrate this, one can use the metaphor of a tapestry of interwoven threads: If it were analyzed into its various strands, it would unravel (Young, Valach, & Collin, 1996). From this perspective, the multiple meanings of career are seen to interweave and overlap; they cannot be separated, indeed they are held simultaneously.

To see career as a tapestry of meanings should not be interpreted as a retreat into subjectivism but as a pragmatic recognition of how career is indeed used "ranging across the spectrum from highly abstract notions of individual actions through time and space to more behaviorally rooted definitions that are grounded in an individual's specific work role" (Blustein et al., 2004, p. 425). This revised view throws light on the essential richness, nuances, and ambiguity of career, which according to Watts (1981, p. 214) is "a major source of its power." It is not "either/or" but "both/and" and "[i]ts inherent ambivalence allows it to reflect the ambiguity and contradictions of its time" (Collin & Young, 2000, p. 296). It produces a complex and synergistic picture of the wholeness, roundness, and oneness of how people experience their lives and how they express that experience as career. Traditional approaches have given us a very flat picture and created a gulf between theory and practice (Savickas & Walsh, 1996) as well as between different domains (see Peiperl and Gunz, Chapter 3). For example, our particular interest might be the organizational career, yet as practitioners know too well, in everyday experience this is inextricably interwoven with the individual's life, a family's life (Collin, 2006), mobility in the labor market, as well as an organization's need to develop, retain, and motivate its staff, its economic viability, and its contribution to the economic viability of a nation (Kanter, 1989). If we recognized the tapestry of career, we could perhaps achieve more effective responses to such complex experiences in a complex and changing context.

THE CHALLENGES TO THE FIELD OF SEEING CAREER AS TAPESTRY

However, this view of the meanings of career offers many challenges for the field, which can only be touched on here. I hope that the inclusion of this examination of the meanings of career in the *Handbook* will prompt further exploration and discussion.

Holistic Conceptualizations of Career

The challenges are difficult to prioritize, but I shall start with the need to find appropriate ways of conceptualizing career holistically. One approach that has long been mooted in the field but until recently not really taken up comes from the biological sciences (Collin, 1985;

Patton & McMahon, 1999). That is systems thinking, which is essentially holistic, being concerned with complex wholes that are themselves part of a greater whole, with interdependence of their parts; relationships between the whole, its parts, and its environment; and interactions and recursions rather than linear causes and effects. The principle of emergence could be particularly helpful in understanding career (see Collin, 2006): Because the total system is synergistic and more than the mechanical arrangement of its parts, interactions between its parts create higher levels of organization at which properties emerge that do not exist at the lower levels. Of course, the systems approach can be used in positivistic ways incompatible with the notion of career as tapestry. What is being recommended here, however, is specifically "soft systems" thinking and methodology (Checkland, 1981; Checkland & Poulter, 2006).

Another appropriate conceptualization might be found in chaos theory and the other new unsettling scientific developments that have been introduced into the career field (Bird, Gunz, & Arthur, 2002; Bright & Pryor, 2005; Pryor & Bright, 2003). As in systems thinking, dynamic complexity, nonlinearity, and recursion are key concepts that could be relevant to conceptualizing the tapestry of career. However, as Bird et al. (2002) point out, there could be pitfalls in translating these ideas from the physical into the social sciences.

Narrative is an approach derived from the humanities that is being used increasingly in the various branches of psychology, including career (Cohen & Mallon, 2001; Polkinghorne, 1988) and in organization studies (Gabriel, 2000). Being holistic, integrating both objective and subjective, in-depth and contextualized views of individual experience, and having as its premise that "composing a narrative is our primary way of making meaning" (Cochran, 1997, p. 4), it offers yet another way of conceptualizing the tapestry of career.

By contextualizing career in interpersonal relationships, the relational approach contrasts with traditional career approaches that are built on the Western view of the individual as a self-contained unit (see Blustein et al., 2004; Hall & Associates, 1996). For example, it emphasizes how individual experiences are embedded in the social and cultural context, and how the mutuality and interdependence of experiences generates a "multiplicity in perspectives and meanings" (Blustein et al., 2004, p. 429). Such interpretations would give insight into the understanding of career as tapestry.

The "grand social theories" discussed by Mayrhofer, Meyer, and Steyrer (Chapter 12) could also have something to offer to this proposed interpretation but, rather than examining that, I want to make a somewhat different point here. That is, that such theories come from a tradition very different from the North American "tributaries" (Moore, Gunz, and Hall, Chapter 2) that dominate the field but, nevertheless, have much to offer. For example, the concept of "habitus" (Bourdieu & Wacquant, 1992), which bridges individual and context, has been fruitfully used in European career studies (Guichard, 2005; Hodkinson & Sparkes, 1997; Vilhjálmsdóttir & Arnkelsson, 2003). Not only does the field need to acknowledge the irrelevance of Western assumptions for the study of career in other cultures highlighted by Thomas and Inkson (Chapter 23), it also needs to be open to the potential contributions of different intellectual traditions around the world.[1]

Interpretation and Social Construction

If the meanings of career are interwoven, simultaneous, and contextualized, then we are always and inevitably making interpretations in using and studying career. Readers/hearers have to interpret—from the context, the inferred perspective of the user—the aspect of career that is being referred to and, whatever may have been intended, they will not only hear echoes of other meanings but have to register any subtle changes in its meaning as it is being used.

It is not just a question of parsing the meanings. We are constructing and deconstructing them, and this renders traditional analytical approaches impotent and makes social constructionism of particular relevance here. This is an antiessentialist and antirealist approach that considers knowledge to be historically and culturally specific and language to be a precondition for thought that constitutes rather than reflects reality (Burr, 1995; Young & Collin, 2004). For example, it encourages us to be aware of how the

simultaneous meanings of career are interpreted and used by different people for different purposes: in other words, of the stakeholders in career (Collin & Young, 2000). Apart from the individual, they include counselors, employers, governments, and society itself. When we recognize their different purposes, our attention is drawn to how career is being used as rhetoric (Collin, 2000b), and this in turn highlights the submerged workings of power in institutions and society (Collin & Young, 2000). It offers the possibility of a critical stance in career studies when examining the managerial/organizational discourses of career, as in this *Handbook,* and the discourses of government policymakers who, following changes in the world of work (e.g., Guest and Sturges, Chapter 16; Arthur & Rousseau, 1996; Storey, 2000), seem to have taken up the construct of career (see Bezanson & O'Reilly, 2002; Organisation for Economic Co-Operation and Development, 2004; Peck, 2004; Watts, Law, Killeen, Kidd, & Hawthorn, 1996).

A further point is that, although we can be aware that multiple meanings of career co-exist, we cannot examine them simultaneously. Whether deliberately or otherwise on the part of the user, they shift and slide, echo and elide, once again explaining why definitions of them are scarce. One way of expressing their complex relationships is in terms of figure and ground. (Parker & Arthur, 2000 also refer to that but to make a different point.) This, according to Gestalt psychology, which, like the systems approach, is concerned with the whole, is a characteristic of perceptual organization. We see either figure or ground, and in relation to one another, as in M. C. Escher's woodcuts (see Boje, 1999). Moreover, we cannot represent the simultaneity of the meanings in conventional literary form. Writing is linear: It can represent before and after but, unlike the plastic arts, not a simultaneous all-round view (Lessing, 1766/1984). This has given rise to the use of the metaphor of the kaleidoscope with Mayrhofer, Meyer, and Steyrer (Chapter 12) seeing the contributions of various theories as kaleidoscopic and Collin (1997) suggesting that contextualism gives "a kaleidoscopic rather than a panoramic view of career and its environment" (p. 444). There is a need to explore further ways to express career's multiple, interwoven, meanings.

This might be done graphically, perhaps in some Escher-like way, or through virtual reality.

Recognition of Underpinning Assumptions

It is disappointing that there are so few discussions (in this *Handbook* as in the literature generally) of the writers' epistemologies and their implications for the construction of their theses. If instead of the traditional approaches in the career field any of the conceptualizations above are adopted and attention is paid to the processes of interpretation, then greater recognition would have to be given to the grounds of knowledge. This would be particularly so when working in an interdisciplinary/transdisciplinary/multidisciplinary way. As Mayrhofer, Meyer, and Styrer (Chapter 12) recognize, there are "epistemological and theoretical" limits to how we can combine multiple views of career.

Research Methodologies

The various conceptualizations, interpretations, and assumptions referred to above challenge many of the accepted research methodologies in the field. There will be a need to look beyond traditional qualitative approaches to interpretative approaches such as action theory (Young & Valach, 1996), discourse analysis (Potter & Wetherall, 1987), hermeneutical approaches (Young & Collin, 1992), narrative (Cochran, 1997; Gabriel, 2000), personal construct theory (Neimeyer, 1992), and soft systems methodology (Checkland & Poulter, 2006). An interpretative methodology that allows the identification of respondents' own constructions would be particularly appropriate.

Lessons From Practitioners

Finally, we should look at how practitioners conceptualize and deal with the lived experiences of their clients' careers. What can they tell us about the simultaneous multiple meanings of career? In addition to illuminating our understanding of the tapestry of career, their answers could lead to the development of the closer relationship between theorists, researchers, and

practitioners that the field appears to need (Collin, 1996).

POSTSCRIPT: THE CURIOUS INCIDENT OF THE DOG IN THE NIGHTTIME

I am suggesting that awareness of the tapestry of simultaneous multiple meanings of career would greatly enrich our field. This could stimulate it to become broader, deeper, and more critical; possibly more able to address a changing world. We still have to explore ways of representing and communicating this interwoven multiplicity, a considerable challenge for theorists, researchers, and scholars, but I have wondered why such a significant understanding of career was not already a major feature in the literature. Could it be that the scarcity of definitions and of discussions of the both/and character of career—the dog that did not bark—was not because that tapestry was *not* recognized in the field but because it was recognized only too clearly and the field shied away from it? That the holistic and interwoven nature of career is widely appreciated not only by practitioners but also by academics, but they do not examine it because its implications are at odds with their traditional analytical and positivist/postpositivist approaches? That it is easier to deal with the issue by sidestepping it and by forgoing definitions than by confronting those implications?

NOTE

1. See, for example, the *International Journal for Educational and Vocational Guidance.*

REFERENCES

Arthur, M. B., Hall, D. T., & Lawrence, B. S. (1989). Generating new directions in career theory: The case for a transdisciplinary approach. In M. B. Arthur, D. T. Hall, & B. S. Lawrence (Eds.), *Handbook of career theory* (pp. 7–25). Cambridge, UK: Cambridge University Press.

Arthur, M. B., & Rousseau, D. M. (Eds.). (1996). *The boundaryless career: A new employment principle for a new organizational era*. New York: Oxford University Press.

Bezanson, L., & O'Reilly, E. (Eds.). (2002). *Making waves: Vol. 2. Connecting career development with public policy*. Ottawa, Ontario: Canadian Career Development Foundation.

Bird, A., Gunz, H. P., & Arthur, M. B. (2002). Careers in a complex world: The search for new perspectives from the "new science." *M@n@gement, 5*(1), 1–14.

Blustein, D. L., Schultheiss, D. E. P., & Flum, H. (2004). Toward a relational perspective of the psychology of careers and working: A social constructionist analysis. *Journal of Vocational Behavior, 64*, 423–440.

Boje, D. M. (1999). Is there reality outside the classroom? Critical postmodern turns in management/OB pedagogy. Retrieved February 17, 2005, from http://business.nmsu.edu/~dboje/bojeobtc99.html.

Bourdieu, P., & Wacquant, L. (1992). *An invitation to reflexive sociology*. Chicago: University of Chicago Press.

Bright, J. E. H., & Pryor, R. G. L. (2005). The chaos theory of careers: A user's guide. *Career Development Quarterly, 53*, 291–305.

Burr, V. (1995). *An introduction to social constructionism*. London: Routledge.

Checkland, P. (1981). *Systems thinking, systems practice*. Chichester: Wiley.

Checkland, P. B., & Poulter, J. (2006). *Learning for action: A short definitive account of soft systems methodology and its use, for practitioners, teachers and students*. Chichester: Wiley.

Cochran, L. (1997). *Career counseling: A narrative approach*. Thousand Oaks, CA: Sage.

Cohen, L., & Mallon, M. (2001). My brilliant career? Using stories as a methodological tool in careers research. *International Studies of Management and Organization, 31*, 48–68.

Collin, A. (1985). The learning circle of a research project on "mid-career change": Through stages to systems thinking. *Journal of Applied Systems Analysis, 12*, 35–53.

Collin, A. (1990). Mid-life career change research. In R. A. Young & W. A. Borgen (Eds.), *Methodological approaches to the study of career* (pp. 197–220). New York: Praeger.

Collin, A. (1996). Re-thinking the relationship between theory and practice: Practitioners as map-readers, map-makers—or jazz players? *British Journal of Guidance and Counselling, 24*, 67–81.

Collin, A. (1997). Career in context. *British Journal of Guidance and Counselling, 25*, 435–446.

Collin, A. (2000a). Dancing to the music of time. In A. Collin & R. A. Young (Eds.), *The future of career* (pp. 83–97). Cambridge, UK: Cambridge University Press.

Collin, A. (2000b). Epic and novel: The rhetoric of career. In A. Collin & R. A. Young (Eds.), *The future of career* (pp. 163–177). Cambridge, UK: Cambridge University Press.

Collin, A. (2006). Conceptualising the family-friendly career: The contribution of career theories and a systems approach. *British Journal of Guidance and Counselling, 34*, 295–306.

Collin, A., & Young, R. A. (2000). The future of career. In A. Collin & R. A. Young (Eds.), *The future of career* (pp. 276–300).Cambridge, UK: Cambridge University Press.

Gabriel, Y. (2000). *Storytelling in organizations: Facts, fictions, and fantasies*. Oxford: Oxford University Press.

Goffman, E. (1959). The moral career of the mental patient. *Psychiatry, 22*, 123–142.

Guichard, J. (2005). Life-long self-construction. *International Journal for Educational and Vocational Guidance, 5*, 111–124.

Gunz, H. P., & Heslin, P. A. (2005). Reconceptualizing career success [Introduction to a special issue]. *Journal of Organizational Behavior, 26*(2), 105–111.

Hall, D. T., & Associates. (1996). *The career is dead: Long live the career: A relational approach to careers*. San Francisco: Jossey-Bass.

Hodkinson, P., & Sparkes, A. C. (1997). Careership: A sociological theory of career decision making. *British Journal of Sociology of Education, 18*, 29–44.

Hughes, E. C. (1937). Institutional office and the person. *American Journal of Sociology, 43*, 404–413.

Kanter, R. M. (1989). Careers and the wealth of nations: A macro-perspective on the structure and implications of career forms. In M. B. Arthur, D. T. Hall, & B. S. Lawrence (Eds.), *Handbook of career theory* (pp. 506–521). Cambridge, UK: Cambridge University Press.

Law, B. (1981). Careers theory: A third dimension? In A. G. Watts, D. E. Super, & J. M. Kidd (Eds.), *Career development in Britain* (pp. 300–337). Cambridge, UK: Hobsons Press.

Lessing, G. E. (1984). *Laocoon: An essay on the limits of painting and poetry* (E. A. McCormick

Trans.). New York: Johns Hopkins Press. (Original work published 1766)

Neimeyer, G. J. (1992). Personal constructs in career counseling and development. *Journal of Career Development, 18,* 163–173.

Organisation for Economic Co-Operation and Development. (2004). *Career guidance and public policy: Bridging the gap.* Paris: Author.

Parker, P., & Arthur, M. B. (2000). Careers, organizing and community. In M. Peiperl, M. B. Arthur, R. Goffee, & T. Morris (Eds.), *Career frontiers: New conceptions of working lives* (pp. 99–121). Oxford: Oxford University Press.

Patton, W., & McMahon, M. (1999). Career development and systems theory: A new relationship. Pacific Grove, CA: Brooks/Cole.

Peck, D. (2004). *Careers services: History, policy and practice in the United Kingdom.* London: Routledge Falmer.

Pepper, S. C. (1942). *World hypotheses.* Berkeley: University of California Press.

Polkinghorne, D. E. (1988). *Narrative knowing and the human sciences.* Albany: State University of New York Press.

Potter, J., & Wetherall, M. (1987). *Discourse and social psychology: Beyond attitudes and behaviour.* London: Sage.

Pryor, R. G. L., & Bright, J. E. H. (2003). Order and chaos: A twenty-first century formulation of careers. *Australian Journal of Psychology, 55*(2), 121–128.

Roberts, R. J. (1980). An alternative justification for careers education: A radical response to Roberts and Daws. *British Journal of Guidance and Counselling, 8,* 158–174.

Savickas, M. L., & Walsh, W. B. (Eds.). (1996). *Handbook of career counseling theory and practice.* Palo Alto, CA: Davies-Black.

Schein, E. H. (1971). The individual, the organization and the career: A conceptual scheme. *Journal of Applied Behavioral Science, 7*(4), 401–426.

Schein, E. H. (1976). Career development: Theoretical and practical issues for organizations. In *Career planning and development*

(Management development series no. 12). Geneva: International Labour Office.

Schein, E. H. (1978). *Career dynamics: Matching individual and organizational needs.* Reading, MA: Addison-Wesley.

Stebbins, R. A. (1970). Career: The subjective approach. *Sociological Quarterly, 11,* 32–49.

Storey, J. A. (2000). "Fracture lines" in the career environment. In A. Collin & R. A. Young (Eds.), *The future of career* (pp. 21–36). Cambridge, UK: Cambridge University Press.

Vilhjálmsdóttir, G., & Arnkelsson, G. (2003). The interplay between habitus, social variables and occupational preferences. *International Journal for Educational and Vocational Guidance, 3,* 137–150.

Watts, A. G. (1981). Career patterns. In A. G.Watts, D. E. Super, & J. M. Kidd (Eds.), *Career development in Britain* (pp. 213–245). Cambridge, UK: Hobsons Press.

Watts, A. G., Law, B., Killeen, J., Kidd, J. M., & Hawthorn, R. (1996). *Rethinking careers education and practice: Theory, policy and practice.* London: Routledge.

Young, R. A., & Collin, A. (Eds.). (1992). *Interpreting career: Hermeneutical studies of lives in context.* Westport, CT: Praeger.

Young, R. A., & Collin, A. (2000). Introduction: Framing the future of career. In A. Collin & R. A. Young (Eds.), *The future of career* (pp. 1–17). Cambridge, UK: Cambridge University Press.

Young, R. A., & Collin, A. (2004). Introduction: Constructivism and social constructionism in the career field. *Journal of Vocational Behavior, 64,* 373–388.

Young, R. A., & Valach, L. (1996). Interpretation and action in career counseling. In M. L. Savickas & W. B. Walsh (Eds.), *Handbook of career counseling theory and practice* (pp. 361–375). Palo Alto, CA: Davies-Black.

Young, R. A., Valach, L., & Collin, A. (1996). A contextual explanation of career. In D. Brown, L. Brooks, & Associates (Eds.), *Career choice and development* (3rd ed., pp. 477–512). San Francisco: Jossey-Bass.

33

Destiny, Drama, and Deliberation

Careers in the Coevolution of Lives and Societies

Nigel Nicholson

The richness of the career field is astonishing, as this volume testifies. Indeed, many contributors point out that there is much more out there that we could be writing about and researching. Casting one's mind back a few decades to the first collected volumes of writings on careers, one is struck by the contrast—then the field was dominated by a few quite distinctive approaches yet with a strong sense of future possibilities. Well, the future arrived, and how much better off are we? Is the field richer or just denser? Where are the big ideas, or is that an immature longing in a field where a thousand flowers are already blooming?

Corollaries of the Concept of Career

If there is a problem, it lies in the seductions of the concept and its inherent difficulties. Candace

Jones and Mary B. Dunn (Chapter 22) remind us of the brave new dawn being hailed by Barley decades ago for its excitement and promise to be at "the vanguard of organization studies" by linking persons and institutions. I have argued similarly that the career concept provides a unique and dynamic link between identities and social structure (Nicholson, 2000; Nicholson & West, 1989). Jones and Dunn do not directly answer the obvious question about whether Barley's prophesy has been fulfilled, but arguably, it has not. Yet the careers field is a cornucopia for sure. The nexus that Jones and Dunn discuss has certainly been a source of the field's fertility and dynamism. It is an intersection that is constantly changing, as social structures evolve, forcing individuals to find new pathways. However, this also makes the notion of career quite hard to keep in focus, and when one looks at the work represented here and elsewhere, one can detect several consequences:

- It is bifocal between individualism and institutionalism. Careers are possessed by individuals and are defined by social structures. Cohorts may share many of the same career sequences and experiences but in the manner of individuals in a bus queue. The concept of the group is almost absent and, most importantly, so is the family, for arguably, families have careers too.
- The field has multiple centers of gravity. One can focus on individual lives, organizational environments, social structures, and a range of processes affecting career development, such as mobility. There is little scope for theoretical integration between these centers.
- It is mainly descriptive. An important role of careers scholars is to chart the shifting landscape of career development and its contexts, but the field badly needs durable theory. Many so-called theoretical forays could be said to be heavily disguised descriptive essays insofar as predictions have quite local and ultimately ephemeral temporal boundary conditions.
- It is pluralistic rather than interdisciplinary in methodologies and approaches. There are exceptions, but for the most part, scholars are drawing on distinctive empirical and theoretical traditions. The most durable contributions are arguably those that are less "careers" oriented than disciplinary in anchorage and contribution. (This, incidentally, is true of many other areas of organization studies, such as marketing, HRM, and strategy).

There is nothing inherently "wrong" in these attributes, but one does wonder where the field of careers will go next—these elements augur centrifugal development, for it seems likely that these properties of the career concept decree that there is little prospect of a common core at the heart of the area around which theory can coalesce and to which empirical approaches can refer for validation.

That being said, there is better research and a greater richness of ideas to be found now in the field than ever before, for which we may all rejoice. They seem to be clustering around some centers of gravity, on which I shall briefly make comment. This I shall undertake, drawing on an evolutionary psychology perspective, under two headings: (a) identity and destiny and (b) context and coevolution.

THEMES IN CAREER RESEARCH

Identity and Destiny

Destiny is an unfashionable and unpopular notion, entirely absent from this volume. Even in its looser usages it is likely to be disliked as overly deterministic. Let us revisit it briefly. Early approaches to the study of careers were more open to the idea, if not the usage, of the concept of destiny. This was to be found in the idea that (a) individual differences are determinants of career destinations and (b) life chances are determined by accidents of birth—that is, social class, place, and resources. The former clearly continues to matter, as is implied by Judge and Kammeyer-Mueller (Chapter 4) in their discussion of personality. The human capital perspective, advanced by many writers here, would seem to discourage the latter idea of life chances being inherited and socially determined. But arguably, as wealth inequalities increase, not just in the West but in many of the emerging markets of the 21st century, the concept of destiny has undiminished relevance inasmuch as it denotes the forces that govern opportunity, choice, and constraints beyond an individual's control. The counterpart to destiny is *drama*—non-normative life events (Baltes, Reese, & Lipsett, 1980) that intervene and disrupt the flow of automaticity in career decisions (Bargh & Chartrand, 1999). Lying in the space between destiny and drama is *deliberation*—that is, the reflective self, the evolved capacity that separates humans from all other species and that makes us uniquely able to apprehend and intervene to change our destiny (Leary, 2004).

The micro level of career analysis should be in this space—the area of self-awareness that leads many people not to submit passively to their "destiny." But many do, and the analysis of their unfolding careers is simple, predictable and of little scholarly interest. So, arguably we should concentrate our attention on those areas where personal development emerges as an unpredictable outcome of choice (Young & Rodgers, 1997). There is almost nothing in the literature on the psychological triggers for such decisions as migration, career change, downshifting, or any other strategies by which individuals lay claim to their careers. At the micro level of analysis, theory and research here could focus on the processes of self-regulation by which people alter their goals, or alter their perceptions and strategies to sustain their goals (Karoly, 1993). Within this domain lie the well-documented snares of cognitive bias and heuristics that also have barely featured in writings on career decision making (Bazerman, 1994; Gigerenzer, Todd, & ABC Research Group, 1999). For that matter, neither have analyses of motives. Careers theory could benefit from renewed attention to this micro level of analysis of cognition and motivation.

At the level of the individual person, the idea that reflexivity is a key to agentic processes in careers falls within the ambit of the study of identity and transitions (Ibarra, 2003). As Moore, Gunz, and Hall (Chapter 2) show, life-space, life-span approaches were once a dominant perspective in the field—the idea of career as part of a life story, possessed by an individual, driven by his or her unique attributes and experiences, and rooted in processes of identity formation. If we are to assume that this volume is representative of the field, it would appear that this biographical approach is seriously out of fashion. There is reason for this. We seem to have little faith in the theoretical presumptions that spawned this early work. However elegant they have been, biographical approaches have often delivered little more than over-interpreted narratives under the dense cover of varieties of personological theorizing. We are no longer content with mere storytelling dressed up as theory.

But there also is a loss here. The virtue of the biographical approach is that it takes cognizance of a variable curiously undervalued in a field that it defines—namely, time (as Lawrence and Tolbert also note in Chapter 20). Taking account of time with respect to the dimensions of a human life has the merit—in a field prone to great abstraction—of dealing with the essential, irreducible, and central elements of career processes. The bottom-line is (a) that our lives are finite, (b) that it takes time to acquire the attributes that will underpin our fitness, and (c) that we will use them for the benefit of ourselves and our kin. This is the true meaning of the Latin tag *Ars longa, vita brevis:* It takes a long investment to develop the arts and skills for living, and life is short.

This paradox embodies one of the most interesting, important, and neglected challenges for career theory: How do people make trade-offs in their life choices? As the gag has it, experience is something you don't get until just after you need it. Lives are interesting because maturation processes are inexorable. The timetables for key life events may have become much more irregular, but they have not ceased to operate sequentially for most people. In many contexts, they conform to quite compelling local norms and, in aggregate, have the appearance of cultural universals—reflecting enduring aspects of the human condition (Brown, 1991). It is all too easy to atomize human attributes in a field that is concerned with lives through time.

My own bias, as an evolutionary psychologist, is for a revival of biographical approaches to careers. We can now be a lot sharper in our analysis of life-span development via the advances in knowledge that have been accruing in the areas of individual differences, self-regulatory processes, and cognition. An overarching question from an evolutionary perspective is how do people attempt to optimize between risk and career success in their life choices. Career success in this context, as I have discussed elsewhere (Nicholson & De Waal-Andrews, 2005), is not so much to do with subjective well-being as the material utilities of status, wealth, and related variables that underpin life expectancy, life quality, and reproductive fitness. This arguably supplies a framework for a more systematic approach to the analysis of lives through time than we have hitherto been able (and willing) to undertake.

Context and Coevolution

There was a stream of books in the last decades of the 20th century foretelling the death of jobs and careers as we know them. The notion of boundarylessness became common currency in the careers field and elsewhere (Arthur & Rousseau, 1996). This volume reflects the degree to which these scenarios were both right and wrong. They were right inasmuch as the expectations, structures, and contracts of employment have altered dramatically in the Western world. The landscape is indeed radically different, with many new opportunities coupled with a loss of the traditional "climbing frames" (as Gunz, 1989, memorably called them) in many occupations and professions. Many chapters in this book supply chapter and verse for the substance of these changes.

Yet, as both Guest and Sturges (Chapter 16) and Prasad, D'Abate, and Prasad (Chapter 10) point out, many traditional occupational patterns persist outside the world of professionals and elites on whose existence the greater part of the careers literature concentrates. But even in these ranks, there is far less mobility and uncertainty than is being assumed by many writers. Cappelli and Hamori (Chapter 17) are surely right to point out that there has been a shift from bureaucratic to human capital orientations, but this has only made some organizations cling more tenaciously to their human assets. Lifetime employment has not disappeared in the Western world, and in many other regions managers continue to expect and receive a contract of loyal and long-term engagement.

But perhaps the important question is not so much which predictions are correct or incorrect as what are the consequences of the changing landscape. This is where theory needs to be built, as several contributors to this volume recognize. In the Darwinian framework, the issue can be construed as one of coevolution (Janicki & Krebs, 1998). The starting point for this analysis is the evidence, from the empirical literature, that we have in contemporary society a greater plurality of career systems and operating models for the design of jobs than ever before. This implies that there is scope for greater selection—the clustering of "people like me," as Lawrence and Tolbert (Chapter 20) put it—in sectors, occupations, organizations, and even national cultures. Again, the missing level of analysis in the careers literature is the group. In many societies, indeed, lurking within our own in the unfashionable yet highly prevalent domain of family business, there are kinship groupings and networks that locate "careers" within systems of shared fate for people whose interests are intimately connected. The individualism of the careers field seems predisposed to conceive of us all as lonely self-willed actors (though this volume also shows the desire to transcend this perspective, as in Greenhaus and Foley's contribution, Chapter 8).

The duality of coevolutionary processes is the cyclical relationship between (a) people selecting, adapting to, and changing environments to achieve an optimal "fit" with them and (b) environments selecting people who will fit into the culture, thereby enhancing the homogeneity of the aggregation of their human capital, i.e. their culture (Chatman, 1991; Graen, 1975; Schneider, 1987). Writers in this volume argue that careers shape organizational culture and capability (Ibarra and Deshpande, Chapter 14; Higgins and Dillon, Chapter 21). It is the case that the opposite perspective—how cultures shape careers, principally via processes of socialization—has previously been somewhat simplistically absorbed with the over-socialized conception of how employee attitudes and orientations are molded, rather than one that comprehends the coevolution of careers and institutions.

Where might a bolder analysis of coevolution take us? Thomas and Inkson (Chapter 23) accuse career theory of both individualism and parochialism, a charge that certainly seems justified by the neglect of cross-cultural perspectives in the field, and their framework is a helpful stimulus to thinking afresh about culture. However, arguably more is needed to help us escape the tendency to lapse into further descriptive analysis. A coevolutionary perspective points to the possibility of explaining, for example, patterns of migration, the convergence of business subcultures around the world, and how the ideologies that characterize industries and occupations evolve to accommodate the orientations of the human assets to which they have access and seek to retain. What are the adaptive processes to be found in cultures that exist to solve fitness problems? Such a research program would consider how values, perceived opportunity structures, and access to networks emerge as communal characteristics and as solutions to the challenge of adjustment to environmental pressures. This would require a genuinely interdisciplinary orientation, bringing together labor economists, sociologists, and psychologists to model these processes.

INTERACTIONS AND INTERVENTIONS

To put these two perspectives together is to entertain a quite sophisticated kind of interactionism, one that applies at various levels of analysis. It implies that the dynamic between individuals, and organizations and institutions is more than a "psychological contract" between notional equivalents. Rather, it is a kind of game played by willed individuals in regulated arenas of interests and incentives. The missing concept of groups—that is, where the interests of economic actors are closely combined, as among couples, families, and communities—also supplies a micro context within which choices are constrained and opportunities created. A notable example of collective careers is to be found in the influential Marwari community of North Indian entrepreneurs, who have been highly instrumental (among other groups) in the wave of economic development that has been driving the subcontinent in recent times. My own recent ethnographic reflections on the Maasai in Northern Kenya make the same point: People's fates are often inextricably intertwined by tight bonds of kinship, social rules, and maturational timetables, leaving spaces (very small in this case) for them to find and then mold their destinies (Nicholson, 2005)—yet many of them do.

The destiny-drama-deliberation model also helps us consider afresh the role of third-party interventions in career development and decision making. There is a long tradition of work on vocational guidance and career counseling that Kidd (Chapter 6) reviews comprehensively. The astonishing growth of executive coaching seems to betoken people's increased determination to make rather than be shaped by their destiny in the face of increased environmental uncertainty. Kidd and other contributors point to the growing role of intermediation, through executive search and similar agencies, mentors (see Chandler and Kram, Chapter 13), and the growing use of the Internet as a labor market place (as discussed by Cappelli and Hamori, Chapter 17). Again, the whole area of third-party interventions seems to be under-theorized, where we might conceive, for example, of analyzing the preconditions, triggers, and facilitators that lead individuals to seek and accept intervention and intermediation.

In the same vein, the approach I am advocating would lead us to take an interest in career errors and failures, and the learning and readjustment that follow them—or should follow them, for often it does not. People's need for emotional self-protection and an escalating commitment to the sunk costs of career investments can easily cause inertia, magical thinking, and self-justification to triumph over analysis, insight, and innovation (Cannon, 1999; Frese, 1995).

END THOUGHT: BEYOND CAREER ILLUSIONS AND DELUSIONS

In brief, I see the need for both a more deterministic *and* a more agentic conceptualization of the careers field than we have at present. We need to confront more fearlessly the fact that much apparent choice is illusory and highly predictable from the givens and knowns in people's lives, and yet by acts of will, people are capable of confounding the forces of destiny.

The deterministic position starts with the idea that choice and decision are often rhetorical games that help sustain the illusion that our futures are more self-determined than they are, or that opportunity and choice are more random than we would like to think. An early shock in my own career research came when we found how executives in a large longitudinal cohort were extremely poor at predicting their own job moves over one calendar year (Nicholson, West, & Cawsey, 1985). Most of those who changed jobs hadn't predicted they would, and most of those who predicted they would change jobs didn't. The only way the Time 1/Time 2 correlation achieved statistical significance was because of the large number of people who predicted no change and were right!

My Darwinian bias tells me to suspect that many narratives are ex-post rationalizations of people who are sleepwalking into the future. Actually, this metaphor is incorrect. It would be more accurate to say we walk backward into the future, seeing only the road behind and only imagining the road ahead. We are adept at bolstering our confidence in our agentic powers and self-regulatory skill through a hardwired hindsight bias (Fischhoff & Beyth, 1975).

If one does the thought experiment of imagining oneself to be a rather superior alien observing, with wry amusement, human destiny, drama, and deliberation from an elevated position and in possession of detached knowledge of the causal forces and contingencies bearing down on the person (i.e., being god-like), then human choice looks rather different. Much of it appears to be a game, where we go through the motions of agonizing deliberation when all along the odds were obviously stacked in the direction of one option over another. Putting together the psychological profile of individuals, the state of their bank balance, the networks of influence they have access to, the time and place of their existence, even observers much less omniscient than a god might not find it hard to predict the choices a person agonizes over. Or to put it another way, we as agents and actors are much more influenced in our prospective choices by our fears and wishes than by dispassionate self-observation and analysis.

Of course, what are not predictable are often the consequences of our choices. So it might be externally more predictable to others than to ourselves that we will choose this partner/job than what this partner/job will turn out to be like for us. It is the adjustment processes to the unintended outcomes of predictable choices that lend the careers field much of its excitement.

The other source of excitement comes more directly from genuine drama and deliberation—where predictable choice is jettisoned, the presumptions of destiny are challenged, and remarkable transformations are achieved by acts of will and choice. It is curious how uninterested careers theory and research seems to be in these events—which often shape the course of human history—compared with our attention to the more commonplace phenomena of career development.

Within the boundaries of destiny, drama, and deliberation, there seems to me to be great scope for theory that will enhance the rich descriptions we are accumulating about the changing content and context of careers.

REFERENCES

Arthur, M. B., & Rousseau, D. M. (1996). (Eds.). *The boundaryless career: A new employment principle for a new organizational era.* New York: Oxford University Press.

Baltes, P. B., Reese, H., & Lipsett, L. (1980). Life span developmental psychology. *Annual Review of Psychology, 31,* 65–110.

Bargh, J. A., & Chartrand, T. L. (1999). The unbearable automaticity of being. *American Psychologist, 54,* 462–479.

Bazerman, M. H. (1994). *Judgment in managerial decision making* (3rd ed.). New York: Wiley.

Brown, D. E. (1991). *Human universals.* Philadelphia: Temple University Press.

Cannon, D. R. (1999). Cause or control? The temporal dimension in failure sense-making. *Journal of Applied Behavioral Science, 35,* 416–438.

Chatman, J. A. (1991). Matching people and organizations: Selection and socialization in public accounting firms. *Administrative Science Quarterly, 36,* 459–484.

Fischhoff, B., & Beyth, R. (1975). "I knew it would happen": Remembered probabilities of once-future things. *Organizational Behavior and Human Performance, 13,* 1–16.

Frese, M. (1995). Error management in training: Conceptual and empirical results. In C. Zuchermaglio, S. Bagnara, & S. U. Stucky (Eds.), *Organizational learning and technological change* (pp. 112–124). Berlin: Springer.

Gigerenzer, G., Todd, P. M., & the ABC Research Group. (1999). *Simple heuristics that make us smart.* Oxford: Oxford University Press.

Graen, G. B. (1975). Role-making processes within complex organisations. In M. D. Dunnette (Ed.), *Handbook of industrial and organisational psychology.* Chicago: Rand McNally.

Gunz, H. (1989). *Careers and corporate cultures.* Oxford: Blackwell.

Humphrey, N. (1980). Nature's psychologists. In B. D. Josephson, & V. S. Ramachandran (Eds.), *Consciousness and the physical world* (pp. 55–75). New York: Pergamon.

Ibarra, H. (2003). *Working identity.* Cambridge, MA: Harvard Business School Press.

Janicki, M., & Krebs, D. (1998). Evolutionary approaches to culture. In C. Crawford & D. Krebs (Eds.), *Handbook of evolutionary psychology.* Mahwah, NJ: Lawrence Erlbaum.

Karoly, P. (1993). Mechanisms of self-regulation: A systems view. *Annual Review of Psychology, 44,* 23–52.

Leary, M. R. (2004). *The curse of the self.* New York: Oxford University Press.

Nicholson, N. (2000). Motivation-selection-connection: An evolutionary model of career development. In M. Peiperl, M. B. Arthur, R. Goffee, & T. Morris (Eds.). *Career frontiers:*

New conceptions of working lives. Oxford: Oxford University Press.

Nicholson, N. (2005). Meeting the Maasai: Messages for management. *Journal of Management Inquiry, 14,* 255–267.

Nicholson, N., & De Waal-Andrews, W. (2005). Playing to win: Biological imperatives, self-regulation and trade-offs in the game of career success. *Journal of Organizational Behavior, 26,* 137–154.

Nicholson, N., & West, M. A. (1989). Transitions, work histories and careers. In M. B. Arthur, D. T. Hall, & B. S. Lawrence (Eds.), *Handbook of career theory* (pp. 181–202). New York: Cambridge.

Nicholson, N., West, M. A., & Cawsey, T. F. (1985). Future uncertain: Expected vs. attained job change among managers. *Journal of Occupational Psychology, 58,* 313–320.

Schneider, B. W. (1987). The people make the place. *Personnel Psychology, 40,* 437–453.

Young, J. B., & Rodgers, R. F. (1997). A model of radical career change in the context of psychosocial development. *Journal of Career Assessment, 5*(2), 167–182.

AFTERWORD

CAREER RESEARCH

Some Issues and Dilemmas

EDGAR H. SCHEIN

I n this essay, I would like to revisit some of the trends that I identified in career research and to comment in a more critical vein on what is left out in the way research is being done today.

As I noted in my Foreword, the field of career studies has grown and diversified to an incredible degree. At the same time, I am struck by the degree to which the division between sociological and psychological approaches seems as strong as ever. Disciplines don't come together easily, but in the career field, the continued isolation of disciplinary research streams hurts the overall understanding of what careers are ultimately all about. Specifically, as one goes through the various chapters of this *Handbook*, it is amazing how little overlap there is in the references at the end of each chapter. The psychological "selection bias" continues to be strong, as can readily be observed in noting that in the research aimed at identifying what careers people will *select*, there continues to be virtually no attention to the role that actual occupational experiences play in the selection process. Hardly anyone refers to the seminal work of Hughes, Becker, Van Maanen, and others who have noted that the nature of the

work to be done is as important as the motivations and skills of the workers if one is to understand career dynamics in their fullest. But there seems to be a strong bias toward treating careers as an individual phenomenon to be analyzed psychologically rather than as a social phenomenon involving economics, political science, anthropology, and sociology.

Many years ago, when I was writing my first book *Career Dynamics* (1978), I noted that the field was "summarized" by the psychologist Samuel Osipow in 1973 without a single reference to any of the sociology of occupations done by Everett Hughes and the Chicago School of Sociology. My observation is that we are not much better off today with various paradigms pursuing their own conception of what career research is without the slightest feeling of responsibility to connect their views to other researchers allegedly in the same field. This kind of compartmentalization is, of course, not limited to the career field, but it is ironic in that the concept of career is itself a bridging concept between the individual and the occupation or organization.

Another disjunctive trend that I see has to do with the nature of research in this field. As much of the research reflects, one can study careers by locating relevant constructs, measuring some abstract surrogate of those constructs, and then correlating the measurements with each other and performing various statistical operations to tease out relationships. If the relationship reaches some criterion of *statistical* significance, it begins to be treated as significant in terms of practical implications, though the correlation may be so small that only a tiny portion of the variance in the thing being studied is actually explained. This paradigm is well established in the management field, generally, as is very evident in the Academy of Management's journal, where literally nine out of every ten articles use virtually identical research methods based on this paradigm of testing relationships between empirical measurements of abstract operational definitions. Research elegance is then often displayed by ever more refined statistical operations rather than careful checking of whether the original operational definitions really reflect the phenomena that the researcher is trying to study.

The good news is that there are at least two other approaches to career research evident in the chapters of this *Handbook*, but they are not yet well integrated with the cross-sectional correlational approach. One important alternative is longitudinal research to discover patterns that occur over longer periods of time in a career. The massive project at AT&T by Doug Bray (Bray, Campbell, & Grant, 1974) was an early example of this kind of work.

My own concept of career anchors (Schein, 1978, 2006) was only discovered by reviewing my data from a panel of MIT Masters alumni when they were 12 to 13 years into their career. The research was originally launched to discover evidence of corporate indoctrination, and it was only by interviewing my panel well into their careers that I discovered the working of career anchors and then also found that the anchors explained why some people adopted business and organizational values readily (the managerially anchored panelists), whereas others actually developed counter-business attitudes (some of the autonomy anchored panelists). Averaging them together as I had done originally obscured the clear patterns that emerged longitudinally (Schein, 1978).

Another research approach is a more case-based clinical analysis focused either on particular career occupants, as exemplified in the Levinson and Vaillant studies, or on a particular occupational role, as exemplified by Becker's classic studies of doctors and Van Maanen's (1973) work on policemen. The bias toward the more popular psychological/cross-sectional/correlational approach reveals very little about the internal dynamics of how people forge their own work identities; neither does it reveal anything about the actual dynamics of the work that is to be done. In other words, correlating certain personality characteristics with success in accounting, for example, illuminates neither the internal psychological dynamics of being in that field with its ethical dilemmas, nor does it tell us anything about the organizational dynamics and variations of those dynamics in the companies in which that individual will work.

Let me provide an example. In recent years, I have focused more on organizational culture, which led to some study of what has come to be called "safety culture" in high hazard industries such as nuclear plants. In that regard, I ran into Snook's (2000) study of the shooting down of a U.S. helicopter by U.S. fighters in the Iraq "no fly zone" in 1994. Twenty-six UN dignitaries were killed in this incident of "friendly fire." What the post mortem of this tragedy reveals has surprising implications for career studies. Specifically, each of the main actors in the tragedy—the helicopter pilots, the fighter pilots, and the members of the overhead surveillance team on board the AWAC were doing their job as best they could, but what they were actually doing reflected what Snook calls "practical drift." Over a period of years, each job occupant evolves ways of doing that job that is most practical and efficient, changing the technology and bending the procedural rules to fit his or her current reality. For example, both the helicopters and fighters changed their communication systems in terms of their immediate needs and did not notice that over a period of years they ended up with different frequencies, making it impossible for the helicopter to respond to the fighter's repeated inquiries of "Who are you, identify yourself." Practical drift occurs in every occupation and represents the reality of how work actually gets done and how careers are actually played out; yet very little research is devoted to that reality.

Another powerful example of a different kind of research comes from Connie Perin's (2005) analysis of a number of close calls in several nuclear plants. What her intense observations and extensive interviews show is that different occupational groups within the organization evolve different worldviews and use different "logics" for decision making. Executives and senior managers tend to be policy oriented and inevitably have to be worried about the financial survival of the organization (Schein, 1996). Though they espouse safety, their control logic must take productivity and reliability into account as well. The designers of the system and the design engineers working in the system use a different logic that I have observed repeatedly. They would like the system to function elegantly, minimize human intervention and, therefore, the possibility of human error, and overdesign for safety where possible. They would use a technical logic for decision making. Finally, there is the group that is actually operating the plant, and they have to deal with immediate reality, which often does not fit what they were trained for. Doing the job therefore is inevitably, to some degree, a matter of improvisation, which leads to practical drift and eventually the institutionalization of deviations from formally prescribed procedures (Vaughan, 1996). The point is that becoming an engineer, or an operator, or an executive involves complex career socialization, which the correlational approach to career research is ill equipped to discover.

As a final example of a different kind of approach to career research, I would like to cite Monica Higgins's (2005) work on "career imprinting," which shows how the strong socialization into one kind of organizational culture leads people who leave that organization to reproduce that culture in their new organizations. Some "originating" organizations can thus spawn a whole industry style through the imprinting of the first generation of employees. To discover such trends requires a combination of historical, ethnographic, and clinical research and enables one to find patterns of evolution over time that would not be visible otherwise. My own example was the analysis of how the

culture of Digital Equipment Corporation both created a successful company and, in the end, was the cause of the financial failure of that company (Schein, 2003).

Another divisive trend is the disjunction between career research clearly geared to young people/career selection and career research that deals with adult evolution and the role that career development plays throughout the lifetime. As I noted in my Foreword, this approach goes all the way back to pilot selection in World War I, and has grown and evolved to the point where interest inventories and aptitude tests have become mature and effective. What is often forgotten, however, is that selection through testing is only effective when the criterion to which you are predicting is clear. Pilot selection is thus effective because we know what skills, etc. a pilot must have. Selection of managers or leaders is less so, primarily because what managers or leaders are supposed to do and how one would judge whether or not they do it well is much less clear. This dilemma becomes clearest in the difficulty we have in helping organizations select their top executives.

Even if those selection problems were solved, the developmental problems of entering and maintaining a career involving occupational or organizational socialization is a focus requiring very different research methods because what the occupation or organization is doing to the student/recruit requires a more sociological analysis. Research in this area highlights the fact that prediction of success is weakened by whether or not a particular organization or occupation actually values the skills that the aptitude test actually measures. Typically, these measures are based on statistical amalgamation of the results from many organizations. The implication for career incumbents is that they must not only choose an occupation or organization, but they must then diagnose whether the culture into which they are entering suits their own value system. One of the most salient characteristics of the early career is the frequency with which people switch organizations within the first few years of employment. The reasons for those switches that are given in exit interviews are usually "seeking a better job" or "higher pay." My own research suggests that a more accurate reason is "My values and the values of the organization did not mesh."

Studies of different socioeconomic groups pose yet another set of issues. First of all, it is much harder to do research on this population than on career entrants. Second, the issues differ in different occupations, especially as a function of whether or not the career occupant is employed in a large organization or is to some degree self-employed. The level of education attained determines to a great degree the kind of career that is possible, and career research to be fully useful must make it a point to study both extreme groups—the educated wealthy elites and the working or unemployed poor. At these extremes, career research becomes political in the sense that the wealthy have things to hide and are, therefore, less accessible, whereas the poor immediately highlight some of the career injustices that society has created, putting the researcher in the difficult position of becoming an advocate.

The problems of late career and retirement also highlight a very important individual psychological problem. Those whose identities have been tied up with organizations are much more vulnerable to depression postretirement than those who have engaged in work that can continue into the later ages. There is not nearly the same amount of late career counseling available as there is for career selection and career entry. And relatively little research has looked at what organizations do (if anything) to facilitate the retirement of their long-time employees. This problem has implications for society in that with the growth of life expectancy because of medical advances many adults have an entire career after retirement.

In conclusion, the growing field of career studies must not only continue to diversify the content of what is studied but, more importantly, must develop more diversity in research approaches. The research methods must be linked more closely to the nature of the problems being studied, and we must get over the obsession with the correlational paradigm that has been overworked in psychology.

REFERENCES

Bray, D. W., Campbell, R. J., & Grant, D. L. (1974). *Formative years in business.* Chichester: Wiley.

Higgins, M. C. (2005). *Career imprints.* San Francisco: Jossey-Bass.

Osipow, S. H. (1973). *Theories of career development* (2nd ed.). Norwalk, CT: Appleton-Century-Crofts.

Perin, C. (2005). *Shouldering risk.* Princeton, NJ: Princeton University Press.

Schein, E. H. (1978). *Career dynamics.* Reading, MA: Addison-Wesley.

Schein, E. H. (1996). Three cultures of management. *Sloan Management Review, 38*(1), 9–20.

Schein, E. H. (2003). *DEC is dead; Long live DEC.* San Francisco: Berrett-Koehler.

Schein, E. H. (2006). *Career anchors* (3rd ed.). San Francisco: Pfeiffer.

Snook, S. A. (2000). *Friendly fire.* Princeton, NJ: Princeton University Press.

Van Maanen, J. (1973). Observations on the making of policemen. *Human Organization, 4,* 407–418.

Vaughan, D. (1996). *The Challenger launch decision.* Chicago: Chicago University Press.

AUTHOR INDEX

Subject Index

ABOUT THE EDITORS

Hugh Gunz is Professor of Organizational Behaviour at the J. L. Rotman School of Management, University of Toronto and Chair of the Department of Management at the University of Toronto Mississauga. He trained as a chemist, first in New Zealand and later in the United Kingdom. After completing his PhD, he worked for some years in the petrochemicals industry and then returned to school to study business, which led to a second PhD and a tenured teaching appointment in organizational behavior at Manchester Business School. He joined the University of Toronto in 1989, serving in a variety of administrative positions, including as an Associate Dean of the Rotman School.

His current research interests include the role of developmental relationships in the acculturation and career success of immigrant workers and the ethical dilemmas faced by professionals in organizational and commercial contexts. He has published articles on managers' careers, the professions, and management education in many scholarly and practitioner journals. He is the author of *Careers and Corporate Cultures* (published in 1989) and coeditor of *Managing Complexity in Organizations* (published in 1999). He is Co-Editor of *M@n@gement* and serves on the editorial boards of *Academy of Management Journal, Journal of Managerial Psychology*, and *Emergence*. A former general secretary and Coordinating Committee member of the European Group for Organizational Studies, he has also served as Program Chair and Division Chair of the Careers Division of the Academy of Management.

Maury Peiperl is Professor of Leadership and Strategic Change at IMD in Lausanne, Switzerland, where he develops executive education programs for global organizations. He also teaches on the MBA program and chairs IMD's Business Advisory Council, a group of HR directors from around the world interested in the development of global executives. He is the author or editor of five books and numerous articles and case studies, primarily in the areas of careers, performance management, and leading change. These include *Career Frontiers* (2000), *Career Creativity* (2002), and the market-leading text *Managing Change: Cases and Concepts* (2003, second edition), as well as articles in *Academy of Management Review, Human Resource Management, Harvard Business Review*, and *Organizational Dynamics*, among others.

He is a long-standing member of the Academy of Management, where he has served as Chair of the Careers Division, and a member of the International Programs Committee. He is a member of the Evian Group Brain Trust, an organization dedicated to promoting free and fair global trade, and also sits on the Alumni Council of the Harvard Graduate School of Arts and Sciences, as well as the boards of several companies. Outside his teaching and research, he is active in amateur radio contests and expeditions and has received numerous awards. He is also a pianist and musical director, most recently for *Gypsy* (in Maryland) and *Follies* (Geneva, Switzerland). He lives in Bougy-Villars, Switzerland, and Silver Spring, Maryland, with his wife, Jennifer Georgia, and their children, Evan and Julia.

About the Contributors

Michael B. Arthur is Professor of Management at Suffolk University, Boston, Massachusetts. His books include the *Handbook of Career Theory, The Boundaryless Career, The New Careers, Career Frontiers, Career Creativity* and *Knowledge at Work: Creative Collaboration in the Global Economy* (with Robert DeFillippi and Valerie Lindsay, 2006). He has also written widely in academic and professional journals and is a developer of the "intelligent career card sort" (ICCS), intended to help people manage their careers in contemporary times. His current work focuses on the relationships among careers, communities, and employment arrangements in the knowledge-based economy.

Silvia Bagdadli, PhD in Management and Organization, is Associate Professor of Organization and Human Resource Management at Bocconi University and at SDA Bocconi School of Management where she is the Director of a Master of Science in Organization and HRM and the Director of an Executive Master in HRM. She is a member of the Academy of Management and of EGOS (coconvenor of the Career track—EGOS, Bergen, 2006). Her research and teaching are in the areas of HRM and career management where she is interested in the intersection of the individual and the organizational perspective and in understanding the relation between HRM, career management, and organizational performance.

Lotte Bailyn is Professor of Management at MIT's Sloan School of Management and Codirector of the MIT Workplace Center. She has long studied and worked on careers as well as the connections of the structure, culture, and practices of work with family, community, and other personal interests and concerns of employees. She is the author of *Breaking the Mold: Women, Men, and Time in the New Corporate World* (1993) and its new and revised edition *Breaking the Mold: Redesigning Work for Productive and Satisfying Lives* (2006) as well as coauthor of *Beyond Work-Family Balance: Advancing Gender Equity and Workplace Performance* (2002).

Richard E. Boyatzis is Professor in the Departments of Organizational Behavior and Psychology at Case Western Reserve University, Cleveland, Ohio, and Adjunct Professor at ESADE in Barcelona. He is the author of more than 150 articles and of several books, including *The Competent Manager*. He is the coauthor of the international best seller *Primal Leadership* with Daniel Goleman and Annie McKee, published in 29 languages, and *Resonant Leadership* with Annie McKee, published in 18 languages. He has a BS in aeronautics and astronautics from MIT and an MS and a PhD in social psychology from Harvard University.

Jon P. Briscoe is Associate Professor in the Department of Management and Adjunct Professor in the Department of Psychology at Northern Illinois University. His research focuses on conceptualizing and measuring career orientations related to boundaryless and protean careers. Another key focus concerns the impact of international culture and generational differences on career transitions and career success. He has held leadership positions in the Careers division of the Academy of Management and is a founder and facilitator of the "5C" Group (The Collaboration for the Cross-Cultural study of Contemporary Careers). He received his DBA from Boston University.

Peter Cappelli is the George W. Taylor Professor of Management at the Wharton School and Director of Wharton's Center for Human Resources. He is also a research associate at the National Bureau of Economic Research in Cambridge and the editor of the *Academy of Management Perspectives.*

Wayne F. Cascio is U.S. Bank Term Professor of Management at the University of Colorado at Denver and Health Sciences Center. His research interests include staffing, development, performance management, compensation, and the economic impact of employee behavior. He has published 21 books and more than 125 articles and book chapters and is an elected fellow of the National Academy of Human Resources, the Academy of Management, and the American Psychological Association.

Dawn E. Chandler is Assistant Professor at California Polytechnic State University, San Luis Obispo. Her primary research interests include careers, mentoring, and action research. Dawn is particularly interested in developmental networks—a group of people who take an active interest in and take action to advance a focal individual's career—and what she terms *relational savvy*, which she defines as "protégé adeptness at initiating and cultivating developmental relationships." Prior to entering academia, she worked in Boston, Massachusetts, and San Jose, California, as a financial recruiter.

Audrey Collin is Professor Emeritus of Career Studies, De Montfort University, Leicester, United Kingdom. She began her career in personnel management, had a family break, made a midlife career change to academia, and pursued her doctorate by part-time study (1984). That developed her interest in systems and interpretative approaches in the study of career, leading to many publications, including articles and two edited books in collaboration with Richard A. Young. She taught organizational behavior and organization studies to Business School postexperience graduate students until her retirement and contributed to an HRM textbook. She has a degree in English and a diploma in anthropology.

Madeline Crocitto (PhD, Baruch College City University of New York) is Associate Professor in the School of Business at the State University of New York College at Old Westbury. She has published extensively in the field of careers and management education, has earned paper, reviewing, and teaching awards, and also consults in the area of health care and career development. She has served on the boards of the Careers Division of the Academy of Management and the Eastern Academy of Management and is a member of the Society for Human Resource Management.

Caroline D'Abate is Assistant Professor of Management and Business at Skidmore College where she teaches organizational behavior, human resource management, introductory business, and the department's senior thesis/research methods course. Her research on employee development and mentoring relationships, the relationship between work/nonwork life realms, personal business on-the-job, careers and diversity, and other topics has been published in journals and presented at national conferences. She holds a PhD in organizational studies from the School of Business, University at Albany, State University of New York.

C. Brooklyn Derr is currently the Staheli Professor in the Organization, Leadership, and Strategy Department at the Marriott School of Management at Brigham Young University, Utah. He has also taught at Harvard, University of California, Los Angeles, IMD (Switzerland), the University of Utah, the Naval Postgraduate School, and has authored 7 books and 60 scholarly articles. His research interests focus on internal career orientations and, in terms of the external career, managing high-potential employees—mostly from a global and cross-cultural perspective. He is also a permanent adjunct faculty member at the Lyon Graduate School of Management (EM Lyon) in France.

Prashant H. Deshpande is a PhD candidate in Organizational Behavior at INSEAD. His research interests include social network analysis, organizational boundaries, and interorganizational relations. The focus of his dissertation is the effect of boundary spanners' social networks and relational styles on the effectiveness of interorganizational relationships. His current empirical research focuses on the role of relationship managers in offshore outsourcing of IT services.

James R. Dillon is a PhD student in Organizational Behavior at Harvard University. His current research explores how group composition and processes lead to learning and performance outcomes in multifunctional teams—especially teams of senior executives. He has a longstanding interest in the process of leadership development, including the effects of career experiences on the performance of leaders and their organizations. Previously, he was a business strategy consultant at Monitor Group and a Research Associate at Harvard Business School. He earned a BS in Accounting from Brigham Young University and an EdM in Mind, Brain, and Education from Harvard University.

Mary B. Dunn is currently Lecturer in the Management Department at the McCombs School of Business at The University of Texas at Austin. Her research interests include professionals' social networks, socialization, and knowledge creation. In particular, she has studied how developmental networks help physician-scientists create scientific knowledge. She completed her PhD in Organization Studies at the Wallace E. Carroll School of Management at Boston College in 2006. She also received an MBA from the University of California, Irvine, and a BA from Colgate University in Hamilton, New York.

Daniel C. Feldman is Synovus Chair of Leadership and Associate Dean for Research at the University of Georgia Terry College of Business. He has served as Editor-in-Chief of *Journal of Management*, Associate Editor for *Human Resource Management* and *Journal of Organizational Behavior*, and Chair of the Careers Division of the Academy of Management. He has published over 100 articles on career topics such as career indecision, socialization, job mobility, job loss, expatriation and repatriation, career plateaus, early retirement, and bridge employment. His most recent book is *Work Careers: A Developmental Perspective* (2002). He has a PhD from Yale University.

Sharon Foley is a full-time student in the Chinese Language Program at Tsinghua University in Beijing, People's Republic of China. She has worked at universities in the United States, the United Kingdom, and Hong Kong. During the 2005 to 2006 academic year, she was a visiting scholar in the management department at The Chinese University of Hong Kong. Her research interests include the "glass ceiling" for women and minorities, organizational fairness, and management practices in the People's Republic of China. She earned her MBA from London Business School and her PhD in Management from University of Connecticut.

Jeffrey H. Greenhaus is Professor and William A. Mackie Chair in the Department of Management at Drexel University's LeBow College of Business. His research focuses on work-family relationships and career dynamics. In addition to journal articles and book chapters on these topics, he has coauthored or coedited *Career Management,* now in its third edition (2000), *Integrating Work and Family: Challenges and Choices for a Changing World* (1997), *Work and Family— Allies or Enemies? What Happens When Business Professionals Confront Life Choices* (2000), and the *Encyclopedia of Career Development* (Sage, 2006).

David E. Guest is Professor of Organizational Psychology and Human Resource Management in the Department of Management at King's College, London. He has written, researched, and published extensively in the areas of human resource management, employment relations and the psychological contract, motivation and commitment, and careers. His current research is concerned with the relationship between human resource management and performance in the private and public sectors; the individualization of employment relations and the role of the psychological contract; flexibility, employment contracts, and worker well-being; partnership at work; and the future of the career.

Douglas T. Hall is the Morton H. and Charlotte Friedman Professor of Management in the School of Management at Boston University. He has recently served as a visiting scholar at Boston College and as Visiting Erskine Fellow at the University of Canterbury in Christchurch, New Zealand. In 2007, he will be the Richardson Visiting Fellow at the Center for Creative Leadership. He is the author of several books and articles on careers and a recipient of the American Psychological Association's Ghiselli Award for research design, the Walter Storey Professional Practice Award from ASTD, and the E. C. Hughes Award from the Academy of Management. He is a fellow of the American Psychological Association and the Academy of Management.

Monika Hamori is Professor of Human Resources Management at the Instituto de Empresa Business School in Madrid, Spain. Her current research focuses on executive career advancement and the role of executive search firms in executive careers. She received her PhD from the Wharton School of the University of Pennsylvania.

Monica C. Higgins is Associate Professor at Harvard University. Her research focuses on leadership and career development. Her book *Career Imprints: Creating Leaders Across an Industry* (2006) focuses on the leadership development of executives in the biotechnology industry. In addition, she has a longitudinal project underway on the Harvard Business School Class of 1996. Before her academic career, she worked at Bain & Company and at Harbridge House, an international organizational change consulting firm. She earned her PhD in Organizational Behavior and MA in Psychology from Harvard's Graduate School of Arts and Sciences and her MBA from Tuck Business School.

Herminia Ibarra is the INSEAD Chaired Professor of Organizational Behavior. Her research interests include identity dynamics, social networks, career development, and women's careers. Her recent book, *Working Identity: Unconventional Strategies for Reinventing Your Career* (2003), describes how people reinvent themselves. Her articles on these topics are published in leading journals, including *Administrative Science Quarterly, Academy of Management Review, Academy of Management Journal*, and *Harvard Business Review.* Prior to joining INSEAD, she had served on the Harvard Business School faculty for 13 years. She received her MA and PhD from Yale University.

Kerr Inkson is semiretired and is Adjunct Professor of Management at the University of Waikato, New Zealand. He has had an academic career of more than 40 years, mainly in New Zealand's business schools. He has published more than 60 refereed journal articles, more than 30 book chapters, and 12 books. His latest books are *Cultural Intelligence* (with David C. Thomas, 2004) and *Understanding Careers* (Sage, 2007). In recent years, his research has focused on careers, and he was Chair of the Careers Division, Academy of Management, 2005 to 2006. He has a PhD from the University of Otago.

Candace Jones is Associate Professor in the Organization Studies Department, Boston College. Her research interests focus on the intersection of creative industries and creative professionals. She examines the careers, social networks, institutions, and project-based organizing within creative industries and professions such as architecture and film. She has recently coedited special issues on creative and cultural industries in *Journal of Organizational Behavior, Research in the Sociology of Organizations, Journal of Management Studies*, and *Creativity and Innovation Management*. She has also published in *Academy of Management Review, Academy of Management Executive, Organization Science, Organization Studies*, and *Human Resource Management.*

Karsten Jonsen is Researcher of Organizational Behaviour and International Management at IMD in Lausanne, Switzerland, where he directs a global research project comparing cultures across nations. His research interests and publications cover a variety of issues in human resource management, including team performance, executive education, virtual teams, stereotyping, and workforce diversity. He earned his bachelor's and master's degrees in organizational behavior and economics from Copenhagen Business School and an MBA from ESCP-EAP in Paris, France. Before coming to IMD in 2002, he held various management positions in the IT industry.

Timothy A. Judge is the Matherly-McKethan Eminent Scholar in the Department of Management at the University of Florida. Previously, he served on the faculties of the University of Iowa and Cornell University. His research interests are in the areas of personality, leadership and influence behaviors, staffing and careers, and job attitudes. He holds a bachelor of business administration degree from the University of Iowa and masters and doctoral degrees from the University of Illinois. Prior to entering graduate school, he worked as a manager at Kohls Department Stores in Wisconsin and Illinois.

John D. Kammeyer-Mueller works at the Warrington College of Business Administration at the University of Florida. His research has focused mostly on topics related to workplace adjustment, including the socialization and adaptation of new organizational members, mentoring, work withdrawal, turnover, and career planning. He has also made occasional research diversions into applied research methods, interpersonal relationships, and personality. His empirical research has appeared in the *Journal of Applied Psychology, Personnel Psychology; the Journal of Vocational Behavior, Industrial Relations*; and the *International Journal of Selection and Assessment*. He received his PhD from the University of Minnesota.

Svetlana N. Khapova is Assistant Professor of Cross-Cultural Management and Organizational Behavior at the Faculty of Economics and Business Administration at the Vrije Universiteit Amsterdam. Her research interests include careers and career behaviors in the knowledge economy and in its related economic contexts of the Internet and the globe. Her publications have appeared in a number of books and in the *Journal of Organizational Behavior*. She holds a PhD degree from the University of Twente, an MBA from the University of Portsmouth, and an MSc (*Cum Laude*) in economics and management from North Caucasus State Technical University.

Jennifer M. Kidd is Reader in the Department of Organizational Psychology, Birkbeck, University of London, where she is the course director for the MSc degree in career management and counseling. She is a coeditor of the *British Journal of Guidance and Counselling* and also a chartered occupational psychologist. Her writing and research in the field of career development and career management span 30 years. Her most recent book is *Understanding*

Career Counselling: Theory, Research and Practice (Sage, 2006), and her current work focuses on career well-being and the role of emotion in careers.

Sharon H. Kim is a PhD student in Organizational Behavior at the Cornell University School of Industrial and Labor Relations. Her research interests include creativity, organizational misbehavior, and careers.

Maria L. Kraimer is Associate Professor and Reader at the University of Melbourne, Australia. Her research interests are in the areas of careers, international assignment success, and the employee-organization relationship. She has received a number of research awards from the Careers Division of the Academy of Management and from the *Academy of Management Journal*. She serves on the editorial board of the *Journal of Applied Psychology* and *Administrative Science Quarterly*. She has previously held academic positions at Cleveland State University and University of Illinois at Chicago. She received her PhD in human resource management from the University of Illinois at Chicago.

Kathy E. Kram is Professor of Organizational Behavior at the Boston University School of Management and the Everett W. Lord Distinguished Faculty Scholar. In addition to her book *Mentoring at Work*, she has published in a wide range of academic and practice-oriented journals on the role of developmental relationships over the life course. She is currently exploring the nature of peer coaching, mentoring circles, and developmental networks. In addition, she is serving a second 3-year term as a member of the Center for Creative Leadership's Board of Governors. She received her BS and MS degrees from MIT Sloan School of Management and a PhD from Yale University.

Barbara S. Lawrence is Professor of Human Resources and Organizational Behavior at the Anderson Graduate School of Management, University of California, Los Angeles. Her current research examines organizational reference groups, the evolution of organizational norms through perceptions, and organizational demography. She served as Chair of the Careers Division of the Academy of Management, was

Senior Editor at *Organization Science,* was coeditor of the *Handbook of Career Theory* (with M. B. Arthur and D. T. Hall), and in 1998, received the Outstanding Publication in Organizational Behavior Award for her work on organizational demography. She received her PhD from the Sloan School of Management at MIT.

Wolfgang Mayrhofer is Professor of Organizational Behavior and Management at the Interdisciplinary Unit for Management and Organisational Behaviour, Department of Management, Wirtschaftsuniversität (WU) Wien, Vienna, Austria. He has previously held research and teaching positions at the University of Paderborn, Germany, and at Dresden University of Technology, Germany. He conducts research in the area of comparative international human resource management and leadership, work careers, and systems theory and management and is a consultant to both private and public sector organizations regularly.

Michael Meyer is Professor of Nonprofit Management at the Institute for Organisation Studies and Organisational Behaviour at Wirtschaftsuniversität Wien (WU), Vienna, Austria. He is the head of the Research Institute for Nonprofit Organisations (NPOs), the academic director of a professional MBA program in social management, and a member of the European network of excellence CINEFOGO (www.cinefogo.org). His current research is on NPOs, the third sector and civil society, careers in NPOs, the social theory of Pierre Bourdieu, text and discourse analysis, and organizational analysis.

Philip H. Mirvis is a Senior Research Fellow of the Boston College Center for Corporate Citizenship. He is an organizational psychologist whose research and private practice concern organizational change and the workforce and workplace and has authored eight books, including *The Cynical Americans, Building the Competitive Workforce,* and *Joining Forces.* His most recent is a business transformation story, *To the Desert and Back.* He has taught at Boston University; Jiao Tong University, Shanghai, China; and the London Business School. He has a BA from Yale University and a PhD in organizational psychology from the University of Michigan.

Celia Moore is Assistant Professor of Organizational Behavior at the London Business School and is completing her PhD in organizational behavior at the University of Toronto's Rotman School of Management. Her research focuses on how power and its abuses are implicated in organizational life. Currently, she is studying how individuals who are morally disengaged navigate corporate hierarchies. Before returning to academia, she spent 8 years as a human resources consultant, working with organizations to build more supportive work environments. She has a master's degree from Columbia University.

Nigel Nicholson is Professor of Organizational Behaviour and a former Research Dean at London Business School. His research and writing have been extensive and wide-ranging, including over 15 books and monographs and over 200 articles in leading academic and practitioner journals. He has been pioneering the application of evolutionary psychology to business, and his current research is on leadership and family business. In addition to his work in the careers field, he has studied absence from work, employee relations, behavioral risk in finance, leadership, and personality. He directs two major leadership programs at London Business School: High Performance People Skills and one of the world's most innovative programs, Proteus.

Anshuman Prasad is Professor of Management at the School of Business, University of New Haven, Connecticut. He brings an interdisciplinary focus in his research, which deals with themes such as workplace diversity and multiculturalism, resistance and empowerment in organizations, strategic action and corporate legitimacy in the global petroleum industry, and epistemological issues. He is the editor of *Postcolonial Theory and Organizational Analysis: A Critical Engagement* (2003) and a coeditor of *Managing the Organizational Melting Pot: Dilemmas of Workplace Diversity* (1997). His articles have appeared in several scholarly journals. He obtained his PhD from the University of Massachusetts, Amherst.

Pushkala Prasad is the Zankel Chair Professor of Management for Liberal Arts Students at Skidmore College. She has also worked at Lund

University in Sweden and at the University of Calgary. Her research interests include the computerization of work, workplace diversity, postpositivist research, and organizational legitimacy. She has published widely in reputed journals such as the *Academy of Management Journal, Organization Science,* the *Journal of Management Studies,* and *Research in the Sociology of Organizations.* She is also a coeditor of *Managing the Organizational Melting Pot* and the *Handbook of Workplace Diversity.* Her most recent publication is *Crafting Qualitative Research: Working in the Post-Positivist Traditions.* She obtained her PhD from the University of Massachusetts, Amherst.

Maria Alejandra Quijada is Assistant Professor in the Department of Management, Loyola Marymount University. Her research interests include work-family integration, careers, and the transformation of the employee-employer relationship. Her current research project looks to understand how issues such as acquisitions and globalization affect software engineers, their teams, and their relation to their employer and profession. She has a PhD in Organization Studies from MIT's Sloan School of Management.

Mark L. Savickas is Professor and Chair in the Behavioral Sciences Department at the Northeastern Ohio Universities College of Medicine and Adjunct Professor of Counselor Education at Kent State University. His 80 articles, 40 book chapters, and 500 presentations to professional groups have dealt with vocational behavior and career counseling. He has served as editor for the *Career Development Quarterly* (1991–1998) and is currently editor for the *Journal of Vocational Behavior* (1999–present). He is a fellow of the National Career Development Association, the American Psychological Society, and the American Psychological Association.

Edgar H. Schein is currently Sloan Fellows Professor of Management Emeritus, MIT Sloan School of Management. After 4 years as a Research Psychologist at the Walter Reed Institute of Research, he joined the Sloan School of Management in 1956 where he taught until his retirement in 2004. His research and writing has concentrated on *Organizational Psychology* (1980), *Organizational Culture and Leadership* (1992, 2004), and *Process Consultation* (1999). His seminal research on careers has led to a third edition of *Career Anchors* (2006), a self-administering instrument for adult career development. He received his PhD in Social Psychology from Harvard University's Department of Social Relations in 1952.

Scott E. Seibert is Associate Professor in the Department of Management and Marketing, University of Melbourne. He has held academic positions at the University of Illinois, Chicago, and the University of Notre Dame, Indiana. His research in careers is informed by his interest in personality, mentoring, and social networks. He has received a number of research awards from the Careers, Entrepreneurship, and Organizational Behavior divisions of the Academy of Management. He serves on the editorial board of the *Academy of Management Journal.* He received his PhD from the New York State School of Industrial and Labor Relations, Cornell University.

Holly S. Slay is on the faculty of the Rochester Institute of Technology's Saunders College of Business. Her current research examines the role of networks and identity in influencing career transition decisions, career decision making at midlife/mid-career, and the impact of race and gender on career behaviors (such as networking) and career outcomes. She received her PhD from University of Maryland's Smith School of Business. Before pursuing her PhD, she worked in industry for over 13 years in a number of diverse technical and management positions.

Johannes Steyrer is Associate Professor of Organizational Behavior at the Institute for Organisation Studies and Organisational Behaviour at Wirtschaftsuniversität Wien (WU), Vienna, Austria. He is the academic director of a professional MBA program in health care management. His current research is on leadership behavior, with a special focus on charismatic leadership, and careers in for-profit and non-profit organizations.

Jane Sturges is Senior Lecturer in Organizational Behavior in the Department of Management at King's College, London. She has researched and published on individual and organizational perspectives of the career, including career success orientations, career capital, and career management. Her current research interests include the employment relationship, contemporary careers in organizations, the psychological contract, and work-life balance.

Sherry E. Sullivan is the coauthor of *The Opt-Out Revolt: Why People Are Leaving Companies to Create Kaleidoscope Careers* (with Lisa Mainiero, 2006), the coeditor of *Winning Reviews: A Guide for Evaluating Scholarly Writing* (with Yehuda Baruch and Haze Schepmyer, 2006), and has published more than 100 journal articles on careers and gender. She is a Fellow of Southern Management Association, has served as the Careers Division Chair (1998) for the Academy of Management, and was recognized with the Academy of Management's Gender & Diversity in Organization Division's Janet Chusmir Award for mentoring and service (2002). She is the Director of the Small Business Institute, Bowling Green State University and earned her PhD from The Ohio State University.

M. Susan Taylor is Dean's Professor of Human Resources and Co-Director of the Center for Human Capital, Innovation and Technology at the Robert H. Smith School of Business, University of Maryland at College Park. Her career interests include managerial career mobility and individuals' self-directed career transitions. Her current research views careers through the lens of the employment relationship and radical organizational change. She expresses her gratitude to the editors and her coauthor for the opportunity to continue learning about careers while preparing this chapter. In 1996, she was very fortunate to coedit *The Rhythms of Academic Life* with the late Professor Peter Frost.

David C. Thomas is currently Professor of International Management in the Faculty of Business Administration at Simon Fraser University, Canada. He previously held positions at The University of Auckland, New Zealand, and at The Pennsylvania State University. He is the author of five books and numerous journal articles concerning cross-cultural interactions in organizational settings. He is currently Associate Editor of the *International Journal of Cross-Cultural Management* and serves on the editorial boards of the *Journal of International Business Studies*, the *Journal of Management*, and the *Journal of World Business*. He has a PhD from the University of South Carolina.

Pamela S. Tolbert is Professor and current Chair of the Department of Organizational Behavior in the Industrial and Labor Relations School at Cornell University. She also serves as an associate editor for the *Academy of Management Review* and is on the editorial boards of several journals. Her research interests have focused on several areas: organizational change processes, occupations and organizations, organizational demography, and work/family relations. These interests are reflected in the articles that she has published in a number of journals, including *Administrative Science Quarterly, Organization Studies, Work and Occupations, Industrial and Labor Relations Review,* and *International Journal of Human Resource Management*, and in various book chapters. She received her PhD in sociology from the University of California, Los Angeles.

Daniel Tzabbar is Assistant Professor of Entrepreneurship and Strategy at the School of Business Administration, University of Central Florida. His research focuses on creating and testing organizational and strategic theories related to the flow of inter- and intraorganizational knowledge, through R&D alliances, scientists' and executives' mobility, and the facilitation of learning and technological change. This research incorporates related interests such as exploring the ways in which individual career experiences, mobility, and network affect entrepreneurial firm competitive viability, strategic alliance formation, and decision-making processes leading to strategic change. He earned his PhD from the Rotman School of Management, University of Toronto.

Monique Valcour is Assistant Professor in the Department of Organization Studies, Carroll School of Management, Boston College. Her research program focuses on career dynamics and on the integration of work and family roles. Her publications have appeared in *Human Relations, Industrial Relations,* and the *International Journal of Human Resource*

Management as well as in several edited volumes. She earned PhD and MS degrees from the School of Industrial and Labor Relations at Cornell University, an MEd from the Harvard Graduate School of Education, and an AB from Brown University.

Yoav Vardi has retired from the Department of Labor Studies at Tel Aviv University where he served since 1980. His main areas of interest are organizational careers and organizational misbehavior. His book on misbehavior *(Misbehavior in Organizations: Theory, Research, and Management,* coauthored with Ely Weitz) was published in 2004. His articles appeared in the *Academy of Management Journal, Academy of Management Review, Journal of Vocational Behavior, Psychological Reports, Organization Science,* and the *Journal of Business Ethics.* He received his PhD in

Organizational Behavior from the New York State School of Industrial and Labor Relations, Cornell University, where he recently spent his sabbatical as Visiting Professor.

Celeste P. M. Wilderom is Professor of Management and Organizational Behavior in the Private and Public Sector (University of Twente, The Netherlands). Her main research focus is on effective organizational change, including leadership and culture. She publishes through a variety of outlets; she is one of the three editors of the award-winning *Handbook of Organizational Culture & Climate* (2000, Sage) and served as an associate editor of *Academy of Management Executive, International Journal of Service Industry Management,* and *British Journal of Management.* She obtained a PhD from the State University of New York, Buffalo, in 1987.